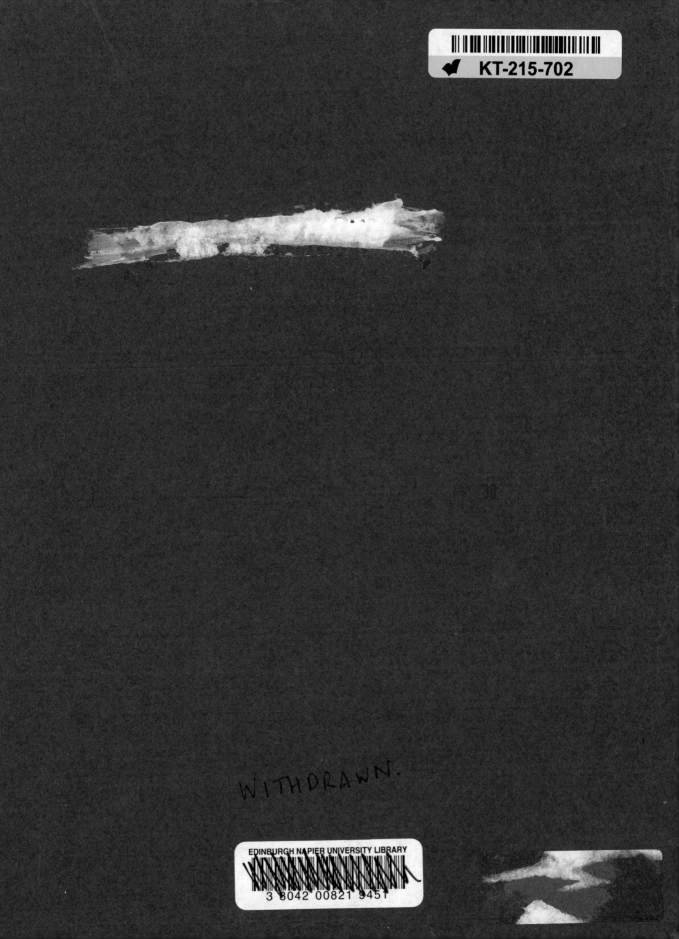

THE
MANAGEMENT
OF
ORGANIZATIONS

STRATEGY

STRUCTURE

BEHAVIOR

THE
MANAGEMENT
OF
ORGANIZATIONS

STRATEGY

STRUCTURE

BEHAVIOR

JAY B. BARNEY
Texas A & M University

RICKY W. GRIFFIN
Texas A & M University

HOUGHTON MIFFLIN COMPANY   BOSTON   TORONTO
Dallas   Geneva, Illinois   Palo Alto   Princeton, New Jersey

To Bill Ouchi, from whom I began to learn about real organizations.
—J.B.B.

To the memory of my grandmother, Mattie Robinson, who taught me to read and to write.
—R.W.G.

Senior Sponsoring Editor: Patrick F. Boles
Senior Development Editor: Paula Kmetz
Senior Project Editor: Paula Kmetz
Assistant Design Manager: Patricia Mahtani
Production Coordinator: Frances Sharperson
Senior Manufacturing Coordinator: Marie Barnes
Marketing Manager: Diane L. McOscar

Cover painting   Robert Feero, "ICA," 1978. Collection of John E. Shore, Cincinnati, Ohio.

Part opener paintings   **Part I** — Robert Feero, "Bascule," 1979. Synthetic resin on canvas. **Part II** — Robert Feero, "Plenum," 1979. Synthetic resin on paper. **Part III** — Robert Feero, "Duece," 1980. Synthetic resin on canvas. **Part IV** — Robert Feero, "Dhow," 1979. Synthetic resin on canvas. **Part V** — Robert Feero, "Sinkona," 1979. Synthetic resin on canvas.

Line Art   Rossi & Associates

Photo Credits   **Chapter 1:** p. 5, © Frank Siteman; p. 14, courtesy Goya Foods; p. 20, © Jon Chase; p. 26, © Nippon Television Network Corporation, Tokyo. **Chapter 2:** p. 41, © Giraudon/Art Resource; p. 56, courtesy Oregon Historical Society (OrHi 56468). **Chapter 3:** p. 76, courtesy DHL International Express Ltd., Ontario; p. 84, © Walter Bibikow; p. 91, © Robin Thomas. **Chapter 4:** p. 114, Savescu/Sipa Press; p. 116, © Bob Krist; p. 121, Wendy Maeda/The Boston Globe; p. 128, courtesy Hewlett-Packard Co. and Saatchi & Saatchi DFS Pacific.
(Photo credits continued on p. 820.)

Printed in the U.S.A.

Library of Congress Catalog Card Number: 91-72002

ISBN: 0-395-57427-7

ABCDEFGHIJ-D-954321

Brief Contents

Contents

Preface

In 1953 George Terry published a textbook entitled *Principles of Management.* He organized his book around a set of basic managerial functions. Under the further influence of Harold Koontz and Cyril O'Donnell's *Principles of Management: An Analysis of Managerial Functions* (1955) and Terry's second edition (1956), professors and researchers in the field came to settle on a pedagogical framework of four basic managerial functions that were thought to comprise the field of management—planning, organizing, directing, and controlling. Almost forty years later, virtually every major survey of management textbook is still organized according to that same basic framework. While there is little empirical research to support this perspective, many authors and instructors still find it effective.

At the same time, however, there is growing disenchantment with this viewpoint. Some instructors argue that the functional approach fails to capture the true essence of managerial work. Others point out that newer topics such as ethics, international management, and stress do not fit easily into the basic functional framework. Still others are concerned with meeting AACSB guidelines and the new imperatives for management education sparked by the Porter and McKibbon report. Perhaps most importantly, the traditional management text is not appropriate for use in the growing number of schools of business that offer combined management and organizational behavior courses.

These concerns about traditionally organized management texts prompted us to write *The Management of Organizations: Strategy, Structure, Behavior.* In particular, our goal was to approach the study of management from a more contemporary and meaningful perspective. Our work together started in 1988 when we visited London, Paris, Munich, Venice, and Geneva with our families and thirty-three undergraduates. In the course of many late-night conversations, we came to agree that the time had come for a new textbook that would respond to the current thinking about management as well as to current trends in management curricula.

Organization of the Book

Rather than focusing on previously defined functions of management (planning, organizing, directing, controlling), we decided to concentrate on how organizations really work. We started by carefully analyzing recent research about organizations. We also consulted extensively with colleagues about their views of how organizations are managed. We studied course outlines from dozens of colleges and universities to see how principles of management courses are taught. From these various sources of inquiry, we were able to discern a clear pattern: many people in the management field conceive of management as being comprised of three fundamental sets of issues—those related to strategy, those related to structure, and those related to behavior. These issues form the framework around which the book is organized.

In *The Management of Organizations*, the topics of strategy, structure, and behavior (covered in Parts II, III, and IV respectively) are given equal weight. This results in a book with greater emphasis on strategy, and fuller coverage of behavior, than virtually any other principles of management textbook. The content of the five parts of the text are outlined in the following paragraphs.

Part I introduces students to organizations and management. This three-chapter part first characterizes the world of organizations, then summarizes the history and theory of organizations, and concludes by identifying important contemporary challenges faced by all organizations. Part II, consisting of six chapters, focuses on the organization's relationship with its environment by discussing the strategic management of organizations. This part first describes environments within which organizations function and then discusses how managers make decisions. Goals and planning are discussed next, followed by in-depth coverage of strategy formulation and implementation. This part concludes with a discussion of individual creativity and organizational innovation.

Part III, also six chapters long, deals more specifically with the organization itself, how it is configured and managed, and especially how it is structured and designed. We first discuss the basic concepts and issues associated with organization structure and design. We then discuss control and information systems. We also describe the management of human resources and of operations management in the last two chapters of Part IV.

In Part IV, we look inside the organization and include six chapters on a variety of issues associated with human behavior in organizational settings. Separate chapters are devoted to individual behavior, motivation, leadership, group dynamics, communication, and conflict and stress. Finally, in Part V we devote separate chapters to areas that serve to integrate strategy, structure, and behavior — ethics and social responsibility, organization change and development, and entrepreneurship and small business management.

Features of the Book

Several carefully planned features of *The Management of Organizations* add to the text's value and to the integrity of its purpose.

- The organizational focus of the book. While we cover virtually all of the basic topics and concepts found in a traditional principles of management book, we cover them from the point of view of the organization rather than that of the individual manager.

- The integration of international management content throughout the book — in textual material, examples, boxed inserts, cases, and photos. We chose to do this rather than relegate international coverage to a single chapter.
- Up-to-date information and examples (along with historical and background information where necessary).
- Most major points are illustrated with real-world examples from today's business press in order to help students apply the knowledge they gain.

A variety of both proven and innovative features serve to make the book both informative and interesting. In Chapter 1 we present the strategy-structure-behavior framework around which the book is organized. A contemporary design also conveys in a visual sense the sophistication of the book. Each part opens with a text introduction that highlights its purpose and contents for the student.

Within each chapter there are several features that enhance its effectiveness. Each chapter begins with a set of learning objectives for students and an outline of chapter contents. An opening vignette then draws the reader into the text discussion. Throughout the text, key terms are boldfaced and major points are highlighted in margin notes. An attractive program of figures and tables, combined with striking photographs with content-driven captions, add visual appeal to the chapters.

Each chapter also has three boxed inserts. One boxed insert, The Global Challenge, highlights an international issue or example. A second boxed insert, The Entrepreneurial Challenge, focuses on start-up and entrepreneurial examples. The Environmental Challenge, the third type of boxed insert, deals with the environment of organizations, often taking an ethical or social responsibility slant.

Each chapter concludes with a learning summary that recalls the key points of the text. Other end-of-chapter learning aids include three types of questions. Review questions ask the student to recall basic points from the chapter. Analysis questions then ask the student to interpret, extend, or synthesize the material from the text. Thus, they assess higher levels of learning. Application exercises then ask the student to use the material in an experiential or applied fashion. The chapters end with two cases. The first focuses on a domestic organization, while the second explores an international organization.

Taken together, the pedagogical framework for the text provides a superior learning package for students.

Instructional and Educational Support Materials

The Management of Organizations: Strategy, Structure, Behavior is accompanied by a substantial ancillary package that facilitates the presentation and testing of the text material for the teacher, and that promotes learning for the student.

Instructor's Resource Manual   For each chapter, the Instructor's Resource Manual provides a chapter summary; a list of learning objectives; a lecture outline; answers to review, analysis, and application questions; a case summary followed by answers to the case discussion questions; and lecture enhancement materials. Also included in the IRM are course outlines, a list of film and video resources by chapter, and approximately 120 transparency masters. The Instructor's Resource Manual is written by Mary Coulter of Southwest Missouri State University.

Test Bank   Written by Robert Wagley of Wright State University, the Test Bank includes over 2,000 multiple-choice, true/false, and essay questions. An item information column in the Test Bank specifies details about each question — the correct answer, the relevant learning objective number, the learning level (knowledge or understanding), and the page number in the text on which the answer is found.

Microcomputerized Test Bank   A microcomputerized version of the printed Test Bank is available on diskette for use on IBM-compatible personal computers. Instructors can generate tests using items of their choice as well as items that they compose themselves.

Transparencies   The instructional package includes 100 color transparencies.

Study Guide   The Study Guide, written by Robert Wagley of Wright State University, assists students in learning, reviewing, and integrating chapter content. The Study Guide includes the learning objectives, a chapter outline, a list of key terms, and multiple-choice, true/false, and matching questions for each chapter. Also provided are answers to all of the questions in the Study Guide, annotated to explain both correct and incorrect answers.

Microcomputerized Study Guide   A microcomputerized version of the printed Study Guide is available on diskette for use on IBM-compatible personal computers.

Acknowledgments

Although the names Jay Barney and Ricky Griffin appear on the cover of this book, there are many other people who played important roles in its creation. First of all, we want to thank the individuals who helped us refine the strategy-structure-behavior framework for application in a survey of management text. Dozens of conversations, telephone calls, informal chats, and formal meetings with colleagues from around the country helped us direct and focus our thinking as we arrived at this approach.

We were also helped by many outstanding reviewers. These busy professional instructors and researchers took substantial time from their schedules to read and critique first- and second-draft manuscript. There are literally dozens of passages throughout the text that were improved as a result of their suggestions. All reviewers responded to our questions with keen insight and concern for enhancing the quality of our presentation. Their names and affiliations are listed below.

Maryann Albrecht
University of Illinois–Chicago

Douglas Baker
Washington State University

William Bommer
Bowling Green State University

Albert Cabral
Nazareth College of Rochester

Stephen J. Carroll
University of Maryland–College Park

Julio De Castro
University of Colorado at Boulder

Donald Conlon
University of Delaware

Richard S. DeFrank
University of Houston

Arthur K. Fischer
Pittsburgh State University

Steve Grover
Indiana University–Bloomington

Bob Gulbro
Jacksonville State University

Lady Hanson
California State Polytechnic University–Pomona

Timothy Harper
Bowling Green State University

J. Kline Harrison
Wake Forest University

Jeffrey Harrison
Clemson University

Eline Hewitt
University of Scranton

Robert Hill
University of Houston

Jaqueline Hood
University of New Mexico–Albuquerque

Steve Iman
California State Polytechnic University–Pomona

David Jalajas
Clarkson University

Daniel G. Kopp
Southwest Missouri State University

Michael Marker
Jacksonville State University

Kurt W. Mikan
University of Montevallo

Edward J. Morrison
University of Colorado at Boulder

Diana D. Mrotek
Sacred Heart University

Helen J. Muller
University of New Mexico–Albuquerque

Jay Nathan
Clarion University of Pennsylvania

John Orife
Indiana University of Pennsylvania

Hugh O'Neill
University of Connecticut at Storrs

Kevin O'Neill
State University of New York at Plattsburgh

James Campbell Quick
University of Texas at Arlington

Alan Raymond
University of South Dakota

Paula L. Rechner
University of Houston

Jaqueline Rowley
University of Alabama

Nirmal Sethia
University of Southern California

Larry Theye
Kearney State College

James Thomas
Pennsylvania State University

Robert Wagley
Wright State University

Patricia Wilkie-Gootman
University of Massachusetts at Boston

We must also acknowledge the outstanding level of professional support we received at Texas A & M University. Don Hellriegel, Head of the Department of Management, and A. Benton Cocanougher, Dean of the College of Business Administration and Graduate School of Business, maintain a culture that fosters and enables this type of work. Our colleagues in the Department of Management also deserve recognition. There is no finer group of people anywhere. We also want to recognize David D. Van Fleet, a former colleague and currently a faculty member at Arizona State University-West. David helped us plan this book and originally intended to be a collaborator. After he left A & M, however, his new commitments forced him to drop off the author team.

We would also like to express our sincere appreciation to a truly outstanding team of professionals at Houghton Mifflin Company. Patrick Boles, Senior Sponsoring Editor, was a believer in this project from its very inception and never faltered in his belief that we could create something special. Nancy Doherty-Schmitt, Editorial Production Manager, has also been a consistent and effective supporter of our work for many years. Karen Donovan took on the challenging task of helping us develop this text and never compromised in her efforts to make every word, sentence, and paragraph as clear and logical as possible. Paula Kmetz, Senior Project Editor, has also made significant contributions to the text. Paula coordinated the entire project, kept us focused on our goals, challenged us to do better, reinforced us when we did, and ran interference for us when it was needed.

Finally, we would like to acknowledge the myriad contributions to this and our other works made by our families. Our wives, Kim and Glenda, provide us with support and companionship. Our children, Lindsay, Kristian, and Erin (Barney) and Dustin and Ashley (Griffin), give us inspiration, hope, and joy. Without them, most of what we do would have little meaning.

J. B. B.
R. W. G.

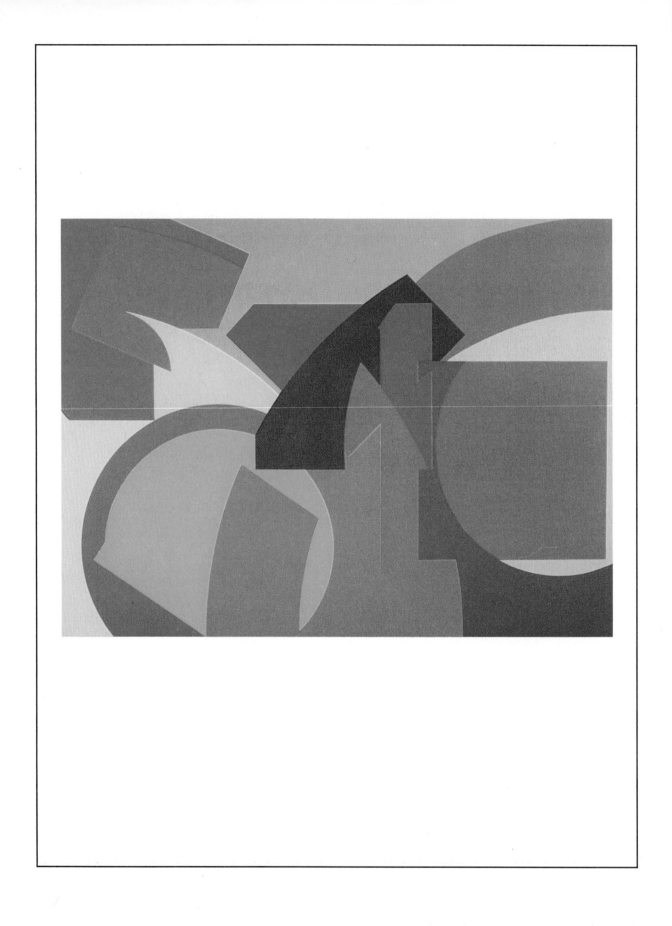

1 Organizations and Management

Organizations, and their managers, constitute a significant portion of contemporary society. From the elementary school down the street to the large multinational companies that make and sell the products we use every day, organizations touch almost every aspect of our lives. Their many activities and practices reflect — and sometimes influence — society's prevailing ideas about how people should best work together to accomplish common goals. This book describes what organizations do and how managers contribute to the success of organizational activities. To help you establish a context for understanding organizations and management, this first section introduces you to the nature of organizations and to some fundamentals of the management process. Subsequent parts examine the major aspects of organizations and management in more detail.

1

The World of Organizations

After studying this chapter, you should be able to:

1. Explain what an organization is and why organizations exist.

2. Identify the various types of managers needed by organizations.

3. Discuss the primary functions of managers that contribute to an organization's competitiveness and productivity.

4. Describe the basic roles and skills that characterize managerial work in organizations.

5. Discuss the role of organizations and managers in the global era.

Microsoft Corp. has quietly become one of the most influential (and successful) firms in American industry. The company's primary product is the Disk Operating System (DOS), the computer operating software that has become the industry standard for personal computers. Its other major products include Microsoft Word (a word-processing package), Excel (a spreadsheet program), and Windows (an alternative operating system rapidly gaining in popularity).

Microsoft was the brainchild of William Gates III, who began writing computer software when he was in junior high school. He dropped out of Harvard in 1975 to establish Microsoft just outside of Seattle. Gates still serves as the firm's chief executive officer and owns 35.8 percent of Microsoft's stock. He is one of the youngest billionaires in the world. A self-proclaimed computer nerd, Gates hardly fits the image of the typical chief executive.

Indeed, from the very beginning, Gates recognized that his talents were in coordinating technological innovation and inspiring others, as opposed to managing the details of a large corporation. Thus he hired a cadre of experienced professional managers to run the company. Today Microsoft has over five thousand employees and annual revenues of $1.5 billion.

Gates's entrepreneurial fervor keeps him always on the alert for new business opportunities, and his strong competitive urge pushes him to stay on top of his competitors. One of Gates's biggest assets is his ability to inspire fierce loyalty in his employees. The organization that he has created functions as a loose collection of small, relatively autonomous businesses beneath the Microsoft corporate umbrella.

Microsoft has also been at the leading edge of international competition in the computer industry. It was one of the first software firms to write programs for foreign markets. As a result, Microsoft dominates virtually every foreign market it has entered and achieves more than half of its sales and profits overseas.[1]

Organizations and the people who run them have a dramatic impact on our standard of living and quality of life. We feel their influence daily and in myriad ways — some positive and others quite negative. For example, Microsoft's products have led to significant improvements in productivity in many industries and allowed people around the world to tap into the potential provided by the personal computer. However, the tremendous increase in computer-related tasks has also led to new occupational diseases resulting from the repetitive movements that characterize prolonged computer use.

This chapter introduces you to organizations and the people who manage them. We first discuss the general nature of organizations and then describe the kinds of managers that are needed to run them. We detail the organizational functions of managers, their roles, and the skills that they must bring to the organization. Finally we describe the increasingly international tenor of organizations and their competitive environments.

The Nature of Organizations

Organizations are collections of people working together in a coordinated and structured fashion to achieve one or more goals.

When most people hear the word "organization," they think "business." A business is indeed an organization, but many other kinds of organizations exist as well. We define an **organization** as a collection of people working together in a coordinated and structured fashion to achieve one or more goals.[2] In the sections that follow we describe how organizations contribute to society, describe the major types of organizations, and highlight the importance of people in those organizations.

The Role of Organizations in Society

Why do organizations exist? Of what use are they to society? As we discuss more fully in Chapter 2, organizations have existed since the dawn of

Organizations play a vital role in society. City Year Inc., a not-for-profit organization started in 1988 in Boston, contributes to society by arranging internships for young people in various profit-seeking organizations. City Year hopes to make tomorrow's managers more sensitive to environmental and social issues. These City Year service corps interns have worked in such organizations as Reebok and New England Telephone.

recorded history. Anthropologists speculating about the earliest days of humankind believe that our ancestors first banded together into tribes. Such tribes had one or more leaders, a division of labor, and a clear set of goals — each a characteristic of modern organizations.

Organizations exist because two people working together can generally accomplish more than they could if they worked individually. Just as our prehistoric ancestors divided up tasks to fit their own strengths and weaknesses, modern managers also try to mesh their strengths and weaknesses with tasks they can perform most effectively. Thus, in modern organizations managers with relatively strong quantitative abilities may concentrate on finance or accounting while others with stronger interpersonal skills may handle human resource activities.

Besides enabling people to get more work done more easily, most organizations also contribute somehow to the society in which they function. Among their goals are activities that society generally deems to be appropriate and useful. For example, in the United States societal norms cause most businesses to support one or more social causes and most universities to provide some sort of community service activities. A society allows an organization to continue as long as the organization's goals are deemed to be appropriate.

People and Organizations

The attitudes, perceptions, and behaviors of the individual members of an organization strongly influence how the organization operates and how effective it is. Organizations have executive jobs, operating jobs, secretarial jobs, and janitorial jobs. They have machinist jobs, staff specialist jobs, supervisory jobs, and programming jobs. Each of these jobs, as well as dozens, hundreds, or even thousands of others, is performed by an individual. Even when organizations automate jobs and replace some operating employees with sophisticated robots, people are still necessary to make sure the robots work correctly.

Because the operation of an organization is the responsibility of its managers, all managers need to develop a keen understanding of people and how they function in organizations.

Types of Organizations

Profit-seeking organizations seek to generate profits for their owners by selling products and services.

Table 1.1 lists several types of organizations and provides some examples of them from around the world. **Profit-seeking organizations** are business firms that sell products and services in order to generate profits for their owners. The largest can be extremely large and can control vast resources. For example, General Motors, the largest industrial firm in the world, had sales in 1990 of over $126 billion. The auto giant has $180 billion in assets and employs 775,100 employees around the world.[3]

Start-up profit-seeking organizations are created by individuals, groups, or firms and have a goal of quickly growing into large organizations.

Start-up profit-seeking organizations are relatively new firms organized by individuals or groups or as subsidiaries of other firms. They often begin small, but their owners and managers may envision their growing into large organizations as quickly as possible. For example, Compaq Computer was started in 1984 by a group of former Texas Instruments engineers. By 1990,

Table 1.1

Types of Organizations

Large Profit-Seeking Organizations

Exxon, General Motors, Sony, British Petroleum, Unilever, IBM, Citicorp, Prudential Insurance, Sears, Kroger Grocery, Delta Air Lines

Start-Up Profit-Seeking Organizations

Compaq Computer, Blockbuster Video, Sharper Image, Hypermart, Intervoice, Sierra On-line

Small Profit-Seeking Organizations

Local hair design shop, neighborhood video rental store, corner pizza parlor, automobile dealership, electronics repair shop, T-shirt shop, neighborhood fruit stand

Government Organizations

Environmental Protection Agency, Internal Revenue Service, Central Intelligence Agency, British Navy, MITI (Japan's industrial planning organization)

Educational Organizations

Stanford University (private), Ohio State University (public), Dallas Independent School District, Mesa Community College

Health Care Organizations

Mayo Clinic, Texas Medical Center, Humana Hospital, university health center, AM/PM Walk-In Clinic

Interest Group Organizations

Sierra Club, Mothers Against Drunk Drivers, Irish Republican Army, neighborhood improvement association, United Auto Workers, American Civil Liberties Union

Religious Organizations

Methodist Church, the Vatican, a neighborhood storefront church

Other Organizations

Fraternity or sorority, drug-running operation, commune, household, agricultural cooperative

Compaq had annual sales of over $3.6 billion and employed 9,500 people.

Small profit-seeking organizations are businesses not intended by their owners to grow rapidly.

By **small profit-seeking organizations** we mean firms never intended for rapid growth by their owners. Many individual entrepreneurs are content to earn enough profit to sustain themselves and their dependents and are not particularly eager to expand their business into a large firm. As noted in Table 1.1, a local hair design shop or pizza parlor may fit this description. In many parts of the world (rural regions of Europe, for example) organizations such as corner fruit stands, bakeries, and fish or meat markets also fall into this category.

Many types of *nonprofit organizations* — organizations with a goal other than earning a profit for owners — also exist, including government, educational, and health care organizations.

As you now know, however, not all organizations are businesses. **Nonprofit organizations** are those organizations that have a goal other than earning a profit for owners. They include government agencies such as the Environmental Protection Agency and the British Navy. Other examples of nonprofit organizations include educational institutions such as your college or university, health care organizations like the Mayo Clinic, and interest groups such as the Sierra Club. Religious institutions like the Vatican and a wide variety of social collectives like communes and cooperatives are also nonprofit organizations.

Regardless of how we categorize them, all organizations share two characteristics: each has one or more goals that its members want to accomplish, and to accomplish their goals each uses coordination and direction.

Managers in Organizations

The *management process* is a set of activities directed at combining resources efficiently and effectively in order to attain the organization's goals.

Organizations can function smoothly only when people within them practice the art and science of management. The **management process** is a set of activities directed at combining resources efficiently and effectively in order to attain the organization's goals. In many cases, the group of people that an organization employs to carry out these activities is also referred to as its "management." Let's look closely at the parts of this definition for the management process.

Organizations use *financial, physical, human,* and *information resources.*

All organizations use four kinds of resources. **Financial resources** are the funds that the organization uses to pay the costs of operations. They are obtained from stockholder investment, sales, bank loans, and various other sources. **Physical resources**, usually obtained from various suppliers, are the materials, tools, buildings, equipment, and raw materials needed by an organization to create its products and services. **Human resources** are the people who make up the organization and include managers, support personnel, and operating employees. **Information resources** include economic forecasts, sales projections, analyses of competitive firms and customer groups, and other information.

Organizations strive to be both *efficient* and *effective.*

To be successful, an organization must use these resources efficiently and effectively. **Efficiency** is the maximization of the quality, quantity, or some other measure of what is created relative to the resources needed to create it. For example, an employee who makes 15 units of a product is more efficient than a second employee who makes only 12 units in the same amount of time and with the same materials.

Effectiveness is the extent to which the activities that the organization undertakes are appropriate, given the context in which they occur. If demand for a new product is increasing while the organization is increasing the number of those products being produced, the organization is being effective. But if demand is declining while more products are being made, the organization is not being effective. (Of course, most production situations are more complex than these simple examples indicate.)

Our definition of the management process includes the concept of goals. A **goal** is a target that the organization wants to reach; without goals, the organization has no clear direction or purpose. The role that goals play in organizations is covered more fully in Chapter 6.

Managers are individuals whose primary activities are to carry out the management process.

Managers are those individuals whose primary activities are to carry out the management process.[4] In a Ford Motors assembly plant, the people who assemble the cars, operate production equipment, and transport materials are vital employees, but they are not responsible for the management process. However, the supervisor who oversees their work, schedules production for the day, and decides how to replace a broken machine is, and each of these activities is part of the management process. We discuss the various managerial roles and skills later in this chapter. Now, however, we turn our attention to the different types of managers that organizations employ.

Types of Managers

We can begin to understand the many important activities included in the management process by examining the variety of managers that many organizations require. Figure 1.1 illustrates two ways to categorize managers: by level and by area.

The three levels of management are *top, middle,* and *first-line.*

Levels of Management   Differentiating managers by level focuses on their position and the extent of their responsibility in the organization. As shown in Figure 1.1, the three levels of managers are top, middle, and first-line.

Top managers are the relatively small set of individuals who provide the main direction and leadership for the entire organization. Their titles include president, chief executive officer (CEO), and vice president (for a business), chancellor and president (for a university), admiral and general (for the military), and director (for a government agency). Top managers are responsible for monitoring the organization's environment, determining the organization's strategies, and making the major decisions that determine what path the organization will follow.[5] John Akers, CEO of IBM, and Ellen Marram, president of Nabisco's grocery division, are top managers.

Middle managers are a large group of people whose positions fall generally in the middle of the organization. Common middle-management titles include plant manager, division head, and district manager (for a business), dean (for a university), major and colonel (for the military), and bureau chief (for the government). The basic tasks of middle managers are to implement the strategies developed by top managers and to oversee the work of first-line managers. During the booming economy of the 1960s many U.S. companies created middle-management positions that weren't really necessary. Increased foreign competition during the 1970s and 1980s led these firms to become more cost conscious and to eliminate some middle-management positions. For example, Du Pont, an international chemical company, reduced its total number of middle-management positions by 15 percent during the last decade; Mobil Corporation cut 17 percent of its middle-management positions during that same period.[6]

First-line managers supervise and coordinate the work of operating employees. Common titles for first-line managers include office manager, foreman, shift supervisor, and sales manager (for a business), department chair (in a university), sergeant (for the military), and supervisor (for the government). Most managers start their careers at this level before advancing into the ranks of middle management.

Areas of Management   We can also discuss managers and their specific activities in terms of the management areas in which they function. Com-

Figure 1.1

Types of Managers by Level and Area

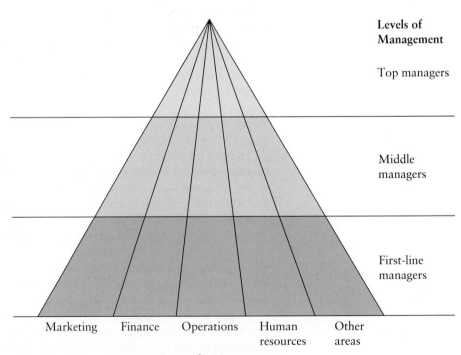

Levels of Management

Top managers

Middle managers

First-line managers

Marketing   Finance   Operations   Human resources   Other areas

Areas of Management

Common areas of management include *marketing, finance, operations,* and *human resources.*

mon areas of management are also illustrated in Figure 1.1. **Marketing managers** are primarily responsible for enhancing the actual and perceived utility of the organization's products or services in the eyes of potential customers. Thus they are involved with new-product (or new-service) development, promotion, distribution of products to customers, and the like.

Financial managers focus on the organization's financial resources. For example, they make sure that funds are borrowed at favorable interest rates, that idle funds are properly invested, and that the organization addresses its financial commitments. **Operations managers** are concerned with the transformation of physical resources into products and services. Thus they are responsible for acquiring the necessary materials and equipment, using those materials and equipment to produce goods and services, storing finished goods until they are shipped to customers, and overseeing related activities.

Human resources managers are responsible for ensuring that the right kinds of people are available and willing to work in the organization. They determine future human resource needs, recruit and hire qualified applicants, and develop procedures for training employees and evaluating their performance and providing appropriate compensation.

Many organizations require additional types of specialized managers. Public relations managers, research and development managers, international specialists, and information managers are becoming increasingly sought after. Hospitals need administrators familiar with both management and health care practices. Many universities employ development officers to assist in fund raising.

Each area of management usually includes top, middle, and first-line managers. For example, the vice president of Procter & Gamble's marketing division is a top manager. The firm's regional sales and advertising directors are middle managers, and the numerous district sales managers and local advertising managers are first-line managers.

Becoming a Manager

Individuals follow a variety of paths to a career in management. The first step is generally an undergraduate degree in business or a related field of study. After getting their degree, most people spend some time working in first-line management positions. After they gain some experience in this way, they may return to school for an advanced degree (for example, an MBA) or continue working toward promotion into the lower levels of middle management.

Periodic training and refresher courses are important parts of many managerial careers. In response to the recent significant trend toward the internationalization of business, many managers are taking special courses to prepare themselves to work in foreign cultures, introduce their products or services in foreign markets, and compete with foreign firms. The Global Challenge describes how one group of executives recently returned to campus to participate in just such a program.

THE GLOBAL CHALLENGE

Becoming a Global Manager

In the "old days," prospective managers went to school, got degrees, and then began the quest for success and advancement. Most people spent their entire managerial careers in a single country, working for a domestic organization concerned almost exclusively with domestic competition. Increasingly, however, managers are having to add an international dimension to their portfolios if they are to succeed.

How do they accomplish this? International assignments and responsibilities will likely be a standard part of the training of younger managers in the years ahead. Senior executives with a solid career track record may need an intensive, in-depth program specifically tailored to enhance their understanding of organizational activities around the globe.

The University of Michigan recently sponsored just such a program. Twenty-one executives from Japan, the United States, Brazil, Great Britain, and India spent five weeks learning to become global managers. During the program they went through a variety of both structured and unstructured activities. One of the first goals of the program was to make the managers sensitive to the differences that existed among them. Attention then shifted to overcoming those differences and working together effectively.

Some differences were apparent almost immediately. For example, the Japanese executives were initially ill at ease and reluctant to communicate. A major roadblock that had to be overcome was clarifying how each person in the group was to be addressed. Some of the Japanese preferred to be addressed by their traditional names; others wanted to be called by American nicknames. Once this problem was resolved, communication improved significantly.

Later in the program, the executives were divided into teams and actually sent to different sites abroad. Each team experienced a variety of activities intended to provide new insights into international business. For example, the team sent to India was assigned to work through the legendary red tape of the Indian government bureaucracy to meet the local managers they had been sent to visit.

How well did the program work? Most of the participants agreed that it was a rousing success. But the participants and the organizers agreed that no one can really learn how to be an international manager in only five weeks. Nevertheless, the program did represent an important first step in enhancing the participants' awareness of the opportunities and challenges of international business.

REFERENCES: Shawn Tully, "The Hunt for the Global Manager," *Fortune*, May 21, 1990, pp. 140–144; Jeremy Main, "How 21 Men Got Global in 35 Days," *Fortune*, November 6, 1989, pp. 71–76; Jeremy Main, "How to Go Global — And Why," *Fortune*, August 28, 1989, pp. 70–76.

Some people start their own firms right out of school. Some work for a large business for a while and then step out on their own. Some spend their entire careers working for one or more large companies. People also change jobs occasionally, to advance or to learn new skills or because they are (or feel they are) no longer needed in their current organization.

Although "job hopping" — working in a job for only a few years before moving to another — has some negative connotations (to people who stay in one organization) and can lead to problems (such as questions about a person's loyalty), many managers change jobs several different times in their careers. For example, Robert Crandall, CEO of American Airlines, worked for Eastman Kodak, Hallmark Cards, Trans World Airlines, and Bloomingdale's before joining American in 1973. In contrast, Donald Petersen, recently retired CEO of Ford Motor Company, spent his entire career working for that organization.

Figure 1.2

The Three Organizational Functions

Managing Strategy
Determining what the organization
wants to do and how it intends to do it

↓

Managing Structure
Creating the framework of jobs, relationships
among jobs, and operational systems and processes
that an organization uses to carry out its strategy

↓

Managing Behavior
Understanding how and why people in
organizational settings behave as they do

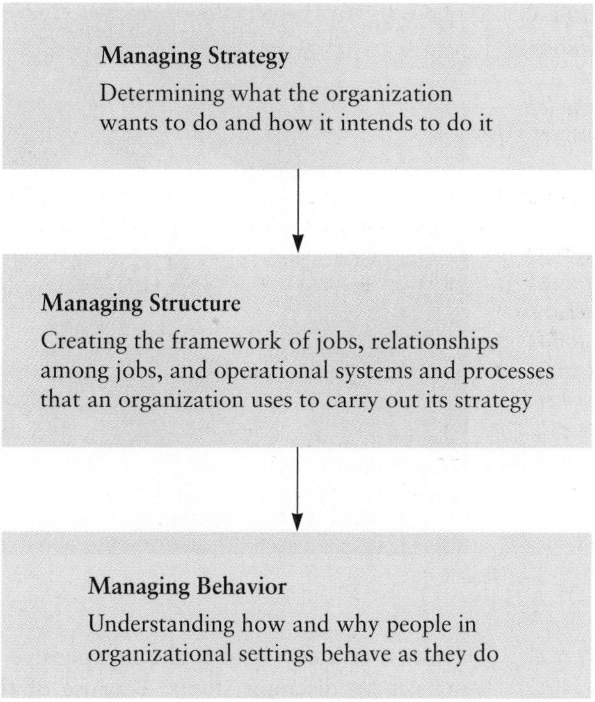

The Three Main Organizational Functions

The three functions of managers in organizations are managing strategy, managing structure, and managing behavior.

Regardless of level, area, or career path, managers carry out three main functions that engage every organization. Recall our description of an organization: a collection of *people* working together in a *coordinated and structured* fashion toward one or more *goals*. This definition reflects the three organizational functions, as Figure 1.2 shows. The first function, *managing strategy,* involves establishing goals and deciding how to reach them through various facets of strategic management. The second function, *managing structure,* focuses on creating and coordinating the means for achieving those goals. The third function, *managing behavior,* includes motivating people to behave in ways that support the organization's strategies.[7] As we explain more fully later, these three organizational functions provide the framework around which this book is organized.

Managing Strategy

A *strategy* is a statement of what the organization wants to do and how it intends to do it.

The first function that any organization must address is managing its strategy. A **strategy** is a statement of what the organization wants to do and how it intends to do it. For example, Rolex and Timex are both in the same industry, but each company has developed a distinct strategy that sets it apart from the other. Rolex's strategy is to make high-fashion, high-quality watches that are sold at premium prices in fine jewelry stores.

A key function that must be addressed by all organizations is managing strategy. Joseph A. Unanue shown here on the left with his brother, Francisco, is CEO of Goya Foods Inc. Goya, a company that specializes in ethnic foods such as olive oil and exotic spices, controls over 80 percent of the Hispanic foods market. Because that market has grown so rapidly, larger food producers like Campbell and CPC are beginning to market ethnic foods as well. Consequently, Goya is having to adjust its strategy to compete with these larger firms.

Strategic management involves positioning the organization in its environment and then formulating and implementing strategy.

Timex's strategy is to make inexpensive watches that are sold to a mass market by discount stores. Because of the differences in their strategies, Rolex and Timex differ markedly in terms of the quality, price, and image of their product lines.

Strategic management is a broad set of activities that includes positioning the organization in its competitive environment and formulating and implementing strategy. Managers must develop and maintain a keen understanding of the environment in which the organization operates, from general economic conditions to the specific actions of competitors. If managers ignore or misjudge an important component of the organizational environment, any number of problems can result. For years U.S. auto firms virtually ignored their Japanese competitors until it was almost too late to regain their competitive standing. In contrast, Microsoft's early entry into foreign markets gave it an edge over other U.S. software manufacturers. A firm that understands and anticipates its environment has a real advantage over its competitors.

The true heart of strategic management consists of the complementary activities of formulating and then devising ways of implementing strategy. A few years ago General Motors determined that it needed to create a new line of cars to compete against Japanese carmakers. During strategy formulation, GM managers decided to establish an entirely new division called Saturn. Implementation of that strategy involved building a new plant, designing the new car, creating a dealer network, and putting the car into production.

Other strategic management activities are making decisions, setting goals and making plans, and managing innovation. Decision making spans all organizational activities, but the decisions made during strategic management have far-reaching effects. Rolex managers long ago decided to stress quality and image; their counterparts at Timex decided to emphasize low price and practicality. These initial decisions still guide both organizations today. Managers also play a prominent role in setting goals and planning ways to achieve them. Businesses set profit goals, and universities set goals for enrollments and research funding levels. Museums set goals for donations, and the military sets goals for re-enlistment rates.

Part of managing strategy is determining how much emphasis the organization will place on innovation and encouraging employee creativity. Some firms, such as Gillette, International Business Machines (IBM), and Procter & Gamble, emphasize innovation and always seek to be at the forefront of development. Other companies, such as Schick, Unisys, and Lever Brothers, tend to let other firms invest in research and development and then follow their lead. Many Japanese firms wait for and adopt American innovations and then use their manufacturing advantages to outsell their American counterparts.

To understand how the various strategic management activities work together, consider the recent history of the Disney organization. When Michael Eisner became CEO of Disney in the early 1980s, the entertainment giant lacked direction and vision. Eisner evaluated the firm and its environment and realized that Disney was not capitalizing on its strengths and competitive advantages. He decided to expand the company aggressively in several different areas, and he formulated several strategies for doing so. To implement those strategies, Disney opened the MGM/Disney Studio at Disney World and Euro Disneyland in France, announced plans for a new park in California, established a new movie studio (Hollywood Pictures), established a new record label (Hollywood Records), built several new hotels, and initiated a variety of other new ventures. For each of these projects Eisner set specific goals for growth.[8]

Managing Structure

Structure is the framework of jobs, relationships among jobs, and operational systems and processes that an organization uses to carry out its strategy.

The second function that any organization must address is developing and managing its structure. **Structure** is the framework of jobs, relationships among jobs, and operational systems and processes that an organization uses to carry out its strategy. Structure is the means by which the organization achieves its goals.

By definition, most organizations are characterized by similar structural components. They all have jobs or tasks that must be performed, and those jobs or tasks must be logically related so that work proceeds efficiently and effectively. Decisions that a manager makes as part of developing organization structure include deciding what jobs must be performed, how they will be performed, and how they relate to one another. Keep in mind, however, that each organization is unique and that the structure that one organization specifically creates and uses effectively may not work for another. Even though both IBM and Unisys make computers, their structures are different. But their structures are more alike than they are similar to the structure of the Ohio State University or the Swiss Army.

Given that the building blocks of any organization are its jobs or tasks, managers must closely attend to the people who perform those jobs or tasks. The management of human resources is a vital part of managing structure. Key issues to address include specifying the types of employees that the organization desires, hiring them, training them, evaluating their performance, and rewarding them.

Just as the jobs and tasks performed by individuals within the organization must be coordinated and linked, so, too, must larger units such as divisions and operating departments. The mechanism for achieving this broader coordination is the flow of information through the organization. Ensuring that information is distributed and used effectively is a crucial aspect of managing structure.

Operations management is also important. Operations is the set of activities that allow the organization to transform inputs into outputs. Manufacturing firms use operations management to transform raw materials into finished products. The U.S. Postal Service uses operations management to process mail, and universities use operations management to schedule classes. Because the structure of the organization reflects relationships among jobs and tasks, it largely determines how operations are managed. Likewise, specific requirements of operations dictate certain aspects of structure.

No structure is perfect. Even if an organization develops a structure that works very well, its effectiveness may eventually subside as the environment or the organization's strategy changes. Hence it is important for organizations to monitor and adjust their structure as appropriate to keep themselves on target toward their goals. This monitoring process is called organizational control.

Managing Behavior

Managing behavior involves understanding how and why people in organizations behave as they do and then using that understanding to benefit both the organization and its people.

The third organizational function that an organization must address is managing the behavior of its members. We have already noted that as part of managing structure the organization hires people and assigns them to jobs. But people are not robots that can be ordered around nonchalantly. To be truly successful, managers must acknowledge and understand the personalities and needs of their subordinates, peers, and superiors. Thus, from an organizational perspective, managing behavior involves understanding the behavior of people in organizational settings and then applying that understanding to benefit both the organization and its people.

As a starting point, organizations must allow for the fact that every human being is unique. People work for a variety of reasons, respond to stimuli differently, and perceive reality in their own ways. Accepting this is the first step in managing behavior.

Leadership skills and the ability to influence others are important tools for managers. Individuals must often be motivated to work in ways that are consistent with the goals and needs of the organization. On any given day, employees may choose to work diligently, just hard enough to get by, or not at all. It is often up to the individual manager both to encourage people to do their best and to be able to recognize whether stress is keeping people from working effectively.

Although an organization's work force is made up of individuals, few of them work in isolation. Employees communicate with one another as they perform their jobs. Managers communicate as they develop plans and make decisions, and managers and employees communicate as they discuss projects, performance, and rewards. Insight into interpersonal communication can help managers understand how people relate to one another in organizations and what makes some groups of people work together well while other groups experience conflict. Group conflict may promote healthy competition and lead to innovative solutions to problems or be divisive and counterproductive. Understanding the nature of conflict and how to handle it is therefore an important part of managing behavior.

All organizations must address three main functions: managing strategy, managing structure, and managing behavior. The Entrepreneurial Challenge describes how Sam Walton carried out these functions when he founded one of the most successful new ventures in American history — Wal-Mart Corporation.

The Strategy and Structure of This Book

We mentioned earlier that the three functions of organizations — managing strategy, managing structure, and managing behavior — define the framework for this book. The plan for the book appears in Figure 1.3, which is an elaboration of Figure 1.2. We have structured the material for this course in order to fulfill our strategy: to provide an integrated picture of the world of organizations.

This chapter is the first of a three-chapter sequence that sets the context for further discussion. Chapter 2 discusses the history and theory of management, and Chapter 3 identifies the challenges that contemporary organizations face. Part II of the book examines the fundamentals of managing strategy. Separate chapters cover the environment of organizations, decision making, goals and planning, strategy formulation, strategy implementation, and innovation and creativity.

Part III focuses on the elements of managing structure. The chapters in this part cover organization structure, design, and control, information systems, human resource management, and operations management. Managing behavior is the subject of Part IV. The topics covered in these chapters are individual behavior, motivation, leadership, group dynamics, communication, and conflict and stress. Part V integrates the discussions of strategy, structure, and behavior with three chapters on ethics and social responsibility, organization change, and entrepreneurship and small business management.

THE ENTREPRENEURIAL CHALLENGE

A Country Start-Up Success Story

Sam Walton was just a single man who wanted to open his own store. He was successfully managing a Ben Franklin variety store in the early 1960s but wanted to do something new. Walton first tried to convince Ben Franklin executives that they should start opening discount stores to compete with the increasing number of K marts that were springing up around the country.

The company rejected his idea, and Walton set out on his own. Conventional wisdom at the time suggested that a retailer needed a population base of 50,000 to succeed with a large discount store. Walton rejected that notion, however, and developed the strategy of opening his stores in small towns. He opened his first Wal-Mart in tiny Rogers, Arkansas, in 1962. The store struggled at first, but its low prices and the entrepreneurial enthusiasm that Walton brought to work every day soon made it profitable.

From the very beginning, Walton insisted on keeping prices lower than the competition and stressing customer service and satisfaction. He plowed all his personal savings into the venture and soon began to open more stores. The time necessary to make a store profitable shortened with each successive opening.

Walton was able to keep his new venture growing because he had planned its organization in advance. He insisted on tight controls so that prices could be as low as possible. He set up an elaborate distribution system and an information system at company headquarters that allowed him to communicate by satellite with every Wal-Mart store in America.

Walton also worked hard to establish good relations with his employees. Wal-Mart employees were among the first in the retailing industry to be called "associates," rather than "clerks" or "checkers." Retailing is generally a low-paying industry, and Wal-Mart is no exception. But the company goes to great lengths to promote from within and give talented people an opportunity to advance.

How successful has the firm been? Wal-Mart is the fastest-growing retailer in the world and recently became the largest. Annual revenues are increasing at a rate of over 40 percent per year. A $1,000 investment in Wal-Mart's first public stock offering in 1970 would be worth half a million dollars today. The incredible part in the story of Wal-Mart's success is that the firm has stores in only twenty-five states! But that, too, is changing, as Wal-Mart expands aggressively throughout the United States.

REFERENCES: John Huey, "Wal-Mart — Will It Take Over the World?" *Fortune*, January 30, 1989, pp. 52–64; Bill Saporito, "Retailing's Winners & Losers," *Fortune*, December 18, 1989, pp. 69–80; "Little Touches Spur Wal-Mart's Incredible Growth," *Wall Street Journal*, September 22, 1989, pp. B1, B4; "Leaders of the Most Admired," *Fortune*, January 29, 1990, pp. 40–54.

Managerial Roles and Skills

Organizations must accomplish the main functions of managing strategy, structure, and behavior, but it falls to individual managers to execute these functions. To do so, they must perform certain roles within the organization and bring certain skills to their jobs. These roles and skills are the focus of this section.

Important Roles of Managers

There are ten *roles* that managers may play as they carry out their jobs.

Research has suggested that many managers may have to fulfill as many as ten roles in their jobs.[9] In this context, a role is a specific set of behaviors that the manager has to exhibit. These roles are shown in Figure 1.4.

The three interpersonal roles are the *figurehead, leader,* and *liaison.*

Interpersonal Roles Three managerial roles involve interactions between the manager and other people. The three roles are called the figurehead, the leader, and the liaison. The **figurehead role** involves representing the organization in a symbolic or ceremonial fashion. For example, Jack Welch, CEO of General Electric, recently attended the ribbon-cutting ceremony

Figure 1.3

The Plan for This Book

(1) World of organizations
(2) History and theory
(3) Organizational challenges

Managing Strategy

(4) Environment
(5) Decision making
(6) Goals and planning
(7) Strategy formulation
(8) Strategy implementation
(9) Creativity and innovation

Managing Structure

(10) Organization structure
(11) Organization design
(12) Organization control
(13) Information systems
(14) Human resources management
(15) Operations management

Managing Behavior

(16) Individual behavior
(17) Motivation
(18) Leadership
(19) Group dynamics
(20) Communications
(21) Conflict and stress

(22) Ethics and social responsibility
(23) Organization change
(24) Entrepreneurship and
    small business management

As president of Radcliffe College, Linda Wilson performs a variety of important roles: decisional, informational, and interpersonal. Leading the Harvard Band, she acts in a figurehead role, representing the organization in a symbolic manner.

for a new manufacturing facility in France. This activity was a part of the figurehead role.

The **leader role** is played whenever the manager carries out the leadership function. It may manifest itself in very specific ways, such as when the manager attempts to inspire and motivate others to perform their jobs more effectively. Welch does this whenever he meets with division heads and exhorts them to enhance the performance of their respective units. The leader role is also carried out in most daily activity as the manager leads her or his subordinates.

The **liaison role** involves coordinating the activities of two or more units or groups. Indeed, without such coordination, work groups might not be working toward the same goals or with the same assumptions. Welch occasionally has to coordinate the activities of some of the businesses that General Electric owns. For example, he might help arrange discounted advertising rates for GE's appliance business on the NBC television network (another GE business). He must also coordinate the activities of various executive committees and task forces.

The three informational roles are the monitor, disseminator, and spokesperson.

Informational Roles   Managers fill three informational roles, which facilitate the transmission of information between people. These three roles are

Figure 1.4

Ten Roles in the Manager's Job

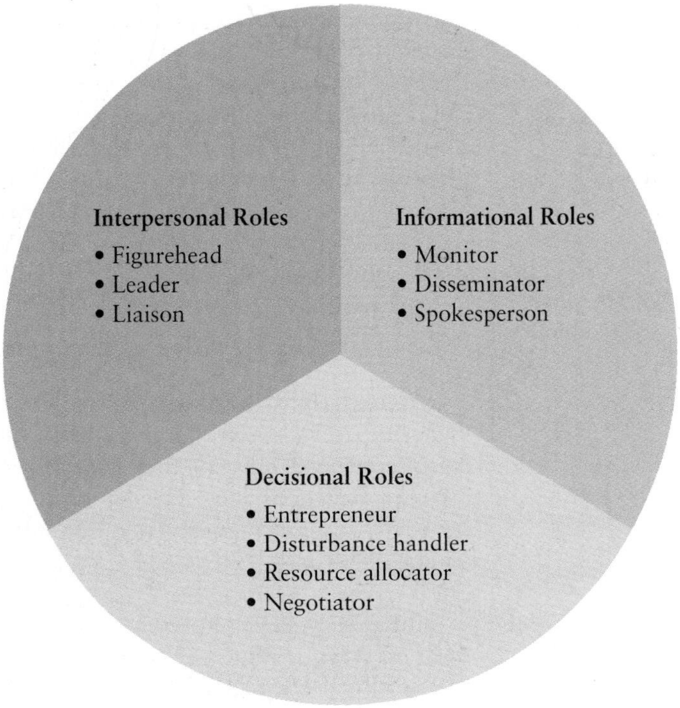

Interpersonal Roles
- Figurehead
- Leader
- Liaison

Informational Roles
- Monitor
- Disseminator
- Spokesperson

Decisional Roles
- Entrepreneur
- Disturbance handler
- Resource allocator
- Negotiator

called monitor, disseminator, and spokesperson. The **monitor role** is played when the manager seeks information that may be of value to the organization. For example, when Jack Welch reads the *Wall Street Journal* or examines government business forecasts for information about inflation projections, he is playing the role of monitor.

The **disseminator role** involves transmitting information to others who may find it useful. For example, suppose Welch comes across an article in the *Wall Street Journal* about a proposed new government regulation that could affect how the firm reports foreign income. When he passes it along to his chief financial officer, he is filling the disseminator role.

The **spokesperson role** is played when the manager speaks for the organization in a substantive fashion (in contrast to serving as a figurehead, which is a purely symbolic role). For example, when Welch appears at a press conference to announce a major new acquisition by GE, he is being a spokesperson for the organization.

The four decisional roles are the *entrepreneur, disturbance handler, resource allocator,* and *negotiator.*

Decisional Roles The four decisional roles of managers are the entrepreneur, the disturbance handler, the resource allocator, and the negotiator. The role of **entrepreneur,** in this context, comes into play when the manager voluntarily works to initiate change within the organization. A few years ago, Jack Welch essentially traded GE's electronics business to the French firm Thomson for that company's medical equipment business. His role was that of entrepreneur.

The role of **disturbance handler** must be played when there is a conflict or major problem within the organization that the manager must address. Deciding how to respond to a union strike threat falls into this category. The **resource allocator** decides how the organization's resources will be divided among people or units. At a large firm such as General Electric, there are always a wide variety of potential uses for funds. Deciding which markets to pursue most vigorously is a part of this role. Finally, the manager must sometimes be a **negotiator**. After Welch decided to exchange businesses with Thomson, the two parties still had to reach detailed agreement on the financial terms, when the changeover would occur, and how certain fringe operations would be handled.

It is important to recognize that the mix of roles varies for different managers, for different organizations, and over periods of time. Some managers spend most of their workday filling only a few of these roles; other managers assume a wider array of roles. These ten roles reflect a large part of many managerial jobs, but they by no means can be considered all-encompassing.

Crucial Managerial Skills

Most successful managers have technical, interpersonal, conceptual, and *diagnostic skills.*

Another determinant of an organization's ability to carry out its basic functions is the skill mix of its managers. In general, most successful managers have a strong combination of technical, interpersonal, conceptual, and diagnostic skills.[10]

Technical skills are necessary to accomplish specialized tasks within the organization.

Technical Skills   **Technical skills** are those skills necessary to accomplish specialized tasks within the organization. Assembling a computer, developing an additive for a laundry detergent, and writing a press release are technical skills. David Packard and Bill Hewlett, founders of Hewlett-Packard, started their careers as engineers, and they still work hard to keep abreast of new technology. Their technical skills are an important part of their success as managers. Other managers with strong technical skills include David Glass (CEO of Wal-Mart), who started his career as a store manager, and William Wrigley (CEO of Wm. Wrigley Corp.), who learned to make gum when he was a child.

Interpersonal skills enable the manager to communicate with, understand, and motivate individuals and groups.

Interpersonal Skills   **Interpersonal skills** enable the manager to communicate with, understand, and motivate individuals and groups. Since managers spend such a large portion of their time interacting with others, it is clearly important for them to be able to relate to, and get along with, other people. Unfortunately, some managers are surprisingly lacking in this area. Thus they come across as aloof and insensitive and fail as leaders because they are not empathetic. Frank Lorenzo, former CEO of Texas Air Corporation, had a reputation for being moody, antagonistic, and sneaky. In contrast, Roy Vagelos, CEO of Merck, is one of the most admired business leaders in America. Part of his success is attributable to the fact that he makes a conscious effort to get acquainted with people in the firm, treats them with dignity and respect, and is always open and direct when he talks to them.[11]

Conceptual skills reflect the manager's ability to think in the abstract.

Conceptual Skills **Conceptual skills** reflect the manager's ability to think in the abstract. A manager with strong conceptual skills is able to see the "big picture." She or he can envision potential or opportunity where others see nothing but roadblocks or problems. Managers with strong conceptual skills can recognize opportunities that others miss. For example, after Steve Wozniak and Steve Jobs designed and built a small computer, Wozniak simply viewed it as a new toy to tinker with in his spare time. Jobs, however, saw far more potential than this and convinced his partner that they should start a company to make and sell the computers. Thus was born Apple Computer, Inc.

Diagnostic skills reflect the manager's ability to understand cause-and-effect relationships and to find the optimal solution to problems.

Diagnostic Skills **Diagnostic skills** reflect the manager's ability to understand cause-and-effect relationships and to recognize the optimal solution to problems. For example, Robert Goizueta, CEO of Coca-Cola, was concerned that the firm's stock price was not as high as he thought it should be. Upon closer analysis, he discovered the reason: the company was focusing too much attention on increasing sales without proper consideration of actual profits. He reoriented the firm's goals toward enhancing returns to shareholders and, as a consequence, has achieved record stock prices. Goizueta needed diagnostic skills to see what needed to be done.[12]

Not every manager has equal measures of these four types of skills, nor are equal measures critical to managerial success. As Figure 1.5 shows, the optimal skills mix tends to vary with the level that the manager occupies

Figure 1.5

Managerial Skill Mixes at Different Levels of the Organization

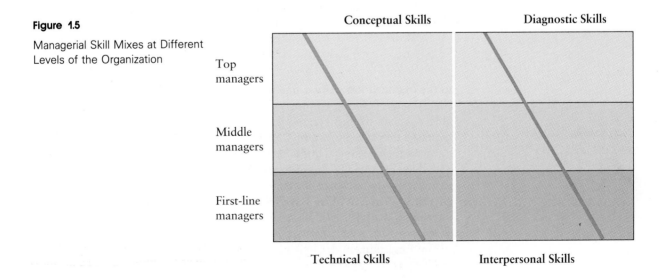

THE ENVIRONMENTAL CHALLENGE

Business Is Where You Find It

Around the world, organizations of every stripe are coming under increasing scrutiny regarding their role in protecting the environment. For years, manufacturers dumped their wastes into the air and into streams and oceans. Packaging for consumer products, such as the Styrofoam containers used by McDonald's and plastic bottles used for many different household products, has also contributed enormously to the waste disposal problems that abound today. Although people associate pollution with large urban centers such as New York and Los Angeles, smaller cities suffer as well. Many cities in eastern Europe are among the most polluted.

But where there are problems, astute managers can often find opportunities. Toxic waste disposal was first recognized as a significant problem around fifteen years ago. In the early 1980s, Alan McKim borrowed $13,000 from friends, bought a specially equipped truck, and opened a waste cleanup business called Clean Harbors Inc. in Massachusetts. Today, McKim's business has a fleet of two hundred trucks and annual revenues exceeding $100 million.

McDonald's has also taken action. Partially in response to negative publicity and partially out of genuine environmental concern, the fast-food giant has become a major proponent of recycling. McDonald's has recently stopped using ozone-depleting Styrofoam

and gone back to paper wrappers. The firm has also made a major commitment to educating the public about environmental issues.

The environmental movement in Europe is profoundly affecting the business community. Some firms, such as Coca-Cola and PepsiCo, have suffered in Europe because of tight packaging restrictions. But others have benefited. Procter & Gamble, for example, has been successful in Great Britain with a disposable diaper made from pulp that is bleached without using toxic chlorine gas.

In every case, managers faced with decisions that affect and are affected by the environment must rely on all their skills to help them make the choice that is best for their organization and the environment. Both 3M and Du Pont, for example, are doing far more than is required by law to combat pollution at their manufacturing facilities. Some might see in this effort merely a profit motive, but society is still likely to benefit from it.

REFERENCES: David Kirkpatrick, "Environmentalism: The New Crusade," *Fortune*, February 12, 1990, pp. 44–52; Stratford P. Sherman, "Trashing a $150 Billion Business," *Fortune*, August 28, 1989, pp. 90–98; Shawn Tully, "What the 'Greens' Mean for Business," *Fortune*, October 23, 1989, pp. 159–164; "The Big Haul in Toxic Waste," *Newsweek*, October 3, 1988, pp. 38–39.

in the organization. A first-line manager, for example, spends a lot of time supervising operating employees. It follows that these managers need to be able to relate to and communicate with those employees and understand the tasks they are performing. First-line managers generally need to depend more on their technical and interpersonal skills and less on their conceptual and diagnostic skills. In contrast, because top managers focus more on strategic issues and broader concerns, conceptual and diagnostic skills are critical to them, and they have somewhat less dependence on technical and interpersonal skills. Middle managers require a more even distribution of skills.

The Environmental Challenge describes how some managers are using these skills to clean up — in an entirely new industry.

The Nature of Managerial Work

Managerial work is characterized by variety, spontaneity, fragmentation, and interruption.

Even though managers play a variety of roles and use a range of skills that can be listed, and even though they are responsible for specific organizational functions, their work is anything but predictable. Indeed, the typical manager's workday is characterized by variety, spontaneity, fragmentation, and interruption.

On average, managers spend around 59 percent of their time in scheduled meetings and another 10 percent in unscheduled meetings. They spend around 22 percent of their time at their desks, reading or writing correspondence or reports, and over 6 percent on the telephone. The remaining time is spent walking around organizational facilities, observing, and talking with people spontaneously. Managers get anywhere from three to four dozen pieces of mail each day and almost as many telephone calls. Less than half of how they will spend their time each day can be predicted beforehand. Even though schedules and agendas can be set in advance, there are always surprises.

All this implies that managers need a great deal of enthusiasm, patience, and flexibility. They must be astute decision makers and warm and caring human beings. They must be efficient, use their time wisely, know when to take action, and know when to sit and wait. Little wonder, then, that so many people find management to be simultaneously a challenging, invigorating, frustrating, rewarding, and demanding profession.

Organizations in the Global Era

In recent years most organizations have increasingly been affected by the emergence of a global marketplace and a global economy. Numerous trends in international business have profoundly changed the way all organizations function. In this section we characterize the nature of global organizations and their managers.

Global Organizations

Not all that long ago the United States was the world's dominant economic power. American firms controlled most major markets, from audio equipment to zippers. In this country "Made in Japan" was a synonym for poor quality, and business executives perceived Europe as a bunch of quaint hamlets with little real industry. No more. Business is booming around the globe, and organizations that don't pay attention are being left behind. We are rapidly moving toward a global economy with a handful of major marketplaces. North America, Europe, Japan, and the Pacific Rim (Taiwan, Australia, South Korea, Singapore, and their Pacific neighbors) collectively dominate this global economy today.

Organizations are increasingly confronting both global threats and global opportunities. In doing so, they often seek joint ventures or other reciprocal projects with organizations in other countries. These partnerships may involve unusual and creative arrangements. Nippon Television Network Corporation is partially funding restoration of Michelangelo's work in the Sistine Chapel in return for temporary reproduction rights to the art.

Four different levels of international activity are represented by *domestic, international, multinational,* and *global organizations.*

Some organizations have operated on a global scale for decades. The Red Cross has maintained operations around the world since it was founded in Switzerland in 1863. In recent years, though, the number and variety of organizations seeking to establish a global identity has dramatically increased. As Figure 1.6 shows, a **domestic organization** is one that acquires its resources and derives its revenues within a single country and is relatively unaffected by international competition. There are few, perhaps no, large purely domestic organizations in existence today. A regional bakery that produces bread and distributes it to local groceries might fit this profile. Many small businesses may seem to be domestic, but most carry foreign products or compete with foreign businesses.

An **international organization** is one that is based in a single country but has some operations in a few other countries. Paramount Communications Corporation is an international organization. Most Paramount movies are made and distributed in the United States. A few are made abroad, however, and most are eventually distributed abroad through foreign distribution networks. A **multinational organization** is an organization that is based in one home country but has extensive operations in several other countries. Ford Motor Company is a U.S. firm, but Ford has subsidiaries and manufacturing facilities all around the world. Ford makes cars in Europe that are never sold in the United States.

A **global organization** is one that transcends national boundaries and operates on a global scale. Just as there are few, if any, purely domestic organizations today, the truly global organization probably does not yet exist. But some organizations are clearly moving in this direction. For example, the Dutch electronics firm Philips derives 94 percent of its sales and has 85 percent of its assets outside the Netherlands. Moreover, 46 percent of its stock is held outside the Netherlands, and the firm has a large contingent of foreign managers at all levels. Although Philips is still considered a Dutch firm, its base of operations is the world.[13]

Internationalization is an organization's progression from domestic to international activity or from international to multinational activity. *Globalization* is the progression of a multinational organization to a truly global one.

Many organizations are moving along the continuum shown in Figure 1.6, from the domestic toward the global. An organization undergoing **internationalization** is attempting to move from domestic to international, or perhaps from international to multinational, activity. In the later stages, as multinational organizations evolve toward the global scope, the process might be more aptly called **globalization.**[14]

A number of factors are behind this trend toward globalization. Increased communication and transportation technologies have made it much easier to do business abroad. Saturated domestic markets have prompted organizations to seek new markets in other countries. As a result, the relative dominance of the world economy by the United States is gradually diminishing. In 1960, 70 of the world's 100 largest businesses were American. By 1970, the figure had dropped to 64 and by 1985 to 45. In 1990, 33 of the world's 100 largest firms were American. Companies like Toyota, Hitachi, Nippon Steel (all based in Japan), Royal Dutch/Shell Group, Daimler-Benz, Renault (based in Europe), Samsung (South Korea), PEMEX (Mexico), and Elders IXL (Australia) are now among the largest businesses in the world. American firms like Coca-Cola, Disney, and Texaco are increasingly looking for foreign markets. Tokyo banks exert enormous influence in world financial markets; medical centers in London and Paris are gaining worldwide respect; and universities are establishing branch campuses abroad.

Global Managers

As the world of organizations becomes increasingly global, managers must adopt a global orientation to be successful. Increasingly, managers are

Figure 1.6

Stages of International Business Activity

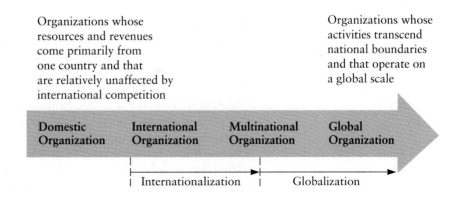

Organizations whose resources and revenues come primarily from one country and that are relatively unaffected by international competition

Organizations whose activities transcend national boundaries and that operate on a global scale

Domestic Organization International Organization Multinational Organization Global Organization

Internationalization   Globalization

studying foreign languages and seeking international assignments. Consider, for example, the case of Jan Prising, a Swedish citizen who runs an American firm based in Italy. He speaks five languages (but not Italian!). After working for Electrolux for twenty-one years, Prising was lured to his current job by a headhunting firm a few years ago. (A headhunter is an organization that identifies prospective managers who can be hired away from other organizations; headhunting itself was almost unheard of outside the United States until recently.)[15] As a result of his background and experiences, Prising almost certainly has a better understanding of international business than many other managers.

Of course, not all managers handle international issues on a day-to-day basis. In locally owned businesses of large multinational organizations, most managers below the very top levels focus primarily on domestic competition. Carnation, for example, owned by the Swiss firm Nestlé, employs many managers who are U.S. born and educated and who deal almost exclusively with the firm's U.S. competitors. The key to succeeding in a global economy is recognizing the importance and pervasiveness of internationalization and, eventually, globalization and being prepared in the event one must confront it.[16]

Many books in the management field discuss international issues in a separate chapter. Since this practice tends to make an artificial distinction between international and global issues and other organizational activities, we have chosen to integrate this discussion throughout the text. Many of the examples reflect international issues, as do many photographs and accompanying captions. Each chapter concludes with two cases, the second of which represents an international organization, and each chapter includes a boxed insert entitled "The Global Challenge."

Learning Summary

Organizations are collections of people working together in a coordinated and structured fashion toward one or more goals. Some are large profit-seeking organizations; some are start-up profit-seeking organizations; and some are small profit-seeking organizations. Others — including government, educational, health care, religious, and interest group organizations — are nonprofit organizations.

The management process is a set of activities directed at combining resources efficiently and effectively and in ways that contribute to the achievement of the organization's goals. All organizations use financial, physical, human, and information resources.

Managers are individuals whose primary activities are to carry out the management process. There are many different kinds of managers. The general levels of management are top, middle, and first-line. Common areas of management are marketing, finance, operations, and human resources.

There are three main functions that all organizations and their managers must address. First, managing strategy is deciding what the organization wants to do and how it intends to do it. Strategic management involves positioning the organization in its competitive environment, formulating strategy, and then implementing that strategy. Second, managing structure is developing the framework of jobs, relationships among jobs, and operational systems and processes that an organization uses to carry out its strategy. Third, managing behavior involves understanding how and why people in organizational settings behave as they do and then using that understanding to benefit both the organization and its people.

Managers are often called upon to play any of ten interpersonal, informational, and decisional roles. They must also rely on conceptual, technical, interpersonal, and diagnostic skills to help them effectively carry out the organizational functions for which they are responsible. Managerial work is often fragmented and unpredictable.

The internationalization and globalization of business and the world's economy are becoming increasingly important issues for all managers. More organizations are becoming international or multinational, and some are evolving toward the global stage. As a result of these trends, many managers have had to become more global in their training and thinking. All managers must at least be aware of the international context in which they now function.

Questions and Exercises

Review Questions

1. Define the terms *organization*, *management process*, and *manager*.
2. Identify the three different levels of managers. List seven different areas of management.
3. What are the three main functions of managers in organizations?
4. Identify ten important managerial roles. Give an example of each.
5. Describe the general nature of managerial work in terms of its routineness and predictability.
6. In what ways are people important to an organization?

Analysis Questions

1. In the text you saw that different managerial skills are important depending on the levels of management. Explain similarly how managerial roles might also vary with management level.
2. Relate the various managerial roles and skills to the three main organizational functions. Which roles and skills are most important in managing strategy? In managing structure? In managing behavior?
3. Identify and briefly describe five different kinds of managers in organizations with which you are familiar (your college or university, a local department store, etc.).

4. If you have an interest in an international management career, what kinds of things might you do now to be well prepared?

5. Describe the similarities and differences among the functions of managing strategy, structure, and behavior for managers of a small locally owned business, a multinational corporation, a university, and a hospital.

Application Exercises

1. Make a list of several different organizations that influence your life in a typical day. Compare your list with a classmate's. How similar or dissimilar are the lists? What examples did your classmate identify that should have been on your list?

2. Think of a manager you know. It might be a parent, a spouse, or a friend. If you don't know any managers, reflect on the job of a manager you have observed — the manager of a local hair salon, bookstore, or fast-food restaurant, for example. Write a general description of that manager's job, including the part it plays in the management of strategy, structure, and behavior as well as the roles and skills most closely associated with it.

Chapter Notes

1. "Opening of 'Windows' Shows How Bill Gates Succeeds in Software," *Wall Street Journal*, May 21, 1990, pp. A1, A6; "Microsoft Rolls Out Windows 3.0," *USA Today*, May 21, 1990, pp. 1B, 2B; "The Billion-Dollar Whiz Kid," *Business Week*, April 13, 1987, pp. 68–76; Brenton Schlender, "How Bill Gates Keeps the Magic Going," *Fortune*, June 18, 1990, pp. 82–89.

2. See Richard Daft, *Organization Theory and Design*, 4th ed. (St. Paul, Minn.: West, 1992), for a review of other definitions.

3. "The Fortune 500," *Fortune*, April 22, 1991, p. 286.

4. See Rosabeth Moss Kanter, "The New Managerial Work," *Harvard Business Review*, November–December 1989, pp. 85–92.

5. For some insightful perspectives on top-management work, see Harry S. Jones III, Ronald E. Fry, and Suresh Srivasta, "The Person of the CEO: Understanding the Executive Experience," *The Academy of Management Executive*, August 1989, pp. 205–215.

6. For details, see Kenneth Labich, "Making over Middle Managers," *Fortune*, May 8, 1989, pp. 58–64; and "When Firms Slash Middle Management, Those Spared Often Bear a Heavy Load," *Wall Street Journal*, April 4, 1990, p. B1.

7. For other perspectives on managerial and organizational functions, see Fred Luthans, "Successful vs. Effective Real Managers," *The Academy of Management Executive*, May 1988, pp. 127–132; William Whitely, "Managerial Work Behavior: An Integration of Results from Two Major Approaches," *Academy of Management Journal*, June 1985, pp. 344–362; Francis Joseph Aguilar, *General Managers in Action* (New York: Oxford University Press, 1987).

8. "Do You Believe in Magic?" *Time,* April 25, 1988, pp. 66–73.
9. Henry Mintzberg, *The Nature of Managerial Work* (New York: Harper & Row, 1973).
10. Robert L. Katz, "The Skills of an Effective Administrator," *Harvard Business Review,* September–October 1987, pp. 90–102.
11. "Leaders of the Most Admired," *Fortune,* January 29, 1990, pp. 40–54.
12. Ibid.
13. "The Stateless Corporation," *Business Week,* May 14, 1990, pp. 98–105.
14. Michael Porter, *The Competitive Advantage of Nations* (New York: Free Press, 1990).
15. Shawn Tully, "The Hunt for the Global Manager," *Fortune,* May 21, 1990, pp. 140–144.
16. Brian Dumaine, "What the Leaders of Tomorrow See," *Fortune,* July 3, 1989, pp. 48–62.

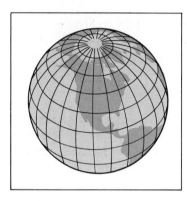

CASE 1.1

Conner Peripherals Earns the Country's Fastest Billion

The computer revolution of the last decade has made many people rich. Start-ups have grown king-size almost overnight. But no company in the history of American industry has grown as fast as Conner Peripherals, a maker of computer disk drives, which reached the billion-dollar mark in record time. In its fourth year of shipping products, Conner's revenues rose to $1.34 billion. The secrets to its success seem well worth investigating.

People, of course, are a big part of the story. Finis Conner's early years showed few indications of what was to come. The fifth son of an Alabama carpenter, he didn't earn a college degree until his late twenties, and then he began selling electronics. John Squires, the company's technical genius and other co-founder, had a somewhat more auspicious genealogy: his father was an innovative scientist who developed methods to seed clouds to make rain.

Luck helped. Conner fell in with Al Shugart, a pioneer in developing the small floppy disk drives that made the personal computer possible. The two men developed a personal relationship that paid off for both. Later, Conner met Squires in a bar during a trade show.

Ideas were crucial. Conner's success rests on one great notion — building faster, smaller, more reliable disk drives to allow ever-smaller computers to store data more efficiently. In the late 1970s, the most compact format for storing more information than a floppy disk would hold was the 8-inch hard disk used by minicomputers. Conner imagined a smaller hard disk for use in the desktop computers that were just beginning to become popular. He took his idea to his old boss, Shugart, and together they founded Seagate Technology. Computer makers loved the new 5¼-inch disk drives.

Vision separated the extraordinary from the merely successful. By 1984, Seagate was doing almost $350 million worth of business a year. The company's other partners were content to build sales with their established products, but Conner wanted to continue innovating. So he quit to go his own way.

Timing was perfect. In December 1985, John Squires called Conner. Squires was looking for help raising money for his latest invention, a smaller, faster disk drive. The two became partners in the new venture.

Connections made all the difference. Backers were wary of Conner Peripherals, one of about seventy companies vying in the small disk drive market at the time. But Conner's friend Rod Canion, CEO of Compaq Computer Corporation, liked the new disk drive and decided to use it in Compaq's computers. The deal gave Conner Peripherals cash to grow on and kept Compaq on the frontier of computer technology. Compaq paid $12 million for about half of Conner and bought all of its first year's output. Four years later, its shares were worth $367 million.

A **new approach** evolved from this relationship. Conner spent its first year designing and building disk drives specifically for Compaq's purposes, and it has developed similar relationships with its forty-odd customers ever since. Rather than designing a product, building it, and then finding a buyer for it, Conner follows the "sell, design, build" principle and keeps inventory to a minimum. First it finds a customer who will purchase the product; then it designs and builds the product to fit that customer's exact needs.

Creative **technology** is at the heart of Conner's success. Squires developed a "smart" drive: every drive has its own microprocessor that can be programmed for particular tasks. The flexibility of this design allows Conner to build a "new" drive to meet a customer's needs by modifying only a few elements of an existing drive. Conner can therefore produce custom-designed drives extremely quickly.

Conner's **innovation** is not limited to the technology of its disk drives. Ignoring industrial tradition, Conner keeps its designers one thousand miles away from its manufacturing engineers, and its manufacturing plants are on the other side of the world. Working in Colorado while the engineers work in California allows Squires and other designers to avoid getting bogged down in the manufacturing problems that engineers might puzzle them with if the two groups worked in close proximity. The company's main manufacturing plant is in Singapore, and when it decided it needed a plant closer to Europe, it found a creative way to get the plant up to speed in record time. Conner flew an entire manufacturing team from Singapore to the company's new building in Scotland, then brought Scottish workers in one at a time. Once a Scot had learned a particular part of the process, the new employee would take over and the Singapore worker would fly home. The new factory shipped its first disk drives less than three months after the company began moving in.

The elements of Conner's miraculous growth may not provide a universal recipe for organizational success, but a young entrepreneur could do much worse than follow in Finis Conner's footsteps.

Discussion Questions

1. Which of the elements of Conner Peripherals' success seem most universally applicable?
2. How many different kinds of innovation did Conner Peripherals use during its rise to the top?
3. What qualities would a manager need to run a high-tech company with such explosive growth?
4. How did Conner manage strategy, structure, and behavior?

REFERENCES: Richard Brandt, "The Disk-Drive Maker That's Driving to a Record," *Business Week*, September 14, 1987, pp. 134–138; "Earnings: Conner Tops $1B for Year," *USA Today*, January 24, 1991, p. 313; Andrew Kupfer, "America's Fastest-Growing Company," *Fortune*, August 13, 1990, pp. 48–54; "North American Profiles," *Datamation*, June 15, 1990, p. 92; "Conner's Drive is Getting a Bit Gummed Up," *Business Week*, April 29, 1991, p. 31.

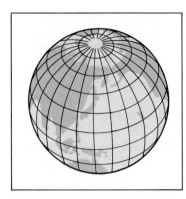

CASE 1.2

Nintendo Plays Hardball with Software

To some parents, Nintendo must seem like a disease. No one had heard of Nintendo before 1986, yet now it has infected at least one person in more than one-quarter of the nation's households. Accounting for 90 percent of U.S. video game sales, by 1990 Nintendo—a Japanese company based in Kyoto—was taking in one out of every five dollars that Americans spent on toys. And it accomplished all this in an era when everyone seemed bored with Atari and some analysts had declared home video games dead.

What is behind this phenomenal rise? The wacky creativity that characterizes the company's games certainly has something to do with it, but perhaps even more important is the company's disciplined approach to its business and its tight—some would say monopolistic—control over its products. Nintendo's success is no accident.

From some angles, Nintendo's product is simple: a small gray box that hooks up to a television set and plays the company's game cartridges. The box sells for about $100, the cartridges from $19 to $50. A Nintendo player can choose from over two hundred game cartridges, most of them more interesting and subtle than the simple shoot-the-aliens style of early video games. The company's most popular game, Super Mario Brothers, features an Italian plumber who has adventures in fantasy worlds and can turn himself into a raccoon. A recent poll showed that American schoolchildren are more familiar with Mario than with Mickey Mouse.

As you might expect, Nintendo keeps research and development designers—two hundred of them—on its payroll. They work long hours, staring at video screens, surrounded by piles of inspiration—comic books, stuffed animals, and toy vehicles.

However, Nintendo's in-house designers come up with only about one-tenth of its games—its software—and it's the company's relations with its creativity contractors that rankles many people in the business. Nintendo has developed a system that forces the contractors to shoulder the risk of developing and marketing new games but allows Nintendo to keep control. Until 1990, Nintendo insisted on manufacturing—for a fee, of course—all games that could be played on its machines, even those that another company designed and sold. Even after it relaxed its grip on making the games, it kept control over the content of the games and their packaging. The contractors still have to pay Nintendo royalties, buy certain parts from Nintendo, and agree not to make the game playable on other makes of machines.

Nintendo insists that it needs to retain such control in order to ensure that the quality of the games remains high and that the marketplace does not become flooded with hundreds of not-so-exciting games. Nintendo is haunted by the fate of Atari, which rode the crest of the first wave of home video popularity. Atari's wave broke, Nintendo thinks, because customers were overwhelmed with low-quality games from designers trying to cash in on the video craze.

Some of Nintendo's independent contractors are not complaining about the system, for when they develop a game that catches on, they can become rich quickly thanks to Nintendo's millions of devotees. That happened to Koichi Nakamura, who at age 22 created Dragonquest. The game has since sold 10 million copies. When a second version was released, Japanese police, fearing massive school absenteeism, requested that it be released for sale on a Sunday.

To avoid the Atari syndrome, Nintendo is not content to stake its future on the sales of new software for its current system. One-third of Nintendo players are adults, and the company aims to increase that figure. It counts on adults to buy its version of Jeopardy and to be attracted to Game Boy, a hand-held machine with its own screen and $20 cartridges. Adults and kids who have been unimpressed with Nintendo's graphics may be more taken with the next generation of Nintendo, which has 16-bit graphics chips, much more powerful than the current 8-bit chips. Nintendo hopes that many game players are itching for a chance to send Mario through a new and better 16-bit world of brilliant colors, solid-looking objects, and stereo sound.

Looking farther into the future, Nintendo is developing a network that will link game players through their telephone lines and perhaps eventually allow them to use the company's banking and investment network, as they do now in Japan. It has given Massachusetts Institute of Technology $3 million to come up with ways of using Nintendo-like products for educational purposes. And when the 16-bit machines take over in the United States, Nintendo will ship its stock of 8-bit machines to Europe to hook the Europeans on the games before introducing them to the new machines.

Learning from the past, looking toward the future, and using both creativity and careful management to make sure everything runs profitably in the present, Nintendo has made itself into an organization well worth watching for the next decade.

Discussion Questions

1. What are the principal challenges that Nintendo's managers must face?
2. What particular characteristics of Nintendo's organization have helped it to become so successful?
3. Nintendo's president, Hiroshi Yamauchi, has said that he doesn't really like video games. Is that attitude a barrier to his ability to manage the company well?
4. Given Nintendo's arrangement with its contractors, how do you think other companies could benefit from Nintendo's success?

REFERENCES: Susan Moffat, "Can Nintendo Keep Winning?" *Fortune,* November 5, 1990, pp. 131–136; Thane Peterson and Maria Shao, "'But I Don't Wanna Play Nintendo Anymore!'" *Business Week,* November 19, 1990, pp. 52–54; G. Pascal Zachary, "Nintendo to Ease Restrictions on U.S. Game Designers," *Wall Street Journal,* October 22, 1990, pp. B1, B4; "Nintendo's Latest Novelty Is a Price-fixing Settlement," *Wall Street Journal,* April 4, 1991, pp. B1, B2.

2

History and Theory of Organizations

LEARNING OBJECTIVES

After studying this chapter, you should be able to:

1. Describe the evolution of organizations from antiquity to the modern era.

2. Discuss historical perspectives on strategy in organizations.

3. Explain how historical perspectives on the structure of organizations have evolved.

4. Compare historical perspectives on behavior in organizations.

The History of Organizations

Organizations in Antiquity

Organizations During the Middle Ages and Renaissance

Organizations During the Industrial Revolution

Modern Organizations

Historical Perspectives on Strategy in Organizations

Adam Smith and *The Wealth of Nations*

The Theory of Perfect Competition

Industrial Organization Economics

The Porter Framework

Ricardian Economics

Theories of Distinctive Competence

Modern Strategic Management Theory

Historical Perspectives on the Structure of Organizations

Early Theories About Organization Structure

Efficiency-based Analyses

Power-based Analyses

Other Approaches to Organization Structure

Modern Theories of Organization Structure

Historical Perspectives on Behavior in Organizations

Scientific Management

The Administrative Management Movement

The Behavioral School

The Human Relations Movement

The Global Imperative

Modern Theories of Organizational Behavior

Revolutions have marked important times of transition and progress in human history. Some, like the American and the Russian revolutions, were violent political upheavals that changed the distribution of power and authority among individuals, groups, and countries. Others, like the Industrial Revolution, were major shifts in technology that altered economic relationships. Even long after a revolution has occurred, it is often difficult to disentangle the strands of political, economic, and technological change.

The period of time from the mid-1960s through the 1990s will probably be seen as a significant revolutionary era. The first steps in this revolution were taken in Holmdale, New Jersey, and Palo Alto, California, where work by small groups of scientists led, in the late 1950s, to the invention of microelectronic circuits, or "chips." They were smaller than a tenth of an inch square, but they fundamentally changed virtually every technological facet of our lives. We use them to communicate (over telephone lines), to cook (in microwave ovens), to transport ourselves (in cars and airplanes), to work (with computers, fax machines, and copy machines), to entertain ourselves (with televisions and video games), to share information (through satellite communications), and to wage war (through "smart" weapons).

While this technological revolution was unfolding, change stirred in another corner of the world. In 1980, in a shipyard in Gdansk, Poland, workers went on strike for higher wages and better working conditions. Their demand for economic self-determination spread, slowly at first, to affect much of eastern Europe. Subsequent economic and political changes culminated in the collapse of the Berlin Wall in 1989 and rearrangements in global power relationships that are still taking place.

It is difficult to know how these two revolutions — the technological and the political — will evolve over the next several decades, but organizations and the people who manage them cannot afford to ignore their implications. Learning to recognize the opportunities and risks faced by organizations in a time of revolutionary change is one of the central managerial challenges of the twenty-first century.[1]

The technological and political changes of recent years have had unpredictable and often surprising results: portable telephones, computers that fit inside a briefcase, McDonald's franchises in the Soviet Union, and Coca-Cola for sale in the People's Republic of China. In such an unpredictable and rapidly changing environment, the decisions that managers face can be pivotal to the survival of an organization. The strategies followed by the organization, the structure supporting those strategies, and the types of behavior by its members that the organization encourages are crucial decision-making areas. Modern managers can learn from the past by observing how organizations adapted to change in earlier revolutionary eras.

This chapter traces the history of organizations, and it examines theories about what organizations are and what they do. We begin by discussing the development of organizations from ancient times to the present. Then we examine how systematic thinking about organizational strategy, structure, and behavior has developed over the last several hundred years. These discussions help set the groundwork for the rest of this book and for an understanding of how strategy, structure, and behavior may best be managed in modern organizations.

The History of Organizations

Organizations of various sizes and characteristics have existed from the very beginning of recorded history. The most basic organization, the family unit, has many attributes of modern-day organizations described in Chapter 1. It consists of people who work together to achieve common goals and objectives, such as economic stability and childrearing.[2] Indeed, in many of the world's societies today, families still provide the core around which business organizations form. From the corporate offices of Du Pont to the mom-and-pop grocery stores in almost every American town, close family ties and business relationships are often indistinguishable.[3]

Organizations in Antiquity

The Sumerians were an ancient people who made extensive use of organizations.

Even in ancient times, however, many organizations existed separately from the family unit. As Figure 2.1 shows, some of the first nonfamily organizations were founded by the Sumerians, a people who settled along the southern part of the Euphrates River around 3500 B.C. Records indicate that Sumerians made extensive use of organizations in their political, religious, and economic lives. At the head of political organizations were the ruling families and other members of the elite, who established the laws of the land, raised armies, and levied taxes. Religious organizations helped define an individual's relationship to the divine and reinforced the moral values of the society. Organizations that produced the goods and services bought and sold in ancient Sumer included farms (often family-run farms), small manufacturing operations, and building associations. Trading organizations moved products from one part of the world to another. Sumerian traders traveled by camel throughout the Middle East, buying, selling, bartering, and in other ways facilitating commerce.

The demands of these organizations led to several crucial inventions. To aid commerce, the Sumerians developed a system of weights and measures,

Organizations in Antiquity	Organizations During the Middle Ages and Renaissance	Organizations During the Industrial Revolution	Modern Organizations

Prehistory	3500 B.C.	1000 B.C.	1500	1800	1900 and beyond
Family units engage in small-scale trade and production.	First nonfamily organizations emerge in Sumer and expand into Egypt, Babylonia, and Assyria. Plato's *Republic* discusses role of organizations in society. Roman Empire develops new organizations, including banks, insurance organizations, military, etc.		Small regional organizations such as guilds replace most large organizations. Catholic church remains a large, highly structured, powerful organization. Renaissance sweeps Europe, encourages new organizational forms, including international trading organizations founded in Venice and later in Amsterdam.	Steam and electrical power create strong incentives for the rise of the factory system, which has negative consequences that still plague many organizations.	New economic, competitive, global, legal, social, and workplace challenges face modern organizations.

Figure 2.1

The History of Organizations

The Greek and Roman empires developed and implemented many sophisticated organizations, some of which are still in existence.

a postal system, and a system of writing called cuneiform. In a similar way, the need for fast and efficient communications in modern organizations has driven the modern electronics revolution.

The organizational forms invented by the Sumerians were copied and extended by other societies in the ancient world. Egyptians elaborated on Sumerian political and production arrangements to manage the construction of the pyramids around 2000 B.C. The Babylonians developed trading organizations that dominated commerce throughout the Mediterranean by around 1200 B.C.[4]

By the rise of the Greek and Roman empires (around 1000 B.C. for the Greeks, around 300 B.C. for the Romans), political, religious, production, and trading organizations were widespread and quite sophisticated. Greek philosophers developed thorough analyses of the moral bases of political and economic organizations. Plato's *Republic* was one of the first books to explain how organizations should be structured and to describe their role in society. The tightly organized Roman Empire eventually assigned separate responsibilities to the church, to the government, and to commerce. The Romans had a highly developed banking system, an efficient insurance industry, courts in which businesses could sue for breach of contract, a strong military, and a political organization that enabled them to dominate the Western world. Indeed, many of the organizational forms invented by the Greeks and Romans are still in use today. For example, the structure of the Roman army, with its clearly delineated hierarchy and lines of authority, is still used by most modern armies. Also, the delegation of authority from Rome to the governors of provinces parallels, in many ways, the relationship between federal and local governments in many modern countries.[5]

The Renaissance brought with it profound changes in the types and character of organizations. During this era Venetian ambassadors to Egypt were given the responsibility for protecting trade between the two governments.

Organizations During the Middle Ages and Renaissance

With the fall of the western Roman Empire in A.D. 476, Rome was no longer the center of world politics and commerce, and the evolution of organizations took a new turn. With the exception of the Roman Catholic church, the large, sophisticated organizations that dominated the Roman world were replaced by numerous smaller organizations. Regional economies developed throughout western Europe, each dominated by local political leaders and local production and trading organizations.

Guilds were groups of medieval craftsmen who joined together to regulate their craft, train the next generation of craftsmen, and restrict the number of craftsmen in a particular location.

A significant development in the history of organizations during the Middle Ages was the guild. The **guild** was a group of craftsmen who joined together to regulate their craft, to train the next generation of craftsmen, and to restrict the number of craftsmen in any particular geographic location. Guilds performed many of the functions of modern-day unions and trade associations. Just as the stone masons guild in A.D. 1100 protected the interests of stone masons and represented those interests to the king (or other local political authority), the United Auto Workers, in the 1990s, attempts to protect the interests of automobile workers, and the American Electronics Association represents the interests of electronics companies to the U.S. government.[6]

The Roman Catholic church developed many organizational policies and practices that are still used in large organizations.

Guilds tended to be small and regional in scope during the Middle Ages. In contrast, the Roman Catholic church remained very large, highly structured, and very powerful. Many characteristics that enabled the Catholic church to survive and prosper from around A.D. 300 to the present were adopted by other organizations. Its hierarchical structure, with clearly defined job descriptions, division of labor, and authority relationships, is characteristic of nearly all modern large organizations.[7]

Trading organizations, a significant organizational development during the Renaissance, led to the invention of a wide variety of modern organizational practices.

Beginning in Italy around 1500, the Renaissance rapidly swept over western Europe, bringing radical changes in the arts, government, religion, and commerce. Scholars and artists alike rediscovered the ideas and values of the Greek and Roman cultures and sought to revive the best of these in the arts, literature, and commerce. Organizations, too, changed during this period. Guilds continued to be a major organizing force, but large international trading organizations headquartered in Venice and Amsterdam began to dominate world trade. Some of these organizations, including the Hudson Bay Company, formed in 1670 in London, still exist. Not surprisingly, organizations during the Renaissance took on many characteristics of ancient Greek and Roman organizations. Banks, insurance organizations, and courts were patterned after Roman models. In addition, Renaissance organizations developed accounting methods, checking accounts, letters of credit, and other tools of modern business. Scholars such as Niccolò Machiavelli and Leonardo da Vinci again began to analyze the role of political and commercial organizations in society and how best to manage them.[8]

Organizations During the Industrial Revolution

Up to the mid-1700s, the production of goods and services was conducted in small, decentralized units, either within homes or in small village workshops. Technology was relatively unsophisticated and widely available (simple hand tools and animal-powered equipment), so there was no need for workers to gather in a single location to engage in production. This changed with the introduction of the steam engine throughout western Europe and North America in the early 1800s. With steam power, and later with electricity, it became economically feasible to gather large numbers of workers together at a single site to operate the new machines that were capable of producing goods at a speed hitherto unknown.

The Industrial Revolution was a period of rapid technological change beginning in the early 1800s. The rise of technology led to the development of the factory system of production.

One of the benchmarks of the Industrial Revolution was the emergence of the factory system. Between 1800 and 1850 factories sprang up all over western Europe and in the Americas. Some of them employed thousands of people, all of whom needed to be assigned job responsibilities, trained, paid, and supervised. The rise of the factory system forced organizations to create management systems to take full advantage of this burgeoning work force.[9]

The Industrial Revolution had a dark side. Brutal working conditions, air and water pollution, concentration of workers in disease-ridden slums, and the general exploitation of men, women, and children were some of its social consequences. Charles Dickens gave a fair representation of the quality of life in a factory town in this passage from *Hard Times* (1854):

> It was a town of red brick, or of brick that would have been red if the smoke and ashes had allowed it; but as matters stood, it was a town of unnatural red and black, like the painted face of a savage. It was a town of machinery and tall chimneys, out of which interminable serpents of smoke trailed themselves for ever and ever, and never got uncoiled. It had a black canal in it, and a river that ran purple with ill-smelling dye, and vast piles of buildings full of windows

where there was a rattling and a trembling all day long, and where the piston of the steam engine worked monotonously up and down, like the head of an elephant in a state of melancholy madness. It contained several large streets all very like one another, and many small streets still more like one another, inhabited by people equally like one another, who all went in and out at the same hours, with the same sound upon the same pavements, to do the same work, and to whom every day was the same as yesterday and tomorrow, and every year the counterpart of the last and the next.[10]

Such conditions led to the publication of the *Communist Manifesto* (1847), by Karl Marx and Friedrich Engels, and Marx's *Das Kapital* (3 vols., 1867, 1885, 1895), as Western intellectuals began searching for alternatives to the horrors of the factory system.

One of the first people to confront some of the negative consequences of the factory system directly was Welsh industrialist Robert Owen. In the 1810's Owen improved working conditions in his cotton mills in Manchester, England, raised the minimum working age for children, provided meals for his employees, and shortened working hours. Two decades later, Andrew Ure, a Scottish chemist and professor, studied successful Scottish organizations and described the results of his research to his classes at Anderson's College in Glasgow. Many of Ure's students went on to create and manage large organizations in Europe and the United States. In America, businessman Daniel McCallum utilized some of Ure's ideas to improve organizations in the railroad industry. McCallum was one of the first to publish organization charts and to write job descriptions.

Managers like Owen, Ure, and McCallum helped organizations evolve in the early years of the Industrial Revolution. Several decades elapsed before the most negative aspects of the factory system were eliminated. Even today, factory work may subject people to repetitive, boring tasks that are harmful to their health. Modern managers' efforts to alleviate these conditions through the redesign of jobs, compensation schemes, and training are discussed in detail in Part IV of this book.[11]

Modern Organizations

Many of the challenges that faced organizations thousands of years ago are still pertinent issues today. But a new set of challenges has also arisen from the social and historical realities of the modern age. These challenges fall into five broad categories: economic, competitive, global, legal and social, and workplace challenges. The problems and opportunities that these challenges present to modern organizations and their managers are discussed in detail in Chapter 3.

The history summarized in Figure 2.1 focuses on the evolution of organizations in the Western tradition, from the "cradle of civilization" in the Middle East, through Greece and Rome, to the Industrial Revolution in western Europe, to the present. The evolution of organizations in Asia followed a somewhat different tradition. The influence of history on modern Asian organizations is discussed in The Global Challenge.

THE GLOBAL CHALLENGE

The Developoment of Asian Organizations

The Far East emerged in the 1980s as a source of managerial ideas. The so-called Five Dragons — Japan, South Korea, Taiwan, Hong Kong, and Singapore — are outperforming the United States and Europe. According to most economic indicators, "Made in Asia" has come to describe high-quality, reliable products at low or reasonably low costs.

Examining the origins of the managerial practices of the Far East provides a basis for understanding the current success of the Five Dragons. The Far Eastern nations have common cultural roots extending far back in history. Confucian origins provide a strong cultural legacy that accounts in part for many of these nations' successful organizational practices. Confucius (Kong Fu Ze), a highly placed civil servant in China around 500 B.C., became revered for his wisdom, and a group of disciples recorded his ideas on scrolls from which they studied and learned. Confucianism has four basic teachings: (1) unequal relationships between people are normal and required for a stable society; (2) the family is the model for all organizations; (3) others should be treated in the same manner as one would like to be treated oneself; and (4) all people should strive to educate themselves, work hard, and spend no more money than is necessary.

Those values, coupled with the emergence of an international marketplace and a political context that fosters economic development, gave rise to the success of the Far East. Managers in the West have been working with and studying their counterparts in the Far East to learn the secrets of this success. Managerial ideas developed in the Far East have been implemented by organizations in the United States and Europe.

Of course, blindly copying managerial practices from the Far East without considering the historical and cultural contexts in which they arose is not likely to lead to success. Only Western managers who have knowledge of the history and culture of the Far East will be able to adapt Far Eastern ideas and practices to the benefit of their organizations.

REFERENCES: David D. Van Fleet and Ricky W. Griffin, "Quality Circles: A Review and Suggested Future Directions," in *1989 International Review of Industrial & Organizational Psychology*, ed. Cary L. Cooper and Ivan Robertson (London: Wiley, 1989), pp. 213–233; Geert Hofstede and Michael Harris Bond, "The Confucius Connection: From Cultural Roots to Economic Growth," *Organizational Dynamics*, Summer 1988, pp. 5–21; Miyamoto Musashi, *A Book of Five Rings*, trans. Victor Harris (Woodstock, N.Y.: Overlook Press, 1974).

Historical Perspectives on Strategy in Organizations

Now that you have an understanding of the broad movements in the history of organizations, we can look more closely at how current ideas about strategy, structure, and behavior have developed. As suggested in Chapter 1, an organization's strategy is what an organization intends to do and how it intends to do it. Throughout the history of thought on organizational strategy, most authors have assumed that organizations have at least two main objectives: to survive over time and to maximize performance. Much of the research about organizational strategy has focused on understanding how organizations successfully accomplish these two objectives.

An organization that survives is performing just well enough to satisfy those who depend on it for goods, services, and a return on investment. An organization that is maximizing its performance is performing at a level greater than what is required for survival. An organization such as Pan American World Airways, which has just barely survived over the last several decades, has been under constant pressure from suppliers, stock-holders, and banks to fulfill its financial obligations. Indeed, Pan Am recently declared bankruptcy and is systematically selling off its assets and using this capital to satisfy the financial demands of these constituents. In contrast, organizations such as Toyota and IBM have consistently performed at a much higher level than what is required for mere survival.[12]

Figure 2.2 summarizes the development of theories about how organizations survive and how they maximize performance. In the sections that follow, we examine each of these theories and trace their integration into modern strategic management theory.

Adam Smith and The Wealth of Nations

One of the first people to describe the workings of organizational strategy was a Scottish economist named Adam Smith. A keen observer of business and commerce, Smith developed a series of simple principles that he believed explained why organizations survive and how they maximize their performance. In 1776 he published his ideas in a book titled *The Wealth of Nations*.[13]

Some of the principles identified by Adam Smith are enduring concepts in the study of organizational strategy. For example, Smith observed that organizations become more efficient as they specialize in specific productive tasks. This concept is called the **division of labor**. As different organizations specialize in different productive tasks, they become more skilled and efficient in accomplishing those tasks, and the cost of production falls below what it would be if the organizations did not specialize. The cost of making footballs at Wilson Sporting Goods is low because Wilson has a factory that specializes in making footballs. If that same factory also made baseballs, Hula-Hoops, dishwashers, and helicopters, the costs of manufacturing all these items would be much higher than at specialized factories.

The use of specialization and the division of labor implies the need for a system to coordinate production and trade among different organizations. In other words, if one organization specializes in manufacturing cars and another specializes in manufacturing tires, then somehow these two organizations must coordinate their activities to produce cars that customers can drive. Adam Smith suggested that there are two ways to coordinate these activities. First, one organization can own both the car manufacturer and the tire manufacturer. Second, the two separate organizations can be coordinated indirectly through the demands of the marketplace. One of Adam Smith's great intellectual contributions was his observation that the "invisible hand" of the marketplace can efficiently coordinate the activities of independent organizations.

Smith's concept of the "invisible hand" was based on his analysis of changes in the supply of and demand for goods and services. As organizations produce more of a certain good or service, the supply of that good or service in the market increases. If demand for that good or service remains constant, its price will fall because supply has grown to outstrip

---

Adam Smith, a Scottish economist, wrote *The Wealth of Nations* in 1776. Two key concepts set forth in this book are: (1) the economic advantages associated with the division of labor and (2) the ability of the "invisible hand" of the market to coordinate production across independent organizations.

According to the principle of the *division of labor*, as organizations specialize in different productive tasks, they become more skilled and efficient in accomplishing those tasks.

According to the principle of the "invisible hand," when organizations adjust their output and prices in response to changes in supply and demand, the independent productive activities of specialized organizations can be coordinated, indirectly, through the market.

demand. On the other hand, if demand for a good or service increases and supply remains constant, prices will rise. When an organization adjusts its level of output in response to changes in the price of its goods or services, it is letting the "invisible hand" of the market coordinate production across

Figure 2.2

The Evolution of Thinking About Organizational Strategy

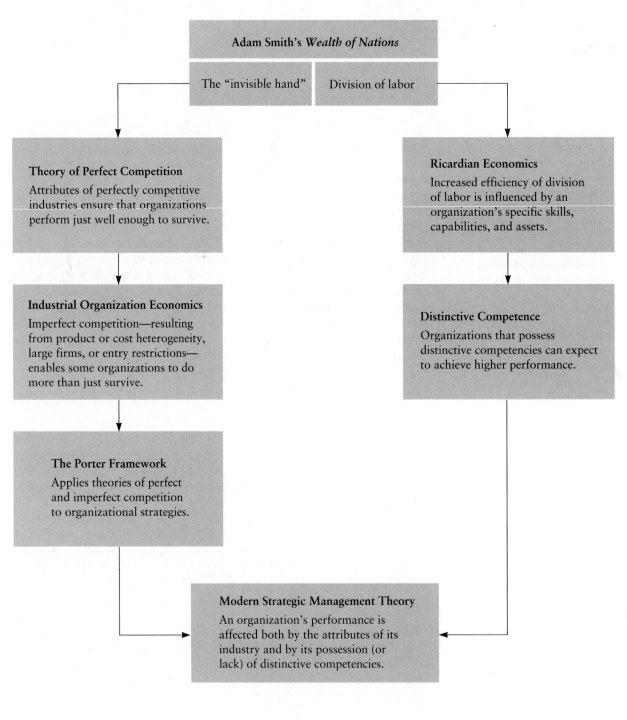

THE ENTREPRENEURIAL CHALLENGE

A Hungarian Miracle: Semilab

The high-stakes game of providing electronic instruments to microchip manufacturers features numerous large and powerful competitors. Huge multinational companies such as Siemens and Hewlett-Packard spend millions of dollars on research and development and dominate most of the market — except for one segment controlled by tiny Semilab, Inc. That a small organization like Semilab has been able to survive, and even prosper, in this highly competitive marketplace is surprise enough. That Semilab was founded in Budapest, Hungary, makes this company truly outstanding. Semilab is among a handful of start-up companies from eastern Europe exporting technology to western Europe and maybe someday to the United States.

Semilab's current product, a deep-level spectrometer, tests for impurities in a microchip. The idea for this instrument occurred to Semilab's founder, George Ferenczi, in 1982. Initially, limited access to technology and eastern European government concern about giving technological developments away to the West hampered the firm's development. Ferenczi was once reduced to selling his instruments from door to door, out of the back of his van. Since 1989, however, reduced trade restrictions have put Semilab in a good position to succeed. In 1990 sales at Semilab were $1 million and profits exceeded $300,000.

Much of Semilab's success can be attributed to the speed with which it has been able to develop new technology, despite technological and government limitations. In fact, Hewlett-Packard — an organization often cited as one of the fastest-moving high technology firms — was investigating the same technology as Semilab. Semilab actually beat Hewlett-Packard and obtained its patent first.

Now that Semilab has had success with one product, it faces the challenge of developing even newer technologies. Ferenczi has committed almost all of Semilab's $300,000 in profits to developing new technologies. The new products will use microwaves to test for impurities in semiconductors. Once again, though, Semilab is confronting government interference. As of 1991, laws prohibit the microwave technology that Semilab needs to complete its product development from being exported to Hungary from the West.

REFERENCES: Gail E. Schares, "Swimming Against the Technology Flow," *Business Week*, June 15, 1990, p. 146; Jonathon B. Levine, "The World's Hottest Chipmaker Is — Siemens?" *Business Week*, June 15, 1990, p. 142; Brian Dumaine, "How Managers Can Succeed Through Speed," *Fortune*, February 13, 1989, pp. 54–57; Brian Dumaine, "Hewlett-Packard's Whip Cracker," *Fortune*, February 13, 1989, pp. 58, 59.

organizations. When prices are low, supply is greater than demand and output needs to be reduced. When prices are high, demand is greater than supply and output can be increased.

By 1776 Adam Smith had already identified the two central features of a successful organizational strategy. First, to be successful, strategies need to exploit the particular skills and capabilities of the organization through the division of labor. Second, organizations must respond simultaneously to the marketplace and to changes in supply and demand. Only when organizations are successful at managing the division of labor and responding to the "invisible hand" of the market can they expect to survive and maximize their performance. A company that has succeeded in combining its special skills with a thorough understanding of the marketplace, despite enormous challenges, is Semilab, a Hungarian electronic instruments company. Semilab is described in detail in The Entrepreneurial Challenge.

The Theory of Perfect Competition

Adam Smith's two insights had an enormous impact on subsequent thinking in economics and organizational strategy. His idea that the "invisible hand" of the marketplace can coordinate the productive activities of thousands of independent organizations received significant early attention. Alfred Marshall, Irving Fisher, and other economists developed a theoretical model of the operation of industries that enables economists to predict the performance of organizations in those industries. This model is called the **theory of perfect competition**. According to this model, perfectly competitive industries have the following three attributes: (1) homogeneous organizations, (2) small organizations, and (3) unrestricted entry.[14]

Perfect competition characterizes an industry in which (1) organizations are homogeneous, (2) organizations are small, and (3) entry is unrestricted. Organizations in this type of industry earn normal levels of economic performance.

When organizations in an industry are homogeneous, they all make the same products, with the same technology, the same inputs, and the same costs. When organizations in an industry are small, their total sales and total productive output are small relative to the sales and output of the industry as a whole. This means that decisions made by any one organization have no impact on the size of total industry sales. Even very large organizations may be small relative to their market. For example, the Swiss food company Nestlé has many thousands of employees and offices all over the globe, yet compared with the market it serves (the worldwide food market), Nestlé is relatively small. Finally, when entry into an industry is unrestricted, an organization outside the industry that identifies an opportunity can enter the industry to take advantage of the opportunity.

Organizations in a perfectly competitive industry earn what is called normal economic performance. **Normal economic performance** is a level of economic performance just high enough for an organization to pay all of its expenses (in hiring employees, buying raw materials, purchasing machines, etc.) and to pay investors (including banks and stockholders). In other words, organizations in perfectly competitive industries perform just well enough to survive.

Normal economic performance is a level of economic performance just high enough for an organization to pay all of its expenses.

The reasoning behind the conclusion that organizations in perfectly competitive industries will just survive is straightforward. Because entry is unrestricted, any opportunity that might come along can be exploited either by organizations already in the industry or by organizations entering for the first time. Among organizations already in an industry and those poised to enter, the supply of a good or service normally equals demand and prices hold at a level that just covers the cost of the organizations' operations. Moreover, since organizations in perfectly competitive industries are small relative to the size of the market, there is little chance that one or two organizations will dominate the market and raise prices.

We should note that the expression "perfect competition" can sometimes cause confusion. "Perfect" in this context does not refer to some moral imperative. It does not suggest that industries with the three attributes listed above are somehow good or right. Rather, it simply refers to a set of industry attributes that can be used to predict the performance of organizations in the industry.

Industrial Organization Economics

Over the years, numerous authors have debated whether any perfectly competitive industries actually exist. Some industries, such as agricultural products and iron ore, seem to approximate perfect competition, but most theorists agree that the vast majority of industries do not. Thus, where early theoretical efforts focused on determining the performance implications for organizations under perfect competition — that is, perfect competition leads to survival — more recent work has explored the performance implications for organizations under imperfect competition. Organizations in imperfectly competitive industries may earn greater than normal economic profits — that is, they may do more than simply survive. **Industrial organization economics** is the group of theories that attempts to understand the performance implications of imperfectly competitive industries.

Industrial organization economics is the branch of economics that attempts to understand how industries can be imperfectly competititve and what impact their imperfections will have on firm performance.

Scholars have investigated different ways in which industries can be imperfectly competitive. For example, Joan Robinson and Edward Chamberlin examined what happens to organizational performance when goods and services sold by organizations within an industry are not homogeneous (*product heterogeneity*). David Ricardo studied what happens to organizational performance when organizations have different operating costs (*cost heterogeneity*). Various authors have examined what happens to performance when organizations in an industry are not small relative to the size of the market. Edward Mason and Joseph Bain studied what happens to the performance of organizations in an industry when entry into that industry is restricted. Each of these authors found that when some (or all) of the characteristics of perfect competition do not exist in an industry, organizations within that industry may experience higher than normal economic performance. Organizations with higher than normal levels of performance can be thought of as maximizing their performance. Thus the theory of perfect competition generates an explanation of how organizations can survive, and the theory of imperfect competition generates an explanation of how firms can maximize their performance.[15]

The Porter Framework

The Porter framework is a set of analytical tools that managers can use to evaluate the competitiveness of their industry and thus estimate the level of economic performance possible in that industry.

In the last several years, scholars have begun to apply industrial organization economics directly to understand organizational strategies. Much of this work has been done by Michael Porter of the Harvard Business School, and the framework that Porter and his colleagues have developed is often called the Porter framework.[16] Since this idea is discussed in detail in Chapters 4 and 7, we need only emphasize here that the Porter framework derives from Adam Smith's concept of the "invisible hand" of the marketplace: it focuses on the impact that an industry has on the performance of organizations within it. Porter's work explores the conditions under which an organization can expect to just survive and the conditions under which an organization will maximize its performance.

One interesting implication of applying the Porter framework is that strategies that improve a particular organization's performance may not be good for society as a whole. How one company, Lotus, has struggled with the ethical as well as the economic consequences of choosing and implementing its strategies is discussed in The Environmental Challenge.

Ricardian Economics

David Ricardo, an English economist, analyzed the economic performance consequences when firms possess different resources and these differences persist over time.

Adam Smith's other important insight — that the division of labor can create organizational efficiency — was explored by a separate group of economists who were interested in what this idea implied for the performance of organizations. One of the first scholars to study organizational efficiency in this way was English economist David Ricardo. Ricardo observed that organizations may have different assets, skills, and capabilities and that the ability of other organizations to acquire these assets, skills, and capabilities may be limited.

Assume, for example, that an organization purchases a piece of land with the intention of using it to grow corn but discovers oil on the land. The price of the land to grow corn is only $10 per acre. The price of the land once oil is discovered on it is hundreds of times more, perhaps $1,000 per acre. The organization may be able to earn above-normal economic performance by taking advantage of its newfound opportunities (purchasing what turned out to be $1,000-per-acre land for only $10 per acre), but when the true value of the land is known, no other organizations will be able to achieve this same level of economic performance (because they will have to pay $1,000 per acre). In *The Principles of Political Economy and Taxation* (1817), Ricardo extended his analysis to explain the relationship between economic performance and a wide variety of assets, skills, and capabilities of organizations.[17]

Theories of Distinctive Competence

An organization's *distinctive competencies* are those skills and capabilities that a firm possesses but competing firms do not possess.

Ricardo's insight was that organizations in the same industry may have different skills and capabilities and that these differences may persist over long periods of time. An organization's **distinctive competencies** are the skills and capabilities that it possesses but competing firms do not possess. The concept of distinctive competence has three distinct parts. First, it describes all of the capabilities that enable an organization to conceive of or implement valuable strategies. Organizational attributes that *prevent* an organization from choosing or implementing valuable strategies, or that lead an organization to choose or implement strategies that are not valuable, cannot be sources of distinctive competence. Second, a distinctive competence results from organizational attributes that are possessed by relatively few competing organizations. Third, the organizational attributes that result in a distinctive competence must be difficult for organizations that do not possess them to obtain.

THE ENVIRONMENTAL CHALLENGE

Lotus Marketplace Software

Lotus Development Corporation is the world's leading manufacturer of spreadsheet programs for personal computers. These programs enable computer users to rapidly calculate and recalculate complicated financial and accounting projections. Lotus's key spreadsheet product, Lotus 1-2-3, represented over 65 percent of the $350 million spreadsheet business in 1990. Lotus 1-2-3 provides over 73 percent of Lotus's corporate sales and is widely acknowledged to be the industry leader in spreadsheet software.

Despite its enormous success, Lotus has a problem. After five years of effort, the company has been unable to develop another product to complement 1-2-3. A recent effort to acquire Novell (a manufacturer of personal-computer network-operating systems) was unsuccessful, as were attempts to develop several new products. Indeed, Lotus even has repeatedly had to delay important upgrades to its flagship 1-2-3 software.

Partly in response to its need for a new product, Lotus formed a partnership with Equifax, Inc., an Atlanta-based credit reporting company. Together, Lotus and Equifax developed a new software package, Lotus Marketplace, which enables users to access a database containing the names, addresses, shopping habits, and likely income of over 80 million households in the United States. This information would be very valuable to organizations seeking to fine-tune their marketing and advertising efforts.

However, making the information available in Lotus Marketplace widely accessible could be an invasion of privacy. Organizations that purchased the software would suddenly have access to information that many consumers might believe is none of their business. Lotus Marketplace caused enormous controversy before it was introduced. Ethics professors at some of the nation's universities questioned whether such a product should be outlawed. In response to this pressure, the corporation abandoned plans to sell Lotus Marketplace, despite strong indications that it would be a highly profitable product.

REFERENCES: John R. Wilke, "Lotus Product Spurs Fears About Privacy," *Wall Street Journal*, November 12, 1990, p. B1; Michael W. Miller, "Lotus Likely to Abandon Consumer Data Project," *Wall Street Journal*, January 23, 1991, p. B1; William M. Bulkeley, "After Years of Glory, Lotus Is Stumbling in Software Market," *Wall Street Journal*, August 30, 1988, p. B1; "Overnight Lotus Blossoms into No. 1," *Business Week*, April 23, 1990, pp. 28–29.

After Ricardo, two groups of scholars examined the performance implications of organizational distinctive competencies. The first person to define the characteristics of such organizations was Arthur Stinchcombe, a sociologist. A second group, centered at the Harvard Business School, also focused on the concept of distinctive competence. Some of these early researchers included C. Roland Christensen, Kenneth R. Andrews, and William D. Guth.[18] All of these people have concluded that organizations that possess distinctive competencies can expect to achieve superior levels of economic performance. The impact of these theories of distinctive competence on our understanding of organizational performance is discussed in detail in Chapter 7.

Modern Strategic Management Theory

As one traces the evolution of thinking about organizational strategy, it seems fitting that Adam Smith's two fundamental insights — that there are advantages to the division of labor and specialization and that the "invisible hand" of the market can coordinate economic activity — have once again been joined in modern strategic management theory. Modern strategic management theory is still concerned with understanding how organizations survive and how they can maximize performance. How these two sets of questions are integrated, by considering the impact both of industry attributes and of distinctive competencies on an organization's performance, is the primary topic of Part II of this book.

Historical Perspectives on the Structure of Organizations

As described in Chapter 1, structure is the framework of jobs, relationships among jobs, and operational systems and processes that an organization uses to carry out its strategy. The study of organization structure has focused on questions such as these: What is the purpose of organization structure? What business activities should an organization engage in? How should different business activities in an organization be related to one another? How should an organization modify its structure in response to changes in its environment?

Early Theories About Organization Structure

As Figure 2.3 shows, modern thinking about the nature and purpose of organization structure, and about how structure should be managed, begins with two very different authors: Adam Smith and Karl Marx. Adam Smith in *The Wealth of Nations* explained that one way to coordinate the activities of specialized manufacturing organizations is to incorporate previously independent organizations into a single organization. In this way, a single organization structure can be used to directly coordinate production. (The other approach to coordination is the "invisible hand" of the market.) According to Adam Smith, organizations provide a valuable social benefit. They enable society to take advantage of the lower costs associated with specialized production, without having to relinquish the advantages of coordinated productive efforts.[19]

Karl Marx argued that prevailing organization structures were the primary mechanism through which workers in a society were exploited. His emphasis on power is common to many models of organization structure.

Karl Marx took a very different perspective on the purpose of organizations. Marx believed that prevailing organization structures were the primary mechanism through which workers in a society were exploited. He held that the owners of organizations exploited workers by extracting high profits from their labor and not sharing any of those profits with the workers. In marked contrast with Smith, Marx saw organizations as instruments of power that make society much worse off.[20] The ideas of these two theorists — that organization structure increases the productive efficiency of society and that organization structure reinforces power relationships — continue to influence thinking about organization structure today.[21]

Efficiency-based Analyses

Organizational economics is the branch of economics that attempts to analyze the efficiency characteristics of alternative ways of organizing firms.

Various authors have examined the characteristics of organization structure that contribute to efficiency. Collectively, this body of work has come to be known as **organizational economics**.[22] One of the earliest organizational economists was Ronald Coase. Coase was interested in understanding why, given the numerous advantages of coordinating production through the "invisible hand" of the market, organization structures should exist at all. His great insight was that there are costs associated with using the market as a coordination mechanism and that sometimes the cost of using an organization to coordinate production is lower than the cost of using a market. When this is true, the use of organization structure is more efficient. These ideas have been developed by a large number of authors, including Oliver Williamson and William Ouchi, as a basis for analyzing organization structure.[23]

Whereas Coase was interested in understanding why organization structures exist, Alfred Chandler was interested in understanding the best ways to link and integrate different business functions within an organization.

Figure 2.3

The Evolution of Thinking About Organization Structure

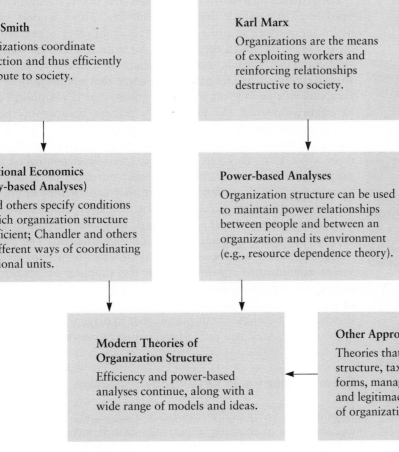

Adam Smith

Organizations coordinate production and thus efficiently contribute to society.

Karl Marx

Organizations are the means of exploiting workers and reinforcing relationships destructive to society.

Organizational Economics (Efficiency-based Analyses)

Coase and others specify conditions under which organization structure will be efficient; Chandler and others specify different ways of coordinating organizational units.

Power-based Analyses

Organization structure can be used to maintain power relationships between people and between an organization and its environment (e.g., resource dependence theory).

Modern Theories of Organization Structure

Efficiency and power-based analyses continue, along with a wide range of models and ideas.

Other Approaches

Theories that link technology and structure, taxonomies of structural forms, managing social acceptability and legitimacy, biological analysis of organizations.

By studying the history of several organizations, Chandler was able to describe the basic organizational forms that can be used to coordinate business functions (these organizational forms are described in detail in Chapter 11). Later authors such as Oliver Williamson, Richard Rumelt, Paul Lawrence, and Jay Lorsche found that organizations that adopted the organizational forms most appropriate for their strategies outperformed organizations that adopted inappropriate forms.[24]

Power-based Analyses

While organizational economists examined organization structure from the point of view of economic efficiency, other researchers looked at how organization structure can be used to maintain power relationships among people. Some of the most influential work in this area began in the 1950s with studies by Peter Blau and Melville Dalton on power relationships among managers in organizations. These ideas were later extended by Jeffery Pfeffer, Gerald Salancik, and several other authors who studied the relationship between a person's position in the organization structure and the ability to influence organizational outcomes.[25]

Resource dependence models are used to examine the relationship between how an organization acquires vital resources and how that organization structures itself.

Power-based analyses of organization structure reached their most developed level in **resource dependence models**. These models assumed that organizations seek to protect themselves from other organizations in their environment on which they depend for critical resources. For example, a steel company depends on the suppliers of iron ore to be able to make steel. Resource dependence theorists argue that organizations like the steel company will go to great lengths to ensure that key suppliers are not able to unfairly exercise the power they possess because of the important resources they supply.

Organizations may address a resource dependence problem in one of three ways. First, they can attempt to gain direct control of the resource supplier. Thus the steel company might purchase the iron ore supplier, thereby reducing dependence. Second, they can attempt to obtain multiple suppliers of the key resource. In this case, the steel company would purchase iron ore from several suppliers. Third, they can attempt to influence the supplier so that it will not take action against them. The steel company might obtain this influence in a variety of ways: by placing its managers in senior administrative positions with the supplier, by encouraging close interpersonal relationships between its members and those of the supplier, or by becoming a major customer of the supplier. According to resource dependence theorists, organizations that manage their power relationships with suppliers well will outperform organizations that do not.[26]

Early theories of organization structure focused considerable attention on power and hierarchical relations. Thomas Nast, the political cartoonist, frequently dealt with the hierarchical positioning of labor and management in organizations. From this cartoon, it is evident that Nast sided with the hard-working employer, not with the labor movement.

Other Approaches to Organization Structure

Although efficiency and power-based analyses are important influences in the evolution of thinking about organization structure, they are not the only influences. Beginning with the work of Joan Woodward and Charles

Perrow, several researchers have studied the effect of an organization's manufacturing and production technology on its structure.[27] A number of scholars in the United Kingdom used complex empirical methods to develop a taxonomy of the basic structural forms that exist in organizations.[28] Several authors have studied how organizations use structure to inform important constituencies that they are behaving in socially acceptable and responsible ways.[29] Even more recently, researchers have applied ideas from biological science to analyze the evolution of organization structure over time.[30]

Modern Theories of Organization Structure

The study of organization structure today is accomplished with a rich array of conceptual tools. Many of the ideas that have dominated this discussion since the days of Adam Smith and Karl Marx are still influential. Organizational economics, resource dependence theories, theories that link technology and structure, theories that analyze organizations by means of a biological analogy, and many other theories all influence the study of organization structure. Many of these ideas are discussed in detail in Part III of this book.

Historical Perspectives on Behavior in Organizations

As described in Chapter 1, once an organization successfully manages its strategy and structure, the important task remaining is managing behavior within the organization. This task requires a threefold recognition: that all individuals within an organization are unique, that leadership styles can affect the motivation of individuals, and that behavior can be affected by the group settings within which people in organizations find themselves. Just as our understanding of organizational strategy and structure has evolved, so has our understanding of the causes and consequences of individual and group behavior in organizations.

Scientific Management

Scientific management is a theory about behavior in organizations that focuses on individual jobs and tries to determine the best way to carry them out.

As Figure 2.4 summarizes, several scholars and managers in the early 1900s became interested in how the design of jobs in organizations affected the motivation and output of employees. The conceptual and management tools that these individuals developed are called **scientific management**. One of the most important proponents of scientific management was Frederick Taylor.[31]

Taylor was an engineer who became interested in labor efficiency. While working as a foreman at the Midvale Steel Company in Philadelphia, he noticed that laborers reduced the pace at which they were working, thereby reducing their productive output. When Taylor discussed this phenomenon

Scientific management and job specialization were cornerstones of early perspectives on behavior in organizations. These salmon cannery workers in Brookfield, Washington performed increasingly specialized and standardized jobs as the company's management attempted to boost efficiency.

with other managers, he was surprised to learn that they were unaware of it. Moreover, they seemed to know very little about the jobs that their employees were performing. Taylor decided that something needed to be done. He studied each job carefully, motion by motion, and determined the most efficient way to perform it. Then he taught that method to workers and installed a piece-rate compensation system, which paid employees for the number of units they produced. The more units workers produced, the higher was their pay. The effect of these changes was striking: productive output soared; employees earned more money and seemed to be more satisfied; and the organization was more profitable.

Taylor gradually developed his ideas about designing jobs, compensation, and performance. The practice of scientific management consists of four distinct steps. The manager (1) studies each job and determines the best way to do it, (2) selects workers who are capable of doing the job and trains them, (3) monitors the work to make sure employees are performing it in the best way, and (4) assumes all planning and organizing responsibilities while the workers carry out their assigned tasks.

Scientific management was not uniformly accepted by all those it touched. Organized labor fought it because its application often put greater demands on laborers, and Congress investigated it because of its impact on labor. Most importantly, scientific management methods can be successfully applied in only a relatively narrow range of jobs. If a job requires repetitious manual activities (for example, installing fenders on automobiles in a manufacturing line or putting bottles into a bottle-filling machine), then the time- and motion-saving tools of scientific management can be quite helpful. For most other kinds of jobs, there seldom is "one best way" of performing the work. Nor is it likely that managers, by themselves, will be able to enumerate the best ways of performing a job. The involvement of people who actually perform the job is usually required.

The Administrative Management Movement

The *administrative management movement* is a group of theories that recognize that managers need to consider the organization as a whole when they attempt to improve performance.

A second important model for thinking about behavior in organizations is known as the **administrative management movement**. Whereas scientific management focused on increased productivity through the work of individual employees, administrative management was concerned with how the organization as a whole should be managed to improve performance. The primary contributors to this perspective were Henri Fayol and Max Weber.

Fayol, a French industrialist, drew on more than fifty years of organizational experience to develop a list of fourteen general guidelines, or principles, of "good" management. Table 2.1 lists and describes these principles. Fayol believed that they were universally valid and that if they were applied they would always enhance organizational performance. Many of Fayol's principles still apply to modern organizations. For example, Principle 11 (Managers should be kind and fair when dealing with subordinates) and Principle 13 (Subordinates should have the freedom to take initiative) are as widely applicable today as they were in Fayol's time.[32]

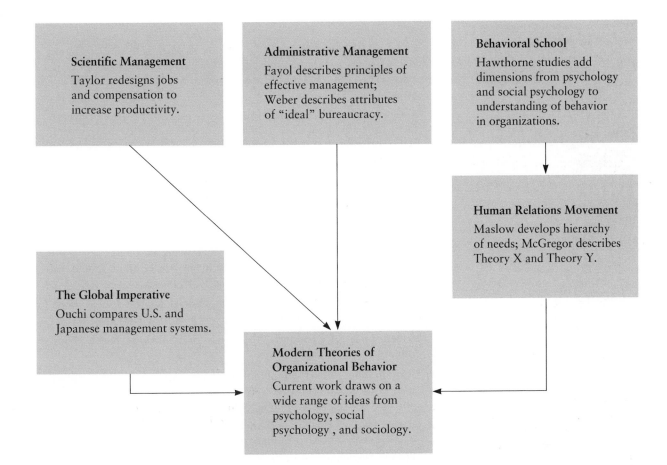

Figure 2.4

The Evolution of Thinking About Behavior in Organizations

Some of Fayol's ideas, however, do not apply as universally as he thought. For example, Principle 12 (High turnover of employees should be avoided) probably does not apply in an organization such as McDonald's, which has very high turnover, or Kelly Temporary Services, which makes temporary employees available to corporate customers. Likewise, Principle 4 (Each subordinate receives orders from one and only one superior) does not apply to complex organizations with teams of managers working on a single project who simultaneously report to several different superiors. Thus, although Fayol's administrative principles may give general guidance to managers, they must be adapted to the specific circumstances in which an organization operates.

Max Weber, a German sociologist, was the first person to describe the administrative benefits of bureaucracy. Weber identified six characteristics of the ideal bureaucracy. Some of these six characteristics, listed in Table 2.2, are similar to Fayol's principles of management. For example, Fayol's Principle 4 (unity of command) is very similar to Weber's first characteristic (Labor is divided with clear lines of authority). Like Fayol's principles, some of Weber's characteristics still apply to many organizations today.

Table 2.1

Fayol's Principles of Management

1. **Division of Work**   The object of division of work is to produce more and better work with the same effort. Managerial and technical work is amenable to specialization. There is, however, a limit to such specialization.

2. **Authority and Responsibility**   Authority is needed to carry out managerial responsibilities. This includes the formal authority to command and also personal authority deriving from intelligence and experience. Responsibility always goes with authority.

3. **Discipline**   Discipline is absolutely essential for the smooth running of business, but the state of discipline depends essentially on the worthiness of the organization's leaders.

4. **Unity of Command**   Each subordinate receives orders from one and only one superior.

5. **Unity of Direction**   Similar activities in an organization should be grouped together under one manager.

6. **Subordination of Individual Interest to General Interest**   Interests of individuals should not be placed before the goals of the organization.

7. **Remuneration of Personnel**   Compensation should be fair to both employees and the organization.

8. **Centralization**   Power and authority tend to be concentrated at upper levels of the organization. The degree must vary according to the situation; the objective is the optimum utilization of all faculties of personnel.

9. **Scalar Chain**   A chain of authority extends from the top to the bottom of the organization. Horizontal communication is, however, necessary for swift action.

10. **Order**   A place for everything and everything in its place; a place for everyone and everyone in his or her place.

11. **Equity**   Managers should be fair when dealing with subordinates.

12. **Stability of Tenure of Personnel**   High turnover of employees should be avoided.

13. **Initiative**   Subordinates should have the freedom to take initiative.

14. **Esprit de Corps**   Harmony, team spirit, and a sense of unity and togetherness should be fostered and maintained.

SOURCE: Adapted from Henri Fayol, *General and Industrial Management*, trans. Constance Storrs (London: Sir Isaac Pitman and Sons, 1949), pp. 19–42. Original French edition published in Paris by Dumod. Copyright © 1949 by Lake Publishing Company, Belmont, CA.

Others seem likely to apply only in certain organizations or in special situations. Indeed, Weber himself did not see bureaucracy necessarily as the "perfect" organizational form. Rather, he considered it one of a variety of tools that organizations can use to manage behavior.[33]

Table 2.2

Weber's Characteristics of an Ideal Bureaucracy

1. Labor is divided with clear lines of authority.

2. Positions are organized in a hierarchy of authority.

3. Promotion is based on merit, assessed by examination.

4. Decisions are recorded in writing.

5. Management is separate from ownership.

6. Managers are subject to rules that are uniformly applied.

SOURCE: Max Weber, *The Theory of Social and Economic Organization*, trans. T. Parsons, (New York: Oxford University Press, 1947).

The Behavioral School

The *behavioral school* is a set of theories about behavior in organizations that apply concepts developed by psychologists, psychiatrists, and social psychologists.

Of all the early approaches to studying behavior in organizations, none is currently more influential than what is now called the **behavioral school**. This approach to understanding organizational behavior applies ideas and concepts developed by psychologists, psychiatrists, and social psychologists. One of the first psychologists to apply his ideas to understanding behavior in organizations was Hugo Munsterberg.[34] Munsterberg first applied theories from psychology to organizational behavior in 1913, but not until a series of experiments conducted at the Hawthorne plant of the Western Electric Company from 1927 to 1932 did the approach of the behavioral school became widely understood and appreciated.[35]

The Hawthorne experiments, conducted at a Western Electric plant near Chicago, demonstrated the importance of psychological and social psychological phenomena to an understanding of behavior in organizations.

Two experiments at the Hawthorne plant were particularly important. In the first, researchers manipulated the workplace lighting for an experimental group of workers and compared their subsequent performance with the performance of a control group for whom lighting had not been changed. As expected, when the lighting in the experimental group was increased, performance in this group also increased. However, what was not expected was that when lighting was *decreased* in the experimental group, performance continued to improve. Reducing the lighting in the experimental group did not reverse the increased productivity until the workplace became so dark that workers could hardly see.

In the second experiment, researchers established a piecework pay system for a particular group of workers. Scientific management was based on the assumption that people are motivated solely by money. If this assumption were true, workers under a piece-rate system should have produced as much as possible in order to be paid as much money as possible. As in the earlier study, however, the results were not as expected. The group, on its own, established a level of acceptable output for its members. People who produced below that level were called "chiselers" and were pressured to do more. People who produced too much were labeled "rate-busters" and were pressured to bring their output into line with that of the rest of the group.

The Hawthorne researchers concluded that social and behavioral factors previously unknown to managers were affecting results. For example, the researchers attributed the results in the lighting study to the fact that the workers in the experimental group were receiving special attention for the first time; their increased productivity was a response to the attention itself, not to the lighting change. The researchers concluded from the piecework experiment that social pressure was a powerful force to be reckoned with in organizations — even more so than increased pay.

The Hawthorne studies gave rise to a new way of thinking about workers, one that focuses on the individual in the workplace. Other efforts at understanding behavior in organizations (including scientific management and the administrative management movement) failed to recognize the full role of individuals, but the behavioral school recognized that people have unique needs and motives that they bring into the workplace with them. While at work, individuals encounter a task, a supervisor, and the resources needed to do their jobs. But work is also a social experience, and the workplace has a social context that includes the possible satisfaction of social needs, such as the need to be accepted and to participate in the camaraderie of the work group.

The Human Relations Movement

The *human relations movement* proposed that workers respond primarily to the social context of the workplace, which includes their social conditioning and their interpersonal situation at work.

The **human relations movement** developed from the Hawthorne studies and was a popular approach to management for many years. The proponents of this view proposed that workers respond primarily to the social context of the workplace, which includes their social conditioning and their interpersonal situation at work. An underlying assumption of the human relations movement was that management concern for the worker would lead to increased satisfaction, which would in turn result in improved performance. Two early writers who helped advance the human relations movement were Abraham Maslow and Douglas McGregor.

Abraham Maslow's hierarchy of needs is a psychological theory that suggests that behavior in organizations depends on meeting certain individual needs.

In 1943, Maslow advanced a theory suggesting that people are motivated by a sequence of needs, including monetary incentives and social acceptance. Maslow's hierarchy of needs, described in detail in Chapter 17, was a primary factor in the increased attention that managers began to give to the work of academic theorists.[36]

Theory X and Theory Y, developed by Douglas McGregor, are two sets of propositions about workers' motives and beliefs that are thought to influence managers' behavior toward subordinates.

Maslow's theory was one of the first in the emerging area of human relations, but Douglas McGregor's Theory X and Theory Y perhaps best represent the theoretical basis for the human relations movement (see Table 2.3). According to McGregor, Theory X and Theory Y represent two opposing sets of assumptions that different managers make about their subordinates. Theory X reflects a relatively pessimistic and negative view of workers. It assumes that subordinates are lazy, must be forced to work, and so forth. Theory Y takes a more positive view of workers and represents the assumptions that human relations advocates make. In McGregor's view, Theory Y was the more appropriate philosophy for managers to adhere to.[37] Work by both Maslow and McGregor has significantly influenced the thinking of many practicing managers.

Table 2.3

McGregor's Theory X and Theory Y

Theory X Assumptions	Theory Y Assumptions
1. People do not like work and try to avoid it.	1. People do not naturally dislike work; work is a natural part of their lives.
2. People do not like work, so managers have to control, direct, coerce, and threaten employees to get them to work toward organizational goals.	2. People are internally motivated to reach objectives to which they are committed.
3. People prefer to be directed, to avoid responsibility, to want security; they have little ambition.	3. People are committed to goals to the degree that they receive personal rewards when they reach their objectives.
	4. People will both seek and accept responsibility under favorable conditions.
	5. People have the capacity to be innovative in solving organizational problems.
	6. People are bright, but under most organizational conditions their potentials are underutilized.

SOURCE: From Douglas McGregor, *The Human Side of Enterprise*, copyright 1960, McGraw-Hill. Used by permission of McGraw-Hill, Inc.

The Global Imperative

One recent line of thinking about behavior in organizations has developed out of the so-called global imperative. As Chapter 1 explained, proponents of this view hold that the world has become a global village and that managers must adopt a global vision regarding all their activities and how they affect behavior in organizations. What this means is that managerial theories, models, and perspectives about behavior in organizations must be reformulated to account for global similarities and differences. Perhaps the most fully developed of such efforts is the Type Z model.[38]

The Type Z model, as argued by William Ouchi in 1981, is an attempt to integrate common business practices in the United States and in Japan into a single middle-ground framework. Ouchi describes the characteristics of traditional American firms (which he calls Type A companies) and traditional Japanese companies (Type J). He states that some American firms have achieved great success by adopting a hybrid form of management, which he calls Type Z.

Figure 2.5 summarizes the basic characteristics of Type A, Type J, and Type Z organizations. It shows that American and Japanese firms are essentially different in seven important dimensions: (1) length of employment, (2) mode of decision making, (3) location of responsibility, (4) speed

Type Z, described by William Ouchi, is a management system that combines attributes from traditional Japanese and American approaches to management.

of evaluation and promotion, (5) mechanisms of control, (6) specialization of career path, and (7) nature of concern for the employee. For example, some Japanese firms feature lifetime employment opportunities and collective decision making, whereas their American counterparts offer short-term employment and rely on individual decision making.

According to Ouchi, a few particularly successful American firms (such as IBM, Hewlett-Packard, and Procter & Gamble) modify the typical American Type A model. The synthesis they evolve borrows one characteristic (individual responsibility) from Type A, incorporates three characteristics (collective decision making, slow evaluation and promotion, and holistic concern) from Type J, and assumes an intermediate stance with respect to the other three dimensions (for instance, they use long-term employment — as opposed to short-term employment in Type A and lifetime employment as in Type J). On average, firms that adopt a Type Z management style should outperform Type A organizations.

Modern Theories of Organizational Behavior

While scientific management and administrative management have declined in influence over the last several years, the approach of the behavioral school, the human relations movement, and theories fueled by the global imperative have flourished. Contemporary theories of organizational behavior apply the most sophisticated ideas from psychology and social psychology to understand how individuals behave within organizations. Part IV of this book discusses these contemporary theories of organizational behavior in detail.

Figure 2.5

Ouchi's Type Z

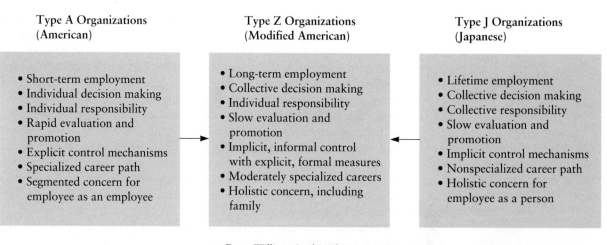

Type A Organizations (American)

- Short-term employment
- Individual decision making
- Individual responsibility
- Rapid evaluation and promotion
- Explicit control mechanisms
- Specialized career path
- Segmented concern for employee as an employee

Type Z Organizations (Modified American)

- Long-term employment
- Collective decision making
- Individual responsibility
- Slow evaluation and promotion
- Implicit, informal control with explicit, formal measures
- Moderately specialized careers
- Holistic concern, including family

Type J Organizations (Japanese)

- Lifetime employment
- Collective decision making
- Collective responsibility
- Slow evaluation and promotion
- Implicit control mechanisms
- Nonspecialized career path
- Holistic concern for employee as a person

SOURCE: From William Ouchi, *Theory Z: How American Business Can Meet the Japanese Challenge* © 1981 by Addison-Wesley Publishing Company, Inc. Adapted with permission of the publisher.

Learning Summary

Organizations have existed since before the dawn of recorded history. The most basic of all organizations is the family unit. Families still play a vital role in a variety of modern organizations.

Beginning around 3500 B.C., the Sumerians made extensive use of political organizations, religious organizations, organizations that produced goods and services, and trading organizations. To support the operation of those organizations, the Sumerians invented a system of weights and measures, a postal system, and a writing system.

The Egyptians and Babylonians adopted and modified many of the organizations invented by the Sumerians. Greek philosophers were the first to think systematically about why organizations exist and their role in society. The Romans developed a variety of organizations that still operate today, including banks, insurance companies, courts of law, and military organizations.

During the Middle Ages, many of the organizational innovations of the Greeks and Romans were lost, replaced by smaller, regional organizations such as guilds. One exception to this pattern was the Roman Catholic church.

During the Renaissance, many of the ideas and values of the Greek and Roman cultures were rediscovered. Renaissance organizations such as international trading companies developed some of the tools of modern business, including accounting practices and checking accounts.

The Industrial Revolution, beginning in the early 1800s, marked the rise of the factory system and the use of new technologies to produce goods.

The study of organizational strategy began with the ideas of Adam Smith. In *The Wealth of Nations,* Smith identified specialization and the coordination of production as central to understanding organizational strategies. A variety of economists later developed Smith's ideas through the theory of perfect competition, and industrial organization economics, to predict the performance of organizations in a particular industry. Other economists examined what happens to firm performance when organizations possess different distinctive competencies. Modern strategic management theory focuses on the impact of both industry structure and distinctive competencies on organizational performance.

The study of organization structure began with work by Adam Smith and Karl Marx. Smith emphasized the social benefits and efficiency of organization structures. Marx focused on how organization structure can be used to exploit workers in a society. This conflict between efficiency-based models of organization structure and power-based models continues today. Modern analysis of organization structure employs a broad range of tools and theories.

The study of behavior in organizations began with the work of Frederick Taylor on scientific management and the work of Henri Fayol and Max Weber on administrative management. Further findings led to the development of the behavioral school and the human relations movement.

Recently, the growth of the global village has forced those who study behavior in organization to acknowledge important differences between countries and cultures. Modern analyses of behavior in organizations apply sophisticated conceptual tools from a variety of social science disciplines, including psychology and social psychology.

Questions and Exercises

Review Questions

1. Describe the major types of organizations in ancient Sumer.
2. Describe the changes that occurred in organizations as a result of the Industrial Revolution.
3. Explain Adam Smith's two major insights about the function of organizations in society.
4. What is *normal economic performance* and how is it related to the concept of *perfect competition*?
5. What is a *distinctive competence*?
6. What was Karl Marx's view of the function of organizations in society?
7. What are the four steps in scientific management?
8. Describe the findings of the Hawthorne studies.
9. What are the major attributes of Type X and Type Y managers? How does McGregor's model of understanding behavior in organizations differ from Ouchi's Type Z organization?

Analysis Questions

1. Describe the relationship between the development of organizations and the invention of writing, banking, and steam power. Can organizational developments lead to such inventions? Can such inventions lead to important organizational developments? If you think so, give examples.
2. As the text suggests, organizations developed significantly during periods of time when scholars and other interested individuals closely analyzed the role of organizations in society — in ancient Greece and Rome and during the Renaissance, for example. Why is this so?
3. Adam Smith and Karl Marx are important figures in the history of thinking about organizations. How do they agree? Disagree?
4. In what context will the application of the principles of scientific management improve organizational performance? When will it hurt organizational performance?

Application Exercises

1. Interview two managers, one in a nonregulated organization and one in a highly regulated organization. Are there differences in the extent to

which these managers emphasize efficiency-based and power-based approaches to analyzing their organization's structure?

2. Think about a group project in which you have participated during the past two years. List the characteristics that enabled your group to complete its task. Then list any characteristics that made it difficult for the group to complete its task. Which of all these characteristics were also observed in the Hawthorne experiments?

Chapter Notes

1. Gerry Blackwell, "The Laptop Reolution," *Computing Canada*, 1990, pp. 35, 44; Bob Johnstone, "Research and Innovation: The Silent Revolution," *Far Eastern Economic Review,* 1990, p. 62; Bob Wallace, "Looking Back: Recalling the Events That Shaped the 80's," *Network World*, 1989, pp. 1, 50, 59; Charles Ganti, "East-Central Europe: The Morning After," *Foreign Affairs,* Winter 1990–1991, pp. 129–145.

2. Melvin Ember, *Marriage, Family, and Kinship: Comparative Studies in Social Organization* (New Haven, Conn.: HRAF Press, 1983).

3. For a discussion of family businesses, see David Bork, *Family Business, Risky Business* (New York: AMACOM, 1986). Some of the unique challenges of managing family businesses are described in Peter Davis, "Wars of Succession," *Business,* September 1990, pp. 100–102; and Joshua Hyatt, "The Parent Trap," *INC,* October 1990, pp. 48–62.

4. See William McKelvey, "The Evolution of Organizational Form in Ancient Mesopotamia," in *Organizational Systematics* (Los Angeles: University of California Press, 1982), pp. 295–335.

5. Allison Burford, *Craftsmen in Greek and Roman Society* (London: Thames and Hudson, 1972); Henry C. Boren, *Roman Society* (Lexington, Mass.: Heath, 1977).

6. Steven Epstein, *Wage and Labor Guilds in Medieval Europe* (Chapel Hill, N.C.: University of North Carolina Press, 1991).

7. See Scott Safranski, *Managing God's Organization* (Ann Arbor, Mich.: UMI Press, 1985), for a discussion of the Roman Catholic church as a modern organization. The classic analysis of the Roman Catholic church in medieval times is Summerfield Baldwin, *The Organization of Medieval Christianity* (New York: Holt, 1929).

8. For a discussion of commerce in the Renaissance, see Richard Ehrenberg, *Capital and Finance in the Age of the Renaissance,* trans. H. M. Lucas (1928; reprint, New York: Kelly, 1963).

9. See Michael B. Katz, Michael J. Doucet, and Mark J. Stern, *The Social Organization of Early Industrial Capitalism* (Cambridge, Mass.: Harvard University Press, 1982).

10. Charles Dickens, *Hard Times* (1854; reprint, New York: Heritage Press, 1966), p. 23.

11. Daniel Wren, *The Evolution of Management Theory,* 3rd ed. (New York: Wiley, 1987).

12. See Jay B. Barney, "Firm Resources and Sustained Competitive Advantage," *Journal of Management,* 1991, pp. 99–120; and Jay B. Barney and William G. Ouchi, *Organizational Economics* (San Francisco: Jossey-Bass, 1986).

13. Adam Smith, *An Inquiry into the Nature and Causes of the Wealth of Nations* (1776; reprint, New York: Modern Library, 1937).

14. Alfred Marshall, *Principles of Economics,* 2nd ed. (London: Macmillan, 1891); Irving Fisher, *Elementary Principles of Economics* (New York: Macmillan, 1912); see also Donald A. Hay and Derek J. Morris, *Industrial Economics: Theory and Evidence* (New York: Oxford University Press, 1985).

15. Joan Robinson, *Economics of Imperfect Competition* (London: Macmillan, 1933); Edward Chamberlin, *The Theory of Monopolistic Competition* (Cambridge, Mass.: Harvard University Press, 1933); David Ricardo, *The Principles of Political Economy and Taxation* (London: Dent and Son, 1817); Edward Mason, "Price and Production Policies of Large-Scale Enterprises," *American Economic Review,* 1939, pp. 61–74; Joseph Bain, *Barriers to New Competition* (Cambridge, Mass.: Harvard University Press, 1956).

16. Michael Porter, *Competitive Strategy* (New York: Free Press, 1980); see also Michael Porter, *Competitive Advantage* (New York: Free Press, 1985), and Michael Porter, "The Contributions of Industrial Organization to Strategic Management," *Academy of Management Review,* 1981, pp. 609–620.

17. David Ricardo, *The Principles of Political Economy and Taxation.*

18. Arthur Stinchcombe, "Social Structure and Organizations," in *Handbook of Organizations,* ed. James G. March (Chicago: Rand McNally, 1965), pp. 142–193; E. P. Learned, C. R. Christensen, K. R. Andrews, and W. D. Guth, *Business Policy* (Homewood, Ill.: Irwin, 1969).

19. Smith, *The Wealth of Nations.*

20. Karl Marx, *Capital,* vol. 1, trans. Ernest Untermann (Chicago: Kerr, 1912).

21. For an example of these perspectives, see the debate between Oliver Williamson and William G. Ouchi, on the side of the efficiency perspective, and Charles Perrow, on the side of the power perspective, in Andy Van de Ven and William Joyce, eds., *Assessing Organization Design and Performance* (New York: Wiley, 1981). The Williamson/Ouchi view is further articulated in Oliver Williamson, *Markets and Hierarchies* (New York: Free Press, 1975). Perrow's view is further developed in Charles Perrow, *Complex Organizations: A Critical Essay,* 3rd ed. (New York: Random House, 1986).

22. Jay Barney and William G. Ouchi, eds., *Organizational Economics* (San Francisco: Jossey-Bass, 1986).

23. Ronald Coase, "The Nature of the Firm," *Economica,* 1937, pp. 386–405; Williamson, *Markets and Hierarchies;* William G. Ouchi, "Markets, Bureaucracies, and Clans," *Administrative Science Quarterly,* 1980, pp. 124–141. Other examples of organizational economic work can be found in Barney and Ouchi, *Organizational Economics.*

24. Alfred Chandler, *Strategy and Structure: Chapters in the History of the American Industrial Enterprise* (Cambridge, Mass.: MIT Press, 1962); Williamson, *Markets and Hierarchies;* Richard Rumelt, *Strategy, Structure, and Economic Performance* (Cambridge, Mass.: Division of Research, Graduate School of Business Administration, Harvard University, 1974); Paul Lawrence and Jay Lorsch, *Organization and Environment: Managing Differentiation and Integration* (Cambridge, Mass.: Graduate School of Business Administration, Harvard University, 1967).

25. Peter Blau, *The Dynamics of Bureaucracy* (Chicago: University of Chicago Press, 1955); Melville Dalton, *Men Who Manage* (New York: Wiley, 1955); Jeffery Pfeffer and Gerald Salancik, *The External Control of Organizations: A Resource Dependence Perspective* (New York: Harper & Row, 1978).

26. Pfeffer and Salancik, *The External Control of Organizations.*

27. Joan Woodward, *Industrial Organization: Theory and Practice* (London: Oxford University Press, 1965); Charles Perrow, "A Framework for the Comparative Analysis of Organizations," *American Sociological Review,* 1967, pp. 194–209.

28. This group of scholars was known as the Aston Group, named after the city in the United Kingdom where much of this work was conducted. Important research papers in this tradition include David Hickson, D. S. Pugh, and Diana Pheysey, "Operations Technology and Organization Structure: An Empirical Reappraisal," *Administrative Science Quarterly,* 1969, pp. 378–397; and C. R. Hinnings, D. S. Pugh, and C. Turner, "An Approach to the Study of Bureaucracy," *Sociology,* 1967, pp. 61–72. A criticism of this approach to studying organizations can be found in Howard Aldrich, "Technology and Organizational Structure: A Reexamination of the Findings of the Aston Group," *Administrative Science Quarterly,* 1972, pp. 26–43.

29. Authors in this tradition include Phillip Selznick, *Leadership in Administration* (New York: Harper & Row, 1957), and Lynn Zucker, "The Role of Institutionalization in Cultural Persistence," *American Sociological Review,* 1977, pp. 726–743.

30. The seminal article in this biological tradition is Michael Hannan and John Freeman, "The Population Ecology of Organizations," *American Journal of Sociology,* 1977, pp. 929–964.

31. Frederick W. Taylor, *Principles of Scientific Management* (New York: Harper, 1911).

32. Henri Fayol, *General and Industrial Management,* trans. J. A. Coubrough (Geneva: International Management Institute, 1930).

33. Max Weber, *Theory of Social and Economic Organization,* trans. T. Parsons (New York: Oxford University Press, 1947).

34. Hugo Munsterberg, *Psychology and Industrial Efficiency* (Boston: Houghton Mifflin, 1913).

35. The Hawthorne studies are described in the works of several authors, including Elton Mayo, *The Human Problems of Industrial Civilization* (New York: Macmillan, 1933); and Fritz J. Roethlisberger and William J. Dickson, *Management and the Worker* (Cambridge, Mass.: Harvard University Press, 1939). Recent criticisms of the Hawthorne studies can be found in J. A. Seiler, "Architecture at Work," *Harvard Business Review,* September–October 1984, pp. 111–121; and Lyle Yorks and David A. Whitsett, "Hawthorne, Topeka, and the Issue of Science Versus Advocacy in Organizational Behavior," *Academy of Management Review,* January 1985, pp. 21–30.

36. Abraham Maslow, "A Theory of Human Motivation," *Psychological Review,* July 1943, pp. 370–396.

37. Douglas McGregor, *The Human Side of Enterprise* (New York: McGraw-Hill, 1960).

38. William G. Ouchi, *Theory Z* (Reading, Mass.: Addison-Wesley, 1981).

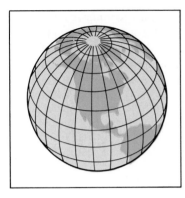

CASE 2.1

Big Changes at Big Steel

USX has been the nation's largest steel producer since it first saw the light of day as U.S. Steel in 1901. But ninety years of tradition mean little to an organization trying to survive in the 1990s. So in 1991 the company that had begun with an exchange of scribbled notes between J. P. Morgan and Andrew Carnegie made official its slow exit from the steel business by effectively splitting itself into two companies, one of which has nothing to do with the steel industry.

The history of U.S. Steel/USX is in many ways a history of industrial organizations in twentieth-century America. The company was created at the turn of the century as the result of two major, and sometimes conflicting, forces in nineteenth-century American business — the ascension of the self-made man and the formation of noncompetitive trusts. Andrew Carnegie had started work in a textile factory at age 13, bought his first stock at age 20 by mortgaging his mother's house, made lucky investments in oil, and bought into steel. By the end of the century, Carnegie Steel Company was producing more steel than all of Great Britain, which had been the world's leader just a decade before.

By that time the steel industry was suffering from overcapacity and sagging profits, which didn't please J. P. Morgan, America's leading banker and backer of Federal Steel. Carnegie had spoken out against the kind of holding companies and trusts that Morgan liked to set up to keep an industry's top companies from undermining each other with competition. But even Carnegie had a price — $480 million — which Morgan was willing to pay, and the nation's largest company was formed — U.S. Steel, proud maker of two-thirds of the nation's steel.

In its birth were the seeds of its downfall, however. U.S. Steel was a dinosaur from the beginning, large and slow moving, a federation of mining companies, steel-making companies, and fabrication companies. The corporation was too big and its holdings too widespread to be managed effectively by then-current organizational systems. Its divisions were essentially autonomous, and all that headquarters did at first was help to set prices and production schedules. Gradually the parent company began taking more control, first simply by getting all its subsidiaries to provide the same accounting information. But the centralization of control didn't begin in earnest until after the death of U.S. Steel's first chairman Elbert H. Gary in 1927.

By 1937, U.S. Steel resembled what we now think of as an old-fashioned industrial giant. It had a large general staff and vice presidents heading departments such as operations, sales, industrial relations, and research and metallurgy. Executives in New York and Pittsburgh handled policy-making, and a production planning department guided the flow of materials through various operations. In 1950 most of the company's steel-making activities were consolidated into Central Operations, which kept a tight grip on activities through departments organized along functional lines.

Unions were playing a major role in U.S. Steel's fortunes by this time, organizing five industry-wide strikes between 1945 and 1959 and gradually raising steelworkers' wages to be among the highest for American factory workers. But these high wages, combined with old plants and a top-heavy bureaucracy, spelled trouble in the late 1970s, as inexpensive imported steel began driving prices down and American producers found that they couldn't sell everything they were producing. Despite government-imposed import restrictions, the entire industry floundered, and U.S. Steel began a major move to diversify and restructure. In 1982 it bought Marathon Oil Company, then the nation's seventeenth-largest oil producer. It began cutting its steel-making capacity and its work force. Between 1982 and 1990, the number of salaried employees dropped from 30,000 to 5,000, the number of steelworkers from 75,000 to 20,000. In 1986, U.S. Steel bought Texas Oil & Gas Corp., a producer of natural gas, sold off some of its divisions, and changed its name to USX Corp.

When it became difficult to make a dollar on steel, USX became an energy company. In 1990, the operating earnings of its Marathon Oil subsidiary exceeded those of the entire steel industry; and some USX stock-holders, led by corporate raider Carl Icahn, began saying that it was time to get rid of the steel business entirely. In 1991 Icahn and the company reached a compromise: USX began offering two different common stocks, one tied to its steel business, the other to its energy businesses. Although it's not clear how long this unusual arrangement will last, USX CEO Charles A. Corry has not hidden his willingness to sell the steel business if he can find a buyer with $5.5 billion.

USX may be eager to get rid of steel. But if it succeeds, an era of American industry will come to an end.

Discussion Questions

1. What factors have most influenced USX?
2. What does the history of USX say about the value of competition in the American economic system?
3. Explain USX's loss of dominance in the U.S. steel industry.
4. Explain the changes in U.S. Steel's organization structure in terms of some of the perspectives discussed in this chapter.

REFERENCES: Clare Ansberry, "As USX Edges Out of the Steel Business, Family Faces Changes," *Wall Street Journal*, February 22, 1991, pp. A1, A5; Clare Ansberry, "Corry Is Moving to Energize USX's Image," *Wall Street Journal*, April 8, 1991, pp. B1, B4; Alfred Chandler, *Strategy and Structure* (Cambridge, Mass.: MIT Press, 1962); Milton Moskowitz, Michael Katz, and Robert Levering, *Everybody's Business* (San Francisco: Harper & Row, 1980), pp. 591–595; Thomas F. O'Boyle, "Icahn Forces the Issue at USX: Is it Time to Get Out of Steel?" *Wall Street Journal*, March 9, 1990, pp. A1, A4.

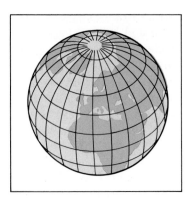

CASE 2.2

Saddled with Tradition

If Americans have heard of only one overseas insurance company, it's bound to be Lloyd's of London. Although Lloyd's is not, in fact, an insurance company — it has no shareholders and is not liable as a corporation for risks insured through its services — it gets in the news because its underwriters insure unusual things. When Scotland's Cardhu distillery wanted to insure the nose of its chief whiskey sniffer for $1.5 million, it turned to Lloyd's. So did a comedian who wanted to insure his mustache and someone else who had put up a large prize for catching the Loch Ness monster and feared that Nessie might actually be caught. Lloyd's also tends to be mentioned in the last paragraph of stories about hurricanes, shipwrecks, and other disasters, for chances are good that some of the victims were insured through Lloyd's.

Lloyd's is proud of its reputation for charting new insurance territory. It was responsible for the first aviation insurance, burglary insurance, and workmen's compensation insurance. It is equally proud of its long and interesting history, now in its fourth century. But that history — one of the reasons Lloyd's is a household word in households that don't care about insurance — is giving Lloyd's trouble in a world very far removed from the seventeenth-century coffee house where Edward Lloyd served ship captains and merchants.

Because there were no marine insurance companies in the seventeenth century, insurance brokers would take a policy around to rich merchants, persuading each to cover part of a ship's total liability, until the ship's entire value was insured. A place where merchants and shipowners went to relax was therefore an ideal setting for such brokers and for potential underwriters, those who actually took on the financial responsibility for an insured vessel. Add to those inducements Edward Lloyd's reputation for providing accurate shipping news, and it is easy to see why his coffee house became the focal point of British marine insurance.

In many ways, Lloyd's today is a direct descendant of the coffee shop that opened in 1688. Lloyd's provides services beyond the coffee and news that Edward Lloyd offered his patrons, but it still does not underwrite insurance. It brings together rich people willing to underwrite a venture and the agents or brokers of those looking for insurance. Lloyd's is much more heavily regulated and scrutinized now, of course. It has been the subject of at least two acts of the British Parliament, the latest in 1982; but as a unique and powerful British institution, Lloyd's is still self-governing to an extent that newer institutions might envy.

The underwriters at Lloyd's — known as "members" or "names" — have long grouped themselves into syndicates. Currently about 30,000 members are divided into about 400 syndicates. Members make money if their syndicate takes in more money in premiums than it disburses for claims. But if a member's syndicate gets hit with a very large claim, members are liable for the entire amount, down to the last cent of their personal wealth.

The possibility that a disaster somewhere could lead to members' bankruptcy is one of the holdovers from former times that is now causing Lloyd's problems. In good years, members earn a good deal more than they could earn through other investments. In fact, the assets that members pledge as collateral stay under their control and can thus earn interest in a bank even as they enable members to share in insurance profits. But few other investments carry such risks. One of Lloyd's biggest worries is the number of members who withdraw from the syndicates each year, no longer willing to risk their personal fortunes.

Other Lloyd's traditions make it relatively easy for more modern, efficient insurance companies or exchanges to win business away from Lloyd's. Lloyd's uses very few computers, in part because competitive syndicates are wary of sharing information, in part because any such change must be approved by a bureaucracy that has grown large over the years. Most business at Lloyd's is still conducted face to face, ink to paper. Thus brokers spend much of their time waiting in line to see underwriters. A broker may have to speak to a dozen or two underwriters before getting a policy completely covered. And getting a claim paid can take months.

Nevertheless, Lloyd's remains the exchange of choice for people wanting to insure unusual things, and its history and unique mode of operation make it an institution without parallel in the insurance world. But although a century ago about half of all the world's insurance was written at Lloyd's, today that figure is less than 2 percent. Lloyd's has played a prominent role in the business world and in the development of organizations for over 300 years, but it will need radical changes if it hopes to celebrate its 400th birthday.

Discussion Questions

1. Could an organization with Lloyd's structure be founded today? Why or why not?
2. Why are history and tradition powerful assets for an institution in the insurance business?
3. What about Lloyd's history or structure has led this organization to be responsible for so many insurance innovations?
4. Can you think of any institutions that seem to be modeled after Lloyd's or that may have learned from some of Lloyd's difficulties?

REFERENCES: Craig Forman, "Lloyd's of London, an Insurance Bulwark, Is a Firm Under Siege," *Wall Street Journal*, October 24, 1989, pp. A1, A18; "Lloyd's of London: A Sketch History," promotional brochure, Publicity and Information Department, Lloyd's of London; Richard A. Melcher, "The New Broom at Lloyd's of London," *Business Week*, January 14, 1991, p. 54; Richard Morais, "The Time Bombs at Lloyd's of London," *Forbes*, December 1, 1986, pp. 114+.

3

Contemporary Organizational Challenges

LEARNING OBJECTIVES

After studying this chapter, you should be able to:

1. Describe some of the changes in the world over the last hundred years that have affected organizations.

2. Identify and explain four main economic challenges faced by organizations.

3. Discuss three sets of challenges that organizations must address in order to remain competitive.

4. Explain why most organizations will have to develop the ability to compete in a global environment.

5. Describe some of the legal challenges that organizations must contend with, and explain some of the new social demands placed on organizations and their managers.

6. Discuss three organizational challenges associated with recent changes in the workplace.

Very few businesses can be characterized as cultural icons. Coca-Cola, Fuller Brush, and Levi Strauss are all likely candidates. Many people would also place The Reader's Digest Association Inc. on the list. The firm has been publishing its flagship magazine *Reader's Digest* — an easy-to-read compendium of general-interest articles on everything from personal health to politics — once a month since 1922. Worldwide circulation of *Reader's Digest* exceeds 28 million. With pass-on readership, it is estimated that more than 100 million people read the magazine every month.

The Reader's Digest organization has confronted a number of issues and challenges in recent years. Rising expenses and increased competition from other publishers have forced the firm to search for new ways to cut costs and increase efficiency. Managers also realized that the firm was not capitalizing on the latest technology. For example, until recently Reader's Digest lacked the computer technology to use its data bank, packed with information about several million current and past subscribers, for much more than printing mailing labels. With a new computer system in place, the firm can now target mailings to different segments of its audience to promote such specialized products as condensed books, anthologies, and videocassettes.

Reader's Digest has also had to contend with many different workplace issues. Many long-time employees have resisted some of the cost-control measures, and some key managers have left following policy and editorial disputes. Some who remain are still not convinced that the firm is making the right choices in its efforts to remain competitive. Still others view the company as a public trust and disapprove of the increased attention being focused on profits. Like many other organizations, Reader's Digest is also facing increasing difficulties caused by dual-career couples and changing worker values.

To complicate the situation further, Reader's Digest has recently recognized that it should work harder to penetrate foreign markets, from which, management believes, much of the firm's future growth will come. The company demonstrated the extent of its new competitive focus after the borders of East Germany were opened. Employees based in Berlin drove throughout the eastern region of the country distributing free copies of the German edition of *Reader's Digest* and enlisting subscribers.[1]

The changes at Reader's Digest highlight many of the contemporary challenges that organizations are having to confront. Pressures to cut costs have forced stern measures ranging from work-force reductions to salary cutbacks. New technological imperatives have provided both opportunities (such as an increased ability to manage information) and problems (such as integrating the activities of people with automated production systems). Changing employee expectations — about compensation, about job assignments, about participation in decision making — have altered the ways in which managers relate to their subordinates. The globalization movement is bringing about profound changes in everything from competition to banking regulations throughout the business world.

These issues and challenges are the focus of this chapter. First we characterize the changing world of organizations. Subsequent sections explore particular economic, competitive, global, environmental, and workplace challenges (and opportunities) that organizations and their managers must address.

The Changing World of Organizations

Although organizations have existed for centuries, big business has been around for less than two hundred years. In the grand scope of human history, large business organizations are relative newcomers. But consider the vast changes that have occurred since their inception. Electric motors, automobiles, airplanes, and telephones were all invented in the last 150 years.[2] Early industrialists such as Cornelius Vanderbilt and Andrew Carnegie could only dream of taking a transcontinental flight from New York to San Francisco. Messages were sent by telegraph. Workers made do with unsophisticated equipment and put in long hours, often with little pay.

Now consider the array of tools and equipment that people in modern organizations have come to rely on. Personal computers, xerographic machines, electronic calculators, overnight delivery services, facsimile machines, videocassette recorders, compact disc players, industrial robots — these and other amenities now commonplace in organizations have been around for only a few decades or in some cases a few years.

To bring the impact of these changes into sharper focus, let's look at the changes faced by a single organization: Ford Motor Company. When Henry Ford started his company in 1903, he did not have to contend with government regulation or organized labor because there were few regulations and no autoworkers' unions. He had a handful of domestic competitors, but demand for his automobiles was so great that quality was not a major concern. Indeed, most early Ford automobiles were not of particularly high quality. The firm produced a single make of car — the Model T — from 1908 until 1927. Ford himself owned the company, so he did not have to wrangle with hostile stockholders. And because his firm was such a large purchaser of raw materials, he could virtually dictate what prices he would pay, when suppliers would deliver materials, and so forth.

One constant in the world of organizations is change. Increased competition, deregulation, and international trade agreements are among the trends that businesses face today. Canadian air express companies are subject to all these conditions. Competition is stiff, price wars are causing decreasing profits, and the potential "open skies" agreement between the United States and Canada may allow unlimited entry into Canada to U.S. giants such as Federal Express. In response to these marketplace changes, shipping companies are making internal changes, such as putting greater emphasis on customer satisfaction and improving tracking and scanning technology.

In the years since 1903, the situation faced by Ford Motor Company has changed in every way imaginable. The organization has operations around the world and must contend with myriad international competitors. The United Auto Workers, a major union, bargains aggressively for wages, benefits, and worker rights, and various government agencies regulate and control many of Ford's activities in areas ranging from pollution to hiring. Quality has become of paramount importance. Suppliers often have several large customers, thus shrinking Ford's relative importance as a purchaser. Consumer tastes and demands continue to change, necessitating regularly updated models and features. Today Ford makes twenty-three different car models, each of which has to be redesigned every few years. The price of gasoline can also dramatically affect demand for different models: when gas prices go up, demand rises for small fuel-efficient cars like the Escort; but when the price of gas goes down or stabilizes, demand jumps for larger cars like the LTD or Lincoln series. In short, the environment that Ford must cope with is vastly more complex and more prone to change today than it was just a few decades ago.

In a sense, the various forces and changes that buffet organizations today must be viewed as real challenges. Competing for resources is seldom easy; if it were, all organizations would be successful and none would ever fail. Thus major economic changes, competition, globalization trends, legal and social issues, and workplace changes are indeed problems to surmount. The organization that does not deal with them effectively will suffer and perhaps fall by the wayside.[3] At the same time, we should also remember

Figure 3.1

Contemporary Organizational
Challenges

that a natural complement to challenge is opportunity. Failing to meet a challenge can have negative consequences; overcoming it or meeting it successfully can lead to increased profitability, effectiveness, and reputation.

As shown in Figure 3.1, many of the changes that organizations have undergone over the last several years can be characterized as the responses to five sets of challenges: economic, competitive, global, legal and social, and workplace. These challenges are clearly related in several ways, but our intent is simply to sensitize you to the basic issues without going too far beyond our focus on organizations and their managers. Our discussion proceeds from the broadest, most general challenges to more specific ones.

> Organizations face five sets of challenges: economic, competitive, global, legal and social, and workplace. These challenges also provide opportunities.

Economic Challenges

Far more complex than the simple supply and demand curves that students learn to interpret, the real economic world of organizations is fraught with perils and opportunities, challenges and payoffs. Economic challenges of organizations are the forces and dynamics associated with the production and distribution of material wealth in the environment within which the organization functions. General economic factors such as inflation rates, levels of unemployment, interest rates, budget deficits or surpluses, and the international balance of trade are all major economic dimensions that affect organizations. Four more specific economic challenges that have become particularly significant are entrepreneurship, downsizing and cutbacks, the emergence of the service sector, and changes in corporate ownership.

> Economic challenges are the forces and dynamics associated with the production and distribution of material wealth in the environment within which the organization functions.

Entrepreneurship

Entrepreneurship is the process of assuming the risk of business ownership.

People decide to engage in **entrepreneurship,** to assume the risk of business ownership, for a variety of reasons. Many want the freedom of setting their own goals and objectives. Others want the challenge of creating something new — their own product, for example. Still others are attracted by opportunities in a family-owned business that may seem safer or more lucrative than working for a big corporation. As we discuss more fully in the next section, many former employees of large businesses that have cut back on their payrolls decide to start their own business or go to work in someone else's small business.

Small businesses play a vital role in the U.S. economy and in the economies of most industrialized nations around the world. For example, over half of all new private-sector jobs created in the United States in the 1980s were in businesses with fewer than one hundred employees (a common benchmark for defining small business).[4] In many eastern European countries just opening their markets to a free enterprise-based system, small businesses are expected to fuel economic growth and development.

Unfortunately, many new businesses fail within a relatively short period of time. Although such failures sometimes carry significant negative consequences (including financial setback, social censure, and damage to reputation), many successful entrepreneurs fail one or more times before they finally get on track. Henry Ford, for example, went bankrupt twice before succeeding with Ford Motor Company.

Many other small businesses survive from the very beginning. They establish a comfortable niche for themselves by serving a well-defined market, and they allow the owner-entrepreneur to set the course for organization development. These businesses may remain small or grow slowly over a period of several years. A few take off and become large businesses within just a few years. The Entrepreneurial Challenge describes the path of one new business. Entrepreneurship and small businesses are the subject of Chapter 24.

Downsizing and Cutbacks

Downsizing is a planned reduction in organizational size. *Cutbacks* are reductions in the scope of operations.

During much of the 1970s and 1980s many firms were forced to go through a period of downsizing and cutbacks, and the trend is continuing in the 1990s. **Downsizing** is a planned reduction in organizational size (number of employees, number of businesses, number of markets served, and so forth). **Cutbacks** are reductions in the scope of an organization's operations (operating budgets, travel expenses, research and development expenditures, expansion plans, and so on).

For years, U.S. firms in particular enjoyed so much demand for their products and services that they didn't really have many concerns about costs. Likewise, quality was of only token importance (i.e., a Ford had to be only as good as a Chevrolet) and prices could be raised as necessary with consideration for only a handful of competitors. This atmosphere

THE ENTREPRENEURIAL CHALLENGE

RV for Success

William J. Rex is on his way toward becoming another American success story. Rex used to work for a company that made recreational vehicles, or RVs. His first job was assembler, but through hard work and drive he worked himself up to plant manager. When the business was sold, he decided to apply the skills he had learned and start his own firm.

In 1986 he convinced his friends to put up part of the investment to start Rexhall Industries and then sank $150,000 into a warehouse and equipment in Saugus, California. He converted the building into an assembly plant and started making the Airex, a sleek but less expensive alternative to the Fleetwood and Winnebago products that dominate the marketplace. Rexhall's RVs sell for $2,000 to $5,000 less than those of competitors and offer a wider variety of options and special features that appeal to customers.

Sales of the Airex soared to $34 million in 1989 while total industry sales declined by 7 percent. A public stock offering raised several million dollars, and the firm is now on sound financial footing. Rexhall still faces some major hurdles, however. For one thing, the organization needs a nationwide distribution and maintenance network if it is going to continue to grow. For another, Rexhall is fast approaching the point where Fleetwood and Winnebago will recognize it as a serious competitor and take steps to regain the market share they have lost to the newcomer.

REFERENCES: "These RVs Are Doing Wheelies Off Dealers' Lots," *Business Week,* May 21, 1990, p. 104; Joe Schwartz, "No Fixed Address," *American Demographics,* July 1988, pp. 50–51; "The Unhappy Campers at Winnebago," *Business Week,* May 28, 1990, p. 28; "This Skyline Is Drawing Crowds," *Business Week,* April 3, 1989, p. 92.

changed dramatically when global competition spread and productivity and quality took on greater importance as competitive advantages. Many U.S. organizations began to experience loss of market share and declining income. They found themselves with excessive payroll costs (too many employees), excess capacity (too many offices and plants), and technology that was far too inefficient and outdated to rise to the competitive challenge.

In response, many organizations closed some plants, refurbished others, and slashed payrolls. They also eliminated hundreds of thousands of jobs. For example, through attrition, layoffs, terminations, and early retirement, Honeywell eliminated 4,000 jobs in 1986; AT&T cut 66,000 people over a three-year period; and General Motors trimmed its salaried work force by 25 percent. General Electric eliminated 100,000 jobs; BankAmerica cut 24,000 jobs; and even IBM (with a strong reputation for job security and employment longevity) has edged thousands of employees toward early retirement.[5]

Many managers agree that most of the big cutbacks are nearing completion, but more may be needed in the 1990s. For example, NYNEX in early 1990 announced a planned cutback of several thousand jobs. Although downsizing has helped many businesses regain a competitive position, it has also undermined workers' confidence in the traditional job security they have long expected from large organizations. As a result, worker loyalty has diminished, and some firms are finding that they must offer additional incentives to employees to make up for reduced job security.

The Emergence of the Service Sector

The service sector has become an increasingly important part of the American economy.

For many decades, American industry sat squarely on its traditional foundation of manufacturing. The manufacturing sector is composed of firms such as automobile companies, steel mills, oil refineries, and computer companies, which make tangible products later sold for profit. In recent decades, however, the service sector has supplanted manufacturing as the basis of the U.S. economy. Services provide utility for consumers, rather than a tangible product. Examples of service firms range from small architectural and accounting partnerships, to neighborhood beauty shops, aerobics studios, and pizza parlors, to giants such as AT&T, Marriott, and Paramount, which have sales in billions of dollars.[6]

In 1947 the service sector accounted for less than half of America's gross national product. By 1975, however, its proportion had grown to 65 percent, and by 1985 it had climbed to over 70 percent. Since the early 1970s, around 90 percent of all new jobs have come from the service sector. Figure 3.2 compares job growth in service-producing industries with that in goods-producing industries.

Changes in Corporate Ownership

Changes in corporate ownership patterns have given some investors more power over the organizations in which they hold an interest.

Corporations sell stock to investors, who then have a share of ownership in the corporation. Until the last few decades, each corporation had so many owners — individual investors — that no single one of them could exert much influence over the firm. Two significant changes in corporate ownership, however, have led to shifts in the way corporations do business.

One change in ownership patterns reflects the emergence of the mutual fund market and the growth of institutional investing. Mutual funds are collections of stocks handled by professional fund managers. Individual investors can choose to put their money in a mutual fund and gain the expertise of a financial professional in deciding what stocks to buy and sell. The fund itself buys and sells stocks, passing along dividends and resale gains to the investors. Since individual mutual funds may have the resources to buy and sell hundreds of millions of dollars in stock, they have much more power than do the individual investors themselves. At the same time, managers who handle investments for institutions (universities, for example) and retirement funds can also control large blocks of stock. Since these managers themselves, however, are responsible for showing a return to their investors, there has been some concern that corporations may feel pressured to focus too much on short-term returns and not enough on long-term strength.[7]

Another change in corporate ownership has been the growth in hostile takeovers. A takeover occurs when one corporation or group of investors buys or trades for enough stock in a company to gain control over it. Such a takeover is considered hostile when the target company does not wish to be taken over. The acquiring firm may want to control the target firm in order to enter a new market, to buttress existing market positions, or to

Figure 3.2

Job Growth in the Service Sector Compared with Job Growth in the Manufacturing Sector

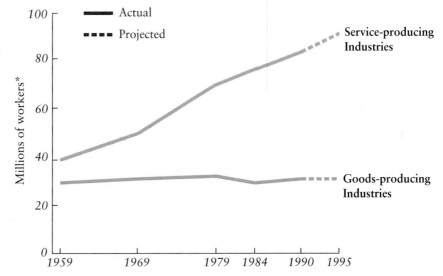

*Includes wage and salary workers, the self-employed, and unpaid family workers

SOURCE: From Ricky W. Griffin/Ronald J. Ebert, *Business,* 2e, © 1991, p. 333. Reprinted by permission of Prentice-Hall, Englewood Cliffs, New Jersey.

achieve other goals. After being acquired, the target firm may be allowed to continue doing what it was already doing; or it may be integrated into the acquiring firm; or it may be broken up and sold, asset by asset, for profit.

Competitive Challenges

Competitive challenges consist of the methods by which organizations attempt to gain advantages over one another in acquiring scarce resources.

Competitive challenges consist of the methods by which organizations attempt to gain advantages over one another in acquiring scarce resources. The major competitors within some industries are quite visible. In the soft-drink market, for example, Coca-Cola and PepsiCo are close competitors. Likewise, well-regarded universities such as Stanford and Harvard compete for the best students, and neighboring states may compete for tourist dollars or industrial development opportunities. Other competitive relationships are more subtle. Two college students with limited entertainment funds on a Saturday night might go out for a pizza or hamburgers. They might go bowling or dancing. They might decide to go to a cinema or to rent a movie and watch it at home. Each of the organizations offering these diverse goods or services is vying for the same consumer dollars.

Virtually all organizations compete with other organizations in some way or another, be it for consumer dollars, student applicants, or budget appropriations. There are several different aspects of effective competition. These are discussed at more length in Chapters 7 and 8. Our concern here is with three sets of challenges that affect an organization's ability to compete effectively: productivity and quality, technology and automation, and innovation and intrapreneurship.

Productivity and Quality

Productivity is a measure of efficiency — how much is created relative to the resources used to create it.

Quality is a measure of value. Both products and services can be judged for quality.

During the last decade organizations around the world have increasingly come to recognize the importance of productivity and quality as ingredients in the recipe for successful competition. **Productivity** is a measure of efficiency — how much is created relative to the resources used to create it. A bank teller who handles 20 customers an hour is more efficient than one who handles only 15 customers an hour. Similarly, if two workers are paid the same wages but the first produces twice as many units each day as the second, the first worker is clearly more productive.

Quality is a measure of value. Consider two wristwatches with the same low selling price. One runs flawlessly for five years, but the other must be discarded after only three. The longevity of the first watch is evidence of its higher quality. Services also have an aspect of quality. Retail customers who are treated cordially and receive a prompt refund for unwanted merchandise might assess the quality of a store's service as high. Customers who are treated rudely are likely to rate the quality of service as poor. As these examples show, productivity and quality can be used to characterize both tangible products and services.

Productivity can be assessed at numerous levels, all the way from the productivity of an individual worker to the productivity of an entire country or economic system. We can talk just as meaningfully about the relative productivity of two bank tellers as we can about the relative productivity of IBM and Compaq Computer or workers in Japan versus workers in France. Productivity helps determine the standard of living enjoyed by the residents of a particular economic system and the relative prosperity of its various businesses. In general, the more productive a country's workers are, the higher the country's standard of living will be and the more profitable its businesses.[8] Although American workers have for years been the most productive in the world, the rate of productivity growth in other industrial countries has outstripped that of the United States. This means that organizations in other countries are rapidly closing the gap on productivity. Figure 3.3 illustrates productivity growth rates for several different countries over the past several years.

At one time, managers believed that quality and productivity were inversely related — that spending more to achieve higher quality resulted in higher total costs and, therefore, lower productivity. Now, however, managers recognize that just the opposite is true. Higher quality means fewer defects, more efficient use of resources, and fewer quality inspections and thus actually boosts productivity.[9] Of course, quality is a relative concept. Most knowledgeable consumers expect a Lincoln Continental to be of higher quality than a Ford Escort. But because there are also major price differences between the two automobiles, each product may be of

Figure 3.3

Recent Productivity Growth Rates
in Different Countries

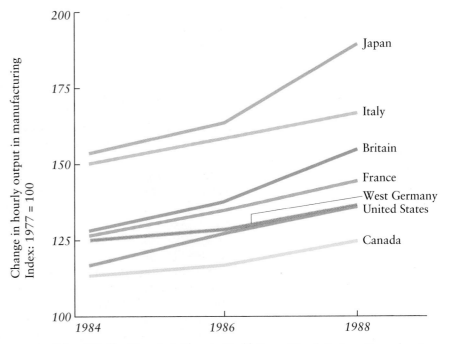

SOURCE: Brian O'Reilly, "America's Place in World Competition," *Fortune,* November 6, 1989. Used by permission of the artist, Anders J. Wenngren.

high quality relative to its price. When assessing quality, then, we must understand that it can have both absolute (as compared to some objective standard) and comparative (as compared to substitute products or services) dimensions.

An organization that falls behind its competitors in either productivity or quality will be hard pressed to catch up. Indeed, more and more organizations are attempting to compete on the basis of productivity and quality. Some of the reasons for this are discussed in Chapters 7 and 8. Other aspects of productivity and quality are covered in Chapter 15.

Technology and Automation

Technology is the set of processes and steps used to transform inputs into outputs. *Automation* is the use of machinery in this process of transformation.

Technology is the set of processes and steps that an organization uses to transform various inputs such as raw materials and component parts into a commodity such as a stereo, a book, or a shirt. **Automation** is the use of machinery, especially computers and robots, in the transformation process.

Technology has become a major focus of the competitive battlefield. Indeed, around the world more firms are finding that intensifying their technology allows them to introduce new products and to improve existing products more effectively than in the past. Much of this advantage flows from extensive use of automation. When Steven Jobs launched his computer firm NeXT, he decided early on that manufacturing and technology would

Technology poses a major competitive challenge for organizations. Michael Kuperstein founded Neurogen Laboratories Inc. in a Boston suburb in January 1988. His firm is working on developing and marketing technology that enables computers to read hand-written numbers. Neurogen's biggest challenge is to match this emerging technology with the rapidly changing technology of the computer industry itself.

be the core of his business. He created an almost fully automated plant that operates with only six hourly workers. Company engineers who design a new circuit board on their office computers can transmit specifications to the plant by modem and pick up the completed board in twenty minutes. The boards are made with such precision that there are less than twenty defects per million units produced.[10]

Many other organizations, both manufacturers and service firms, are recognizing that robotics and other approaches to automation can help them boost productivity and quality while also lowering costs. At the same time, however, automation sometimes eliminates jobs and makes other jobs less challenging than before. We discuss this paradox again in Chapter 15.

Innovation and Intrapreneurship

Innovation is the set of steps that an organization uses to create and develop new products or services and to identify new uses for existing products or services.

Innovation is the set of steps that an organization uses to create and develop new products or services and to identify new uses for existing products or services. Without innovation, firms stagnate as competitors continue to grow. One of the most innovative U.S. firms, 3M, based in Minnesota, has a goal of generating 25 percent of its profits from products less than five years old. Recent successes for 3M include Post-it Note Pads and removable Scotch Magic Tape. Post-it notes were a new product; the removable tape was an extension of an existing product.

Americans have typically been among the world leaders in innovation. All too frequently, however, U.S. scientists have achieved new-product breakthroughs only to see organizations in other countries devise better ways of exploiting them for a mass market. This has been the case for a wide range of products ranging from televisions and cameras to hard disks. In recent years, however, many American businesses have renewed their commitment to not only developing new products but applying innovative methods to manufacturing and marketing as well.[11] For example, Eastman Kodak, IBM, and Merck have all made significant commitments in the last few years to increase spending on R&D, automate plants, and strive for greater innovation.

An *intrapreneur* is an individual who initiates ventures within a large organization.

Many firms are also finding that intrapreneurship is an effective approach to stimulating innovation. An **intrapreneur** is an individual who initiates ventures within a large organization, instead of starting a brand-new business. He or she develops new ideas and then champions them through the various organizational channels that lead to their introduction into the marketplace. At 3M it was an intrapreneur who developed the Post-it Note Pad and then fought for it over the objections of his boss, who didn't think it was a good idea. Many organizations are actively encouraging and rewarding intrapreneurship. Some firms even allow engineers and scientists a fixed amount of time each week to pursue pet projects. Both innovation and intrapreneurship are described more fully in Chapter 9.

Global Challenges

Global challenges include new marketplace and competitive pressures associated with the movement toward a global economy.

Global challenges to organizations include new marketplace and competitive pressures associated with the movement toward a global economy. Chapters 1 and 2 noted the trends toward globalization of business. This section examines the organizational challenges associated with this trend.

The Globalization Movement

Some organizations began to function on a worldwide scale by means of business tools and practices developed during the Renaissance. Christopher Columbus, for example, was seeking a new Spanish trade route to the Orient when he landed in the West Indies. The British Empire also grew, at least in part, in response to competitive business pressures. But since most markets were small and transportation and communication were slow, global operations were the exception rather than the rule for the vast majority of organizations until the middle of the twentieth century.

After World War II, when many of the industrialized countries lay in ruins, international trade began to take on renewed importance. For many European countries, the United States was the only viable supplier of goods, and many American firms began to recognize the true potential of international business. Because American firms had few competitors, international business opportunities were relatively easy for them to exploit. As the industrialized nations rebuilt, however, their businesses also came to

Figure 3.4

Major Marketplaces of the World

Figure 3.4 *(cont.)*

The Pacific Rim

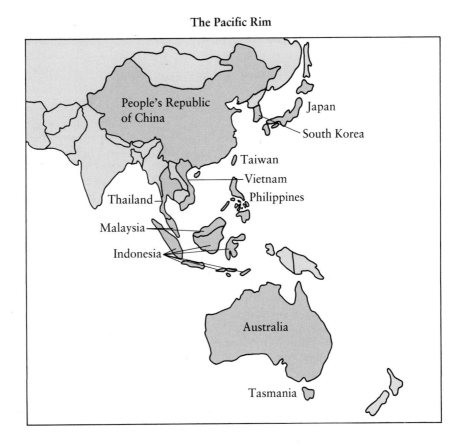

vie for international opportunities. International trade grew, and well-defined marketplaces — geographic regions in which firms compete — began to emerge. A few marketplaces still follow national boundaries, but three major marketplaces currently dominate the global economy.

As Figure 3.4 shows, North America, the European Community, and Japan and the Pacific Rim are generally seen as the dominant markets today. Most large global organizations are based in one of these marketplaces and do business in the others. South America, Africa, the Soviet Union, and China are also becoming important marketplaces. The Global Challenge discusses some of the challenges and opportunities for business associated with recent economic changes in the Soviet Union. The dramatic changes there in the last few years have provided managers with a new potential market in which to compete.

Many organizations today really have no choice but to adopt a global perspective on doing business. Even if a company targets only a single small national market, competitors that draw on global financial resources, design and technology breakthroughs, and production efficiencies are quite likely to enjoy a marked advantage. Thus the effects of the globalization movement are so pervasive that many organizations must participate in that movement or else gradually lose their ability to compete at all.

THE GLOBAL CHALLENGE

Challenges and Opportunities in the Soviet Union

Until the late 1980s, the USSR was a closed market-place. All businesses were state owned, and foreign business was allowed in only under rigid conditions. The thriving Soviet underground economy sometimes found ways to circumvent state control, but "official" businesses always operated under strict government vigilance.

With the advent of President Mikhail Gorbachev's policy of *perestroika,* the Soviet economy embarked on a dramatic, and predictably bumpy, road to change. Under the emerging "semi-free" market system, private ownership of business will be possible, and foreign business will have more opportunities to enter the Soviet marketplace. The question facing many international businesses is whether to enter this marketplace and, if so, how quickly. On the one hand, profits are still likely to be several years away, and there are no guarantees that government economic policies will remain committed to an open market. On the other hand, moving aggressively today might give an organization a significant advantage over more conservative competitors.

The few U.S. firms with a history to draw on provide mixed signals. PepsiCo has operated in the USSR since the early 1960s but employs very few people there. The firm reports that its operations are still only marginally profitable. McDonald's, in contrast, opened its first store in Moscow in 1990 and reported tremendous success in just a short time.

Despite the uncertainties, many organizations are making commitments to the Soviet marketplace. Gillette, for example, is building a new razor-blade plant outside Moscow, and Estée Lauder has opened a perfume store near Red Square. Ford and General Motors are both exploring joint-venture opportunities in the USSR, as are firms from Japan and various European nations. All in all, it appears as though the Soviet Union will be a major competitive battleground for business in the 1990s.

REFERENCES: "Crash Courses in Capitalism for Ivan the Globe-Trotter," *Business Week,* May 28, 1990, pp. 42–44; "U.S. Ideas Creep into Soviet Union," *USA Today,* May 11, 1990, pp. B1, B2; James B. Hayes, "Wanna Make a Deal in Moscow?" *Fortune,* October 22, 1990, pp. 113–115.

Competing in a Global Environment

Organizations competing in a global environment face myriad challenges and opportunities. At the simplest level, an organization must determine which market to enter and how to enter it. One way is to hire a foreign broker to sell the firm's goods in the chosen market. Another is to license a company already in the market to both make and sell the firm's products. Some organizations might decide to build a new plant in that foreign market and make their own products there. Others might enter into a joint venture with another firm to help get a foothold.

To better understand global competition today, Harvard professor Michael Porter has recently described the factors that lead companies in different countries to succeed. His "diamond" of national competitive advantage is shown in Figure 3.5. In the past, many managers associated the success of a country's economic system with the traditional factors of production: natural resources, human resources, capital, and entrepreneurs. Porter, however, claims that industry competition within a country is the real key to global success. Although factors of production are important, so too are company strategy (what businesses want to do), structure (how they are designed), and rivalry (how they compete). Other important aspects of competitiveness are demand conditions (local demand for products and services) and related and supporting industries (for example, the availability of parts manufacturers for auto companies).[12]

To present evidence for his claim, Porter points to Japan, generally considered today to be a model competitive system. U.S. auto companies have to compete with Japanese automakers for market share in the United States. Some American managers object that Japanese businesses are overly protected by Japanese government trade restrictions, but according to Porter people with this perspective are ignoring other aspects of competition. Nissan, Toyota, and Honda are fierce rivals in Japan, in the United States, and in Europe. They compete with General Motors, Ford, Fiat, and Audi, but they also compete with each other.

Table 3.1 identifies the number of Japanese rivals in selected industries. In the United States, there are essentially three domestic automakers (General Motors, Ford, and Chrysler) and two domestic camera makers (Eastman Kodak and Polaroid). In Japan, however, there are no less than nine major automobile companies and fifteen major camera companies! Porter argues that the fierce internal competition within Japan is a major reason Japanese firms compete so well abroad. They must strive for efficiency, productivity, and quality to survive at home, and the skills they have learned there put them at a considerable advantage abroad.

Figure 3.5

Porter's Diamond of National Competitive Advantage

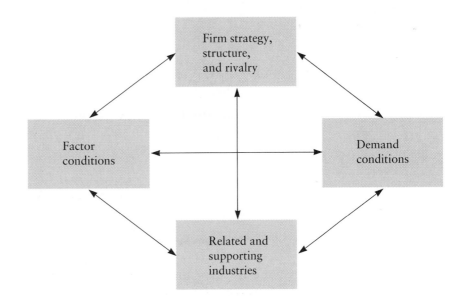

SOURCE: Reprinted by permission of *Harvard Business Review.* An exhibit from "The Competitive Advantage of Nations" by Michael E. Porter (March/April 1990). Copyright © 1990 by the President and Fellows of Harvard College; all rights reserved.

Legal and Social Challenges

Legal challenges are guidelines or prohibitions that an organization is required by law to recognize in its practices. Social challenges are the prevailing expectations that a society has about the roles organizations

Table 3.1

Estimated Number of Japanese Rivals in Selected Industries

Industry	Number of Domestic Rivals
Air conditioners	13
Audio equipment	25
Automobiles	9
Cameras	15
Car audio	12
Carbon fibers	7
Construction equipment	15
Copiers	14
Facsimile machines	10
Large-scale computers	6
Lift trucks	8
Machine tools	112
Microwave equipment	5
Motorcycles	4
Musical instruments	4
Personal computers	16
Semiconductors	34
Sewing machines	20
Shipbuilding	33
Steel	5
Synthetic fibers	8
Television sets	15
Truck and bus tires	5
Trucks	11
Typewriters	14
Videocassette recorders	10

SOURCE: Adapted by permission of *Harvard Business Review*. An exhibit from "The Competitive Advantage of Nations" by Michael E. Porter (March/April 1990). Copyright © 1990 by the President and Fellows of Harvard College; all rights reserved.

A variety of legal and social challenges must be addressed by all organizations. When Yvonne Scruggs-Leftwich left her career in government to pursue other interests, she decided to start a business that would also serve a useful social function. After a careful study of business opportunities and community needs, Scruggs-Leftwich established a nondepository bank in downtown Buffalo where inner-city residents could handle many of their daily business transactions without having to drive to the suburbs.

Legal challenges are guidelines or prohibitions that an organization is required by law to recognize in its practices. Social challenges are the prevailing expectations that a society has about the roles organizations should or should not play in community life.

should or should not play in community life. The two are often closely related and sometimes overlap. One important challenge is the call for ethical behavior in organizations. Another concerns government regulation. Still another is public pressure on business to assume more responsibility in protecting the natural environment. Each of these challenges has both legal and social aspects.

The Ethical Dilemma

Ever since the advent of large businesses, people have questioned the morals and ethics of those who run them. Nineteenth-century U.S. industrialists such as Vanderbilt, Carnegie, and Rockefeller were called "robber barons" because they were perceived to be padding their pockets at the expense of the general public and would stop at nothing to further their own ambitions and gains. On the one hand, they took considerable personal risks in establishing their businesses in an atmosphere unrestrained by today's norms of business etiquette. On the other hand, they did in fact break laws and injure people in the pursuit of their goals.

The ethical standards of individual managers have come under increased scrutiny in recent years.

Much of the recent demand for ethics in organizations was stimulated by the behavior of a few individuals during the 1980s. Ivan Boesky, David Levine, and Michael Milken were all involved in widely publicized Wall

Street scandals.[13] E. F. Hutton, the investment company, was charged with check kiting; General Electric employees admitted to faking time sheets to cheat the government; and the Bank of Boston was involved in a money-laundering scheme. Those practices are illegal, but many instances of legal but ethically questionable behavior also arose. Nor were such problems confined to the United States. Major ethical scandals plagued Japan, Great Britain, and West Germany as well.

All managers face ethical dilemmas as an inherent part of decision making. Both organizations and the managers who work for them must strive to identify the ethical context in which decisions get made. For example, consider the case of a manager deciding what to do about employee safety. His plant is within guidelines established by the Occupational Safety and Health Administration (OSHA). He recognizes, however, that some hazards still exist for workers in the plant. One choice he has is to do nothing and accept the risk still present on the grounds that he is within federal guidelines. Another choice is to make a modest investment to reduce some of the risk. Yet another choice is to make a major investment to eliminate virtually all risk in the plant. Depending on the context of the decision, such as the availability of funds and the nature of the risks involved, compelling arguments can be made for each of these three choices.

Managers must make countless decisions every day about how to treat employees and how to interact with suppliers, customers, lenders, regulators, and competitors. Virtually all of these decisions have an ethical component to them. We return to issues of ethics and social responsibility in Chapter 22.

Government Regulation

In theory, free-market economies are characterized by relatively little government regulation: businesses are free to compete as they see fit. In planned economies (socialistic or communistic economies, for example), government regulation plays a much greater role: the government plans what is supposed to happen within the economy and then regulates business toward that end.

Even though the United States has a free-market economy, an abundance of government regulation both proscribes and prescribes business activity. Government regulation of American business has been considered necessary for a variety of reasons. For one, large and powerful firms have sometimes tried to drive weaker competitors out of business by using unfair business practices. For another, government regulation is sometimes necessary to support various laws such as the Occupational Safety and Health Act and the Environmental Protection Act. There is also a feeling among some people that the government should strive to maintain a reasonable level of competition for the public good. Finally, many people believe that unscrupulous business people will resort to unethical and illegal behavior on a regular basis if they are not regulated.

Government regulation of business is a contentious issue for supporters of a free-market economy.

Critics of regulation argue that if the United States is indeed a free-market economy, businesses in America should be free to do whatever they want. The logic behind this argument is that if a business does something that people object to, the people will "punish" the business by not buying its products or services. In the United States, there has been a trend to reduce or lower regulation of business. For example, in recent years much regulation of the airline, financial, and trucking industries has been softened. What has been the result? In the airline industry many weak carriers have been absorbed by larger ones, but fares are considerably lower than they were during the days of extreme regulation. In the financial industry, however, managers in many savings and loan organizations took advantage of decreased regulation and prompted one of the biggest financial crises in American history.

Still, many managers believe that government regulation is excessive and costs everyone more money. For example, Goodyear Tire & Rubber recently generated 345,000 pages of computer printout to comply with one new OSHA regulation. The firm also spends over $35 million each year to comply with various government regulations and devotes thirty-four employee-years annually to filling out required forms associated with those regulations.[14]

The degree of government regulation varies dramatically around the world. Some countries, such as Australia and the United States, have relatively little regulation. Other countries, such as the Soviet Union and China, have far more. However, as more and more regulated economies move toward a free-market system, regulation in general is declining in countries such as the Soviet Union, Poland, and Yugoslavia. Still, government regulation of organizational practices is likely to remain a significant issue for the next decade.

The Natural Environment

Concerns about the natural environment and the role of business in protecting it are another focus of legal and social challenges to organizations.

Concerns about pollution and the environment have been raised for decades, but they are coming to center stage.[15] Increasing consumer awareness, growing alarm about problems ranging from global warming to the closing of landfills, and media attention on events such as the Exxon *Valdez* oil spill have sensitized the public to these issues. Organizations of all types must address a variety of controversial environmental issues, from air pollution to toxic waste disposal to water pollution. For example, some environmentalists protest the plastic containers that many firms use to package their products. The Environmental Challenge describes steps that Mobil Corporation is taking to help overcome these criticisms.

Still another issue that has emerged is the widespread organizational practice of promoting products as being environmentally sound. Sometimes the marketing claims are legitimate, but at other times they are overstated. After examination by the Federal Trade Commission, Procter & Gamble had to drop claims that its disposable diapers were biodegradable.

THE ENVIRONMENTAL CHALLENGE

Mobil Enters the Recycling Business

One of the biggest problems facing business today is determining how to respond to the groundswell of consumer interest in recycling. Many communities nationwide have initiated curbside recycling of aluminum, glass, and paper. Still at issue, however, is an item that has been a packaging staple for years — the plastic grocery sack.

American grocery stores dispense around 12 billion plastic grocery bags each year. The problem is that the bags are not biodegradable. Moreover, it is expensive to recycle them. Environmentalists have started a movement to ban or limit the use of these bags. This spells trouble (lost profits, for example) for the firms that make them.

Mobil Corporation is the second largest producer of plastic bags in the United States. To stave off pressures to ban the bags, the firm recently announced a plan to handle expensive recycling of them itself. Gro-

cery stores like the bags because they are cheaper than paper and take up less storage space. Thus Mobil plans to enlist their help in collecting the bags for eventual recycling.

Customers will be encouraged to return their plastic bags to the grocery stores. Kroger, for example, has placed large bins at the front of its stores with signs asking customers to return their plastic bags. Mobil will collect the bags and recycle them for other use. Of course, the program is highly dependent on consumer acceptance. The recycling effort will work only if enough people return their bags to make it cost-effective.

REFERENCES: "Mobil to Recycle Flimsy Plastic Grocery Bags," *Wall Street Journal,* May 16, 1990, pp. B1, B6; Jennifer Lawrence, "Mobil," *Advertising Age,* January 29, 1991, pp. 12–13; "Suddenly, Green Marketers are Seeing Red Flags," *Business Week,* February 25, 1991, pp. 74–76.

Citizens from many countries are concerned about the extent to which businesses around the world are acting irresponsibly toward the environment. For example, many environmentalists decry the unregulated fishing practices in Japan and the fact that Japanese fishing fleets hunt whales or destroy dolphins while catching tuna. The Canadian government has for years tried to get the United States to curb the pollution that results in forest-destroying acid rains. Others worry that Brazil is destroying its vital rain forests for the sake of industry and expansion. Many countries in eastern Europe suffer from the worst industrial pollution on Earth. For example, 70 percent of the rivers in Czechoslovakia are heavily polluted; one-third of Bulgaria's forests are damaged by unrestricted air pollution; and the area that formerly was East Germany has major toxic waste problems.[16]

Workplace Challenges

The relationships among organizations and their managers and operating employees give rise to workplace challenges.

The relationships among organizations and their managers and operating employees give rise to several workplace challenges. Here we focus on three: employee expectations and rights, workplace democracy, and labor market trends and forces.

Employee Expectations and Rights

Employee expectations and rights have changed in recent years, posing a significant workplace challenge for organizations.

In the early days of scientific management, as detailed in Chapter 2, organizations operated on the assumption that all workers were only economically motivated. Later, with more emphasis on human relations, it was thought that personal satisfaction was the driving force in motivation. Eventually, managers came to recognize that employee motivation is actually a very complex process and that each individual has his or her own unique set of needs and perceptions of how best to fulfill them. These needs continue to change over time. Now that more fathers want to participate in raising children and more women seek professional careers, contemporary organizations are finding it necessary to be more flexible in how they treat their employees.[17] Many allow workers more say in selecting and performing jobs and provide more information to workers about future organization plans.

Managers seeking to motivate, enhance the performance of, and help develop their organization's work force must understand the needs of employees. Some managers even argue that organizations should help employees with drug or alcohol problems. Critics of this viewpoint, however, raise concerns about worker rights and privacy.[18] They assert that individual behavior outside the workplace is private and that organizations should not intervene as long as employees meet performance expectations.

Workplace Democracy

Workplace democracy is the practice of allowing workers a greater voice in how the organization is managed.

Some organizations have gradually recognized that letting workers have a say in organizational practices enhances worker commitment while also improving overall effectiveness. Workers, in turn, feel more valued as members of the organization. **Workplace democracy** is the practice of allowing workers a greater voice in how the organization is managed.

As you will see in Chapters 11 and 17, many firms have begun to increase the participation of workers in determining how they do their own jobs. Employees who participate in such programs expect to have a greater voice in a wide variety of other areas, including but not limited to working hours, organizational practices, and hiring and compensation decisions. Sometimes this voice becomes legitimized in very specific ways. For example, the United Auto Workers union was granted a seat on Chrysler's board of directors in return for wage concessions made during the automaker's financial crisis in the early 1980s.

In some parts of the world, workplace democracy has been part of organizational life for a long time. In Germany, organizations are required by law to have a specified number of operating employees and managers on their governing boards. In the United States, however, workplace democracy is a relatively new concept that managers are just beginning to address. For example, in traditional General Motors plants, workers are gradually gaining a bigger voice. However, in the firm's new Saturn division, workers started out with a significant role in deciding how work will be done.

Worker councils review an array of activities and projects and make recommendations to Saturn management about whether to adopt them.

Labor Market Trends and Forces

In the United States, union membership is decreasing. More women and members of minority groups are entering the workplace. More people are seeking part-time or temporary work as a way of increasing their leisure time or modifying their lifestyle. At the same time, the average age of the work force is increasing, and people are changing jobs more frequently.

The U.S. labor market will grow increasingly more diverse in the coming years.

As a result of these changes, organizations are having to cope with increasingly diverse and transient work forces. Fifty years ago, a typical first-line manager might have been responsible for a group of white male unionized workers with an average work history in the organization of ten or more years. The manager in that same role today supervises both male and female workers of many races and ethnicities. Most will have a shorter work history with the organization than did employees in years past.

Although few could argue against the merits of this diversity, it does pose unique challenges for the organization. Simply understanding the basic assumptions that all members of the organization have about work takes special care. Language barriers may need to be surmounted, and managers may require training in order to be sensitive to cultural differences in interpersonal relations. The essential point to remember is that just as the external environment of organizations has grown increasingly complex over the past half-century, so too has the internal environment. We return to a discussion of organizational environments in Chapter 4.

Learning Summary

Organizations today operate in an ever-changing world. As part of this change they must confront a variety of issues. This confrontation carries with it both challenge and opportunity. Five sets of contemporary organizational challenges are economic, competitive, global, legal and social, and workplace issues.

Economic challenges are the forces and dynamics associated with the production and distribution of material wealth in the environment within which the organization functions. Some of the most important economic challenges are entrepreneurship, downsizing and cutbacks, the emergence of the service sector, and changes in corporate ownership.

Competitive challenges consist of the methods by which organizations attempt to gain advantages over one another in acquiring scarce resources. Three competitive challenges that organizations have to address today are productivity and quality, technology and automation, and innovation and intrapreneurship.

Global challenges include new marketplace and competitive pressures associated with the movement toward a global economy. The globalization movement has led to the emergence of three major world marketplaces: North America, the European Community, and Japan and the Pacific Rim. Managing in a global environment requires an understanding of the factors that affect global competition.

Legal challenges are guidelines or prohibitions that an organization is required by law to recognize in its practices. Social challenges are the prevailing expectations that a society has about the roles organizations should or should not play in community life. Key legal and social challenges today focus on the ethical standards of managers, government regulation, and the relationship between business and the natural environment.

Workplace challenges are posed by the relationships among organizations, their managers, and their operating employees. Employee expectations and rights, workplace democracy, and labor market trends and forces are important areas of challenge.

Questions and Exercises

Review Questions

1. Identify and briefly describe the five sets of organizational challenges discussed in this chapter.
2. What are some of the main economic challenges facing organizations today?
3. How are productivity and quality different, and how are they related? Can you change one without changing the other?
4. Why is innovation important to organizations?
5. What are some of the arguments for and against government regulation of business? Can a "free market" truly exist? Why or why not?

Analysis Questions

1. How is entrepreneurship affected by organizational downsizing and cutbacks?
2. What issues would a plant manager consider before installing a fully automated assembly line?
3. It is fairly easy to identify American firms, such as automakers, that have stiff international competition. Identify some American firms that appear to have no direct foreign competitors, at least not in North America.
4. What are some recent controversies that have arisen regarding the relationship between the natural environment and business? Give specific examples, and describe the issues involved in each.

5. Suppose you have a subordinate who has a drug problem. The subordinate is capable of performing well on the job but seems to be having personal problems resulting from the drug use. Should you try to help, or should you stay out of it? What if your supervisor is experiencing a drug problem?
6. Identify examples of situations in which legal, global, and organizational challenges might be interrelated. That is, think of a specific opportunity or problem an organization might face that has legal, global, and organizational implications.

Application Exercises

1. Ask a local manager to identify the biggest challenges faced by her or his organization. Explain how these challenges relate to those described in the chapter.
2. Describe how each of the challenges discussed in the chapter applies to a nonbusiness organization such as a hospital, a university, or a local charity. Do these organizations face any different challenges?
3. Develop a list of ten personal challenges that interest you. Which challenges do you presently feel most equipped to address? Which do you feel least equipped to address?

Chapter Notes

1. "The Man Who Rewrote Reader's Digest," *Business Week*, June 4, 1990, pp. 148–149; Gary Hoover, Alta Campbell, and Patrick J. Spain, eds., *Hoover's Handbook — Profiles of Over 500 Major Corporations* (Austin, Tex.: The Reference Press, 1990), p. 454; Benjamin H. Cheever, "Bad Days in Pleasantville," *The Nation*, May 7, 1990, pp. 628–632; "Pulp Profits," *The Economist*, October 20, 1990, pp. 84–86; "Reader's Digest Still Hot a Year Later," *USA Today*, February 14, 1991, p. 3B.
2. See Alvin Toffler, *Future Shock* (New York: Random House, 1970).
3. "Managing Now for the 1990s," *Fortune*, September 26, 1988, pp. 44–47.
4. "Small-Business Hiring, a Locomotive for the Economy in the '80s, Is Slowing," *Wall Street Journal*, March 16, 1990, pp. B1, B3.
5. Anne B. Fisher, "The Downside of Downsizing," *Fortune*, May 23, 1988, pp. 42–52.
6. "The Service 500," *Fortune*, June 4, 1990, p. 304.
7. John J. Curran, "Companies That Rob the Future," *Fortune*, July 4, 1988, pp. 84–89.
8. Terence P. Pare, "Why Some Do It the Wrong Way," *Fortune*, May 21, 1990, pp. 75–76.
9. Joel Dreyfuss, "Victories in the Quality Crusade," *Fortune*, October 10, 1988, pp. 80–88.
10. Joel Dreyfuss, "Getting High Tech Back on Track," *Fortune*, January 1, 1990, pp. 74–77.

11. Christopher Knowlton, "What America Makes Best," *Fortune,* March 28, 1988, pp. 40–53.
12. Michael Porter, *The Competitive Advantage of Countries* (New York: Free Press, 1990).
13. " 'Guilty, Your Honor,' " *Business Week,* May 7, 1990, pp. 32–37.
14. "Many Businesses Blame Governmental Policies for Productivity Lag," *Wall Street Journal,* October 28, 1980, pp. 1, 22.
15. See Jeremy Main, "Here Comes the Big New Cleanup," *Fortune,* November 21, 1988, pp. 102–118; David Kirkpatrick, "Environmentalism: The New Crusade," *Fortune,* February 21, 1990, pp. 44–52.
16. "Eastern Europe's Big Cleanup," *Business Week,* March 19, 1990, pp. 114–115.
17. "Flexible Formulas," *Wall Street Journal,* June 4, 1990, pp. R34, R35.
18. "Is Your Boss Spying on You?" *Business Week,* January 15, 1990, pp. 74–75.

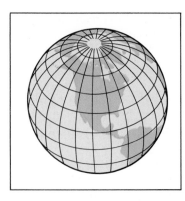

CASE 3.1

Big ITW Thinks Small

Illinois Tool Works (ITW) is a big company. A maker of thousands of products from screws to valves to adhesives, it commands the number-one or number-two spot in dozens of small market niches. Its sales top $2 billion a year, and it has operations in more than thirty countries. Yet its executives will tell you that the secret of its success is thinking small.

Only one hundred people work at company headquarters near O'Hare Airport, where they occupy just one-and-a-half stories of a nondescript building. At the top of the largest of the company's nine groups — the construction products group — are three central administrators: a president, a controller, and a secretary who works for both. Top-heavy this company isn't.

ITW likes it that way. In fact, if it had a mascot, it would probably be the amoeba, which multiplies by dividing itself in two. The company's nine groups comprise ninety divisions, each in charge of its own research and development, manufacturing, and marketing, and none with annual revenues over $30 million. In response to customers' changing needs, engineers and marketers in these divisions are constantly coming up with new products; and if a product looks promising, it and the people who work on it are split off to become a new division.

For instance, in the mid-1980s a customer of the Fastex division wanted a buckle for life jackets. The buckle that Fastex came up with was so durable and safe that its uses quickly multiplied. Soon it became the focus of a new unit, Nexus, which now sells millions of dollars of buckles for everything from bicycle helmets to pet collars. ITW engineers also developed plastic six-pack collars, which soon earned a division of their own. That division has been working on twelve-pack collars and using photodegradable plastic so that the discarded collars do less harm to animals and to the environment.

Such extreme decentralization allows each unit to know its market very well and to be ready to fill any niche that competitors haven't discovered. Most of ITW's salespeople are engineers who learn the manufacturing processes of their customers and work closely with ITW research and development people to come up with a steady stream of products that will improve the work that their customers do. ITW's Buildex division, for example, heard that insurance companies were going to start discouraging the use of adhesive to fasten insulation to the roofs of commercial buildings. So it came up with small plates that take the place of the adhesive. Not satisfied with that step, Buildex invented a tool to install the plates; the tool can be worked by one person instead of the two that the job used to require.

Since ITW owns 2,400 active U.S. patents and ITW designers are coming up with new ideas every day, no one knows precisely how many products the company makes. This tremendous diversity has forced ITW's production engineers to think both big *and* small. Recently ITW reshuffled some of its factory operations to take advantage of both economies of scale and more customized production.

One of ITW's factories manufactured only "self-drilling" screws that fasten two pieces of automotive sheet metal together, creating their own hole. But that one type of product actually came in 2,500 varieties, and it could take a single screw months to emerge from the six processes involved in its manufacture. ITW discovered that it could rearrange assembly lines so that one worker could perform all six processes. But it also discovered that the new "in-lining" setup was efficient only for large batches of a particular type of screw. So it began sorting out the products that got ordered in large quantities from those that sold only in small quantities.

By segregating production, ITW simplified and speeded manufacturing. Many high-volume products are now made in small "focus factories," where a few workers make a single product on a highly automated assembly line. These factories are not just efficient; they are also good places to work. Individual employees can see that they are making a contribution, and they are often given a good deal of responsibility over factory operations.

ITW pursues its small-and-innovative approach even when handling acquisitions. In 1986 it bought Signode Industries, a maker of specialty packaging, and immediately began to break Signode into smaller units. Within months, the new units had come up with twenty new products, including the first battery-operated power nailing tool.

By taking a chance in order to fill a market niche ignored by others, ITW may "make a lot of mistakes,"* as Chairman John Nichols says, but the thinking-small philosophy doesn't appear to be one of them. And that philosophy certainly seems appropriate for a company that first gained attention by patenting the lowly lock washer.

Discussion Questions

1. Why is a decentralized organization structure particularly appropriate for a company with ITW's types of products?
2. Do you think that engineers and designers would enjoy working for a division of ITW? Why or why not?
3. What are the potential drawbacks to the amoeba-like growth of ITW's divisions?
4. What types of organizational challenges has ITW successfully faced?

---

* Quoted in John Merwin, "Think Small and Grow," *Forbes*, January 11, 1988, p. 147.

REFERENCES: Ronald Henkoff, "The Ultimate Nuts & Bolts Co.," *Fortune*, July 16, 1990, pp. 70–73; Suzanne Loeffelholz, "Illinois Tool Works: Waiting for Godot," *Financial World*, April 18, 1989, pp. 15; John Merwin, "Think Small and Grow," *Forbes*, January 11, 1988, p. 147.

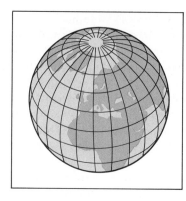

CASE 3.2

SAS Leads the Pack

As Pan Am, Continental, and Eastern Air Lines have recently discovered, it's difficult for an international airline to succeed even when it is based in the country of frequent fliers and has spent years amassing impressive international routes. Think, therefore, of how much more difficult it is for Jan Carlzon and his airline, Scandinavian Airlines System (SAS), based in Sweden. Sweden has a population about the size of New York City's; it's not exactly a hub of international travel; and its people are used to being well paid. And in the two years prior to Carlzon's takeover in 1981, SAS had lost $30 million.

SAS's current success—it made almost $200 million in 1989—is a testament to Carlzon's ability to alter radically the way his company views its business and to plan intelligently for the changes to come. Carlzon believes that after the predicted deregulation of European airlines in 1992, large carriers will elbow smaller ones out of business, as happened in the United States in the years following deregulation there. Carlzon plans for his airline to be one of the survivors.

When Carlzon took over SAS, he was worried about surviving not into the next century but into the next year. A jump in oil prices had shaken the entire industry; American airlines were in turmoil following deregulation; and SAS's reputation was deteriorating. Because of its high union wages, Carlzon knew his airline couldn't compete in the fare wars. So he looked to his company's strength—his well-paid work force and Scandinavia's worldwide reputation for quality. And he staked the company's survival on its ability to attract business customers, many of whom are less concerned with a flight's cost than with its amenities.

To turn itself into a business traveler's dream, SAS devoted up to 60 percent of its seats to EuroClass, a business class with wide leather seats and VIP treatment. SAS also went all-out to improve its customers' experiences on the ground. It linked itself to hotels around the world, improved its lounges, and made more computers and fax machines available to business customers who want to work while they wait.

Most importantly, Carlzon set out to change the way his employees deal with customers. "We used to fly planes," he says; "now we transport people."* Carlzon sees the most important employee-customer interactions—which he calls "moments of truth"—as occurring during check-in and boarding and whenever a problem arises. If employees handle such moments well, he reasons, travelers will feel good about the airline and will return to it. So SAS gave its employees the power to handle such difficult moments themselves, making a refund or offering free drinks without a lot of red tape. Carlzon sees the job of management as supporting its front-line employees, communicating with them, making their jobs easier, removing the barriers that get in the way of the best possible customer service.

Carlzon's strategy worked and turned SAS around. But he wasn't content just to fine-tune this one successful strategy. He foresaw the problems that his relatively small airline would face as airline regulations disappeared, but he also knew that to grow SAS had to gain access to the routes from which the company was currently cut off. So he began making cooperative agreements with other airlines. With Swiss Air, Finnair, and Austrian Airlines, SAS formed the European Quality Alliance. Alliance members work to coordinate such things as their schedules of flights to eastern Europe, and they hope to win better treatment from airplane manufacturers by cooperating in high-volume purchases.

SAS now has similar agreements or ownership stakes in airlines around the world. It owns 35 percent of LAN Chile Airlines and connects with its flights in São Paulo, Brazil. Its 25 percent ownership of British Midland gives it a foothold in Great Britain, and cooperative agreements give it routes to Tokyo, Toronto, and Bangkok. In 1990, SAS made its biggest move by buying a significant share in struggling Continental Airlines. Although Continental may have to sell off many of its foreign routes, SAS is most eager for access to its domestic routes in the United States. Within months of the purchase, SAS passengers were pouring through the new international terminal in Newark, New Jersey.

Ten years after SAS set a new standard for how airlines treat their customers, U.S. airlines are bombarding Americans with ads demonstrating how well *they* treat their business customers. And some people in the industry hope that other Carlzon innovations will catch on. After SAS bought a piece of Continental, the U.S. Department of Transportation turned down a request by Continental's board to make Carlzon Continental's chairman. Apparently the board knows a good man when it sees one.

Discussion Questions

1. What major organizational challenges has SAS faced?
2. Why has SAS succeeded where many American airlines have failed?
3. What environmental and government pressures are likely to affect SAS in the 1990s?
4. Does SAS's experience seem to contradict the general view that to succeed in tough economic times, a company must cut its labor costs?

* Quoted in Michael Maccoby, "Three Firms That Changed," *Research Technology Management*, January–February 1990, p. 44.

REFERENCES: "Four-Airline European Cooperative Alliance Sets Sights on Eastern European Market," *Aviation Week & Space Technology*, May 14, 1990, pp. 95–98; Kenneth Labich, "An Airline That Soars on Service," *Fortune*, December 31, 1990, pp. 94–96; Kenneth Labich, "Goodbye, Frank, Hello, Jan," *Fortune*, September 10, 1990, p. 11; Michael Maccoby, "Three Firms That Changed," *Research Technology Management*, January–February 1990, pp. 44–45.

II The Strategic Management of Organizations

To survive and prosper, organizations need to manage their strategies, structure, and behavior carefully. Managing an organization's strategy includes analyzing the environment, setting goals and objectives, and formulating and implementing strategies. When these multiple strategic processes are effectively integrated and managed, an organization is well positioned for long-term survival and prosperous operations. This section discusses how firms choose and implement their strategies.

4

Organizational Environments

After studying this chapter, you should be able to:

1. Describe the major components of an organization's general and task environments.

2. Describe the five forces model of industry structure, and use it to predict the economic performance of organizations in different kinds of industries.

3. Explain how organizations both adapt to and influence their environment.

E arly in the 1970s Winnebago, the world's leading manufacturer of motor homes, was flying high. It had cash in the bank and growing orders for its products. Then the Middle East oil embargo hit the United States.

To understand the link between economic and political events in the Middle East and the fate of Winnebago, it is important to recognize that motor homes, though a comfortable way to tour the countryside, are not economical on gasoline. In an era of cheap and plentiful oil, poor gas mileage was not viewed as an obstacle by purchasers of motor homes. But as political tensions mounted in the Middle East, members of OPEC (Organization of Petroleum Exporting Countries) stopped shipments of oil to the United States and other Western economies. The result was long lines at service stations, fuel shortages, and gasoline costing up to $2.00 per gallon. Throughout the 1970s, the price of a barrel of crude oil increased about fifteenfold, and the demand for Winnebago motor homes dropped steeply.

The late seventies and early eighties were a time of adjustment and struggle for Winnebago. Eventually, though, two factors combined to improve the economic outlook for the company. First, Winnebago radically changed the design of its motor homes, emphasizing aerodynamics, light-weight construction, and fuel efficiency. Second, the price of gasoline in the United States fell to approximately one-half of its highest level. By 1985, Winnebago had recovered to the point where sales topped $400 million and net earnings were almost $20 million.

Earnings remained positive for another two years. However, in 1988, Winnebago once again faced declining sales due to reduced demand for motor homes. That and a costly investment in the satellite communications business combined to generate negative net earnings for Winnebago in 1988, 1989, and 1990.

Winnebago's ability to weather the economic storm created by the oil boycott of the 1970s had been impressive. But by 1990, managers at Winnebago once again had to demonstrate their ability to adjust to new economic conditions.[1]

OPEC's decision to restrict the flow of oil to the Western economies transformed Winnebago from a high-flying darling of Wall Street into a struggling enterprise. After years of adjustment, Winnebago was able to reorganize into a strong and financially sound organization. Now it faces yet another financial crisis, once again brought on — at least in part — by environmental factors.

Shifts in the environments in which organizations function affect the fortunes of all organizations to some degree. On occasion, the disruption can be great, but most often the effects are less pronounced and less sudden, although no less significant. For example, as the average age of consumers in the United States, Europe, and Japan continues to increase, the demand for such products as Clearasil (to treat acne), Swatch watches, and *Seventeen* (a magazine for teenage girls) is likely to decline. Organizations that produce these products must anticipate and respond to this change in their environment in order to survive.[2] Of course sometimes environmental shifts can significantly improve a firm's position. The same increase in the age of consumers that is likely to hurt organizations that cater to younger customers may benefit organizations with older customers, such as companies that own and manage retirement communities, that sell hearing aids, and that offer cruise ship vacations.

This chapter examines the relationship between an organization's environment and its economic performance. We begin by discussing the major components of an organization's environment. Next we explore the impact that an organization's environment can have on its performance. In the final section we examine the actions that organizations can take to adapt to their environments, and to influence their environments, in order to maintain or improve performance.

Components of the Organizational Environment

The organizational environment consists of all the factors and conditions outside the organization that may affect the organization. This definition is deceptively simple, because it is sometimes difficult to decide whether an organization is being influenced by internal forces, such as an incompetent sales force, or by external forces, such as declining product demand or financial pressures that cut consumer spending.

The *general environment* comprises broad trends and conditions that indirectly affect an organization.

The *task environment* comprises individuals, groups, and organizations that directly affect a particular organization but are not part of it.

The components of an organization's environment can be grouped into two categories, the general environment and the task environment. The **general environment** comprises broad trends and conditions that indirectly affect an organization. The **task environment** comprises individuals, groups, and organizations that directly affect a particular organization but are not part of it. The components of the task environment relate to the specific tasks undertaken by an organization. Figure 4.1 depicts the relationships between an organization and its general and task environments.[3]

The General Environment

As Figure 4.1 shows, the major components of the general environment are technology, social and cultural dimensions, the economic climate, legal and political dimensions, and international events and trends.

Figure 4.1

Relationship Between an Organization and Its General and Task Environments

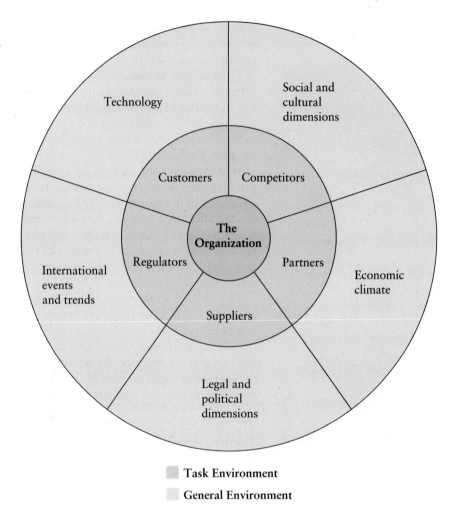

Task Environment

General Environment

The major components of the general environment are technology, social and cultural dimensions, the economic climate, legal and political dimensions, and international events and trends.

Technology   Technology, as we saw in Chapter 3, is the set of tools that organizations use to transform resources into products or services. The technology available to modern organizations, both new machines and new ways to use them, has evolved rapidly. Indeed, as Chapter 2 suggested, organizations in the last few decades have been part of a technological revolution.

Sometimes, however, organizations fail to keep up with important advances in technology. When this happens, they face the real prospect of technological obsolescence. In the United States, the steel industry did not make crucial investments in new steel-manufacturing technology in the 1960s and 1970s. Many U.S. steel companies thereby became technologically obsolete in the 1980s. This hurt their profitability, because firms from other countries, using new technology, could make and sell steel for less.[4]

Social and Cultural Dimensions   Another important component of an organization's general environment is the social and cultural dimensions of

THE ENVIRONMENTAL CHALLENGE

Women in Japanese Organizations

Over the last two decades in the United States and elsewhere, attitudes toward women in organizations have undergone major change. Although there are still numerous examples of sexual discrimination in the workplace, more women are being fully accepted into organizations and accorded the same responsibilities, opportunities, and incomes as men. But this cannot yet be said of women in Japanese organizations. Japanese women receive essentially the same education as their male counterparts. They study as hard, take the same entrance examinations, and attend the same colleges and universities. Upon graduation, they are employed by the same companies. At this point, however, the equal treatment of men and women in Japanese organizations ends.

Once hired, men in the largest Japanese organizations can expect very high job stability. Because of a practice known as *life-time employment,* it is virtually impossible for newly hired Japanese men to be laid off or fired. Japanese women, in contrast, have much less job stability. After working for a couple of years (usually as a secretary, receptionist, or administrative assistant, but rarely as a manager), many college-trained women take a leave of absence to have a family. After the children are grown, these women may return to work. But upon returning, they are treated as temporary employees, even if they work for the organization for the rest of their lives. As temporary employees, women in Japanese organizations are subject to layoffs during bad economic times and rarely receive managerial promotions. Men are not subject to layoffs and receive managerial promotions. One result is that very few managers in Japanese organizations are women.

Some have suggested that external pressures stemming from trade with international companies that have a different attitude toward women may begin to change these Japanese management practices. However, this change is taking place very slowly, if at all. The cultural values that underlie these management practices are deep-seated and not subject to a great deal of influence.

REFERENCES: William G. Ouchi, *Theory Z* (Reading, Mass.: Addison-Wesley, 1980); Urgan Lehner and Kathryn Graven, "Japanese Women Rise in Their Workplaces, Challenging Tradition," *Wall Street Journal,* September 6, 1989, pp. A1, A11; Sally Solo, "Japan Discovers Woman Power," *Fortune,* June 19, 1989, pp. 153–158.

the society or societies in which the organization operates. Social and cultural dimensions are the customs, values, and demographic characteristics of a society. Customs and values define what are, and are not, acceptable organizational practices and individual behaviors in different countries.

The world is almost unimaginably diverse culturally. What is regarded as helpful behavior in one country may be considered rude in another. For example, in the United States, bringing the thumb and the forefinger together to make a circle means "OK," but in Brazil this sign is considered quite vulgar. In the United States, brides typically wear white; in China, white is the color of mourning and is worn at funerals. In the United States, two parties file suit against each other in court in order to facilitate dispute resolution. In Japan, the filing of a legal suit is seen as an admission of failure and should be avoided at almost any cost.[5] Other Japanese customs and values determine the treatment of women in the workplace. The Environmental Challenge discusses the way working women are treated in Japan and speculates about whether these traditions are changing.

Demographics is the distribution of individuals in a society in terms of age, sex, marital status, income, and other characteristics that determine buying patterns.

Another aspect of the social and cultural dimensions of an organization's general environment is demographics. **Demographics** is the distribution of individuals in a society in terms of age, sex, marital status, income, and other characteristics that determine buying patterns. Demographics can have an important impact on an organization, because people at different stages of life have different needs and tastes. Rap music, faddish clothing, and roller skates are not likely to appeal to older consumers. Similarly, the needs of single adults (stereo and video equipment, high-fashion clothes) are very different from the needs of young families (disposable diapers, car seats, preschools). Needs continue to evolve over people's lives. Organizations must be aware of the changing demographics of their environment in order to produce the goods and services needed by potential customers. One organization that has been very skilled in this regard is described in The Entrepreneurial Challenge.

Economic Climate   The economic climate is the overall health of the economic systems within which an organization operates. The health of an economy varies over time in a distinct pattern: periods of relative prosperity, when demand for goods and services is high and unemployment is low, are followed by periods of relatively low prosperity, when demand for goods and services is low and unemployment is high. When activity in an economy is low, the economy is said to be in a *recession*. A severe recession, with very low demand for goods and services and very high unemployment, is called a *depression*. This alternating pattern of prosperity followed by recession, followed by prosperity, is called the **business cycle.**[6]

The *business cycle* is an alternating pattern of prosperity, followed by recession, followed by prosperity, and so on.

Some industries — making, distributing, and showing movies, for example — are relatively immune to the business cycle. During recessionary periods, people often look for ways to forget their troubles, and movies are a relatively inexpensive form of entertainment. During prosperous times, people are willing to spend even more on entertainment such as movies.[7]

On the other hand, the health of some organizations is closely linked to the business cycle. When the overall economy worsens, these businesses can suffer significantly. Construction and lumber are industries that are both highly dependent on the number of new houses built in any year. When the economy is in a recession, the demand for new housing falls, and organizations in the construction and lumber industries usually see a significant reduction in demand for their products. The same is true for the steel and automotive industries.[8]

Legal and Political Dimensions   The legal and political dimensions of an organization's general environment are the laws and the legal system's impact on business, together with the general nature of the relationship between government and business. These vary substantially from country to country. In the United States, the relationship between business and government has fluctuated significantly over the last several years. During the Carter administration (1976–1980) many business people complained of an antibusiness attitude in the government — an attitude reflected in

THE ENTREPRENEURIAL CHALLENGE

Hammacher Schlemmer and Sharper Image: Appealing to Affluent Baby Boomers

Hammacher Schlemmer and Company was founded in 1848 to sell exotic products to eccentric (and wealthy) customers. Some of the products it has sold over the years still stretch the imagination — and the pocketbook. For example, to protect snow skiers from strained vocal chords, Hammacher Schlemmer sells ski helmets with built-in two-way radios, for only $450. For sedate golfers, Hammacher Schlemmer sells a motorized, self-propelled golf bag for $1,299. And for the owners of aging puppies, Hammacher Schlemmer sells a specially designed orthopedic foam cushion for dogs, for just $47.

By focusing on unusual products for its targeted customers, Hammacher Schlemmer was able to build a small but loyal clientele. Most of this clientele lived in Manhattan and frequented Hammacher Schlemmer's seven-story Manhattan store.

Meanwhile, significant demographic changes were occurring in the United States. In particular, the baby boomers were growing up — and growing up wealthy. Upon graduation from college, they represented an important, and affluent, segment of the economy. They also had an interest in the kinds of products that Hammacher Schlemmer specialized in. Somehow, though, Hammacher Schlemmer failed to notice. It remained focused on its traditional client base.

However, the demographic shift was not lost on Richard Thalheimer and his firm, Sharper Image, founded in 1979. Now with retail stores in sixty-seven cities, it offers almost exactly the same kinds of high-technology gadgets that Hammacher Schlemmer has sold since 1848. However, Sharper Image currently has revenues of $208.6 million and employs 1,200 people. By building its retail outlets and investing heavily in catalog sales, Sharper Image was able to find a place in the market and grow rapidly. Recently, Hammacher, too, has begun to invest in a retail distribution network — and to emphasize catalog sales.

REFERENCES: Jeffery A. Tannenbaum, "Hammacher Aims for Sharper Image," *Wall Street Journal,* May 16, 1990, p. B1; "The Sharper Image Leaves Imitators in the Dust," *Catalog Age,* September 1990, pp. 140–141; Ronnie Gunnerson, "Retail and Mail Order—a Marriage Made in Heaven?" *Target Marketing,* September 1986, pp. 10, 12; Nathaniel Frey, "Hammacher Gets a Face Lift," *Catalog Age,* March 1991, pp. cover, 52.

vigorous enforcement of antitrust laws and the development of new and tough environmental standards. The perception changed dramatically during the Reagan administration (1980–1988), which was seen as adopting a probusiness perspective. Signs of this new perspective were loosened antitrust regulation and relaxed or delayed environmental standards. The Bush administration is generally perceived as occupying a moderate position between these two extremes.[9]

In the United Kingdom prior to the election of Margaret Thatcher as prime minister, the British government was widely perceived as antibusiness, and during this time the government purchased many private businesses. Mrs. Thatcher and her conservative successors reversed this approach, sold off most government-owned enterprises, and adopted a more supportive attitude toward private enterprise and business in the United Kingdom.[10]

In Japan the relationship between business and government has been relatively stable and quite positive over the last several decades. Indeed, the Japanese government has instituted a wide range of laws that help Japanese organizations succeed in national and international markets. For example, if there is substantial excess manufacturing capacity in a Japanese industry, the Japanese government will allow firms in that industry to cooperate to reduce capacity efficiently and thereby keep prices at a level high enough to ensure an organization's survival (this is not legal in the United States).[11] Also, in an effort to protect domestic markets from foreign imports, the Japanese government has instituted a variety of trade barriers. These range from **quotas**, which restrict the number of certain products that can be imported to Japan; to **tariffs**, which charge foreign organizations a tax for exporting their products to Japan (thereby increasing the price of these products to Japanese consumers); to **nontariff barriers** such as long quarantine periods for imported foods and long inspection periods for imported American cars.[12]

Trade barriers protect domestic organizations from international competition. Examples include quotas, which restrict the number of certain products that can be imported into a country; tariffs, which charge foreign organizations a tax for importing their products; and nontariff barriers, which include long quarantine periods for food and long inspection periods for products.

International Events and Trends   Of all the components of an organization's general environment, none is currently more volatile than the international setting. As we saw in Chapter 2, the last few years may be remembered as an important period of international political and economic change. Beginning with the Soviet Union, under the leadership of Mikhail Gorbachev, many **command economies**, in which the government largely plans the production and distribution of goods and services and sets prices, are being replaced by **market-based economies**, in which organizations themselves choose what to sell and consumers choose what to buy. Poland, Czechoslovakia, Bulgaria, Romania, and other countries seem to be moving away from a command economy toward a more market-based economy.

In command economies the government largely plans the production and distribution of goods and services and sets prices. In market-based economies, organizations themselves choose what to sell and consumers choose what to buy.

An important component of an organization's environment is international events. Nowhere have international events in the last few years been more rapid and unpredictable than in eastern Europe. Businesses around the world are alert to the possible opportunities that may exist due to the opening of markets in countries formerly behind the iron curtain. De Fonseca is a family-owned fashion store based in Italy, which in April 1990 opened a store in Bucharest, Romania. The store is a cooperative project between De Fonseca and ICECOOP-ILEIM of Romania.

How these economies will actually evolve is difficult to anticipate, as are the potential economic opportunities that will be associated with these changes. However, what seems very clear is that these changes, however they unfold, are likely to generate enormous opportunities for organizations in the United States, western Europe, Japan, and elsewhere.

The Task Environment

The major components of the task environment are the organization's customers, competitors, partners, suppliers, and regulators.

As shown in Figure 4.1, the major components of the task environment are the organization's customers, competitors, partners, suppliers, and regulators. Unlike the general environment, which tends to be more or less similar for most organizations, the task environment varies significantly among organizations. Consider, for example, the task environments of the two organizations compared in Figure 4.2. The task environment of International Business Machines (IBM) includes customers such as General Electric, competitors such as Hewlett-Packard and Unisys, partners such as Microsoft Corporation (developers of the MS-DOS operating system for IBM personal computers), suppliers such as Intel Corp. (suppliers of semiconductor chips to IBM), and regulators such as the Environmental Protection Agency (EPA) and the Occupational Safety and Health Administration (OSHA).

The task environment of INSEAD, a well-known college of business in Fountainbleau, France, is a completely different constellation. INSEAD's customers are the organizations that hire its graduates, and among its competitors are Harvard Business School and Bocconi University in Milan,

Figure 4.2

The Task Environments of IBM and INSEAD

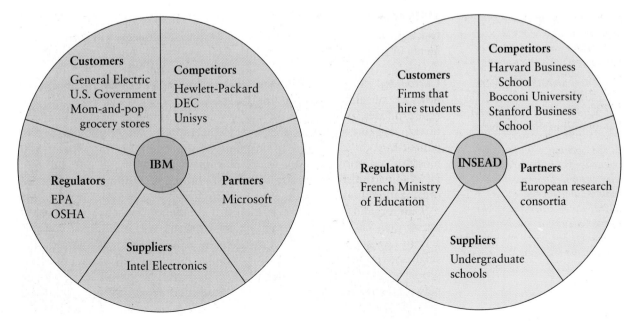

As a component of the task environment, customers can significantly influence an organization's performance. Two farmers that understand this are Kerry and Barbara Sullivan, who manage a 10-acre farm in Kimberton, Pennsylvania. By guaranteeing that synthetic, non-organic chemicals will not be used in growing their vegetables, the Sullivans appeal to an ever-growing population of health-conscious consumers. This has allowed the Sullivans to sell their full crop of vegetables to eager "shareholders" even before the seeds are planted.

Italy. Numerous European corporations have joined with INSEAD as partners in research efforts; undergraduate schools throughout the world supply students; and regulators come from the French Ministry of Education.

Although each organization's task environment is unique, similar organizations (including those in the same industry) tend to operate with similar task environments. Let us examine the major components of task environments in more detail.

Customers are the individuals, groups, and other organizations that acquire the goods or services that an organization produces.

Customers   An organization's **customers** are the individuals, groups, and other organizations that acquire the goods and services that the organization produces. Automobile purchasers are the customers of car manufacturers; airplane travelers are the customers of airline companies; and patients are the customers of hospitals. Without customers of some sort, most organizations — even nonprofit organizations — will not survive. Developing the ability to attract, satisfy, and retain customers is a central organizational task.

Some organizations have developed a reputation for always trying to satisfy their customers. Frito-Lay is one of them. It is not uncommon for a Frito-Lay delivery person to travel many miles just to make sure that a small convenience store receives its supplies of Fritos and other Frito-Lay products. By putting customer needs first, Frito-Lay can rely on a loyal network of retail outlets committed to selling its products.[13]

Competitors, or *rivals*, are other organizations that compete directly for a particular organization's resources, customers, or both.

Competitors   An organization's **competitors** are other organizations that compete directly for its resources, customers, or both. Competitors are also known as **rivals**. It is usually not difficult to specify an organization's direct competitors. Nike, L.A. Gear, and Reebok all directly compete in the sports-shoe market. The National Broadcasting Company (NBC) and the Fox Broadcasting Company directly compete in the television viewing market. The University of Minnesota, Pennsylvania State University, and the University of California compete for quality faculty and students.

Sometimes an organization's competitors are not so obvious. For example, Ford clearly competes with Chrysler, General Motors, Toyota, and Honda. However, Ford also competes with IBM, General Electric, Phillips Petroleum, and other large corporations for capital with which to run and expand its business. Ford also competes to a lesser extent with Schwinn (a bicycle manufacturer), Greyhound, American Airlines, Amtrak, and the New York City subway system, all of which provide alternative sources of transportation. When a person living on the island of Manhattan does not buy a Ford because taking the subway, the bus, or a taxi is preferable, then suppliers of these substitute forms of transportation are Ford competitors.

Partners are two or more people or organizations working in a cooperative effort or joint venture.

Partners   **Partners** are two or more people or organizations working in a cooperative effort or joint venture. The number of partnerships has risen dramatically over the last few years. Some well-known business partnerships include Sematech, a group of microelectronics firms in the United States designed to improve manufacturing in semiconductor technology, and NUMMI, a venture between General Motors and Toyota to assemble cars in Fremont, California.[14]

Partnerships allow firms to reduce the financial risks associated with engaging in new business activities. They are particularly valuable when the partners have complementary strengths and weaknesses. For example, as a partner in NUMMI, Toyota obtains access to GM's broad distribution system in the United States and also reduces the threat of political and economic sanctions for importing too many cars into the United States. For its part, GM can learn how to manufacture high-quality small cars in a profitable way by working with Toyota in the NUMMI plant. Thus both parties benefit from the partnership.[15]

Suppliers are organizations that provide tangible and intangible resources to other organizations.

Suppliers   **Suppliers** are organizations that provide tangible and intangible resources to other organizations. Each of the hundreds of thousands of products and services that organizations use to produce their own products or services is, in turn, produced by an organization. Some supplies the organization produces itself. But most supplies — from pencils to computer printers, from shovels to bulldozers, and from desks to office buildings — are obtained from other organizations. The availability of quality supplies is crucial to an organization's success.

Japanese firms often treat suppliers as business partners. It is not uncommon in Japan for suppliers to locate manufacturing facilities physically next door to customers. These suppliers also make significant investments in manufacturing products that meet the needs of only one particular customer. In return for this commitment, the customer stands by its suppliers in good times and bad. In one instance, a wire and cable supplier to the Fujitsu Electronics Company became unprofitable, but rather than let its supplier go out of business, Fujitsu invested several hundred million dollars to transform the organization into a supplier of semiconductor chips. In this way, Fujitsu obtained a very loyal business partner and supplier.[16]

Regulators are outside organizations that have the ability to control or influence an organization's internal policies and practices. Examples include *government regulatory agencies* and *private interest groups*.

Regulators   A final component of an organization's task environment is regulators. **Regulators** are outside organizations that have the ability to control or influence an organization's internal policies and practices. There are two important kinds of regulators in an organization's task environment: government regulatory agencies and private interest groups.

Government regulatory agencies are units of national or local governments that influence and control the actions of organizations, usually to ensure that they are consistent with national or local policies and laws. In the United States, important government regulatory agencies include the Securities and Exchange Commission (SEC) (regulates the sale and purchase of an organization's stock and debt), the Environmental Protection Agency (EPA) (regulates the amount and types of pollutants that organizations can release), the Occupational Safety and Health Administration (OSHA) (regulates on-the-job hazards), and the Internal Revenue Service (IRS) (collects taxes).

The impact of government regulatory agencies on organizations is hotly debated in many countries. In the United States, some scholars have argued that regulation has led to a steady decline in the competitiveness of U.S. companies. Others believe that government regulatory agencies have been "captured" by the organizations they are supposed to regulate. These observers argue, for example, that the influence of the savings and loan industry on the very commissions designed to regulate it led directly to the multi-billion-dollar savings and loan crisis.[17] Still other authors have argued that the emergence of Japan as a dominant economic force in the world can be traced, in part, to the regulatory efforts of such Japanese government agencies as the Ministry of International Trade and Industry (MITI).[18]

The relationship between organizations and their government regulators can be complicated. Nevertheless, the managers of organizations, both business and nonbusiness, must be aware of this aspect of their task environment and be able to respond to the demands of government regulators.

Private interest groups are private, nongovernment groups that attempt to influence an organization's policies and procedures. One example is the Sierra Club, whose goal is environmental conservation, among other objectives. This interest group lobbies Congress for legislation to reduce the amount of pollutants released by manufacturing facilities. Another group, Mothers Against Drunk Drivers (MADD), has pressured beer companies to put warning labels on beer cans. Still another is the Better Business Bureau, an association of business firms that attempts to monitor and discourage unethical business practices.

The power of these interest groups to affect organizations can sometimes be very great. In the late 1980s, a worldwide coalition of environmental action groups called for a consumer boycott of tuna until tuna companies changed their fishing methods, which were needlessly killing thousands of dolphins. This boycott forced significant changes. For example, both Star-kist and Chicken of the Sea now fish for tuna in areas where dolphins are less likely to live. They also have redesigned their product labels to indicate that their methods are "dolphin safe." Recently, McDonald's yielded to the pressure of health-oriented interest groups and introduced a new, low-fat hamburger.[19]

Impact of the Environment on Organizational Performance

Understanding how the general and task environments can affect an organization is vital for managers. With such an understanding, managers can watch for trends in the general and task environments and enable the organization to respond appropriately.

Recently, however, it has become possible for managers to pinpoint the critical components of a particular organization's environment. By adapting some of the ideas from Chapter 2 — specifically, the theory of perfect competition and concepts from industrial organization economics — we may predict with some certainty the average level of economic performance of organizations in an industry by evaluating certain attributes of that industry's structure. These ideas allow managers to predict when organizations in an industry can expect to achieve only normal economic performance, and when they can expect to achieve higher than normal economic performance.[20]

The Five Forces Model of Industry Structure

Industry structure consists of the characteristics and attributes of the industries within which an organization operates.

The five forces in Porter's model of industry structure are level of rivalry, power of suppliers, power of buyers, threat of substitute products, and threat of new entrants.

Industry structure consists of characteristics and attributes of the industries within which an organization operates. As briefly mentioned in Chapter 2, Professor Michael Porter of the Harvard Business School has developed a framework that describes the impact that an industry has on the performance of organizations within it. Known as the *five forces model of industry structure,* Porter's framework is presented in Figure 4.3.[21]

By comparing the five forces in Figure 4.3 with the attributes of a perfectly competitive industry discussed in Chapter 2, we see that Porter's model demonstrates the different ways in which an industry can be imperfectly competitive, and thus the different ways the organizations in the industry may achieve greater than normal economic performance. Let's look at the elements of Porter's model.

Figure 4.3

The Five Forces Model of Industry
Structure

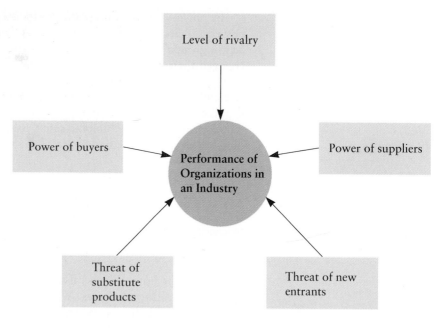

The *level of rivalry* among firms
in an industry is the intensity of
competition in that industry.

Level of Rivalry   The **level of rivalry** among firms in an industry is the
intensity of competition in that industry. In industries with very high levels
of rivalry, organizations (on average) can expect to earn only normal
economic profits. This is because any action that an organization in a
competitive industry takes to create greater than normal economic profits
will instantly be duplicated by numerous rivals, thus restoring conditions
of perfect competition. On the other hand, when rivalry in an industry is
low, actions taken by one organization may not be duplicated by rivals,
and above-normal economic performance may be possible.

The fast-food industry is characterized by a high level of rivalry. Every
price reduction or advertising campaign that McDonald's develops is countered by a sale or promotion by Burger King. McDonald's has its Ronald
McDonald mascot; Burger King has its Burger King. When Burger King
uses a promotional tie-in with the movie *Teen-Age Mutant Ninja Turtles*,
McDonald's develops a promotional tie-in with the movie *The Little Mer-
maid*. The soft-drink industry is similar. PepsiCo contracts for exclusive
sales at Burger King, and Coca-Cola does the same at McDonald's. In these
industries, every competitive action leads to a very quick and competitive
reaction.[22]

Although defense system contractors do compete for government business, their industry is characterized by a low level of rivalry. For example,
defense firms like McDonnell Douglas and General Dynamics often cooperate in attempting to obtain major contracts from the U.S. government.
Such cooperation is indicative of low levels of competitive rivalry.[23]

The *power of suppliers* is the
degree to which the suppliers to
organizations in an industry can
influence the policies and operations of those organizations.

Power of Suppliers   The **power of suppliers** is the degree to which the
suppliers to organizations in an industry can influence the policies and
operations of those organizations. When the power of suppliers is great,

The level of rivalry is an important determinant of the economic performance of individual firms within an industry. Some organizations still start new business ventures in industries characterized by high rivalry, however. John Hoagland is moving the organization he heads, The Christian Science Monitor, in this direction with his plans to begin a 24-hour cable news network. Hoagland believes this is necessary, despite the intense competition in the cable industry and several direct rivals (including CNN and the Financial News Network), to meet the Monitor's objective of providing objective, thoughtful news to the world.

organizational performance is, on average, likely to be around normal. This is because powerful suppliers can demand (and obtain) the full value of the resources they are selling. As the price of resources rises, the economic performance of organizations being supplied is kept at normal levels.

The power of an organization's suppliers can depend on several factors, but two are particularly important: (1) the number of suppliers that provide the most important resources and (2) the importance of those resources to an organization. In an industry such as manufacturing of aluminum products, where only a few organizations control all the aluminum ore from which aluminum is extracted, the power of suppliers is great and can restrict the potential for above-normal performance. In an industry such as food retailing, where the number of suppliers of food products (farmers) is very large, the power of suppliers is low and thus does not restrict the performance of food retailers.[24]

The *power of buyers* is the ability of the customers of organizations in an industry to influence the policies and operations of those organizations.

Power of Buyers In the same way that the power of suppliers can affect an organization's performance, so can the power of buyers. The **power of buyers** is the ability of the customers of organizations in an industry to influence the policies and operations of those organizations. When buyers are powerful, they can demand lower prices or higher quality from organizations. Both lower prices and higher quality can restrict an organization's economic performance to normal.

The power of buyers depends most critically on how many different customers the organizations in an industry have and what percentage of an organization's product or service is purchased by each of its customers.

If organizations have only one customer, then that customer will be a powerful buyer. Organizations that sell military hardware and defense-related services to the U.S. government usually have few other customers. As a result, the U.S. government has a very large impact on the kinds of products these organizations produce, the prices they charge for these products, and the level of profitability of these firms.[25]

Another example of an industry within which buyers have had significant power is the international banking industry. The extent of this power, and how one bank, Citibank, responded to it, are described in The Global Challenge.

Threat of Substitute Products   Another force that Porter identifies is the threat of substitute products. **Substitute products** are goods or services that may be used in place of a particular product. Tea is a substitute for coffee as an after-dinner beverage. Organizations in industries where many substitutes exist generally have normal economic performance. Organizations in industries not threatened by substitute products may achieve above-normal economic performance.

Substitute products are goods or services that may be used in place of a particular product.

Virtually all the products or services that organizations provide have substitutes. Some of these substitutes are very close. For example, some people believe that NutraSweet is a near-perfect substitute for sugar, that soybean-based frozen drinks (sold at McDonald's and Wendy's) are near-perfect substitutes for milk shakes, and that fluorescent lights are a near-perfect substitute for incandescent lights. When a product or service has close substitutes, then customers can choose to forgo it in favor of the substitute. To make their goods and services more attractive than close substitutes, organizations must keep their prices low, though doing so reduces economic performance.

On the other hand, some substitute products or services are very imperfect. Driving a car and walking are both forms of transportation, but few would argue that they are perfect substitutes for each other. The same can be said for sprinklers as substitutes for swimming pools, slide rules as substitutes for electronic calculators, and telegraph machines as substitutes for telephones. When organizations are operating in industries with only imperfect substitutes, the performance of these organizations, on average, will be higher than normal.

Threat of New Entrants   The last of Porter's five forces is the threat of new entrants. **New entrants** are organizations that can or do enter an industry and begin to compete with organizations already in the industry. When new entrants enter, they obtain any above-normal profits that might potentially exist in an industry. Obviously, if new entry into an industry is great, the level of rivalry in the industry is very high. Thus the greater the threat of new entrants, the more likely are organizations in the industry to achieve only normal economic performance.

New entrants are organizations that can or do enter an industry and begin to compete with organizations already in the industry.

The threat of new entry varies significantly from industry to industry. In the microcomputer software industry, new entrants arrive virtually every day. Almost all that is required to begin operation in this industry is a

THE GLOBAL CHALLENGE

Citibank Responds to Third World Customers

Through the 1970s, Citibank was one of a large number of banks throughout the world that lent money to less developed countries (LDCs) to encourage economic growth. In the late 1970s, world interest rates soared to a level six times higher than before. Many LDCs could no longer afford to pay the interest on their loans. In 1982, for example, Mexico almost defaulted on $82 billion in loans. In 1985, Peru announced that it would devote no more than 10 percent of its revenues from exports to pay its foreign debt. Since that time, Peru has been paying interest on only a small percentage of its total foreign debt.

The amounts involved in this LDC debt are staggering. In 1987, the total foreign debt owed by LDCs totaled $437 billion. Citibank's share of this debt was also staggering: $10.4 billion. Much of this money was at risk. Investors in Citibank and other U.S. banks saw the risks of this foreign debt and discounted the stock market value of these organizations.

Not to respond to these threats from their customers would have hurt Citibank severely. An appropriate response was implemented by John Reed, president of Citibank. Reed decided that Citibank was going to have to put the LDC debt crisis behind it. On May 19, 1987, Reed announced the creation of a special reserve fund against possible losses from loans to LDCs. The amount of money placed in the fund was $3 billion.

What were the results of this bold move? First, placing $3 billion in a reserve fund led Citibank to lose $2.5 billion in the second quarter of 1987. This is the largest one-quarter loss of any U.S. bank ever. However, rather than decreasing the value of Citibank, Reed's move actually enhanced the value of the company. Setting up this reserve improved the long-term viability of Citibank. As important, this action allowed Citibank to begin to exploit other opportunities in the credit card business. The results were that on the same day that Citibank announced a $2.5 billion loss, its stock price went from $48 per share to just over $55 per share.

REFERENCES: "A Stunner from the Citi," *Business Week,* June 1, 1987, pp. 42–43; Jaclyn Fierman, "John Reed's Bold Stroke," *Fortune,* June 22, 1987, pp. 26–32; "All That Plastic Is Still Fantastic for Citibank," *Business Week,* May 28, 1990, pp. 90–92.

small group of programmers, a few microcomputers, access to software sales outlets, and some ideas about software design. In the automobile industry, where a great deal of capital is required to start operations, entry is more difficult and less frequent, although it can still occur. Hyundai, Yugo, Suzuki, and several other car manufacturers have recently entered the U.S. automobile industry. In the mainframe computer industry, new entry is virtually unknown. Except for some Japanese firms that have entered this industry in partnership with established firms, the organizations that dominated this industry in the early 1960s still dominate it.[26]

Applying the Five Forces Model

Taken together, the five attributes of industry structure that Porter identified can be used to estimate the level of performance of firms operating in different kinds of environments. Table 4.1 shows how the five forces would be expected to affect performance in three different industries.

Table 4.1

The Expected Level of Performance of Organizations in Three Industries

	Type of Industry		
	Electronic Parts Distribution	Automobile Manufacturing	Pharmaceuticals
Level of rivalry	High	Moderate	Moderate
Power of suppliers	High	Moderate	Low
Power of buyers	High	Moderate	Low
Threat of substitutes	High	Low	Low
Threat of new entrants	High	Moderate	Low
Expected level of performance	Normal	Normal to above normal	Above normal

Organizations in the electronic parts distribution industry specialize in purchasing electronic components from manufacturers and distributing these components to wholesale customers. Organizations in this industry include Pioneer, Hall-Mark, Bell Industries, and Jaco Electronics. The level of rivalry in this industry is very high; there are numerous distribution organizations and they compete neck and neck for even the smallest sales contracts. The power of suppliers in this industry is very high, because only a small number of organizations manufacture and sell the electronic components that distribution companies purchase for resale to their customers. The power of buyers is high, because buyers can easily shift from one distributor to another, thus forcing distributors to keep their prices very low. The threat of substitutes is also high, because the original manufacturers can, at any time, begin selling their components to wholesale customers directly, thereby by-passing the distribution companies. Finally, the threat of entry is high. To begin operations in this industry, all that is required is a small warehouse, some telephone lines, and a few salespeople. Given these industry attributes, the expected performance of organizations in the electronic parts distribution industry is, at best, normal economic performance. Research on the performance of firms in this industry is consistent with these expectations.[27]

For organizations in the automobile industry — GM, Ford, Honda, Toyota, and the others — rivalry is moderate. There are relatively few firms in this industry; and although they often compete on the basis of design, quality, guarantees, and so forth, there is reluctance to compete solely on the basis of price. Suppliers, including steel companies and tire firms, are plentiful, so they are not particularly powerful. Because auto companies sell most of their cars to their own dealer networks, they are highly dependent on those networks. However, there are enough retail dealers so that if some dealers in the network start causing difficulties, the auto companies can simply give priority to other dealers. This practice moderates the power of buyers. There are few close substitutes for automobiles, and the threat of new entry is moderate. Given this analysis of the automobile industry, the expected performance of organizations in this industry ranges from normal to above normal.[28]

The pharmaceutical industry consists of organizations that develop, patent, and distribute drugs, such as Merck, Johnson & Johnson, and Abbott Laboratories. Since the number of organizations in this industry is not large, rivalry is moderate. The power of both suppliers and buyers is low, because pharmaceutical firms acquire their supplies and raw materials from numerous sources and sell their products to numerous retail outlets. Once a pharmaceutical firm has developed a drug that cures a disease, there are usually few substitutes. Strong drug patent protection lessens the threat of new entrants, as does the research and development skill of successful pharmaceutical companies, which is difficult to duplicate. Given these industry attributes, the expected performance of firms in this industry is above normal.[29]

Impact of Organizational Strategies on the Environment

From the foregoing, it might be possible to conclude that an organization is simply a passive agent, completely subject to the forces in its environment. However, as the story of Winnebago clearly demonstrates, organizations need not passively accept their environment. Sometimes they are able to adapt constructively to changes in their environment. At other times they can actively influence their environment.

Adapting to the Environment

Organizations can adapt to their environment by forecasting and planning and by maintaining flexibility.

Organizations adapt to their environment by anticipating and adjusting to the impact that the environment is likely to have on their economic performance. Organizations enhance their adaptability by forecasting and planning for changes and by remaining flexible.

Forecasting is projecting the future of an organization's environment. Three forecasting techniques are *trend analysis, modeling,* and *scenario building.*

Forecasting and Planning Many organizations use forecasting and planning as a means to anticipate changes in their environment and to determine the effects of those changes. **Forecasting** is projecting the future of an organization's environment. Perhaps the simplest form of forecasting is trend analysis. In **trend analysis**, current trends in an environment are simply extended out into the future. An example of trend analysis is shown by the straight line in the graph in Figure 4.4. Demand for this organization's products has grown at a steady rate of 6 percent per year for the last five years. Trend analysis suggests that demand will continue to grow at this 6 percent rate for the foreseeable future.

Figure 4.4

Two Techniques for Forecasting Growth in Product Demand

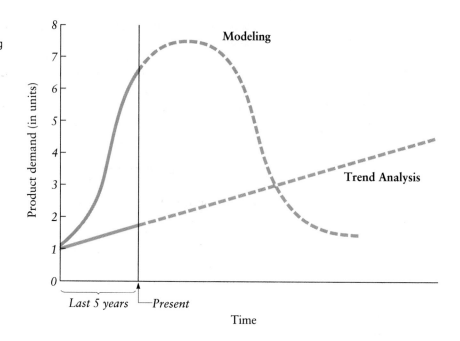

One weakness of trend analysis is that few environmental trends remain perfectly constant over time. Thus it is usually preferable to use more sophisticated modeling techniques. In **modeling**, it is recognized that current trends in an organization's environment may shift. An example of modeling is shown by the curved line in Figure 4.4. The growth rate in demand for this organization's product is expected to level off and then decline.

Another forecasting technique is called **scenario building**. A scenario is a complex description of a possible future situation. An organization typically postulates a number of environmental scenarios, each encompassing several interrelated trends. The organization then plans a response to each scenario, so that it is prepared to act if one of the scenarios becomes reality.

One organization that depends heavily on scenario building is Royal Dutch/Shell Group, an oil company headquartered in Amsterdam. In the mid-1970s, Royal Dutch Shell began to devise a variety of scenarios concerning the future of the world oil market. Some of these scenarios anticipate what would happen if OPEC were able to reduce the supply of crude oil. Another scenario examines what would happen to world oil supplies if Israel went to war with some of its Arab neighbors. With multiple scenarios prepared, Royal Dutch/Shell was able to develop plans for responding to different possible futures. If one of the scenarios actually came true, the company would be well positioned to respond.[30]

Of course, forecasting is helpful only if it leads to a plan for adjusting to the environment. The planning process and its impact on organizational performance are discussed in more detail in Chapter 6.

Maintaining Flexibility   No matter how much effort organizations expend, their forecasts are rarely perfect. Some environmental events are

Flexibility is a characteristic of organizations that are able to change their strategy, structure, and behavior quickly in light of changes in their environments.

just about impossible to anticipate and plan for; the startling revolutionary change in eastern Europe discussed in Chapter 2 is only one example. When faced with these kinds of events, organizations can improve their performance by remaining flexible. **Flexibility** is a characteristic of organizations that are able to change their strategy, structure, and behavior quickly in light of changes in their environments. Specific techniques that organizations use to maintain flexibility are described in Part III.

Influencing the Environment

Organizations can not only anticipate and plan for changes in their environment, they can also attempt to actively bring about change. Although any one organization has limited ability to influence the general environment, it can effectively influence its task environment and the structure of the industry in which it functions.

Organizations can influence their task environment and their industry structure.

Advertising is a message that an organization creates about its products or services, or about itself, and publicizes in a variety of media.

Product differentiation occurs when an organization makes its products or services seem much different from those of its competitors, through adding new features and through advertising.

Influencing the Task Environment   Organizations engage in a variety of activities to directly influence each component of their task environment. Some of the methods they use are listed in Table 4.2. To influence customers, organizations invest in advertising. **Advertising** is a message that an organization creates about its product or service, or about itself, and publicizes in a variety of media. Effective advertising campaigns can actually change the tastes and preferences of customers, making one organization's goods or services more attractive than another's. In the 1960s, Timex's "Takes a Licking, But Keeps on Ticking" and BIC's "Writes first time, every time" product campaign slogans helped sales dramatically. In the 1980s, "Where's the Beef" ads enabled Wendy's to establish a solid position in the fast-food industry.

Organizations influence competitors by making their own products seem much different from those of their competitors, through adding new features and through advertising. Competitors must then decide whether to respond to a firm's differentiation efforts. This tactic is called **product differentiation**. Braun (a German electric shaver manufacturer) has utilized

Table 4.2

Influencing the Task Environment

Component of Task Environment	Method of Influence
Customers	Advertising
Competitors	Product differentiation
Partners	Joint ventures
Suppliers	Second sources
Regulators	Political lobbying

Organizations can use advertising to influence their task environment. They often do this by linking their products or services with appealing images. Hewlett-Packard employs this strategy in this ad for its LaserJet IIP printer. As well as emphasizing the high quality and reasonable price of its product, HP also features the image of a loyal, patient, irresistible dog. Just as one feels almost compelled to pick up the leash and take this dog for a walk, one also might feel compelled to purchase and use a Hewlett-Packard printer.

this approach by emphasizing the high-technology construction and modern design of its product compared to other electric razors. Product differentiation is discussed in more detail in Chapter 7.

Organizations can influence partners through **joint ventures**. For example, in the late 1970s, five Japanese electronics organizations (Nippon Electric, Toshiba, Hitachi, Mitsubishi, and Fujitsu) formed a research and development organization to develop integrated circuit technology. Top managers in each of these organizations attempted to influence the course of the partnership in ways that would help their own organization the most. They did this by sending verbal, highly talented engineers to the joint venture in the hope that these engineers would be able to dominate design discussions.

Joint ventures are cooperative efforts between separate organizations.

One way in which organizations can influence suppliers is by insisting on second sources. A **second source** is a second supplier for an organization's key resources. Suppose that a computer company wants to use a semiconductor firm's newly designed microprocessor but can purchase that microprocessor only from the one semiconductor firm. If the computer company designs its entire computer around this chip, it will be at the mercy of the semiconductor firm. If the supplier wants to increase the price of the chip, the computer company can do little, if anything, to prevent it from doing so. Before the company designs its computer around this chip, it will take the protective measure of insisting that the semiconductor firm license another firm — a second source — that can also sell the chip.

A *second source* is a firm, beyond the initial supplier, that supplies some vital resource to an organization.

Political lobbying is an attempt by organizations to directly influence government policies. Lobbying can be done by representatives of an individual organization or through *trade associations.*

Organizations can influence regulators in their task environment through political lobbying. **Political lobbying** is an attempt by organizations to directly influence government policies. Lobbying can be done by representatives of an individual organization who contact government and regulatory officials to argue for or against specific government policies. Lobbying can also be accomplished through trade associations. **Trade associations** are groups of organizations, typically in the same industry, with similar interests that attempt to influence government policies.

Political lobbying can be quite effective. In the late 1980s, organizations in the electronics industry had a strong common interest in changing federal tax laws to encourage more investment in start-up companies. Several firms, including Hewlett-Packard and National Semiconductor, lobbied the federal government directly. These firms also joined together under the leadership of a trade association, the American Electronics Association (AEA). Because of these lobbying efforts, the tax laws were changed in ways that directly benefited electronics organizations in the United States.[31]

Lobbying is an important method of influence in other countries, too. Strong lobbying by Fiat Motor Company in Italy has influenced government policy regarding the Italian automobile industry. Lobbying by banks in Hong Kong, including the Hong Kong–Shanghai Bank, has been important in keeping financial regulations to a minimum in Hong Kong. In Japan, a strong farmers' lobby has kept trade barriers for agricultural products high, despite international pressure.

Influencing Industry Structure   Many methods that organizations use to influence their task environment can also influence industry structure. However, organizations can take several additional actions to influence industry structure in ways that enhance organizational performance. Some of these are listed in Table 4.3.

Table 4.3

Influencing Industry Structure

Component of Industry Structure	Method of Influence
Level of rivalry	Horizontal acquisitions
Power of suppliers	Acquire suppliers or engage in business of suppliers
Power of buyers	Acquire buyers or engage in business of buyers
Threat of substitutes	Advertising
Threat of new entrants	Barriers to entry: product loyalty and patents

A *horizontal acquisition* occurs when an organization purchases a competitor.

To reduce rivalry, organizations can directly purchase a competitor. This tactic is called **horizontal acquisition**. Because the level of rivalry in an industry depends, in part, on the number of organizations in the industry, horizontal acquisitions can reduce rivalry. They have become common in the airline industry; recently Texas Air acquired Continental and USAir acquired Piedmont. Horizontal acquisitions in the banking industry, whereby firms such as NCNB, Citibank, and Security Pacific Bank have acquired financially troubled banks in Texas, Massachusetts, and California, have also had the effect of reducing rivalry.

In addition to insisting on second sources, organizations can influence the power of suppliers by acquiring them or by engaging in their business activities. General Motors purchased Electronic Data Systems (EDS) instead of continuing to purchase EDS's computing services. In a similar way, both Sony and Home Box Office (HBO) have begun producing their own movies. Sony accomplished this by acquiring Columbia Pictures. Columbia now produces movies that Sony eventually releases on videocassette.

To influence the power of buyers, organizations can engage in the business activities of formally independent customers. Recently, several movie studios have opened their own theaters. Mitsubishi's decision to open its own distribution network for auto sales in the United States (as opposed to selling cars only through its partner, Chrysler) reduced the power of its buyers.

Certain types of advertising can reduce the threat of substitute products. The objective of this advertising is not simply to convince customers that a particular organization's goods or services are better than those of a rival but that they are better than substitutes. For example, an entire industry focuses on providing male customers with ways to deal with the problem of thinning hair. Some organizations in the industry argue that toupees are best; others argue that hair transplants are best; and still others argue that new drugs are best. In their commercials, each organization suggests that its product or service is better than the alternative: going bald.

Finally, organizations can restrict new entry to an industry by erecting barriers. Two that have been particularly effective are product (or brand) loyalty and patents. **Product** or **brand loyalty** is the feeling of commitment that customers have toward a particular organization and its products. The automobile industry is characterized by extensive product loyalty. Some customers are "Ford people"; others love Chrysler products; and still others cannot imagine purchasing anything but a Honda. It is very difficult for new entrants into an industry to overcome intense product loyalty toward existing products.

Product or *brand loyalty* is the feeling of commitment that customers have toward a particular organization and its products. *Patents* are legal protections that prevent other organizations from duplicating a firm's goods or services. Both loyalty and patents can be used to reduce the threat of new entrants.

Patents are legal protections that prevent other organizations from duplicating a firm's goods or services. Organizations that have patent protection are able to earn above-normal economic performance without attracting new entrants to the industry, because new entrants are prohibited by law from entering and selling the same product. Organizations that have used patents to achieve high economic performance include Polaroid (in instant cameras), Xerox (in copy machines), and Merck (in pharmaceuticals).

Learning Summary

The organizational environment can be grouped into general and task environments. The general environment consists of broad trends and conditions that indirectly affect an organization. Important components of the general environment are technology, social and cultural dimensions, the economic climate, legal and political dimensions, and international events and trends. The task environment consists of individuals, groups, and organizations that directly affect an organization but are not part of it. Important components of the task environment are an organization's customers, competitors, partners, suppliers, and regulators.

Porter's five forces model of industry structure describes how components of an organization's environment can directly affect its performance. The five forces included in Porter's framework are level of rivalry, power of suppliers, power of buyers, threat of substitutes, and threat of new entrants.

Organizations can adapt to their environment through forecasting and planning. Important forecasting techniques are trend analysis, modeling, and scenario building. Organizations can increase their adaptability by remaining flexible — by being able to change quickly. Organizations can influence their task environment through advertising, product differentiation, joint-venture partnerships, second sources, and political lobbying. Organizations can influence industry structure through horizontal acquisition, acquiring or engaging in the business activities of suppliers, acquiring or engaging in the business activities of buyers, advertising, and erecting barriers to entry such as product and brand loyalty and patents.

Questions and Exercises

Review Questions

1. What are the major components of an organization's general environment? Can organizations directly influence their general environment? Why or why not?
2. What are the major components of an organization's task environment? What can organizations do to influence each of these components?
3. Describe the elements in the five forces model of industry structure, and explain how each is related to economic performance.

Analysis Questions

1. According to the five forces model, why would an organization that invents a new and valuable product want to patent it?
2. Sometimes it is very difficult for organizations to predict trends in their general environment. In such situations, what are the advantages and

disadvantages of forecasting and planning? What are the advantages and disadvantages of remaining flexible?

3. Consider this scenario. Political upheavals force hundreds of thousands of people to leave Southeast Asia. Thousands of these refugees come to the United States, where increased demand for housing leads to a small housing boom. This housing boom increases the demand for concrete and in turn increases the demand for the cement supplied by an organization in the Midwest. This organization's economic performance improves. Is that improvement due to a change in the general environment, in the task environment, in the industry structure, or in some combination of all three? Explain.

4. Baseball-card collecting has recently increased in popularity. Given the five forces model, and assuming that firms currently selling baseball cards are quite profitable, do you think the number of firms selling baseball cards is likely to increase, decrease, or remain the same? Why?

Application Exercises

1. Read a history of some organization (for example, International Business Machines or General Motors) and trace how changes in its task environment, general environment, and industry structure have affected its performance.

2. Interview five managers in at least two different organizations to discover which aspects of the environment get most of their attention: (1) the general environment, (2) the task environment, or (3) industry structure.

Chapter Notes

1. David Greising, "The Unhappy Campers at Winnebago," *Business Week,* May 28, 1990, p. 28; Richard C. Beercheck, "Recreational Vehicles: Comfort Plus Advanced Engineering," *Machine Design,* 1988, pp. 94–100; Robert L. Rose, "Winnebago Dismisses Conner as Chief, as Founder Again Is Tough to Please," *Wall Street Journal,* April 13, 1990, p. B6; Christi Harlan, "The Curious Tale of a Spendthrift Heir," *Wall Street Journal,* May 16, 1989, p. B1.

2. Barbara E. Van Gorder, "The Maturing of America," *Credit,* March–April 1991, pp. 10–12; Richard C. Leventhal, "The Aging Consumer: What's All the Fuss About Anyway?" *Journal of Consumer Marketing,* Winter 1991, pp. 29–34.

3. For classic treatments of organizational environments, see James D. Thompson, *Organizations in Action* (New York: McGraw-Hill, 1967), and Richard H. Hall, *Organizations: Structure and Process,* 2nd ed. (Englewood Cliffs, N.J.: Prentice-Hall, 1977). For a general review, see John W. Meyer and W. Richard Scott, eds., *Organizational Environments* (Beverly Hills: Sage, 1983). For more recent treatments, see Gregory G. Dess and Donald W. Beard, "Dimensions of Organizational Task Environments," *Administrative Science Quarterly,* March

1984, pp. 52–73, and Donald W. Beard and Gregory Dess, "Modeling Organizational Species' Interdependence in an Ecological Community: An Input-Output Approach," *Academy of Management Review*, July 1988, pp. 362–373.

4. See James M. Uterback, "Corporate Renewal," *International Journal of Technology Management*, 1989, pp. 625–630; John H. Steinbreder, "The Smokestacks Steam Again," *Fortune*, December 21, 1987, pp. 47–48; James W. Brock, "Bigness Is the Problem, Not the Solution," *Challenge*, July–August 1987, pp. 11–16.

5. The role of the courts in Japanese business has been discussed by William G. Ouchi, *The M-Form Society* (Reading, Mass.: Addison-Wesley, 1984).

6. The business cycle has been studied by economists for centuries. For early discussions, see Alvin H. Hansen, *Fiscal Policy and the Business Cycle* (New York: Norton, 1941), and J. A. Schumpeter, *Business Cycles* (New York: McGraw-Hill, 1939). The classic technical description of the causes and consequences of the business cycle is Milton Friedman, "The Optimum Quantity of Money," in *The Optimum Quantity of Money and Other Essays*, ed. Milton Friedman (Hawthorne, N.Y.: Aldine, 1969).

7. Stewart Toy, Gregory L. Miles, Ronald Grover, David Lieberman, and Joan Hamilton, "1989 Industry Outlook: Defense, Steel, Entertainment, Health Care," *Business Week*, January 9, 1989, pp. 75–82. For an academic discussion of resistance to business cycles, see Schumpeter, *Business Cycles*.

8. Histories of the construction, lumber, steel, and automobile industries give strong evidence of the effect of the business cycle on organizations in these industries. See, for example, Walter J. Mead, *Competition and Oligopsony in the Douglas Fir Lumber Industry* (Berkeley: University of California Press, 1966); The Federal Trade Commission, *The United States Steel Industry and Its International Rivals* (Washington, D.C.: Government Printing Office, 1977); and Lawrence J. White, *The Automobile Industry Since 1945* (Cambridge, Mass.: Harvard University Press, 1971).

9. For a discussion of the orientation toward business of the Carter, Reagan, and Bush administrations, see Richard Levine, "Unfinished Business: Reagan's Regulatory Relief," *Management Review*, March 1989, pp. 18–23, and Marshall Yates, "The Bush Administration: A New Environmental Focus," *Public Utilities Fortnightly*, January 5, 1989, pp. 26–28.

10. See "The Thatcher Record: To the Victor These Spoils," *The Economist*, November 24, 1990, pp. 17–20.

11. See Ouchi, *The M-Form Society;* Chalmers Johnson, *MITI and the Japanese Miracle* (Stanford, Calif.: Stanford University Press, 1982), and Ezra Vogel, "Guided Free Enterprise in Japan," *Harvard Business Review*, May–June 1978, pp. 161–170.

12. See James K. Weekly and Raj Aggarwal, *International Business: Operating in the Global Economy* (New York: Dryden, 1987).

13. Frito-Lay is often cited as one of the best-managed companies in the United States. See Tom Peters and Robert Waterman, *In Search of Excellence* (New York: Harper & Row, 1982).

14. Kathryn Harrigan, *Managing for Joint Venture Success* (Lexington, Mass.: Lexington Books, 1986), Kathryn Harrigan, *Strategies for Joint Ventures* (Lexington, Mass.: Lexington Books, 1985).

15. For a discussion of the NUMMI joint venture, see Clair Brown and Michael Reich, "When Does Union-Management Cooperation Work? A Look at NUMMI and GM–Van Nuys," *California Management Review*, Summer 1989,

pp. 26–44; and Lowell Turner, "Three Plants, Three Futures," *Technology Review,* January 1989, pp. 38–45. Joint-venture theory is summarized in Harrigan, *Managing for Joint Venture Success.*

16. This, and other cooperative efforts with suppliers, are described in Ouchi, *M-Form Society;* "Inside the Charmed Circle: Japan's Industrial Structure," *The Economist,* January 5, 1991, p. 54; and John McMillan, "Managing Suppliers: Incentive Systems in Japanese and U.S. Industry," *California Management Review,* Summer 1990, pp. 38–55.

17. See Edward Conry, *The Legal Environment of Business,* 2nd ed. (Boston: Allyn and Bacon, 1990), and Robert E. Norton, "Can Business Win in Washington?" *Fortune,* December 3, 1990, pp. 75–84.

18. See Johnson, *MITI and the Japanese Miracle.*

19. Phyliss Berman, "McDonald's Caves In," *Forbes,* February 4, 1991, pp. 73–74.

20. Recall that normal economic performance is a level of performance just great enough for a firm to pay its financial obligations and survive; above-normal economic performance is a level of performance greater than what is required for survival. See Jay Barney, "Firm Resources and Sustained Competitive Advantage," *Journal of Management,* 1991, pp. 99–121, and Michael Porter, *Competitive Strategy* (New York: Free Press, 1980).

21. Porter, *Competitive Strategy.* The five forces framework is summarized in Michael Porter, *Competitive Advantage* (New York: Free Press, 1985).

22. See Ian Williams, "Burger Bun-Fight," *Business,* May 1990, pp. 76–78; Brian Bremmer, "McDonald's Stoops to Conquer," *Business Week,* October 30, 1989, pp. 120, 124; Patricia Winters, "BK Resumes Burgher Wars, Mulls Smaller Whopper," *Advertising Age,* October 13, 1986, pp. 3, 103; Walecia Konrad, "The Real Thing Is Getting Real Aggressive," *Business Week,* November 26, 1990, pp. 94–104; and "Coke's Game Plan," *Advertising Age,* November 7, 1988, p. 4.

23. See F. M. Scherer, *Industrial Market Structure and Economic Performance,* 2nd ed. (Boston: Houghton Mifflin, 1980). Classic discussions of cooperation in the defense industry can be found in M. J. Peck and F. M. Scherer, *The Weapons Acquisition Process: An Economic Analysis* (Boston: Harvard Business School, Division of Research, 1962), and F. M. Scherer, *The Weapons Acquisition Process: Economic Incentives* (Boston: Harvard Business School, Division of Research, 1964). Recent cooperative efforts are described in Michael A. Dornheim, "Lockheed Team Unveils YF-22A Fighter Prototype," *Aviation Week,* September 3, 1990, pp. 41–42, and Thomas G. Donlan, "Victory Bandwagon: Will the Defense Industry Get a War Dividend?" *Barron's,* March 18, 1991, pp. 10–11, 30–34.

24. See M. J. Peck, *Competition in the Aluminum Industry: 1945–1958* (Cambridge, Mass.: Harvard University Press, 1961); Michael Schroeder, "Has Alcoa Found a Way to Foil the Aluminum Cycle?" *Business Week,* January 8, 1990, pp. 36–37; Russell Mitchel, Lois Therrien, and Gregory Miles, "ConAgra: Out of the Freezer," *Business Week,* June 25, 1990, pp. 24–25; and Bruce W. Marion, Willard F. Mueller, et al., *The Profit and Price Performance of Leading Food Chains, 1970–1974* (Washington D.C.: Government Printing Office, 1977).

25. See Peck and Scherer, *The Weapons Acquisition Process: An Economic Analysis,* and Scherer, *The Weapons Acquisition Process: Economic Incentives.*

26. See Ron Glen, "Software Directions: Reflections on 1990," *Canadian Data Systems,* December 1990, pp. 34–35; Keith Hammonds, "Spreadsheet Wars:

When Will Lotus Do Windows?" *Business Week,* January 14, 1991, p. 42; Lawrence J. White, *The Automobile Industry Since 1945* (Cambridge, Mass.: Harvard University Press, 1971); Yu Inaba, "The Final Battle: Japan Takes on the US Luxury Car Market," *Tokyo Business Today,* February 1990, pp. 26–31; and Gerald W. Brock, *The US Computer Industry* (Cambridge, Mass.: Ballinger, 1975).

27. Michael Porter, "Note on the Electronic Component Distribution Industry," Harvard Business School, Case No. 9-380-384, 1979.

28. See White, *The Automobile Industry Since 1945;* Inaba, "The Final Battle"; and Robert J. Browning, "Detroit '89: Forging Foreign Alliances," *Machine Design,* January 12, 1989, pp. 86–95.

29. Porter, *Competitive Strategy.*

30. Hank A. Becker and Joseph Van Doorn, "Scenarios in an Organizational Perspective," *Futures,* December 1987, pp. 669–677.

31. See Ouchi, *The M-Form Society.*

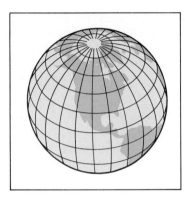

CASE 4.1

Mercedes Struggles to Keep Its Place

Mercedes-Benz cars, made by Daimler-Benz of Germany, have long been unique status symbols in the United States. Without conveying the ultra-rich image associated with Rolls-Royces or the frustrated-racer image that Porsches carry, Mercedes for most of this century have said to Americans, "The owner of this car has both money and good sense." They were reliable *and* luxurious, durable *and* stylish. And they held a firm position as the best-selling luxury import in the United States. That enviable position has been changing, however, as a result of a number of environmental factors and of Daimler-Benz's own dubious decisions.

During the 1980s, every automaker wanted to get into the American luxury car market. Sales of cars costing $20,000 or more doubled within the decade, reaching 1.2 million in 1987. Such growth attracted auto-makers, for more expensive cars mean higher profits. General Motors might make 10 or 20 times as much profit on a top-of-the-line Cadillac as on a subcompact Chevette. This inducement was particularly important for Jap-anese automakers, who for four years voluntarily limited their exports to the United States. A company that was going to send only 100,000 cars to the United States wanted each of those vehicles to yield as much profit as possible.

Carmakers from around the world began producing models to compete with Lincolns, Cadillacs, and Mercedes for the American luxury car market. Honda, Toyota, and Nissan introduced new lines — Acura, Lexus, and Infiniti, respectively — that were sold from separate showrooms that didn't carry the companies' lower-priced cars. Most of the ads for Acura, Lexus, and Infiniti didn't even mention the parent companies. Yet Honda, Toyota, and Nissan let customers know that these were Japanese cars built to the same exacting quality standards that make lower-priced Japanese cars so popular in America. As if that competition wasn't enough, Daimler-Benz's German rival, BMW, greatly expanded its own line of luxury cars.

Moreover, Daimler-Benz suddenly had to deal with internal changes. It went through a major diversification in the mid-1980s, buying companies that made aircraft engines, aerospace equipment, and electrical products, and becoming West Germany's biggest industrial company. The acquisi-tions promised to bring Mercedes-Benz new technologies in the years to come, but the sudden growth seems to have distracted Daimler management from the business of making cars. Daimler was much slower than its competitors to come out with new models, and the models it did produce had uncharacteristic problems with technical quality. While other car-makers were radically expanding their production of luxury cars — Toyota increased Lexus production from 16,000 in 1989 to 70,000 in 1990 — Daimler actually cut production of Mercedes.

The Wall Street crash of 1987 began changes in the luxury car market that the recession of 1990 and the 1991 tax law accelerated. Beginning in January 1, 1991, anyone spending more than $30,000 on a car had to pay a luxury tax equal to 10 percent of the amount over $30,000. So someone buying a Mercedes for $50,000 had to pay $2,000 extra. The so-called gas-guzzler tax levied on fuel-inefficient cars also rose sharply — a buyer of a Mercedes 560 SEL had to pay $2,600, double the amount of the previous year. These changes, and a general sense of frugality brought on by economic uncertainty, highlighted the differences between Mercedes and its Japanese rivals. The Japanese luxury cars have always been less expensive and more efficient than most European models, and those differences became harder for customers to ignore. Mercedes sales dropped 27 percent in the first quarter of 1991, and the company began advertising its 190E 2.3 sedan as an "affordable" luxury car, priced just under the $30,000 cut-off point.

Daimler-Benz is trying to make its product more affordable through the kinds of deals that would have been unthinkable a few years ago. To help customers avoid the luxury tax, Mercedes has been offering discount leasing rates — a 190E 2.3 sedan for $375 a month. It has also gone into the used-car business, operating "preparation centers" that make used Mercedes look and run better before they're sent to dealers for resale. Some reconditioned Mercedes even come with two-year warranties.

It will be difficult for Mercedes to regain its comfortable position at the top of the American luxury car market. Concern about energy conservation may fade again, or the company may successfully turn its engineering genius to the problem of making its cars run more efficiently. But powerful competition from the Japanese automakers is here to stay.

Discussion Questions

1. What environmental forces changed the fortune of Mercedes cars in the past decade?
2. How could Daimler-Benz have reacted better to the changes in its environment?
3. Use the five forces model to make sense of what has happened to Mercedes-Benz.
4. How can Daimler-Benz influence its environment? Would you advise the company simply to adapt?

REFERENCES: "Diverse Daimler Versus Brilliant BMW," *The Economist,* June 3, 1989, pp. 65–66; Krystal Miller, "European Luxury Auto Makers Resort to Discounts in Drive to Jump Start Sales," *Wall Street Journal,* April 29, 1991, pp. B1, B3; Alex Taylor III, "Detroit vs. New Upscale Imports," *Fortune,* April 27, 1987, pp. 69–77.

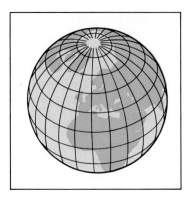

CASE 4.2

Guinness Bucks the Trend and Survives the Scandal

Some corporate catastrophes are a matter of bad luck, bad timing, or environmental changes that no one could foresee or control. Others result from gross human error, often motivated by greed or pride — the kinds of very human factors that cause catastrophes for individuals. Recently, Anglo-Irish brewer and distiller Guinness has had to contend with both sources of problems. That the company survived and, in fact, is doing well is a testament to how much good management can do for an organization.

Guinness, famous for its dark, foamy beer, is now Britain's largest brewer and distiller, producing about 40 percent of the world's Scotch. The trouble is, people aren't drinking as much Scotch as they used to. Scotch shipments to the United States fell 40 percent between 1978 and 1988, and worldwide shipments dropped 12 percent in the same period. Other hard liquor has suffered the same fate as health consciousness and the battle against drunk driving have led many people to turn to softer drinks.

Guinness's other big problem in the 1980s was wholly of its own creation. While making an acquisition that impressed the financial world even in an era of mergers and buyouts, Guinness tried a little too hard and wound up on the wrong side of a number of civil and criminal cases.

Guinness's chairman at the time, Ernest Saunders, had done a remarkable job of revitalizing the company. When he took over in 1981, sales were slowing and profits were down because the company had been diversifying into unrelated businesses. Profits almost tripled in Saunders's first four years, but that wasn't enough; Saunders wanted Guinness to become a major force in the worldwide liquor market. His big chance came when whiskey maker Distillers Corp., the prize Saunders really hungered for, came to him for help in fighting off a hostile takeover by Argyll Group, owners of a supermarket chain. Guinness mounted its own takeover attempt, even though Distillers was almost three times as large a company as Guinness. Since both Guinness and Argyll were offering stock as partial payment in the deal, the competition hinged on which buyer's stock price did better. In the month before the bidding closed, the price of a share of Guinness rose 25 percent, and Guinness completed the $4 billion buyout.

Saunders might have been hailed as a financial genius and gone on to knighthood if the British government hadn't started looking into that 25 percent stock price rise. British investigators may have been tipped off by Ivan Boesky, an American financial wizard who was being prosecuted for insider trading in the United States and may have received easier treatment for turning in other traders who had broken the law. Apparently Saunders had persuaded investors as disparate as Boesky and Switzerland's oldest bank to buy Guinness shares at the crucial time, thus raising the price. Saunders's most persuasive — and illegal — tools were guarantees that the company would buy the shares back at the same price and arrangements that left buyers with millions of dollars in commissions. Guinness ended up paying a large fine to Distillers' shareholders, and Saunders wound up with a five-year prison sentence for what the judge called "dishonesty on a massive scale."

In the two months after the investigation began in late 1986, the price of Guinness stock dropped 14 percent, and many thought that Guinness itself would become the target of a hostile takeover. But Guinness quickly moved to distance itself from Saunders and the others implicated in the scandal and hired a new CEO, Anthony Tennant.

Under Tennant, the company revived, eventually becoming the world's most profitable spirits company. It sold off its news dealers and health food stores to concentrate on its two main businesses, brewing and distilling. It began buying distributors and by 1990 owned three-quarters of its own distribution network, up from one-quarter in 1986. This change allowed Guinness not only to pocket the middleman's fee but also to control the mix and marketing of brands in particular areas. It pulled thirty of its Scotch brands off American shelves in order to concentrate on its large sellers. And it used advertising and its distribution control to encourage drinkers to move up to its more expensive — and considerably more profitable — brands like Johnnie Walker Black Label. The results have been impressive: profits have more than doubled since 1986.

If there's a lesson in Guinness's self-created catastrophe, it may be to look carefully into a new executive's background. Before moving to Guinness, Saunders had run Nestlé's infant-food division at a time when Nestlé's subsidiary, Beech-Nut, was selling fake apple juice for American babies and Nestlé itself was accused of marketing its infant formula in a way that resulted in the deaths of thousands of Third World babies. When those who had followed Nestlé's infant-food problems read about Saunders's problems at Guinness, they said, "What did you expect?" Perhaps some catastrophes *can* be foreseen.

Discussion Questions

1. What environmental factors have most affected Guinness's ability to make a profit?
2. How is Guinness adapting to its changed environment?
3. Use the five forces model to account for both of Guinness's big problems.
4. How do environmental factors affect a person's honesty?

REFERENCES: Richard I. Kirkland Jr., "Britain's Own Boesky Case," *Fortune,* February 16, 1987, pp. 85–86; Richard A. Melcher and Mark Maremont, "How Guinness Suddenly Fell from Grace," *Business Week,* February 9, 1987, pp. 44–46; Mark Maremont, "Guinness: A Lesson in Dealing with Drier Times," *Business Week,* June 27, 1988, pp. 52–54; Barbara Toman, "Guinness Learns to Keep Up Its Spirits," *Wall Street Journal,* December 20, 1990, p. A10.

5

Decision Making in Organizations

LEARNING OBJECTIVES

After studying this chapter, you should be able to:

1. Explain the differences between programmed and nonprogrammed decisions and between certain, risky, and uncertain decisions.

2. Describe how decisions change at different levels in the organizational hierarchy.

3. Identify the steps in the classical decision-making model, and discuss why an understanding of behavioral aspects of decision making is important.

4. Discuss the advantages and disadvantages of group decision making.

5. Explain three techniques for quantitative decision making.

I n 1986, Robert Campeau was a successful and respected Canadian real estate developer. By 1988 he headed one of the largest retail-store corporations in the world. A mere one year later, however, Campeau was unemployed, and his retail empire was in disarray. Having filed for bankruptcy, Campeau's organization was saddled with several billion dollars' worth of debt and had little prospect of short-term financial health.

Campeau's first involvement in retailing came through the acquisition of Allied Stores Corporation, a diversified owner of twenty-one respected chains. Supported by high-interest loans of almost $3.6 billion, Campeau acquired Allied on Halloween in 1986. To pay off this enormous debt, Campeau began selling some of Allied's respected retail chains, including Ann Taylor and Brooks Brothers. However, before the debt could be reduced, Campeau announced a takeover offer for Federated Department Stores. Initially set at $47 per share, Campeau's bid for Federated was challenged by several other companies, including Macy's and May Department Stores. Campeau's final bid was $73.50 per share ($12.50 per share higher than the next highest offer), for a total of $6.5 billion. Most of this money was also borrowed, at very high interest rates. The deal was completed on April Fool's Day in 1988.

With the completion of the Federated acquisition, the end of Campeau's retail-store empire was near. Not enough cash was being generated by Allied and Federated to pay the interest payments on the debt used to buy these companies. In the end, bankruptcy became as inevitable as death and taxes. Looking back on Campeau's crumbled empire, observers could only ask why so many bankers, lawyers, business people, and other experts had been so wrong about investing in Campeau's firms. Were these rational but risky business decisions that had simply not turned out well, or had other nonrational and emotional elements crept into the decision-making process?[1]

Decisions are the means by which organizations turn ideas into action. Some decisions are very important and have large implications for an organization's performance. Robert Campeau's decision to invest $6.5 billion of borrowed money in the purchase of Federated Department Stores had an enormous negative impact on his company, as well as on its suppliers and customers. Important decisions may have positive results that are equally sizable, however. Marriott's decision to manage, rather than own, hotel properties led it to record levels of profitability. Acura's decision to build and sell the NSX sports car has added both prestige and sales to that organization.

This chapter describes different types of decisions made in organizations and discusses the individuals who are generally responsible for making these decisions. We examine the model of classical decision making and the important decision-making behaviors that often limit its use. The chapter ends by introducing several important techniques used to improve group decision making in organizations. An appendix describes three important quantitative decision-making techniques.

Types of Decisions Made in Organizations

A *decision* is a choice made from among a set of alternatives. *Decision making* is the process of identifying, evaluating, and selecting among alternatives.

A **decision** is a choice made from among a set of alternatives, and **decision making** is the process of identifying alternatives, evaluating alternatives, and selecting an alternative.[2] It is often helpful to characterize the decisions made in organizations in terms of two dimensions: (1) whether a decision is programmed or nonprogrammed and (2) whether a decision is made under certain, risky, or uncertain conditions. The degree to which decisions are programmed depends on the number of times similar decisions have been made in the past. The extent of risk and uncertainty in decision making depends on the possible future outcomes of the decisions.

Programmed and Nonprogrammed Decisions

Programmed decisions are decisions that occur often enough in an organization that standardized decision rules are used to make them.

Programmed Decisions   **Programmed decisions** are decisions that occur often enough in an organization that standardized decision rules are used to make them.[3] Consider, for example, the string of decisions required in order to get an airplane aloft — a process repeated hundreds of times every day by large airline companies such as United, American, and TWA. Starting the engines, checking the electronic equipment, communicating destinations and flight plans, and informing passengers about safety are just a few of the tasks in this complicated process.

To ensure that these tasks are performed smoothly and consistently each time, airline companies (in coordination with the Federal Aviation Administration and aircraft-manufacturing companies like Boeing and McDonnell Douglas) have developed long check lists that pilots and co-pilots must go through to prepare for takeoff. By working through this highly programmed list of tasks, pilots automatically follow the correct procedure for starting and flying their aircraft. Pilots even have check lists for handling certain types of emergencies.

Nonprogrammed decisions are decisions that occur infrequently enough in an organization that standardized decision rules cannot be used to make them.

Nonprogrammed Decisions   **Nonprogrammed decisions** are decisions that occur infrequently enough in an organization that standardized decision

Programmed decisions are not unimportant decisions. Racing teams in NASCAR's Winston Cup series understand that the speed and efficiency with which they service their cars during races can have an important impact on the outcome of the race. Because of this, pit crews spend hundreds of hours practicing their highly programmed tasks, such as changing tires and adding fuel.

rules cannot be used to make them. Instead of looking to decision guidelines, standard operating procedures, or check lists, managers must rely more on their own experience and intuition to make a nonprogrammed decision. Just as some in-flight emergencies occur frequently enough to warrant the development of a check list, other emergencies are so infrequent that pilots must rely on their skills and training to be able to handle them.

Electronic Data Systems (EDS) faced a nonprogrammed decision in 1979 in Iran. That year the shah of Iran was forced out of power and replaced by the Ayatollah Khomeini. As this change in political power occurred, some members of the new Iranian government came to believe that EDS, a major supplier to the shah's regime, had somehow cheated them. Two EDS employees were arrested and jailed. As it became clear that most Western businesses were going to have to leave Iran, Ross Perot, founder and president of EDS, had to decide whether EDS should attempt to rescue the jailed employees. Perot consulted lawyers, international business experts, and his top-management team for advice. His final decision — to go ahead and rescue his employees — was his alone. It was ultimately based on his commitment to the safety and well-being of his employees — a commitment that had always been at the core of EDS's management philosophy. The uniqueness of this decision situation suggests just how nonprogrammed a decision can be.[4]

Rarely are nonprogrammed decisions as extreme as Perot's decision to rescue EDS employees. However, whenever IBM decides to invest in a new computer technology, or Procter & Gamble decides to bring out a new household product, or Toyota decides to build a new automobile plant, those decisions are at least partially nonprogrammed. In each case, previous experience with similar decisions is only an imperfect guide to making the

THE ENVIRONMENTAL CHALLENGE

When the Phones Hung Up

January 15, 1990, began like any other day at the American Telephone and Telegraph Network Operations Center in New Jersey. At Network Operations, AT&T monitors and routes long-distance telephone calls to ensure the fastest and clearest connections possible. The core of Network Operations is a room with two-story video screens on one wall. These video screens normally show maps of the continental United States, with red and blue lines extending from city to city. The red and blue lines, almost like electronic veins and arteries, represent well-functioning and efficient long-distance telephone lines.

By the afternoon of January 15, what started out as a normal day of routing and rerouting long-distance phone calls had turned into a complete disaster. A minor change in one computer program had taken large sections of AT&T's network out of operation. Only half of AT&T's normal load of 80 million long-distance phone calls were connected that day. Some AT&T executives called it the worst communications crisis in the organization's 114-year history.

The emergence of this computer problem turned a series of highly programmed decisions (switching long-distance phone calls) into a situation that called for a nonprogrammed decision. At 7 A.M. the morning after the crisis, AT&T executives met to decide what to tell the press about the network breakdown. Recalling Johnson & Johnson's experience with the Tylenol poisonings, AT&T decided to describe the communications problem as clearly as possible, to take full responsibility for the problem, to establish a task force to make sure the problem did not recur, and, finally, to give all customers affected by the problem a 33 percent discount on long-distance service on Valentine's Day.

Fast decisions helped AT&T re-establish good relations with its customers, but competitors took advantage of the crisis. Both MCI and Sprint immediately began an aggressive marketing campaign, arguing that even though AT&T was working to reduce the chance of further network breakdowns, customers should have access to a second long-distance network in case another crisis developed.

REFERENCES: "Glitch Imperils AT&T's Marketing Edge," *Wall Street Journal,* January 17, 1990, p. B1; "The Day That Every Phone Seemed off the Hook," *Business Week,* January 29, 1990, p. 39; John J. Keller, "The January Glitch: AT&T Discloses What Happened," *Wall Street Journal,* February 14, 1990, p. B1.

current decision. For example, IBM has invested in new computer technology before and knows something about managing this process. The familiar aspect of the decision is programmed. However, whether or not the particular technology being invested in is going to work, appeal to customers, be cost competitive, and so forth, is unique to this particular decision and thus is not programmed. The same is true for Toyota building a new plant and Procter & Gamble bringing out new products. The organizations have made similar decisions in the past, but these *particular* decisions contain some unique and thus nonprogrammable elements.

Sometimes an organization has a great deal of experience in making highly programmed decisions, such as AT&T's routing of long-distance phone calls. Then, without warning, unexpected events inside or outside the organization occur, and the decision suddenly becomes highly nonprogrammed. When transformation of a decision type occurs, organizations must make decisions quickly. AT&T faced exactly this kind of situation when its long-distance telephone network failed. The problem and AT&T's response are described in The Environmental Challenge.

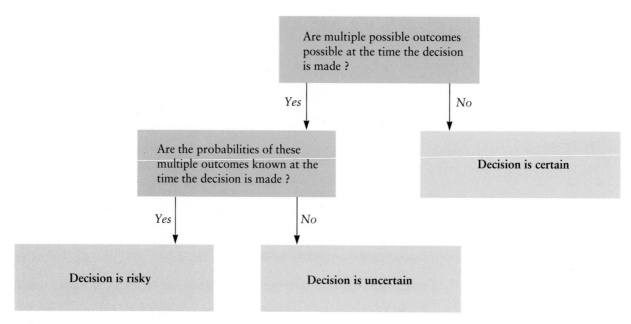

Figure 5.1

Distinguishing Between Certain,
Risky, and Uncertain Decisions

Certain, Risky, and Uncertain Decisions

Another way to describe decisions depends on whether the conditions under which the decisions are made are certain, risky, or uncertain.[5] Figure 5.1 distinguishes among these three types of decisions.

A decision is certain when, at the time it is made, it is known to have only a single likely outcome.

Certain Decisions   A decision is certain when, at the time it is made, it is known to have only a single likely outcome. This kind of decision is a "sure thing"; the probability that such a decision will work out as anticipated is very high.

Relatively few decisions in organizations are perfectly certain. Sometimes, however, they come pretty close. For example, the BIC Pen Company, which sells inexpensive ballpoint and other pens, manufactures, on average, over 3 million pens a day. In this manufacturing setting, any new machine that BIC uses to reduce its costs, even by a fraction of a penny per pen, will yield huge dividends. If a new machine saves only one-tenth of a cent per pen, that will mean a savings of $3,000 per day [$3,000 = (.1 × 3,000,000)/100]. Running the machine 360 days a year means a savings of $1,095,000 per year ($1,095,000 = 360 × $3,000). Thus, as long as BIC continues to sell at least 3 million pens a day (which the company has been doing since at least 1973), and as long as the new machine costs less than $1,095,000 per year, then the decision to add this machine to the manufacturing process will almost certainly generate positive economic dividends.[6] In this case the decision (whether BIC should purchase the machine) has only one known outcome (it will save money), and that outcome is extremely likely.

A decision is risky when, at the time it is made, the probabilities of several alternative outcomes' occurring are known.

Risky Decisions   A decision is risky when, at the time it is made, the probabilities of several alternative outcomes' occurring are known. Risky decisions thus have two characteristics. Several different outcomes are possible, and the probability of each outcome's actually occurring is known when the decision is made.

One example of a risky decision in organizations concerns the promotion of managers. There are three possible outcomes of promoting a manager. The individual (1) will excel in the new position, (2) will be an average performer, or (3) will turn out to be incompetent. Senior managers in an organization carefully evaluate candidates for promotion in an attempt to estimate the probability that the individual promoted will excel, will be an average performer, or will be incompetent. Since the multiple possible outcomes of the decision are known, and the probability of each outcome can be estimated, such a decision is classified as risky.

Many decisions in organizations are risky decisions.[7] When an electronic instruments company such as Hewlett-Packard spends money on research and development (R&D), it is taking a risk. Sometimes, investing in R&D leads to the invention of products and services that make companies like Hewlett-Packard a great deal of money. Sometimes, investing in R&D does not generate any financial benefits for an organization. From its past experience, Hewlett-Packard is able to predict, on average, that some of its research projects will financially benefit the organization and that some will not (although it cannot predict which *particular* projects will succeed or fail).

Risky decisions are often very important for organizations. In some industries organizations must make risky decisions in order to succeed. If they do not, they may fall behind, become technologically outmoded, and suffer severe financial setbacks. In these settings (described in detail in Chapter 9) the risky decisions that do not work well for an organization are simply a cost of operations.[8]

A decision is uncertain when, at the time it is made, the range of possible outcomes is not known, and thus the probability of these different outcomes' occurring is not known.

Uncertain Decisions   A decision is uncertain when, at the time it is made, the range of possible outcomes is not known, and thus the probability of these different outcomes' occurring is not known. As we saw earlier, for certain decisions, the outcome is known. For risky decisions, the range of outcomes and each of their probabilities are known. For uncertain decisions, neither the range of outcomes nor the probability of each of them occurring is known.[9]

Ross Perot's decision to rescue EDS employees from Iran is an example of an uncertain decision. When Perot made this decision, he could not anticipate the possible full range of outcomes or the probability that each would occur. General Motors' decision to acquire Perot's company Electronic Data Systems (EDS) was also uncertain. The outcome that Perot, as a member of the GM board of directors, would publicly criticize GM management and be removed from the board, could not have been anticipated at the time the acquisition decision was made.[10]

When managers make certain decisions, they know what the outcome will be. When they make risky decisions, they know the range of outcomes and can carefully manage the risk associated with different outcomes. But when managers make uncertain decisions, they do so without knowing — whether for sure or probabilistically — what the outcomes might be. Managers make these kinds of decisions because they believe the decisions are the right thing to do. Once managers make uncertain decisions, their task becomes working hard to make the decisions come out the way they want them to. They do this by marshaling the resources of an organization, including its structure and the behavior of its people, to make an uncertain decision turn out well.

One example of working hard to make an uncertain decision turn out well is Disney's decision to produce the movie *Dick Tracy*. At the time this decision was made, it was not at all clear that a movie about an old-fashioned comic-strip hero would appeal to modern audiences. The film might be very appealing; it might appeal to a limited audience; or it might appeal to no one. The probability of these different events' occurring was simply not known. To make this decision work, Disney made a series of related decisions — marketing related Dick Tracy products, selling video rights, and so forth — that transformed this uncertain decision into a certain one. By the time *Dick Tracy* was released, Disney was certain that it would at least break even on this investment. Only the level of profitability remained uncertain.[11]

Responsibility for Decision Making

Not everyone in organizations makes the same kinds of decisions. Some kinds of decisions are handled by executives in an organization's hierarchy. Other kinds of decisions are reserved for individuals at different levels and in different areas. The relationship between an individual's position in an organization's hierarchy and the types of decisions made is summarized in Figure 5.2.

In general, the higher one goes in an organization's hierarchy, the more likely that the decisions made are both nonprogrammed and uncertain. For example, when Sony's president, Akio Morita, decided to acquire Columbia Pictures, he was making a type of acquisition that had never been made before (the acquisition of a U.S. film company by a Japanese electronics firm). It was thus a nonprogrammed decision. Also, the outcome of this decision was highly uncertain. How much was Columbia worth as a stand-alone company? How much was it worth in combination with Sony? How would the traditional conservative management style of a Japanese company interact with the high-energy, risk-taking management style of a movie studio? Would the key individuals in the two organizations get along and form a productive team? All these questions were directly relevant to the

Top-level decision makers have broad responsibilities in organizations. As chairman of Johnson & Johnson's Consumer Sector, Pierre J. Dupasquier's responsibilities include reviewing and approving television commercials for many of Johnson & Johnson's consumer products.

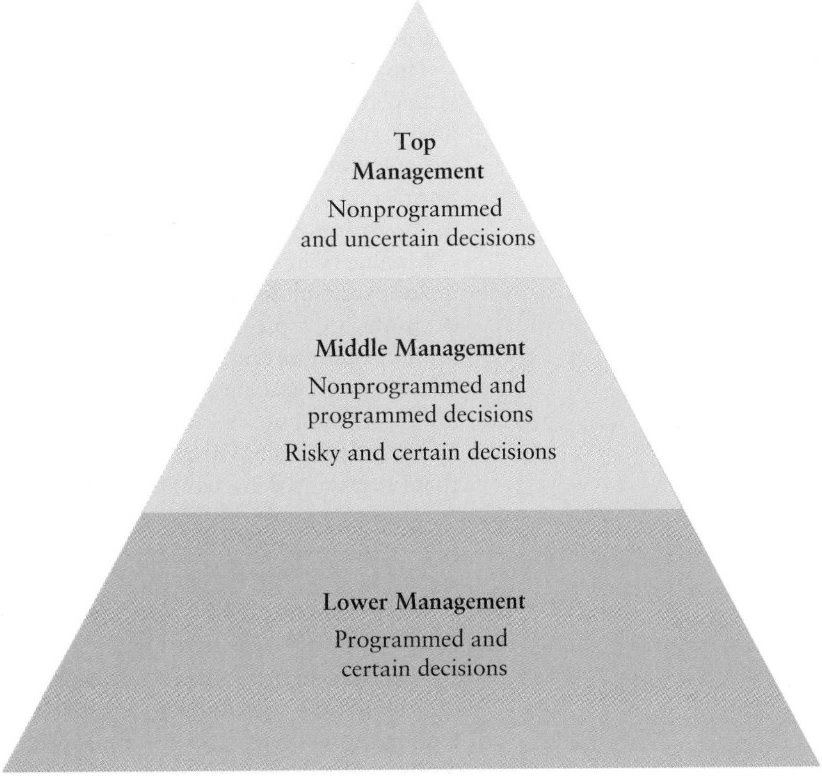

Figure 5.2

Types of Decisions Made at Different Levels in the Organizational Hierarchy

Top Management
Nonprogrammed and uncertain decisions

Middle Management
Nonprogrammed and programmed decisions
Risky and certain decisions

Lower Management
Programmed and certain decisions

success of the Columbia acquisition but could not be answered at the time the acquisition decision was made. Indeed, the only thing Morita could anticipate was that the acquisition would create unanticipated challenges and opportunities. As with most uncertain decisions, Morita's job was to find the people needed to make the acquisition work, no matter what occurred.[12]

Managers in the middle levels of an organization's hierarchy make programmed and nonprogrammed decisions and risky and certain decisions. Indeed, managers at this level of the hierarchy are often charged with transforming nonprogrammed decisions into programmed decisions by developing explicit criteria, policies, and procedures through which decisions are made. Thus, for example, a middle manager who develops an employee evaluation procedure is taking what may have been an ad hoc, nonprogrammed decision (how to evaluate an employee) and turning it into a routine, programmed decision.

In a similar way, middle managers are often given the assignment of transforming risky decisions into certain ones. They accomplish this task by carefully analyzing possible decision outcomes and taking steps to eliminate unfavorable alternatives. For example, a manager can transform a risky decision about purchasing a new piece of manufacturing equipment by negotiating a low price. With this low price, what was risky (will this new equipment generate a profit?) can be transformed into a certainty (with the price we paid for this equipment, it will certainly generate a profit).

The only kind of decision that middle managers generally do not make is uncertain decisions. Uncertain decisions usually require a great deal of active support from the entire organization to make them successful. A manager in the middle of an organization's hierarchy is usually not well positioned to muster this kind of organization-wide support, but managers in the top levels of the hierarchy are.

Managers in the lowest levels of an organization's hierarchy generally make programmed and certain decisions. Although the outcomes of these decisions are typically known before the decisions are made, these decisions are not unimportant. Airline pilots make the highly programmed and certain decisions associated with flying an airplane, but without these decisions airlines could not serve customers. Home-plate umpires make programmed and certain decisions about balls and strikes at a baseball game, but without these decisions there would be no game.

The Decision-making Process

All decision makers at every level of an organization engage in a process of identifying alternatives, evaluating alternatives, and selecting from among those alternatives the appropriate decision. This process may follow the prescribed logic of the classical decision-making model, but significant behavioral aspects of decision making may cause deviations from the model.

The Classical Decision-making Model

The six steps in the classical decision-making model are (1) recognizing the need to make a decision, (2) diagnosing the situation, (3) developing alternatives, (4) selecting an alternative, (5) implementing the alternative, and (6) exercising control and follow-up.

The classical decision-making model is a highly rational six-step procedure for making decisions.[13] It begins when an individual or organization recognizes the need for a decision. The next steps are to diagnose the situation, to develop alternatives, to select a particular alternative, and to implement the alternative. The final step is to exercise control and follow-up regarding the decision made. Figure 5.3 depicts the classical decision-making process. The text that follows explains the steps in this process and examines Perrier's use of classical decision making to solve a problem.

Recognize Need   In order to recognize that a decision must be made, those charged with making decisions must understand that there is a gap between the actual state of the organization and the desired state. The greater the gap between what is and what should be, the greater is the probability that decision makers will recognize the need for a decision.[14] Recognizing this gap is the crucial first step in solving the problem. This was certainly true for Perrier.

For years, Perrier has advertised the purity of its sparkling water, taken from a spring in the heart of the French Alps. In early 1990, however, researchers at the firm discovered that this pure water was becoming tainted with minute amounts of benzene. Although the levels of benzene involved were unlikely to create a significant health hazard, a gap nevertheless existed between the way Perrier wanted to be perceived by the public and the way it was being perceived. It wanted to be perceived as the bottler of the purest, best spring water in the world. But the perception was that it was selling polluted water. A decision had to be made.[15]

Diagnose Problem   The purpose of diagnosis is to understand *why* a gap between an actual state and a desired state of an organization exists.

Figure 5.3

Steps in Classical Decision Making, with Perrier as an Example

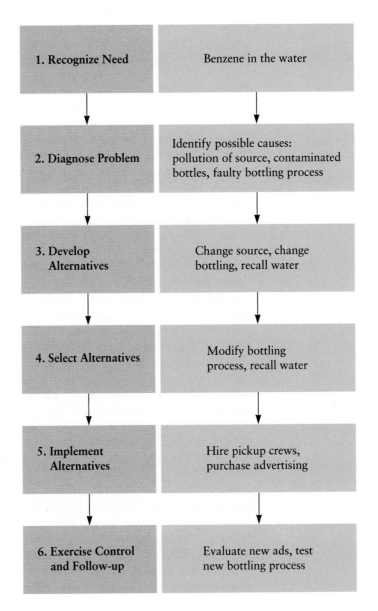

1. Recognize Need	Benzene in the water
2. Diagnose Problem	Identify possible causes: pollution of source, contaminated bottles, faulty bottling process
3. Develop Alternatives	Change source, change bottling, recall water
4. Select Alternatives	Modify bottling process, recall water
5. Implement Alternatives	Hire pickup crews, purchase advertising
6. Exercise Control and Follow-up	Evaluate new ads, test new bottling process

Usually, there are several plausible explanations. Diagnosis involves collecting data and information about each of these plausible explanations, to discover which of them are contributing to the perceived gap. Once the causes are isolated, alternative solutions can be developed.

For Perrier, several possible explanations existed. The source of water could have become polluted with benzene. The bottling process could have introduced the benzene. Perhaps the problem was in the bottles—the chemicals used to turn the glass green might have traces of benzene in them, or the benzene might come from the cap. Maybe some demented individual had injected traces of benzene into Perrier's water. To choose from among all these possibilities the explanation that accounted for the benzene in the water, Perrier began carefully investigating each possibility. Tests revealed that the water source, the glass, and the caps were not a source of contamination. Further research revealed that benzene was being introduced in the bottling process.[16]

Develop Alternatives   Once an organization identifies the cause of a problem, it can begin to develop alternative solutions. In classical decision making, it is important for organizations to explore all possible alternative solutions. Otherwise, some potentially effective ways of addressing the "gap" between the organization's actual and desired states may go untried.

Given Perrier's diagnosis (benzene contamination was occurring in the bottling process), several alternative solutions immediately suggested themselves. One was to shut down the entire bottling process and develop a new one. Another was to isolate the problem in the current process and fix it. Perrier had other alternatives to consider as well. Should it attempt to reassure customers that the level of benzene in the water would not pose a health hazard? Should it stop shipping water? Should it recall all the Perrier already shipped and attempt to restock with pure water? What were the ethical implications of each of these actions?[17]

Select Alternatives   Once decision makers have explored all the alternative solutions for solving a problem, they must next decide which of those alternatives to implement. In classical decision making, the alternatives that organizations select for implementation are called optimal solutions. **Optimal solutions** are alternatives that address a particular problem in the most complete way possible but at the lowest cost.[18]

In practice, selecting an optimal solution often involves some difficult choices. Sometimes very effective alternatives are either too expensive or not technically feasible. At other times, the only actions that an organization can take to solve a problem are not likely to be very effective. In many circumstances, however, an organization is able to select alternatives that address the problems at hand cost-efficiently.

Perrier faced some of these challenges in deciding what it should do. One choice Perrier made was simple: to modify the current bottling process to avoid any additional benzene contamination. Thus developing an entirely new bottling process was not necessary. This first alternative was both effective and not very costly. Many of Perrier's other alternatives were more

Optimal solutions are alternatives that address a particular problem in the most complete way possible but at the lowest cost.

difficult. Perrier also decided to recall *all* of its product, even though the level of benzene contamination would not pose a health hazard. The firm decided that its reputation for purity, and its ability to sell water in the future, required it to accept the very large losses associated with a recall.[19]

Implement Alternatives Once an organization selects from among its alternatives, it has, in one sense, made a decision. What counts, however, is not the "*announced*" decision but the *implemented* decision. Implementation occurs when the ideas and principles represented in a decision are actually put into operation by members of an organization, its suppliers, and its customers. For Perrier, decision implementation meant modifying the bottling process and sending its representatives out to grocery stores and restaurants throughout the world to physically pick up its product. Implementation also required notifying the public through paid advertising that the benzene problem had been located and solved and that all currently available Perrier products should not be purchased or consumed.[20]

Exercise Control and Follow-Up Once a decision has been made and implemented, organizations following the classical decision-making model complete this process by exercising control and follow-up. Table 5.1 lists several critical tasks in this stage of decision making. First, organizations need to ensure that the decisions selected for implementation are actually being implemented. Second, they need to ensure that the implemented decisions are having the desired effect—that is, closing the gap between the actual state of the organization and its desired state. Third, organizations need to ensure that the implemented decisions do not have any unintended consequences. A decision has an unintended consequence when, in addition to addressing problems it was intended to address, it addresses problems it was not intended to address or creates problems it was not intended to create. Finally, organizations need to anticipate other actions that they need to take to further narrow the gap between where they would like to be and where they are.[21]

Perrier has engaged in most of the control and follow-up tasks listed in Table 5.1. First, Perrier made certain that its recall order was carried out by developing an advertising campaign that asked consumers *not* to buy Perrier, by hiring extra employees to pick up recalled Perrier from stores, and so forth. Perrier also invested in a redesign of its bottling facilities.

Table 5.1

Exercising Control and Follow-Up in Classical Decision Making

1. Ensure that the decision selected is being implemented.
2. Ensure that the decision is having the desired effect.
3. Ensure that the decision has no unintended consequences.
4. Anticipate additional actions.

THE ENTREPRENEURIAL CHALLENGE

Decision Making at Compaq

Founded in 1980 in Houston, Texas, Compaq Computer is one of the fastest-growing companies in the United States. Compaq's sales swelled to $111 million in 1983, to $1.2 billion in 1987, and to $2.1 billion in 1988. A leading manufacturer of personal computers, Compaq is widely respected for its engineering and technological excellence.

One might think that a fast-growing organization like Compaq would be characterized by very unstructured decision making. An unstructured approach is the norm at some of Compaq's competitors, including Apple and Sun Microsystems. However, decision making at Compaq is anything but informal. Founded by managers who had left Texas Instruments, Compaq has adopted a very structured, very thorough decision-making process that closely follows the classical decision-making model.

At Compaq, organization size has never made much of a difference in decision making. Early in its history the company regarded itself not as a small organization but as a large organization in its "formative stages."

Anticipating its development into a large firm, Compaq implemented state-of-the-art accounting, management information, and finance systems. As the firm has grown, these systems have guided its increasingly complex decisions.

Compaq is counting on classical decision making to sustain it as it competes more directly with IBM and other large companies. But the dynamics of the computer industry already have begun to strain this decision-making approach. Although Compaq is well tuned to bringing out one or two new products a year, the firm has found it necessary recently to bring out four or five new products a year. The time needed to utilize classical decision making may simply no longer be available in the personal-computer industry.

REFERENCES: Stuart Gannes, "America's Fastest Growing Companies," *Fortune,* May 23, 1988, pp. 28–40; Brenton R. Schlender, "Who's Ahead in the Computer Wars," *Fortune,* February 12, 1990, pp. 59–66; Karen Blumenthal and Robert Tomsho, "An IBM Tagalong Sets Independent Course, with Plenty of Risks," *Wall Street Journal,* April 21, 1989, pp. A1, A5.

Perrier's efforts to pull its product from the market were successful. Perrier also began to anticipate the time when it would reintroduce its product to the market. A new label (emphasizing the purity of the water) was designed. An advertising campaign to reintroduce Perrier water was implemented, and pure Perrier once again became available to customers, less than six months after the original product had been pulled from the market.[22]

Classical decision making sounds as though it is well suited for large bureaucratic organizations, and often it *is* adopted by large firms. However, even smaller organizations, like Compaq Computer, can gain from this highly structured approach. Compaq's experience with classical decision making is discussed in The Entrepreneurial Challenge.

Behavioral Aspects of Decision Making

The classical decision-making process is a very logical, very linear way of making decisions. However, limits on the information-processing capabilities of decision makers sometimes make it impossible to use classical decision making. At times, there is simply too much information for individuals or groups in the organization to digest. At other times, the costs of

Table 5.2

Decision Making in Theory and in Practice

Assumptions of Classical Decision-making Model	Behavioral Aspects of Decision Making in Practice
1. Decision makers have unlimited information-processing capability.	1. Decision makers are subject to bounded rationality.
2. Optimizing evaluates all possible solutions.	2. Satisficing evaluates only a subset of plausible solutions.
3. Decision making does not take into account social and psychological processes.	3. Decision making is affected by social and psychological processes.

collecting and analyzing all the information needed for classical decision making are simply too high. Social and psychological phenomena in organizations also tend to make complete application of classical decision making rare. Table 5.2 summarizes the assumptions of the classical decision-making model and compares them with some behavioral aspects of decision making in practice.

Bounded Rationality in Organizations   One important attribute of classical decision making is its assumption that decision makers have an unlimited capacity for processing information. The model assumes that no matter how complicated a decision is, how many alternatives exist, or how complex the tradeoffs and subtle the relationships, decision makers will be able to weigh the tradeoffs effectively and choose the optimal course of action.

Many decision makers simply do not have this unlimited capacity. Even when they are supported by extremely intricate management information systems, computers, and support staffs, the complexity of some decisions simply overwhelms the ability of decision makers to process information. **Bounded rationality** is a term that describes the limited capacity of decision makers to process information. Most decisions in organizations are made under conditions of bounded rationality.[23]

Bounded rationality describes the limited capacity of decision makers to process information.

To see how bounded rationality affects decision making, consider some relatively straightforward decisions you may now be facing. For example, what sort of work will you decide to do upon graduation? For some of you (those planning to enter a family business or those already employed), this decision is perhaps clear. For others, the decision is not at all clear because it depends on events about which you do not yet have full information: your performance in school, the kinds of jobs offered, the companies you might interview with. If you were not subject to the condition of bounded rationality, you would be able to understand and anticipate all the events in your life and make an accurate prediction about where you will work upon graduation. Given your condition of bounded rationality, however, the answer to this question is something of a guess.

In general, the more complex a decision is, or the farther off in the future the consequences of a decision will be known, the more decision makers are limited by bounded rationality. Simple decisions about actions taken tomorrow (such as what time to get out of bed and what clothes to wear) can usually be arrived at through classical decision making because all the alternatives for these decisions can be listed and the best alternative selected. However, complex decisions that have consequences far into the future are difficult to analyze so completely.

Satisficing Versus Optimizing   Given the condition of bounded rationality, how can organizations best make complex decisions that have consequences far into the future? Typically, organizations abandon the search for optimal solutions — a search that considers *all* possible alternatives — and look instead for satisfactory solutions. The search for optimal solutions is called **optimizing**, and the search for satisfactory solutions is called **satisficing**.[24] In satisficing, decision makers list only a subset of alternatives and select from among this list.

Optimizing is the search for optimal solutions. *Satisficing* is the search for satisfactory solutions.

Acknowledgment of bounded rationality is not the only reason that decision makers might abandon optimizing in favor of satisficing. Sometimes, using classical decision making can be expensive in terms of money and resources.

Satisficing may also be more appropriate when a decision needs to be made quickly. Sometimes, opportunities present themselves to organizations for only brief periods of time. Organizations that use classical decision making may find the opportunity gone by the time they decide to take advantage of it. In the dynamic field of microelectronics, small, fast-acting companies like Silicon Solutions and Sun Microsystems sometimes outmaneuver larger organizations like IBM and General Electric. In telecommunications, MCI, Sprint, and other smaller providers are able to make decisions faster than AT&T. Although AT&T may have more complete decision-making processes, the speed of satisficing gives the smaller firms advantages.[25]

Social and Psychological Factors   Social and psychological factors that exist in organizations tend to limit the application of classical decision making. Three such powerful factors are escalation of commitment, organizational politics, and managerial intuition.

Escalation of commitment is a psychological process whereby decision makers become increasingly committed to their chosen course of action even as the ineffectiveness of that action becomes more obvious. One implication of escalation of commitment is that decision makers are reluctant to abandon or change their bad decisions. Instead, they spend more time, money, and other organizational resources trying to turn a bad decision into a good one. Sometimes this effort is successful. More often than not, the inappropriate decision remains inappropriate, and the additional resources spent are wasted.[26]

Escalation of commitment is a psychological process whereby decision makers become increasingly committed to their chosen course even as the ineffectiveness of that action becomes more obvious.

Escalation of commitment occurs often in organizations. Winnebago seems committed to an investment in satellite communications even though most observers and experts believe this investment will never yield positive dividends. Robert Campeau continued to push for the acquisition of Federated for $73.50 a share even though the next best offer for Federated was only $67 per share. *Fortune* ultimately called this acquisition the "Biggest, Looniest Deal Ever."[27] In the 1980s, the Canadian province of British Columbia remained committed to hosting a world's fair (Expo '86) even though deficit projections rose from $6 million in 1978 to over $300 million in 1985.[28]

Several organizational forces may give rise to escalation of commitment. Decision makers have strong incentives to see their choices succeed, not the least of which is concern for career and income. Also, once an organization puts administrative apparatus in place to implement a decision, it is often difficult to dismantle since all the managers, workers, and suppliers who depend on it for their livelihood will resist change. The more resources an organization commits to implement a decision, the more difficult it is to back out, even if the decision is apparently a bad one.[29]

These organizational pressures for escalation of commitment are complicated by the fact that sometimes it is not clear whether a decision is appropriate or not. A decision may look inappropriate, but individuals committed to it may credibly claim that a few more resources could turn the situation around. Such an optimistic outlook tends to increase commitment to the decision even more.[30]

Organizational politics is a set of individual or group activities carried out for the specific purpose of acquiring, developing, and using power to influence the outcomes of decisions.

Another factor that tends to interfere with the orderly operation of classical decision making is organizational politics. **Organizational politics** is a set of individual or group activities carried out for the specific purpose of acquiring, developing, and using power to influence the outcomes of decisions.[31] When organizational politics is introduced into decision making, rational questions such as "What is the situation?" and "What are the alternatives?" are supplemented by politically attuned questions such as "Whose interests are served by this decision?" and "Who is likely to be offended by this decision?"

The influence of organizational politics on decision making is widespread. In a recent survey one-third of managers said that organizational politics plays a role in salary decisions, and 28 percent said that organizational politics influences hiring decisions. Most managers agreed that learning how to manage organizational politics is very important for managers to be successful in the top levels of organizations.[32] How political influence is used, and abused, in organizations is discussed in more detail in Chapter 18.

Organizational politics can make itself felt at the lowest or highest levels of an organization. Apple Computer ran into trouble when, as part of a new marketing effort, it hired the former president of PepsiCo, John Sculley, to be president and CEO. Almost as soon as he arrived, Sculley began having differences with Steven Jobs, one of the original Apple founders. These two battled each other for a couple of years, until Jobs finally left Apple to found NeXT, Inc.

Managerial intuition is the ability of decision makers to make successful decisions while drawing on incomplete, inconclusive, and contradictory information.

Managerial intuition is the ability of decision makers to make successful decisions while drawing on incomplete, inconclusive, and contradictory information. Intuition in decision making is widespread. By drawing on their years of experience, intuitive managers such as Jack Welch, president and CEO at General Electric, and John Young, president of Hewlett-Packard, are able to make correct decisions that go well beyond the information they currently possess.[33]

To summarize, although classical decision making has a logical appeal, and although it can be successfully applied in some situations, it offers a limited description of how decisions are actually made in organizations. Because of bounded rationality, decision makers often cannot achieve the level of sophisticated analysis assumed by classical decision making. Often, the cost of optimizing is too high or the timing too long, so satisficing is more appropriate. In addition, factors such as escalation of commitment, organizational politics, and managerial intuition tend to interfere with or even supplant the classical decision-making model.

Group Decision Making

Group decision making is any decision-making process that is performed by several individuals.

Managers can use a variety of quantitative and group decision-making techniques to improve decision making. Three important quantitative techniques are described in the appendix to this chapter. **Group decision making** is any decision-making process that is performed by several individuals. Thus, when Allen Neuharth, chief executive of Gannett Co., the publisher of *USA Today,* gathers his top editorial staff to decide the content of an issue, he is using group decision making. Table 5.3 lists some advantages and disadvantages of group decision making.[34]

Advantages of Group Decision Making

By including more individuals in the decision-making process, organizations increase the amount of information and experience available and thus may improve the quality of the final decision. In addition, because group decision

Table 5.3

Advantages and Disadvantages of Group Decision Making

Advantages	Disadvantages
1. Increases the amount of experience and information available for decision making.	1. Increases the amount of time needed to reach a decision.
2. Generates more alternatives to evaluate and select from.	2. Forces compromises when strong action is required.
3. Broadens communication and acceptance of the decision throughout the organization.	3. Encourages groupthink.

Group decision making is very common in organizations. This form of decision making enables an organization to capitalize on the unique skills of diverse individuals when decisions are made. At General Mills, business unit director John Halberg (l.) brought together the marketing, production, sales, product-development, and business-management skills represented by the other people pictured here to maximize the success of the Cheerios family of breakfast cereals. The result of their efforts was a more than 1 percent market share increase in 1990 alone.

Group decision making has three advantages: (1) it can increase the amount of information available for making a decision; (2) it can generate more alternatives, thus increasing the chances of optimization; and (3) it increases the likelihood that a decision will be accepted and implemented by organization members.

Group decision making has three disadvantages: (1) it takes a great deal of time; (2) it may lead to compromises where strong action is required; and (3) it may lead to groupthink.

making tends to generate more alternatives to consider, it may enable organizations to optimize more, as in the classical decision-making model.

Group decision making also increases communication and understanding throughout an organization about the reasons for a particular decision. This, in turn, increases the likelihood that individuals will accept the decision and enthusiastically support and implement it. Chapter 19 discusses the link between group decision making and implementation in detail.

Disadvantages of Group Decision Making

Group decision making takes longer than individual decision making. Gathering people together, reaching a consensus about the nature of a problem, generating alternative solutions, evaluating those solutions, and so forth, takes time. In industries characterized by brief periods of opportunity, such as microelectronics and the record business, the time needed to use group decision making may not be available.

Group decision making can also force compromises in an organization when what is required is strong, decisive action and direction. This is especially the case for organizations facing a crisis. When Lee Iaccoca took over at Chrysler, he avoided this disadvantage by taking a variety of decisive steps to ensure the short-term survival of the firm. He did not allow his clear vision of what was required to be compromised by pressures from different groups inside the company.

Groupthink is a phenomenon that emerges in a group when group members' desire for consensus and cohesion overwhelms their desire to make the best decision.

Finally, group decision making can encourage the development of group-think. **Groupthink** is a phenomenon that emerges in a group when group members' desire for consensus and cohesion overwhelms their desire to make the best decision.[35] This phenomenon arose among President John F. Kennedy and his advisers in 1961 as they were attempting to decide whether or not to support a U.S. invasion of Cuba. Kennedy's advisers were more worried about offending the president than about determining whether the invasion should be supported. To preserve the appearance of harmony, they avoided asking tough, noncompromising questions about the motives and goals of the plan. The result was that a bad decision was made, and the invasion—now often called the Bay of Pigs "fiasco"—was doomed to failure before it started.[36]

Even organizations with a great deal of experience in group decision making sometimes fall victim to these disadvantages. Japan's Ministry of International Trade and Industry (MITI) has gained an international reputation for the quality of its decisions. Yet, as discussed in The Global Challenge, even this organization makes mistakes.

Techniques for Group Decision Making

The effective techniques for group decision making are the interacting group technique, the nominal group technique, and the role-assigning technique.

To avoid some of the disadvantages of group decision making while still exploiting all of its advantages, organizations can use specific techniques. Three of the most important are the interacting group technique, the nominal group technique, and the role-assigning technique.

Interacting Group Technique   An **interacting group** is a decision-making group in which members openly and freely discuss, argue about, or agree on the best alternative. Of all group techniques, the interacting group is the least structured. It is appropriate when participants have a great deal of experience in group decision making or in interacting with one another. If participants do not have such experience, however, the lack of structure in an interacting group can create two main decision-making problems: (1) group members feel uncomfortable sharing their ideas or experiences, especially when their ideas and experiences conflict with those of the group majority; and (2) one individual, or one point of view, can dominate discussion. If either of these problems appears in an interacting group, it may be appropriate to introduce more structure into the decision process.[37]

Nominal Group Technique   A more structured group technique is the nominal group. In a **nominal group**, members do not talk freely with one another. Instead, a group leader describes the decision situation as he or she currently understands it. Then individual members write down as many alternatives as they can think of to address the problem. The alternatives are read out loud and listed on a chalkboard or flip chart. Discussions are limited to clarifications of what different alternatives mean. Finally, group members individually write down and rank their preferred alternatives. The group leader collects the rankings and uses them to make a decision.[38]

THE GLOBAL CHALLENGE

MITI's Mixed Record

The Ministry of International Trade and Industry (MITI) in Japan is widely seen as one of the world's most effective government organizations. Some have credited MITI with the Japanese postwar economic miracle. MITI credits its success to working carefully with Japanese organizations to focus research and development efforts on new products and technologies that seem to have high economic potential. In this way, MITI helped establish the very successful Japanese microelectronics industry, consumer electronics industry, and computer industry.

However, some of MITI's decisions have been somewhat less successful. For example, MITI strongly recommended that Honda not enter the automobile business because there were already enough good Japanese carmakers and another one would not succeed. Fortunately, Honda ignored MITI's advice.

MITI was also very concerned about the lead that U.S. microelectronics firms had in high-density memory chips. Japanese firms had been able to duplicate the 64K memory chip, but they were unable to duplicate the 256K memory chip. MITI formed a special research group consisting of five companies — Nippon Electric Company (NEC), Toshiba, Hitachi, Mitsubishi, and Fujitsu — whose task was to develop the 256K chip. Oki Electronic Industry, a firm that MITI did not allow to join the research group, worked on its own and developed the new chip before the MITI-sponsored group did. It would have been better for MITI to include Oki as a member of the research group.

MITI has invested in a remote-controlled undersea oil drilling rig ($36 million), an electric car ($46 million), a nuclear-powered blast furnace for steel making ($110 million), and a process for deriving petrochemicals from carbon monoxide ($84 million). All of these projects failed. When asked why some of their decisions do not work out, MITI officials admit that bad decisions usually result when MITI does not follow its standard process of decision making. This process emphasizes group involvement, consensus building, and discussion.

REFERENCES: Carla Rapoport, "Great Japanese Mistakes," *Fortune,* February 13, 1989, pp. 108–111; William G. Ouchi, *The M-Form Society* (Reading, Mass.: Addison-Wesley, 1984); Chalmers Johnson, *MITI and the Japanese Miracle* (Stanford, Calif.: Stanford University Press, 1982).

The responsibility of a *devil's advocate* is to continuously disagree with the majority opinion and to muster arguments about why the majority opinion is incorrect.

The responsibility of a *group facilitator* is to ensure that every group member feels free to express opinions, even if the opinions are controversial, and to make sure that no one person dominates the group.

Role-assigning Technique   Interacting groups have very little structure and nominal groups sometimes have too much structure. Role assignment comes between these two extremes. The different roles assigned to specific group members serve as structure to keep the group focused on its decision making. Role assignment usually does not inhibit discussion, as can be the case with the nominal group technique.[39]

Two roles are particularly important in group decision making. The responsibility of a **devil's advocate** is to continuously disagree with the majority opinion and to muster arguments about why the majority opinion is incorrect, regardless of their own individual beliefs. They prevent the group from coming to a decision too early and help avoid the problem of groupthink.[40]

The responsibility of a **group facilitator** is to ensure that every group member feels free to express opinions, even if the opinions are controversial. The group facilitator also makes sure that no one person dominates a group. This facilitator role is discussed in detail in Chapter 19.[41]

Learning Summary

A decision is a choice made from among a set of alternatives. The decisions made in organizations can be programmed or nonprogrammed. Programmed decisions have been made enough times in an organization so that standard rules or procedures for making them have been developed. Nonprogrammed decisions have no such rules associated with them. Decisions can also be certain, risky, or uncertain. Certain decisions have only one outcome, which is known at the time the decision is made. Risky decisions have several possible outcomes, the probability of which is known at the time the decision is made. Uncertain decisions are decisions for which neither the range nor the probability of possible outcomes is known at the time the decision is made.

Different individuals in an organization tend to make different types of decisions. Those at the top of an organization's hierarchy make nonprogrammed and uncertain decisions. Those in the middle of the hierarchy make risky and certain decisions. Those at the bottom of the hierarchy tend to make programmed and certain decisions.

The classical decision-making model is a highly rational and logical procedure for developing and selecting alternatives. A variety of behavioral factors tends to limit the application of the classical decision-making model. These factors include bounded rationality, satisficing, escalation of commitment, organizational politics, and managerial intuition.

Group decision making offers several advantages. It increases the amount of experience and information available for decision making, generates more alternatives to evaluate and select from, and broadens communication and acceptance of the decision throughout the organization. The disadvantages are that it takes a great deal of time, forces inappropriate compromises, and can encourage groupthink. Techniques that may overcome some of the disadvantages of group decision making are use of an interacting group, use of a nominal group, and assignment of devil's advocate and group facilitator roles to group members.

Questions and Exercises

Review Questions

1. What are some important differences between programmed and non-programmed decisions? Give examples of each.
2. What are some important differences between risky decisions and uncertain decisions? Give some examples of each.
3. What are the major steps in classical decision making?
4. Define each of the following:
   a. escalation of commitment
   b. organizational politics
   c. intuitive decision making
   d. interacting group
   e. nominal group
   f. groupthink
   g. devil's advocate
   h. group facilitator

Analysis Questions

1. What happens in organizations when a programmed decision suddenly becomes a nonprogrammed decision? Give an example of when this might occur.
2. Identify each of the following decisions as certain, risky, or uncertain. Explain.
   a. An organization hires new employees.
   b. An organization decides to market a brand-new product that is based on a technology that the organization has never before used.
   c. An organization reduces the number of its employees without affecting its product or service.
   d. An organization builds a fourth manufacturing plant.
3. In which kinds of industries is classical decision making likely to be most effective? In which are behavioral aspects of decision making likely to have the most effect?
4. How can group decision making improve the quality of decision making? How can it negatively affect the quality of decision making?

Application Exercises

1. Evaluate the thought process you followed to choose your major. Did you use classical decision making? Were there important behavioral aspects to your decision making? Describe them.
2. Think about the most recent group study session you attended (for this class or for any other). Which of the disadvantages of group decision making did you observe?

Chapter Notes

1. Steven Kaplan, "Campeau's Acquisition of Federated: Value Destroyed or Value Added?" *Journal of Financial Economics*, 1989, pp. 191–212; "Deal and Misdeals: A Sampling of M&A Hits and Strikeouts in the 1980s," *Mergers and Acquisitions*, 1990, pp. 100–119; Carol Loomis, "The Biggest, Looniest Deal Ever," *Fortune*, June 18, 1990, pp. 48–72.
2. For recent reviews of decision making, see E. Frank Harrison, *The Managerial Decision Making Process*, 3rd ed. (Boston: Houghton Mifflin, 1987), and David J. Hickson, Richard J. Butler, David Cray, Geoffrey R. Mallory, and David C. Wilson, *Top Decisions* (San Francisco: Jossey-Bass, 1986).
3. The distinction between programmed and nonprogrammed decisions is discussed by George Huber, *Managerial Decision Making* (Glenview, Ill.: Scott, Foresman, 1980).
4. The story of the rescue of the EDS managers is told in Ken Follet, *On Wings of Eagles* (New York: Signet, 1983).
5. See Huber, *Managerial Decision Making*. The distinction between certain, risky, and uncertain decisions was first discussed by Frank Knight, *Risk, Uncertainty, and Profit* (New York: Harper & Row, 1965).

6. See C. Roland Christensen, Kenneth R. Andrews, Joseph L. Bower, Richard G. Hamermesh, and Michael Porter, "BIC Pen (A)," *Business Policy: Text and Cases,* 5th ed. (Homewood, Ill.: Irwin, 1982), pp. 136–159.

7. See, for example, Avi Feigenbaum and Howard Thomas, "Attitudes Toward Risk and the Risk-Return Paradox: Prospect Theory Explanations," *Academy of Management Journal,* March 1988, pp. 85–106; Jitendra K. Singh, "Performance, Slack, and Risk Taking in Organizational Decision Making," *Academy of Management Journal,* September 1986, pp. 562–585; and James G. March and Zur Shapira, "Managerial Perspectives on Risk and Risk Taking," *Management Science,* November 1987, pp. 1404–1418.

8. Michael Porter, *Competitive Strategy* (New York: Free Press, 1980), describes the conditions under which risky decision making may be required for organizational survival.

9. See Huber, *Managerial Decision Making.* See also David W. Miller and Martin K. Starr, *The Structure of Human Decisions* (Englewood Cliffs, N.J.: Prentice-Hall, 1976), and Alvar Elbing, *Behavioral Decisions in Organizations,* 2nd ed. (Glenview, Ill.: Scott, Foresman, 1978).

10. Thomas Moore, "Make or Break Time for General Motors: 'How I Would Turn Around GM,'" *Fortune,* February 15, 1988, pp. 32–50.

11. J. Egan, "Hollywood's Numbers Game," *U.S. News and World Report,* April 12, 1990, pp. 39–42; B. Kanner, "Will Crime Pay for Dick Tracy?" *New York,* June 25, 1990, pp. 20+.

12. Andrea Rothman, "Sony Is Out to Be the World's One-Stop Shop for Entertainment," *Business Week,* March 25, 1991, pp. 64–74.

13. For recent reviews of the classical decision-making model, as well as a discussion of some of its limitations, see Paul C. Nutt, "Types of Organizational Decision Processes," *Administrative Science Quarterly,* September 1984, pp. 414–450, and Lawrence T. Penfield, "A Field Evaluation of Perspectives on Organizational Decision Making," *Administrative Science Quarterly,* September 1986, pp. 365–388.

14. See R. T. Lenz and Jack L. Engledow, "Environmental Analysis Units and Strategic Decision Making: A Field Study of Selected 'Leading Edge' Corporations," *Strategic Management Journal,* 1986, pp. 69–89, for a recent analysis of how decision situations are recognized. One of the first scholars to describe the importance of recognizing a need for change was Kurt Lewin, "Frontiers in Group Dynamics: Concept, Method, and Reality in Social Science," *Human Relations,* June 1947, pp. 5–41.

15. Daniel Butler, "Perrier's Painful Period," *Management Today,* August 1990, pp. 72–73; Bruce Crumely, "French Cola Wars: Pepsi Battles Coke; Fight Perrier over Distribution," *Advertising Age,* December 17, 1990, p. 22; Fred Pfaff, "The Search for Perrier's Single Source," *Marketing and Media Decisions,* July 1990, pp. 28–29; Jatiana Pouschine, "Perrier, Your Bubbles Are Too Big," *Forbes,* May 1, 1989, pp. 106–112.

16. Pfaff, "The Search for Perrier's Single Source"; Bruce Crumley, "Fizzzz Went the Crisis," *International Management,* April 1990, pp. 52–53.

17. Stewart Toy and Lisa Driscoll, "Can Perrier Purify Its Reputation?" *Business Week,* February 26, 1990, p. 45.

18. Methods for making optimum decisions are discussed in James L. McKenney and Richard Rosenbloom, *Cases in Operations Management* (New York: Wiley, 1969), and Barry Render and Ralph M. Stair, *Cases and Readings in Quantitative Analysis for Management* (Boston: Allyn and Bacon, 1982).

19. Patricia Sellers, "Perrier Plots Its Comeback," *Fortune,* April 23, 1990, pp. 277–278.

20. Patricia Winters, "Perrier's Back: Whimsical Campaign to Support Its Return," *Advertising Age*, April 23, 1990, pp. 1, 84; Toy and Driscoll, "Can Perrier Purify Its Reputation?"

21. Following up on both the intended and the unintended consequences of decisions is emphasized by Huber, *Managerial Decision Making.* Of course, not all unintended consequences of decisions will be bad for a firm. This is discussed by Henry Mintzberg, "Patterns in Strategy Formulation," *Management Science*, 1978, pp. 934–948.

22. Winters, "Perrier's Back"; Toy and Driscoll, "Can Perrier Purify Its Reputation?"

23. The concept of bounded rationality was first defined by Herbert Simon, *Administrative Behavior* (New York: Free Press, 1945). Simon's ideas have been refined and revised in Herbert Simon, *Administrative Behavior,* 3rd ed. (New York: Free Press, 1976), and Herbert Simon, "Making Management Decisions: The Role of Intuition and Emotion," *The Academy of Management Executive,* February 1987, pp. 57–63. Professor Simon won the Nobel Prize in Economics for his work on bounded rationality.

24. See Simon, *Administrative Behavior,* for a discussion of the relationship between bounded rationality and satisficing.

25. Other reasons, besides bounded rationality, that organizations may engage in satisficing are described by Richard Cyert and James March, *A Behavioral Theory of the Firm* (Englewood Cliffs, N.J.: Prentice-Hall, 1963); Roy Radner, "A Behavioral Model of Cost Reduction," *Bell Journal of Economics,* Spring 1975, pp. 196–215; and James Brian Quinn, "Managing Strategies Incrementally," in *Competitive Strategic Management,* ed. R. Lamb (Englewood Cliffs, N.J.: Prentice-Hall, 1984), pp. 35–61.

26. See Barry M. Staw, "Good Money After Bad," *Psychology Today,* February 1988, pp. 30–33; Michael G. Bowen, "The Escalation Phenomena Reconsidered: Decision Dilemmas or Decision Errors?" *Academy of Management Review,* January 1987, pp. 52–66; and Ed Bukszar and Terry Connolly, "Hindsight Bias and Strategic Choice: Some Problems Learning from Experience," *Academy of Management Journal,* September 1988, pp. 628–641.

27. Loomis, "The Biggest, Looniest Deal Ever."

28. David Greising, "The Unhappy Campers at Winnebago," *Business Week,* May 28, 1990, p. 28; Loomis, "The Biggest, Looniest Deal Ever"; Jerry Ross and Barry Staw, "Expo86: An Escalation Prototype," *Administrative Science Quarterly,* 1986, pp. 274–297.

29. Barry Staw and Jerry Ross, "Knowing When to Pull the Plug," *Harvard Business Review,* March–April 1987, pp. 68–74.

30. See Bukszar and Connolly, "Hindsight Bias and Strategic Choice," and Daniel Kahneman, Paul Slovic, and Amos Tversky, eds., *Judgment Under Uncertainty* (Cambridge, England: Cambridge University Press, 1982).

31. See Jeffrey Pfeffer, *Power in Organizations* (Marshfield, Mass.: Pittman, 1981).

32. Victor Murray and Jeffrey Gandz, "Games Executives Play: Politics at Work," *Business Horizons,* December 1980, pp. 11–23; Jeffrey Gandz and Victor Murray, "The Experience of Workplace Politics," *Academy of Management Journal,* June 1980, pp. 237–251.

33. See Simon, "Making Management Decisions."

34. See Marvin E. Shaw, *Group Dynamics: The Psychology of Small Group Behavior,* 3rd ed. (New York: McGraw-Hill, 1981); Edwin A. Locke, David M. Schweiger, and Gary P. Latham, "Participation in Decision Making: When Should It Be Used?" *Organizational Dynamics,* Winter 1986, pp. 65–79; and Nicholas Baloff and Elizabeth M. Doherty, "Potential Pitfalls in Employee

Participation," *Organizational Dynamics,* Winter 1989, pp. 51–62.

35. See Irving L. Janis, *Groupthink,* 2nd ed. (Boston: Houghton Mifflin, 1982).

36. Ibid.

37. See Shaw, *Group Dynamics.*

38. Douglas Anderson, "Increased Productivity Through Group Decision Making," *Supervision,* September 1990, pp. 6–10; James Thomas, Reuben McDaniel, Michael Dooris, "Strategic Issue Analysis: NGT + Decision Analysis for Resolving Strategic Issues," *Journal of Applied Behavioral Science,* 1989, pp. 189–200; William M. Fox, "The Improved Nominal Group Technique," *Journal of Management Development,* 1989, pp. 20–27.

39. Fox, "The Improved Nominal Group Technique."

40. Richard Cosier and Charles R. Schwenk, "Agreement and Thinking Alike: Ingredients for Poor Decisions," *The Academy of Management Executive,* February 1990, pp. 69–74; Charles Schwenk, "Effects of Devil's Advocacy on Escalating Commitment," *Human Relations,* 1988, pp. 769–782.

41. The facilitator role was first described by Robert Freed Bales, *Interaction Process Analysis: A Method for the Study of Small Groups* (Reading, Mass.: Addison-Wesley, 1950).

APPENDIX

Techniques for Quantitative Decision Making

Quantitative techniques are particularly helpful to decision makers who need to understand the economic consequences of a decision. Three techniques that have been particularly valuable in organizations are expected value analysis, breakeven analysis, and net present value analysis.

Expected Value Analysis

Expected value analysis is a quantitative technique that evaluates decision alternatives by integrating information about the probability of outcomes with information about the value of outcomes.

Expected value analysis evaluates decision alternatives by integrating information about the probability of outcomes with information about the value of outcomes. In order for expected-value analysis to be an appropriate decision-making technique, a decision must have the following attributes: (1) there must be several discrete alternative outcomes; (2) each outcome must have a known probability of occurrence; and (3) each outcome must have known economic consequences. Given these requirements, we can see that expected value analysis can be applied to risky decisions.

Consider three possible alternative outcomes that Sony faced in its decision to acquire Columbia Pictures in 1990. First, Columbia could successfully resist the acquisition. Second, Columbia could decide to resist but fail to stop the acquisition. Third, Columbia could enthusiastically welcome the acquisition.

Each of these alternative outcomes would have very different economic consequences for Sony. If Columbia successfully resisted (alternative 1), Sony could expect to lose approximately $50 million. If Columbia resisted but did not prevent the acquisition (alternative 2), Sony could expect to break even: there would be little financial impact on Sony. If Columbia encouraged the acquisition (alternative 3), Sony could expect to earn $200 million.

Of course, these different alternatives were not all equally likely. The probability of an event's occurring is simply the likelihood of that event, expressed as a percentage. If a particular event is likely to occur 80 times out of 100, then that event has a probability of 0.8 of occurring. Probabilities range from 0 (no chance of occurrence) to 1.0 (100 percent chance of occurrence). For the three alternatives that Sony faced, let's say that Sony concluded that the probability of alternative 1 was 0.1, the probability of alternative 2 was 0.3, and the probability of alternative 3 was 0.6. These probabilities reflect Sony's subjective assessments of Columbia's likely response to a takeover attempt.

Now that we know the expected economic consequences of the three different alternatives, and the probability of each one's occurring, we can estimate the expected value of Sony's decision to attempt to take over

Columbia. The *expected value* of a decision is equal to the sum of the economic consequences of all decision alternatives multiplied by their likelihood of occurring. For Sony's decision about whether to take over Columbia, the expected value is

$$\text{Expected value} = .1(-50,000,000) + .3(0) + .6(200,000,000)$$
$$= -5,000,000 + 0 + 120,000,000$$
$$= 115,000,000$$

Because the expected value of Sony's takeover of Columbia is a positive number, Sony should go ahead with the acquisition. Although there is a chance that the acquisition effort will hurt Sony (0.1), and a chance that it will not help Sony (0.3), the chance that it will help Sony (0.6) and the size of the payoff ($200 million) are large enough to justify this decision.

The usefulness of expected value analysis depends on how well decision makers specify and evaluate the probabilities of a decision's outcomes. If, for example, the actual probability of alternative 1 is 0.6, and the actual probability of alternative 3 is 0.1, then the expected value of this decision changes radically:

$$\text{Expected value} = .6(-50,000,000) + .3(0) + .6(200,000,000)$$
$$= -30,000,000 + 0 + 20,000,000$$
$$= -10,000,000$$

This negative expected value suggests that Sony should not attempt to acquire Columbia Pictures.

Likewise, what if the payoffs associated with different alternatives are changed? If the economic consequences of alternative 1 are $-500,000,000$, and the economic consequences of alternative 2 become $+5,000,000$, the expected value calculation also changes:

$$\text{Expected value} = .1(-50,000,000) + .3(0) + .6(5,000,000)$$
$$= -50,000,000 + 0 + 3,000,000$$
$$= -47,000,000$$

As you can see, great care must go into specifying the probabilities and economic consequences in decision alternatives when expected value analysis is being used.

Breakeven Analysis

Breakeven analysis is a quantitative technique that establishes the level of revenues that a business decision must generate in order to offset its costs.

Breakeven analysis is a quantitative technique that establishes the level of revenues that a business decision must generate in order to offset its costs. Early in Chapter 5 an informal analysis established that a new manufacturing process that costs BIC Pen exactly $1,095,000 is a breakeven investment because its benefit ($1,095,000 saved) is exactly equal to its cost.

A more formal breakeven analysis is shown for the hypothetical King Kong Rescue Company (the world's leading manufacturer of high-altitude rescue equipment) in Figure 5.A1. At this time, King Kong is trying to decide whether to introduce a new line of rescue aids. In Figure 5.A1, the number of new rescue aids that King Kong might be able to sell is listed on the horizontal axis, and the sales revenues and costs associated with the sale of different quantities of rescue aids is listed on the vertical axis.

There are two lines on this graph. The solid line depicts the relationship between the number of new rescue aids that King Kong sells and the revenues that it receives from selling those products. This line is called the *total-revenue line*. It starts at point zero (because an organization that sells no products generates no revenues) and continues upward and to the right. Thus, if King Kong is able to sell 20 new rescue aids, it will obtain $4,000 of revenue. If it sells 60 new rescue aids, it will obtain $12,000 of revenue. King Kong is planning to sell its new rescue aids for $200 each. The higher the price of an organization's products, the steeper the total-revenue line will be in the breakeven analysis.

The dashed line in Figure 5.A1 is called the *total-cost line*. Notice that the total-cost line does not start at point zero. Even when an organization does not sell any products, it still has costs that it must pay. For example, King Kong must pay for its factory, salaries of its employees and managers, and general office expenses even if it does not sell any new rescue aids. For King Kong, these basic costs of operation are about $7,000.

Figure 5.A1

Breakeven Analysis for King Kong
Rescue Company

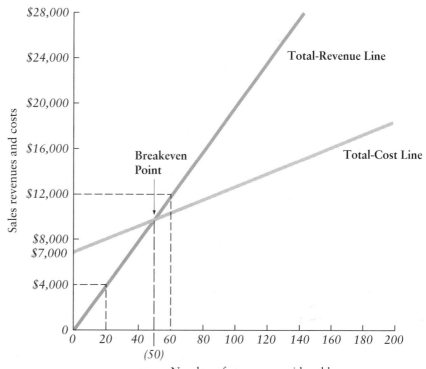

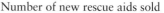
Number of new rescue aids sold

Just like the total-revenue line, the total-cost line moves upward and to the right. This means that the more an organization sells, the higher its total costs will be. This makes sense, because in order to manufacture and sell products, organizations must buy raw materials, pay workers, and pay salespeople. The more products an organization sells, the more of these expenses it has to pay for and thus the higher are its total costs. The total costs to King Kong if it sells 60 new rescue aids is about $10,000, and its total costs if it sells 120 new rescue aids is about $12,000.

Although the total-cost line in Figure 5.A1 moves upward and to the right, it usually is not as steeply sloped as the total-revenue line. The reason is that as organizations sell more products, their costs *per product* usually fall and thus their total costs increase less rapidly. Whenever an organization's total costs are greater than (above) its total revenues, the organization is losing money. When total revenues are greater than total costs, the organization is earning a profit.

The point at which the total-cost and total-revenue lines cross is an organization's **breakeven point**. This is the point where sales generate just enough revenues to cover an organization's costs. For King Kong, the breakeven point is 50 new rescue aids. If King Kong sells 50 new rescue aids, it will generate total revenues of $10,000, and its total costs will be $10,000. If King Kong sells more than 50 new rescue aids, then this business enterprise will earn a profit. Breakeven analysis suggests that if King Kong can sell 50 new rescue aids (at $200 each), then it should introduce this new product line. If it can sell only 30 new rescue aids (at $200 each), then it should not.

Any organization can determine its breakeven point by computing total-cost and total-revenue lines. Decision makers can use this information as a basis for deciding whether to take advantage of a business opportunity. Breakeven analysis can also be used to evaluate the economic impact of decisions that increase an organization's revenues or decrease its costs. Both of these outcomes have the effect of shifting breakeven points to the left. Such decisions may make new business opportunities that have high breakeven points appear much more feasible.

Net Present Value Analysis

Net present value analysis is a quantitative technique that calculates the current economic value of all of a decision's economic consequences over the entire life of that decision.

Net present value analysis calculates the current economic value of all of a decision's economic consequences over the entire life of that decision. In calculating the lifetime value of a decision, this technique compares the value of money earned today with the value of money that a decision may earn sometime in the future.

Net present value analysis begins with the simple observation that "A bird in the hand is worth two in the bush." In economic terms, this means that $100 earned today is worth more than $100 earned five years from now. The reason is simple. The $100 earned today can be invested in a business, put in a bank, or invested in other ways to earn a return. In five years, the money earned today may actually be worth $150 ($100 plus $50 earned by investing the $100), but the $100 earned five years hence will be worth only $100. That money earned in the future is not as valuable as the same amount of money earned now suggests that the value of money depends on when one earns it.

With this in mind, it is possible to show that any decision generates a pattern of economic consequences for an organization over time. One common pattern appears in Figure 5.A2. In this example, it is expected that a decision, when it is made, will cost an organization more money than it generates. In Figure 5.A2, the size of the initial investment is expected to be $1,000. However, after an initial period of investment, the decision is expected to begin to generate more money for an organization than it costs. In Figure 5.A2, the decision is expected to generate $500 in its first year and $1,000 in its second, third, and fourth years. In its fifth year, the decision is expected to generate no net positive cash for the organization. To see if the decision will help or hurt an organization's overall economic performance, it seems logical that one should simply compare the total investment required by the decision to the total amount expected to be generated. In Figure 5.A2 this is done by summing the following:

$$-1,000 + (500 + 1,000 + 1,000 + 1,000 + 0) = 2,500$$

Figure 5.A2

Net Present Value Analysis

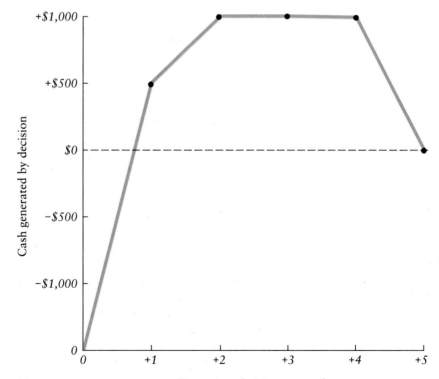

Since the total amount of money generated is greater than the total investment, the decision in Figure 5.A2 looks like a good idea.

Remember, however, that "A bird in the hand is worth two in the bush." The dollars that a decision is expected to generate in its fourth and fifth years are not as valuable as the dollars that an organization is required to invest to implement the decision. Thus simply comparing the total investment to the money expected to be generated does not reflect the true economic consequences of the decision. The money generated later must be *discounted* to reflect its true current value.

How much these future revenues should be discounted depends on how much money the organization could earn by not making the investment in Figure 5.A2, but rather making some other investment. If an organization could earn, say, a 20 percent return on some other investment, then it would need to earn *at least* a 20 percent return on the investment depicted in Figure 5.A2 for it to add to the firm's economic position. If this decision generates less than a 20 percent return, the organization would be better off investing its money another way.

The formula for discounting a decision's economic consequences and for computing a decision's net present value is

$$\text{Net present value} = \sum_{t=1}^{N} \frac{\text{net cash}_t}{(1 + k)^t} - I$$

where t is the number of years since the decision is made, N is the expected life of the decision (in Figure 5.A2, $N = 5$), net cash$_t$ is the amount of cash (positive or negative) generated by a decision in year t, I is the initial investment required to implement a decision (in Figure 5.A2, I is 1,000), and k is the discount rate (in Figure 5.A2, $k = 20\%$). The net present value (*NPV*) of the decision in Figure 5.A2 is calculated as follows:

$NPV = [(500/(1+.2)^1)$ Positive cash, year 1
$+ (1,000/(1+.2)^2)$ Positive cash, year 2
$+ (1,000/(1+.2)^3)$ Positive cash, year 3
$+ (1,000/(1+.2)^4)$ Positive cash, year 4
$+ (0/(1+.2)^5)]$ Zero cash, year 5
$- 1,000$ Initial investment
$= [500/1.2 + 1,000/1.44 + 1,000/1.73 + 1,000/2.07 + 0/2.49]$
    $- 1,000$
$= [416 + 694 + 578 + 483 + 0] - 1,000$
$= 1,171$

Thus the net present value of the decision in Figure 5.A2 is $1,171. A decision with a positive net present value generates a return greater than that of all alternative investments that the organization could make. A decision with a zero net present value generates the same return as alternative investments. A decision with a negative net present value generates a return less than the return that an organization could obtain in some alternative investments. Decision makers should generally seek to make positive net present value decisions and avoid negative net present value decisions. Since the net present value of the decision in Figure 5.A2 is greater than zero, this decision is a good one for an organization to pursue.

Application Exercise

Discuss the application of quantitative decision-making techniques with some managers. Do these managers use the techniques discussed in this appendix? Do they use some other quantitative techniques? Which do they think work best for them, and why?

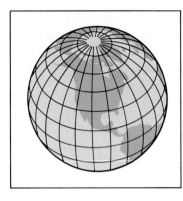

CASE 5.1

What *Is* CBS Up To?

Sometimes when a major company makes an unexpected decision, competitors and stock analysts assume that the company is up to something clever and everyone waits eagerly for the company's next move. Many felt that way when CBS fired CEO Thomas Wyman in 1986 and put Laurence Tisch in his place. Tisch made some bold and unexpected moves; but he had amassed a fortune with such maneuvers as CEO of Loews Corporation, so observers waited expectantly for the payoff. As the years have gone by, however, CBS's decisions have not seemed to add up, and it has become clear that the company doesn't really know what it wants to be.

Tisch's takeover of CBS was typical of the dramatic shifts that many corporations underwent in the mid-1980s. He moved into a position of power when Loews bought almost 25 percent of CBS's common stock; he engineered the removal of Wyman; and then he began the trimming of personnel that became common in companies trying to become leaner and more efficient. He eventually got rid of about 1,200 employees, including 215 in the news division, 14 of them on-air correspondents. And he amassed a cash hoard of some $3 billion by selling off the company's music-publishing, magazine, and records divisions. He seemed well on his way to making CBS an energetic organization, ready for expansion.

The trouble was, CBS wasn't an ordinary organization. Tisch couldn't just call together his pared-down staff and say, "Okay, now let's make more widgets." He had already sold off the kinds of businesses that a television network might logically expand into, but it didn't seem as though the sales were an attempt to get the company to refocus on its basic business. Eventually the company simply bought a big chunk of its own stock. This move showed faith in the future of CBS, but it did nothing to clarify CBS's direction.

For years, many people would have had no trouble saying what CBS stood for — the best news organization in the broadcast business. The radio reports of Edward R. Murrow, covering the blitz of London, may have been the most famous reporting of the Second World War. And CBS's foremost television anchor, Walter Cronkite, became one of the most respected public figures in the United States. He is given some credit for turning public opinion against the Vietnam War by voicing his doubts about it on the air. But in the Persian Gulf War, CBS coverage was so poor that it became the butt of jokes on other networks. CBS had about half as many people in the Gulf as its competitors, and archrival ABC News drew a 50 percent larger audience during the first week of the war.

The problems at CBS News, however, went well beyond the war coverage and in fact reflected the company's overall state of indecision. Between 1984 and 1991, CBS News had six different presidents, four of them since Tisch took over. The news division was split into two camps. Journalists, headed by news anchor Dan Rather, believed that their job was to gather hard news and broadcast it seriously. On the other side, many of CBS's top executives preferred prime-time features and special programs that cost less than hard news reporting and allow producers to spice up the stories. The group that planned the initial coverage of the Persian Gulf War didn't even include Rather. And the whole division may still be smarting from Tisch's sudden firing of so many veterans of the department, a move that even Tisch now admits was poorly executed.

If CBS is no longer *the* news network, it seems determined to become *the* sports network. In 1989, CBS signed agreements to spend over $1.5 billion to broadcast baseball and the Winter Olympics, paying over half a billion dollars more than its rival networks were willing to spend. Even the architects of the deals seem to admit that CBS will lose money on the broadcasts, but they hope for ancillary benefits: good press, loyalty from contented affiliates, happy advertisers, and the chance to reach a large audience and tell them about CBS's other programs.

Yet even the choice of "other programs" on CBS seems confused. Alone among the major networks, CBS targets an older audience, virtually ignoring the 18 to 34 crowd that most interests advertisers and that might give CBS a chance to climb out of the ratings cellar. Within the past decade, both ABC and NBC came from behind in the ratings war by airing experimental programs, such as NBC's *Hill Street Blues* and ABC's *thirtysomething,* that gradually built a large audience. But CBS seems content to please its most loyal audience — the over-55 age group.

It's easy to say with hindsight that Tisch's moves were misguided. All three of the big CBS divisions that he sold were resold for a lot more money within months. But the important question now is, Can CBS's executives develop a coherent strategy on which to base their decisions and rebuild the network's image?

Discussion Questions

1. What types of decisions are involved in the televison business?
2. What unique characteristics of a television network might make the ordinary business decision-making process inappropriate?
3. Given what you know about CBS and its strengths and weaknesses, how do you think the company should go about making sound plans for the future?
4. If you were a program director for CBS, what groups would you consult in order to make programming decisions about a new season?

REFERENCES: Kevin Goldman, "Weak War Coverage Isn't the Only Problem at CBS Evening News," *Wall Street Journal,* February 7, 1991, pp. A1, A11; Dennis Kneale, "Seeking Ratings Gains, CBS Pays Huge Sums for Sports Contracts," *Wall Street Journal,* October 10, 1989, pp. A1, A6; Kenneth Labich, "Has Larry Tisch Lost His Touch?" *Fortune,* February 26, 1990, pp. 99–104; Bill Powell and Jonathan Alter, "The Showdown at CBS," *Newsweek,* September 22, 1986, pp. 54–58; Richard Turner, "CBS Gears Fall Lineup to Older Viewers," *Wall Street Journal,* September 29, 1989, p. B1.

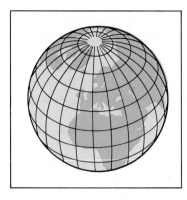

CASE 5.2

Decision Making in a Global Economy

"Technology is destroying time and space, the two remaining barriers for the human being,"* says Carlo De Benedetti, Italy's most famous deal-maker. As a result, he says, exporting will become obsolete because it is too slow. Businesses will look to find the solutions to their problems close to home, where they are available immediately. And that means decisions must be made rapidly and without wavering.

This sounds like a tall order for the manager of the future, but De Benedetti can preach such a gospel because he lives it already himself. His style, his decisiveness, and his personal success have captured Europe's attention, as has his unusual ability to run one company and build others at the same time.

De Benedetti got his start in the family's metal-hose-making business, which his father rebuilt in 1945 after the Second World War. Carlo took over from his father at age 33 and built the 50-employee business into the largest independent auto-component producer in Italy, employing 1,600. Such success attracted the interest of the Agnelli family, owners of Fiat, Italy's largest industrial company. The Agnellis made De Benedetti Fiat's youngest CEO ever. But after they rejected his bold plan to transform the company, De Benedetti abruptly left after only three months on the job. Four years later, Fiat finally restructured, using, De Benedetti claims, most of the elements of his plan.

Never one to sit still, De Benedetti began building his own empire through several holding companies and in 1978 agreed to run Olivetti, a typewriter maker that was losing $8 million a month and seemed headed for bankruptcy. Moving with his usual speed and decisiveness, De Benedetti bought a 20 percent share in the company, laid off workers, started investing heavily in research and development, and replaced most of the company's top management by moving subordinates up. Part of De Benedetti's doctrine is that nationalistic companies cannot survive against huge multinationals like IBM. His strategy is to link his companies with others around the world. Olivetti has worked with AT&T to develop and market computers, with Electronic Data Systems to provide Europe with computer services, and with Canon to make copiers. By 1986, Olivetti's sales had reached five times their 1978 level.

With Olivetti running profitably, De Benedetti turned his attention to expanding his empire, buying into companies that sell everything from pasta to high-fashion clothes to financial services. His style remained the same: make quick, perfectly timed decisions and stand behind them; then hire top executives to run the companies and get out of their way. After he bought 37 percent of Yves Saint Laurent Parfums Corp., Saint Laurent's partner described De Benedetti as "an artist" with "the ability and need to make quick decisions." The two made a deal over lunch in Milan, and "Not a comma needed to be changed later."†

De Benedetti's timing and sense of drama draw big headlines in Europe but can also make him enemies. In one of his failed takeover attempts, De Benedetti secretly bought up shares of SGB, a large Belgian holding company, then fought in board rooms and in courts to win control of the whole company. Knowing that the Belgian government would not be pleased to have an Italian control SGB, De Benedetti made his key moves when the Belgian government had fallen, so there was, in effect, no government to oppose him. Although clever, this ploy heightened nationalistic sentiments against him, and he eventually lost control to a Belgian-French group.

De Benedetti also occasionally blunders with his quick decisions. He passed up a chance to buy 25 percent of Apple Computer in 1979, when he could have made the deal of his life. And when he sold his stock and left his position as vice chairman in a small bank just before its collapse, many thought that the timing was a little too perfect. He has also lost deals because of his refusal to make alliances with Italian politicians.

Many of Olivetti's managers still don't fully accept De Benedetti's vision of the business world, and his fast-paced, high-risk style does not guarantee a smooth future for the company that is still his home base. The agreement with AT&T did not work out well for either company, and when the financial markets cooled off in the late 1980s, Olivetti's earnings dropped steadily. De Benedetti's critics say that his constant dealmaking and his restructuring of Olivetti distracted its management's attention.

These problems may have more to do with De Benedetti's attempt to perform as both a CEO and an entrepreneur than with his decision-making style. Certainly as the barriers of time and distance fall, more and more managers will have to adopt De Benedetti's approach.

Discussion Questions

1. How do you think the major events of De Benedetti's youth have affected De Benedetti's own style and decision making?
2. How should the decision-making style of a CEO differ from that of an entrepreneur?
3. What advantages do De Benedetti's dealmaking, entrepreneurial talents bring to Olivetti? What disadvantages?
4. Would all group decision making be impossible in De Benedetti's vision of the business world of the future? Why or why not?

* Quoted in Philip Revzin and Laura Colby, "Olivetti Chief Stresses Software and Services in World Market Push," *Wall Street Journal,* April 7, 1987, p. 1.
† Pierre Berge, quoted ibid., p. 22.

REFERENCES: Jonathan Kapstein and Frank J. Comes, "How De Benedetti Botched the 'Battle of Belgium,'" *Business Week,* March 7, 1988, pp. 44–46; Philip Revzin, "Italian Tycoons Push European Unity, Then War over Home Turf," *Wall Street Journal,* April 3, 1990, pp. A1, A16; Philip Revzin and Laura Colby, "Olivetti Chief Stresses Software and Services in World Market Push," *Wall Street Journal,* April 7, 1987, pp. 1, 22; William C. Symonds, "Dealmaker De Benedetti," *Business Week,* August 24, 1987, pp. 42–47.

6

Goals and Planning in Organizations

LEARNING OBJECTIVES

After studying this chapter, you should be able to:

1. Describe the relationship between goals and objectives.

2. Identify and explain the major functions of goals and objectives.

3. Discuss the different types of goals and objectives in an organization, and indicate how they are related to one another.

4. Describe three different goal-setting processes and their advantages and disadvantages.

5. Explain the relationship between the planning hierarchy and the hierarchy of goals and objectives.

Alfred Checchi, chairman of Northwest Airlines, could look back on 1989 as a time of radical change. Only one year earlier, Checchi and several close associates had been successful senior managers at the Marriott Corporation and had helped that firm become one of the most well-respected hotel and lodging companies in the world. Through carefully planned diversification, Marriott had taken advantage of its reputation for high-quality service and accommodation by opening three other chains, Courtyard Marriott, Fairfield Inn, and Residence Inn.

In 1989, however, Checchi and his associates set aside the relative security of managing for Marriott. They quit their jobs, borrowed $3.3 billion, and purchased Northwest Airlines. At the time of this purchase, Northwest was still recovering from a poorly planned and executed merger with Republic Airlines. It had an aging fleet of planes, the worst on-time record of any major airline, and very poor employee morale. Comedians, including Jay Leno of "The Tonight Show," regularly lambasted Northwest. Among the traveling public, Northwest was known as "Northworst Airlines" and "None Worse Airlines."

To address these problems, Northwest's new management set some very specific goals and objectives. In the short term, the firm needed to reduce financial demands stemming from the $3.3 billion debt repayment. By selling planes and then leasing them back, and by liquidating Northwest's valuable real estate holdings in Japan, Northwest raised over $400 million to pay back its debt.

But short-term efforts, no matter how successful, would not result in a financially healthy Northwest Airlines unless they were linked with long-term goals and objectives. Northwest thus set itself a major goal: to have the best on-time record of any major airline. Another goal was to put people — customers and employees — ahead of cutting costs. Northwest's overall goal was, within five years, to be the preferred airline to fly.

By 1990 Northwest was well on its way to accomplishing these goals. That summer, Northwest had the best on-time record of the six largest airlines. It had implemented employee and customer involvement programs that improved customer satisfaction and employee morale. All signs indicated that if Northwest continued striving to attain its goals, it would emerge in the 1990s a viable competitor in the airline industry.[1]

Much of Northwest's turnaround resulted from its new management's ability to set identifiable goals and objectives and then work to implement them. Without these goals and objectives, Northwest would have been less efficient in reducing its debt in the short term. Northwest also would have been less capable of addressing its poor on-time record and customer and employee relations, problems that seriously threatened the firm's recovery and success.

Without clearly articulated goals and objectives, organizations may not recognize where they are headed and certainly will have difficulty planning their activities. Goals and objectives provide organizations with an all-important map that lays out a course of action and often anticipates changes in the environment to which an organization may need to respond. This chapter discusses the closely related concepts of organizational goals, objectives, and planning.

The Nature of Organizational Goals and Objectives

A *goal* is a desired future state that an organization attempts to realize. An *objective* is a specific short-term target for which measurable results can be obtained.

Organizational goals and objectives are closely related. A **goal** is a desired future state that an organization attempts to realize. Northwest Airlines set a goal when it decided to become the preferred airline of the traveling public. Likewise, Cable News Network (CNN) set a goal when it decided to provide high-quality 24-hour TV news service throughout the world, and Nissan set a goal when it decided to re-enter the high-performance sports car market with the Nissan 300ZX. An **objective** is a specific short-term target for which measurable results can be obtained. Objectives should support an organization's goals. They may be thought of as the concrete steps that the organization takes to reach its goals. Organizations monitor their attainment of objectives as a way to evaluate their progress toward goals.[2] Thus, Northwest Airlines met its objectives when it had the best on-time record among its competitors.

As Table 6.1 shows, for each of an organization's goals, there are usually several corresponding objectives. For example, one of Hewlett-Packard's goals is to remain at the cutting edge of high technology. Specific objectives that support this goal might include introducing a specific number of new products each year, applying for a specific number of new patents each year, and presenting a specific number of scientific papers at research meetings each year. Objectives that support Cadillac's goal to re-establish itself in the luxury car market might include introducing a restyled Cadillac in 1992, designing a completely new car in 1993, building prototypes in 1994, and manufacturing and selling the new car in 1995. Objectives that supported NASA's goal to reach the moon by 1970 included testing rocket safety and durability in the Mercury program, examining the effects of weightlessness on astronauts and evaluating the feasibility of docking in the Gemini program, and testing the technology for traveling to the moon in the Apollo program.[3]

Table 6.1

Goals and Objectives for Three Organizations

	Goal	Objectives
Hewlett-Packard	Maintain leadership in high technology.	• Introduce a specific number of new products each year. • Apply for a specific number of new patents each year. • Deliver a specific number of scientific papers each year.
Cadillac	Re-establish share in luxury car market.	• Redesign current cars for 1992. • Begin design of new car by 1993. • Build prototypes by 1995. • Begin manufacturing by 1995. • Sell 300,000 units in 1995.
NASA	Put an astronaut on the moon by 1970.	• Mercury program: test rocket design and safety. • Gemini program: test effects of weightlessness and test docking procedure. • Apollo program: test technology for traveling to the moon.

The Function of Organizational Goals

The four functions served by organizational goals are (1) to provide guidance and unified direction, (2) to facilitate planning, (3) to motivate and inspire employees, and (4) to aid in evaluation and control.

Organizational goals serve four important functions: they provide guidance and unified direction; they facilitate planning; they motivate and inspire employees; and they aid evaluation and control.[4] The following sections explain these functions in detail.

Providing Guidance and Unified Direction

Organizations need clearly articulated goals to make sure that employees know where the organization is headed and why. Hewlett-Packard (HP) has been very successful in articulating its goals. Every Hewlett-Packard employee receives a small pamphlet titled "The HP Way," which summarizes Hewlett-Packard's key goals and objectives. Whenever employees need to make a decision, they can refer to this pamphlet to renew their understanding of the "HP Way" of doing business. Managers at Hewlett-Packard are thus able to conduct business in a unified and organized manner, and this ability has helped the organization become one of the most successful electronics companies in the world.[5]

Facilitating Planning

Planning is the process that organizations use to decide how they will attain their goals.

Organizational goals facilitate planning by providing managers with specific targets at which to aim. **Planning** is the process that organizations use to decide how they will attain their goals. Goals specify where an organization is going, and planning specifies the means by which organizations will get there.

Cadillac, for example, is in the midst of a planning effort to re-establish its position in the luxury car market. It lost this position in the mid-1980s because of increased competition from European and Japanese automakers and by failing to design distinctive automobiles. To recapture its market position, Cadillac has decided to introduce a distinctive new line of cars in the mid-1990s. The plan General Motors has adopted to accomplish this goal gives the Cadillac division complete autonomy in the design, test, and production of the new cars. Cadillac is the only division in all of General Motors that has this autonomy. It is thought that by maintaining this autonomy, Cadillac will be able to design a distinctive line of products to compete with BMW, Mercedes, Lexus, Infiniti, and other luxury cars.[6]

Two functions of organizational goals are to facilitate planning and to motivate employees. The American Ballet Theater has always had a goal of providing world-class ballet performances to its audiences. This goal helps Jane Hermann, the Ballet Theater's co-director, plan a season of performances that will both appeal to broad audiences and challenge the dancers to extend the bounds of their art.

Motivating and Inspiring Employees

Early in the 1960s, President John Kennedy gave the National Aeronautics and Space Administration (NASA) a very challenging goal: to land a man on the moon and bring him back safely to Earth, before the decade was over. The results of setting that goal were remarkable. NASA changed from a relatively small government agency into a large, aggressive organization with a prestigious reputation. It attracted the best managers and scientists, invested in the latest technology, and developed partnerships with some of the best aerospace and technology companies in the United States. For many employees, working at NASA became a mission. Despite numerous setbacks, NASA succeeded in reaching its goal when Neil Armstrong, commander of Apollo 11, stepped onto the lunar surface on July 20, 1969.

Although NASA had notable subsequent achievements, including the Skylab space station, numerous planetary probes, and the space shuttle, none of these projects has captured the public imagination as much as the moon launch did. Indeed, after the explosion of the shuttle *Challenger,* investigations revealed that work at NASA had become dull and bureaucratic, hardly the spirit that had dominated the agency in the 1960s. NASA's new goal, a manned exploration of Mars by the year 2019, may re-energize the organization and allow it to attract once again the best and the brightest minds in the United States.[7]

Aiding Evaluation and Control

Goals help organizations evaluate and control performance. An organization can compare its actual performance with its goals and decide if more needs to be done. For example, if the Cadillac division at GM does not bring out an entirely new car by the mid-1990s, it will not have reached its goal, and more work will be required. If Northwestern continues to have financial difficulties while simultaneously being "roasted" on national talk shows, it will not have reached its goals, and more work and effort will be required.

Sometimes managers in organizations focus more on their personal goals than on the organization's goals. When this happens, the organization's performance almost always suffers. One example of this situation is described in The Global Challenge.

Types of Goals and Objectives

Organizations set numerous types of goals and objectives. The most important of these can be arranged in the hierarchy depicted in Figure 6.1. At the top of the hierarchy is a statement of the organization's mission, which in turn is supported by an organization's strategic goals, tactical goals and objectives, and operational goals and objectives.[8]

THE GLOBAL CHALLENGE

Becoming a Star Banker to the Stars

At first, it looked like a good investment. Credit Lyonnais, a French bank, was relatively small, and only moderately profitable. Through its acquisition of the Dutch bank, Slavenberg's Bank N.V., Credit Lyonnais gained access to a small portfolio of loans made to independent movie producers in Hollywood. Though small in size, this portfolio of loans was quite profitable. Frans Afman, former head of Slavenberg's international lending operations, assured the managers of Credit Lyonnais that it would be able to expand its Hollywood loans to obtain even greater levels of economic profit.

With Afman taking the lead, Credit Lyonnais began an aggressive program of loans to Hollywood producers. Some of the biggest names in Hollywood— including Dino De Laurentis and Arnold Kopelson— lined up to get money from Credit Lyonnais to support some of Hollywood's most successful movies— including *Platoon, The Fabulous Baker· Boys,* and *Crimes of the Heart.* The size of Credit Lyonnais' investment in producers soared to over $300 million. Afman was often seen in Malibu and Cannes, partying with the stars. When Arnold Kopelson accepted the best picture Oscar for producing *Platoon,* he thanked his banker, Mr. Afman, for his support during the making of this film.

Along with these successes, there were failures as well. Credit Lyonnais provided capital for several big losers, including the movie *Pirates,* which starred Walter Matthau. However, even more ominous were signs that the maintenance of Afman's and the bank's relationships with movie producers was becoming a higher priority than ensuring the safety and security of Credit Lyonnais' investments. Money for one French miniseries was made available even before loan doc-

uments were complete. Afman accepted salaried positions with several corporate bank customers, including the Cannon Group, Inc., Carolco Pictures, Inc. (producers of *Rambo*), and Scotti Brothers Entertainment Industries, Inc., the total value of which was over $350,000 per year. Government regulators questioned whether Afman could objectively evaluate the creditworthiness of companies from which he was receiving this amount of remuneration. Ultimately, Afman was forced to sever his relationship with Credit Lyonnais.

Over time, Credit Lyonnais has become more and more involved with Hollywood producers. They have lent $20 million to Fries Entertainment, $37.5 million to Epic Pictures, $60 million to Weintraub Entertainment, $99 million to Nelson Entertainment, $95 million to Live Entertainment, $85 million to Carolco Pictures, and over $1 billion to MGM-Pathe Communications Company. Unfortunately, all these firms (except Carolco and Live Entertainment) are currently suffering severe financial setbacks. A variety of government investigations, both in the United States and in France, are currently underway to determine if Credit Lyonnais exercised proper due diligence in making these loans, or if personal relationships between Credit Lyonnais bankers and Hollywood producers outweighed concern for the bank's profitability.

REFERENCES: Kathleen A. Hughes and Charles Fleming, "How a French Bank Went to Hollywood—And Found Trouble," *Wall Street Journal,* June 19, 1991, pp. A1+; George Anders, "In U.S., Credit Lyonnais Is Only Bank That Still Buys Things Like Junk Bonds," *Wall Street Journal,* June 19, 1991, pp. A8; John B. Matthews, Kenneth E. Goodpaster, and Laura L. Nash, *Policies and Persons: A Casebook in Business Ethics,* 2nd ed. (New York: McGraw-Hill, 1991).

Organizational Mission

An *organizational mission* is an organization's fundamental reason for existence. A *mission statement* is a broad written definition of an organizational mission.

An **organizational mission** is an organization's fundamental reason for existence. It is the specific duty or series of purposes that an organization has imposed on itself. It often reflects the core values of managers in an organization. A **mission statement** is a broad written definition of an organizational mission.[9]

Figure 6.1

Hierarchy of Organizational Goals
and Objectives

Organizational missions, and associated mission statements, are as varied as organizations themselves. Figure 6.2 shows three sample corporate statements. NCR's mission statement emphasizes the organization's obligations to its many stakeholders. Hershey Foods' mission statement emphasizes commitment to the food industry and describes the firm's effort to develop those aspects of its business. MCI's mission statement emphasizes commitment to the telecommunications business and defines the company's focus on quality.[10]

Mission statements reflect the individuality of each particular organization, but they often share several common components. Table 6.2 identifies five typical components of mission statements and shows how NCR, Hershey, and MCI address these components.[11] (Note that not all mission statements have all these attributes in common.) One organization whose mission broadly influences all of its strategies is The Body Shop. This organization, and the personal values of its founder, Anita Reddick, are described in The Environmental Challenge.

Strategic Goals and Objectives

Strategic goals are organization-wide goals that directly support the implementation of an organizational mission.

The eight types of strategic goals that organizations should possess are (1) market standing, (2) innovation, (3) productivity, (4) physical and financial resources, (5) profitability, (6) manager performance development, (7) worker performance and attitude, and (8) public responsibility.

Strategic goals are organization-wide goals that directly support the implementation of an organizational mission. Strategic goals apply to an organization as a whole, rather than to one department or division within an organization.

Peter Drucker has described eight types of strategic goals that organizations should possess. Table 6.3 lists these eight types of goals along with some strategic goals that might support the mission statement of Hershey Foods Corporation.[12] Strategic goals that support Hershey's mission of becoming a "major, diversified food company" could include (1) controlling 30 percent of the chocolate market in the United States by 1995 (market standing), (2) reducing average manufacturing costs by 3 percent each year

Figure 6.2

Samples of Corporate Mission Statements

NCR's Mission Statement

At NCR, we've found that in order to create value, we must first satisfy the legitimate expectations of every person with a stake in our company. We call these people stakeholders, and we attempt to satisfy their expectations by promoting partnerships in which everyone is a winner.

We believe in building mutually beneficial and enduring relationships with all our stakeholders, based on conducting business activities with integrity and respect.

We take customer satisfaction personally: we are committed to providing superior value in our products and services on a continuing basis.

We respect the individuality of each employee and foster an environment in which employees' creativity and productivity are encouraged, recognized, valued , and rewarded.

We think of our suppliers as partners who share our goal of achieving the highest standards and the most consistent level of service.

We are dedicated to creating value for our shareholders and financial communities by performing in a manner that will enhance the return on their investment.

Hershey Foods Corporation Mission Statement

Hershey Foods Corporation's Mission is to become a major diversified food company and a leading company in every aspect of our business as:

• The No. 1 confectionery company in North America, moving toward worldwide confectionery market share leadership.

• A respected and valued supplier of high quality, branded, consumer food products in North America and selected international markets.

This Mission will be carried out in accordance with the Statement of Corporate Philosophy and pursued through the objectives and strategies of the Corporate Strategic Plan.

MCI Communication Corporation (1980s)

MCI's mission is leadership in the global telecommunications service industry. Profitable growth is fundamental to that mission, so that we may serve the interests of our stockholders and our customers.

To maintain profitable growth, MCI will: provide a full range of high-value services for customers who must communicate or move information electronically throughout the United States and the world; manage a business so as to be the low cost provider of services; make quality synonymous with MCI to our growing customer base; set the pace in identifying and implementing cost-effective technologies and services as we expand our state-of-the-art communications network; continue to be an entrepreneurial company, built of people who can make things happen in a competitive marketplace.

SOURCE: Reprinted by permission of NCR Corporation. Courtesy of Hershey Foods Corporation. The mission statement is reprinted by permission of the copyright owner, Hershey Foods Corporation, Hershey, Pennsylvania, U.S.A. Reprinted by permission of MCI Communications, Inc.

Organizations have both long-term strategic goals, and shorter-term objectives that support those goals. Claudio and Gianfranco Castiglioni, owners of Cagiva Group, have the long-term goal of re-establishing a European presence in the world motorcycle market. They plan to do this by selling both top-of-the-line showcase models and less expensive racing bikes. However, to obtain this long-term goal, the Castiglionis must first accomplish a variety of shorter-term objectives, including increasing the company's technical expertise, attracting equity partners, and focusing on styling and marketing.

(productivity), (3) increasing value added per employee by 7 percent in 1994 (physical and financial resources), and (4) investing 0.1 percent of net income in 1996 in programs to help slow the destruction of the rain forests (public responsibility).

Tactical Goals and Objectives

Tactical goals and *objectives* specify the results expected from major divisions and departments within an organization.

Whereas strategic goals apply to an entire organization, **tactical goals** and **objectives** specify the results expected from major divisions and departments within an organization. Tactical goals and objectives must support the organization's overall strategic goals. For example, if an organization has a strategic goal of growing 20 percent in sales each year, tactical goals at the divisional level must generate a sales increase of 20 percent or more.[13]

Table 6.4 shows how tactical goals might support three of the hypothetical strategic goals for Hershey presented in Table 6.3. In each case, the goals and objectives of Hershey's divisions support the broader strategic goals. For example, the strategic goal "increase return on assets by 5 percent in 1994" is supported by four tactical goals. Each of four divisions is expected to increase its return on assets by a specific percentage in 1994. Adding the percentages together and computing their average [(7% + 3% + 6% + 4%)/4 = 5%] reveals that the tactical goals support the strategic goal of 5 percent growth in return on assets in 1994.

Notice that not all strategic goals can be directly identified with tactical goals within a specific division. Some goals apply to the corporation as a whole. For example, the strategic goals of increasing Hershey's stock appreciation and investing 0.1 percent of net income to help save the rain forests are corporate strategic goals that do not have specific divisional counter-

Table 6.2

Common Components of Corporate Mission Statements

Target Customers and Markets

NCR: "We take customer satisfaction personally"
HERSHEY: "a major diversified food company"
MCI: "global telecommunications service industry"

Geographic Domain

NCR: (not specified)
HERSHEY: "North America and worldwide" markets
MCI: "throughout the United States and the world"

Concern for Survival, Growth, and Profitability

NCR: "to create value, we must first satisfy the legitimate expectations [of stakeholders]"
HERSHEY: "moving toward worldwide confectionery market share leadership;" to be "a leading company in every aspect of our business"
MCI: "profitable growth"

Company Philosophy

NCR: "we attempt to satisfy [stakeholders'] expectations by promoting partnerships in which everyone is a winner"
HERSHEY: to offer "high quality, branded, consumer food products"
MCI: "continue to be an entrepreneurial company, built of people who can make things happen in a competitive marketplace"

Desired Public Image

NCR: "promoting partnerships"
HERSHEY: "a respected and valued supplier"
MCI: "make quality synonymous with MCI"

parts. Although the performance of divisions certainly may help the corporation reach these goals, divisional performance relative to these goals cannot be calculated separately.

Operational Goals and Objectives

Operational goals and *objectives* apply to specific individuals or subunits within divisions or departments.

The final level of goals and objectives in an organization is the operational level. Whereas tactical goals and objectives apply to an entire division or department within an organization, **operational goals** and **objectives** apply to specific individuals or subunits within divisions or departments. Table 6.5 presents specific operational goals that could support some of Hershey's tactical goals. Notice that these tactical goals focus on the individual responsibilities of people. Thus, to support Division II's tactical goal of increasing return on assets by 3 percent in 1994, the sales manager, man-

Table 6.3

Strategic Goals for Well-managed Companies

Strategic Goals Should Address	Possible Strategic Goals to Support Hershey's Mission
1. **Market standing:** An indication of the percentage of market share desired by the firm or the specification of a competitive niche.	Control 30% of chocolate market in the United States by 1995. Control 15% of European chocolate market by 1997.
2. **Innovation:** Recognition of the need to develop new services or products.	Introduce 3 new brands of food each year in the United States.
3. **Productivity:** An efficiency measure that relates resources used to output generated.	Reduce manufacturing costs for all product lines by 3% per year.
4. **Physical and financial resources:** The acquisition and efficient use of physical and financial resources.	Increase return on assets by 5% in 1994. Increase value added per employee by 7% in 1994.
5. **Profitability:** An indication of the firm's profitability as measured by one or more financial indexes, such as return on investment.	Increase return on investment by 8% in 1995. Increase stock value appreciation 5% more than overall U.S. stock market in 1995.
6. **Manager performance development:** Effective conduct of the managerial roles and development of potential in the individual.	Increase the number of hours of management training by 6% in 1993.
7. **Worker performance and attitude:** Effective conduct of the operational roles and maintenance of positive attitudes on the part of employees.	Conduct an employee attitude survey in 1992. Redo the survey in 1994. Obtain an average increase of overall employee satisfaction of 10% between these two years.
8. **Public responsibility:** A consideration for the firm's impact on society.	Reduce pollutants by 10% in 1995. Invest 0.1% of net income in 1996 in programs to slow the destruction of the rain forests.

SOURCE: Adapted from Peter F. Drucker, *The Practice of Management* (New York: Harper & Row, 1954).

THE ENVIRONMENTAL CHALLENGE

The Greening of Cosmetics: The Body Shop

There are now two ways to market cosmetics: the traditional way and the Body Shop way. The traditional approach emphasizes glamour, high fashion, and sex appeal. Hair coloring advertises eternal youth; skin conditioners promise wrinkle-free skin; and perfumes hold out hope for universal attractiveness. The Body Shop approach emphasizes ecological awareness, the plight of the Third World, and deforestation in Brazil.

The Body Shop is a chain of stores in western Europe and the United States that sell cosmetics and other body- and skin-care products. Founded by Anita Roddick in Great Britain in 1986, The Body Shop has grown from a handful of stores to more than 578 Body Shops in 37 countries in 1990. Each store sells over 300 natural products in refillable containers with labels printed on recycled paper. Decorated in green, each Body Shop is plastered with political posters decrying acid rain, animal testing, and other ecologically aware causes. This combination of products and social consciousness netted The Body Shop over $341 million in worldwide sales in 1989 and made Anita Roddick one of the five richest women in the United Kingdom.

The Body Shop's success stems from a combination of good timing and strong commitments. Roddick opened her Body Shop stores just as the entire Western world seemed almost overnight to become more aware of the physical environment and each person's responsibility to protect that environment. High-quality products mean that Body Shop customers obtain all the benefits of traditional cosmetics and body care products. But customers can also feel good about the contribution they are making to maintaining a quality environment.

One of the most impressive attributes of The Body Shop is that the organization has remained loyal to its socially aware strategy, despite its growth and success. Much of the reason for this commitment can be traced directly to Roddick's personal goals and objectives. For her, it isn't enough to sell products and generate profits if the world as a whole does not also benefit. This personal goal has infused all those associated with Body Shops with a social commitment that is unusual in an industry traditionally dominated by glamour, fashion, and superficial images.

REFERENCES: Jeannie Ralston, "Cosmetics with a Conscience," *American Way*, March 15, 1991, pp. 84–89; Faye Brookman, "Specialty Cosmetic Stores Hit with Frustrated Consumers," *Advertising Age*, March 4, 1991, p. 32; Bo Burlingham, "Body Shop Bares Its Soul," *Business*, December 1990, pp. 82–85; Hilary Seward, "Establishing a Social Conscience at Work," *New England Business*, November 1990, pp. 97–98.

ufacturing manager, and purchasing manager in Division II all have operational goals and objectives. In the same way, Division III's tactical goal of reducing pollutants by 10 percent in 1995 is supported by operational goals for the manufacturing and research and development managers in the division.[14]

The Hierarchy of Goals and Objectives Revisited

Earlier, we saw that different types of goals and objectives in an organization can be arranged in a hierarchy. Figure 6.1 depicts that hierarchy in its simplest form. Now, using the foregoing discussion of missions, strategic goals, tactical goals and objectives, and operational goals and objectives at

Table 6.4

Possible Tactical Goals and Objectives Supporting Hershey's Strategic Goals

Strategic Goals	Possible Tactical Goals and Objectives
1. Introduce 3 new brands of food each year in the United States.	Division I: Introduce 1 new brand of food each year in the United States. Division II: Introduce 2 new brands of food each year in the United States. Division III: Introduce no new brands.
2. Increase return on assets (ROA) by 5% in 1994.	Division I: Increase ROA by 7% in 1994. Division II: Increase ROA by 3% in 1994. Division III: Increase ROA by 6% in 1994. Division IV: Increase ROA by 4% in 1994.
3. Reduce amount of pollutants released from manufacturing facilities by 10% in 1995.	Division I: Reduce pollutants by 12% in 1995. Division II: Reduce pollutants by 8% in 1995. Division III: Reduce pollutants by 10% in 1995.

Hershey Foods, Figure 6.3 presents a more complete version of the hierarchy of goals. As before, each level in the hierarchy supports and reinforces the levels above it. Organizations that are able to create a complete hierarchy of goals have significantly increased the probability that they will accomplish their mission.

Choosing Goals and Objectives

The goals and objectives that an organization chooses significantly determine its performance. Because managers are typically responsible for choosing goals, the process of decision making that managers follow in choosing goals is important. Faulty decision making may result in inappropriate or vaguely defined goals, goals not tied to a specific time period, or contradictory goals. How can organizations increase the probability of choosing appropriate goals and objectives?

Table 6.5

Possible Operational Goals and
Objectives Supporting Hershey's
Tactical Goals

Tactical Goals	Possible Operational Goals and Objectives
1. **Division I:** Introduce 1 new brand of food each year in the United States.	Marketing Manager: Conduct a market survey of customer needs in the United States each year.
	Sales Manager: Interview salespeople concerning market needs in the United States each year.
	R&D Manager: Develop 5 product prototypes each year.
2. **Division II:** Increase ROA by 3% in 1994.	Sales Manager: Increase sales by 8% in 1994.
	Manufacturing Manager: Reduce overtime costs by 9% in 1994.
	Purchasing Manager: Reduce costs of supplies by 3% in 1994.
3. **Division III:** Reduce pollutants by 10% in 1995.	Manufacturing Manager: Increase number of times antipollution devices are cleaned from 2 times a year in 1994 to 5 times a year in 1995.
	R&D Manager: Investigate alternative ways to reduce pollutants in 1994.

Evaluating Goals and Objectives

Table 6.6 lists important questions to ask in evaluating the potential of specific goals and objectives to enhance an organization's effectiveness.[15]

Evaluating Goals   The first question, whether proposed goals cover important dimensions of an organization's performance, is an important one. It seeks to avoid the possibility of an organization's accomplishing its goals only to discover that the goals do not fully account for some vital aspect of performance. In the mid-1970s, Polaroid decided to build the best, most convenient instant photography system in the world. It spent over $3 billion to research and develop this camera, called the SX-70. Although successful in developing a truly remarkable piece of technology, Polaroid's management somehow overlooked the fact that selling the camera at a price attractive to customers was also an important consideration. The SX-70 camera met all of Polaroid's technical requirements but could not be sold at a price that generated consumer interest. In the end, the camera had to be redesigned and simplified so that its price could be substantially reduced.[16]

The second question, whether a goal is realistic, is vital to address because organizations sometimes choose unattainable goals. The result is that employees lose motivation because they cannot reach the goals no matter how hard they try. Andy Grove, president of Intel Corp., recently described some unrealistic goal setting in his organization.[17]

Figure 6.3

Partial Hierarchy of Goals and Objectives for Hershey Foods

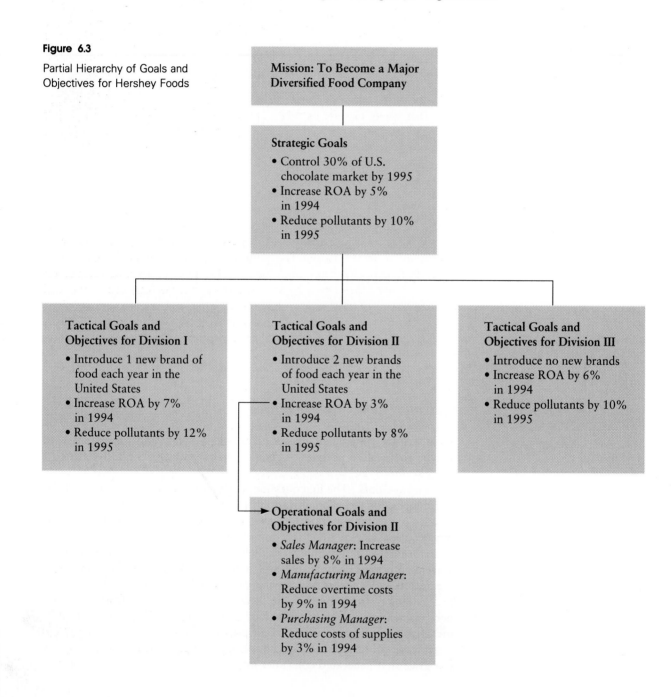

Managers must ensure that their organization's goals are ambitious. Airbus Industrie, the European commercial aircraft company, has established a goal of becoming a major actor in the world commercial aircraft industry — and especially of making inroads in the U.S. market. This is an ambitious goal because the aircraft industry is dominated by two giants: McDonnell Douglas and Boeing. Boeing alone holds 53 percent of the world market share. However, Airbus has made great strides: six years ago, it had orders for only 200 planes; as of 1991 its backlog totaled 1,600 planes.

Each time middle managers at Intel proposed some production goals, senior managers insisted that they increase the goals. The final goals were raised to the point where they were technologically and managerially unattainable. The following year, new goals were set, increased, and once again proved to be unattainable. The pattern of production goals and actual production at Intel is depicted in Figure 6.4. Notice that actual production closely followed the originally proposed goals, but the final goals remained unattainable. Unfortunately, Intel based hiring and investment decisions not on the proposed production goals but on the final production goals. As a result, the company had far too much staff and too much production

Table 6.6

Questions for Evaluating Goals and Objectives

Goals
Do the goals cover all important dimensions of the organization's performance?
Are the goals realistic? Will they seem attainable?
Are the goals ambitious? Will they motivate employees?
Objectives
Are the objectives specific and measurable?
Do the objectives support the organization's goals?
Are the objectives linked to a specific time period?
Are the objectives linked to rewards?

SOURCE: Max D. Richards, *Setting Strategic Goals and Objectives*, 2nd ed. (St. Paul, Minn.: West, 1986).

Figure 6.4

Gap Between Actual Production
and Final Goals at Intel

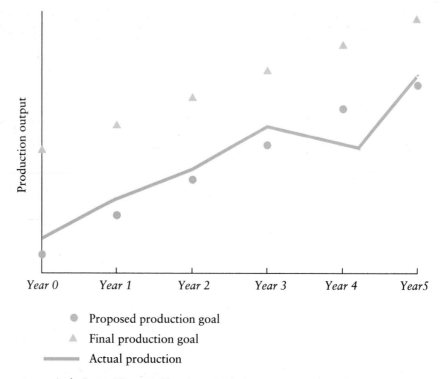

● Proposed production goal

▲ Final production goal

━━━ Actual production

SOURCE: Andy Grove, "Strategic Planning at Intel" (Presentation given at the Annual Meeting of the Strategic Management Society, San Francisco, September 1989).

capacity and in the fifth year had to substantially reduce its work force through early retirements and layoffs.

The final question in evaluating the quality of a goal is whether the goal is ambitious. Goals that are not ambitious are not very motivating because individuals in the organization do not have to work hard to accomplish them.[18] However, an ambitious goal, like NASA's moon launch, can capture the imagination of employees and lead them to work hard and creatively to attain it. Another example of an organization that is attempting to implement some ambitious goals is Pentech. Pentech, and its ambitious founder, Norman Melnick, are described in The Entrepreneurial Challenge.

Evaluating Objectives   As we have seen, objectives should support and reinforce an organization's goals. *Specific* objectives indicate precisely what behaviors or actions members of an organization are expected to engage in or accomplish. *Measurable* objectives have a quantitative component that allows the organization to measure not only whether an objective has been accomplished but by how much. The objective "to improve performance" is neither specific nor measurable. The objective "to increase sales by 3 percent next quarter" is both specific (it refers to sales next quarter) and measurable (it specifies a quantity).[19]

Specific objectives indicate precisely what behaviors or actions members of an organization are expected to engage in or accomplish. *Measurable* objectives have a quantitative component that allows the organization to measure not only whether an objective has been accomplished but by how much.

THE ENTREPRENEURIAL CHALLENGE

Making Waves in Writing Instruments

Writing instruments are boring. At least that is what most people thought — except Norman Melnick, founder and president of Pentech, Inc. Melnick is looking to turn this industry upside down by introducing more new kinds of writing instruments, at a faster pace, than ever before.

Like many industries, the writing-instrument industry has historically moved through periods of rapid technological change followed by relative stability. The invention of the ball-point pen in the 1950s marked the beginning of a period of rapid technological change in this industry. This invention was quickly followed up by the introduction of the inexpensive (19-cent) ball-point by BIC, the porous-point (or felt-tip) pen by Gillette, and the razor-point pen by a variety of firms. However, by the late 1970s, the pace of technological change had slowed. Most of the big players in the writing-instruments industry, including Paper Mate, BIC, Fisher, and Faber-Castell, seemed satisfied to introduce one or two new writing products a year and to focus instead on reducing manufacturing costs and exploiting untapped markets such as cigarette lighters and disposable razors.

Norman Melnick, however, was not satisfied with the status quo. The inventor of instant-drying ink for ball-point pens, Melnick has always been an innovator. After making a fortune selling his ink (through his Chemolene Corporation), Melnick acquired and turned around a series of companies, including Zip-Mark Products, Magic Marker, and Doral Industries. In 1983, Melnick began his newest venture, Pentech.

In starting Pentech, Melnick had only one goal — to create the most innovative writing-instruments company in the world. He has set the goal of introducing *at least* twenty-four new writing instruments each year. Melnick's ideas include cloth-covered pens (the Fiberx pen), an easy-to-hold pencil for children (the Grip Stick), and a fluorescent erasable highlighter.

Melnick's aggressive goals have generated positive returns for Pentech. Since its founding, Pentech has achieved an average annual growth rate of at least 25%. Pentech currently sells around 250 million pens, pencils, and markers a year and generates annual sales revenues of approximately $30 million. While Pentech is still a relatively small piece of the overall $2 billion writing-instruments industry, it may not be small for long if Melnick has his way.

REFERENCES: Bob Weinstein, "Pointed Matters," *Continental Profiles,* June 1991, pp. 22+; C. Roland Christensen, Norman A. Berg, and Malcolm S. Salter, "Note on the Mechanical Writing Instruments Industry," *Policy Formulation and Administration,* 8th ed. (Homewood, Ill.: Irwin, 1980), pp. 127–145; C. Roland Christensen, Norman A. Berg, and Malcolm S. Salter, "BIC Pen Corporation (A)," *Policy Formulation and Administration,* 8th ed. (Homewood, Ill.: Irwin, 1980), pp. 146–171.

It is not uncommon for there to be a mismatch between goals and objectives, but often the discrepancy is hard to recognize. Even the best objectives sometimes, perhaps inadvertently, do not support an organization's goals. When this occurs, the organization needs to refocus its efforts. **Means-end inversion** is a term that describes a situation in which accomplishing an objective becomes more important than accomplishing a goal.

A means-end inversion occurs when accomplishing an objective becomes more important than accomplishing a goal.

To reach its goal of delivering very high-quality semiconductors to its customers, a semiconductor manufacturer instituted a comprehensive quality-control and product-test program. In the meantime, it also instituted aggressive production objectives. Over the years, the high production objectives were consistently met, and high levels of quality were also reported.

However, a new production manager interested in the total manufacturing capacity of her production line discovered, much to her surprise, that running full-time, twenty-four hours a day, with no mistakes and no machine downtime, her line could not reach both the production and the quality objectives set for it. Apparently, in order to meet the high production objectives, employees had not been fully testing the quality of the products. The overall goal of shipping high-quality products to customers thus had been replaced by the objective of producing large numbers of products.[20]

Objectives should be linked to a specific time period. Given enough time, almost all objectives can be accomplished. However, an objective that takes too long to accomplish may end up not supporting an organization's goal. For example, it is not enough for Cadillac to design a new car. If the design is not completed until 1998, the Cadillac division will almost certainly be bankrupt. For Cadillac to turn itself around financially, it must complete its objectives in a timely manner.[21]

Objectives should also be linked to rewards. Without rewards, employees have reduced incentives to work hard to attain objectives. It is not uncommon for an organization to fail to connect objectives with a system of rewards or to mismatch objectives and rewards. For example, many organizations that have the objective of investing in long-term success (for example, investing in research and development) reward only short-term behaviors (for example, maximizing sales in the present quarter).[22]

Building a Consensus in Goal Setting

Once evaluation is complete, there are at least three processes that organizations can use to choose their goals and objectives. Goal setting can be top-down, bottom-up, or interactive.

Top-down goal setting is the process by which individuals at higher levels in the organization determine the goals of individuals at lower levels.

Top-Down Goal Setting   As Figure 6.5 shows, **top-down goal setting** is the process by which individuals at higher levels in the organization determine the goals of individuals at lower levels. Senior management establishes the organizational mission and then decides what the strategic goals will be. Given these strategic goals, managers at the next level dictate the tactical goals and objectives to divisional or departmental managers, who in turn dictate the operational goals and objectives to individuals. In strict top-down goal setting, no negotiation or discussion occurs about the goals and objectives passed down the organizational hierarchy.[23]

Top-down goal setting has two advantages. First, it ensures that an organization's operational goals, tactical goals, strategic goals, and mission support one another, because these goals are all set by senior managers. Second, top-down goal setting can lead to ambitious goals, for senior managers sometimes ask for more output than workers would ask from themselves.

These advantages are often countered by three disadvantages. First, because the most senior managers may be very far removed from the day-

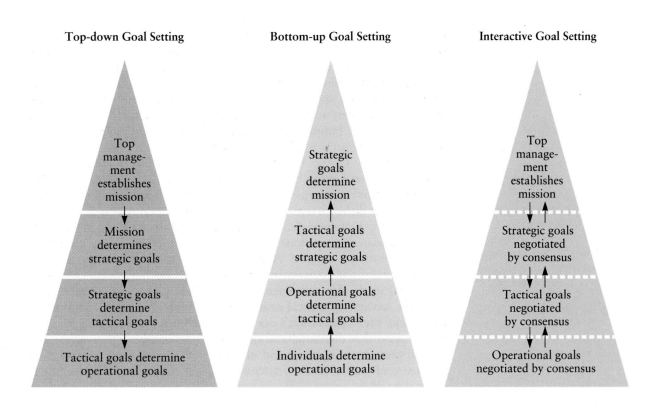

Top-down Goal Setting

Top management establishes mission

↓

Mission determines strategic goals

↓

Strategic goals determine tactical goals

↓

Tactical goals determine operational goals

Bottom-up Goal Setting

Strategic goals determine mission

↑

Tactical goals determine strategic goals

↑

Operational goals determine tactical goals

↑

Individuals determine operational goals

Interactive Goal Setting

Top management establishes mission

↓↑

Strategic goals negotiated by consensus

↓↑

Tactical goals negotiated by consensus

↓↑

Operational goals negotiated by consensus

Figure 6.5

Goal-setting Processes in Organizations

Bottom-up goal setting is a process by which individuals at lower levels in the organization determine the goals and objectives of individuals at higher levels.

to-day activities of individuals in the organization, the goals they set may be quite unrealistic. Unrealistic goals, as suggested earlier, tend to be very nonmotivating for people. Second, if senior managers have not kept abreast of changes in organizational performance, the goals they suggest may be outmoded. Third, top-down goal setting fails to encourage significant commitment, or "buy-in," among members of an organization. As Chapter 23 discusses in more detail, individuals in an organization must feel committed to goals and objectives in order to feel motivated to accomplish them. This commitment grows when individuals are involved in the creation of goals and objectives.[24]

Bottom-Up Goal Setting   Bottom-up goal setting, as depicted in Figure 6.5, is a process by which individuals at lower levels in the organization determine the goals and objectives of individuals at higher levels. In bottom-up goal setting, individual operational goals and objectives are aggregated to generate tactical goals and objectives, and tactical goals and objectives are aggregated to generate strategic goals. The organizational mission is then derived from the strategic goals.[25]

The advantages and disadvantages of bottom-up goal setting are the converse of those for top-down goal setting. In bottom-up goal setting, goals are likely to be very realistic because they are set by those who are going to implement them. They are also likely to reflect up-to-date changes in organizational performance. Finally, because it allows individuals at different levels to formulate goals and objectives, bottom-up goal setting encourages commitment. However, the goals chosen in this process sometimes do not challenge an organization because they are not sufficiently ambitious. More importantly, goals and objectives generated by bottom-up goal setting may support one another only accidentally. Organizations that use a strict bottom-up process sometimes lack clear direction and purpose.

Interactive Goal Setting   The third goal-setting process depicted in Figure 6.5 is interactive goal setting. **Interactive goal setting** is a process by which individuals at different levels in the organizational hierarchy negotiate goals and objectives and then reach a consensus about which goals and objectives are appropriate. This process often begins with top management's view of the organizational mission. How that mission is translated into strategic goals depends on the outcome of discussions and debates among individuals at several levels of management. Once strategic goals are agreed to, discussions concerning tactical goals and objectives can begin. These discussions keep the organization's mission in mind but also recognize the vital information that divisional and departmental managers can contribute to the process of setting goals and objectives. With a consensus reached on tactical goals and objectives, discussions begin concerning individual operational goals.[26]

Interactive goal setting is a process by which individuals at different levels in the organizational hierarchy negotiate goals and objectives and then reach a consensus about which goals and objectives are appropriate.

Interactive goal setting has all the advantages of the bottom-up process with few of the disadvantages. The interactive process ensures that goals are realistic and up-to-date. Since it necessarily requires much involvement from individuals at all levels of the organization, it generates the commitment needed to attain goals and objectives. Interactive goal setting also has many of the benefits of the top-down process. Guidance from higher levels in an organization ensures that goal setting is coordinated and that goals and objectives support one another. Importantly, negotiations among individuals at different organizational levels increase the probability that goals will be realistic and ambitious and thus motivate achievement.

In fact, compared to top-down and bottom-up goal setting, interactive goal setting has only two real weaknesses. First, negotiation and consensus building can be very time consuming. Second, interactive goal setting is a complicated process to manage. If not managed very carefully, its top-down or its bottom-up aspects can dominate. Despite these two drawbacks, most organizations most of the time use interactive goal setting. This is particularly the case in Japanese organizations.[27]

Planning to Reach Goals and Objectives

Carefully selecting goals and objectives at all levels in an organization is an important step in ensuring strong organizational performance. However, well-formulated goals and objectives are not much use without a plan for

A *plan* is the means by which an organization intends to pursue its goals and objectives.

realizing them. A **plan** is the means by which an organization intends to pursue its goals and objectives.

The Planning Hierarchy

As pictured in Figure 6.6, the hierarchy of an organization's plans and planning processes echoes the hierarchy of the organization's goals and objectives. Strategic plans specify how an organization's strategic goals will be accomplished. Tactical plans specify how an organization's tactical goals and objectives will be accomplished. Operational plans specify how an organization's operational goals and objectives will be accomplished.

Strategic plans are general plans that outline decisions regarding resource allocation, business and investment priorities, and action steps necessary to reach strategic goals.

Strategic Plans **Strategic plans** are general plans that outline decisions regarding resource allocation, business and investment priorities, and action steps necessary to reach strategic goals.[28] These plans are set by top managers in an organization, generally take a long time to accomplish, and span all of an organization's departments and divisions. Hershey Foods included important components of its strategic plan in its mission statement. As you recall from Figure 6.2, Hershey Foods' mission is to become "a major, diversified food company." Its mission statement specified the plan

Figure 6.6

The Planning Hierarchy and Its Relationship to the Hierarchy of Goals and Objectives

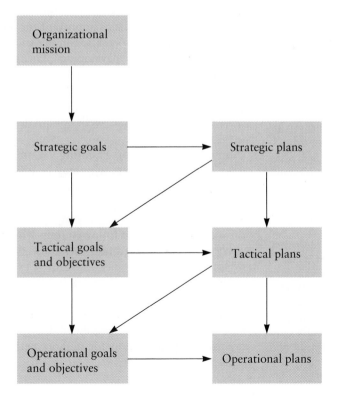

the corporation would follow for accomplishing this: (1) to increase growth of current products in their current markets, (2) to introduce new products, (3) to expand distribution of current products, and (4) to make acquisitions and other alliances.

An important attribute of strategic plans is that they not only specify what an organization will do to reach its mission and strategic goals, but they also specify what an organization will *not* do. It is very unlikely that Hershey will enter, say, the personal-computer business or the market for personal grooming products. Each of these areas holds significant potential for some firms, but Hershey's efforts are to position itself in the food market. The reasons a firm like Hershey tries to remain focused in its strategic goals and plans are discussed in more detail in Chapter 7.

Tactical plans specify how an organization will reach its tactical goals; *operational plans* specify how it will reach its operational goals.

Tactical and Operational Plans   **Tactical plans** specify how an organization will reach its tactical goals and objectives, and **operational plans** specify how an organization will reach its operational goals and objectives. Both tactical and operational plans are set by middle- and lower-level managers in response to the strategic plans developed by top managers. Both focus on near-term actions that different groups within an organization must take to help accomplish an organization's strategic plans.[29]

The Planning Process

The process that an organization uses to develop its strategic, tactical, and operational plans is just as important for the ultimate success of those plans as the goal-setting process is for the success of goals and objectives. The first consideration in developing plans is to decide whether the process should be top-down, bottom-up, or interactive. Not surprisingly, interactive planning tends to be more successful than strictly top-down or bottom-up planning. However, in choosing a planning process, managers must consider two other issues as well: comprehensiveness and timing.

Comprehensive planning involves all individuals inside a firm who may be affected by a plan, and it emphasizes complete information acquisition, rational calculation, and discussion before plans are decided upon.

Comprehensiveness of Planning   **Comprehensive planning** involves all individuals inside a firm who may be affected by a plan, and it emphasizes complete information acquisition, rational calculation, and discussion before plans are decided upon. It is a very long and complicated process. Since valuable management time is expended in comprehensive planning, this process should be followed only when it is likely to have a significant payoff for an organization — that is, only when it is likely to improve performance.

Noncomprehensive, or *incremental, planning* is less complete, collects less information, involves fewer individuals, and expends fewer organizational resources than comprehensive planning. It provides a general organizational direction for a short period of time.

Noncomprehensive planning is less complete, collects less information, and involves fewer individuals. It also expends fewer organizational resources. Noncomprehensive planning is also known as **incremental planning** because plans generated in this process tend to provide a general organizational direction for a short period of time, after which they are replaced by other plans.[30]

Some recent research suggests that, in highly turbulent and changing environments, organizations that use noncomprehensive planning usually outperform organizations that use comprehensive planning. This may be because, just as an organization completes expensive comprehensive planning, the environment suddenly shifts and the plan developed is no longer relevant or appropriate. The organization that uses noncomprehensive, incremental planning is able to more rapidly adjust to changed circumstances. However, research also suggests that comprehensive planners outperform noncomprehensive planners in environments that are relatively stable over time. In these environments, stability works to the benefit of comprehensive planning, and thus the costs of such planning are justified.[31]

Research suggests that comprehensive planning is most effective in stable environments and noncomprehensive planning is most effective in unstable environments.

Planning Time Horizon   A **time horizon** is the period of time for which plans are thought to apply. Different types of plans are associated with different time horizons. As Figure 6.7 shows, strategic plans generally have the longest time horizon, sometimes more than five years. Tactical plans have time horizons of between two and four years; operational plans, one to two years. The longer the time horizon, the more difficult it is to develop a plan, and thus the more uncertain it is that the organization will accomplish its goals and objectives. This uncertainty stems from the numerous unanticipated changes in environment that may affect the organization's goals, objectives, and therefore its plans.[32]

*A plan's *time horizon* is the period of time for which the plan is expected to apply.*

In the 1960s, AT&T's mission was to provide low-cost, high-quality telephone service to private and business customers. AT&T expected to continue to do this in a highly regulated environment. However, in the late 1970s MCI entered the long-distance telephone market, and AT&T, which had been forced to divest its regional telephone companies (e.g., Pacific Telephone, New Jersey Bell), found itself competing in a complex and rapidly changing market. It is quite unlikely that AT&T's original strategic plan allowed for the radical changes that AT&T would undergo in the 1970s and 1980s. Likewise, Atlantic Richfield Company (ARCO) probably could not have anticipated the dramatic fluctuations in oil prices in the 1970s, 1980s, and early 1990s.

Figure 6.7

Planning Time Horizons

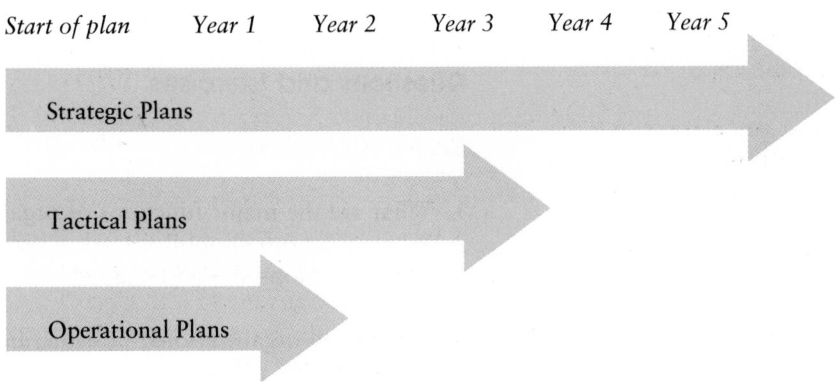

Start of plan   Year 1   Year 2   Year 3   Year 4   Year 5

Strategic Plans

Tactical Plans

Operational Plans

Learning Summary

An organizational goal is a desired future state that an organization attempts to realize. An objective is a specific short-term target that should support and reinforce an organization's goals. The main functions of organizational goals are (1) to provide guidance and a unified direction in a firm, (2) to facilitate planning, (3) to motivate and inspire members of an organization, and (4) to aid evaluation and control. Objectives support and reinforce these goals.

Organizations form a hierarchy of goals and objectives that consists of the organization's mission, strategic goals, tactical goals and objectives, and operational goals and objectives. Organizational goals must cover all important dimensions of organizational performance and must be realistic and ambitious. Organizational objectives must be specific and measurable, must support organizational goals, and must be linked with specific time periods and specific rewards.

Choosing goals and objectives almost always involves making difficult tradeoffs. Three processes for making these choices are top-down goal setting, bottom-up goal setting, and interactive goal setting. In most situations, interactive goal setting is the best way to choose organizational goals and objectives.

Plans are the means by which organizations reach their goals. In the planning hierarchy, strategic plans specify how an organization will attain its strategic goals, tactical plans specify attainment of tactical goals, and operational plans specify attainment of operational goals. The same advantages and disadvantages of top-down, bottom-up, and interactive goal setting pertain to the planning process. In general, interactive planning is most effective.

Research suggests that organizations in highly turbulent environments should adopt noncomprehensive planning, and organizations in stable environments should adopt more comprehensive planning. Strategic planning generally requires long time horizons, often greater than five years. Tactical planning requires time horizons of three to five years, and operational planning requires short-term planning of one to two years.

Questions and Exercises

Review Questions

1. What are the major functions of organizational goals?
2. What questions should one ask when evaluating *organizational goals*? What questions should be asked when evaluating *organizational objectives*?
3. What is an organizational mission, and what impact can it have on an organization's performance?
4. What are the specific advantages and disadvantages of top-down, bottom-up, and interactive processes for goal setting and planning?

5. Explain the relationship between organizational goals and planning. Can goals be effective without planning? Why or why not? Can planning be effective without goals? Why or why not?

Analysis Questions

1. AT&T had a successful venture in Iran called American Bell International. When the shah of Iran was overthrown, this business had to close quickly and sell off many of its assets far below their market price. Was this "fire sale" necessarily an example of poor planning at American Bell International? Why or why not?
2. Horace A. Boscoe, president of Boscoe Brothers, Inc., believes that goal setting and planning are very important in his organization. Mr. Boscoe believes that the Midwest division always seems to set goals and objectives that are quite different from those set by other company divisions. What are some possible ways in which these discrepancies could create problems for Mr. Boscoe's company?
3. Suppose that an organization has decided to focus on satisfying customers and shareholders in its goal setting and planning. When will it not be possible to satisfy both groups? Why?
4. Why might some organizations choose poorly designed goals and objectives? What personal motives might a manager have for choosing these kinds of goals and objectives?

Application Exercises

1. Outline a possible hierarchy of goals and objectives for MCI Communications. Use Figure 6.3 as a model.
2. For each of the following goals, suggest a specific and measurable objective:
   a. maximize shareholders' wealth
   b. stay on the cutting edge of technology
   c. satisfy customers
   d. engage in no layoffs
   e. reduce operating costs

Chapter Notes

1. Doug Carroll, "Seeking New Heights: LBO Team Redirecting Northwest," *USA Today,* July 23, 1990, pp. B1, B2; Michael Oneal and Kevin Kelly, "Even After a Shakeout, the Airlines May Be Shaky: All Al Checchi Needs Now Is Cash," *Business Week,* February 25, 1991, pp. 38–39; Gail DeGeorge and Seth Payne, "The Law of the Jungle Takes to the Skies," *Business Week,* February 4, 1991, p. 49; James Ott and Christopher Fotos, "Northwest Airlines: Developing a New Image," *Aviation Week,* April 9, 1990, pp. 64–72.

2. Organizational goals and objectives have been examined by a large number of authors, including George Steiner, *Top Management Planning* (New York: Macmillan, 1969); John E. Dittrich, *The General Manager and Strategy Formulation* (New York: Wiley, 1988); and Max D. Richards, *Setting Strategic Goals and Objectives,* 2nd ed. (St. Paul, Minn.: West, 1986).

3. For a discussion of Hewlett-Packard's goal to be at the leading edge of technology, see Nancy Herther, "Turning Raw Technology into Real Products," *Laserdisk Professional,* January 1990, pp. 28–35, and Paul Carter and Cedric Lunsdon, "How Management Development Can Improve Business Performance," *Personnel Management,* October 1988, pp. 49–52. For a discussion of goals and objectives at the Cadillac division of General Motors, see Mike Knepper, "Saving Cadillac," *American Way,* July 1, 1990, pp. 34–38. For a discussion of the evolution of goals and objectives at NASA, see Jim Shahin, "Can NASA Get Us There?" *American Way,* July 13, 1990, pp. 43–50.

4. Richards, *Setting Strategic Goals and Objectives.*

5. For a discussion of the "HP Way," see William G. Ouchi, *Theory Z* (Reading, Mass.: Addison-Wesley, 1980), and Kathleen Wiegner, "Goodbye to HP Way?" *Forbes,* November 26, 1990, pp. 36–37.

6. Knepper, "Saving Cadillac"; Jerry Flint, "GM — Yes It's For Real," *Forbes,* November 28, 1988, pp. 42–43.

7. Shahin, "Can NASA Get Us There?"; William David Compton, *Where No Man Had Gone Before* (Washington, D.C.: NASA, 1989).

8. This hierarchy of goals and objectives was originally described by Charles H. Granger, "The Hierarchy of Objectives," *Harvard Business School,* May–June 1964, pp. 63–74. Since that time, it has been a central organizing framework in a great deal of research and practice. See, for example, Charles Hofer and Dan Schendel, *Strategy Formulation: Analytical Concepts* (St. Paul, Minn.: West, 1978); R. McLellan and G. Kelly, "Business Policy Formulation: Understanding the Process," *Journal of General Management,* Autumn 1980, pp. 38–47; and Arthur A. Thompson, Jr., and A. J. Strickland, *Strategic Management: Concepts and Cases,* 4th ed. (Plano, Tex.: Business Publications, 1987).

9. John A. Pearce and Fred David, "Corporate Mission Statements: The Bottom Line," *The Academy of Management Executive,* May 1987, p. 109.

10. NCR's mission statement was prominently featured in NCR corporate advertising campaigns in the 1980s. Hershey Foods' and MCI Communications' mission statements are reproduced in Thompson and Strickland, *Strategic Management,* pp. 6–7.

11. Pearce and David, "Corporate Mission Statements."

12. Peter F. Drucker, *The Practice of Management* (New York: Harper & Row, 1954).

13. Thompson and Strickland, *Strategic Management.*

14. See Robert D. Pritchard, Philip L. Roth, Steven D. Jones, Patricia J. Galgay, and Margaret D. Watson, "Designing a Goal Setting System to Enhance Performance: A Practical Guide," *Organizational Dynamics,* Summer 1988, pp. 69–78, for a discussion of how operational goals and objectives affect individual behavior and performance.

15. Richards, *Setting Strategic Goals and Objectives.*

16. See C. Roland Christensen, Norman A. Berg, and Malcolm Salter, "Polaroid-Kodak," *Policy Formulation and Administration,* 8th ed. (Homewood, Ill.: Irwin, 1980), pp. 330–359.

17. Andy Grove, "Strategic Planning at Intel" (Presentation given at the Annual Meeting of the Strategic Management Society, San Francisco, September 1989).

18. Richards, *Setting Strategic Goals and Objectives.*

19. See Richards, *Setting Strategic Goals and Objectives,* and Edwin A. Locke, "The Ubiquity of the Technique of Goal Setting," *Academy of Management Review,* July 1978, pp. 594–602.

20. Lee Perry and Jay Barney, "Performance Lies Are Hazardous to Organizational Health," *Organizational Dynamics,* Winter 1981, pp. 68–80.

21. See Knepper, "Saving Cadillac."

22. This emphasis on measuring short-term performance while asking for longer-term investments has been cited as one of the major reasons many U.S. firms are unable to compete successfully with Japanese firms. See, for example, Robert H. Hayes and William J. Abernathy, "Managing Our Way to Economic Decline," *Harvard Business Review,* July–August 1980, pp. 67–77.

23. See Richards, *Setting Strategic Goals and Objectives;* E. A. Locke and G. P. Latham, *Goal Setting: A Motivational Technique That Works!* (Englewood Cliffs, N.J.: Prentice-Hall, 1984); and H. Levinson, "Management by Whose Objectives?" *Harvard Business Review,* July–August 1970, pp. 125–135.

24. For further discussions of the limitations of top-down goal setting, see D. J. Fellner and B. Sulzer-Azaroff, "A Behavioral Analysis of Goal Setting," *Journal of Organizational Behavior Management,* 1984, pp. 33–51; M. Erez and F. H. Kanfer, "The Role of Goal Acceptance in Goal Setting and Task Performance," *Academy of Management Review,* 1983, pp. 454–463; and G. P. Latham and T. P. Steele, "The Motivational Effects of Participation Versus Goal Setting on Performance," *Academy of Management Journal,* 1983, pp. 406–414.

25. Richards, *Setting Strategic Goals and Objectives.*

26. See Richards, *Setting Strategic Goals and Objectives;* Locke and Latham, *Goal Setting;* and L. P. Cusella, "Feedback, Motivation, and Performance," in *Handbook of Organizational Communication,* ed. F. J. Jablin, L. L. Putnam, K. H. Robers, and L. W. Porter (Newberry Park, Calif.: Sage, 1987), pp. 624–678.

27. For a discussion of goal setting in Japanese organizations, see Ouchi, *Theory Z,* and Richard Pascal and Anthony Athos, *The Art of Japanese Management* (New York: Simon and Schuster, 1981).

28. See Charles Hill and Gareth Jones, *Strategic Management: An Integrated Approach,* 2nd ed. (Boston: Houghton Mifflin, 1992).

29. Ibid.

30. The distinction between comprehensive and noncomprehensive planning was first suggested by J. W. Fredrickson, "The Comprehensiveness of Strategic Decision Making Processes: Extensions, Observations, Future Directions," *Academy of Management Journal,* 1984, pp. 445–466; and J. W. Fredrickson and T. R. Mitchell, "Strategic Decision Processes: Comprehensiveness and Performance in an Industry with an Unstable Environment," *Academy of Management Journal,* 1984, pp. 399–423. The closely linked concept of incremental planning has been discussed by a large number of scholars, including Herbert Simon, *Administrative Behavior,* 3rd ed. (New York: Free Press, 1976); Charles Lindbloom, *The Strategy of Decision* (New York: Free Press, 1963); and Charles Lindbloom, "The Science of Muddling Through," *Public Administration Review,* Spring 1959, pp. 79–88.

31. See Fredrickson, "The Comprehensiveness of Strategic Decision Making Processes," and Fredrickson and Mitchell, "Strategic Decision Processes."

32. See Hill and Jones, *Strategic Management.*

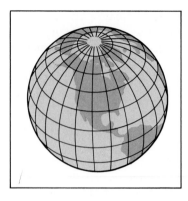

CASE 6.1

It's Not Easy Being Number One

Boeing has one clear goal: to retain its position as the largest maker of commercial aircraft. It first reached that position in the late 1950s, when it introduced the first passenger jet, the 707. Since then it has made about six out of every ten commercial aircraft now flying and has a $97 billion backlog of business (1,768 planes), which will keep its factories busy until close to the year 2000. The Boeing 747 is so popular that airline companies wait five years to get one. Yet despite its firm grasp on its world-leader position, Boeing is undergoing the changes and self-scrutiny associated with much less successful organizations — but not because the industry leader fears complacency. Boeing is demonstrating what it takes to stay on top.

Boeing must keep taking big risks even though its goal is in hand. Boeing must always know where it is headed and why. Developing a new airplane costs so much that Boeing management in effect bets the company each time it develops a new model. That may be one reason that the 747 is still the only jumbo jet made by Boeing. Economic shifts, fluctuations in oil prices, and world events can overnight raise airline ticket prices or convince travelers to stay home, and during an airline slump Boeing could see many of its contracts canceled.

Success itself caused Boeing serious problems in the late 1980s. Boeing has always prided itself on delivering its planes on time and on offering customers an almost unlimited number of options. But the popularity of Boeing's 747 — the aircraft of choice for the rapidly expanding airlines of the Pacific Rim — led Boeing to overextend itself. It hired hundreds of new, inexperienced workers to try to meet a frantic production schedule. Suddenly problems started showing up, especially in the planes' plumbing and wiring. The $120 million 747-400 has 175 miles of wires, 17 lavatories, and a newly redesigned cockpit, and every 747 customer seems to want a different placement of seats, galleys, and lavatories. Boeing's assembly process was slowed even more because the 1,500 suppliers of the 747-400's six million parts weren't prepared for the deluge of orders.

After fixing these problems on the 747, Boeing set out to change. In the short term, it brought in more experienced workers by transferring some from its military aircraft divisions and hiring others from Lockheed. In the long term, it decided to slow its production increases and invest more heavily in training. And it has radically changed the way it plans to build its next major airplane, the 777.

Although the company can't hope to produce a 777 until 1995, the new plane already represents a big risk because it will absorb some $5 billion in development money. Boeing hopes to use new production and design concepts to simplify its designs and make its production more efficient. Japanese-style teams will design and build the 777. Representatives from marketing, engineering, manufacturing, finance, and service departments will work together at all stages, rather than waiting for "their turn." On the largest IBM mainframe ever put together for design work, the teams will assemble and test three-dimensional computer models, cutting down drastically on the reworking that needs to be done on the factory floor. The 777 will have an unusual support structure that will enable changes in cabin design to be made more easily and with less cost than in the 747. If an airline wants all its bathrooms up front and its galleys in the rear, the changes won't cause engineering nightmares. Boeing has involved eighteen major suppliers in the design, hoping to dramatically reduce the six hundred requests for custom design changes that it gets on most models. The company is hoping that the 777 will provide a maximum of customization at a minimum of cost.

A look at Boeing's assembly facility gives some sense of why the company wants to simplify post-design changes. Boeing's plant in Everett, Washington, is the largest building in the world, covering 63 acres with one roof. Behind its 11-story-high doors, 8,000 people and one robot turn out one new jet about every three days. So any design change that can simplify work-flow layout is greeted with enthusiasm. One way Boeing keeps from going overboard in new technology is by giving customers the technology they want but letting other manufacturers experiment with technology that is so new that no one knows whether it's needed.

Boeing hopes that the new elements of the 777 production will allow it to become more profitable. Although the company's revenues are impressive, its profit margins are not. And despite its backlog of orders, it can't just raise prices, because McDonnell Douglas and Europe's Airbus Industrie offer competitive planes in almost every category. Either company would love to take some of the order backlog off Boeing's hands. But with its considerable resources focused on staying at the top, Boeing will be hard to beat.

Discussion Questions

1. Which of Boeing's objectives and recent changes do you find surprising for a company that has already reached its goal?
2. What general differences in approach would you expect between a company trying to be number one and a company trying to maintain its position?
3. How does the unique nature of Boeing's business affect its planning?
4. What seem to be the objectives behind Boeing's plans for the 777?

REFERENCES: Howard Banks, "Running Ahead, but Running Scared," *Forbes*, May 13, 1991, pp. 38–40; Marc Beauchamp, "No More Weekend Stands," *Forbes*, September 17, 1990, pp. 191–192; Anthony Ramirez, "Boeing's Happy, Harrowing Times," *Fortune*, July 17, 1989, pp. 40–48; Maria Shao, "Trying Times at Boeing," *Business Week*, March 13, 1989, pp. 34–36; Dori Jones Yang and Michael Oneal, "How Boeing Does It," *Business Week*, July 9, 1990, pp. 46–50.

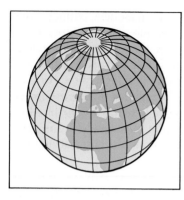

CASE 6.2

Trying to Stick to the Goal at Nestlé

Nestlé Enterprises is the world's largest food company, and for the 1990s it has one principal goal: to extend its dominance into the United States, where its $7 billion in operations still leave it far behind Kraft General Foods and ConAgra. But although in 1990 Nestlé finally made some positive moves toward its goal, it spent much of the 1980s sidetracked in controversy, most of it associated with baby foods.

Once thought of as a slow-moving Swiss chocolate maker, Nestlé began to gain world prominence in 1981 when Helmut Maucher took over. Within five years, Nestlé's earnings almost doubled, and other executives were taking lessons from Maucher on how to create a globally successful organization. Maucher thinks long term and is willing to accept years of losses in a particular country in order to establish a brand. This patience is one of the secrets of Nestlé's ability to take a product that's successful in one market and get it to catch on in another.

For instance, Lean Cuisine was already a hit in the United States when Nestlé decided to introduce it to Great Britain in 1985, replacing the dull, low-margin frozen offerings that it had been selling there. The introduction faced several major difficulties. For one, the British are as contemptuous of weight-watching as Americans are addicted to it. For another, Nestlé's frozen-food plant in Britain wasn't going to be fully operational until a year after the introduction, so the company had to ship its frozen entrées in refrigerated ships all the way from Canada. It took four years for Lean Cuisine to show a profit in Great Britain, but during that time it captured one-third of the fast-growing frozen-dinner market in that country.

The ability to spread a successful product around the globe allows Nestlé to get maximum benefit out of its four research laboratories and the $50 million a year that the company spends perfecting flavors, colors, and aromas. Nestlé is showing that even a food business needs to be capital-intensive and based on high technology if it wants to be successful worldwide. It now has plants in more than sixty countries and is number one in the world in coffee, powdered milk, frozen dinners, and candy.

But its push to become number one in the United States has been hampered by bad publicity surrounding the way Nestlé has marketed its products for its youngest consumers. The most serious charge leveled against Nestlé is that its infant-formula marketing led to the deaths of thousands of babies in the Third World. Nestlé's ads and free hospital samples convinced new mothers in poor countries to feed their babies formula instead of nursing them. Then, when their own milk dried up, the new mothers found that they had neither the clean water to make the formula nor the money to pay for it, and in some cases their babies starved. Groups around the world boycotted Nestlé products, and Maucher gave in to the demands of the World Health Organization.

That wasn't, however, the end of Nestlé's baby problems. In the middle 1980s, the American public learned that Nestlé's subsidiary Beech-Nut had sold flavored sugar water as "100% pure apple juice" for babies from 1978 to 1983. Beech-Nut's top officers were eventually convicted of hundreds of violations of the Federal Food, Drug and Cosmetic Act, and Beech-Nut's market share plummeted.

In 1988, Nestlé's recently acquired subsidiary, Carnation, ran afoul of several state attorneys general by advertising its new infant formula as "hypoallergenic" when in fact it caused severe allergic reactions in some babies. Perhaps having learned a lesson from the other scandals, Carnation changed its labels just two weeks after nine states began investigating the formula.

Despite this poor start, Carnation is a key ingredient in Nestlé's recipe for increasing its share of the American food market. Nestlé bought Carnation for $3 billion in 1985 and for the balance of the decade seemed content to allow it to continue to sell its old line of products, some of which duplicated other Nestlé brands. Under pressure from competition and changes in the supermarket environment, in 1990 Nestlé finally created Nestlé USA, a single holding company to coordinate all of Nestlé's U.S. business. The new company can eliminate redundant distribution and administrative costs and offer customers better service, combining all its products into single shipments instead of saddling customers with large inventories of products from infrequent shipments. The new structure also allows Nestlé to react more quickly to changes in public tastes and in its customers. As supermarket chains become more powerful, they can demand better service and distribution, which only a unified company can offer. It still has a long way to go, but if the single, integrated Nestlé USA can avoid further blunders with its baby products, it may reach its goal.

Discussion Questions

1. In what ways could the baby-products scandals, which concerned only a tiny portion of Nestlé's products, affect the entire company?
2. What objectives should Nestlé set in order to reach its overall goal of dominance of the American market?
3. How would planning for a national company like Nestlé USA differ from planning for a global company like Nestlé Enterprises?
4. What conflicting goals or objectives may have led Nestlé into its baby-products problems?

REFERENCES: Alix M. Freedman, "Unit of Nestlé Settles Dispute on Infant Ads," *Wall Street Journal*, July 7, 1989, p. B3; Zachary Schiller, "Nestlé's Crunch in the U.S.," *Business Week*, December 24, 1990, pp. 24–25; Zachary Schiller, "Timm Crull," *The 1991 Business Week 1000*, p. 92; Shawn Tully, "Nestlé Shows How to Gobble Markets," *Fortune*, January 16, 1989, pp. 74–78; Shawn Tully, "Stirring the Coffee Pot," *Fortune*, August 3, 1987, p. 44; Betty Wong, "Conviction of Nestlé Unit's Ex-President Is Overturned on Appeal in Juice Case," *Wall Street Journal*, March 31, 1989, p. B5.

7

Formulating Organizational Strategy

LEARNING OBJECTIVES

After studying this chapter, you should be able to:

1. Discuss the importance of strategy formulation.

2. Describe how to use SWOT analysis in formulating strategy.

3. Discuss the difference between business- and corporate-level strategies.

4. Identify and describe three categories of business-level strategies.

5. Describe three corporate diversification strategies.

The strategy of American Express Company rests on two management pillars: quality and synergy. The "rule" at American Express, strongly emphasized by CEO James D. Robinson III, is, Never promise more than you can deliver, but deliver more than you promised. This focus on quality is reinforced through an aggressive employee-training program and a variety of company publications, one of which describes extraordinary acts of service that American Express employees have performed for their customers. The company's emphasis on synergy reflects Robinson's belief that the future of the financial services market belongs to organizations that provide an integrated range of services, including credit cards, savings and investment programs, insurance programs, financial planning, brokerage services—even real estate and travel planning.

In the 1980s, American Express reaffirmed its twenty-year reputation for quality management by implementing a far-sighted, aggressive strategy that positioned it as a major player in the international financial services market. The firm purchased Investors Diversified Services (IDS) to obtain savings and investments expertise, and it purchased Shearson Lehman Hutton to enter into stock and bond brokerage.

American Express's two-pronged strategy of quality and synergy received wide praise until 1987, when the stock market crashed over 500 points. Increased uncertainty in international equity markets sent investors scurrying off to more secure investments, leaving brokerage houses like Shearson struggling for survival and desperate for customers. By 1990, Shearson faced as much as $2.5 billion in losses due to bad loans and other investments. To support Shearson, American Express had to invest nearly $1.35 billion in the first few months of 1990. It also purchased the rest of Shearson's publicly available stock.

The short-term financial impact of these events on American Express was undoubtedly negative, but the long-term implications of these events were not so clear. The organization's senior managers had to answer a difficult question: was the trouble at Shearson just a temporary downturn, or was the fundamental strategy that led American Express to purchase Shearson fatally flawed? In early 1990, all indications were that American Express was not going to abandon its quality and synergy strategy, although it might be forced to slow the pace of implementation.[1]

Strategy is a comprehensive plan for accomplishing an organizational mission.

American Express faces a challenge common to many organizations: deciding whether short-term fluctuations in performance represent only a temporary setback or a serious flaw in strategy. **Strategy** is a comprehensive plan for accomplishing the organizational mission. Deciding what strategies an organization should adopt, and when it should change its strategies, has an enormous impact on organizational performance. Indeed, much research suggests that an organization's strategic decisions largely determine its economic value.[2]

This chapter discusses the formulation of organizational strategies. It begins by examining the nature of strategic management and then describes the kinds of analyses needed for firms to formulate their strategies. Finally, the major strategic options facing firms at the business and corporate levels are discussed.

The Nature of Strategic Management

Strategic management is a comprehensive and ongoing management process aimed at formulating and implementing effective strategies.

In Chapter 6 we described a strategic plan as a general plan outlining decisions of resource allocation, priorities, and action steps necessary to reach strategic goals. Strategic management, however, is much more than this. It is a way of thinking about management — and a way of approaching business opportunities and challenges. **Strategic management** is a comprehensive and ongoing management process aimed at formulating and implementing effective strategies that promote a superior alignment between the organization and its environment and the achievement of strategic goals.[3] To fully understand how strategic management is practiced, it is first necessary to understand the components of strategy and the distinction between strategy formulation and strategy implementation.

The Components of Strategy

Strategies should address an organization's distinctive competencies, its scope, and its resource deployment.

In general, a well-conceived strategy addresses three areas of concern: distinctive competence, scope, and resource deployment. A distinctive competence is something the organization does exceptionally well. The Limited, a large clothing chain, stresses its distinctive competence of speed in moving inventory. It tracks consumer preferences daily with point-of-sale computers, uses facsimile machines to transmit orders to suppliers in Hong Kong, charters 747s to fly products to the United States, and has products in stores forty-eight hours later. Since other retailers take weeks or sometimes months to accomplish the same things, The Limited relies on this distinctive competence to stay ahead of its competition.[4]

The *scope* of a strategy specifies the range of markets in which an organization will compete.

The **scope** of a strategy specifies the range of markets in which an organization will compete. Hershey has essentially restricted its scope to the confectionery business, with a few related activities in other food-processing areas. In contrast, its biggest competitor, M&M/Mars, has adopted a broader scope by competing in the pet-food business and the electronics industry, among others. Some organizations, called *conglomerates,* compete in dozens or even hundreds of markets.[5]

Resource deployment refers to how an organization distributes its resources across the areas in which it competes.

A strategy should also include an outline of the organization's projected **resource deployment** — how it will distribute its resources across the areas in which it competes. Raytheon, for example, has used profits from its large defense-contracting business to support growth in its publishing (D. C. Heath) and appliance (Amana, Speed Queen, and Caloric) businesses. The company could have chosen to reinvest those profits in its defense businesses and let the other units stand alone. Instead, it chose a different deployment.[6]

Strategy Formulation and Implementation

Strategy formulation is the set of processes involved in creating or determining the strategies of the organization. It focuses on the content of strategies. *Strategy implementation* is the methods by which strategies are operationalized or executed within the organization. It focuses on the processes through which strategies are achieved.

It is instructive to draw a distinction between strategy formulation and strategy implementation. Simply stated, **strategy formulation** is the set of processes involved in creating or determining the strategies of the organization, and **strategy implementation** is the methods by which strategies are operationalized or executed within the organization. The primary distinction is along the lines of content versus process: the formulation stage determines what the strategy is, and the implementation stage focuses on how the strategy will be achieved. Strategy implementation is discussed in detail in Chapter 8.

Using SWOT Analysis to Formulate Strategy

SWOT is an acronym that stands for Strengths, Weaknesses, Opportunities, and Threats.

To choose from among all possible ways of accomplishing its mission, an organization should engage in SWOT analysis. **SWOT** (which only *sounds* like a way to fight off flies and insects) is an acronym that stands for Strengths, Weaknesses, Opportunities, and Threats. As shown in Figure 7.1, SWOT analysis is a very careful evaluation of an organization's internal strengths and weaknesses, and its environmental opportunities and threats. In SWOT analysis, the best strategies accomplish an organization's mission by (1) exploiting an organization's opportunities and strengths while (2) neutralizing its threats and (3) avoiding (or correcting) its weaknesses. Strategies that do not exploit an organization's opportunities and strengths, that do not neutralize its threats, or that do not avoid its weaknesses are unlikely to improve its performance.[7]

According to SWOT analysis, the best strategies (1) exploit an organization's opportunities and strengths while (2) neutralizing its threats and (3) avoiding (or correcting) its weaknesses.

Evaluating an Organization's Strengths

Organizational strengths are skills and capabilities that enable an organization to conceive of and implement its strategies.

Organizational strengths are skills and capabilities that enable an organization to conceive of and implement its strategies. Different strategies call upon different skills and capabilities. For example, Matsushita Electric Industrial Co. has demonstrated strengths in manufacturing and selling

Figure 7.1

Using SWOT Analysis in Strategy Formulation

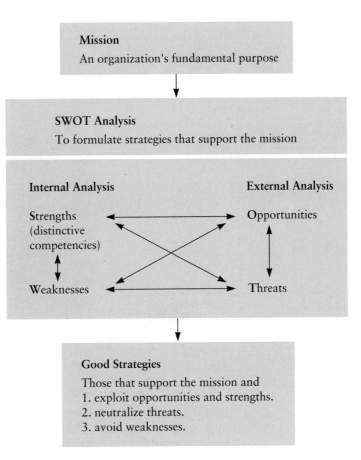

consumer electronics under the brand name Panasonic. However, Matsushita's strength in consumer electronics does not ensure success if the firm expands into insurance, swimming-pool manufacture, or retail. Different strategies such as these require different organizational strengths.[8] SWOT analysis divides organizational strengths into two categories: common strengths and distinctive competencies.

Common strengths are skills and capabilities held by numerous competing firms. *Competitive parity* exists when strategies exploit only common strengths.

Common Organizational Strengths   A **common strength** is an organizational capability possessed by a large number of competing firms. For example, all the major Hollywood film studios possess common strengths in lighting, sound recording, set and costume design, and makeup. As Figure 7.2 shows, **competitive parity** exists when large numbers of competing firms are able to implement the same valuable strategy. In this situation organizations generally attain only normal levels of economic performance. Thus a film company that exploits only its common strengths in choosing and implementing strategies is not likely to go beyond normal economic performance.[9]

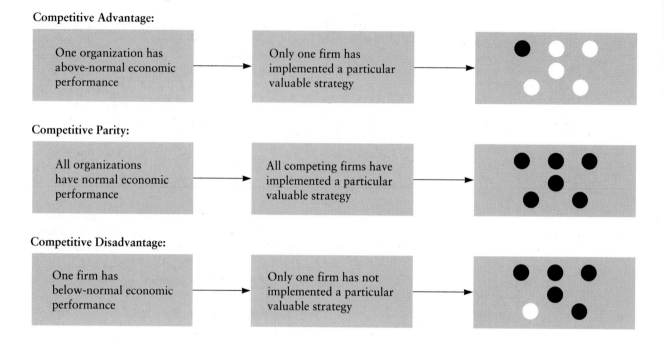

Competitive Advantage:

| One organization has above-normal economic performance | → | Only one firm has implemented a particular valuable strategy | → | |

Competitive Parity:

| All organizations have normal economic performance | → | All competing firms have implemented a particular valuable strategy | → | |

Competitive Disadvantage:

| One firm has below-normal economic performance | → | Only one firm has not implemented a particular valuable strategy | → | |

Figure 7.2

Ways in Which Implementing a Valuable Strategy Affects Organizational Performance

A *distinctive competence* is an organizational strength possessed by only a small number of competing firms. Firms that exploit distinctive competencies in choosing and implementing their strategies can expect to obtain a *competitive advantage.*

Distinctive Competencies   A **distinctive competence** is an organizational strength possessed by only a small number of competing firms. Distinctive competencies are rare among a set of competitors. George Lucas's well-known company Industrial Light and Magic (ILM), for example, has brought the cinematic art of special effects to new heights. Some of ILM's special effects can be produced by no other organization; these rare special effects are thus ILM's distinctive competencies.

Organizations that exploit their distinctive competencies often obtain a **competitive advantage,** in that they are able to implement valuable strategies that other organizations cannot implement. As suggested in Figure 7.2, organizations with a competitive advantage usually attain above-normal economic performance.[10]

A main purpose of SWOT analysis is to discover an organization's distinctive competencies so that the organization can choose and implement strategies that exploit its unique organizational strengths. Thus Industrial Light and Magic, which has a distinctive competence in cinematic special effects, should exploit this competence by signing on to films that require numerous special effects. ILM probably should not work on films that require no special effects, since it possesses no unusual skills or distinctive competencies in any other areas.

ILM might have the financial capability of engaging in a different strategy, but such a move would generate only average performance at best. So far, ILM has continued to exploit its distinctive competencies and avoided competitive arenas in which it possesses only common strengths.[11]

Strategic imitation is the practice of duplicating another organization's distinctive competence and thereby implementing a valuable strategy.

A *sustained competitive advantage* is a competitive advantage that exists after all attempts at strategic imitation have ceased.

Imitation of Distinctive Competencies An organization that possesses distinctive competencies and exploits them in the strategies it chooses can expect to obtain a competitive advantage and above-normal economic performance. However, as suggested in the discussion of new entrants in Chapter 4, its success will lead other organizations to duplicate these advantages. **Strategic imitation** is the practice of duplicating another firm's distinctive competence and thereby implementing a valuable strategy.

Many distinctive competencies can be imitated, but some cannot be. When a distinctive competence cannot be imitated, strategies that exploit these competencies generate sustained competitive advantages. A **sustained competitive advantage** is a competitive advantage that exists after all attempts at strategic imitation have ceased.[12]

There are three reasons why a distinctive competence might not be imitated. First, the acquisition or development of the distinctive competence may depend on unique historical circumstances that other organizations cannot replicate. Caterpillar Tractor, for example, obtained a sustained competitive advantage when it was granted a long-term contract with the United States Army. The Army felt obligated to offer this long-term contract because of the acute international construction requirements created by World War II. Caterpillar's current competitors, including Komatsu, J.I. Case, and John Deere, cannot re-create these circumstances.[13]

Second, a distinctive competence might be difficult to imitate because its nature and character might not be known or understood by competing firms. Procter & Gamble, for example, considers that its sustained competitive advantage is based on its manufacturing practices. Large sections of Procter & Gamble's plants are screened off to keep this information secure. ILM also refuses to disclose how it creates some of its special effects.[14]

Finally, a distinctive competence can be difficult to imitate if it is based on complex social phenomena, like organizational teamwork or culture. In this case, competing organizations may know, for example, that a firm's success is directly traceable to the teamwork among its managers but, because teamwork is a difficult thing to create, may not be able to imitate this distinctive competence. Why socially complex organizational phenomena are sometimes difficult to change and imitate is discussed in detail in Chapter 23.[15]

The VRIO framework summarizes the characteristics of organizational skills and abilities that are the source of different levels of competitive advantage. These requirements include (1) is the skill or ability valuable, (2) is it rare, (3) is it difficult to imitate, and (4) is the firm organized to take advantage of this skill or ability.

The VRIO Framework By concentrating on the value, rareness, and imitability of an organization's skills and abilities, it is possible to estimate the kind of competitive advantage and economic performance these abilities can generate for an organization. How well an organization exploits these skills and abilities also has an impact on firm performance. These four questions about an organization's skills and resources (value? rareness? imitability? organization?) are combined in the VRIO framework presented in Table 7.1.

A skill or ability is valuable when it takes advantage of an opportunity, or neutralizes a threat, in an organization's environment. Skills or abilities that are not valuable can be expected to generate below-normal economic performance for a firm. If a skill or ability is valuable but not rare, then it is a common strength, a source of competitive parity and normal economic performance. If a skill or ability is valuable and rare but can be imitated, then it is a source of competitive advantage and above-normal economic performance. However, that advantage will ultimately be competed away. Finally, if an organization's skill and abilities are valuable, rare, and difficult to imitate, they will be sources of sustained competitive advantage and above-normal economic performance. All these conclusions depend on an organization's successfully organizing itself to implement its strategies. An organization that otherwise has the potential for above-normal economic performance may actually forfeit that performance by failing to organize itself for successful strategic implementation.[16]

Evaluating an Organization's Weaknesses

Evaluating an organization's weaknesses is similar to evaluating its strengths. **Organizational weaknesses** are skills and capabilities that do not enable an organization to choose and implement strategies that support its mission. An organization has essentially two ways of addressing weaknesses. First, it may need to make investments to obtain the strengths required to implement strategies that support its mission. Second, it may need to modify its mission so that it can be accomplished with the skills and capabilities that the organization already possesses.

Organizational weaknesses are skills and capabilities that do not enable an organization to choose and implement strategies that support its mission. A firm with organizational weaknesses either can make investments to improve its weaknesses, or it can change its mission.

Table 7.1

The VRIO Framework for Evaluating the Performance Implications of an Organization's Skills and Abilities

Are these skills and abilities valuable?	Are these skills and abilities rare?	Are these skills and abilities difficult to imitate?	Does the firm organize itself to implement strategies that exploit these skills and abilities?	Competitive Consequences	Economic Performance Implications
No	—	—	No	Competitive disadvantage	Below-normal performance
Yes	No	—		Competitive parity	Normal performance
Yes	Yes	No		Competitive advantage	Above-normal performance
Yes	Yes	Yes	Yes	Sustained competitive advantage	Above-normal performance

Sony has invested heavily to overcome its weaknesses and accomplish its mission, which is to become an integrated consumer electronics company. To fulfill its goals in video electronics, Sony needed access to recently released films and television shows. Because the firm had no in-house video production capabilities, it had to rely on film and video work produced by other organizations. Sony addressed this weakness by purchasing Columbia Pictures, thereby acquiring high-quality in-house film and television-show production capability.[17]

The March of Dimes changed its mission rather than try to acquire new strengths. Originally founded to fund research in discovering a cure for polio, over the years the March of Dimes became extremely skilled at fund raising. In the early 1950s, a cure for polio was discovered. To continue to capitalize on its fund-raising capabilities, the organization adopted a new mission and now raises funds to support research into the causes and cure of birth defects. By changing its mission, the March of Dimes deployed its organizational strengths in a new and valuable way.[18]

In practice, organizations have a difficult time focusing on weaknesses, in part because organization members are often reluctant to admit that they may not possess all the skills and capabilities needed. Evaluating weaknesses also calls into question the judgment of managers who chose the organization's mission in the first place and who failed to invest in the skills and capabilities needed to accomplish that mission. Organizations that fail either to recognize or overcome their weaknesses are likely to suffer from competitive disadvantages. An organization has a **competitive disadvantage** when it is not implementing valuable strategies that are being implemented by competing organizations. Organizations with a competitive disadvantage can expect to attain below-normal levels of economic performance.[19]

An organization has a competitive disadvantage when it is not implementing valuable strategies that are being implemented by competing organizations.

Evaluating an Organization's Opportunities and Threats

Whereas evaluating strengths and weaknesses focuses attention on the internal workings of an organization, evaluating opportunities and threats requires analysis of an organization's environment. **Organizational opportunities** are events or phenomena in an organization's environment that, if exploited, may generate above-normal economic performance. **Organizational threats** are events or phenomena in an organization's environment that make it difficult for an organization to create or maintain above-normal economic performance, or even normal economic performance. The tools of environmental analysis presented in Chapter 4 are directly relevant here. In particular, Porter's five forces model of the competitive environment can be used to characterize the extent of opportunity and threat in an organization's environment.

Organizational opportunities are events or phenomena in an organization's environment that, if exploited, may generate above-normal economic performance.

Organizational threats are events or phenomena in an organization's environment that make it difficult for an organization to create or maintain above-normal economic performance, or even normal economic performance.

As reviewed in Table 7.2, Porter's five forces are level of rivalry, power of suppliers, power of customers, threat of substitutes, and threat of new entrants. In general, when the level of rivalry, the power of suppliers and customers, and the threat of substitutes and new entrants are all high, an

Table 7.2

Using Porter's Five Forces Model to Characterize the Level of Opportunities and Threats in an Industry

	High Opportunity Low Threat	Low Opportunity High Threat
Level of rivalry	Low	High
Power of suppliers	Low	High
Power of customers	Low	High
Threat of substitutes	Low	High
Threat of new entrants	Low	High
Potential performance	Above-normal economic performance	Normal economic performance

The five forces in Porter's model that determine the level of opportunity and threat in an industry are (1) level of rivalry, (2) power of suppliers, (3) power of consumers, (4) threat of substitutes, and (5) threat of new entrants.

industry has relatively few opportunities and numerous threats. Firms in these types of industries typically have the potential to earn only normal economic performance. On the other hand, when the level of rivalry, the power of suppliers and customers, and the threat of substitutes and new entrants are all low, then an industry has numerous opportunities and relatively few threats. These industries hold the potential for above-normal performance for organizations in them.[20]

As we saw in Chapter 4, an industry with relatively low opportunity is electronic parts distribution. Organizations in this industry buy electronic components from large manufacturers such as Intel and National Semiconductor and resell these components to small customers. There are literally hundreds of organizations in this distribution business, and they usually follow very aggressive price-cutting policies to obtain sales. These actions are indicative of very high rivalry. Electronic parts distributors purchase products from a few very powerful suppliers and sell them to numerous demanding customers. Since parts manufacturers often sell directly to end users, they also act as a substitute for the service provided by parts distributors. Because not much investment is necessary, the threat of new entrants is very high. On average, organizations in this industry show normal economic performance.[21]

The pharmaceutical industry has greater opportunities. Although there is significant competition in developing new and effective drugs and medicines, once an organization develops and patents a product, rivalry in the marketplace is substantially reduced. Suppliers to the pharmaceutical industry (mostly chemical companies) are not powerful, nor are customers. Because of drug patent protections, substitute products are unavailable; and given the enormous research and development skills and facilities required, the threat of new entrants into this industry is low, although generic (nonbranded) drugs are becoming more popular. On average, organizations in this industry show above-normal performance.[22]

To suggest that, on average, a particular industry has normal or above-normal performance potential does not imply that all competitors will

Successful organizational strategies neutralize environmental threats to a firm's performance. Restaurants that accept the American Express card have threatened to boycott its use because of the higher-than-average merchant's fee AmEx collects from the restaurant for every meal charged by a dining customer. AmEx responded to this threat in the short term by reducing its merchant's fee. In the long term, Kenneth I. Chenault, president of American Express's U.S. consumer card group, has been given the responsibility of seeking strategies that will keep restaurants in the AmEx fold without excessively reducing the merchant's fees.

attain these levels of performance. The extent of performance depends on the opportunities and threats of the industry and the distinctive competencies of the particular organization. To illustrate, most observers would agree that the metal-container industry does not have great performance potential. The level of rivalry is very high. Major competitors include Continental Can, American Can, and National Can. The power of suppliers is very high, because a key resource in this industry is aluminum and the aluminum industry is dominated by a small number of companies. Indeed some of these aluminum companies, such as Alcoa, have begun manufacturing their own cans. The power of customers is also high, as some large users of cans (for example, Campbell Soup) are now making their own cans. Substitutes for cans are common, including glass, plastic, and paper containers. Not surprisingly, the threat of new entrants is not particularly great, and in fact many of the competitors in the metal-container industry have substantially reduced their financial commitment. However, one organization, Crown Cork & Seal, has remained committed to this industry and has prospered. It is able to do so, despite the industry's normal performance potential, because it holds distinctive competencies in manufacturing, service, and management.[23]

Types of Strategic Alternatives

SWOT analysis suggests that an organization should choose strategies that support its mission, that exploit opportunities and strengths while neutralizing threats, and that avoid weaknesses. However, what strategic options and alternatives are available to an organization? SWOT analysis tells organizations how they should choose among these alternatives, but it does not specify what these alternatives are.

Research on strategic alternatives focuses on two general areas: business strategies and corporate strategies. **Business-level strategy** is the set of strategic alternatives that an organization chooses from as it conducts business in a particular industry or a particular market. **Corporate-level strategy** is the set of strategic alternatives that an organization chooses from as it manages its operations simultaneously across several industries and several markets.[24]

At the business level, for example, American Express might focus attention on increasing consumer use of the American Express Card (strategy in one industry or market). At the corporate level, the firm might focus attention on applying its skills and capabilities in the credit card business to selling insurance policies and annuities (strategy across multiple industries and markets). The rest of this chapter examines strategy formulation at the business and corporate levels.

Business-level strategy is the set of strategic alternatives that an organization chooses from as it conducts business in a particular industry or market. *Corporate-level strategy* is the set of strategic alternatives that an organization chooses from as it manages its operations simultaneously across several industries and several markets.

Examining Business-Level Strategies

A number of authors have classified the major strategic alternatives that organizations should consider when choosing their business-level strategies. Three important classification schemes are Porter's generic strategies, the Miles and Snow typology, and strategies based on the product life cycle.

Porter's Generic Strategies

Porter has argued for three generic business strategies: differentiation, overall cost leadership, and focus.

An organization that pursues a *differentiation strategy* seeks to distinguish itself from competitors through the quality of its products or services.

An organization implementing an *overall cost leadership strategy* attempts to gain a competitive advantage by reducing its costs below the costs of competing firms.

According to Michael Porter, organizations may pursue a differentiation, overall cost leadership, or focus strategy at the business level.[25] Table 7.3 summarizes each of these strategies. An organization that pursues a **differentiation strategy** seeks to distinguish itself from competitors through the quality of its products or services. Firms that successfully implement a differentiation strategy are able to charge more for their products or services because customers are willing to pay more to obtain the extra value they perceive.

Rolex pursues a differentiation strategy in the watch industry. Rolex watches are handmade of gold and stainless steel and are subjected to strenuous tests of quality and reliability. The firm's reputation enables it to charge up to $15,000 for one of its wristwatches. Other organizations that implement differentiation strategies are Mercedes-Benz in automobiles, Nikon in cameras, Cross in writing instruments, and Hewlett-Packard in hand-held calculators.

An organization implementing an **overall cost leadership strategy** attempts to gain a competitive advantage by reducing its costs below the costs of competing firms. By keeping costs low, the organization is able to sell its products at low prices and still make a substantial profit. In the

Table 7.3

Porter's Generic Strategies

Strategy Type	Definition	Examples
Differentiation	Distinguish products or services	Rolex (watches) Mercedes-Benz (automobiles) Nikon (cameras) Cross (writing instruments) Hewlett-Packard (hand-held calculators)
Overall Cost Leadership	Reduce manufacturing and other costs	Timex Hyundai Kodak BIC Texas Instruments
Focus	Concentrate on specific regional market, product market, or group of buyers	Longines Fiat, Alpha Romeo Polaroid Waterman Pens Fisher Price

watch industry, Timex uses an overall cost leadership strategy. For decades, this firm has specialized in manufacturing relatively simple, low-cost watches for the mass market. The price of Timex watches, which starts around $19.95, is low because of the company's efficient high-volume manufacturing capacity. Other organizations that implement overall cost leadership strategies are Hyundai in automobiles, Kodak in cameras, BIC in writing instruments, and Texas Instruments in hand-held calculators.

An organization pursuing a **focus strategy** concentrates on a specific regional market, product line, or group of buyers. This strategy may have either a differentiation focus, whereby the organization attempts to differentiate its products or services in the focus market, or an overall cost leadership focus, whereby the organization attempts to manufacture and sell its products at low cost in the focus market. In the watch industry, Longines follows a focus differentiation strategy by selling highly jeweled watches to wealthy female consumers. Fiat follows a focus cost leadership strategy by selling its automobiles only in Italy and in selected regions of Europe; Alpha Romeo uses focus differentiation to sell its high-performance cars in these same markets. Fisher Price uses focus differentiation to sell electronic calculators with large, brightly colored buttons to the parents of preschoolers.

Porter argues that organizations should choose one of these three strategies and concentrate on implementing it. Porter suggests that organizations that attempt to implement more than one type of strategy are "stuck in the middle," as depicted in Figure 7.3, and generally do not perform as

An organization pursuing a *focus strategy* concentrates on a specific regional market, product line, or group of buyers.

Organizations that are "stuck in the middle" attempt to implement more than one generic strategy and often fail to implement any strategy very well.

An organization implementing a focus strategy concentrates on a particular geographic area or market segment — employing either a cost-leadership or a differentiation strategy. Matson, a shipping company, differentiates itself by specializing in frequent, high-quality service to, from, and within Hawaii only. It's claim to be as familiar as the fish with Hawaii's waters emphasizes to customers the advantages of its focus.

well as firms that implement a differentiation strategy *or* an overall cost leadership strategy, or as well as firms that implement a focus differentiation strategy *or* a focus cost leadership strategy.[26]

Although Porter's analysis of generic strategies can be very helpful, misapplying these ideas can create problems for organizations. The questionable differentiation strategies used by the National Football League to compete with the United States Football League are described in The Environmental Challenge.

The Miles and Snow Typology

Miles and Snow suggest that business-level strategies fall into four categories: *prospector, defender, analyzer,* and *reactor.*

A second classification of strategic options available to organizations was developed by Raymond Miles and Charles Snow.[27] These authors suggested that business-level strategies generally fall into one of four categories: prospector, defender, analyzer, and reactor. Table 7.4 summarizes each of these strategies.

An organization that follows a **prospector strategy** is a highly innovative firm that is constantly seeking out new markets and new opportunities and is oriented toward growth and risk taking. 3M is an excellent example of a firm that uses prospector strategies. Over the years, it has prided itself

Figure 7.3

An Organization That Implements More Than One Generic Strategy May Get Stuck in the Middle

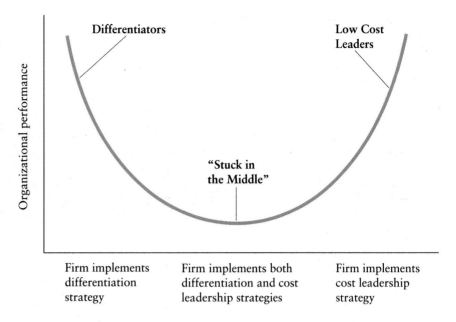

Firm implements differentiation strategy

Firm implements both differentiation and cost leadership strategies

Firm implements cost leadership strategy

on being one of the most innovative major corporations in the world. Employees at 3M are constantly encouraged to develop new products and ideas in a creative and entrepreneurial way. This focus on innovation has led 3M to develop a wide range of new products and markets, including invisible tape and antistain fabric treatments.[28] Another example of an organization following a prospector strategy is Piccone Apparel, a swimwear manufacturer described in The Entrepreneurial Challenge.

Rather than seeking new growth opportunities and innovation, an organization that follows a **defender strategy** concentrates on protecting its current markets, maintaining stable growth, and serving current customers. BIC Corporation uses defender strategies, despite its history as an innovative firm (the original BIC "crystal" and the BIC "biro" pen were significant innovations in the writing instruments industry). Since the late 1970s, with the maturity of the market for writing instruments, BIC has adopted a less aggressive, less entrepreneurial style of management and has chosen to defend its substantial market share in the industry. It has done this by emphasizing efficient manufacturing and customer satisfaction.[29]

An organization that follows an **analyzer strategy** both maintains market share and seeks to be innovative, although usually not as innovative as an organization that uses a prospector strategy. Most large companies fall into this third category, because they want both to protect their base of operations and to create new market opportunities. International Business Machines (IBM), a manufacturer of mainframe computers, uses analyzer strategies. Thousands of customers have purchased IBM computers over the last several decades. It is in IBM's interest to keep these customers satisfied and to introduce new products and services that update their computer facilities. Whenever IBM introduces a new computer system, for

THE ENVIRONMENTAL CHALLENGE

The NFL vs. the USFL

The United States Football League (USFL) began operating in 1983. Originally the league was designed to run its games during the spring season and to consist of teams that offered only restricted salary scales to players. Before long, however, the USFL switched to a fall schedule and began competing head-to-head with the National Football League (NFL). Competition for the best players drove salaries higher and higher, until one player, Steve Young, was offered a contract worth over $40 million by the Los Angeles Express, a USFL team.

Increased competition from the USFL was hurting the more established NFL, so NFL team owners gathered together to develop a response. They hired Michael Porter, a professor at Harvard Business School, to help them formulate a strategy to beat back the USFL challenge. The two-day strategy formulation session was as hard-hitting as an NFL linebacker. NFL team owners talked about how they could "destroy" the USFL, "wipe out" the upstart league, and in other ways prevent this competitive entry.

In response to this NFL strategizing session, the USFL sued, charging the NFL with attempting to monopolize the game of professional football. A long and complicated jury trial ensued, during which the NFL was found guilty of attempting to unfairly exclude the USFL from this marketplace. The jury determined that the extent of the damages caused by the NFL to the USFL was $1. Because the NFL was found guilty under antimonopoly laws, the total fine was three times the amount of damages, or $3.

Although the NFL was fortunate to have to pay only a $3 fine, this story illustrates the point that not all strategies that an organization can implement are legal. Strategies designed to maintain monopolies, fix prices, or reduce competition can lead to substantial fines and even jail terms. Obviously, organizations formulating their strategies must obtain competent legal advice to ensure that they are not subject to legal liability.

REFERENCES: Vance H. Fried and Benjamin M. Oviatt, "Michael Porter's Missing Chapter: The Rise of Antitrust Violations," *The Academy of Management Executive,* February 1989, pp. 49–50; W. O. Johnson, "Can the USFL Cut the Mustard?" *Sports Illustrated,* January 16, 1984, pp. 76+; W. Nack, "Give the First Round to the USFL," *Sports Illustrated,* July 7, 1986, pp. 22–24; E. Bowen, "Sacked," *Time,* August 11, 1986, pp. 12–13.

example, it develops procedures that help its customers move from the older system to the new system. In this way IBM maintains its customer base. However, IBM also tries to create new markets. Its line of personal computers represents an effort to expand beyond its traditional product base of mainframe computers. IBM also has invested in biotechnology, superconductivity technology, and other projects that are very innovative.[30]

According to Miles and Snow, an organization that follows a **reactor strategy** has no consistent strategic approach; it drifts with environmental events, reacting to but failing to anticipate or influence those events. Not surprisingly, these organizations usually do not perform as well as organizations that implement prospector, defender, or analyzer strategies. Most organizations would probably deny using reactor strategies. However, International Harvester (IH) during the 1960s and 1970s followed this approach. At a time when IH's market for trucks, construction equipment, and agricultural equipment was booming, IH failed to invest in research and development, in improvements in manufacturing, or in improvements in distribution. By the time a recession cut demand for its products, it was

Table 7.4

The Miles and Snow Typology

Strategy Type	Definition	Examples
Prospector	Is innovative and growth oriented, searches for new markets and new growth opportunities, encourages risk taking	3M
Defender	Protects current markets, maintains stable growth, serves current customers	BIC
Analyzer	Maintains current markets and current customer satisfaction with moderate emphasis on innovation	IBM
Reactor	No clear strategy, reacts to changes in the environment, drifts with events	International Harvester in the 1960s and 1970s, Joseph Schlitz Brewing Co., W. T. Grant

too late for IH to respond, and the company lost millions of dollars. Indeed, at one time IH had the largest annual loss of any company in the history of the world. In the last ten years, IH has had to sell off virtually all of its businesses, except its truck-manufacturing business. IH has moved from being a dominant firm in trucking, agriculture, and construction to a medium-sized truck manufacturer because it failed to anticipate changes in its environment.[31]

Strategies Based on the Product Life Cycle

The *product life cycle* is a model that portrays how sales volume for products changes over the life of products. The four stages of the model are *introduction, growth, maturity,* and *decline.*

The **product life cycle** is a model that portrays how sales volume for products changes over the life of products. An understanding of the four stages in the product life cycle helps managers recognize that strategies need to evolve over time. As Figure 7.4 shows, the cycle begins when a new product or technology is introduced by the first organization to manufacture and sell it. In the **introduction stage**, demand may be very high and sometimes outpaces the organization's ability to supply the product. At this stage, managers need to focus their efforts on "getting product out the door" without sacrificing quality. Managing growth by hiring new employees and managing inventories and cash flow are also significant concerns during this stage of the life cycle.

During the **growth stage**, more firms begin producing the product, and sales continue to grow. Key management issues include ensuring quality

Figure 7.4

Stages in the Product Life Cycle

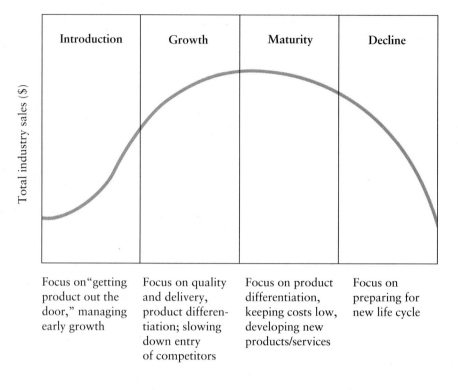

and delivery, plus beginning to differentiate an organization's product from competitors' products. Entry into the industry during the growth stage may threaten an organization's competitive advantages; thus strategies to slow the entry of competitors are important.

After a period of growth, products enter a third phase. During this **mature stage**, overall demand growth for a product begins to slow down and the number of new firms producing the product begins to decline. The number of established firms producing the product may also begin to decline. This period of maturity is key if an organization is going to survive in the long run. Product differentiation concerns are still important during this stage. However, keeping costs low and beginning the search for new products or services are also important strategic considerations.

In the **decline stage**, demand for the product or technology decreases, the number of organizations producing the product drops, and total sales drop. The decline in demand is often due to the fact that all those who might have an interest in purchasing a particular product have already done so. Organizations that failed to anticipate the decline stage in earlier stages of the life cycle may go out of business. Those that differentiated their product, kept their costs low, or developed new products or services may do well during this stage.

Virtually every product has a life cycle. Sometimes the cycle revolves quickly. In the 1970s, for example, "pet rocks" moved through the product life cycle in less than two months. At first many people were intrigued by

THE ENTREPRENEURIAL CHALLENGE

Neoprene Rubber as a Fashion Statement

A trend toward skimpy bathing suits may appeal to some consumers, but for active, sports-minded women these suits are just not practical. Enter Robin Piccone, a designer from southern California looking to combine fashion and function in a swimsuit line. Her solution? Neoprene rubber.

When asked about which fabrics and materials they are most likely to consider for women's swimsuits, most designers don't point to neoprene rubber. This material is made in sheets about one-quarter inch thick and has traditionally been used in the manufacture of wet suits. Historically, neoprene rubber came in only one color — black — and had limited fashion appeal.

However, Robin Piccone discovered that it was possible to cut neoprene rubber in a variety of ways and to color it in a range of vivid hues — from Day-Glo orange to tangerine to lemon yellow. Armed with her designing skills, honed at Los Angeles Trade Technical College and during stints as an apprentice designer at Cole of California and Bobbie Brooks in New York, Piccone produced a line of neoprene swimsuits.

Rather than run this business on her own, Piccone entered into a partnership with Body Glove International, a leading manufacturer of wet suits. By putting the Body Glove name on each of her suits, Piccone had instant credibility among sports-minded women. In return, Body Glove receives royalties of between 7 and 12 percent on each of the suits Piccone sells.

And she sells a lot of suits. By 1990, Piccone Apparel had sales of almost $12 million, with suits ranging in price from $48 to $120. Rather than take her success in neoprene bathing suits for granted and expand into other sportswear markets, Piccone has renewed focus on her unusual product — a line of swimming suits that seem well designed for many women in the 1990s.

REFERENCES: Samuel Greengard, "Queen of Neoprene," *American Way,* July 15, 1990, pp. 20–24; Susan Smarr, "Swimwear: Marketers Make the Biggest Waves," *Bobbin,* February 1990, pp. 40–50; Susan Smarr, "Retail Now: Remembering the Forgotten Women," *Bobbin,* February 1990, pp. 24, 26.

a rock in a box with printed instructions for care and feeding, but this fad soon faded. In the early 1980s demand for Coleco's Cabbage Patch dolls increased so dramatically that near riots occurred at toy stores that ran out of stock. Now, Cabbage Patch dolls can be purchased for one dollar at most garage sales. Even high-technology products have a life cycle. Each time a new integrated circuit is developed, demand rises suddenly, followed by growth, maturity, and finally decline as newer integrated circuits take its place.[32]

Examining Corporate-Level Strategies

Most large organizations are engaged in several businesses, industries, and markets. An organization such as General Electric operates hundreds of different businesses, making and selling products as diverse as jet engines, nuclear power plants, and light bulbs. Even organizations that sell only one product may operate in several distinct markets. McDonald's sells only fast food, but it occupies markets as diverse as the United States, western Europe, the Soviet Union, Japan, and South Korea.

Diversification refers to the number of different businesses that an organization is engaged in and the extent to which these businesses are related to one another.

Decisions about which businesses, industries, and markets an organization will enter, and how to manage these different businesses, are based on an organization's corporate strategy. Research suggests that the most important strategic issue at the corporate level concerns the extent and nature of organizational diversification. **Diversification** is a term that describes the number of different businesses that an organization is engaged in and the extent to which these businesses are related to one another. The following sections discuss three types of diversification strategies: single-product strategy, related diversification, and unrelated diversification.[33]

Single-Product Strategy

An organization that pursues a *single-product strategy* manufactures just one product or service and sells it in a single geographic market.

An organization that pursues a **single-product strategy** manufactures just one product or service and sells it in a single geographic market. The WD-40 Company, for example, manufactures only a single product, WD-40 spray lubricant, and sells it in just one market, North America. WD-40 has considered broadening its market to Europe and Asia, but it continues to center all manufacturing, sales, and marketing efforts on one product.[34]

The single-product strategy has one enormous strength and one enormous weakness. By concentrating its efforts so completely on one product and market, an organization is likely to be very successful in manufacturing and marketing the product. Because it has staked its survival on a single product, the organization works very hard to make sure the product is a success. It may turn out, though, that the firm's product is simply not accepted by the marketplace. If so, the organization will likely go out of business. This happened to slide-rule manufacturers when electronic calculators became widely available, to companies that manufactured only black and white televisions when color televisions became available, and to companies that manufactured only mechanical watches when electronic watches became available.[35]

Related Diversification

An organization that pursues a strategy of *related diversification* operates in several businesses that are somehow linked with one another.

Given the disadvantage of the single-product strategy, most organizations operate in several different businesses, industries, or markets. If the businesses are somehow linked, that organization is implementing a strategy of **related diversification**. Approximately 490 of the 500 largest organizations in the United States implement related diversification.

Bases of Relatedness   Organizations link their different businesses, industries, or markets in different ways. Table 7.5 gives some typical bases of relatedness. In organizations such as Philips, a European consumer electronics company, a similar type of electronics technology underlies all the businesses. A common technology in aircraft design links Boeing's commercial and military aircraft divisions, and a common computer design technology links Digital's various computer products and peripherals.

Organizations implementing a related diversification strategy engage in a set of businesses that are linked by some common attribute. Dairy Crest Limited, Britain's largest dairy processor and one of Europe's ten largest dairy companies, is an example of such an organization. Its two hundred work sites include creameries, regional bottling dairies, and distribution depots for both commercial and household delivery.

Organizations such as Philip Morris, RJR Nabisco, and Procter & Gamble operate multiple businesses related by a common distribution network (grocery stores) and common marketing skills (advertising). Disney and Universal rely on strong brand names and reputations to link their diverse businesses, which include movie studios and theme parks. Pharmaceutical firms such as Merck sell numerous products to a single set of customers: hospitals, doctors, patients, and drugstores. Similarly, AMF-Head sells snow skis, tennis rackets, and sportswear to a single set of active, athletic customers.[36]

Table 7.5

Bases of Relatedness in Implementing Related Diversification

Basis of Relatedness	Examples
Similar technology	Philips, Boeing, Westinghouse, Digital
Common distribution and marketing skills	RJR Nabisco, Philip Morris, Procter & Gamble
Common brand name and reputation	Disney, Universal
Common customers	Merck, IBM, AMF-Head

Advantages of Related Diversification   However an organization links its businesses, pursuing a strategy of related diversification has three primary advantages. First, it reduces an organization's dependence on any one of its business activities and thus reduces economic risk. Even if one or two of an organization's businesses lose a great deal of money, the organization as a whole may still survive because the healthy businesses will generate enough cash to support the others.[37]

Second, by managing several businesses at the same time, an organization can reduce the overhead costs associated with managing any one business. In other words, if the normal administrative costs required to operate any business, such as legal services, personnel services, and accounting, can be spread over a large number of businesses, then the overhead costs *per business* will be lower than they would be if each business had to absorb all costs itself. Thus the administrative and other overhead costs of businesses in a related diversified firm are usually lower than those of similar businesses that are not part of a larger corporation.[38]

Third, related diversification allows an organization to exploit its strengths and capabilities in more than one business. When organizations do this successfully, they capitalize on synergies, which are complementary effects that exist among their businesses. **Synergy** exists among a set of businesses when the businesses' economic value together is greater than their economic value separately. Disney has been very skilled at creating and exploiting synergies. Every time Disney produces a successful animated motion picture, it incorporates the lead characters in the film into its theme parks. Children and adults who became familiar with Snow White, Peter Pan, and Roger Rabbit in the movies can remember that pleasant experience by seeing Snow White, Peter Pan, and Roger Rabbit walking around Disneyland, Disney World, Tokyo Disneyland, and Euro Disneyland. They can even take those memories home with them in the form of Snow White dresses, Peter Pan magic wands, and Roger Rabbit shirts. Disney's recent attempt to acquire Jim Henson's Muppets is another effort to exploit synergies.[39]

Because organizations that implement a strategy of related diversification take on less risk, have lower costs, and are able to more widely exploit their unique strengths and capabilities, they tend, on average, to outperform firms that have a single product.

Unrelated Diversification

An organization that pursues a strategy of *unrelated diversification* operates in several businesses that are either unintentionally related or not related at all.

Organizations that implement a strategy of **unrelated diversification** operate multiple businesses that are either unintentionally related or not related at all. Unrelated diversification was a very popular strategy in the 1960s and early 1970s. During this time, organizations such as International Telephone and Telegraph (ITT) and Transamerica grew very large and very diversified by acquiring literally hundreds of other organizations and then running these numerous businesses as completely independent entities. Even if there are important potential synergies between their different businesses, organizations implementing a strategy of unrelated diversification do not attempt to exploit them.[40]

In principle, unrelated diversification has two advantages. First, an organization that implements this strategy will have very stable economic performance over time. If, during any given time period, one or two businesses in this organization are in a cycle of decline, one or two will probably be in a cycle of growth. This is the case because the businesses in question are not linked in any fundamental way.

Unrelated diversification is also thought to have resource allocation advantages. Every year, when a corporation allocates capital, people, and other resources among its various businesses, it must evaluate information about the future of those businesses so that it can place its resources where they have the highest return potential. Given that it owns the businesses in question and thus has full access to information about the future of those businesses, an organization implementing unrelated diversification should be able to allocate capital to maximize corporate performance.

Despite these theoretical advantages, research suggests that unrelated diversification usually does not lead to high performance, for two reasons. First, corporate managers in such an organization usually do not know enough about the unrelated businesses to provide helpful strategic guidance or to allocate capital appropriately. In fact, if their guidance is forthcoming at all, it more often than not actually detracts from each business's ability to compete in its marketplace. To make strategic decisions about investments in areas such as research and development, management training, and advertising, managers must have complete and subtle understanding of a business and its environment. Since corporate managers often have difficulty fully evaluating the economic importance of investments for all the businesses under their wing, they tend to concentrate only on a business's current performance. This narrow attention at the expense of broader planning eventually hobbles the entire organization. Many of International Harvester's problems stem from an emphasis on current performance at the expense of investments for the future success of the firm.

Second, because organizations that implement unrelated diversification fail to exploit important synergies, they are at a competitive disadvantage compared to organizations that use related diversification. Disney theme parks would be at a disadvantage if their managers had to spend additional resources to develop original characters, rather than employing characters already developed by Disney filmmakers.

For these reasons, almost all organizations have abandoned unrelated diversification as a corporate-level strategy. ITT and Transamerica have sold off numerous businesses and now concentrate on a core set of related businesses and markets. Large corporations that have not concentrated on a core set of businesses eventually have been acquired by other companies and then broken up. Research suggests that these organizations are actually worth more when broken up into smaller pieces than they are when joined.[41]

THE GLOBAL CHALLENGE

Related Diversification in Japan

Mitsubishi Chemical, Mitsubishi Electric, Mitsubishi Gas, Mitsubishi Heavy Industries, Mitsubishi Metal, Mitsubishi Cement, Mitsubishi Oil — the list of businesses bearing the name Mitsubishi seems endless. But Mitsubishi is not the only name used in large numbers in Japanese organizations. There is Mitsui Construction, Mitsui Mining, Mitsui Petrochemicals, Mitsui Real Estate, Mitsui Sugar, and so forth, as well as Sumitomo Chemical, Sumitomo Coal, Sumitomo Construction, Sumitomo Light Metals, Sumitomo Precision Products, and on and on.

At first glance, all these organizations with similar names appear to overcome the limitations of unrelated diversification. And they would, if one large corporation owned all these diverse businesses. However, looks can be deceiving. Although all these organizations share similar names, they are, in fact, independent businesses that work in a close cooperative network. To understand the part these networks play in the Japanese economy, it is necessary to recall the unique history of Japan.

Before the Second World War, Japan's economy was dominated by less than a dozen large, integrated organizations called *zaibatsu* (pronounced "zi-bot-soo"). These organizations were definitely implementing an unrelated diversification strategy, but they were small enough to avoid many of the liabilities of this strategic choice. Moreover, they were able to obtain many of the benefits of vertically integrated production and sales.

After the war, the Allied military government, headed by General Douglas MacArthur, determined that the *zaibatsu* were anticompetitive and inconsistent with democracy in Japan. These organizations were broken up and sold to a variety of individual and institutional investors. Other businesses in the former *zaibatsu* could purchase small ownership positions in these businesses, and they were allowed to keep their old name — Mitsubishi, Mitsui, Sumitomo, and so forth. Thus an affiliation continued among these different businesses based on a common history, a common name, and overlapping ownership, but each business was managed as a separate economic entity. This new set of affiliated organizations came to be known as *keiretsu* (pronounced "kay-ret-soo").

MacArthur's decision to disband the *zaibatsu* and replace them with the *keiretsu* forced Japanese organizations to abandon a strategy of unrelated diversification and adopt related diversification. Given the numerous advantages of the latter, MacArthur's action may have unwittingly helped propel Japanese business into the forefront of the international economic scene.

REFERENCES: Daiwa Securities Research Institute, *Analyst's Guide, 1989* (Tokyo: Daiwa Securities, 1989); William G. Ouchi, *The M-Form Society* (Reading, Mass.: Addison-Wesley, 1984); Robert Neff, Paul Magnusson, and William Holstein, "Rethinking Japan," *Business Week,* August 7, 1989, pp. 44–52.

One apparent exception to this trend is organizations in Japan. From the outside these organizations appear to be implementing unrelated diversification. However, as is explained in The Global Challenge, appearances can be deceiving.

Learning Summary

Strategy is a comprehensive plan for accomplishing the organization's mission. Strategic management is a comprehensive and ongoing process aimed at formulating and implementing effective strategies. Effective strategies address three organizational issues: distinctive competence, scope, and resource deployment. Strategy formulation is the set of processes involved in creating or determining the strategies of an organization. Strategy implementation, the process of executing strategies, is discussed in Chapter 8.

SWOT analysis considers an organization's strengths, weaknesses, opportunities, and threats. Using SWOT analysis, an organization chooses strategies that support its mission and (1) exploit its opportunities and strengths, (2) neutralize its threats, and (3) avoid its weaknesses.

Organizational strengths are skills and capabilities that enable an organization to conceive of and implement its strategies. Common strengths are strengths held by large numbers of competing organizations. Distinctive competencies are strengths held by just a few competing organizations. Exploiting distinctive competencies can lead to competitive advantages and above-normal economic performance. Organizational weaknesses are skills and capabilities that do not enable an organization to choose and implement strategies that support its mission.

Organizational opportunities are events or phenomena in an organization's environment that, if exploited, may generate above-normal economic performance. Organizational threats are events or phenomena in an organization's environment that make it difficult for an organization to create or maintain above-normal, or even normal, economic performance. The performance potential of an organization depends both on the industry environment and on the organization's ability to exploit its distinctive competencies.

A business-level strategy is the plan an organization uses to conduct business in a particular industry or market. According to Porter, organizations may pursue a product differentiation strategy, an overall cost leadership strategy, or a focus strategy at the business level. According to Miles and Snow, organizations may choose one of four business-level strategies: prospector, defender, analyzer, or reactor. Business-level strategies may also take into account the stages in the product life cycle.

A corporate-level strategy is the plan an organization uses to manage its operations across several businesses. A firm that does not diversify is implementing a single-product strategy. An organization pursues a strategy of related diversification when it operates a set of related businesses. Related diversification reduces the financial risk associated with any particular product, reduces the overhead costs of each business, and enables the organization to create and exploit synergy. An organization pursues a strategy of unrelated diversification when it operates a set of unrelated businesses. In practice, this strategy rarely generates superior economic performance.

Questions and Exercises

Review Questions

1. What is a "good" strategy according to SWOT analysis?
2. According to Porter, what are the attributes of an industry that has the potential to achieve above-normal economic performance?

3. What are the two main types of strategic alternatives available to an organization?
4. List and describe Porter's generic strategies and the Miles and Snow typology of strategies.
5. What is the difference between a single-product strategy, a related diversification strategy, and an unrelated diversification strategy?

Analysis Questions

1. Common strengths among firms cannot give one firm a competitive advantage. Does this mean that an organization should ignore its common strengths in choosing and implementing its strategies? Why or why not?
2. Suppose that an organization does not have any distinctive competencies. If the organization is able to acquire some distinctive competencies, how long are these strengths likely to remain distinctive competencies? Why?
3. Suppose that an organization moves from a single-product strategy to a strategy of related diversification. How might the organization use SWOT analysis to select attributes of its current business to serve as bases of relatedness among its newly acquired businesses?
4. Suppose that an organization is attempting to implement related diversification but is unable to create synergies. How is this organization likely to perform? Why?

Application Questions

1. Interview a manager and categorize the business- and corporate-level strategies of his or her organization according to Porter's generic strategies, the Miles and Snow typology, and extent of diversification.
2. Read the history of International Telephone and Telegraph, and describe how ITT's strategies evolved from unrelated diversification in the 1960s to related diversification in the 1990s.

Chapter Notes

1. John Meehan and John Friedman, "The Failed Vision: Jim Robinson's Big Plans for American Express Aren't Working," *Business Week,* March 19, 1990, pp. 108–113; "American Express and Its Broker, Shearson Lehman: Not Doing Nicely," *The Economist,* February 3, 1990, pp. 84, 86; and Anthony Bianco, "Do You Know Me? An Intimate Profile of Jim Robinson, CEO at American Express," *Business Week,* January 25, 1988, pp. 72–82.
2. See, for example, Michael Porter, *Competitive Strategy* (New York: Free Press, 1980), and Richard P. Rumelt, "How Much Does Industry Matter?" *Strategic Management Journal,* 1991, pp. 167–186.

3. For early discussions of strategic management, see Kenneth Andrews, *The Concept of Corporate Strategy*, rev. ed. (Homewood, Ill.: Dow Jones–Irwin, 1980); Igor Ansoff, *Corporate Strategy* (New York: McGraw-Hill, 1965); and E. P. Learned, C. R. Christensen, K. R. Andrews, and W. D. Guth, *Business Policy* (Homewood, Ill.: Irwin, 1969).

4. Stephen Phillips, "Is There No Limit to The Limited's Growth?" *Business Week,* November 6, 1989, pp. 192–199.

5. Joseph Weber, "Why Hershey Is Smacking Its Lips," *Business Week,* October 30, 1989, p. 140; Bill Saporito, "Uncovering Mars' Unknown Empire," *Fortune,* September 26, 1988, pp. 98–104; Catherine Bond, "Chocolate Wars: Sweet Stakes," *Marketing,* May 5, 1988, pp. 17, 20.

6. Harlan Byrne, "Raytheon Co.: In Diversifying Years Ago — 'We Did the Right Thing,'" *Barron's,* April 2, 1990, pp. 61–62.

7. Learned et al., *Business Policy.*

8. Andrew Tanzer, "We Do Not Take a Short Term View," *Forbes,* July 13, 1987, pp. 372–374; "Matsushita Electric Industrial Company," *Wall Street Journal,* June 29, 1988, pp. 18–19.

9. This discussion of competitive parity and normal economic performance refers back to the discussion of performance in Chapters 2 and 4. Recall that normal economic performance is a level of performance just large enough to enable an organization to pay all of its financial obligations. Firms earning this level of performance survive but do not prosper. See also Jack Hirshliefer, *Price Theory and Applications* (Englewood Cliffs, N.J.: Prentice-Hall, 1980), and Jay Barney, "Firm Resources and Sustained Competitive Advantage," *Journal of Management,* 1991, pp. 99–120.

10. Barney, "Firm Resources and Sustained Competitive Advantage"; Porter, *Competitive Strategy.*

11. "Great New Indy Jones Special Effects Created by Industrial Light and Magic," *Popular Mechanics,* July 1989, p. 18; T. G. Smith, "Reel Illusions," *Omni,* June 1987, pp. 70–79.

12. Jay Barney, "Strategic Factor Markets," *Management Science,* 1986, pp. 1231–1241.

13. Classic discussion of the impact of unique historical circumstances on firm strategies can be found in F. A. Hayek, "The Use of Knowledge in Society," *American Economic Review,* 1945, pp. 519–530, and Edith Penrose, *The Theory of the Growth of the Firm* (New York: Wiley, 1958). More recent discussions can be found in Barney, "Firm Resources and Sustained Competitive Advantage," and Ingmar Dierickx and Karel Cool, "Asset Stock Accumulation and Sustainability of Competitive Advantage," *Management Science,* 1989, pp. 1504–1511.

14. See Steve Lippman and Richard Rumelt, "Uncertain Imitability: An Analysis of Interfirm Differences in Efficiency Under Competition," *Bell Journal of Economics,* 1982, pp. 418–453; R. B. Mancke, "Causes of Interfirm Profitability Differences: A New Interpretation of the Evidence," *Quarterly Journal of Economics,* 1974, pp. 1–9; and Jay Barney, "Organizational Culture: Can It Be a Source of Sustained Competitive Advantage?" *Academy of Management Review,* 1986, pp. 656–665.

15. See Dierickx and Cool, "Asset Stock Accumulation and Sustainability of Competitive Advantage"; Barney, "Organizational Culture"; and Barney, "Firm Resources and Sustained Competitive Advantage."

16. This framework is presented in Barney, "Organizational Culture," and Barney, "Firm Resource and Sustained Competitive Advantage."

17. Andrea Rothman, "Sony Is Out to Be the World's One-Stop Shop for Entertainment," *Business Week,* March 25, 1991, pp. 64–74.
18. William Olcott, "Taking Care of America: 50 Years of Philanthropy," *Direct Marketing,* May 1988, pp. 98–102; Gwen Kinkead and Patricia Langan, "America's Best Run Charities," *Fortune,* November 9, 1987, pp. 145–150.
19. The psychological processes that make it difficult for managers to recognize their organization's weaknesses are described in Daniel Kahneman, Paul Slovic, and Amos Tversky, eds., *Judgment Under Uncertainty* (Cambridge, England: Cambridge University Press, 1982).
20. See Porter, *Competitive Strategy.*
21. Michael Porter, "Note on the Electronic Component Distribution Industry," *Cases in Competitive Strategy* (New York: Free Press, 1979), pp. 1–19.
22. Porter, *Competitive Strategy.*
23. C. Roland Christensen, Kenneth R. Andrews, Joseph L. Bower, Richard G. Hamermesh, and Michael Porter, "Crown Cork & Seal," *Business Policy: Text and Cases,* 6th ed. (Homewood, Ill.: Irwin, 1987), pp. 170–196.
24. For a discussion of this distinction, see Arthur A. Thompson and A. J. Strickland, *Strategic Management: Concepts and Cases,* 4th ed. (Plano, Tex.: Business Publications, 1987), and Charles Hill and Gareth Jones, *Strategic Management: An Integrated Approach,* 2nd ed. (Boston: Houghton Mifflin, 1992).
25. Porter, *Competitive Strategy.* Recent research on the Porter framework includes Aneel Karnani, "Generic Strategies: An Analytical Approach," *Strategic Management Journal,* 1984, pp. 367–380; R. T. Lenz and Jack L. Engledow, "Environmental Analysis: Applicability of Current Theory," *Strategic Management Journal,* 1986, pp. 329–346; Gregory Dess and Peter Davis, "Porter's Generic Strategies as Determinants of Strategic Group Membership and Organizational Performance," *Academy of Management Journal,* 1984, pp. 467–488; Lynn Phillips, Dae R. Chang, and Robert Buzzell, "Product Quality, Cost Position, and Business Performance: A Test of Some Key Hypotheses," *Journal of Marketing,* 1983, pp. 26–43; Peter Wright, "A Refinement of Porter's Strategies," *Strategic Management Journal,* 1987, pp. 93–101; and Theodore T. Herbert and Helen Deresky, "Generic Strategies: An Empirical Investigation of Typology Validity and Strategy Content," *Strategic Management Journal,* 1987, pp. 135–147.
26. Porter, *Competitive Strategy.*
27. Raymond E. Miles and Charles C. Snow, *Organizational Strategy, Structure, and Process* (New York: McGraw-Hill, 1978). This approach to strategic analysis and generic strategies has also been applied by numerous authors, including Edward Zajac and Stephen M. Shortell, "Changing Generic Strategies: Likelihood, Direction, and Performance Implications," *Strategic Management Journal,* 1989, pp. 413–430; Don Hambrick, "Some Tests of the Effectiveness and Functional Attributes of Miles & Snow's Strategic Types," *Academy of Management Journal,* 1983, pp. 5–26; and Charles Snow and Don Hambrick, "Measuring Organizational Strategies," *Academy of Management Review,* 1980, pp. 527–538.
28. See Tom Peters and Robert Waterman, *In Search of Excellence* (New York: Harper & Row, 1982), for a discussion of 3M.
29. C. Roland Christensen et al., "BIC Pen (A)," *Business Policy,* pp. 136–159.
30. Gene Bylinsky, "America's Hot Young Scientists," *Fortune,* October 8, 1990, pp. 56–69; Personal conversation with IBM's chief scientist, Fall 1984.
31. C. Roland Christensen et al., "International Harvester (A)," *Business Policy,* pp. 758–792.

32. Allison Cowan, "Ken Hakuta: Black Ink from a Rubber Octopus," *Business Week,* September 15, 1986, p. 138; Susan Benway, "Coleco: Out of the Cabbage Patch and into the Fire," *Business Week,* March 30, 1987, p. 54; Porter, "Note on the Electronic Parts Distribution Industry."

33. Much current work on diversification is founded on the seminal research of three authors: Alfred Chandler, *Strategy and Structure: Chapters in the History of the American Industrial Enterprise* (Cambridge, Mass.: MIT Press, 1962); Richard Rumelt, *Strategy, Structure, and Economic Performance* (Cambridge, Mass.: Division of Research, Graduate School of Business Administration, Harvard University, 1974); and Oliver Williamson, *Markets and Hierarchies* (New York: Free Press, 1975). Recent work in the area includes Allen Michel and Israel Shaked, "Does Business Diversification Affect Performance?" *Financial Management,* Winter 1984, pp. 18–25; Ron Bird and Mark Tippett, "Naive Diversification and Portfolio Risk," *Management Science,* 1986, pp. 244–251; Joel D. Goldhar and Mariann Jelinek, "Plan for Economies of Scope," *Harvard Business Review,* November–December 1983, pp. 141–148; and C. K. Prahalad and Richard Bettis, "The Dominant Logic: A New Linkage Between Diversity and Performance," *Strategic Management Journal,* 1986, pp. 485–501.

34. Williamson, *Markets and Hierarchies.*

35. See J. A. Schumpeter, *Capitalism, Socialism, and Democracy,* 3rd ed. (New York: Harper & Row, 1950).

36. See Rumelt, *Strategy, Structure, and Economic Performance,* and Prahalad and Bettis, "The Dominant Logic," for insightful discussions of the bases of relatedness.

37. See Chandler, *Strategy and Structure,* and Yakov Amihud and Baruch Lev, "Risk Reduction as a Managerial Motive for Conglomerate Mergers," *Bell Journal of Economics,* 1981, pp. 605–617.

38. Chandler, *Strategy and Structure;* Williamson, *Markets and Hierarchies.*

39. Prahalad and Bettis, "The Dominant Logic."

40. Williamson, *Markets and Hierarchies.*

41. See Jay Barney and William G. Ouchi, *Organizational Economics* (San Francisco: Jossey-Bass, 1986), for a discussion of the limitations of unrelated diversification. Some recent research suggests that unrelated diversification may be a viable alternative for a small set of firms that have a distinctive competence in buying and selling companies and in managing companies. These organizations (e.g., Hanson Trust) tend to operate in very mature industries (e.g., shoe manufacturing, shovel and garden tools). See Cynthia Montgomery and Birger Wernerfelt, "Diversification, Ricardian Rents, and Tobin's q," *Rand Journal of Economics,* 1988, pp. 623–632, for a discussion of these unusual firms.

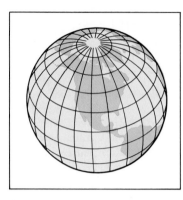

CASE 7.1

Anheuser-Busch Switches Strategies and Still Wins

As any American with a television knows, Anheuser-Busch makes beer. In fact, it makes more beer than anyone else in the world, more than its two largest rivals combined, twice as much as it made a decade ago. And it sells this huge amount of beer to a society in which per capita beer consumption has been steadily dropping for years. Anheuser-Busch got where it is today by using classic marketing strategies, but recently, when the competition changed, Anheuser-Busch changed with it, proving that it knows more than one way to sell beer.

Today's young beer drinkers may not realize it, but beer companies didn't always sponsor sporting events and fill TV screens with scantily clad young women and with men who like gusto. Although Anheuser-Busch is clearly the king of such advertising now, spending close to half a billion dollars a year on it, it did not invent it. When Philip Morris bought Miller Brewing Company in 1971, it brought to beer the advertising style that had sold billions of cigarettes. The company created "Miller Time," the time when America's traditional heavy beer drinkers, blue-collar men, get off work and head for a cold beer.

Anheuser-Busch was slow to respond. In fact, it might have lost the number-one spot to Miller if August Busch III, then 37, hadn't taken over the business from his father in 1975 and begun using Miller's tactics. Busch, the great-grandson of the man who founded the company in 1864, is still personally involved in Anheuser-Busch's daily business, tasting samples from each of the company's eleven breweries every evening and making the final decisions on many of Anheuser-Busch's now-famous ad campaigns. Despite opposition from other Anheuser-Busch executives, he chose "This Bud's for you" from a long list of new slogans, and it became one of the most successful advertising lines ever.

More importantly, he has played a major role in the company's highly successful target marketing. Anheuser-Busch's ads and sponsorship of events are aimed at very specific consumers. They saluted waiters and waitresses with the line "This Bud's for everyone that serves them up cold," and they aimed for armed forces personnel and other patriots by thanking "all the men and women in uniform who proudly serve this great country." Anheuser-Busch runs ads aimed at Californians, immigrants, computer lovers, and auto-racing buffs. It divides the United States into 210 geographical markets, funneling most of its money into the 33 areas where three-quarters of its beer is drunk. Before national brands like Budweiser forced small regional brands out of business, many towns had their own brands that locals drank with fierce loyalty. Now Anheuser-Busch hopes beer drinkers will view Budweiser with the same sense of identity and loyalty.

Anheuser-Busch knows how to create a lasting image for its product through manipulating familiar scenes and characters. August Busch insists that all Busch beer advertisements include real cowboys, a black stallion, a stream, and the "head for the mountains" theme. Apparently consistency, or repetition, works. The same may be true of Anheuser-Busch's relationship with sports: many avid television sports watchers must know Anheuser-Busch's ads by heart. Anheuser-Busch spends about 70 percent of its advertising budget on sports programs and has exclusive advertising deals with almost all major league baseball teams, three-quarters of the NFL teams, and three hundred college sports teams. It sponsors everything from triathlons to softball teams to bowling matches to rodeos, making sure that beer drinking has an active, young, outdoorsy image without a whiff of the lifetime of alcoholic despair that critics contend such sponsorship and ads encourage young drinkers to begin.

Despite its impressive success, its 40-plus percent domination of the American beer market, and the obvious effectiveness of its strategy, Anheuser-Busch wasn't afraid to change that strategy in 1989 when its competitors began significantly discounting their products. Anheuser-Busch could have stayed above the fray, but it recognized the importance of market share in a maturing industry, and it saw its sales slow as other companies discounted their products. Every beer company and investor knows the stories of Schlitz and Pabst, formerly large-selling brands that tried to become inexpensive and wound up with reputations for just being cheap. So the day after Anheuser-Busch announced that it was joining the price war, its stock lost $1.2 billion in value.

But Anheuser-Busch was in a strong position to win, even though it was playing a new game. Its operating profits per barrel of beer are three times as high as Miller's or Coors's so it does not suffer when discounting lowers profits but raises volume. Its wholesalers are twice as profitable as competitors' and can therefore more easily absorb their half of the discount. Anheuser-Busch didn't want a price war, but it was ready with a strategy to win one.

Discussion Questions

1. Which of Porter's generic strategies has been most important to Anheuser-Busch's growth?
2. What do you think Philip Morris learned about selling beer from selling cigarettes?
3. Do Anheuser-Busch's shifting strategies indicate a change in its product's life cycle?
4. What does a SWOT analysis of Anheuser-Busch reveal?

REFERENCES: James P. Miller, "Anheuser-Busch, Slugging It Out, Plans to Cut Prices," *Wall Street Journal*, October 26, 1989, pp. B1, B6; Patricia Sellers, "Busch Fights to Have It All," *Fortune*, January 15, 1990, pp. 81–88; Patricia Sellers, "How Busch Wins in a Doggy Market," *Fortune*, June 22, 1987, pp. 99–111.

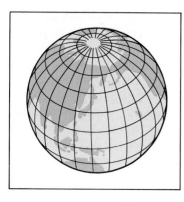

CASE 7.2

Nissan's New Strategies

Back in the 1970s, cars that Americans knew as Datsuns earned a reputation similar to Toyota's—rugged and practical though not necessarily stylish. Then in 1982, Datsun disappeared and a new Japanese name, Nissan, began showing up on cars that looked like Datsuns. Although the inevitable identity confusion wasn't the only problem that the Japanese automaker faced, it became symbolic of a mid-1980s slump for the company that is number two in its native country but seemed to be losing ground to everyone in the United States. Starting in 1986, Nissan set out to reverse the trend with a fistful of new strategies covering every aspect of its business from company culture to design to advertising.

Cultural changes had to come first, for Nissan's rigid corporate rules had a lot to do with the company's tendency to produce boxy cars that didn't capture the imagination of the American buying public. Nissan had dress codes, prohibitions against employees' driving competitors' cars, and name tags that included each employee's date of hire. Seniority was everything: the most senior interior designer got to work on the dashboard; new hires might be given one instrument to play with. In meetings, young and enthusiastic employees had to wait until everyone with more seniority had spoken.

In December 1986, as Nissan management prepared to announce that the company had become the first Japanese automaker to post an operating loss since Japan's postwar recovery, top executives led the way in admitting that the company had problems and needed radical change. They eliminated the seniority systems, transferred five thousand middle managers, opened the first co-ed dorm in Japanese corporate history, and began sending employees out in groups to observe competitors and popular haunts in Tokyo, trying to get new ideas.

These changes in culture and the unchaining of young designers and engineers led to a spate of new ideas and products. Nissan began creating new car lines and improving the styling and engineering on others. It revamped its Maxima, making it sleeker and more powerful and winning "most trouble-free car in America" awards in the process. It also updated its sporty 240SX and 300ZX cars. All three easily outsold their predecessors and competed well in their classes, but they did relatively little for Nissan's overall market share, since all three—and especially the sports models—are specialty cars, appealing only to a small slice of car buyers.

Borrowing a strategy from Honda and Toyota, Nissan developed a new luxury car line that is largely dissociated from the parent company. Nissan's Infiniti is the biggest, most powerful, most expensive Japanese car ever sold in the United States; and to establish it, Nissan began running ads in the United States eight months before the cars were available. The unusual ads seldom showed a car at all but focused on trees and cows and fences, creating an image and an atmosphere and generating a lot of attention, though only some of it was positive. Dealers weren't always pleased with the ads or with customers' initial responses to the cars, but the company said it was in no hurry to sell them. "Infiniti is Nissan's big business move for the 21st century,"* the head of Infiniti's development team says.

Nissan's greatest problem has been getting customers interested in its small efficient cars, still the sales leaders for most Japanese manufacturers. To prove that its Sentra compares favorably with Honda's Civil and Toyota's Corolla, Nissan ran ads showing the three (among others) driving around a track in a fuel-economy contest that the Sentra eventually won. And in a significant break with tradition, the ads emphasized that the Sentra is "American-built." Other Japanese automakers with plants in the United States have been reluctant to advertise where their cars are built because they worried about the perception that plants in Japan produce better cars, and thus customers would choose Japanese cars built in Japan over Japanese cars built in the United States. But Nissan wanted to attract customers in the Midwest, home of the auto plants and of many patriotic buyers.

Nissan's highest hopes rest on a new compact family car with radical new styling that the company hopes will catch on as did Ford's Taurus. The car, a replacement for the Stanza, was designed in California and engineered in Michigan and is built in Tennessee. It is indicative of another way in which Nissan is trying to differentiate itself: by designing, engineering, and building cars in each of its three major markets — Europe, North America, and Japan. Nissan is already ahead of its competitors in establishing such geographically independent units, and if these units are successful, they may pull the entire company back into the auto world's top rank even if all its other strategies fail.

Discussion Questions

1. Which of the terms defined in the chapter best apply to Nissan's various new strategies?
2. Given the changes that Nissan has made, what seems to be the company's perception of its own strengths and weaknesses?
3. Which automaker strategies most attract you as a car buyer or a potential car buyer?
4. What advantages does Nissan stand to gain by having self-contained design, engineering, and production units in each of its three major markets?

* Takashi Oka, quoted in Paul Ingrassia and Kathryn Graven, "Nissan Shakes Free of Hidebound Ways to Mount a Comeback," *Wall Street Journal*, November 1, 1989, p. A6.

REFERENCES: Paul Ingrassia and Kathryn Graven, "Nissan Shakes Free of Hidebound Ways to Mount a Comeback," *Wall Street Journal*, November 1, 1989, pp. A1, A6; Mark Landler, "No Joyride for Japan," *Business Week*, January 15, 1990, pp. 20–21; Jacqueline Mitchell, "Honda and Nissan Push American Roots of Some Models in a Major Tactical Shift," *Wall Street Journal*, February 26, 1991, pp. B1, B5; Alex Taylor III, "Nissan's Bold Bid for Market Share," *Fortune*, January 1, 1990, pp. 99–101.

8

Implementing Organizational Strategy

LEARNING OBJECTIVES

After studying this chapter, you should be able to:

1. Explain the differences between deliberate strategies and emergent strategies.

2. Describe how organizations integrate five organizational functions to implement Porter's list of generic business-level strategies.

3. Describe how organizations implement Miles and Snow's strategies.

4. Explain the three ways in which an organization may diversify, and discuss the major portfolio management techniques used to manage diversification.

I n 1981, Ted Turner's announced goal of creating a worldwide television news network that would provide information twenty-four hours a day in competition with the major commercial networks hardly seemed realistic. After all, the three major networks had all the resources, all the key personnel, and a rich history of quality news reporting. All Ted Turner had was a name — Cable News Network (CNN) — and a dream.

In its first decade, however, CNN grew from an upstart, fourth-rate news service to become one of the best-known and most powerful news organizations in the world. In every way, CNN rivaled — and sometimes surpassed — the news gathering and reporting of NBC, CBS, and ABC. And then war broke out in the Persian Gulf.

Of all the television news services, CNN was uniquely well positioned to cover the war in the Persian Gulf. CNN had built a fully international news-reporting capability. It had established its credibility throughout the world, and especially in the Middle East, as an objective news-reporting organization. CNN had also hired experienced war correspondents and stationed them in Baghdad. Most importantly, only CNN, among all the American television networks, had leased a direct line to Amman, Jordan, then to a satellite — thus by-passing Iraq's telephone system.

The results of this planning were spectacular, both in the quality of the news reported and in the size of the CNN audience. Few viewers will forget the pictures of the first bombing of Baghdad on January 17, 1991, as described by CNN correspondents Bernard Shaw, Peter Arnett, and others. Within minutes, it became clear that CNN was going to be able to deliver information about this war that the other networks could not. Both Secretary of Defense Richard Cheney and General Norman Schwarzkopf later said that the best information they had about the effectiveness of the bombing came from CNN, and many network affiliates disconnected their network news feeds in favor of feeds from CNN.

Once the Persian Gulf War ended, however, CNN faced some large questions. Would it be able to retain the viewers that it had gained during its war coverage? Could those viewers be convinced to turn to CNN throughout the day for news updates and, most importantly, in the evening as replacement for the news programs of major network competitors NBC, CBS, and ABC?[1]

Strategy implementation is the allocation of resources in an organization to support chosen strategies. To realize its strategy of being a world leader in oil and gas production, Chevron spends billions of dollars each year to develop new exploration and drilling technologies. These technologies are being employed by Chevron in the Gulf of Mexico, where it has started production in twelve new natural gas fields, some of them over 1,000 feet deep.

As CNN's competitors have discovered, what ultimately counts is not an organization's formulated strategy but its implemented strategy. When CNN began broadcasting over ten years ago, its announced goal of becoming a leader in the news business hardly seemed a real threat to the major television networks. However, by carefully implementing strategies to support that goal, CNN has been very successful. Events in Iraq further solidified CNN's position in the news industry.

This chapter discusses the important relationship between strategy formulation, strategy implementation, and organizational performance. It then examines implementation of some of the business-level strategies introduced in Chapter 7, including Porter's generic strategies and Miles and Snow's strategies. A discussion of techniques for implementing the corporate strategy of diversification ends the chapter.

The Nature of Strategy Implementation

Strategy implementation is the process of allocating resources to support chosen strategies.

Traditionally, the relationship between strategy formulation, strategy implementation, and organizational performance has been depicted as shown in Figure 8.1(a).[2] In this model, organizations begin strategy formulation by carefully specifying their mission, goals, and objectives, and then they engage in SWOT analysis to choose appropriate strategies. **Strategy implementation,** then, is the process of allocating resources to support the chosen strategies. Organizations that formulate and implement strategies better than competitors can expect to gain a competitive advantage. Organizations that follow the process shown in Figure 8.1(a) only as well as competitors will experience competitive parity, and organizations that do not complete this process as well as competitors will experience a competitive disadvantage.

Henry Mintzberg suggests that the traditional way of thinking about strategy implementation focuses only on deliberate strategies. A **deliberate strategy** is a plan of action that an organization chooses and implements in order to support its mission and goals.[3] Texas Instruments (TI) excels at formulating and implementing deliberate strategies. TI follows a planning process that assigns most senior managers two distinct responsibilities: an operational, short-term responsibility and a strategic, long-term responsibility. For example, one manager may be responsible for both increasing the efficiency of semiconductor manufacture over the next year (operational, short term) and investigating new materials for semiconductor manufacture in the twenty-first century (strategic, long term). TI's aim is to increase the probability that managers make short-term operational decisions while keeping in mind longer-term goals and objectives.[4]

Although the process that Figure 8.1(a) depicts is a common one, not all organizations choose and implement strategies in this manner. Mintzberg claims that some organizations begin implementing strategies before they clearly articulate mission, goals, or objectives and before they conduct formal SWOT analyses. In this case, as Figure 8.1(b) shows, strategy implementation actually precedes strategy formulation. Mintzberg calls strategies that unfold in this way emergent strategies. An **emergent strategy** is a pattern of action that develops over time in an organization in the absence of missions and goals, or despite missions and goals.[5] Implementation of emergent strategies involves the allocation of resources even though an organization has not explicitly chosen its strategies.

A *deliberate strategy* is a plan of action that an organization chooses and implements in order to support its mission and goals.

An *emergent strategy* is a pattern of action that develops over time in an organization in the absence of missions and goals, or despite missions and goals.

Figure 8.1

Relationship Between Strategy Formulation, Strategy Implementation, and Organizational Performance

Deliberate Strategies

Strategy formulation
- *Specify mission, goals, objectives*
- *Complete SWOT analysis*
- *Choose strategies*

→

Strategy implementation
- *Allocate resources to support strategies*

→

Organization performance
- *Competitive advantage*
- *Competitive parity*
- *Competitive disadvantage*

Emergent Strategies

Strategy implementation
- *Allocate resources to support strategies*

→

Strategy formulation
- *Specify mission, goals, objectives*
- *Complete SWOT analysis*
- *Choose strategies*

→

Organization performance
- *Competitive advantage*
- *Competitive parity*
- *Competitive disadvantage*

McDonnell Douglas is one organization that has successfully exploited emergent strategies. In its ongoing effort to design and build state-of-the-art military aircraft, McDonnell Douglas invested heavily over the years in computer and information-processing capabilities. In the mid-1960s, some of the firm's managers concluded that it might be possible to apply this expertise in computer and information technology to business settings other than the construction of military aircraft. Slowly the company started to sell its information-processing services to other firms. Over time, McDonnell Douglas became a leading information services company, with a competitive advantage in providing information-processing systems for hospitals. Once its information-processing business was well established in the marketplace, McDonnell Douglas transformed emergent strategy into deliberate strategy by organizing a special division devoted to information processing and by acquiring Tymeshare, another information-processing company.[6]

Similarly, 3M has at times implemented strategies in spite of existing missions, goals, or objectives. The invention of invisible tape, for instance, gave rise to emergent strategies. Entrepreneurial engineers working independently took the invention to their boss, who concluded that it did not have significant market potential because it was not part of an approved research and development plan. Managers higher up rejected the product for the same reason. Only when the product was evaluated at the highest levels in the organization was it accepted and made part of 3M's product mix. Of course, 3M's Scotch tape became a major success, despite the fact that it arose outside of the firm's established practices. 3M now counts on emergent strategies to help expand its numerous businesses.[7]

Most organizations make use of both deliberate and emergent strategies. Whether deliberate or emergent, however, a strategy has little effect on an organization's performance until it is implemented. We now examine several ways of implementing business- and corporate-level strategies.

Implementing Business-Level Strategies

The implementation of business-level strategies involves the integration of five organizational functions: *marketing, sales, accounting* and *finance, manufacturing,* and *organizational culture.*

To implement strategy at the business level, organizations must integrate the functions of several different organizational areas, as Figure 8.2 shows. The function of **marketing** is to promote the organization's products or services, and the overall public image of the organization, often through various types of advertising. The function of **sales** is to price the organization's products or services, directly contact customers, and make sales. **Accounting** and **finance** control the flow of money both within the organization and from outside sources to the organization, and **manufacturing** creates the organization's products or services. An **organizational culture** is a set of central values and beliefs by which the organization is managed and organized. Culture in organizations is a major topic in Chapter 11. The discussion in this chapter focuses only on how culture affects the implementation of business-level strategies.

Figure 8.2

Organizational Functions That
Support Business-Level Strategies

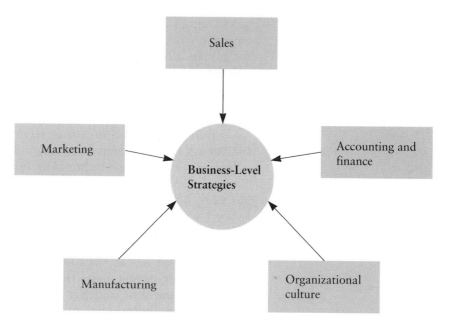

Once marketing, sales, accounting, finance, manufacturing, and organizational culture are working together to support strategy, an organization is well on the way to implementation. The next sections of the chapter examine how these organizational functions are integrated to implement Porter's generic strategies and Miles and Snow's strategies.

Implementing Porter's Generic Strategies

As you recall from Chapter 7, Porter described three strategic options available to firms at the business level: differentiation strategies, overall cost leadership strategies, and focus strategies.[8] In the following sections we describe key organizational functions necessary to implement these strategies.

Differentiation Strategy   An organization implements a differentiation strategy when it seeks to distinguish itself from competitors through the high quality of its products or services. Table 8.1 summarizes the main emphasis of each organizational function in support of a differentiation strategy.

To support differentiation, marketing must emphasize the high-quality, high-value image of the organization's products or services. Quality, product performance, perceived quality, and even snob appeal are much more important components of the marketing effort than is a concern for low price. Neiman-Marcus, a department store for well-heeled consumers, has excelled at using marketing to support its differentiation strategy. One does not go to Neiman-Marcus just to buy clothes or to shop for home elec-

Organizations implementing a differentiation strategy emphasize high quality and high value in marketing, avoid price competition in sales, avoid discouraging creativity in the finance and accounting functions, emphasize quality in manufacturing, and have a culture that emphasizes customer satisfaction.

Table 8.1

How Organizational Functions
Support a Differentiation Strategy

Function	Main Emphasis	Examples
Marketing	Emphasizes high-quality product performance, perceived value, snob appeal; avoids focusing on low prices	Neiman-Marcus, Chanel, Calvin Klein, Bloomingdale's
Sales	Avoids price competition; builds on personal relationships, quality reputation, and perceived image	Avon, General Motors, State Farm, Sears
Accounting and Finance	Controls without stifling creativity, innovation, and customer service	IBM, Honda, Sony, Procter & Gamble
Manufacturing	Focuses on quality, meeting customer needs, high inventory, customization	Rolex, Toyota
Organizational Culture	Encourages innovation, creativity, and customer responsiveness	Lands' End, Frito-Lay, Mitskoshi Department Store

tronics. Instead, a trip to Neiman-Marcus is advertised as a "total shopping experience." Customers who want to shop for $3,000 dog houses, $50,000 mink coats, and a $7,000 exercise machine—and perhaps be seen by all the "right" people in the process—should shop at Neiman-Marcus. Other organizations that have used their marketing function to implement a differentiation strategy include Chanel Inc., Calvin Klein, and Bloomingdale's.[9] How U.S. automobile firms have used new safety devices as a way to differentiate their product is described in The Environmental Challenge.

In sales, an organization implementing a differentiation strategy needs to avoid, wherever possible, competition solely on the basis of the product's price. Such **price competition** emphasizes a product's price over its other attributes, including its value for customers. Instead, the function of sales is to build on personal relationships between salesperson and customer, on the product's reputation for high quality, or on the public image of the organization created by its marketing staff. The sales pitch that supports differentiation strategy is more often, "Buy this product because of what it can do for you and because of our reputation," and less often, "Buy this product because it costs less."

Avon uses personal relationships to facilitate sales and implement a differentiation strategy. Rather than distributing its products through stores, Avon employs numerous salespeople to contact their friends and neighbors about purchasing Avon products. Sales meetings occur in the homes of potential customers and emphasize the convenience and quality of Avon

THE ENVIRONMENTAL CHALLENGE

Selling Safety in the Automobile Industry

Since the 1960s, consumer advocate Ralph Nader has been in constant conflict with the "big three" U.S. automakers — General Motors, Ford, and Chrysler. Since the publication of Nader's scathing criticism of the industry's safety record in *Unsafe at Any Speed,* Nader and the auto companies have clashed over mandatory anticrash bumpers, mandatory seat belts, mandatory air bags, and a host of other safety issues. Nader consistently argued that U.S. autos must be made safer, while the auto companies complained that mandated safety devices were expensive and that consumers did not want them.

Then came the nineties. Volvo began to run advertisements stressing the structural integrity of its cars in crashes, and automobile companies in the United States and abroad started selling safety. Mercedes-Benz emphasized auto-body design that protects occupants during a head-on collision. General Motors advertised the crash barriers welded in its doors. Chrysler publicized the installation of driver-side air bags in all of its U.S.-made cars.

Observers wondered why the car companies had changed their tune. Gary Trudeau parodied Chrysler's chairman, Lee Iaccoca, in a *Doonesbury* comic strip. Iaccoca is pictured at a press conference, describing the safety features of Chrysler products and ignoring reporters' questions about the firm's historical reluctance to invest in safety.

Most observers agree that U.S. automobile companies are now selling safety because safety sells cars. The reason safety sells cars now but did not thirty years ago has more to do with demographic shifts than with anything else. Millions of baby boomers are growing older and having their own children. Suddenly, the safety of those children is a high priority. Safer cars look like good alternatives to these consumers.

REFERENCES: James B. Treece, "Can Detroit Hold Its Lead in Safety?" *Business Week,* November 26, 1990, pp. 127, 130; Ray Hutton, "Underselling Safety Features," *Business,* September 1989, pp. 44–45; Ralph Nader, Clarence Ditlow, and Joyce Kinnard, *The Lemon Book* (Ottawa, Ill.: Caroline House, 1980).

---

products. Even organizations as diverse as General Motors, State Farm Insurance, and Sears try to build sales efforts on personal relationships with customers. GM does this by appealing to the positive experience of repeat customers, State Farm by emphasizing its convenient network of insurance agents, and Sears by recalling its long history of serving U.S. homeowners.[10]

The function of accounting and finance in an organization that is implementing a differentiation strategy is to control the flow of funds without discouraging the creativity needed to constantly develop new products and services to meet customer needs. If keeping track of and controlling the flow of money become more important than determining how money and resources are best spent to meet customer needs, then no organization, whether high-technology firm or fashion designer, will be able to implement a differentiation strategy effectively.

One organization that has been very successful at balancing the need to control the flow of money with the need to encourage creativity and responsiveness to customer needs in order to implement differentiation strategy is International Business Machines (IBM). IBM has developed an extensive current business in computers and information technology, but it also continues to invest in risky, cutting-edge research for the future. Some of this effort, including research on quantum physics and biophysics, may go on for decades before it results in profitable products. Still, IBM's ability to reconcile short-term profitability with longer-term research and development may have intermediate payoffs: in the process, two IBM scientists have received the Nobel Prize. This research puts IBM in the position to meet its customer needs for decades to come.[11] Other organizations that have been able to control their flow of funds efficiently, without reducing their ability to meet customer needs, include Honda Motor Company, Sony, and Procter & Gamble.

In manufacturing, an organization implementing a differentiation strategy must emphasize quality and meeting specific customer needs, rather than simply reducing costs. Manufacturing may sometimes have to keep inventory on hand so that customers will have access to products when they want them. Manufacturing also may have to engage in costly customization in order to meet customer needs.

Rolex uses a differentiation strategy. The organization's manufacturing function supports this strategy well. The body of a Rolex watch is not welded together from separate parts. Instead, it is stamped in one piece from a bar of solid gold, so it has no leaks, no seams, and no possible flaws. Customers have come to expect such high-quality manufacturing from Rolex. Toyota's manufacturing function also supports a differentiation strategy. In every Toyota manufacturing plant, workers who spot a recurring defect in cars pull on a signal rope. This action stops the manufacturing line until the problem can be isolated and resolved. Halting the line can reduce output and productivity, but it helps ensure that Toyota manufactures one of the highest-quality cars in the world.[12]

The organizational culture of a firm implementing a differentiation strategy, like the firm's other functions, must emphasize creativity, innovation, and response to customer needs. Lands' End's organizational culture puts the needs of customers ahead of all other considerations. This organization, which sells men's and women's leisure clothes through a catalog service, offers a complete guarantee on merchandise. Dissatisfied customers may return clothes for a full refund or exchange, no questions asked. Lands' End takes orders twenty-four hours a day and will ship most orders within twenty-four hours. Replacements for lost buttons or broken zippers are sent immediately. The priority given to customer needs is typical of an organization that is successfully implementing a differentiation strategy.[13] Other "customer-first" companies include Frito-Lay and the Mitskoshi Department Store in Tokyo.

Overall Cost Leadership Strategy   An organization implements an overall cost leadership strategy when it attempts to gain a competitive advantage by reducing its costs below the costs of competing firms. Table 8.2 summarizes the main emphasis of each organizational function in support of a cost leadership strategy.

To support cost leadership, marketing is likely to focus on simple product attributes and how these product attributes meet customer needs in a low-

Organizations implementing an overall cost leadership strategy emphasize simple products that meet customer needs in marketing, focus on a product's price and value in sales, emphasize cost control in the accounting and finance functions, produce large runs of highly standardized products in manufacturing, and have a culture that focuses on improving internal efficiency.

cost and effective manner. These organizations are very likely to engage in advertising. However, throughout this effort, emphasis is on the value that an organization's products provide for the price, rather than on the special features of the product or service. Advertising for BIC pens ("Writes first time, every time"), Timex watches ("Takes a licking and keeps on ticking"), and Wal-Mart ("Always the low price brands you trust always") has helped these firms implement cost leadership strategies.

The sales function is consistent with marketing: it emphasizes the product's price and value. In general, an organization that chooses a cost leadership strategy sells a mass-produced product to large numbers of customers and provides strong incentives to its salespeople to increase the volume of sales. High sales volume allows the organization to reduce its costs even further. The sales function at Charles Schwab Corporation (a discount stock brokerage), Emerson Electric (a consumer electronics manufacturer), and K mart (a discount department store) helps these organizations implement cost leadership strategies.

Proper emphasis in accounting and finance is also pivotal. Since the success of the organization depends on having costs lower than the competitors', great care must be taken to reduce costs wherever possible. Tight financial and accounting controls at Wal-Mart, Price Club, and MCI have helped these organizations implement cost leadership strategies.

To support this strategy, manufacturing typically emphasizes large runs of highly standardized products. Products are designed both to meet customer needs and to be easily manufactured. Manufacturing emphasizes increased volume of production to reduce the per unit costs of manufacturing. Organizations such as Toshiba (a Japanese semiconductor firm),

Table 8.2

How Organizational Functions Support a Cost Leadership Strategy

Function	Main Emphasis	Examples
Marketing	Features simple product attributes, meeting customer needs, value for price	BIC Pen, Timex, Wal-Mart
Sales	Focuses on price and value, standardized product, high volume of sales	Schwab, Emerson Electric, K mart
Accounting and Finance	Sets tight cost controls, strong budgets	Wal-Mart, Price Club, MCI
Manufacturing	Stresses large runs of standardized products, ease of manufacture in product design	Toshiba, GEO, Texas Instruments
Organizational Culture	Strong cultural orientation toward control	Wal-Mart, Texas Instruments, Fujitsu

GEO (a South Korean car manufacturer in partnership with General Motors), and Texas Instruments have used this type of manufacturing to implement cost leadership strategies.

The organizational culture of organizations implementing cost leadership strategies tends to focus on improving the efficiency of manufacturing, sales, and other business functions. Managers in these organizations are almost fanatical about keeping their costs low. Wal-Mart appeals to its customers to leave shopping carts in its parking lot with signs that read "Please — help us keep *your* costs low." Fujitsu Electronics, in its Tokyo manufacturing facilities, operates in plain, unpainted cinder-block and cement facilities in order to keep its costs as low as possible.

One organization that is attempting to implement a cost leadership strategy is Hypermart USA, a division of Wal-Mart. Hypermart's inability to do this successfully, and the financial implications of the effort, are discussed in The Entrepreneurial Challenge.

The organizational functions that support a differentiation focus strategy are the same as those that support a differentiation strategy; the organizational functions that support a cost leadership focus strategy are the same as those that support a cost leadership strategy.

Focus Strategy   An organization implements a focus strategy when it uses either a differentiation strategy or an overall cost leadership focus strategy in a particular market segment or geographic area. Thus the organizational functions that support a differentiation focus strategy are the same as those summarized in Table 8.1. The organizational functions that support a cost leadership focus strategy are the same as those summarized in Table 8.2.

Implementing Miles and Snow's Strategies

As you also recall from Chapter 7, Miles and Snow's typology identifies four business-level strategies: prospector, defender, analyzer, and reactor. The attributes of organizations that implement those strategies are summarized in Table 8.3.

Prospector firms encourage creativity and flexibility and are often decentralized.

Prospector Strategy   Organizations implementing a prospector strategy are innovative, seek new market opportunities, and take numerous risks. To implement this strategy, organizations need to encourage creativity and flexibility. Creativity helps an organization perceive, or even create, new opportunities in its environment; flexibility enables it to change quickly to take advantage of these new opportunities. Organizations often increase creativity and flexibility by adopting a decentralized organization structure. An organization is decentralized when major decision-making responsibility is delegated to middle- and lower-level managers. The conditions under which an organization should adopt a decentralized structure are discussed in detail in Chapters 10 and 11.

Johnson & Johnson links decentralization with a prospector strategy. Each of the firm's different businesses is organized into a separate unit, and the managers of these units hold full decision-making responsibility and authority. Often, these businesses develop new products for new markets. As the new products develop, and sales grow, Johnson & Johnson reorganizes so that each new product is managed in a separate unit.[14]

THE ENTREPRENEURIAL CHALLENGE

Hyping Hypermart: When Low Costs Aren't That Low

Hypermarkets are huge (over 220,000 square feet, or greater than five football fields) retail stores that carry everything from groceries to electronics to sporting goods and hardware — all at rock-bottom prices. The concept of a hypermarket was invented by the French firm Carrefour in 1960. This concept swept Europe, and by 1990 Carrefour owned some 600 hypermarkets in France alone, which account for 14 percent of that country's total retail trade.

Although popular in Europe, hypermarkets have never truly caught on in the United States. In this country, a broad range of discount department stores, including Wal-Mart, K mart, and Target, already exists. There are even numerous specialty discount stores. Stores such as Highland sell electronics at discount prices. Stores such as Marshall's do a brisk business in discount clothing. Thus the competition facing hypermarkets in the United States is much stronger than it is in Europe.

Nevertheless, Sam Walton, founder of the Wal-Mart empire, concluded in 1987 that the time had come for hypermarkets in America. Walton formed a company called Hypermart USA and built his first store outside Dallas in 1988. K mart soon followed with American Fare, a hypermarket joint venture with Bruno's, a southeastern grocery store chain. Carrefour has opened its first U.S. hypermarket, as have several other European firms.

Unfortunately, the results of these openings have not met expectations. Hypermarkets specialize in very low prices. Whereas a typical discount department store such as Wal-Mart may have a gross margin (as a percentage of sales) of 25 percent, hypermarket stores operate on a gross margin of only 15 percent. To be able to charge these low prices, hypermarkets must have very low costs, which they obtain by volume buying (purchasing large amounts of a supplier's product at a discount); restricting variety in the products they sell (only white paint, two types of refrigerators); keeping the design of stores simple; and limiting customer service.

These practices may keep a hypermarket's costs low and enable it to charge low prices, but they also make hypermarkets less attractive places to shop. Some consumers are willing to pay a little more money for a greater variety of products, for technical advice when choosing from among sophisticated items, and for better checkout service.

Overall, hypermarkets have been unable to attract the number of customers they need to be successful. The first hypermarket in the United States, owned by the French firm Euromarché, lost $9 million in its first three years of operation. Most of Walton's Hypermart USA stores are merely breaking even. Indeed, in early 1990, both Wal-Mart and K mart announced that they would not be building any more hypermarkets.

REFERENCES: Barbara Rudolf, "Here Come Malls Without Walls," *Time,* February 8, 1988, p. 50; "K mart in Hypermarket Venture," *Advertising Age,* June 27, 1988, p. 76; Kevin Kelly, "Wal-Mart Gets Lost in the Vegetable Aisle," *Business Week,* May 28, 1990, p. 48; Christy Fisher and Patricia Strand, "Wal-Mart Pulls Back on Hypermarket Plans," *Advertising Age,* February 19, 1990, p. 49.

Defender firms focus on lowering costs and improving the performance of current products.

Defender Strategy   Organizations implementing a defender strategy attempt to protect their market from new competitors. They tend to downplay creativity and innovation in bringing out new products or services and focus their efforts instead on lowering costs or improving the performance of current products.

Often a firm implementing a prospector strategy will switch to a defender strategy. This happens when the firm successfully creates a new market or business and then attempts to protect its market from competition. A good example is Mrs. Fields Inc. One of the first firms to introduce high-quality, high-priced cookies, Mrs. Fields sold its product in special cookie stores

Table 8.3

Attributes of Organizations That Implement Miles and Snow's Strategies

Strategy	Organizational Attributes	Examples
Prospector	Creative, innovative, flexible, decentralized, new-product emphasis	Johnson & Johnson
Defender	Efficient, low-cost emphasis on maintaining position of older products	Mrs. Fields Cookies
Analyzer	Simultaneous emphasis on improving operations in current business *and* encouraging creativity, innovativeness, flexibility, and decentralization	Procter & Gamble
Reactor	Attributes tend to vary significantly over time	Honeywell's Large Information Systems division

and grew very rapidly. This success, however, encouraged numerous other companies to enter the market. Increased competition, plus reduced demand for high-priced cookies, has threatened Mrs. Fields's market position. To maintain its profitability, the firm has slowed its growth and is now focusing on making its current cookie operation more profitable. This behavior is consistent with the defender strategy.[15]

Analyzer firms attempt to maintain their current businesses and to be somewhat innovative in new businesses.

Analyzer Strategy   Organizations implementing analyzer strategies attempt to maintain their current businesses and to be somewhat innovative in new businesses. Because the analyzer strategy falls somewhere between prospector strategy (with focus on innovation) and defender strategy (with focus on maintaining and improving current businesses), the attributes of organizations implementing the analyzer strategy tend to be similar to both of these other types of organizations. They have tight accounting and financial controls and high flexibility, efficient production and customized products, creativity and low costs. It is difficult for organizations to maintain these multiple and contradictory processes.

One organization that has been able to successfully balance the need for innovation with the need to maintain current businesses is Procter and Gamble (P&G). As a major food products company, P&G has established numerous brand-name products, such as Crest toothpaste, Tide laundry detergent, and Sure deodorant. It is important for P&G to continue to invest in its successful products, in order to maintain financial performance. But P&G also needs to encourage the development of new products and brand names. In this way, it can continue to expand its market presence and have new products to replace those whose market falls off. Through these efforts, P&G can continue to grow.[16]

A firm following an analyzer strategy both maintains its current market and seeks to be innovative. McDonald's is a highly visible firm that has provided an example of this strategy by adding pizza to its traditional menu of hamburgers and French fries. This is, in fact, not a new strategy for McDonald's: since 1980 the number of its menu items has grown by 25%, and top managers hint at more innovative additions to come.

Reactor firms have no consistent approach.

Reactor Strategy   Organizations that follow a reactor strategy have no clear purpose or direction. Sometimes these organizations are innovative, sometimes they attempt to reduce costs, and sometimes they do both. They tend to drift from one strategy to another, implementing no strategy very well. These organizations typically do not perform very well.

During the 1970s and 1980s the Large Information Systems division of Honeywell seemed to follow a reactor strategy. As a relatively small manufacturer of mainframe computers, Honeywell sometimes tried to be very innovative in its research and development efforts and sometimes tried to reduce its costs as much as possible. Sometimes it focused on very innovative software, and sometimes it laid off hundreds of skilled workers. Not until Honeywell entered into joint ventures with some Japanese and European firms did it begin to focus its strategic efforts.[17]

Implementing Corporate-Level Strategies

Whereas business-level strategy is concerned with how an organization operates within a particular business or market, corporate-level strategy focuses on how organizations manage their operations across multiple businesses and markets. As Chapter 7 discussed, the most important cor-

Two issues are important for implementing corporate strategies: (1) how firms become diversified and (2) how firms manage diversification.

porate strategy decision that organizations need to make concerns the type and degree of corporate diversification.

In implementing a diversification strategy, organizations face two important questions. First, how will the organization move from a single product strategy to some form of diversification? Second, once the organization diversifies, how will it manage diversification effectively? Each of these questions is discussed below.

Becoming a Diversified Firm

Most organizations do not start out completely diversified. Rather, they begin operations in a single business, pursuing a particular business-level strategy. Success in this strategy then creates resources and strengths that the organization can use in related businesses. Ideally, these related businesses generate additional resources and strengths. Over time, as Figure 8.3 shows, cumulative success leads firms to adopt a diversification strategy.[18]

Honda is an example of an organization that followed this path to diversification. Relying on its traditional strength in the motorcycle market, over the years Honda learned how to make fuel-efficient, highly reliable small engines. As Figure 8.4 shows, Honda began to apply its strengths in a new business, manufacturing small, fuel-efficient cars for the Japanese domestic market. These vehicles were first sold in the United States in the late 1960s. Honda's success in U.S. exports led the company to increase the size and improve the performance of its cars. Over the years, Honda has introduced automobiles of increasing quality, culminating in the Acura line of luxury cars. While diversifying into the market for automobiles, Honda also applied its engine-building strengths to produce a line of all-terrain vehicles, portable electric generators, and lawn mowers. In each case, Honda was able to parlay its strengths and resources into successful new businesses.[19]

Firms can become diversified by means of internal development, replacing suppliers and customers, and mergers and acquisitions.

Organizations can move along the path depicted in Figure 8.3 by developing new products internally, by replacing suppliers and customers, or by engaging in mergers and acquisitions. Each of these alternatives is discussed below.

Internal Development of New Products   Apple Computer, like Honda, became diversified by developing its own new products and services within the boundaries of its traditional business operations. Apple had significant success selling the Apple I, Apple II, and Apple III computers, but when IBM introduced its own personal computer, Apple needed to develop a new and revolutionary product in order to remain successful in the industry. Whereas Apples I, II, and III had been refinements of a single design, the new product needed to break significantly with the past. Steve Jobs, then president of Apple, decided to form a special team of engineers and scientists to develop it. This internal development process led Apple to introduce the first user-friendly personal computer, the Macintosh.[20]

One way organizations can implement a related diversification strategy is through mergers and acquisitions. Sony, the Japanese electronics giant, has made steps toward providing what one top manager terms "total entertainment" by acquiring Columbia Pictures, Columbia Pictures Television, Tri-Star Pictures, and Sony Studios. Recently these different businesses have been organized into one unit called Sony Pictures Entertainment.

Backward vertical integration occurs when an organization begins the business activities formerly conducted by its suppliers.

Forward vertical integration occurs when an organization begins the business activities formerly conducted by its customers.

A *merger* occurs when one firm purchases another firm of approximately the same size. An *acquisition* occurs when one of the organizations involved is considerably larger than the other.

Another organization that has used internal development of new products to implement a diversification strategy is the Japanese firm Nissei Build Kogyo. This organization is described in The Global Challenge.

Replacement of Suppliers and Customers   Organizations can also become diversified by replacing their former suppliers and customers. An organization that stops buying supplies (either manufactured goods or raw materials) from other companies and begins to provide its own supplies has diversified through **backward vertical integration**. An organization that stops selling to one customer and sells instead to that customer's customers has diversified through **forward vertical integration**.

One organization that used backward vertical integration to diversify is Campbell Soup Company. Campbell once bought soup cans from several different manufacturers, but in the 1970s the firm began manufacturing its own cans. In fact, Campbell is currently one of the largest can-manufacturing companies in the world, although almost all the cans it makes are used in its soup operations.[21]

G. H. Bass & Co. used forward vertical integration to diversify its operations. In the past, Bass sold its shoes and other products only to retail outlets. However, throughout the 1980s Bass opened numerous factory outlet stores, which now sell products directly to consumers, although Bass has not abandoned its former customers, retail outlets.

Mergers and Acquisitions   Another common way for organizations to become diversified is through mergers and acquisitions — that is, through purchasing another organization. Such a purchase is called a **merger** when the two organizations being combined are approximately the same size. It is called an **acquisition** when one of the organizations involved is considerably larger than the other.

Figure 8.3

The Path to Organizational Diversification

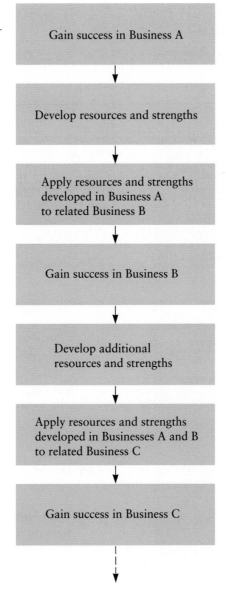

Organizations engage in mergers and acquisitions to diversify through vertical integration by acquiring former suppliers or former customers. General Motors used mergers and acquisitions to achieve backward vertical integration. For years, GM had purchased millions of dollars' worth of computing services from its supplier, Electronic Data Systems (EDS). GM decided to integrate these computing services into its ongoing operations, and it accomplished this goal by acquiring EDS.[22]

Complementary products and *complementary services* are products or services linked by a common technology and common customers.

Most organizations use mergers and acquisitions to acquire **complementary products** or **complementary services**, which are products or services linked by a common technology and common customers. In the acquisition

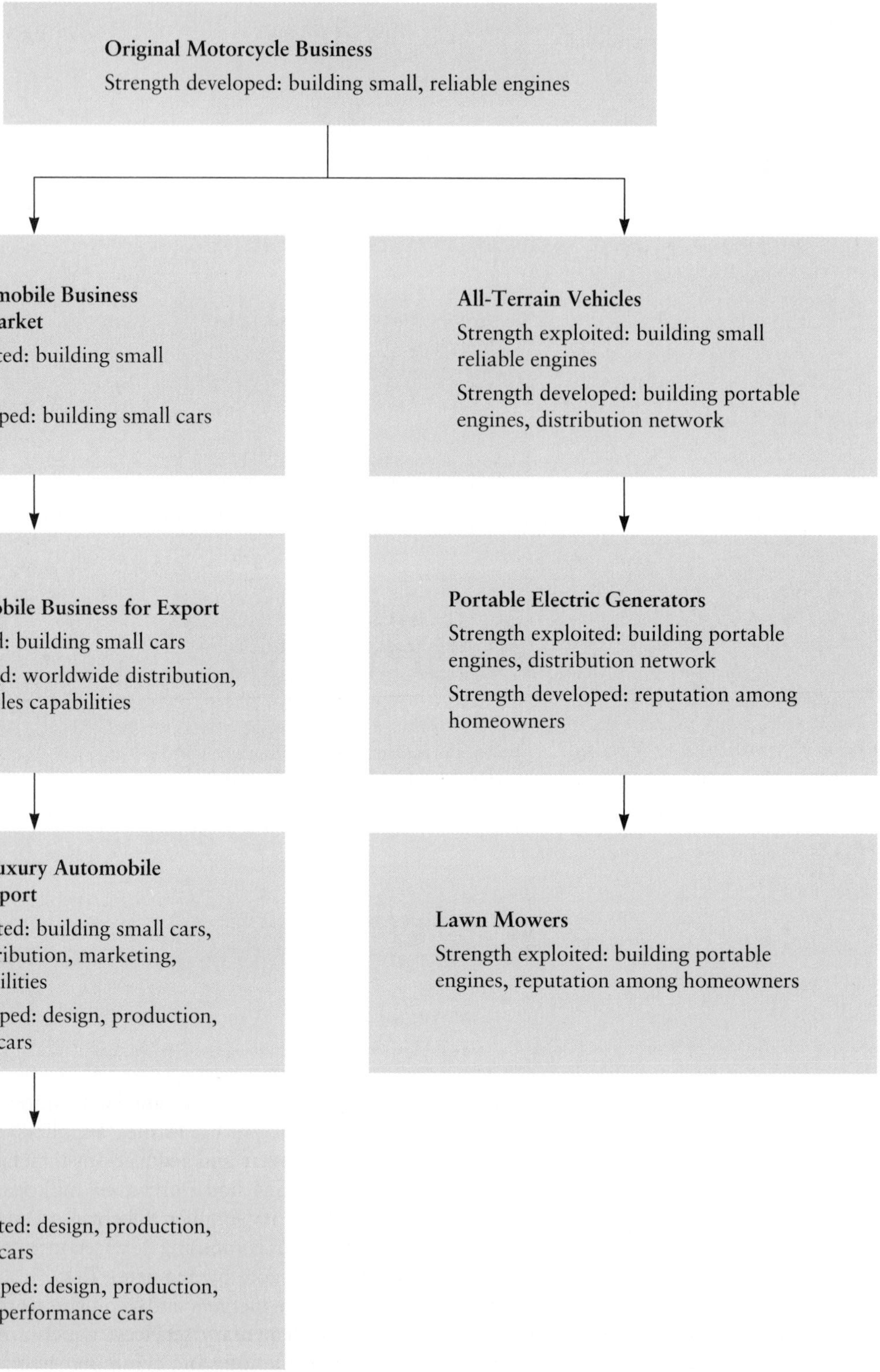

Figure 8.4

Honda's Path
to Diversification

Original Motorcycle Business

Strength developed: building small, reliable engines

**Low-End Automobile Business
for Japanese Market**

Strength exploited: building small
reliable engines

Strength developed: building small cars

All-Terrain Vehicles

Strength exploited: building small
reliable engines

Strength developed: building portable
engines, distribution network

Low-End Automobile Business for Export

Strength exploited: building small cars

Strength developed: worldwide distribution,
marketing, and sales capabilities

Portable Electric Generators

Strength exploited: building portable
engines, distribution network

Strength developed: reputation among
homeowners

**Medium and Luxury Automobile
Business for Export**

Strength exploited: building small cars,
worldwide distribution, marketing,
and sales capabilities

Strength developed: design, production,
sales of luxury cars

Lawn Mowers

Strength exploited: building portable
engines, reputation among homeowners

Acura Division

Strength exploited: design, production,
sales of luxury cars

Strength developed: design, production,
sales of luxury performance cars

THE GLOBAL CHALLENGE

Parking in Japan's Crowded Cities

Anyone who has ever visited Japan's major cities, including Tokyo, Osaka, and Yokohama, knows just how crowded they are. The population density of Japan is 825.4 people per square mile. The United States, with only 65.9 people per square mile, seems practically uninhabited by comparison.

The crowded conditions in Japanese cities have led to some unusual product innovations. For example, to indulge the public's passion for golf, organizations in this land-poor country have built multistory driving ranges in downtown Tokyo. Few such innovations have been as important as the development of the elevator-served parking garage, however. Parking cars in Japan is notoriously difficult. Traditional multistory garages help alleviate this problem, but the ramps used to drive between floors take up valuable space that could be used for cars.

Hireshi Morioka, president of Nissei Build Kogyo, knew there had to be a way to save that space. At the time, Nissei Build Kogyo was a relatively small supplier of small, prefabricated steel-frame buildings for temporary shelters at construction sites. Morioka saw that it would be possible to take the same pre-fabricated steel-frame technology that the firm used to make these temporary buildings and apply it in making parking garages. His important insight was to propose replacing the large and inefficient access ramps with car elevators that would service all floors. Now Tokyo car owners drive into an elevator and are whisked to their floor in less time than it would take to drive up a ramp. Elevator-served garages more than doubled Nissei Build Kogyo's sales in 1989 to $24 million.

Morioka is looking to expand his organization's products even further, always building on skills and technologies that his firm already possesses. For example, Nissei Build Kogyo may apply its parking technology to the construction of so-called vertical warehouses, in which elevators largely replace forklifts for moving stored inventory. Morioka is also considering joint ventures to move his car-parking technology into the United States and Europe.

REFERENCES: *The 1989 Almanac* (Boston: Houghton Mifflin), pp. 218, 290; Ted Holden, "Parking Garages That Tower over the Competition," *Business Week,* May 21, 1990, p. 128; Urban C. Leshner, "Japanese May Be Rich, but Are They Satisfied with Quality of Life?" *Wall Street Journal,* January 9, 1990, pp. A1, A12.

of Kraft (dairy products) by Philip Morris (tobacco products, food products), of Nabisco (food products) by R. J. Reynolds (tobacco products, food products), and of Federated (retail department stores) by Campeau (retail department stores), the acquiring organization was seeking to obtain complementary products or services.

The objective of most mergers and acquisitions is the creation or exploitation of synergies. As explained in Chapter 7, synergy exists between two organizations if their value as a combined organization is greater than their value as separate organizations. Synergy can reduce the combined organization's costs of doing business; it can increase revenues; and it may open the way to entirely new businesses for the organization to enter. Before engaging in a merger or acquisition, organizations must determine whether synergies exist between them. If there is no advantage to combining organizations, then why do it?[23]

The existence of synergies between two organizations by itself, however, is not sufficient to motivate a merger or acquisition. As Figure 8.5 shows, two other questions are important: (1) is the price of the acquisition less

In deciding whether to engage in a merger or an acquisition, three questions are important: (1) is there synergy between the two firms; (2) is the price of the acquisition less than the value of the acquisition; and (3) will the combined organization actually be able to exploit the synergy?

than the value of the acquisition, and (2) will the combined organization actually be able to exploit the synergy?

Deciding how much an acquisition is worth is a complicated problem, and paying too much may severely limit the combined organization's ability to perform. Suppose Organization A has a value (as a stand-alone enterprise) of $10,000 and Organization B a value (as a stand-alone enterprise) of $7,000. If synergy exists between these two organizations, then their combined value will be greater than their value as stand-alone enterprises. Since their value as stand-alone enterprises is $17,000 ($10,000 + $7,000), their combined value must be greater than $17,000, say $22,000, for synergy to exist. (Combined value is determined by means of the net present value techniques discussed in the appendix to Chapter 5.)

Suppose that the combined value of these firms actually is $22,000, and thus a synergy worth $5,000 exists: $22,000 − ($10,000 + $7,000) = $5,000. If Organization A decides to acquire Organization B and to pay $7,000 for B, then Organization A will make $5,000 on the acquisition. This is a matter of simple arithmetic: Organization B is worth $12,000 to Organization A ($7,000 as a stand-alone enterprise plus $5,000 because of the synergy between Organizations A and B). The difference between the value that Organization B adds to Organization A once B is acquired ($12,000 in total value) and what Organization A pays for Organization B ($7,000) is Organization A's profit for completing the acquisition ($5,000).

Figure 8.5

Evaluating the Performance Potential of Mergers and Acquisitions

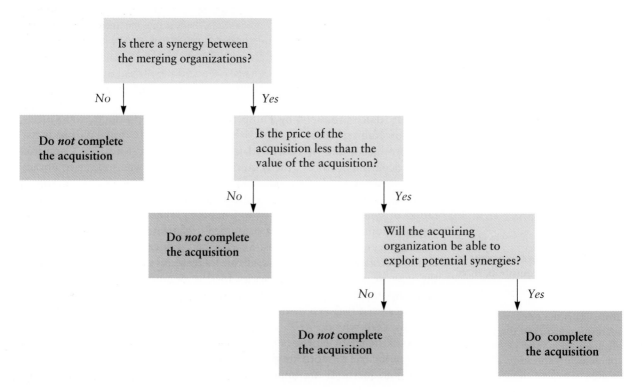

Of course, this scenario changes drastically if Organization A miscalculates the value of Organization B. If, for example, Organization A makes a mistake and pays $15,000 for Organization B when Organization B brings only $12,000 worth of value, then the acquisition will severely reduce the combined organization's performance. In fact, Organization A will lose $3,000 on its acquisition of B even though the synergy between these two organizations is worth $5,000. Often, organizations do pay too much for acquisitions. Campeau paid $6.5 billion for Federated Department Stores and this huge investment ultimately led Campeau to file for bankruptcy.[24]

Even if a merger or an acquisition is priced correctly, organizations still face one final challenge: integrating the two organizations to exploit the synergies created. A great deal of research indicates that it is often very difficult for formerly independent organizations to integrate their operations quickly. Different telephone systems, computer programs, compensation policies, and conflicting organizational cultures, among other factors, can complicate efforts toward integration. Nevertheless, numerous organizations have been able to integrate sufficiently so that the merger or acquisition becomes a successful strategy of diversification.[25]

Managing Diversification

Portfolio management techniques are methods that diversified organizations use to determine which businesses to engage in and how to manage these businesses to maximize corporate performance.

However an organization implements diversification — whether through internal development, vertical integration, or mergers and acquisitions — it must monitor and manage its strategy. The two major tools for managing diversification are (1) organization structure and (2) portfolio management techniques. How organization structure can be used to manage a diversification strategy is discussed in detail in Chapter 11. **Portfolio management techniques** are methods that diversified organizations use to make decisions about what businesses to engage in and how to manage these multiple businesses in order to maximize corporate performance. Two important portfolio management techniques are the BCG matrix and the GE Business Screen.

The BCG matrix evaluates businesses relative to the growth rate of their market and the organization's share of the market.

BCG Matrix   The BCG (for Boston Consulting Group) matrix provides a framework for evaluating the relative performance of businesses in which a diversified organization operates. It also prescribes the preferred distribution of cash and other resources among these businesses.[26] The BCG matrix uses two factors to evaluate an organization's set of businesses: the growth rate of a particular market and the organization's share of that market. The matrix suggests that fast-growing markets in which an organization has the highest market share are more attractive business opportunities than slow-growing markets in which an organization has small market share. Dividing market growth and market share into two categories (low and high) creates the simple matrix shown in Figure 8.6.

The matrix classifies the types of businesses that a diversified organization can engage in as pets, cash cows, question marks, and stars. **Pets** are businesses that have a very small share of a market that is not expected to

Figure 8.6

The BCG Matrix for Managing
Diversified Organizations

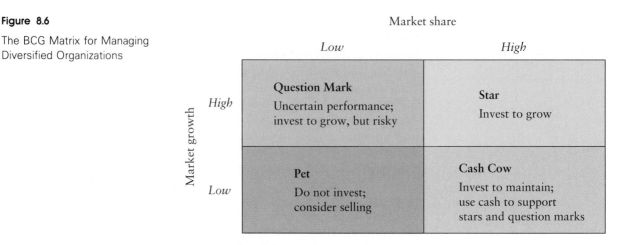

SOURCE: Adapted from *The Product Portfolio Matrix*, © 1970, The Boston Consulting Group, Inc. Used by permission.

The BCG matrix classifies businesses into four categories: *dogs* (small market growth, small market share), *cash cows* (small market growth, large market share), *question marks* (large market growth, small market share), and *stars* (large market growth, large market share).

grow. Since these businesses do not hold much economic promise, the BCG matrix suggests that organizations either should not invest in them or should consider selling them as soon as possible. **Cash cows** are businesses that have a large share of a market that is not expected to grow substantially. These businesses characteristically generate high profits that the organization should use to support question marks and stars. (Cash cows are "milked" for cash to support businesses in markets that have greater growth potential.) **Question marks** are businesses that have only a small share of a quickly growing market. The future performance of these businesses is uncertain. A question mark that is able to capture increasing amounts of this growing market may be very profitable. On the other hand, a question mark unable to keep up with market growth is likely to have low profits. The BCG matrix suggests that organizations should carefully invest in question marks. If their performance does not live up to expectations, question marks should be reclassified as pets and divested. **Stars** are businesses that have the largest share of a rapidly growing market. Cash generated by cash cows should be invested in stars to ensure their pre-eminent position.

International Telephone and Telegraph (ITT) invested profits from its cash cows in stars and new acquisitions and became one of the largest organizations in the world during the 1970s. However, ITT's performance in the 1980s reflects the main weakness of the BCG matrix technique: it may be too narrowly focused. Other factors besides market growth and market share determine the performance of a business. By relying so closely on the BCG matrix, ITT failed to recognize several promising business opportunities in businesses that it had classified as pets or cash cows. Other organizations recognized these opportunities and took advantage of them. Recently, ITT has explicitly abandoned the BCG matrix and no longer regards its businesses as pets or cash cows simply on the basis of market growth and market share.[27]

The GE Business Screen evaluates businesses along two dimensions: (1) industry attractiveness and (2) competitive position. In general, the more attractive the industry and the more competitive the position, the more an organization should invest in a business.

GE Business Screen   In response to the narrow focus of the BCG matrix, General Electric (GE) developed the GE Business Screen. The Business Screen is a portfolio management technique that can also be represented in the form of a matrix. Rather than focusing solely on market growth and market share, however, the GE Business Screen considers industry attractiveness and competitive position. These two factors are divided into three categories, to make the 9-cell matrix shown in Figure 8.7.[28]

As Figure 8.7 shows, both market growth and market share appear in a broad list of factors that determine the overall attractiveness of an industry and the overall quality of a firm's competitive position. Other determinants of an industry's attractiveness (in addition to market growth) include market size, capital requirements, and competitive intensity. In general, the greater the market growth, the larger the market, the smaller the capital requirements, and the less the competitive intensity, the more attractive an industry will be. Other determinants of an organization's competitive position in an industry (besides market share) include technological know-how, product quality, service network, price competitiveness, and operating costs. In general, businesses with large market share, technological know-how, high product quality, a quality service network, competitive prices, and low operating costs are in a favorable competitive position.

Figure 8.7

The GE Business Screen for Managing Diversified Organizations

Competitive position

	Good	Medium	Poor
High	Winner	Winner	Question mark
Medium	Winner	Average business	Loser
Low	Profit producer	Loser	Loser

Industry attractiveness

Competitive Position
1. Market share
2. Technological know-how
3. Product quality
4. Service network
5. Price competitiveness
6. Operating costs

Industry Attractiveness
1. Market growth
2. Market size
3. Capital requirements
4. Competitive intensity

SOURCE: Reprinted by permission from *Strategy Formulation: Analytical Concepts* by C. W. Hofer and D. Schendel. Copyright © 1978 by West Publishing Company. All rights reserved.

Think of the GE Business Screen as a way of applying SWOT analysis to the implementation and management of a diversification strategy. The determinants of industry attractiveness are similar to the environmental opportunities and threats in SWOT analysis, and the determinants of competitive position are similar to organizational strengths and weaknesses. By conducting this type of SWOT analysis across several businesses, a diversified organization can decide how to invest its resources to maximize corporate performance. In general, organizations should invest in winners and in question marks (where industry attractiveness and competitive position are both favorable), should maintain the market position of average businesses and profit producers (where industry attractiveness and competitive position are average), and should sell losers.

Learning Summary

What counts ultimately is not an organization's announced strategy but its implemented strategy. Strategy implementation is the process of allocating resources to support the organization's chosen strategies. Most organizations implement both deliberate and emergent strategies.

Strategy implementation at the business level takes place in the areas of marketing, sales, accounting and finance, and manufacturing. Organizational culture also influences strategy implementation. Implementation of Porter's generic strategies (differentiation, cost leadership, and focus) requires different emphases in each of these organizational areas. Implementation of Miles and Snow's strategies (prospector, defender, analyzer, and reactor) affects organization structure and practices.

Strategy implementation at the corporate level addresses two issues: the type of organizational diversification and the way that an organization is managed once it has diversified. In general, organizations become diversified by building strengths and capabilities in one industry that they then exploit in other industries. Organizations accomplish this in three ways: developing new products internally, replacing suppliers (backward vertical integration) or customers (forward vertical integration), and engaging in mergers and acquisitions.

Most mergers and acquisitions are designed to exploit synergy between merging organizations. However, for this type of diversification to have a positive impact on economic performance, synergy must exist, the price of acquiring the synergy must be less than the value of the synergy, and the combined organization must be able to exploit the synergy.

Organizations manage diversification through the organization structure that they adopt and through portfolio management techniques. The BCG matrix classifies an organization's diversified businesses as dogs, cash cows, question marks, or stars according to market share and market growth rate. The GE Business Screen classifies businesses as winners, losers, question marks, average businesses, or profit producers according to industry attractiveness and competitive position.

Questions and Exercises

Review Questions

1. Which is more important for an organization's performance, its announced strategy or its implemented strategy? Why?
2. How does a deliberate strategy differ from an emergent strategy?
3. How do the five organizational functions support the implementation of differentiation, cost leadership, and focus strategies?
4. Identify the attributes of organizations that implement prospector, defender, analyzer, and reactor strategies.
5. Describe the process that organizations typically go through to become diversified.
6. Define *backward vertical integration* and *forward vertical integration*.
7. What is *synergy,* and what conditions must exist for a merger or acquisition to have a positive impact on an organization's performance?
8. According to the BCG matrix and the GE Business Screen, when should a diversified organization invest in, maintain, or sell its businesses?

Analysis Questions

1. The Environmental Challenge discusses the recent trend among U.S. automobile companies to advertise their cars' safety features. Is this use of advertising an example of a deliberate or an emergent strategy? Why?
2. Your company is worth $60,000 as a stand-alone business, and Westridge Electric Supply Company is worth $100,000 as a stand-alone business. The two businesses combined are worth $180,000. Is there synergy between these two businesses? If you want to maximize the economic performance of your company, should you buy Westridge Electric for $90,000? For $110,000? For $130,000? Why or why not?
3. For decades now, Ivory Soap has advertised that it is 99% pure. Ivory has refused to add deodorants, facial creams, or colors to its soap. It also packages its soap in plain paper wrappers — no foil or fancy printing. Is Ivory implementing a product differentiation, low cost, focus strategy, or some combination? Explain your answer.

Application Exercises

1. Is implementing a differentiation strategy always going to improve an organization's performance? Give three real-world examples in which differentiation did not seem to improve an organization's performance, and describe why it did not. What do these "errors" have in common?
2. Read a history of a major recent takeover (for example, RJR's takeover of Nabisco or Du Pont's takeover of Conoco). Referring to the questions posed in Figure 8.5, do you believe the acquisition is likely to improve the performance of the acquiring firm?

Chapter Notes

1. "Bombs over Baghdad," *Newsweek,* Special Issue, *America at War,* Spring–Summer 1991, pp. 66–74; "The Shrinking World of Totalitarian TV," *Broadcasting,* September 10, 1990, p. 96; "Getting Video Home from the Persian Gulf via Satellite," *Broadcasting,* September 3, 1990, pp. 23–24.

2. The traditional model of strategy formulation, implementation, and performance is described in Arthur Thompson and A. J. Strickland, *Strategic Management: Concepts and Cases,* 4th ed. (Plano, Tex.: Business Publications, 1987), and Charles Hill and Gareth Jones, *Strategic Management: An Integrated Approach,* 2nd ed. (Boston: Houghton Mifflin, 1992). This traditional view was first developed by a variety of scholars, including E. P. Learned, C. R. Christensen, K. R. Andrews, and W. D. Guth, *Business Policy* (Homewood, Ill.: 1969), and K. Andrews, *The Concept of Corporate Strategy* (New York: Dow Jones–Irwin, 1971).

3. Mintzberg discusses the distinction between deliberate and other types of strategies in Henry Mintzberg, "Patterns in Strategy Formulation," *Management Science,* 1978, pp. 934–948; Henry Mintzberg, "Strategy Making in Three Modes," *California Management Review,* 1973, pp. 44–53; and Henry Mintzberg, D. Raisinghani, and A. Theoret, "The Structure of Unstructured Decision Processes," *Administrative Science Quarterly,* 1976, pp. 246–275.

4. "Texas Instruments Incorporated: Management Systems," 9-172-054 (Revised 9/75), Harvard Business School, Boston, Mass.

5. See Mintzberg, "Patterns in Strategy Formulation."

6. Stewart Toy, "Can McDonnell Douglas Make Its Computers Fly?" *Business Week,* May 14, 1987, pp. 121–122.

7. Tom Peters and Robert Waterman, *In Search of Excellence* (New York: Harper & Row, 1982).

8. Michael Porter, *Competitive Strategy* (New York: Free Press, 1980).

9. E. Morley and H. Lane, "Neiman Marcus," Harvard Business School, Boston, Mass., 1974.

10. Jay Palmer, "Avon's Calling," *Barron's,* February 4, 1991, pp. 14–15, 43.

11. John W. Verity, "Doing Pure Research Is Only Common Sense," *Business Week,* June 15, 1990, p. 62.

12. Allan J. Magrath, "Segmentation and Differentiation Positioning Strategies Are Timeless," *Marketing News,* October 24, 1988, p. 18; Cassandra Jardine, "Timeless Mystique at Rolex," *Business,* February 1988, pp. 114–117; John F. Krafcik, "Triumph of the Lean Production System," *Sloan Management Review,* Fall 1988, pp. 41–52.

13. Jeff Haggin and Bjorn Kartomten, "Breaking the Rules Can Pay Off: Catalogs That Dare to Be Different May Succeed Where Followers Fail," *Catalog Age,* August 1989, pp. 73–74.

14. Kenneth Labich, "The Innovators," *Fortune,* June 6, 1988, pp. 50–64; "At Johnson and Johnson, a Mistake Can Be a Badge of Honor," *Business Week,* September 26, 1988, pp. 126–128.

15. Tom Richman, "Mrs. Field's Secret Ingredient," *Inc.,* October 1987, pp. 65–72.

16. Spencer C. Hapoienu, "The Rise of Micromarketing," *Journal of Business Strategy,* November–December, 1990, pp. 37–42; Laurie Freeman, "P&G Food Unit Back in the Black," *Advertising Age,* September 17, 1990, p. 16.

17. Sarah Glazer, "Taking Bull by the Horns," *CFO,* March 1991, pp. 40–46.

18. For a discussion of this evolution of diversification based on the accumulation of strengths and capabilities, see C. K. Prahalad and Richard Bettis, "The Dominant Logic: A New Linkage Between Diversity and Performance," *Strategic Management Journal,* 1986, pp. 485–501.

19. James Cook, "We Are the Target," *Forbes,* April 7, 1986, pp. 54, 56; Alex Taylor III, "Here Come Japan's New Luxury Cars," *Fortune,* August 12, 1989, pp. 62–66.

20. Clare C. Swanger, "Apple Computer, Inc. — Macintosh (A)," Case no. S-BP-234, Graduate School of Business, Stanford University, 1984.

21. "Crown Cork & Seal, Inc.," in C. Roland Christensen, Kenneth R. Andrews, Joseph L. Bower, Richard G. Hamermesh, and Michael Porter, *Business Policy,* 6th ed. (Homewood, Ill.: Irwin, 1987), pp. 170–196.

22. William Hampton, Todd Mason, and Russell Mitchell, "GM Hasn't Bought Much Peace/The Risks of Running EDS Without Perot," *Business Week,* December 15, 1986, pp. 24–27.

23. See Jay Barney, "Returns to Bidding Firms in Mergers and Acquisitions," *Strategic Management Journal,* 1988, pp. 71–78, for a discussion of the impact of pricing acquisitions on returns to acquisitions. Other examples of this pricing issue are discussed in Christopher James and Peggy Wier, "Returns to Acquirers and Competition in the Acquisition Market: The Case of Banking," *Journal of Political Economy,* 1987, pp. 355–370, and Peter Dodd and Richard Ruback, "Tender Offers and Stockholder Returns: An Empirical Analysis," *Journal of Financial Economics,* 1977, pp. 351–373.

24. A discussion of how bidders in mergers and acquisitions might pay too much for a target firm can be found in John Kagel and Dan Levin, "The Winner's Curse and Public Information in Common Value Auctions," *American Economic Review,* 1986, pp. 894–920.

25. See, for example, M. Salter and W. Weinhold, *Diversification Through Acquisition: Strategies for Creating Economic Value* (New York: Free Press, 1979).

26. See Barry Hedley, "A Fundamental Approach to Strategy Development," *Long Range Planning,* December 1976, pp. 2–11, and Bruce Henderson, "The Experience Curve — Reviewed. IV: The Growth Share Matrix of the Product Portfolio," *Perspectives,* no. 135 (Boston: Boston Consulting Group, 1973).

27. For a discussion of the limitations of the BCG matrix, see Bruce Henderson, "The Application and Misapplication of the Experience Curve," *Journal of Business Strategy,* 1984, pp. 3–9, and P. Haspeslagh, "Portfolio Planning: Uses and Limits," *Harvard Business Review,* January–February 1983, pp. 58–73.

28. Michael G. Allen, "Diagramming G.E.'s Planning for What's WATT," in Robert J. Allio and Malcolm W. Pennington, eds., *Corporate Planning: Techniques and Applications* (New York: AMACOM, 1979). Limits of this approach are discussed in R. A. Bettis and W. K. Hall, "The Business Portfolio Approach: Where It Falls Down in Practice," *Long Range Planning,* 1983, pp. 95–105.

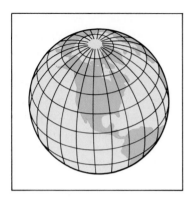

CASE 8.1

Fattening and Slaughtering Beatrice

Beatrice is one of the largest companies that Americans have never heard of. Its brands — Peter Pan, Hunt's, Butterball, Wesson, La Choy — are in every American kitchen, yet few consumers identify the individual products with a larger corporate entity. That's probably just as well, for since the mid-1980s, when Beatrice was taken private in a leveraged buyout, Beatrice has been carved into pieces like one of its own Butterball turkeys. And when ConAgra, the nation's second largest food company, bought the carcass in 1990, it seemed fitting that one identity-less conglomerate would be absorbed by another.

Beatrice did originally have an identity and a strategy. It began in 1894 in Beatrice, Nebraska, where two enterprising men began buying eggs, butter, and poultry from local farmers and shipping them to markets throughout the Midwest. The scheme that made them rich involved butter making. They gave hand-powered cream separators to farmers on credit, made butter out of the farmers' cream, and sold the butter to hotels, restaurants, and grocery stores, making money on both the separators and the butter. By the turn of the century, the company was churning out close to a million pounds of butter a year and soon created its own brand — Meadow Gold, the first butter to be advertised in a national magazine.

The company continued to expand into other dairy products — principally milk and ice cream — and might still be a focused business except that the federal government felt that it was buying too many local dairies and stopped it from buying any more. So in 1943, Beatrice bought its first nondairy business — La Choy Food Products. Under a new CEO in the 1950s, Beatrice became the grand acquisitor of its time but still kept its acquisitions related to food — Thos. Richardson (candy) and Bond (pickles) in 1957, Rosarita Mexican Foods (1961), and Fisher Nut (1962).

But soon Beatrice's appetite for acquisitions became less focused. In the 1960s and 1970s, it began buying companies overseas and moved into chemicals, metals, and consumer products. Although some of its name-brand acquisitions were food related (Martha White Foods in 1975, Tropicana in 1978), it also bought unrelated businesses: Culligan (water softeners) in 1978 and Samsonite (luggage) in 1973. At the end of the 1970s, Beatrice ranked number one in food processing, yogurt, and ready-to-drink orange juice, and number two in dairy products, nuts, and Oriental foods.

In the 1980s, big conglomerates, especially those that, according to investors, had parts worth more than the present value of the whole, became targets for leveraged buyouts. In such a buyout, the takeover group typically put up very little of its own money and borrowed the bulk of the purchase price, often selling junk bonds, assuming that it could sell parts of its acquisition to pay off the debt. Thus when a group led by Kohlberg Kravis Roberts & Co (KKR), a New York investment firm, spent $6.9 billion to buy Beatrice and take it private in 1986, everyone assumed that pieces of the company would soon be up for sale. And they were right.

People who have bought a company simply as a short- to medium-term investment have very different ideas about what the goals and strategies for that company should be than do employees or managers of the company who are interested in its long-term growth. The differences may be analogous to the differences between the way an auctioneer views a house and its furnishings and the way a homeowner sees the same property. KKR and Donald Kelly, one of the investors and CEO of Beatrice, were interested in breaking up Beatrice into the right parcels and selling them off at the right time to produce the maximum amount of cash. So the company began a multi-billion-dollar sell-off that included its Coca-Cola bottling operations and Playtex in 1986, its international division in 1987, and Tropicana in 1988. Donald Kelly left his CEO position in 1987 to run E-II Holdings, a spin-off of Beatrice's nonfood operations. Finally, pared down to mostly food operations (but minus its dairy division, which had already been sold), Beatrice was sold to ConAgra in 1990 for $1.34 billion.

Altogether, the sales from the pieces of Beatrice netted the KKR limited partners what amounted to a 50 percent rate of return on their investment. The joining of Beatrice and ConAgra created a diversified company, but its businesses are more related than those formerly owned by the larger Beatrice. ConAgra's frozen food lineup fits well with some of Beatrice's remaining brands like Hunt's tomato products and Wesson oils. Beatrice's grocery-store distribution network also fills a ConAgra need. So the remaining Beatrice brands may have found a home where they will be treated as something more than assets. ConAgra may develop a strategy that uses the strengths of both companies' products.

Discussion Questions

1. Supporters argue that many leveraged buyouts are healthy because they trim the acquired firm back to its core businesses. Do you think the KKR buyout was good for Beatrice?
2. When Beatrice diversified beyond food products, what advantages and disadvantages did it have that it doesn't have now as part of a larger food products company?
3. Does a food products company need complementary products? Does it have to worry about business cycles and sales slumps?
4. If you had run Beatrice in 1980, what strategy would you have chosen, and how would you have implemented it?

REFERENCES: Gary Hoover, Alta Campbell, and Patrick J. Spain, eds., *Hoover's Handbook* (Austin, Tex.: Reference Press, 1991), p. 121; Jay McCormick, "A Smaller Spin-off Goes Public in June," *USA Today*, May 21, 1987, pp. 1B, 2B; Russell Mitchell, Lois Therrien, and Gregory L. Miles, "ConAgra: Out of the Freezer," *Business Week*, June 25, 1990, pp. 24–25; Milton Moskowitz, Michael Katz, and Robert Levering, *Everybody's Business* (San Francisco: Harper & Row, 1980), pp. 1–5; Ford S. Worthy, "Beatrice's Sell-off Strategy," *Fortune*, June 23, 1986, pp. 44–49.

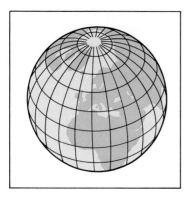

CASE 8.2

France's Thomson Buys American to Battle the Japanese

Can you name the two companies that made the greatest number of color TVs in the late 1980s? Not Sony or Hitachi or Toshiba — in fact, neither leader is Asian. Philips, which most Americans know because of its light bulbs, was in first place, followed by Thomson.

Thomson? Yes, Thomson, France's state-owned leader in defense and consumer electronics. It attained its surprising position in world electronics through its 1986 purchase of 80 percent of General Electric's GE and RCA brands. The purchase, which doubled Thomson's consumer electronics sales, was part of a risky strategy that combined business considerations with nationalism. So far the strategy has demonstrated more of the liabilities than the assets of such a mixture.

General Electric's sale of its consumer electronics business left Zenith as the only American maker of television sets, the high quality and reasonable price of Japanese TVs having gradually driven American manufacturers out of the market. But while most Americans do no more than grumble about sending their dollars overseas as they lug home their new Sony or Sanyo, many people in France, including some in the government, view with horror the possibility of a total Japanese takeover of a major product area. Because of this attitude, the GE purchase assured Thomson of a continuing of government backing for such costly new projects as the development of high-definition television.

But whether the move made good sense from a strictly business perspective is a different question. Thomson argues that the GE purchase did make sense because only a company with huge volume, a global presence, and tremendous research and development resources could hope to compete with Japanese manufacturers. Thomson knew well that despite a decade of cost-cutting and quality-enhancing measures, most Western consumer electronics firms still could not sell their products as inexpensively or make as much profit as their Japanese rivals.

Thomson also is aiming to be ready for the next audio-visual revolution, in which high-definition television and digital TV and stereo will replace current technologies. Thomson intends to lead this revolution, and it is starting with an advantage, at least in Europe. The European Community has adopted MAC, a signal-transmission standard developed by Philips and Thomson, rather than a Japanese alternative.

With this type of government help, moving into consumer electronics might seem like a good strategy if the company's other businesses could be assured of stable growth. But the end of the cold war is having the same negative effect on Thomson's defense electronics business as it is on the American defense industry. The company expects its income from defense sales — $7.3 billion — to fall 20 percent by 1993, and it has been cutting its defense work force.

Thomson took a giant step towards leadership in consumer electronics when it introduced its Space Station television early in 1991. The timing seemed somewhat ironic, as the U.S. recession had led to a slump in American consumer electronics buying, and the world was in economic and political turmoil due to the Persian Gulf War. The company insists that the timing wasn't a mistake, however, because for once it wanted to beat Japanese companies to the punch. The 34-inch Space Station is a forerunner of high-definition television (HDTV). It picks up current signals but is ready for the high-definition signals of the future. Thomson hopes that selling the Space Station now will create demand for HDTV and the MAC transmission standard as well as give the company a new, high-class image, which could improve sales of its entire product line.

Of course, the Space Station itself is another gamble. Comparably sized TVs account for only 1 percent of current sales of color sets in Europe, and at $7,000 the Space Station costs 25 percent more than the competition. Feature films are about the only things now broadcast in the wide-screen format, although the Space Station does allow viewers to expand standard TV signals to fill the screen, which gives a wide-screen effect.

Thomson has announced that it plans to enter the European market for telephones and answering machines, a move likely to please those who feel that Thomson's main businesses are too risky. Because the market for telephone equipment is mature, Thomson probably won't make much money selling standard phone equipment, but it hopes to use its initial entry to break into higher-growth areas like fax machines and cellular telephones. And although it did not ask the government for financial assistance for the new venture, it did quickly win a contract from the national telecommunications authority to make a central electronic component for a new video-telephone system. Such strides into high tech, building on the company's established strengths, may provide some ballast for an organization that is otherwise at the mercy of national, international, and competitive forces.

Discussion Questions

1. Why would Thomson feel that only a huge global company could compete against the likes of Sony and Hitachi?
2. Does diversifying from defense electronics into consumer electronics make sense to you as a strategy for Thomson?
3. How have Thomson's connections with the French government affected its business strategies?
4. How might you change Thomson's strategy in consumer electronics to help offset the problems inherent in its defense businesses?

REFERENCES: Jonathan Levine, "The Heat on Alain Gomez," *Business Week*, March 11, 1991, pp. 66–67; Thane Peterson, "Overnight, Thomson Has the Stuff to Take on the Titans," *Business Week*, August 10, 1987, pp. 36–37; "Thomson to Enter European Market for Telephone Gear," *Wall Street Journal*, February 5, 1991, p. B4.

9

Individual Creativity and Organizational Innovation

LEARNING OBJECTIVES

After studying this chapter, you should be able to:

1. Discuss the importance of creativity and innovation for modern organizations.

2. Identify the attributes of a creative individual, and describe the creative process.

3. Discuss the steps in the innovation process.

4. Describe different types of innovations in organizations.

5. Explain why organizations sometimes fail to innovate and how they might promote innovation.

The Nature of Creativity and Innovation

Individual Creativity
The Creative Individual
The Creative Process

Organizational Innovation
The Innovation Process
Types of Innovations in Organizations
The Failure to Innovate

Ways of Promoting Innovation in Organizations
The Reward System
Intrapreneurship
Organizational Culture

Perched on a mountainside in Colorado Springs, Colorado, tiny Ramtron International Corp. has set itself an ambitious goal—to revolutionize the entire microelectronics industry. Founded by former University of Colorado researchers, Ramtron hopes to base its revolution on a relatively simple idea—computer chips made with ceramics instead of with pure silicon.

Most microelectronic devices manufactured today are made with pure silicon. To turn the silicon into electronic devices, manufacturers etch minute yet precise patterns of impurities into it. These patterns of impurities are the electronic circuits that enable computer chips to operate.

What the scientists at Ramtron discovered was that a silicon chip coated with a thin layer of ceramic material has two distinct advantages over one made of pure silicon: its molecular structure allows for a much tighter packing of electronic instructions, and the information stored in a ceramic device does not disappear when the electricity is turned off. The tighter packing means that electronic devices can be smaller and operate faster (because signals do not have so far to travel). The ability of ceramic chips to "remember" without electricity means that memory devices required for silicon chips (such as floppy disks) will not be needed.

Although Ramtron successfully uncovered the many advantages of ceramic circuits, these basic ideas required a great deal of development. Since Ramtron did not have all the resources required for product development, it obtained $3.5 million from an Australian venture capital company and formed development partnerships with ITT Semiconductors, Seiko Epson Corp., TRW, and Japan's NMB Semiconductor. Ramtron (in association with its partners) currently is producing memory chips for the European and defense markets.

Even as manufacturing begins, however, ceramic technology still meets with skepticism from the makers of silicon-based chips. An alternative ceramic technology has been developed by Krysalis Corporation; and an entirely new approach to semiconductor manufacture that preserves data with nitride-oxide film has been invented. Certainly, creativity and innovation in the microelectronics industry are a risky proposition.[1]

Ramtron is an innovative organization that has been able to exploit the creative skills of its managers and scientists. Over the last three decades, the ability of many other organizations to be creative and innovative has revolutionized the way we communicate, travel, and live. In the past, it was possible for an organization to survive and perhaps even prosper without being innovative, but today, to lack the capacity for innovation is to fall behind. Never has the management of creativity and innovation been a more critical factor in organizational performance. In these days of vast research and development complexes, highly integrated teams of scientists, and networks of joint-venture relationships between firms, individual creativity is a vital ingredient. More and more, though, to turn ideas into products, individual creativity must be supported by organizational policies and practices.

This chapter begins by discussing the relationship between creativity and innovation. It then examines some characteristics of creative people and describes the steps in the creative process. Next we see how an organization's innovation process transforms a creative idea into a marketable product. The chapter ends by describing ways organizations may promote innovation and creativity.

The Nature of Creativity and Innovation

Creativity is the ability of an individual to generate new ideas or to conceive of new perspectives on existing ideas. *Innovation* is the managed effort of an organization to develop new products or services or new uses for existing products or services.

The concepts of creativity and innovation are closely linked, but they are not the same. **Creativity** is the ability of an individual to generate new ideas or to conceive of new perspectives on existing ideas. **Innovation** is the managed effort of an organization to develop new products or services or new uses for existing products or services. Thus creativity is an individual process that may or may not occur in an organization. Innovation is an organizational activity aimed at managing and stimulating the creativity of employees.[2]

Figure 9.1 depicts the relationship between creativity and innovation and the ability of organizations to introduce new products or services. In general, the most new products and services are developed in organizations that have very creative people and that support innovative activity. Organizations that employ creative people but have no resources to support or take advantage of their creativity have less ability to develop new products

Figure 9.1

The Relationship Between Creativity, Innovation, and the Development of New Products and Services

Does the organization employ creative individuals?

	Yes	No
Yes	**Very high** levels of new products/ services	**Moderate** levels of new products/ services
No	**Moderate** levels of new products/ services	**Low** levels of new products/ services

Does the organization support innovative activity?

or services. These organizations need to develop an environment in which creativity is encouraged. Likewise, organizations that provide a supportive environment for creativity but have no creative employees are less successful at developing new products or services. These organizations need to employ more creative individuals or to assist their current employees in becoming more creative. Finally, organizations that neither employ creative individuals nor support creative activity develop the fewest new products and services.

3M is an organization that employs creative people and provides them with an environment supportive of innovation. Rather than emphasizing research and development plans developed by top management and delegated to scientists and engineers to implement, 3M encourages all its employees to think independently and creatively about innovative products. As a result of this creative effort, 3M sells almost sixty-thousand different kinds of products a year, a substantial percentage of which are brand-new products. 3M encourages this level of creativity by financially rewarding employees who develop new products and by not firing or otherwise punishing employees who develop new products that are not successful.[3]

Not all organizations possess this ideal combination of creative people and innovative organizational environment. Some are unable to take advantage of the new and exciting ideas that their employees may generate. Over the years at Xerox's research and development facility in Palo Alto, California, for example, scientists developed a broad range of exciting new products, many of which now dominate their industries. Xerox scientists invented the "mouse" as a tool for operating personal computers, sophisticated software to make personal computers easier to use, and advanced computer graphics capabilities. Unfortunately, Xerox did not introduce any of these inventions to the market, even though reports indicated that Xerox managers were aware of the economic potential they held. Other organizations built on Xerox's ideas, brought them to market, and obtained the substantial profits that Xerox might have garnered had it been able to support the creativity of its employees.[4]

Often, creative individuals working in a noninnovative organization must leave in order to bring their ideas to fruition. For example, Steve Jobs was working for Atari (a computer game manufacturer) and Steve Wozniak for Hewlett-Packard when they first conceived of the idea of a personal computer. Because these engineers were unable to interest either of their companies in this product, they began to develop it on their own. Similarly, the movement of skilled creative people away from Texas Instruments has led to the founding of Ramtron, Compaq Computer, and many other successful electronics businesses.

Individual Creativity

Individual creativity is a core requirement for organizations whose aim is to introduce new and exciting products and services into the marketplace. What makes a person creative? How do people become creative? How

Venezuelan-born Carolina Herrera is an individual who has utilized her creative talents to the fullest. Using her insights into consumer taste and fashion design, she has developed a line that is marketed in the United States, Canada, and Mexico. She has also developed a signature fragrance that sells even more widely: in England, France, and South America, as well as in the United States.

does the creative process work? Although psychologists have not yet discovered complete answers to these questions, examining a few general patterns can help us understand the sources of individual creativity within organizations.

The Creative Individual

Individual creativity depends on background experiences, personality traits, and cognitive abilities.

Numerous researchers have focused their efforts on attempting to describe the common attributes of creative individuals. These attributes generally fall into three categories: background experiences, personality traits, and cognitive abilities.[5]

Background Experiences and Creativity   Background experiences are the events that people live through during childhood and young adulthood. Researchers have noticed that many creative individuals were raised in an environment in which creativity was perceived and rewarded.[6] Mozart, one of the greatest composers of all time, was raised in a family of musicians and began composing and performing music at age 6. Pierre and Marie Curie, great scientists in their own right, also raised a daughter, Irene, who won the Nobel Prize in Chemistry. Thomas Edison's renowned creativity was nurtured by his mother.

However, people with background experiences very different from theirs have also been creative. The African-American abolitionist and writer Frederick Douglass was born into slavery in Tuckahoe, Maryland, and had very

Table 9.1

Personality Traits Shared by Most Creative People

1. Broad interests
2. Attraction to complexity
3. High levels of energy
4. Independence and autonomy
5. Strong self-confidence
6. Belief in personal creativity

limited opportunities for education. Nonetheless, Douglass became one of the most influential figures of the Civil War era. His powerful oratory and creative thinking helped lead to the Emancipation Proclamation, which outlawed slavery in the United States.

Personality and Creativity   Various personality traits have been linked with individual creativity. As listed in Table 9.1, the personality traits shared by most creative people are broad interests, attraction to complexity, high levels of energy, independence and autonomy, strong self-confidence, and a strong belief that one is, in fact, creative.[7] Individuals who have these personality characteristics are more likely to be creative than people who do not have them.

Different industries tend to attract different numbers of highly creative people. One industry that seems to attract a large number of these people is the fashion industry. Indeed, the fashion industry thrives on the creativity of individuals. One firm that has taken full advantage of creative individuals in this industry is described in The Entrepreneurial Challenge.

Cognitive abilities are an individual's power to think intelligently and to analyze situations and data effectively.

Cognitive Abilities and Creativity   **Cognitive abilities** are an individual's power to think intelligently and to analyze situations and data effectively. Research suggests that intelligence may be a precondition for individual creativity, which means that although most creative people are highly intelligent, not all intelligent people necessarily are creative.[8] Creativity is also linked with the ability to think divergently and convergently. **Divergent thinking** is a skill that allows people to see differences between situations, phenomena, or events. **Convergent thinking** is a skill that allows people to see similarities between situations, phenomena, or events. Creative people are generally very skilled at both divergent and convergent thinking.[9]

Some of the decisions made by Lee Iaccoca after he assumed the presidency of Chrysler illustrate the interplay between divergent and convergent thinking. As he joined Chrysler, the company was losing millions of dollars, laying off numerous employees, and on the verge of bankruptcy. Once the organization was stabilized financially with the help of government loans, Iaccoca turned to improving the products available to potential Chrysler customers. The first task was to catalog what a range of different customers might want in a car in terms of size, performance, cost, and styling. Describ-

THE ENTREPRENEURIAL CHALLENGE

Yes Women, Yes Men

The fashion industry is a hotbed of creativity — some would say chaos. Almost daily, highly eccentric, idiosyncratic designers all over the world come up with new fabrics and styles, old fabrics used in new ways, and old styles renewed and revitalized. Fabrics as varied as neoprene rubber, plastic, and polyester are now featured in high-fashion apparel.

In this changeable environment, it was probably inevitable that a fabric once limited to leotards would be featured in bandeau tops, blouses, pants, skirts, and even dresses. Bringing this fabric — Spandex — out of the gym and onto the fashion floor was the creative inspiration of George Randall and Moshe Tsabag, co-founders of Yes Clothing Co. Now over half of the Yes line features Spandex.

Spandex, a Du Pont fabric, is best known for its clinging properties, but from the perspective of fashion design, it has additional advantages. Vivid colors and patterns are relatively easy to print on it, and it provides designers with opportunities for designs that are not available with other fabrics. Unfortunately for Yes, other organizations have also discovered the fashion

potential of Spandex. Some, including Beeba's Creations and L.A. Gear, have brought out their own Spandex fashions. In fact, demand has been so great that Du Pont has had to allocate what Spandex it can make. Yes tries to keep on top of this expanding market through close interaction with its retail outlets and a creative manufacturing strategy that focuses on making Yes garments in the United States, where changes in fashion can be instantly included in new lines of clothing.

So far, the strategy at Yes seems to be working. Total sales for the firm are up 55 percent since 1989 and topped $50 million in 1990. Product plans in 1992 include the introduction of Spandex clothes for men — Yes men, that is.

REFERENCES: Larry Armstrong, "Splashing Spandex Togs for the Suntanned Masses," *Business Week,* May 21, 1990, p. 105; Raye Rudie, "Men's Wear Favors Comfort and Style," *Bobbin,* October 1990, pp. 54–57; Monica Roman, "How Du Pont Keeps 'Em Coming Back for More," *Business Week,* August 20, 1990, p. 68.

ing these diverse and sometimes contradictory customer needs is an example of divergent thinking. One of Iaccoca's insights was that it might be possible to meet all these different customer needs by manufacturing different versions of one basic automobile design. This design became known as the "K-car." It was the result of using convergent thinking to find a common solution to numerous problems.[10]

The Creative Process

The creative process often moves through a series of four stages: *preparation, incubation, insight,* and *verification.*

Although creative people often report that ideas seem to come to them "in a flash," individual creative activity actually tends to progress through a series of stages.[11] Figure 9.2 summarizes the major stages of the creative process. Not all creative activity has to follow these four stages, but much of it does.

Preparation   The creative process normally begins with a period of **preparation,** which may include education and formal training. In Edison's time (the late 1800s to early 1900s) a highly creative person with a high school

Figure 9.2

The Creative Process

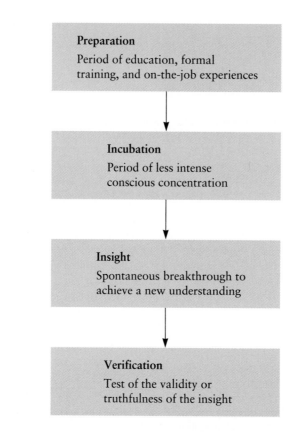

education or less could make significant creative contributions to technology. Many inventors during that time were self-taught. Since the majority of the population knew relatively little about science and technology, creative people did not need formal training or education to be successful.

Because of the growth in science and technology over the last century, we now know a great deal more about both how the world works and how to apply this knowledge to engineer new products and services. Formal education and training are usually the most efficient ways of becoming familiar with this vast amount of research and knowledge. Currently, most practicing scientists in organizations have Ph.D.s in their scientific discipline, and many have additional postdoctoral training.[12]

Moreover, the requirement for increased preparation through formal education and training is not limited to the physical and life sciences such as physics, chemistry, and biology. Understanding of the economic and business world has also grown more sophisticated over the years. To make a creative contribution to business management or business services, individuals must usually receive formal training and education in business. This is one reason for the increasing demand for undergraduate and master's level business education. Formal business education can be an effective way for an individual to get "up to speed" and begin making creative contributions quickly.

Experiences that scientists and managers have on the job after their formal training has finished can also contribute to the creative process. In an important sense, the education and training of creative people never really ends. It continues as long as they remain interested in the world and curious about the way things work.

Incubation   The second phase of the creative process is incubation. **Incubation** is a period of less intense conscious concentration during which the creative person is able to let the knowledge and ideas acquired during preparation mature and develop. From the outside, it may look as though nothing is happening; few major breakthroughs occur during incubation. Slowly, however, behind the scenes, often on a subconscious level, the creative individual is linking ideas together and generating new concepts.

A curious aspect of incubation is that it is often helped along by pauses in concentrated rational thought. Some creative people rely on physical activity such as jogging or swimming to provide a "break" from thinking. Others may read or listen to music. Sometimes sleep may even supply the needed pause. While out rowing one day, David Morse, a research scientist at Corning, hit on the answer to a long-sought-after product improvement. Morse had a special interest in a new line of cookware called Visions. These glass pots and pans had many advantages over traditional cookware, but no one at Corning had yet succeeded in putting a nonstick surface on the glass. Looking for a solution to this problem, Morse put in many long days in the laboratory, but it was during his hours of rowing that the ideas and concepts that would enable him to devise a nonstick coating began to come together and mature. Morse may never have been able to solve this technical problem if he had not taken the time to let his ideas incubate.[13]

Insight   Usually occurring after preparation and incubation, **insight** is a spontaneous breakthrough in which the creative person achieves a new understanding of some problem or situation. Insight represents a coming together of all the scattered thoughts and ideas that were maturing during incubation. It may occur suddenly or develop slowly over time. Insight can be triggered by some external event, such as a new experience or an encounter with new data that forces the individual to think about old issues and problems in new ways, or it can be a completely internal event in which patterns of thought finally coalesce in ways that generate new understanding.

One manager's key insight led to a complete restructuring of Citibank's Back Room Operations. "Back Room Operations" refers to the enormous avalanche of paperwork that a bank must process in order to serve its customers — listing checks and deposits, updating accounts, and preparing bank statements. Historically, Back Room Operations at Citibank had been managed as if they were part of the regular banking operation. When then Vice President John Reed arrived on the scene, he realized that Back Room Operations had less to do with banking and more to do with manufacturing. Reed's insight was that Back Room Operations could be managed as a paper-manufacturing process. On the basis of this insight, he hired former manufacturing managers from Ford and other automobile companies. By reconceptualizing the nature of Back Room Operations, Reed was able to substantially reduce the costs of these operations for Citibank.[14]

Verification   Once an insight has occurred, **verification** determines the validity or truthfulness of the insight. For many creative ideas, verification includes scientific experiments to determine whether or not the insight actually leads to the results expected. In David Morse's case, the insight concerning how to apply a nonstick coating on glass pots was verified in several important experiments and practical trials. Without these experiments and trials Morse's idea would have remained an interesting concept with little practical application.

Verification may also include the development of a product or service prototype. A **prototype** is one (or a very small number) of products built just to see if the ideas behind this new product actually work. Product prototypes are rarely sold to the public but are very valuable in verifying the insights developed in the creative process. Once the new product or service is developed, verification in the marketplace is the ultimate test of the creative idea behind it.

> A *prototype* is one (or a very small number) of products built to see if the ideas behind this new product actually work.

Organizational Innovation

As shown in Figure 9.1, individual creativity is a determining factor in an organization's ability to bring new products and services to the market. In order for an organization to be highly successful in introducing new products and services, however, individual creativity must be linked with innovation. Innovative organizations are able to attract, nurture, and develop creative individuals and, in turn, to take advantage of the new products and services they create.

The Innovation Process

Organizations that employ creative individuals often have the benefit of possessing numerous ideas for many new products and services. They may also possess several product prototypes that verify the insights of their creative employees. However, to turn these ideas and prototypes into real products and services that can be sold to customers, an organization must marshal other resources to develop and sell the innovation. The process of developing, applying, launching, growing, and managing the maturity and decline of a creative idea is called the innovation process.[15] This process is depicted in Figure 9.3.

> The organizational innovation process often proceeds through six steps: *innovation development, innovation application, application launch, application growth, innovation maturity,* and *innovation decline.*

Innovation Development   Once a creative insight is verified and, where appropriate, product prototypes are built, then an innovation is developed. Most ideas do not emerge from the creative process ready to be instantly transformed into new products or services. **Innovation development** is the stage in which an organization evaluates, modifies, and improves on a creative idea before turning that idea into a product or service to sell.

Figure 9.3

The Innovation Process

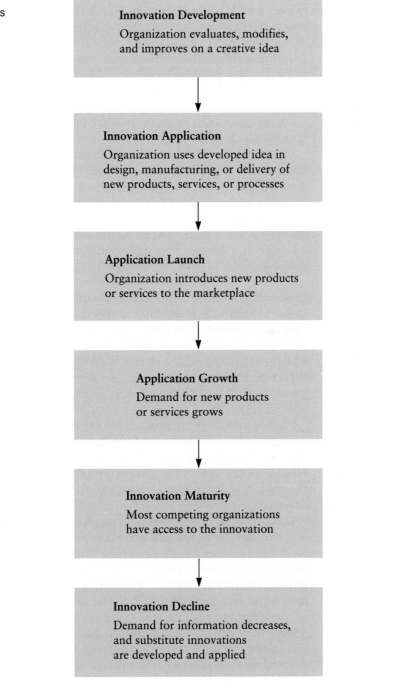

Innovation Development
Organization evaluates, modifies, and improves on a creative idea

Innovation Application
Organization uses developed idea in design, manufacturing, or delivery of new products, services, or processes

Application Launch
Organization introduces new products or services to the marketplace

Application Growth
Demand for new products or services grows

Innovation Maturity
Most competing organizations have access to the innovation

Innovation Decline
Demand for information decreases, and substitute innovations are developed and applied

Innovation development can transform a product or service with only modest potential into a product or service with significant potential. Parker Brothers (manufacturers of the board games Monopoly, Risk, and Life), for example, decided during innovation development not to market an indoor volleyball game but instead sell separately the appealing little foam ball designed for the game. The firm will never know how well the volleyball game would have sold, but the Nerf ball and numerous related products have generated millions of dollars in revenues for Parker Brothers.[16]

Innovation Application   Even after development, the idea has yet to be applied to real products or services. **Innovation application** is the stage in which an organization takes a developed idea and uses it in the design, manufacturing, or delivery of new products, services, or processes. At this point the innovation emerges from the laboratory and is transformed into tangible goods or services.

One example of innovation application is the use of radar-based focusing systems in Polaroid's instant cameras. The idea of using radio waves to discover the location, speed, and direction of moving objects was first applied extensively by Allied forces during World War II. As radar technology developed over the following years, the electrical components needed became smaller and more streamlined. Researchers at Polaroid hit on radar as a creative idea and applied this well-developed technology in a new way.[17]

Application Launch   **Application launch** is the stage in which an organization introduces new products or services to the marketplace by contacting potential customers, making sales arrangements, and delivering the new products and services. Verification in the creative process focuses on whether or not a creative insight is scientifically correct — does it work as expected? In application launch, the key question is not "Does the innovation work?" but "Will customers want to purchase the innovative product and service?"

History is full of creative ideas that did not generate enough interest among customers to be successful. Some notable innovation failures include the Edsel automobile (with its notoriously homely front end), the movie *Heaven's Gate* (which lost almost $100 million before it was pulled from theaters), and Polaroid's SX-70 instant camera (which cost $3 billion to develop but never sold more than 100,000 units in a year). Despite individual creativity, development, and application, it is still possible for products and services to fail at the application launch phase of innovation.[18]

Application Growth   Once an innovation has been successfully launched, it then enters the stage of **application growth**, where demand for the innovation increases. This is a period of high economic performance for an organization, because there is often more demand for the product or service than supply. Organizations that fail to anticipate this stage may unintentionally limit their growth, as Coleco did by not anticipating demand for its Cabbage Patch dolls in the late 1980s, and as Nintendo did by not anticipating demand for its "Super Mario Brothers" video games in the late 1980s and early 1990s.

At the same time, overestimating demand for a new product or service can be just as detrimental to performance. This occurred for many western-wear manufacturers in the early 1980s after the enormous popularity of the John Travolta movie *Urban Cowboy* suddenly but very briefly increased demand for cowboy boots, shirts, and other clothes. Many of these organizations lost a great deal of money anticipating higher demand than what actually existed and purchasing a great deal of western-wear inventory that took years to dispose of.

Innovation Maturity   After a period of growing demand, an innovative product or service often enters a period of maturity. **Innovation maturity** is the stage in which most organizations in an industry have access to an innovation and are applying it in approximately the same way. The technological application of an innovation during this stage of the innovation process can be very sophisticated. However, because most firms have access to the innovation, either because they have developed the innovation on their own or have copied the innovation of others, it does not provide competitive advantage to any one of them.

The time that elapses between innovation development and innovation maturity varies significantly depending on the particular product or service. Whenever an innovation involves the use of complex technical or social skills (such as a complicated manufacturing process or highly sophisticated teamwork), it will take longer to move from the growth phase to the maturity phase. Using language introduced in Chapter 7, we can say that these innovations have already been shown to be valuable (in the launch and growth stages). If, in addition, the skills needed to implement these innovations are rare and difficult to imitate, then strategic imitation may be delayed, and the original innovating organization may enjoy a period of sustained competitive advantage.

One innovation that has taken a very long time to move from growth to maturity (and may not have matured even yet) is the user-friendliness of Apple's Macintosh computer. When the Macintosh was first introduced in the early 1980s, it immediately provided a level of user-friendliness that was unique in the personal-computer industry. Over the years, efforts to make other types of PCs as user-friendly as the Macintosh have not succeeded. Only recently has Microsoft's Windows software begun to address user-friendliness as effectively. During all this time, customers who wanted to purchase user-friendly personal computers were limited to Apple's Macintosh.[19]

On the other hand, when the implementation of an innovation does not depend either on rare or on difficult-to-imitate skills, then the time between the growth and maturity phases can be very brief. In the market for computer memory devices, for example, technological innovation by one firm can be very quickly duplicated by other firms, because the skills needed to design and manufacture these electronic devices are widespread. Computer memory devices thus move very rapidly from growth to maturity.

Innovation Decline   Every successful innovation bears the seeds of its own decline. Since an organization does not gain a competitive advantage from an innovation at maturity, it must encourage its creative scientists, engineers, and managers to begin looking for new innovations. Thus the individual creative process depicted in Figure 9.2 begins again and leads again to the innovation process. It is this continued search for competitive advantage that usually leads new products and services to move from the creative process through innovation maturity and finally to innovation decline. **Innovation decline** is the stage during which demand for an innovation decreases and substitute innovations are developed and applied.

First described by Joseph Schumpeter, the *cycle of creative destruction* suggests that as organizations innovate to create competitive advantage, they simultaneously destroy the innovations of other organizations.

This continuing cycle of creativity, innovation, and decline was originally described by Joseph Schumpeter. Schumpeter called it the cycle of "creative destruction," for each creative act at least partly destroys the value of previous innovations while simultaneously creating new sources of value for organizations. As depicted in Figure 9.4, the **cycle of creative destruction** has been widely cited as the main reason for the enormous technological progress over the last one hundred years. To gain competitive advantage, firms encourage individual creativity, which in turn leads to innovation. As innovations mature, competitive advantage disappears, and the search for creative new sources of advantage must begin again.[20]

One organization that is using the cycle of creative destruction to explicitly address important societal needs is Success Source, Inc., as described in The Environmental Challenge.

Types of Innovations in Organizations

Each creative idea that an organization develops poses a different challenge for the innovation process. Innovations can be radical or incremental, technical or managerial, and product or process. Each of these types of innovations is discussed below.

Radical innovations are new products or technologies that completely replace existing products or technologies. *Incremental innovations* are new products or technologies that modify existing products or technologies.

Radical Versus Incremental Innovations   **Radical innovations** are new products or technologies developed by an organization that completely replace the existing products or technologies in an industry. **Incremental innovations** are new products or processes that modify existing products or technologies. Organizations that implement radical innovations funda-

Figure 9.4

The Cycle of Creative Destruction

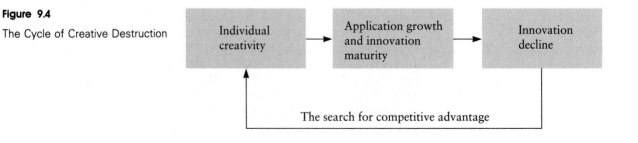

THE ENVIRONMENTAL CHALLENGE

Marketing Success to Middle-Class African-Americans

At first glance, the multimedia products and marketing services of Success Source, Inc., do not sound that unusual. They include a national speakers bureau (Success Net), a direct-mail service for firms selling to professionals (Success Mail), a nationally syndicated radio program (*For Your Success*), a self-help newsletter (*Success Notes*), and a resource book for purchasing high-quality products and services (*Success Guide*). The themes of career improvement, and of access to the "good life" that such improvement creates, permeate all Success Source products. These business themes are also present in the products and services of companies such as SyberVision (which markets self-improvement video and audio tapes) and Sharper Image and Hammacher Schlemmer (which market expensive products for affluent professionals).

What makes Success Source different is that it markets its services and products to African-American professionals and managers and has as one of its key objectives the development of black entrepreneurs throughout the United States. So far, Success Source's $3 million in revenues after just three years of operation testifies to the economic value of this entrepreneurial effort.

Founder George C. Fraser seeks in several ways to reach his business goal of developing the skills and competencies of fellow black entrepreneurs. First, by identifying African-Americans who are successful entrepreneurs (through his *Success Guide* books, radio shows, and speaking tours), Fraser helps publicize important role models to other aspiring African-Americans. Second, by helping corporations market products to the black middle class, Success Source helps corporations take advantage of the economic potential of this large group. Finally, Fraser seeks partners in cities throughout the United States to develop and publish regional versions of *Success Guide*. These business people, Fraser hopes, will pass on the message of African-American entrepreneurship and professionalism. Fraser is one of a growing number of entrepreneurs who recognize profit potential in selling the idea of African-American business success.

So far, Fraser has been successful in encouraging fourteen entrepreneurs in seven cities to participate in Success Source. By 1995, Fraser hopes to have helped establish twenty-five independent black-owned businesses in the United States.

REFERENCES: Lisa Gitlin, "George C. Fraser: A Voice for African Americans," *Continental Profiles*, May 1991, p. 26; Meg Whittemore, "Franchising: Expanding Opportunities for Minorities and Women," *Nation's Business*, December 1990, p. 58; Glen Macnow, "Business Is the Emancipator," *Nation's Business*, September 1990, pp. 41–44.

mentally shift the nature of competition and the interaction of firms within their environments. Organizations that implement incremental innovations alter, but do not fundamentally change, competitive interaction in an industry.[21]

Many radical innovations have been introduced by organizations over the last several years. For example, compact disc technology is now replacing long-playing vinyl records in the recording industry, and high-definition television seems likely to replace regular television technology (both black and white and color) in the near future. Whereas radical innovations like these tend to be very visible and public, incremental innovations actually are more numerous. One example is General Motors's aerodynamic minivan, the Lumina. Manufacture of this sleek product pioneered the use of plastic auto-body panels and employed a new process for forming the front windshield. However, although the van's exterior is the result of innovation, the engine, drive train, and other mechanical parts remain quite standard.

Radical innovations have higher potential for economic return than do incremental innovations. This is because an organization that is able to successfully implement a radical innovation will have an important competitive advantage. Associated with this higher economic potential, however, is greater economic risk and uncertainty. As defined in Chapter 5, *economic risk* exists when, at the time a decision is made, several possible outcomes are possible and the probability of each occurring is known. *Economic uncertainty* exists when, at the time a decision is made, both the range of possible outcomes and their likelihood of occurring are not known. Highly risky and uncertain radical innovations have a much greater chance of failing to meet expectations than do less risky and uncertain incremental innovations. In general, the riskier and more uncertain an innovation, the greater the potential economic return must be in order to balance the risks that the organization bears.[22]

Technical innovations are changes in the physical appearance or performance of a product or service or changes in the physical processes through which a product or service is manufactured.

Technical Versus Managerial Innovations   **Technical innovations** are changes in the physical appearance or performance of a product or service or changes in the physical processes through which a product or service is manufactured. Many of the most important innovations over the last fifty years have been technical. For example, the serial replacement of the vacuum tube with the transistor, the transistor with the integrated circuit, and the integrated circuit with the microchip has greatly enhanced the power, ease of use, and speed of operation of a wide variety of electronic products.

Not all innovations developed by organizations are technical, however. **Managerial innovations** are changes in the management processes by which products and services are conceived, built, and delivered to customers. Managerial innovations do not necessarily affect the physical appearance or performance of products or services directly, but they can. Many Japanese firms have used managerial innovations to improve the quality of their products or services. One of the most important of these innovations developed in the last thirty years, called the *quality circle,* helped Oki Electronics become one of the premier electronics companies in the world. Organizations that have been able to incorporate quality circles and total quality management, in which small groups of concerned workers discuss how to improve product quality, have found that quality improves dramatically and the costs of operations decrease.[23]

Other managerial innovations have been important for firms selling in international markets. One of these innovations, called *counter trade,* is described in The Global Challenge.

Managerial innovations are changes in the management processes by which products or services are conceived, built, and delivered to customers.

Product innovations involve either changes in the physical characteristics or performance of existing products or services or the creation of brand-new products or services. *Process innovations* are changes in the way products or services are manufactured, created, or distributed.

Product Versus Process Innovations   Perhaps the two most important types of technical innovations are product innovations and process innovations. **Product innovations** involve either changes in the physical characteristics or performance of existing products or services or the creation of brand-new products or services. **Process innovations** are changes in the way products or services are manufactured, created, or distributed. Whereas

Innovation is critical to the success of most organizations. This is particularly true of organizations in rapidly changing environments, such as the microelectronics industry. T. J. Rodgers, chief executive of Cypress Semiconductors, uses a computer system to track the innovation goals and objectives of each of Cypress's 1,500 employees. This takes him four hours to do, and he does it weekly. This way he can efficiently manage the innovative goals within his company and offer help where needed to accomplish them.

Organizations may fail to innovate because (1) they lack the necessary resources, (2) they fail to recognize the potential of particular innovations, and (3) they resist change.

managerial innovations generally affect the broader context of development, process innovations directly affect the manufacturing process.

One very important process innovation that many organizations have adopted over the last several years is the use of robots. The careful utilization of robots in the manufacturing of products as diverse as automobiles, steel, and semiconductors can increase quality, speed, and efficiency and simultaneously free workers to concentrate on less repetitive and boring tasks.

As Figure 9.5 shows, the effect of product and process innovations on economic return depends on the stage of the innovation process that a new product or service occupies. At first, during development, application, and launch, the physical attributes and capabilities of an innovation most affect organizational performance. Thus product innovations are particularly important during these beginning phases. Later on, as an innovation enters the phases of growth, maturity, and decline, an organization's ability to develop process innovations such as fine-tuning manufacturing, increasing product quality, and improving product distribution becomes important to maintaining economic return.[24]

Japanese organizations have often excelled at process innovation. The market for 35-mm cameras was dominated by German and other European manufacturers when, in the early 1960s, Japanese organizations such as Canon and Nikon began making cameras. Some of the early Japanese-made products were not very successful, but these companies continued to invest in their process technology and eventually were able to increase quality and decrease manufacturing costs. Now these Japanese organizations dominate the worldwide market for 35-mm cameras, and the German companies, because they were not able to maintain the same pace of process innovation, are struggling to maintain market share and profitability.[25] By focusing efforts on refining the manufacturing process, organizations that do not have a competitive advantage when innovations are introduced may develop a competitive advantage over time.

The Failure to Innovate

The cycle of creative destruction depicted in Figure 9.4 sends an unambiguous signal to modern organizations: to remain competitive in today's economy, it is necessary to be both creative and innovative. And yet many organizations that should be creative and innovative are not successful at bringing out new products or services, or do so only after innovations created by others are very mature. There are at least three reasons why organizations may fail to innovate: (1) they lack the necessary resources; (2) they fail to recognize the potential of particular innovations; and (3) they resist change.

Lack of Organizational Resources

Implementing an innovation strategy can be expensive in dollars, time, and energy. If a firm does not have sufficient money to fund a program of innovation, or does not currently

THE GLOBAL CHALLENGE

Turning Sesame Seeds into Pepsi-Cola

Imagine the following hypothetical commercial. The sun is beginning to set as six teenage boys finish their game of basketball. The final score was close, but the losers have promised to buy the winners a cool drink — Pepsi-Cola. The heat of the day still rises, shimmering from the blacktop, as the losing team goes into the store to buy their Pepsis. The refrigerator in the store is overflowing with Pepsi — regular, diet — and all sorts of flavored soft drinks. The boys make their selection, take it to the counter, reach into their pockets, and pull out a handful of sesame seeds and give them to the cashier. "Thanks, boys. See you tomorrow," he replies as he stores the seeds in the register. The boys take their drinks outside and walk slowly to their homes in the Sudanese desert, refreshed by a drink made in the United States.

It sounds far-fetched — sesame seeds for Pepsi-Cola — but this is exactly the kind of innovative trading that PepsiCo and many other U.S. firms have resorted to in order to sell their products to Third World countries. Countries with underdeveloped economies are shackled by enormous debts and have very little foreign currency with which to buy foreign products. A country like the Sudan, for example, has a literacy rate of 20 percent and a gross national product of $200 per person per year.

PepsiCo and other firms sell their products to such countries in exchange for not worthless domestic currency but products for export. In the Sudan, PepsiCo takes sesame seeds as payment for its soft drinks and, in turn, sells the sesame seeds on the world market to obtain a profit. In Mexico, Pepsi accepts pineapples for payment; in Tanzania, Pepsi receives sisal (a component of rope); and in Nicaragua, Pepsi sells its drinks for sesame seeds and molasses. This process, called *counter trade,* is one of the few ways that U.S. firms can sell to the cash-starved economies of the Third World. Many companies may find they have to practice counter trade in order to do business with the Soviet Union and cash-starved eastern European countries.

REFERENCES: Louis Kraar, "How to Sell to Cashless Buyers," *Fortune,* November 7, 1988, pp. 147–154; James K. Weekly and Raj Aggarwal, *International Business: Operating in the Global Economy* (New York: Dryden, 1987), p. 27; *The 1990 Almanac* (Boston: Houghton Mifflin), pp. 260, 278.

employ the kinds of creative individuals that it needs to be innovative, it may find itself lagging behind in innovation.

Even a highly innovative organization cannot become involved in every new product or service that its employees think up. As we saw earlier, for example, numerous other commitments in the electronic instruments and computer industry forestalled Hewlett-Packard from investing in Steve Jobs and Steve Wozniak's idea for a personal computer. With infinite resources of money, time, and technical and managerial expertise, HP might have entered this market early. However, because the firm did not have this flexibility, it had to make some difficult choices about which innovations to invest in.[26]

Failure to Recognize Opportunities   Since organizations cannot pursue all innovations, they need to develop the capability to carefully evaluate innovations and to select the ones that hold the greatest potential. In order to obtain a competitive advantage, an organization usually must make investment decisions before the innovation process reaches the mature stage.

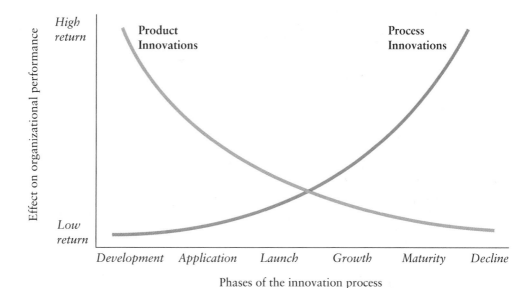

Figure 9.5

The Effect of Product and Process Innovation on Economic Return

However, as suggested above, the earlier the investment, the greater is the risk. If organizations are not skilled at recognizing and evaluating opportunities, they may be overly cautious and fail to invest in innovations that turn out later to be successful for other firms.

Resistance to Change   There is a tendency in many organizations to resist change. Innovation means giving up old products and old ways of doing things in favor of new products and new ways of doing things. These kinds of changes can be personally difficult for managers and other members of an organization. As we indicate in detail in Chapter 23, resistance to change can slow the innovation process.

Ways of Promoting Innovation in Organizations

Three of the best ways to encourage innovation in organizations are (1) using the reward system, (2) using intrapreneurs, and (3) using organizational culture.

A wide variety of management techniques for promoting innovation in organizations has been developed over the years. Most of these management tools encourage individuals and groups within organizations to be open and flexible to change and innovation. Because these tools are so closely linked to the management of change in organizations, they are discussed in detail in Chapter 23. Three of the most effective ways of promoting innovation, however, are described below.

The Reward System

An organization's reward system is the financial and nonfinancial means that the organization uses to encourage and discourage certain behaviors by employees. Key components of the reward system include salaries, bonuses, and perquisites, such as a company car and a large office. Using the reward system to promote creativity and innovation is a fairly mechanical but nevertheless effective management technique. The idea is to provide financial and nonfinancial rewards to people and groups that develop innovative ideas. Once the members of an organization understand that they will be rewarded for creative activities, they are more likely to work creatively. With this end in mind, Monsanto Company gives a $50,000 award each year to the scientist or group of scientists that develops the biggest commercial breakthrough.[27]

It is important for organizations to reward creative behavior, but it is vital to avoid punishing creativity when it does not result in highly successful innovations. It is the nature of the creative and innovative processes that many new product ideas will simply not work out in the marketplace. Each process is fraught with too many uncertainties to generate positive results every time. An individual may have prepared herself to be creative, but an insight may not be forthcoming. Or managers may attempt to apply a developed innovation, only to gradually recognize that it does not work. Indeed, some organizations operate according to the assumption that if all their innovative efforts succeed, then they are probably not taking enough risks in research and development. At 3M, nearly 60 percent of the creative ideas suggested each year do not succeed in the marketplace.

Organizations need to be very careful in responding to innovative failure. Certainly, if innovative failure is due to incompetence, systematic errors, or managerial sloppiness, then an organization should respond appropriately, perhaps by withholding raises or by reducing promotion opportunities. However, creative people who act in good faith to develop an innovation that simply does not work out should not be punished for failure. If they are, they will probably not be creative in the future. A punitive reward system will discourage people from taking risks and therefore reduce the organization's ability to obtain competitive advantages.

To avoid punishing failure inappropriately, managers must thoroughly understand both the skills and capabilities of a creative individual and the goal that the individual was attempting to accomplish. By developing this understanding, managers will be able to distinguish among creative activities that simply do not work out and other activities that reflect managerial incompetence, stupidity, or poor judgment. The role that a reward system plays in an organization is discussed in more detail in Chapters 14 and 17.

Intrapreneurship

The use of intrapreneurs also helps organizations encourage innovation. As we saw in Chapter 3, intrapreneurs are similar to entrepreneurs, except that they develop a new business in the context of a larger organization.

There are three intrapreneurial roles in large organizations.[28] To successfully use intrapreneurship to encourage creativity and innovation, the organization must find one or more individuals to perform these roles. The

Edgar Woolard (center), chief executive of Du Pont, is particularly dedicated to creating an organizational culture that supports creativity, innovation, and risk taking. The culture at Du Pont is influenced by his understanding that all employees genuinely want to make a contribution. Here he visits research scientists to emphasize his support of their work.

An *inventor* is a person who actually conceives of and develops a new idea, product, or service. A *product champion* is a middle manager who becomes aware of an innovation and helps in its development. A *sponsor* is a top-level manager who approves of and supports a project.

inventor is the person who actually conceives of and develops the new idea, product, or service by means of the creative process. However, because the inventor may lack the expertise or motivation to oversee the transformation of the product or service from an idea into a marketable entity, a second role comes into play. A **product champion** is usually a middle manager who learns about the project and becomes committed to it. He or she helps overcome organizational resistance and convinces others to take the innovation seriously. The product champion may have only limited understanding of the technological aspects of the innovation. However, product champions are skilled at knowing how the organization works, whose support is needed to push the project forward, and where to go to secure the resources necessary for successful development. A **sponsor** is a top-level manager who approves of and supports a project. This person may fight for the budget needed to develop an idea, overcome arguments against a project, and use organizational politics to ensure the project's survival. With a sponsor in place, the inventor's idea has a much better chance of being successfully developed.

Several firms have embraced intrapreneurship as a way to encourage creativity and innovation. Colgate-Palmolive has created a separate unit, Colgate Venture Company, staffed with intrapreneurs who develop new products. General Foods developed Culinova Group as a unit to which employees can take their ideas for possible development. S. C. Johnson &

Son established a $250,000 fund to support new product ideas, and Texas Instruments refuses to approve an innovative project unless it has an acknowledged inventor, champion, and sponsor.

Organizational Culture

An organization's culture is the set of values, beliefs, and symbols that help guide behavior. A strong, appropriately focused organizational culture can serve numerous purposes. We saw in Chapter 8 that managers can use culture to help implement business-level strategies. They can also use it to support creative and innovative activity. A well-managed culture can communicate a sense that innovation is valued and will be rewarded and that occasional failure in the pursuit of new ideas is not only acceptable but even expected. In addition to reward systems and intrapreneurial activities, firms such as 3M, Corning, Monsanto, Procter & Gamble, Texas Instruments, Johnson & Johnson, and Merck are all known to have strong, innovation-oriented cultures. These cultures value individual creativity, risk taking, and inventiveness.[29] The importance of culture to organizational behavior and performance is discussed in more detail in Chapter 11.

Learning Summary

Creativity and innovation are both important for modern organizations. Creativity is the ability of an individual to generate new ideas or to conceive of new perspectives on existing ideas. Innovation is an organization's managed effort to develop new products or services or new uses for existing products or services. The successful introduction of new products and services depends critically on an organization having creative people and supporting those people in a context that encourages, nurtures, and rewards their creativity.

Many creative individuals come from backgrounds in which their creativity was perceived and rewarded. They often share certain personality traits and cognitive skills. Among the most important of these is the ability to think divergently and convergently.

The creative process is complex but often proceeds through four stages. During preparation, creative individuals obtain the education and training needed to develop their creativity. During incubation, the ideas and questions obtained during preparation are allowed to ferment quietly, as the creative person begins to make connections and linkages. During insight, these ideas and connections coalesce, forming a new understanding. Finally, in verification, the creative person tests the idea to make sure that it actually works as predicted.

To be able to introduce new products and services, an organization must usually link individual creativity with organizational innovation. The innovation process has six steps: development, application, launch, growth, maturity, and decline. Radical innovations completely replace existing products or technologies in an industry. Incremental innovations modify products or technologies. Technical innovations are changes in the physical appearance or performance of a product or service or changes in the physical processes through which a product or service is manufactured. Managerial innovations are changes in the management policies and practices through which products and services are conceived, built, and delivered to customers. Finally, product innovations involve either changes in the physical characteristics of old products or services or the creation of brand-new products or services. Process innovations are changes in the way products or services are manufactured, created, or distributed. In the early stages of the innovation process, product innovations have the most effect on organizational performance. In the later stages, process innovations become more important.

Despite the importance of creativity and innovation, many organizations fail to introduce new products or services. These organizations may lack the required creative individuals, be committed to too many other creative activities, fail to recognize opportunities, or resist the change that creativity and innovation may require.

Organizations can use a variety of tools to overcome these problems, including the reward system, intrapreneurship, and organizational culture. Organizations that use intrapreneurs should encourage the development of inventor, product champion, and sponsor roles.

Questions and Exercises

Review Questions

1. Define the terms *individual creativity* and *organizational innovation*.
2. What is the relationship between individual creativity and organizational innovation?
3. What personality traits do creative individuals commonly share?
4. What cognitive skills are often possessed by creative people?
5. What are the steps in the creative process?
6. What are the steps in the innovation process?
7. What kinds of innovations exist in organizations? Give an example of each.
8. Why do some organizations resist innovation, and what can be done to overcome this resistance?

Analysis Questions

1. Steve Jobs and Steve Wozniak both worked for large electronics companies when they developed the concept of the personal computer. Does the fact that two large firms did not take advantage of Jobs's and Wozniak's ideas necessarily mean that those companies made a mistake? Why or why not?

2. Creative individuals are often different from other managers in background, personality, and cognitive style. This difference can sometimes lead to conflicts between creative and noncreative people in an organization. What might some of these conflicts be, and how might they be managed?
3. Suppose you are a manager in a highly innovative organization, and you are in charge of a group of creative scientists. How can you tell the difference between a scientist who is going through the incubation process and one who is wasting time?

Application Exercises

1. In your own experience as a student or an employee, have you ever developed a creative new idea or approach? If you have, analyze your experience in terms of the creative process outlined in the chapter. If you have not, speculate about why you have not had a creative experience. Do you have the attributes of a creative person? Have you been a member of an organization that encourages creativity?
2. Think about an organization that you know well — your university, a firm you worked for, your church. Are there creative people in this organization? Why or why not? Does this organization take advantage of the creative individuals in it? Why or why not?

Chapter Notes

1. William C. Symonds, "Ramtron's Revolution: Circuits on Ceramics," *Business Week,* June 15, 1990, p. 64; Michael Bloom, "Advanced ICs: A Memory to Remember," *ESD,* October 1989, pp. 38–44; David Bondurant and Fred Gnadinger, "Ferroelectrics for Nonvolatile RAMs," *IEEE Spectrum,* July 1989, pp. 30–33; Joe Evans, "Ferroelectric Memories," *ESD,* August 1988, pp. 29–35.
2. The distinction between individual creativity and organizational innovation is discussed in T. M. Amabile, "A Model of Creativity and Innovation in Organizations," in *Research in Organizational Behavior,* vol. 10, ed. B. M. Staw and L. L. Cummings (Greenwich, Conn.: JAI Press, 1988); F. Barron, *Creative Person and Creative Process* (New York: Holt, Rinehart and Winston, 1969); and L. L. Cummings, "Organizational Climates for Creativity," *Academy of Management Journal,* 1965, pp. 220–227.
3. Kenneth Labich, "The Innovators," *Fortune,* June 6, 1988, pp. 60–64.
4. "Xerox Unveils a Wide Ranging Package of Computers and Software — The Company Is Attempting to Shed Its Outdated Image," *Wall Street Journal,* September 20, 1990, pp. A1+.
5. For a discussion of these three categories, see Richard Woodman, John Sawyer, and Ricky Griffin, "Organizational Creativity: A Proposal for Research on Creativity in Complex Social Systems" (Department of Management, Texas A&M University, College Station, 1991); and R. T. Brown, "Creativity: What Are We to Measure?" in *Handbook of Creativity,* ed. J. A. Glover, R. R. Ronning, and C. R. Reynolds (New York: Plenum, 1989), pp. 3–32.

6. The study of the impact of background characteristics on creativity has a long tradition stemming from the work of Francis Galton, *Hereditary Genius* (London: Macmillan, 1869). More recent work on background and creativity can be found in C. E. Schaefer and A. Anastasi, "A Biographical Inventory for Identifying Creativity in Adolescent Boys," *Journal of Applied Psychology,* 1968, pp. 42–48; D. K. Simonton, "Biographical Typicality, Eminence, and Achievement Styles," *Journal of Creative Behavior,* 1986, pp. 14–22; and B. Singh, "Role of Personality Versus Biographical Factors in Creativity," *Psychological Studies,* 1986, pp. 90–92. This entire approach to understanding creativity has been criticized by F. B. Barron and D. M. Harrington, "Creativity, Intelligence, and Personality," *Annual Review of Psychology,* 1981, pp. 439–476.

7. For summaries of this personality trait literature, see Barron and Harrington, "Creativity, Intelligence, and Personality," and Richard Woodman and Lyle Schoenfeldt, "An Interactionist Model of Creative Behavior," *Journal of Creative Behavior,* 1990, pp. 10–20.

8. The link between intelligence and creativity is discussed by H. G. Gough, "Studying Creativity by Means of Word Association Tests," *Journal of Applied Psychology,* 1976, pp. 348–353, and Barron and Harrington, "Creativity, Intelligence, and Personality."

9. The relationship between convergent thinking, divergent thinking, and creativity has been discussed by M. Basadur, G. B. Graen, and S. G. Green, "Training in Creative Problem-solving: Effects on Ideation and Problem Finding and Solving in an Industrial Research Organization," *Organizational Behavior and Human Performance,* 1982, pp. 41–70; M. Basadur and C. T. Finkbeiner, "Measuring Preference for Ideation in Creative Problem Solving Training," *Journal of Applied Behavioral Science,* 1985, pp. 37–49; and M. Kirton, "Adaptors and Innovators: A Description and Measure," *Journal of Applied Psychology,* 1976, pp. 622–629.

10. See Lee Iacocca (with William Novak), *Iacocca: An Autobiography* (New York: Bantam, 1984). Other cognitive abilities thought to be associated with individual creativity are discussed in J. B. Carrol, "Domains of Cognitive Ability" (Paper presented at the American Association for the Advancement of Science, Los Angeles, May 1985); H. A. Witkin, R. B. Dyk, H. F. Paterson, D. R. Goodenough, and S. A. Karp, *Psychological Differentiation* (New York: Wiley, 1962); J. P. Guilford, *Way Beyond IQ: Guide to Improving Intelligence and Creativity* (Buffalo, N.Y.: Creative Education Foundation, 1977); J. P. Guilford, "Transformation Abilities or Functions," *The Journal of Creative Behavior,* 1983, pp. 75–83; and J. P. Guilford, "Varieties of Divergent Production," *The Journal of Creative Behavior,* 1984, pp. 1–10.

11. See Thomas V. Busse and Richard S. Mansfield, "Theories of the Creative Process: A Review and a Perspective," *Journal of Creative Behavior,* 1980, pp. 91–103, for a discussion of this and other models of the creative process.

12. This is true in the United States, Japan, and Europe. See John Carey, Robert Buderi, and Emily Smith, "Innovators: United States Scientists," *Business Week,* June 15, 1990, pp. 52, 56, 58; Otis Port and Neil Gross, "Innovators: Japanese Scientists," *Business Week,* June 15, 1990, pp. 90, 94, 98; and Jonathan Levine, Thane Peterson, and Rose Brady, "Innovators: European Scientists," *Business Week,* June 15, 1990, pp. 136, 138, 140.

13. Labich, "The Innovators."

14. Jay W. Lorsch, Cyrus F. Gibson, and John A. Seeger, "First National City Bank Operating Group (A)," Case no. 9474165, Harvard Business School, Boston, Mass., 1975.

15. The organizational innovation process is discussed by L. B. Mohr, "Determinants of Innovation in Organizations," *American Political Science Review,* 1969, pp. 111–126; G. A. Steiner, *The Creative Organization* (Chicago: University of Chicago Press, 1965); M. J. Kirton and S. Pender, "The Adaptation-Innovation Continuum, Occupational Type, and Course-Selection," *Psychological Reports,* 1982, pp. 882–886; L. L. Cummings and M. J. O'Connell, "Organizational Innovation," *Journal of Business Research,* 1978, pp. 33–50; R. Duncan and A. Weiss, "Organizational Learning: Implications for Organizational Design," in *Research in Organizational Behavior,* vol. 1, ed. B. M. Staw (Greenwich, Conn.: JAI Press, 1979), pp. 75–123; and J. E. Ettlie, "Adequacy of Stage Models for Decisions on Adoption of Innovation," *Psychological Reports,* 1980, pp. 991–995.

16. Beth Wolfensberger, "Trouble in Toyland," *New England Business,* September 1990, pp. 28–36.

17. See Alan Patz, "Managing Innovation in High Technology Industries," *New Management,* 1986, pp. 54–59.

18. An excellent guide to these kinds of management errors is Robert F. Hartley, *Management Mistakes and Successes,* 3rd ed. (New York: Wiley, 1991).

19. John Dunkle, "The Windows Payoff: Macintosh Still Holds Graphical Edge," *Computer World,* March 4, 1991, pp. SR16–SR17; Brian Nielson, "Doing Windows," *Online,* September 1990, pp. 105–107.

20. Schumpeter described this cycle of creative destruction in J. A. Schumpeter, *Capitalism, Socialism, and Democracy,* 3rd ed. (New York: Harper & Row, 1950). His initial insights have been studied by a wide range of economists, including R. R. Nelson and S. Winter, *An Evolutionary Theory of Economic Change* (Cambridge, Mass.: Harvard University Press, 1982); Edith Penrose, *The Theory of the Growth of the Firm* (New York: Wiley, 1958); and Jay Barney, "Types of Competition and the Theory of Strategy," *Academy of Management Review,* 1986, pp. 791–800.

21. See Schumpeter, *Capitalism, Socialism, and Democracy,* for a discussion of radical and incremental innovations.

22. The need to increase expected returns as a compensation for accepting higher levels of risk is a central tenet of economic reasoning. See, for example, F. M. Scherer, *Industrial Market Structure and Economic Performance,* 2nd ed. (Boston: Houghton Mifflin, 1980), and Kathleen Conner, "A Historical Comparison of Resource Based Theory and Five Schools of Thought Within Industrial Organization Economics: Do We Have a New Theory of the Firm?" *Journal of Management,* 1991, pp. 121–154.

23. See William G. Ouchi, *Theory Z* (Reading, Mass.: Addison-Wesley, 1980), for a discussion of quality circles at Oki Electronics.

24. The relative importance of product and process innovations at different stages has been discussed by Robert Hayes and Steven Wheelwright, "Link Manufacturing Process and Product Life Cycles," *Harvard Business Review,* January–February, 1979, pp. 133–153; Robert Hayes and Steven Wheelwright, "The Dynamics of Process-Product Life Cycles," *Harvard Business Review,* March–April, 1979, pp. 127–136; and Robert Hayes and Steven Wheelwright, "Competing Through Manufacturing," *Harvard Business Review,* January–February, 1985, pp. 99–109.

25. Terutomo Amano, "Minolta Camera: Autofocus Perfected," *Tokyo Business Today,* August 1988, pp. 57–58; Tome Lester, "Canon Fires on All Cylinders," *Marketing,* March 20, 1986, pp. 22–24.

26. Clare C. Swanger, "Apple Computer, Inc. — Macintosh (A), Case no. S-BP-234, Graduate School of Business, Stanford University, 1984.

27. The impact of the reward system on innovation is discussed by Fariborz Damanpour, "The Adoption of Technological, Administrative, and Ancillary Innovations: Impact of Organizational Factors," *Journal of Management,* Autumn 1987, pp. 675–688, and Andre Delbecq and Peter Mills, "Managerial Practices That Enhance Innovation," *Organizational Dynamics,* Summer 1985, pp. 24–34.

28. See Gifford Pinchot III, *Intrapreneuring* (New York: Harper & Row, 1985).

29. See Steven P. Feldman, "How Organizational Culture Can Affect Innovation," *Organizational Dynamics,* Summer 1988, pp. 57–68.

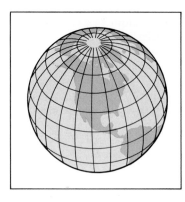

CASE 9.1

Alcoa's Two Very Different Innovators

Moving into the 1980s, everyone agreed that Alcoa (Aluminum Company of America) needed revitalization — a new direction or at least a new way to make a profit. For over a century, aluminum had been Alcoa's only major business, and it still accounted for 85 percent of its revenues. The world's largest aluminum producer, Alcoa made about 17 percent of the world's aluminum and easily outpaced its American rivals. But just as aluminum had once replaced steel in many applications, primarily because it is lighter, aluminum was being replaced by even lighter plastics, composites, and ceramics. World growth in aluminum consumption was slowing to 3 percent per year, and the aluminum industry was suffering many of the same problems that the steel industry had gone through. Alcoa could no longer grow simply by increasing its volume of output. The company clearly needed an innovator with a new strategy.

During the 1980s, Alcoa got not one but two new CEOs with innovative ideas and energy to back them up. Charles W. Parry, who took over in 1983, had spent his entire working life with Alcoa and was one of the company's most popular executives. He set about shaking up the company in two ways: through restructuring its present and re-envisioning its future. He changed Alcoa's highly centralized structure and gave plant managers more power, reduced headquarters staff, and closed some of the company's most expensive plants. At the same time, he began investing heavily in businesses and technologies only tangentially related to aluminum.

Boasting that by 1995, half of Alcoa's revenues would come from non-aluminum sources, he put half a billion dollars into a dozen acquisitions, the largest of which, TRE Corp., is an aerospace and defense contractor. One of TRE's products — a helicopter blade made of 17 different materials and costing $50,000 — is the kind of high-tech, high-price product that Parry saw in Alcoa's future. Parry also beefed up Alcoa's research and development department, hiring hundreds of new Ph.D.s to work at Alcoa's 2,300-acre R&D center. Many of the researchers are working on perfecting Alithalite, Alcoa's alloy of aluminum and lithium, which is 10 percent lighter than other alloys and may therefore play a major role in the next generation of commercial jets. Other researchers have nothing to do with metallurgy but instead are experts in ceramics, ancient materials for which exotic new uses have recently been developed.

Both at Alcoa and within the larger investment community, this innovation excited some people, who saw that Parry was forging for Alcoa a legitimate escape from its reliance on aluminum. But others at Alcoa, particularly members of the board of directors, were wary of Parry's strategies and shocked at his plan to move so quickly away from Alcoa's primary business. Managers within the company grumbled that Parry was squeezing profits out of aluminum to pay for his new high-tech projects. The company's new Materials Science Division began to consume one-third of Alcoa's R&D budget while producing only $200 million in sales.

By 1987, the board had had enough of Parry's brand of innovation. It accepted Parry's offer to retire early and replaced him with one of its own members, Paul O'Neill, who was at the time president of International Paper Company.

O'Neill quickly declared that Alcoa's business was aluminum, and although he didn't scrap all of Parry's innovations, he refocused the company's energies on its main product. However, he also earned a reputation for his own innovative, unorthodox moves. A firm believer in continuous quality improvements, O'Neill shocked the company when he declared that the top item on his agenda was safety. He was determined to lower the company's already low injury rate to zero. He knew that in the process of investigating why accidents happen, the company would discover ways to improve its work processes and the quality of its products.

His emphasis on quality rather than on price or short-term profit led him to an innovative approach to the aluminum industry's demand and price cycles. When the industry experienced a downturn and all the other makers of aluminum for cans lowered their prices, O'Neill refused to budge. When stockholders complained about Alcoa's loss of profits and market share, he said, "The emphasis on quarterly results is ridiculous."* Far from oblivious to the company's financial fortunes, however, he took the unusual step of linking both shareholders' dividends and employees' bonuses to Alcoa's profits. He eliminated most of the symbols of status within the company, solicited and acted on employee suggestions, backed Alcoa's drive to produce an all-aluminum car, and looked for ways to spread Alcoa's industry dominance overseas. So far he seems to have the company — and the directors — behind him.

Discussion Questions

1. Why do you think Alcoa rejected Charles Parry's innovative approach to rescuing the company from reliance on aluminum?
2. How might Paul O'Neill's innovations help his company grow when overall demand for aluminum is increasing so slowly?
3. What differences can you discern between the two CEOs' approaches to promoting innovation at Alcoa?
4. Parry spent his whole adult life with Alcoa, whereas O'Neill was an outsider. Would you expect fresh, creative ideas to come from someone who knew the company well or from someone approaching it as a newcomer? Why?

* Quoted in Thomas F. O'Boyle and Peter Pae, "O'Neill Recasts Alcoa with His Eyes Fixed on a Decade Ahead," *Wall Street Journal,* April 9, 1990, p. A1.

REFERENCES: Gregory L. Miles and Matt Rothman, "Alcoa: Recycling Itself to Become a Pioneer in New Materials," *Business Week,* February 9, 1987, pp. 56–58; Thomas F. O'Boyle and Peter Pae, "O'Neill Recasts Alcoa with His Eyes Fixed on a Decade Ahead," *Wall Street Journal,* April 9, 1990, pp. A1, A16; Michael Schroeder, "The Quiet Coup at Alcoa," *Business Week,* June 27, 1988, pp. 58–65; Thomas A. Stewart, "A New Way to Wake Up a Giant," *Fortune,* October 22, 1990, pp. 90–103.

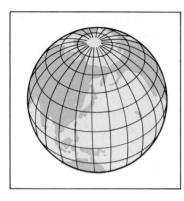

CASE 9.2

Sony Tries Again

Most Americans know Sony because of its successes — its Trinitron television, its Walkman, its tape recorders of all styles and varieties. But they tend to forget that Sony has also suffered some colossal failures, including its Betamax VCR system and its early personal computers. In light of such failures, Sony's ability to continue to break new ground is impressive, especially considering its size and the ease with which it could simply coast on its top-selling products.

In the past, Sony thrived on inventing new products that created their own markets, like the Walkman. When Sony created a truly personal tape player — small enough to put in a pocket and complete with headphones to avoid offending the person sitting next to you on the bus — it seemed to be an idea that people had been waiting for. Suddenly everyone wanted a Walkman, and although numerous imitators quickly flooded the market, Sony kept ahead of the crowd by offering, at last count, about one hundred different varieties, including solar-powered, waterproof Walkmen for the beach and tiny, radio-only Walkmen that joggers can clip to their sweatbands. Sony still claims almost one-third of the worldwide personal tape player market, which is valued at over $1.3 billion.

Sony's experience with its Betamax, however, demonstrates what can happen when an innovation strategy doesn't quite work. The Betamax was the first commercial VCR, and it might still be the dominant VCR system if Sony had played its cards differently. In 1977, RCA wanted to sell Sony VCRs under the RCA name. Sony refused, and RCA joined a number of other companies looking for an alternative technology. Sony's rival, Victor Company of Japan (JVC), came up with VHS, and backing by companies like RCA meant that VHS soon became the industry standard, leaving Betamax an also-ran.

Sony's recent entries in video recording demonstrate how its approach to innovation has changed, or at least expanded. Sony scored another trend-setting success when it came out with its 8-mm camcorder line in 1985. Its cameras were much smaller and lighter than the existing VHS camcorders, and Sony kept making them better, holding on to an 80 percent share in the 8-mm market. At the same time, Sony was learning to be more humble and sometimes play a game that others had invented. After sticking with its Betamax line for a decade and thus becoming only a minor player in the VCR market, in 1988 Sony began making its own VHS system VCR. Some viewed the switch as a final announcement of the defeat of Betamax, but Sony insisted that Betamax was still very much alive and still a better technology. It wanted to build a VHS recorder, it said, in order to make use of idle Betamax-making capacity and to please dealers who wanted to sell an all-Sony entertainment system to customers with VHS tapes.

Sony has also learned from its earlier failures in the computer business. It began selling word processors in 1980, just when personal computers began making dedicated word processors obsolete. Its own PC came out in 1982, but it, too, was about a year behind, and it was incompatible with the industry-standard IBM PC. By the mid-1980s, much of the Sony bureaucracy was terrified of another computer failure, so Toshi Doi, head of Sony's R&D, had to take an unusual route to develop a new computer. He put together a group of what he describes as "misfits" and gave them the freedom to develop whatever computer they wanted. They designed the kind of machine that they dreamed of using themselves — a workstation dubbed "News" for Net Work Station. The small team worked feverishly to come up with a prototype, but the production people then said that producing the prototype would take two years. In desperation, Doi appealed to Sony's president, Norio Ohga, who came up with the $6 million that Doi needed to speed up production. The News workstation came to market in Japan four months before its major new competitor. It was cheaper and faster than other workstations and quickly captured an impressive chunk of the Japanese workstation market. Doi had battled what he called "Big Company Syndrome," but Sony's top brass had demonstrated that they could still support new, risky ideas.

Sony's next round of innovations will almost certainly take advantage of the organization's diverse holdings in the entertainment business. Sony has been working in joint ventures with small American companies to develop such things as a new television camera lens, while at the same time it has spent over $5 billion to buy CBS Records and Columbia Pictures. Industry analysts expect the next wave of technology for the home to use all of these assets: computers will do work *and* use discs to play music or show movies. When you go shopping for your first such multimedia station, you're likely to find the Sony name on every one of its components.

Discussion Questions

1. Why do large companies seem to have more trouble staying innovative than smaller ones?
2. What factors does the Sony story demonstrate are necessary to turn good innovations into successes?
3. For years Sony guarded its technological secrets carefully, but now it is sharing them with small American companies. Why do you think Sony made such a change?
4. Besides technological expertise, what kinds of knowledge do Sony employees need in order to come up with a new and successful Sony product?

REFERENCES: Larry Armstrong, "How Sony Became a Home-Movie Superstar," *Business Week,* June 11, 1990, p. 72; Neil Gross, "How Sony Pulled Off Its Spectacular Computer Coup," *Business Week,* January 15, 1990, pp. 76–77; Udayan Gupta, "Sony Adopts Strategy to Broaden Ties with Small Firms," *Wall Street Journal,* February 28, 1991, p. B2; Andrea Rothman, "Media Colossus," *Business Week,* March 25, 1991, pp. 64–74; David E. Whiteside, "Sony Isn't Mourning The 'Death' of Betamax," *Business Week,* January 25, 1988, p. 37.

III The Structure and Design of Organizations

The second major function of managers in organizations is managing structure. The purpose of this function is to create a coordinated and logical framework through which the organization can achieve its goals. To do this effectively, managers must understand the elements of structure and how those elements may be fitted into an overall design for the organization. They must understand organizational control and the management of information. Two other components of managing structure are human resources and operations management.

10 √

The Elements of Structure in Organizations

After studying this chapter, you should be able to:

1. Describe the elements of organization structure.

2. Discuss job specialization, and identify alternative approaches to designing jobs.

3. Describe the common forms of departmentalization.

4. Explain how the chain of commmand and the span of management result in tall or flat organizations.

5. Describe the relationship between delegation and the extent to which an organization is centralized or decentralized.

6. Discuss interdependence and the methods that organizations use to coordinate their activities.

7. Describe the difference between line and staff positions.

Weyerhaeuser, a large forest products concern based in Tacoma, Washington, makes a variety of paper products and building materials and also owns real estate development and financial services businesses. In 1990, with annual sales of almost $10 billion, the firm ranked fifty-fourth on the *Fortune 500* listing of the largest U.S. industrial firms. Weyerhaeuser has about 41,000 people on its payroll, making it one of the largest employers in the state of Washington.

Like many other American companies, Weyerhaeuser has begun to recognize the importance of enhancing the quality of its products and services. To that end, the firm has started using the team approach to solving problems and making decisions. Mustering groups of employees to perform jobs, rather than assigning jobs to individuals who are then supervised by managers, the team approach has often been found to be quite effective in improving quality.

Until recently, individual managers at Weyerhaeuser made virtually all decisions and then dictated the results to subordinates, who had little or no say in what happened. Workers and managers often found themselves at odds with one another over the best way to get work done. Now many Weyerhaeuser employees come together to find innovative ways of conducting business and improving the quality of the firm's operations. Managers serve as facilitators rather than as overseers.

One team of employees was charged with examining Weyerhaeuser's corporate law department's filing system to detect inefficiencies. The team consisted of a secretary, a file clerk, a paralegal, an attorney, and a quality manager. One of their accomplishments was substantially reducing the time it takes to retrieve filed documents. Other teams have improved the effectiveness of Weyerhaeuser's reforesting programs, its methods of harvesting trees, and numerous other areas of business operations.[1]

In its move toward a team-based approach, Weyerhaeuser has made several significant changes in how it conducts business. The firm changed the way many people do their jobs, giving them more autonomy. It changed how jobs are arranged (from isolated individuals to groups), and it changed reporting relationships between employees and their managers, making them partners rather than adversaries. Each of these changes, as well as several others, affects relationships among parts of the company's overall structure.

This chapter introduces the six elements of organization structure. We first describe what organization structure is and why it is important. We then discuss how jobs are designed and grouped to create departments and work units. Next we focus on how organizations create a hierarchy between managers and subordinates and distribute authority among positions. We then address how organizations coordinate activities. Finally, we discuss line and staff positions in organizations.

The Nature of Organization Structure

As the previous five chapters of Part II described, the first function that an organization must carry out is determining strategy. In many ways, the purpose of the second organizational function, developing structure, is to carry out that strategy. In several basic ways the implementation of strategy leads to the development of organization structure.

Organization structure is the basic framework of positions, groups of positions, reporting relationships, and interaction patterns that an organization adopts to carry out its strategy.

Organization structure is the basic framework of positions, groups of positions, reporting relationships, and interaction patterns that an organization adopts to carry out its strategy. For example, consider the fundamental strategy of Ford Motor Company: to make and sell cars for profit. In order to implement this strategy, Ford must organize its 366,000 employees scattered around the world so that everyone knows who does what and when, and who has the final responsibility for a decision. A further problem for a company the size of Ford is to work out the ways in which activities at one facility are coordinated with activities at another facility. As Figure 10.1 shows, there are six elements of organization structure: designing jobs, forming departments and work units, creating a hierarchy, distributing authority, coordinating and integrating activities, and differentiating between positions. These six elements are covered fully in the rest of this chapter.

Designing Jobs

The first element of organization structure is designing the jobs people perform so that both workers and managers understand what they are expected to do for the organization. **Job design** specifies the boundaries of a job by describing what tasks the job does and does not involve, the responsibilities and expectations of the job holder, and the authority of the job holder to make decisions.

Job design specifies the boundaries of a job by describing what tasks the job does and does not involve, the responsibilities and expectations of the job holder, and the authority of the job holder to make decisions.

Job Specialization

When Walt Disney first started his animation business, he did everything from drawing cartoons to marketing them to movie studios to keeping

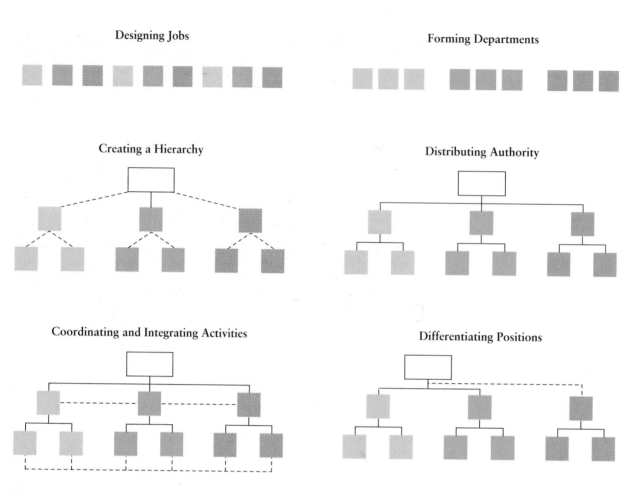

Figure 10.1

The Six Elements of Organization Structure

Job specialization is the process of breaking jobs into small component parts and assigning specialists to perform each part.

track of his finances. As his business grew, however, he eventually had to hire some help. He employed artists to assist him in drawing, sales representatives to market the cartoons to distributors and theaters, and a financial planner to manage the firm's money. Eventually the jobs became even more specialized. Some artists began drawing only the major cartoon characters, and others drew only backgrounds. Still others became specialists in developing new colors or drawing techniques. Finally, some artists drew only one specific character such as Mickey Mouse or Donald Duck.[2]

What happened at Disney illustrates a typical pattern that organizations follow as they grow and expand — dividing the overall "job" of the organization into increasingly smaller parts. This pattern is called job specialization. **Job specialization** is the process of breaking jobs into small component parts and assigning specialists to perform each part.

As described in Chapter 2, the eighteenth-century economist Adam Smith was among the first to point out the advantages of job specialization.[3] He observed how workers at a pin factory divided the making of pins into small component tasks. One man drew out the wire; another sharpened it; another filed the point; and still others performed each of the remaining

Job specialization is an important element in organization structure. The crew members that operate commercial aircraft have moderately specialized jobs. The pilot and copilot of this Lufthansa flight, for example, each have specific tasks that must be executed to successfully complete the flight.

steps to finish the pins. Smith argued that if each man had performed each step himself he would have been able to produce only a few dozen pins a day. Working together and using job specialization, however, a group of 10 men made 48,000 pins a day.

Virtually all of the mass-production industries in the early years of this century used job specialization on the assembly line. Henry Ford, for example, separated the assembly of his Model T into hundreds of distinct operations, and each operation — from bolting on a headlamp to painting a fender — was performed repeatedly by one worker. Frederick W. Taylor, as explained in Chapter 2, identified job specialization as a logical outgrowth of the manager's scientific study of each job.

Of course, specialization is also used in many non-manufacturing jobs as well. A McDonald's restaurant employs some people to cook food, some to take and fill customer orders at the counter, some to work in the drive-in window, and still others to clean up. Likewise, a textbook such as this one is produced with the talents of an author, a developmental editor, a copy editor, an art editor, a permissions editor, and a production editor.

As Adam Smith noted, the benefits to productivity are a compelling advantage of job specialization. First, job holders can develop tremendous skill in performing a narrowly defined and specialized task. If all a worker does all day is bolt on headlamps, he or she can become a real expert in doing that job. Second, workers who do not have to stop one task and start another lose no work time. Third, equipment that further increases productivity can be more easily developed for highly specialized jobs than for less specialized jobs. Finally, training people to perform highly specialized jobs is relatively easy. Teaching someone to bolt on a headlamp is simpler than teaching someone to assemble an entire engine.

However, many organizations have found that job specialization also has some undesirable consequences. Some workers quickly become bored with simple, specialized jobs. They experience little intrinsic satisfaction and feel no pride in carrying out tasks that they see as relatively trivial. Such workers come to feel like cogs in a machine and have little or no chance to grow, develop, and learn. As a consequence, workers with highly specialized jobs often have high levels of absenteeism, leave the organization in search of more meaningful or fulfilling jobs, express high levels of job dissatisfaction, and may develop antagonistic relationships with supervisors.[4]

Large organizations cannot exist without some degree of specialization, and specialization is likely to be beneficial even to small organizations. Nevertheless, it is possible to carry job specialization too far. Excessive specialization can result in so many undesirable outcomes that any gains to the organization are offset. The key, then, is to achieve a moderate or optimal level of specialization that allows the organization to capitalize on its advantages without incurring its disadvantages.

Some organizations have experimented with a variety of ways of designing jobs so as to make them more enjoyable, interesting, and meaningful to employees. The goal of these alternative approaches is to increase worker motivation to perform the job effectively. Each involves specialization, but each also attempts to moderate that specialization to keep it from becoming extreme.

Because job specialization has some undesirable consequences, organizations often seek alternative approaches to job design.

Alternatives to Specialization

There are four alternatives to specialization in job design: job rotation, job enlargement, job enrichment, and the use of job characteristics.

Job rotation is the systematic movement of people from one job to another.

Job Rotation   **Job rotation** is the systematic movement of people from one task to another. It does not involve any modification to the employee's job description itself.

Consider the job of preparing men's dress shirts for shipment to department stores. The first task is to fold the shirt. The second is to pin the folds to keep the shirt straight. The third is to insert cardboard supports around the collar. The fourth task is to attach size and price labels. The last task is to put the shirt in a plastic bag. Under normal job specialization individual workers are assigned to perform each task — one worker folds, one pins, and so on.

If the firm adopts job rotation, however, workers do not perform the same task all the time. One worker folds on Monday, pins on Tuesday, and so forth. A second worker pins on Monday and inserts cardboard on Tuesday. Each worker rotates across the five tasks every week. The problem with job rotation is that since the job descriptions do not change, people are still performing simple, routine tasks, and are still doing only one job all day long. Because of unsatisfactory experiences with job rotation at Bethlehem Steel, Prudential Insurance, and other firms in the 1950s, today it is used primarily as a training device. Job rotation allows people to become familiar with a wide array of jobs but may provide little motivational incentive.

Job enlargement is the practice of giving workers more tasks to perform.

Job Enlargement   Popular in the 1960s, **job enlargement** actually does involve changes in the employee's job description. Specifically, workers are given more tasks to perform on any given day. The shirt maker described above might allow each worker to do all five of the tasks involved in preparing dress shirts for shipment, rather than just one.

After some initial promise at Maytag, the U.S. Civil Service, and IBM, job enlargement also fell from favor. Doing a large number of simple tasks doesn't make the job any more motivating or enjoyable than doing fewer simple tasks. In response to criticism of job enlargement and job rotation, organizations began to realize that neither of these alternatives to specialization added to worker involvement, control, and autonomy. Thus other solutions were sought.

Job enrichment gives workers more tasks and more control and autonomy over how to perform them.

Job Enrichment   Popular in the late 1960s and early 1970s, **job enrichment** is a two-pronged approach to modifying jobs. (Job enrichment is based on a popular model of motivation called the two-factor theory, which we cover in Chapter 17.[5]) As in job enlargement, the starting point in job enrichment is simply giving workers more tasks to perform. In addition, though, they are also given more control over how they do their tasks.

In the shirt company, one worker may feel that he can be more effective by pinning the shirts as they are folded, rather than treating pinning as a separate step. Another may think that putting the tags on first is easier. If job enrichment is being used, each worker can decide how to do the job, as long as the end result is acceptable to the manager. Thus workers experience more responsibility, are more accountable for their efforts, and feel a greater degree of job ownership. Firms such as Texas Instruments, General Foods, and IBM have all had generally favorable experiences with job enrichment. At Texas Instruments, for example, job enrichment resulted in significant savings in the firm's maintenance department. Still, job enrichment does not always work, and some managers have been frustrated in trying to use it because some jobs do not easily lend themselves to individual worker control and autonomy.

The *job characteristics theory* identifies five dimensions along which jobs can be modified: skill variety, task identity, task significance, autonomy, and feedback.

Job Characteristics   The current approach to designing individual jobs relies on the **job characteristics theory**, illustrated in Figure 10.2.[6] This theory focuses on the following five job dimensions:

1. Skill variety — the number of tasks in the job
2. Task identity — the extent to which the worker does a meaningful part of the total job
3. Task significance — the perceived importance of the job
4. Autonomy — the degree of control the worker has over how he or she performs the job
5. Feedback — the extent to which the worker knows how well he or she is performing the job

Figure 10.2

The Job Characteristics Theory

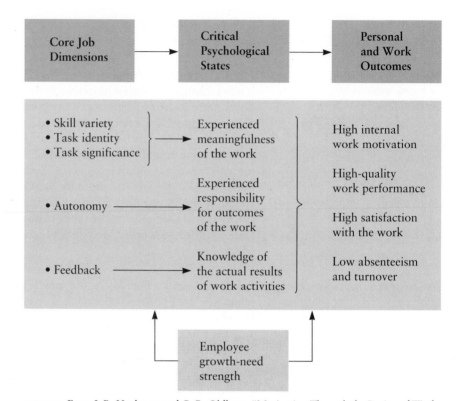

SOURCE: From J. R. Hackman and G. R. Oldham, "Motivation Through the Design of Work: Test of a Theory," *Organizational Behavior and Human Performance,* vol. 16. Copyright © 1976 by Academic Press, Inc. Used by permission of Academic Press and J. R. Hackman.

The basic idea of the job characteristics theory is that if organizations improve each job dimension, three critical psychological states will be created in workers. These psychological states are the experienced meaningfulness of the job, the experienced responsibility for outcomes, and knowledge of results. If employees experience these psychological states, they will presumably exhibit more motivation, satisfaction, and performance, and less turnover and absenteeism.

Another component of the job characteristics theory is the recognition that not everyone responds to job conditions in the same way. The theory acknowledges that some people (those with high growth-need strength) respond favorably to the presence of additional job characteristics and others (with low growth-need strength) are indifferent. Because of its greater specificity and consideration of individual differences, the job characteristics theory seems to work better than any of the other approaches discussed. To date, organizations like Prudential Insurance and AT&T have reported positive results from using the job characteristics approach with a wide variety of operating jobs.

Designing Jobs for Groups

Organizations find that designing jobs for groups can remove some of the negative effects of job specialization.

As we saw with Weyerhaeuser's experience, an increasingly popular approach to designing jobs is to assign a collection of tasks to a group of workers and let the group itself decide how best to perform them. This gives workers the feeling of greater control over their work, participation in decision making, and a sense of involvement in what the organization is doing. One early approach to using groups was the concept of autonomous work groups. The Volvo plant in Kalmar, Sweden, which opened in 1971, uses groups of workers to do each of the major sets of tasks necessary to assemble automobiles. Instead of passing through a large number of discrete workstations where individual workers perform tasks, cars pass through large work areas where entire groups of workers perform several different tasks at the same time. Each group decides which tasks each member will perform each day. The Volvos made at Kalmar are of especially high quality but cost somewhat more to produce than Volvos manufactured elsewhere.

A recent refinement to this concept involves self-managed teams. Whereas autonomous work groups have considerable latitude over how they do their tasks, their control is generally limited to task-related activities. Self-managed teams, in contrast, usually do much more. Such teams often schedule their own work, order supplies and materials, interview and hire replacement members for the group, and set quality standards. They may even evaluate their own performance and set their own rewards.

At a General Mills cereal plant in California self-managed teams have greatly increased productivity and output while simultaneously reducing costs. Indeed, they are working so well that no managers are on duty during the night shift. Aetna Life & Casualty set up several teams, also eliminating the need for several managers. Aetna has reduced the ratio of middle managers to workers from 1:7 to 1:30 while simultaneously improving customer service.[7] Many firms in Japan and Germany are also using self-managed teams. The Entrepreneurial Challenge explains how Johnsonville Foods used self-managed teams to boost productivity at its Wisconsin factory. We discuss self-managed teams again in Chapter 19.

Forming Departments and Work Units

After organizations have determined how to structure various jobs, they must decide how to put them into logical groups or units. The organization needs to develop structural arrangements wherein job families are created. For example, an insurance company may group everyone working on automobile insurance together, everyone working on life insurance together, and so forth. This grouping is useful because it facilitates coordination, helps integrate the activities of different people in a unified manner, and provides administrative convenience.

THE ENTREPRENEURIAL CHALLENGE

Johnsonville Foods Profits from Designing Jobs for Groups

Johnsonville Foods, based in Sheboygan, Wisconsin, has enjoyed tremendous benefits since it decided to design jobs for groups rather than for individuals. Johnsonville is a small food-processing firm specializing in sausages and other meat products.

In 1986 a major food distributor asked Johnsonville CEO Ralph Stayer if his firm would accept a contract to make sausage under its own private label for national distribution. Stayer's initial reaction to the proposal was to say no because he thought the firm was too small to handle such a large contract. After more consideration, however, he decided to poll his workers. At the time, Johnsonville paid all its employees a year-end bonus based on profits. Although the contract would mean a lot of additional work (the reason for Stayer's reluctance to accept it), it could also mean bigger bonuses for everyone.

The workers debated the proposal for several days and then told Stayer that they wanted to accept the contract. They also recommended that he redesign all facets of their jobs, arranging workers into teams of five to twenty members each. They reasoned that they could work more efficiently under such an arrangement.

Stayer agreed and gave the work groups virtually total control over how they proceeded. During the next few months they decided what extra equipment they needed, how many new employees needed to be hired, and how to meet daily production quotas. In late 1986 they started work on the new contract. Since then they have increased their productivity by 50 percent, increased profits (and their bonuses) by an even greater amount, and taken on two additional contracts similar to the first one. Several factors have no doubt contributed to the success enjoyed by Johnsonville, but Stayer and his workers put the work group concept at the top of the list.

REFERENCES: Brian Dumaine, "Who Needs a Boss?" *Fortune*, May 7, 1990, pp. 52–60; Patricia Galagan, "Work Teams That Work," *Training and Development Journal*, November 1986, pp. 33–35; "The Payoff from Teamwork," *Business Week*, July 10, 1989, pp. 56–62.

Departmentalization is the basis on which jobs are grouped together.

At the upper levels of an organization (i.e., the corporate level), grouping arrangements may be called *divisions, product groups,* or *units.* At middle and lower levels, they are more often called *departments.* We define **departmentalization** as the basis on which jobs are grouped together within an organization. In the discussion that follows we identify common forms of departmentalization and then discuss how organizations use multiple forms of departmentalization.[8]

Common Forms of Departmentalization

Organizations usually employ one or more forms of departmentalization: by function, product, customer, and location. Figure 10.3 illustrates each form of departmentalization for a hypothetical computer firm.

Functional departmentalization groups jobs on the basis of common functions such as marketing and finance.

Functional Departmentalization   Because it is the simplest and easiest to coordinate, most new and small businesses use **functional departmentalization**, which groups jobs on the basis of common functions. As Figure 10.3 shows, the typical functions include marketing, operations (or production), finance, and human resource management. Jobs in each of these

Organizations group jobs together into natural work units. The Seattle Police Department has initiated a novel response to the problems it was experiencing in responding to calls in heavy city traffic: it created teams of mountain-bicycle police that patrol many high-crime areas of the city. The police officers keep in touch via radio and, because of their increased maneuverability, are able to respond to calls much more quickly than before.

functional areas are defined as a work unit or department. Blackwell Manufacturing, a moderate-size oil field equipment firm in Houston, uses these exact departments.

Functional departmentalization allows the organization to rely on specialized experts in each area, and it facilitates supervision and coordination. Blackwell is able to get by with a relatively small human resources department because the department handles all human resource–related functions for the entire organization. However, functional departmentalization leads to slow decision making, focuses attention on functional specialties at the expense of the overall organization, and obscures accountability. Blackwell has recently experienced some cost overruns, but because so many different individuals are involved, pinpointing the exact source of the problem has been difficult.

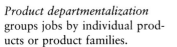

Product departmentalization groups jobs by individual products or product families.

Product Departmentalization   **Product departmentalization** groups jobs by individual products or product families. Functional specialists are then located within each product department. Because it allows an organization to achieve the benefits of functional departmentalization within product groups while simultaneously overcoming some of its limitations, most large businesses adopt product departmentalization. For example, Borden has one department for dairy products, one for pasta, one for snack foods, and so forth.

Product departmentalization facilitates coordination and integration, speeds up decision making, and eases the assessment of unit performance. Borden feels that it can respond quickly to environment changes, for example, and can readily determine the relative performance of each of its departments. However, the organization needs to employ specialists in the various functional areas, and managers tend to focus too narrowly on their product responsibilities to the exclusion of the overall organization. Borden,

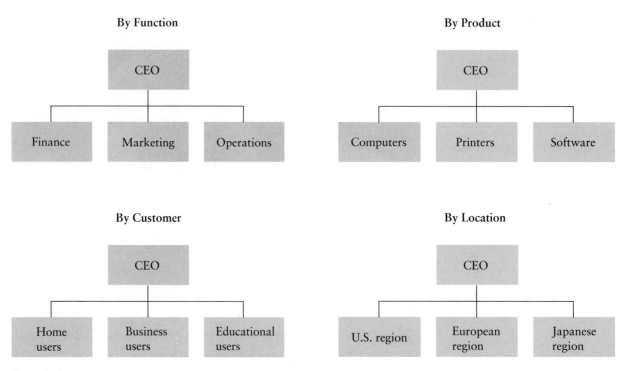

Figure 10.3

Common Forms of Departmentalization

for example, has to employ human resource specialists within each of its departments in order to allow those departments to function with reasonable autonomy.

Departmentalization by customer groups jobs that are associated with customers or customer categories.

Customer Departmentalization   As shown in Figure 10.3 **departmentalization by customer** groups jobs that are associated with specific customers or customer categories. For example, a local bank might have one department for individual nonbusiness customers, one for small businesses, and one for large businesses. Likewise, the retail stores of Furrow's Building Centers have one department to serve private homeowners and another to serve contractors and building professionals.

The biggest advantage of this approach is that it allows the organization to tailor its activities to the specific needs of individual customers. At the local bank, for example, one lending department can become knowledgeable about the specific financial needs of small businesses while another can focus on the more complex needs of larger businesses. On the downside, a large staff component is required (the bank will need to have loan officers on duty in each department at all times), and coordination costs are high (each department must be continually updated on the dollar volume and the risk on loans made by the other).

Departmentalization by location groups jobs on the basis of geographic location.

Location Departmentalization   **Departmentalization by location** groups jobs on the basis of geographic location. For example, the Federal Reserve Bank is organized around several regional banks. Many multinational

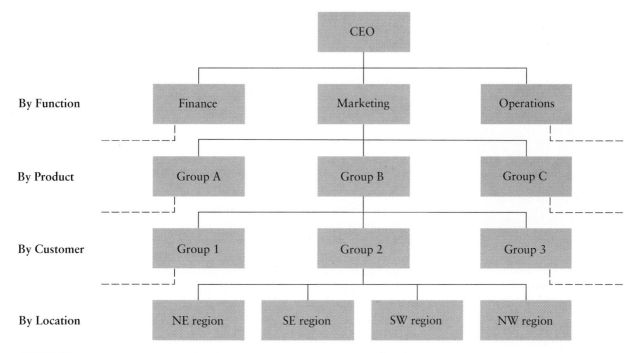

Figure 10.4

Multiple Forms of Departmentalization

organizations also base at least some portion of their operations on location. Ford, for example, has located wholly owned subsidiaries within many of its major marketplaces.

Departmentalization by location is most effective when organizational activities occur in a geographic area with unique characteristics and circumstances. By means of its seven regional banks, the Federal Reserve can respond to the fact that economic conditions vary significantly across the United States. Again, however, a large staff may also be necessary to provide services at each location. Ford still retains a marketing research group within each of its worldwide subsidiaries to assess local customer needs and preferences.

Using Multiple Forms of Departmentalization

Most large organizations use multiple forms of departmentalization.

Because they tend to grow complex and diverse with time, most organizations eventually must use multiple forms of departmentalization within their single overall structure. Complex environmental factors and demands at different organizational levels and within different areas, for example, often necessitate unique approaches to grouping jobs. Figure 10.4 illustrates how one large corporation might use different multiple forms of departmentalization at different levels.

Wal-Mart is an excellent example of a firm that uses multiple forms of departmentalization. At the corporate level Wal-Mart is departmentalized

All organizations determine (and periodically re-examine) the form of hierarchy that will be most appropriate in reaching their goals. For over thirty years, W. L. Gore, a family-owned plastics company, has been experimenting with a hierarchical model that is as flat as they come: a so-called "lattice" system. In this system, all employees are called "associates," and "leaders" (not "bosses") head teams in plants or staff departments. Anyone in the organization can take ideas or questions to anyone else without fear of violating the chain of command—because in effect there isn't one!

A *hierarchy* is the pattern of reporting relationships between individuals in positions throughout an organization.

The *chain of command* is the line of authority that extends from the position with ultimate authority for decision making down to the operating level.

by function. The buying and purchasing function, however, is organized by product: some buyers handle apparel; some handle hardware; and some handle other products. Wal-Mart also has regional divisions that report to district managers who are grouped on the basis of location. Finally, within a given Wal-Mart store, departmentalization is generally by customer, with some sales associates specializing in men's clothing, other associates in children's clothing, and still others in women's clothing.

Creating a Hierarchy

Once it determines its bases of departmentalization, the organization then develops a network of reporting relationships. This involves the creation of a hierarchy. A **hierarchy** is the pattern of reporting relationships between individuals in positions throughout an organization. The organization's hierarchy has two purposes: to specify which positions are responsible for which areas of operations and to specify the authority of different positions relative to one another.

For example, if a small-business owner hires a sales representative and a financial analyst, it is likely that each will report directly to the owner. Suppose that one day the owner is out and a decision has to be made. Which of the two employees has final control over and responsibility for the decision? This and related questions are answered by employees' relative position in a hierarchy. Creating a hierarchy requires the organization to define a chain of command and determine a desirable span of management. These two characteristics of the hierarchy, in turn, play a major role in determining the overall shape of the organization's structure.

The Chain of Command

The **chain of command** in an organization is the line of authority that extends from the position with ultimate authority for decision making (such as the board of directors or the CEO) down to the operating level. The idea of the chain of command has its roots in the military; it was applied to nonmilitary organizations in the United States during the early days of this century. Figure 10.4, introduced previously to illustrate multiple bases of departmentalization, also demonstrates the chain of command. The chain follows the various vertical lines from the top position in the organization all the way to the bottom.

The chain of command specifies lines of accountability. Virtually everyone in an organization is accountable to someone else. The chain of command helps clarify who can assign work to someone else, who will be evaluating the performance of a given employee, and to whom an employee should turn with questions or for additional direction.

The popular saying "The buck stops here" echoes the logic underlying the concept of chain of command. For example, suppose a local charity

THE ENVIRONMENTAL CHALLENGE

Missing Links in the Chain of Command

Several years ago, a Citicorp manager named David Edwards learned that the bank was engaging in a variety of illegal banking practices involving foreign currency exchange. Edwards told his boss, who seemed uninterested and recommended that Edwards just forget it. After several other conversations with his boss, Edwards then went to his boss's boss, who also ignored the problem. After eventually going all the way to the upper echelons of the organization, Edwards finally reported his findings to the board of directors. They took action against the illegal practices but also fired Edwards for being disruptive.

What exactly did Edwards do to warrant termination? Only those involved know all the details, but one of his biggest "mistakes" was going over his boss's head. As we will discuss more fully in Chapter 22, what Edwards did is called "whistle blowing" — reporting an incident of illegal or unethical behavior to upper management or to the press. Other widely reported instances of whistle blowing to higher-level organizational officials have occurred at Beech-Nut, General Dynamics, and Lockheed.

But people sometimes bypass the chain of command for other reasons as well. Perhaps they don't trust their boss. Perhaps they are engaging in political behavior to gain power or to diminish their boss's power. They may be asking for a raise or new job assignment that their boss won't grant, or they may be complaining about ineffective leadership on the part of their boss. Regardless of the reason, most managers are resentful when a subordinate takes a problem or issue to someone higher in the organization. They may also feel betrayed or threatened. Unfortunately, even when the subordinate's actions are clearly justified, and even when there is an equitable settlement reached, hidden anger and resentment are likely to linger for a long time.

REFERENCES: "Think Before You Blow the Whistle," *Business Week,* May 18, 1987, p. 161; "Nestlé Quietly Seeks to Sell Beech-Nut, Dogged by Scandal of Bogus Apple Juice," *Wall Street Journal,* July 6, 1989, p. B4; Roy Rowan, "The Maverick Who Yelled Foul at Citibank," *Fortune,* January 10, 1983, pp. 46–56.

wants to solicit contributions from the employees of a local business. The charity organizer may ask the firm's public relations manager for permission to contact employees. If that individual lacks the authority to make such a decision, she will pass the request up the hierarchy to her boss, who may have to pass it on as well. Eventually, it will come to rest on the desk of someone with the authority and responsibility for dealing with it. As described in The Environmental Challenge, breakdowns in the chain of command can sometimes lead to unfortunate consequences.

The Span of Management

The *span of management* is the number of people who report to a particular manager.

The **span of management** is the number of people who report to a particular manager. Organizations must determine whether the span of management should be relatively wide (many subordinates per manager) or relatively narrow (few subordinates per manager). Once it was assumed that a single, ideal span of management would work for all organizations, and many managers sought to identify that ideal. Lyndall Urwick, a management pioneer who published his ideas in the early 1900s, suggested that a span of six subordinates for each manager was optimal. Other managers and writers, such as A. V. Graicunas and Ralph Davis, provided similar prescriptions.

Since then, however, managers have realized that no single span is always correct. Indeed, the span that works best for any given organization actually depends on a number of different factors, as described in Table 10.1. For example, a wide span of management is appropriate if both supervisor and subordinates are highly skilled and trained or if the work to be done encompasses many standardized procedures. An experienced manager can supervise a large number of highly trained workers who are performing routine and highly structured tasks. But if the manager is inexperienced or if subordinates need a great deal of training and supervision, a narrow span of management may be more appropriate.[9]

Tall and Flat Organizations

The span of management partially determines how tall the structure of the organization is. Wide spans result in flat organizations, and narrow spans result in tall structures.

The span of management is a major determinant of how "tall" or "flat" the organization's structure is. A tall organization structure has many levels of management in its hierarchy; a flat organization structure has fewer levels of management. An organization that uses very narrow spans of management tends to have a tall structure because it requires numerous managers to supervise employees. Wider spans of management result in flatter structures because fewer managers are involved in the supervision of employees.

Table 10.1

Factors Influencing the Span of Management

1. Basic competence of manager and subordinates. The greater the competence, the wider the span can be.

2. Physical dispersion of work and subordinates from one another and from the manager. The lower the dispersion, the wider the span can be.

3. Amount of nonsupervisory work the manager must perform. The lower the amount of nonsupervisory work, the wider the span can be.

4. Degree of interaction required between manager and subordinates. The less interaction required, the wider the span can be.

5. Number of standardized procedures for performing work. The more standardized procedures, the wider the span can be.

6. Similarity of tasks being supervised. The more similar the tasks, the wider the span can be.

7. Frequency of new problems. The lower the frequency, the wider the span can be.

8. Personal preferences of manager and subordinates.

Figure 10.5 shows two organization structures, one relatively tall and one relatively flat. Notice that the narrower spans in the taller structure result in more levels of management, whereas the wider spans in the flatter structure result in fewer levels of management. Essentially, a decision to use narrow spans of management is a decision to have a tall structure. In contrast, a decision to employ wide spans of management is a decision to have a flatter structure.

Figure 10.5

Tall Versus Flat Organizations

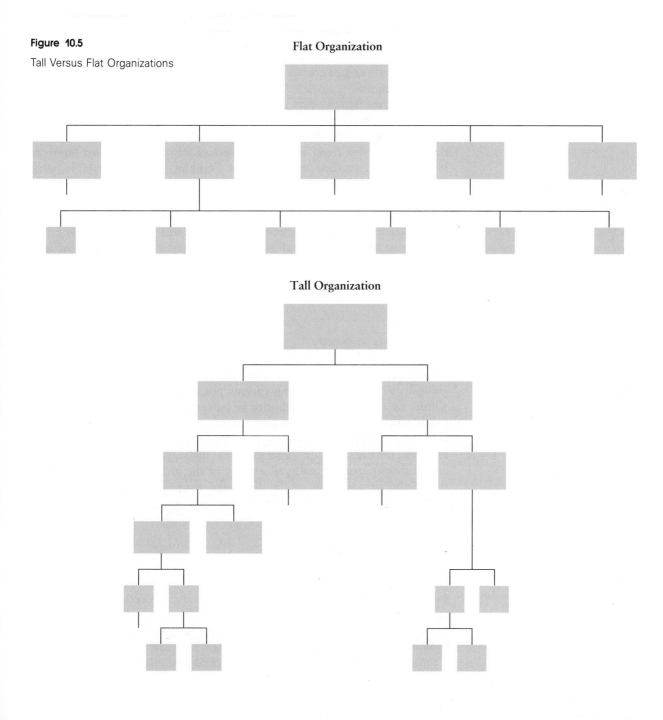

What differences does it make how tall or flat an organization's structure is? One study by James Worthy at Sears found that eliminating two levels of management, thereby creating a relatively flat structure, led to higher levels of employee morale and productivity.[10] Taller structures tend to require more managers (increasing administrative overhead costs) and make communication more difficult (because information must pass through more people as it goes up and down the organization).

A flatter organization structure tends to make communication up and down the organization easier, faster, and more accurate. This promotes quicker decision making. It also allows the organization to give individuals at lower levels in the hierarchy more power and control over their jobs and to give all managers a greater understanding of what is going on throughout the organization.

During the last ten years there has been a marked trend toward flatter organization structures, which are achieved by widening the span of management. IBM and the Franklin Mint were just two of the many companies that followed this trend in the late 1980s. Each eliminated two layers of management from their structures. The Franklin Mint, for example, went from six layers to four and simultaneously doubled sales.[11] In the United States especially, organizations are finding that flattening their structures increases flexibility. Japanese organizations have traditionally had relatively flat structures, so they have been unaffected by this trend. But many European firms, with relatively tall structures, are beginning to follow the lead of U.S. firms. The Royal Dutch/Shell Group and the Unilever Group, for example, have recently eliminated one or more layers of management.

Distributing Authority

Authority is power created and granted by the organization.

Another element of creating a structure is determining how authority is going to be distributed among various positions, levels, and departments within an organization. **Authority** is power created and granted by the organization. A key question that organizations must address is how to distribute authority between managers and those who report to them. For example, the organization might grant the manager of a work group absolute authority over virtually all aspects of the group's activities. Alternatively, the organization might grant the manager final say but allow subordinates a significant voice in how work will be done.

Delegation in Organizations

Delegation is the process of distributing authority between manager and subordinates.

Delegation is the process of distributing authority between manager and subordinates. Delegation is essentially a three-step process between a manager and one or more subordinates. The first step is to assign responsibility. The manager gives a subordinate a job or task to perform, and the subordinate accepts the assignment. A manager may ask her assistant to chair a committee to develop new grievance procedures, instruct her work group to start scheduling its own assignments, or tell a staff member to draft a report about the organization's expansion plans.

The next step is to grant authority. The manager must give the subordinate the power necessary to get the job done. The manager's assistant must have the power to schedule the committee's first meeting. The work group must be allowed to develop and submit its revised work schedule, and the staff member must be given access to the information needed to write the expansion report.

The final step is to create accountability, which obligates the subordinate to fulfill the task assigned. Successful completion of the assignment may result in rewards, and failure may result in punishment or other sanctions. If the assistant develops the new grievance procedures, he has met his obligations and may receive a bonus or other reward. If the work group makes too many mistakes or leaves workstations unattended because of poor scheduling, it has not met its obligations. In this case, the manager may have to help the group get its schedule straightened out. If the staff member fails to complete the report on time, he may be reprimanded.

Delegation is an important process in all organizations because most managers have jobs that are simply too big for them to do alone. Of course, in most instances managers and their subordinates do not mechanically and formally go through the three steps just described. Instead, they often share an implicit understanding of how the work is to be divided, the boundaries of the subordinate's authority, and the manager's expectations about performance. A simple frown or smile may convey the outcome of accountability — that the supervisor is displeased or pleased with what the subordinate has done.

Occasionally, problems may disrupt the delegation process. For example, some managers may not know how to delegate effectively, giving their subordinates either too much or too little to do. They may also fear that if their subordinates perform too well, their own position in the organization will be threatened. In these cases, the organization must help managers better understand how to delegate responsibility and how to overcome the fear of being overshadowed.

The organization should also be sure that managers recognize the limitations of individual performance. When performance breaks down, the fault is not necessarily the subordinate's. Suppose a manager requests that his assistant review and interpret some sales data within the next week. Unfortunately, the assistant is ill on Monday and Tuesday. On Wednesday, the company's computer goes down. A higher-priority task has to be finished by Thursday. As a result of these factors, the manager will likely need to give the assistant an extension on the sales data project.[12]

Decentralization and Centralization

Decentralization is the systematic delegation of authority to middle and lower levels of the organization. *Centralization* is the systematic retention of authority at higher levels.

Decisions about how to distribute authority throughout the organization result in decentralization or centralization. **Decentralization** is the systematic delegation of power and responsibility to middle and lower levels of the organization. **Centralization** is the systematic retention of power and responsibility at higher levels of the organization. Centralization and decentralization represent extremes. Few organizations are fully centralized or decentralized; some are relatively more decentralized, others relatively more centralized.[13]

In general, centralization allows top managers to exercise control over the organization. They can stay attuned to everything the organization is doing and make sure that decisions are being made according to their preferences. However, centralization slows decision making and inhibits innovation, for in a centralized organization decisions are made by a relatively small number of people.

Decentralization distributes control more evenly throughout the organization by giving more managers the authority to make decisions. It also increases the speed of decision making and makes the organization more flexible and responsive. Decentralization, however, allows more opportunities for error or incorrect decisions, for more inexperienced managers are involved in making decisions.

Several factors influence whether an organization opts for decentralization or for centralization. If the environment of the organization is relatively simple and predictable, centralization is more feasible because such environmental factors allow for slower and more considered decision making. Smaller firms, especially those still run by their founder, often tend to remain centralized, as do organizations going through a period of retrenchment, cutbacks, and decline. When the organization is watching costs and cutting back, centralization allows top managers to control expenditures.

In contrast, firms that operate in a dynamic and complex environment that requires flexibility are likely to be decentralized. Decentralization allows managers directly involved with operations to make decisions quickly without having to get approval from top management. Large organizations and organizations that are widely diversified are also likely to be decentralized because of the complexity and range of decisions that have to be made. Rapidly growing organizations also usually adopt decentralization, in part because top management may be so busy managing growth that lower-level managers are called upon to make more day-to-day decisions. Still another reason that organizations opt for decentralization is to allow middle and lower-level managers to learn and develop managerial and decision-making abilities as they are groomed for future advancement.

Many very successful organizations, such as McDonald's, K mart, British Airways, and Toyota, have always been relatively centralized. Top managers at K mart opt for centralized control despite the firm's dynamic and uncertain environment. To benefit from the cost advantages of centralized purchasing, all K mart stores tend to carry the same merchandise. Thorough market research dictates the best way to display that merchandise, and individual store managers have little authority to depart from the recommended layout. On the other hand, firms such as General Electric, Nestlé, and Unilever have tended to be more decentralized. Top managers at General Electric, for example, believe that managers at the operating levels should have considerable control over how they do their jobs and in making decisions that affect their performance.

THE GLOBAL CHALLENGE

Decentralization in Japan

For decades, U.S organizations such as General Electric and Ford and European firms such as Unilever and Nestlé have practiced decentralization. As part of their corporate strategies, these organizations systematically give managers based in other countries considerable autonomy in conducting their local operations.

Many Japanese firms, though, have remained extremely centralized. In contrast with American and European firms, which often set up research and develoment facilities in foreign locations to support local operations, virtually all Japanese firms have kept their R&D facilities in Japan. Japanese firms also grant very little decision-making control to their foreign managers, even over relatively minor things like local advertising or work schedules. Foreign managers routinely make grueling trips to Japan to present decisons for approval.

In response to these restrictive practices, some managers have started looking for greener pastures.

Mazda's two top American managers, for example, recently resigned because they were being left out of key decisions. Top managers at several other U.S. subsidiaries of Japanese firms have also resigned.

A few Japanese organizations are beginning to recognize the potential advantages of decentralization, however, and are starting to move in that direction. Sony, for example, wants to develop a cadre of international managers who both understand local markets and who can make high-level decisions. Honda allows its U.S. subsidiary considerable discretion in marketing and production decisions.

REFERENCES: "Can Japan's Giants Cut the Apron Strings?" *Business Week*, May 14, 1990, pp. 105–106; "Japan Cuts the Middle-Management Fat," *Wall Street Journal*, August 8, 1989, p. B1; "Can Japan Cope?" *Business Week*, April 23, 1990, pp. 46–53; Carla Rapoport, "Who Runs Japan?" *Fortune*, August 28, 1989, pp. 113–114.

Because the environment of most organizations seems to be becoming more complex, many firms are moving toward decentralization. For example, IBM has granted middle managers much more authority in making decisions than they had previously.[14] As The Global Challenge describes, many Japanese firms, which have historically been centralized, are trying to become more decentralized.

Coordinating and Integrating Activities

Creating a hierarchy and distributing authority generally involve establishing vertical relationships up and down the organization structure. However, since individuals and groups must often work together in order to carry out an organization's functions, attention must also be devoted to managing horizontal relationships, across the organization structure. The fifth element of organization structure is coordinating activities, making sure that they are integrated and synchronized with one another.[15] The degree of coordination that an organization needs is determined by the extent to which the people and groups in it are interdependent — that is, how much they must rely on one another to get their work done. Three levels of interdependence exist in most organizations.[16]

The degree of coordination that an organization needs is determined by the extent of interdependence.

Types of Interdependence

Most organizations must coordinate pooled, sequential, and reciprocal interdependence.

Pooled interdependence, by which each person or group performs its activities separate from the activities of others, requires the simplest forms of coordination. Both Kentucky Fried Chicken and Frito-Lay are units of PepsiCo. But the two businesses operate independently of one another. Their profits (or losses) are pooled at the corporate level, but each business is otherwise separate. What KFC does has no affect on Frito-Lay and vice versa. Thus PepsiCo does not need to worry too much about coordination between the two units.

Sequential interdependence, in which work flows in one direction from one person or group to the next, is characteristic of an assembly line. The output of one station serves as the direct input for the next station on the line. If the first unit's work is of poor quality or is below production quotas, the second group may have trouble getting its own work done. Note that since the work flow is one-way, the first group is not affected if the second group's work is poor, but the third group is. In the case of sequential interdependence, coordination is moderately important.

Reciprocal interdependence requires the highest degree of coordination because the flow of work, resources, or information is two-way — that is, each person or group is dependent on the other. For example, the marketing department of a cellular telephone company is dependent on the manufacturing department to maintain sufficient inventory of cellular telephones to satisfy customer needs and to meet appropriate quality standards. At the same time, the manufacturing department is dependent on marketing for demand forecasts and customer feedback about the telephones. Given the complexities of reciprocal interdependence, a great deal of coordination is necessary.

How Coordination Is Achieved

Common methods of achieving coordination are using the hierarchy, rules and procedures, liaisons, task forces, and integrating departments.

Table 10.2 describes several ways in which organizations can achieve coordination. The first two methods listed in the table — using the hierarchy and establishing rules and procedures — are useful primarily for managing the routine and predictable forms of coordination typical of pooled interdependence. For example, the registrar's office in a university has a set of rules that it uses to create class schedules and assign classrooms to different departments. A designated campus official settles disputes about preferred class times or classrooms. These two methods of coordination are also likely to be effective in smaller, more centralized organizations.

Using rules and procedures and the third method described in Table 10.2 — assigning liaisons — are most useful when interdependence is sequential. Rules and procedures can establish priorities about which activities take precedence over others, and a liaison can facilitate the transition of work from one unit to the next. For example, at the Compaq Computer plant in Houston partially completed computers that leave one workstation are accompanied by the name of a contact person from that unit. If there

Table 10.2

Common Methods of Achieving Coordination

1. **Using the hierarchy**   One manager supervises a variety of interdependent activities among subordinates.

2. **Establishing rules and procedures**   Standard operating procedures and priorities set the guidelines for interdependence.

3. **Assigning liaison roles**   One individual provides the lateral link among interdependent functions.

4. **Forming task forces**   Interfunctional groups (composed of members from different functional areas) facilitate coordination among interdependent activities by managing information flowing between areas.

5. **Integrating departments**   A permanent organizational unit promotes coordination among interdependent activities.

are problems with the quality of the work that has been performed, the next group knows whom to contact for assistance.

The other two methods for achieving coordination — forming task forces and integrating departments — are most useful when interdependence is reciprocal. Similarly, they also work best in large, complex organizations that are somewhat decentralized. For example, the work teams used by Weyerhaeuser help facilitate coordination by functioning as task forces that explore better ways of working together and achieving more efficient levels of coordination.

Differentiating Between Positions

The final element of organization structure is differentiating between positions. All organizations rely on a variety of positions to carry out their mission. Some of these positions are central to the organization's work; others provide more support and indirect contribution. Although organizational positions can be differentiated in several different ways, the traditional approach classifies positions as being either line or staff.

Line and Staff Positions

Line positions are directly involved in the organization's operations and contribute directly to the creation of goods and services.

A **line position** is directly involved in the organization's operations and directly contributes to the creation of goods and services. For example, at Xerox purchasing managers buy materials to make photocopy machines, plant managers oversee the actual production of those machines, and sales managers market the machines to businesses. Each of these managers is involved in creating and selling photocopiers, and his or her contributions to the organization can be directly assessed.

Staff positions serve the organization's goals indirectly by providing auxiliary or support services.

In contrast, a **staff position** serves the organization's goals indirectly by providing auxiliary or support services to line functions. Members of the legal staff at Xerox, for example, do not make direct contributions to making or selling photocopy machines. Instead, they review contracts, provide legal opinions, and interpret government regulations that might affect the company. Likewise, financial analysts, human resources managers, and public relations officials are often considered to be staff positions. Although the contributions of these positions are important, they are often difficult to measure and evaluate.

Recent Trends in Administrative Intensity

A large number of the human resources cutbacks that occurred in many American firms in the 1980s came at the expense of staff positions. During the relatively prosperous 1950s, 1960s, and early 1970s, many firms added extra staff members to offer support and provide specialized services for line managers. When profits were growing rapidly, it was fairly easy to justify the extra expense, and some line managers aggressively sought to add staff positions in their departments as a way of increasing their own power and influence.

Often, however, organizations went too far and added more staff positions than they really needed. Many U.S. firms created large corporate planning units employing dozens of staff members. Although these staff employees provided valuable services to line managers, they sometimes took over so much of the planning function that line managers saw their own participation in planning diminish to practically nothing.

Administrative intensity is the ratio of staff managers to line managers.

When U.S. prosperity began to decline in the late 1970s, many organizations were forced to confront their inflated payrolls. For example, in 1986 IBM cut its corporate staff from 7,000 to 2,700. Burlington Northern, the largest railroad in the United States, learned during this same period that it could function effectively with a corporate staff of only 77 — down from several hundred in the mid-1970s. To help avoid the errors of the past, many organizations now calculate and monitor a measure of **administrative intensity**, which is the ratio of staff managers to line managers. The higher the ratio, the more staff managers the organization has; and the lower the ratio, the smaller is the number of staff managers. If the ratio of administrative intensity deviates too much from optimum, organizations may start to question the need for additional staff positions.

Learning Summary

Organization structure is the basic framework of positions, groups of positions, reporting relationships, and interaction patterns that an organization adopts to carry out its strategy. Organization structure can be characterized in terms of six elements.

Job design specifies the boundaries of a job. Job specialization breaks jobs down into small component parts. Because extreme specialization may result in boredom and monotony, organizations have tried alternative methods of designing jobs, including job rotation, job enlargement, job enrichment, focusing on job characteristics, and designing jobs for groups.

Departmentalization is the basis on which jobs are grouped together in organizations. Common bases of departmentalization are by function, product, customer, and location. Each of these bases has advantages and disadvantages. Most large organizations use multiple bases of departmentalization within their single overall structure.

Organizations also create a hierarchy as a part of their structure. A hierarchy is the pattern of reporting relationships between positions in an organization. The chain of command is the line of authority that extends from the position with ultimate authority for decision making down to the operating level. The span of management is the number of people who report to a manager. Several factors influence the most effective span of management. The span of management also determines whether the organization is relatively tall or flat.

Authority is power that is created and granted by the organization. The process of distributing authority between a manager and her or his subordinates is called delegation. At the organizational level, delegation results in decentralization or centralization.

The degree to which an organization must coordinate its activities is determined by the extent of interdependence among its people and groups. Depending on whether the interdependence is pooled, sequential, or reciprocal, coordination may be achieved through use of the hierarchy, rules and procedures, liaisons, task forces, and integrated departments.

Organizations often differentiate positions by classifying them as either line or staff. A line position is directly involved in the organization's operations and directly contributes to the creation of goods and services. A staff position serves the organization's goals indirectly by providing auxiliary or support services to line functions. In order to avoid creating too many staff positions, organizations sometimes monitor their ratio of administrative intensity.

Questions and Exercises

Review Questions

1. What are the six elements of organization structure?
2. Why have organizations sought alternatives to job specialization? What are the most common alternatives?
3. Identify the four common forms of departmentalization. What are the advantages and disadvantages of each?
4. Why is there no optimal span of management? What factors should be considered when a span of management is being established?

5. Explain the delegation process.
6. What forms of interdependence exist in organizations? How do they affect coordination needs?
7. What is the difference between line and staff positions in organizations?

Analysis Questions

1. Suggest some ways of combining the alternatives to job specialization to offset the negative effects of specialization.
2. Explain the connection between job design and forms of departmentalization. Do some approaches to job design work better in one type of department than in another?
3. A classical principle of hierarchy is that subordinates should have one and only one boss. Do you think this idea is still relevant today? Why or why not?
4. Would you prefer to work in an organization that uses decentralization or in one that uses centralization? If you worked for a boss who did not delegate effectively, how might you change things?
5. Give some examples of interdependence beyond those discussed in the text.
6. Would you prefer to work in a line position or in a staff position? Why?

Application Exercises

1. Study your college or university. Describe how it handles each of the six elements of organization structure.
2. Write a description of an organization that you might create. Start with yourself as an individual entrepreneur. Discuss how you would address each of the six structural elements as your organization grows. For example, when you hire your first employee, what part of your job will you assign to him or her? What form of departmentalization will you adopt as your organization grows bigger? Will you use decentralization or centralization?

Chapter Notes

1. "Companies Putting Teamwork to Work" (a Knight-Ridder News Service story), *Bryan–College Station Eagle,* May 20, 1990, p. 6C; "The *Fortune 500* Largest Industrials," *Fortune,* April 23, 1990, p. 346; "Weyerhaeuser's Real Worry," *Business Week,* July 16, 1990, pp. 50–51.
2. Christopher Finch, *The Art of Walt Disney* (New York: Abrams, 1983).
3. Adam Smith, *An Inquiry into the Nature and Causes of the Wealth of Nations,* (1776; reprint New York: Modern Library, 1937).
4. See Ricky W. Griffin, *Task Design — An Integrative Approach* (Glenview, Ill.: Scott, Foresman, 1982), for a review.

5. See Frederick Herzberg, *Work and the Nature of Man* (Cleveland: World, 1966).

6. J. Richard Hackman and Greg R. Oldham, "Motivation Through the Design of Work: Test of a Theory," *Organizational Behavior and Human Performance*, 1976, pp. 250–279.

7. Brian Dumaine, "Who Needs a Boss?" *Fortune*, May 7, 1990, pp. 52–60.

8. See Richard L. Daft, *Organization Theory & Design*, 3rd ed. (St. Paul, Minn.: West, 1989).

9. David D. Van Fleet, "Span of Management Research and Issues," *Academy of Management Journal*, September 1983, pp. 546–552.

10. James C. Worthy, "Factors Influencing Employee Morale," *Harvard Business Review*, January 1950, pp. 61–73.

11. Jeremy Main, "The Winning Organization," *Fortune*, September 26, 1988, pp. 50–60.

12. See Carrie Leana, "Predictors and Consequences of Delegation," *Academy of Management Journal*, December 1986, pp. 754–774, for a review of recent findings about delegation.

13. See Daft, *Organization Theory & Design*.

14. "IBM Unveils a Sweeping Restructuring in Bid to Decentralize Decision Making," *Wall Street Journal*, January 29, 1988, p. 3.

15. Bart Victor, "Coordinating Work in Complex Organizations," *Journal of Organizational Behavior*, 1990, pp. 187–199.

16. James Thompson, *Organizations in Action* (New York: McGraw-Hill, 1967).

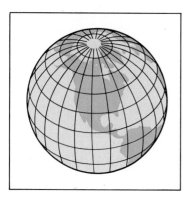

CASE 10.1

Digital Is No Longer a One-Chief Company

Digital Equipment Corporation (DEC) is a huge company — the second largest American computer manufacturer after IBM — yet it is still controlled by its founder, Kenneth H. Olsen. For thirty years, Olsen ran the company almost as though it were an entrepreneur's start-up, without a chairman, chief executive officer, or chief operating officer. No one on Wall Street complained, however, as DEC became the fastest-growing computer company, largely on the strength of its VAX minicomputers. But when sales of the minis began slumping in the late 1980s and earnings dropped for the first time, Olsen and his company followed the lead of IBM and restructured, shifting much of DEC's decision making away from its headquarters in Maynard, Massachusetts.

With the goal of producing more sales with less overhead, Olsen first imposed a wage freeze and then tried to trim Digital's payroll. The company has a long-standing no-layoffs tradition, but it hopes that severance bonuses will encourage eight or nine thousand of its 126,000 employees to quit voluntarily. Such moves are painful and don't immediately produce positive results. Similar slimming at IBM took four or five years to pay off.

In the first phase of the reorganization, Olsen eliminated separate and sometimes competing divisions organized around particular products and markets. All 30,000 marketing, sales, and service employees were combined into one unit focused on selling computers. No executive from headquarters was given control of the branch offices of this sales army; instead, a regional manager was put in charge. Because of this decentralization, much of the decision making moved to the field.

In Digital's new departmentalization, the regional managers coordinate all employees — including engineers, programmers, and salespeople — who cater to a particular industry. For instance, a manager in New York now oversees everyone from Digital who does business with the financial services industry. Such targeting of specific industries — from health care to manufacturing — should make DEC more responsive to customer needs. It is complemented by DEC's "competency centers," where members of target groups meet with the company's product engineers to figure out together how DEC products can best serve these groups. Altogether, DEC plans to create eighteen industry-targeting organizations, thirteen more than IBM created in its reorganization. Each DEC group will have a budget ranging from $500,000 to $1 million dollars and will be responsible for setting its own budgets and quotas and making its own profit.

Taking another cue from IBM, DEC shifted three or four thousand workers from staff jobs at headquarters to line jobs in the field, where they can more directly affect sales. IBM's augmented sales force in the field helped make its latest minicomputer a success, and DEC hopes that its new sales teams can do the same for an array of new Digital products.

Although Olsen clearly still holds the company's reins, he delegated considerable responsibility during the reorganization, and his choices of executives reflect his perception of what the company needs. David W. Grainger, new vice president of U.S. sales and marketing, proved himself by, among other things, beating out the other vice presidents in a race to unpack and assemble a DEC computer system. Such hands-on knowledge is important if the new decentralized decision making is to work. John F. Smith, senior vice president for operations and the company's new number-two man, is known for his decisiveness and willingness to make decisions from the top. Credited with keeping the company's old VAX design competitive, Smith avoids DEC's traditional consensus building, preferring to make decisions himself. Since he was the twelfth person hired at DEC, other employees can hardly accuse him of not understanding the company's culture. Peter J. Smith (no relation) coordinates the eighteen industry-targeting organizations, having proved himself by running the company's successful demonstration centers. Besides familiarizing potential customers with DEC products, the centers encourage software developers to write more programs for the VAX.

While undergoing all these structural changes, DEC has also had to make major product changes. Customers are no longer satisfied with machines based on a company's proprietary software, as DEC's VAX line has been. So Digital has tried to take the lead in creating computer systems that can link, rather than exclude, other machines and programs. Its new Network Application Support software allows most major personal computers, including Apple Macintosh and IBM PC, to share data and use VAX services. No doubt some engineers balked at making DEC machines "talk" to their competitors, just as some staff employees at the Massachusetts headquarters objected to being sent to Brown University to be taught how to sell computers. But analysts agree that without such major changes accompanying the restructuring, DEC could have become a bloated giant ready to be overtaken by nimbler competitors.

Discussion Questions

1. What kind of job design changes does Digital's reorganization make necessary?
2. Why is it rare for one person to take a company from start-up to industry leader?
3. How did Digital's departmentalization apparently change during the reorganization?
4. Why was decentralization of decision making a key step for Digital?

REFERENCES: Leslie Helm, "DEC Has One Little Word for 30,000 Employees: Sell," *Business Week,* August 14, 1989, p. 86; Gary McWilliams, "Can DEC Beat the Big Blue Blues?" *Business Week,* August 13, 1990, pp. 114–115; Gary McWilliams, "DEC Is Changing with the Times — A Little Late," *Business Week,* April 9, 1990, pp. 76–78; John R. Wilke, "At Digital Equipment, Slowdown Reflects Industry's Big Changes," *Wall Street Journal,* September 15, 1989, pp. A1, A12; John R. Wilke, "Smith Coolly Mans Digital's 'Hot Seat,'" *Wall Street Journal,* July 5, 1990, p. B6.

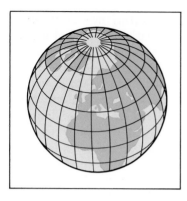

CASE 10.2

Imperial Chemical Industries Goes Global

Since its formation in 1926, the result of a merger of four companies, Imperial Chemical Industries (ICI) has been one of Britain's industrial success stories. Manufacturing chemicals, pharmaceuticals, film, plastics, and related products, it became Britain's largest industrial company, turning a profit every year for over half a century.

But then in 1980, a bad year for the chemical industry in general, ICI reported its first loss. To recover, the company put into high gear changes that had already been taking place, though at an agonizingly slow pace. It changed its worldwide organization and focus, acquired subsidiaries and partners around the globe, and moved various operations to more strategic locations. In the process, it became one of the most truly global of companies. No longer a strictly British organization with imperial tentacles reaching around the world, ICI has moved many of its operations overseas, and they provide most of its growth. The word "imperial," which conjures up images of a mighty empire firmly based in England, may no longer be appropriate.

ICI actually started to become a global company back in 1936, when it began to invest in pharmaceutical research and development. Because of difficulty in making its pharmaceuticals division profitable, the company soon learned a lesson that some of its competitors didn't learn until the 1980s: the more it costs to develop a product, the more important it is to have a global market for that product. Developing a drug from the first research to the market entry may now take over a decade and cost over $250 million. No company wants to pay these costs to bring out a drug in, say, Great Britain, and then go through the whole process again when trying to introduce the drug into the United States. From the outset, a global company tries to make a product universally acceptable.

Expanding on this early lesson, ICI gradually built a network of business, manufacturing, and research and development units around the globe, from Australia to Uruguay, from Scotland to Chile. An Australian now runs ICI Americas from Wilmington, Delaware. The formerly all-British board of directors now boasts members from Canada, the United States, Japan, and Germany, and over one-third of the top 180 people in the company are non-British.

ICI continues to change along two fronts. Bucking the trend toward selling off subsidiaries, ICI has been expanding around the world by purchasing companies like Glidden paint and Beatrice's chemical and specialty plastics business. It recognizes that its traditional chemical business is cyclical and not particularly attractive to investors, so it is diversifying into more glamorous products. But ICI's most important changes occurred during a major restructuring in the 1980s. Recognizing that it was employing many more workers than other top chemical companies, ICI laid off one-third of its British work force. Just as important, the company clarified its historically blurry definitions of managerial responsibility and authority.

Before the restructuring, different groups battled to win development money from ICI headquarters. Now a single person heads the company's worldwide efforts to make a particular product successful. Managers who previously focused their attention solely on maximum production efficiency are now aiming to exploit new markets and create new products. Whole layers of middle managers were eliminated to allow top managers to communicate more directly with operations. And major parts of ICI's business were reshuffled into new groups.

The new focus on products means that the company has dedicated the majority of its resources to support its strongest products and has moved many of its plants and laboratories to the center of a product's market. Its advanced materials research unit moved to Phoenix, close to defense-industries clients. Its leather dye research moved near customers in southern France. In all, four of the nine new business units that the company began developing in 1983 are located outside Great Britain.

These structural changes have allowed ICI to speed up product development and to cut the time it takes to introduce a product to new markets. In the past, it could take five or six years for a drug that succeeded in Great Britain to be introduced in America. ICI has cut that period to one or two years and hopes eventually to introduce drugs simultaneously around the world.

Simultaneous introduction would be another step in demonstrating ICI's desire to treat the world's countries as it once treated Britain's cities — as geographically distinct parts of the same market. While the company grows at a measly 2 to 3 percent rate in Britain, it is advancing ten times that fast in the United States. If home is where the activity is, ICI may need to change "Imperial" to "Global."

Discussion Questions

1. Why does product departmentalization often make sense for a global company?
2. What new skills does an ICI product manager have to acquire in order to handle the demands of the new structure?
3. Is there a "best" departmental form for a large transnational corporation like ICI? Why or why not?

REFERENCES: Stephanie Cooke, "ICI Wants to Be a Household Word in the U.S.," *Business Week,* September 1, 1986, p. 40; Geoffrey Foster, "The Legacy of Harvey-Jones," *Management Today,* January 1987, pp. 35–86; Jeremy Main, "How to Go Global — And Why," *Fortune,* August 28, 1989, pp. 70–76.

11

The Design of Organizations

LEARNING OBJECTIVES

After studying this chapter, you should be able to:

1. Describe the nature of organization design.

2. Summarize two historical views of organization design, and discuss their relevance for today's organizations.

3. Explain how situational factors such as technology, environment, and life cycle play a role in determining appropriate organization design.

4. Identify and describe the major contemporary forms of design that organizations use today.

5. Discuss the role of participation, flexibility, and sociocultural factors in organization design.

6. Discuss the meaning and importance of organizational culture, and explain how it is created, maintained, and changed.

The Nature of Organization Design

Historical Views of Organization Design

The Bureaucratic Model

System 1 and System 4

Situational Determinants of Organization Design

Technology

Environment

Organization Size and Life Cycle

Contemporary Forms of Organization Design

The U-Form Organization

The H-Form Organization

The M-Form Organization

The Matrix Organization

The Global Organization

Hybrid Designs

Emerging Issues in Organization Design

Employee Participation and Work Teams

Organizational Flexibility

Sociocultural Factors

Organizational Culture

The Meaning and Importance of Culture

Creating, Maintaining, and Changing Culture

The Toyota Motor Corporation was founded in Japan in 1926 as Toyoda Automatic Loom Works by Sakichi Toyoda. As its original name suggests, the firm started out making looms. Before his death in 1930, Toyoda sold the rights to the loom to another firm and gave the profits to his son, Kiichiro. Kiichiro changed the firm's name to Toyota (for clarity in spoken Japanese) and started making automobiles.

The firm grew slowly until the end of World War II. At that time, it started making major commitments to research and development and began to grow rapidly. By the beginning of this decade Toyota controlled 40 percent of the Japanese automobile market, was the third largest automaker in the world, and was closing in on Chrysler for the number-three position in the United States.

For most of its existence, Toyota has been a tall, bureaucratic organization. Decision making has been slow; advancement has been based on senority; and the firm has been highly centralized. Beginning in the late 1980s, however, Toyota started to see that it had become complacent and sluggish. Its growth was slowing, and costs were starting to creep up. In response, the firm has made several fundamental changes in its structure. Two layers of middle management were eliminated, and those managers were reassigned to other jobs. The company also announced plans to increase decentralization.

Toyota is also rearranging several of its divisions. Some are being combined, and new ones are being created. In addition, Toyota is taking steps to reduce its bureaucracy by giving more people the authority to make decisions. The firm is also trying to enhance its ability to process information, modify its structure to better fit the global automobile marketplace, and increase its flexibility.[1]

Instead of focusing on just a few components, Toyota is changing virtually everything about its structure. Indeed, these changes are so far-reaching and comprehensive that they will redefine the overall character of the firm. When multiple structural components are being revised simultaneously, as at Toyota, a shift in organization design is occurring.

This chapter explains the importance of organization design and examines its historical roots. We discuss several factors that determine the optimal design for an organization and compare five contemporary approaches to organization design. We then describe emerging issues in organization design and conclude with a discussion of organizational culture.

Organizations are like jigsaw puzzles, comprised of many different pieces that have to be fitted together into a viable design. Some organizations are beginning to employ anthropologists to help them better achieve an optimal design. Lucy Suchman, shown on the left, is one of a growing number of anthropologists who are applying their expertise to business issues. Suchman works for Xerox Corporation's Palo Alto Research Center. Her work focuses on how people in organizations can work together efficiently and effectively.

The Nature of Organization Design

Organization design is the overall configuration of structural components that define jobs, groupings of jobs, the hierarchy, patterns of authority, approaches to coordination, and line-staff differentiation into a single, unified organizational system.

Organization design is the overall configuration of structural components that defines jobs, groupings of jobs, the hierarchy, patterns of authority, approaches to coordination, and line-staff differentiation into a single, unified organizational system. In some ways the various structural components discussed in Chapter 10 are like pieces of a jigsaw puzzle. They can be arranged in a number of ways to create a wide variety of organization designs.

Consider, for example, the differences in organization design that might exist between a computer manufacturer and a university. Because the computer manufacturer has to respond to frequent technological breakthroughs and changes in its competitive environment, it is likely to have a relatively flat, decentralized design. The university, in contrast, has a somewhat more stable environment and is less affected by technology. Thus it may have a taller, more centralized structure with numerous rules and regulations.

Even firms that function in the same environment can create quite different designs. For example, Coca-Cola and Pepsi-Cola are fierce competitors in the soft-drink market. But the two businesses look as different as day from night. Coca-Cola Company has relatively specialized jobs, uses functional departmentalization, and has narrow spans of control and a relatively tall and centralized hierarchy. PepsiCo, in contrast, has less specialization, uses product departmentalization, and has wide spans of control and a flat decentralized hierarchy.

Historical Views of Organization Design

Organizations have long been concerned with how to create effective designs for themselves. Some of the approaches popularized in this century tried to identify ideal forms of organization design that could be used in a wide variety of settings with equal effectiveness. These models were called universal approaches to organization design because they were presumed to be universally appropriate. Two of the most important universal approaches were the bureaucratic model and the System 4 approach.

The Bureaucratic Model

For many people, the term *bureaucracy* conjures up images of an inflexible and monolithic organization manned by unsmiling clerks and technicians entangled in a thicket of red tape. Some bureaucractic organizations do indeed seem to take on these characteristics, but the original concept of the bureaucracy was really very different from this stereotype.

The *bureaucratic model* is an idealized approach to organization design based on a rational set of guidelines and procedures.

Although its roots go back several centuries, the **bureaucratic model** of organizations is most often associated with the work of German sociologist Max Weber.[2] As we saw in Chapter 2, Weber was trying to describe an ideal approach to structuring organizations based on a rational set of guidelines and procedures. He suggested that organizations should have a clear division of labor. Consistent rules should be developed to guide all activities, and a hierarchy of positions should define a clear chain of command from the top to the bottom of the organization. All business should be transacted in an impersonal fashion, and employment and advancement should be based on technical expertise.

The general idea underlying the bureaucratic model is that bureaucracy can enhance efficiency, logic, and rationality in large organizations. Many universities and government organizations still use variations of the bureaucratic model today, in part because it allows them to deal with a large number of routine transactions involving many different people in an objective and impartial way.

However, just as its critics charge, the bureaucratic model does indeed lead to organizations that are inflexible and rigid. This inflexibility and rigidity, in turn, lead to slow decision making and a general inability to respond to rapid change or unexpected circumstances. Thus many businesses, as well as other types of organizations, have generally found the bureaucratic model to be less than ideal. Consequently, organizations began to seek approaches to organization design that would allow them to be more flexible and responsive. A noteworthy early alternative to the bureaucratic model was the System 4 approach.

System 1 and System 4

Organizational theorist Rensis Likert developed a second universal approach to organization design by drawing a distinction between System

System 4 is an informal and flexible approach to organization design.

1 and System 4 organizations.[3] He described the traditional bureaucratic organization and labeled it **System 1**. He then went on to describe a form of organization design that is the antithesis of System 1; he labeled this second form **System 4**. Table 11.1 summarizes the characteristics of System 1 and System 4 organizations. Note that whereas a System 1 organization is relatively formal, rigid, and mechanistic, a System 4 organization is more likely to be informal and flexible.

Likert's model strongly suggests that organizations that are like System 1 should try to change their design to be more like System 4. Since such a dramatic change is likely to be difficult to manage, he also describes

Table 11.1

System 1 and System 4 Organizations

System 1 Organization	System 4 Organization
1. **Leadership process** includes no perceived confidence and trust. Subordinates do not feel free to discuss job problems with their superiors, who in turn do not solicit their ideas and opinions.	1. **Leadership process** includes perceived confidence and trust between superiors and subordinates in all matters. Subordinates feel free to discuss job problems with their superiors, who in turn solicit their ideas and opinions.
2. **Motivational process** taps only physical, security, and economic motives through the use of fear and sanctions. Unfavorable attitudes toward the organization prevail among employees.	2. **Motivational process** taps a full range of motives through participatory methods. Attitudes are favorable toward the organization and its goals.
3. **Communication process** is such that information flows downward and tends to be distorted, inaccurate, and viewed with suspicion by subordinates.	3. **Communication process** is such that information flows freely throughout the organization — upward, downward, and laterally. The information is accurate and undistorted.
4. **Interaction process** is closed and restricted; subordinates have little effect on departmental goals, methods, and activities.	4. **Interaction process** is open and extensive; both superiors and subordinates are able to affect departmental goals, methods, and activities.
5. **Decision process** occurs only at the top of the organization; it is relatively centralized.	5. **Decision process** occurs at all levels through group processes; it is relatively decentralized.
6. **Goal-setting process** is located at the top of the organization; discourages group participation.	6. **Goal-setting process** encourages group participation in setting high, realistic objectives.
7. **Control process** is centralized and emphasizes fixing of blame for mistakes.	7. **Control process** is dispersed throughout the organization and emphasizes self-control and problem solving.
8. **Performance goals** are low and passively sought by managers who make no commitment to developing the human resources of the organization.	8. **Performance goals** are high and actively sought by superiors who recognize the necessity for making a full commitment to developing, through training, the human resources of the organization.

SOURCE: Adapted from Rensis Likert, *The Human Organization*, copyright © 1967, McGraw-Hill. Used by permission of McGraw-Hill.

intermediate and evolutionary stages called — logically enough — System 2 and System 3. In one widely publicized experiment studying the effectiveness of his model, Likert transformed a General Motors plant in Atlanta from a System 1 to a System 4 organization. Findings from the study indicated that the transformation reduced labor costs, scrap, and tool-breakage rates while also increasing quality.[4]

At the same time, however, several other organizations were unsuccessful when they attempted to adopt a System 4 design. As a consequence, managers and researchers alike learned that blindly adopting a System 4 design was no more a guarantee of success than was relying purely on the bureaucratic model. Most now recognize that the most appropriate design for any organization is likely to be determined by a number of variables that characterize the overall situation in which the organization functions. Our next section identifies and discusses some of these variables.

Situational Determinants of Organization Design

We noted earlier that Coca-Cola and PepsiCo use very different forms of organization design even though they compete in the same industry. Although there may be several explanations for their differences, a major factor is organizational environment. Coca-Cola is largely a single-product firm, and Pepsi-Cola is actually only one division of a larger corporation, PepsiCo. This parent organization also owns three fast-food restaurant chains (Pizza Hut, Taco Bell, and Kentucky Fried Chicken) and the Frito-Lay snack-foods business. Thus the environment serves as a situational determinant that partially defines the organization design most appropriate for a business. As Figure 11.1 shows, the key situational determinants of organization design are technology, the organizational environment, and organization size and life cycle.

> Key situational determinants of organization design are technology, the organizational environment, and organization size and life cycle.

Technology

As defined in Chapter 3, technology is the set of processes that an organization uses to transform various resources (such as materials and labor) into products or services. Technology can have a major impact on any of the structural components discussed in Chapter 10. The term *technology* conjures up images of manufacturing plants, robots, and smokestacks, and indeed, manufacturing firms such as Monsanto and Fiat do use plants and equipment to make their products. At the same time, however, service firms such as Hyatt, CBS, and Pizza Hut also use technology. Moreover, technology can involve the conversion of information.

One of the first people to see the link between technology and organization design was the British researcher Joan Woodward.[5] Woodward led a team of researchers in a study of one hundred manufacturing firms in southern England. They observed significant differences in both technology

Figure 11.1

Situational Determinants of Organization Design

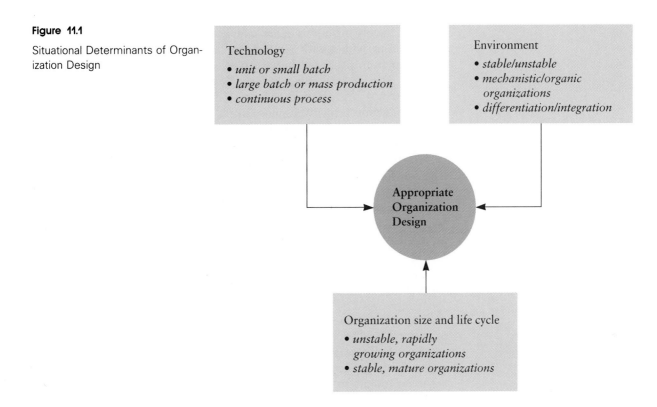

Woodward identified three forms of technology — *unit* or *small batch, large batch* or *mass production*, and *continuous process* — that seemed to affect organization design.

and organization design among the various firms. In particular, Woodward defined three basic types of technology.

1. In unit or small-batch technology, products are either custom-made to customer specifications or produced in small quantities. Examples of firms that use unit or small-batch technology are printing shops (like Kinko's Graphics), portrait studios (such as Olan Mills), and aircraft manufacturers (like Boeing).
2. In large-batch or mass-production technology, products are manufactured in assembly-line fashion by combining component parts to create finished goods. Examples of firms that use large-batch or mass-production technology are home appliance manufacturers (Maytag), automakers (Honda), and computer companies (Apple).
3. In continuous-process technology, products are transformed from raw materials into finished goods through a series of machine transformations that change the composition of the materials themselves. Examples of firms that use continuous-process technology are petroleum refineries (British Petroleum), food processors (Nestlé), and chemical manufacturers (Bayer).

Woodward viewed unit or small-batch technology as the least complex, and continuous process as the most complex. She found that when she classified the organizations in her sample according to their technology, the organizations within each set had similar designs but the designs varied somewhat from set to set. In particular, she found that organizations that used the most or least complex technology tended to have designs similar to a System 4 organization and those in the middle (the large-batch or mass-production firms) were more like a System 1 organization. This pattern of findings led Woodward to conclude that different forms of technology are likely to dictate different types of organization design.

Unfortunately, several issues have limited the value of Woodward's findings. For one thing, all the organizations she studied were relatively small: many employed fewer than one hundred people. For another, some of the research measures employed in the study were weak. Overall, however, Woodward's research played an important role in spotlighting technology as an important situational determinant of organization design.

Environment

The environment also influences the type of design an organization is likely to adopt. As Chapter 4 discusses, the environment of an organization consists of all the factors and conditions outside of the organization that might affect it. The specific aspects of the task and general environments are useful points to recall when considering the relationships between an organization and its environment.

Tom Burns and G. M. Stalker, two British scholars, were among the first to recognize a relationship between an organization's environment and its design.[6] They classified environments into two categories. Stable environments are relatively placid and do not change very much. Unstable environments are more volatile and are prone to rapid and major changes. Burns and Stalker then studied a variety of organizations in each of the two environmental conditions and found major differences in their design.

Burns and Stalker identified two types of organization design. *Organic designs* seem to work best for organizations in unstable environments. *Mechanistic designs* seem to work best for organizations in stable environments.

Organizations in unstable environments took on the basic characteristics of System 4 organizations. Burns and Stalker called them **organic organizations**. In contrast, organizations in more stable environments resembled System 1 organizations; these the researchers called **mechanistic organizations**. Profiles of each type of organization are presented in Table 11.2.

These ideas were extended and studied again by two American researchers, Paul R. Lawrence and Jay W. Lorsch.[7] Lawrence and Lorsch found that just as the overall organization adapts to its environment, so too do its various subunits or departments. Say, for example, that the marketing and manufacturing units within the same organization confront quite different types of environments. The manufacturing unit uses standard technology with reliable equipment and fairly predictable work demands and therefore has a stable environment. The marketing unit, in contrast, is implementing a new communications system and faces intense competition so its environment is dynamic and less predictable. Each unit should attempt to match the unique characteristics of its own environment while simultaneously making sure its activities are properly coordinated with other organizational units.

Differentiation is the extent to which the organization is broken down into subunits or departments.

As a result of their study, Lawrence and Lorsch identified two important concepts, differentiation and integration. **Differentiation** is the extent to which the organization is broken down into subunits or departments. When an organization increases its differentiation, it is adding departments. Decreasing differentation means eliminating departments.

According to Lawrence and Lorsch, the more unstable and dynamic the environment, the more differentiation the organization should establish. If the organization's environment is relatively stable and predictable, less differentiation is appropriate. Organizations that have too much or too little differentiation relative to the demands of their environment will be less effective than those that achieve the right amount of differentiation.

Table 11.2

Mechanistic and Organic Organizations

Mechanistic	Organic
1. Tasks are highly fractionated and specialized; little regard paid to clarifying relationship between tasks and organizational objectives.	1. Tasks are more interdependent; emphasis on relevance of tasks and organizational objectives.
2. Tasks tend to remain rigidly defined unless altered formally by top management.	2. Tasks are continually adjusted and redefined through interaction of organizational members.
3. Specific role definition (rights, obligations, and technical methods prescribed for each member).	3. Generalized role definition (members accept general responsibility for task accomplishment beyond individual role definition).
4. Hierarchic structure of control, authority, and communication. Sanctions derive from employment contract between employee and organization.	4. Network structure of control, authority, and communication. Sanctions derive more from community of interest than from contractual relationship.
5. Information relevant to situation and operations of the organization formally assumed to rest with chief executive.	5. Leader not assumed to be omniscient; knowledge centers identified where located throughout organization.
6. Communication is primarily vertical between superior and subordinate.	6. Communication is both vertical and horizontal, depending upon where needed information resides.
7. Communications primarily take form of instructions and decisions issued by superiors, of information and requests for decisions supplied by inferiors.	7. Communications primarily take form of information and advice.
8. Insistence on loyalty to organization and obedience to superiors.	8. Commitment to organization's tasks and goals more highly valued than loyalty or obedience.
9. Importance and prestige attached to identification with organization and its members.	9. Importance and prestige attached to affiliations and expertise in external environment.

SOURCE: Adapted from Tom Burns and G. M. Stalker, *The Management of Innovation,* copyright © 1961. Used by permission of the publisher, Tavistock Publications (London).

Integration is the degree of coordination among organizational subunits.

Integration is the extent to which the subunits created through differentiation must coordinate their activities and functions. Lawrence and Lorsch suggest that the more an organization differentiates, the more integration is required to achieve an efficient design. Integration can be enhanced through any or all of the coordination techniques discussed in Chapter 10. Again, too much or too little integration will adversely affect organizational effectiveness. Too much can result in rigidity and slow decision making. Too little can lead to poor communication and inefficient operations.

Like the research on technology, studies linking environment and organization design have contributed to our understanding of organizations. Some of the work on strategy formulation and implementation discussed in Chapters 7 and 8, for example, draws from this perspective.

Organization Size and Life Cycle

Organization size is the number of full-time employees. The organization's *life cycle* is its relative maturity.

Organization size refers to how large the organization is, usually in terms of the number of its full-time employees. **Life cycle**, discussed more fully below, is the organization's maturity relative to that of other organizations.

Size can affect organization design in many different ways. A group of researchers at the University of Aston in England, for example, found that large organizations tend to have more job specialization, more standard operating procedures, more rules, more regulations, and more decentralization than small organizations.[8] The researchers suggested that these are normal and predictable characteristics that organizations adopt as they grow in order to handle more employees and a more complicated set of activities. Thus as organizations grow in size, they should be prepared to adapt their design accordingly.

To illustrate the importance of this adaptation, consider the stories of two U.S. firms, People Express Airlines and Tandem Computers. Each started as a relatively small firm. Each espoused a casual, democratic, and highly participative approach to management — and each grew rapidly. As both became larger, however, problems set in. Costs started to increase unexpectedly; decision making slowed; and customers started to complain. Although there are always several possible explanations for organizational troubles, a likely one is that People Express and Tandem simply grew too large for the informal and casual management styles they were using.

Managers at People Express stubbornly refused to change, and the organization was eventually bought by Texas Air Corporation. Managers at Tandem Computers initiated a number of changes designed to formalize the organization's design. A structured hierarchy was created and drawn in an organization chart, and precise job descriptions were written for all top managers. As a result, Tandem overcame its problems and is again a fast-growing and profitable enterprise.

An organization's life cycle is related to its size. Organizations tend to follow a fairly predictable pattern of growth. After they are created, they

THE ENTREPRENEURIAL CHALLENGE

Managing Growth at Sun Microsystems

Sun Microsystems was one of the fastest growing businesses in the world during the 1980s. The firm's main product is high-performance technical workstations used by engineers and scientists. Sun was formed in 1982 in California's Silicon Valley. By the close of the decade, Sun had achieved annual sales of $2.4 billion, reflecting an annual growth rate of a phenomenal 114 percent.

In its early days Sun operated with a loose and informal design. Reporting relationships were often not specified; virtually anyone could make any decision that had to be made; and the firm operated with no staff managers. Along the way Sun also developed a strong albeit odd culture. Some observers have likened it to a college fraternity. One night, for example, some engineers emptied the CEO's office, brought in a load of dirt, and built a miniature golf course.

As Sun grew, it had to change. CEO Scott McNealy saw the first signs of strain when the company posted its first quarterly loss in 1989. One of his first actions was to create a completely new design for the organization. He clarified reporting relationships, specified where various decisions were to be made, and hired a handful of financial analysts to help keep tabs on operations. So far his efforts seem to be paying off. Sun's profits have returned, and its growth rate shows no signs of leveling off.

REFERENCES: William E. Sheeline, "Avoiding Growth's Perils," *Fortune,* August 13, 1990, pp. 55–58; "Will Sun Also Rise in the Office Market?" *Business Week,* May 21, 1990, p. 44; Stuart Gannes, "America's Fastest Growing Companies," *Fortune,* May 23, 1988, pp. 28–40; "Sun Microsystems on the Rise Again," *USA Today,* April 27, 1990, p. 3B.

grow for some period of time and then eventually stabilize as a mature organization. This stable period of maturity characterizes most large businesses today. Some, like IBM, Exxon, Toyota, and Unilever, grew slowly and reached maturity only after several decades. Others, like Reebok, Wal-Mart, Liz Claiborne, and Compaq Computer, have grown rapidly and are still not fully mature. The Entrepreneurial Challenge explains how another fast-growing company, Sun Microsystems, used an unusual form of organization design in its early days.

To summarize, the organization design needed by a small but rapidly growing business is different from the organization design needed by an established and entrenched industry giant growing at a stable and predictable rate. An organization's life cycle and growth rates are directly linked to the strategy that the organization is pursuing. This relationship is explored more fully in a later section of this chapter.

Contemporary Forms of Organization Design

Every organization has its own unique design. As we saw above, depending on the technology it uses, the limits and potentials of its environment, and the life cycle stage it occupies, each organization creates varying configurations of specialization, departmentalization, and coordination that best fit its circumstances. In the midst of all this uniqueness, however, we can still discern five basic structural arrangements that generally describe the designs adopted by many organizations. These are discussed in the sections that follow.[9]

The U-Form Organization

The *U-form organization* uses a design based on functional departmentalization to implement the strategy of a single-product firm.

The **U-form organization** (the U stands for unity), also called *functional design,* relies almost exclusively on the functional approach to departmentalization as explained in Chapter 10: members of the organization who perform the same functions are grouped together into work units or departments.[10] A pure U-form organization uses functional departmentalization at all levels. In order for such an organization to operate smoothly, a lot of attention must be devoted to coordination, which in most cases is the responsibility of the CEO. The U-form design is used to implement the single-product corporate strategy discussed in Chapter 7.

Figure 11.2 shows a hypothetical U-form organization — a small manufacturing firm. One particularly noteworthy characteristic of this design is that each unit is highly dependent on the others. For example, the marketing unit cannot take care of its responsibilities if the production department doesn't supply it with products to sell or if the finance department doesn't allocate funds to market them.

The U-form design has several important advantages. It allows the organization to staff each department with experts at lower cost than is possible with other organization designs. It also facilitates wide spans of manage-

Figure 11.2

Design of a U-Form Organization

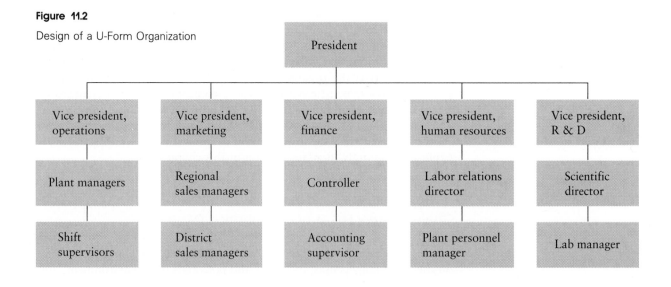

ment (since tasks within each functional unit are somewhat similar) and allows the CEO to maintain centralized authority. However, the U-form design slows decision making. Also, employees within each unit may concentrate on their own function so much that they lose sight of overall organizational goals. Finally, the U-form design tends to make it hard for the organization to monitor the performance of individual managers within each functional area.

Small organizations commonly use a U-form design, as did Compaq and Reebok early in their life cycles, because its advantages can serve a small organization very well. But as they grow, organizations often find that the disadvantages of the U form tend to become more significant. As a result, they adopt different designs as they evolve through their life cycles.

The H-Form Organization

The *H-form organization,* also called a conglomerate, uses a design based on product departmentalization to implement a strategy of unrelated diversification.

The **H-form organization** (the H stands for hybrid) is sometimes called a *conglomerate.* This design relies loosely on product departmentalization, with the various products actually constituting different businesses. The decision to use the H-form design usually results from the corporate strategy of unrelated diversification discussed in Chapter 7. In an H-form organization, each business is headed by a separate company president or division leader who operates autonomously and reports directly to top management of the corporation. The defining characteristic of the H-form organization is that the activities of each business are generally unrelated.

Figure 11.3 shows a simplified version of a real H-form organization, Teledyne, Inc., one of the largest conglomerates in the United States. Note that Teledyne's various businesses bear little similarity to one another—one in the camera industry, one in insurance, and one in the aerospace industry, for example. An H-form organization might own only two or three or as many as several hundred unrelated businesses.

The H-form design has two advantages. First, such an organization can protect itself from cyclical fluctuations in a single industry. Suppose a conglomerate owns a chain of toy stores and a swimming pool supply company. The toy stores will generate most of their revenues during the pre-Christmas season and will produce less revenue the rest of the year.

Figure 11.3

Design of an H-Form Organization (Teledyne)

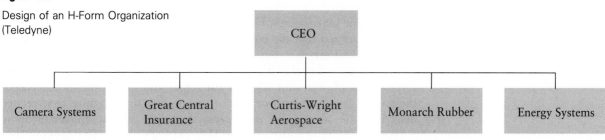

The pool company will generate most of its revenue in the spring and summer. Thus, in the course of a year, the conglomerate will have revenues in one business increasing as revenues in the other are falling. A second advantage is that the organization can buy and sell its individual businesses with little or no disruption to the others. The conglomerate described above might sell the toy stores and buy a computer manufacturer without necessarily affecting operation of the pool supply firm.

There are, however, notable drawbacks to the H-form design. For example, research by Michael Porter has suggested that the typical H-form organization is likely to achieve only average-to-weak financial performance.[11] The reason is that an H-form organization is so complex and diverse that top managers of the corporation have difficulty staying abreast of all its activities. A top executive who understands the toy industry may be at a loss to understand the swimming pool or computer industry. In the late 1970s, there was a strong trend toward the H-form design. In more recent times, the trend has reversed itself. There are still dozens of H-form organizations, but their numbers are gradually diminishing.

The M-Form Organization

The *M-form organization* uses a design based on product departmentalization to implement a strategy of related diversification.

In contrast, the M-form organization is increasing in popularity both in the United States and around the world. The **M-form organization**, also called the *divisional design,* is similar to the H-form design but has one notable distinction: most or all of its businesses are in the same or related industries. For example, a corporation with an M-form design might own one business that makes automobile batteries, another that makes tires, and still another that makes car polish. Each is distinct from the others but also related in that each makes products of value to automobile owners. Thus the M-form design is used to implement a corporate strategy of related diversification. The Global Challenge details how Arnault & Associés is using the M-form design to implement its related diversification strategy.

A primary advantage of the M-form organization is that it can achieve a great deal of synergy in its operations. A consumer familiar with a firm's batteries, for example, may be inclined to buy its tires and car polish. Moreover, because the various units are in the same or related industries, it is easy for top managers to understand, coordinate, and control them.

However, if the businesses are too closely related, the organization is no longer buffered from cyclical trends. A few years ago, the parent company of United Air Lines bought Hertz Corporation and Westin Hotel Company. The CEO argued that the company would be able to offer travelers a full range of travel services, but the board of directors quickly realized that a downturn in the travel industry could be devastating. As a result, the board forced the CEO out and sold the car rental and hotel operations. Nevertheless, in general, organizations are beginning to recognize that related diversification often makes more sense than does unrelated diversification.

Figure 11.4 shows how a large U.S. clothing chain, The Limited Inc., uses an M-form organization. Each of the chains operated by The Limited

THE GLOBAL CHALLENGE

Luxury at Arnault & Associés

The name Arnault & Associés means little to the average person. To many international high rollers, however, the products made by the firm are basic necessities — Louis Vuitton luggage, Dom Pérignon champagne, and Hennessy cognac, among others.

Arnault & Associés is the largest luxury products firm in the world. Founded in 1984 by French financial wizard Bernard Arnault, the company enjoys annual revenues exceeding $5 billion. Its most recent acquisition, Moët Hennessy Louis Vuitton, prompted Arnault to create a new design for his organization. Arnault & Associés is now an M-form organization with seven divisions.

One division handles luggage and leather goods. Its name brands include Louis Vuitton and Loewe, French Co. A second division consists of several retailing operations, including Givenchy, Christian Dior, and Céline. The clothing, accessories, and toiletries division consists of a variety of Christian Dior, Givenchy, and Christian Lacroix products. The firm's champagne division includes Dom Pérignon, Merceir, and Ruinart. The spirits division consists of Johnnie Walker, Dewars, and White Horse scotch. The California wine division has only two brand names, Domaine Chandon and Simi. The cognac division includes Hennessy and Hine.

Arnault believes that even though some of the businesses he owns seem to be unrelated, in reality they are all highly interrelated. The common thread, he argues, is luxury. He thinks the name brands controlled by his organization have across-the-board snob appeal to individuals who don't mind paying $2,200 for a suitcase or $2,700 for a woman's suit.

REFERENCES: "Meet Monsieur Luxury," *Business Week,* July 30, 1990, pp. 48–52; "Avant le Déluge at Moët Hennessy Louis Vuitton," *Business Week,* April 24, 1989, p. 44; "King of Chic — And Artful Deals," *Fortune,* January 2, 1989, p. 40.

are in the same industry, and some even compete directly with one another. But the firm also achieves considerable benefits from having a centralized buying function, sharing transportation facilities, and developing a large database of consumer preferences and trends across a variety of retail outlets. Indeed, the opportunities for coordination and shared resources within an M-form organization are so great that research has found it to be among the most effective approaches to organization design.[12]

Figure 11.4

Design of an M-Form Organization (The Limited Inc.)

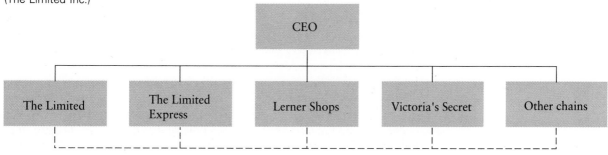

The Matrix Organization

A *matrix organization* is created by overlaying product-based departmentalization onto a functional structure.

A **matrix organization** is created by overlaying product-based departmentalization onto a functional structure. A matrix design is seldom used for an entire organization; it is most often used for a portion of it. Figure 11.5 shows a matrix design. The functional basis of the matrix appears across the top of the diagram, and down the side is an array of project managers.

As the figure shows, each member of a matrix organization has a functional "home." This functional position resides within a traditional department where the individual has regular responsibilities tied to her or his functional specialty. At any given time, however, the individual may also be part of one or more groups working on special projects such as a new product, a new product line, or a joint venture.

For example, in Figure 11.5 project managers A and B both lead groups consisting of one member from each functional area: engineering, produc-

Figure 11.5

Design of a Matrix Organization

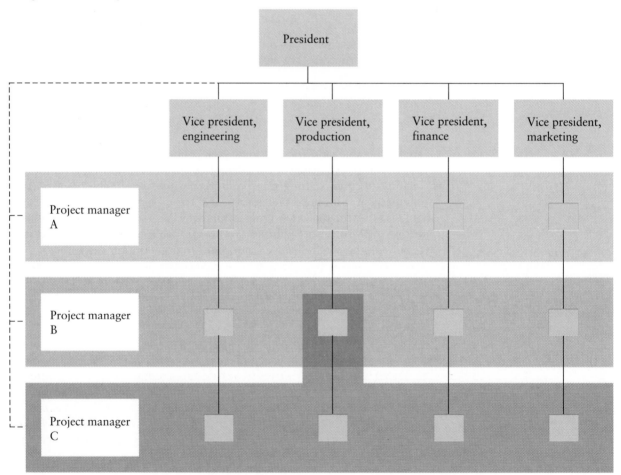

tion, finance, and marketing. Project manager C's group has two representatives from production, one of whom is also a member of B's group. Project manager C may need two representatives from production because her project has a heavier production component than do the other projects. The one individual working in two different project groups may be serving as a liaison between them or may have been selected because he has a relatively light load in his functional department right now.

A matrix design allows an organization to capitalize on the advantages of both functional and product departmentalization. In the early 1980s Ford used a matrix design in planning its highly successful Taurus automobile. Team Taurus, as the group was called, consisted of designers, engineers, production specialists, marketing specialists, and experts from other functional areas all working on a single project.

Of course, the matrix design also has some drawbacks. For one, since such an organization lacks a clear chain of command, confusion may result about which manager has authority over a given employee. Project groups may take longer to complete work and may be prone to more conflict as each member represents the interests of his or her functional area. Finally, the organization also has to devote more resources to coordination because of the high levels of interdependence that result from a matrix.

Many organizations have used the matrix design successfully, including NCR, Monsanto, and NASA. Others have found it less useful. Citicorp dropped its matrix design because it was too costly, and Texas Instruments scaled back its matrix because it wasn't achieving the innovations that the company had anticipated. In general, managers seem to agree that a matrix design is less useful when an organization has a simple and stable environment, when internal coordination is not important, and when a product-based design (such as an H-form or M-form) is already in place.

The Global Organization

A *global organization design* is necessary for organizations that are moving toward multinational status. Such a design is likely to be a modified version of the U-, H-, or M-form design.

An organization that is entering foreign markets or evolving to full multinational status must modify and adapt its design to allow it to function effectively. A **global organization design** is necessary for organizations that are moving toward or have achieved multinational status. There is no single such design, since all global organizations typically confront a unique series of design-related questions and issues. However, most global organizations adopt modified versions of the U-, H-, or M-form design.

Nestlé, for example, is one of the most multinational of businesses, but it is also highly decentralized. Its organization design is like an umbrella. The entire corporation is run by a relatively small group of executives based in Vevey, Switzerland. Each of Nestlé's operating companies scattered around the world is operated by its own general manager, who is empowered with a great deal of autonomy and authority to make decisions. In effect, Nestlé is really almost a confederation of independent operating companies. Its design is similar to the M form, but because the operating units are so far apart there is little synergy.

In contrast to Nestlé, Matsushita Electric Industrial Company, also a global business, is relatively centralized. Surprisingly routine decisions such as local pricing policies and advertising slogans must still be cleared in Japan by top management before they can be implemented. Subsidiaries have relatively little autonomy. Yet Nestlé and Matsushita are both outstanding performers by any measure.

Figure 11.6 shows the locations of the various operations of ICI — Imperial Chemical Industries — a large British multinational firm. The map underscores the complexities involved in developing a global design for this type of organization. ICI's business unit headquarters, manufacturing plants, and R&D centers are located all over the world. The map does not show the many locations for marketing, human resource, and financial management functions. The key to creating a design for an organization such as this is to create a framework that will coordinate and direct organizational efforts while also maintaining flexibility and autonomy. In other words, the organization must find ways to allow local managers the autonomy they need to respond to local conditions while also maintaining an appropriate level of corporate-level oversight and control.

Figure 11.6

The Global Organization (Imperial Chemical Industries)

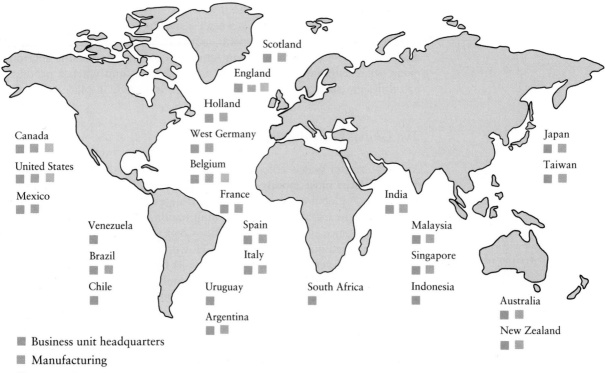

 Business unit headquarters

◾ Manufacturing

◾ R & D Centers

SOURCE: From *Fortune*, August 28, 1989. © 1989 The Time Inc. Magazine Company. All rights reserved.

Hybrid Designs

In Chapter 10 we described how organizations can use multiple forms of departmentalization. Similarly, most organizations use designs that are hybrids of the several idealized designs discussed above. Say, for example, a corporation pursuing a strategy of related diversification adopts an M-form design at the corporate level. One of the businesses within this corporate umbrella might subsequently adopt a matrix design, and another might use a U-form design.

The key point to remember is that there is no one best form of design that all organizations should adopt. Each organization has to carefully assess its own strategy, its strengths and weaknesses, its history, its technology, environment, life cycle, and size. It must then choose a design that fits these elements most effectively. But that design will also need to be further tailored. An organization may choose an M-form design but will subsequently need to modify that design to meet its own specific needs.

Emerging Issues in Organization Design

In recent years, several other issues related to organization design have become important. Two have to do with some aspects of structure touched on in the previous chapter: employee participation and work teams, and organizational flexibility. A third issue is the recognition of sociocultural factors as another situational determinant of organization design.

Employee Participation and Work Teams

Many early views of organization design, such as the bureaucratic model, took what might be termed a top-down approach to management: managers were supposed to make the decisions, and subordinates were supposed to carry them out. Stimulated in part by general changes in managerial philosophy and in part by Japanese models of management, American firms have begun to increase employee participation at many organizational levels. In many cases, this participation is achieved through the use of work teams.[13]

Work teams are groups of employees who are allowed to function as a unit with very little and sometimes no supervision.

[Work teams are groups of employees who are allowed to function as a unit with very little and sometimes no supervision.] For example, the Aid Association for Lutherans (AAL), a nonprofit insurer, recently adopted work teams as a way to eliminate bureaucracy and red tape. All AAL operating employees are grouped according to function, and each group develops its own work procedures, hires new members, and schedules its own work hours. As a result, productivity at AAL has increased by 20 percent, and processing time for claims has dropped by 75 percent.[14] We discuss participation more fully in Chapter 17 and work teams again in Chapter 19.

Employee participation in decision making can occur in almost any area. When managers in U.S. firms initially began to allow participation, it was often narrowly confined to such areas as developing work rules and routine procedures. Over time, however, the trend has been to allow employee participation in a wider variety of areas ranging from workplace issues like scheduling and job assignments to more general issues such as strategy and organization change.[15] The German firms BMW and Siemens and the Asian giants Samsung and Sony have been pioneers in employee participation. In the United States, Ford, Delta, Merck, Philip Morris, and 3M have been leaders in the move toward participation.

Organizational Flexibility

Organizations based on the bureaucratic model were rigid and relatively inflexible. They were slow to respond to environmental forces and hard to change. As described in Chapter 4, the environment faced by organizations today is both dramatically volatile and incredibly complex. As a result, organizations have been forced to become more responsive and flexible.

Organizational flexibility allows the organization to respond quickly to its environment.

To increase flexibility, organizations change their design regularly, always on the lookout for faster ways to get things done. Until recently, for example, Ford needed five years to bring a new model automobile from concept sketch to dealer showroom. The development cycle is important because it determines how quickly a firm can react to consumer tastes and moves by competitors. To shorten the cycle, Ford gave designers and engineers more autonomy (by decentralizing decision-making authority) and adopted a modified matrix design. Ford has shortened its development cycle to four years, but Honda can still beat Ford to the showroom by a year. Ford has set a new goal of paring development to two years by the end of the 1990s.

Sociocultural Factors

Sociocultural factors must be considered by organizations that establish operations in different cultures.

Managers are beginning to realize that sociocultural differences among employees may constitute an important influence on organization design. For example, organizations in the United States often emphasize individual achievement and distribute rewards on the basis of individual accomplishment, whereas in Japan the achievements of the group take precedence. Individual Japanese workers who are singled out may become embarrassed or make light of their contributions in order to direct attention back to group achievements. As a result, then, organizations with operations in both countries should recognize that accountability and rewards need to be structured in quite different ways.

In theory, sociocultural factors can influence virtually any aspect of organization design. For example, in some cultures extreme centralization might be acceptable because workers are uncomfortable making decisions

Organizations with international operations or which employ large numbers of foreigners have to account for the influence of sociocultural factors as they explore new and better forms of design. These Kuwaiti managers, for example, must blend Jordanians, Palestinians, Egyptians, and other foreigners into a cohesive and coordinated work force in order to effectively compete in the world marketplace.

and expect managers to make them. In other cultures, workers may have great expectations about participation in decision making and subsequently expect decentralization.

The sociocultural differences among some countries — the United States, Canada, and England, for example — are comparatively small, thus making design variations also relatively minor. Sociocultural differences are more profound among other counties — South Korea, India, and Arab nations, for example — potentially dictating greater design differences among organizations that operate in each of them. Given the increased level of international business activity, organizations will almost certainly begin to account for sociocultural factors in their design.

Organizational Culture

In the last ten years or so the relationship between an organization's own internal culture and its design has been more clearly understood. Culture is not strictly a part of design, but culture and design must be complementary in order for an organization to function smoothly. We first highlight the meaning and importance of culture and then discuss how it is created, maintained, and changed.

Organizational culture is a powerful but elusive phenomenon. To effectively manage its organizational culture, Fred Meyer, Inc. (a west-coast retail chain with annual sales of over $2 billion) established the Fred Meyer Institute (FMI). The FMI has a two-pronged mission: to develop a clearer understanding of the company's culture among Fred Meyer employees, and to develop ways to use that culture to enhance organizational effectiveness. These FMI employees are creating training sessions to increase employee motivation.

The Meaning and Importance of Culture

Organizational culture is the set of values that defines for members what the organization stands for, how it operates, and what it considers important.

Organizational culture is the set of values that defines for members what the organization stands for, how it operates, and what it considers important. For example, Texas Instruments (TI) has what its managers call a "shirt sleeve" culture. The message is that hard work and focusing on the job at hand are more important qualities than an expensive-looking wardrobe or a fancy office. The firm's managers and engineers seldom wear formal business attire. And only upper-level managers have large private offices. Thus, the culture at TI is clear and well defined but quite different from the culture at a firm such as IBM, where business suits and office perquisites are more the norm.

Culture plays a very significant role in any organization by communicating information about acceptable and unacceptable behavior. The new TI employee who wonders about the company's dress code need only look around. Culture can communicate whether the organization expects its managers to be aggressive or conservative in making decisions, to provide generous or modest support for social causes, or to be ruthless or amiable in their competitive dealings.

Some organizations have clear, strong, and well-defined cultures. Others have ambiguous, weak, and poorly defined cultures. Most managers agree that a strong and clear culture is preferable because it helps provide a common frame of reference for managerial decision making and a wide variety of other organizational activities.[16] We should again note that no one culture is always preferable. IBM and TI, for example, are both quite successful despite their different cultures.

Creating, Maintaining, and Changing Culture

An organization's culture generally takes shape over time and is often deeply influenced by the values of the firm's founders. Walt Disney, for example, left an indelible imprint throughout the Disney corporation. When Disney managers today face tough decisions, many ask themselves, "What would Walt have done?" Likewise, the values of James Case Penney, Henry Ford, and Bill Hewlett and David Packard still permeate the organizations that bear their names.

As organizational culture evolves, various symbols, stories, heroes, slogans, and ceremonies also come into being. These then serve to maintain and perpetuate the culture through subsequent generations of employees. A new Texas Instruments employee gets a white name badge. After one year of service the white badge is exchanged for a green one. Five years of service brings a blue badge. Everyone in the organization knows the meanings of the different colors: seniority and longevity in the firm. These characteristics, in turn, carry meaning for everyone. A red badge (twenty or more years), for example, earns its wearer a strong measure of respect from junior employees.

Levi Strauss has an informal and casual culture. Several years ago, the firm moved into larger headquarters in a tall office building in downtown San Francisco. Employees didn't like the new offices, however, because they seemed so formal. Within a short time, the firm bought out its lease and moved into other facilities that more closely resemble a college campus. The Environmental Challenge summarizes a new effort at Levi Strauss to further clarify its values.

Of course, it is sometimes necessary to change culture. Change is most often needed when the organization has lost its effectiveness and is struggling either to carry out its strategic goals or perhaps to change them altogether. For example, when Helmut Maucher became CEO of Nestlé in 1981, he decided that the firm was too bureaucratic and lacked a strong commitment to creativity and new ideas. He immediately adopted the slogan "Let's have more pepper and less paper." This was his way of telling people to start shaking things up and stop spending so much time on administrative paperwork.

Learning Summary

Organization design is the overall configuration of structural components that define jobs, groupings of jobs, the hierarchy, patterns of authority, approaches to coordination, and line-staff differentiation into a single, unified organizational system. Each organization has to create the design that best fits its own unique set of circumstances.

The bureaucratic model describes an idealized form of design based on rational guidelines and procedures. Later work identified an alternative

THE ENVIRONMENTAL CHALLENGE

The Aspirational Culture at Levi Strauss

Levi Strauss has always had a strong and well-defined culture. In recent years, CEO Robert Haas has taken steps to make it even clearer and to enhance its concerns about values and social responsibility. He recently set forth this "Aspirations Statement":

ASPIRATIONS STATEMENT

We all want a company that our people are proud of and committed to, where all employees have an opportunity to contribute, learn, grow, and advance based on merit, not politics or background. We want our people to feel respected, treated fairly, listened to, and involved. Above all, we want satisfaction from accomplishments and friendships, balanced personal and professional lives, and to have fun in our endeavors.

When we describe the kind of Levi Strauss & Co. we want in the future, what we are talking about is building on the foundation we have inherited: affirming the best of our company's traditions, closing gaps that may exist between principles and practices, and updating some of our values to reflect contemporary circumstances.

What type of leadership is necessary to make our Aspirations a Reality?

New Behaviors: Leadership that exemplifies directness, openness to influence, commitment to the success of others, willingness to acknowledge our own contributions to problems, personal accountability, teamwork, and trust. Not only must we model these behaviors but we must coach others to adopt them.

Diversity: Leadership that values a diverse work force (age, sex, ethnic group, etc.) at all levels of the organization, diversity in experience, and diversity in perspectives. We have committed to taking full advantage of the rich backgrounds and abilities of all our people and to promoting a greater diversity in positions of influence. Differing points of view will be sought; diversity will be valued and honesty rewarded, not suppressed.

Recognition: Leadership that provides greater recognition — both financial and psychic — for individuals and teams that contribute to our success. Recognition must be given to all who contribute: those who create and innovate and also those who continually support the day-to-day business requirements.

Ethical Management Practices: Leadership that epitomizes the stated standards of ethical behavior. We must provide clarity about our expectations and must enforce these standards through the corporation.

Communications: Leadership that is clear about company, unit, and individual goals and performance. People must know what is expected of them and receive timely, honest feedback on their performance and career aspirations.

Empowerment: Leadership that increases the authority and responsibility of those closest to our products and customers. By actively pushing responsibility, trust, and recognition into the organization, we can harness and release the capabilities of all our people.

REFERENCE: Reprinted with permission of Levi Strauss & Co.

model of organization design called System 4. The System 4 design is more informal and flexible.

The appropriateness of any design for an organization depends on several different situational factors, including technology, the organizational environment, and organization size and life cycle.

The U-form organization is based on functional departmentalization and is commonly used by single-product firms. The H-form organization is based on product departmentalization and a strategy of unrelated diversification. The M-form organization is based on product departmentalization and a strategy of related diversification. A matrix design overlays a product-based design onto a functional one. Global organizations can adapt any of these designs to meet their own circumstances. Organizations usually use hybrid designs that combine different aspects of the basic forms, and modify their designs as their situations evolve.

To increase employee participation, the use of work teams, and flexibility, an organization may need to change parts of its design. Sociocultural factors must be addressed in the design of multinational organizations.

Organizational culture is the set of values that defines for members what the organization stands for, how it operates, and what it considers important. A strong culture is an advantage because it provides a common frame of reference for members of the organization.

Questions and Exercises

Review Questions

1. What is the difference between organization structure and organization design?
2. Compare and contrast the bureaucratic and System 4 models of organization design.
3. Summarize the basic characteristics of an M-form and an H-form organization.
4. Summarize the primary situational determinants of organization design.
5. Compare and contrast the major contemporary forms of organization design.
6. Describe emerging issues in organization design.
7. What is an organization's culture? Why is it important?

Analysis Questions

1. Describe circumstances in which the bureaucratic model might be the most appropriate design for an organization to use.
2. Why should organizations that do *not* use the bureaucratic model know what it is?
3. Identify two organizations that use very different forms of technology, and then draw inferences about how those differences might affect their organization design.
4. Describe how a domestic M-form organization might adapt its design to fit a more global orientation.
5. Explain how participation, flexibility, and sociocultural factors are related to the major situational factors that affect organization design.

6. Why might it be useful or necessary for an organization to change its culture? How might a top manager go about implementing such a change?

7. How are organization design and organization culture related? That is, can you think of characteristics of an organization's design that affect its culture? How might culture affect the design of an organization?

Application Exercises

1. Many business schools use a matrix design in which functional academic departments like management and accounting are overlaid with program units like the undergraduate program and the graduate program. Research and describe the organization design that your college uses.

2. Assume that you are about to graduate and begin your career with a large organization such as Mobil or Sheraton. Describe the ideal culture you would like to experience in the organization.

3. Research a major international organization to gain an understanding of its organization design. Which form of organization design described in the chapter comes closest to representing the design of this organization?

Chapter Notes

1. Gary Hoover, Alta Campbell, and Patrick J. Spain, eds., *Hoover's Handbook — Profiles of Over 500 Major Corporations* (Austin, Tex.: The Reference Press, 1990), p. 537; "Japan Cuts the Middle-Management Fat," *Wall Street Journal,* August 8, 1989, p. B1; "Toyota Wants More Managers Out on the Line," *Wall Street Journal,* August 2, 1989, p. A8.

2. Max Weber, *Theory of Social and Economic Organization,* trans. T. Parsons (New York: Free Press, 1947).

3. See Rensis Likert, *New Patterns in Management* (New York: McGraw-Hill, 1961), and Rensis Likert, *The Human Organization* (New York: McGraw-Hill, 1967), for overviews of this approach.

4. William F. Dowling, "At General Motors: System 4 Builds Performance and Profits," *Organizational Dynamics,* Winter 1975, pp. 23–28.

5. See Joan Woodward, *Industrial Organization: Theory and Practice* (London: Oxford University Press, 1965).

6. Tom Burns and G. M. Stalker, *The Management of Innovation* (London: Tavistock, 1961).

7. Paul R. Lawrence and Jay W. Lorsch, *Organization and Environment* (Homewood, Ill.: Irwin, 1967).

8. See Derek S. Pugh and David J. Hickson, *Organization Structure in Its Context: The Aston Program I* (Lexington, Mass.: Heath, 1976), for an overview of this research.

9. See Richard L. Daft, *Organization Theory & Design,* 3rd ed. (St. Paul, Minn.: West, 1990), for a review.

10. Oliver Williamson, *Markets and Hierarchies* (New York: Free Press, 1975).

11. Michael Porter, "From Competitive Advantage to Corporate Strategy," *Harvard Business Review,* May–June 1987, pp. 43–59.

12. See Robert E. Hoskisson, "Multidivisional Structure and Performance: The Contingency of Diversification Strategy," *Academy of Management Journal,* December 1987, pp. 625–644.

13. Donald F. Barkman, "Team Discipline: Put Performance on the Line," *Personnel Journal,* March 1987, pp. 58–63.

14. "Work Teams Can Rev Up Paper-Pushers, Too," *Business Week,* November 28, 1988, pp. 64–72.

15. See Dean Tjosvold, "Participation: A Close Look at Its Dynamics," *Organizational Dynamics,* Autumn 1987, pp. 739–750.

16. See Jay B. Barney, "Organizational Culture: Can It Be a Source of Sustained Competitive Advantage?" *Academy of Management Review,* July 1986, pp. 656–665.

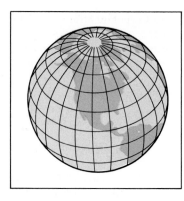

CASE 11.1

Nike Sprints into the Lead

The U.S. sneaker wars of the 1980s were as hard fought a two-company rivalry as the soda wars. Venerable Nike led in the early 1980s but was soon passed by upstart Reebok, which helped make athletic shoes a fashion item. But reinvigorated by its Air Jordan basketball sneakers and its emphasis on performance, Nike won back the lead in 1989 and has been trying to show Reebok its dust ever since. Reebok tends to view the rivalry with humor, but Nike is dead serious about competition. The organization is built to win.

Much of Nike's winning attitude comes from its co-founder, Phil Knight, who ran middle distances with the University of Oregon's track team in the late 1950s. Knight and his coach, Bill Bowerman, enjoyed experimenting with new shoe designs, and in 1964 they created Blue Ribbon Sports with $1,000 of their own money. The company distributed Japanese-made Tiger shoes until 1972, when it started making its own shoes (with the distinctive "swoosh" on the side) and named them for Nike, the Greek goddess of victory.

With this background, and continuing ties to the individualistic, performance-oriented sport of track and field, it is no wonder that Nike developed a corporate culture based on a belief in the superiority of its products. Nike sees itself as the only major athletic shoe company that is devoted to athletic performance rather than to good looks or gimmicks. It was particularly galling, therefore, when rival Reebok sped past Nike in 1986. By Nike's standards, Reebok did everything the wrong way. Rather than stress how fast customers would go in Reeboks, the upstart told customers how good they would look and feel. Reebok offered a wide variety of fashionable colors. Movie stars wore Reeboks on formal occasions, and the shoes swept the country on the crest of the aerobics craze, which Nike ignored until it found itself in second place.

Nike fought back by putting more emphasis on colors and styles, but it also relied on the strength of its technological edge and on the flexibility of its matrix structure. For technical advancements, Nike counts on its APEs — advanced product engineers — who constantly tinker with shoe designs. The company's Air Force basketball shoes were a result of an APEs basketball game — the teams kept stopping to trim unnecessary rubber and leather off their shoes and ended up with a new lightweight design. Although Nike derides Reebok's current "pump" model, it too is constantly looking for ways to make its shoes fit better and to increase their shock absorbency.

Company executives at headquarters outside Portland, Oregon, describe the company's matrix structure as a cross between a traditional hierarchy and Japanese-style consensus management. The structure means that even big decisions like which shoe designs or ads to approve are made by relatively low-level managers.

A flexible structure is particularly important for shoe makers now because national ad campaigns like Nike's successful "Bo knows" series have changed the way people make decisions about their sneakers. Instead of buying whatever retailers recommend, most people go to shoe stores looking for the brands they have seen on TV. But Nike's relationships with retailers continue to be the envy of the industry and to keep the company in the top spot. Rather than count on independent sales representatives, as do most other shoe companies, Nike has three hundred of its own sales reps on its payroll, and fifty other representatives visit retailers solely to explain the latest technical advantages of Nike's products.

Nike's special relationship with retailers calls for unusual commitments from both sides. Nike reps let their retailers know in advance of problems with orders or changes in models. For their part, retailers must commit themselves to large orders at least six months in advance. Having gotten stuck with 22 million unsold running shoes in the mid-1980s, Nike now makes certain that demand stays ahead of the supply produced by its Asian manufacturers. Retailers are willing to make long-range commitments because Nike gives them a guaranteed price and because Nike's high-price, high-profit shoes like the Air Jordan tend to sell themselves.

Having missed the aerobics craze, Nike is determined not to be caught napping again, and its matrix organization allows it to be ready for the next fad. It pioneered the concept of a "cross-training" shoe, which has become the new hot category. Apparently having accepted the fact that only one in ten buyers of athletic shoes uses the shoes solely for sports, Nike began running ads in 1989 targeting sports *fans,* not athletes. In 1990 Nike passed Germany's Adidas as the world's top maker of sporting shoes and apparel, and now, like a good runner, it is keeping its eyes on the finish line and not looking over its shoulder.

Discussion Questions

1. Does Nike's organizational culture seem appropriate for its products? How do you imagine Reebok's culture might be different from Nike's?
2. Why does an athletic shoe company need to have a flexible organization?
3. Explain in your own terms how, as Nike executives put it, a matrix design combines a traditional corporate hierarchy with Japanese consensus management.
4. What situational determinants have a particularly strong effect on Nike's organization design?

REFERENCES: James Cox, "Confidence Keeps Firm Running," *USA Today,* August 2, 1990, pp. B1, B2; Mark Dolliver, "Beyond 'Just Do It': Now Nike Asks Us to Just Buy It," *Adweek's Marketing Week,* January 29, 1990, p. 63; Marcy Magiera, "Nike Again Registers No. 1 Performance," *Advertising Age,* January 29, 1990, p. 16; Fleming Meeks, "The Sneaker Game," *Forbes 400,* October 22, 1990, p. 114.

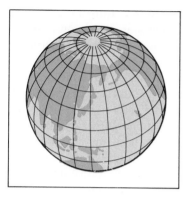

CASE 11.2

Entrepreneurship and Amoebas at Kyocera Corporation

Americans often accuse Japanese high-tech companies of being imitators, taking good product ideas developed by American research and then figuring out how to make the product better or more cheaply. At first glance, Japan's Kyocera Corporation might seem to deserve such criticism, since much of the basic technology for its most important products — industrial ceramics — was pioneered by American Lava Company. But a closer look reveals that Kyocera breaks this and other stereotypes about Japanese companies. Providing what may be a glimpse of corporations of the future, Kyocera combines many of the best elements of Japanese and American organizations.

Kyocera's claim to be an innovator, not an imitator, is well recognized, at least in Japan. Surveys in Japan consistently show that Kyocera's entrepreneurship and technological progress are the most admired in the country. Company officials estimate that 90 percent of the products that Kyocera makes originated in its own laboratories.

In fact, the driving force behind Kyocera, Kazuo Inamori, has been making a name for himself as an entrepreneur and an innovator ever since he got a doctorate in chemical engineering and went to work for Sofu Industries. Rejecting the Japanese tradition of deference to superiors, he argued with his research director at Sofu, quit, and founded Kyoto Ceramics in 1959 (the name was soon shortened to Kyocera). Now the head of a company with over $2.5 billion in sales each year, Inamori is still breaking the rules. Kyocera recently took on American computer giants IBM and Hewlett-Packard, and in the mid-1980s Inamori started the only Japanese company to compete successfully with Nippon Telegraph & Telephone, which used to have a monopoly in Japan. He even established a foundation that hands out the Kyoto Prize to innovators in fields not covered by the Nobel awards.

Inamori's American-style entrepreneurial bent is combined with some typically Japanese elements, such as the regimented early-morning employee exercises in the parking lot, and with some ideas that are purely Inamori's own, such as "amoebas." Kyocera's amoebas take the concept of autonomous work teams to its logical extreme. They form and dissolve according to the needs of a particular project, and they may include from two to hundreds of people. Every foreman and virtually every executive is in charge of an amoeba. Each amoeba makes its own decisions about purchases and suppliers, although it needs permission to spend money. Kyocera calculates an amoeba's profit or loss by computing how much each hour put in by each member adds to the value of the project or product that the amoeba is working on.

This kind of financial responsibility makes amoebas very cost conscious, for the boss can find out at any time how the amoeba is doing, and he does not hesitate to lecture amoebas whose work is not going well. As is traditional in Japan, everyone is expected to work for the benefit of the group, so the heads of even top-performing amoebas are rewarded only with points toward promotions. As a booklet about Inamori's philosophy puts it, "We don't buy individuals' loyalty with monetary incentives or titles."*

Kyocera's name is not yet as well known as Sony's or Toyota's, in part because of the products it makes, in part because its products often appear with other companies' names on them. Kyocera produces almost two-thirds of the world's ceramic housings for semiconductor chips, but few people can explain what such housings are, much less tell you who made the ones in their computers. Kyocera is also a top maker of solar cells and of virtually everything else that can be made from ceramics — from artificial teeth and hips to industrial cutting tools. It developed some of the first laptop computers, but they were sold in America under the Tandy name. In a break from the tradition of anonymity, Kyocera recently took on America's high-tech giants by entering the personal laser printer market with a machine that carries the Kyocera name. Reviewers were impressed by the printer's speed, but they worried about its proprietary laser engine and other unique features.

This kind of response to its printer is something that Kyocera may have to deal with more often as it continues to become more vertically integrated. It has been buying up other companies in related industries and moving into larger products and systems that use the components it has traditionally made. To convince buyers that they should buy a Kyocera computer made with Kyocera parts, Inamori is going to have to increase his company's visibility and name recognition. But that may not be too hard, given the company's excellent reputation among corporate American buyers. It is known for high quality, superior service, and willingness to deal with any company, no matter how small. Soon you too may make your life easier with a product developed by an amoeba.

Discussion Questions

1. What forces make it difficult for most large corporations to foster entrepreneurial activity?
2. Would "amoebas" work in any organization? Why or why not?
3. What advantages and disadvantages does a high-tech company face by becoming vertically integrated?
4. What difficulties does an organization face when its organizational culture is at odds with the culture in the society at large?

* Quoted in Gene Bylinsky, "The Hottest High-Tech Company in Japan," *Fortune*, January 1, 1990, p. 86.

REFERENCES: Gene Bylinsky, "The Hottest High-Tech Company in Japan," *Fortune*, January 1, 1990, pp. 82–88; "Cult of Personality," *Business Month*, August 1990, pp. 42–44; Stanford Diehl and Stan Wszola, "Laser Printers Get Personal," *BYTE*, July 1990, pp. 138–156.

12

Control in Organizations

LEARNING OBJECTIVES

After studying this chapter, you should be able to:

1. Explain the purpose of control, identify different types of control, and describe the steps in the control process.

2. Identify and explain the three forms of operations control.

3. Describe budgets and other tools of financial control.

4. Identify and distinguish between two opposing forms of structural control.

5. Discuss the relationship between strategy and control, including international strategic control.

6. Identify characteristics of effective control, why people resist control, and how managers can overcome this resistance.

The Nature of Control in Organizations

The Purpose of Control

Types of Control

Steps in the Control Process

Operations Control

Preliminary Control

Screening Control

Postaction Control

Financial Control

Budgetary Control

Other Tools of Financial Control

Structural Control

Bureaucratic Control

Clan Control

Strategic Control

Integrating Strategy and Control

International Strategic Control

Managing Control in Organizations

Characteristics of Effective Control

Resistance to Control

Overcoming Resistance to Control

I n 1988 the Baltimore Orioles had the worst team in professional baseball and seemed headed nowhere but down. Attendance and local television revenues — and thus profits — were down, and the team showed no signs of improvement. A few baseball experts, however, believed that the Orioles were poised for a major turnaround. As it turned out, the experts were right.

Professional sports teams such as the New York Islanders, the Houston Astros, the Chicago Bears, and the Los Angeles Lakers face many of the same challenges and risks as American Airlines, Teledyne, Apple Computer, and other businesses. A major concern for any organization, including a professional sports franchise, is costs. Team owners must buy equipment, pay transportation costs, and cover stadium operating expenses.

As the owners of the Orioles were painfully aware, the biggest expense in baseball is player salaries. In 1988 the team roster was made up of fading stars with high salaries carried over from their glory years. Not only were the players' skills eroding, their salaries were chewing up a disproportionate chunk of the team's revenues. Indeed, the organization was only barely turning a profit.

Between 1988 and 1989, the Orioles traded or released eighteen older players and replaced them with younger players from the Orioles' farm system. By so doing, the team reduced its average salary per player from $425,000 to $234,000. The new young players brought fresh enthusiasm to the team and won far more games than anyone dared expect. As a result of the team's newfound competitiveness, ticket sales and television revenues also jumped sharply.

In 1992 the Orioles move into a new stadium. Because of its larger capacity and more comfortable seating, attendance should climb even higher. The new contract also gives team owners a bigger percentage of stadium revenues. In addition, major league baseball's new television contract goes into effect and will give the Orioles still another boost in revenues. All things considered, then, the Orioles seem to have succeeded in turning their operation around.[1]

The Baltimore Orioles team has regained its financial standing — if not its first-place standing in the pennant race — through a combination of increasing revenues and lowering costs. Baltimore improved the quality of its on-field performance and lowered its salary expenses. As a result, the profitability of the organization improved. Any business can enhance its financial health by taking the same steps, although each organization must work with its own particular configuration of revenues and costs. The general framework for achieving and maintaining financial health is called *control.*

In the first section of this chapter we explain the purpose of control. We then look at types of control and the steps in the control process. The rest of the chapter examines the four levels of control that most organizations must employ in order to remain effective: operations, financial, strutural, and strategic control. We conclude by discussing the characteristics of effective control, noting why some people resist control and describing what organizations can do to overcome this resistance.

The Nature of Control in Organizations

Control is the regulation of organizational activities so that some targeted element of performance remains within acceptable limits.

Control is the regulation of organizational activities so that some targeted element of performance remains within acceptable limits. Without this regulation, organizations have no indication of how well they perform in relation to their goals. Control, like a ship's rudder, keeps the organization moving in the proper direction. At any point in time, it compares where the organization is in terms of performance (financial, productive, or otherwise) to where it is supposed to be.

Also, like a rudder, control provides an organization with a mechanism for adjusting its course if performance falls outside of acceptable boundaries. For example, Federal Express has a performance goal of delivering 99 percent of its packages on time. If on-time deliveries fall to 97 percent, control systems will signal the problem to managers so they can make necessary adjustments in operations to regain the target level of performance. An organization without effective control procedures is not likely to reach its goals — or if it does reach them, to know that it has!

The Purpose of Control

Control helps the organization adapt to environmental change, limit the accumulation of error, cope with organizational complexity, and minimize costs.

As Figure 12.1 illustrates, control provides an organization with ways to adapt to environmental change, to limit the accumulation of error, to cope with organizational complexity, and to minimize costs. These four functions of control are worth a closer look.

Adapting to Environmental Change In today's complex and turbulent business environment, all organizations must contend with change.[2] If managers could establish goals and achieve them instantaneously, control would not be needed. But between the time a goal is established and the time it is reached, many things can happen in the organization and its environment to disrupt movement toward the goal — or even to change the

Figure 12.1

The Purpose of Control

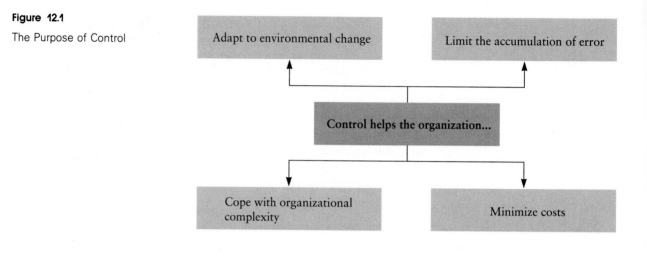

goal itself. A properly designed control system can help managers antici-pate, monitor, and respond to changing circumstances. In contrast, an improperly designed system can result in organizational performance that falls far below acceptable levels.

For example, Michigan-based Metalloy Foundry Co., a 43-year-old family-run metal-casting company, recently signed a contract to make engine-seal castings for NOK, a big Japanese auto parts maker. Metalloy was satisfied when its first 5,000-unit production run yielded 4,985 accept-able castings and only 15 defective ones. NOK, however, was quite unhappy with this performance and insisted that Metalloy raise its standards. Global quality standards had shifted so dramatically that managers at Metalloy had lost touch with how high their own standards had to be in order to remain competitive.[3] A properly designed control system would have kept Metalloy's managers better attuned to rising standards. The Environmental Challenge contrasts the effectiveness of the control exercised by the two banking companies that recently merged to form NationsBank.

Limiting the Accumulation of Error   Small mistakes and errors do not often seriously damage the financial health of an organization. Over time, however, small errors may accumulate and become very serious. For exam-ple, in 1986 Whistler Corporation, a large manufacturer of radar detectors, was faced with such rapidly escalating demand that it essentially stopped worrying about quality. The defect rate rose from 4 percent to 9 percent to 15 percent and eventually reached 25 percent. One day, a manager realized that 100 of the firm's 250 employees were spending all their time fixing defective units and that $2 million worth of the firm's radar detectors was awaiting repair. If the company had adequately controlled quality while it responded to increased demand, the problem would have never reached such proportions.[4]

THE ENVIRONMENTAL CHALLENGE

Value of Control Evident to Creators of NationsBank

In July 1991 NationsBank was born. The third-largest U.S. banking company, NationsBank resulted from a merger of two large regional banking companies, one that had effectively used control throughout its existence to adapt to its environment and another that had used control less successfully.

NCNB Corporation, the more effective organization in terms of control, was itself created by a merger of two North Carolina banks in 1960. Led by Hugh McColl, who was named to the post of CEO in 1982, NCNB grew rapidly into the largest bank outside the states of New York and California. NCNB fueled its growth by investing heavily in the creation of a sophisticated and intricate control system that allowed its managers to stay on top of virtually every aspect of the banking industry. This control system gave NCNB valuable insights about tax law as it prepared to bid for several failing banks put up for auction by the FDIC in the late 1980s. As a result, NCNB bid wisely and acquired many new banks, while avoiding those banks that were not good investments. These acquisitions furthered the growth of the firm's market share.

The second bank had not fared nearly as well. C&S/Sovran, based in Virginia and Georgia, also acquired new banks during the 1980s. Some of these, however, proved to be much less attractive than the banks bought by NCNB. The firm had also made some poor decisions regarding the management of its loan portfolio and had millions of dollars in bad loans that had to be written off.

It will most likely take several years to achieve a completely integrated bank corporation from the two firms that joined to create NationsBank. New and even more elaborate control systems will be needed by the new organization. But with Hugh McColl and his managers in charge of this potential financial powerhouse, bankers from the east to the west coasts may well be looking over their shoulders.

REFERENCES: Gary Hector, "The Brash Banker Who Bought Texas," *Fortune*, August 27, 1990, pp. 54–62; "NCNB May Make Bid for Southeast 'In Near Future'," *Wall Street Journal*, April 23, 1991, p. A1; "Deal is $4.1B Marriage of Convenience," *USA Today*, July 23, 1991, pp. 1B, 2B.

Coping with Organizational Complexity   When a firm purchases only one raw material, produces one product, has a simple organization design, and enjoys constant demand for its product, its managers can maintain control with a very basic and simple system. But a business that produces many products from myriad raw materials and has a large market area, a complicated organization design, and many competitors needs a sophisticated system in order to maintain adequate control. Emery Air Freight was quite profitable until it bought Purolator Courier Corporation in 1987. The new Emery that resulted from the acquisition was much bigger and more complex, but no new controls were added to operations. Consequently, Emery began to lose money and market share, costs increased, and service deteriorated until the company was on the verge of bankruptcy. There is still some question as to whether Emery will regain its former levels of performance or if it will eventually go under.[5]

Minimizing Costs   When it is practiced effectively, control can help reduce costs and boost output. For example, Georgia-Pacific Corporation, a large wood products company, recently learned of a new technology that could be used to make thinner blades for its saws. The firm's control system was used to calculate the amount of wood that could be saved from each cut made by the thinner blades relative to the cost of replacing the existing blades. The results were impressive: the wood saved by the new blades each year would fill eight hundred railcars.[6] As Georgia-Pacific discovered, effective control systems can eliminate waste, lower labor costs, and improve output per unit of input.[7]

Types of Control

The examples of control given thus far have illustrated the regulation of several organizational activities, from producing quality products to coordinating complex organizations. Organizations practice control in a number of different areas and at different levels, and the responsibility for managing control is widespread.

Organizations control physical, human, information, and financial resources.

Areas of Control Control can focus on any area of an organization. Most organizations define areas of control in terms of the four basic types of resources they use: physical, human, information, and financial resources. Control of physical resources includes inventory management (stocking neither too few nor too many units in inventory), quality control (maintaining appropriate levels of output quality), and equipment control (supplying the necessary facilities and machinery). Control of human resources includes selection and placement, training and development, performance appraisal, and compensation. Control of information resources includes sales and marketing forecasting, environmental analysis, public relations, production scheduling, and economic forecasting. Financial control involves managing the organization's debt so that it does not become excessive, ensuring that the organization always has enough cash on hand to meet its obligations but does not have excess cash in a checking account and ensuring that receivables are collected and bills paid on a timely basis.

In many ways, the control of financial resources is the most important area. This is because financial resources are related to the control of all the other resources in an organization: too much inventory leads to storage costs; poor selection of personnel leads to termination and rehiring expenses; inaccurate sales forecasts lead to disruptions in cash flows. Financial issues tend to pervade most control-related activities. Indeed, financial issues are at the root of the problem faced by Emery Air Freight. Various inefficiencies and operating blunders put the company in a position where it lacked the money to service its debt (make interest payments on loans), had little working capital (cash to cover daily operating expenses), and was too heavily leveraged (excessive debt) to borrow more money.

Organizations practice operations, financial, structural, and strategic control.

Levels of Control Just as control can be broken down by area, it can also be broken down by organizational level, as Figure 12.2 shows. At the lower levels, operations control focuses on the processes that the organization uses to transform resources into products or services. Quality control is one type of operations control. Financial control is concerned with the organization's financial resources. Monitoring receivables to make sure customers are paying their bills on time is an example of financial control.

At a higher level, structural control is concerned with how the elements of the organization's structure are serving their intended purposes. Monitoring administrative intensity to make sure staff expenses do not become excessive is a type of structural control. Finally, strategic control focuses on how effectively the organization's corporate, business, and functional strategies are helping the organization meet its goals. For example, if a corporation has been unsuccessful in implementing its strategy of related diversification, its managers need to identify the reasons and either change the strategy or renew their efforts to implement it.[8] We discuss these four levels of control more fully later in this chapter.

All managers are responsible for control. The controller is a specialized managerial position created to oversee financial control.

Responsibilities for Control   Traditionally, managers have been responsible for overseeing the wide array of control systems and concerns in organizations. They decide which types of control the organization will use, and they implement control systems and take actions based on the information provided by control systems. Thus ultimate responsibility for control rests with all managers throughout an organization.

Most large organizations also have one or more specialized managerial positions called *controller*. A controller is responsible for helping line managers with their control activities, for coordinating the organization's overall control system, and for gathering and assimilating relevant information. Many businesses that use an H-form or M-form organization design have several controllers: one for the corporation and one for each division.[9] The job of controller is important and often leads to advancement within an

Figure 12.2

Levels of Control

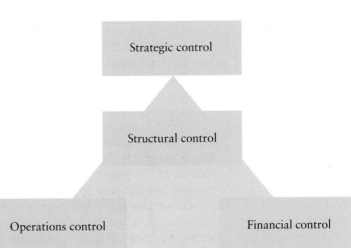

organization. For example, within the last ten years former controllers have held the position of CEO at such corporations as Cooper Industries, Singer Corporation, FMC Corporation, CPC International, General Motors, Pfizer, and Fruehauf.[10]

Nevertheless, more and more organizations are also beginning to call upon operating employees to help maintain effective control. As we discuss more fully in Chapters 15 and 17, employee participation is often used as a vehicle for allowing operating employees an opportunity to help facilitate organizational effectiveness. For example, Whistler Corporation increased employee participation in an effort to turn its quality problems around. As a starting point, the quality-control unit, formerly responsible for checking product quality at the end of the assembly process, was eliminated. Next, all operating employees were encouraged to check their own work and were made responsible for correcting their own errors. As a result, Whistler eliminated its quality problems and is highly profitable once again.

Steps in the Control Process

Regardless of the type or levels of control systems an organization needs, there are four fundamental steps in any control process.[11] These are displayed in Figure 12.3.[12]

Establishing Standards   The first step in the control process is establishing standards. A **control standard** is a target against which subsequent performance will be compared. Employees at Taco Bell fast-food restaurants, for example, work toward the following service standards:

1. A minimum of 95 percent of all customers will be greeted within three minutes of their arrival.
2. Preheated tortilla chips will not sit in the warmer more than thirty minutes before they are served to customers.
3. Empty tables will be cleaned within five minutes after being vacated.

Standards established for control purposes should be expressed in measurable terms. Note that standard 1 above has a time limit of three minutes and an objective target of 95 percent of all customers. In standard 3, the objective target is implied: "all" empty tables.

Control standards should also be consistent with the organization's goals. Taco Bell has organizational goals involving customer service, food quality, and restaurant cleanliness. A control standard for a retailer like Home Depot should be consistent with its goal of increasing its annual sales volume by 25 percent within five years. A hospital trying to shorten the average hospital stay by a patient will have control standards that reflect current average stays. A university reaffirming its commitment to academics might adopt a standard of graduating 80 percent of its student athletes within five years of their enrollment. Control standards can be as narrow or as broad as the activity to which they apply.

A *control standard* is a target against which subsequent performance will be compared.

A final aspect of establishing standards is to identify performance indicators. Performance indicators are measures that provide information about how well the activity is being controlled. For example, suppose an organization is building a new plant on a tight schedule and needs to monitor closely each step in the project. Relevant performance indicators might be the dates for buying a site, selecting a building contractor, and ordering equipment. The Sharper Image, a chain of up-scale specialty shops, recently set two performance standards for yearly sales: stores in operation for more than a year should increase sales by 5 percent from the previous year, and overall sales, including revenues from new stores, should increase by 25 percent. Monthly sales figures from both existing and new stores were then used as performance indicators to provide the organization with an ongoing assessment of its efforts to meet the overall sales standards.[13]

Performance measurement is a constant, ongoing activity for most organizations.

Measuring Performance The second step in the control process is measuring performance. Performance measurement is a constant, ongoing activity for most organizations. For control to be effective, performance measures must be valid. Daily, weekly, and monthly sales figures measure sales

Figure 12.3

Steps in the Control Process

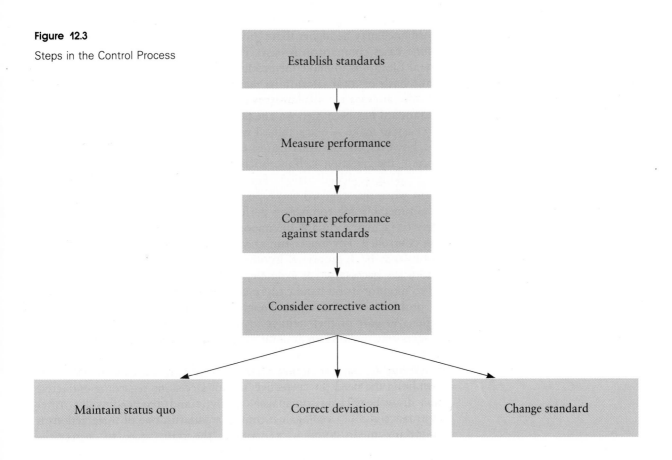

performance, and production performance may be expressed in terms of unit cost, product quality, or volume produced. Employee performance is often measured in terms of quality or quantity of output, but for many jobs measuring performance is not so straightforward. A research and development scientist at Merck, for example, may spend years working on a single project before achieving a breakthrough. A manager who takes over a business on the brink of failure may need months or even years to turn things around.

Valid performance measurement, however difficult to obtain, is nevertheless vital in maintaining effective control, and suitable performance indicators usually can be developed. The scientist's progress, for example, may be partially assessed by peer review, and the manager's success may be evaluated by her ability to convince creditors that she will eventually be able to restore profitability. At the end of its fiscal year, The Sharper Image measured both total sales and individual store sales. The results indicated that overall sales did indeed reach the desired 25 percent increase but individual store sales (which did not include sales from new stores) declined by 7 percent.

After performance is measured, it is compared against established standards.

Comparing Performance Against Standards   The third step in the control process is comparing measured performance against established standards. Performance may be higher than, lower than, or identical to the standard. In some cases comparison is easy. The goal of each product manager at General Electric is to make the product either number one or number two (on the basis of total sales) in its market. Since this standard is clear and total sales are easy to calculate, it is relatively simple to determine whether this standard has been met. At The Sharper Image, comparisons were also fairly easy to make — one standard was met and the other was not. Sometimes, however, comparisons are less clear-cut. If performance is lower than expected, the question is how much deviation from standards to allow before taking remedial action. For example, is increasing sales by 7.9 percent when the standard was 8 percent close enough?

The timetable for comparing performance to standards depends on a variety of factors, including the importance and complexity of the activity being controlled. For longer-run and higher-level standards, annual comparisons may be appropriate. In other circumstances, more frequent comparisons are necessary. For example, a business with a cash shortage may need to monitor its on-hand cash reserves daily. We noted earlier the cash-flow problems that Emery Air Freight faced after it purchased Purolator Courier. As part of their efforts to improve the firm's control, Emery's managers eventually started monitoring their cash reserves weekly.

Considering Corrective Action   The final step in the control process is determining the need for corrective action. Decisions regarding corrective action draw heavily on a manager's analytic and diagnostic skills. After performance is compared against control standards, one of three actions is appropriate: to do nothing, or maintain the status quo; to correct the deviation; or to change the standard. Maintaining the status quo is preferable when performance essentially matches the standard. To correct a deviation from the standard, some action is likely to be needed. Managers at The Sharper Image diagnosed a clear problem with individual store sales and took corrective action: they increased advertising, brought in new products, and started paying more attention to the product line. As a result, sales eventually increased.

Sometimes, performance that is higher than expected may also cause problems for organizations. For example, when Mazda introduced its new Miata sports car in 1989, demand was so strong that there were waiting lists and many customers were willing to pay more than the suggested retail price to obtain a car. The company was reluctant to increase production, in part because it feared demand would eventually drop, and in part because it wanted to build a mystique for the car. At the same time, however, it didn't want to alienate potential customers. Consequently, Mazda decided to reduce its advertising. This cutback curtailed demand a bit and limited customer frustration.

Changing an established standard usually is necessary if the standard was set too high or too low at the outset. A standard is too low if large numbers of employees routinely beat it by a wide margin, too high if no employees ever meet it. Also, standards that seemed perfectly appropriate when they were established may need to be adjusted because circumstances have changed. One cause cited for The Sharper Image's sales problems was increased competition from other specialty chains and from department stores. Thus the company eventually may need to reassess and lower its standard to better reflect marketplace realities.

Operations Control

Operations control is control of the processes that the organization uses to transform resources into products or services.

As mentioned, most organizations practice four levels of control. **Operations control** is control of the processes that the organization uses to transform resources into products or services. As Figure 12.4 shows, the three forms of operations control — preliminary, screening, and post-action — occur at different points in relation to the transformation processes used by the organization.[14]

Preliminary Control

Preliminary control focuses on the resources that the organization brings in from the environment.

Preliminary control (also called *steering control* or *feedforward control*) focuses on the resources — financial, material, human, and information — that the organization brings in from the environment. Preliminary control attempts to monitor the quality or quantity of these resources before they enter the organization.[15] Firms such as PepsiCo and General Mills hire only college graduates for their management training programs, and even then only after applicants satisfy several interviewers and selection criteria. In this way, they practice preliminary control of human resources. When Sears orders merchandise to be manufactured under its own brand name, it specifies rigid standards of quality, thereby controlling physical inputs. Organizations similarly control financial and information resources. For example, privately held companies such as United Parcel Service and M&M/Mars limit the extent to which outsiders can buy their stock. Television networks such as ABC and CBS verify the accuracy of news stories before they are broadcast.

Screening Control

Screening control focuses on meeting standards for product or service quality or quantity during the transformation process itself.

Screening control (also called *yes/no control* or *concurrent control*) focuses on meeting standards for product or service quality or quantity during the transformation process itself. Screening control relies heavily on feedback processes. For example, in a Compaq factory, computer system components are checked periodically as each unit is assembled. This is done to ensure that all the components assembled up to that point are working properly. The periodic quality checks provide feedback to workers so they know what, if any, corrective actions to take. Because they are widely applicable and useful in identifying the cause of problems, screening controls tend to be used more often than other forms of control.

More companies are adopting screening controls because they are an effective way to promote employee participation and catch problems early in the overall transformation process. For example, Corning recently adopted screening controls for use in manufacturing television glass. In the

Figure 12.4

Operations Control

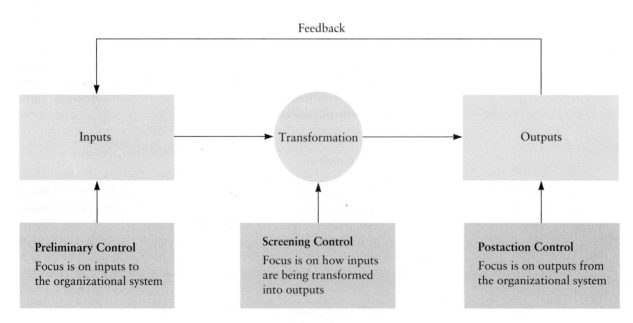

Operations control focuses on the processes used by the organization to transform resources into products or services. Nearly 70 percent of the candies made by Godiva Chocolatier (headquartered in Brussels) are hand-decorated. Thus, operations control at Godiva is concerned with the people who do the decorating and the technology that is used by them as they carry out this delicate work.

past, television screens were inspected only after they were finished. Unfortunately, over 4 percent of them were later returned by customers because of defects. Now the glass screens are inspected at each step in the production process rather than at the end, and the return rate from customers has dropped to .03 percent.[16]

Postaction Control

Postaction control focuses on the outputs of the organization after transformation is complete.

Postaction control (sometimes called *feedback control*) focuses on the outputs of the organization after transformation is complete. Although Corning abandoned postaction control in favor of screening control, this still may be an effective method, primarily if a product can be manufactured in only one or two steps or if the service is fairly simple and routine. Although postaction control alone may not be as effective as preliminary or screening control, it can provide management with information for future planning. For example, if a quality check of finished goods indicates an unacceptably high defective rate, the production manager knows that he or she must identify the causes and take steps to eliminate them. Postaction control also provides a basis for rewarding employees. Recognizing that an employee has exceeded personal sales goals by a wide margin, for example, may alert the manager that a bonus or promotion is in order.[17]

Most organizations use more than one form of operations control. For example, Honda's preliminary control includes hiring only qualified employees and specifying strict quality standards when ordering parts from other manufacturers. Honda uses numerous screening controls in checking the quality of components during assembly of cars. A final inspection and test drive as each car rolls off the assembly line is part of the company's postaction control. Organizations employ a wide variety of techniques to facilitate operations control. We discuss more of those techniques, as well as other dimensions of operations management, in Chapter 15.

As the term suggests, financial control deals with the organization's financial resources. Franklin A. Thomas, shown here in his office, is president of the Ford Foundation. He and the organization he heads are responsible for distributing nearly $2 billion each year to support nonprofit activities around the world. As part of its financial control system, the Foundation closely monitors how each recipient uses the awards and the outcomes that it subsequently achieves.

Financial Control

Financial control is control of financial resources as they flow into the organization, are held by the organization, and flow out of the organization.

Financial control is control of financial resources as they flow into the organization (i.e., revenues, shareholder investments), are held by the organization (i.e., working capital, retained earnings), and flow out of the organization (i.e., expenses). Business organizations such as United Parcel Service, Delta Air Lines, and Apple Computer must manage their finances so that revenues are sufficient to cover expenses and still return a profit to the firm's owners. Not-for-profit organizations such as universities and government agencies have the same concerns: their revenues (from tax dollars or tuition) must cover operating expenses and overhead. A complete discussion of financial management is beyond the scope of this discussion, but we will examine the control provided by budgets and other financial tools.

Budgetary Control

A budget is a plan expressed in numerical terms.

A **budget** is a plan expressed in numerical terms.[18] Organizations establish budgets for work groups, departments, divisions, and the whole organization. The usual time period for a budget is one year, although breakdowns of budgets by the quarter or month are also common. Budgets are generally expressed in financial terms, but they may occasionally be expressed in units of output, time, or other quantifiable factors.

Because of their quantitative nature, budgets provide yardsticks for measuring performance and facilitate comparisons across departments, between levels in the organization, and from one time period to another. Budgets serve four primary purposes. They help managers coordinate resources and projects (because they use a common denominator, usually dollars). They help define the established standards for control. They provide clear guidelines about the organization's resources and expectations. Finally, budgets enable the organization to evaluate the performance of managers and organizational units.

Types of Budgets   Most organizations develop and make use of three different types of budgets: financial, operating, and nonmonetary. Table 12.1 summarizes the characteristics of each of these.[19]

A financial budget indicates where the organization expects to get its cash for the coming time period and how it plans to use it. Since financial resources are critically important, the organization needs to know where those resources will be coming from and how they are to be used. Usual sources of cash include sales revenue, short- and long-term loans, the sale

Table 12.1

Types of Budgets

Type of Budget	What Budget Shows
Financial budget	**The sources and uses of cash**
Cash-flow or cash budget	All sources of cash income and cash expenditures in monthly, weekly, or daily periods
Capital expenditures budget	Costs of major assets such as a new plant, machinery, or land
Balance sheet budget	Forecast of the organization's assets and liabilities in the event all other budgets are met
Operating budget	**Planned operations in financial terms**
Sales or revenue budget	Income the organization expects to receive from normal operations
Expense budget	Anticipated expenses for the organization during the coming time period
Profit budget	Anticipated differences between sales or revenues and expenses
Nonmonetary budget	**Planned operations in nonfinancial terms**
Labor budget	Hours of direct labor available for use
Space budget	Square feet or meters of space available for various functions
Production budget	Number of units to be produced during the coming time period

of assets, and the issuance of new stock. A few years ago MCA realized that revenues from its new Universal Studios theme park in Florida were going to be significantly lower than expected. As a result, the firm moved quickly to modify its financial budget to reflect lower revenues. Common uses of cash are operating expenses, debt repayment, purchase of new assets, retained earnings, and stock dividends. Heavily leveraged companies such as Continental Airlines must commit much of their cash to debt repayment. MCA further revised its financial budget by cutting back on planned expansion.

An operating budget is concerned with planned operations within the organization. It outlines what quantities of products or services the organization intends to create and what financial resources will be used to create them. IBM draws up an operating budget that specifies how many of each model of its personal computer will be produced each quarter.

A nonmonetary budget is simply a budget expressed in nonfinancial terms, such as units of output, hours of direct labor, machine hours, or square-foot allocations. Nonmonetary budgets are most commonly used by managers at the lower levels of an organization. For example, a plant manager can schedule work more effectively knowing that he or she has 8,000 labor hours to allocate in a week, rather than trying to determine how to best spend $76,451 in wages in a week.

Developing Budgets   Traditionally, budgets were developed by top management and the controller and then imposed on lower-level managers. Although some organizations still follow this pattern, many contemporary organizations now allow all managers to participate in the budget process. As a starting point, top management generally issues a call for budget requests, accompanied by an indication of overall patterns the budgets may take. For example, if sales are expected to drop in the next year, managers may be told up front to prepare for cuts in operating budgets. Likewise, departments can expect a budget increase if sales are rising.

As Figure 12.5 shows, the heads of each operating unit typically submit budget requests to the head of their division. An operating-unit head might be a department manager in a manufacturing or wholesaling firm or a program director in a social service agency. The division heads might include plant managers, regional sales managers, or college deans. The division head integrates and consolidates the budget requests from operating-unit heads into one overall division budget request. A great deal of interaction among managers usually takes place at this stage, as the division head coordinates the budgetary needs of the various departments.

Division budget requests are then forwarded to a budget committee. The budget committee is usually composed of top managers. The committee reviews budget requests from several divisions and, once again, duplications and inconsistencies are corrected. Finally, the budget committee, the controller, and the CEO review and agree on the overall budget for the organization as well as specific budgets for each operating unit. These decisions are then communicated back to each manager.

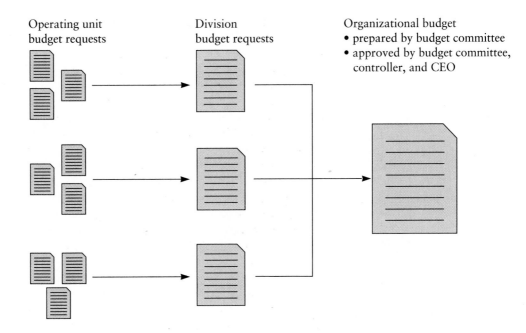

Operating unit
budget requests

Division
budget requests

Organizational budget
• prepared by budget committee
• approved by budget committee,
  controller, and CEO

Figure 12.5

Developing Budgets in Organizations

Strengths and Weaknesses of Budgeting   Budgets offer a number of advantages, but they have weaknesses as well. On the plus side, budgets do
facilitate effective control. Placing dollar values on operations enables managers to monitor operations better and to pinpoint problem areas. Budgets
also facilitate coordination and communication between departments
because they express diverse activities in a common denominator (dollars).
Budgets help maintain records of organizational performance and are a
logical complement to planning. As managers develop plans they should
simultaneously consider control measures to accompany them. Organizations can use budgets to link planning and control by first developing
budgets as part of the plan and then using those budgets as a part of
control.

Some managers apply budgets too rigidly. Budgets are intended to serve
as frameworks, but managers sometimes fail to recognize that changing
circumstances may warrant budget adjustments. The process of developing
budgets can also be very time consuming. Finally, budgets may limit innovation and change. When all available funds are allocated to specific operating budgets, it may be impossible to procure additional funds to take
advantage of an unexpected opportunity.[20]

Indeed, for these very reasons, some organizations are working to scale
back their budgeting system. Although most organizations are likely to
continue to use budgets, the goal is to make them less confining and rigid.
For example, Xerox, 3M, and Digital Equipment are all cutting back on
their budgeting systems by reducing the number of budgets they generate

THE GLOBAL CHALLENGE

The CEO Who Sees Beyond Budgets

Many U.S. managers are ripping up confining, old-fashioned budgets, but few of the budget bashers have gone further faster than Europe's Jean-Marie Descarpentries. A portly Frenchman with a Rabelaisian taste for ribald jokes and country cooking, he runs the Franco-British CMB Packaging (1989 sales: $4.6 billion) as a federation of entrepreneurs who strive to multiply sales, profits, and productivity as fast as they can. For Descarpentries, 54, following a formal budget would mean curbing his epic ambitions. "If the budget is the basis of your plan, you content yourself with an extrapolation of the past," he says. "How can you budget the 26%-a-year compound growth we've achieved?"

By reaching for the sky, Descarpentries has turned in one of the best corporate performances of the 1980s. When he took over a debt-laden French tin-can maker called Carnaud in 1982, its market value was $19 million. Now, after a 1989 acquisition, the rechristened CMB is worth $3 billion.

In lieu of binding budgets, Descarpentries sets dramatic targets designed to make managers stretch for the seemingly unreachable. Each year he asks the heads of 94 profit centers to project their best possible performance if everything, including product demand, goes just right. Those estimates become the budget. "Then we promptly forget about them," he says. "The purpose is to get managers to dream the impossible dream."

Unlike most companies, CMB doesn't measure managers against the budget. Descarpentries says that removes budgeting's biggest evil, aiming too low:

"Normally, managers try to negotiate easy targets so they can surpass them and earn big bonuses. The guy who sets an ambitious goal and just misses is penalized."

Instead, CMB rates its managers mainly on how they did this year vs. last year, and how they stack up against the best managers in the industry. Besides growth in sales and operating profits, the main criteria are productivity, debt levels, and hours spent on training. Each month the division heads get a chart comparing their performance on each criterion. "It's management by pride," says Descarpentries. "They all want to be first."

Money is also at stake. Each year CMB rates the 94 profit-center heads on a scale ranging from a low of −5 to a maximum of 15. Poor performers often get no bonus at all, while the stars receive bonuses equal to 30% of their salary, plus lucrative stock options. How does Descarpentries fit in? "My job is offering consulting advice — not orders — and choosing people," he says. If a manager posts consistently low ratings for 18 months, Descarpentries replaces him.

Last year, during a 10-day company outing in the Jordanian desert, he exploited the surrealistic setting to unveil his new goal: a monumental $17 billion in sales by 2000. Reaching it will require huge effort. But for Descarpentries — and the managers he taught to substitute dreams for budgets — nothing seems impossible.

SOURCE: Shawn Tully, "The CEO Who Sees Beyond Budgets," *Fortune,* June 4, 1990. © 1990 The Time Inc. Magazine Company. All rights reserved.

and by injecting more flexibility into the budgeting process.[21] The Global Challenge describes how one European firm has taken an extreme position in its efforts to overcome some of the weaknesses of budgeting.

Other Tools of Financial Control

Although budgets are the most common means of financial control, other useful tools are financial statements, ratio analysis, and financial audits.

A *financial statement* is a profile of some aspect of the organization's financial circumstances. The *balance sheet* and *income statement* are common financial statements.

Financial Statements   A **financial statement** is a profile of some aspect of an organization's financial circumstances. There are commonly accepted and required ways to prepare and present financial statements.[22] The two most basic financial statements prepared and used by virtually all organizations are a balance sheet and an income statement.

The **balance sheet** lists the assets and liabilities of the organization at a specific point in time, usually the last day of an organization's fiscal year. A balance sheet might summarize the financial condition of an organization on December 31, 1992. Most balance sheets are divided into current assets (assets that are relatively liquid, or easily convertible into cash), fixed assets (assets that are longer term in nature and less liquid), current liabilities (debts and other obligations that must be paid in the near future), long-term liabilities (payable over an extended period of time), and stockholders' equity (the owners' claim against the assets).

Whereas the balance sheet reflects a snapshot profile of an organization's financial position, the **income statement** summarizes financial performance over a period of time, usually one year. An income statement might be for the period January 1, 1992, through December 31, 1992. It adds up all income to the organization and then subtracts all expenses, debts, and liabilities. The "bottom line" of the statement represents net income, or profit. Information from the balance sheet and income statement is used to compute important financial ratios.

Ratio analysis is the calculation of one or more financial ratios to assess some aspect of the organization's financial health. *Liquidity ratios, debt ratios, return ratios, coverage ratios,* and *operating ratios* are often calculated.

Ratio Analysis   Financial ratios compare different elements of a balance sheet or income statement to one another. **Ratio analysis** is the calculation of one or more financial ratios to assess some aspect of the financial health of an organization. Organizations use a variety of different financial ratios as part of financial control. For example, **liquidity ratios** indicate how liquid (easily converted into cash) an organization's assets are. **Debt ratios** reflect ability to meet long-term financial obligations. **Return ratios** show managers and investors how much return the organization is generating relative to its assets. **Coverage ratios** help estimate the organization's ability to cover interest expenses on borrowed capital. **Operating ratios** indicate the effectiveness of specific functional areas rather than the effectiveness of the total organization.

Audits are independent appraisals of an organization's accounting, financial, and administrative procedures. Audits may be conducted by experts external or internal to the organization.

Financial Audits   **Audits** are independent appraisals of an organization's accounting, financial, and administrative procedures. The two major types of financial audit are the external audit and the internal audit.

External audits are financial appraisals conducted by experts who are not employees of the organization.[23] The organization contracts with certified public accountants (CPAs) for this service. The CPA's main objective is to verify for stockholders, the Internal Revenue Service, and other interested parties that the methods used by the organization's financial managers and accountants to prepare documents and reports are legal and proper. External audits are so important that publicly held corporations are required by law to have external audits done regularly, as assurance to investors that the financial reports are reliable. An external audit at U.S.

Shoe Corporation recently discovered some significant accounting irregularities in one of the firm's divisions. As a result, the firm was fined and had to revamp its entire accounting system.[24] Of course, as The Entrepreneurial Challenge explains, auditing results themselves are sometimes open to different interpretations.

Some organizations are also starting to employ external auditors to review other aspects of their financial operations. Some auditing firms now specialize in checking corporate legal bills. An auditor for the Fireman's Fund Insurance Company uncovered several thousand dollars in legal fee errors. Other auditors are beginning to specialize in real estate, employee benefits, and pension plan investments.[25]

An **internal audit** is handled by employees of the organization. Its objective is the same as that of an external audit: to verify the accuracy of financial and accounting procedures. Internal audits also examine these procedures for efficiency and appropriateness. Because the staff members who conduct them are a permanent part of the organization, internal audits tend to be more expensive than external audits. But because employees are more familiar than external auditors with the organization's practices, they may point out other details about the accounting system besides its technical correctness. Large organizations such as Dresser Industries, Dow Chemical, and Eastman Kodak have internal auditing staffs that spend all their time conducting audits of different divisions and functional areas of the organizations. Smaller organizations may assign accountants to an internal audit group on a temporary or rotating basis.

Structural Control

Structural control focuses on how well an organization's structural elements serve their intended purpose.

Structural control focuses on how well an organization's structural elements serve their intended purpose. Organizations can create designs for themselves that result in very different approaches to control. Two major forms of structural control, bureaucratic control and clan control, represent opposite approaches, as shown in Figure 12.6.[26] Organizations characterized by these opposite approaches to control differ structurally in terms of goals, degree of formality, performance focus, organization design, reward system, and level of participation. Although a few organizations use one approach or the other exclusively, most tend toward one but have specific characteristics of both.

Bureaucratic Control

Bureaucratic control is characterized by formal and mechanistic structural arrangements.

Bureaucratic control is an approach to organization design characterized by formal and mechanistic structural arrangements. As the term suggests, it follows the bureaucratic model. The goal of bureaucratic control is employee compliance. Organizations that use it rely on strict rules and a rigid hierarchy, insist that employees meet minimally acceptable levels of

THE ENTREPRENEURIAL CHALLENGE

Debatable Financial Control at Blockbuster

Blockbuster Entertainment Corporation, based in Fort Lauderdale, Florida, has grown to become the largest video rental chain in the United States. Indeed, the firm's growth rate has been nothing short of phenomenal. In 1988, 258 Blockbuster Video stores produced $216 million in revenues. In 1990, 1,525 Blockbuster stores generated $1.25 billion in revenues. Blockbuster's goal is to have 3,000 stores in operation by 1995.

Blockbuster's performance has not gone unnoticed on Wall Street. The firm's stock price has increased sevenfold since 1987 and continues to rise steadily. Some skeptics, however, believe that Blockbuster's financial performance is overstated and attributable in part to some liberal accounting practices.

Blockbuster was audited in 1988 by Kellogg Associates, a Los Angeles–based accounting firm. Kellogg announced that Blockbuster's accounting practices were all legal but did have the effect of overstating present earnings. More recently other auditors have reached similar conclusions. For example, whenever Blockbuster grants a new franchise, it collects a hefty fee. Moreover, the franchisee has to buy a large initial inventory of seven thousand titles from Blockbuster.

Thus there is a large one-time-only infusion of cash to the corporation each time a new store opens. If growth ever starts to slow, so too will this income.

Blockbuster has also bought several small regional video rental chains. Whenever it does so, it amortizes the cost of the acquired firm's "good will" over a 40-year period. This practice has the effect of lowering the short-term expense of the acquisition (thus keeping profits higher), but it affects earnings negatively for a longer period.

Although these practices are all perfectly legal, auditors have repeatedly pointed out that Blockbuster's financial profile looks better than it really is. Investors seem not to be concerned, however. Indeed, some experts think that Blockbuster is on its way to becoming the McDonald's of the video rental industry — with a store on every corner.

REFERENCES: "Will This Video Chain Stay on Fast-Forward?" *Business Week,* June 12, 1989, pp. 72–75; "Video Giant Got Bargain, Analysts Say," *USA Today,* November 20, 1990, pp. 1B, 2B; "After Frantic Growth, Blockbuster Faces Host of Video-Rental Rivals,"*Wall Street Journal,* March 21, 1991, pp. A1, A6.

performance, and often have a tall structure. They reward individual performance and allow only limited and formal employee participation.

NBC applies structural controls that reflect many elements of bureaucracy. The television network relies on highly detailed rules to regulate employee travel, expense accounts, and other expenses. A new performance appraisal system precisely specifies minimally acceptable levels of performance for all workers. The organization's structure is considerably taller than the structures of the other major networks, and rewards are based on individual contributions. Perhaps most significantly, many NBC employees have argued that they have too small a voice in how the organization is managed.[27]

Clan Control

Clan control is characterized by informal and organic structural arrangements.

Clan control is an approach to organization design characterized by informal and organic structural arrangements. As Figure 12.6 shows, its goal is employee commitment to the organization. Accordingly, it relies heavily on group norms and a strong corporate culture and gives employees the responsibility for controlling themselves. Employees are encouraged to perform beyond minimally acceptable levels. Organizations using this approach are usually relatively flat. They direct rewards at group performance and favor widespread employee participation.

Levi Strauss practices clan control. The firm's managers use groups as the basis for work and have created a culture wherein group norms help facilitate high performance. Rewards are subsequently provided to the best-performing groups and teams. The company's culture also reinforces contributions to the overall team effort, and employees feel strong loyalty to the organization. Levi Strauss has a flat structure, and power is widely shared. Employee participation is encouraged in all areas of operation.[28]

Figure 12.6

Two Forms of Structural Control

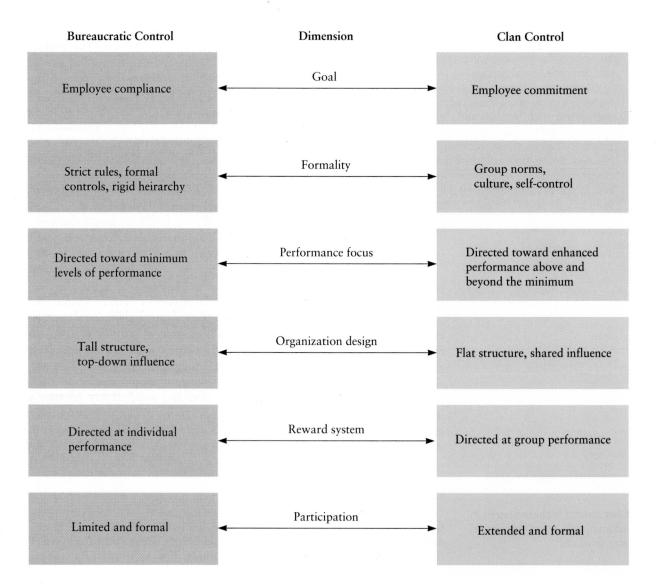

Bureaucratic Control	Dimension	Clan Control
Employee compliance	Goal	Employee commitment
Strict rules, formal controls, rigid heirarchy	Formality	Group norms, culture, self-control
Directed toward minimum levels of performance	Performance focus	Directed toward enhanced performance above and beyond the minimum
Tall structure, top-down influence	Organization design	Flat structure, shared influence
Directed at individual performance	Reward system	Directed at group performance
Limited and formal	Participation	Extended and formal

Strategic Control

Strategic control focuses on how effectively an organization's strategies result in the attainment of goals.

Strategic control focuses on how effectively an organization's strategies result in the attainment of goals. As we saw in Part II, formulating and implementing strategy are vital activities, but it is also important to assess how well the strategy works.[29] Doing this requires the organization to integrate strategy and control. This is especially true for a global organization.

Integrating Strategy and Control

Strategic control generally turns on one or more of the following aspects of an organization: its structure, leadership, technology, human resources, and information and operations control systems. These aspects are often viewed as avenues through which strategies are or are not being effectively implemented. For example, an organization should periodically examine its structure to determine whether it facilitates the attainment of strategic goals. Suppose a firm using a functional (U-form) design has an established goal of achieving a 20 percent sales growth rate per year. Performance indicators show it is currently growing at a rate of only 10 percent per year. Detailed analysis might reveal that the current organization structure is inhibiting growth in some way (perhaps by slowing decision making and discouraging innovation) and that a divisional (M-form) design is more likely to bring about the desired growth (by speeding decision making and promoting innovation).

In this way, strategic control focuses on the extent to which implemented strategy achieves the organization's strategic goals. If, as outlined above, one or more avenues of implementation do not facilitate the attainment of goals, that avenue should be changed. Consequently, the firm might find it necessary to alter its structure, replace key leaders, adopt new technology, modify its human resources, or change its information and operations control systems.[30]

The board of directors at Borden recently realized that the company was not meeting its strategic goals for growth and profitability and was not providing stockholders with an adequate return on their investment. The board took action by changing the company's leadership. The new CEO, Romeo Ventres, continued to adjust strategic controls. He shifted the company's structure from an H-form to an M-form, implemented a variety of innovative manufacturing techniques to enhance productivity (change in technology), brought in several managers from other organizations (change in human resources), installed a new information system, and mandated new levels of product quality (change in operational control). As a result, Borden has attained record levels of sales growth and profitability.[31]

International Strategic Control

Because of both their relatively large size and the increased complexity associated with international business, global organizations must take an especially pronounced strategic view of their control systems. One basic question that has to be addressed is whether to establish centralized or decentralized control. Under a centralized system, each organizational unit around the world is responsible for frequently reporting the results of its performance to headquarters. Managers from the home office often visit foreign branches to observe firsthand how the units are functioning.

British Petroleum, Unilever, Procter & Gamble, and Sony use this approach. They believe centralized control is effective because it allows the home office to keep informed about the performance of foreign units and to maintain control over how decisions are made. For example, British Petroleum (BP) recently discovered that its Australian subsidiary was not billing its customers for charges as quickly as were its competitors. By shortening the billing cycle, BP now receives customer payments five days faster than before. BP managers believe that they discovered this oversight only because of a centralized financial control system.

Organizations that use a decentralized control system require foreign branches to report less frequently and in less detail. For example, each unit may submit summary performance statements on a quarterly basis and provide full statements only once a year. Similarly, visits from the home office are less frequent and less concerned with monitoring and assessing performance. IBM, Ford, Royal Dutch/Shell, and IRI Group (a large Italian food-processing firm) all use this approach. Because Ford practices decentralized control of its design function, European designers have developed several innovative automobile design features. Managers at Ford believe that if they had been more centralized, designers would not have had the freedom to develop their new ideas.

Managing Control in Organizations

Effective control, whether at the operations, financial, structural, or strategic level, successfully regulates and monitors organizational activities. To use the control process, managers must recognize the characteristics of effective control and understand how to identify and overcome occasional resistance to control.

Characteristics of Effective Control

Effective control systems are integrated with planning and are flexible, accurate, timely, and objective.

Control systems tend to be most effective when they are integrated with planning and when they are flexible, accurate, timely, and objective.

Integration with Planning   Control should be linked with planning. The more explicit and precise the linkage, the more effective is the control system. The best way to integrate planning and control is to account for control as plans develop. In other words, as goals are set during the planning process, attention should be paid to developing standards that will reflect how well the plan is realized.

A few years ago managers at Champion Spark Plug Company decided to broaden their product line to include a full range of automotive accessories—a total of twenty-one new products. As part of this plan, managers decided what level of sales they wanted to realize from each product for each of the next five years. They established these sales goals as standards against which actual sales would be compared. Thus, by accounting for their control system as they developed their plan, managers at Champion did an excellent job of integrating planning and control.[32]

Flexibility   The control system itself must be flexible enough to accommodate change. Consider, for example, an organization whose diverse product line requires seventy-five different raw materials. The company's inventory-control system must be able to manage and monitor current levels of inventory for all seventy-five materials. When a change in product line changes the number of raw materials needed, or when the required quantities of the existing materials change, the control system should be flexible enough to handle the revised requirements. The alternative—designing and implementing a brand-new control system—is an avoidable expense.

Champion's control system included a mechanism that automatically shipped products to major customers to keep their inventory at predetermined levels. The firm had to adjust this system when one of its biggest customers, Montgomery Ward, decided not to stock the full line of Champion products. Because Champion's control system was flexible, modifying it for Montgomery Ward was relatively simple.

Accuracy   Managers base a surprisingly large number of decisions on inaccurate information. Field representatives may hedge their sales estimates to make themselves look good. Production managers may hide costs to meet their targets. Human resources managers may overestimate their minority recruiting prospects to meet affirmative action goals. In each case the information that other managers receive is inaccurate, and the results of inaccurate information may be quite dramatic. If sales projections are inflated, a manager might cut advertising (thinking it is no longer needed) or increase advertising (to further build momentum). Similarly, a production manager unaware of hidden costs may quote a sales price much lower than desirable. Or a human resources manager may speak out publicly on the effectiveness of the company's minority recruiting, only to find later that these prospects have been overestimated. In each case, the result of inaccurate information is inappropriate managerial action.

Timeliness   Timeliness does not necessarily mean quickness. Rather, it describes a control system that provides information as often as necessary. Since Champion has a wealth of historical data on its spark-plug sales, it may not need information on spark plugs as frequently as it needs sales feedback for its newer products. Retail organizations usually need sales results daily so that they can manage cash flow and adjust advertising and promotion. In contrast, they may require information about physical inventory only quarterly or annually. In general, the more uncertain and unstable the circumstances, the more frequently measurement is needed.

Objectivity   The control system should provide information that is as objective as possible. To appreciate the need for objective information, imagine the task of a manager responsible for control of his organization's human resources. He asks two plant managers to submit reports. One manager notes that morale at his plant is "okay," that grievances are "about where they should be," and that turnover is "under control." The other reports that absenteeism at her plant is running at 4 percent, that sixteen grievances have been filed this year (compared with twenty-four last year), and that turnover is 12 percent. The second report will almost always be more useful than the first. Of course, managers also need to look beyond the numbers when assessing performance. For example, a plant manager may be boosting productivity and profit margins by putting too much pressure on workers and by using poor materials. As a result, impressive short-run gains may be overshadowed by longer-run increases in employee turnover and customer complaints.

Resistance to Control

Managers may sometimes make the mistake of assuming that the value of an effective control system is self-evident to employees. This is not always so, however. Many employees resist control if they feel overcontrolled, if they think control is inappropriately focused or rewards inefficiency, or if they are uncomfortable with accountability.

Overcontrol   Occasionally, organizations try to control too many things. Overcontrol becomes especially problematic when the control directly affects employee behavior. An organization that instructs its employees when to come to work, where to park, when to have morning coffee, and when to leave for the day exerts considerable control over people's daily activities. Yet many organizations attempt to control not only these but other aspects of work behavior as well. Troubles arise when employees perceive these attempts to limit their behavior as being unreasonable. Employees at Chrysler used to complain because if they drove a non-Chrysler vehicle they were forced to park in a distant parking lot. People felt that this effort to control their personal behavior was excessive. Managers eventually removed that control and now allow open parking.

Inappropriate Focus   The control system may be too narrow, or it may focus too much on quantifiable variables and leave no room for analysis or interpretation. A sales standard that encourages high-pressure tactics to maximize short-run sales may do so at the expense of good will from long-term customers. Such a standard is too narrow. A university reward system that encourages faculty members to publish large numbers of articles but fails to consider the quality of the work is also inappropriately focused. Employees resist the intent of the control system by focusing their efforts only at the performance indicators being used.

Rewards for Inefficiency   Imagine two operating departments that are approaching the end of the fiscal year. Department 1 expects to have $5,000 of its budget left over; department 2 is already $3,000 in the red. As a result, department 1 is likely to have its budget cut for the next year ("They had money left, so they obviously got too much to begin with"), and department 2 is likely to get a budget increase ("They obviously haven't been getting enough money"). Thus department 1 is punished for being efficient, and department 2 is rewarded for being inefficient. As with inappropriate focus, people resist the intent of this control and behave in ways that run counter to the organization's intent.

Too Much Accountability   Effective controls allow managers to determine whether or not employees successfully discharge their responsibilities. If standards are properly set and performance is accurately measured, managers know when problems arise and which departments and individuals are responsible. People resist control when they do not want to be answerable for their mistakes or do not want to work as hard as their boss might like them to work. For example, American Express has a new computer system that provides daily information on how many calls each of its operators handles. If one operator works at a slower pace and handles fewer calls than other operators, that individual's deficient performance can be pinpointed easily.

Overcoming Resistance to Control

Perhaps the best way to overcome resistance to control is to create effective control to begin with. If control systems are properly integrated with organizational planning and if the controls are flexible, accurate, timely, and objective, the organization will be less likely to overcontrol, to focus on inappropriate standards, or to reward inefficiency. Two other ways to overcome resistance are encouraging participation and developing verification procedures.

Encouraging Employee Participation   Chapter 11 notes that participation can help overcome resistance to change. By the same token, when employees are involved with planning and implementing the control system, they are less likely to resist it. For instance, employee participation in planning, decision making, and quality control at the Chevrolet Gear and Axle plant in Detroit has resulted in increased employee concern for quality and a greater commitment to meeting standards.[33]

Developing Verification Procedures   Multiple standards and information systems provide checks and balances and allow the organization to verify the accuracy of performance indicators. Suppose a production manager claims that she failed to meet a certain cost standard because of increased prices of raw materials. A properly designed inventory-control system will

A key ingredient in managing control is the involvement of the organization's employees. Such involvement increases the effectiveness of the control, as well as decreasing resistance to it. These employees at Jamestown Advanced Products, a small metal-fabricating business in New York (shown here with company founder and president Jon W. Wehrenberg) help set their own production standards, are responsible for monitoring the quality of their own work, and participate in setting company policies.

either support or contradict her explanation. Suppose an employee who was fired for excessive absences argues that he was not absent "for a long time." An effective human resources control system should have records that support the termination. Resistance to control declines because these verification procedures protect both employees and management. If the production manager's claim about the rising cost of raw materials is supported by the inventory-control records, she will not be held solely accountable for failing to meet the cost standard, and some action will probably be taken to lower the cost of raw materials.

Learning Summary

Control is the regulation of organizational activities so that some targeted element of performance remains within acceptable limits. Control provides ways to adapt to environmental change, to limit the accumulation of error, to cope with organizational complexity, and to minimize costs. Organizations control financial, physical, information, and human resources. Control is the function of managers, the controller, and, increasingly, of operating employees.

Operations control focuses on the processes that the organization uses to transform resources into products or services. Common forms of operations control are preliminary, screening, and postaction control. Most organizations need multiple control systems because no one system alone can provide adequate control.

Financial control focuses on controlling the organization's financial resources. The foundation of financial control is budgets, which are plans expressed in numerical terms. Financial statements, ratio analysis, and external and internal audits are also important tools that organizations use to exercise financial control.

Structural control addresses how well an organization's structural elements serve their intended purpose. Bureaucratic control is relatively formal and mechanistic, whereas clan control is informal and organic. Most organizations use a form of organizational control somewhere in between these two extremes.

Strategic control focuses on how effectively the organization's strategies result in the attainment of goals. The integration of strategy and control is generally achieved through organization structure, leadership, technology, human resources, and information and operations control systems. For multinational organizations, international strategic control is necessary as well.

One way to increase the effectiveness of control is to fully integrate planning and control. The control system should also be flexible, accurate, timely, and as objective as possible. Employees may resist organizational controls because of overcontrol, inappropriate focus, rewards for inefficiency, and a desire to avoid accountability. Managers can overcome this resistance by improving the effectiveness of controls and by allowing employee participation and developing verification procedures.

Questions and Exercises

Review Questions

1. Why do organizations use control?
2. What are the basic areas and levels of control?
3. Describe the four steps in the control process.
4. Identify and describe three forms of operations control.
5. What are the strengths and weaknesses of budgets?
6. What are the two forms of structural control?
7. Why do people resist control? How can organizations overcome this resistance?

Analysis Questions

1. Identify how the purposes of control relate to your college or university.
2. Develop a set of examples to illustrate levels of control for each area of control.
3. Discuss the four steps in the control process as applied to each type of operations control.
4. Do you use a budget for your personal finances? Relate your experiences with budgeting to the discussion in the chapter.

5. Discuss the relative importance of the characteristics of effective control for each type of operations control.
6. Do you resist control? If so, why? If not, what characteristics of a control system might make you start to resist?

Application Exercises

1. Invite the controller from your college or university to class as a guest speaker. Ask questions to learn more about the role she or he plays in control.
2. Develop a control system for use in your class. Include within the system the four steps in control, and describe how the system overcomes resistance.

Chapter Notes

1. "For the Orioles, Less Is More — It's First Place," *Business Week,* July 10, 1989, p. 34; "Baltimore Isn't About to Let the Orioles Fly the Coop," *Business Week,* August 1, 1988, p. 34; "So You Wanna Own a Baseball Team," *Business Week,* July 22, 1991, p. 80; "Eli Jacobs, Financier and Orioles Owner, Covers All the Bases," *Wall Street Journal,* May 15, 1991, pp. A1, A8.
2. Peter F. Drucker, *Managing in Turbulent Times* (New York: Harper & Row, 1980).
3. Joel Dreyfuss, "Victories in the Quality Crusade," *Fortune,* October 10, 1988, pp. 80–88.
4. Ibid.
5. "Why Emery Is Biting Its Nails," *Business Week,* August 29, 1988, p. 34.
6. "America's Leanest and Meanest," *Business Week,* October 5, 1987, pp. 78–84.
7. Ronald Henkoff, "Cost Cutting: How to Do It Right," *Fortune,* April 9, 1990, pp. 40–49.
8. James P. Walsh and James K. Seward, "On the Efficiency of Internal and External Corporate Control Mechanisms," *Academy of Management Review,* July 1990, pp. 421–458.
9. Vijay Sathe, "Who Should Control Division Controllers?" *Harvard Business Review,* September–October 1978, pp. 99–104.
10. "The Controller — Inflation Gives Him More Clout with Management," *Business Week,* August 15, 1977, pp. 85–87, 90, 95.
11. Edward E. Lawler III and John G. Rhode, *Information and Control in Organizations* (Pacific Palisades, Calif.: Goodyear, 1976).
12. Robert N. Anthony, *The Management Control Function* (Boston, Mass.: Harvard Business School Press, 1988).
13. "The Sharper Image May Need to Refocus," *Business Week,* November 21, 1988, p. 84.
14. See Stephen G. Green and M. Ann Welsh, "Cybernetics and Dependence: Reframing the Control Concept," *Academy of Management Review,* April 1988, pp. 287–301.

15. Harold Koontz and Robert W. Bradspies, "Managing Through Feedforward Control," *Business Horizons*, June 1972, pp. 25–36.
16. Dreyfuss, "Victories in the Quality Crusade."
17. Anthony, *The Management Control Function*.
18. See Belverd E. Needles, Jr., Henry R. Anderson, and James C. Caldwell, *Principles of Accounting*, 4th ed. (Boston: Houghton Mifflin, 1990).
19. John Dearden, "Measuring Profit Center Managers," *Harvard Business Review*, September–October 1987, pp. 84–88.
20. Christopher K. Bart, "Budgeting Gamesmanship," *The Academy of Management Executive*, November 1988, pp. 285–294.
21. Thomas A. Stewart, "Why Budgets Are Bad for Business," *Fortune*, June 4, 1990, pp. 179–190.
22. Needles, Anderson, and Caldwell, *Principles of Accounting*.
23. Ibid.
24. "Questions About U.S. Shoe Corp. Continue to Mount," *Wall Street Journal*, April 5, 1990, p. A4.
25. "Auditors of Corporate Legal Bills Thrive," *Wall Street Journal*, February 13, 1991, p. B1.
26. William G. Ouchi, "The Transmission of Control Through Organizational Hierarchy," *Academy of Management Journal*, June 1978, pp. 173–192; Richard E. Walton, "From Control to Commitment in the Workplace," *Harvard Business Review*, March–April 1985, pp. 76–84.
27. "As NBC News Cuts Costs Will It Clobber Quality?" *Business Week*, December 5, 1988, pp. 137–138.
28. "The Push for Quality," *Business Week*, June 8, 1987, pp. 130–135.
29. Peter Lorange, Michael F. Scott Morton, and Sumantra Ghoshal, *Strategic Control* (St. Paul, Minn.: West, 1986).
30. For other perspectives, see Georg Schreyogg and Horst Steinmann, "Strategic Control: A New Perspective," *Academy of Management Review*, January 1987, pp. 91–103.
31. Walter Guzzard, "Big Can Still Be Beautiful," *Fortune*, April 25, 1988, pp. 50–64.
32. "Champion Is Starting to Show a Little Spark," *Business Week*, March 21, 1988, p. 87.
33. Charles G. Burck, "What Happens When Workers Manage Themselves," *Fortune*, July 27, 1981, pp. 62–69.

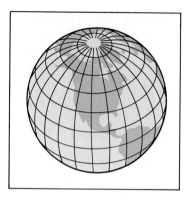

CASE 12.1

Is Chrysler Out of Control?

The past decade has not been easy on American automakers. Foreign car companies, under pressure from the U.S. government to stop exporting so many vehicles to the United States, have been building factories in America, adding to general domestic production overcapacity. Because the growth in demand for cars is slow, for every new Toyota or Honda plant constructed, it almost seems a Ford, Chrysler, or GM plant closes. Ford and GM fall back on profits from their European operations during bad years in the domestic car market, but Chrysler has no such cushion.

During the last major slump for American automakers, Chrysler flirted with bankruptcy and was saved only by a massive federal loan guarantee in 1979. In the 1980s the name of Chrysler chairman Lee Iacocca became familiar to every American as Chrysler scored successes with its K-car, minivan, and Jeep (the last acquired when Chrysler bought American Motors in 1987). But toward the end of the decade Chrysler's profits and market share began slipping alarmingly. With popular products in some crucial market niches, how did Chrysler go wrong? Both the problems and the potential solutions have to do with control.

Financial Control Chrysler seemed to learn its lesson about costs in the early 1980s as it struggled desperately to stay alive. But between 1986 (before the American Motors acquisition) and 1988, its total costs soared from $23 billion to over $33 billion. Chrysler still could boast a lower cost-per-vehicle rate than the other domestic automakers, but such a boast sounded hollow because neither GM nor Ford was making much money domestically. So in 1989 Chrysler undertook an ambitious financial control program, aiming to cut $1 billion from its yearly costs. Its first step was to trim its bureaucracy by 2,300 white-collar positions, about 8 percent of the total. Chrysler also involved top executives in the cost-cutting process by asking them to wager up to one-tenth of their pay on the cost-control program. If the company reached its goal within sixteen months, each manager would get twice the wager back, plus bonuses. If Chrysler did not reach its goal, the executives would lose their wager.

Further cost cutting at Chrysler is even more difficult than it would be at many other American corporations because Chrysler has already trimmed the fat out of its work force, both white and blue collar. So the corporation is looking at the costs of health care and supplies. In a recent letter to suppliers, Iacocca gave an example of the kinds of small decisions that have to be made to control costs. Chrysler was using a parking-brake cable that functions at 60 degrees below zero. Since Chrysler sells few vehicles that will ever encounter that low temperature, Iacocca reasoned that the company could save money and still offer customers good value by using a cable that works at 40 below.

Strategic Control Some observers blame Chrysler's problems on lack of strategic control, citing mistakes with the Omni/Horizon subcompacts as a good example. These cars sold well in 1986 after Chrysler cut their options and prices. But then Chrysler moved Omni production from Belvidere, Illinois, to Kenosha, Wisconsin, to make room for a new model at the Belvidere plant. This move stopped production for six months. Then, less than two years later, Chrysler halted production again for three months and closed the Kenosha plant. The Omni/Horizon resurgence died.

Chrysler is betting much of its future on its new LH car platform, due out in 1992. The new platform will accommodate front-, and rear-, and all-wheel drive models, and Chrysler hopes that it will ease its reliance on sales of vans, minivans, Jeeps, and pickups, which now outsell its cars. But because Chrysler cut its research and development budget in the 1980s to control costs, it has little new to offer buyers before the LH models come out. So in this round of cost cutting, Chrysler has left alone the $15 billion budgeted for product development for the first half of the 1990s.

Structural Control   Chrysler's changes for the new decade include some major shakeups at the top. In 1990, two vice presidents left, and then vice chairman Gerald Greenwald, who appeared ready to take over the chairmanship from Lee Iacocca, resigned to head an employee buyout of United Air Lines (the buyout attempt failed). Less than a day after Greenwald resigned, Iacocca announced a restructuring of top management, splitting up Greenwald's duties. This shakeup was a fitting culmination to a series of shuffles that had seen each of Iacocca's four top executives hold at least three different titles in the previous four years. "We were having a little trouble managing success," Greenwald says.* Chrysler may not have the luxury of managing success again for a while; now it just hopes that it can once again succeed at managing for survival.

Discussion Questions

1. Why might some managers find it easier to establish and maintain controls during difficult economic times than during good economic times?
2. What control mistakes has Chrysler apparently made?
3. After Chrysler cut a significant portion of its white-collar employees, would you expect the remaining managers to resist or welcome control?
4. How would you evaluate Chrysler's program to get its executives to gamble on the company's cost-cutting success?

* Quoted in Melinda Grenier Guiles, "Chrysler Corp., Facing Rough Stretch Again, Struggles to Cut Costs," *Wall Street Journal*, November 29, 1989, p. A6.

REFERENCES: Melinda Grenier Guiles, "Chrysler Corp., Facing Rough Stretch Again, Struggles to Cut Costs," *Wall Street Journal*, November 29, 1989, pp. A1, A6; Melinda Grenier Guiles, "With Sales Falling, Chrysler Takes on Honda in New Ads," *Wall Street Journal*, May 8, 1990, pp. B1, B4; James R. Healey, "Chrysler Cuts: $1B a Year, Jobs," *USA Today*, July 28, 1989, p. B1; Paul Ingrassia, "Chrysler to Cut White-Collar Work Force to Cope with Deepening Slump in Sales," *Wall Street Journal*, July 24, 1989, p. A3; James B. Treece and Wendy Zellner, "The Flashing Signal at Chrysler: Danger Dead Ahead," *Business Week*, June 18, 1990, pp. 44–46.

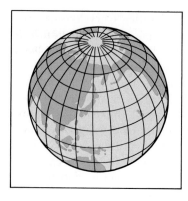

CASE 12.2

Japanese Banking Control Changes Hands

Until recently, banking in Japan was heavily regulated by the Japanese government. Regulators tried to ensure that big banks didn't force small ones out of the market by offering more services, and they kept a tight lid on the interest rates that banks could pay depositors. Despite often earning less than 2 percent interest, the Japanese people, especially the older ones who believed in the traditional savings ethic, deposited a large percentage of their earnings in the banks. With their profitability limited, the banks saw expansion as their only route to growth, and they racked up some impressive numbers. By the end of 1988, Japanese banks had $1.7 trillion in overseas loans, handling almost 40 percent of total international lending, dominating lists of the world's largest banks.

In effect, Japanese banks spread themselves far and wide because government control and the financial climate at home kept them from reaching up for profits. When the Tokyo Stock Exchange was at its peak, the shares of major Japanese banks traded at prices that equaled 40 to 60 times their earnings, far higher than American banks could expect. Such ratios meant that Japanese banks had a far easier time raising capital than their American counterparts.

With the huge infusion of capital from stock sales, Japan's positive international balance of payments, and traditional Japanese savers, Japanese banks became known for offering loans to borrowers worldwide at rates slightly lower than those offered by Western banks. Thus Japanese banks grabbed a huge share of world banking, but not of banking profits. By 1990, eight out of the ten largest banks in the world were Japanese, but Japanese banks did not figure at all among the ten most profitable.

But with gradual deregulation—and a sharp drop in the Tokyo Stock Exchange and in the value of the yen—all that is changing. As they take control of their own futures, the banks are experiencing many of the growing pains felt by many American banks in the early 1980s. For the first time, Japanese bankers are paying as much attention to ratios and profit percentages as their American counterparts do. The drop in stock values made Japanese bank managers particularly aware of one ratio that is always on the minds of American financial planners: price-to-earnings.

Most Japanese banks have shifted their focus to domestic finances. Responding to free-market forces, the rates that banks pay their Japanese depositors have been steadily edging up. At the same time, the banks have been reacting to international pressure to raise their bank reserves to a level acceptable to the Bank for International Settlements, a Swiss bank that sets international banking standards. Meeting the reserve standards means that the banks need more cash on hand.

As a result, banks' strategies are changing radically, as are the ways they measure their success. They now actively pursue profit, not market share. Their return on assets, which stood at about 0.25 percent in 1990, is expected to edge up toward the 1 percent ratio that American and British banks generally earn. Banks are also restraining their rate of growth; the huge 20 to 30 percent annual growth rates of the past few years may drop to below 10 percent during the 1990s. Like the world's other banks, Japanese banks now look much more closely at the rate of return on an investment before signing an agreement.

Although this new focus means that Japanese banks will compete even more fiercely with Western banks to make profitable loans, they have also shifted more of their attention to making domestic consumer loans, which are the most profitable and fastest-growing segment of their business. In a break from tradition fueled by the banks' desire to lend to consumers, many Japanese are now saving less and spending more. The Fuji Bank is making loans called *jukatsu* — "brighten your lifestyle."

Government regulations that ensured strong distinctions between the banking and securities industries are also disappearing, giving banks a chance to specialize. Under regulation, most Japanese banks tended to have similar strategies, chasing growth wherever they could find it. Now, some are choosing to become largely domestic retail banks, and others are using their contacts in the Japanese industrial world to specialize in investment banking.

These changes have forced Japanese bankers to adopt very different styles of thinking in a short period of time. But if bankers prove to be as adaptable as Japanese manufacturers, they will not lose much time figuring out how to manage best under the new conditions. Under regulation, the financial statements of Japanese banks didn't even include a column for return on assets. Now, return on assets and asset-liability management quickly become the focus of any conversation among bankers. It seems that Japanese managers are aware that changes in the environment require changes in strategy *and* in strategic controls.

Discussion Questions

1. What financial controls have gained and lost in importance as a result of Japan's banking deregulation?
2. Many Japanese banks have recently hired Americans to handle sophisticated international financial engineering. Why?
3. Why would Japanese banks submit voluntarily to the standards set down by the Bank for International Settlements?
4. Do you think the changes described here will lead to changes in structural control? Why or why not?

REFERENCES: "Back to the Streets," *The Economist*, November 3, 1990, pp. 97–98; William M. Isaac, "Is Bigger Better?" *FW*, July 24, 1990, p. 90; "Japan's Banks Change Their Style Abroad," *The Economist*, July 28, 1990, pp. 61–62; Carla Rapoport, "Tough Times for Japan's Banks," *Fortune*, July 16, 1990, pp. 66–69.

13

Information Systems in Organizations

LEARNING OBJECTIVES

After studying this chapter, you should be able to:

1. Describe the role of information in organizations, management, decision making, and the environment.

2. Explain the characteristics that make information useful for organizations.

3. Identify the basic components of information systems.

4. List and describe four kinds of information systems.

5. Outline the steps in establishing an information system.

6. Discuss the growing importance of global information systems.

7. Describe some advances in electronic communications.

Managers at Frito-Lay, a division of PepsiCo, faced a growing problem—and they didn't have a solution. Sales of the firm's Tostitos corn chips were starting to drop in many south Texas markets. Since sales of the popular chips were increasing in the rest of the country, the organization knew that the decline in south Texas was a local phenomenon of some sort. Prior to 1986, it would have taken Frito-Lay a minimum of three months to identify the cause of the sales decline and at least another six months to figure out what to do about it. But that year the firm made a decision that would allow sales managers to address this problem faster than they ever could have done before.

During the late 1980s, Frito-Lay spent over $40 million developing an elaborate computer-based information system that keeps daily track of individual product sales at each location (broken down by region, city, or individual store). The system also collects a wealth of information about competitors, including their product prices, packaging sizes, shelf space, and estimated sales.

When managers addressed the Tostitos problem, they found the culprit in one day. A regional competitor had introduced El Galindo, a white-corn tortilla chip that was taking business away from Tostitos. Less than three months after this discovery, Frito-Lay had introduced its own white-corn chip and regained most of its lost market share.[1]

In 1986 Frito-Lay began to address a need that more and more organizations have to confront: the effective management of information. In today's complex environment, organizations face a bewildering array of information about all facets of their operations. Some of this information is unimportant; some is potentially important; and some is critically important. Organizations must develop ways to sort, store, and use this information. As a maker of consumer products, Frito-Lay, for example, must stay in touch with consumer tastes, retailing patterns, and actions of competitors. Frito-Lay's information management system allows the firm to stay abreast of developments in these and other areas.

This chapter examines a variety of perspectives on information systems in organizations. An **information system** is an operational set of procedures that an organization uses to gather data, create information, and then disseminate that information to those who need it. We start by describing the nature of information and the way it permeates organizational activities. We identify the components of information systems and discuss the basic kinds of systems that most organizations use. We then discuss various aspects of how organizations manage their information systems. Next we

> An *information system* is an operational set of procedures that an organization uses to gather data, create information, and disseminate information to those who need it.

briefly examine the role of information systems in managing global organizations. Finally, we note some recent advances in information management that continue to affect how organizations and their managers function.

The Role of Information in Organizations

Information plays a vital role in communication, in decision making, and in the relationship between an organization and its environment.

Organizations rely on information in every phase of their operations. They create more information as they function, and they disseminate information to their environment. The importance of information, and therefore the need to manage it well, continue to grow rapidly. To appreciate this importance, we need to understand the role that information plays in the manager's job as a communicator, in decision making, and in the relationship between an organization and its environment.

Information and Management

Communication is a major part of every manager's job. Indeed, managers spend most of their day in scheduled and unscheduled meetings, reading and writing, and talking (to other managers, customers, bankers, and other constituents) on the telephone. Given that information is a vital part of communication, it follows that information is a critical resource that managers must use to perform their functions in organizations. Indeed, it is possible to characterize management itself as a series of steps involving the reception, processing, and dissemination of information. As Figure 13.1 illustrates, the manager is constantly bombarded with information and must make myriad decisions about what to do with it.

Figure 13.1

Managing the Flow of Information

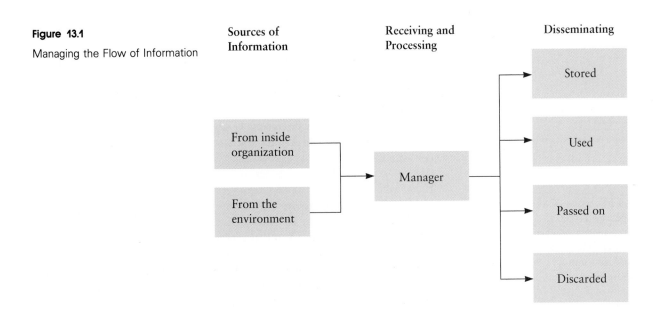

Information plays a key role in decision making. Sound decisions about where to drill for oil and gas are crucial to a firm such as Union Pacific Resources: an incorrect decision can cost the firm large amounts of money; a correct decision results in new drilling opportunities. These Union Pacific geophysicists use computers to organize vast quantities of seismic data that are vital to their decision making.

For example, during the course of a normal day, a marketing manager for a large manufacturing firm receives a great many pieces of information from meetings, telephone calls, personal observation, letters, reports, memos, trade publications, and formal and informal conversations. She reads a report from a subordinate that explains exactly how to solve a pressing problem, so she calls the subordinate and tells him to put the solution into effect immediately. She scans a copy of a report prepared for another manager, sees that it has no relevance to her, and discards it. She notes an article in a recent issue of *Fortune* that she knows a colleague in operations should see, so she passes it on to him. She glances at yesterday's sales report, but since she knows she won't need to analyze it for another week, she files it.

Information and Decision Making

A subset of every manager's job is decision making. Recall from Chapter 5 that decision making is the process of identifying alternatives, evaluating them, and then selecting one for implementation. Without the right information in the right form and at the right time, it is difficult to make correct decisions.[2]

For example, information from the environment, from managers, from customers, from employees, or from other sources alerts the organization that a decision needs to be made. Subsequent information about the decision context helps the organization generate alternatives to consider. Managers then use information about the nature of the alternatives to evaluate them. On the basis of their assessment they select one alternative for implementation. Information about the results also helps the organization assess the quality of the decision after it has been implemented.

Information and the Environment

As discussed in Chapter 4, all organizations must strive to make sense of their environment and to position themselves effectively within it. Individual managers and groups of managers, especially at the boundaries of the organization (in sales and other areas in close contact with the external environment), need to be alert to useful and potentially useful information from the environment.

The organization itself needs to ensure that its operating and control systems are properly integrated, that the necessary information is flowing in, and that they can supply other necessary information to individual managers.[3] Frito-Lay was able to respond so effectively to its competitive challenges because its information systems provided all of these benefits. The Entrepreneurial Challenge explains how several new ventures profit by helping large organizations manage information from their environments.

Characteristics of Useful Information

Data are isolated figures and facts without an associated context.

We can begin to understand the usefulness of information by distinguishing it from data. **Data** are isolated figures and facts without an associated context. Consider the following four facts: (1) a plant has 42 numerical control machines; (2) each machine is capable of producing 2,000 units of output per day; (3) current and projected future demand for the units is 55,000 per day; and (4) workers sufficiently skilled to run the machines make $17 an hour. By itself, each of these pieces of data is relatively meaningless because we have no context within which to evaluate it.

Information is data presented in a context that yields meaning.

Information is data presented in a context that yields meaning. By putting the preceding four pieces of data together into a single context, we create information. For example, we can see that the plant can produce 84,000 units per day but that it needs to be producing only 55,000 units per day to meet demand. Given the high cost of the labor involved, the organization is incurring unnecessary costs. This information has meaning to the organization and provides a basis for action. In this case, the plant manager might decide to moth-ball the extra machines and transfer some of the operators to other jobs.[4] Similarly, the fact that a certain convenience store sold 7 bags of Ruffles potato chips in one day tells Frito-Lay very little. A second piece of data, that the average daily sale for this store used to be

THE ENTREPRENEURIAL CHALLENGE

Small Firms Capitalize on Information Explosion

It is no secret that organizations have more information to contend with than ever before. There's an interesting paradox, however, in the fight to manage this burgeoning amount of data. More organizations use computers to help process information, but computerized data banks, on-line information networks, and electronic bulletin boards themselves provide even more information that organizations may need to consider.

In response, a new industry has emerged — small firms that help organizations manage information. For example, Desktop Data Inc., based in Waltham, Massachusetts, scans wire services looking for stories with key words provided by its customers. Relevant stories are then transmitted directly to the organization's information system. One customer, a Chicago-based investment firm, receives articles featuring the words *takeover, merger, junk bonds*, and *acquisition* so that it can monitor possible merger activity.

Another firm uses a product jointly developed by Lotus Development Corporation and a small software company called NewsEdge to monitor international information. The system accepts stories about countries where the firm has investments and filters out other international stories.

Still another information management firm, Beyond, Inc., markets software that allows organizations to refine their own information systems. The software automatically prioritizes information according to who is sending it or requesting it. Thus managers know which messages to read first and which to set aside for later reading.

REFERENCES: "Fighting Back Against Data Overload," *Wall Street Journal,* October 20, 1989, p. B1; "Lotus Isn't Wasting Time Weeping at the Altar," *Business Week,* June 4, 1990, pp. 108–110; "Creating New Software Was Agonizing Task for Mitch Kapor Firm," *Wall Street Journal,* May 5, 1990, pp. A1, A14.

Valuable information is accurate, timely, complete, and relevant.

15 bags, tells a little more. Add a report that average daily sales in other stores in the same area have also declined, and the information value increases again and may prompt a manager to take some action.

For information to be of real value to organizations, it should be accurate, timely, complete, and relevant.[5] These criteria are similar to the characteristics of effective control discussed in Chapter 12. They distinguish good or valuable information from bad or less valuable information.

Accuracy   Information must provide a reliable and valid picture of reality. A few years ago, managers at Gulf Oil (now a part of Chevron) were planning a new factory to make plastic garbage bags. The information they gathered suggested that no new technological breakthroughs were expected in the industry. Accordingly, they started construction on a plant that relied on current technology. Less than one year after the plant was completed, however, Union Carbide unveiled a new manufacturing process that cut production costs of the plastic by 20 percent. To remain competitive, Gulf had no choice but to retool its plant at enormous cost and inconvenience.

Timeliness   What constitutes timeliness in information is largely a function of the organization's environment. In the fast-paced world of computer technology, IBM, Compaq, and Apple need virtual daily updates on one another's plans. By contrast, when Marriott was gathering information for its Fairfield Inns project, managers decided that they could spend six months collecting data. Because change in the hotel industry occurs relatively slowly, timeliness was less of an issue. Thus they decided that six months would enable them to get the information they needed while not delaying other phases of the project too much.[6]

Completeness   Information must tell a complete story. If it doesn't, the manager will get a distorted picture of reality. When Coca-Cola made its ill-fated decision a few years ago to change the formula of its famous soft drink, it relied on incomplete information. Market research about the proposed formula had focused solely on taste. Left out of the research was the powerful emotional attachment people had with the Coke image. The New Coke bombed, and the firm had to quickly reintroduce the original formula as Coca-Cola Classic.

Relevance   The relevance of information depends on the needs and circumstances of particular management areas. Operations managers need information on costs and productivity; human resources managers need information on hiring needs and turnover rates; and marketing managers need information on sales projections and advertising rates. One of Frito-Lay's biggest competitors is Borden. Information about new Borden snack foods, including their prices, is very relevant to Frito-Lay. However, Borden sells many other products, ranging from pasta to Elmer's glue. Information about Borden's pasta sales is less relevant to Frito-Lay, and information about sales of Elmer's glue is not relevant at all.

Components of Information Systems

Information systems have five components: *input medium, processor, storage device, output medium*, and *operating system*.

To help manage information, organizations create information systems. As defined earlier, an information system is used to gather data, create information, and disseminate that information to those who need it. Information systems can be either manual or computer based, but they all have five basic components, as Figure 13.2 shows.

The **input medium** is a device used to add data and information to the system. A personal computer uses a keyboard to input data. Scanners in grocery stores like Kroger and Safeway are also input devices. The data entered into the system typically flow first to a processor. The **processor** organizes, manipulates, sorts, or performs calculations with the data. For example, the processor tallies the number of bags of Frito-Lay products sold each day and provides information about total sales. Thus it plays a big role in transforming data into information. Most systems also have one or more **storage devices** where data and information can be kept for later use. Floppy disks, hard disks, magnetic tapes, and optical disks are the most common storage devices. As data are processed into a usable form,

Figure 13.2

Components of Information Systems

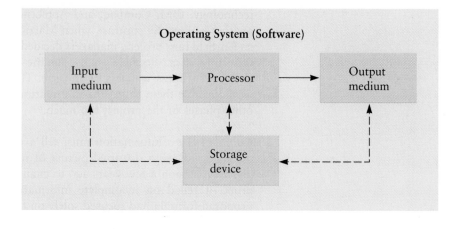

the resultant information is communicated via an **output medium**. Common ways to display output are to display it on video screens, to print it onto paper, and to transfer it other computers.

Input, processing, storage, and output are operated by an overall **operating system**, most often called *software*. Small information systems can use off-the-shelf software such as Microsoft Word, WordPerfect, and WordStar. Lotus 1-2-3 and Microsoft Excel are popular spreadsheet programs, and dBASE III is frequently used for database management. More elaborate information systems used by larger businesses require a special customized operating system, especially when the organization links computers together into a network. For example, Frito-Lay managers can communicate with one another through their information system because their computers are linked together by a common operating system.

As noted earlier, information systems need not be computerized. Some small organizations such as local video rental stores, restaurants, and barber shops can still function with a manual system using paper documents, routing slips, file folders, file cabinets, and typewriters. Increasingly, however, even small businesses are abandoning their manual systems for computerized ones. As hardware prices continue to drop and software becomes more and more powerful (able to handle more information), computerized information systems will likely be available for any type of business.

Types of Information Systems

Many organizations, especially large ones, often find that they need several different kinds of systems in order to manage their information effectively. Their need is due to the wide array of information that is processed in organizations and the variety of information users within organizations. As Figure 13.3 illustrates, the four main types of information systems are transaction-processing systems, management information systems, decision support systems, and executive information systems.[7]

In general, the different types of systems are used at different organizational levels. As shown in Figure 13.3, executive information systems are used by top managers, transaction-processing systems are used by first-line managers and operating employees, and decision support systems and management information systems are used by middle managers. As the arrows suggest, information can sometimes pass between the different systems. For example, the user of a decision support system may be able to access information from a transaction-processing system or provide information to add to an executive information system.

Transaction-processing Systems

A *transaction-processing system (TPS)* handles large numbers of routine and recurring transactions.

A **transaction-processing system,** or **TPS,** is an information system designed to handle routine and recurring transactions. A TPS is most useful for organizations that must process a large number of highly similar transactions, such as customer billing, bank transactions, and point-of-sale records. American Express uses a TPS to record charges to individual credit accounts, to credit payments made on the accounts, and to send monthly bills to customers. Frito-Lay's TPS begins with the data that each delivery salesperson records on a hand-held computer. At every stop on the delivery route, the salesperson inputs sales for each product. This information is stored by the hand-held computer until the end of the day, when it is

Figure 13.3

Types of Information Systems in Organizations

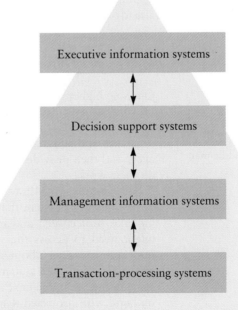

Organizations use many different types of information systems. Transaction-processing systems handle routine and recurring transactions. A common type of transaction-processing system is the laser scanning device now used in many grocery stores. Such systems, which scan bar codes on products, keep track of exactly what is being sold and help retailers reorder efficiently.

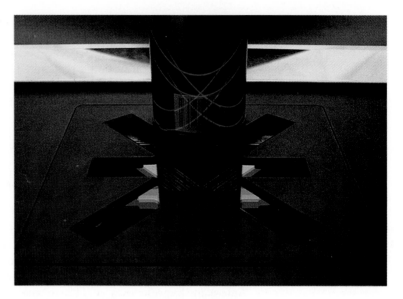

downloaded (transferred) to the organization's mainframe computer. Each day, Frito-Lay records 14 million transactions this way.

A TPS is especially helpful in summarizing large amounts of data into manageable forms of information. A given transaction recorded for any single American Express cardholder will not be useful to a bank loan officer who must decide whether to grant credit to a new customer. More useful is information about each cardholder's average number of purchases, average daily balance, or average monthly finance charge. In general, then, as already noted, a TPS is most useful to first-line managers.

Management Information Systems

A *management information system (MIS)* gathers more comprehensive data and organizes and summarizes it for middle managers.

One step higher in many organizations is a somewhat more complex system called a **management information system**, or **MIS**. An MIS gathers data that are somewhat more comprehensive than data handled by a TPS. It organizes and summarizes data in a form that is of value to middle managers and then provides those managers with the information they need to do their work.

For example, an MIS for a manufacturing firm might include a computerized inventory system that keeps track of both anticipated orders (based on sales projections) and inventory on hand. A marketing representative might need to access the system to check current inventory in order to inform a customer about anticipated delivery dates. Likewise, the plant manager can use the system to determine how much of the firm's product to manufacture in the next week or the next month by comparing inventory on hand with projected demand.

Frito-Lay's district managers, each of whom might be responsible for ten, twenty, or even thirty sales routes, use an MIS to scan and review information from many different sales routes at once. The system groups the information for each route and provides a wide array of sales information for single products or product lines across all retail outlets in the region.

Decision Support Systems

A *decision support system (DSS)* automatically searches for, manipulates, and summarizes information that managers need to make decisions.

A **decision support system**, or **DSS**, is a newer, more elaborate, and more powerful system that automatically searches for, manipulates, and summarizes information that managers need to make decisions. Like an MIS, a DSS is used most often by middle managers. An MIS, however, simply provides information for the manager to use; a DSS is considerably more flexible and can help users cope with nonroutine problems and decisions.[8] Decision support systems take considerable time and resources to develop and maintain, and managers must learn how to use them. But a DSS also holds considerable potential for improving the quality of information available for decision making.

Say, for example, a manager needs to know the likely effects of 5, 7, and 10 percent price increases for a product her firm sells. In the past, she might have relied on intuition and the advice of others in the organization. With a properly designed DSS, however, the system already has a record of the pricing history for the product, the prices charged by competitors and their most recent price changes, the effects of price on sales, seasonal variations in demand and price, inflation rates, and other relevant pieces of information. Once the manager inputs the three alternative price-increase values, the system calculates projected sales, market share, and profit profiles for each of the potential price-increase levels.

Frito-Lay's information system includes a DSS that compiles and stores aggregate sales data and flags potential problems or opportunities for managers. For example, if product sales start to decline within a region, the DSS recognizes this trend earlier than individual managers might be able to detect it and creates a report signaling that a decision may be necessary. Likewise, if sales of a new product exceed expectations, the system will quickly highlight this trend. Frito-Lay spent $40 million on its integrated network of information systems but estimates that the network is now saving the firm $39 million annually. Thus, even though a DSS has high initial costs, those costs may very well be repaid in a short period of time.

Executive Information Systems

An *executive information system (EIS)* summarizes information for review by top managers.

A type of information system that has become popular in the last few years is the **executive information system**, or **EIS**. An EIS is an information system designed for the special information-processing needs of top managers in an organization. Information systems were not initially used by many top managers. For one thing, many top managers lacked even the most basic computer literacy skills. For another, those who did know how to operate a computer faced an array of information so vast that figuring out how to use it took too much time.

A sophisticated EIS solves both of these problems. The system itself is capable of managing large quantities of information but very simple to operate. It also allows top managers to by-pass the large quantities of detailed information that others may need and to focus instead on overall patterns and trends that affect strategic decisions. When a district sales manager at Frito-Lay uses an MIS to scan sales, the first thing he or she sees is a listing of individual product sales at individual outlets. From there, the data can be aggregated and combined for further review. An EIS works in the opposite manner: it dramatically summarizes information for executive review. The executive first sees the aggregate figures and can then work down to more specific levels as circumstances warrant.[9]

Managing Information Systems

Without well-designed information systems, managers would be confronted with a staggering amount of data to sift through in order to make decisions and get things done. Fortunately, the managers of many organizations are now able to rely on information systems to help them do their work effectively and efficiently. But getting to this point is not easy. Organizations must expend considerable effort and resources to develop information systems. Even after a system is installed, the organization must monitor its effectiveness and continue to upgrade and refine it as circumstances warrant. The main considerations in managing an information system are shown in Figure 13.4 and discussed more fully in the sections that follow.

Determining Information System Needs

An organization's information system needs are determined by its environment and size and by functional area and organizational level.

The first step in planning an information system is determining the organization's needs for information processing. The factors that define these needs fall into two categories: the environment and size of the organization and the functional area and organizational level in which the information system will be used.[10]

Environment and Size   In Chapter 4 we noted that the environment affects an organization in many different ways. The relationship between an organization's environment and its information-processing needs is very straightforward: the more uncertain and complex the environment, the greater is the need to manage information systematically. Given that virtually all organizations face at least some degree of uncertainty, it might be argued that all organizations need to manage information. At the very least, organ-

Figure 13.4

Managing Information Systems

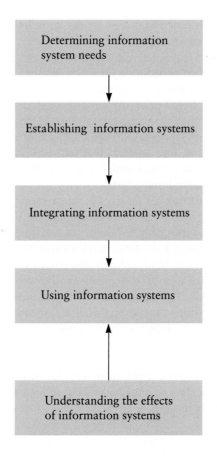

izations such as Hewlett-Packard and IBM, which operate in extremely uncertain environments, have strong needs for structured and comprehensive information management. These organizations must attend to a large quantity of information that changes rapidly.

Also, the larger an organization is, the greater are its needs to manage its information systematically. Thus Citicorp has greater information management needs than does its domestic banking division alone, and each division has greater needs than does a single Citicorp bank. The effects of size may be mitigated by organization design. A large U-form organization, for example, has slightly less pressure for information management than does a multidivisional H-form or M-form organization.

Area and Level   Each functional area has its own set of information management needs. Human resources, for example, needs complete demographic data on all current employees, job grade information, and affirmative action statistics. Marketing needs data on current prices, market share, and advertising expenditures. Finance needs information about accounts receivable and accounts payable. Operations needs information about raw materials and finished-goods inventory levels.

If each functional area works completely on its own, and coordination is handled by the managerial hierarchy, each area can function with its own self-contained information system. However, if different areas are expected to coordinate their activities, their information systems also need to be coordinated. For example, if marketing projects 10 percent more sales next year than previously expected, an integrated information system can use that information to provide the other functional areas with an indication of increased needs. Operations then will project additional output needed; human resources will project additional workers needed; and finance will project additional working capital needed to support higher wage and materials costs.

Organizational level also determines the information management requirements of the organization, because managers at different levels use different types of information and make different types of decisions. Managers at the top of the organization need broad, general information across different time frames to help them with strategic planning. Middle managers need more specific information with a shorter time frame to help them with tactical decisions. First-line managers need highly specific information with a very short time frame to help them with operational decisions. For example, the vice president of marketing at Kellogg Company might need to know projected demand for eight different cereal products over the next five years. A divisional sales manager might need to know projected demand for two of those cereal products for the next one-year period. And a district sales manager might need to know how much of one cereal is likely to be sold next month.

Establishing Information Systems

After determining its information system needs, the organization can focus on actually developing the system. The steps in creating an information system are outlined in Figure 13.5.[11] The first step is to establish goals for what is to be achieved with the proposed system and determine the information needs of the organization. Goals should specify who will have access to the system, what types of information it will contain, and how that information will be managed. The project must have full support and financial commitment from top management in order to be successful. Once the decision has been made to develop and install an information system, a task force is usually constituted to oversee all phases of system development. System users must be well represented on this task force because they will have a better understanding of their own information-processing needs than anyone else.

The next three tasks can be done simultaneously. One task is to assemble a data base. A **data base** is the total set of information that the system contains. Most organizations already possess the information they need for an information system, but it is often not in the correct form. The Pentagon is spending large sums of money to transform paper records into computer records, and many other branches of the government are computerizing

Figure 13.5

Establishing an Information
System

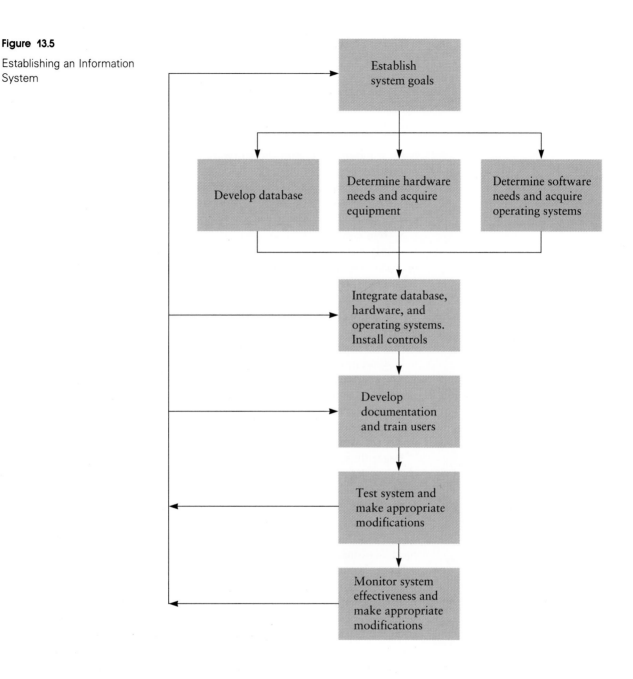

their own data as well.[12] The paper documents have simply become too
numerous to be properly managed.

At the same time, the organization needs to determine its computer
hardware needs and acquire the appropriate equipment. Some systems rely
solely on one large mainframe computer; others are increasingly using
personal computers. Many organizations obtain hardware from such large
manufacturers as IBM, Sun, Compaq, and Digital.

The organization must also define its software needs. Most organizations, for example, select one word-processing package and one spreadsheet package to serve as the company "standard." In addition, the organization needs to choose an operating system (such as DOS or Windows) for its information system. Again, off-the-shelf packages will sometimes work, although most companies find it necessary to customize software.

In the next step, the information system is created by integrating the data base, the hardware, and the software. The equipment is installed. Cables are strung between units. The data are entered into the system. The operating system is installed and tested. During this phase, the organization usually relies on the expertise of outside consulting firms (such as private systems analysts) and the vendors who provide the system components.

System controls are also installed at this point. In this context, a control is simply a characteristic of the information system that limits certain forms of access or use. For example, top managers who want to limit access to certain sensitive data may give selected people private passwords that they must use when entering the system. A large number of people may be able to use the system, but only those with the password can gain access to the sensitive data. It is also important to make sure that data cannot be accidentally erased by someone who happens to press the wrong key.

Following installation, the organization must document how the information system works and train people in how to use it for different purposes. Documentation takes the form of manuals, computerized help programs, diagrams, and instruction sheets. Hands-on training sessions are also commonly held, since they allow users to practice using the system under the watchful eye of experts.

Regardless of how well planned the installation is, there will almost certainly be operating glitches, so the system must be tested and modified if necessary. Typical adjustments include making sure the system will generate all the reports that managers need, in the appropriate formats, and will allow users the required access to data. In most cases, the consultants or internal computer support group that installed the system make these modifications.

Since information management is a continuous process, organizations must monitor its effectiveness. Even after the information system begins normal operation, modifications may still be necessary, since information needs will change over time. For example, after Black & Decker acquired General Electric's small-appliance business, it had to overhaul its own information system to accommodate all the information associated with its new business.

Integrating Information Systems

Because their information needs tend to be complex, very large organizations must integrate all the information systems they use. For example, some information may be needed in all four types of information system. Rather than duplicate it in all four systems, it may be more efficient to

A major challenge faced by many organizations is how to integrate diverse information systems. The Digital Equipment Corporation has invested heavily in recent years in the development of new computer systems and software that help businesses integrate their information systems. This ad, for example, focuses on how Digital's open systems architecture has enabled ICI Pharmaceuticals Group to better manage its information.

store the information in only one system but set the other systems up so that users can obtain data from any system as needed.

Organizations may achieve this integration by linking the information systems of their own separate functional areas so that, for example, marketing and operations are able to communicate with each other. They may also integrate systems with those of other organizations.[13] Wal-Mart, The Limited, and other retailers link up with their suppliers, who can tap directly into the retailer's information system and monitor sales and inventory levels of their products. According to contractual arrangements, the supplier automatically ships more merchandise when inventory drops to a predetermined level.

Unfortunately, linking systems together is no easy task, mainly because functional areas often choose different hardware and software.[14] If operations uses a Digital system and marketing uses an IBM system, differences in technology and operating systems might make later integration difficult or even impossible. There are two ways of addressing this problem. One is to develop all information systems at once, but this is expensive, and managers often can't anticipate exactly what their technology needs will be in the future. The second way is for the organization to adopt a standard technology so that subsequent additions fit it properly. Even then, however, breakthroughs in information system technology may still make it necessary to change approaches in midstream.

Using Information Systems

The real test of an information system's value is in its use. Using an information system should be simple: one should not have to be a computer expert. Ideally, managers should be able to access a modern information system by turning on a computer and pressing certain keys in response to menu prompts. They should be able to enter new data and request access to data already stored in the system's files. The requested information might first be displayed on a computer monitor and then printed out on paper. Managers should be able to easily store the information back in the system for their own use or for use by others.

The Travelers Corporation has made effective use of its information system by hiring trained nurses to review health insurance claims. The nurses use the company's information system to analyze the medical diagnoses provided with each claim. They use this information to determine, for example, whether a second opinion is warranted before a particular surgical procedure is approved. They enter their decision directly into the system. When the claim form is printed out, it contains a provision that spells out whether the claimant must seek a second opinion before proceeding with a particular treatment.[15] The company feels that this practice saves money and improves efficiency.

Understanding the Effects of Information Systems

Information systems in modern organizations affect performance, structure and design, and employee behavior.

Information systems are an integral part of most modern organizations, and their effects are felt in a variety of ways. They affect organizational performance, structure and design, and employee behavior. Despite their broad usefulness, however, information systems are limited in what they can do.

Effects on Performance   Organizations install information systems because they promise to make the organization more effective and efficient. Over the past fifteen years, more than 40 percent of all capital spending by U.S. companies has been on information systems technology — over a trillion dollars.[16] Has the expense been worthwhile? Some experts say yes, but others have their doubts. Information systems speed up an organization's ability to crunch numbers and generate documents, but it is difficult to measure whether this increased speed is always worth the enormous costs involved. Many organizations, ranging from Ford to Wal-Mart to Frito-Lay, claim that their information systems have improved the performance of their managers. There seems to be a growing consensus that information systems do pay for themselves over time, although it may take many years.

Effects on Organizational Structure and Design   These effects generally happen in two ways. First, most organizations find it useful to create a separate unit to handle the information management system. Some even create a new top management position, usually called the chief information officer, or CIO.[17] This manager and her or his staff are responsible for maintaining the information system, upgrading it when appropriate, finding new applications for it, and training people in its use.

Second, information systems allow organizations to eliminate layers in the managerial hierarchy because each manager can stay in touch with large numbers of subordinates. As we noted in Chapter 10, flat organizations tend to make faster decisions and to be more responsive to environmental change than tall organizations. IBM eliminated an entire layer of middle management because of improved efficiencies achieved through its information management system. Some experts have suggested that in the future managers will be able to coordinate the work of as many as two hundred subordinates.[18]

Effects on Behavior   Information systems have both positive and negative effects on the behavior of people in organizations. On the one hand, information systems usually improve individual efficiency. Some people enjoy their work more because they are intrigued with new technology. Social groups can even form across organizational boundaries through the use of computerized bulletin boards and electronic mail.

On the other hand, information systems can lead to isolation as people have everything they need to do their jobs without interacting with others. Managers with personal computers can work at home easily. As a result they may be unavailable to co-workers or removed from key parts of the social system within the organization. Computerized working arrangements also tend to be a bit impersonal. For example, a computer-transmitted "pat on the back" may be less satisfying than a real one. Researchers are just beginning to determine how individual behaviors and attitudes are affected by information systems. One very interesting approach to using information systems to structure meetings is described in The Environmental Challenge.

Limitations of Information Systems   Table 13.1 lists the significant limitations of information systems.[19] As already noted, information systems are expensive and difficult to develop. Organizations that try to cut too many corners or install a system piecemeal may not end up with an effective system. Also, information systems are simply not suitable for some tasks or problems. Complex problems requiring human judgment must still be addressed by humans. This is why information systems are useful tools for managers but can seldom actually replace managers.

Managers may rely too much on information systems, losing touch with the real-world problems they need to be concerned about. Their personal insights and intuition may become numbed by a constant reliance on computers and numbers. In addition, the information the system supplies may not be as accurate, timely, complete, or relevant as it appears. People tend to think that because a computer performed the calculations, the answer must be correct—especially if it is calculated to several decimal places. But if the initial information is flawed, all computations using it are likely to be flawed as well.

Managers may have other unrealistic expectations of information systems. They may believe, for example, that the first stage of implementation will result in a sophisticated and flawless communications network that a

THE ENVIRONMENTAL CHALLENGE

Silent Meetings

Computerized information systems have affected managerial behavior in a variety of ways. Some organizations have recently started exploring a new and unusual use for computerized information systems — the silent meeting.

Most organizational meetings are characterized by a lot of talk and discussion. Although this talk and discussion are important, some people are reluctant to voice their feelings or opinions fully and to speak freely in a group. There is also a lot of digression as conversations wander away from the central topic of the meeting.

To get around these problems, IBM has developed an electronic meeting system. People sit around a conference table, but no one talks. Instead, participants keyboard their ideas or opinions into a personal computer. The information system sorts messages by topic and displays them onto a large monitor at the front of the room for everyone to see. The system even includes icons through which people can express their emotions: one symbol for a smile, one for a frown, one for anger, one for a wink, and so forth.

Greyhound Corporation has found IBM's system to be very effective. In one recent meeting employees expressed their feelings about their boss. As a result, managers learned a great deal about how their subordinates perceived them. One enrolled in an interpersonal skills program, and another agreed to devote more time to planning.

Research has suggested that silent meetings are 55 percent faster than conventional ones. And more people do seem willing to express their opinions. However, since the system makes all communication confidential, no one gets the credit for a good idea. Some people also find the silent method too sterile and argue that such meetings lack the richness of face-to-face interchange.

REFERENCES: "At These Shouting Matches, No One Says a Word," *Business Week*, June 11, 1990, p. 78; "IBM Pulling Out of Big Blue Funk," *USA Today*, October 4, 1990, p. 3B; Marc Beauchamp, "Under the Gun," *Forbes*, June 13, 1988, pp. 90–92.

child could use. When forced to confront the flaws and limits in the system, managers may be disappointed and not use the system as effectively as they otherwise might have done. Finally, it is important to remember that information systems are subject to sabotage, computer viruses, or downtime. Disgruntled employees, for example, have been known to deliberately enter false data.[20] A company that relies too much on a computerized information system may also find itself paralyzed in the event of a simple power outage.

Global Information Systems

Consider the case of a domestic firm that must integrate the flow of information between headquarters in New York, a sales office in St. Louis, and a manufacturing plant in Dallas. Buying the computer hardware from a single supplier is a wise first step. Likewise, the organization can adopt an integrated software system to operate its information system. The system will have to handle only a one-hour difference in time zones and will operate between all three locations in a common language and a common currency.

Table 13.1

Some Limitations of Information Systems

1. Information systems are expensive and difficult to develop and implement.

2. Information systems are not suitable for all tasks or problems.

3. Managers sometimes rely on information systems too much.

4. Information provided to managers may not be as accurate, timely, complete, or relevant as it appears.

5. Managers may have unrealistic expectations of what the information system can do.

6. The information system may be subject to sabotage, computer viruses, or downtime.

Major differences in time zones, language, currency, and available equipment complicate the use of information systems by global organizations.

Now consider the case of a firm trying to integrate information flows between New York, Tokyo, and Munich. Vastly different time zones, currency, and language complicate the task. So, too, does the availability of equipment and software. For example, the Tokyo branch might have to buy NEC computers, the Munich branch Olivetti computers, and the New York branch IBM computers. Linking the various locations is also more complicated. Communication between Dallas and New York can be run through telephone lines, but communication between New York and Munich is most efficient if routed by satellite.

International delivery firms such as Federal Express, brokerage firms such as Merrill Lynch, and airlines such as British Airways have had to invest huge sums of money to link their international operations. In general, such organizations adopt one of two extreme approaches for managing information. One approach is to develop a central information-processing network based on a single mainframe computer. All other organizational units around the world are linked to this mainframe by telephone or satellite hookups. Since the computer can function twenty-four hours a day, time zones become less important. Managers from any spot on the globe can access the system at any time. They can also use the system for electronic mail. Thus, when a manager in New York goes to work in the morning he can immediately review messages that Tokyo colleagues left for him during the night. Federal Express uses this approach, locating its central computer in Memphis.

The alternative approach is to create several decentralized information systems that are tied into an integrated system. For example, an organization might create one system in Tokyo, one in New York, and one in Munich. A central information system at headquarters then serves as a central link. New York managers cannot communicate directly with Tokyo managers through such a system, but each can communicate with the central system in Munich. Interestingly, the Japanese remain at a disadvantage in the important area of information systems. The Global Challenge explains why.

THE GLOBAL CHALLENGE

The Japan Paradox

Japanese firms are among the leaders in most global industries, and Japanese management techniques have been widely imitated. But in one area Japanese firms do not have an advantage — indeed, they have a significant disadvantage: the electronic information systems industry.

The root of the problem is the Japanese language. Because the Japanese "alphabet" is far more complex and has far more characters than most other alphabets, developing keyboards to accommodate it has taken a long time. Also, because most Japanese managers were not exposed to "typing" as part of their education, they are more reluctant to adopt computer-based information systems than are their counterparts in other areas of the world.

To complicate things even more, nuances of the Japanese language require that computers have significantly more memory and processing capability than are needed for other languages. Even computer print-ers have to be more elaborate to reproduce the intricate Japanese language symbols.

Computer manufacturers are forging ahead and achieving breakthroughs that will no doubt enhance information system capabilities in Japan. Apple, for example, is investing heavily in new computer technology for Japanese use. Lotus is translating its English-based software into Japanese in only about six months, as opposed to the three years it took just a few years ago. Ironically, American firms are reaping the benefits of a Japanese weakness, but at the same time they are giving Japanese firms more organizational tools for the future.

REFERENCES: "Japan's Offices Buy Personal Computers in a Race to Catch Up," *Wall Street Journal,* October 31, 1989, pp. A1, A4; "Apple's Point Man in the Fight to Catch Up Overseas," *Business Week,* February 10, 1986, pp. 43–44; Joel Dreyfuss, "IBM's Vexing Slide in Japan," *Fortune,* March 28, 1988, pp. 73–77.

Electronic Communication

Because of the enormous promise of information systems, and despite their occasional limitations, research continues to uncover new and even more sophisticated approaches to managing information. This section highlights some of the most interesting ones.

Telecommunications

New advances in *telecommunications, networks,* and *expert systems* will continue to change the way organizations manage information.

Great strides have been made in **telecommunications**, which is communication that involves video as well as audio transmissions. Several forms of telecommunications have been or are being developed. Videoconferencing allows people in different locations to see and talk to one another by means of computers, telephones, and television monitors. For example, Sam Walton often uses teleconferences to talk directly with the 300,000 Wal-Mart employees all over the nation during their normal Saturday morning meetings.[21] Electronic mail systems allow managers to send messages to one another through computer linkups. Electronic bulletin boards allow people to "post" messages for other interested people to read. Voice messaging allows voice messages to be stored and transferred between computers. These applications save time for managers and improve the accuracy of messages.

Networks and Expert Systems

Networks are interconnected computers or computer systems that can communicate directly with one another. Networks are efficient ways for organizations to link together computers used by different managers. Networking enables them to use more powerful operating systems, to communicate more easily with one another, and to transfer information back and forth between a central storage device. Even computer systems with very different operating systems are becoming increasingly able to link together in networks. Although there are still a variety of "standard" operating systems, as each is more finely developed it can interface with others more effectively.

Expert systems are also beginning to have more practical applications in organizational activities. An **expert system** is an information system created to imitate the thought processes of a human being.[22] There are several reasons why organizations might want to use expert systems. For one thing, such systems can follow the logical thought processes of human beings without falling victim to errors caused by distractions or fatigue. For another, they free up managerial time by taking over complex but programmable decisions. Finally, expert systems can serve as sophisticated tools that managers can use for a wide variety of activities.

The starting point in developing an expert system is to identify all the "if-then" contingencies that pertain to a given organizational activity. These contingencies form the knowledge base for the system. Table 13.2 summarizes the knowledge base for a hypothetical firm's pricing policy. The facts and if-then contingencies outlined in the table help the manager make decisions about the organization's pricing policy.

The statements in boldface represent the current situation facing the company. Thus a manager could query the system with the question "What is price policy?" The system would respond, "Price policy is increase price." The manager could then further query the system and ask why, and the system would answer, "Price policy is increase price because margin is low and demand is strong."

Organizations are developing increasingly complex and useful expert systems. For example, Campbell Soup developed an expert system to re-create the thought processes of one of its key employees, a manager who was very familiar with operations of the seven-story soup kettles used to cook soup. The manager, Aldo Cimino, knew so much about how the kettles worked that the company feared that after he retired no one else could learn the job as well as he. So it hired Texas Instruments to study his job, interview him and observe him at work, and create an expert system that could mimic his experience. The resultant system, containing over 150 if-then rules, still helps operate the kettles.[23]

Table 13.2

Knowledge Base for a Hypothetical Expert System

Factual Knowledge

Price is $50.00.
Cost is $45.00.
Demand is 1,121.
Margin is (price − cost).

Process Knowledge

1. If margin is high and demand is weak, then price-policy is decrease-price.
2. If margin is normal and demand is steady, then price-policy is maintain-price.
3. **If margin is low and demand is strong, then price-policy is increase-price.**
4. If margin is greater-than 25, then margin is high.
5. **If margin is less-than 10, then margin is low.**
6. If margin is-not high and margin is-not low, then margin is normal.
7. **If demand is greater-than 1,100, then demand is strong.**
8. If demand is less-than 900, then demand is weak.
9. If demand is-not strong and demand is-not weak, then demand is steady.

SOURCE: From David B. Paradice and James F. Courtney, Jr., "Intelligent Organizations," *Texas A&M Business Forum*, Fall 1988. Used by permission of the College of Business, Texas A&M University.

Learning Summary

Managing information is a vital organizational function because of information's role in communication, in decision making, and in the relationship between the organization and its environment. An information system is an operational set of procedures that an organization uses to gather data, create information, and then disseminate that information to those who need it.

Data are isolated figures and facts without an associated context. Information is data presented in a context that gives it meaning. Information and data are related, but information enhances the meaning of data. For information to be useful, it must be accurate, timely, complete, and relevant.

All information systems, whether manual or computerized, contain five components: input medium, processor, storage device, operating system, and output medium. There are four types of information systems: transaction-processing systems, management information systems, decision support systems, and executive information systems. Transaction-processing systems are generally found at the lowest levels of an organization. Executive information systems are used at the highest levels. The other two types of information systems are used most often by middle managers.

An organization's information system needs are determined by its environment and size, and by functional area and organizational level. The steps in establishing an information system are establishing goals, selecting a task force to oversee the project, developing a data base, acquiring hardware and an operating system, integrating and installing the system, and establishing system controls. Information systems affect organizational performance, structure and design, and employee behavior.

Establishing an information system for a global organization poses additional challenges because of distances, time zones, and language. Recent advances in information systems include breakthroughs in telecommunications, networks, and expert systems.

Questions and Exercises

Review Questions

1. What is an information system?
2. How do data and information differ?
3. Identify the characteristics of information that make it useful.
4. Identify the five components of an information system.
5. Define and give an example of each of the four main types of information systems.
6. List the steps that organizations follow when developing information systems.
7. What recent advances have been made in electronic communication?

Analysis Questions

1. Explain the ways in which information management is a complementary activity to organizational control.
2. List examples of different types of information you use that vary in terms of accuracy, timeliness, completeness, and relevance.
3. The text describes in detail a computerized information system (pages 419–420). Describe the components of a similar system from start to finish that does not rely on a computer.
4. Select an organization that you know something about (e.g., a fast-food restaurant or a clothing store), and describe how the organization might use each type of information system discussed in the chapter.
5. What are the information management needs of your college or university?
6. How have recent advances in electronic communication affected managerial work?

Application Exercises

1. Develop a hypothetical information system that your instructor could use to manage his or her classroom information.

2. Assume you have been hired by a small clothing firm as an information consultant. Describe how you would go about determining the firm's information management needs. Then describe how you would go about establishing an information system for the organization.

Chapter Notes

1. Patricia Sellers, "Pepsi Keeps on Going After No. 1," *Fortune,* March 11, 1991, pp. 62–70; "How Software Is Making Food Sales a Piece of Cake," *Business Week,* July 2, 1990, pp. 54–55; "Scanner Data System Helps Frito-Lay Stay on Top" (a Knight-Ridder News Service story), *Bryan–College Station Eagle,* September 9, 1990, p. 2C; "Frito-Lay's Cooking Again, and Profits Are Starting to Pop," *Business Week,* May 22, 1989, pp. 66–70.
2. See George Huber, "A Theory of the Effects of Advanced Information Technologies on Organizational Design, Intelligence, and Decision Making," *Academy of Management Review,* January 1990, pp. 47–71. See also Carol Saunders and Jack William Jones, "Temporal Sequences in Information Acquisition for Decision Making: A Focus on Source and Medium," *Academy of Management Review,* January 1990, pp. 29–46.
3. Robert G. Lord and Karen J. Maher, "Alternative Information-processing Models and Their Implications for Theory, Research, and Practice," *Academy of Management Review,* January 1990, pp. 9–28.
4. Lynda M. Applegate, James I. Cash, Jr., and D. Quinn Mills, "Information Technology and Tomorrow's Manager," *Harvard Business Review,* November–December 1988, pp. 128–136.
5. Charles A. O'Reilly, "Variations in Decision Makers' Use of Information Sources: The Impact of Quality and Accessibility of Information," *Academy of Management Journal,* December 1982, pp. 756–771.
6. Brian Dumaine, "Corporate Spies Snoop to Conquer," *Fortune,* November 7, 1988, pp. 68–76.
7. V. Thomas Dock and James C. Wetherbe, *Computer Information Systems for Business* (St. Paul, Minn.: West, 1988).
8. Applegate, Cash, and Mills, "Information Technology and Tomorrow's Manager."
9. Jeremy Main, "At Last, Software CEOs Can Use," *Fortune,* March 13, 1989, pp. 77–83.
10. See Jesse B. Tutor, Jr., "Management and Future Technological Trends," *Texas A&M Business Forum,* Fall 1988, pp. 2–5.
11. See George W. Reynolds, *Information Systems for Managers* (St. Paul, Minn.: West, 1988), for a detailed description of developing information systems.
12. "Computerizing Uncle Sam's Data: Oh, How the Public Is Paying," *Business Week,* December 15, 1986, pp. 102–103.
13. Cornelius H. Sullivan, Jr., and John R. Smart, "Planning for Information Networks," *Sloan Management Review,* Winter 1987, pp. 39–44.
14. "Linking All the Company Data: We're Not There Yet," *Business Week,* May 11, 1987, p. 151.
15. "Office Automation: Making It Pay Off," *Business Week,* October 12, 1987, pp. 134–146.
16. Ibid.

17. John J. Donovan, "Beyond Chief Information Officer to Network Managers," *Harvard Business Review,* September–October 1988, pp. 134–140.

18. Jeremy Main, "The Winning Organization," *Fortune,* September 26, 1988, pp. 50–60.

19. See Reynolds, *Information Systems for Managers.*

20. "Computer Headaches," *Newsweek,* July 6, 1987, pp. 34–35.

21. John Huey, "Wal-Mart — Will It Take over the World?" *Fortune,* January 30, 1989, pp. 52–61.

22. Dorothy Leonard-Barton and John J. Sviokla, "Putting Expert Systems to Work," *Harvard Business Review,* March–April 1988, pp. 91–98.

23. "Turning an Expert's Skills into Computer Software," *Business Week,* October 7, 1985, pp. 104–108.

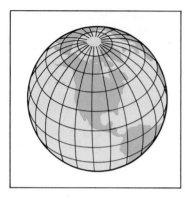

CASE 13.1

Information Systems, IBM Style

IBM is no longer the unassailable leader in information technology. Although its revenues are still almost five times those of runner-up Digital Equipment Corporation, the 1980s was not a good decade for Big Blue. Smaller companies consistently beat IBM to the market with products that were generally cheaper than IBM's and often just as good. But after a major restructuring in the late 1980s, IBM entered the 1990s confident that its products still offered customers the best way to improve their information transfer and therefore their business.

IBM is often one of the best customers for its own information systems. For instance, the company is hooked on its own professional office system — PROFS. The system allows 350,000 IBM employees in 130 countries to send and receive electronic notes, plan projects, schedule meetings, and gather information about the company. IBM's American employees actually use PROFS more often than they use their telephones. By improving communication among IBM employees around the world, PROFS has made IBM's far-flung divisions easier to manager and more efficient. IBM estimates that PROFS has increased the productivity of its employees by almost 12 percent and has returned about 42 percent on its investment over five years.

The benefits of IBM's favorite information technology extend well beyond the limits of the company itself. PROFS has played a major role in communication between nations. For instance, in the late 1980s, IBM and the U.S. government were negotiating with the government of South Korea about extending copyright protection to computer software, an important step for any computer company wanting to do business in Korea. Because the negotiating was going on in Korean, the South Korean negotiators expected that IBM would need weeks to translate and get legal opinions on each of their amendments to the proposal. Instead, IBM surprised everyone by getting responses to the amendments to the negotiating table the next day. It translated the documents into English in its Seoul headquarters, then sent them around the globe via PROFS to legal experts who used PROFS to relay their opinions back to Korea.

Of course, PROFS is only one of many current information technologies that IBM offers. The company's "interenterprise connection" allows vendors and suppliers to communicate instantaneously with IBM, placing and taking orders when needed, making "just-in-time" manufacturing possible and eliminating the need for large inventories of parts and products. In addition, customers can use IBM's Information Network to get technical information or check on order status or billing.

A particularly customer-pleasing aspect of IBM's information technology is its computers' ability to call for help before a problem affects the computer's function. IBM's largest mainframes come with a device that activates when it detects a malfunction. The device identifies the problem, sends information to another IBM location, and notifies a service representative.

Without the device, the customer may be unaware of a problem that could cripple the computer.

This self-fixing computer is an example of IBM's new focus on customer needs. IBM readily admits that during much of the last decade it was concerned more with its own needs than with those of its customers. Thus it was slow to respond to customer demands for personal computers, laptops, and PC networks, preferring instead to concentrate on its highly profitable mainframe lines. Eventually, however, IBM saw that it was getting so out of touch with customers that both its stock price and its once-impeccable reputation were falling.

So now IBM is taking in information from customers as well as providing customers with the technology to manipulate information. It has heard the message that customers are tired of dealing with proprietary systems — hardware and software that are incompatible with other companies' products. People want "open systems" — networks of different kinds of computers that share software. So IBM has been working with a number of software vendors (another new step) to develop products for its Office-Vision integrated office automation line, which allows IBM computers to communicate with each other.

IBM's reorganization has also improved Big Blue's responsiveness to customers and brought about advances in information technology. Under the old system, different IBM units worked on similar products without communicating with each other. Thus some technology got delayed because one IBM branch was assuming, incorrectly, that another branch was solving a particular problem. Now all product development for IBM communications systems is grouped under one general manager, Ellen Hancock, who says proudly, "If there's something in telecommunications and we're not doing it, it's probably not being done."* IBM may never be able to regain its pre-eminence in the field of information technology, but at least it has proven that it can listen, as well as help others communicate.

Discussion Questions

1. Why do you think IBM's American employees use PROFS more than they use their phones?
2. Why might a huge company like IBM have trouble keeping up with customers' needs and the latest trends in information technology?
3. Why should a computer company produce computers that can "talk" with other computers?
4. With access to a system like PROFS, why would anyone write a formal memo or make a phone call?

* Quoted in Joel Dreyfuss, "Reinventing IBM," *Fortune*, August 14, 1989, p. 34.

REFERENCES: Joel Dreyfuss, "Reinventing IBM," *Fortune*, August 14, 1989, pp. 30–39; "International Business Machines Corp.," *Datamation*, June 15, 1990, p. 53; Terence R. Lautenbach, "MIS at IBM: Improving the Business Through Better Communications," *The Academy of Management Executive*, May 1989, pp. 26–28.

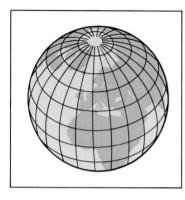

CASE 13.2

UPS Takes On the World

American children who mistake the brown-uniformed United Parcel Service driver for the "mailman" have good reason to be confused. The company's 62,000 drivers seem as ubiquitous as mail carriers: they make daily stops at over 1.1 million American accounts and occasional deliveries to millions more. But UPS is no longer content to be the most profitable and respected package delivery company in the United States. It has set its sights on the world, and its success at expanding around the globe will depend in large part on information systems, both traditional and new.

Until recently, UPS was known as an old, conservative company that changed with all the speed and abruptness of a glacier. Founded in 1907, UPS has always operated "by the watch," changing only when its engineers found new ways to make the delivery process more efficient, like beveling the fronts of the drivers' seats so drivers can slide out of trucks quickly.

But in the early 1980s, UPS's rate of change began to increase as Big Brown realized that Federal Express's overnight delivery posed a significant threat. UPS made a belated entry into overnight delivery in 1982, and although it still trails Federal Express in that area, it has established a healthy edge over all other competitors. Now, with the growth of overnight delivery slowing, both Federal Express and UPS are looking to overseas package delivery as the next big growth area.

The superiority of Federal's information systems has been a major factor in Federal Express's ability to retain its lead in overnight service. For years, Federal packages have carried bar codes that can be read by drivers' hand-held scanners and thus enable Federal to know where a package is at any given time. UPS, meanwhile, was content with its traditional manual tracking system. Now, both to catch up to Federal and to expand overseas, UPS is turning to technology that it hopes will top Federal's.

UPS's $1.4 billion computerization budget has produced a "dense code," a variation of the bar code. In an area less than an inch square, the fingerprint-like swirls of dense code hold twice as much information as a normal bar code. Thus a scanner on a conveyor or in a delivery truck can read a package's origin, destination, contents, and price without anyone having to contact headquarters. The dense codes and scanners should improve the flow of packages, especially at the company's central hubs, and they will give UPS the ability to tell a customer where a particular package is at any time.

UPS is also testing a computer that can read address labels. And a small subsidiary in Los Angeles, a messenger service, recently experimented with an entire electronic tracking system. Tracking devices allow headquarters to know where all the company's vehicles are at any time and to send messages to a particular vehicle. Drivers can get directions electronically and carry a computerized clipboard to record transactions electronically. If UPS can successfully transfer this system to its huge fleet, UPS drivers may one day present package recipients with the traditional "sign at the

X" clipboard, then at the end of the day plug the clipboard into a central computer and send all the transaction information, including a copy of each customer's signature, to headquarters.

UPS is able to take such strides in information technology in part because of its history of conservative financing. When it wanted to enlarge its air fleet in 1987, it paid cash for 110 planes worth $1.8 billion, instantly becoming the tenth largest American airline. It took a decade for UPS's first foreign venture, in West Germany, to become fully functional and profitable, but when UPS decided to move into Europe in a big way in the late 1980s, it purchased its Italian partner outright and bought nine other small courier airlines. In 1985 UPS had major operations in the United States and Canada and only a toehold in Europe; now it boasts operations in 180 countries.

Most of UPS's foreign operations are not yet profitable, however, as UPS faces a hurdle that creates problems for all countries that set up operations overseas: culture shock. The slow, steady growth of the company has always been fed by promotions from inside. Everyone who rose into managerial positions had long ago accepted the company's unusual policies, such as its prohibitions against beards and coffee at work desks. Now, however, the company is trying to absorb employees from different corporate and national cultures. Teaching these new employees how to become successful members of the Big Brown team will no doubt take a lot of low-tech information transfer. But the success of UPS may very well depend on it.

Discussion Questions

1. Why are innovations in information technology especially important for a company trying to expand around the globe?
2. Would a company's high-tech information system help the company communicate its corporate culture to outsiders? Why or why not?
3. What advances in electronic communication might help UPS gain some business from other overnight package deliverers?
4. Would UPS be better off establishing a centralized information system in the United States or a number of regional centers around the world?

REFERENCES: Resa W. King, "UPS Isn't About to Be Left Holding the Parcel," *Business Week*, February 13, 1989, p. 69; Kenneth Labich, "Big Changes at Big Brown," *Fortune*, January 18, 1988, pp. 56–64; Daniel Pearl, "UPS Takes on Air-Express Competition," *Wall Street Journal*, December 20, 1990, p. A4; Todd Vogel, "Can UPS Deliver the Goods in a New World?" *Business Week*, June 4, 1990, pp. 80–82.

14

Human Resources in Organizations

LEARNING OBJECTIVES

After studying this chapter, you should be able to:

1. Explain the strategic and legal importance of human resources management.

2. Discuss how organizations forecast their need for human resources and how they match labor supply and demand.

3. Describe the process of recruiting and selecting human resources.

4. Discuss the steps in training and development, and identify some training methods that organizations use.

5. Discuss the common methods that organizations use to appraise employee performance.

6. Describe the role of compensation and benefits in organizational reward systems.

7. Explain how employees form unions, and identify the issues typically addressed in collective bargaining.

F ederal law stipulates that organizations cannot discriminate on the basis of race or sex when they hire new employees or promote current employees to new positions. Like many other firms, Ortho Pharmaceutical Corporation assumed that it was in full compliance with this legislation. Thus Ortho executives were quite surprised to learn recently that most of their black and female employees were working at jobs for which they were overqualified.

The discovery came when a new human resources executive commissioned an external audit of Ortho's human resource practices. The firm had not discriminated against either group in hiring; it had nevertheless failed to provide them with the same promotion opportunities as their white male colleagues. Managers immediately set out to correct the problem.

Closer study determined that the discrimination was not intentional but instead resulted from the fact that the organization was using inappropriate evaluation standards. But intentional or not, discrimination is illegal. Ortho was not treating its employees fairly and was also leaving itself open to possible lawsuits and fines.

To get things back on track, Ortho created a Diversity Advisory Committee. The purpose of the committee was to help the organization learn more about how to manage a diverse work force comprising both sexes and multiple ethnic groups. In addition, all Ortho executives underwent training to help them avoid unintentional discrimination in the future. Mindful of the legal and moral issues involved, Ortho executives equate this human resources error to buying an expensive piece of equipment and then using it to only 80 percent of its capabilities. Today Ortho has changed all of its promotion practices in order to give everyone an equal opportunity for advancement and to use all of its human resources effectively.[1]

Ortho Pharmaceutical Corporation learned a valuable human resources lesson — before a lawsuit forced it to. Managing human resources well is a crucial factor in organizational effectiveness. Financial, physical, and information resources are obviously important. But human resources, because of their potential for contributing to the organization, and because of legal requirements and changing societal norms, are of special concern.

Human resources management (HRM) is the set of organizational activities directed at attracting, developing, and maintaining an effective work force.

This chapter covers **human resources management,** or **HRM,** the set of organizational activities directed at attracting, developing, and maintaining an effective work force. We begin by looking at human resources management from strategic and legal points of view. We then focus on the five-

Figure 14.1

The Sequence of Human
Resources Management

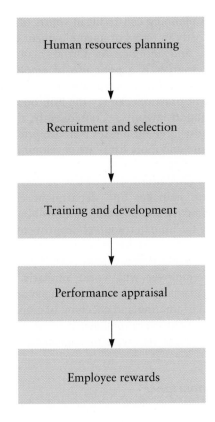

part sequence of ongoing HRM illustrated in Figure 14.1: human resources planning, recruitment and selection, training and development, performance appraisal, and employee rewards. We conclude with a discussion of labor relations.

The Importance of Human Resources Management

Human resources management is important for both strategic and legal reasons.

Human resources management (or personnel, as it is sometimes called) was once relegated to second-class status in many organizations. Recognition of its importance has grown dramatically in the last three decades, however, as a result of legal complexities, the value of human resources as a means for increasing productivity, and the costs associated with poor management of human resources.[2] Human resources management has both strategic and legal importance.

Strategic Importance

Organizations today acknowledge that the effectiveness of human resources management substantially affects bottom-line performance. Poor human resources planning can result in spurts of hiring followed by layoffs. That cycle is costly in terms of unemployment compensation payments, training expenses, and morale. As Ortho managers discovered, underutilizing human resources is a poor use of employees. Haphazard compensation systems do not attract, keep, and motivate good employees, and outmoded recruitment practices can lay the firm open to expensive and embarrassing discrimination lawsuits.[3] Consequently, the chief human resources executive of most large businesses is a vice president directly accountable to the CEO. More and more firms are developing strategic human resources plans and integrating them with other strategic planning activities.[4]

Even organizations with as few as two hundred employees usually have a separate manager and department charged with overseeing human resources activities. However, responsibility for these activities is invariably shared by the human resources department and line managers. For instance, the human resources department may recruit and initially screen candidates, but the final selection is usually made by managers in the department where the new employee will work. Similarly, although the human resources department may establish performance appraisal policies and procedures, the actual evaluating and coaching of employees is done by their immediate superiors. Thus every manager is involved in and needs to understand the basics of human resources management.

Legal Importance

Federal laws govern equal employment opportunity, compensation and benefits, labor relations, and employee health and safety.

Federal laws in the United States regulate several different aspects of employee-employer relations, most notably equal employment opportunity, compensation and benefits, labor relations, and employee health and safety. The major laws are listed in Table 14.1.

Equal Employment Opportunity   Several laws forbid unfair discrimination by employers, but the most important is **Title VII of the Civil Rights Act of 1964.** Title VII forbids discrimination on the basis of sex, race, color, religion, or national origin in all areas of the employment relationship, including hiring, layoff, discharge, discipline, compensation, access to training, and promotion. The intent of Title VII is to ensure that employment decisions are based on an individual's qualifications for a particular job, rather than on the personal biases of the individual making decisions about hiring or promotions.

This legislation has also curbed less overt forms of discrimination. For instance, the use of employment tests that white job candidates pass at a higher rate than black candidates is forbidden unless the employer can document that the test is a valid predictor of job performance. Many height and weight standards for police officers and firefighters have also been eliminated because they excluded a disproportionate number of female, Hispanic, and Asian applicants and could seldom be proved necessary for success on the job. Such requirements are said to have an *adverse impact* on minorities and women when such individuals pass the selection standard at a rate less than 80 percent of the pass rate for others. Tests or other standards that have an adverse impact on protected groups can be used only when there is solid evidence that they effectively identify individuals who are better able than others to do the job.[5] The Equal Employment Opportunity Commission is charged with ensuring that Title VII is enforced.[6]

The **Age Discrimination in Employment Act**, passed in 1967 and amended in 1978, outlaws discrimination against people between the ages of 40 through 69. Individuals cannot be forced to retire before age 70 except for documented health- or performance-related reasons. People under the age of 40 who are discriminated against because they are too young have no protection under this federal law (some states, however, have broader age discrimination acts that may provide relief).

Both the Age Discrimination Act and Title VII require passive nondiscrimination, or equal employment opportunity. These laws do not require employers to seek out and hire large numbers of older employees or minority group members, but they must treat fairly all who apply. However, a series of executive orders requires employers holding government contracts to engage in **affirmative action**, which is the practice of intentionally seeking qualified or qualifiable employees from racial, sexual, and ethnic groups that are underutilized or underrepresented in the organization.

Ideally, an employer's work force should reflect the racial, sexual, and ethnic makeup of the relevant labor market. Employers with federal contracts worth over $100,000 per year must have a written affirmative action plan that spells out employment goals for each underutilized group and the company's plans for meeting these goals. The plans might include recruiting

Affirmative action is the practice of intentionally seeking qualified or qualifiable employees from racial, sexual, and ethnic groups that are underutilized or underrepresented in the organization.

Table 14.1

Important Human Resources Legislation

Equal Employment Opportunity

Title VII of the Civil Rights Act of 1964
Age Discrimination in Employment Act
Executive orders requiring affirmative action

Compensation and Benefits

Fair Labor Standards Act
Equal Pay Act
Employee Retirement Income Security Act (ERISA)

Labor Relations

National Labor Relations Act (Wagner Act)
Labor-Management Relations Act (Taft-Hartley Act)

Health and Safety

Occupational Safety and Health Act (OSHA)

at largely minority schools or making special efforts to attract women into apprenticeship programs.[7] Employers with government contracts are also required to act affirmatively in hiring Vietnam-era veterans and qualified handicapped individuals.

Compensation and Benefits   A number of important state and federal laws also regulate the payment of wages and the provision of benefits to employees. The wage law with the widest impact is the **Fair Labor Standards Act**, passed in 1938 and amended frequently since then. Among many other provisions, this law sets the "minimum wage" and requires the payment of overtime rates for work in excess of forty hours per week. Not all employees are covered. Salaried professional, executive, and administrative employees are "exempt" from the minimum hourly wage and overtime provisions.

Another important law is the **Equal Pay Act** of 1963, requiring that men and women be paid the same amount for doing the same jobs (assuming the jobs demand equal skill, effort, and responsibility and are performed under the same working conditions). Attempts to circumvent the law by assigning different job titles and pay rates to men and women who perform essentially the same work (she is the "head secretary," he the "office manager") are also illegal. However, it is both legal and reasonable to base an individual's pay on seniority, performance, or qualifications, even if this results in a particular man and woman being paid different amounts for doing the same job. The Equal Pay Act overlaps with Title VII in that both cover pay discrimination on the basis of sex.

The provision of benefits is also regulated in some ways by state and federal law. Certain benefits are mandatory — unemployment compensation for employees who are laid off and workers' compensation insurance for employees who are injured on the job, for example. Employers who provide a pension plan for their employees are subject to the **Employee Retirement Income Security Act** of 1974 (ERISA). This law sets standards for pension plans and provides federal insurance if pension funds go bankrupt. The primary goals of ERISA are to ensure that employees receive the pension benefits due them when they retire and that they do not lose accrued benefits if they change employers.

Labor Relations   Union activities and management behavior toward unions constitute another heavily regulated area. Before the 1930s, federal laws generally inhibited unionization, and unions were often prosecuted as "conspiracies in restraint of trade." However, during the New Deal era, new laws affirmed the right of unions to exist and the obligation of management to bargain collectively with them. The **National Labor Relations Act** (Wagner Act), passed in 1935, set up a procedure for employees of a firm to decide by vote whether to have a union. If they vote for a union, management is required to bargain collectively with the union. The Wagner Act lists certain "unfair labor practices": firing or otherwise punishing employees known to be pro-union, threatening or bribing employees to vote against the union, attempting to control the union, and sending spies to union meetings. The National Labor Relations Board was established by the Wagner Act to enforce its provisions.

Following a series of severe strikes in 1946, the **Labor-Management Relations Act** (Taft-Hartley Act) was passed in 1947 to limit union power. First, the law lists unfair labor practices by unions, such as refusing to bargain in good faith, harassing both union members and nonmembers, and charging excessive dues and fees. Second, it gives management more rights to speak out against the union during an organizing campaign, though management must still be careful not to threaten employees. Finally, the Taft-Hartley Act contains the national emergency strike provision. This allows the president of the United States to obtain a court injunction to prevent or end a strike that endangers the national health and safety. The injunction has a duration of up to eighty days — in hopes that the strike can be settled during this cooling-off period. During the Reagan administration this provision was invoked during a railroad strike. A new labor agreement was reached during the cooling-off period, and a strike was averted.

Health and Safety   The **Occupational Safety and Health Act** of 1970 (**OSHA**) directly mandates the provision of safe working conditions. OSHA is undoubtedly the most influential occupational safety law. It requires employers to provide a place of employment free from recognized hazards that may cause death or serious physical harm and to obey the safety and health standards established by the Occupational Safety and Health Administration. Safety standards are intended to prevent accidents (such as being injured by a moving piece of machinery), and occupational health standards are concerned with preventing occupational disease (due to long-term exposure to hazards such as excessive noise, carcinogenic chemicals, and other contaminants.)[8] Some standards, for example, limit the concentration of cotton dust in the air, because this contaminant has been associated with lung disease in textile workers. Standards are enforced by OSHA inspections, which are conducted when an employee files a complaint of unsafe conditions or when a serious accident occurs. Spot inspections of plants in especially hazardous industries are also made. Employers who fail to meet OSHA standards may be fined.[9]

Emerging Legal Issues   Several other areas of legal concern have emerged during the past few years. One is sexual harassment on the job. Technically, sexual harassment is covered under Title VII, but it has received additional attention in the courts as more victims decide to confront their harassers publicly. In addition, recent court rulings have tended to define alcoholics and drug addicts as handicapped, protecting their right to a job under the same laws that protect the rights of other handicapped people. AIDS victims also are most often protected under these laws.

Organizations with international operations must also contend with an even more complex network of legal issues. Most countries, for example, have their own laws and regulations that govern employment practices. An organization with operations in six countries must therefore understand

Human resources planning is an important activity for all organizations. Skip Marsden, shown here on the ladder, manages the largest maintenance business in Minneapolis. He knows that if he employs too many workers, he will incur excessive labor costs and cut his profits. If he has too few workers on hand, however, he will not be able to keep his customers satisfied. Marsden also planned well in choosing the site of his business: the pool of workers in Minneapolis/St. Paul is well-educated (the area has the best high school graduation rate in the United States) and has a strong work ethic.

and follow six different sets of legal constraints. For this reason, most global organizations decentralize their human resources practices so that local human resources experts can be hired to follow domestic laws and practices.

Human Resources Planning

Human resources planning consists of forecasting future needs for employees in different jobs, forecasting the availability of such employees, and taking steps to match supply and demand.

Human resources planning consists of forecasting future needs for employees in different jobs, forecasting the availability of such employees, and then taking steps to match supply and demand. Figure 14.2 shows this process. Short-range planning (one to two years) to guide immediate recruiting needs is most common, but mid- and long-range planning (up to ten years) can also be helpful, especially for managerial jobs. More and more organizations are increasing their human resources planning activities. Systematic planning of this type results in improved efficiency and effectiveness throughout the organization.[10] Before any forecasting takes place, however, the organization must analyze the types of jobs it needs to fill.

Job Analysis

Job analysis is a procedure for collecting and recording information about jobs.

Job analysis is a procedure for collecting and recording information about jobs. A job analysis is usually made up of two parts. The job description lists the duties of a job, its working conditions, and the tools, materials, and equipment used to perform it. The job specification lists the skills (such as typing), abilities (such as manual dexterity), and other credentials (a college degree or chauffeur's license) needed to do the job. There are many methods of collecting and presenting job analysis data, from simple home-made forms to standardized and computer-scored questionnaires.[11]

Job analysis information is used in many human resources activities. For instance, it is necessary to know about job content and job requirements to develop appropriate selection methods and job-relevant performance appraisal systems and to set equitable compensation rates across jobs. Job analysis information is also used in the development of training programs.[12]

Forecasting the Supply of and Demand for Human Resources

Organizations need a great deal of information to accurately forecast future demand for employees.[13] They need to consider past use of human resources, future organizational plans, and general economic trends. A sales forecast is often a good beginning, especially for small organizations. Historical ratios (for example, sales volume per employee) can then be used to predict demand for staff workers and sales representatives. Large organizations use more complicated models to predict their future need for

Figure 14.2

Human Resources Planning

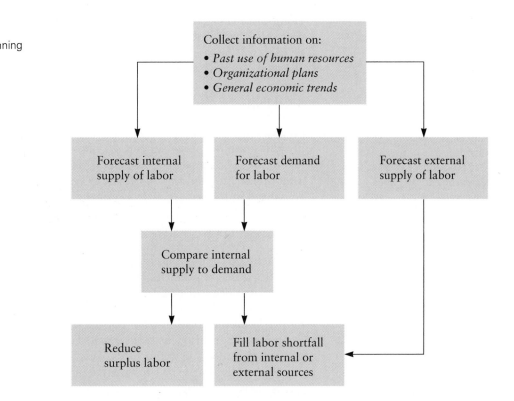

human resources. However, most models rely on basic assumptions about the future. Forecasting the supply of labor is actually two tasks: forecasting the internal supply (the number and type of employees who will be in the firm at some future date) and forecasting the external supply (the number and type of people who will be available for hiring in the labor market at large).

Forecasting Internal Supply of Labor   The simplest approach to forecasting the internal supply of labor merely adjusts present staffing levels for anticipated turnover and promotions. More sophisticated models apply this simple forecasting procedure simultaneously to all jobs in the organization and can predict staffing conditions more than one year in advance. General Foods, for example, has a complex forecasting system that monitors both present and future professional and managerial positions. The system can spot areas in the organization where too many qualified professionals will eventually be competing for too few promotions or, conversely, where too few qualified people will be available to fill important positions.

Forecasting models predict demand and supply of human resources in the aggregate. For example, if Federal Express forecasts a need for one hundred new drivers next year, knowing exactly who these people are is of no real concern today. However, at higher managerial levels, organizations need to plan more specifically for certain people and positions. This planning most commonly employs a **replacement chart**, which lists each important managerial position, who occupies it, how long he or she will probably stay in it before moving on, and who (by name) is now qualified or soon will be qualified to move into the position. This type of planning allows the organization ample time to include appropriate training experiences for individuals identified as potential successors to pivotal managerial jobs.

Both to facilitate planning and to identify employees for transfer or promotion, some organizations also use an **employee information system**, or **skills inventory**. Such systems are often computerized and contain information on each employee's education, skills, work experience, and career aspirations. An employee information system could quickly locate all the employees in a large organization qualified to fill a position requiring, for instance, a degree in chemical engineering, three years of experience in an oil refinery, and fluency in Spanish.

Forecasting External Supply of Labor   Forecasting the external supply of labor is a different problem. How can an organization predict, for example, how many chemical engineers will be seeking work in Minnesota three years from now? To get an idea of the future availability of labor, planners must rely on information from outside sources, such as state employment commissions, government reports, and figures supplied by colleges on the number of students in major fields. Organizations with international operations generally focus their forecasting on each area where they have operations. It is sometimes necessary to move new employees in if there is a local shortage of qualified employees.

Useful tools for forecasting the internal supply of labor include the *replacement chart* and the *employee information system,* or *skills inventory.*

THE GLOBAL CHALLENGE

Japan Grapples with Labor Shortage

Japanese organizations are enjoying tremendous success in the world economy, but they confront a gnawing problem at home: a labor shortage. Several factors have combined to create this shortage. For one thing, growth in the Japanese economy has created large numbers of new jobs. But because the Japanese birthrate started dropping significantly in the mid-1960s, fewer new workers are entering the labor market. To make things worse for Japanese employers, many workers are beginning to take more time off for vacations, sabbaticals, and leaves of absence in order to enjoy their prosperity.

Competition for workers has become fierce in Japan. In 1990 almost one hundred firms went out of business simply because they could not find qualified employees. Bigger companies are going to extraordi-

nary lengths to recruit college graduates. For example, most Japanese students receive recruiting videotapes from the country's largest employers during their senior year in school.

Some organizations look for ways around the labor shortage by investing more heavily in automation. Others are hiring more women and placing them in jobs traditionally held only by men. Older workers are being lured out of retirement. One American firm in Japan, Kentucky Fried Chicken, has even started offering new employees a free trip to Hawaii after they have worked six months.

REFERENCES: "Hang Up the Help-Wanted Sign," *Newsweek*, July 16, 1990, p. 39; "Help Wanted," *Business Week*, August 10, 1987, pp. 48–53; "A Japanese Import That's Not Selling," *Business Week*, February 26, 1990, pp. 86–87.

Matching the Supply of and Demand for Human Resources

After forecasting the internal supply of and demand for human resources, organizations plan ways to resolve predicted staff shortfalls or overstaffing. If a shortfall is expected, the organization can hire new employees, retrain and transfer current employees into the understaffed area, tempt individuals approaching retirement to stay on by offering additional benefits, or install labor-saving or productivity-enhancing systems. Forecasts of the external supply of labor help determine how extensively to recruit new employees, depending on whether the individuals needed are readily available or scarce in the labor market.

If overstaffing is expected, the organization has the options of transferring the extra employees, not replacing individuals who quit, encouraging early retirement, and laying people off.[14] Many organizations like Apple and Tektronix hire temporary workers during peak production times to help balance demand and supply.[15] The Global Challenge explains some of the hurdles that Japanese employers face because of a labor shortage in Japan.

Recruitment and Selection

Recruiting is the process of attracting individuals to apply for job openings. Most organizations use both internal and external recruiting.

Once an organization has determined its human resources needs, the next step is usually attracting new employees. **Recruiting** is the process of attracting individuals to apply for job openings.[16] The goal is to attract the right number of qualified candidates. Too few candidates means the organization has less choice among applicants and may have to leave openings unfilled. Having too many candidates is also undesirable, since evaluating job applicants is costly and time consuming, particularly when it requires individual testing or interviews.

Recruiting Human Resources

Where do recruits come from? Some are found internally; others come from outside the organization. **Internal recruiting** is the practice of considering present employees as candidates for job openings. Such a policy of promotion from within can help build morale and keep high-quality employees from leaving the firm. The procedures for notifying unionized employees of internal job-change opportunities, called "job posting and bidding," are usually spelled out in their union contracts. A skills inventory system may be used to identify internal candidates for management positions, or superiors may recommend individuals to consider. One disadvantage of internal recruiting is its ripple effect. When a current employee moves to a different post, someone else must be found to take her or his old job. If this replacement is already an employee, then that now-vacant job must also be filled. In one organization, 454 job movements were necessary as a result of filling 195 initial openings![17] Although internal recruiting gives many employees a chance to move up, it also increases training costs.

External recruiting is the practice of attracting individuals outside the organization to apply for jobs. This is accomplished through a number of methods, including advertising, campus recruiting, public or private employment agencies or executive search firms, union hiring halls (union-sponsored offices where interested employees apply for jobs in the organizations represented by the union), referrals by present employees, and hiring "walk-ons" or "gate-hires" (people who show up without being solicited). It is important to select the most appropriate recruiting method. For instance, an organization would probably not go to the local state employment service office to locate a top executive but would go there to find blue-collar workers. Private employment agencies can be a reliable source of clerical and technical employees, and executive search firms specialize in locating top-management talent. Because newspaper ads reach a very diverse audience, they reinforce affirmative action programs.

As a recruiting method, newspaper ads are quite inexpensive compared with executive search firms or campus recruiting. But organizations must consider both costs and results. One New York City bank studied the quality of tellers hired through each of their seven recruiting methods. Three of the methods (newspaper advertising, major private employment agency, and public agencies) produced tellers who were more likely to quit than the tellers produced by other methods (rehiring former employees, acting on referrals from high schools, acting on referrals from present employees, and hiring walk-ons). Analyses showed that the bank could save over $50,000 per year in hiring and training costs by using only the four most effective recruiting methods.[18]

Recruiting decisions often go both ways — the organization is selecting an employee, but the prospective employee is also selecting a job. Thus organizations treat applicants with dignity and strive for a suitable fit between person and job. Recent estimates suggest that hiring the "wrong" operating employee — one who flops and either quits or must be fired — costs organizations $5,000 in lost productivity and training (for a manager, as much as $75,000).[19] One way to facilitate a suitable person-job fit is through a **realistic job preview**, or **RJP**.[20] The RJP provides an applicant with a real picture of what it is like to perform the job that the organization is trying to fill. An RJP might include showing applicants a video of people actually performing the job, asking applicants to read descriptions of the job written by current employees, or even having them perform the job on a trial basis for a day or two.

A *realistic job preview (RJP)* provides an applicant with a real picture of what it is like on the job.

Selecting Human Resources

Once recruiting has attracted a pool of applicants, the next step is to select someone to hire. The intent of the selection process is to gather information from applicants that will predict their job success and then to hire the candidate or candidates predicted to be most successful. Organizations collect information about candidates in many ways, using application blanks, tests, interviews, and reference checks.

Organizations gather information about job candidates by using application blanks, tests, interviews, and reference checks.

In order to avoid discrimination on the basis of nonrelevant criteria, selection devices must measure only the factors that predict future performance. Organizations prove that a selection device is predictive of future job performance through a process called validation. **Predictive validation** is collecting the scores of employees or applicants on the selection device and correlating these scores with actual job performance. A strong correlation indicates that the device is a valid predictor of job performance. For instance, the SAT test is used as a selection device by many colleges because scores on it are correlated with later academic performance.

Organizations use *predictive validation* and *content validation* to prove that their selection devices predict future job performance.

Content validation establishes that the selection device measures the exact skills needed for successful job performance. Content validation relies on careful job analysis showing exactly what duties are required for the job. A work-sample test is then developed to measure the applicant's ability to perform those duties. For example, for a job that requires a great deal of typing of tables and figures, a typing test including such material is content-valid. Figure 14.3 illustrates a sample selection process.

Application Blanks   As a typical first step in selection, application blanks are an efficient method for gathering information about the applicant's work history, educational background, and other job-related demographic data. Because of legal restrictions, however, they should not contain questions about sex, religion, national origin, or other areas not related to the

Figure 14.3

A Sample Human Resources
Selection Process

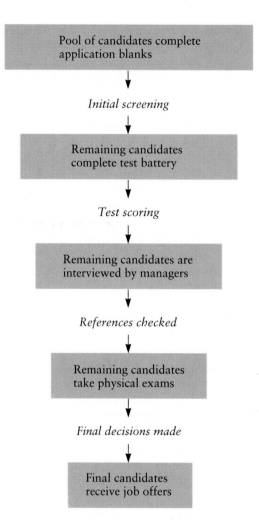

job. Information from application blanks is generally used informally to decide whether a candidate merits further evaluation, and it is used by interviewers to familiarize themselves with candidates before interviews.

Tests   Tests of ability, skill, aptitude, or knowledge that is relevant to the particular job are usually the best predictors of performance, although tests of general intelligence or personality are occasionally useful. Tests must be validated and must be administered and scored consistently: all candidates should be given the same directions, the same amount of time, and the same testing environment (temperature, lighting, noise level). The Entrepreneurial Challenge describes how one entrepreneur has found a profitable niche by providing employment testing for organizations.

Interviews   The interview is a popular selection device because, besides evaluating the applicant, the interviewer can tell the applicant about the

THE ENTREPRENEURIAL CHALLENGE

Testing Nuances Provide Business Opportunities

Employment tests are widely considered to be a valuable and important selection technique. Nonetheless, the legal issues involved in validating employment tests, as well as the complexities of administering them and interpreting the results, have caused some organizations to avoid using tests.

Kathy Kolbe, a Phoenix-based management consultant, has founded a successful business that performs the testing service for other organizations. In 1983 Kolbe developed a test she called the Kolbe Conative Index, or KCI. Most employment tests are either personality inventories or intelligence tests. The KCI purports to measure an individual's inclinations or desires to do something. Based on her initial successes with the KCI, she founded KolbeConcepts Inc.

The test itself consists of thirty-six multiple-choice questions. It assigns people a score on each of four traits. Kolbe is then able to interpret the scores and recommend to organizations the types of jobs for which an applicant is best suited.

Many of Kolbe's clients report successful experiences with the KCI. For example, Honeywell's Industrial Automation and Control Division uses the test as part of the hiring process for all its engineers. The test, however, has its share of critics. Motorola's Government Electronics Group has found the KCI to be useful in training and development programs but does not rely on it when making hiring decisions.

REFERENCES: "New Test Quantifies the Way We Work," *Wall Street Journal,* February 7, 1990, pp. B1, B6; "Personality Testing Is Entering the 1980s," *Wall Street Journal,* September 13, 1989, pp. A1, A6; "The Price of Discrimination May Well Go Up," *Business Week,* August 13, 1990, p. 34.

company. Unfortunately, interviews are often poor predictors of job success.[21] There are many reasons for this, most of them stemming from biases inherent in the way people perceive and judge others on first meeting.[22] Organizations can improve interview validity by training interviewers to be aware of potential biases and to structure the interview effectively.

Interviews of managerial or professional candidates can be somewhat less structured than interviews of nonmanagers, because of the wider array of experiences and responsibilities involved. The interviewer plans question areas and information-gathering objectives in advance, but the actual questions asked vary with the candidate's background. Trammell Crow, a real estate development firm, uses a novel interviewing approach in hiring managers. Applicants are interviewed not only by two or three other managers but also by a secretary or young leasing agent, who provide information about how the prospective manager interacts with nonmanagers.[23]

Assessment Centers   Assessment centers, rapidly gaining in popularity, are used primarily to select managers and are particularly good for selecting current employees for promotion into management. The assessment center simulates key parts of the managerial job. A typical center lasts two to three days, with groups of six to twelve individuals participating in a variety of managerial exercises. Most assessment centers include an "in-basket test" of individual decision making and group exercises to assess interpersonal skill. Centers may also include an interview, public speaking, and

THE ENVIRONMENTAL CHALLENGE

Background Checks Growing in Importance

More organizations are using background checks as a tool in the selection of new employees. Indeed, a whole new industry has been created to supply background information about job applicants. These research firms dig into an individual's past and sell any pertinent information to prospective employers, who consider it before making someone an offer of employment.

Although an organization cannot base a hiring decision on race, sex, or marital status, it can consider such diverse information as a person's credit history, workers' compensation claims, record of criminal convictions, and moving violations and automobile accidents. Organizations argue that this type of information speaks volumes about the responsibility, values, and ethics of job applicants. These considerations are especially important for organizations whose employees have access to sensitive information, cash, and other marketable commodities.

Such firms as Equifax, Fidelifacts, and Apscreen have all become extremely successful at tracking down background information and selling it to organizations. Many organizations report major cost savings from using their services. One convenience store chain, for example, was experiencing turnover of 300 percent per year and employee thefts of over $4 million per year. After the firm started using background check data, its turnover dropped down to 97 percent, and its losses to employee theft were more than halved.

Still, critics argue that the information provided by these firms is not always accurate or relevant. Moreover, when errors are made, they may never be discovered—and even if discovered may be hard to correct. One man, for example, was denied a job because a background check indicated that he had been charged with cocaine possession. Even though he was able to prove a case of mistaken identity (he had the same first name as the convicted drug user), it took him several months to get the information corrected.

REFERENCES: "More Employers Check Credit Histories of Job Seekers to Judge Their Character," *Wall Street Journal*, August 30, 1990, pp. B1, B5; "Looking for a Job? You May be Out Before You Go In," *Business Week*, September 24, 1990, pp. 128–129; "Many Businesses Responding Too Slowly to Rapid Work Force Shifts, Study Says," *Wall Street Journal*, July 20, 1990, pp. B1, B9.

standardized ability tests. Candidates are assessed by several trained observers, usually managers several levels above the job for which the candidates are being considered. Assessment centers are quite valid if properly designed and have been shown to overcome potential discriminatory effects that plague other methods.[24] However, assessment centers are expensive to create and operate. AT&T pioneered the assessment center concept and still uses it.

Other Selection Devices   Polygraph tests, once very popular, have recently been declared illegal for most jobs. Some organizations are requiring that final job candidates take physical exams. Drug tests are also increasingly used, especially when drug-related performance problems could create serious safety hazards.[25] The Environmental Challenge describes how some organizations are using credit and other background checks in their hiring decisions.

Training and development are a vital component of human resources management. Singapore Airlines is the world's most profitable airline and the one that customers consistently rate as the best managed. One key to the firm's success is an outstanding training program for all its employees. This cabin crew is taking a refresher course in handling emergencies.

Training and Development

After choosing an individual for hiring or promotion, the organization's next step is often to provide some form of training. In human resources management, **training** usually refers to teaching operational or technical employees how to do the job for which they were hired. **Development**, in contrast, refers to teaching managers and professionals the skills needed for both present and future jobs. Most organizations provide regular training and development programs for managers and employees.[26] For example, IBM spends $750 million annually on training and development programs and even has a vice president in charge of employee education. American business overall spends $30 billion each year on training and development programs away from the office or shop floor, not counting wages and benefits paid to employees while they are participating in such programs.[27]

Training refers to teaching operational or technical employees how to perform their jobs. Development refers to teaching managers and professionals the skills needed for both present and future jobs.

Steps in Training and Development

The first step in developing a training plan is to determine what needs exist. For instance, if employees do not know how to operate machinery required to do their jobs, a training program is clearly needed. But when a group of office workers is performing poorly, training may not be the answer. The problem could be lack of motivation, aging equipment, poor supervision, inefficient work design, or a deficiency of skills and knowledge. Only the last cause could be remedied by training the office workers.

If after careful investigation the problem does seem to require training, the organization should thoroughly assess the present level of employees' skill and knowledge and then define the desired level in concrete, measurable terms. For example, an organization might set the following objective for a training program in word processing: "Trainees will be able to type from handwritten copy at 60 words per minute with no more than one error per page." After the training is completed, performance is assessed against the objectives. Because training programs are costly, they should always be evaluated and should be modified or discontinued if judged not effective.

Methods of Training and Development

Job content is probably the most important element in determining a training method. When the content is factual material (such as company rules or how to fill out forms), then assigned reading, programmed learning, and lecture methods work well. However, when the content is human relations or group decision making, organizations must use a training method that allows interpersonal contact, such as role playing or case discussion groups. When the content to be learned is a physical skill, methods allowing practice and the actual use of tools and material are needed, as in on-the-job training or vestibule training (a simulated work setting). Interactive video is also becoming popular for training. This approach, relying on a computer-video hookup, is a promising method for combining several of the other methods into one. Xerox, Massachusetts Mutual Life Insurance Co., and Ford have all reported tremendous success with this method. Other issues to consider in selecting a training method are cost, time, number of trainees, and whether the training is to be done by in-house trainers or contracted to an outside training firm.

International organizations often face special training problems. For example, many organizations move their production facilities to areas where labor is inexpensive. But the local employees may have underdeveloped skills and abilities, necessitating a large investment in training. Japanese firms setting up production facilities in the United States have had to provide training to American workers in quality management.

Performance Appraisal

Performance appraisal is a formal assessment of how well an employee is doing his or her job.

Once employees are trained and settled into their jobs, the next concern is performance appraisal. **Performance appraisal** is a formal assessment of how well an employee is doing his or her job. There are many reasons to regularly evaluate employee performance. Evaluation may be necessary for human resources research efforts, such as validating selection devices or assessing the impact of training programs. Performance appraisal helps supervisors make decisions about pay raises, promotions, and training and provides employees with feedback that may aid them in career choices. Because evaluations often determine wages and promotions, they must be fair and nondiscriminatory.

Common Appraisal Methods

Three common methods of appraisal are objective methods, subjective methods, and management by objectives.

Objective methods of performance appraisal measure actual
employee output.

Objective Methods Objective methods of appraisal measure an employee's actual output (i.e., number of units produced), scrappage rate, dollar volume of sales, number of claims processed, or other work produced. To represent each individual's performance accurately, it is often necessary to adjust raw performance figures for the effect of opportunity bias. For example, if one sales representative has a territory with 100 potential customers and another has a territory with only 75 potential customers, the first will likely attract more customers than will the second. Thus, when comparing the performance of the two sales representatives it is necessary to account for differences in potential as well as in actual performance.

Another type of objective measure is the special performance test, which assesses each employee under standardized working conditions. This kind of appraisal also eliminates opportunity bias. General Telephone Company, for example, tests operators with a series of prerecorded calls; the operators are graded on speed, accuracy, and courtesy in handling the calls. The problem with performance tests is that they measure ability but not the extent to which an individual is motivated to use that ability on the job. Therefore, special performance tests must be supplemented by other appraisal methods to provide a complete picture of performance.

Subjective methods of performance appraisal involve the assessment of performance through the
eyes of someone else. Subjective
methods include *performance
ranking, performance rating,* and
*behaviorally anchored rating
scales.*

Subjective Methods By far the most common way to measure performance is through subjective methods, including ranking and rating techniques. By subjective, we mean that performance is assessed through the eyes of someone else. **Performance ranking** compares employees directly with each other and orders them from best to worst, usually on the basis of overall performance. Ranking has a number of drawbacks. First, it is difficult to use for large groups, because the persons in the middle of the distribution may be hard to distinguish from one another accurately. Second, intervals are unequal between ranks. Number one is better than number two, but by a lot or a little? This kind of information is not conveyed by ranks. Third, comparison of people in different work groups is impossible. Each group has a person ranked first, but which first is best? Finally, ranking focuses on "overall" goodness or badness compared with others. This is a bit simple-minded in that each employee certainly has both good and bad points.

Another problem with ranking is that the subjective criteria that each evaluator uses in arriving at a global judgment may vary. One evaluator may consider quantity of performance above all else, whereas another may attend more to quality or cooperativeness. Furthermore, rankings do not provide useful information for feedback. To be told that one is ranked third is not nearly so helpful as to be told that the quality of one's work is outstanding, its quantity is satisfactory, one's punctuality could use improvement, and one's paperwork is seriously deficient.

Performance rating differs from ranking in that it compares each employee with a fixed standard rather than with other employees. A rating scale provides the standard. Figure 14.4 gives examples of three graphic rating scales for a grocery checker. Such scales are very commonly used. They consist of a performance dimension to be rated (such as punctuality, congeniality, and accuracy) followed by a scale on which to make the rating. In constructing graphic rating scales, it is extremely important to select performance dimensions that are relevant to job performance. In particular, they should be focused on job behaviors and results, rather than on personality traits or attitudes (unless, of course, attitudes are an important consideration in performance).

The **behaviorally anchored rating scale (BARS)** is a very sophisticated and useful rating method. BARS provides examples of specific and observable behaviors to illustrate the various levels of achievement for each performance dimension evaluated. BARS can be an effective appraisal

Figure 14.4

A Sample Graphic Rating Scale for a Grocery Checker

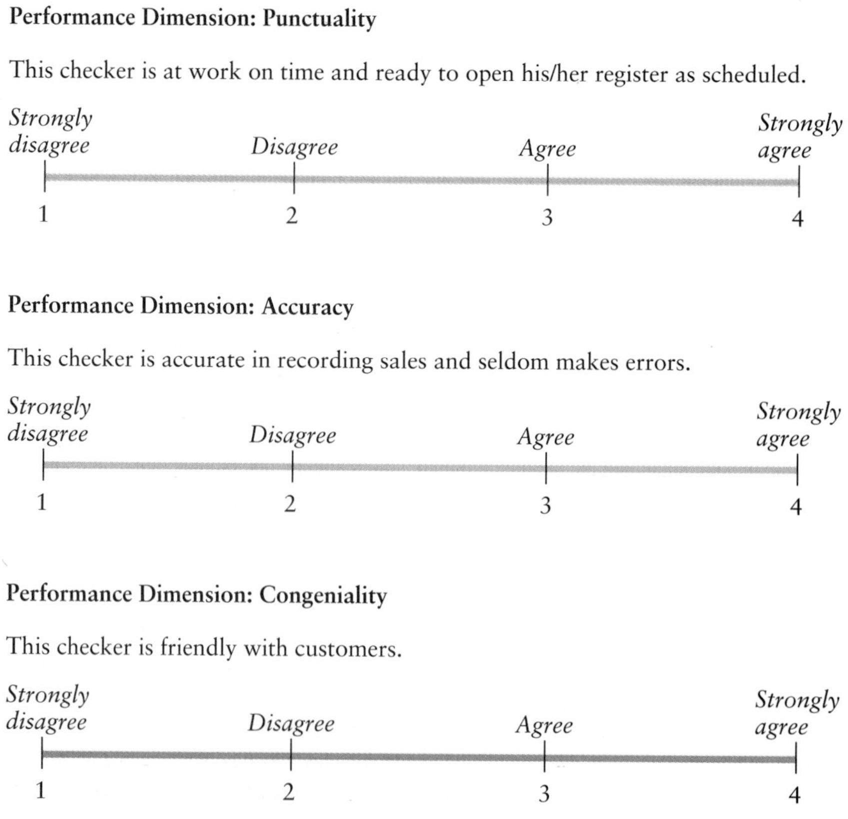

Performance Dimension: Punctuality

This checker is at work on time and ready to open his/her register as scheduled.

Strongly disagree	*Disagree*	*Agree*	*Strongly agree*
1	2	3	4

Performance Dimension: Accuracy

This checker is accurate in recording sales and seldom makes errors.

Strongly disagree	*Disagree*	*Agree*	*Strongly agree*
1	2	3	4

Performance Dimension: Congeniality

This checker is friendly with customers.

Strongly disagree	*Disagree*	*Agree*	*Strongly agree*
1	2	3	4

method because of the care required to construct the scales and because it provides objective criteria for supervisors to use. It is costly, however, because outside expertise is usually needed and because scales must be developed for each unique job within the organization.

In any kind of rating or ranking system, judgmental errors or biases can occur. One common problem is recency error, which is the tendency to base judgments on an employee's most recent performance because it is most easily recalled. Since rating or ranking is often intended to evaluate performance over a period of time, such as six months or a year, recency error does distort appraisal. Another error is to overuse one part of the scale, being too lenient or too severe or giving everyone a rating of "average." Halo error is allowing assessment of an employee on one dimension to "spread" to ratings of that employee on other dimensions. For instance, if an employee is outstanding on quality of output, a rater might tend to give her or him higher marks than deserved on other dimensions. Additional judgment errors can occur because of race, sex, or age discrimination, either intentional or unintentional.[28]

Management by objectives is an appraisal system in which objectives agreed to in advance by both employee and supervisor serve as individualized performance standards by which the employee is evaluated.

Management by Objectives   In a management by objectives (MBO) both supervisor and subordinate agree on performance objectives. The objectives are characterized as goals that the employee will work toward. At the end of the planning period, supervisor and subordinate meet again to assess the extent to which the subordinate met the objectives. The agreed-upon objectives become individualized performance standards, just as rating scales provide generalized performance standards. If MBO is to be effective, employee rewards must be tied directly to goal attainment.

Performance Feedback

The last step in performance appraisal is giving feedback to subordinates about their performance. This is usually done in a private meeting between supervisor and subordinate. The discussion should generally be focused on the facts — the assessed level of performance, how and why that assessment was made, and how it can be improved in the future. Feedback interviews are not easy to conduct. Many managers are uncomfortable with the task, especially if feedback is negative and subordinates are disappointed by what they hear. Proper training, however, can help managers conduct effective feedback interviews.[29]

Compensation and *benefits* are the rewards that organizations provide to their employees in exchange for their time, effort, and other contributions.

Employee Rewards

Compensation is the financial remuneration that the organization gives to its employees in exchange for their work. **Benefits** are other things of value that the organization provides to its workers.

Compensation

Compensation is an important and complex part of the relationship between an organization and its employees. Basic minimum levels of compensation are necessary to provide employees with the means to maintain a reasonable standard of living. Beyond this, however, compensation also provides a tangible measure of the individual's value to the organization. If employees do not earn enough to meet their basic economic goals, they will seek employment elsewhere. Likewise, if they feel that their contributions are undervalued, they may leave or exhibit poor work habits, low morale, and little commitment to the organization. Thus it is clearly in the organization's best interests to design an effective compensation system.[30] The motivational aspects of rewards are considered in Chapter 17.

A good compensation system can help attract qualified applicants, retain present employees, and stimulate high performance at a cost that is reasonable for the organization's industry and geographic area. To set up a successful system, organizations must make decisions about wage levels, the wage structure, and individual wages. These steps in determining compensation are illustrated in Figure 14.5.

Wage Levels   The wage-level decision is an organizational policy decision about whether to pay above, at, or below the going rate for labor in the industry or the geographic area. The wage level generally follows from the organization's strategy. Most organizations choose to pay near the average. Large, successful firms may like to cultivate the image of being "wage leaders" by intentionally paying more than average and thus attracting and keeping high-quality employees. IBM, for example, pays top dollar to attract the employees it wants. As a result, going to work for IBM is a prestigious opportunity for many people, and the organization is able to get some of the top college graduates each year. The amount of unemployment in the labor force also affects wage levels: pay declines when labor is plentiful (that is, in periods of high unemployment) and increases when labor is scarce (in periods of low unemployment).

Once it sets wage-level policy, the organization needs outside information to help set the actual wage rates it will pay for specific jobs. Pay administrators need to know what the maximum, minimum, and average wages are for particular jobs in the appropriate labor market. This information is collected by means of a wage survey, which may be conducted by individual firms or by local human resources or business associations. Professional and industry associations often conduct regional or nationwide surveys and make the results available to employers.

Survey data, however, do not provide enough information for setting all wage rates. It is unlikely that wage-rate data will be available for every single job in an organization. Moreover, paying average or above-average rates based on survey data creates external equity — employees feel fairly paid relative to others in the community, industry, or profession doing the same work. But it does not address the issue of internal equity — whether different jobs within the firm are fairly paid relative to each other. A

Figure 14.5

Steps in Determining Compensation

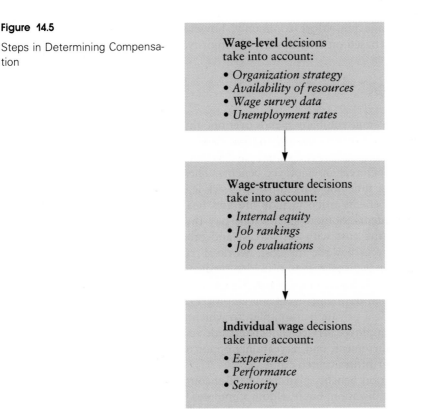

Wage-level decisions
take into account:

- *Organization strategy*
- *Availability of resources*
- *Wage survey data*
- *Unemployment rates*

Wage-structure decisions
take into account:

- *Internal equity*
- *Job rankings*
- *Job evaluations*

Individual wage decisions
take into account:

- *Experience*
- *Performance*
- *Seniority*

perception of internal inequity may arise when production workers earn as much as or more than their supervisors. This can happen if workers are on incentive plans or put in a lot of overtime while supervisors on fixed salaries are "exempt" from the overtime-pay requirement of the Fair Labor Standards Act.

Job evaluation assesses the worth of each job relative to the worth of other jobs in the organization.

Wage Structure   The pay differentials among different jobs within an organization constitute the wage structure. Wage structures are usually established through a procedure called **job evaluation**, which assesses the worth of each job relative to the worth of other jobs in the organization. A committee made up of several managers and a few nonmanagerial employees usually does the evaluating. The simplest method is to rank jobs from those that should be paid the most (for example, the president) to those that should be paid the least (for example, a mail clerk or a janitor). In a small firm with few positions, this method is quick and practical, but medium-sized and large firms with many job titles require a more sophisticated approach.

Individual Wages   Once wage levels, rates, and structure are set, there is only one more issue to address: how much to pay each employee in a particular job. The easiest solution is to pay the same to everyone doing the same job. More commonly, however, organizations pay differential wages based on criteria such as seniority, experience, and performance.

Benefits

The average company spends over one-third of its cash payroll on employee benefits. Little wonder, then, that they are no longer called "fringe" benefits.[31] An average individual paid $18,000 per year receives about $6,588 more per year in employee benefits. These benefits come in several forms. Pay for time not worked includes sick leave, vacation, and holidays. Insurance benefits often include life and health insurance for employees and dependents. Some organizations pay the entire cost of insurance; others share the cost with employees; and others negotiate group rates but let employees pay the full cost. Workers' compensation is a legally required insurance benefit that provides medical care and disability income for employees injured on the job. Social Security is a government pension plan to which both employers and employees contribute. Many employers also provide a private pension plan to which they and their employees contribute. Employee service benefits include such things as credit unions, tuition reimbursement, and recreational opportunities such as a company softball field or fitness center.

A good benefits plan may help encourage people to join and stay with an organization, but it seldom stimulates high performance because benefits are tied more to membership in the organization than to performance. To ensure that they are spending benefits dollars wisely, organizations should shop carefully (for example, to select the best insurance provider), avoid redundant coverage, and provide only those benefits that employees want. Benefit programs should also be clearly explained to employees so that they can use benefits wisely and appreciate the organization's commitment.

Some organizations have instituted "cafeteria benefit plans," which provide basic coverage for all employees but then allow employees to choose additional benefits (up to a cost limit based on salary). An employee with five children might choose medical and dental coverage for dependents; a single employee might prefer more vacation time; an older employee might elect increased pension benefits. Such a flexible system is expected to encourage people to stay in the organization and perhaps to help the company attract new employees.[32]

Some companies have started to offer innovative benefits as a way of accommodating even more employee needs. For example, on-site child care, mortgage assistance, and generous paid leave programs are becoming popular.[33] At the same time, however, J. C. Penney, Chrysler, Allied-Signal, Genentech, and other companies have eliminated some benefits because of the escalating cost of insurance.[34] Although it is too early to assess how widespread the latter trend may become, it seems safe to say that because of their high costs, benefits will continue to be closely monitored and scrutinized by organizations.

Boston-area construction firms and labor unions recently worked together to develop a new program aimed at increasing on-the-job safety, called Work-Safe. Its goals are to reduce construction accidents and to control the cost of workers' compensation. Such collaborative efforts between management and labor are an important element in labor relations.

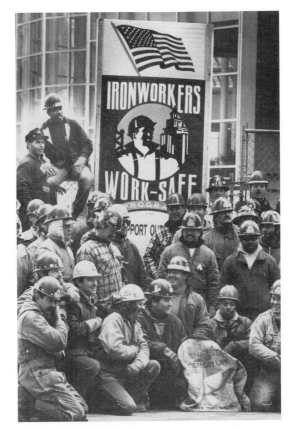

Labor Relations

Labor relations is the set of activities through which an organization structures its relationship with employees who are represented by a union.

Labor relations is the set of activities through which an organization structures its relationship with employees who are represented by a union. As we noted at the beginning of the chapter, nonmanagement employees have the legal right to organize and bargain collectively with management. In this section we discuss how unions are formed and the process of collective bargaining.

How Unions Are Formed

For a new local union (i.e., a local affiliate of a national union) to be formed, several things must occur. First, employees must become interested in having a union. This interest may be stimulated by worker discontent or simply by a perception among workers that they would be better off if they were represented by a union. Low wages or concerns about job security are common motives among workers considering unionization. Professional organizers employed by a national union (such as the Teamsters or United

Auto Workers) sometimes generate interest simply by making speeches and distributing literature outside the workplace. Employees who want a union will try to convince other workers of the benefits of a union.

Second, a sufficient number of employees must sign authorization cards stating that the signer wishes to have a vote about union representation. Thirty percent of the employees in the potential bargaining unit must sign these cards to show the National Labor Relations Board (NLRB) that there is sufficient interest to justify holding an election. The **bargaining unit** consists of all employees who will be eligible to vote in the election and to join and be represented by the union if one is formed. The bargaining unit must be defined as a logical grouping of employees, such as "all nonmanagement employees at the Acme plant in Cleveland" or "all clerical employees at State University."

> A *bargaining unit* is the set of all employees eligible to join and be represented by a particular union.

The election is supervised by an NLRB representative and is conducted by secret ballot. If a simple majority of those voting (not of all those eligible to vote) votes for the union, then the union is certified as the official representative of the bargaining unit.[35] The new union then organizes itself by officially signing up members and electing officers, and it is soon ready to negotiate the first contract.

An organization usually prefers that employees not be unionized because unions limit the organization's freedom in many areas. Union contracts may stipulate wage increases, how overtime is to be assigned, and which employees will perform which jobs — decisions that the organization itself would like to control. Thus an organization may wage its own campaign to convince employees to vote against the union, and it is at this point that "unfair labor practices" are often committed. For instance, it is an unfair labor practice for organizations to interrogate employees about their feelings toward unions and to discriminate in hiring, firing, or layoffs on the basis of participation in union activities. It is also an unfair labor practice to promise to give employees a raise (or any other benefit) if the union is defeated.

International organizations must confront labor relations issues wherever they do business. In some countries, such as South Korea and Great Britain, unions are much stronger than they are in the United States. In others, such as Japan, unions are less powerful. Japanese organizations doing business in the United States have been successful at avoiding unions by paying above-average wages, by treating employees fairly, and by working closely with labor to facilitate employee participation in decision making.

Collective Bargaining

> *Collective bargaining* is the process of negotiating a labor contract that is acceptable to both management and the union.

The intent of **collective bargaining** is to negotiate a labor contract that is acceptable to both management and the union. The contract contains agreements about wages, hours, and other conditions of employment, including promotion, layoff, discipline, benefits, methods of allocating overtime, vacations, rest periods, and the grievance procedure. A no-strike clause is also usually included, stating that the union will not strike during the term of the contract (usually three years). The union (unless it is a union of federal, state, or municipal workers) can still strike before the contract is approved or after it expires if a new one has not been agreed on. The process of bargaining may go on for weeks or months, with representatives of management and the union meeting to make proposals and counterproposals. The resulting agreement must be ratified by the union membership. If it is not approved, the union may strike to put pressure on management, or it may choose not to strike and simply continue negotiating until a more acceptable agreement is reached.

A grievance procedure is the means through which a labor contract is enforced.

The **grievance procedure** is the means by which the contract is enforced. When employees feel that they have not been treated fairly under the contract they file a grievance to correct the problem. For instance, if the contract says that the most senior person will be given the first chance to work overtime but a supervisor offers the overtime to a less senior employee first, the more senior employee can file a grievance.

The first step in a grievance procedure is for the aggrieved employee to discuss the alleged contract violation with her or his immediate superior. Often the grievance is resolved at this stage. However, if the employee still believes that he or she is being mistreated, the grievance can be appealed to the next higher level, perhaps the foreman. A union official may help an aggrieved employee present her or his case. If the foreman's decision is also unsatisfactory to the employee, additional appeals to successively higher levels of management are made, until finally all in-company steps are exhausted. The final step is to submit the grievance to binding arbitration. An arbitrator is a labor law expert who is paid jointly by the union and management. The arbitrator studies the contract, hears both sides of the case, and renders a decision that both parties must obey. The grievance system for resolving disputes about contract enforcement is intended to prevent any need to strike during the term of the contract.[36]

Learning Summary

Human resources management, or HRM, is the set of organizational activities directed at attracting, developing, and maintaining an effective work force. It has both strategic and legal importance to organizations. Key human resources legislation covers equal employment opportunity, compensation and benefits, labor relations, and health and safety. HRM consists of a sequence of five activities: planning, recruitment and selection, training and development, performance appraisal, and employee rewards.

Human resources planning is forecasting the organization's future need for employees, forecasting the availability of employees both within and outside the organization, and planning programs to ensure that the proper number and type of employees will be available when needed. Job analysis typically includes both job description and job specification.

Recruitment and selection are the processes by which job applicants are attracted, evaluated, and hired. Most organizations rely on both internal and external recruiting. Methods for selecting applicants include application blanks, tests, interviews, and assessment centers. Selection methods should be properly validated.

Training is teaching employees how best to perform their present jobs. Development is teaching employees the skills needed for both present and future needs. Performance appraisals are important for determining training needs, deciding pay raises and promotions, and providing helpful feedback to employees. Most organizations use both objective and subjective methods of appraisal.

Compensation and benefits are the rewards that organizations provide employees for the work they do. Compensation rates must be fair compared with the rates of other jobs within the organization and with the rates of the same or similar jobs in other organizations in the labor market. Properly designed compensation systems can encourage high performance, and a good benefit program can help attract and retain employees.

Labor relations is the set of activities through which an organization structures its relationship with employees who are represented by a union. If a majority of a company's nonmanagement employees so desire, they have the right to be represented by a union. Management must engage in collective bargaining with the union in an effort to agree on a contract. While the contract is in effect, employees do not strike but use the grievance system to settle disputes with management.

Questions and Exercises

Review Questions

1. Identify the major pieces of legislation that affect human resources management.
2. What are the major issues to address in human resources planning?
3. Describe the selection techniques that organizations use in hiring new employees.
4. Summarize the basic steps in training and development. Why is training important?
5. How do organizations appraise employee performance?
6. Explain how an organization determines the compensation that it will provide to its workers.
7. List the steps that employees must take if they want to establish a union.

Analysis Questions

1. Have you or a friend ever been discriminated against in a hiring decision? If so, what did you do about it?

2. Some people argue that anti-discrimination legislation has the effect of reverse discrimination against white males. Do you agree or disagree with this assertion?
3. Whenever you have sought a job, what methods did you use to find out about potential opportunities? When you graduate, how will you go about searching for a job?
4. What sort of training do you think you will need most in your first job?
5. What benefits do you think are most important?
6. Some people think that unions in the United States have outlived their usefulness. What do you think? Have you ever belonged to a union? If so, include some of your reflections on that experience.

Application Exercises

1. Interview someone in your campus human resources department about the selection procedures that your school uses in hiring new employees. Develop a flow diagram of the procedures used and compare it to Figure 14.3.
2. Assume that you and your classmates have organized a union. Negotiate a collective-bargaining agreement with your instructor.

Chapter Notes

1. "Past Tokenism," *Newsweek,* May 14, 1990, pp. 37–43; "The Price of Discrimination May Well Go Up," *Business Week,* August 13, 1990, p. 34; "Many Businesses Responding Too Slowly to Rapid Work Force Shifts, Study Says," *Wall Street Journal,* July 20, 1990, pp. B1, B9.
2. Thomas A. Mahoney and John R. Deckop, "Evolution of Concept and Practice in Personnel Administration/Human Resources Management (PA/HRM)," *Journal of Management,* Summer 1986, pp. 223–241.
3. Brian D. Steffy and Steven D. Maurer, "Conceptualizing and Measuring the Economic Effectiveness of Human Resources Activities," *Academy of Management Review,* April 1988, pp. 271–286.
4. For recent reviews, see Randall S. Schuler, "Repositioning the Human Resource Function: Transformation or Demise?" *Academy of Management Executive,* August 1990, pp. 49–60, and Cynthia A. Lengnick-Hall and Mark L. Lengnick-Hall, "Strategic Human Resources Management: A Review of the Literature and a Proposed Typology," *Academy of Management Review,* July 1988, pp. 454–470.
5. David P. Twomey, *A Concise Guide to Employment Law* (Dallas: Southwestern Publishing, 1986).
6. Equal Employment Opportunity Commission, "Uniform Guidelines on Employee Selection Procedures," *Federal Register,* August 25, 1978, pp. 38290–38315.
7. Robert Calvert, Jr., *Affirmative Action: A Comprehensive Recruitment Manual* (Garrett Park, Md.: Garrett Park Press, 1979). For recent perspectives on affirmative action, see "Affirmative Action Faces Likely Setback," *Wall Street Journal,* November 30, 1988, p. B1.

8. "Workplace Injuries Proliferate as Concerns Push People to Produce," *Wall Street Journal,* June 16, 1989, pp. A1, A8.

9. "OSHA Awakens from Its Six-Year Slumber," *Business Week,* August 14, 1987, p. 27.

10. Lee Dyer, "Strategic Human Resources Management and Planning," in *Research in Personnel and Human Resources Management,* ed. Kendrith M. Rowland and Gerald R. Ferris (Greenwich, Conn.: JAI Press, 1985).

11. For more information on job analysis methods, see Ernest J. McCormick, *Job Analysis: Methods and Applications* (New York: AMACOM, 1979).

12. "New Test Quantifies the Way We Work," *Wall Street Journal,* February 7, 1990, pp. B1, B6.

13. Thomas H. Stone and Jack Fiorito, "A Perceived Uncertainty Model of Human Resources Forecasting Technique Use," *Academy of Management Review,* July 1986, pp. 635–642.

14. Leonard Greenhalgh, Anne T. Lawrence, and Robert I. Sutton, "Determinants of Work Force Reduction Strategies in Declining Organizations," *Academy of Management Review,* April 1988, pp. 241–254.

15. David Kirkpatrick, "Smart New Ways to Use Temps," *Fortune,* February 15, 1988, pp. 110–116.

16. Sara L. Rynes and Alison E. Barber, "Applicant Attraction Strategies: An Organizational Perspective," *Academy of Management Review,* April 1990, pp. 286–310.

17. Michael R. Carrell and Frank E. Kuzmits, *Personnel: Human Resources Management,* 3rd ed. (Westerville, Ohio: Merrill, 1989).

18. Martin F. Gannon, "Sources of Referral and Employee Turnover," *Journal of Applied Psychology,* June 1971, pp. 226–228.

19. Brian Dumaine, "The New Art of Hiring Smart," *Fortune,* August 17, 1987, pp. 78–81.

20. Mary K. Suszko and James A. Breaugh, "The Effects of Realistic Job Previews on Applicant Self-Selection and Employee Turnover, Satisfaction, and Coping Ability," *Journal of Management,* Fall 1986, pp. 513–523.

21. John F. Binning, Mel A. Goldstein, Mario F. Garcia, and Julie H. Scattaregia, "Effects of Preinterview Impressions on Questioning Strategies in Same- and Opposite-Sex Employment Interviews," *Journal of Applied Psychology,* February 1988, pp. 30–37.

22. Neal Schmitt, "Social and Situational Determinants of Interview Decisions: Implications for the Employment Interview," *Personnel Psychology,* Spring 1976, pp. 79–102. For an opposing view, see M. Ronald Buckley and Robert W. Eder, "B. M. Springbett and the Notion of the 'Snap Decision' in the Interview," *Journal of Management,* March 1988, pp. 59–67.

23. Dumaine, "The New Art of Hiring Smart."

24. Paul R. Sackett, "Assessment Centers and Content Validity: Some Neglected Issues," *Personnel Psychology,* Fall 1987, pp. 13–25.

25. Abby Brown, "To Test or Not to Test," *Personnel Administrator,* March 1987, pp. 67–70.

26. See Bernard Keys and Joseph Wolfe, "Management Education and Development: Current Issues and Emerging Trends," *Journal of Management,* June 1988, pp. 205–229, for a recent review.

27. Michael Brody, "Helping Workers to Work Smarter," *Fortune,* June 8, 1987, pp. 86–88.

28. Jerry W. Hedge and Michael J. Kavanagh, "Improving the Accuracy of Performance Evaluations: Comparison of Three Methods of Performance

Appraiser Training," *Journal of Applied Psychology,* February 1988, pp. 68–73; Gregory H. Dobbins, Robert L. Cardy, and Donald M. Truxillo, "The Effects of Purpose of Appraisal and Individual Differences in Stereotypes of Women on Sex Differences in Performance Ratings: A Laboratory and Field Study," *Journal of Applied Psychology,* August 1988, pp. 551–558; and Clinton O. Longnecker, Dennis A. Gioia, and Henry P. Sims, Jr., "Behind the Mask: The Politics of Employee Appraisal," *The Academy of Management Executive,* August 1987, pp. 183–194.

29. James S. Russell and Dorothy L. Goode, "An Analysis of Managers' Reactions to Their Own Performance Appraisal Feedback," *Journal of Applied Psychology,* February 1988, pp. 63–67.

30. Edward E. Lawler III, "The Design of Effective Reward Systems," in *Handbook of Organizational Behavior,* ed. Jay W. Lorsch (Englewood Cliffs, N.J.: Prentice-Hall, 1987), pp. 255–271; and Robert J. Greene, "Effective Compensation: The How and Why," *Personnel Administrator,* February 1987, pp. 112–116.

31. "Ouch! The Squeeze on Your Health Benefits," *Business Week,* November 20, 1989, pp. 110–116.

32. "To Each According to His Needs: Flexible Benefits Plans Gain Favor," *Wall Street Journal,* September 16, 1986, p. 29.

33. "The Future Look of Employee Benefits," *Wall Street Journal,* September 7, 1988, p. 21.

34. "Firms Forced to Cut Back on Benefits," *USA Today,* November 29, 1988, pp. 1B, 2B.

35. John A. Fossum, "Labor Relations: Research and Practice in Transition," *Journal of Management,* Summer 1987, pp. 281–300.

36. For recent research on collective bargaining, see Wallace N. Davidson III, Dan L. Worrell, and Sharon H. Garrison, "Effect of Strike Activity on Firm Value," *Academy of Management Journal,* June 1988, pp. 387–394; John M. Magenau, James E. Martin, and Melanie M. Peterson, "Dual and Unilateral Commitment Among Stewards and Rank-and-File Union Members," *Academy of Management Journal,* June 1988, pp. 359–376; and Brian E. Becker, "Concession Bargaining: The Meaning of Union Gains," *Academy of Management Journal,* June 1988, pp. 377–387.

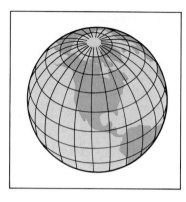

CASE 14.1

Who's Driving Greyhound?

For years, thousands of Greyhound buses have crisscrossed the United States, providing public transportation to places too small and out of the way to have air or rail service. Greyhound's slogan was "Leave the driving to us," and its customers did just that, assuming that America's only national bus line was too big and too important to run into trouble. But Greyhound's image—and, along with it, its ridership and perhaps its future—changed in 1990 as a long and at times violent strike by the Amalgamated Transit Union led to lawsuits, bitter feelings, and a widening gap between labor and management. Many passengers were left wondering, "Who's driving this bus?"

Greyhound changed hands in 1987 when a group led by Fred G. Currey took over the company through a leveraged buyout. At first, relations between Greyhound workers and their new boss seemed ideal. For months, Currey met with drivers and ticket agents, collecting ideas about how the company should be restructured. He put on banquets to honor model workers and promised better times ahead.

At the same time, Greyhound worked to spruce up the decrepit terminals and clean the filthy bus bathrooms that kept many people from "going Greyhound." The company renovated many of its terminals, increased its advertising by 50 percent, and began using a computerized reservation system. These changes began paying off in 1989, when passenger miles increased 10 percent from the previous year and the company showed a slim net profit after a $17 million loss in 1988.

But then in March 1990, 9,400 drivers, mechanics, and clerks went on strike, and the company's future began to grow dimmer. Each side blamed the other for the strike and for putting the company on the road to financial disaster. The drivers were angry at Currey for proposing that Greyhound consolidate many of its routes, a plan that would eliminate 2,000 jobs. The drivers wanted a 20 percent pay raise over three years, which would, the company claimed, cost more than $140 million. Greyhound and some industry analysts complained that the union was refusing to face the harsh reality of the company's financial situation. When the company cut its original offer and proposed a four-year pay freeze, the union said the offer was an insult. Union officials later said that the heart of the disagreement was grievance procedures, not money.

If the union overestimated the company's willingness and ability to increase wages, the company overestimated drivers' willingness to cross picket lines. Union officials believe that Currey expected half of the company's 6,000 drivers to cross the lines; but as the strike stretched on into months, only about 10 percent of the drivers returned to work. The strike turned ugly: buses were shot at, and pickets carried signs reading "Drop Dead Fred." Although the union deplored the violence, company officials accused the union of using violence to scare off replacement drivers.

Hiring nonunion replacements to augment the few drivers who had crossed the picket lines, Greyhound managed to get buses back on the road, covering 85 percent of its prestrike miles and carrying 95 percent of its former ridership by the end of 1990. It cut its overall work force by one-third and was reducing costs by canceling leases on buses and terminals, becoming a leaner, potentially more profitable company.

But these changes may have come too late. Greyhound had filed for Chapter 11 bankruptcy protection in June, only three months after the strike had begun. At the end of the year, the company and the union were waiting for a judgment on a National Labor Relations Board charge that Greyhound had brought on the strike by not bargaining sufficiently before imposing a new contract. If the charge is upheld, Greyhound could be liable for over $80 million in back pay. Some creditors began pressuring the company to solve its problems with the union peacefully, seeing that course of action as the only way to keep the company afloat. Union members searched for their own solution by hiring an investment banking firm in an attempt to buy the company themselves.

The mess at Greyhound reminded many observers of what had happened at Continental and Eastern airlines under Frank Lorenzo. On the one side was a powerful man trying to keep a struggling company afloat, claiming that the company's survival depended on employees' willingness to sacrifice. On the other side were employees who felt that they had already sacrificed enough and worried that management was deceiving them and was really intent on breaking their union. These situations seem to represent a turning point for American unions and, more generally, for labor-management relations. Consistent management victories might signal the end of union power; union victories could mean a resurgence of organizing. But at the moment at Greyhound, both sides are losing.

Discussion Questions

1. What went wrong in the way Greyhound dealt with its employees?
2. Is it possible to tell who is truly at fault in the Greyhound situation? If you were called in to arbitrate, what would you try to do?
3. What steps could a company like Greyhound take to try to avoid such a disastrous strike?
4. Are workers' desires for good pay and working conditions incompatible with the company's desire to cut costs and make a profit?

REFERENCES: James Cox, "Strike-forced Chapter 11 Is a Bitter Pill," *USA Today,* June 6, 1990, pp. 1B, 2B; Kevin Kelly, "Greyhound May Be Coming to the End of the Line," *Business Week,* May 21, 1990, p. 45; Robert Tomsho, "Greyhound Head Holds Secret Talks with Union Group," *Wall Street Journal,* May 10, 1990, p. B6; Robert Tomsho, "Greyhound Lines Takes Hard-Line Stand on Hiring Amid Bitter Strike by Drivers," *Wall Street Journal,* March 5, 1990, p. A4; Wendy Zellner, "Labor May Still Have Greyhound Collared," *Business Week,* November 26, 1990, p. 60.

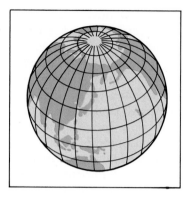

CASE 14.2

Screening and Training the Mazda Way

As Japanese automakers have moved production facilities to the United States to avoid quotas on Japanese cars and to be closer to their customers, they have faced the problem of hiring and training American workers to do things the Japanese way. Ironically, the performance of workers in the country that used to scorn everything "made in Japan" generally doesn't match the performance of their counterparts in Japan, at least according to Japanese bosses. Executives from Mazda and Toyota complain that American workers aren't dedicated, skip work a lot, and aren't interested in teamwork or quality. So Japanese automakers have been spending as much as $13,000 per employee to find and train the best workers the American Midwest has to offer.

The traditional American auto assembly plant reflects the American love of individualism. Each worker performs a specific, defined task and then sends the car down the line to the next worker. At Mazda, however, individuals are rewarded not for their individual performance but for their contribution to the team and the company. Teamwork is not just encouraged but required. Interpersonal skills and an ability to get along with others are prized more highly than technical skills. Mazda wants workers who have the motivation and aptitude to learn new approaches to work.

To make sure that it hires good team workers, Mazda puts job applicants through an unusual series of tests. Applicants learn a new skill — such as how to change a vacuum-cleaner dust bag — and then are assessed on their ability to explain the process to someone else. To practice being group leaders, applicants are presented with a pile of memos that they must deal with in forty minutes. And they are put on a mock assembly line to see how well they can perform the plant's main tasks. While supervisors look on, applicants struggle to install heater fans and floor mats or attach hoses to the right spots in simulated engines.

At the new Diamond-Star plant in Illinois, a joint venture of Chrysler and Mitsubishi, selection processes are also rigorous. Written, medical, and drug tests eliminate a quarter of the applicants, and 40 percent of the rest are screened out during the testing and training process. Even with this kind of selectivity, Diamond-Star still has more than twenty qualified applicants for every job available.

When Mazda opened its new plant in Flat Rock, Michigan, it hired 1,300 people from 10,000 applicants. Once hired, Mazda employees must participate in a number of team-building exercises and discussions. A group learning about interpersonal relations might focus on a worker's problems with her children rather than on gripes about co-workers — it's the principle that's important. Groups learn how to encourage free thought by trying to come up quickly with twenty-five ways to improve a bathtub. Many American automakers have traditionally wanted their workers just to perform a single, repetitive task; but Mazda and the other Japanese automakers want workers to be able to perform several different jobs, give and receive constructive criticism, and make the suggestions that are the basis of *kaizen,* continual improvement.

As workers progress through the training, they form teams that compete with each other. In one session, groups assemble twenty-five flashlights in just over three minutes, then try to achieve the same accomplishment with one less worker. They practice what they've learned by trying to balance the tasks so that they can be completed in the same amount of time as when the team had the extra worker. The team is held responsible for all aspects of the job, including quality and paperwork. Team members may never assemble a flashlight again, but the company hopes that employees will transfer the skills learned in such practice to their new jobs. And these are just the general training sessions. Line workers may spend six more weeks undergoing more specific training and then work under supervision for a month.

The results of all this screening and training have generally been successful, though not everyone is happy. Not all American workers can get used to the idea that they're supposed to take up the slack when one of their team members is sick. Many Japanese automakers have avoided American unions, but Mazda's Flat Rock plant is unionized, to the distress of some Japanese managers. A number of top American managers at Flat Rock have quit, complaining that they can rise only so high in Mazda's hierarchy and expressing frustration at how little responsibility and decision-making latitude they are given. Unionized workers have been ignoring the suggestion box and complain that *kaizen* is just a fancy term for trying to squeeze ever more work out of each employee. Although some American workers have taken to the Japanese way as though it were a religion, others see their work as just another job and still refuse to drive Japanese cars. Clearly, Mazda's screening and training efforts are extensive, but they're not 100 percent successful.

Discussion Questions

1. If you were a human resources manager at Mazda, what personal characteristics or accomplishments would you look for in Americans applying for line jobs?
2. How might Mazda encourage individualistic American workers to be better team players?
3. Would American automakers be wise to adopt Mazda's screening and training techniques?
4. Why do most Japanese automakers stay away from unions? Are union goals always going to clash with those of Japanese management?

REFERENCES: William J. Hampton, "How Does Japan Inc. Pick Its American Workers?" *Business Week,* October 3, 1988, pp. 84–88; Louis Kraar, "Japan's Gung-Ho U.S. Car Plants," *Fortune,* January 30, 1989, pp. 98–108; Gregory A. Patterson, "Mazda-UAW's Michigan Honeymoon Is Over," *Wall Street Journal,* April 17, 1990, p. B1.

15

Operations Management

LEARNING OBJECTIVES

After studying this chapter, you should be able to:

1. Discuss the importance of operations management for manufacturing and service organizations.

2. Describe the different decisions that organizations must make in designing operations management systems.

3. Discuss some of the techniques that organizations use to control operations and inventory.

4. Explain the importance of productivity and how it can be enhanced.

5. Define *quality*, and explain why quality is a strategic concern for organizations.

6. Identify the methods by which organizations may enhance the speed and flexibility of operations.

National Cash Register (now NCR Corporation) began life in 1882. As its original name suggests, the organization made cash registers, as well as adding machines and other business equipment. The firm dominated its industry during the first several decades of the twentieth century but failed to anticipate the emergence of computers as replacements for the mechanical and electrical machines it was making. By 1971 National Cash Register was on the verge of bankruptcy.

In 1972 a new CEO, William Anderson, was hired to save the company. He changed its name to NCR as a way of changing the firm's image. He also reoriented the firm toward the production of automated teller machines, retail scanners, and computers. Within just a few years NCR regained its financial health and is today a leader in innovation and the development of new technology. A good example to illustrate this point is NCR's adoption of concurrent engineering, or CE.

Many American businesses design and develop new products in a sequential, or linear, fashion. The product is designed first, then tested and modified. Next comes planning for production, accompanied by still other modifications. Production processes are tested next, and they, too, often dictate changes. Finally, actual production is started. This sequential process takes a long time and errors or changes have a ripple effect that can be devastating.

With CE, all these activities except actual production take place at one time. When used properly, CE shortens the time necessary to start production and simultaneously eliminates many of the errors or changes that were once commonplace. NCR has adopted concurrent engineering in a variety of areas. One of the firm's major products today is point-of-sale terminals. NCR decided to experiment with CE in the development of its newest model at its Atlanta factory. Everything was finished in twenty-two months — half the time NCR managers had expected. The new terminal had 85 percent fewer parts than the previous model and could be assembled in one-fourth the time.[1]

NCR has rediscovered that operations management is a critical ingredient in organizational effectiveness. American business got its start by taking advantage of mass-production techniques and manufacturing technology such as the assembly line. During the 1960s and 1970s, however, many American businesses began to concentrate more on marketing, and they targeted increasing market share as a major goal. Meanwhile organizations in Japan, Germany, and other countries remained focused on improving efficiency, productivity, and quality. These improvements are often achieved though operations management. Things have now come full circle in the United States, however, and organizations are increasingly recognizing the importance of operations.

This chapter discusses the process of operations management. We first explore the nature of operations management in the manufacturing and service sectors and discuss its strategic value to organizations. We then describe the various decisions that go into designing operations systems. Next we discuss four different avenues for using operations systems. We then discuss in detail three other related topics — productivity, quality, and speed and flexibility — and explain how they can be enhanced.

Operations Management in Organizations

Operations refers to the set of organizational activities used to transform resource inputs into products and services. *Operations systems* control the transformation processes within the organization.

Operations management is the set of managerial activities directed at achieving effective and efficient operations.

Operations refers to the set of organizational activities used to transform resource inputs into products and services.[2] **Operations systems**, which control these transformation processes, include procedures for everything from receiving and handling inventory to performing the steps in manufacturing a product or providing a service. **Operations management** is the set of managerial activities directed at achieving effective and efficient operations. NCR uses operations management when it designs new point-of-sale terminals, buys and assembles electronic components, and then ships the finished product to customers. Likewise, a Taco Bell employee who puts in an order for food and beverage supplies or makes burritos for customers does so according to guidelines spelled out by operations management.

Operations is an important functional concern for any organization. Efficient and effective operations go a long way toward ensuring organizational success. If a firm makes products that are in demand in the marketplace (effectiveness) and produces them in ways that allow them to be sold for reasonable profits (efficiency), the organization will likely succeed. Inefficient or ineffective operations can be disastrous. Making products that consumers do not want (ineffectiveness) or making them in such a way that little or no profit can be achieved (inefficiency) can only cause difficulties for an organization.

From the perspective of economics, operations management creates utility, or value. If the product is a physical item, such as a Yamaha motorcycle, operations provides form utility by combining many dissimilar inputs (sheet metal, rubber, paint, combustion engines, and human craftsmanship) to produce the desired output. The inputs are converted from their incoming forms into a new physical form; this conversion typifies operations in manufacturing organizations.

If the product is a service, operations management provides other types of utility. A service such as British Airways provides time and place utility, since it transports passengers and freight according to agreed-on times and places of departure and arrival. A Miller beer distributorship or The Gap retail chain provides place and possession utility, since it brings products made by others together with customers. Although the organizations in these examples produce different kinds of products or services, it is important to note that their operations processes share many important features.[3]

Operations Management in the Manufacturing Sector

Manufacturing organizations are businesses that combine and transform resource inputs and other resources into tangible goods that are then sold to others.

Operations management used to be called production management because much of American industry was once concentrated in manufacturing. **Manufacturing organizations** are businesses that combine and transform resource inputs and other resources into tangible goods that are then sold to others. Bridgestone Corporation and Goodyear Tire & Rubber Company are manufacturers because they combine rubber and chemical compounds, use blending equipment and molding machines, and create tires. Emerson Electric Company and Sony Corporation are manufacturers because they combine electronic components, wood, plastic, and glass to make stereos, radios, televisions, and other electronic products.

During the 1970s, manufacturing entered a long period of decline in the United States. The major cause of this decline was American industry's inability to compete with foreign companies. Steel companies in the Far East, for example, were able to produce high-quality steel for much lower

Stanley Works, a U.S.-based firm that specializes in manufacturing tools and hardware, has used operations management to compete more effectively against foreign firms. Faced with a tide of cheap imports, the firm automated its plants, increased worker participation, and boosted significantly the quality of its products. This plant uses high-tech, nonpolluting manufacturing processes to chrome-coat tape measure cases better than any other company in the world.

prices than were American companies like Bethlehem Steel and U.S. Steel (now USX). The electronics and automobile industries fared similarly.

Faced with a marketplace battle, many American companies underwent a difficult period of change. The ones that survived transformed themselves into leaner, more efficient and responsive entities. They reduced their work forces dramatically, closed antiquated or unnecessary plants, and modernized their remaining plants. Slowly their efforts have begun to pay off. U.S. steel companies, for example, now use over 80 percent of their production capacity, whereas they once were mired at less than 50 percent. Because they are making better use of their resources, they are operating more efficiently. In copper, paper, textiles, and rubber, American industry has once again become competitive with that of other nations.[4]

Operations Management in the Service Sector

Service organizations transform resources into services that are then sold to customers.

During the decline of the manufacturing sector in the 1970s, one factor that kept the American economy as a whole from declining at the same rate was tremendous growth in the service sector.[5] **Service organizations** transform resources into services that are then sold to customers. When you purchase a service, you are paying someone to do something for you. For example, investors pay Dean Witter to handle their stock transactions, travelers pay Avis to lease them a car, individuals and firms pay Federal Express to transport their documents and packages.

As we saw in Chapter 3, the service sector was responsible for almost 90 percent of all new jobs created in the United States during the 1980s. Today, even though manufacturing is once again on the upswing, the service sector has continued its strong growth.[6] Why has this sector of the economy grown so rapidly? For one thing, people tend to use services when they are made available. When a town has no car wash, people wash their own cars. But when a car wash is installed, many of those same people start paying someone to perform the service for them. Likewise, when a town has no cable television service, people have no choice but to rely on standard reception media. But when cable comes to town, many people subscribe. The increase in the number of service organizations has thus been accompanied by an increased demand for those services.

Another reason for the boom in services is the rise in disposable income in the United States: as people earn more money, they are more willing to pay for services. Still another factor is the increased number of dual-career couples and single-parent families. When both parents work full-time, families are more prone to eat out, to contract their housecleaning, and to pay for laundry services. Thus restaurants, house-cleaning companies, and laundromats — all service organizations — enjoy increased demand for their product.

Operations management is as important to service organizations as it is to manufacturing organizations. The manager of a jet engine manufacturer and the manager of a hospital both must decide how to design their facility, identify the best location for it, and determine optimal capacity. They must

THE ENTREPRENEURIAL CHALLENGE

Fast-Forward for a British Video Chain

Britain has long been a nation of shopkeepers. But when David A. Quayle surveys the charming shop windows, he sees inefficiency and a chance to make money. Quayle pioneered Britain's do-it-yourself industry with a chain of warehouse stores that offered wider selection and cheaper prices than the village hardware store. Now he's at it again. As chief executive of Britain's No. 1 video rental chain, Cityvision PLC, Quayle has been busy acquiring every small retail outlet that comes his way.

With a consortium of investors behind him, Quayle, 53, began by buying a money-losing video distributor in 1986. He shook up the company and raised fresh cash on the London stock exchange to begin his acquisition drive. Today, Cityvision's chain of Ritz video stores numbers 730, and Quayle plans to have 1,000 by the end of this year.

Quayle breezed past the mom-and-pop stores by using computerized ordering and by keeping his stores open long after the shopkeepers have headed for the pubs. Sales soared from $7 million in 1987 to $74 million in 1989, while operating earnings jumped from $1 million to $20.5 million.

But with two out of every three British households owning a videocassette recorder, new competition is looming. The biggest threat to Cityvision is the recent arrival from the United States of Blockbuster Entertainment Corp., which plans to open 400 of its huge stores in Britain by the mid-1990s.

Quayle is confident he can keep it growing. He is sitting on a cash cushion of $25 million and has recently assembled a team of seasoned retailers to guide the chain's expansion. And while he thinks the British video market has five more years of solid growth, he's exploring Spain and Italy for video outlets and eyeing new retailing concepts. Among them: offering candy and popcorn in his stores and opening a new chain that sells rather than rents videos. That's good news for the growing ranks of British couch potatoes.

SOURCE: Reprinted from May 21, 1990 issue of *Business Week* by special permission, copyright © 1990 by McGraw-Hill, Inc.

decide how to store inventory, set procedures for purchasing raw materials, and set standards for productivity and quality. The Entrepreneurial Challenge describes how effective operations management has made Cityvision Britain's number-one video rental chain.

The Strategic Context of Operations Management

Operations management is of sufficient importance to organizations that it must be addressed at every level, starting at the top. Operations managers face myriad decisions that must be integrated with the organization's strategy. For example, the seemingly simple strategic decision of whether to stress high quality regardless of cost, lowest possible cost regardless of quality, or some intermediate combination has complicated implications for operations. The first alternative may require state-of-the-art technology, rigorous control of product design and materials specifications, and thorough quality checks throughout the production process. The second and third alternatives might require lower-grade technology, less concern about product design and materials specifications, and fewer quality checks.

Just as strategy affects operations management, so too does operations management affect strategy. Suppose, for example, a firm decides to upgrade the quality of its products or services. The ability of the organization to implement this strategic decision depends in part on current production capabilities and other resources. If existing technology will not permit higher-quality work, and if the organization lacks the resources to replace its technology, increasing quality to the desired new standards will be very difficult.

Designing Operations Management Systems

The goal of operations management is both efficiency and effectiveness (recall from Chapter 1 that efficiency is a measure of resource utilization, whereas effectiveness is the appropriateness of an organization's activities).[7] All organizations have a variety of questions to address as they design the system of operations management that they will use. The crucial questions generally pertain to the acquisition and utilization of resources for conversion of raw materials into finished goods or services. Of course, even after an operations management system is designed, periodic adjustments may be necessary as the circumstances and strategies of the organization change. Table 15.1 shows four categories of design decisions.

Product/Service Design Decisions

Product/service design decisions determine what products or services the organization will provide to customers.

Product/service design decisions determine what products or services the organization is going to offer to customers. Subsidiary questions cover actual product design, packaging, and related considerations. Colgate-Palmolive, for example, makes regular, tartar-control, and gel formulas of Colgate toothpaste and packages them in several different sizes of tubes and pumps. These decisions should flow logically from the various strategies (corporate and business strategies) discussed in Chapters 7 and 8.

Table 15.1

Decision Areas in Designing Operations Management Systems

Product/service design decisions	Facilities decisions
• product line	• location
• quality	• layout
• cost	**Technology decisions**
• design	• traditional methods
Capacity decisions	labor-intensive technology
• demand	capital-intensive technology
• variation and flexibility	• FMS/CIM
	• CAD/CAM

Organizational strategy also helps determine the level of quality, the optimal cost, and the design of each product or service. As noted at the beginning of the chapter, NCR has made the decision to manufacture, among other products, point-of-sale terminals. The firm reduced the number of parts in its terminals by 85 percent and then combined this product-design decision with other operating innovations to cut production time significantly. A key part of this breakthrough was making many of the parts interchangeable. The various decisions that NCR has made about what products to produce and how to produce them are a part of its product/service design decisions.

Capacity Decisions

Capacity decisions determine how much volume of output the organization wants to be capable of creating.

Capacity decisions determine how much volume of output the organization wants to be capable of creating. This decision involves choosing the amount of conversion capacity appropriate for the organization.[8] Determining whether to build a factory capable of making 5,000 or 8,000 units per day is a capacity decision. So, too, is deciding whether to build a restaurant with seating for 100 or 150 patrons or a bank with 5 or 10 teller stations. The capacity decision offers high risk because of the uncertainties of future product demand and the large monetary stakes involved. The organization may build capacity that exceeds its needs and requires resource commitments (capital investment) that may never be recovered. Many American firms made this mistake during the 1960s and 1970s. Or the organization may build capacity that does not meet demand. This error may result in lost market opportunities, but it may also free capital resources for use elsewhere in the organization.

A key consideration in determining capacity is estimating demand. A company operating in a stable environment with fairly constant monthly demand might build a plant capable of producing an amount each month roughly equivalent to that demand. But if its market is characterized by seasonal fluctuations, it might be better advised to build a smaller plant to meet normal demand and then plan to add extra shifts during peak periods. Likewise, it would probably be unwise for a restaurant that needs 150 seats for Saturday night but never more than 100 at any other time to expand to 150 seats. During the rest of the week, the restaurant must still pay to light, heat, cool, and clean the excess capacity. Expanding capacity to 150 seats might be a good idea, however, if demand will or can be increased in the near future.

Facilities Decisions

Facilities are the physical surroundings in which products or services are created or stored and from which they are distributed.

Facilities are the physical surroundings in which products or services are created and stored and from which they are distributed.

Location   Facilities location must be determined by the needs and requirements of the organization. For example, because General Motors relies heavily on railroads to transport raw materials and finished goods, most of its facilities are located close to rail facilities. In contrast, because Weyerhaeuser relies on trucks, its facilities tend to be located near major highway arteries. Of course, different organizations in the same industry often made different facilities-location decisions. Benetton, for example, uses only one distribution center for the entire world. K mart, in contrast, has several distribution centers in the United States alone. Each decision takes the organization's particular environment and product strategy into account.

Common facilities layouts are product, process, and fixed-position layouts.

Layout The physical configuration, or the layout, of facilities depends on previous decisions about product or service line, capacity, and location. The three layout alternatives shown in Figure 15.1 help demonstrate the importance of this decision. A **product layout** is appropriate when an organization makes large quantities of a single product. It makes sense to custom design a straight-line flow of work for this one product, in which a specific task is performed at each work station as each unit flows through. Most large-scale assembly lines, such as in Compaq Computer factories, use product layout.

Process layout is appropriate for organizations that create a variety of products. Auto repair shops and health care clinics are good examples; each automobile and each individual is a separate "product." Only the

Figure 15.1

Common Facilities Layouts

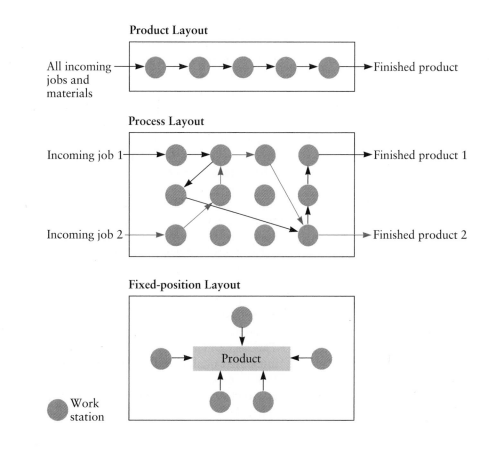

Product Layout

All incoming jobs and materials → Finished product

Process Layout

Incoming job 1 → Finished product 1

Incoming job 2 → Finished product 2

Fixed-position Layout

Product

Work station

general nature of each job is known in advance, and detailed product specifications cannot be determined until the customer's arrival. The needs of each incoming job are diagnosed as it enters the operations system, and the job is routed through the unique sequence of work stations needed to create the desired finished product. In process layout, each type of conversion task is centralized in a single work station or department. A patient who needs x-rays and blood tests, for example, will be sent to different locations to have these performed and then return to the physician's examining room.

Fixed-position layout is used by organizations that create a few very large and complex products. Aircraft manufacturers like Airbus and shipbuilders like Newport News use this method. Because an assembly line capable of moving a passenger airliner would require an enormous plant, the airplane itself remains stationary and people and machines move around it as it is assembled.

Technology Decisions

Operations technology is the set of procedures through which the organization transforms resources into products or services.

Operations technology is the set of procedures through which the organization transforms resources into products or services. Machines that transform crude oil into gasoline for Royal Dutch/Shell are part of its technology. Technology varies from highly labor-intensive to highly capital-intensive. A home-cleaning service, a software design firm, and a professional football team are highly labor-intensive: people do the work. An automated factory or oil refinery, however, is more capital-intensive: expensive machinery does the work. The degree of mechanization and automation that an organization chooses greatly affects output quality, production costs, labor and management skills required, and operations flexibility (the organization's ability to alter its operations procedures).

Although the technologies of most service organizations continue to be highly labor-intensive, relatively more capital-intensive options have evolved. Especially with increasing applications of computers, traditionally labor-intensive professional services such as medicine, law, and education and other service industries such as commercial banking have adopted more capital-intensive technologies for creating and delivering their products. For example, physicians rely more heavily on sophisticated equipment than they once did.

New technologies that have had a significant impact on organizations include flexible manufacturing systems (FMS), computer-integrated manufacturing (CIM), computer-aided design (CAD), and computer-aided manufacturing (CAM).

New technologies have also had a significant impact on organizations over the last few years.[9] **Flexible manufacturing systems** (**FMS**) rely on computers to coordinate and integrate automated facilities.[10] Computers control the flow of resources through the plant, and robots perform many of the tasks. The system is flexible in that resources can be routed several different ways and many robots can perform several different functions. This technology is closely related to another approach called **computer-integrated manufacturing** (**CIM**). At Allen-Bradley in Milwaukee, an IBM mainframe computer controls a manufacturing system that produces six hundred units per hour — with only four technicians in the whole plant.

Another new technology is **computer-aided design (CAD)**, usually used in conjunction with **computer-aided manufacturing (CAM)**. As the term suggests, CAD is use of computers to design new products and services. General Electric uses CAD to redesign its circuit breakers, and Benetton uses CAD to design new clothing styles and product specifications. A properly designed CAD system can tie directly into a CAM system. For example, when a Benetton store needs to order some new blue sweaters, the information is transmitted to a Benetton mainframe computer in Italy. The CAD system, which has a record of all the product specifications, relays the order to a knitting machine, which actually makes the new sweaters. Meanwhile another machine prints out an address label and a copy of the original order. Only when everything is done does a human being step in to provide a final check for quality and accuracy.[11]

Using Operations Systems

Operations systems control operations in accordance with organizational strategy.

Operations systems are created to control the transformation processes within the organization in accordance with the strategic goals of quality, costs, and so forth. In Chapter 12 we noted that three forms of operations control are preliminary, screening, and postaction control. In practice, operations systems apply these forms of control to a number of organizational activities, including materials acquisition, inventory management, and quality control.

Controlling Operations

Operations control ensures that resources and activities attain primary goals such as a high percentage of on-time deliveries, low unit-production cost, or high product reliability. The control system should focus on the elements that are most crucial to goal attainment. For example, if product quality is an important concern (as for a Mountblanc pen), the firm might adopt screening controls to continually monitor the product as it is being created. If quantity is a more pressing goal (as for a BIC pen), postaction controls might be used to identify defects at the end of the system without disrupting the manufacturing process itself. The particular technology adopted by the organization will greatly effect design of the control system.

One way of using operations management as control is to coordinate it with other organizational functions, such as marketing. Monsanto, for example, established a consumer products division that mass-produces and distributes a line of fertilizers and lawn chemicals. This division is a well-defined entity within the corporation. The operations function of the division is organized as an autonomous profit center responsible for defined profit goals. Monsanto finds this useful and effective, because its manufacturing group has the authority to determine not only the costs of creating the product but also the product price and the marketing programs.

Divisions like the one established by Monsanto should be accountable only for the activities over which they have decision-making authority. Under a bureaucratic form of organizational control, this accountability is spelled out in rules and regulations. Under clan control, it is likely to be simply understood and accepted by everyone. It would probably be inappropriate to make operations accountable for profitability in an organization with a marketing-dominated competitive strategy, since marketing will determine prices (a determinant of profitability). Such misplaced accountability results in ineffective organizational control. Depending on the strategic role of operations, operations managers are accountable for different kinds of results.

Techniques for Controlling Operations

Some of the most important techniques of operations control are materials resource planning, statistical quality control, and PERT.

Materials Resource Planning   One important part of controlling operations is coordination, the process of planning what resources to buy and when to have them delivered in order to do the work of the organization effectively. Say, for example, a contractor about to begin construction of a new house needs 2-×-4–inch lumber for framing the walls. Obviously the contractor does not order lumber one piece at a time but instead determines in advance how much lumber will be required and when it will be needed. If the 2-×-4s are delivered too early, they may get stolen or scattered, but construction will be delayed if they are delivered too late.

Materials requirements planning (MRP) is a computerized ordering system that keeps track of inventory on hand and orders additional inventory as needed to maintain minimum levels.

The importance of materials resource planning has become increasingly apparent in recent years as organizations have come to realize that when done properly it can save the organization money. One popular control technique is called **materials requirements planning (MRP)**. An MRP system, as shown in Figure 15.2, is a computerized ordering system that keeps track of current inventory levels and reorders to maintain predefined minimum levels. For example, an organization might decide that it always needs to keep 1,000 units (pounds, gallons, or other measures) of a certain raw material on hand. Every time units are removed from inventory, the system reduces its inventory count accordingly. If the average usage is around 100 units per week and it takes two weeks for new orders to arrive, the system will automatically place a new order for materials when current supplies drop below 1,200 units.

A *just-in-time (JIT) delivery system* delivers parts for assembly just as they are needed.

Organizations have also started relying more and more on **just-in-time (JIT) delivery systems**. A JIT system arranges for parts to be delivered to an assembly plant just as they are needed, in contrast to the traditional method of ordering in large quantities and storing resources until needed. An advantage of both MRP and JIT is that they lower storage facility requirements and thus costs, since they enable organizations to function with smaller warehouses and storerooms. On the other hand, these systems require considerable coordination and integration. Arriving materials are

Figure 15.2

Sample MRP System

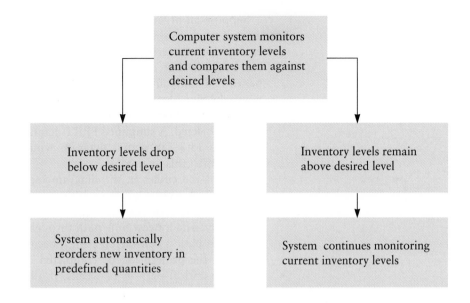

Computer system monitors current inventory levels and compares them against desired levels

Inventory levels drop below desired level

Inventory levels remain above desired level

System automatically reorders new inventory in predefined quantities

System continues monitoring current inventory levels

often sent directly to where they will be used, and the organization may have to temporarily stop production if arriving shipments are delayed.

Statistical quality control (SQC) is a set of statistical procedures developed to help organizations monitor quality. Two SQC methods are acceptance sampling and in-process sampling.

Statistical Quality Control   As the term suggests, **statistical quality control** (**SQC**) is a method of managing quality. It is actually a set of specific statistical techniques used to monitor quality. Acceptance sampling is the sampling of finished goods to ensure that quality standards have been met. It is therefore a form of postaction control. The foundation of effective acceptance sampling is determining what percentage of the products should be tested (for example, 2, 5, or 25 percent). This decision is especially important when the test renders the product useless (for example, flash cubes, wine, and collapsible steering wheels).

Another SQC method is in-process sampling. In-process sampling involves evaluating the products during production so that needed changes can be made. It is therefore a type of screening control. The painting department of a furniture company may periodically check the tint of the paint it is using and adjust the color as necessary to conform to customer standards. The advantage of in-process sampling is that it allows problems to be detected before they accumulate.

PERT is an operations control technique for managing the total length of time needed to complete a project.

PERT   **PERT** is an operations control technique that establishes a network of activities and their interrelationships in order to highlight critical time intervals that affect the length of the overall project. An acronym for Program Evaluation and Review Technique, PERT was developed in 1958 by the U.S. Navy to help coordinate the activities of three thousand contractors during the development of the Polaris nuclear submarine. It was credited with saving two years of work on that project and has subsequently been used by most large companies.

Suppose an organization wants to use PERT to plan the construction of a small machine shop. Some activities must be performed in sequence. For example, a concrete slab must be poured before the frame for the building can be built. But other activities, such as wiring and plumbing, can be performed simultaneously. Each activity is plotted on a flow diagram, or network, that identifies the sequence in which the activities will be done and the interrelationship of activities. The time interval between activities is also projected. A simplified PERT diagram for the machine shop is shown in Figure 15.3 (an actual diagram would be much more complex and detailed than this example).

Each of the circles in the diagram represents an activity that must be completed. Activities connected by lines must be completed in sequence. Each line carries an estimate of the amount of time necessary to complete an activity. The longest time path through the network is called the *critical path*. This path is considered critical because it represents the shortest time in which the project can be completed. For the project shown in Figure 15.3, the critical path is 12 weeks. If all activities remain on schedule, it will take 12 weeks to get the new facility operational.

A starting point in using PERT is to look for ways to refine the network. For example, suppose the organization needs to have the machine shop operational in 11 weeks. By reallocating resources, the organization may be able to shorten the critical path. For example, if the vendor installing the equipment can be persuaded to accelerate installation by one week, the critical path will be shortened from 12 to 11 weeks. Installing the plumbing in less than a week wouldn't help, because that activity is not on the critical path. Monitoring progress along the critical path also serves as a useful control function. If an activity along the path is two weeks behind schedule, that time must be made up or else the project completion date will slip. For example, if it takes the organization 2.5 weeks to get the roof built, the entire project falls behind schedule by half a week.

Managing Materials Acquisition

Materials acquisitions management, or purchasing management, is the procedure of buying the materials or resources that the organization needs to function.

Materials acquisitions management, or **purchasing management,** is the procedure of buying the materials and resources needed to produce the organization's products and services.[12] The purchasing manager for a local clothing store is responsible for buying the merchandise that the store will sell. The purchasing manager for a manufacturer buys raw materials, parts, and machines needed by the organization. Large organizations like General Motors, IBM, and Westinghouse have large purchasing departments.

Materials acquisition is a game of balance. Buying too much of a particular material or product ties up capital and increases storage costs. Buying too little might lead to shortages and higher reordering costs. For example, when the organization orders in small quantities, it may not qualify for quantity discounts offered by suppliers, or it may have to pay extra shipping costs in order to get the order delivered quickly. The quality of the materials must meet the organization's needs; the supplier must be reliable; and the financial terms must be acceptable.

Figure 15.3

Simplified PERT Diagram for
Building a Small Machine Shop

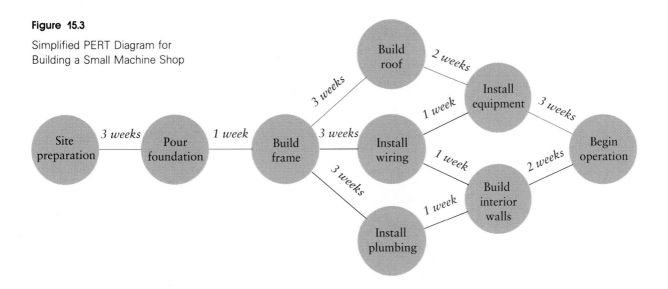

Many firms have recently changed their approach to purchasing in order to lower costs and improve quality and productivity. Rather than relying, as they did in the past, on hundreds or even thousands of suppliers, many companies have reduced the number of suppliers and negotiated special production and delivery arrangements with them. For example, the Honda plant in Marysville, Ohio, negotiated an agreement with a local business-man. He agreed to start a new company to mount car stereo speakers into plastic moldings. He delivers finished goods to the Honda plant three times a day, and Honda buys all he can manufacture. Thus he has a stable sales base; Honda has a local and reliable supplier; and both companies benefit.[13]

Ford, Sears, and other companies have streamlined their purchasing systems, choosing to restrict the number of suppliers in exchange for greater cooperation and higher quality standards from the suppliers they retain. For example, Ford can now tell a supplier that it will be getting more business (because Ford will buy only from that one supplier) if it raises its quality standards or lowers its prices. In addition to the cost and quality benefits, Ford can also manage with a smaller purchasing staff because it is dealing with fewer suppliers.

Managing Inventory

Inventory control, or materials control, is concerned with managing raw materials, work-in-process, finished goods, and in-transit inventories.

Inventory control, also called **materials control**, focuses on managing the various inventories held by an organization.[14] The four kinds of inventories are raw materials, work-in-process, finished-goods, and in-transit inventories. As shown in Table 15.2, the sources of control over these inventories are as different as their purposes.

Raw materials inventory constitutes the resources the organization has on hand for use in producing goods and services. For example, the raw materials inventory for a furniture manufacturer consists of wood, cloth,

Table 15.2

Inventory Types, Purposes, and
Sources of Control

Type of Inventory	Purpose	Source of Control
Raw materials	Provides the materials needed to make the product	Purchasing models and systems
Work-in-process	Enables overall production to be divided into stages of manageable size	Shop-floor control systems
Finished goods	Provides ready supply of products upon customer demand and enables long, efficient production runs	High-level production-scheduling systems in conjunction with marketing
In-transit	Distributes products to customers	Transportation and distribution control systems

glue, nails, and other materials used to make sofas and chairs. Control of raw materials is achieved through purchasing systems and is the responsibility of the purchasing department.

Work-in-process inventories consist of products that are partially completed and need further processing. A sofa frame that has not yet been covered with upholstery would be a part of the organization's work-in-process inventory. Shop managers are responsible for controlling work-in-process through work schedule and sequencing.

Finished goods are products that have been completed and are awaiting sale or distribution. The quantities and costs of finished-goods inventories are under the control of the overall production-scheduling system, which is determined by higher-level planning decisions. Completed sofas and chairs would be the finished-goods inventory for the furniture company.

Finally, in-transit inventories are completed products that have been shipped to but not yet received by customers. A truck full of sofas and chairs en route to a furniture retailer is considered to be in-transit inventory for the manufacturer, since the shipper is responsible for goods that are lost or damaged before the customer takes possession of them. In-transit inventories are controlled by the transportation and distribution system.

Each of these inventories has its own goals regarding materials cost and quantity. Organizations should monitor inventories and take action to correct significant deviations from these goals.

Like most other areas of operations management, inventory management has been the source of much change in recent years. JIT delivery has enabled organizations to reduce investment in both storage space and inventory on hand, but it requires high levels of coordination and cooperation between the company and its suppliers. Johnson Controls, which makes automobile seats for Chrysler and then ships them by small truckloads to a Chrysler plant seventy-five miles away, schedules each shipment to arrive two hours before it is needed. If the seats arrive too early, Chrysler has no place to store them. If they arrive too late, the entire assembly line may have to be shut down, resulting in enormous expense (Chrysler does maintain a small buffer stock, but only enough for assembling a few cars). When properly designed and used, however, JIT delivery is a very effective method for controlling inventory.

Managing Productivity

Productivity has been a topic of considerable discussion, research, and debate over the past several years. American workers are still the most productive in the world, but workers in other countries achieve greater productivity growth rates than their U.S. counterparts.

The Nature of Productivity

Productivity is an economic measure of efficiency that summarizes what is produced in relation to the resources used to produce it.

As we saw briefly in Chapter 3, **productivity** is an economic measure of efficiency that summarizes what is produced in relation to the resources used to produce it.[15] Productivity may be assessed at different levels and in different forms.

Levels of Productivity Figure 15.4 shows five different levels of productivity. The most basic level is the productivity of each individual worker in an organization. Unit productivity reflects the efficiency of organizational units such as plants or divisions. Organizational productivity reflects the efficiency and profitability of the overall firm. Industry productivity is the total productivity achieved by all the firms in a particular industry. Aggregate productivity is the total productivity achieved by a country.

Forms of Productivity There are many different forms of productivity.[16] Total factor productivity is an overall indicator of how well an organization uses all of its resources to create all of its products and services. It is determined by this formula:

$$\text{Total Factor Productivity} = \frac{\text{Outputs}}{\text{Labor + Capital + Materials + Energy Inputs}}$$

The biggest problem with total factor productivity is that for the formula to be meaningful, all the ingredients must be quantified in the same terms — dollars (it is meaningless to add hours of labor to number of units of a raw material). This measure also gives little insight into how to improve productivity. Consequently, most organizations find it more useful to calculate a partial productivity ratio focusing on a single form of productivity.

Figure 15.4

Levels of Productivity

Aggregate
productivity

Industry
productivity

Organizational
productivity

Unit
productivity

Individual
productivity

Such a ratio uses only one category of resource. For example, direct labor productivity is calculated by a simpler formula:

$$\text{Direct Labor Productivity} = \frac{\text{Outputs}}{\text{Direct Labor}}$$

(Direct labor is labor that contributes to the actual production of goods or services, as opposed to the indirect labor of office staff, sales representatives, and so forth.)

This measure has several advantages. Using it, an organization need not transform the units of input — labor hours — into some other unit. Moreover, an organization can monitor the ratio over time to see trends in productivity among its labor force or to compare the organization's ratio to industry standards. Simply put, direct labor productivity provides a direct indicator of productivity in relation to a single type of resource.

The Importance of Productivity

Productivity determines an organization's profitability and ultimately its ability to survive. Suppose two tool manufacturers have significantly different levels of productivity. The firm with higher productivity will have more products to sell, can sell them at lower prices, and will have more profits to reinvest in growth and expansion. The firm with lower productivity, on the other hand, will be making fewer products, will have to charge higher prices to cover costs, and will have fewer profits to invest in other operations.

Productivity is also important because it partially determines the living standards of people. The goods and services that organizations create can be used by citizens or be exported for sale in other countries. The more goods and services the businesses within a country can produce, the more goods and services a country's citizens will have. Exported goods and services bring financial resources flowing back into the country. Thus the citizens of a highly productive country are likely to have higher living standards than are the citizens of a country with low productivity.

The United States has the highest productivity in the world. In 1990, each worker in America produced goods or services worth $39,200. The second best productivity was achieved by Canada ($37,400).[17] These statistics give only a partial picture, though. An alarming trend beginning in the 1960s and continuing into the early 1980s showed that the rate of productivity growth (increases in annual productivity per worker) in the United States had stalled, especially in comparison with rates in other industrialized countries. For example, from 1966 to 1976, productivity growth in the United States averaged only 1.6 percent per year, and from 1976 to 1981 it grew only 0.7 percent each year. In contrast, during this same period productivity grew at a much faster pace in many other industrialized countries.

Recognition of this trend spurred many U.S. businesses and industries to retrench, retool, and become more competitive in the world marketplace. Consequently, productivity in this country has rebounded strongly. Although there are still differences across industries, productivity growth rates in the United States are once again competitive with those of other industrialized nations. The Global Challenge discusses how the Cummins Engine Company has responded to international competition.

Enhancing Productivity

How does a business or industry improve its productivity? Perhaps the two most significant actions **that** an organization can take are to improve operations and to increase employee involvement.

THE GLOBAL CHALLENGE

Cummins Fights Back

The Cummins Engine Company was founded in 1919. The firm started out making diesel engines for manufacturers of tractors and trucks. It grew to be a large and highly profitable enterprise, with annual sales of over $3.5 billion. But like many other American companies, Cummins has been hard hit by increased Japanese competitiveness.

CEO Henry Schacht, however, was astute enough to see international competition on the horizon. He decided to anticipate it, rather than wait and react to it. While other American firms gave up their markets or tried to differentiate themselves from Japanese competitors, Cummins planned from the very beginning to beat them at their own game.

First of all, Schacht toured Japanese plants to see firsthand how they functioned. He then spent over $1 billion overhauling Cummins's technology by building new plants and modernizing old ones. In the mid-1980s, the competitors arrived—and Cummins was ready. Two Japanese firms, Nissan Motor Co. and Komatsu, Ltd., introduced diesel engines into the United States at prices 25 percent lower than those charged by Cummins. But Schacht was able to match their prices and demonstrate that his engines were of higher quality. Cummins's customers remained loyal, and the firm actually increased its market share.

The competitive threat is not past. Continued efforts by Japanese firms to enter the American market have sliced Cummins's profit margins so thin that the company's stock prices have started to drop. This makes the firm a ripe target for a takeover. But Schacht isn't giving up. He recently lined up three big investors to help reduce the firm's debt and thus increase its profits once again. All things considered, it looks as though Cummins is here to stay.

REFERENCES: "Turning Cummins into the Engine Maker That Could," *Business Week,* July 30, 1990, p. 20; Gary Hoover, Alta Campbell, and Patrick J. Spain, eds., *Hoover's Handbook—Profiles of Over 500 Major Corporations* (Austin, Tex.: The Reference Press, 1990), p. 196; "Cummins Hits Turnaround Roadblock," *Wall Street Journal,* September 25, 1989, p. A6.

Improving Operations   Organizations that improve operations find ways to enhance the kinds of products they make or the processes they use to make products. One way to improve operations is to increase spending on research and development. R&D spending helps identify new products, new uses for existing products, and new methods for making products, all of which contribute to productivity. Bausch & Lomb fell behind in the market for extended-wear contact lenses because the firm had neglected R&D. Recognizing its mistake, it made R&D a top-priority item. As a result, the company has made several significant scientific breakthroughs, shortened the time needed to introduce new products, and greatly enhanced both total sales and profits—and all with a smaller work force than the company used to have.[18]

Organizations can also boost productivity by reassessing and revamping their facilities. Many American factories are older than Japanese factories. Investing in newer and and more efficient plants may increase U.S. competitiveness. Although simply building a new factory is no guarantee of success, IBM, Ford, Allen-Bradley, Caterpillar, and many other American businesses have achieved dramatic productivity gains by revamping their production facilities. Facilities refinements are not limited to manufacturers.

For example, many McDonald's restaurants have added two features that increase productivity by speeding up customer service: drive-up windows, and soft-drink dispensers out on the restaurant floor that allow customers to pour their own drinks.

Increasing Employee Involvement Many organizations are adopting participative management techniques, since evidence suggests that employee involvement often increases productivity (we discuss this more fully in Chapter 17).[19] This involvement might range from giving individual workers a greater voice in how they do their jobs to formal cooperation between management and labor to instituting employee involvement throughout the entire organization. For example, at one General Electric factory most supervisory positions have been eliminated, and most of the control has been put in the hands of workers. That plant is now turning out more units than six plants did previously. Various other participative management techniques have also been shown to enhance productivity.

Managing Quality

The catalyst for the emergence of quality as a mainstream management concern for U.S. firms was the gain made by foreign businesses. Nowhere was this gain more visible than in the auto industry. During the energy crisis in the late 1970s, many people purchased automobiles made by Toyota, Honda, and Datsun (now Nissan) because they were more fuel

Quality can be an unexpected— as well as important—issue with many products. Take, for example, Legos, the ubiquitous plastic building blocks that are a staple of many children's toy boxes. Lego makes billions of the little plastic blocks each year, and each one has to snap together perfectly with all the others. To ensure this end, each piece has to undergo a host of quality tests, including one that simulates the bite of a small child!

efficient than their American counterparts. Consumers soon discovered that the Japanese-made cars were also of higher quality. Parts fit together better; the trim work was neater; and the cars were more reliable. After the energy crisis subsided, the Japanese cars remained formidable competitors because of their reputation for quality.

The Nature and Importance of Quality

Quality is the total set of features and characteristics that determine the ability of a product or service to satisfy needs.

The American Society for Quality Control defines **quality** as the totality of features and characteristics that bear on the ability of a product or service to satisfy stated or implied needs.[20] Quality is an important concern for organizations because of its role in competition, productivity, and cost control.[21]

Competition   Today, quality is a selling point. Ford, Chrysler, and General Motors each argues that its cars are highest in quality. IBM, Apple, and Digital each stresses the quality of its products. A business that fails to maintain product quality may find itself falling behind both its foreign and its American competitors. The Environmental Challenge summarizes how one restaurant has used quality to its competitive advantage for years.

Productivity   Organizations have come to recognize the positive relationship between quality and productivity. If a firm is able to enhance the quality of what it produces, three outcomes are likely. First, the number of defects will decrease, so there will be fewer returns from customers. Second, as the number of defects goes down, resources (materials and people) dedicated to reworking flawed output will decrease. Third, making workers more responsible for quality reduces the need for quality inspectors. Since the organization is now able to produce its product with fewer resources, productivity will increase.

Costs   Improved quality lowers costs. Poor quality results in higher returns from customers, high warranty costs, and even lawsuits filed over faulty products. It also damages future sales. An organization with quality problems often has to increase inspection expenses just to catch defective products. For example, as a result of its successful efforts to enhance product quality, IBM now uses 25 percent fewer quality-control inspectors than it did just five years ago. This reduction translates into lower labor costs.[22]

Enhancing Quality

The starting point for quality is a strategic commitment by top management. This commitment is often referred to as **total quality control**—a real and meaningful effort by an organization to change its strategy to make quality a guiding factor in everything it does. Strategic commitment is important for several reasons. First, the organizational culture must change to reflect the recognition that quality is not just an ideal but a goal

THE ENVIRONMENTAL CHALLENGE

Quality Makes Steak King

What role does quality play in a restaurant's success? Most customers have a pretty good idea — reasonable prices, good food, cleanliness, and a courteous staff. The trend in the restaurant industry has been toward small, specialized eating areas catering to a well-defined clientele. It certainly seems as if this type of place could do a better job of quality control than could a large, full-menu restaurant that attracts all kinds of customers.

But for fifty-four years the Hilltop Steak House right outside Boston has defied the experts. Each year approximately 2.4 million people make the trek to the outskirts of the city to eat at Hilltop. The restaurant seats 1,400 people and serves over 4,000 meals on a good Saturday night.

What's Hilltop's secret? Quality. Hilltop's owner, 73-year-old Frank Giuffrida, insists on nothing but fresh, top-quality meat — including 40,000 pounds of beef every week. He also keeps prices low, with an average tab of $15 per person. The staff is trained to strict standards of cleanliness, higher even than those set by the health department. Courtesy is stressed in every training program that the organization sponsors for its employees.

Hilltop combines this approach to quality with a concern for efficiency. Giuffrida has set up two lines for servers to pick up food from the kitchen. They enter through one of two middle doors, pick up their orders, and then go back out through side doors. Giuffrida has recently decided to take his magic to new venues. He and a partner have opened three smaller Hilltop restaurants in other New England locations and plan to open several more during the next few years.

REFERENCES: "Quantity Reigns at Hilltop," *USA Today,* August 22, 1990, pp. B1, B2; "Making the Grade with the Customer," *Wall Street Journal,* November 12, 1990, pp. B1, B8; Patricia Sellers, "Getting Customers to Love You," *Fortune,* March 13, 1989, pp. 38–49.

to pursue. Second, a decision to pursue the goal of quality carries with it some real costs — new equipment, facilities, and employee training. Without a commitment from top management, quality improvement will prove to be just a slogan or a gimmick, with little or no concrete change in operations.

Employee Involvement   We noted earlier the importance of employee involvement in enhancing productivity. It is no less important in improving quality. Virtually all successful quality enhancement programs involve making the person responsible for doing the job also responsible for making sure it's done right.[23]

Technology   New forms of technology often improve quality. Robots, for example, can often make products more precisely and consistently than can people. CAD/CAM systems in particular are good ways to enhance quality because they overcome human limitations and errors in intricate design and manufacturing operations. Investing in higher-grade machines that enable operators to do jobs more precisely and reliably often improves quality. AT&T has achieved significant improvements in product quality by replacing many of its manufacturing machines, some of them decades old, with newer equipment.[24]

Materials   Organizations can improve product quality by improving the quality of raw materials. Suppose, for example, a company that assembles stereos buys electronic chips and circuits from a supplier. If the chips have a high failure rate, consumers will return defective stereos to the company that assembled them, not to the chip supplier. Many firms have increased the quality requirements they impose on their suppliers as a way of improving the quality of their own products and services.

Operating Methods   Operating methods are the actual procedures and systems that the organization uses during the transformation process. Shearson Lehman Hutton, a large brokerage firm owned by American Express, found that its offices were late in redeeming customer bonds 80 percent of the time and that the amount of the redemption was wrong 20 percent of the time. The firm studied and then improved operating methods in use. The results have been impressive: the time needed to redeem customer bonds has been cut in half, and the accuracy of those redemptions has increased to 98 percent.[25] Another way to improve operating methods is statistical quality control, which we discussed earlier in this chapter.

Managing Speed and Flexibility

Speed and flexibility are strategic concerns for contemporary organizations. Philips, a Dutch electronics firm, introduced the first VCR in 1972, three years before Japanese firms. Because it was first, Philips did not concern itself too much about product refinements or new versions. Soon, however, Japanese-made VCRs flooded the market. By the time Philips got around to introducing its second-generation machine in 1979, Japanese VCR makers had already gone through three generations of products and defined VHS as the industry standard. Today, Philips is an also-ran in the VCR industry.

But the firm learned an important lesson. When Philips introduced the first compact disc player in 1983, it already had plans for a second-generation model under development, and one team of engineers was sketching designs for the third-generation machine. This time, because the firm remained at the forefront of innovation, its technology became the industry standard. Philips still controls over 20 percent of the world market for CD players.[26]

The Nature and Importance of Speed and Flexibility

Speed is the organization's ability to develop and introduce new products or services on a timely basis. *Flexibility* is the organization's ability to adapt and modify its operations systems.

Speed refers to the organization's ability to develop and introduce new products or services on a timely basis. **Flexibility** is the organization's ability to adapt and modify its operations systems. One recent survey identified speed as the number-one strategic issue confronting managers in the 1990s.[27]

Speed is fast becoming a major ingredient of competitive success between businesses around the world. Kodak, a company historically viewed as quite hierarchical, has given work teams the power and responsibility to identify areas where productivity and speed could be improved. This team cut the production time needed to make X-ray cassettes by almost two-thirds. In another Kodak facility—the precision components manufacturing division—a team figured out how to cut the time needed to accomplish a certain quantity of work from three shifts to one.

An emphasis on speed can be directed at any functional area, including developing, making, and distributing products or services. General Electric once needed three weeks to design and manufacture a custom-made industrial circuit breaker. At the time, GE also had six plants making the breakers and relied on 28,000 parts. Today, GE can deliver higher-quality breakers in three days. One factor in this dizzying increase in speed has been the flexibility gained by relying on only 1,275 parts.[28]

Enhancing Speed and Flexibility

Table 15.3 identifies methods that some companies have developed to help increase the speed of their operations. General Electric, for example, found it better to start from scratch with a totally remodeled plant. The firm wiped out delay-causing approvals by eliminating most managerial positions and now uses teams as a basis for organizing work. Taking schedules seriously helped Motorola build a new plant and start production of a new product in only eighteen months. Benetton, a paragon of streamlined distribution, has only one warehouse to serve 5,000 stores in 60 countries. But the state-of-the-art facility, which cost $30 million to build, ships 230,000 pieces of clothing daily — and employs only eight people! Finally, organizations must instill an appreciation for speed in their corporate culture. Honda started to sponsor Formula One car racing only a few years ago, but by rotating new engineers through the Formula One team, the organization has made speed an important element of its culture.

Table 15.3

Methods for Increasing Speed of Operations

1. Start from scratch (it's usually easier than trying to do what the organization does now but in a faster way).

2. Minimize the number of approvals needed to do something (the fewer people who have to approve something, the faster it will get done).

3. Use work teams as a basis for organization (teamwork and cooperation work better than individual effort and conflict).

4. Develop and adhere to a schedule (a properly designed schedule can greatly increase speed).

5. Don't ignore distribution (making something faster is only part of the battle).

6. Integrate speed into the organization's culture (if everyone understands the importance of speed, things will naturally get done quicker).

SOURCE: From Brian Dumaine, "How Managers Can Succeed Through Speed," *Fortune*, February 13, 1989. © 1989 The Time Inc. Magazine Company. All rights reserved.

Flexibility can be enhanced through any number of different technologies. Implementing a flexible manufacturing system by definition enhances organizational flexibility. So, too, does using CAD/CAM. Many organizations increase the flexibility of their work force by training employees to perform a number of different jobs. Such crosstraining allows the firm to function with fewer workers, because individuals can be transferred easily to areas where they are most needed. For example, at the Lechmere department store in Sarasota, Florida, a single employee can operate a forklift in the stockroom, serve as a cashier, or provide customer service on the sales floor. At one Motorola plant, 397 out of 400 employees have learned at least two skills under a similar program.

An important part of making worker flexibility successful is rewarding people for learning new skills and using them proficiently. At Motorola, workers who master a new skill are then assigned to a job in that area for a five-day period. If they perform with no defects, they move to a higher pay grade and then alternate between two jobs as they are needed. If their performance drops, they return for more training and practice. Although this approach is fairly new, anecdotal evidence suggests that it can increase productivity significantly.[29] Many unions resist crosstraining programs, however, because they threaten job security and reduce worker identification with one skill or craft—the basis around which unions are typically structured.[30]

Learning Summary

Operations is the set of organizational activities used to transform inputs into products and services. Operations management is the set of managerial activities directed at achieving effective and efficient operations. Operations management is important to both manufacturing and service organizations and plays an important role in an organization's strategy.

The starting point in operations management is to design operations management systems. Organizations must make decisions about the products or services they will offer and about the capacity, facilities, and technology they will use to create those products or services.

Once an operations system has been designed and put into use, it is used to control the organization's transformation processes. Various techniques are used for controlling operations, including materials resource planning, statistical quality control, and PERT. Major activities in the use of operations systems are materials acquisition and inventory control.

Productivity, a growing concern of U.S. businesses, is a measure of how efficiently an organization uses its resources to create products or services. Productivity can be assessed at different levels and expressed in different forms. Although the United States still leads the world in productivity, other industrialized nations are catching up. Productivity can be enhanced by improving operations and increasing employee involvement.

Quality is the totality of features and characteristics that bear on the ability of a product or service to satisfy needs. Quality affects competition, productivity, and costs. A strategic commitment by top management, employee involvement, technology, materials, and operating methods can all contribute to improving quality.

Speed is an organization's ability to develop and introduce new products or services on a timely basis. Flexibility is the organization's ability to adapt and modify its operations systems. Both speed and flexibility are becoming important issues that organizations have to address.

Questions and Exercises

Review Questions

1. How do manufacturing organizations and service organizations differ? Identify three examples of each.
2. What are the four types of decisions that have to be made in designing operations management systems?
3. Describe three common alternatives for facilities layout.
4. Identify and describe the four types of inventory that most organizations use.
5. What are productivity and quality? How are they related?
6. Why is productivity important?
7. What do *speed* and *flexibility* mean in an organizational context?

Analysis Questions

1. Can you identify some organizations that are both manufacturing and service? What services do you use most often?

2. What special decisions do international organizations have to make in the design of their operations management systems?

3. Do service organizations have the same types of inventories as manufacturing organizations?

4. Productivity in the many parts of the service sector is harder to measure than is typically the case in manufacturing. Identify some service organizations whose productivity seems hard to assess.

5. U.S. businesses would like consumers to believe that they are making higher-quality products than they made just a few years ago. Do you think they are? Why or why not?

6. In what types of organizations is speed especially important? Are there some organizations that do not need to worry much about speed?

Application Exercises

1. Analyze from the perspective of operations management the registration system that your college or university uses. How is the system designed? How is it used?

2. Select an organization in your local community with which you have some familiarity (your favorite restaurant, a bookstore, a video rental store, etc.). Analyze the organization from the standpoint of operations management system design and use. How productive do you think its workers are relative to those of its competitors? Is quality an issue? If so, how does the organization measure up?

Chapter Notes

1. "A Smarter Way to Manufacture," *Business Week,* April 30, 1990, pp. 110–117; Peter F. Drucker, "The Emerging Theory of Manufacturing," *Harvard Business Review,* May–June 1990, pp. 94–102; Gary Hoover, Alta Campbell, and Patrick J. Spain, eds., *Hoover's Handbook — Profiles of Over 500 Major Corporations* (Austin, Tex.: The Reference Press, 1990), p. 397.

2. See Everett E. Adam, Jr., and Ronald J. Ebert, *Production and Operations Management,* 4th ed. (Englewood Cliffs, N.J.: Prentice-Hall, 1989), for a review.

3. Richard B. Chase and Eric L. Prentis, "Operations Management: A Field Rediscovered," *Journal of Management,* Summer 1987, pp. 351–366.

4. Sylvia Nasar, "America's Competitive Revival," *Fortune,* January 4, 1988, pp. 44–52.

5. Richard B. Chase and Warren J. Erikson, "The Service Factory," *The Academy of Management Executive,* August 1988, pp. 191–196.

6. James Brian Quinn and Christopher E. Gagnon, "Will Service Follow Manufacturing into Decline?" *Harvard Business Review,* November–December 1986, pp. 95–103.

7. See Everett Adam, "Towards a Typology of Production and Operations Management Systems," *Academy of Management Review,* July 1983, pp. 365–375,

for a full discussion. See also Byron J. Finch and James F. Cox, "Process-oriented Production Planning and Control: Factors That Influence System Design," *Academy of Management Journal,* March 1988, pp. 123–153.

8. Adam and Ebert, *Production and Operations Management.*
9. Jack R. Meredith, "Strategic Control of Factory Automation," *Long Range Planning,* Fall 1987, pp. 106–112.
10. Patricia L. Nemetz and Louis W. Fry, "Flexible Manufacturing Organizations: Implications for Strategy Formulation and Organization Design," *Academy of Management Review,* October 1988, pp. 627–638.
11. Brian Dumaine, "How Managers Can Succeed Through Speed," *Fortune,* February 13, 1989, pp. 54–59.
12. Adam and Ebert, *Production and Operations Management.*
13. Louis Kraar, "Japan's Gung-Ho U.S. Car Plants," *Fortune,* January 30, 1989, pp. 98–108.
14. See Chan K. Hahn, Daniel J. Bragg, and Dongwook Shin, "Impact of the Setup Variable on Capacity and Inventory Decisions," *Academy of Management Review,* January 1988, pp. 91–103.
15. John W. Kendrick, *Understanding Productivity: An Introduction to the Dynamics of Productivity Change* (Baltimore: Johns Hopkins University Press, 1977).
16. Adam and Ebert, *Production and Operations Management.*
17. U.S. Department of Labor, *Monthly Labor Review,* January 1991, p. 112.
18. "Bausch & Lomb Is Correcting Its Vision of Research," *Business Week,* March 30, 1987, p. 91.
19. See Brian Dumaine, "Who Needs a Boss?" *Fortune,* May 7, 1990, pp. 52–60.
20. Ross Johnson and William O. Winchell, *Management and Quality* (Milwaukee: American Society for Quality Control, 1989).
21. W. Edwards Deming, *Out of the Crisis* (Cambridge, Mass.: MIT Press, 1986).
22. Joel Dreyfuss, "Victories in the Quality Crusade," *Fortune,* October 10, 1988, pp. 80–88.
23. "The Push for Quality," *Business Week,* June 8, 1987, pp. 130–135.
24. "How to Make It Right the First Time," *Business Week,* June 8, 1987, pp. 142–143.
25. Dreyfuss, "Victories in the Quality Crusade."
26. Bro Uttal, "Speeding New Ideas to Market," *Fortune,* March 2, 1987, pp. 62–66.
27. Dumaine, "How Managers Can Succeed Through Speed."
28. Ibid.
29. Norm Alster, "What Flexible Workers Can Do," *Fortune,* February 13, 1989, pp. 62–66.
30. Ibid.

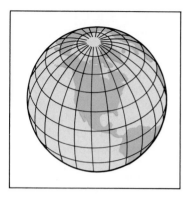

CASE 15.1

High-Quality Service

The 1990s promises to be a decade of quality and service. American manufacturers are striving to overcome the perception that American goods aren't as well made as goods from Japan and Europe. And service industries continue to become more important to the American economy. Studies have shown that companies perceived to give excellent service and high quality can charge 10 percent more than their competitors. Most such companies agree about a few basic principles.

Be human.   Computers now handle correspondence, answer telephones, and even make solicitation calls. But people don't like dealing with machines. They want a human being taking their order or listening to their complaint. Surveyed customers of banking, high-tech, and manufacturing companies say that "the personal touch" is more important than convenience, delivery speed, or product quality. Burger King's customers used to care most about speed of service. Now they care about courtesy.

Use technology to help you be human.   The importance of the personal touch doesn't mean that companies have to throw their computers in the junk heap. They just need to be careful about assigning appropriate tasks to people and to machines. A new $4 million computer system boosted American Savings Bank's rankings among the country's consumer banks, but customers never deal with the computer directly. It helps people help others. It gives bank employees immediate access to all the bank's information about a customer's accounts, allowing the bank to resolve customer account problems with one phone call 93 percent of the time. Instead of being put on hold for more than two minutes, the average customer now holds for only twenty-eight seconds.

Make customers and *employees happy.*   Some companies concentrate on pleasing their customers. Others are known for how well they treat their workers. Now many companies are finding that the key to keeping one group happy is making the other group happy. At American Express Travel Related Services Co., each employee used to perform a separate function in the complaint-handling chain. One might write a response while another tracked down information. Now, one employee deals with every aspect of a complaint. The results: resolving the average complaint takes 6 days instead of 35; customers are much happier; and employee turnover dropped 30 percent in three months. Employees get satisfaction out of seeing a job through to the end, and everyone likes to deal with contented customers.

Don't let customers get away.   Keeping a customer generally costs about one-fifth as much as attracting a new one. MBNA America Bank, a credit card company, spends on average $100 to attract a new customer. A customer who has had an MBNA card for five years brings the company $100 of profit; a ten-year cardholder, $300. The company has a Card Retention Department, with 68 employees who contact every card member who wants to close an account and does whatever is necessary — including waiving fees — to get customers to change their minds.

Fidelity Investments demonstrates as well as any company what it means to live by these and other principles of high-quality service. Fidelity offers 185 mutual funds, managing $112 billion of its 6 million customers' money. Although Fidelity's largest fund, Magellan, has been the most successful in the business for the last fifteen years, overall Fidelity's funds do just slightly better than average. Fidelity keeps its position as the world's largest mutual fund company not by making customers millionaires but by treating them as though they were. It takes care of the details. Its phone system can handle 672 calls simultaneously, routing a call to a free operator anywhere in the country. Customers can write checks on their money market funds, do business over the phone twenty-four hours a day, and always reach a well-educated and knowledgeable operator.

Fidelity's proactive stance toward customers' needs was demonstrated in 1990 when the manager at the Magellan Fund, Peter Lynch, quit. Worried that investors might panic at the loss of their guru, Fidelity had already amassed a large stock of cash to be ready to redeem Magellan shares. The morning of the announcement, it supplied each of its one thousand telephone operators with a script providing answers to questions that it expected investors to ask. It hired extra operators, polled investors all day, and prepared newspaper ads to remind investors of all the other Fidelity funds. But telling evidence of the relationship between the company and its customers came at the end of the day when Fidelity discovered that the number of people who had called was actually lower than on an average day. High-quality service pays off.

Discussion Questions

1. What trends led companies away from providing personal service?
2. In the short run, what extra costs might be incurred by a company trying to provide high-quality service?
3. Why is customer relations very important to a mutual fund company?
4. What decisions have you made recently because of a company's quality of service?

REFERENCES: Jaclyn Fierman, "Fidelity's Secret: Faithful Service," *Fortune,* May 7, 1990, pp. 86–92; Stephen Phillips and Amy Dunkin, "King Customer," *Business Week,* March 12, 1990, pp. 88–94; Patricia Sellers, "Getting Customers to Love You," *Fortune,* March 13, 1989, pp. 38–49; Patricia Sellers, "What Customers Really Want," *Fortune,* June 4, 1990, pp. 58–67.

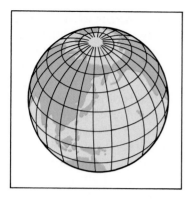

CASE 15.2

Bridgestone Inherits an Identity Crisis

The growth of the service sector in the United States has induced some companies that formerly focused on manufacturing to shift their orientation to service. Under chairman John J. Nevin during the 1980s, Firestone Tire & Rubber was making just such a shift. Nevin cut the company's work force by almost half, closed ten of Firestone's seventeen North American tire plants, and invested heavily in the company's 1,500 MasterCare auto service centers. These moves yielded short-term profits and pleased shareholders, but they angered Firestone dealers and workers. And when Bridgestone, Japan's largest tire maker, bought Firestone in 1988 primarily for its tire-making capabilities, it found that it owned a company with a severe identity problem.

Even before the Firestone purchase, Bridgestone was the world's third largest tire manufacturer, after Goodyear and Michelin. Bridgestone makes almost half of all the tires sold in Japan, but before the Firestone purchase it was a virtual unknown in the American marketplace. It bought a truck tire plant in Tennessee from Firestone in 1983, poured $348 million into upgrading it, enlisted employees in improving production methods, and after six years tripled production per employee. After it bought the whole company five years later, Bridgestone hoped to achieve the same sort of transformation at Firestone's other plants, gain a significant share of the American market, and resolidify its intimate relations with Japanese automakers that had started buying American tires for their models made in the United States.

But the sudden change in ownership brought about a shift in focus and philosophy from which the combined companies may not soon recover. John Nevin's focus on MasterCare — in effect, his desire to turn Firestone into a service company — had an impact on the company's manufacturing abilities that will not be easy to reverse. The shrinking of Firestone brought the company profit and made it more efficient but angered manufacturing unions. And the company's special deals with MasterCare outlets — which allowed MasterCare to undersell Firestone's tire dealers — angered many of the dealers in Firestone's network. Just before Bridgestone's purchase became final, General Motors announced that it was dropping Firestone as a supplier because its quality and service were not up to the standard of GM's other tire suppliers.

The loss of GM business hurt Firestone's reputation and its balance sheet — GM had been buying about one-fifth of Firestone's North American tire production. So to make Firestone a major manufacturing force once again, Bridgestone will have to improve significantly Firestone's manufacturing and its employee relations. After years of neglect, the Firestone plants are about half as productive as Bridgestone plants. Bridgestone keeps raising its estimate of how much money will be needed to boost Firestone's production quality up to Bridgestone's standards — perhaps as much as Bridgestone paid for Firestone in the first place.

Bridgestone has sent mixed messages about how it intends to run its new acquisition. At first it seemed ready to let Americans continue to oversee the operation, but then it sent its chairman Teiji Eguchi to Akron, Ohio, to keep an eye on the business. Bridgestone doesn't have enough engineers to go around, and within months of the purchase it scaled back its plans to expand American manufacturing capacity. The American tire industry is already operating at only about 84 percent of capacity, and both Michelin and Goodyear have laid off workers in Europe and the United States.

The first signs of manufacturing improvement began to appear in June 1990: productivity rose 4 percent over the previous year; quality improved; and the plants scrapped fewer tires. But rebuilding manufacturing equipment slows production and costs millions of dollars, and reducing personnel is taking longer than anticipated.

There is also hope for the company's relations with the United Rubber Workers (URW). The union had been outraged by the Firestone plant closings. URW was thus delighted with Bridgestone's plans to increase Firestone's American tire production and even more pleased when Bridgestone returned to workers concessions amounting to more than a dollar an hour that Firestone had extracted from the union in 1987. Such a move was a big step toward building trust with Bridgestone's new employees. Bridgestone took another step when it announced that it would not eliminate any jobs as a result of workers' increased productivity.

At the moment, Bridgestone is engaged in a delicate balancing act, trying to keep Firestone as both a manufacturing and a service company. Its purchase of Firestone — the largest Japanese acquisition of an American manufacturer — is yielding many lessons about the difficulties of cross-cultural operations management.

Discussion Questions

1. Would you advise Firestone to emphasize service, manufacturing, or both? Why?
2. Why do you think Bridgestone bought Firestone rather than just build itself some plants in America?
3. Analysts sometimes generalize that Japanese firms are primarily interested in market share and American companies are primarily interested in profits. In what ways does this generalization apply to the Bridgestone/Firestone situation?
4. How would you characterize the types of decisions that Bridgestone made during its akeover of Firestone?

REFERENCES: Zachary Schiller, "Can Bridgestone Make the Climb?" *Business Week,* February 27, 1989, pp. 78–79; Zachary Schiller, "So Far, America Is a Blowout for Bridgestone," *Business Week,* August 6, 1990, pp. 82–83; Zachary Schiller, "Why Bridgestone's Chairman Is Making Tracks to Akron," *Business Week,* November 20, 1989, pp. 32–33; "Wheels Within Wheels," *The Economist,* March 12, 1988, pp. 62–65.

IV Behavior in Organizations

The third major function of managers in organizations is managing behavior. The purpose of this function is to motivate and channel the behavior of individuals and groups in directions that are consistent with the organization's goals and objectives. The direction should be derived from the strategy of the organization and must be defined within the context of organization structure. The critical components of managing behavior include understanding individuals, motivation, leadership, interpersonal and group dynamics, interpersonal communication, and conflict and stress.

16

Individuals in Organizations

LEARNING OBJECTIVES

After studying this chapter, you should be able to:

1. Explain the nature of the relationship between individuals and the organization.

2. Discuss the different physical and intellectual qualities that individuals bring to organizations.

3. Define *personality,* and describe personality attributes that affect behavior in organizations.

4. Discuss individual attitudes in organizations, and indicate how they affect behavior.

5. Describe basic perceptual processes and the role of attributions in organizations.

6. Discuss needs and motives and their role in determining individual behavior in organizations.

7. Explain how workplace behaviors can directly or indirectly influence organizational effectiveness.

Elizabeth Morgan and Sherman McCarter both work for FirstCity Bancorporaion of Texas, based in Houston. Elizabeth and Sherman work in the company's loan servicing department. They and the others in the department answer customer questions about such things as payment due dates and loan balances, and they also handle the closing paperwork when a loan has been paid off.

Elizabeth and Sherman started working for FirstCity around the same time, and each does a very good job. But that's just about where the similarities end. Elizabeth is 38 years old, white, and married, and she worked for two other banks before starting her present job. Sherman is 24, black, and single, and this is his first job since graduating from college.

Elizabeth is very outgoing and seems to have many different friends at work. She usually goes to lunch with a big group and socializes with many of her co-workers on the weekend. Sherman is well liked by his colleagues but is quiet and has only a couple of close friends at work. He usually brings his lunch and eats by himself. Elizabeth says she loves her job and sees FirstCity as the ideal place to work. Sherman is somewhat less enthusiastic. He has no specific complaints about his job, but he thinks he might be happier in a different organization.

Both Elizabeth and Sherman were hired as part of the organization's affirmative action program. Elizabeth never seems to think about this, however, and believes she was the top candidate for her job. Sherman is also confident about his abilities, but he still occasionally wonders about whether he would have been hired if he had been white. He sometimes worries that people won't respect him for his abilities.

As for the future, having worked for two other banks, Elizabeth believes she has found the ideal place. She says that she wants to stay at FirstCity forever. Although Sherman has no specific timetable, he expects to leave FirstCity in the near future. He thinks that after he gets another year or so of experience he will be able to get a better job in another bank. He plans to look first at opportunities in the Northeast.[1]

Erin Young is the supervisor in charge of loan servicing at FirstCity in Houston. She is the manager who hired both Elizabeth Morgan and Sherman McCarter. Erin also hired seven of the other twenty employees in the department. One of the biggest challenges she faces as a manager is supervising and coordinating the work of the people in her department. Her oldest employee is 62, her youngest 22. The group has a few more males than females (Erin has hired most of the females), and the majority of them are white. Several employees are Hispanic; a few are black; and one is Asian. One employee is physically handicapped.

Some of the employees in Erin's group are dedicated and hard working; others do just enough to get by. Some are pleasant and congenial; others are unpleasant and complain about the organization. Some are happy with their job and expect to stay for a long time. Others are less satisfied and plan to leave someday. Still others are ambitious enough to want to advance to better jobs within the organization. Some of Erin's employees see her as a strong manager and leader and have great respect for her managerial abilities. A few, however, complain about her hiring practices and think she gives favorable treatment to women.

When dealing with the employees in loan servicing, Erin has to walk a fine line. To start with, she has to treat everyone the same. She can't legitimately award a pay increase or a better job assignment because she likes someone, because someone is female, because someone is black, or because someone is pleasant. She has to provide fair and equitable treatment for all her employees. But the people in the group are not the same. They behave in different ways, expect different things, and see the world in very different ways. Erin can legitimately treat higher-performing employees differently than she does lower-performing employees. But she has to make sure that the basis for her treatment is job related.

This chapter discusses individuals in organizations and is the first of several chapters designed to develop a more complete perspective on how behavior in organizations can be understood and managed. The first section investigates the relationship between individuals and organizations. We then discuss the variety of physical and intellectual qualities that individuals bring to the workplace. The next section introduces the concept of personality and discusses several important personality attributes that can influence behavior in organizations. We then examine the effect of individual attitudes, needs, and motives on behavior. Finally, we describe a number of workplace behaviors that influence organizational effectiveness.

Understanding Individuals in Organizations

As a starting point in understanding the behavior of people in organizational settings we must consider the relationship between individuals and organizations. We must also gain an appreciation of the nature of individual differences.

The Psychological Contract

Whenever people buy a car or sell a house, both buyer and seller sign a contract that specifies the terms of the sales agreement. A standard legal

Figure 16.1

The Psychological Contract

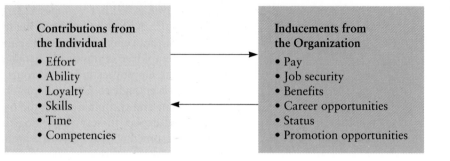

Contributions from
the Individual

- Effort
- Ability
- Loyalty
- Skills
- Time
- Competencies

Inducements from
the Organization

- Pay
- Job security
- Benefits
- Career opportunities
- Status
- Promotion opportunities

A *psychological contract* is the overall set of expectations that an individual holds with respect to his or her contributions to the organization and the organization's response to those contributions.

Contributions are what the individual provides to the organization, and *inducements* are what the organization provides to the individual.

contract spells out what each signer may expect from the other. Most people, when they begin a working relationship with an organization, similarly formulate (more or less consciously) a psychological contract with their employer. A **psychological contract** is the overall set of expectations that an individual holds with respect to his or her contributions to the organization and the organization's response to those contributions.[2] A psychological contract is not written down nor are all of its terms explicitly negotiated.

Figure 16.1 illustrates the essential nature of a psychological contract. The individual makes a variety of **contributions** to the organization — effort, skills, ability, time, loyalty, and so forth. These contributions presumably satisfy various needs and requirements of the organization. It is reasonable for an organization to expect that an individual hired for her skills will subsequently display those skills in the performance of her job.

In return for contributions, the organization provides **inducements** to the individual. Some inducements, such as pay and career opportunities, are tangible rewards. Others, such as job security and status, are intangible. Just as the contributions available from the individual must satisfy the organization's needs, the inducements must serve the individual's needs. If a person accepts employment with an organization because he thinks he will earn an attractive salary and have an opportunity to advance, he will subsequently expect that those rewards will actually be forthcoming.

If both the individual and the organization consider the psychological contract fair and equitable, they will be satisfied with the relationship and will likely continue it. If either party perceives an imbalance or inequity in the contract, it may initiate a change. For example, the individual may request a pay raise or promotion, decrease her contributed effort, or look for a better job elsewhere. The organization might initiate change by requesting that the individual improve his skills through training, by transferring the person to another job, or by terminating the person's employment altogether.

A major challenge faced by an organization, then, is to manage psychological contracts. The organization must ensure that it is getting value from its employees. At the same time, it must also be sure that it is providing employees with appropriate inducements. If the organization is underpaying

It is important that organizations strive to create a good fit between people and their jobs. These trainers work with Shamu the killer whale at San Diego's Sea World marine life park. The trainers obviously need to possess the technical skills and expertise to work with large marine mammals. But they also need to have a temperament suited to working in a highly public place and dealing with the thousands of visitors who pass through the park daily.

its employees for their contributions, for example, they may perform poorly or leave for better jobs elsewhere. If employees are overpaid relative to their contributions, the organization is incurring unnecessary costs.

The Person-Job Fit

The *person-job fit* is the extent to which the contributions made by the individual match the inducements offered by the organization.

One specific aspect of managing psychological contracts is managing the person-job fit. The **person-job fit** is the extent to which the contributions made by the individual match the inducements offered by the organization. In theory, each employee has a specific set of needs to fulfill and a set of job-related behaviors and abilities to contribute. If the organization can take complete advantage of those behaviors and abilities and exactly fulfill the employee's needs, it will have achieved a perfect person-job fit.[3]

Of course, such a precise level of person-job fit is seldom achieved. For one thing, organizational selection procedures are imperfect. Organizations can approximate employee skill levels during hiring and can improve them through training. But even simple aspects of performance are hard to measure objectively and validly.

In addition, the needs and requirements of both people and organizations change. An individual who finds a new job stimulating and exciting may find the same job boring and monotonous after performing it for a few years. An organization that adopts new technology changes its skill requirements. Still another reason for imprecision in the person-job fit is that each individual is unique. Measuring skills and performance is difficult enough, but assessing needs, attitudes, and personality is far more complex. Each of these individual differences serves to make matching individuals with jobs more of an art than a science.

The Nature of Individual Differences

Every individual has a unique psychological and emotional life. Elizabeth Morgan and Sherman McCarter differ in terms of sex, race, age, and various other demographic characteristics, but these are only observable differences. These two individuals also see their work environment in different ways, hold different attitudes toward their jobs and the organization, want different things from the organization, and have different personalities and attitudes. Each of these factors represents a potentially important individual difference.

Individual differences are personal attributes that vary from one person to another.

Individual differences are personal attributes that vary from one person to another. Individual differences may be physical, psychological, and emotional. Taken together, all of the individual differences that characterize any specific person serve to make that individual unique from everyone else. Figure 16.2 illustrates the five categories of individual differences that we discuss in this chapter: physical and intellectual qualities, personality, attitudes, perception, and needs and motives. First, however, we need to note the importance of the work situation in assessing the behavior of individuals.

Are the specific differences that characterize given individuals good or bad in themselves? Do they contribute to or detract from performance? The answer, of course, depends on the circumstances. One person may be very dissatisfied, withdrawn, and negative in one job setting but very sat-

Figure 16.2

Categories of Individual Difference in the Workplace

The Individual

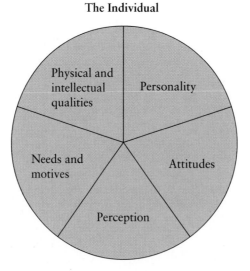

THE GLOBAL CHALLENGE

McDonald's Comes to Russia

McDonald's and its familiar golden arches have become as ubiquitous a symbol of America as the Coca-Cola bottle or Mickey Mouse. McDonald's now has successful restaurant operations in such diverse countries as Switzerland, Singapore, Malaysia, and Mexico. Indeed, over half of all new McDonald's restaurants are now being built outside the United States. But as the hamburger giant expands its global reach into increasingly exotic foreign markets, it is also having to learn more about human behavior, among both its employees and its customers. For each country in which it operates, McDonald's must design acceptable reward and performance appraisal systems. In addition, the firm often has to adjust its menus to accommodate local tastes.

Recently, McDonald's accepted perhaps its biggest marketplace challenge: the Soviet Union. Soviet workers, long accustomed to being told where they can work, how they are to behave, even when they can smile, have been caught up in the infectious atmosphere at the new Moscow McDonald's. But when they tell their friends how satisfied they are with their jobs, they often get blank stares in return — the concept of job satisfaction has no meaning to someone who has never experienced it. Moreover, not every Soviet worker wants to, either. Many Soviets look down on those who have chosen to work under the golden arches because they think they have "sold out" to the capitalists.

In part because of the workers and the good will that the corporation tries to convey in its advertising, customers at McDonald's feel quite welcome. This, too, is a new experience for many residents of Moscow. At many other restaurants, workers treat customers like a nuisance that has to be endured. At McDonald's, however, the customer is king. This explains why over three hundred people line up outside the door every day before the restaurant even opens.

REFERENCES: "U.S. Ideas Creep into Soviet Union," *USA Today,* August 11, 1990, pp. B1, B2; "Inside the Golden Arches," *Newsweek,* December 18, 1989, pp. 46–47; "McWorld?" *Business Week,* October 13, 1986, pp. 78–86; "A Great Place to Invest — If You Don't Mind the Wait," *Business Week,* October 1, 1990, p. 145.

isfied, outgoing, and positive in another. Working conditions, co-workers, and leadership are all important influences on individual behavior. Sherman McCarter's general discontent with his job, for example, may be attributable to a variety of factors, such as his lack of experience, his unmet expectations, or the circumstances under which he was hired. He may find his next job worse, the same, or better in terms of each of these factors.

Whenever an organization attempts to assess or account for individual differences among its employees, it must consider the situation in which behavior occurs. Individuals who are satisfied or productive workers in one context may prove to be dissatisfied or unproductive workers in another context. Assessing both individual differences and contributions in relation to inducements and contexts, then, is a major challenge for organizations as they attempt to establish effective psychological contracts with their employees and achieve optimal fits between people and jobs. The Global Challenge describes the cultural differences that McDonald's has had to account for in managing its new store in Moscow.

Physical and Intellectual Qualities

Physical differences among individuals are the most visible of all differences. They are also relatively easy to assess or document. Intellectual differences are somewhat more difficult to discern, but they too can be assessed by fairly objective means. The abilities, skills, and competencies that organizations require of employees call on both physical and intellectual qualities.

Abilities are individual capacities for performing well in one or more areas of activity.

Abilities are an individual's capacities to perform well in one or more areas of activity, such as physical, mental, or interpersonal work.[4] Individuals with numerical ability, for example, can be trained to apply their ability in a wide array of occupations, such as engineering, accounting, and computer science. Abilities develop from an individual's natural aptitudes and subsequent learning opportunities.[5] Aptitudes are relatively enduring capacities for performing some activity effectively.[6] Learning opportunities translate aptitudes into abilities through practice and experience and formal training. Fixed aptitudes such as reaction time and finger dexterity tend to be less valuable to organizations than are aptitudes that can be developed through training, such as interpersonal or diagnostic abilities.

Skills are task-specific capabilities—the results of applying ability to specialized areas.

Skills are generally thought of as being more task-specific than abilities.[7] For example, an individual with the ability to work with numerical data who goes to school to learn about accounting develops a numerical skill specific to that field. Applying ability to a specialized area (for example, to pass the CPA exam) is a reflection of skill.

Competencies are skills associated with specialization.

Competencies are skills that have been refined by practice and experience and that enable the individual to specialize in some field. For example, suppose the accountant described above takes a position in the taxation department of a public accounting firm. As time passes, he develops more and more competency as a tax specialist. A colleague who specializes in auditing will have different competencies, although her similar abilities and skills would allow her to also develop competencies as a tax expert, given training and time.

Physical and mental abilities, which are an individual's primary productive capabilities, are thought to interact with social capability to determine individual earning potential.[8] Most organizations have a sizable financial interest in enhancing the productive capabilities of all of their employees. Since experience plays such a major part in the development of abilities, skills, and competencies, these organizations try to structure and plan work experiences that help employees continue to develop throughout their careers.

Physical abilities such as strength, flexibility, coordination, endurance, and stamina can be developed with exercise and training. Mental abilities such as reasoning, memory, visualization, and comprehension, and interpersonal abilities such as motivating subordinates and relating with colleagues, can also be developed through practice and education. Even in the absence of such formal programs, many individuals manage their own careers in such a way as to continually upgrade their abilities, skills, and competencies in order to remain valuable to their organizations and marketable to other organizations as well.

Personality

Personality is the relatively stable set of psychological and behavioral attributes that distinguish one person from another.

If physical differences are relatively easy to observe and assess, personality differences are just the opposite. **Personality** is the relatively stable set of psychological and behavioral attributes that distinguish one person from another.[9] Understanding these attributes is important for managers because they affect people's behavior in organizational situations, people's perceptions of and attitudes toward the organization, and the needs and motives that people bring to the organizational environment.[10]

Personality Formation

The personality of an individual is solidly formed before he or she ever becomes a member of an organization. Indeed, personality formation starts at birth and continues throughout adolescence. Hereditary characteristics (e.g., body shape and height) and the social context (family and friends) and cultural context (religion and values) in which people grow up interact to shape personality. As people grow into adulthood, their personalities become very clearly defined and generally stable.

But an individual's personality can still be affected by organizational experiences. For example, a manager subjected to prolonged periods of stress or conflict at work may become withdrawn, anxious, and irritable. Removal of the stressful circumstances may eventually temper these characteristics, but the individual's personality may also reflect permanent changes. On the other hand, continued success, accomplishment, and advancement at work may cause an individual to become increasingly self-confident and outgoing. Circumstances outside work can also affect personality and behavior in unexpected ways. For example, an honest employee may be tempted to steal money from the organization if he or she is experiencing severe financial pressures.

These extreme examples aside, managers should recognize that they can do little to change the personalities of their subordinates. Instead, they should make an effort to understand the nature of their subordinates' personalities and how personality attributes affect the behavior of individuals in the workplace.

Personality Attributes in Organizations

Over the past few decades a considerable amount of research has been conducted to identify and further understanding of personality attributes that are relevant to organizations.[11] Several of the most important attributes that have been identified and studied are listed and defined in Table 16.1.

Locus of control is the degree to which an individual believes that his or her behavior has a direct impact on the consequences of that behavior.[12] Some people, for example, believe that if they work hard they are certain to succeed. They also may believe that people who fail do so simply because

Table 16.1

Personality Attributes Relevant to Organizations

Locus of control   The degree to which an individual believes that his or her behavior has a direct impact on the consequences of that behavior.

Authoritarianism   The extent to which an individual believes that status and power differences are appropriate within hierarchical social systems such as organizations.

Dogmatism   The rigidity of a person's beliefs and her or his openness to other viewpoints.

Self-monitoring   The extent to which a person pays close attention to and subsequently emulates the behavior of others.

Self-esteem   The extent to which a person believes that he or she is a worthwhile and deserving individual.

Risk propensity   The degree to which an individual is willing to take chances and make risky decisions.

they lack ability or motivation. Because these people believe that each individual is in control of his or her life, they are said to have an internal locus of control.

By contrast, some people think that what happens to them is a result of fate, chance, luck, or the behavior of other people. For example, an employee who fails to get a promotion may attribute that failure to a politically motivated boss or just bad luck, rather than to a lack of skills or a record of poor performance. Because these individuals think that forces beyond their control dictate what happens to them, they are said to have an external locus of control.[13]

As a personality attribute, locus of control has clear implications for organizations. For example, individuals with an internal locus of control may have a relatively strong desire to participate in the governance of their organizations and have a voice in how they do their jobs. Thus they may prefer a decentralized organization and a leader who provides them freedom and autonomy. They may be more likely to resist control, and they may be most comfortable with a reward system that recognizes individual performance and contributions. People with an external locus of control, by contrast, are likely to prefer a more centralized organization where decisions are taken out of their hands. They may gravitate to structured jobs where standard procedures are defined for them. Similarly, they may also prefer a leader who makes most of the decisions and may prefer a reward system that puts a premium on seniority.

Authoritarianism is the extent to which an individual believes that power and status differences are appropriate within hierarchical social systems like organizations.[14] For example, a person who is highly authoritarian may unquestioningly accept directives or orders from someone with more authority purely because the other person is "the boss." A person who is not highly authoritarian may agree to carry out appropriate and reasonable directives from the boss but is also likely to raise questions, express disagreement with the boss, and even refuse to carry out requests if they are for some reason objectionable. A manager who is highly authoritarian may be relatively autocratic and demanding; subordinates who are also highly authoritarian will be likely to accept this behavior from their leader. A manager who is less authoritarian may allow subordinates a bigger role in making decisions, and less authoritarian subordinates will respond positively to this behavior.[15]

Dogmatism is the rigidity of a person's beliefs and his or her openness to other viewpoints.[16] The popular terms "close-minded" and "open-minded" describe people who are more and less dogmatic in their beliefs. For example, suppose a manager has such strong beliefs about how certain procedures should be carried out that he or she is unwilling to even listen to a new idea for doing something more efficiently. We might say that this person is close-minded, or highly dogmatic. A manager in the same circumstances who is very receptive to hearing about and trying out new ideas might be seen as more open-minded, or less dogmatic. Dogmatism can be either beneficial or detrimental to organizations, but given the degree of change in the nature of organizations and their environments, individuals who are not dogmatic are most likely to be useful and productive organizational members.

Self-monitoring is the extent to which a person pays close attention to and subsequently emulates the behavior of others.[17] A highly self-monitoring person pays very close attention to the behavior of others for cues about how to act in different situations. For example, this person may tend to dress like others, imitate their work behaviors, and so forth. Thus he or she tends to be somewhat of a conformist and is not likely to initiate change. A less self-monitoring person, in contrast, will be more independent and will freely choose different forms of behavior. This person will pay less attention to how others dress, their work behaviors, and so forth. Such an individual is also more likely to be an initiator of change.

Self-esteem is the extent to which a person believes that he or she is a worthwhile and deserving individual.[18] A person with high self-esteem is likely to seek high-status jobs, be confident in his or her ability to achieve high levels of performance, and derive great intrinsic satisfaction from his or her accomplishments. In contrast, a person with less self-esteem may be more content to remain in a lower-level job, be less confident of his or her ability, and focus more on extrinsic rewards.

Risk propensity is the degree to which an individual is willing to take chances and make risky decisions. A manager with a high risk propensity might be expected to experiment with new ideas, to gamble on new products, and to lead the organization in new directions. This manager might also be a catalyst for innovation. Of course, this individual might jeopardize the continued well-being of the organization if the risky decisions prove to be bad ones. The potential consequences of risk propensity heavily depend on the organization's environment. Thus a manager with low risk propensity might either lead to a stagnant and overly conservative organization or help the organization successfully weather turbulent and unpredictable times by maintaining stability and calm.

Attitudes in Organizations

In a way, attitudes are conceptually similar to personality attributes. We noted that personality attributes are shaped early in life and are difficult to change. Some attitudes also fit this description, but other attitudes can be quickly formed or changed. We define **attitudes** as complexes of beliefs and feelings that people have about specific ideas, situations, or other people.

Attitudes are complexes of beliefs and feelings that people have about specific ideas, situations, or other people.

Attitudes are important because they are the mechanism through which most people express their feelings. An employee's statement that he feels underpaid by the organization reflects his attitude about his pay. Similarly, when a manager says that she likes the new advertising campaign, she is expressing her attitude about the organization's marketing efforts.

Attitudes have three components,[19] as Figure 16.3 shows. The affective component of an attitude reflects feelings and emotions that an individual has toward a situation. The cognitive component of an attitude is derived from knowledge that an individual has about a situation. It is important to note that cognition is subject to individual perceptions (something we discuss more fully later). Thus one person might "know" that a certain political candidate is better than another, while someone else might "know" just the opposite. Finally, the intentional component of an attitude reflects how an individual expects to behave toward or in the situation.

To illustrate these three components, consider the case of a manager who places an order for his organization with a new office supply firm. Suppose many of the items he orders are out of stock, others are overpriced, and

Figure 16.3

Components of Individual Attitudes

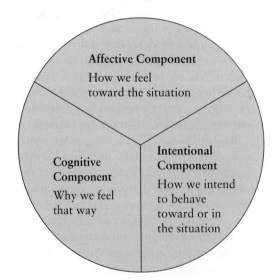

still others arrive damaged. When he calls someone at the supply firm for assistance, he is treated rudely and gets disconnected before his claim is resolved. When asked to describe his attitude toward the new office supply firm, he responds, "I don't like that company (affective component). They are the worst office supply firm I've ever dealt with (cognitive component). I'll never do business with them again (intentional component)."

Cognitive dissonance is caused when an individual has conflicting attitudes.

People try to maintain consistency among the three components of their attitudes as well as among all their attitudes. However, circumstances sometimes arise that lead to conflicts. The conflict that individuals may experience among their own attitudes is called **cognitive dissonance**.[20] Say, for example, a woman who has vowed never to work for a big, impersonal corporation intends to open her own business and be her own boss. But a series of financial setbacks gives her no choice but to take a job with a large company and work for someone else. Cognitive dissonance occurs: the affective and cognitive components of the individual's attitude conflict with intended behavior. In order to reduce cognitive dissonance, which is usually an uncomfortable experience for most people, the woman described above might tell herself that the situation is only temporary and that she can go back out on her own in the near future. Or she might revise her cognitions and decide that working for a large company is more pleasant than she had ever expected.

Attitude Formation and Change

Individual attitudes form over time as a result of repeated personal experiences with ideas, situations, or people. The situational view of attitude formation suggests that strong attitudes evolve from the socially constructed realities in which people live, such as educational, family, or work situations.[21] Students who attend a college class, for instance, receive from fellow students and from the instructor situational information about what is expected of them and what will happen in the class. This information helps shape their attitudes about the class, the instructor, and the other students. Because the situational information differs in every class, the attitudes in each specific class may also vary.

Looking closely at attitudes that are situationally specific and learned is one very important way to understand individual behavior in organizations. For example, suppose an organization is considering moving its headquarters to a new location. If the manager recognizes that employees have a positive attitude toward the current facility because they live nearby and because they find it to be warm and comfortable, he might realize that they will resist the move and that many may quit. But if employees have a negative attitude toward the current facility because it is in an unsafe neighborhood and they find it cramped and uncomfortable, they are likely to welcome a move.

As noted earlier, attitudes are not as stable as personality attributes. For example, attitudes may change as a result of new information. A manager may have a negative attitude about a new colleague because of his lack of job-related experience. After working with the new person for a while, however, the manager may come to realize that he is actually very talented and subsequently may develop a more positive attitude toward him. Attitudes can also change as a result of changes in the object of the attitude. For example, if employees have a negative attitude about their pay because they feel underpaid, a salary increase may result in more positive attitudes about their pay.

Attitude change can also occur when the object of the attitude becomes less important or less relevant to the person. For example, suppose an employee has a negative attitude about his company's health insurance. When his spouse gets a new job with an organization that has outstanding health insurance benefits, his attitude toward his own insurance may become more moderate simply because he no longer has to worry about it. Finally, as noted earlier, individuals may change their attitudes as a way of reducing cognitive dissonance.[22]

Deeply rooted attitudes that have a long history are, of course, very difficult to change. For example, over a period of years top executive Frank Lorenzo developed a reputation in the airline industry for being anti-union and for cutting wages and benefits. As a result, employees throughout the industry came to dislike and distrust him. When Lorenzo took over Eastern Air Lines, Eastern employees had such a strong attitude of distrust toward him that they could never agree to cooperate with any of his programs or ideas. Some of them actually cheered months later when Eastern went bankrupt, even though bankruptcy was costing them their own jobs!

Work-related Attitudes

People in an organization form attitudes about many different things — about their salary, promotion possibilities, their boss, employee benefits, the food in the company cafeteria, and the color of the company softball team uniforms. Of course, some of these attitudes are more important than others.

Important work-related attitudes are job satisfaction *or* dissatisfaction, organizational commitment, *and* job involvement.

Job Satisfaction or Dissatisfaction   **Job satisfaction** or **dissatisfaction** is an attitude that reflects the extent to which an individual is gratified by or fulfilled in his or her work. Extensive research conducted on job satisfaction has indicated that personal factors such as an individual's needs and aspirations determine this attitude, along with group and organizational factors such as relationships with co-workers and supervisors, working conditions, work policies, and compensation.[23]

A satisfied employee tends to be absent less often than someone who is dissatisfied, to make positive contributions, and to stay with the organization. A dissatisfied employee may be absent often, may experience stress that disrupts co-workers, and may be continually looking for another job. Strong feelings of job satisfaction do not necessarily lead to high levels of performance, however. Moreover, one recent survey has indicated that,

Job satisfaction is an attitude that reflects the degree to which a person is fulfilled by his or her job. These researchers work at a Procter & Gamble test facility near Cincinnati. As long as they remain satisfied with their work, they are likely to remain with the firm and continue to make important contributions. If they become less satisfied, however, their special training and experience would enable them to find employment elsewhere. It is clearly in the firm's best interests to do what it can to promote positive attitudes.

contrary to popular opinion, Japanese workers are less satisfied with their jobs than are their American counterparts.[24]

Organizational Commitment and Job Involvement   Two other important work-related attitudes are organizational commitment and job involvement. **Organizational commitment** is an attitude that reflects an individual's identification with and attachment to the organization itself. A person who feels strong commitment is likely to see herself as a true member of the organization (referring to the organization in personal terms by saying things like "We make high-quality products"), to overlook minor sources of dissatisfaction with the organization, and to see herself remaining a member of the organization. In contrast, a person with less organizational commitment is more likely to see himself as an outsider (referring to the organization in less personal terms by saying things like "They don't pay their employees very well"), to express more dissatisfaction, and to see himself as only a short-term member of the organization. Research suggests that Japanese workers may be more committed to their organizations than are American workers.[25]

Job involvement results in an individual's tendency to exceed the normal expectations associated with his or her job. An employee who feels little involvement will regard a job as just something to do in order to earn a living. All of her motivation has an extrinsic source (money), and she has little or no interest in learning how to perform the job better. A person who feels strong involvement will derive intrinsic satisfaction from the job itself and will want to learn how to perform the job more effectively.

Richard Steers has demonstrated that organizational commitment and job involvement strengthen with an individual's age, years with the organization, sense of job security, and participation in decision making.[26] Employees who feel committed to an organization and involved with their jobs have highly reliable habits, plan a long tenure with the organization, and muster more effort in performance. Although there are few definitive actions that organizations can take to promote these attitudes, a few specific guidelines are helpful. For one thing, if the organization treats its employees fairly and provides reasonable rewards and job security, employees are more likely to be satisfied and committed. Allowing employees to have a say in company procedures can also help. In particular, designing jobs so that they are interesting and stimulating can enhance job involvement.

Perception in Organizations

As noted earlier, individual perceptions strongly influence the cognitive component of people's attitudes. Since perception plays a role in a variety of workplace behaviors, managers need to have a general understanding of basic perceptual processes. The role of attribution is also important.

Basic Perceptual Processes

Perception is the set of processes by which an individual becomes aware of and interprets information about the environment.

Perception is the set of processes by which an individual becomes aware of and interprets information about the environment. As shown in Figure 16.4, two perceptual processes that are particularly relevant to organizations are selective perception and stereotyping.

Selective Perception   Selective perception is the process of screening out information that we are uncomfortable with or that contradicts our beliefs. For example, suppose a manager has a very positive attitude about a particular worker and thinks he is a top performer. One day the manager notices that the worker seems to be goofing off. Selective perception may cause the manager to quickly disregard what he observed. Suppose another manager has formed a very negative attitude about a particular worker. She thinks this worker is a poor performer and never does a good job. When she happens to observe an example of high performance from the worker, she, too, may not remember it for very long.

In one sense, selective perception is beneficial because it allows us to disregard minor bits of information. If selective perception causes managers

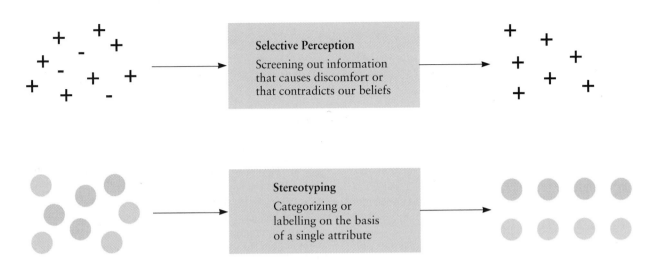

Figure 16.4

Perceptual Processes

to ignore important information, however, it can become quite detrimental. The Environmental Challenge describes the effects that selective perception may have on individual ethical behavior.

Stereotyping   Stereotyping is the process of categorizing or labeling people on the basis of a single attribute. Perceptions based on stereotypes about people's race or sex exist more or less in most workplaces, although they are inaccurate and can often be harmful. Typically these perceptions lead to the belief that an individual's race or sex determines which tasks he or she will be able to perform. A human resources manager who bases hiring decisions on stereotypes about the sex or race of job applicants is (1) costing the organization valuable talent, (2) violating federal antidiscrimination law, and (3) behaving unethically.

Sometimes, though, certain forms of stereotyping can be helpful. Suppose, for example, a manager believes that communication skills are important for a particular job and that speech communication majors tend to have exceptionally good communication skills. As a result, whenever he interviews candidates for jobs, he pays especially close attention to speech communication majors. To the extent that communication skills truly predict job performance and that majoring in speech communication does indeed provide those skills, this form of stereotyping can aid the manager in finding suitable workers.

Perception and Attribution

Attribution is the process of observing behavior and attributing causes to it.

Perception is also closely linked with another process, called attribution. **Attribution** is a mechanism through which we observe behavior and then attribute causes to it.[27] The observed behavior may be our own or that of others. For example, an individual realizes that she is working fewer hours,

THE ENVIRONMENTAL CHALLENGE

Selective Perception and Ethics

Ethics are an individual's beliefs about what is right and wrong behavior. The ethical standards of individuals vary almost as much as their personalities and attitudes. What one person sees as correct behavior may be seen by someone else as wrong.

From the standpoint of managing individuals in organizations, there are two distinct perspectives to take in regard to ethics. One considers the extent to which people are willing to adhere to ethical norms in the conduct of business. Some individuals are willing to follow ethical standards regardless of personal costs. They may speak out publicly when other members of the organization behave improperly, talk customers out of buying more than they need, or commit additional funds to increase the safety of a new product. Other people, however, may not choose this type of behavior, wishing instead to avoid angering their colleagues or jeopardizing their jobs. They may perceive behavior as unethical but not take any action to correct it.

The second perspective considers the extent to which people actually perceive an ethical component to behavior. Many people follow ethical standards consistently, but define them differently. For example, consider two salespeople in an electronics store selling VCRs to different customers. One salesperson tells his customer that the VCR she is considering is going on sale next week and that she can save money by waiting a few days to make the purchase. The other salesperson goes ahead with the sale, on the assumption that the customer wants the VCR today, not next week. The different behavior of these two individuals relates more to perception than to personal values. The second salesperson, when criticized for not being completely honest with a customer, might argue that his behavior was in fact ethical, since it was none of his business whether the customer wanted to buy the VCR today or next week.

REFERENCES: "Unfuzzing Ethics for Managers," Fortune, November 23, 1987, pp. 229–234; Richard P. Nielsen, "Changing Unethical Organizational Behavior," The Academy of Management Executive, August 1989, pp. 123–130; "The Business Ethics Debate," Newsweek, May 25, 1987, p. 36.

that she talks less about her work, and that she calls in sick more frequently. She might conclude from this observation that her job is no longer interesting enough to her and subsequently decide to look for another job. Thus she observed her own behavior, attributed a cause to it, and developed what she thought was a consistent response.

The manager of the individual described above might form exactly the same attribution from her behavior. Alternatively, he might conclude that she has a chronic illness, that she is experiencing too much stress, that she has a drug problem, or that she is having family problems.

People form attributions for behavior by recognizing three types of patterns: consensus (the extent to which other people in the same situation behave the same way), consistency (the extent to which the same person behaves the same way at different times), and distinctiveness (the extent to which the same person behaves the same way in different situations). For example, suppose a manager observes that an employee is late for a meeting. The manager might realize that this employee is the only one who is late (low consensus), recall that he is often late for other meetings (high consistency), and subsequently recall that the same employee is sometimes late for work and late returning from lunch (low distinctiveness). This pattern of attributions might cause the manager to decide that the individual's behavior is something that should be changed. At this point, the manager might meet with the subordinate to establish some punitive consequences for future tardiness.

Needs and Motives in Organizations

Individual needs and motives are often derived from personality attributes and attitudes and are affected by perceptions. They also have a direct bearing on individual behavior.

The Nature of Needs and Motives

A *need* is anything that a person requires or wants.

A **need** is simply anything that an individual requires or wants.[28] Not surprisingly, most people have a large number of needs.[29] Primary needs are the physiological necessities that people require in order to survive, such as food, water, and shelter. Secondary needs are more psychological in character and are learned by individuals from the society and culture in which they live. Examples of secondary needs include the needs for achievement, autonomy, power, order, affiliation, and understanding. Secondary needs often seem to manifest themselves in organizational settings, so they are important to consider in any examination of individual behavior. For example, if an individual is to be satisfied with her psychological contract, the inducements that the organization offers must be consistent with her needs. Offering a nice office and job security may not be sufficient if the individual is primarily seeking income and promotion opportunities.

It is also important to note that people's needs will change with time. An individual may be satisfied with his compensation this year, but if he does not receive a raise for several years, he may begin to feel a need for more compensation. This means that from an organizational perspective programs designed to elicit certain behavior may lose their effectiveness as employees satisfy one set of needs and begin to identify another set of needs. Cafeteria-style benefits programs, discussed in Chapter 14, are one way organizations can satisfy an array of different needs.

A *motive* is the individual's reason for choosing a certain behavior.

A **motive** is the individual's reason for choosing a certain behavior. Motives are derived from needs in that most behaviors are undertaken to satisfy one or more needs. For example, suppose an individual just graduating from college wants to get a good starting job in her field. She has been offered two positions, roughly equivalent in salary. Coincidentally, one is with a firm in her hometown. One of her motives in choosing the job near home might be to stay close to family and friends during her first few years of work. Her motive in choosing the job away from home might be to increase her feeling of independence. The reasons for either choice, then, reflect the individual's motive.

Needs, Motives, and Behavior

Motives typically arise in the context of satisfying a need. The manifestation of a motive is actual behavior. For example, suppose an individual wants to advance his career in order to gain income and prestige (needs). He decides to work harder and do higher-quality work in order to impress his boss (motives). Thus he works late each evening, comes into the office on Saturday, and pays special attention to detail as he strives for recognition (behaviors).

People's motives can vary considerably in the degree of conscious deliberation with which they are formed and in complexity. Where to have lunch, for example, is a decision about behavior that most people make without a great deal of careful thought. On the other hand, a decision about behavior that affects an individual's career or family may take much longer and involve many other considerations. The Entrepreneurial Challenge explores the needs and motives that often contribute to the success or failure of people who start their own businesses. We also discuss needs more completely in the next chapter.

Types of Workplace Behavior

Workplace behavior is a pattern of action by the members of an organization that influences organizational effectiveness.

Now that we have looked closely at how individual differences — physical and intellectual qualities, personality, attitudes, perception, needs, and motives — can influence behavior in organizations, let's turn our attention to workplace behavior. **Workplace behavior** is a pattern of action by the members of an organization that directly or indirectly influences organizational effectiveness. One way to talk about workplace behavior is to describe its impact on performance and productivity, absenteeism and turnover, and organizational citizenship.

Performance Behaviors

Performance behaviors are the total set of work-related behaviors that the organization expects the individual to display. They derive from the psychological contract. For some jobs, performance behaviors can be narrowly defined and easily measured. For example, an assembly-line worker who sits by a moving conveyor and attaches parts to a product as it passes by has relatively few performance behaviors. He or she is expected to remain at the work station and correctly attach the parts. Performance can often be assessed quantitatively by counting the percentage of parts correctly attached.

For many other jobs, however, performance behaviors are more diverse and much more difficult to assess. Consider the case of a research and development scientist at Merck. The scientist works in a lab trying to find new scientific applications that have commercial potential. The scientist

THE ENTREPRENEURIAL CHALLENGE

The Entrepreneurial Motive

Why would someone with a secure job and a good salary give it all up to start a risky business that promised no security and a limited income? Ask the hundreds of people who have made just this choice. Ask Bill Elliott, for example. A graduate of the Harvard Business School, Elliott recently left a lucrative investment banking position to start his own trucking company. Today his salary is about half of what he was making on Wall Street, and he has to work longer hours than before. He says he's having the time of his life.

Or ask Rose Kane. Kane left a secure position at Tenneco Corporation to start her own employment agency. She simply wanted to be her own boss. She's actually making more today than when she worked for Tenneco but must still face the uncertainties of the entrepreneurial life. Her income isn't secure, and she doesn't have the luxury of delegating work: she has to do most things herself. But she, too, says she's never been happier.

What is it about these people that sets them apart from many others who prefer the stability and security that come from a corner office in a big corporation? For one thing, people who choose entrepreneurship seem to have a strong desire for independence: they want to be their own boss and to set their own agenda. For another, they feel the need to create something themselves. They are willing to live with less security and often less income in return for other things that they think are more important.

REFERENCES: Kenneth Labich, "Breaking Away to Go on Your Own," *Fortune,* December 17, 1990, pp. 40–56; "Entrepreneurs and Second Acts," *Wall Street Journal,* May 17, 1989, p. B1; Jeremy Main, "Breaking Out of the Company," *Fortune,* May 25, 1987, pp. 82–88.

must apply knowledge learned in graduate school with experience gained from previous research. Intuition and creativity are important ingredients in this work. The desired breakthrough may take months or even years to occur. As we discussed in Chapter 14, organizations rely on a number of different methods for evaluating performance. The key is to match the evaluation mechanism to the job being performed.

Withdrawal Behaviors

Two types of withdrawal behaviors are absenteeism and turnover. Absenteeism occurs when an individual does not show up for work. The cause (illness, jury duty, death in the family) may be legitimate or feigned — reported as legitimate but actually just an excuse to stay home. When an employee is absent, her or his work does not get done at all, or a substitute must be hired to do it. In either case, the quantity or quality of actual output is likely to suffer.[30] Obviously, some absenteeism is expected. The key concern of organizations is to minimize feigned absenteeism and reduce legitimate absences as much as possible. High absenteeism may be a symptom of other problems, however, such as job dissatisfaction and low morale on the part of employees.

Organizations are increasingly recognizing the connection between their own success and citizenship behaviors of their employees. General Motors's advertising campaign for its Saturn division stresses how all Saturn employees are committed to making high-quality products. The assembly line worker in this ad, for example, demonstrates organizational citizenship in her comments about product quality and teamwork.

You're really a part of the full process.
Because the next team down the line won't accept your work if it's not completely right.
And why should they?
No customer out there will accept anything less. They'll go buy a Toyota or something.

That's why every single person at Saturn has a responsibility to make sure every piece fits the way it should. Makes sense to me.
I've always thought someone's going to pay good money for a car I've built. I have a car payment. I know what that's like.... **"**

A DIFFERENT KIND *Of* COMPANY. A DIFFERENT KIND *Of* CAR.

If you'd like to know more about Saturn, and our new sedans and coupe, please call us at 1-800-522-5000.

Turnover occurs when people quit their jobs. An organization usually incurs costs when replacing individuals who have quit, but if turnover involves productive people, it is especially costly. Turnover seems to result from a number of factors, including aspects of the job, the organization, the individual, the labor market, and family influences. In general, a poor person-job fit is also a likely cause of turnover.

Efforts to manage turnover directly are frequently fraught with difficulty, even in organizations that concentrate on rewarding good performers.[31] Of course, some turnover is inevitable, and in some cases it may even be desirable. For example, if the organization is trying to cut costs by reducing its staff, having people voluntarily choose to leave is preferable to having to terminate their employment. The organization may also benefit from turnover if the people who choose to leave are low performers or express strong job dissatisfaction.

Organizational Citizenship

Organizational citizenship is individual behavior that makes a positive overall contribution to the organization.

Organizational citizenship is individual behavior that makes a positive overall contribution to the organization.[32] Consider, for example, an employee who does work acceptable in terms of quantity and quality but refuses to work late, will not take time to help newcomers, and is generally unwilling to contribute to the organization beyond the strict performance of her job. This person may be seen as a good performer but may not be considered a good organizational citizen. In contrast, a second employee who performs comparably but who also usually works late when requested, makes time to help newcomers learn their way around, and is perceived as committed to the organization's success is likely to be considered a good organizational citizen.

The extent of people's organizational citizenship is determined by a complex mosaic of individual, social, and organizational variables. In order to be a good citizen, an individual must have the personality, attitudes, and needs that are consistent with citizenship behaviors. Similarly, the social context, or group in which the individual works, needs to facilitate and promote such behaviors (we discuss group dynamics in Chapter 19). Importantly, the organization itself, especially its culture, must be capable of promoting, recognizing, and rewarding citizenship behaviors if they are to be maintained. Although the study of organizational citizenship is still in its infancy, preliminary research suggests that it may play a powerful role in organizational effectiveness.[33]

Learning Summary

Understanding individuals in organizations is an important consideration for all managers. The psychological contract is the set of expectations that people hold with respect to what they will contribute to the organization and what they will receive in return. Organizations strive to achieve an optimal person-job fit, but this process is complicated by the existence of individual differences.

Individuals' different physical and intellectual qualities contribute to their different abilities, skills, and competencies. Organizations, and individuals themselves, often invest heavily in developing abilities and enhancing skills and competencies.

Personality is the relatively stable set of psychological and behavioral attributes that distinguish one person from another. Managers can do little to alter personality but should strive to understand the effects of key personality attributes such as locus of control, authoritarianism, dogmatism, self-monitoring, self-esteem, and risk propensity.

Attitudes are based on emotion, knowledge, and intended behavior. Whereas personality is relatively stable, some attitudes can be formed and changed easily. Others are more constant. Job satisfaction or dissatisfaction, organizational commitment, and job involvement are important work-related attitudes.

Perception is the set of processes by which an individual becomes aware of and interprets information about the environment. Perceptual processes that come into play in the workplace are selective perception and stereotyping. Attribution is closely related to perception.

Individual needs are anything that an individual requires or wants. Thus they serve as a catalyst for behavior. Motives are an individual's reasons for choosing a certain behavior. They explain how an individual attempts to satisfy a need.

Workplace behavior is a pattern of action by the members of an organization that directly or indirectly influences organizational effectiveness. Performance behaviors are the set of work-related behaviors that the organization expects the individual to display in order to fulfill the psychological contract. Two withdrawal behaviors are absenteeism and turnover. Organizational citizenship is behavior that makes a positive overall contribution to the organization.

Questions and Exercises

Review Questions

1. What is a psychological contract between an individual and an organization?
2. Identify examples of abilities and skills that are primarily physical. Identify others that are primarily intellectual. Finally, identify others that are both.
3. Identify and describe five personality attributes.
4. What are the components of an individual's attitude?
5. How does perception affect behavior?
6. How does a need differ from a motive?
7. Identify and describe several important workplace behaviors. How do these behaviors influence organizational effectiveness?

Analysis Questions

1. How do psychological contracts evolve? What role do they play in organizations?
2. Identify a job that you would like to have. What skills and abilities are necessary for that job?
3. An individual was heard to describe someone else as having "no personality." What did this individual actually mean?
4. Describe a circumstance in which you formed a new attitude about something.
5. What stereotypes do you form about people? Are they good or bad?
6. What needs do you want to satisfy in this class? How do they differ from the needs you will want to satisfy in your first job after you finish school?
7. As a manager, how would you go about trying to encourage someone to be a better organizational citizen?

Application Questions

1. Write the psychological contract that you have in this class. What do you contribute, and what inducements are available? Compare your contract with the contracts of some of your classmates. In what ways are they similar, and in what ways is yours unique?
2. Assume you are going to hire three new employees for the department store you manage. One individual will sell shoes; one will manage the toy department; and one will work in the stockroom. Identify the characteristics that you want in each of the people in order to achieve a good person-job fit.

Chapter Notes

1. These examples were drawn from actual interviews with FirstCity employees by Ricky W. Griffin. The names have been disguised, but the actual individuals and the characteristics attributed to them in this vignette are real.
2. Denise M. Rousseau, "Psychological and Implied Contracts in Organizations," *Employee Responsibilities and Rights Journal,* Spring 1989, pp. 121–139.
3. See Jennifer A. Chatman, "Improving Interactional Organizational Research: A Model of Person-Organization Fit," *Academy of Management Review,* July 1989, pp. 333–349.
4. E. A. Fleishman, "On the Relation Between Abilities, Learning, and Human Performance," *American Psychologist,* December 1972, pp. 1018–1025.
5. Hugh J. Arnold and Daniel C. Feldman, *Organizational Behavior* (New York: McGraw-Hill, 1986).
6. Benjamin Schneider, A. E. Richers, and T. M. Mitchell, "A Note on Some Relationships Between the Aptitude Requirements and Reward Attributes of Tasks," *Academy of Management Journal,* December 1982, pp. 567–574.
7. Fleishman, "On the Relation Between Abilities, Learning, and Human Performance."
8. J. Hertog, "Earnings and Capability Requirements," *Review of Economics and Statistics,* June 1980, pp. 230–240.
9. Lawrence Pervin, "Personality," in *Annual Review of Psychology,* vol. 36, ed. Mark Rosenzweig and Lyman Porter (Palo Alto, Calif.: Annual Reviews, 1985), pp. 83–114; S. R. Maddi, *Personality Theories: A Comparative Analysis,* 4th ed. (Homewood, Ill.: Dorsey, 1980).
10. Lawrence Pervin, *Current Controversies and Issues in Personality,* 2nd ed. (New York: Wiley, 1984).
11. Pervin, "Personality."
12. J. B. Rotter, "Generalized Expectancies for Internal vs. External Control of Reinforcement," *Psychological Monographs,* Vol. 80, 1966, pp. 1–28; Bert De Brabander and Christopher Boone, "Sex Differences in Perceived Locus of Control," *The Journal of Social Psychology,* July 1990, pp. 271–276.
13. H. Levinson, "Reliability and Validity of the I, P, and C Scales: A Multidimensional View of Locus of Control" (Paper presented at the meeting of the American Psychological Association, Montreal, September 1973).

14. T. W. Adorno, E. Frenkel-Brunswick, D. J. Levinson, and R. N. Sanford, *The Authoritarian Personality* (New York: Harper & Row, 1950).
15. "Who Becomes an Authoritarian?" *Psychology Today*, March 1989, pp. 66–70.
16. Edward Necka and Malgorzata Kubiak, "The Influence of Training in Metaphorical Thinking on Creativity and Level of Dogmatism," *Polish Psychological Bulletin*, Vol. 20, 1989, pp. 69–78; A. F. Kostin, "The Truth of History and Stereotypes of Dogmatism," *Soviet Studies in History*, Vol. 27, 1988, pp. 85–96.
17. Mark Snyder and Nancy Cantor, "Thinking About Ourselves and Others: Self-Monitoring and Social Knowledge," *Journal of Personality and Social Psychology*, April 1980, pp. 222–234.
18. Barbara Foley Meeker, "Cooperation, Competition, and Self-Esteem: Aspects of Winning and Losing," *Human Relations*, March 1990, pp. 205–220; Jiing-Lih Farh and Gregory H. Dobbins, "Effects of Self-Esteem on Leniency Bias in Self-Reports of Performance: A Structural Equation Model Analysis," *Personnel Psychology*, Fall 1990, pp. 835–860; Jon L. Pierce, Donald G. Gardner, and Larry L. Cummings, "Organization-based Self-Esteem: Construct Definition, Measurement, and Validation," *Academy of Management Journal*, September 1989, pp. 622–648.
19. Charles E. Kimble, *Social Psychology: Studying Human Interaction* (Dubuque, Iowa: Wm. C. Brown, 1990); Frank E. Saal and Patrick A. Knight, *Industrial/Organizational Psychology* (Belmont, Calif.: Brooks/Cole, 1988).
20. Leon Festinger, *A Theory of Cognitive Dissonance* (Stanford, Calif.: Stanford University Press, 1957).
21. Gerald Salancik and Jeffrey Pfeffer, "An Examination of Need-Satisfaction Models of Job Attitudes," *Administrative Science Quarterly*, June 1977, pp. 427–456; Gerald Salancik and Jeffrey Pfeffer, "A Social Information Processing Approach to Job Attitudes and Task Design," *Administrative Science Quarterly*, March 1978, pp. 224–253.
22. For an example of an attitude change effort see Deborah A. Byrnes and Gary Kiger, "The Effect of a Prejudice-Reduction Simulation on Attitude Change," *Journal of Applied Social Psychology*, August 1990, pp. 341–353.
23. Patricia C. Smith, L. M. Kendall, and Charles Hulin, *The Measurement of Satisfaction in Work and Behavior* (Chicago: Rand McNally, 1969).
24. James R. Lincoln, "Employee Work Attitudes and Management Practice in the U.S. and Japan: Evidence from a Large Comparative Study," *California Management Review*, Fall 1989, pp. 89–106.
25. Ibid.
26. Richard M. Steers, "Antecedents and Outcomes of Organizational Commitment," *Administrative Science Quarterly*, March 1977, pp. 46–56.
27. See H. H. Kelley, *Attribution in Social Interaction* (Morristown, N.J.: General Learning Press, 1971), for a classic treatment of attribution.
28. H. A. Murray, *Explorations in Personality* (New York: Oxford University Press, 1938).
29. D. C. McClelland and R. E. Boyatzis, "Leadership Motive Pattern and Long-Term Success in Management," *Journal of Applied Psychology*, November 1982, pp. 737–743; J. W. Atkinson and N. T. Feather, *A Theory of Achievement Motivation* (New York: Wiley, 1966); D. C. McClelland, *The Achieving Society* (Princeton, N.J.: Van Nostrand, 1961); Murray, *Explorations in Personality*.

30. "Controlling Absenteeism: How to Motivate Good Attendance," *Small Business Report,* September 1989, p. 30.
31. Robert P. Steel, W. H. Hendrix, and S. P. Balogh, "Confounding Effects of the Turnover Base Rate on Relations Between Time Lag and Turnover Study Outcomes: An Extension of Meta-Analysis Finding and Conclusions," *Journal of Organizational Behavior,* May 1990, pp. 237–251; Muhammad Jamal, "Relationship of Job Stress and Type-A Behavior to Employees' Job Satisfaction, Organizational Commitment, Psychosomatic Health Problems, and Turnover Motivation," *Human Relations,* August 1990, pp. 727–738.
32. See Dennis W. Organ and Mary Konovsky, "Cognitive Versus Affective Determinants of Organizational Citizenship Behavior," *Journal of Applied Psychology,* February 1989, pp. 157–164, for recent findings regarding this behavior.
33. Ibid.

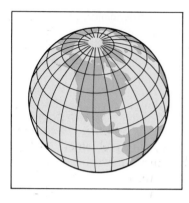

CASE 16.1

Contrasting Successes in the Airline Industry

Since the airline deregulation of the early 1980s, many airlines have struggled and a number have declared bankruptcy. But in an industry noted for cutthroat competition and tough executives, a few airlines and their bosses can boast consistent records of success. Chief among them are Robert L. Crandall, chairman of AMR Corp., parent of American Airlines, and Herbert D. Kelleher, chief executive of Southwest Airlines Co. Success is just about the only thing these two men share.

Southwest has grown to become the nation's eighth largest airline under Kelleher, and it was one of only three U.S. airlines to make a profit in 1990. Yet Kelleher is anything but the distant tyrant that many people associate with lean and profitable companies. To many Southwest employees, the chairman is not "Mr. Kelleher" but "Uncle Herb" or "Herbie." In fact, Kelleher doesn't fit the stereotype in a number of ways. If it's Friday, Southwest's "fun uniform" day, Kelleher may wear khaki pants and a bright red sweatshirt even if he's going to a bank board meeting. To celebrate the opening of Sea World in San Antonio, Kelleher painted one of the company's 737s to look like a killer whale. And he's been known to spend time on baggage duty or behind a ticket counter and to show up for a flight in jungle-print jams.

Robert Crandall, by contrast, is a no-nonsense workaholic. He regularly puts in fourteen-hour days, holds marathon meetings, and is the first to arrive and the last to leave. He is a fanatic for detail, and his background in finance and computers makes a budget meeting with him an appointment to be feared. He makes *Fortune* magazine's list of the ten toughest bosses, and although he doesn't like to be interviewed about such things, he is probably pleased by the selection. "The airline business," he likes to say, "is the closest thing there is to legalized warfare — and we regard winning as essential."*

These two very different leaders have one important attribute in common: both are very good at using their personal strengths to develop innovative ways to trim waste and make their companies more efficient. Southwest makes money by keeping its operating costs the lowest in the business. Southwest's no-frills approach pleases customers, employees, and stockholders. First-time Southwest flyers may be surprised at the lack of in-flight meals, but low ticket prices attract customers, and the company's no-layoff and profit-sharing policies keep employees happy and motivated to work productively. Southwest has an unusually low turnover rate (10 percent), and though 85 percent of its employees are unionized, both sides sign new contracts without any fuss. Up to 80 percent of promotions come from within the company, and to most of Southwest's 8,200 employees in 33 cities, the company feels like a family.

After a bitter battle between Crandall and American's pilots in 1990, few American employees are likely to mistake their company for a family. But Crandall is persuasive, and he knows his details. In 1983, he persuaded pilots to accept the industry's first two-tier pay scale, assuring them that the company's growth would reward them with rapid promotions. His background in computers and finance proved valuable when he helped develop American's Sabre computerized reservation system. The idea revolutionized the industry and generates income for American every time a travel agent uses one of Sabre's 85,500 terminals in 47 countries. Another American innovation under Crandall was the industry's first "frequent flier" program. Crandall's obsession for details has also paid off in minor ways — when, for instance, he saved American $40,000 by eliminating olives from the company's in-flight salads. And he courts international fliers by discovering and catering to their idiosyncracies: American flight attendants make sure to address German passengers by formal titles (like "Herr Doktor") and are careful not to touch Japanese passengers.

The success of these radically different executives in the same industry demonstrates that there are many right ways to run a company. But that doesn't stop the two men from ribbing each other when they meet. At one such meeting, Kelleher remarked that tiny Southwest was like Finland to American's mighty Russia, to which Crandall replied, "There's only one difference. I ain't reducing the troops."† On another occasion, after hearing about Southwest's killer whale 737, Crandall called Kelleher to congratulate him on his clever marketing but asked what he would do with the killer whale waste. On the following Monday, during a staff meeting at American, a messenger appeared with Kelleher's response: a huge bowl of chocolate mousse and a spoon. Maybe a little bit of Kelleher will rub off on Crandall, a change that might please American's employees.

Discussion Questions

1. Do you think that Herb Kelleher is able to maintain his style of leadership only because his airline is relatively small?
2. Which man would you rather work for? Which airline would you rather invest money in?
3. What qualities do you think the two men share besides those noted here?
4. Does the ability of such different people to be equally successful mean that it is impossible to generalize about which personal traits allow a manager to succeed? Explain.

* Quoted in Kenneth Labich, "Bob Crandall Soars by Flying Solo," *Fortune,* September 29, 1986, p. 118.

† Quoted in Kevin Kelly, "American Aims for the Sky," *Business Week,* February 20, 1989, p. 54.

REFERENCES: Kevin Kelly, "American Aims for the Sky," *Business Week,* February 20, 1989, pp. 54–58; Kevin Kelly, "Southwest Airlines: Flying High with 'Uncle Herb,'" *Business Week,* July 3, 1989, pp. 53–55; Kenneth Labich, "American Takes on the World," *Fortune,* September 24, 1990, pp. 40–48; Kenneth Labich, "Bob Crandall Soars by Flying Solo," *Fortune,* September 29, 1986, pp. 118–124; Peter Nulty, "America's Toughest Bosses," *Fortune,* February 27, 1989, pp. 40–54.

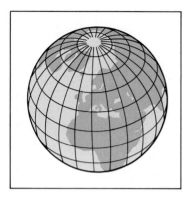

CASE 16.2

The Hatchet (and Radar) Take on BP's Bureaucracy

How does a stodgy old British oil company with dwindling reserves prepare for the 1990s? Winston Churchill himself chose British Petroleum (BP) to fuel the Royal Navy, and for years the company coasted on its past glory and on its huge oil reserves. But when BP began to see its own fuel gauge dropping, it decided to revive itself with a brash, almost American image, and it chose a man nicknamed "The Hatchet" to make the company lean and efficient. The mixture of an aggressive, forward-looking individual and a complacent company has caught the interest of many organizational experts.

BP is the world's fourth largest private oil company. It sells $50 billion worth of oil and gas each year and owns about 5 billion barrels of oil reserves, mostly in the huge oil fields in Prudhoe Bay, Alaska, and the North Sea. But the productivity of BP's big fields is dropping by about 10 percent per year, and though the two fields account for only about one-sixth of the company's revenues, they bring in over 40 percent of its operating profits. In other words, the rest of the company is not in good shape.

To make sure that BP has a future, the company chose Robert B. Horton as its new chairman and also gave him the un-British title of chief executive, one of many moves aimed at making the company more attractive to American consumers and investors. Horton spent the 1980s as the company's top troubleshooter, earning the nickname "Horton the Hatchet." First he turned the company's refining and chemical division around; then he moved to Cleveland to trim the fat from Standard Oil of Ohio (Sohio), which BP had just finished acquiring. He has the invaluable skill of carrying out his "hatchet" duties without creating too much resentment. He is so adept at dealing with people one on one that he had a teleconferencing studio installed near his office so he could talk directly to BP employees around the world. When he takes with one hand, he tries to give with the other: while cutting Sohio's charitable contributions by $4 million, he joined the boards of the Cleveland Orchestra and the fledgling Rock 'n' Rol Hall of Fame.

Already, BP has radically altered the way it spends its oil exploration money. In general, large oil companies drill most of their new wells in areas with proven reserves rather than take a risk on new areas. But new wells in an old field are not as profitable as successful wells in a new field. So rather than join the crowd in well-drilled areas, BP is spending half of its $1 billion yearly exploration budget on "frontier" exploration, going to places like Papua New Guinea and Ethiopia to look for new fields that will turn a profit into the next century.

Just as important to Horton's strategy is a major restructuring of BP's bureaucracy. One of the reasons that BP's profits were not keeping pace with its revenues was that the company was burdened with a huge hierarchical bureaucracy, a relic from the days when oil production was a very different business. To succeed in its risky, innovative strategy, BP must be lean and flexible, able to make decisions quickly. New structure must accompany the new strategy.

Horton saw how necessary restructuring was when he returned to Britain from Cleveland and viewed BP with fresh eyes. He was appalled at the levels of distrust and second-guessing in the old, slow-moving bureaucracy. In his first year, Horton cut corporate staff from about 2,500 to less than 380, working to decentralize responsibility, increase trust, openness, and teamwork, and involve employees in directing the changes. Responding to employee criticisms, Horton abolished six of BP's eleven bureaucratic layers and divided the work previously done by eighty standing committees among individuals and small, flexible teams that report directly to Horton or to the heads of the company's four major divisions. Along with the new responsibilities, managers have new authority. They can now spend two-and-a-half times as much as they used to without authorization, and spending requests that do require authorization now need only two or three signatures instead of a dozen.

Horton is also working to make Americans aware of BP. The company has raised the BP logo at all of its 7,700 American gas stations, which used to carry names like Boron, Gulf, and Sohio. It is letting Americans know that BP pumps more North American crude than any other company. And it is trying to convey the image of a company with a sense of humor. That's where M*A*S*H's Radar O'Reilly — Gary Burghoff — comes in. BP made seven television ads with Burghoff, including a $1 million extravaganza done by Steven Spielberg's cinematographer. If The Hatchet can do the real work behind the scenes, the company is betting that Radar can do what he always did so effectively on M*A*S*H — spread the word.

Discussion Questions

1. What problems might someone with Horton's personality encounter trying to change an old, bureaucratic organization like BP?
2. Why would British Petroleum want to change its image to seem more American?
3. What elements of Horton's background make him seem particularly well suited to make the changes necessary at BP?
4. Why did BP need to change its structure in order to pursue its new exploration strategy?

REFERENCES: "BP Signals a New Direction," *Petroleum Economist,* April 1990, p. 106; Peter Nulty, "Batman Shakes BP to Bedrock," *Fortune,* November 19, 1990, pp. 155–162; Caleb Solomon, "BP America's Gas Stations to Get a Single Brand Name," *Wall Street Journal,* January 6, 1989, p. B5; Allanna Sullivan and Joann S. Lublin, "British Petroleum Goes American in Its Quest for Bigger World Role," *Wall Street Journal,* February 13, 1990, pp. A1, A4.

17

Motivation in Organizations

After studying this chapter, you should be able to:

1. Explain how the concept of individual motivation in organizations has evolved over time.

2. Discuss the need hierarchy, the dual-structure approach to motivation, and acquired needs.

3. Discuss the expectancy and equity theories of motivation in organizations, and explain how they address the process of motivation.

4. Discuss the four types of reinforcement contingencies and describe how that reinforcement can be provided.

5. Identify and describe two new approaches to motivation in organizations.

6. Explain how reward systems affect motivation, and discuss the advantages and disadvantages of incentive reward systems.

The Nature of Motivation in Organizations

    Motivation and Performance in Organizations

    Historical Views of Motivation

Need-based Approaches to Motivation

    Need Hierarchies

    The Dual-Structure Approach to Motivation

    Acquired Needs

Process-based Approaches to Motivation

    Expectancy Theory

    Equity Theory

Reinforcement-based Approaches to Motivation

    Reinforcement Contingencies

    Providing Reinforcement

New Approaches to Motivation in Organizations

    Goal-setting Theory

    The Japanese Approach to Motivation

Enhancing Motivation in Organizations

    Organizational Reward Systems

    Interventions for Enhancing Motivation

Nordstrom, Inc., is one of the fastest-growing retailers in America. The Seattle-based firm operates a variety of specialty clothing stores in six states, primarily in the West. Its sales increased 600 percent during the 1980s, and the chain currently has around thirty-thousand employees.

Part of Nordstrom's success has been achieved through customer service. Nordstrom employees are said to be among the industry's friendliest and most enthusiastic, and they go to great lengths to keep their customers satisfied. They write personal thank-you notes to customers, for example, and they have been known to deliver customers' purchases to their homes and warm up customers' cars in the store parking lot on wintry days.

The basis for many of these behaviors is Nordstrom's reward system. Most salespeople are paid on a complicated commission system that allows them to earn considerably more money than the industry average. Some earn in excess of $80,000 a year. Nordstrom salespeople also receive bonuses and surprise rewards for doing an especially good job.

Recent allegations, however, reveal a dark side to the Nordstrom system of rewards. Many workers say that they are encouraged to work long hours without pay after they have finished their day's sales work. Some claim that the individual commission system that Nordstrom uses encourages cut-throat competition among clerks anxious to increase their personal income. Although they appreciate the occasional surprise bonuses of $5, $10, or $100, they also claim that they work under constant threat of dismissal if their sales drop. Indeed, one salesperson recently claimed that Nordstrom's carrot-and-stick system was a lot more stick than carrot.[1]

By most objective measures Nordstrom has been incredibly successful. Many of its employees are satisfied and highly motivated. They believe that they are personally responsible for their own performance and that they can earn large rewards by working hard and doing what the organization expects of them. But other Nordstrom employees complain that the organization takes advantage of them and treats them unfairly. The crux of this conflict is individual difference: each Nordstrom employee responds differently to the firm's reward system.

This chapter addresses motivation in organizations. We begin by examining the nature of employee motivation and looking at how perspectives on motivation have developed historically. The next sections explore the three major theoretical approaches to motivation: need-based, process-based, and reinforcement-based approaches. We then discuss some emerging approaches to motivation and conclude by describing the various interventions and reward systems that organizations adopt in an effort to enhance motivation.

The Nature of Motivation in Organizations

Motivation is the set of forces that cause people to choose certain behaviors from among the alternatives open to them.

We define **motivation** as the set of forces that cause people to choose certain behaviors from among the many alternatives open to them.[2] On any given day, for example, an employee may choose to work very hard, to do only an acceptable amount of work, or to do just enough to get by. What causes one employee to choose the first behavior and another the third? This is the basic question that an understanding of employee motivation seeks to answer.

Motivation and Performance in Organizations

Motivation, along with ability and the work environment, determines the performance of an individual employee.

In most instances, the performance of an individual employee is determined by three things: motivation (the person's desire to do the job), ability (the person's capability to do the job), and the work environment (the availability of the necessary tools, materials, opportunity to perform, and information needed to do the job). If an employee lacks ability, the organization can take action — either providing training or replacing the worker. If there is an environmental problem, the organization again can act — altering the environment to promote higher performance. But if motivation is the problem, the task for the organization is more challenging. Individual behavior is a complex phenomenon, and managers may be hard-pressed to figure out the precise nature of the problem and how to solve it. Thus motivation is important because of its significance as a determinant of performance and because of its intangible character.[3]

The motivation framework in Figure 17.1 is a good starting point for understanding how people choose certain behaviors. The motivation process begins with needs that individuals identify for themselves. Say, for example, a worker feels that he is underpaid. This deficiency becomes a need that the worker seeks to satisfy, perhaps by asking for a raise, by working harder to earn a raise, or by seeking a new job. Once he chooses to pursue one or more of these options and then enacts them (working harder while simultaneously looking for a new job, for example), he evaluates his success. If his hard work resulted in a pay raise, he probably feels satisfied and will continue to work hard. But if no raise has been provided, he is likely to try another option. Since people have many different needs, the satisfaction of one need or set of needs is likely to give rise to the identification of other needs. Thus the cycle of motivation is being constantly repeated.

Figure 17.1

Framework for the Motivation Process

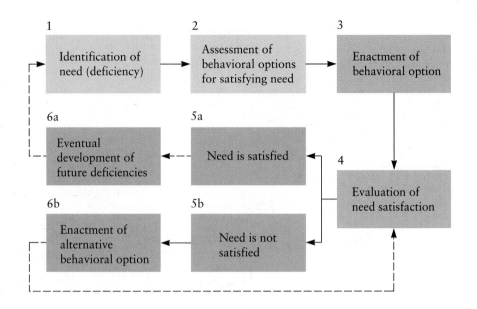

Historical Views of Motivation

To appreciate what we know (and don't know) about employee motivation, it is helpful to review some of the early ideas about this concept. In general, motivation theory has evolved through three different stages: scientific management, the human relations movement, and the human resource approach.

Scientific Management   This approach to understanding employee motivation is best represented by the work of Frederick W. Taylor.[4] As discussed in Chapter 2, Taylor suggested the use of an incentive pay system. Nordstrom's commission system is an incentive pay system. Taylor believed that management knew more about the jobs being performed than the workers did, and he assumed that economic gain was the primary motivation for every worker. Other assumptions of scientific management were that work is inherently unpleasant for most people and that the money they earn is more important to employees than the nature of the job they are performing. Hence, people could be expected to perform any kind of job if they were paid enough. Although the role of money as a motivating factor cannot be dismissed, proponents of scientific management took too narrow a view of the role of monetary compensation and failed to consider other motivational factors.

Human Relations Movement   The human relations movement (also discussed in Chapter 2) grew out of research done at Western Electric Company by Elton Mayo and his associates.[5] The human relationists emphasized the role of social processes in the workplace. They assumed that employees want to feel useful and important and want to belong to a social group,

The human resource approach to motivation often involves employee participation throughout the organization. These members of the Flint, Michigan, Transportation Problem Solving team helped develop a proposal to improve drainage in Grand Trunk Works's Flint rail yard. They are shown here surveying the results of their plan after it was implemented by GTW.

and that these needs are more important than money in motivating employees. Advocates of the human relations movement advised managers to make workers feel important, to keep them informed, and to allow them a modicum of self-direction and self-control in carrying out routine activities. Subsequent feelings of involvement and importance were expected to satisfy workers' basic social needs and result in higher motivation to perform.

Human Resource Approach   The human resource approach to motivation carries the concepts of human needs and motivation one step further. Whereas the human relationists believed that even the illusion of contribution and participation would enhance motivation, the human resource view assumes that the actual contributions themselves are valuable, both to individuals and to organizations. It assumes not only that people want to contribute but that they are able to make genuine contributions. The organization's task, then, is to encourage participation and to create a work environment that makes full use of the human resources available. This philosophy guides most contemporary thinking about employee motivation. At Ford, Westinghouse, Texas Instruments, and Hewlett-Packard, for example, work teams are called on to solve a variety of problems and to make substantive contributions to organizational effectiveness.[6]

Each of the perspectives described above provides some insights into employee motivation. Money (as suggested by Taylor) and the social context of work (as suggested by the human relations movement) are each important in motivation. Moreover, as argued by the human resource approach, people do make substantive contributions to organizational effectiveness. At the same time, each of these viewpoints tells only part of the story. Although the human resource approach represents the philosophy that guides most thinking about motivation today, three integrative approaches have been developed to conceptualize more completely the complex process of motivation. These are the need-based, the process-based, and the reinforcement-based approaches to motivation.

Need-based Approaches to Motivation

Need-based approaches to motivation attempt to determine the set of factors that cause people to choose certain behaviors.

Need-based approaches to motivation address the first part of the motivation process depicted in Figure 17.1 — identification of needs and deficiencies. Need-based approaches try to answer the question "What factor or factors motivate people to choose certain behaviors?" Thus they address boxes 1 and 2 in the figure. Labor leaders, for example, often argue that workers can be motivated by more pay, shorter working hours, and improved working conditions. Meanwhile, some behavioral scientists suggest that motivation can be enhanced by providing employees with more autonomy and greater responsibility. Both of these views represent need-based views of motivation. The former asserts that motivation is a function of pay, working hours, and working conditions; the latter suggests that autonomy and responsibility are the causes of motivation.[7] Two widely known need-based approaches to motivation are need hierarchies and the dual-structure approach.

Need Hierarchies

Maslow's hierarchy of needs specifies five levels of human needs that motivate behavior.

Many different need hierarchies have been proposed, but the version most popular in the management field was developed by Abraham Maslow in the 1940s.[8] **Maslow's hierarchy of needs** assumes that people are motivated to satisfy five levels of needs: physiological, security, belongingness, esteem, and self-actualization needs. According to Maslow's hierarchy, physiological needs for food, sex, and air represent basic issues of survival and biological function. In organizational settings, most physiological needs are satisfied by adequate wages and by the work environment itself, which provides employees with restrooms, adequate lighting, comfortable temperatures, and ventilation.

Next are security needs — the requirements for a secure physical and emotional environment. Examples include the desire for adequate housing and clothing, the need to be free from worry about money and job security, and the desire for safe working conditions. Security needs are satisfied for many people in the workplace by job continuity (no layoffs), a grievance system (to protect against arbitrary supervisory actions), and an adequate insurance and retirement benefit package (for security against illness and provision of income in later life). Even today, however, depressed industries and general economic decline can put people out of work and restore the primacy of security needs. This perspective is discussed more fully in The Environmental Challenge.

THE ENVIRONMENTAL CHALLENGE

Employees Seek New Avenues for Security

Many people have strong security needs. These needs include the desire to have a safe and protected life and to be free from worry. They also include a need for job security. In recent years, however, increasing threats to job security have caused many workers to reassess the role of job security in their work lives.

For decades American workers had a pretty clear vision of their future — get an education, get a good job, buy a home, and live happily ever after. Cutbacks and massive layoffs throughout American industry, however, have shattered this vision for millions. Moreover, these changes have caused many workers to reassess their priorities and to redefine the meaning of job security. But even having a job and a reasonable degree of security is no longer enough to guarantee someone a claim on the American dream.

Worker loyalty has been shaken, and firms that have traditionally afforded great job security — IBM, General Motors, and Hewlett-Packard, for example — lost this distinction with more and more layoffs on into the 1990s. Thus today's new workers are likely to worry about their long-term prospects with any employer.

Some worry but do nothing about it. Others, however, are taking steps to increase their own personal value — if not to their present employers, then to other prospective employers in the event they lose their jobs.

Highly skilled technical workers are projected to be in great demand during the rest of this decade. Jobs that once used unskilled workers now require people who can operate computers and sophisticated electronic equipment and who know the meaning of productivity and quality. By going back to school, by seeking technical training, and by developing new competencies, today's workers are ensuring themselves a better job tomorrow. This new-found mobility is helping them satisfy their security needs in ways that stable employment satisfied the security needs of their parents.

REFERENCES: Jaclyn Fierman, "Shaking the Blue-Collar Blues," *Fortune,* April 22, 1991, pp. 209–218; Anne B. Fisher, "The Downside of Downsizing," *Fortune,* May 23, 1988, pp. 42–52; "How Safe Is Your Job?" *Newsweek,* November 5, 1990, pp. 44–47.

Belongingness needs are related to the social aspect of human life. They include the need for love and affection and the need to be accepted by one's peers. For most people these needs are satisfied by a combination of family and community relationships outside of work and friendships on the job. Managers can help ensure the satisfaction of these important needs by allowing social interaction and by making employees feel like part of a team or work group. Managers can also be sensitive to the probable effects (such as absenteeism or low performance) when an employee has family problems or interpersonal conflict with others at work.

Esteem needs actually comprise two different sets of needs: the need for a positive self-image and self-respect and the need for recognition and respect from others. Organizations can help address esteem needs by providing a variety of extrinsic symbols of accomplishment such as job titles, spacious offices, and similar rewards as appropriate. At a more intrinsic level, organizations can also help satisfy esteem needs by providing employees with challenging job assignments that carry with them a sense of accomplishment.

At the top of the hierarchy are what Maslow calls the self-actualization needs. These involve realizing one's potential for continued growth and individual development. Because they are highly individualized and personal, self-actualization needs are perhaps the most difficult for managers to address. In fact, it can be argued that individuals must meet these needs entirely by themselves. Organizations can help, however, by promoting a climate wherein self-actualization is possible. For instance, an organization can promote the fulfillment of these needs by providing employees with a chance to participate in making decisions about their work and with the opportunity to learn new things about their jobs and the organization. The processes of contributing to actual organizational performance (through decision making) and learning more about the organization are likely to help people experience the personal growth and development associated with self-actualizing.

Maslow suggests that the five levels of needs are arranged in order of importance, starting at the bottom of the hierarchy. An individual is motivated first and foremost to satisfy physiological needs. As long as these needs remain unsatisfied, the individual is motivated to fulfill only them. When satisfaction of physiological needs is achieved, however, this first level of needs ceases to act as the primary motivation, and the individual "moves up" the hierarchy and becomes concerned with security needs. This "moving up" process continues until the individual reaches the self-actualization level.

Maslow's concept of the need hierarchy has a certain intuitive logic and has been accepted by many managers. But research has revealed several shortcomings in the theory. For example, some research has found that five levels of needs are not always present and that the order of the levels is not always the same as postulated by Maslow.[9] Moreover, it is difficult for organizations to use the need hierarchy to enhance employee motivation. Thus, although Maslow's view of motivation provides a logical framework for categorizing needs, it does not supply a full picture.

In response to the criticisms directed at Maslow's work, Clayton Alderfer has proposed an alternative hierarchy of needs called the **ERG theory of motivation**.[10] The letters *E, R,* and *G* stand for existence, relatedness, and growth. ERG theory, as Figure 17.2 shows, collapses the need hierarchy developed by Maslow into three levels. Existence needs correspond to the physiological and security needs of Maslow's hierarchy. Relatedness needs focus on how people relate to their social environment. In Maslow's hierarchy, they would encompass both the need to belong and the need to earn the esteem of others. Growth needs, the highest level, include the needs for both self-esteem and self-actualization.

Although ERG theory assumes that motivated behavior follows a hierarchy in somewhat the same fashion as suggested by Maslow, there are two important differences. First, ERG theory suggests that needs at more than one level can cause motivation at the same time. For example, it allows for the possibility that people can be motivated by a desire for money (existence), friendship (relatedness), and the opportunity to learn new skills (growth) all at once.

Second, ERG theory has what has been called a frustration-regression element that is missing from Maslow's need hierarchy. Maslow maintained that one need must be satisfied before an individual can progress to needs

The *ERG theory of motivation* specifies three levels of human needs and describes the frustration-regression process.

at a higher level (from security to belongingness, for instance). The individual then is motivated by those higher-level needs until they are satisfied. This might be termed the satisfaction-progression process, since people are presumed to progress up the hierarchy as they become satisfied. Although the ERG theory includes this same process, it also suggests that if needs remain unsatisfied at some higher level, the individual will become frustrated, regress to a lower level, and begin to pursue those lower-level needs again.

Say, for example, a worker previously motivated by money (existence needs) is awarded a pay raise sufficient to satisfy those needs. Suppose that he or she then attempts to establish more friendships to satisfy relatedness needs. If for some reason the employee finds that it is impossible to become better friends with others in the workplace, he may eventually become frustrated and regress to being motivated to earn even more money.

The ERG theory is relatively new compared with Maslow's need hierarchy, but research suggests that it may be a more valid account of motivation in organizations.[11] Organizations should not, of course, rely too heavily on any one particular perspective to guide their thinking about employee motivation. There are, however, two key insights to be gleaned from the need hierarchy view. The first is simply that some needs may be more important than others. The second is that people may change their behavior after any particular set of needs has been satisfied.

The Dual-Structure Approach to Motivation

The *dual-structure approach* to motivation suggests that one set of factors influences satisfaction and a different set of factors influences dissatisfaction.

Another popular need-based approach to motivation is the **dual-structure approach** developed by Frederick Herzberg.[12] Herzberg developed this approach after interviewing two hundred accountants and engineers in

Figure 17.2

The ERG Theory of Motivation

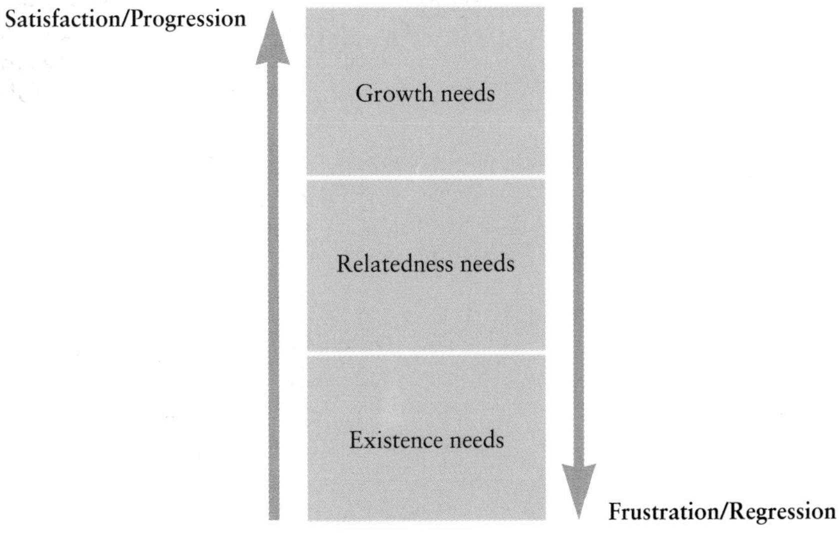

Satisfaction/Progression

Growth needs

Relatedness needs

Existence needs

Frustration/Regression

Pittsburgh. He asked them to recall occasions when they had been especially satisfied with their work and highly motivated and occasions when they had been dissatisfied and less motivated. He found that entirely different sets of factors were associated with satisfaction and with dissatisfaction. An individual who identified "low pay" as causing dissatisfaction did not necessarily mention "high pay" as a cause of satisfaction. Instead, different kinds of factors, such as recognition or accomplishment, were cited as causing satisfaction.

This finding led Herzberg to conclude that the conventional model of job satisfaction and motivation was incomplete. That view suggests that satisfaction and dissatisfaction are at opposite ends of a single continuum. Employees would therefore be satisfied, dissatisfied, or somewhere in between. But Herzberg's interviews suggested a more complex situation. Thus he argued that attitudes and motivation consist of a dual structure. One structure involves a set of factors that result in feelings ranging from satisfaction to no satisfaction. The other structure involves a set of factors that result in feelings ranging from dissatisfaction to no dissatisfaction. This dual-structure approach is illustrated in Figure 17.3.

Figure 17.3 shows the two sets of factors that Herzberg identified as causing either satisfaction or dissatisfaction. Note that the factors influencing the satisfaction continuum—called **motivation factors**—are related specifically to the job itself. The set of factors presumed to cause dissatisfaction—called **hygiene factors**—relate to the work environment in which the job is performed.

Herzberg argued that there are two stages in the process of motivating employees. First, the organization must ensure that the hygiene factors are not deficient. Pay and security must be appropriate, working conditions must be safe, technical supervision must be acceptable, and the like. By

The two sets of factors influencing satisfaction are called *motivation factors* and *hygiene factors*.

Figure 17.3

The Dual-Structure Approach to Motivation

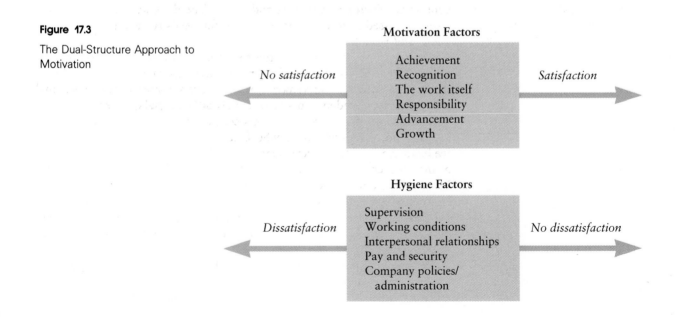

providing these factors at an appropriate level, the organization does not stimulate motivation but merely ensures that employees are "not dissatisfied." Employees whom an organization attempts to "satisfy" by means of hygiene factors alone will usually do just enough to get by.

Thus organizations should proceed to stage two — giving employees the opportunity to experience motivation factors such as achievement and recognition. The result is predicted to be high levels of satisfaction and motivation. Herzberg also goes a step further than most theorists and describes exactly how to use the dual-structure approach in the workplace. Specifically, he recommends job enrichment (discussed in Chapter 10) as a means of enhancing the availability of motivation factors.

Although widely accepted by many managers, Herzberg's dual-structure approach is not without its critics. One criticism is that the findings in Herzberg's initial interviews are subject to different explanations. Another charge is that his sample was not representative of the general population and that subsequent research has often failed to uphold the theory.[13] At the present time, Herzberg's theory is not held in high esteem by researchers in the field of motivation. The theory has had a major impact on managers, however, and has played a key role in increasing their awareness of motivation and its importance in the workplace.

Acquired Needs

Individual needs for achievement, affiliation, and power are learned, or acquired, from the social environment.

Need hierarchies and the dual-structure approach to motivation identify a number of individual needs and then attempt to arrange them in some kind of order of importance. Other need-based views of motivation have focused more on the important needs themselves without being concerned about ordering them. In particular, some needs are learned as a result of the social context in which a person lives and works. The three acquired needs most often discussed from this perspective are the needs for achievement, affiliation, and power.[14]

The need for achievement, the best known of the three, reflects an individual's desire to do something more effectively than in the past. People with a high need for achievement generally have a desire to assume personal responsibility, a tendency to set moderately difficult goals, a need for specific and immediate feedback, and a preoccupation with their task. David C. McClelland, the psychologist who first identified this need, suggests that we learn the need for achievement when we are young. He argues that only a small percentage of the U.S. population has a high need for achievement. Because such a need is assumed to be important for success in organizations, he has devised a training program for increasing one's need for achievement. McClelland's research has suggested that people who complete this achievement training may make more money and receive promotions faster than other managers.[15]

The need for affiliation is less well understood. Like Maslow's belongingness need, the need for affiliation is a desire for human companionship and acceptance. People with a strong need for affiliation are likely to prefer (and perform best in) a job that entails a good deal of social interaction and offers opportunities to make friends. The need for power has recently received considerable attention as an important ingredient in managerial success.[16] The need for power might be defined as the desire to be influential in a group and to control one's environment. Research suggests that people with a strong need for power are likely to be superior performers, have good attendance records, and occupy supervisory positions. At the same time, the quest for power may also promote conflict and come at the expense of organizational effectiveness. One study found that managers as a group tend to have a stronger need for power than does the general population and that successful managers tend to have a stronger need for power than do less successful managers.[17]

In summary, the major need-based approaches to motivation focus on individual needs. Maslow's need hierarchy, the ERG theory, the dual-structure approach, and a focus on acquired needs all provide useful insights into factors that cause motivation. What they do not do is shed much light on the process of motivation. They do not explain why some people might be motivated by one factor rather than by another, or how people might try to satisfy the different needs. These questions pertain to behaviors or actions, goals, and feelings of satisfaction — concepts that are addressed by various process-based approaches to motivation.

Process-based Approaches to Motivation

Process-based approaches to motivation attempt to determine how motivation occurs and to explain why people choose certain behaviors.

Process-based approaches to motivation are concerned with how motivation occurs. As shown in boxes 3 and 4 of the motivation framework in Figure 17.1, process-based approaches focus on why people choose to enact certain behavioral options to fulfill their needs and how they evaluate their satisfaction after they have attained these goals. Two of the most useful process-based approaches to motivation are expectancy theory and equity theory.

Expectancy Theory

Expectancy theory suggests that motivation is determined by how much people want a particular outcome and how likely they think they are to get it.

The expectancy theory of motivation has many different forms and labels. We describe it from a general perspective and in the form most easily understood. Basically, **expectancy theory** suggests that motivation depends on two things: how much we want something and how likely we think we are to get it. Assume for a moment that you are approaching graduation and therefore are looking for a job. You see in the want ads that the New York Yankees are looking for a new center fielder and are offering a starting salary of $500,000 per year. Even though you might want the job, you probably do not apply because you realize that you have little chance of getting it. The next ad you see is for someone to pull staples out of hall bulletin boards for $4.00 an hour. Even though you realize that you could probably get the job, you do not apply because you do not want it. Then you see an ad for a management trainee for a big company with a starting salary of $30,000. You apply for this job because you want it and because you think you have a reasonable chance of getting it.

The formal framework of expectancy theory as we now recognize it was developed by Victor Vroom.[18] Expectancy theory rests on four assumptions. First, the theory assumes that behavior is determined by a combination of forces in the individual and in the environment. Second, it assumes that people make decisions about their own behavior in organizations. The third assumption is that different people have different types of needs, desires, and goals. Finally, expectancy theory assumes that people make choices from among alternative plans of behavior based on their perceptions of the extent to which a given behavior will lead to desired outcomes.[19]

Figure 17.4 summarizes the expectancy model of employee motivation. The model suggests that motivation leads to effort and that effort, when combined with employee ability and environmental factors, results in performance. Performance, in turn, leads to various outcomes — each of which has an associated value (called its *valence*). The most important parts of the expectancy model cannot be truly illustrated in the figure, however. They are the individual's expectation that effort will lead to high perform-

Figure 17.4

The Expectancy Theory of Motivation

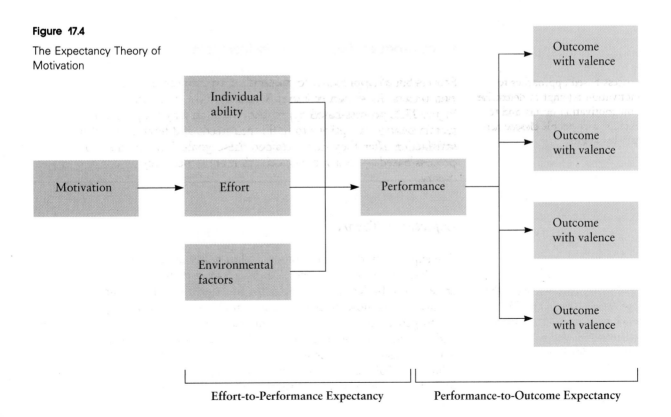

Wisconsin is one of the several states that have recently adopted a choice program, wherein parents — using public money — can choose the school in which they enroll their children. Half the first graders shown here have entered this private school in Milwaukee through the choice program. Like employees in organizations, students in school are motivated by expectancy theory, in that they choose to expend effort, trusting that hard work will result in a high level of performance in the classroom, and that this in turn will lead to desired outcomes: good grades and the approval of their teacher and parents.

ance, that performance will lead to outcomes, and that each outcome will have some kind of value. According to the model, individuals develop some sense of these expectations before they exhibit motivated or nonmotivated behavior.

The *effort-to-performance expectancy* is an individual's perception of the probability that effort will result in high performance.

Effort-to-Performance Expectancy   The **effort-to-performance expectancy** is an individual's perception of the probability that effort will result in high performance. When the individual believes that effort will lead directly to high performance, expectancy is quite strong (close to 1.00). When the individual believes that effort and performance are unrelated, the effort-to-performance expectancy is very weak (close to 0). The belief that effort is somewhat but not strongly related to performance carries with it a moderate expectancy (somewhere between 0 and 1).

The *performance-to-outcome expectancy* is an individual's perception of the probability that performance will result in a specific outcome.

Performance-to-Outcome Expectancy   The **performance-to-outcome expectancy** is an individual's perception of the probability that performance will result in a specific outcome. For example, an individual who believes that high performance will lead to a pay raise has a high performance-to-outcome expectancy (approaching 1.00). An individual who believes that high performance may possibly lead to a pay raise has a moderate expectancy (between 1.00 and 0). And an individual who believes that performance has no relationship to rewards has a low performance-to-outcome expectancy (close to 0).

Outcomes are the consequences of behavior. *Valence* is the relative attractiveness of a certain outcome for a particular person.

Outcomes and Valences   Expectancy theory recognizes that an individual may experience a variety of **outcomes** (consequences of behavior) in an organizational setting. A high performer, for example, may get big pay raises, fast promotions, and praise from the boss. But she may also be subject to a lot of stress and incur resentment from co-workers. Each of these outcomes has an associated value, or **valence** — an index of how much an individual desires a particular outcome. If the individual wants the outcome, its valence is positive. If the individual does not want the outcome, its valence is negative. If the individual is indifferent to the outcome, its valence is zero.

It is this part of expectancy theory that goes beyond the need-based approaches to motivation. As we saw in Chapter 16, different people have different needs, and they try to satisfy these needs in different ways. For an employee who has a high need for achievement and a low need for affiliation, the pay raise and promotions cited above as outcomes of high performance might have positive valences, the praise and co-worker resentment zero valences, and the stress a negative valence. In contrast, for an employee who has a low need for achievement but a high need for affiliation, the pay raise, promotions, and praise might all have positive valences, and the resentment and stress might have negative valences.

For motivated behavior to occur on the part of any one individual, then, three conditions must be met. First, the effort-to-performance expectancy must be greater than zero (the individual must believe that if effort is expended, high performance will result). The performance-to-outcome expectancy must also be greater than zero (the individual must believe that if high performance is achieved, certain outcomes will follow). And the sum of the valences for all relevant outcomes must be greater than zero. (One or more outcomes may have negative valences if they are more than offset by the positive valences of other outcomes. For example, the attractiveness of a pay raise, a promotion, and praise from the boss may outweigh the unattractiveness of more stress and resentment from co-workers). Expectancy theory maintains that when all of these conditions are met, the individual is motivated to expend effort. At Nordstrom, efforts are made to provide employees with pay as an outcome accompanied by clear effort-to-performance and performance-to-outcome expectancies.

Porter and Lawler argued that high performance, if followed by equitable rewards, may lead to high satisfaction.

The Porter-Lawler Extension   An interesting extension to expectancy theory has been proposed by Porter and Lawler.[20] Recall from Chapter 2 that the human relationists assumed employee satisfaction causes good performance, but we noted that research has not supported such a relationship. Porter and Lawler suggest that there may indeed be a relationship between satisfaction and performance but that it goes in the opposite direction! In other words, high performance may cause high satisfaction. Performance results in various rewards for an individual. Some of these are extrinsic (such as pay and promotions); others are intrinsic (such as self-esteem and a feeling of accomplishment). The individual then evaluates the equity, or fairness, of the various rewards relative to the effort expended and the level of performance attained. If the rewards are felt to be equitable, the individual is satisfied.

Implications for Managers   Expectancy theory can be useful for organizations attempting to improve the motivation of their employees. Nadler and Lawler suggest a series of steps in applying the basic ideas of the theory. First, managers should determine the outcomes that each employee is likely to want. Next they should decide what kinds and levels of performance are needed to meet organizational goals, making sure that the desired levels of performance are attainable. Managers should ensure that desired outcomes and desired performance are linked. They should also analyze the complete work situation for conflicting expectancies. Finally, they need to make sure that the rewards are large enough and that the total system is equitable (fair to all).[21]

Of course, expectancy theory has its limitations. Although the theory makes sense and has been generally supported by empirical research, it is quite difficult to apply.[22] To apply this theory completely in the workplace, for example, it would be necessary to identify all the potential outcomes for each employee, to determine all relevant expectancies, and then to balance everything somehow to maximize employee motivation. Expectancy theory also assumes that people are rational — that they will systematically consider all of the potential outcomes and their associated expectancies before selecting a particular behavior. But few people actually make decisions in such a precise, rational manner.

Equity Theory

After needs have stimulated the motivation process and the individual has chosen an action that is expected to satisfy those needs, the individual assesses the fairness, or equity, of the resultant outcome. Much of the current thinking on this stage of assessment has been shaped by the **equity theory** of motivation developed by J. Stacy Adams. Adams contends that people are motivated to seek social equity in the rewards they receive for performance.[23] **Equity** can be defined as an individual's belief that he or she is being treated fairly relative to the treatment of others.

Like expectancy theory, equity theory takes into consideration an array of job-related outcomes, including pay, recognition, promotions, social relationships, and intrinsic rewards. To gain these rewards, the individual makes inputs to the job, such as time, experience, effort, education, and loyalty. The theory suggests that people view their outcomes and inputs as a ratio and then compare their ratio to the ratio of someone else. This other "person" may be someone in the work group or some sort of group average or composite.

An individual develops a sense of these ratios in a qualitative, subjective way. Comparison of the two ratios is likewise imprecise but affects the individual's attitudes nonetheless. Three attitudes are possible: the individual may feel equitably rewarded, underrewarded, or overrewarded. The individual will experience a feeling of equity when the two ratios are equal. This may occur even though the other person's outcomes are greater than the individual's own outcomes — provided that the other's inputs are also proportionately greater. Suppose that Mark has a high school education

Equity theory suggests that people are motivated to seek social equity in the rewards they receive for performance. *Equity* is the individual's belief that he or she is being treated fairly relative to the treatment of others.

and earns only $15,000. He may still feel equitably treated relative to Susan, who earns $20,000, because she has a college degree.

People who feel underrewarded try to reduce the inequity. Such an individual might decrease her inputs by exerting less effort, increase her outcomes by asking for a raise, distort the original ratios by rationalizing, try to get the other person to change his outcomes or inputs, leave the situation, or change the object of comparison. Rickey Henderson, one of the top players in major league baseball, signed a new four-year contract with the Oakland Athletics in 1990 that would pay him $3 million a year. This put him among the highest-paid players in the league, and he said he was very pleased. He had an outstanding season in 1990 and was named the Most Valuable Player in the league. By 1991, however, several other players had signed contracts for even more money, and Henderson showed up for spring training complaining that he was underpaid. He hinted that if his contract was not renegotiated to increase his pay (an attempt to increase his outcomes), he might not try as hard (a threat to decrease his inputs).

An individual may feel overrewarded relative to the other person. This feeling is not likely to be terribly disturbing to most people, but research suggests that some people who experience inequity under these conditions are somewhat motivated to reduce it.[24] Under such a circumstance, the person might increase his inputs by exerting more effort, reduce his outcomes by producing fewer units (if paid on a per unit basis), distort the original ratios by rationalizing, or try to reduce the inputs or increase the outcomes of the other person.

The single most important idea for managers to remember about equity theory is that if rewards are to motivate employees, they must be perceived as being equitable and fair. If the individual achieves various intrinsic and extrinsic rewards as a result of performance and regards these rewards as equitable, satisfaction will result. A second implication of equity theory is that managers need to consider the nature of the "other" to whom the employee is comparing herself or himself. In recent years, for example, the number of dual-career couples has increased dramatically. Since husbands and wives know a great deal about each other's inputs and outcomes, it is only natural for them to use each other as comparison others. Such equity comparisons have ruined both marriages and careers.[25]

The research support for equity theory is better than that for need-based theories but is still somewhat mixed.[26] The concepts of equity and social comparisons are certainly important for the manager to consider, but it is also apparent that managers should not rely only on this framework in attempting to manage employee motivation.

Reinforcement-based Approaches to Motivation

A final approach to the motivation process, also depicted in Figure 17.1, focuses on why some behaviors are maintained over time and why other behaviors change. As we have seen, need-based approaches identify the

Reinforcement-based approaches to motivation attempt to determine how behaviors in organizations are maintained over time.

needs that stimulate behavior. Process-based approaches, in turn, explain why people choose various behaviors to satisfy needs and how they evaluate the equity of the rewards they get for those behaviors. Reinforcement-based approaches explain the role of those rewards as they cause behavior to change or remain the same over time. Specifically, reinforcement theory is based on the fairly simple assumption that behavior that results in rewarding consequences is likely to be repeated, whereas behavior that results in punishing consequences is less likely to be repeated. Boxes 5a, 5b, 6a, and 6b in Figure 17.1 reflect these alternatives. This approach to explaining behavior was originally tested on animals, but B. F. Skinner and others have been instrumental in demonstrating how it also applies to human behavior.[27]

The starting point in reinforcement theory is a need that serves as a stimulus. For example, because an employee's rent has gone up, she sees that she needs a pay raise. Thus she chooses the response of working harder in hopes of getting a raise. As a result of this response, the individual experiences various consequences. Perhaps one of them is the raise she needs. The value of the consequences affects future responses. If the consequences are pleasant or desirable, the individual will probably choose the same response the next time she encounters the same stimulus. But if the consequences are unpleasant or undesirable, a different response is more likely the next time. Thus, if her efforts lead to a raise, the next time her rent increases she will probably work even harder to get another raise. But if her efforts are futile, the next rent increase may instead cause her to engage in organizational politics, look for a new job, or choose another alternative. There are similarities between expectancy theory and reinforcement theory, in that both consider the processes by which an individual chooses behaviors in a particular situation. However, the former focuses more on behavior choices and the latter is more concerned with the consequences of those choices.[28]

Reinforcement Contingencies

Four reinforcement contingencies in organizations are *positive reinforcement, avoidance, punishment,* and *extinction.*

Reinforcement contingencies are the possible outcomes that an individual may experience as a result of her or his choice of behaviors. The four types of reinforcement contingencies that can affect individuals in an organizational setting are positive reinforcement, avoidance, punishment, and extinction.[29]

Two reinforcement contingencies strengthen or maintain behavior, whereas the other two weaken or decrease behavior. **Positive reinforcement,** a method of strengthening behavior, is a reward or a positive outcome after a desired behavior is performed. When a manager observes an employee doing an especially good job and offers praise, the praise serves to positively reinforce the behavior of good work. Other positive reinforcers in organizations include pay raises, promotions, and awards. Employees who work at General Electric's customer service center receive clothing, sporting goods, and even trips to Disney World as rewards for outstanding perform-

THE ENTREPRENEURIAL CHALLENGE

Small Firms Profit from Reinforcement

Organizations and managers who wish to use positive reinforcement have a reasonable number of rewards to use. The most obvious ones are increased pay and special recognition, such as a compliment or a handshake. More inspired managers might offer a bonus day off or extra vacation time. But there are limits to what even the most creative managers can come up with for reinforcement.

They need rack their brains no longer. Not surprisingly, several new businesses have recently begun to offer a variety of incentives, tokens, and prizes that organizations can use to positively reinforce their workers. For example, Totally Chocolate, based in Valencia, California, sells organizations chocolate bars in one-, two-, and three-pound sizes. An organization can have the bars embossed with the company logo and award them to high-performing employees.

Seattle Select Smoked Seafood, which markets salmon packed in vacuum containers that keep the fish fresh for one year, is also promoting its products to businesses as incentives for top employees. Some companies even offer a plan for applying reinforcement. The New York Steak Company, for example, sells a game that workers can play at work. Each day of attendance or perfect work earns the employee a game token (thus the focus is on reducing absenteeism or improving quality). On a monthly basis winners receive an assortment of fresh steaks.

Of course, some companies may appear to go to extremes. Take the product offered by Back Inc. of Lindenhurst, New York, called the Congratulator. You wear it on your shoulder. When you pull the string, a wooden hand pats you on the back!

REFERENCES: "Need a Motivator for Weary Worker? Try a 'Congratulator,'" *Wall Street Journal*, May 4, 1990, pp. A1, A7; Everett T. Suters, "Show and Tell," *Inc.*, April 1987, pp. 111–112; "Creating Incentives for Hourly Workers," *Inc.*, July 1986, pp. 89–90.

ance.[30] Nordstrom uses pay and periodic bonuses as positive reinforcement. The Entrepreneurial Challenge describes how some new businesses have profited by providing organizations with a wide array of positive reinforcers that might be used to maintain employee motivation.

The other reinforcement contingency that can strengthen desired behavior is **avoidance**. This occurs when the individual chooses a certain behavior in order to avoid unpleasant consequences. An employee may come to work on time to avoid a reprimand. In this instance, the employee is motivated to choose the behavior of punctuality to avoid an unpleasant consequence that is likely to follow tardiness. Some Nordstrom employees complain that they have to work hard in order to avoid getting into trouble or even getting fired.

Punishment, another reinforcement contingency, is used by some managers to weaken undesired behaviors. When an employee is loafing, coming to work late, doing poor work, or interfering with the work of others, the manager might choose to reprimand, discipline, or fine the employee. The logic is that the unpleasant consequence will reduce the likelihood that the employee will choose that particular behavior again. Given the counterproductive side effects of punishment (such as resentment and hostility), it is often advisable for managers to use positive reinforcement or avoidance if at all possible.[31] **Extinction** can also be used to weaken behavior, especially behavior that has previously been rewarded. When an employee tells an off-color joke and the boss laughs, the laughter reinforces the behavior and the employee may continue to tell off-color jokes. By simply ignoring this behavior and not reinforcing it, the boss can cause the behavior to subside and eventually become "extinct."

Positive reinforcement and punishment are the most common reinforcement contingencies practiced by organizations. Since positive reinforcement generally results in continued productive behavior, most managers prefer to use it whenever possible. Moreover, since punishment may be met with resentment and hostility, it should be used judiciously. Avoidance and extinction are generally used only in specialized circumstances. An important thing to remember, however, is that extinction can also occur inadvertently. For example, if a manager shapes the behavior of a subordinate by means of positive reinforcement but then stops providing the reinforcement (i.e., starts taking the subordinate for granted), the new behavior will likely subside and eventually become extinct.

Providing Reinforcement

Reinforcement can be provided according to *fixed-interval, variable-interval, fixed-ratio,* and *variable-ratio schedules.*

There are four basic strategies for the scheduling of reinforcement. The **fixed-interval schedule** provides reinforcement at fixed intervals of time, regardless of behavior. A good example of reinforcement on a fixed-interval schedule is the weekly or monthly paycheck. This method provides the least incentive for good work, because employees know they will be paid regularly regardless of their effort or lack of it. A **variable-interval schedule** also uses time as the basis for reinforcement, but the time interval varies from one reinforcement to the next. This schedule is appropriate for praise or other rewards based on visits or inspections. When employees do not know when the boss is going to drop by, they tend to maintain a reasonably high level of effort all the time.

A **fixed-ratio schedule** gives reinforcement after a fixed number of behaviors, regardless of the time that elapses between behaviors. This results in an even higher level of effort. For example, when Sears is recruiting new credit card customers, salespersons get a small bonus for every fifth credit application they get customers to fill out. Under this arrangement, motivation will be high because each application gets the person closer to the next bonus. The **variable-ratio schedule**, the most powerful in maintaining desired behaviors, varies the number of behaviors needed for each reinforcement. A supervisor who praises an employee for her second order, the seventh order after that, the ninth after that, then the fifth, and then the third is using a variable-ratio schedule. The employee is motivated to increase the frequency of the desired behavior because each performance increases the probability of receiving a reward. Of course, a variable-ratio schedule is difficult (if not impossible) to use for formal rewards such as pay because it would be too complicated to keep track of who was rewarded when.

New Approaches to Motivation in Organizations

New approaches are emerging to supplement the established models and theories of motivation. Two of the most promising are goal-setting theory and the Japanese approach.

Goal-setting Theory

Goal-setting theory suggests that difficult and specific goals that employees accept and commit to, and that are tied to rewards, will increase motivation.

Organizational goal setting was explored fully back in Chapter 6. Edwin Locke and his associates have made use of similar concepts and ideas in their theory of goal setting for individuals.[32] Goal-setting theory suggests that managers and subordinates should set goals for the individual on a regular basis (as also suggested by MBO). These goals should be moderately difficult and very specific and of a type that the employee will accept and make a commitment to accomplishing. Rewards should be tied directly to accomplished goals.

The basic framework of goal-setting theory is illustrated in Figure 17.5. Because goal-setting theory allows managers to tailor rewards to individual needs, to clarify expectancies and maintain equity, and to provide reinforcement consistently, it provides a comprehensive framework for integrating the other approaches to motivation. For the most part, the research support for goal-setting theory is more consistently favorable than is the case for any other single approach to employee motivation.[33] In all likelihood, then, goal-setting theory will become increasingly popular in organizations.[34]

Figure 17.5

The Goal-setting Theory of Motivation

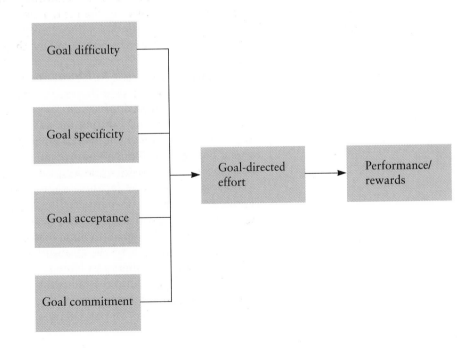

THE GLOBAL CHALLENGE

Japan's Motivated Work Force

The popular U.S. media have created a stereotype of Japanese workers as highly dedicated and committed employees doing their all for the benefit of the company: joining in early morning exercises and company songs and relentlessly pursuing quality and low cost. In some ways, this stereotype is accurate. Part of what makes the Japanese worker different from the American worker stems from cultural differences. In the United States, history and culture emphasize individual achievement and accomplishment. In contrast, Japanese culture puts a premium on group accomplishment. Thus Japanese workers experience the most satisfaction and other positive feelings whenever their group is effective.

These differences are further reflected in hiring standards. American firms stress the potential of the individual and look at the applicant's grades, past work history, test scores, and so forth. Japanese companies look more closely at how well the individual will fit into the work group. Japanese workers are asked to give a lot to their jobs, including extraordinarily high organizational commitment and long working hours. In return, they receive extremely strong job security and enjoy a spirit of teamwork that is found nowhere else in the world today.

There are signs, however, that things may be changing a bit. Japanese workers are giving more thought to leisure time than ever before and are recognizing that they may be paying too high a price for their jobs. Some Japanese workers are quitting their high-stress jobs and taking lower-paying ones that require less commitment to the organization. Indeed, part-time work in Japan has jumped sharply over the past ten years. Job hopping, once rare in Japan, is also becoming more acceptable. Some workers are even seeking contract work — jobs that have a specified starting and ending date. Although the group emphasis is still predominant in Japan, more Japanese workers do seem to be looking for a different sort of work life.

REFERENCES: "Japanese Workers Aren't All Workaholics," *Wall Street Journal,* May 8, 1989, p. A10; "Toyota Takes Pains, and Time, Filling Jobs in Its Kentucky Plant," *Wall Street Journal,* December 1, 1987, pp. 1, 19; Walter Kiechel III, "The Workaholic Generation," *Fortune,* April 10, 1989, pp. 50–62.

The Japanese Approach to Motivation

The Japanese approach to motivation involves getting managers and workers to work together as partners toward the best interests of the organization.

The so-called Japanese approach to motivation has gained increasing popularity around the world during the past few years. This approach is not really a theory or model but instead a philosophy of management. In many ways, it parallels the human resource approach to motivation. It also shares concepts from participative management.

The basic tenet of the Japanese approach is that managers and workers should work together as partners. In the United States, the relationship between managers and workers historically has varied from antagonism to sheer indifference. In Japan, though, managers and workers see themselves as one group; and as a result, all members are committed and motivated to work in the best interests of the organization. The Global Challenge provides more insight into the motivation of Japanese workers.

One U.S. company that practices the Japanese approach to motivation is Domino's Pizza. No one at Domino's is called an employee. Instead, everyone is a team member, team leader, or coach. A large percentage of the company's profits are distributed back to workers, and everyone owns stock. This encourages everyone at the company to work together for Domino's best interests.[35] Like goal-setting theory, the Japanese approach is likely to become more common in businesses throughout the world.

Enhancing Motivation in Organizations

Managers trying to enhance the motivation of their employees can, of course, draw on any of the theories described in this chapter. They may in practice adopt specific interventions derived from one or more theories, or they may influence motivation through the organization's reward systems.

Organizational Reward Systems

An organization's *reward system* consists of the formal and informal mechanisms by which employee performance is defined, evaluated, and rewarded.

The basic structural mechanism through which an organization attempts to motivate its workers is its reward system. An organization's **reward system** consists of the formal and informal mechanisms by which employee performance is defined, evaluated, and rewarded. The primary rewards in most organizations are compensation, promotions, benefits, and status. We

Organizations seek numerous ways to enhance the motivation of their employees. These executives work for US West, a southwestern telecommunications firm. They recently went on a retreat to Tucson, the goal of which was to instill in each manager a better understanding of how cultural diversity both complicates and enriches the work environment of the organization. This understanding is expected to help them do a better job of motivating their increasingly diverse work force.

discussed the formal and structural elements of rewards in Chapter 14; our concern here is the motivational aspects of rewards.

An organization's primary purpose in giving rewards is, of course, to influence employee behavior. Research has shown that extrinsic rewards affect employee satisfaction, which, in turn, plays a major role in determining whether an employee will remain on the job or seek a new one. Reward systems also influence patterns of attendance and absenteeism. Also, if rewards are based on actual performance, employees tend to work harder to earn those rewards.

Effects of Organizational Rewards   Organizational rewards can affect individual attitudes, behaviors, and motivation. Thus managers must clearly understand and appreciate their importance. As we saw in Chapter 16, for example, employee attitudes such as satisfaction contribute to (or discourage) absenteeism and also affect turnover. They also help establish the climate, or internal environment, of the organization. Edward Lawler has advanced four major generalizations about employee attitudes toward rewards.[36] First, employee satisfaction is influenced by how much individuals think they should receive and how much they do receive. Employee expectations thus play a key role. Second, employee satisfaction is affected by comparisons with rewards received by others. This assertion is closely related to equity theory. Third, employees often misperceive the rewards received by others. This suggestion also has implications from equity theory. When one employee believes that another employee makes more money than he or she really does make, the potential for dissatisfaction increases. Finally, overall job satisfaction is affected by how satisfied employees are with both the extrinsic and the intrinsic rewards they derive from their jobs.

The effects of reward systems are perhaps best understood from the perspective of expectancy theory. The effort-to-performance expectancy is strongly influenced by the performance appraisal that is often a part of the reward system. An employee is likely to put forth more effort if he or she knows that performance will be measured, evaluated, and rewarded. The performance-to-outcome expectancy is affected by the extent to which the employee believes that performance will be followed by rewards. As expectancy theory predicts, each reward or potential reward has a somewhat different value for each individual. One person may want a promotion more than benefits; someone else may want just the opposite.

Designing Effective Reward Systems   Lawler has also identified four major characteristics of an effective reward system.[37] The reward system must meet individual needs for food, shelter, and other basic necessities. These needs include the physiological and security needs identified by Maslow and Alderfer and the hygiene factors identified by Herzberg. The rewards should compare favorably with those offered by other organizations. Unfavorable comparisons with people in other settings could result in feelings of inequity. The distribution of rewards within the organization must also be equitable. When some employees feel underpaid compared with others in the organization, the probable results are low morale and poor perform-ance. (People are more likely to compare their situation with that of others in their own organization than with that of outsiders.) Finally, the reward system must recognize that different people have different needs and choose different paths to satisfy those needs. Insofar as possible, a variety of rewards and a variety of methods for achieving them should be made available to employees.

Performance-based Reward Systems   Organizational reward systems have traditionally been one of two kinds: a fixed salary or hourly rate or an incentive system. Salaried employees receive a fixed sum of money on a weekly or monthly basis. Although some reductions may be made for absences, the amount is usually the same regardless of whether the individ-ual works less than or more than a normal amount of time.[38] Hourly employees are paid a fixed wage (based on job demands, experience, or other factors) for each hour they work.

To increase motivation, fixed rewards can be tied more directly to per-formance through merit pay raises. In a merit system people get different pay raises at the end of the year, depending on their overall job perform-ance.[39] Organizations that have a well-designed performance appraisal sys-tem can make use of merit pay to maintain long-term performance.

More organizations today, though, are experimenting with various kinds of incentive systems. Incentive systems attempt to reward employees in proportion to their accomplishments. A piece-rate pay plan is an incentive system (such systems are not new, of course; Taylor introduced them in the early years of the twentieth century). In a factory manufacturing lug-gage, for example, each worker may be paid 50 cents for each handle and set of locks installed on a piece of luggage. There is incentive for the employee to work hard, since the more units produced, the higher the pay. Four increasingly popular incentive systems are profit sharing, gain sharing, lump-sum bonuses, and pay for knowledge.[40] Each of these has advantages and disadvantages.

Profit sharing provides a varying annual bonus to employees based on corporate profits. The biggest advantage of profit sharing is that it unites workers and management toward the same goal — higher profits. A draw-back is that there can be equity problems in deciding how to allocate the profits. Ford, USX, and Alcoa all have profit-sharing plans.[41] Gain sharing is a group-based incentive system whereby all group members receive bonuses when predetermined performance levels, negotiated by managers and workers, are exceeded. This system facilitates teamwork and trust, but it may also encourage workers to focus too narrowly on attaining the specific goals needed for the bonus while neglecting other parts of their jobs.

A lump-sum bonus is a one-time cash payment, rather than an increase in base salary. Not having to increase base salaries enables an organization to control its fixed costs, but employees sometimes feel resentful that their increase is for one year only. Aetna Life and Casualty, Timex, and B. F. Goodrich have successfully used this approach. On the other hand, Boeing workers are trying to get the firm to abolish the lump-sum plan it has been using since 1983.[42] Pay-for-knowledge systems allow an organization to pay the individual rather than the job. Under a standard arrangement, two workers doing the same job are paid the same rate regardless of their skills. Under pay for knowledge, people are advanced in pay grade for each new skill or set of skills they learn. This reward system increases training costs but also results in a more highly skilled work force. Schoolteachers often receive higher pay for increased training. General Foods and Texas Instruments have also experimented with this method and have had favorable results.

Interventions for Enhancing Motivation

Three of the most common motivational interventions are behavior modification, the modified workweek, and work redesign.

Behavior Modification   Behavior modification, or OB Mod (for organizational behavior modification), is a technique for applying the concepts of reinforcement theory in organizational settings.[43] An OB Mod program typically proceeds through five stages. First, the manager specifies behaviors to be increased (such as producing more units) or decreased (such as coming to work late). Second, these target behaviors are measured to establish a baseline against which to assess the effectiveness of OB Mod. Third, the manager analyzes the situation to ascertain what rewards subordinates value most and how best to tie these rewards to the target behaviors. Fourth, action plans and strategies revolving around reinforcement contingencies are implemented so that desired behaviors have pleasant consequences and undesirable behaviors have unpleasant consequences. Fifth, the target behaviors are measured again and compared with baseline behaviors to determine the value of the program.

Although many firms (such as Procter & Gamble, Warner-Lambert, and Ford) have used OB Mod, the best-known application has been at Emery Air Freight. Management felt that workers were not packing the containers used to consolidate many small shipments into fewer large ones efficiently enough. Through a system of self-recorded feedback (to enable workers to see the results of their own performance) and rewards, Emery increased container usage from 45 percent to 95 percent and saved over $3 million during the first three years of the program.[44]

Modified Workweek   Organizations also frequently use the modified workweek as a way to increase employee motivation. A modified workweek can be any work schedule that does not conform to a traditional eight-hours-a-day (9 A.M.–5 P.M.) five-days-a-week (Monday–Friday) format. The modified workweek helps individuals satisfy higher-level needs by providing more personal control over one's work schedule. It also provides an opportunity to fulfill several needs simultaneously.

One alternative is the compressed workweek, whereby people work forty hours in less than the traditional five full workdays, most commonly working ten hours a day for four days. Another popular method is the flexible work schedule, or flextime. In this approach, employees are required to work during a certain core period, but they can choose what other hours to work. Thus an individual can come in early and leave early, come in late and leave late, or come in early, take a long lunch, and leave late. Finally, work at home and job sharing are becoming more popular. Now that computers are a widespread feature of organizational life, many people can put in full workdays on a home computer linked by modem to the workplace. Job sharing allows individuals to minimize their work hours while still providing the organization with the benefit of a full-time "worker."[45]

Many companies, including John Hancock Mutual Life Insurance, ARCO, General Dynamics, Metropolitan Life Insurance, Control Data Corporation, and IBM, have experimented successfully with one or more types of modified workweeks. By allowing employees more independence in deciding when they come to work and when they leave, managers acknowledge and show respect for the employees' ability to exercise self-control. The organization's goal is that employees will respond with more motivation. At the same time, there are also costs to these kinds of work schedules. Organizing modified schedules may be complicated, for example, and some individuals who lack personal discipline may use modified work schedules as a way to avoid supervision and do less work.

Work Redesign   Changing the nature of people's jobs is also being used more as a motivational technique. The idea here is that managers can use any of the alternatives to job specialization described in Chapter 10 — job rotation, job enlargement, job enrichment, the job characteristics approach, autonomous work groups — as part of a motivational program. Expectancy theory helps explain the role of work redesign in motivation.[46] The basic premise is that employees will improve their performance if they believe that doing so will lead to intrinsic rewards. Studies have shown that improvements in the design of work do often result in higher motivation. One study at Texas Instruments, for example, found that job redesign for maintenance workers resulted in decreased turnover and improved employee motivation.[47]

Learning Summary

Motivation is the set of forces that cause people to choose certain behaviors. Motivation is an important consideration for managers because it combines with ability and environmental factors to determine the performance of individuals in the organization. Thinking about motivation has evolved from the viewpoint of scientific management through the human relations movement to the human resource approach.

Need-based approaches to motivation attempt to identify the factor or factors that cause motivation. Popular need-based theories include need hierarchies such as Maslow's hierarchy of needs and the ERG theory. The dual-structure approach is also important. Individuals have acquired needs for achievement, affiliation, and power.

Process-based approaches to motivation attempt to explain how motivation occurs. Expectancy theory suggests that people are motivated to perform if they believe that their effort will result in high performance, that performance will lead to rewards, and that the positive aspects of the outcomes outweigh the negative aspects. Equity theory is based on the premise that people are motivated to achieve and maintain equity.

Reinforcement-based approaches attempt to describe how motivation is maintained. Its basic assumption is that behavior that results in rewarding consequences is likely to be repeated, whereas behavior resulting in negative consequences is less likely to be repeated. Reinforcement contingencies are positive reinforcement, avoidance, punishment, and extinction, and each type can occur on a fixed-interval, variable-interval, fixed-ratio, or variable-ratio schedule.

One newly emerging approach to employee motivation is goal-setting theory. Goal-setting theory involves helping employees set difficult and specific goals. When rewards are tied to goal attainment, research is finding strong support for goal-setting theory. Another new perspective on motivation is the Japanese approach. This approach relies on managers and employees working together in the best interests of the organization.

Organizational reward systems are the primary mechanisms that managers have for managing motivation. Performance-based reward systems include merit systems and various kinds of incentive systems. Organizations often adopt behavior modification, modified workweeks, and work redesign to enhance motivation.

Questions and Exercises

Review Questions

1. Describe the three historical views of motivation.
2. What are the five different needs included in Maslow's hierarchy?
3. Identify and summarize the basic elements of expectancy theory.
4. List the four reinforcement contingencies. What schedules can be used to provide reinforcement?
5. Explain goal-setting theory.
6. Identify and describe some performance-based reward systems.

Analysis Questions

1. Describe situations in which two of the three determinants of performance (motivation, ability, work environment) are satisfactory but the third is deficient. Outline a strategy for addressing each situation.
2. Compare and contrast Maslow's hierarchy of needs and the ERG theory.

3. Use equity theory to explain the motivation of students in a classroom setting.
4. Identify examples of each of the four reinforcement contingencies that you have experienced.
5. What are some of the difficulties associated with trying to adopt the Japanese approach to motivation in an existing organization?
6. Assume you are about to go to work for an organization that uses a performance-based reward system. Which system do you think you would be most satisfied with? Which system do you think you would be least satisfied with? Why?

Application Exercises

1. Design a reward system, based on one or more of the theories discussed in the chapter, that an instructor could use in a class.
2. Select a recent significant behavioral choice that you made (choice of a major, a job, an apartment, etc.). Describe the dynamics that went into your choice from the perspectives of need-based, process-based, and reinforcement-based approaches to motivation.

Chapter Notes

1. "At Nordstrom Stores, Service Comes First — But at a Big Price," *Wall Street Journal,* February 2, 1990, pp. A1, A14; Gary Hoover, Alta Campbell, and Patrick J. Spain, eds., *Hoover's Handbook — Profiles of Over 500 Major Corporations* (Austin, Tex.: The Reference Press, 1990), p. 409; Patricia Sellers, "How to Handle Customers' Gripes," *Fortune,* October 24, 1988, pp. 88+.
2. Richard M. Steers and Lyman W. Porter, *Motivation and Work Behavior,* 4th ed. (New York: McGraw-Hill, 1987).
3. Jeremiah J. Sullivan, "Three Roles of Language in Motivation Theory," *Academy of Management Review,* January 1988, pp. 104–115.
4. Frederick W. Taylor, *Principles of Scientific Management* (New York: Harper, 1911).
5. Elton Mayo, *The Social Problems of an Industrial Civilization* (Cambridge, Mass.: Harvard University Press, 1945); Fritz J. Roethlisberger and William J. Dickson, *Management and the Worker* (Cambridge, Mass.: Harvard University Press, 1966).
6. "A Humble Hero Drives Ford to the Top," *Fortune,* January 4, 1988, pp. 22+.
7. See Kenneth A. Kovach, "What Motivates Employees? Workers and Supervisors Give Different Answers," *Business Horizons,* September–October 1987, pp. 58–65.
8. Abraham H. Maslow, "A Theory of Human Motivation," *Psychological Review,* July 1943, pp. 370–396; Abraham H. Maslow, *Motivation and Personality* (New York: Harper & Row, 1954).
9. See Craig Pinder, *Work Motivation* (Glenview, Ill.: Scott, Foresman, 1984), for a review. See also Steers and Porter, *Motivation and Work Behavior.*
10. Clayton P. Alderfer, *Existence, Relatedness, and Growth* (New York: Free Press, 1972).

11. For an example, see Clayton P. Alderfer, "An Empirical Test of a New Theory of Human Needs," *Organizational Behavior and Human Performance,* April 1969, pp. 142–175. See also Pinder, *Work Motivation.*

12. Frederick Herzberg, Bernard Mausner, and Barbara Snyderman, *The Motivation to Work* (New York: Wiley, 1959); Frederick Herzberg, "One More Time: How Do You Motivate Employees?" *Harvard Business Review,* January–February 1987, pp. 109–120.

13. Robert J. House and Lawrence A. Wigdor, "Herzberg's Dual-Factor Theory of Job Satisfaction and Motivation: A Review of the Evidence and a Criticism," *Personnel Psychology,* Winter 1967, pp. 369–389; Victor H. Vroom, *Work and Motivation* (New York: Wiley, 1964). See also Pinder, *Work Motivation.*

14. David C. McClelland, *The Achieving Society* (Princeton, N.J.: Van Nostrand, 1961); David C. McClelland, *Power: The Inner Experience* (New York: Irvington, 1975).

15. David McClelland, "That Urge to Achieve," *Think,* November–December 1966, p. 22; John G. Nicholls, "Achievement Motivation: Conceptions of Authority, Subjective Experience, Task Choice, and Performance," *Psychological Review,* July 1984, pp. 328–346.

16. E. Cornelius and F. Lane, "The Power Motive and Managerial Success in a Professionally Oriented Service Company," *Journal of Applied Psychology,* January 1984, pp. 32–40.

17. David McClelland and David H. Burnham, "Power Is the Great Motivator," *Harvard Business Review,* March–April 1976, pp. 100–110.

18. Vroom, *Work and Motivation.*

19. David A. Nadler and Edward E. Lawler III, "Motivation: A Diagnostic Approach," in *Perspectives on Behavior in Organizations,* 2nd ed., ed. J. Richard Hackman, Edward E. Lawler III, and Lyman W. Porter (New York: McGraw-Hill, 1983), pp. 67–78.

20. Lyman W. Porter and Edward E. Lawler III, *Managerial Attitudes and Performance* (Homewood, Ill.: Dorsey Press, 1968).

21. Nadler and Lawler, "Motivation: A Diagnostic Approach."

22. Terence Mitchell, "Expectancy Models of Job Satisfaction, Occupational Preference, and Effort: A Theoretical, Methodological, and Empirical Appraisal," *Psychological Bulletin,* December 1974, pp. 1053–1077; John P. Wanous, Thomas L. Keon, and Jania C. Latack, "Expectancy Theory and Occupational/ Organizational Choices: A Review and Test," *Organizational Behavior and Human Performance,* August 1983, pp. 66–86.

23. J. Stacy Adams, "Towards an Understanding of Inequity," *Journal of Abnormal and Social Psychology,* November 1963, pp. 422–436; Richard T. Mowday, "Equity Theory Predictions of Behavior in Organizations," in Steers and Porter, *Motivation and Work Behavior,* pp. 91–113.

24. For a review, see Paul S. Goodman and Abraham Friedman, "An Examination of Adams' Theory of Inequity," *Administrative Science Quarterly,* September 1971, pp. 271–288.

25. "Pay Problems: How Couples React When Wives Out-Earn Husbands," *Wall Street Journal,* June 19, 1987, p. 19.

26. Richard A. Cosier and Dan R. Dalton, "Equity Theory and Time: A Reformulation," *Academy of Management Review,* April 1983, pp. 311–319; Richard C. Huseman, John D. Hatfield, and Edward W. Miles, "A New Perspective on Equity Theory: The Equity Sensitivity Construct," *Academy of Management Review,* April 1987, pp. 222–234.

27. B. F. Skinner, *Beyond Freedom and Dignity* (New York: Knopf, 1971).

28. See E. Leroy Plumlee and Kenneth S. Keleman, "A Proposal for the Convergence of the Behavior Modification and the Expectancy Theories of Work Motivation," *Business Review,* Winter 1987, pp. 13–17.

29. Fred Luthans and Robert Kreitner, *Organizational Behavior Modification and Beyond: An Operant and Social Learning Approach* (Glenview, Ill.: Scott, Foresman, 1985).

30. Patricia Sellers, "How to Handle Customers' Gripes," *Fortune,* October 24, 1988, pp. 88–100.

31. Mel E. Schnake, "Vicarious Punishment in a Work Setting," *Journal of Applied Psychology,* May 1986, pp. 343–345.

32. Edwin Locke, "Toward a Theory of Task Performance and Incentives," *Organizational Behavior and Human Performance,* Fall 1968, pp. 157–189.

33. For recent developments, see Gary P. Latham, Miriam Erez, and Edwin A. Locke, "Resolving Scientific Disputes by the Joint Design of Crucial Experiments by the Antagonists: An Application to the Erez-Latham Dispute Regarding Participation in Goal Setting," *Journal of Applied Psychology,* November 1988, pp. 753–772.

34. See Mark E. Tubbs and Steven E. Ekeberg, "The Role of Intentions in Work Motivation: Implications for Goal-Setting Theory and Research," *Academy of Management Review,* January 1991, pp. 180–199.

35. "When Are Employees Not Employees? When They're Associates, Stakeholders . . . ," *Wall Street Journal,* November 9, 1988, p. B1.

36. Edward E. Lawler III, *Pay and Organizational Development* (Reading, Mass.: Addison-Wesley, 1981). See also Edward E. Lawler III, *Pay and Organizational Effectiveness: A Psychological View* (New York: McGraw-Hill, 1971).

37. Lawler, *Pay and Organizational Development.*

38. Robert J. Greene, "Effective Compensation: The How and Why," *Personnel Administrator,* February 1987, pp. 112–116.

39. "Grading 'Merit Pay,'" *Newsweek,* November 14, 1988, pp. 45–46; Frederick S. Hills, K. Dow Scott, Steven E. Markham, and Michael J. Vest, "Merit Pay: Just or Unjust Desserts," *Personnel Administrator,* September 1987, pp. 53–59.

40. Nancy J. Perry, "Here Come Richer, Riskier Pay Plans," *Fortune,* December 19, 1988, pp. 50–58.

41. "Watching the Bottom Line Instead of the Clock," *Business Week,* November 7, 1988, pp. 134–136.

42. "Plans Become Labor's Latest Battleground," *USA Today,* October 7, 1989, pp. B1, B2.

43. Luthans and Kreitner, *Organizational Behavior Modification and Beyond;* W. Clay Hamner and Ellen P. Hamner, "Behavior Modification on the Bottom Line," *Organizational Dynamics,* Spring 1976, pp. 2–21.

44. "At Emery Air Freight: Positive Reinforcement Boosts Performance," *Organizational Dynamics,* Winter 1973, pp. 41–50.

45. Allan R. Cohen and Herman Gadon, *Alternative Work Schedules: Integrating Individual and Organizational Needs* (Reading, Mass.: Addison-Wesley, 1978).

46. Ricky W. Griffin, *Task Design — An Integrative Approach* (Glenview, Ill.: Scott, Foresman, 1982).

47. Earl D. Weed, "Job Environment 'Cleans Up' at Texas Instruments," in *New Perspectives in Job Enrichment,* ed. J. R. Maher (New York: Van Nostrand, 1971), pp. 55–77.

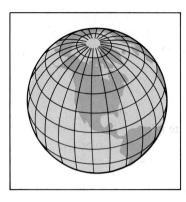

CASE 17.1

Motivating Slow-Track Managers at Hyatt

Back in the 1960s, when Hyatt was a young, quickly expanding chain of hotels, a new, well-educated employee with good motivation could look forward to rapid advancement and the chance to manage a hotel within as little as three years. But now that Hyatt's expansion has slowed and the company's hierarchy is top-heavy with aging baby-boomer managers, even a good management prospect may have to wait eight years or more to run even a small Hyatt hotel. Keeping such employees happy, loyal, and motivated has become a major challenge for Hyatt, as it has for many other companies that face a glut of managers just when they're trimming middle-management positions.

The rise to the top may take today's new managers twice as long as it took current CEOs, and instead of tripling their salaries in ten years, as did managers starting out in the 1970s, managers of the 1990s will be lucky to double their pay in a decade. Still, American businesses have found a number of ways to retain their managers. Some offer them lateral moves or overseas positions. Managers used to worry that such moves would result in career stagnation, but now they're making them to ward off boredom. Companies are allowing managers to say no to transfers more than they used to, aware that many managers forced to choose between family stability and company loyalty will now opt for family. Many corporations are also challenging managers by giving them more power or responsibility or by sending them back to school.

Like many other organizations, Hyatt has found that it can retain managers if it gives them a chance to live out their entrepreneurial dreams. Traditionally many of America's best business minds have been fascinated with starting something new, creating something. Hyatt keeps such people from being lured away to start their own companies by finding ways to let them exercise their creativity without breaking their ties with Hyatt.

John Allegretti, for instance, was a switchboard operator and assistant housekeeping manager for two years at a Chicago Hyatt. He wanted to be a hotel manager and was getting tired of waiting for positions to open up above him, so he began pursuing his other interest — helping the environment — by sending résumés to waste-recycling companies. A Hyatt vice president recognized Allegretti's motivation and interest and asked him to work on reducing waste at the 2,000-room hotel. Allegretti's success at this project convinced the company to set up a new waste-consulting company for him to run, International ReCycleCo, which soon had twenty-four clients in eight states in addition to several large Hyatts.

In such cases, Hyatt typically gives the employee the capital to get the business started but retains ultimate control. It gave James E. Jones, Hyatt's director of sales development, $780,000 to start a business to offer the kind of catering and entertainment services that Hyatt often hired professional party planners to provide. Jones was no whiz at drawing up his first business plan, but Hyatt recognized the value of his contacts in professional sports and encouraged him to rewrite the plan. Within a year, Regency Productions by Hyatt had won contracts to manage corporate hospitality tents at the 1991 Superbowl and handle catering at the 1991 U.S. Open golf tournament.

Such ventures are in some ways a logical extension of Hyatt's management policy, which has always sought consistency, not uniformity, among its hotels. The Hyatt Corporation is still privately held by the Pritzker family of Chicago, but individual hotels are often designed, built, operated, and at least partially owned by local investor groups. Mirroring Hyatt's own decentralized management approach, these local owners often give their employees a good deal of autonomy.

Not all employee ventures are successful, of course, but Hyatt feels it is important to accept the failures in order to encourage future attempts. The recent tales of two Hyatt restaurants demonstrate the point. Assistant food and beverage manager Michael O. Smith opened Hyttops at the Hyatt Regency in New Orleans as a sports bar, counting on the hotel's proximity to the Superdome to bring in business. He figured that another typical hotel restaurant couldn't hope to compete with New Orleans's famous eateries. With donated sports paraphernalia and the patronage of sports stars, the bar quickly became a success. In suburban Chicago, meanwhile, a Hyatt manager opened a club and disco without company approval, naming them after himself. Company executives were embarrassed to discover a new disco so close to headquarters, but Hyatt let the manager stay on. Evidently the company figured that if it wanted to keep managers who had the urge to step out on their own, it shouldn't punish them for stepping too far.

Discussion Questions

1. What risks does Hyatt run by encouraging its employees to start their own Hyatt ventures?
2. What theories of motivation explain the success of Hyatt's approach?
3. Could smaller companies that provide a narrower range of services make use of employees' entrepreneurial urges in similar ways?
4. If you were a manager with no hope of quick promotions or pay raises, what would motivate you to keep working for the same company?

REFERENCES: James E. Ellis, "Feeling Stuck at Hyatt? Create a New Business," *Business Week,* December 10, 1990, p. 195; Rick Lyke, "Hyttops Turns Vacant Space into Bar Bucks," *Hotel & Motel Management,* June 25, 1990, pp. 37–38; Ron Zemke, *The Service Edge* (New York: New American Library, 1989), pp. 129–131.

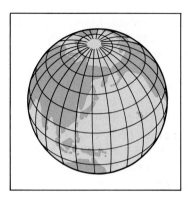

CASE 17.2

Honda Motivates Marysville

Until the last decade, Japanese automakers were outsiders, every Japanese car was an import, and some Americans felt it was unpatriotic to drive a Toyota or a Subaru. That began to change in 1982, when Honda began to build cars in Marysville, Ohio. Now, all of Japan's top automakers have plants in the United States, and American automakers are watching as the Japanese confront perhaps their greatest challenge: motivating American workers to reach the same heights of quality and productivity that Japanese workers achieve.

The whole American auto industry is suffering from overcapacity, and the big three American automakers have been shutting plants as the Japanese have been opening new ones. The competition is fierce, and the overall quality of automobiles is improving, with some Japanese cars nearing the zero-defect level. The company that can most effectively engage its workers in this competition is likely to come out on top.

From their first interactions with job applicants, Japanese automakers do things differently. They scrutinize applicants for line jobs with an intensity that most American companies reserve for potential managers. Toyota, for instance, reduces its huge applicant pool with tests of general knowledge and attitude, then puts the top 30 percent through an assessment of interpersonal skills and a manufacturing execise. The few who are finally hired feel not like the traditional cog-in-a-wheel of American assembly lines but like members of an elite group specially chosen to do a special job.

The Japanese automakers strive to keep that feeling alive. Instead of the narrow job classifications common in Detroit, the Japanese give workers broad titles — "associates" at Honda, "team members" at Toyota and Mazda — and put them into teams responsible for the quality of the work they do and for improving the production process. The teams often make what Americans think of as management decisions — deciding who should do what when and who should work overtime. Production workers' importance is reflected in their symbolic equality with management. Everyone eats in the same cafeteria, parks in the same parking lot, wears the same uniforms. Because production workers can't drink coffee on the job, neither can their managers.

Honda had a head start in treating its workers as important people. Founded by an engineer, the company has always viewed the people who perform a process day after day as being experts on that process. Most of Honda's American managers start as production workers and move up the ladder thanks to their technical expertise and endless company training. Even when they've earned the right to one of the company's open-air offices, they're still often found down on the factory floor, helping out.

Honda also works very hard at rewarding its workers and constantly demonstrating its commitment to teamwork. Each worker gets a share of Honda's worldwide earnings, and six times a year individuals are singled out for suggesting the best improvements. The company's two top Ohio executives spend a fifteen-hour day walking through the Marysville plant, congratulating and *listening to* workers who had the best ideas. The more traditional awards banquet at night just reinforces the message.

One measure of the success of Honda's efforts is the degree to which many American workers have accepted and fervently believe in the Honda system. John L. Michel, a Marysville native, won an award for making a suggestion about job rotation that meant everyone got an equal shot at the easiest jobs and no one got bored. His team also persuaded the company to build a tougher test track so customers wouldn't complain of rattles in their new dashboards. Michel even turned the tables on a Japanese manager who rebuffed Michel's suggestion about a new quality-control form. When the manager asked, "Who are you? What's your title?" Michel replied "I'm the person who wants to fix this, so my title doesn't matter." There wasn't much the Japanese manager could say.

Honda also makes it easier for its patriotic American employees to drive the cars they make. It has led all other Japanese automakers in "Americanizing" its cars — increasing the percentage of parts that are made in the United States. It encourages local companies to build parts for Honda and is aiming to make its American operations more self-sufficient. Its newly designed 1990 Accord boasted engines and transmissions made in Ohio. That means it's a domestic car, according to government and industry standards. And in 1989, Soichiro Honda, the company's founder, took his place in the Automotive Hall of Fame, next to Henry Ford and Billy Durant of General Motors. Honda hopes that one day its founder's name will be as linked to worker motivation and product quality as Ford's is to mass production.

Discussion Questions

1. Using the terminology in the chapter, how would you describe Honda's motivational strategy?
2. Why would a company's hiring practices affect employee motivation?
3. From your experience, what motivational factors make working on a team different from working alone?
4. Why would Honda want to find local suppliers rather than rely on its proven Japanese suppliers?

REFERENCES: Louis Kraar, "Japan's Gung-Ho U.S. Car Plants," *Fortune,* January 30, 1989, pp. 98–108; Bradley A. Stertz, "Big Three Boost Car Quality but Still Lag," *Wall Street Journal,* March 27, 1989, p. B1; Joseph B. White, "Aggressive Expansion at Honda Is Straining Both Staff and Finances," *Wall Street Journal,* October 9, 1989, p. A1; Joseph B. White, "Honda Takes Aim at Detroit's Heart," *Wall Street Journal,* September 18, 1989, p. B1.

18

Leadership and Influence Processes

LEARNING OBJECTIVES

After studying this chapter, you should be able to:

1. Explain the nature of influence, the meaning of leadership, and the difference between leadership and management.

2. Discuss two historical approaches to studying leadership in organizations.

3. Explain three major models of leadership theory.

4. Identify and describe three emerging perspectives on leadership.

5. Discuss power and political behavior in organizations and explain how they can be managed.

merson Electric Company, a St. Louis–based firm, is the world's seventh-largest manufacturer of electrical and electronic products — electric motors, thermostats, machine motors, chemical measuring devices, and thousands of other related products. When Charles Knight became CEO of Emerson in 1973, the firm was already quite successful. But Knight wasn't interested in maintaining the status quo.

Since Knight took over, Emerson's annual sales have increased from $940 million to over $7 billion. Profits have also increased substantially. To achieve this dramatic growth, Knight has relied on a leadership style that combines ruthless managerial acumen with concern for employees. One of his first actions, for example, was to eliminate dozens of staff jobs at the firm's headquarters. He had to do this, he felt, to cut costs. At the same time, he helped the terminated employees find new jobs and promised those who remained that their jobs were secure.

In 1984, Knight realized that Japanese competitors were cutting into Emerson's market share and threatening the organization's future. In response, he initiated a major program to cut costs, trim unnecessary operations, and simultaneously improve quality and productivity. Has Emerson succeeded? Eighty-four percent of the organization's products are number one or two in their markets.

Knight attributes much of this success to the well-honed expertise of Emerson's managers. Under his close guidance, they regularly attend to detail and search for new and better ways to get things done. They must submit monthly reports on all their operations and be ready to defend at a moment's notice any decision they make. Knight bases his demanding approach not on threats of reprisal but on a deep commitment to thoroughness. Only through exhaustive preparation, he believes, will Emerson be able to compete in the global economy.[1]

Charles Knight has a rare combination of skills that set him apart from many other CEOs. He is both an astute leader and a fine manager, and he recognizes the challenges that come with each role. He understands when it is necessary to make tough decisions. He also recognizes the importance of valuing the work of employees and managers.

This chapter examines the qualities of people like Knight and describes the vital part that leadership plays in organizations. We first characterize the nature of influence and introduce the concept of leadership. We next look at some of the historical conceptions of leadership. Our attention is then devoted to examining various models of leadership behavior. We next describe emerging perspectives on leadership. We conclude by discussing the roles of power and political behavior in organizations.

Leadership and Influence in Organizations

In Chapter 17, on motivation in organizations, we saw that organizations attempt to influence the behavior of people. Leadership, too, provides a way to influence the behavior of others. After we examine the nature of influence, we define leadership and distinguish it from management.

The Nature of Influence

Influence is the ability to affect the perceptions, attitudes, or behaviors of others.

Influence is the ability to affect the perceptions, attitudes, or behaviors of others.[2] A political candidate makes use of influence to convince voters that he is competent (perception), that he is the best person for the job (attitude), and that they should vote for him (behavior). Influence can reside in individuals, groups, or entire organizations. For example, an individual manager may be able to influence her subordinates so that they work harder. Similarly, a firm's advertising department may be able to influence decisions made by other groups within the organization, such as the manufacturing department. Entire organizations such as IBM and General Motors are able to influence other firms in their industry through pricing practices or other actions.

In some ways an organization can be thought of as a system of influence. Many of the things managers do are directed at influencing others. For example, during the course of the day a manager might try to influence her boss to increase her operating budget, her subordinate to improve work quality, and a group of her peers to support her proposal for a new set of organizational policies. She may also try to influence a supplier to lower prices, another subordinate to work overtime, and her secretary to spend less time on the telephone.

Influence can be attempted in a variety of ways. Sometimes it is obvious and direct: "Will you give me a salary increase?" At other times it may be more subtle and indirect: "The cost of living sure has gone up a lot this year!" It can also be directed at different audiences on different organizational levels. People in organizations try to influence the behaviors of their peers, their boss, committee members, and constituents such as stockholders, suppliers, and customers. One major channel for influence is leadership.

Leadership is the use of noncoercive influence to shape the goals of a group or organization, to motivate behavior toward the achievement of those goals, and to help define group or organization culture.

The Meaning of Leadership

Leadership can be defined as both a process and a property.[3] As a process, **leadership** is the use of noncoercive influence to shape the goals of a group

Robin Burns, president and CEO of Estée Lauder USA, seems to be one of those rare individuals who is both a strong leader and an effective manager. Burns's strengths include inspiring tremendous effort and loyalty from others in the organization, and understanding the cosmetics industry and how to compete in it as well as anyone. This photo was taken during one of the week-long sessions she conducts for selected employees on the Vassar College campus. Employees are immersed in exercise, self-improvement, competition techniques, and the Lauder corporate culture.

or organization, to motivate behavior toward the achievement of those goals, and to help define group or organization culture.[4] As a property, leadership is the set of characteristics attributed to those who are perceived to be leaders. Thus leaders are people who are able to influence the behaviors of others without having to rely on threats or other forms of force. Importantly, leaders are people whom others accept as leaders.

Leadership Versus Management

From those definitions, it should be clear that although leadership and management are related, they are quite different concepts.[5] A person can be a good manager but not a good leader, or a good leader but not a good manager. Table 18.1 shows some of the basic distinctions between management and leadership.

At the left side of the table are four categories of activity. The two columns show how each activity differs when considered from a management and a leadership point of view. For example, the management side of creating an agenda consists of determining steps for achieving results and then allocating resources to achieve those results. The leadership side of creating an agenda involves developing a vision of the future and conceptualizing strategies for producing the change needed to achieve that vision. Thus Charles Knight's cost-cutting programs at Emerson involved management, and his strategic vision for the firm reflects leadership.

To be effective, organizations need both management and leadership. Leadership is needed to create change, and management is needed to create orderly results. The two work together in that management in conjunction with leadership can produce orderly change, and leadership in conjunction with management can keep the organization in synch with its environment.[6] The Entrepreneurial Challenge describes how Paul Fireman practices both management and leadership at Reebok.

Historical Concepts of Leadership

The phenomenon of leadership in organizations has been extensively studied for years. Two major historical approaches are centered on the search for leadership traits and the search for leadership behaviors.

The Search for Leadership Traits

During the first several decades of this century, literally hundreds of studies were conducted to identify important leadership traits. This approach to studying leadership attempted to analyze the personal, psychological, and physical traits of strong leaders. The underlying assumption was that some basic trait or set of traits differentiates leaders from nonleaders. If those

Table 18.1

Distinctions Between Management and Leadership

	Management	Leadership
Creating an agenda	**Planning and Budgeting.** Establishing detailed steps and timetables for achieving needed results; allocating the resources necessary to make those needed results happen	**Establishing Direction.** Developing a vision of the future, often the distant future, and strategies for producing the changes needed to achieve that vision
Developing a human network for achieving the agenda	**Organizing and Staffing.** Establishing some structure for accomplishing plan requirements, staffing that structure with individuals, delegating responsibility and authority for carrying out the plan, providing policies and procedures to help guide people, and creating methods or systems to monitor implementation	**Aligning People.** Communicating the direction by words and deeds to all those whose cooperation may be needed, so as to influence the creation of teams and coalitions that understand the vision and strategies and accept their validity
Execution	**Controlling and Problem Solving.** Monitoring results vs. plan in some detail, identifying deviations, and then planning and organizing to solve these problems	**Motivating and Inspiring.** Energizing people to overcome major political, bureaucratic, and resource barriers to change by satisfying very basic, but often unfulfilled, human needs
Outcomes	Produces a degree of predictability and order, and has the potential of consistently producing key results expected by various stakeholders (e.g., for customers, always being on time; for stockholders, being on budget)	Produces change, often to a dramatic degree, and has the potential of producing extremely useful change (e.g., new products that customers want, new approaches to labor relations that help make a firm more competitive)

SOURCE: Reprinted with permission of The Free Press, a Division of Macmillan, Inc., from *A Force for Change* by John P. Kotter, Inc.

traits could be defined, potential leaders could be identified. Researchers thought, for example, that leadership traits might include intelligence, assertiveness, above-average height, good vocabulary, attractiveness, and self-confidence.[7]

THE ENTREPRENEURIAL CHALLENGE

Reebok Relies on Management and Leadership

Reebok was a small British shoe company until 1979. That year Paul Fireman purchased a license from the firm to make and sell shoes with the Reebok label in the United States. Fireman introduced new products on an aggressive schedule and used his marketing flare to transform Reebok USA into one of the fastest-growing companies in the United States. He bought the firm's British parent company in 1985.

Part of Reebok's success is due to Fireman's understanding of the differences between leadership and management. He himself led the firm during its formative years. He kept his employees highly motivated and focused on overtaking Nike for industry leadership. Fireman acted like a coach, a cheerleader, and a quarterback all at once as he exhorted his employees to ever greater heights. By the early 1980s, Reebok passed Nike and became the market leader.

About the same time, however, Fireman decided that Reebok had grown too large to be run with the laissez-faire approach he favored. So he hired a professional manager to take over everyday operations. The new president formalized Reebok's organization design and set up an elaborate control system. This new approach helped cut costs and stabilized many of Reebok's activities.

New challenges by Nike and L.A. Gear, however, suddenly began to erode Reebok's market share, and by the end of the 1980s Nike had again taken over the top spot in the industry. Fireman decided that Reebok now needed leadership rather than professional management and so again took charge. He is more involved in daily operations than he was in his earlier stint running the firm but still sees his primary task as motivating and stimulating his employees. Reebok seems to have regained its momentum and is closing the gap on Nike.

REFERENCES: "Can Paul Fireman Put the Bounce Back in Reebok?" *Business Week,* June 18, 1990, pp. 181–182; "Reebok Enrages Nike by Gibing Endorsers," *Wall Street Journal,* February 6, 1991, p. B4; "Where Nike and Reebok Have Plenty of Running Room," *Business Week,* March 11, 1991, pp. 56–57; Gary Hoover, Alta Campbell, and Patrick J. Spain, eds., *Hoover's Handbook — Profiles of Over 500 Major Corporations* (Austin, Tex.: The Reference Press, 1990), p. 456.

For the most part, the results of the studies were disappointing. For every set of leaders who possessed a common trait, a long list of exceptions was also found, and the list of suggested traits soon grew so long that it had little practical value. There were even alternative explanations for traits that initially appeared to predict leadership. For example, researchers observed that many leaders have good communication skills and are assertive. However, rather than being the cause of leadership, those traits were possibly the result — that is, perhaps people begin to display those traits after they have achieved leadership positions.

As it was determined that the qualities of leadership vary with the situation, many researchers gave up trying to identify certain traits as predictors of leadership ability. Still, many people continue explicitly or implicitly to make this identification. Suppose, for example, that a manager is hiring someone to lead a new division that the company is establishing. After narrowing the applicant pool to two roughly equivalent candidates, he might be predisposed to hire the taller of the two if he associates height with leadership ability.

Employee-centered behavior was seen historically as one end of a leadership behavior continuum. While newer models of leadership have moved beyond this earlier behavioral approach, many leaders still believe that concern for employee welfare is a key to organizational effectiveness. Karl Friberg and Lyn Peterson, founders of Motif Designs, believe that being obsessive about work leads to negative results. They encourage their employees to leave work at a reasonable time every day, to exercise, and to spend time with their families.

The Search for Leadership Behaviors

Spurred on by their lack of success in identifying useful leadership traits, researchers next began to investigate other variables, especially the behaviors or actions of leaders. The new hypothesis was that the behaviors of effective leaders were somehow different from the behaviors of less effective leaders. Thus the goal was to develop a fuller understanding of leadership behaviors.

The Michigan Studies   Researchers at the University of Michigan, led by Rensis Likert, began studying leadership in the late 1940s.[8] Based on extensive interviews with both leaders and followers (that is, managers and subordinates) the Michigan studies identified two forms of leader behavior. The first was called **job-centered leader behavior**. When using this behavior, the leader pays close attention to the work of subordinates, explains work procedures, and is keenly interested in performance. The second behavior was identified as **employee-centered leader behavior**. In this case, the leader is interested in developing a cohesive work group and ensuring that employees are satisfied with their jobs. Thus the leader's primary concern is the welfare of subordinates.

The two styles of leader behavior were presumed to lie at opposite ends of a single continuum. Although the notion of a continuum suggests that leaders may be extremely job-centered, extremely employee-centered, or somewhere in between, Likert studied only the two end styles for contrast. He found that employee-centered leader behavior generally tended to be

The Michigan studies identified two basic forms of leader behavior: *job-centered leader behavior* and *employee-centered leader behavior*.

more effective. We should note the similarities between Likert's leadership research and his Systems 1 through 4 organization design (discussed in Chapter 11). Job-centered leader behavior is associated with the System 1 design, whereas employee-centered leader behavior is more consistent with the System 4 design. When Likert talks about moving organizations from System 1 to System 4, he is also advocating a transition from job-centered to employee-centered leader behavior.

The Ohio State Studies   At about the same time that Likert was beginning his work at Michigan, a group of researchers at Ohio State also began studying leadership.[9] Extensive questionnaire surveys conducted during the Ohio State studies again suggested that there are two basic leader behaviors or styles. The first was called **initiating-structure behavior**. When using this behavior, the leader clearly defines the leader-subordinate role so that everyone knows what is expected; the leader also establishes formal lines of communication and determines how tasks will be performed. The second leadership style was identified as **consideration behavior**. In this instance, the leader shows concern for subordinates and attempts to establish a warm, friendly, and supportive climate.

The job-centered and employee-centered behaviors identified at Michigan are similar to the initiating-structure and consideration behaviors recognized at Ohio State, but they are in some ways significantly different. The most obvious difference is that the Ohio State researchers did not position their two forms of leader behavior at opposite ends of a single continuum. Rather, they assumed the behaviors to be independent variables. This assumption meant that a leader could exhibit varying degrees of initiating structure and consideration at the same time.

At first, the Ohio State researchers thought that leaders who exhibit both behaviors would tend to be more effective than other leaders. A study at International Harvester (now Navistar International Corp.) suggested a more complicated conclusion.[10] Researchers found that employees with supervisors who ranked high on initiating structure were better performers but expressed less satisfaction. Conversely, employees with supervisors who ranked high on consideration had lower performance ratings but also fewer absences from work. Later research isolated yet other variables that make consistent prediction difficult and determined that situational factors influence how employees respond to leader behaviors.

The Michigan and Ohio State leader-behavior theories played an important role in the development of contemporary thinking about leadership (the Leadership Grid, a related model of leadership, is discussed in Chapter 23). In particular, they urge us to concentrate not on what leaders are (the trait approach) but to concentrate on what leaders do (their behaviors). Unfortunately, these theories eventually fell prey to the trap of making universal prescriptions about what constitutes effective leadership. In complex social systems composed of complex individuals, there are few if any consistently predictable relationships, and certainly there are no infallible formulas for success. Yet the behavior theorists tried to identify consistent relationships between leader behaviors and employee responses, in the hope of finding a dependable prescription for effective leadership. As we might

The Ohio State studies identified two basic leader behaviors: initiating-structure behavior and consideration behavior.

expect, they often failed, so other approaches to understanding leadership were needed. A few theorists realized that interpersonal and task-oriented behaviors might be useful for describing leadership but not useful for predicting or prescribing it. The next step in the evolution of leadership theory was the creation of contingency models.[11]

Contingency Approaches to Leadership

Contingency approaches to leadership assume that appropriate leader behavior varies from one situation to another.

The main assumption of all contingency approaches is that appropriate leader behavior varies from one situation to another. The goal of a contingency theory is to identify key situational factors and to specify how they interact to determine appropriate leader behavior. When William Marriott interacts with operating employees in a hotel that bears his name, he is low-key, unassuming, and open to different opinions. He finds that this down-to-earth behavior helps relax employees who might otherwise be nervous about interacting with the CEO. When dealing with top management, however, he is much more task-oriented and directive. Since other executives are less likely to be nervous around him, he doesn't have to worry about putting them at ease and instead can focus on the business at hand. Contingency theory explains why Marriott's two approaches are both remarkably successful.

Before discussing the three major contingency theories, we should first note an important early model that laid the foundation for subsequent developments. In 1958 Robert Tannenbaum and Warren H. Schmidt proposed a continuum of leadership behavior in the decision-making process. Their model is much like the original Michigan framework.[12] However, besides purely job-centered behavior ("boss-centered" behavior, as they termed it) and employee-centered behavior ("subordinate-centered"), they identified several intermediate behaviors in which a manager might engage. These are shown on the leadership continuum in Figure 18.1.

This continuum of behavior moves from one extreme, where the manager alone makes the decision, to the other extreme, where employees make the decision with minimal guidance. Each point on the continuum represents a different interaction of contingency factors concerning the manager, the subordinates, and the situation. Managerial factors include the manager's value system, confidence in subordinates, personal inclinations, and feelings of security. Subordinate factors include the subordinates' need for independence, readiness to assume responsibility, tolerance for ambiguity, interest in the problem, understanding of goals, knowledge, and experience. Situational factors that affect decision making include the type of organization, the degree of group effectiveness, the problem itself, and time pressures.

Although Tannenbaum and Schmidt pointed out the importance of contingency factors, their framework was simply speculative. It remained for others to develop more comprehensive and integrated theories. In the following sections, we describe the three most important and most widely accepted contingency theories of leadership: the LPC model, the path-goal model, and the Vroom-Yetton-Jago model.

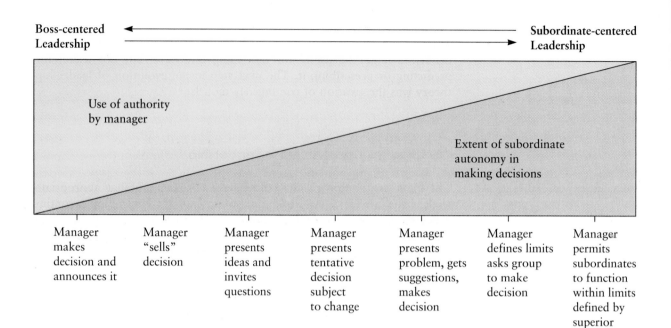

Boss-centered
Leadership

Subordinate-centered
Leadership

Use of authority
by manager

Extent of subordinate
autonomy in
making decisions

| Manager makes decision and announces it | Manager "sells" decision | Manager presents ideas and invites questions | Manager presents tentative decision subject to change | Manager presents problem, gets suggestions, makes decision | Manager defines limits asks group to make decision | Manager permits subordinates to function within limits defined by superior |

Figure 18.1

Tannenbaum and Schmidt's Leadership Continuum

SOURCE: Reprinted by permission of *Harvard Business Review*. An exhibit from "How to Choose a Leadership Pattern" by Robert Tannenbaum and Warren Schmidt (May/June 1973). Copyright © 1973 by the President and Fellows of Harvard College; all rights reserved.

The LPC Model

Fiedler's *LPC model of leadership* suggests that leader behavior tends to be either task-oriented or relationship-oriented.

Fred Fiedler's **LPC model of leadership** was the first true contingency theory of leadership.[13] Beginning with a combined trait and behavior approach, Fiedler identifies two styles of leadership: task-oriented (analogous to job-centered and initiating-structure behavior) and relationship-oriented (similar to employee-centered and consideration behavior). However, he goes beyond the leadership behavior approaches by arguing that the style of leader behavior is a reflection of the leader's personality (and thus is rooted in traits) and is basically constant for any person. In other words, a leader is presumed to be task-oriented or relationship-oriented all of the time.

Fiedler's *least preferred co-worker (LPC)* questionnaire measures leader style.

Fiedler uses a controversial questionnaire called the **least preferred co-worker (LPC)** to measure leader style. A manager or leader is asked to describe characteristics of the type of person with whom he or she is able to work least well — the LPC — by marking a set of sixteen scales anchored at each end by a positive or negative adjective. For example, three of the scales Fiedler uses in the LPC are:*

* Used by permission of Dr. Fred E. Fiedler, University of Washington.

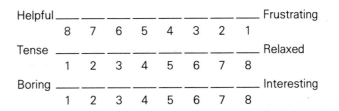

The manager's LPC score is then calculated by adding up the numbers below the line checked on each scale. Notice that in these three examples the higher numbers are associated with the "good" words (*helpful, relaxed,* and *interesting*), whereas the "bad" words (*frustrating, tense,* and *boring*) have low point values. A high total score is assumed to reflect a relationship orientation and a low score a task orientation on the part of the leader. The LPC measure is controversial because researchers disagree about its validity. Some of them question exactly what an LPC measure reflects and whether the score is an index of behavior, personality, or some other unknown factor.[14]

According to the LPC model, appropriate leader behavior is determined by the favorableness of the situation.

Favorableness of the Situation   As already noted, the underlying assumption of contingency models of leadership is that appropriate leader behavior varies from one situation to another. According to Fiedler, the key contingency factor is the favorableness of the situation from the leader's point of view. This factor is determined by leader-member relations, task structure, and position power.

Leader-member relations refers to the nature of the relationship between the leader and the work group. If the leader and the group enjoy mutual trust, respect, and confidence, and if they like one another, relations are assumed to be good. If there is little trust, respect, or confidence, and if they do not like one another, relations are assumed to be bad. Good relations are assumed to be favorable and bad relations unfavorable.

Task structure is the degree to which the group's task is well defined. When the task is routine, easily understood, and unambiguous, and when the group has standard procedures and precedents to rely on, structure is assumed to be high. A task with low structure is the opposite: nonroutine, ambiguous, complex, with no standard procedures or precedents. High structure is more favorable for the leader; low structure is more unfavorable. If task structure is low, the leader will have to play a major role in guiding and directing the group's activities. If task structure is high, the leader will not have to get so involved.

Position power is the power vested in the leader's position. If the leader has the power to assign work, administer rewards and punishment, and recommend employees for promotion or demotion, position power is assumed to be strong. If the leader must get job assignments approved by someone else, does not administer rewards and punishment, and has no voice in promotions or demotions, position power is weak. From the leader's point of view, strong position power is favorable, and weak position power is unfavorable.

Favorableness and Leader Style   Fiedler and his associates conducted numerous studies linking the favorableness of various situations to leader style and group effectiveness.[15] Figure 18.2 shows the results of these studies within the overall framework of the theory.

To interpret this figure, look first at the contingency factors. Notice that good or bad leader-member relations, high or low task structure, and strong or weak position power can combine to yield eight unique situations. For example, good relations, high structure, and strong position power (at the far left) are presumed to define the most favorable situation (for the leader). Bad relations, low structure, and weak power (at the far right) define the least favorable situation (for the leader). The other combinations of factors reflect intermediate levels of favorableness.

Associated with each situation is a form of leader behavior found to be most strongly related to effective group performance in that situation. When the situation includes good relations, high structure, and strong power, Fiedler has found that a task-oriented leader is most effective. However, when relations are good but task structure is low and position power is weak, a relationship-oriented leader is predicted to be most effective. Notice that a task-oriented leader is presumed most effective both when the situation is very favorable and when the situation is least favorable. A relationship-oriented leader is most effective in the intermediate situations.

Figure 18.2

The LPC Model of Leadership

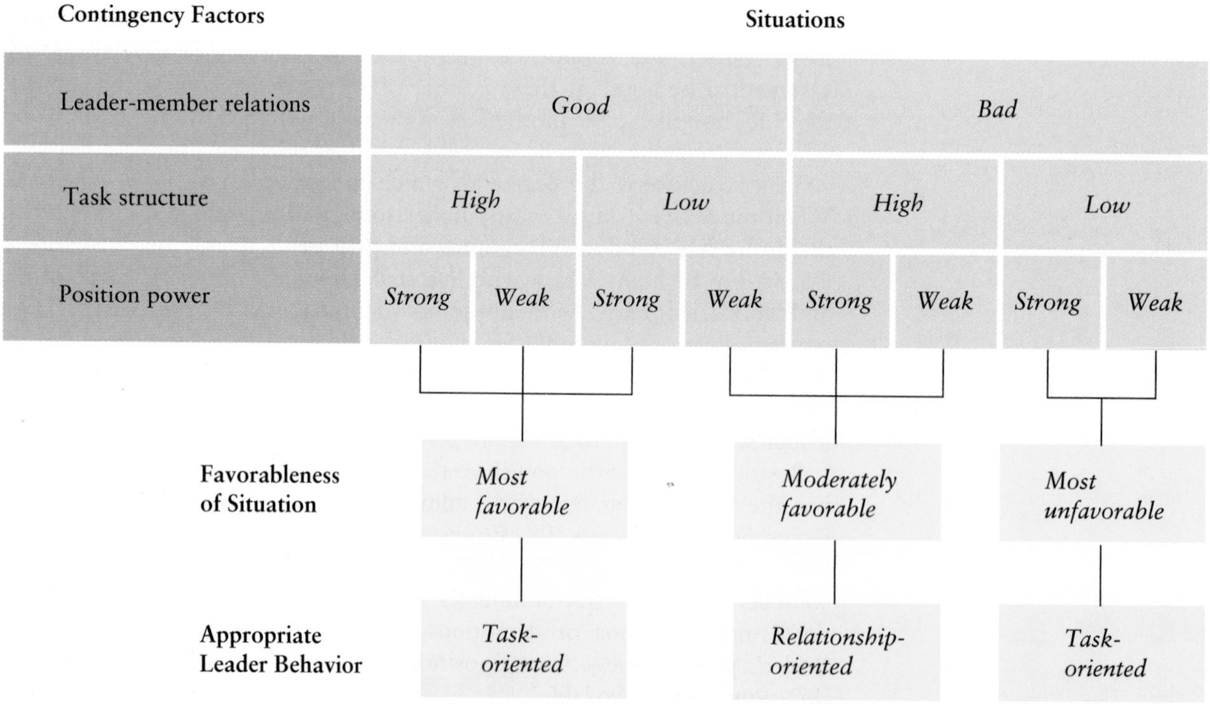

Contingency Factors	Situations							
Leader-member relations	*Good*				*Bad*			
Task structure	*High*		*Low*		*High*		*Low*	
Position power	*Strong*	*Weak*	*Strong*	*Weak*	*Strong*	*Weak*	*Strong*	*Weak*
Favorableness of Situation	*Most favorable*		*Moderately favorable*				*Most unfavorable*	
Appropriate Leader Behavior	*Task-oriented*		*Relationship-oriented*				*Task-oriented*	

Flexibility of Leader Style   A final point about Fiedler's theory concerns his view about the inflexibility of leader style. Fiedler argues that a leader's style, as measured by the LPC, is essentially fixed and cannot be changed: a leader cannot change her or his behavior to fit a particular situation. According to Fiedler, leaders' styles are either task-oriented or relationship-oriented. When a leader's style and the situation do not match, Fiedler argues, the situation should be changed to fit the leader's style. For example, when leader-member relations are good, task structure is low, and position power is weak, the leader style most likely to be effective is relationship-oriented. If the leader is task-oriented, a mismatch exists. According to Fiedler, the leader can make the elements of the situation more congruent with his or her style by structuring the task (by developing guidelines and procedures, for instance) and increasing power (by requesting additional authority or by other means).

Fiedler's contingency theory has been attacked on the grounds that it is not always supported by research, that research findings are subject to other interpretations, that the LPC measure lacks validity, and that the assumptions about the inflexibility of leader behavior are unrealistic.[16] Nevertheless, Fiedler's theory was among the first to help managers recognize the contingency factors they must contend with, and it fostered additional thinking about the contingency nature of leadership.

The Path-Goal Model

The *path-goal model of leadership* matches leader behaviors with several subordinate and environment characteristics. In contrast to the LPC model, the path-goal model assumes leaders can change their own behavior to match the situation.

The **path-goal model of leadership,** associated most closely with Martin Evans and Robert House, is a direct extension of the expectancy theory of motivation discussed in Chapter 17.[17] Recall that according to expectancy theory, motivation turns on the likelihood of a subordinate's attaining various outcomes and the value associated with those outcomes. The path-goal model suggests that the primary functions of a leader are to make valued or desired rewards available in the workplace and to clarify for subordinates the kinds of behavior that will lead to goal accomplishment and valued rewards. In other words, the leader should clarify the paths leading to goal attainment.

Leader Behavior   The most fully developed version of the path-goal model identifies four kinds of leader behavior. Directive leaders let subordinates know what is expected of them, give guidance and direction, and schedule work. Supportive leaders are friendly and approachable, show concern for subordinates' welfare, and treat all group members as equals. Participative leaders consult subordinates, solicit suggestions, and allow participation in decision making. Achievement-oriented leaders set challenging goals, expect and encourage subordinates to perform at high levels, and show confidence in subordinates' abilities.

In contrast to Fiedler's theory, the path-goal model assumes that leaders can change their style or behavior to meet the demands of a particular situation. For example, when first encountering a new group of subordinates and a new project, the leader may be directive in establishing work procedures and in outlining what needs to be done. Next, he may adopt supportive behavior in an effort to foster group cohesiveness and a positive climate. As the group becomes more familiar with the task and as new problems are encountered, the leader may exhibit participative behavior to enhance the motivation of group members. Finally, the leader may use achievement-oriented behavior to encourage continued high performance.

Contingency Factors   Like other contingency theories of leadership, the path-goal model suggests that appropriate leader style depends on contingency factors. Two general categories of contingency factors that receive special attention in the path-goal model are the personal characteristics of subordinates and the environmental characteristics of the workplace.

Subordinates' personal characteristics are their perception of their own ability and their locus of control. If people perceive themselves to be lacking in ability, they may prefer directive leadership to help them understand path-goal relationships. If employees perceive themselves to have a lot of ability, however, they may resent directive leadership. As we saw in Chapter 16, people who have an internal locus of control believe that what happens to them is a function of their own efforts and behavior. Those who have an external locus of control assume that fate or luck or "the system" determines what happens to them. A person with an internal locus of control may prefer participative leadership, whereas a person with an external locus of control may prefer directive leadership. Managers can do little or nothing to influence the personal characteristics of subordinates, but they can shape the environment to take advantage of these personal characteristics.

Environmental characteristics are factors outside the subordinate's control. Task structure is one such factor. When structure is high, directive leadership is less effective than when structure is low. Subordinates do not usually need their boss to continually tell them how to do an extremely routine job. The system of authority (i.e., the degree of centralization within the organization) is another environmental characteristic. Again, the more formal the system of authority, the less subordinates will accept directive leader behavior. Finally, the nature of the work group affects appropriate leader behavior. When the work group provides the individual with social support and satisfaction, supportive leader behavior is less critical. But when social support and satisfaction cannot be derived from the group, the individual may look to the leader for this support.

The path-goal model as illustrated in Figure 18.3 shows that different leader behaviors affect subordinates' motivation to perform. The interplay of personal and environmental characteristics determines which behaviors lead to which outcomes. The path-goal model of leadership is dynamic and incomplete. Its original intent was to depict the theory in general terms so that researchers could explore a variety of interrelationships and modify the theory as a result of their findings. Completed research suggests that the path-goal model is a reasonably good description of the leadership

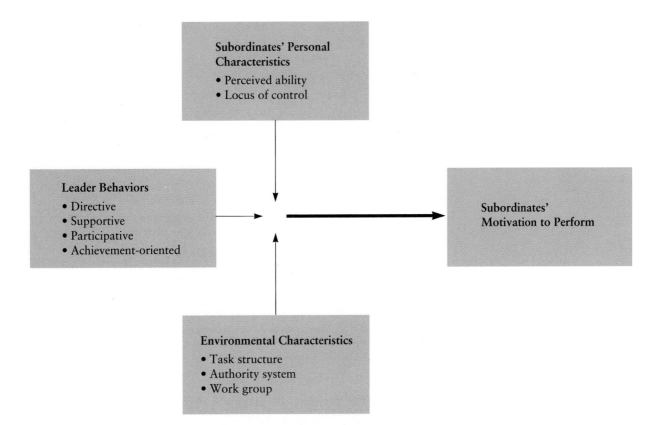

Figure 18.3

The Path-Goal Model of Leadership

process and that future investigations along these lines should enable us to discover more about the link between leadership and motivation.[18]

The Vroom-Yetton-Jago Model

The *Vroom-Yetton-Jago model* of leadership focuses on how much participation a leader should allow subordinates to have in making decisions.

The **Vroom-Yetton-Jago model** was first proposed by Victor Vroom and Philip Yetton in 1973 and was revised and expanded in 1988 by Vroom and Arthur G. Jago.[19] The VYJ model is somewhat narrower than the other contingency theories in that it focuses on only one part of the leadership process: how much participation in decision making to allow subordinates. Drawing from the Tannenbaum and Schmidt continuum of leadership behaviors, the model predicts the degree of group participation required in different situations. The VYJ model, then, sets norms or standards for including subordinates in decision making.

Basic Premises The VYJ model argues that decision effectiveness is best gauged by the quality of the decision and by employee acceptance of that decision. Decision quality is the objective effect of the decision on performance. Decision acceptance is the extent to which employees accept and are

Table 18.2

Decision-making Styles in the VYJ Model

Decision Style	Description
AI	Manager makes the decision alone.
AII	Manager asks for information from subordinates but makes the decision alone. Subordinates may or may not be informed about what the situation is.
CI	Manager shares the situation with individual subordinates and asks for information and evaluation. Subordinates do not meet as a group, and the manager alone makes the decision.
CII	Manager and subordinates meet as a group to discuss the situation, but the manager makes the decision.
GII	Manager and subordinates meet as a group to discuss the situation, and the group makes the decision.

A = autocratic; C = consultative; G = group

SOURCE: Reprinted from *Leadership and Decision-making* by Victor H. Vroom and Philip W. Yetton, by permission of the University of Pittsburgh Press. © 1973 by the University of Pittsburgh Press.

committed to the decision. To maximize decision effectiveness, the VYJ model suggests that managers adopt one of five decision-making styles. The appropriate style, in turn, depends on the situation. As summarized in Table 18.2, there are two autocratic styles (AI and AII), two consultative styles (CI and CII), and one group style (GII).

The situation is defined by a series of questions about the characteristics or attributes of the problem under consideration. To address the questions, the manager uses one of four decision trees. Two of the trees are for use when the problem affects the entire group (for example, a decision about new office facilities for the entire group), and the other two are appropriate when the decision affects a single individual (for example, a new office for that individual). Moreover, one of each is to be used when the decision has to be made quickly (because of some urgency in the situation), and the others are to be used when the decision can be made more slowly and the manager wants to use the opportunity to develop subordinates' decision-making abilities.

The tree for problems that involve the entire group and where time is important is shown in Figure 18.4. The problem attributes defining the situation are arranged above the tree and are expressed as questions. To use the tree, the manager starts at its left side and asks the first question —in this case, whether the decision involves a quality requirement. The answer determines the path to the second node, where another question is asked. The manager continues in this fashion until reaching a terminal node where the appropriate decision style is indicated. Each prescribed decision

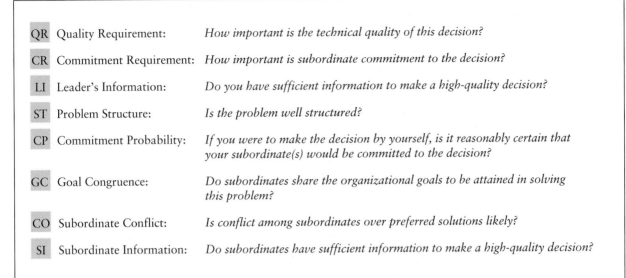

QR Quality Requirement: *How important is the technical quality of this decision?*

CR Commitment Requirement: *How important is subordinate commitment to the decision?*

LI Leader's Information: *Do you have sufficient information to make a high-quality decision?*

ST Problem Structure: *Is the problem well structured?*

CP Commitment Probability: *If you were to make the decision by yourself, is it reasonably certain that your subordinate(s) would be committed to the decision?*

GC Goal Congruence: *Do subordinates share the organizational goals to be attained in solving this problem?*

CO Subordinate Conflict: *Is conflict among subordinates over preferred solutions likely?*

SI Subordinate Information: *Do subordinates have sufficient information to make a high-quality decision?*

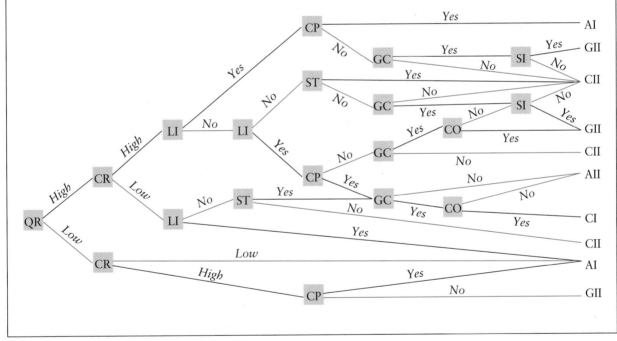

Figure 18.4

Decision Tree for the VYJ Model: Time-driven Group Problem

SOURCE: Reprinted from *The New Leadership: Managing Participation in Organizations* by Victor H. Vroom and Arthur G. Jago, 1988, Englewood Cliffs, NJ: Prentice Hall. Copyright 1987 by V. H. Vroom and A. G. Jago. Used with permission of the authors.

style is designed to protect the original goals of the process (decision quality and subordinate acceptance) within the context of the group versus individual and time versus subordinate development framework.

Evaluation   The original version of the VYJ model has been widely tested. Indeed, one recent review concluded that it had received more scientific support than any other leadership theory.[20] The original version, however, was criticized because of its complexity, and the revised VYJ model is far more complex than the original. For example, it includes four decision trees rather than one. Computer software has been developed to aid managers in defining the situation, answering the questions about problem attributes, and developing a strategy for decision-making participation.[21] In addition, a consulting firm has developed a detailed training program that teaches managers how to use the VYJ model with reasonable efficiency. Still, the inherent complexity of the VYJ model presents a problem for many managers.

Other Contingency Approaches

In addition to these three major theories, other contingency models have also been developed in recent years. Two of the best known are the vertical-dyad linkage model and the life cycle model.

Vertical-Dyad Linkage Model   Most leadership models focus on the relationship between a leader and her or his group of followers. The **vertical-dyad linkage model** stresses the fact that leaders actually have different kinds of relationships with different subordinates.[22] For example, the leader of a work group might respect one subordinate and also enjoy his company. The leader may respect another subordinate but not enjoy her company. Finally, the leader might neither respect nor like a third subordinate. In all likelihood, the leader will have a differerent kind of working relationship with each of these three subordinates.

> The *vertical-dyad linkage model* addresses the specific relationships that leaders have with each of their subordinates.

Each manager-subordinate relationship represents one vertical dyad. The VDL model suggests that leaders establish special working relationships with a handful of subordinates based on some combination of respect, trust, and liking. These people constitute the in-group. Other subordinates whom the leader does not respect, trust, or like remain in the out-group. Those in the in-group receive more of the manager's time and attention and also tend to be better performers. Although the VDL model is not yet a major theory of leadership, research on its effectiveness is quite promising.

Life Cycle Model   The **life cycle model** suggests that appropriate leader behavior depends on the maturity of the followers.[23] In this context, maturity includes motivation, competence, and experience. The model suggests that as followers become more mature, the leader needs to move gradually from high to low task orientation. Simultaneously, the leader's employee-oriented behavior should start low, increase at a moderate rate, and then decline again.

> The *life cycle model* suggests that appropriate leader behavior depends on the maturity of the followers.

The life cycle model was developed and popularized by management consultants. As a result of their many presentations to organizations and in articles in applied management publications, it is quite well known among practicing managers. Moreover, because it is both simple and logical, many managers are familiar with the life cycle theory. However, it has received little scientific support from researchers.[24]

Emerging Perspectives on Leadership in Organizations

Because of its importance in organizational effectiveness, leadership continues to be the focus of a great deal of research, theory building, and speculation. Three new perspectives that have attracted attention are the concepts of substitutes for leadership, transformational leadership, and leadership and diversity.

Substitutes for Leadership

The concept of *substitutes for leadership* identifies situations in which characteristics of the subordinate, the task, and the organization neutralize or replace leader behaviors.

The concept of **substitutes for leadership** was developed in response to the fact that existing leadership models and theories do not account for situations in which leadership is not needed.[25] They simply try to specify what kind of leader behavior is appropriate. The substitute concepts, in contrast, identify situations in which characteristics of the subordinate, the task, and the organization neutralize or replace leader behaviors. For example, when a patient is delivered to a hospital emergency room, the professionals on duty there do not wait to be told what to do by a leader. Nurses, doctors, and attendants all go into action without waiting for directive or supportive leader behavior from the emergency room supervisor.

Several characteristics of the subordinate may serve to neutralize leader behavior. For example, employees with much ability and experience may not need to be told what to do. Similarly, a strong need for independence by the subordinate may render leader behavior ineffective. A strong adherence to professional norms may also neutralize leader behavior. Finally, if an employee is for whatever reason indifferent toward organizational rewards controlled by the leader, attempts to influence behavior with those rewards will be unsuccessful.

Characteristics of the task that may substitute for leadership include routineness, the availability of feedback, and intrinsic satisfaction. When the job is routine and simple, for example, the subordinate may not need direction. When the task is challenging and otherwise intrinsically satisfying, the subordinate may not need or want social support.

Organizational characteristics that may substitute for leadership include formalization, group cohesion, inflexibility, and a rigid reward structure. When policies and practices are formal and inflexible, for example, leadership may not be needed. Likewise, a rigid reward system may decrease the leader's reward power. Preliminary research has provided support for the concept of substitutes for leadership.[26]

Transformational Leadership

Transformational leadership transmits a sense of mission, stimulates learning experiences, and inspires new ways of thinking.

Another new concept of leadership goes by a number of labels — charismatic leadership, inspirational leadership, symbolic leadership, and transformational leadership. We use the term **transformational leadership** to describe leadership that transmits a sense of mission, stimulates learning experiences, and inspires new ways of thinking.[27] Transformational leaders are increasingly being seen as vital to the success of business.

One popular-press article identified seven keys to successful leadership: trust your subordinates, develop a vision, keep your cool, encourage risk, be an expert, invite dissent, and simplify things.[28] Even though this list was based on a very simplistic reading of the leadership literature, it is quite consistent with the premises underlying transformational leadership. So, too, is the case of Gerald Tsai, Jr. Tsai took over American Can Company in the early 1980s and set about turning it into an entirely different company. He sold twenty-six businesses, including the canning operation, and bought almost as many more, mostly in the financial services industry. Today the company is known as Primerica and is a Wall Street powerhouse. It took transformational leadership to conceptualize what needed to be done, to figure out how to do it, and then to pull this huge undertaking off.[29] Given both its theoretical appeal and its practical significance, the notion of transformational leadership is destined to become more popular.

Leadership and Diversity

Organizations in this country were once relatively homogeneous. Managers were primarily male and white; clerks and secretaries were primarily female and white; most employees were American-born; people at each level were about the same age. Now, however, organizations are much more heterogeneous — and are becoming increasingly more so all the time. Although remnants of these earlier stereotypes remain, many U.S. firms are likely to have employees of all colors, races, ages, sexes, and ethnic origins working throughout the organizational hierarchy. Below we look at some of the international and demographic issues that this increasing diversity presents to concepts of leadership.

International leadership is a growing concern for organizations.

International Issues   With the increase in multinational corporations and the global economic trend, the concept of international leadership in organizations is growing in importance. For example, essentially all of the leadership theory and research that we discuss in this book was developed by U.S. researchers studying U.S. managers in U.S. organizations. The question now to ask is, To what extent are leadership processes and approaches similar and different in other cultures? Since little research is available on this question, we can only highlight its importance without giving any answers.

One way to begin thinking about the role of the international leader is to regard aspects of different cultures as important contingency factors.

THE GLOBAL CHALLENGE

Stormin' Norman Takes Charge

When General H. Norman Schwarzkopf III was placed in charge of coalition military operations in the Persian Gulf in 1990, he accepted a challenge of bewildering proportions. The task seemed clear: to drive the occupying Iraqi army out of Kuwait. But the leadership required to accomplish this task was mind-boggling.

For one thing, Schwarzkopf was directing several large groups from very diverse cultures — England, France, Egypt, the United States, and thirty-seven others. For another, each group had its own military traditions and was no doubt wary of being subordinate to the American command. To complicate things further, much of the military operation was based in a country (Saudi Arabia) with highly restrictive cultural norms. Finally, the U.S. media were scrutinizing Schwarzkopf's every move.

The situation had all the potential for a military disaster. Skeptics prophesied that the coalition would disintegrate, that Saudi Arabia would withdraw its support, that there would be huge coalition casualties. What actually happened was a military victory for the coalition that surpassed the expectations of even the most optimistic U.S. observers. The Iraqi army re-

treated completely, and Iraqi president Saddam Hussein was forced to agree to a list of postwar conditions and reparations.

A number of individuals shared responsibility for this success — President George Bush, Secretary of Defense Richard Cheney, and Chairman of the Joint Chiefs of Staff Colin Powell, for example — but none played a bigger daily role than Schwarzkopf. He displayed remarkably astute leadership behaviors at every juncture. He treated the officers and troops from every coalition group with equal dignity and respect. He also treated his Saudi "hosts" in the same way. Schwarzkopf appeared so direct and honest with the press, and displayed such a strong balance of confidence, resolve, compassion, and piety, that after the war he was being touted for both executive positions and political office.

REFERENCES: "A Soldier of Conscience," *Newsweek,* March 11, 1991, pp. 32–34; "Schwarzkopf for President?" *Newsweek,* April 1, 1991, p. 24; "'Storming' Norman' Takes Command," *Newsweek,* September 10, 1990, p. 25; "General's Command Performance Has Corporate America in a Swoon," *Wall Street Journal,* March 1, 1991, pp. B1, B2.

Suppose an individual successful as both a manager and a leader is asked to accept a new assignment in a different culture. What elements of that culture will he or she need to consider in choosing behavior appropriate to the new organization? The Global Challenge provides some insights into the leadership challenges faced by General Norman Schwarzkopf during the Persian Gulf War. Leaders will increasingly be called on to address culturally related issues in our increasingly global economy.

Demographic Issues   The demographic shifts that have occurred in organizational populations have dramatically highlighted several questions about leadership. One such question is the role of gender differences in leadership. The debate over whether males and females have different leadership styles has raged for decades. Some researchers believe that although male and female leaders may perceive that they behave differently, they actually exhibit the same behaviors.[30] In contrast, others suggest that there are substantive differences in leadership behaviors between men and women.[31]

Similar questions have been raised about differences in leadership behavior attributable to the racial composition of the group and leader.[32] Attention has also been directed at age-related issues, such as the problems of managers directing the work of subordinates older than themselves.[33] It is likely, of course, that all of these potential differences are a function of cultural norms that shape our beliefs about how different types of people should behave. The question, therefore, becomes one of understanding why perceptions of difference arise and how organizations can most effectively handle behavior that is based on those perceptions. This task becomes all the more important when the perceptions are clearly inaccurate.

Power and Political Behavior in Organizations

Leadership is one dominant method of influence in organizations. Two others are the use of power and political behavior. Although leaders have power and may engage in political behavior, it is also possible to have power or use political behavior without being a leader.

Power and Influence

Power is a resource-based use of influence. The five types of power in organizations are *legitimate, reward, coercive, referent,* and *expert power.*

Power is a resource-based use of influence — that is, one individual has power over another when he or she controls resources valued by the other. It is important to recognize that a person can have power without actually using it. In organizational settings, there are usually five kinds of power: legitimate, reward, coercive, referent, and expert power.[34]

Legitimate Power   **Legitimate power** is power granted to people occupying a particular position in the organizational hierarchy. The resource controlled by a person with legitimate power is organizational approval. A manager with legitimate power can direct a subordinate to perform a task that is a normal part of that subordinate's job. Performing the task will result in approval — positive effects on performance appraisal, acceptance by the manager, and so forth. Refusing the task can mean a reprimand or termination. Legitimate power, then, is the same as authority.

All managers, by virtue of their position in the organizational hierarchy, have legitimate power over their subordinates. The mere possession of legitimate power, however, does not by itself make someone a leader. In many cases, subordinates will follow orders only if they are strictly within the letter of organizational rules and policies. Asked to perform a task outside their defined domain, they might refuse or do a slipshod job. In such cases, their manager is exercising authority but not leadership.

Reward Power   **Reward power** is the power to give or withhold rewards. Rewards that may be under the control of an individual manager include salary increases, bonuses, promotion recommendations, praise, recognition, and interesting job assignments. The resources being controlled consist of the actual rewards themselves. In general, the more rewards a manager controls and the more important the rewards are to subordinates, the greater is the manager's reward power. If subordinates value only the formal organizational rewards provided by their manager, then there is little managerial leadership. However, if subordinates also desire and appreciate such informal rewards as praise, gratitude, and recognition, then the manager is likely exercising leadership.

Coercive Power   **Coercive power** is the power to force compliance by means of psychological, emotional, or physical threat. Coercion very rarely takes the form of physical punishment. In most organizations the available means of coercion are limited to verbal reprimands, written reprimands, disciplinary layoffs, fines, demotion, and termination. The resource controlled in this case is escape from threat. Some managers occasionally go so far as to use verbal abuse, humiliation, and psychological coercion in an attempt to manipulate subordinates. James Dutt, former CEO of Beatrice, reportedly once told a subordinate that if his wife and family got in the way of his working twenty-four hours a day, seven days a week, he should get rid of them.[35]

The more punitive the manager's control and the more significant it is to subordinates, the more coercive power the manager possesses. But the more a manager uses coercive power, the more likely he is to provoke resentment and hostility — and the less likely he is to be seen as a leader. The Environmental Challenge describes another arena of coercive power: sexual harassment.

Referent Power   Compared with legitimate, reward, and coercive power, which are relatively concrete and grounded in objective facets of organizational life, **referent power** is more abstract. It is based on identification, imitation, or charisma. The resource controlled by means of referent power is the status and prestige of the person being emulated. Subordinates may react favorably to a manager because they identify in some way with his or her personality, background, or attitudes. Some employees may even imitate a manager with referent power by wearing the same kinds of clothes, working the same hours, or espousing the same management philosophy. Referent power is also associated with charisma, an intangible attribute in the leader's personality that inspires loyalty and enthusiasm.

Expert Power   **Expert power** is based on information or expertise. That information, therefore, is the resource being controlled. A manager who knows how to handle an eccentric but important customer, a scientist capable of achieving a rare important technical breakthrough, and a secretary skilled at unraveling bureaucratic red tape all have expert power over anyone who needs that information. The more important the information and the fewer the people with access to it, the greater is the degree of expert power possessed by any one individual. In general, people who are both leaders and managers tend to have a lot of expert power.

THE ENVIRONMENTAL CHALLENGE

Coercion in the Extreme

Perhaps the least acceptable form of power in organizations is coercive power, which is the ability of one individual to force compliance by another through psychological, emotional, or physical threat. One especially intolerable use of coercive power is sexual harassment.

Sexual harassment can take a variety of forms. At one extreme, managers have been known to offer rewards to subordinates in exchange for sexual favors or to threaten punitive action if such favors are not forthcoming. Sexual harassment also includes suggestive glances, unwanted sexual compliments, unnecessary physical contact, and the telling of sexual or suggestive jokes and stories. The common case of sexual harassment involves a male manager and a female subordinate. However, there have also been numerous cases in which the subordinate was male and the manager female, in which both parties were of the same sex, and in which both parties were at the same organizational level.

Sexual harassment is both illegal and unethical. In recent years organizations have increased their efforts to curtail this insidious use of coercive power. Corning, for example, requires all of its employees to complete a four-hour course dealing with diversity issues, and sexual harassment is a major course component. Honeywell and Digital Equipment have also implemented new education programs to help employees deal with sexual harassment. At CBS, the CEO sends out a yearly memo reminding employees that sexual harassment will not be tolerated. Although sexual harassment may never be completely eliminated from organizations, many firms seem to be taking steps to minimize it.

REFERENCES: "Ending Sexual Harassment: Business Is Getting the Message," *Business Week,* March 18, 1991, pp. 98–100; Walter Kiechel, "The High Cost of Sexual Harassment," *Fortune,* September 14, 1987, pp. 147–152; "Tisch Wins Praise for Fast Action at CBS," *Wall Street Journal,* October 3, 1986, p. 6.

Managing Power

In practice, power can be managed in several ways. Most day-to-day interactions between managers and subordinates take the form of a legitimate request. The manager requests subordinates to comply in recognition of the manager's legitimate power. Another typical interaction results in instrumental compliance with reward power. This bears out the reinforcement theory of motivation. Suppose a manager assigns a subordinate a task outside the range of his normal duties, such as working extra hours on the weekend, terminating a relationship with a long-standing buyer, or delivering bad news. When the subordinate complies, he reaps praise and a bonus from the manager. The next time the subordinate is asked to perform a similar activity, he will recognize that compliance is instrumental in gaining more rewards. Hence the basis of instrumental compliance is clarifying important performance-reward contingencies.

A manager who suggests or implies that subordinates will be punished, fired, or reprimanded if they do not comply with a request is practicing coercion. Although managers may feel justified using coercive power with subordinates who are particularly recalcitrant, an alternative is rational persuasion, whereby the manager convinces subordinates that compliance is in their best interest. For example, a manager might argue that the subordinate should (or should not) accept a transfer because it would (or would not) be good for the subordinate's career. Elements of expert power are also present in that the manager may be seen as a knowledgeable person.

A manager who enjoys referent power may use it to shape the behavior of subordinates by modeling desired behaviors for them. Managers can sometimes induce employee compliance through an inspirational appeal to a set of ideals or values. A plea for loyalty often represents an inspirational appeal. Referent power plays a role in determining the extent to which an inspirational appeal succeeds, because its effectiveness depends largely on the persuasive abilities of the leader.

Lastly, a dubious method of using power is through information distortion. A manager may withhold or distort information to influence the behavior of subordinates. For example, suppose a manager withholds some of the credentials of qualified applicants so that subordinates choose her own candidate for membership in a work group. Like coercion, this use of power is dangerous. Beyond the fact that it may be unethical, if subordinates discover that they have been deliberately misled, they will lose their confidence in the manager's leadership.[36]

Political Behavior and Influence

Political behavior is an informal attempt at influence undertaken outside the organizational hierarchy for the specific purpose of obtaining one's preferred outcomes.

As we saw in Chapter 5, political behavior is a common phenomenon in organizations, although it is often a less appealing method of influencing people than is leadership. We define **political behavior** as an informal attempt at influence undertaken outside the organizational hierarchy for the specific purpose of obtaining one's preferred outcomes.[37]

Decisions ranging from the location of a manufacturing plant to the location of the company coffee pot are subject to political behavior. Regardless of the issue, people may engage in political behavior to further their own ends, to protect themselves from others, to further goals they sincerely believe to be in the organization's best interest, or simply to acquire and exercise power. As a result, instances of political behavior will vary dramatically in terms of their ethical nature. For example, trying to convince the organization to donate more to social causes and trying to convince the organization to make illegal campaign contributions may both be approached by means of political behavior.

Four common forms of political behavior are inducement, persuasion, creating an obligation, and coercion.

Research has identified four common forms of political behavior that can be identified in organizations.[38] One form is inducement. Inducement occurs when a manager offers support or rewards to someone in return for something. For example, a manager seeking a promotion might try to induce her subordinates to support her by pledging to help them secure promotions of their own. A second tactic is persuasion, which relies on an appeal to logic. An operations manager who has personal reasons for

Persuasion is one form of political behavior. Faith Wohl, a Du Pont executive, prefers persuasion to confrontation as a management style. Her title is an unusual one: director of work force partnering. It is her responsibility to champion programs that address employees' personal and social concerns. She recently persuaded top management to spend $1.5 million on day-care centers at Du Pont sites around the country.

constructing a new plant on a certain site might try to persuade others to support his goal on grounds that seem purely objective and logical.

A third political behavior is creating an obligation. Say one manager supports a recommendation made by another manager for a new advertising campaign even though he has no deep commitment to the project. He may be offering his support in order to incur a debt from the other manager that he can "call in" at a time when he wants support for one of his own projects. A fourth political behavior, coercion, is the use of force to get one's way (this is essentially the use of coercive power, as described earlier). For example, a manager may threaten to withhold support, rewards, or other resources as a way to influence someone else.

Managing Political Behavior

Managers should recognize that political behavior exists in virtually all organizations and that it should not be ignored. It can, however, be managed in such a way that it will seldom inflict serious damage on the organization, and it may even prove useful. For example, political behavior might be used to help get a worthy colleague promoted, to channel funds in constructive new ways, or to bring about other worthwhile changes that are for some reason being resisted.

How can managers handle political behavior so that it does not do excessive damage? By its very nature, political behavior is tricky to approach rationally and systematically, but some practical guidelines have been suggested. First, managers should be aware that even if their actions are not politically motivated, others may assume that they are. Avoiding the use of power helps managers avoid charges of political motivation. By providing subordinates with autonomy, responsibility, challenge, and feedback, a manager can reduce the likelihood of political behavior by employees. In addition, it is wise to bring disagreements out into the open so that subordinates will have less opportunity to manipulate conflict for their own purposes. Finally, avoid covert activities. Behind-the-scene activities imply political intent even if none really exists. Other guidelines include clearly communicating the bases and processes for performance evaluation, tying rewards directly to performance, and minimizing resource competition among managers.[39]

Learning Summary

Influence is the ability to affect the perceptions, attitudes, or behaviors of others. Influence is practiced through leadership, power, and political behavior. As a process, leadership is the use of noncoercive influence to shape the goals of a group or organization, to motivate behavior toward the achievement of those goals, and to help define group or organization culture. As a property, leadership is the set of characteristics attributed to those who are perceived to be leaders. Leadership and management are related concepts but are different in important ways.

The trait approach to leadership assumed that some basic trait or set of traits differentiated leaders from nonleaders. The leadership behavior approach assumed that the behaviors of effective leaders were somehow different from those of nonleaders. Research identified two forms of leadership behavior, one concentrating on work and performance and the other concentrating on employee welfare and support.

Contingency approaches to leadership recognize that appropriate leadership behavior varies with the situation. The LPC model suggests that a leader's behaviors should be either task-oriented or relationship-oriented, depending on the favorableness of the situation. The path-goal model suggests that directive, supportive, participative, or achievement-oriented leader behaviors may be appropriate, depending on the personal characteristics of subordinates and the environment. The Vroom-Yetton-Jago model maintains that leaders should vary the extent to which they allow subordinates to participate in making decisions as a function of problem attributes. The vertical-dyad linkage model and the life cycle theory are two new contingency theories.

Emerging perspectives on leadership include the concepts of substitutes for leadership, transformational leadership, and the relationships between leadership and diversity.

Power is a resource-based use of influence. Both managers and leaders use legitimate, reward, coercive, referent, and expert power. Political behavior is an informal attempt at influence undertaken outside the organizational hierarchy for the specific purpose of obtaining one's preferred outcomes. Inducement, persuasion, creating an obligation, and using coercion are all political behaviors.

Questions and Exercises

Review Questions

1. Define *influence, leadership, power,* and *political behavior.*
2. Summarize the basic forms of leader behavior identified in early research studies.
3. What is meant by the expression "contingency approaches to leadership"?
4. Summarize the major contingency theories of leadership.
5. What is a transformational leader?
6. Identify and describe five kinds of power.

Analysis Questions

1. Compare and contrast the concepts of management and leadership.
2. Identify traits that you think some people associate with leadership.
3. Compare and contrast the LPC and the path-goal models of leadership.
4. What do you think practicing managers should know about the major contingency approaches to leadership?
5. Give examples from your experience that illustrate each type of power.
6. Is it all right to use political behavior if you truly think the outcome you are championing is in the best interests of the organization? Give reasons for your answer.

Application Exercises

1. Identify several people who you think are managers but not leaders. Identify others who you think are leaders but not managers. Identify the factors that led you to your classification, and then compare and contrast the people on your two lists.
2. Suggest several decisions that your instructor might have to make about your class during a semester. Use the VYJ model to identify suggested degrees of student participation that your instructor might allow for each decision.

Chapter Notes

1. Bill Saporito, "Companies That Compete Best," *Fortune,* May 22, 1989, pp. 36–44; Gary Hoover, Alta Campbell, and Patrick J. Spain, eds., *Hoover's Handbook — Profiles of Over 500 Major Corporations* (Austin, Tex.: The Reference Press, 1990), p. 224; Robert Wrubel, "Power Alley," *Financial World,* August 9, 1988, pp. 26–32.

2. See Robert P. Vecchio and Mario Sussmann, "Choice of Influence Tactics: Individual and Organizational Determinants," *Journal of Organizational Behavior,* March 1991, pp. 73–80.

3. Arthur G. Jago, "Leadership: Perspectives in Theory and Research," *Management Science,* March 1982, pp. 315–336.

4. Gary A. Yukl, *Leadership in Organizations,* 2nd ed. (Englewood Cliffs, N.J.: Prentice-Hall, 1989), p. 5.

5. John P. Kotter, "What Leaders Really Do," *Harvard Business Review,* May–June 1990, pp. 103–111.

6. John P. Kotter, *A Force for Change* (New York: Free Press, 1990).

7. Bernard M. Bass, *Bass & Stogdill's Handbook of Leadership,* 3rd ed. (Riverside, N.J.: Free Press, 1990).

8. Rensis Likert, *New Patterns of Management* (New York: McGraw-Hill, 1961); Rensis Likert, *The Human Organization* (New York: McGraw-Hill, 1967).

9. The Ohio State studies stimulated many articles, monographs, and books. A good overall reference is Ralph M. Stogdill and A. E. Coons, eds., *Leader Behavior: Its Description and Measurement* (Columbus, Ohio: Bureau of Business Research, Ohio State University, 1957).

10. Edwin A. Fleishman, E. F. Harris, and H. E. Burt, *Leadership and Supervision in Industry* (Columbus, Ohio: Bureau of Business Research, Ohio State University, 1955).

11. See Jan P. Muczyk and Bernard C. Reimann, "The Case for Directive Leadership," *The Academy of Management Executive,* November 1987, pp. 301–309, for a recent update.

12. Robert Tannenbaum and Warren H. Schmidt, "How to Choose a Leadership Pattern," *Harvard Business Review,* March–April 1958, pp. 95–101.

13. Fred E. Fiedler, *A Theory of Leadership Effectiveness* (New York: McGraw-Hill, 1967).

14. Recent critiques include Ramadhar Singh, "Leadership Style and Reward Allocation: Does Least Preferred Co-Worker Scale Measure Task and Relation Orientation?" *Organizational Behavior and Human Performance,* October 1983, pp. 178–197; D. Hosking, "A Critical Evaluation of Fiedler's Contingency Hypothesis," *Progress in Applied Psychology,* January 1981, pp. 103–154; and Chester A. Schriesheim, B. D. Bannister, and W. H. Money, "Psychometric Properties of the LPC Scale: An Extension of Rice's Review," *Academy of Management Review,* April 1979, pp. 287–294.

15. Fiedler, *A Theory of Leadership Effectiveness;* Fred E. Fiedler and M. M. Chemers, *Leadership and Effective Management* (Glenview, Ill.: Scott, Foresman, 1974).

16. For recent reviews and updates, see Lawrence H. Peters, Darrell D. Hartke, and John T. Pohlmann, "Fiedler's Contingency Theory of Leadership: An Application of the Meta-Analysis Procedures of Schmidt and Hunter," *Psychological Bulletin,* March 1985, pp. 274–285, and Fred E. Fiedler, "When to Lead, When to Stand Back," *Psychology Today,* September 1987, pp. 26–27.

17. Martin G. Evans, "The Effects of Supervisory Behavior on the Path-Goal Relationship," *Organizational Behavior and Human Performance,* May 1970, pp. 277–298; Robert J. House and Terence R. Mitchell, "Path-Goal Theory of Leadership," *Journal of Contemporary Business,* Autumn 1974, pp. 81–98. See also Yukl, *Leadership in Organizations.*

18. See Yukl, *Leadership in Organizations,* for a thorough review.

19. Victor H. Vroom and Philip H. Yetton, *Leadership and Decision-making* (Pittsburgh: University of Pittsburgh Press, 1973); Victor H. Vroom and Arthur G. Jago, *The New Leadership* (Englewood Cliffs, N.J.: Prentice-Hall, 1988).

20. Yukl, *Leadership in Organizations.*

21. Vroom and Jago, *The New Leadership.*

22. Fred Dansereau, George Graen, and W. J. Haga, "A Vertical Dyad Linkage Approach to Leadership Within Formal Organizations: A Longitudinal Investigation of the Role-Make Process," *Organizational Behavior and Human Performance,* Fall 1975, pp. 46–78; Richard M. Dienesch and Robert C. Liden, "Leader-Member Exchange Model of Leadership: A Critique and Further Development," *Academy of Management Review,* July 1986, pp. 618–634.

23. Paul Hersey and Kenneth H. Blanchard, *Management of Organizational Behavior,* 3rd ed. (Englewood Cliffs, N.J.: Prentice-Hall, 1977).

24. Yukl, *Leadership in Organizations.*

25. Steven Kerr and John M. Jermier, "Substitutes for Leadership: Their Meaning and Measurement," *Organizational Behavior and Human Performance,* December 1978, pp. 375–403.

26. See Jon P. Howell, David E. Bowen, Peter W. Dorfman, Steven Kerr, and Philip M. Podsakoff, "Substitutes for Leadership: Effective Alternatives to Ineffective Leadership," *Organizational Dynamics,* Summer 1990, pp. 20–38.

27. James MacGregor Burns, *Leadership* (New York: Harper & Row, 1978). See also John J. Hater and Bernard M. Bass, "Superiors' Evaluations and Subordinates' Perceptions of Transformational and Transactional Leadership," *Journal of Applied Psychology,* November 1988, pp. 695–702; Karl W. Kuhnert and Philip Lewis, "Transactional and Transformational Leadership: A Constructive/Developmental Analysis," *Academy of Management Review,* October 1987, pp. 648–657.

28. Kenneth Labich, "The Seven Keys to Business Leadership," *Fortune,* October 24, 1988, pp. 58–66.

29. Tatiana Pouschine and Carolyn T. Geer, "Be Careful When You Buy from Gerry Tsai," *Forbes,* April 15, 1991, pp. 84–87.

30. Cynthia Epstein, "Ways Men and Women Lead," *Harvard Business Review,* January–February 1991, pp. 150–160.

31. Judy B. Rosener, "Ways Women Lead," *Harvard Business Review,* November–December 1990, pp. 119–125.

32. David A. Thomas, "The Impact of Race on Managers' Experiences of Developmental Relationships (Mentoring and Sponsorship): An Intra-Organizational Study," *Journal of Organizational Behavior,* November 1990, pp. 479–492.

33. "Older Workers Chafe Under Young Managers," *Wall Street Journal,* February 26, 1990, p. B1.

34. John R. P. French and Bertram Raven, "The Bases of Social Power," in *Studies in Social Power,* ed. Dorwin Cartwright (Ann Arbor: University of Michigan Press, 1959), pp. 150–167.

35. Hugh D. Menzies, "The Ten Toughest Bosses," *Fortune,* April 21, 1980, pp. 62–73.

36. For more information on the bases and uses of power, see Philip M. Podsakoff and Chester A. Schriesheim, "Field Studies of French and Raven's Bases of Power: Critique, Reanalysis, and Suggestions for Future Research," *Psychological Bulletin,* December 1985, pp. 387–411; Robert C. Benfari, Harry E. Wilkinson, and Charles D. Orth, "The Effective Use of Power," *Business Horizons,* May–June 1986, pp. 12–16; and Yukl, *Leadership in Organizations.*

37. Jeffrey Pfeffer, *Power in Organizations* (Marshield, Mass.: Pitman, 1981), p. 7.

38. Don R. Beeman and Thomas W. Sharkey, "The Use and Abuse of Corporate Power," *Business Horizons,* March–April 1987, pp. 26–30.

39. Ibid.

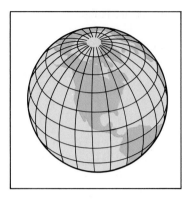

CASE 18.1

Beyond Cost Cutting

Reuben Mark has earned himself quite a reputation for reversing the fortunes of Colgate-Palmolive Co. Since he took over as chairman in 1984, Colgate's earnings have risen at a steady 15 percent per year, return on equity has doubled, and Colgate's stock price has more than tripled and in 1991 was trading at 16 times earnings. But as Colgate reshuffled its strategy for a new decade, everyone wondered whether its leader, so successful at creating an efficient company, could now create an innovative one.

Colgate is the world's leading toothpaste maker, but in the packaged-goods business it has long been a distant third behind Unilever and Procter & Gamble. It makes well-known brands like Palmolive, Ajax, and Irish Spring, but until Mark took over, the company was known for being slow moving and stodgy and having a bloated bureaucracy. Like many 1980s business leaders, Mark saw his first priority as trimming the bureaucracy and making the company leaner and more efficient. He eliminated one layer of management, gave lower-level managers more responsibility for decision making, and encouraged an entrepreneurial spirit throughout the company. The company's numbers quickly responded and have looked good ever since.

Mark's personality made him a leader to watch. He proved quickly that he could fire people when he needed to, and he earned the respect of his fellow CEOs. But he also made a point of keeping in touch with Colgate's factory workers, calming nervous workers in the company's Mexico City plant, for instance, by joking with them in Spanish. He began using company stock to reward workers for innovative and cost-cutting suggestions, and for the first time executives, too, got incentive bonuses. He sent employees postcards on their birthdays and earned a reputation for being humane and direct. In a significant departure from his predecessor's approach, he met often with Wall Street analysts and institutional investors, who reacted by supporting Mark when the company was threatened by a takeover.

Wall Street liked Mark's ideas and applauded as Colgate sold many of the companies it had bought during the 1970s and focused on its three main businesses: household and personal care products, health care, and specialty marketing. Analysts were impressed by his ability to squeeze more profit out of Colgate's domestic products by spending less on trade promotions and raising prices on some of the company's best sellers. Colgate's overseas performance made up for flagging domestic sales. In 1990 Colgate's U.S. operations showed no gain, but overseas sales grew by 18 percent.

But now Colgate needs to take some very different steps, and analysts have been watching with interest to see if a leader in the cause of efficiency can once again turn his company around and make it an innovator. As Colgate has discovered, cost cutting can take a company only so far. Although Colgate's price increases boosted profits, they also led to a sagging market share. Its detergents, for instance, make more money than they did in 1985, but their share of the market has dropped from over 13 percent then to less than 8 percent today.

Mark particularly needs to build a fire under Colgate's research and development people. One of its few recent innovations was its 1987 introduction of Fab 1 Shot, a laundry detergent and fabric softener that came in premeasured packets but was a washout in American supermarkets. Rumor has it that two decades ago Colgate worked on a combination shampoo and conditioner but never brought it to market. When Procter & Gamble introduced its version, in 1985, it became the number-one shampoo. Colgate has never done much with its baking-soda toothpaste, but Church & Dwight (maker of Arm & Hammer baking soda) has made baking soda seem to be a vital ingredient not only in toothpaste but in detergent and carpet deodorizer. Colgate spends less than 2 percent of its revenues for research and development. In contrast, Procter & Gamble spends almost 3 percent and L'Oréal almost 5 percent.

Colgate doesn't seem to take advantage of its well-known brand names. It has avoided forays into the domestic shampoo and skin care markets even though its competitors find beauty creams to be the most profitable of their lines. Colgate's only real domestic success to speak of, and the source of most of its domestic profit, is Hills Pet Products, diet pet food sold by veterinarians.

Colgate has not been as timid in overseas markets, from which it gets two-thirds of its operating profits. But competition abroad is increasing, and Colgate seems to be gaining only in such areas as toothbrush sales. Mark explains his company's reluctance to be innovative in domestic products by saying, "This country is the most expensive to launch new products in, and is the most fragmented market."* But Colgate's fortunes, it seems, rest on Mark's ability to lead his company into that risky market with the same decisiveness and confidence that enabled him to revive ailing Colgate in the 1980s.

Discussion Questions

1. What particular leadership qualities are needed to make a company innovative?
2. Would you expect a cost-cutting expert to be able to lead a company in new directions?
3. What are Reuben Mark's strengths as a leader?
4. Have you read about other leaders who would be well suited for the task that Colgate now faces? Explain.

* Quoted in Gretchen Morgenson, "Is Efficiency Enough?" *Forbes,* March 18, 1991, p. 109.

REFERENCES: Bruce Hager, "Can Colgate Import Its Success from Overseas?" *Business Week,* May 7, 1990, pp. 114–116; Bruce Hager, "The Pet Food That's Fattening Colgate's Kitty," *Business Week,* May 7, 1990, p. 116; Gretchen Morgenson, "Is Efficiency Enough?" *Forbes,* March 18, 1991, pp. 108–109; H. John Steinbreder, "The Man Brushing Up Colgate's Image," *Fortune,* May 11, 1987, pp. 106–112.

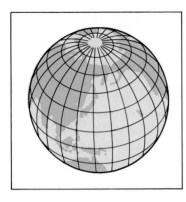

CASE 18.2

Taking Back the Power at Daewoo

One of the most popular buzzwords in modern corporate America is "decentralization." Many companies are trying to trim the lumbering, centralized bureaucracies of the past and give power and responsibility to managers of small units in the field who can make decisions quickly and with the advantages of local knowledge. But Kim Woo-Choong, one of South Korea's richest and most successful business leaders, is moving in the opposite direction, taking control back into his own hands. Whether his centralization of power is viewed as a step backward or a step into the future will depend on Chairman Kim's ability to reverse the recent fortunes of Daewoo, Korea's fourth-largest business group.

South Korean business is dominated by four large business conglomerates, or *chaebol*. Samsung, Hyundai, Lucky-Goldstar, and Daewoo all started out as family businesses, and they remain largely controlled by their founders even though each does over $15 billion in sales each year. Kim founded Daewoo, the newest of the four, in 1967 to make shirts for Sears, Roebuck. In the next two decades he expanded the Daewoo empire with phenomenal speed. In 1988 it included twenty-eight companies involved in trade, financial services, construction, and the manufacture of everything from machine guns to ships to fax machines.

As his business grew, Kim, like many entrepreneurs-turned-corporate-leaders, gradually gave up control of many Daewoo companies, often to fellow graduates of Seoul's Yonsei University. He spent much of his time traveling around the world, looking for new markets. Government protection, the low cost of Korean labor, and the undervalued Korean currency made Korean goods popular on world markets. To spur growth, the South Korean government often lent the *chaebol* money at special rates and helped them import technology from abroad cheaply.

But trouble began brewing for the *chaebol* in the late 1980s under President Roh Tae-Woo. At a time when former president Chun Doo Hwan's close ties with the *chaebol* were the subject of sensational televised hearings, Roh decided to end the government's long-standing support of the four big groups and to give smaller companies a chance to compete. Kim was forced to sell off some of Daewoo's prime properties to get government help in saving Daewoo Shipbuilding & Heavy Machinery, Korea's second-largest shipbuilder.

Changes in the government's support were not Kim's only problem. The increase in democracy in South Korea and violent strikes by some workers ended years of cheap and docile Korean labor. Some of Korea's trade barriers have begun to come down; the currency has been revalued; and the debt that the *chaebol* built up while amassing market share has now become a burden. From a Western perspective, the *chaebol* were overly diversified and poorly managed.

So in 1990, Kim began what he calls a "revolution" at Daewoo. In early January, five thousand of Daewoo's top managers came to Seoul Hilton International for their yearly meeting with the chairman, but the usual spirit of self-congratulation was missing. Many of them had already received letters from Kim criticizing their "poor performance and easy-going manner." Scores had been "retired."

Under Kim's pressure, Daewoo's bureaucracies began to change. At Daewoo's Seoul Hilton International, two hundred middle managers lost their jobs, and the Daewoo trading company cut one-third of its middle managers. Kim personally replaced the head of Daewoo Electronics with a mechanical engineer trained at MIT.

Kim actually began the changes himself when he personally took charge of Daewoo Shipbuilding during its crisis in 1988. He found that managers were ignoring a tenfold increase in labor costs over the past decade and many lacked "the spirit needed to save a company that was near-bankrupt."* Kim saved $8 million a year simply by ending the company policy of providing workers with free haircuts; then he slashed thousands of positions. His reputation grew as Daewoo Shipbuilding turned itself around and began showing a profit.

Amid the soul-searching that usually accompanies major corporate restructuring, Kim admits that he made a mistake by underestimating the importance of establishing the Daewoo brand name. Many of Daewoo's products were sold in the United States, but under brand names like General Motors, Boeing, and Caterpillar. Finally, in 1991, Daewoo started selling its own personal computer in Europe.

Although Kim's personal takeover of power seems old-fashioned to American managers, his ability to shrink the bureaucracy and make companies profitable again impresses observers. And if there is anyone who can revive the image of the corporate leader as a driven, tireless one-man show, it is Kim. During the 1990 Thanksgiving holiday, Kim's son, a graduate student at MIT, was killed in a traffic accident in Boston. On the day after the funeral, a Sunday, Kim showed up for work. As the title of his current best-seller puts it, "It's a Big World, and There's Lots to Be Done."

Discussion Questions

1. Why do we usually associate decentralization with downsizing?
2. What are Kim Woo-Choong's strengths as a leader?
3. From what you've read about South Korean culture and business, do you think a South Korean business leader could be equally successful in the United States?
4. What particular problems does Kim face as he tries to exert more personal control over a group that still includes nineteen companies?

* Quoted in Laxmi Nakarmi, "At Daewoo, a 'Revolution' at the Top," *Business Week*, February 18, 1991, p. 69.

REFERENCES: "Do or Be Done For," *The Economist*, December 9, 1989, pp. 74–79; Laxmi Nakarmi, "At Daewoo, a 'Revolution' at the Top," *Business Week*, February 18, 1991, pp. 68–69; Laxmi Nakarmi, "Korea's Conglomerates Face Life Without a Safety Net," *Business Week*, November 28, 1988, p. 51.

19

Interpersonal and Group Dynamics

LEARNING OBJECTIVES

After studying this chapter, you should be able to:

1. Discuss the interpersonal character of organizations.

2. Identify and describe three types of groups in organizations.

3. Explain why people join groups, and describe the stages of group development from immaturity to maturity.

4. Discuss four important characteristics of mature groups.

5. Describe special types of groups that organizations often use.

Federal Express virtually invented the overnight package delivery business. The firm's founder, Frederick Smith, first proposed the idea in a term paper for an economics class. He received a C. Undeterred, he invested his inheritance in the idea and started delivering packages in 1973. After a slow start, Federal Express quickly grew to become a large firm. Today, the firm deploys its 255 planes and 24,000 computerized delivery vans to deliver around 1 million items a day for customers worldwide. It has annual sales approaching $5 billion.

In recent years, however, new competitors have started chipping away at the company's market share. In addition, facsimile machines are often more economical to use than is Federal Express for delivery of letters and other brief documents. Thus the firm has had to look for innovative ways to continue its stellar performance.

One new approach is the use of superteams. Superteams are groups of employees brought together to help an organization solve special problems. Typically consisting of between 3 and 30 workers, superteams can get around corporate bureaucracy and work together in surprisingly efficient ways. Federal Express has organized its 1,000 clerical workers into super-teams of from 5 to 10 people each. How successful have they been? For one thing, the firm cut service errors (incorrect bills, lost packages, and so forth) by 13 percent in 1989 alone. One team discovered a glitch in the firm's billing system that was costing Federal Express over $2 million a year.[1]

Managers at Federal Express have recognized and taken advantage of what many experts increasingly see as a tremendous resource for all organizations: people working together in groups. Rather than operate as individual performers reporting to a supervisor, employees at Federal Express now function as members of a group and work with only minimal supervision. Group members schedule their own work hours, identify problems they want to address, and decide how best to approach those problems. They also develop loyalty and commitment to the other members of their group, which promotes synergy and gives individuals a greater sense of belonging.

This chapter is about interpersonal and group dynamics in organizations. We begin by describing the interpersonal character of organizations and the types of groups found in them. Subsequent sections explain group formation, the characteristics of mature groups, and special types of groups in organizations.

The Interpersonal Character of Organizations

We noted in Chapter 1 that much of a manager's job consists of scheduled and unscheduled meetings, telephone calls, and related activities. Indeed, a great deal of what managers do is interact with other people, both inside and outside the organization. To illustrate the extent of this interaction, the schedule that follows shows how Robert Lutz, at that time a vice president at Chrysler, spent one typical day.*

8:04 A.M. Lutz meets with a special design team at a Jeep/Truck Engineering facility in Detroit.

10:00 A.M. The meeting ends on schedule. Lutz stays a few minutes and goes over some details with individual members of the design team. He then attends another meeting with Tom Gale, Chrysler's design vice president. Lutz visits the facility every week.

12:10 P.M. Lutz leaves Gale's office and drives to Chrysler's executive office building for a lunch meeting with three division heads and a controller.

1:45 P.M. Lutz leaves the lunch meeting five minutes late and heads to his office for the first time. After he enters, he summons the head of Chrysler's international operations and four associates. This group discusses a variety of options the company is considering in the international arena.

2:29 P.M. The meeting ends, but Lutz and the international director have a private conversation.

3:05 P.M. Lutz hurries to another meeting with the project review committee. This meeting ends at 4:30.

4:30 P.M. Lutz has an unscheduled meeting with Bennett Bidwell, chairman of Chrysler Motors.

5:00 P.M. Lutz returns to his office to greet a company vice president who has been waiting to see him. The two men discuss a proposed new advertising campaign for Plymouth.

5:25 P.M. The meeting ends and Lutz turns to the stacks of paperwork awaiting him.[2]

Interpersonal dynamics are the patterns of interaction that take place between the members of an organization.

This highly compressed outline does not include several telephone calls and brief conversations that Lutz had with his secretary and with other people in the organization. As Lutz's schedule shows, interpersonal dynamics are a pervasive part of all organizations and a vital part of all managerial activities.[3] **Interpersonal dynamics** are the patterns of interaction that take place between the members of an organization.

* Alex Taylor III, "How a Top Boss Manages His Day," *Fortune*, June 19, 1989. © 1989 The Time Inc. Magazine Company. All rights reserved.

Interpersonal Dynamics in Organizations

The flavor of interpersonal dynamics in an organization is as varied as the individual members themselves. Personality, attitudes, abilities, needs, and goals — all these individual differences affect social interaction. At one extreme, interpersonal dynamics can be personal and positive. This might occur when the parties know each other, share mutual respect and friendship, and enjoy interacting with one another. Two managers who have known each other for years, jog together on weekends, and are close personal friends are likely to interact at work in a relaxed and effective fashion. At the other extreme, interpersonal dynamics can have a negative cast. This is most likely the case when the parties dislike one another, do not have mutual respect, and do not enjoy interacting with one another. Suppose, for example, one manager has fought openly for years to block the advancement of another manager within the organization. If the second manager eventually gets promoted nonetheless, relations between them are likely to be strained and difficult.

Most interpersonal dynamics fall between these extremes, as members of the organization interact in a professional way focused almost exclusively on goal accomplishment. A professional relationship is more or less formal and structured and highly task-directed. Two managers may respect each other's work and recognize the professional competence that each brings to the job. The fact that they may have few common interests and little to talk about other than the job they are doing will probably not be a factor in the quality of their work.

Interpersonal dynamics, whether positive and professional or negative, may occur among individuals, among groups, or among individuals and groups. They can also change over time. The two managers in the second scenario above, for example, might eventually resolve their dispute and gain a more professional relationship. Similarly, the managers in the third example might expand their mutual professional respect into friendship.

Consequences of Interpersonal Dynamics

The particular nature of an organization's interpersonal dynamics can have important effects. Recall from Chapter 17, for example, that numerous perspectives on motivation suggest that people have belongingness or affiliation needs. For individuals with a strong need for affiliation, good interpersonal dynamics represents an important positive element in the workplace. When confronted with poor working relationships, however, these same individuals may experience job dissatisfaction. Outright conflict, in which people leave an interpersonal exchange feeling angry or hostile, may have severe and long-lasting effects on an organization. Conflict in organizations is discussed fully in Chapter 21.

Interpersonal dynamics serve as a solid basis for social support in an organization. When people offer reassurance and encouragement to one another, they are providing social support. Suppose an employee receives a poor performance evaluation or is denied a promotion. Others in the organization can commiserate because they share a common frame of reference — the organization's culture, an understanding of the causes and consequences of the event, and so forth.[4]

Good interpersonal relations throughout an organization can be a tremendous source of synergy. People who support one another and who work well together can accomplish much more than people who do not. One factor cited for the success of the superteams at Federal Express is the commitment that participants make to cooperate and to make the new approach work. In the next section, we look more closely at the ways in which groups of people operate in organizations.

The Nature of Organizational Groups

Groups are a ubiquitous part of organizational life. They are the mechanism through which much of the work gets done, and they evolve both inside and outside the normal structural boundaries of the organization. For example, we can identify formal groups created by the organization's design. In addition, however, organizations have many other groups made up of people from different work areas.

Definition of a Group

A group is two or more people who perceive themselves to be a group and who interact regularly to accomplish a common purpose or goal.

Groups can be defined in terms of perceptions, needs, motives, composition, and a variety of other characteristics. For our purposes, we define a **group** as two or more people who perceive themselves to be a group and who interact regularly to accomplish a common purpose or goal.[5] If the individual members do not see themselves collectively as a group, a true group does not exist. Also, although a group must contain at least two people, when the size of a group increases past a certain point, usually around twenty members, it often formally or informally breaks up into smaller groups. When a group gets too large, it is difficult for members to interact sufficiently.

The common goal or purpose shared by group members may range from preparing a new advertising campaign to sharing information to making important decisions to fulfilling their social needs to be with friends. This goal may be formally stated (for example, when the organization creates a group and assigns it a specific goal) or simply implied (such as when people decide to go to lunch together). Regardless of how it is formed, however, a common goal is vital to group identity. The goal or purpose of the group is a primary factor in distinguishing among different types of groups in organizations.[6]

All organizations contain within them many different types of groups, some of which may evolve and change in nature over time. José Agosto, Shirley Dong, and Sharon Hall are the presidents of the Avon Hispanic Network, Avon Asian Network, and Black Professionals Assn., respectively. These groups, now organized self-help groups within the New York Headquarters of Avon Products Inc., started independently as informal social groups.

Types of Groups

In general, there are three types of groups in organizations: functional groups, task groups, and informal or interest groups.[7] These are illustrated in Figure 19.1. Much of this chapter examines the dynamics and characteristics of groups according to this categorization. In the final section, however, we shift our classification scheme slightly to look more specifically at some special groups currently in use in contemporary organizations.

Functional groups are created by the organization to accomplish a number of organizational purposes within an unspecified time.

Functional Groups   A **functional group** is a group created by the organization to accomplish a number of organizational purposes within an unspecified time. The advertising department of Federal Express, the management department of Ohio State University, and the nursing staff of the Mayo Clinic are all functional groups. The goals of the advertising department at Federal Express are to plan effective advertising campaigns, increase market share, increase product identification, and develop a unique identity for the company. It is assumed that the functional group will remain in existence after it attains its current objectives.[8]

Task groups are created by the organization to accomplish a relatively narrow range of purposes within a stated or implied time.

Task Groups   A **task group** is a group created by the organization to accomplish a relatively narrow range of purposes within a stated or implied time. Ad hoc committees, task forces, work teams, and your class are all task groups. The organization specifies group membership and assigns a relatively narrow set of goals, such as developing a new product, evaluating a proposed grievance procedure, or studying the field of management. The time horizon for accomplishing these purposes is either specified (your class ends at the end of the term) or implied (the project team disbands when the new product is developed). The superteams used at Federal Express disband and reform in new configurations every few months.

Figure 19.1

Types of Groups in Organizations

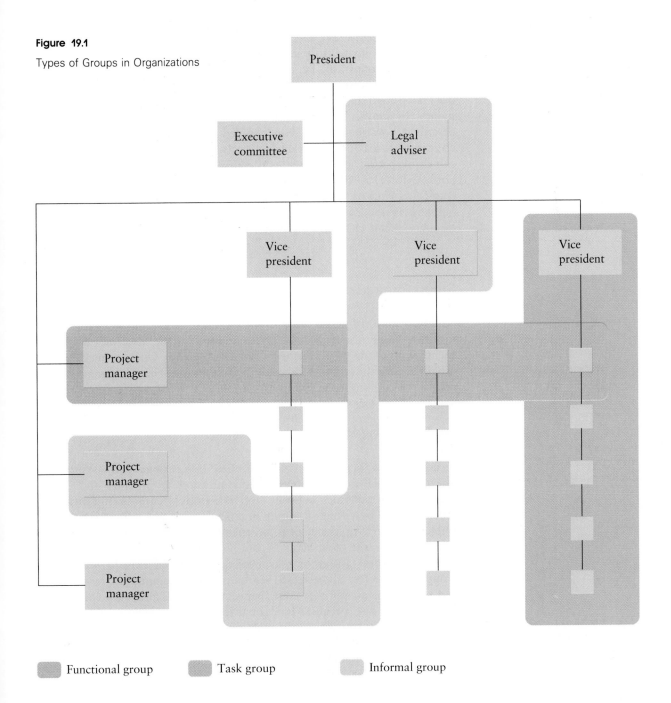

Functional group   Task group   Informal group

Informal or *interest groups* are created by their members for purposes that may or may not be relevant to the organization's goals.

Informal or Interest Groups   **Informal** or **interest groups** are created by their members for purposes that may or may not be relevant to the organization's goals. They also have an unspecified time horizon. Four or five managers who go to lunch together every day constitute an informal group, since the members choose to participate and are not told to do so. An informal group forms spontaneously and disbands relatively quickly; an interest group continues over time. As long as the managers enjoy one another's company, they will continue to meet for lunch. Other people may periodically be invited to join the group.

Informal groups can be a powerful force that organizations cannot ignore. At lunch, for example, the group of managers noted above may be discussing anything from how to improve productivity to how to embezzle money. In another example, dissatisfied workers in an automobile plant described how they engaged in planned sabotage, such as not welding critical spots, leaving out gaskets and seals, not tightening bolts, and sealing soft-drink bottles inside doors.[9] Of course, informal groups can also be a positive force, as demonstrated several years ago when Delta Air Lines employees worked together to buy a new plane to demonstrate their commitment to the company. We pay special attention to informal groups throughout this chapter.

Group Formation

Groups can form when people with similar goals and motives come together. The Entrepreneurial Challenge, for example, describes how two friends with similar goals formed a business together. Once formed, groups usually evolve through a number of discrete stages. The following sections discuss major patterns in group formation.

Organizational Motives to Join Groups

As noted earlier, organizations are composed of functional and task groups. The use of such groups allows the organization to structure and group organizational activities logically and efficiently. People join functional groups simply by virtue of joining organizations. Once individuals accept employment to earn money or to practice their chosen profession, they are assigned jobs in the group. Usually, but not always, functional-group membership precedes task-group membership. People in existing functional groups volunteer or are asked to serve on ad hoc committees, task forces, and teams. The members of superteams at Federal Express are volunteers. Each member has a regular functional job but also devotes considerable time every week to the goal or goals of the superteam. After those goals have been achieved, the employee may return full time to her or his functional job or join another superteam.

THE ENTREPRENEURIAL CHALLENGE

Ben & Jerry's Homemade, Inc.

Ben Cohen and Jerry Greenfield became friends in the seventh grade. They met while running track one day. By their own admission they were the two slowest and chubbiest kids in school and immediately began to help each other cope with taunts and catcalls from their classmates about their "blazing speed."

Another thing they had in common was a love for ice cream. As their friendship deepened, Ben and Jerry decided to go into business together when they finished school. Given their love for ice cream, what better business to enter?

They started in 1978 by enrolling in a $5 correspondence course on how to make ice cream. They then rented an abandoned gas station in Vermont and set up their operation. Like many new entrepreneurs, Ben and Jerry started out small. They made their ice cream in small batches and delivered it to local retailers in an old Volkswagen.

They also acknowledged that they knew little about business. One day they closed to pay their bills, and they put a sign in their window that said, "We're closed because we're trying to figure out what's going on." Eventually they hired a professional manager to take care of their finances and devoted their own attention to creating new flavors and expanding their market.

Their unique flavors (such as White Russian and Cherry Garcia) and commitment to high quality soon began to catch on, and demand for the firm's ice cream soared. Today Ben & Jerry's Homemade, Inc., is an international firm with 90 franchise stores and annual sales approaching $60 million. Cohen and Greenfield have remained best friends throughout the firm's growth. Indeed, their biggest disagreement ever was over what size chunks to put into a new flavor of ice cream they were testing.

REFERENCES: "Calories of the Rain Forest," *Newsweek,* December 3, 1990, p. 61; "Ben & Jerry's Big Chill," *U.S. News and World Report,* April 4, 1988, pp. 52–53; "For New Age Ice-Cream Moguls Ben and Jerry, Making 'Cherry Garcia' and 'Chunky Monkey' Is a Labor of Love," *People Weekly,* September 10, 1990, pp. 73–76.

Personal Motives to Join Groups

People also choose to join informal or interest groups, often for subtle reasons.[10] Because joining these groups is voluntary, various personal motives affect membership. Joining may be prompted by a single motive or by several different motives at the same time. Some of these are shown in Figure 19.2 and discussed below.

Interpersonal Attraction One reason people come together to form informal or interest groups is that they are attracted to each other. Many different factors contribute to interpersonal attraction.[11] When people see a lot of one another, day in and day out, pure proximity increases the likelihood that friendships will develop among them. Attraction is increased when individuals have similar attitudes, personality, or economic standing.

Interest in Group Activities Individuals may also be motivated to join an informal or interest group because the activities of the group appeal to them. Playing volleyball or bridge, bowling, discussing current events or

Figure 19.2

Personal Motives to Join Groups

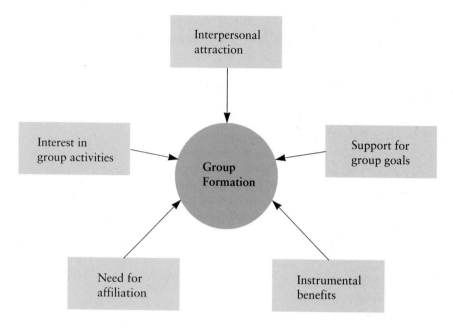

contemporary literature — all these are group activities that people enjoy. Many larger firms such as Exxon and Apple have intracompany football, softball, or bowling leagues. Individuals may join in with group activities whether or not they feel strongly attracted to other group members, but if the interpersonal attraction of the group is very low, they may choose to forgo the activity rather than join the group.

Support for Group Goals   The goals of a group may also motivate people to join. The Sierra Club, which is dedicated to environmental conservation, is a good example of this kind of interest group, as are other public-minded charities. Other groups that attract members because of their goals include political and fund-raising groups. Individuals join groups such as these in order to donate their time or money to advance goals they believe in and to meet other people with similar values.

Need for Affiliation   Another reason people join groups is to satisfy their need for affiliation. Residents new to a community may join the Newcomers Club simply to be around other people. Likewise, newly divorced individuals often join support groups in order to enjoy the companionship of people in a similar situation.

Instrumental Benefits   Group membership is sometimes seen as instrumental in providing other benefits to an individual. For example, it is fairly common for college students entering their senior year to join several professional clubs or associations in an effort to improve their chances of getting a good job. Similarly, a manager might join a health and racquet

One reason people join groups is to reap the instrumental benefits they may provide. Janet Thompson, vice president of marketing at Mazda Motor of America, has found that playing golf is a good way to make business contacts. She joined the Newport Beach (California) Country Club for two reasons: because she enjoys playing golf, and for the opportunity to establish and strengthen business relationships.

Most groups pass through four stages of development: *mutual acceptance, communication and decision making, motivation and productivity,* and *control and organization.*

club primarily because she feels that being a member of this club will lead to important and useful business contacts. Individuals may join civic groups such as Kiwanis and Rotary clubs for similar reasons, though women are occasionally excluded from joining such groups. Workers also join unions like the United Auto Workers because they think that union membership may increase their income or job security.

Stages of Group Development

Imagine the differences between a group of five people who have just met each other and a group of people who have worked together for years. Members of a new group are unfamiliar with one another's personalities and intentions and are tentative in their interactions. In the experienced group, however, members know one another's strengths and weaknesses and are more secure in their roles. The new group is generally considered to be immature; the experienced group, mature. To progress from the immature to the mature phase, a group must go through certain stages of development, which are depicted in Figure 19.3.

The first stage of group development is called **mutual acceptance.** During this stage, the members of the group get acquainted with one another and begin to test which interpersonal behaviors are acceptable and which are unacceptable to the other members of the group. This stage may occur very quickly (if there is a lot of initial interaction) or slowly (if interaction is sporadic). At this point group members are very dependent on each other to provide cues about acceptable behaviors and attitudes. The basic ground rules for the group are established, and a tentative group structure may emerge.

The group then evolves to **communication and decision making,** the second stage of development. During and after the first stage there may be a general lack of unity and uneven patterns of interaction between group members. With time, however, some members of the group may begin to exert themselves to gain recognition as a group leader and to play a role in shaping the group's agenda. As a consequence, the group begins to develop a structure for itself. Through communication and decision making, this structure becomes clear, and the group moves to the third stage.

Stage 3, **motivation and productivity,** is characterized by a shared acceptance among members of what the group is trying to do. Each person begins to recognize and accept her or his role and to understand the roles of others. Members also become more comfortable with each other and develop a sense of group identity and unity. In stage 4, **control and organization,** the members enact the roles they have accepted and direct their group efforts toward goal attainment. The structure of the group is no longer at issue but has become a mechanism for accomplishing the purpose of the group.

In reality, this developmental sequence varies from group to group. Time, personal characteristics of group members, and frequency of interaction, for example, can all affect how the group matures. Note also in Figure 19.3 that the transition between stages is not always smooth. Recent research, for example, has found that stages 1 and 3 are often characterized by periods of inertia or by a lack of momentum but stage 2 is often marked by a concentrated burst of activity that facilitates evolution to stage 3. Stage 4 itself tends also to be characterized by much activity as the group works to accomplish its goals.[12]

Figure 19.3

Stages of Group Development

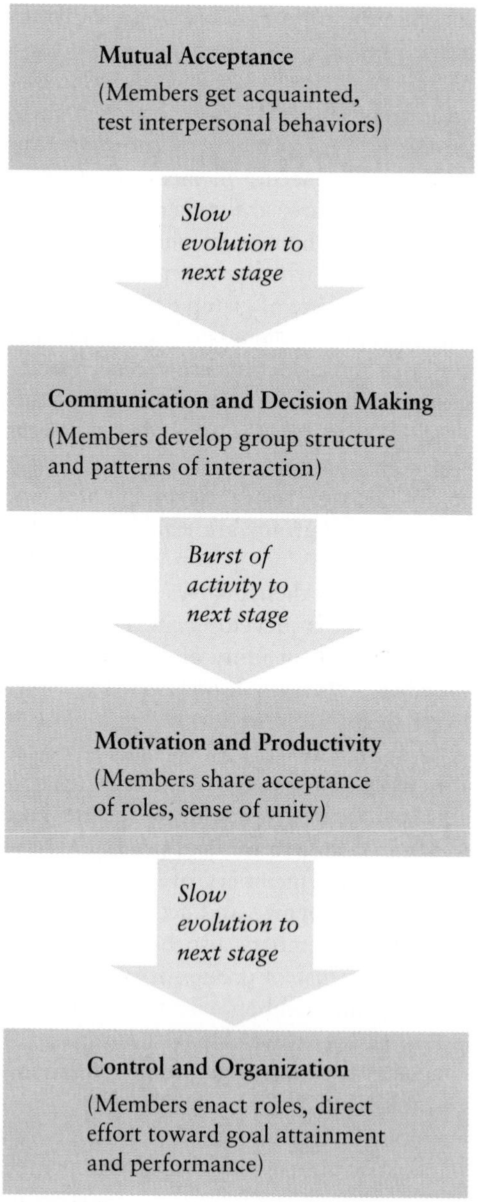

Mutual Acceptance

(Members get acquainted, test interpersonal behaviors)

Slow evolution to next stage

Communication and Decision Making

(Members develop group structure and patterns of interaction)

Burst of activity to next stage

Motivation and Productivity

(Members share acceptance of roles, sense of unity)

Slow evolution to next stage

Control and Organization

(Members enact roles, direct effort toward goal attainment and performance)

Characteristics of Mature Groups

Mature groups are characterized by role structure, behavior norms, cohesiveness, and informal leadership.

As groups pass through the stages of development to maturity, they begin to exhibit four characteristics: a role structure, behavioral norms, cohesiveness, and informal leadership. Understanding these characteristics of mature groups is important for managers because these characteristics largely determine how effective the group is in accomplishing its goals and how easy or difficult the group is to lead and manage.

Role Structures

A *role* is the part that a person plays in a group. *Role structure* is the set of defined roles and interrelationships among those roles that the group members define and accept.

Each individual member of a group has a part to play — a **role** — in helping the group reach its goals. Some people are leaders, some focus on the group's task, some interact with other groups, and so on. For example, a person may take on a task-specialist role (concentrating on getting the group's task accomplished) or a socioemotional role (providing social and emotional support to others in the group). A few group members, usually the leaders, fill both roles, but others may fill neither. The group's **role structure** is the set of defined roles and interrelationships among those roles that the group members define and accept. Each of us belongs to many groups and therefore plays multiple roles — in work groups, classes, families, and social organizations.[13]

Perhaps the easiest way to understand the concept of role structures is to describe the development of a role. As Figure 19.4 illustrates, development begins with the expected role, which is what the members of a group expect an individual to do. The expected role then gets translated into the sent role, which consists of the messages and behavioral cues that group members use to communicate the expected role to the individual. The perceived role is what the individual perceives the sent role to mean. Finally, the enacted role is what the individual actually does in the role. The enacted role, in turn, influences future role expectations of the group.

To illustrate, consider the case of a new employee joining a mature work group in a factory. Over the years, the members of this group have set informal standards for how much work each will produce: if an individual produces too much, the boss may think everyone else is underproducing; but producing too little also gets the boss's attention. The existing group

Figure 19.4

The Role Episode

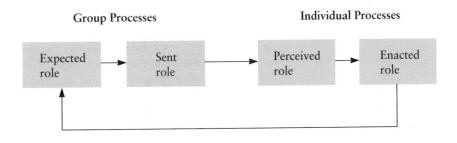

Group Processes   Individual Processes

Expected role → Sent role → Perceived role → Enacted role

members want the newcomer to accept their standards for production (expected role), so they provide behavioral cues such as glaring or making critical comments if the newcomer works too hard (sent role). The newcomer, however, may misinterpret these cues as a show of hostility to an outsider (perceived role) and work even harder to become accepted (enacted role). Finally, a group member might openly explain the situation, thus clarifying the sent role and causing the newcomer to perceive and enact the role the group expects him to play.

At each step of role development, distortions may creep in. The existing group members may not send the expected role accurately. The new group member may not perceive messages and cues correctly, as was the case above. Or the enacted role may deviate from the expected role because the individual either does not have the ability or does not choose to carry out the expected role. These breakdowns in role development result in role ambiguity, role conflict, and role overload, which are summarized in Table 19.1. These characteristics, in turn, lead to a weak and poorly defined role structure for the group.

Role ambiguity occurs when the sent role is unclear.

Role Ambiguity   Role ambiguity occurs when the sent role is unclear. In work settings, role ambiguity can stem from poor job descriptions, vague instructions from a supervisor, or unclear cues from co-workers. The result is likely to be a subordinate who does not know what to do. For example, a new employee instructed to "prepare a report on organizational turnover" will likely suffer role ambiguity if not also informed about the report's due date and intended audience. Role ambiguity can be a significant problem both for the individual who must contend with it and for the organization that expects the employee to perform well.

Role conflict occurs when the messages and cues composing the sent role are clear but contradictory or mutually exclusive.

Role Conflict   Role conflict occurs when the messages and cues composing the sent role are clear but contradictory or mutually exclusive. Role conflict is of particular concern to managers. Research has shown that conflict may occur in a variety of situations and lead to adverse consequences such as stress, poor performance, and rapid turnover.[14]

There are a number of different forms of role conflict.[15] One common form is interrole conflict, or conflict between roles. Many people experience interrole conflict when their work lives and family lives compete for the same time.[16] In organizations with a matrix design, interrole conflict often arises between the roles that a single individual plays in different task groups and in functional groups.

Intrarole conflict occurs when an individual must juggle conflicting demands from different sources within the context of the same role. For instance, a manager's boss may expect her to pressure subordinates to follow new work rules while, at the same time, her subordinates expect her to make exceptions to the rules. Thus the cues are in conflict, and the manager may be unsure about which course to follow.

Intrasender conflict occurs when a single source sends clear but contradictory messages. If the boss says one morning that there can be no more overtime for the next month but after lunch tells someone to work late

Table 19.1

Results of Breakdown in Role Development

> **Role ambiguity**   Sent role is unclear.
>
> **Role conflict**   Messages and cues of the sent role are contradictory or mutually exclusive.
>
> - *Interrole conflict* is conflict between two or more different roles.
> - *Intrarole conflict* is conflict from different sources within the context of the same role.
> - *Intrasender conflict* is conflict that occurs when the same source provides contradictory cues.
> - *Person-role conflict* is conflict between the person's values, attitudes, or needs and the requirements of the role.
>
> **Role overload**   Role expectations exceed the individual's capabilities.

that same evening, intrasender conflict is evident. Person-role conflict results from a discrepancy between role requirements and an individual's ethical standards, attitudes, and needs. An individual directed to do something unethical or illegal, or distasteful (for example, firing a close friend), may experience person-role conflict. This sort of role conflict may also arise for employees with families when the organization is requiring so much of the employee's time and energy that it infringes on the individual's personal life.

Role overload occurs when expectations for the role exceed the individual's capabilities.

Role Overload   A final consequence of a weak role structure is **role overload,** which occurs when expectations for the role exceed the individual's capabilities. If a manager gives an employee several major assignments at once while also increasing her regular workload, the employee will probably experience role overload. Role overload may also result when an individual voluntarily takes on too many roles at one time. For example, a person trying to work extra hard at his job, run for election to the school board, be active in church, coach Little League baseball, maintain an active exercise program, and be a contributing member to his family will probably experience role overload.

Implications   Managers can take steps to avoid role ambiguity, role conflict, and role overload. Having clear and reasonable expectations and sending clear and straightforward cues in functional or task groups go a long way toward eliminating role ambiguity. Encouraging employees to seek feedback and clarity can also be useful. Consistent expectations that take into account the employee's other roles and personal value system may minimize role conflict. Role overload can be avoided if managers recognize each individual's capabilities and limits. In informal and interest groups, role structures are likely to be less formally defined so the possibility of role ambiguity, conflict, or overload may not be very great. However, if a role breakdown does occur, it may be more difficult to resolve, because individuals cannot turn to a formal authority or a written job description to clarify their roles. Although informal sources of information may be somewhat useful, they may also be inaccurate or incomplete.

Behavioral Norms

Norms are standards of behavior that the group accepts for its members.

Norms are standards of behavior that the group accepts for its members. Above we saw how an existing work group might communicate its norms for production to a new member. Most committees also develop norms governing their discussions. In some committees, for example, an individual who talks too much may be perceived as pushy or as a showoff. In response, other committee members may ignore this individual's comments, may roll their eyes, and may otherwise "punish" the individual for violating the norm.

Norms define the boundaries between acceptable and unacceptable behavior.[17] Some groups develop norms that limit the upper bounds of behavior to "make life easier" for the group: don't make more than two comments in a committee discussion; don't produce any more than you have to; don't hurry to greet customers. These norms generally are counterproductive for the organization. Other groups may develop norms that limit the lower bounds of behavior: don't come to committee meetings unless you've read the reports to be discussed; produce as much as you can; greet every customer with a smile. These norms tend to reflect motivation, commitment to the organization, and high performance. Organizations can sometimes encourage the development of preferred norms through their reward systems. The Environmental Challenge describes how Du Pont is doing this.

Uniqueness of Group Norms   The norms of one group cannot be easily generalized to another group. Some college departments, for example, have a dress code that suggests male faculty members wear a coat and tie on teaching days. Men who fail to observe this norm may be "punished" by sarcastic remarks or even formal reprimands. In other departments the norm may be jeans and casual shirts, and the person unfortunate enough to wear a tie may be criticized just as vehemently. Some differences are due primarily to the composition of the groups. However, even very similar work groups may develop different norms. One group may strive always to produce more than its assigned quota; another may maintain productivity just below its quota. The members of one group may be friendly with their supervisor, whereas those of another group may remain aloof.

Norm Variation   Because norms prescribe different roles for different group members, norms may sometimes dictate role structures. The least senior member of a group may be expected to perform the most unpleasant or trivial tasks, such as waiting on customers who are known to be small tippers, attending to complaints, or handling the line of merchandise that carries the lowest commission. At the other end, certain individuals, especially informal leaders, may be allowed to violate norms with impunity.

THE ENVIRONMENTAL CHALLENGE

Du Pont Uses Norms to Advantage

One of the biggest problems that many businesses face is employee safety and health. For both legal and ethical reasons organizations are striving to reduce industrial accidents and to make the workplace a safer environment for everyone.

One major obstacle to safer working conditions is the employees themselves. Old habits are hard to eliminate, and workers are sometimes accustomed to behaving in ways that increase hazards. For example, smoking around toxic fumes and forgetting to wear safety glasses can each lead to accidents.

Du Pont is having some success, however, by making safety a behavioral norm within the company. In the past, most companies focused their efforts on catching and punishing people who violated safety rules. Du Pont decided to try a different approach and start rewarding people who follow the rules. The firm also decided to involve employees in enforcing the rules.

Du Pont has started assigning safety goals to each work group within its chemical plants. Groups that function without accidents for six months receive a prize that can range from cash payments to a day off from work. Each member of the group is encouraged to help the other members understand and follow all relevant safety rules. Group members are encouraged to sign up for voluntary safety classes, and many Du Pont workers agree they are more concerned with safety than ever before.

So far the plan seems to be working. Du Pont has cut its accident rate to about half of the industry average and estimates that it has saved $150,000 in medical claims, lawsuits, and lost work time resulting from accidents. An even more important outcome, of course, is the number of people whose health has been safeguarded.

REFERENCES: "Companies Turn to Peer Pressure to Cut Injuries as Psychologists Join the Battle," *Wall Street Journal,* March 29, 1991, pp. B1, B3; Gary Hoover, Alta Campbell, and Patrick J. Spain, eds., *Hoover's Handbook — Profiles of Over 500 Major Corporations* (Austin, Tex.: The Reference Press, 1990), p. 215; "Du Pont's Missed Opportunities," *Financial World,* May 30, 1989, p. 68.

Latecomers to meetings may be regularly chastised, but if the informal leader arrives a few minutes late the group will probably not object. People with expert power may also be allowed to violate norms.

Norm Conformity   Norms have the power to force a certain degree of conformity — accepting and adhering to the behaviors defined by those norms — among group members. The power of norm conformity was dramatically demonstrated in a now-classic experiment by Solomon Asch.[18] Asch set up a situation in which groups of people were asked to indicate which of three lines was the same length as another line. All the group members except one were Asch's confederates — they only pretended to be subjects. When all the confederates agreed on an answer that was obviously incorrect, the real subject went along with the rest of the group more than one-third of the time, even when he or she had already decided to give the correct answer!

Several factors contribute to norm conformity. Because of the personalities of key members, some groups may simply exert more pressure for conformity than others. The history of the group and its members also plays a part in conformity. For example, if the group has always been successful by following certain behaviors, new group members may be pressured to adopt those behaviors. If the group was not successful in the past, a new group member may have greater freedom to exhibit other behaviors. Individual traits such as intelligence determine the individual's propensity to conform (more intelligent people are often less susceptible to pressure to conform), as do group size and the degree of unanimity.[19]

As individuals begin to recognize the norms of a group they have just joined, they may respond in one of several ways. They may simply accept the norms and subsequently obey them. The new male professor who notices that all the other men in the department dress up to teach would also start wearing a suit. An alternative is to obey the "spirit" of the norm while still asserting individuality. Thus the professor might recognize the norm by wearing a tie — along with sport shirt, jeans, and sneakers.

In some cases individuals may choose to ignore a norm, which may have several consequences. At first the group may increase its communication with the deviant individual to try to bring her back in line. If this does not work, communication may cease. Over time, the group may begin to exclude the individual from its activities. If the norm is especially powerful and fraught with emotional overtones, the group may even resort to physical coercion. People who cross union picket lines during a labor strike, for instance, are occasionally subjected to physical abuse for violating the powerful norm of union solidarity. During a recent strike at Greyhound, picketing drivers threw rocks and bricks and reportedly even shot at other drivers who agreed to drive buses for the company.[20]

Cohesiveness

Cohesiveness is the extent to which group members are loyal and committed to the group and to each other.

Cohesiveness is the extent to which group members are loyal and committed to the group and to each other. In a highly cohesive group, the members work well together, support and trust one another, and are generally effective at achieving their chosen goal. A group that lacks cohesiveness will not be very coordinated. Its members will not necessarily support one another, and they may have a difficult time reaching their goals. Managers should develop an understanding of the factors that increase and reduce group cohesiveness, since the performance of an organization largely depends on how well its various groups function.

Determinants of Cohesiveness   As summarized in Table 19.2, there are five main factors that can increase group cohesiveness. One of the strongest is its competitiveness with other groups. When two or more groups are directly competing for rewards — for example, three sales groups competing for top sales honors — each group itself is likely to become more cohesive. Interpersonal attraction among group members enhances cohesiveness, as does favorable evaluation of the group by outsiders. Thus, once a sales group wins the sales contest, recognition and praise from a superior will strengthen its cohesiveness. Members of cohesive groups also tend to agree on their goals and to interact frequently. Managers who want to foster

Table 19.2

Factors That Determine Group Cohesiveness

Factors That Increase Cohesiveness	Factors That Decrease Cohesiveness
Competitiveness with other groups	Large group size
Interpersonal attraction	Disagreement on goals
Favorable evaluation from outsiders	Competitiveness within group
Agreement on goals	Domination by one or more members
Frequent interaction	Unpleasant experiences

group cohesiveness might do well to establish some form of intergroup competition, to consider interpersonal attraction when making group assignments, to provide opportunities for groups to succeed, to establish goals that all members will be able to accept, and to allow ample opportunity for group interaction.

There are also several factors that can decrease cohesiveness. We noted earlier in this chapter that size is a significant element of groups and that once groups reach a certain size (perhaps around twenty members), subgroups tend to emerge. As Table 19.2 shows, cohesiveness tends to decline as group size increases. Cohesiveness also may decrease if group members disagree on what the goals of the group should be. Importantly, intragroup competition reduces cohesiveness. When members compete among themselves for rewards or recognition, they focus more on their own objectives than on those of the group. In addition, domination of the group by one or more persons may cause other members to feel that they have few opportunities to interact and contribute, and they may become less attracted to the group as a consequence. Unpleasant experiences that result from group membership also may reduce cohesiveness. A sales group that scores last in a company contest or a work group continually reprimanded for poor-quality output may lose cohesiveness.

Consequences of Cohesiveness   In general, as groups become more cohesive, their members tend to conform more to group norms and grow more satisfied with the group. Cohesiveness itself may strengthen group performance, but performance is also highly influenced by the group's performance norms. Figure 19.5 shows how cohesiveness and performance norms interact to help shape group performance.

When cohesiveness and performance norms are both high, high performance should result. The group wants to perform at a high level and its members are committed to working together toward that end. When performance norms are high and cohesiveness is low, performance will be moderate. Although the group wants to perform at a high level, its members are not necessarily working well together. When performance norms are low, performance will be low, regardless of group cohesiveness. The least desirable situation from an organizational perspective is a group that combines low performance norms with high cohesiveness. In this case all group members enthusiastically embrace the standard of restricting performance (the low performance norm), and the group is united in its efforts to maintain that standard (owing to high cohesiveness). If cohesiveness were low, a manager might be able to raise performance norms by establishing group goals and rewarding goal attainment or by bringing in new group members who were strong performers. But a highly cohesive group is likely to resist these interventions.[21]

Informal Leadership

> An *informal leader* is a person who engages in leadership activities but whose right to do so has not been formally recognized.

A formal leader is one appointed by the organization or officially chosen by the group itself. An **informal leader** is a person who engages in leadership activities but whose right to do so has not been formally recognized. We noted in Chapter 18 the distinction between leadership and management. The distinction here is similar. A formal leader is like a manager in that she or he has been given power by the organization. An informal leader, in contrast, has no formal power.

Informal leaders are designated as such by members of the group themselves, and even when a formal leader is appointed, the group may look to others for real leadership. The formal and the informal leader in any group may be the same person, or they may be different people. We noted earlier the distinction between the task-specialist and socioemotional roles within groups. An informal leader is quite likely to be a person capable of carrying out both roles effectively. If the formal leader can fulfill one role but not the other, an informal leader often emerges to supplement the formal

Figure 19.5

Interaction Between Cohesiveness and Performance Norms

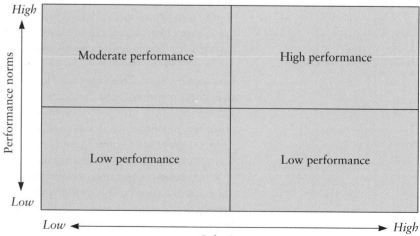

leader's functions. If the formal leader cannot fill either role, one or more informal leaders may emerge to carry out both sets of functions.

Is informal leadership desirable? In many cases informal leaders are quite powerful because they draw from referent or expert power. When they are working in the best interest of the organization, they can be a tremendous asset. However, when informal leaders work to counter the goals of the organization, they can cause significant difficulties. For example, if an informal leader is unhappy with something in the organization and has sufficient power, he or she may be tempted to try to change that something by exercising power rather than by using formal channels. Such leaders may lower performance norms, instigate walkouts or wildcat strikes, or otherwise disrupt the organization.

Special Types of Groups in Organizations

To manage groups in organizations effectively, managers face a twofold challenge. They must understand the complex interpersonal aspects of group behavior, and they must see how group behavior and performance interlock with and further organizational goals. In this section we discuss two types of groups that organizations commonly use to get work done: committees and work teams. We also consider some of the social and cultural aspects of managing special groups.

Committees

Almost everyone has heard the quip about the camel being a horse designed by a committee. The truth is that committees are very common in most organizations — and they offer an effective means for managing group decision making. A **committee** is a special group assembled to make a decision, submit a recommendation, conduct an investigation, or solve a problem. Ad hoc committees, standing committees, and task forces are the most frequently used types of committees.

An ad hoc committee is a committee created for a relatively narrow and short-run purpose, although that purpose may be extremely important to the organization. For example, an ad hoc committee might be appointed by a chief executive officer to evaluate a proposal to merge with another company. An ad hoc committee might also be created to deal with routine problems such as listing new-equipment needs or reviewing employee benefit packages. When its purpose has been fulfilled, such a committee is normally dissolved.

A standing committee, as the name implies, is a relatively permanent committee. The membership of a standing committee is relatively long term and stable. Some standing committees, such as budget review committees, handle the same set of issues on a continuous basis. One special kind of standing committee is the executive committee, composed of top managers

A *committee* is a special group assembled to make a decision, submit a recommendation, conduct an investigation, or solve a problem. Common forms of committees are ad hoc committees, standing committees, and task forces.

and primarily concerned with strategy and policy. General Motors makes effective use of its executive committee to explore the reasons for the company's success or lack of success in various activities. This committee also annually reviews the work of all of the company's top managers.

In many ways, a task force is similar to an ad hoc committee. It usually has a relatively narrow purpose and a limited time horizon, but it also has some unique characteristics. First, a task force is generally associated with the integration or coordination of activities between units. Task forces often function to integrate units that are highly interdependent. Second, the membership of a task force may change regularly as new skills and abilities are needed. For example, in its early stages, a new-product-development task force may need more production and engineering people to develop technical specifications, cost estimates, and the like. Marketing people become more important later, as promotion and advertising campaigns are planned. Task forces are often used to initiate and manage innovation.

The use of committees carries advantages and disadvantages similar to those discussed for group decision making in Chapter 5. The advantages of making decisions by committee are the availability of more information, increased acceptance of the group's recommendation, better communication, and (perhaps) improved quality of the decision. The disadvantages are lengthy, and thus costly, deliberations, the possibility of too much compromising or of domination of the decision making by one person, and the chance that committee members will succumb to groupthink.[22]

Work Teams

Common types of work teams are *autonomous work groups, quality circles,* and *cross-functional teams.*

A great deal of work in organizations is done by various kinds of work teams: autonomous work groups, quality circles, and cross-functional teams. Organizations are increasingly recognizing that (the use of work teams can boost both productivity and quality.)

Autonomous work groups are created in an effort to structure jobs around groups rather than around individuals. For example, in the Volvo plant at Kalmar, Sweden, small groups of workers assemble cars rather than relying on a traditional assembly-line arrangement. The members may rotate jobs among themselves and are often rewarded for group performance rather than for individual performance. The group leader at Volvo is seen more as a facilitator than as a supervisor. Volvo credits this strategy with a dramatic improvement in product quality.

Quality circles, another form of work team increasingly being used in American organizations, are small groups of volunteer employees who meet regularly to identify and discuss quality-related problems in the organization. These circles have been very successful in saving organizations money, but generally they limit their focus to problem solving. Most American businesses have adopted quality circles because of their success in Japan. Many Japanese firms and some American ones go far beyond quality circles by using cross-functional teams.

Cross-functional teams at Federal Express were described at the beginning of the chapter. Chaparral Steel's experiences are described in The

The use of work teams within manufacturing organizations is becoming increasingly common. Volvo, a pioneer in the use of autonomous work groups, is now experimenting with various types of work teams in some of its factories. At the plant in Uddevalla, which opened in 1988, teams spend two to three hours performing various tasks on a single automobile before moving on to the next. In contrast, at the Kalmar factory, tasks are divided such that teams spend twenty-five to thirty minutes with each car. Volvo executives are keeping a close watch on productivity levels as one means of measuring the relative effectiveness of these groups.

Global Challenge. Organizations use these teams to bring together functional expertise from several areas to work on a single project. To create a team, the organization selects representatives from appropriate departments (such as finance, marketing, and production) and assigns them to a particular project, such as introducing a new product. Teams are the bases of the matrix form of organization design discussed in Chapter 11. The project managers in a matrix are actually creating and managing cross-functional teams. They can also be used by nonmatrix organizations for special projects.

This entire approach to managing teams is derived from Japanese experiences. To generate maximum effectiveness from teams, the organization needs to achieve an integration of structurally defined groups that function in the context of a well-defined culture based on cooperation and trust between labor and management. In many ways, the cross-functional teams adopted by Federal Express and other organizations are the beginning of this approach in that they foster a group-based work environment.

A good example of the effectiveness of the Japanese approach to teams is the Toyota–General Motors joint venture in California — New United Motor Manufacturing, Inc. (NUMMI). The facility was originally opened and operated by GM but was shut down in 1982 because of problems with poor quality and abysmal labor relations. GM later entered into a joint venture with Toyota wherein the plant would be reopened under Japanese management. The new management team came in and trained each of the plant's 2,500 workers in group harmony, trust, and cooperation. The organization developed a team-based approach to work in conjunction with a new culture based on participation and cooperation. The result? The plant now makes higher-quality Chevrolets and Toyotas than any other GM plant — even higher than at some Toyota plants in Japan.[23]

THE GLOBAL CHALLENGE

Chaparral Competes with Teams

Chaparral Steel Company, based in Midlothian, Texas, is a model for how firms of all sizes can use teams effectively to confront international competition. During the 1970s the U.S. steel industry was brought to its knees by foreign competition. The entire industry had to change if it was going to survive.

Managers at Chaparral decided that if they wanted to compete internationally they had to understand what their foreign competitors were doing. Since Chaparral had always practiced participative management and was already using work teams, the organization decided to involve its workers in this effort as well.

To start, it selected one team of workers to tour new steel mills in Europe, Asia, and South America. After team members developed an understanding of how new technology was being used in these locations, Chaparral then sent the same team back out to buy new equipment for a Chaparral plant.

The team selected the equipment and then over-saw its installation. Most industry experts at the time projected that buying and installing the equipment would take about three years and that another six months would be needed to get all the bugs worked out. But in less than one year after the search started, Chaparral's new technology was in operation.

Using teams in this way, and throughout its entire manufacturing process, has allowed Chaparral to become a world-class competitor in the steel industry. For example, Chaparral was recently allowed to put the Japanese Industrial Standard mark for quality on its products. It is the first U.S. steel firm to be permitted to do so.

REFERENCES: Brian Dumaine, "Who Needs a Boss?" *Fortune,* May 7, 1990, pp. 52–60; Kurt Eichenwald, "America's Successful Steel Industry," *Washington Monthly,* February 1985, p. 42; "Chapparal Quality Cited by Japanese," *Journal of Manufacturing,* July 1990, p. 4.

Managing Organizational Socialization

Socialization is norm conformity that develops as a person makes the transition from being an outsider to being an insider.

To fully implement such a significant change, as well as to ensure that new employees understand it, organizations need to manage socialization. **Socialization** is norm conformity that develops as a person makes the transition from being an outsider to being an insider. A newcomer to an organization, for example, gradually begins to learn the organizational norms regarding appropriate dress, working hours, interpersonal relations, and so forth. As he adopts these norms, he becomes socialized into the organizational culture. Some organizations, such as Texas Instruments and IBM, actively manage the socialization process for new employees; others leave it to happenstance.[24]

If socialization is managed properly, everyone benefits. The individual is able to fit in easily, becomes a part of the team, and is able to function well with others. He develops a clear understanding of what the organization expects, what is necessary to succeed, and so forth. If socialization is handled poorly, the individual may not feel a part of the team, may not understand what is expected of him, and may be in constant conflict with others.

The key to managing organizational socialization is providing newcomers with information and maximizing communication. This ranges from very simple acts, such as giving the new employee an organization telephone directory, to more complex issues, such as explaining reporting relationships. Assigning the newcomer a mentor is another popular approach (a mentor is a senior employee who helps a newcomer learn the organizational ropes). The idea is that if people know what behavior is expected of them they can make informed choices about whether and how to comply.

Because groups are an important element of an organization's culture, group membership is a very powerful vehicle for socialization. The experiences, trials, and tribulations of groups help shape culture, and group norms help transmit culture. In turn, as shown by NUMMI's success, organizational culture can affect group processes. One reason cross-functional teams work so well for Federal Express may be that the firm has had a long-standing culture of employee participation. The success of those teams convinced team members to go further in tackling the problems they identify.

Learning Summary

Interpersonal dynamics — whether positive and personal, professional, or negative — pervade organizations. Such interaction satisfies affiliation needs, provides social support, is a source of both synergy and conflict, and results in group formation.

A group is two or more people who perceive themselves to be a group and who interact regularly to accomplish a common purpose or goal. Three types of groups in organizations are functional groups, task groups, and informal or interest groups.

People join functional or task groups when they join an organization and are assigned to jobs. They join informal or interest groups because they are attracted to the group's members, activities, goals, or potential instrumental benefits. Groups generally pass through four stages as they evolve toward maturity.

Four important characteristics of mature groups are role structures, behavioral norms, cohesiveness, and informal leadership. Role structures define task and socioemotional specialists. Role ambiguity, role conflict, or role overload can weaken role structure. Behavioral norms are standards of behavior for group members. Cohesiveness describes the extent to which members are loyal and committed to the group and to one another. Group performance is highly influenced by the relationship between group performance norms and cohesiveness. Informal leaders are the leaders whom the group members themselves choose to follow.

Organizations use a variety of special types of groups, including committees and work teams. Organizations must manage socialization and can use groups as part of this process.

Questions and Exercises

Review Questions

1. What are some of the potential consequences of interpersonal dynamics in organizations?
2. Define a group, and identify basic types of groups in organizations.
3. Why do people join groups? What stages of development do groups go through?
4. Describe four characteristics of mature groups.
5. What are two special types of groups that organizations use?

Analysis Questions

1. Identify several groups that you belong to. What type of group is each one?
2. Think of occasions when you have joined groups for each of the reasons discussed in this chapter.
3. Have you ever experienced role ambiguity, role conflict, or role overload? What problems did it cause?
4. Identify some group norms that you have encountered.
5. Imagine that you are the manager of a group that is highly cohesive but has low performance norms. How would you try to change things?

Application Exercises

1. Identify a group that you can observe and interview — a campus club, an intramural athletic team, and so on. Ask why people joined the group, and identify its roles, its norms, and its level of cohesiveness.
2. Think of all the television shows that you watch each week that dramatize scenarios in which people work together. Characterize each group in terms of its norms, cohesiveness, and informal leadership.

Chapter Notes

1. "Federal Express Wasn't an Overnight Success," *Wall Street Journal,* June 6, 1989, p. B2; "Christmas Rush: How Firm Delivers," *USA Today,* December 14, 1989, pp. B1, B2; Brian Dumaine, "Who Needs a Boss?" *Fortune,* May 7, 1990, pp. 52–60.
2. Alex Taylor III, "How a Top Boss Manages His Day," *Fortune,* June 19, 1989, pp. 95–100.
3. See John J. Gabarro, "The Development of Working Relationships," in *Handbook of Organizational Behavior,* ed. Jay W. Lorsch (Englewood Cliffs, N.J.: Prentice-Hall, 1987), pp. 172–189.

4. See Marcelline R. Fisilier, Daniel C. Ganster, and Bronston T. Mayes, "Effects of Social Support, Role Stress, and Locus of Control on Health," *Journal of Management,* Fall 1987, pp. 517–528.

5. See Gregory Moorhead and Ricky W. Griffin, *Organizational Behavior,* 3rd ed. (Boston: Houghton Mifflin, 1992), for a review of definitions of groups.

6. Marilyn E. Gist, Edwin A. Locke, and M. Susan Taylor, "Organizational Behavior: Group Structure, Process, and Effectiveness," *Journal of Management,* Summer 1987, pp. 237–257.

7. Dorwin Cartwright and Alvin Zander, eds., *Group Dynamics: Research and Theory,* 3rd ed. (New York: Harper & Row, 1968).

8. See Gregory P. Shea and Richard A. Guzzo, "Group Effectiveness: What Really Matters?" *Sloan Management Review,* Spring 1987, pp. 25–31, for a discussion of performance in functional groups.

9. Bill Watson, "Counter Planning on the Shop Floor," in *Organizational Reality,* 2nd ed., ed. Peter Frost, Vance Mitchell, and Walter Nord (Glenview, Ill.: Scott, Foresman, 1982), pp. 286–294.

10. Marvin E. Shaw, *Group Dynamics — The Psychology of Small Group Behavior,* 4th ed. (New York: McGraw-Hill, 1985).

11. Rupert Brown and Jennifer Williams, "Group Identification: The Same Thing to All People?" *Human Relations,* July 1984, pp. 547–560.

12. See Connie J. G. Gersick, "Marking Time: Predictable Transitions in Task Groups," *Academy of Management Journal,* June 1989, pp. 274–309.

13. David Katz and Robert L. Kahn, *The Social Psychology of Organizations,* 2nd ed. (New York: Wiley, 1978), pp. 187–221.

14. See Richard G. Netemeyer, Mark W. Johnston, and Scot Burton, "Analysis of Role Conflict and Role Ambiguity in a Structural Equations Framework," *Journal of Applied Psychology,* May 1990, pp. 148–157.

15. Robert L. Kahn, D. M. Wolfe, R. P. Quinn, J. D. Snoek, and R. A. Rosenthal, *Organizational Stress: Studies in Role Conflict and Role Ambiguity* (New York: Wiley, 1964).

16. For recent research in this area, see Arthur G. Bedeian, Beverly G. Burke, and Richard G. Moffett, "Outcomes of Work-Family Conflict Among Married Male and Female Professionals," *Journal of Management,* September 1988, pp. 475–485.

17. Daniel C. Feldman, "The Development and Enforcement of Group Norms," *Academy of Management Review,* January 1984, pp. 47–53.

18. Solomon E. Asch, "Effects of Group Pressure upon the Modification and Distortion of Judgment," in *Group, Leadership, and Men,* ed. H. Guetzkow (Pittsburgh: Carnegie Press, 1951), pp. 177–190.

19. Shaw, *Group Dynamics.*

20. "Greyhound May Be Coming to the End of the Line," *Business Week,* May 21, 1990, p. 45.

21. See Paul F. Buller and Cecil H. Bell, Jr., "Effects of Team Building and Goal Setting on Productivity: A Field Experiment," *Academy of Management Journal,* June 1986, pp. 305–328, for an example of how to increase cohesiveness.

22. Paul D. Lovett, "Meetings That Work: Plans Bosses Can Approve," *Harvard Business Review,* November–December 1988, pp. 38–44.

23. "Hands Across the Workplace," *Time,* December 26, 1988, pp. 14–17.

24. Walter Kiechel III, "Love, Don't Lose, the Newly Hired," *Fortune,* June 6, 1988, pp. 271–274.

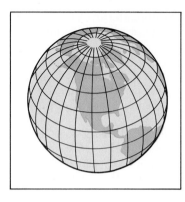

CASE 19.1

Expert Teams at General Mills

General Mills, the nation's number-two producer of breakfast cereals, used to arouse little more interest in the business world than did its flagship product, Cheerios. But luck, fortuitous preparation, and management innovations have changed that image and brought General Mills increasingly into the news. First the company sold off $3 billion of businesses to concentrate on cereals and on restaurants like the Red Lobster and Olive Garden chains. Then suddenly in the second half of the 1980s, the media began buzzing with studies that claimed that oat bran could contribute to a healthy heart and lower blood cholesterol. General Mills, which uses oats in about 40 percent of its cereals, was quick to take advantage of the new health craze. It came out with new brands including Honey Nut and Apple Cinnamon varieties of Cheerios, which gained three percentage points in market share in just a year to become America's best-selling dry cereal. General Mills began catching up to its main rival, Kellogg, which makes only 20 percent of its cereals from oats.

But perhaps the most revolutionary recent development at General Mills has been taking place not in the boardroom or in the research and development department but on the factory floor in such places as Lodi, California. The company's Lodi plant processes, packages, and distributes such products as cereals, cake mixes, and frostings. A tour of the plant might not reveal anything unusual — some of the equipment is new, some a half-century old — unless someone asked to talk to a manager. Especially if the tour arrived during the night shift, the questioner might be told that there wasn't a manager in the building. To a surprising extent, the employees run the plant themselves.

Factory workers at the Lodi plant are organized into self-managing, cross-functional teams that make decisions about everything from scheduling to maintenance. If there is a manager on the team, he or she is likely not to supervise but to provide the team with a particular kind of expertise — on management techniques — and to act as a liaison between the team and headquarters.

General Mills created these teams not as part of a management experiment or to make workers happier but to increase productivity. And in fact, the company says that productivity at its team-oriented plants is as much as 40 percent higher than at its traditional plants. Instituting the team concept at a new factory can take eighteen months, and transforming an old factory to rely on teams can take several years. But the teams eliminate the need for scores of managers and often set higher productivity goals than management would, thus contributing to higher productivity. At a General Mills plant in Carlisle, Pennsylvania, that management felt was running at full capacity, teams changed equipment and found ways to increase the plant's production of Squeezit juice by 5 percent. Team members at General Mills pride themselves on what they call their "championship quality."

General Mills teams aren't content just to improve existing processes. At Lodi, teams have developed a new maintenance training program that ensures that the company has an adequate number of people with the necessary skills to meet all its maintenance needs. All the plant's maintenance people must be proficient at troubleshooting, maintaining, and repairing a large variety of devices, but the plant also needs experts who can fix a particular new, complex machine.

The Maintenance Training and Selection Committee created core task teams (each with one member from management and one from labor) and subteams of from three to five maintenance employees—the experts. To assess the importance of particular maintenance skills, the teams asked the experts to rate hundreds of competencies in terms of difficulty and of importance to both present and future plant requirements.

The wealth of information gathered from these questionnaires led the committee to create a three-level training program. All maintenance employees must complete the core curriculum. Then they are chosen for either the electrical or the mechanical track and get specific training at level II. Finally, after about four years of experience, employees move into specialties such as advanced electronics and pipefitting. The committee decided not to try to create superemployees who could perform all maintenance functions.

The General Mills maintenance training program illustrates a number of aspects of successful teamwork. From the beginning, teams were made up of members from all levels and from all areas of the factory. They had real power over decisions; they weren't just asked to carry out management decrees. They drew heavily on the expertise of the on-the-floor workers both to define the skills necessary and to rate those skills. With the energy and commitment created by group collaboration and support, superteams like these may one day replace the isolated individual as the basic unit of organizational activity.

Discussion Questions

1. What steps could General Mills take to ensure that its employees are motivated to work hard on its teams?
2. Why might some employees at the Lodi plant say they feel more pressure under the team system?
3. What difficulties might arise among team members on a self-managing team?
4. Do you think General Mills would benefit from expanding its teams to include people in research and development and purchasing?

REFERENCES: Brian Dumaine, "Who Needs a Boss?" *Fortune,* May 7, 1990, pp. 52–60; James R. Hanlin and Nancy J. Johns, "Championship Training," *Training and Development Journal,* February 1991, pp. 56–62; Russell Mitchell, "Big G Is Growing Fat on Oat Cuisine," *Business Week,* September 18, 1989, p. 29; Patricia Sellers, "General Mills A Go-Go," *Fortune,* June 5, 1989, p. 173.

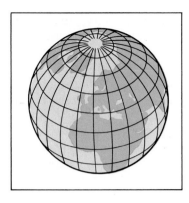

CASE 19.2

IBM-Europe Tries Top-Management Teams

IBM-Europe is not just a minor offshoot of its American parent. It does $28 billion of business, and in good years it generates about half of IBM's total profits. It employs over 100,000 workers and is among Europe's ten biggest taxpayers. In 1985, it accounted for about 25 percent of Europe's total computer-related trade. But in the late 1980s IBM-Europe's market share began slipping. Some European customers complained that all of IBM-Europe's decisions were made at IBM headquarters in Armonk, New York, and the European Community's antitrust regulators investigated claims that IBM-Europe kept its market share by making it difficult for competitors to connect their machines to IBM's. IBM sees Europe as the biggest foreign market for information technology, and it is competing for that market against not just Europe's own companies but huge Japanese computer companies as well. To deal with this competition and the changing European environment, IBM-Europe has had to change strategies several times recently, first emphasizing decentralization, then trying to think regionally rather than nationally, as Europe prepared for trade barriers to come down.

To make such strategic changes, respond quickly to customers' needs, and try to win back market share, IBM-Europe's top management has been using a team planning technique called process quality management (PQM). PQM creates a coherent unit out of an organization's top executives and focuses the team's attention on the basics of its business — its goals, strengths, and weaknesses.

PQM must begin at the top — with the CEO of a company or the head of a division — and it must involve everyone in the management group. The CEO must be ready to change. And IBM-Europe's teamwork consultants recommend postponing the PQM if even one of the ten or twelve top-management people cannot attend. If the team is to succeed, all of its members must be committed both to its goals and to its methods. The team should arrange for a leader or facilitator from outside the company, or at least outside the team's division, so that the facilitator does not have political or financial ties to any team members.

The team members' first goal is to come up with a mission statement, three or four sentences describing what the team collectively is paid to do. The statement needs to be explicit enough so that after a specified period of time the team will know whether it has succeeded and whether it deserves a reward.

To prepare for the next step and continue learning the process of working as a team, team members then brainstorm for ten minutes, listing everything they can think of that might affect the team's ability to achieve its mission. The team next concentrates on identifying critical success factors (CSFs), the things that the company must accomplish in order to achieve its mission. Studies have shown that managers in successful companies agree much more often about their CSFs than do managers in less successful companies, so the team tries to narrow its list of CSFs as much as possible. Each CSF should be *necessary* to the mission, and together the CSFs must be *sufficient* to achieve the mission.

The team then must define the business processes necessary for the company to meet its critical success factors. To accomplish the CSF "We must have excellent suppliers," the necessary business processes might include "monitor competition," "select and certify vendors," and "define new product requirements." Again, each individual process must be necessary to accomplish a CSF, and together all CSFs must be sufficient. Each process must also have an "owner" on the team, someone responsible for carrying out the process.

Next, the facilitator puts the CSFs and the business processes on a matrix, and the team decides how important each process is to each CSF. Team members also rate how well the company currently performs each process. The company can most profitably invest time and money into processes that are important to the greatest number of CSFs and are currently being handled least well.

This practice not only helps the company decide what it needs to concentrate on, it also commits the management team, and therefore the entire organization, to the same goals and the same strategies. The group as a whole is responsible for having selected the CSFs, and each individual accepts ownership of one or more business processes, so each part is strongly linked to the whole. Follow-up is crucial, and the team may need to repeat process quality management every year or so until the company's efforts are closely allied to its mission. IBM-Europe is betting that the tactics and strategies yielded by PQM may be as important as the company's new hardware in enabling Big Blue to continue to dominate Europe's information technology market.

Discussion Questions

1. Would the PQM technique used by IBM-Europe be useful for a team of shop-floor workers? Why or why not?
2. What common interpersonal and political differences does PQM attempt to overcome?
3. Why is it important for each business process to be "owned" by one of the team members?
4. Why not have the company CEO control PQM?

REFERENCES: Maurice Hardaker and Bryan K. Ward, "How to Make a Team Work," *Harvard Business Review,* November–December 1987, pp. 112–119; Richard L. Hudson, "To Europe, IBM Is No Longer Invincible," *Wall Street Journal,* December 16, 1988, p. B4; Jonathan B. Levine, "IBM Europe Starts Swinging Back," *Business Week,* May 6, 1991, pp. 52–53; Thane Peterson, "Mike Armstrong Is Improving IBM's Game in Europe," *Business Week,* June 20, 1988, pp. 96–101.

20

Communication in Organizations

LEARNING OBJECTIVES

After studying this chapter, you should be able to:

1. Explain the concept of effective communication and the role of communication in management.

2. Discuss the advantages and disadvantages of oral and written communication.

3. Identify the major patterns of group communication networks.

4. Describe two forms of vertical communication, and explain the role of the organizational grapevine.

5. Discuss three types of nonverbal communication.

6. Describe the barriers to communication in organizations, and suggest ways to overcome them.

7. Explain the impact of electronic technology on communication in organizations.

The computer industry is one of the most competitive arenas in the world today. Computer firms are especially sensitive about maintaining secrecy and confidentiality regarding product design, since the wrong information falling into the wrong hands can quickly cost a firm technological advantage and market share. Apple Computer has in the past been plagued with a series of harmful information leaks.

It's not always easy to know where company secrets begin to break down. For some people, having access to sensitive information is a sign of power and importance, and they may use that information in an undisguised attempt to gain influence. Then again, secrecy may be breached more innocently. A group of managers who meet socially after work may well get into some office gossip and wind up throwing around confidential information to impress their listeners in a game of "can you top this?"

Apple's problems started a few years ago as more and more of its inside secrets were being leaked to outsiders and, in some cases, to the press and to competitors. To combat the problem, the firm started passing out buttons and hanging up posters that request workers to maintain secrecy. Unfortunately, many of the firm's more discrete employees have come to resent the program because they feel that the company no longer trusts them.[1]

The problems faced by Apple represent two very important aspects of communication in organizations. Mismanaged information may be very destructive, but when organizations try to manage information more effectively, a single misstep can compound the problem. Well-managed communication is a vital asset for all organizations.

This chapter begins by discussing the role of communication in organizations. We then examine the different forms of interpersonal, group, and organizational communication. We describe several ways in which organizational communication can be effectively managed and conclude by considering some of the recent effects of technology on communication.

The Role of Communication in Organizations

As we saw in Chapter 19, communicating through meetings, telephone calls, and correspondence is a necessary part of every manager's job. On what he said was a typical Monday, Nolan Archibald, CEO of Black & Decker, once attended five scheduled meetings and two unscheduled meetings, had fifteen telephone conversations, received twenty-nine letters, memos, and reports, and dictated ten letters of his own.[2] Managers usually spend well over half of their time involved in some form of communication.

Elements of Communication

Communication is the process of transmitting information from one person to another.

We define **communication** as the process of transmitting information from one person to another.[3] Three conditions are necessary for communication to occur. First, at least two people must be involved, although they need not be in close proximity. Two managers having a discussion in an office engage in communication, but so do a student reading a book written five hundred years ago and the Renaissance philosopher who wrote it. Of course, many more than two people can take part in communication, such as when a CEO makes a speech to a group of stockholders.

Second, there must be information to be communicated. Recall from Chapter 13 that information is data presented in a context that yields meaning. In the context of communication, meaning can take the form of facts, ideas, or opinions. Managers discussing next year's profit projections, for example, are dealing with information.

Third, some attempt must be made to transmit this information. Knowing something but being unwilling or unable to communicate it to others results in a lack of communication. A CEO who speaks in English to a roomful of foreign investors may be unable to transmit much accurate information without relying on a translator.

Effective communication occurs when the meaning of the message received is as close as possible to the meaning intended.

To extend this idea of communication, we define **effective communication** as the process of sending a message so that the meaning of the message received is as close as possible to the meaning intended. Effective communication is characterized by consistency of meaning. Meaning is the content of the message — the idea that the sender wishes to convey.

Suppose an individual traveling to a distant city for a business meeting has asked her office for a weather forecast in order to know how to dress. She might receive three different messages: (1) the high tomorrow will be only 35 degrees; (2) it will be cold tomorrow; and (3) you won't need a jacket. Most people would understand the meaning of the first statement and would know how to respond in terms of appropriate dress. But the second statement is somewhat less clear because cold is a relative condition and can mean different things to different people. Is a light jacket all right, or is heavier winter gear necessary? The third message is similarly unclear and contains even less information because it doesn't mention the expected weather at all. It is the breakdown in consistency of meaning that differentiates simple communication from effective communication.

Communication and Management

As a starting point for understanding the importance of effective communication in management, imagine trying to fill any of the ten managerial roles discussed in Chapter 1 without communicating (see Figure 1.4).[4] Interpersonal roles require managers to interact with supervisors, subordinates, peers, and others outside the organization. Decisional roles require managers to seek out information for use in making decisions and to communicate those decisions to others. Informational roles are played when managers acquire and disseminate information.

Without communication, organizations could not exist. Mike Walsh, CEO of Union Pacific Railroad, clearly understands the importance of communication as a management tool. After he became chief in 1986, he conducted numerous "town hall meetings" with employees in numerous locations across the country. In these meetings, he explained the state of the industry and company strategy. He also solicited employee ideas and answered questions and concerns. Town hall meetings have continued throughout the years, as have numerous small-group sessions. Walsh's communication skills are undoubtedly only one reason, but company profits, customer satisfaction, and employee morale are all high at Union Pacific.

Communication underlies the main organizational functions of determining strategy, developing structure, and directing behavior. Environmental assessment, formulating and implementing strategy, and decision making all necessitate the effective exchange of information among people. Organizations also rely heavily on communication to address such structural issues as delegation, coordination, control, and operations management and such behavioral issues as reward systems and leadership. Clearly, communication is a pervasive part of virtually all organizational activities.

A Model of Communication

We are now ready to look at an expanded model of the communication process. Figure 20.1 illustrates the eight steps in which communication generally takes place between people. The communication cycle begins when one person (called the *sender*) wants to transmit meaning — a fact, idea, opinion, or other information — to someone else. Let's say that Denise Fabian, a marketing representative at Edsel Copiers, recently landed a new account and wants to tell her boss about it. The content of this message constitutes her meaning, shown as box 1 in Figure 20.1.

The next step is to encode the meaning into a form appropriate to the situation. The encoding might take the form of words, facial expressions, gestures, or even artistic expressions and physical actions. (Indeed, most communication involves a combination of these.) For example, Fabian might say, "I just landed the Whitson account" or "We just got some good news from Whitson" or "I just spoiled Xerox's day." The encoding process is influenced by the content of the message, the familiarity of sender and receiver, and other situational factors.

After the message has been encoded, it is transmitted through the appropriate channel or medium. (The channel by which an encoded message is being transmitted to you at this moment is the printed page.) Common channels or media in organizations include face-to-face communication, memos, letters, reports, and telephone calls. Denise Fabian might write her boss a note, call him on the telephone, or drop by his office to convey the news in person.

In step 4, the person to whom the message is sent (the *receiver*) decodes the transmitted information into meaningful form. As noted earlier, the meaning the receiver understands may be the same as, almost the same as, or quite different from the meaning intended by the sender. On hearing Fabian's phone message, the sales manager at Edsel might think, "This'll mean a big promotion for both of us" or "This is great news for the company" or "She's blowing her own horn too much again."

In many cases, understanding the sender's meaning (step 5) prompts a response by the receiver, and the communication cycle continues when the

Figure 20.1

A Model of the Communication Cycle

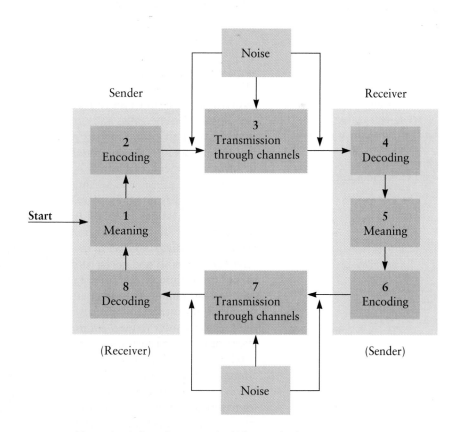

The numbers indicate the sequence in which steps take place.

receiver sends a new message by the same steps back to the original sender (steps 6, 7, and 8). The manager might call the sales representative to offer congratulations, write her a personal note of praise, or send a formal letter of acknowledgment.

As Figure 20.1 also depicts, "noise" may disrupt the communication cycle at any step. **Noise** is any type of disturbance that reduces the clearness of the message being transmitted. Thus it might be something that keeps the receiver from paying close attention, such as someone coughing, a truck driving by, or other people talking close at hand. It can also be a disruption such as a letter being lost in the mail, a telephone line going dead, or one of the participants in a conversation being called away before communication is complete. If the note that Fabian's boss writes gets lost, she might feel that her efforts are unappreciated.

Forms of Interpersonal Communication in Organizations

Managers need to understand several types of communication. Oral and written communication are primarily interpersonal in nature, so we discuss them together here. Various forms of group and organizational communication are addressed in later sections.

Oral Communication

Oral communication takes place in face-to-face conversation, group discussions, telephone calls, and other circumstances in which people use the spoken word to communicate meaning.

Oral communication takes place in face-to-face conversation, group discussions, telephone calls, and other circumstances in which people use the spoken word to communicate meaning. Henry Mintzberg demonstrated the importance of oral communication when he found that the managers in his study spent between 50 and 90 percent of their time talking to people.[5] There are several reasons why oral communication is so prevalent. One primary advantage is that it promotes prompt feedback in the form of verbal questions or agreement, facial expressions, and gestures (we discuss nonverbal communication later in this chapter). Thus managers can present their ideas and get a quick response. Oral communication is also relatively easy (all one needs to do is talk); it can be engaged in with little preparation (though careful preparation is advisable in certain situations); and writing implements or equipment are not required. There is another potential advantage: In one survey, 55 percent of the executives sampled felt that their own written communication skills were fair or poor, so they chose oral communication to avoid embarrassment![6]

However, oral communication has its drawbacks. It can be very inaccurate at transmitting meaning if the speaker chooses the wrong words or leaves out pertinent details, if noise disrupts the process, or if the receiver forgets part or all of the message. A two-way discussion seldom allows time for a thoughtful, considered response or for introducing many new facts. And there is no permanent record of what has been said. After the

People in organizations use different forms of interpersonal communication to exchange information with one another. These teams of Knight-Ridder employees are engaged in group discussions, brainstorming ways to increase customer satisfaction. A possible weakness of oral communication — the lack of a permanent record — is being overcome here by using the blackboard to record ideas and by taking written notes.

invasion of Kuwait by Iraq in August 1990, for example, there were discrepant reports about a conversation between the U.S. ambassador to Iraq and President Saddam Hussein just prior to the invasion. Hussein claimed that the ambassador indicated that the United States would take no action if his army invaded Kuwait, and the ambassador denied making such a statement. However, since there was no written transcript of the meeting, no one can prove what truly transpired.

Written Communication

Written communication relies on notes, letters, memos, reports, and other written formats.

"Putting it in writing" can address many of the problems inherent in oral communication. Nevertheless, and perhaps surprisingly, written communication is not as common as one might imagine, nor is it a mode of communication much respected by managers. One sample of managers indicated that only 13 percent of the mail they received was of immediate use to them.[7] Over 80 percent of the managers who responded to the survey mentioned in the preceding section indicated that the written communication they received was of fair or poor quality.

The biggest single drawback of written communication is that it inhibits feedback and interchange and is usually more difficult and time consuming. When one manager sends another manager a letter, it must usually be written or dictated, typed, mailed, received, routed, opened, and read. If there is a misunderstanding, it may take several days for it to be recognized, let alone rectified, whereas a phone call might settle the whole matter in just a few minutes.

Of course, written communication also has its advantages. It is often quite accurate at transmitting meaning, and it provides a permanent record of communication. The sender can take the time to collect and assimilate the information and can draft and revise it before it is transmitted. The receiver can take the time to read through it carefully and can refer to it repeatedly, as needed. For these reasons, written communication is generally preferable when many details are involved and when it is important to one or both parties to have a written record available as "evidence" of exactly what took place. Julie Regan, founder of Toucan-Do, an importing company based in Honolulu, relies heavily on formal business letters in establishing contacts and buying merchandise from vendors in Southeast Asia. She believes that such letters give her an opportunity to think through what she wants to say, to tailor her message to each individual, and to avoid misunderstandings later.[8]

Which form of interpersonal communication should managers use? The best medium is determined by the situation. Oral communication is often preferred when the message is personal, unusual, and brief. Written communication is usually best when the message is more impersonal, routine, and longer.[9] Managers can also combine media to capitalize on the advantages of each. For example, a quick telephone call to set up a meeting is easy and prompts an immediate response. Following the call up with a reminder note helps ensure that the recipient will remember the meeting and provides a record of the agreed-upon date. Written communication can also be used to formalize the details of unusual messages. As we discuss more fully later, mobile telephones, facsimile machines, and computer networks blur the distinctions between oral and written communication and enhance their effectiveness.

Forms of Group Communication in Organizations

The group communication that occurs in organizations also makes use of oral and written messages. Now, however, communication extends to a number of people within and between groups. As shown in Figure 20.2, groups transmit information by means of communication networks and lateral communication. The members of each group communicate among themselves through networks, and lateral communication links the groups to each other.

Communication Networks

A *communication network* is the pattern of information exchange used by the members of a group.

A **communication network** is the pattern of information exchange used by the members of a group. Researchers studying group dynamics have discovered several typical networks in groups numbering three, four, and five members.[10] Representative types of networks among members of five-member groups are shown in Figure 20.3.

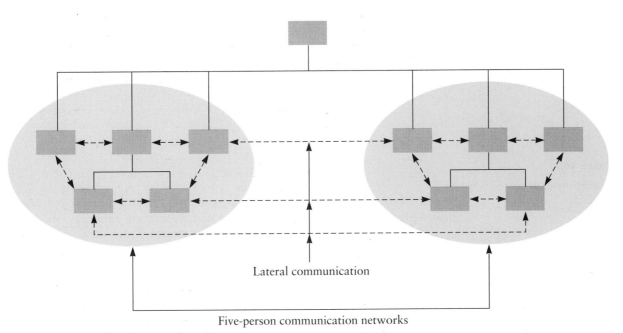

Lateral communication

Five-person communication networks

Figure 20.2

Forms of Group Communication
in Organizations

In the wheel, all communication tends to flow through one central person. This individual is probably the group's formal or informal leader. In a sense this is the most centralized network because one person receives and disseminates all information. The Y is slightly less centralized because two different people communicate with at least two others.

The chain begins to offer a more even flow of information among members, although there are two people (the ones at each end) who interact with only one other person. This communication pathway is completed in the circle network. Finally, the all-channel network allows a free flow of information among all group members. This network is the most decentralized: all members participate equally, and the group's leader, if there is one, is not likely to have excessive power.

Research conducted on networks suggests some interesting connections between the type of network and group performance. For example, when the group's task is relatively simple and routine, the centralized networks tend to perform with greater efficiency and accuracy. The dominant leader facilitates performance by coordinating information flows. When a group of accounting clerks is logging incoming invoices and distributing them for payment, for example, one centralized leader can coordinate tasks efficiently. (If that leader has complete control over the extent of centralization, however, employee satisfaction may suffer.)   When a task is complex and nonroutine, such as making a major decision about organizational strategy, decentralized networks tend to be more effective. Open channels of communication permit more interaction and a more efficient sharing of relevant information. The group should be able to assemble its informational

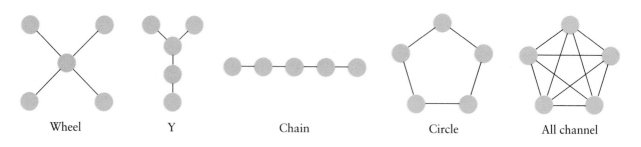

Wheel	Y	Chain	Circle	All channel

Figure 20.3

Typical Types of Communication
Networks

resources effectively and bring to bear a wide array of perspectives. Managers should recognize the effects of communication networks on group and organizational performance and try to structure such networks accordingly.

Lateral Communication

Lateral communication consists of messages transmitted among colleagues and peers at the same levels of an organization.

Lateral communication consists of messages transmitted among colleagues and peers at the same levels of the organization. For example, a production manager might communicate to a marketing manager that inventory levels are running low and that projected delivery dates should be extended by two weeks. Lateral communication probably occurs more among managers than among nonmanagers simply because managerial work is more likely to be interdependent than is the work of operating employees.

Lateral communication serves a number of purposes. First, it facilitates coordination among interdependent units. One Motorola manager who recently was researching the strategies and activities of Japanese semiconductor firms in Europe found a great deal of information relevant to his assignment. He also uncovered some additional information that was potentially important to another department, so he passed it along to a colleague who used it to improve his own operations.[11] Lateral communication can be used for joint problem solving, as when two plant managers at Westinghouse got together to work out a new method to improve productivity. It also plays a major role in matrix designs (as described in Chapter 11 in our discussion of organization structure) and in committees with representatives drawn from several departments (as discussed in Chapter 19).

Forms of Organizational Communication

Although interpersonal and group forms of communication pertain even at the broadest organizational levels, they do not sufficiently describe the paths of all messages transmitted in organizations. As shown in Figure 20.4, individuals can send and receive messages across whole organizational levels and departments by means of vertical communication or the informal communication network. Nonverbal communication is also important and can be a part of interpersonal, group, and organizational communication.

Vertical Communication

Vertical communication flows both up and down the organizational hierarchy.

Vertical communication is communication that flows both up and down the organizational hierarchy, usually along formal reporting lines. This communication typically takes place between managers and their superiors and subordinates. Vertical communication may involve only two people, or it may flow through several different organizational levels.

Upward Communication Upward communication consists of messages moving up the hierarchy from subordinates to superiors. Usually subordinates send messages to a direct superior, who then sends a message to his direct superior, and so on. An occasional message might by-pass a particular superior on its way to the final recipient. The content of upward communication usually includes requests, suggestions, or complaints, information the subordinate thinks is of importance to the superior, responses to requests, and financial information.

Research has shown that upward communication is subject to much distortion because subordinates may withhold or distort information that makes them look bad. The greater the gap in status between superior and subordinate, and the greater the degree of distrust, the more likely the subordinate is to suppress or distort information.[12] For example, when Harold Geneen was CEO of ITT, subordinates routinely withheld problems

Figure 20.4

Organizational Communication

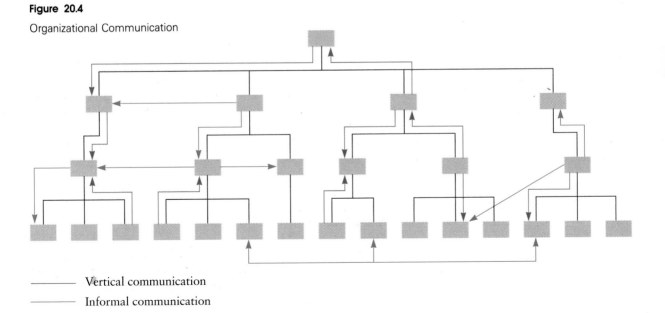

——— Vertical communication

——— Informal communication

from him if they thought the news would make him angry and if they thought they could solve the problem themselves without the necessity of his ever knowing.[13]

Downward Communication   Downward communication consists of messages moving down the hierarchy from superiors to subordinates. The content of downward communication often includes directives, assignments, performance feedback, and information that the superior thinks is of value to the subordinate. We should note, of course, that vertical communication can, and usually should, be two-way. Two-way communication allows managers and their subordinates to exchange feedback and to ensure that they agree on the basic content of their communication exchange.

The Informal Communication Network

The *grapevine* is the informal communication network that exists in most organizations.

Another term for the informal communication network that exists in most organizations is the **grapevine**. Informal networks are found in all organizations except the very smallest, and they often do not coincide with the formal channels of authority represented by vertical communication. Our opening vignette about information leaks at Apple pointed out some of the problems that an informal communication network may create for an organization.

Research has identified several types of informal networks, but the two most common are the gossip chain and the cluster chain.[14] In the gossip chain, one person spreads a message to as many others as possible, who may either keep the information to themselves or pass it on to others. The content of gossip is likely to be personal information. In the cluster chain, one person passes information only to a few selected individuals, some of whom pass it to a few other individuals while the others keep it to themselves. Cluster chains often carry information about the organization itself.

There is some disagreement about the extent to which information carried by the informal network can be accurate. But research is finding it to be fairly accurate, especially when the information is based on fact rather than on idle speculation. Indeed, one recent study found that the grapevine may be between 75 percent and 95 percent accurate in the information it relays.[15] (Of course, the remaining inaccuracies can still be potentially damaging.) That same study also found that informal communication is growing in many organizations for two reasons. One arises from the recent increase in merger, acquisition, and takeover activity. Since this activity can greatly affect the members of an organization, it follows that they may spend more time talking about it. The second reason is that more and more corporations are moving their office facilities from urban centers to surrounding suburbs. As a result employees spend less time outside the organization during the day (for example, since there may be fewer restaurants nearby, people may eat in the company cafeteria more frequently) and may tend to talk more to one another than they would otherwise (since there are fewer external distractions).

Fortunately, managers have some control over the informal network. For example, the grapevine in an organization may be carrying harmful information (e.g., a rumor about impending layoffs that is hurting morale), inaccurate information (e.g., false reports about wage cuts), or politically motivated information (e.g., information that a key manager may be looking for another job when, in fact, the manager has no intention of leaving). When these kinds of rumors are being spread, managers may need to intervene. They can hold open meetings and objectively discuss the issues that are being informally discussed already. Alternatively, they might issue a clearly worded and very specific memo or report that states the facts. Hence, by maintaining open communication channels and responding vigorously to inaccurate information, they can help minimize the damage that the informal network can do. As managers at Apple saw, though, an incorrect response can make matters worse.[16]

Managers can also obtain valuable information from the grapevine and use it to improve decision making. For example, if a manager hears a rumor that a valuable employee is going to leave for a better job, she may be able to dissuade the person from leaving by offering a promotion or higher salary.

Nonverbal Communication

Nonverbal communication is communication that does not use words at all or that uses words to carry more than just literal meaning.

Nonverbal communication is any communication exchange that does not use words at all or that uses words to carry more than just literal meaning. Nonverbal communication can be either intentional or unintentional. It is a powerful but little-understood form of communication in organizations. It often takes the form of facial expressions, body movements, physical contact, and gestures. One study found that as much as 55 percent of the content of a message is transmitted by facial expression and body posture and that another 38 percent derives from inflection and tone of voice. The words account for only 7 percent of the content of the message![17]

Research has identified three important aspects of nonverbal communication practiced by managers: images, settings, and body language.[18] In this context, images are the "pictures" that people paint with words. The expression "Damn the torpedoes, full speed ahead" means essentially the same as "Even though there are some potential hazards, we should proceed with this course of action." Yet the image contained in the first expression may help portray the speaker as a maverick, a courageous hero, an individualist — or a reckless and foolhardy adventurer. The speaker of the second expression, in contrast, might be perceived as forceful, diligent, or resistant to change. In short, our very choice of words conveys much more than literal meaning.

The setting of a message — boundaries, familiarity, home turf — plays a major role in nonverbal communication. Much has been written about symbols of power in organizations. The size and location of an office, the kinds of furniture in it, and the accessibility of its occupant all communicate nonverbal messages. When H. Ross Perot was CEO of Electronic Data

Systems, he positioned his desk so that it was always between him and a visitor. This setup kept him in charge. When he wanted a less formal dialogue, he moved around to the front of the desk and sat beside his visitor. Jim Treybig of Tandem Computers places his desk facing a side window so that when he turns around to greet a visitor there is never anything between them.[19]

Body language consists of the gestures, postures, and facial expressions that may accompany or substitute for speech. It is a powerful form of nonverbal communication.[20] For instance, the distance two people stand apart from each other while talking has meaning. In the United States, standing very close to someone you are speaking to generally signals either familiarity or aggression. In contrast, English and German people tend to stand farther apart than Americans, and Arab, Japanese, and Mexican people stand closer together.[21] (Consider the confusion that can result when individuals unaware of these different conversation customs try to communicate with each other!) Eye contact is another effective means of nonverbal communication, but depending on the situation, prolonged eye contact might suggest either hostility or romantic interest. Other kinds of body language include body and arm movement, pauses in speech, and mode of dress.

Managers should be aware of the importance of nonverbal communication and recognize its potential impact. Giving an employee good news about a reward with the wrong nonverbal cues can destroy the reinforcement value of the reward. Likewise, reprimanding an employee but providing inconsistent nonverbal cues can limit the effectiveness of the sanctions. The tone of the message, where and how it is delivered, facial expressions, and gestures can all amplify or weaken a message or even change its content altogether.

Other Forms of Communication

A few other forms of group and organizational communication warrant mention. One that has become especially popular of late is rather colloquially labeled "management by wandering around."[22] The basic idea is that some managers keep in touch with what's going on by wandering around and talking with people — immediate subordinates, subordinates far down the organizational hierarchy, delivery people, customers, and anyone else involved with the company in some way. Bill Marriott, for example, frequently visits kitchens, loading docks, and custodial work areas whenever he tours a Marriott hotel. He claims that the talks he has with people performing those jobs give him new ideas and a better feel for the entire company.

Another form of communication is the kind of informal interchange that takes place outside the normal work setting among members of an informal or interest group. Employees attending the company picnic, playing on the company softball team, or taking fishing trips together almost always spend

THE ENVIRONMENTAL CHALLENGE

Avon Stoops to Conquer

When is thievery not thievery? When is trash not trash? The answers to these and related questions are of considerable importance to two archrivals in the beauty products industry — Mary Kay Cosmetics and Avon Products.

It all started in 1988 when Mary Kay representatives approached Avon about a possible merger. When Avon said no, Mary Kay launched a hostile takeover attempt. Mary Kay was unsuccessful in the takeover but wound up holding a large block of Avon stock. Avon managers ever since have been concerned about future manuevers by Mary Kay. But some Mary Kay executives have charged that Avon goes too far in its quest for information about their plans.

Some claim that Avon employees have questioned close friends and associates of Mary Kay executives, have spread harmful rumors about Mary Kay products, and have followed Mary Kay employees. Most recently, they have accused Avon of hiring a private detective to sort through Mary Kay's trash bins looking for letters, reports, or memos that might mention the company's plans. Mary Kay has filed a lawsuit to get its garbage back but has so far been unsuccessful. In the meantime, the firm has posted a 24-hour security detail around its trash bins and has resorted to shredding all correspondence before throwing it out.

REFERENCES: "Dumpster Raids? That's Not Very Ladylike, Avon," *Business Week,* April 1, 1991, p. 32; "Avon's Calling," *Barron's,* February 4, 1991, pp. 14–15, 43; "Doesn't Everyone Want to Smell Like Cher?" *Forbes,* April 2, 1990, pp. 142–144; "Avon Is Calling on New Tactics," *Advertising Age,* January 7, 1991, p. 3.

part of their time talking about work. This is the type of communication that plagued Apple Computer.

Engineers at the Texas Instruments facility in Lewisville, Texas, often frequent a local bar in town after work. On any given evening, they talk about the Dallas Cowboys, the company's newest government contract, the weather, their boss, the company's stock price, local politics, and problems at work. There is no set agenda, and the key topics of discussion vary from group to group and from day to day. These gatherings serve an important role. They promote a strong culture and socialize people to the organization's values and practices (see Chapter 19). A controversial use of informal communication is described in The Environmental Challenge.

Managing Organizational Communication

Given the importance and the pervasiveness of communication in organizations, it is vital for managers to understand how best to manage the communication process.[23] Managers should understand how to maximize the potential benefits of communication and minimize the potential problems. We begin our discussion by considering the factors that might disrupt effective communication and then describing how to handle them. We end by noting some special problems in international communication.

Barriers to Communication

Barriers to effective communication may be associated with the sender, with the receiver, with interpersonal dynamics between sender and receiver, and with environmental factors.

Several factors may disrupt the communication process or serve as barriers to effective communication.[24] As shown in Table 20.1, these may be divided into four classes: characteristics of the sender, characteristics of the receiver, interpersonal dynamics occurring between the sender and the receiver, and environmental factors.

Characteristics of the Sender   Three characteristics of the sender may disrupt effective communication. One common problem is conflicting or inconsistent signals. A manager sends conflicting signals when she says on Monday that things should be done one way but then prescribes an entirely different procedure on Wednesday. A manager sends inconsistent signals when he encourages employees to perform at their best but then fails to acknowledge it when they do so.

Credibility problems arise when the sender is not considered a reliable source of information. He may not be trusted or may not be perceived as knowledgeable about the subject at hand. A politician caught withholding information or a manager responsible for a series of bad decisions may lose credibility with others.

Table 20.1

Enhancing Communication Effectiveness in Organizations

Barriers to Effective Communication	Methods for Overcoming the Barriers
Characteristics of the sender • Conflicting or inconsistent signals • Credibility about the subject • Reluctance to communicate	**Techniques for the sender** • Encourage two-way communication • Be aware of language and meaning • Maintain credibility • Be sensitive to the receiver's perspective
Characteristics of the receiver • Poor listening habits • Predispositions about the subject	**Techniques for the receiver** • Develop listening skills • Be sensitive to the sender's perspective
Interpersonal dynamics between sender and receiver • Semantics • Status/power differences • Different perceptions	**Techniques for both sender and receiver** • Follow up • Regulate information flow • Understand the appropriateness and nonverbal character of different channels
Environmental factors • Noise • Overload	

Finally, some people may simply be reluctant to initiate communication. A manager may be reluctant to talk with subordinates about an impending budget cut because she knows they will be unhappy about it. Likewise, a subordinate may be reluctant to communicate with a superior for fear of reprisal or because the effort appears futile.[25]

Characteristics of the Receiver   Two common characteristics of the receiver that impede effective communication are poor listening habits and predispositions about the subject at hand. Poor listeners may daydream, look around, read, or listen to another conversation while being spoken to. Because they are not concentrating on what the sender is saying, they may not comprehend part or all of the message. Sometimes they may think they are paying attention, only to realize later that they cannot remember parts of the conversation.

Receivers who bring certain predispositions to the communication process already have their minds made up and are determined that nothing the sender says will add to or change their perspective. Consider the recent labor problems between Frank Lorenzo, former CEO of Texas Air, and labor leaders at Eastern Air Lines. When Lorenzo bought Eastern, the unions assumed that they were in for a battle because of Lorenzo's previous anti-union activities at Continental. Lorenzo no doubt expected problems with the unions because of their earlier firm stands on various labor issues. Each side approached the bargaining table predisposed to fight the other, and that is precisely what they did.

Interpersonal Dynamics   Communication problems sometimes develop because the individual characteristics of a sender conflict with those of a receiver. Senders and receivers may clash over semantics, differences in status and power, and disparate perceptions of a situation. Semantics becomes a problem when words have different meanings for different people. For example, when a company executive discusses a new program of cutbacks and downsizing with a group of investors, they are likely to accept the message as one aimed at cutting costs and raising profits. But when the executive uses the same words with a group of operating employees, they will focus more on the loss of job security and threat of layoffs and terminations.

People of different status or power also may have difficulty when they try to communicate with each other. A company president who discounts a suggestion from an operating employee may be thinking, "How can someone at that level help me run my business?" Workers may be reluctant to offer suggestions at all because of their lower status. Even two people with the same official status in an organization may experience a power differential that disrupts communication. A marketing vice president who has more power than the human resources vice president may not feel required to attend closely to a staffing report submitted by human resources.

Senders and receivers may also have completely different perceptions of the same situation. For example, two managers may interpret a third manager's absence from a meeting in radically different ways: she is very busy and previous commitments kept her from attending the meeting, or she is avoiding the issues being discussed at the meeting. If they need to discuss her in some official capacity, their different perceptions, one positive and one negative, may distort the communication.

Environmental Factors   Factors such as noise and overload may also disrupt effective communication. A lost memo or misunderstanding created by a poor telephone connection may disrupt communication. Overload occurs when the receiver is sent more information than he can effectively handle. For example, when a manager returns from a vacation or an extended business trip, he will likely have a large stack of letters, memos, notes, and telephone messages waiting on his desk. One might be a note from his boss urgently requesting a meeting at 9:00 on his first morning back. Because of the sheer volume of communication, the manager may not come across the message from his boss until later in the day.

Improving the Effectiveness of Communication

Considering how many factors can disrupt communication, it is fortunate that managers can resort to several techniques for improving communication effectiveness.[26] As also shown in Table 20.1, these techniques may be used by the sender, the receiver, or both.

Techniques for the Sender   The sender should bear in mind four fundamentals that can improve communication effectiveness: feedback, awareness of words, credibility, and sensitivity. Feedback, perhaps the most important of these, is facilitated by two-way communication. The more complicated the message, the more useful two-way communication is, because it allows the receiver to ask questions, request clarification, and express opinions that let the sender know whether she has been understood.

As noted earlier in our discussion of semantics, the sender should be aware of the meanings that different receivers might attach to words. The sender also should try to maintain credibility. The sender can do this by not pretending to be an expert when he is not, by doing his "homework" and checking facts, and by otherwise being as accurate and honest as possible. Finally, the sender should remain sensitive to the receiver's perspective. A manager who must tell a subordinate that she has not been recommended for a promotion should recognize that the subordinate may feel frustrated and unhappy and should choose the content of the message and its method of delivery accordingly. The manager should be ready to accept a reasonably angry response from the subordinate without becoming angry in return.[27]

Techniques for the Receiver   There are two especially good techniques that managers can use to develop their effectiveness as receivers: being a good listener and being sensitive to the sender's perspective. Being a good listener requires that the individual be prepared to listen, not interrupt the speaker, concentrate on both the words and the meaning being conveyed, be patient, and ask questions as appropriate.[28] Good listening skills are so vital that companies such as Delta Air Lines, IBM, and Unisys conduct training programs for their managers on how to be better listeners.

Another technique for the receiver is to be sensitive to the sender's point of view. Suppose an employee tells her boss that her son has just been admitted to a drug rehabilitation center for treatment. The manager should understand that she may be angry or depressed for a while. Thus he might make a special effort to offer his support or to ignore some degree of irritability or preoccupation on her part.

Techniques for Both Sender and Receiver   Three actions for both the sender and the receiver can enhance the effectiveness of communication: following up, regulating the flow of information, and understanding the nonverbal character of different message channels. Following up is simply checking at a later time to be sure that the message has been received and understood. After a manager mails a report to a colleague, she might call a few days later to make sure that it has arrived. If it has, she might ask whether the receiver has any questions about it. (Too much follow-up, of course, can be bothersome.)

Regulating the flow of information is taking steps to ensure that overload does not occur. For the sender, this could mean not passing too much information through the system at one time. For the receiver, this might amount to notifying superiors when the workload becomes unmanageable. Many managers limit the influx of information by periodically weeding out the list of journals and routine reports they receive or asking a secretary to screen phone calls and visitors. A manager leaving on a trip might ask his secretary to sort his mail and messages by priority so that when he returns he will be able to handle the most important things first.

Both parties should also understand the appropriateness and nonverbal character of different channels and media. When a manager must lay off a subordinate temporarily, the message should probably be delivered in person. A face-to-face exchange gives the manager an opportunity to explain the situation and answer questions. (Unfortunately, some managers avoid such meetings just because they are unpleasant.) When the purpose of the message is to grant a pay increase, however, written communication may be appropriate because it can be more objective and precise. The manager could then follow up the written notice with personal congratulations. Nonverbal communication plays a role when the content or form of the message is delivered improperly. For example, when a smiling manager delivers bad news, the receiver may become more angry at the manager's perceived happiness than at the content of the message. Likewise, a formal letter of commendation that contains a misspelled word loses some of its effectiveness.

Using Information Systems to Manage Communication

As discussed more thoroughly in Chapter 13, information systems provide an important method of managing organizational communication. The managerial approach to information systems begins with the creation of a position usually called the chief information officer, or CIO.[29] For example, Burlington Industries created the position of CIO and made the individual hired for it responsible for managing every facet of the organization's information-management needs. The CIO is responsible for developing a keen understanding of the information-processing needs and requirements of the organization and then for installing systems that facilitate smooth and efficient communication.

The operational approach to information systems, which is often a part of the CIO's efforts, forges communication links among all relevant managers, departments, and facilities in the organization. For example, in the absence of such a system, a marketing manager may need to telephone a warehouse manager to find out how much of a particular product is in stock before promising shipping dates to a customer. An effective information system can allow the marketing manager to obtain the information more quickly, and probably more accurately, by plugging directly into a computerized system that provides the necessary information. Whether computerized or not, a properly designed and implemented information system can help any organization manage its communication effectively.

Special Problems in International Communication

As organizations become increasingly global, three special types of communication problems arise. The Global Challenge provides a graphic illustration of these problems.

Time   Time differences complicate communication in a global organization. When a manager in New York needs to talk to a colleague in Los Angeles, there is a three-hour time difference to consider. This time difference may cause inconvenience, but it can be overcome because morning hours in Los Angeles correspond to afternoon hours in New York. For managers in Los Angeles and London, however, time differences are difficult to surmount because at no time will both managers be in their offices during regular business hours.

Distance   Some international communication is done by means of written media or the telephone, but face-to-face meetings are also needed. When a New York–based manager needs to visit the Boston office, when a Houston executive has an appointment in Dallas, or when a manager working in Los Angeles has a business commitment in San Diego, only a few hours of travel time are involved. Even when a manager must visit a site across the country, the distance may require only a single day of travel. But when a manager has to attend meetings in Chicago, Sydney, Singapore, and Amsterdam, the distances involved dictate days of travel. Thus the costs of face-to-face communication in a global organization can be great.

Language and Culture   Other communication problems for the international organization arise from differences in language and culture. Sending

THE GLOBAL CHALLENGE

Ford and Mazda Share the Driver's Seat

Ford Motor Company and Mazda Motor Company recently teamed up in one of the most complex international partnerships ever constructed. In 1983 Ford commissioned Mazda to engineer a new version of Ford's popular compact, the Escort. The idea behind the agreement was that Mazda would design the inside of the car (the engine and other technical systems) and Ford would design the outside of the car. Ford would then use a combination of Japanese and American parts to construct the Escorts at one of its U.S. plants.

The rationale for the deal was that Mazda could provide the technical knowledge that has led Japanese automakers to their strong market positions. But Ford would end up getting much of the credit — and most of the profits from sales of the cars.

One of the biggest problems turned out to be communication between the liaison teams in Detroit and Hiroshima. The head of the U.S. design team had to make over 150 trips to Japan between the inception of the agreement and February 1990, when the first new Escort rolled off the assembly line. The Japanese team was also frustrated over lost time. A common complaint was that Japanese workers couldn't contact their U.S. counterparts to iron out problems because of the time differences between the two countries.

Cultural barriers were another sore point. At first the Japanese managers refused to let Ford representatives into the Mazda design facility because it was restricted to "employees only." After extended deliberations they finally agreed to let the Americans in — but then only in small groups of seven per day.

REFERENCES: "How Ford and Mazda Shared the Driver's Seat," *Business Week,* March 26, 1990, pp. 94–95; "Ford to Emphasize Quality, Not Price, of Its New Escort," *Wall Street Journal,* March 30, 1990, p. B3; "Ford Pulls Out Stops in Launch of New Escort," *Wall Street Journal,* April 26, 1990, pp. B1, B5.

a French manager to run an operation in Brazil, for example, may require the organization to provide extensive language training. But even after the manager has achieved a basic level of language proficiency, it will still be some time before he can effectively communicate with local officials about such detailed information as legal restrictions, tax codes, and labor laws. Some cultures put a premium on punctuality, and others take a more casual approach to time. In Japan it is considered rude to start talking about business before the individuals have become acquainted.

Table 20.2 provides several other examples of language and cultural differences that may lead to significant communication problems for managers engaged in international activities. With increasing numbers of multilingual managers, language problems may become less troubling. Nevertheless, as more and more organizations begin to do business in foreign markets, these and other cultural and social differences will continue to affect communication.

The Technology of Communication

Over the last decades, the nature of managerial and organizational communication has changed dramatically, mainly because of breakthroughs in

Table 20.2

Communication Problems in
Global Organizations

Source of Problem	Example
Language	One firm, trying to find a name for a new soap powder, tested the chosen name in 50 languages. In English, it meant "dainty." In other languages it meant "song" (Gaelic), "aloof" (Flemish), "horse" (African), "hazy or dimwitted" (Persian), and "crazy" (Korean).
	"Coca-Cola" in Chinese became "Bite the head of a dead tadpole."
	Idioms cannot be translated literally: "to murder the King's English" becomes "to speak French like a Spanish cow" in French.
Nonverbal signs	Shaking your head up and down in Greece indicates "no"; swinging it from side to side indicates "yes."
	In most European countries, it is considered impolite to have both hands on the table.
	The American sign for "OK" is an obscenity in Spain.
Colors	Green: Popular in Moslem countries Associated with disease in jungle-covered countries Associated with cosmetics in France, Sweden, Netherlands
	Red: Blasphemous in African countries Signifies wealth and masculinity in Great Britain
Product	Campbell Soup was unsuccessful in Britain until the firm added water to its condensed soup so it would appear to be the same amount of canned soup the British were used to purchasing.
	Long-life packaging, which is used commonly for milk in Europe, allows milk to be stored for months at room temperature if it is unopened. Americans are still wary of it.
	Coca-Cola had to alter the taste of its soft drink in China when the Chinese described it as "tasting like medicine."

SOURCE: Adapted from David A. Ricks, *Big Business Blunders: Mistakes in Multinational Marketing* (Homewood, Ill.: Dow Jones–Irwin, 1983); Nancy Bragganti and Elizabeth Devine, *The Traveler's Guide to European Customs and Manners* (St. Paul, Minn.: Meadowbrook Books, 1984); several *Wall Street Journal* articles.

Technological advances are playing a large part in improving the possibilities of communication. Hewlett-Packard relies heavily on communication systems to help manage its global operations. Shown here are managers communicating with their counterparts in Japan via in-house video teleconferencing facilities.

electronic technology. Electric typewriters and photocopying machines were early breakthroughs that allowed managers to distribute written material to large numbers of people in less time. The use of computers has accelerated communication even more. A manager based in New York can type a letter or memorandum into a computer terminal, press a few keys, and have the memo printed out in San Francisco. Managers can easily retrieve highly detailed information from large computer data banks. Electronic mail and other innovations also make it increasingly easy for people to communicate with one another. The Entrepreneurial Challenge describes how one firm, InterVoice, has profited from the trend toward electronic communications.

The advent of computers in the workplace has revised the meaning of the term "cottage industry," which originally described the small-scale production of goods by families who worked together at home. The new electronic cottage industry is peopled with "telecommuters," who work at home on their computers and transmit their product to the company by means of telephone modems. David L. Hoffman, a partner in a Chicago law firm who lives in Telluride, Colorado, is such a telecommuter. He consults with clients over the phone, sends them reports by modem or by Federal Express, and has calls to his Chicago office electronically routed to Telluride. Recent estimates suggest that as many as 7 million Americans use telephones, computers, and couriers to work outside their conventional offices.[30]

THE ENTREPRENEURIAL CHALLENGE

Big Operators in Phone-Answering Equipment

Hello and welcome to InterVoice Inc. To learn more about the company, press 1. To hear how the company's earnings jumped 233%, to $7 million, on $24.4 million in sales, press 2. To hear how it's riding the crest of a $460 million market that's growing at a 75% annual clip, read on.

Sound familiar? Some people find them infuriating, but those automated voice answering systems are popping up everywhere. InterVoice, with its Robot-Operator system, can hardly keep pace. It's the brainchild of two Dallas telecommunications consultants, Daniel D. Hammond and Michael Tessarowicz, who founded InterVoice in 1984. They were joined by President Allen D. Fleener in 1985. "We have the right product at the right price at the right time," says Hammond, a 38-year-old engineer. Tessarowicz, 46, is a Polish émigré and also an engineer. The two happened to share an office — and a knack for tinkering — in the early 1980s.

Why the mad dash to bounce human operators? Well, consider that a RobotOperator can handle four lines at once for a onetime price of about $20,000,

compared with the $28,000 or so in annual salary for the human variety. One Dallas-based department store figures that it will save $900,000 a year on its 344-line RobotOperator system.

InterVoice's system works with a common IBM Personal System/2 computer, so the company doesn't face the same research and development costs shouldered by rivals with custom-made systems. InterVoice makes the circuit boards that plug into the PCs — a lucrative niche that accounts for its lofty 41% pretax margins last year.

Still, InterVoice will need to stay nimble-footed. Competition is heating up, and there are now 40 companies chasing the market, including mighty AT&T. Even so, InterVoice is sitting atop a $42 million pile of cash from a secondary stock offering last year, and it's on the prowl for acquisitions. And, funny, when Hammond and Tessarowicz run into a phone-answering device, they don't find it irritating at all.

SOURCE: "Big Operators in Phone-Answering Equipment." Reprinted from May 21, 1990, issue of *Business Week* by special permission, copyright © 1990 by McGraw-Hill, Inc.

Cellular telephones and facsimile machines make communication quick and convenient. Many managers use cellular phones to place calls while commuting to and from work. Some even tote them along in a briefcase in order to receive calls while at lunch. Facsimile machines enable people to exchange written messages with almost the speed of oral messages. Thanks to teleconferencing, it is now even possible for managers from several different cities to "meet" over television monitors without ever leaving their offices.[31]

At the same time, though, psychologists are beginning to discover some problems associated with these new advances in communication. For one thing, managers such as David Hoffman, who are seldom in their "real" offices, are more likely to fall behind in their fields and to become victimized by organizational politics. Since they're not around to keep in touch with the organizational grapevine, they miss out on much of the informal communication that goes on. Using electronic communication at the expense of face-to-face meetings and conversations also makes it harder to build a strong organizational culture, develop solid working relationships, and create a mutually supportive atmosphere of trust and cooperation.[32]

Learning Summary

The communication process consists of a sender encoding meaning and transmitting it to one or more receivers who receive the message and decode it into meaning. In two-way communication the process continues as the receiver then sends back a response. Noise can disrupt any part of the cycle. Communication is effective when the meaning of the message to the receiver is the same as the meaning intended by the sender.

Two common forms of interpersonal communication are oral and written. Each form has unique advantages and disadvantages, so managers should carefully consider their pros and cons. Communication networks and lateral communication are the most common forms of group communication. Communication networks are recurring patterns of communication among members of a group. Lateral communication takes place among peers and colleagues at the same level in the organization.

Individuals can send messages across whole organizational levels by means of vertical communication and the informal communication network. Vertical communication between superiors and subordinates may flow up or down the hierarchy, although two-way communication is generally preferable. The informal communication network is often called the grapevine. Nonverbal communication includes facial expressions, body movement, physical contact, gestures, and inflection and tone of voice.

Managing the communication process necessitates recognizing the barriers to effective communication and understanding how to overcome them. It is possible for both sender and receiver to learn and practice effective techniques for improving communication. Organizations also use information systems to manage communication. International communication poses special problems for global organizations.

The technology of communication, represented by computer networks, cellular telephones, facsimile machines, and the like, has had a profound effect on managerial and organizational communication and will continue to do so in the years to come.

Questions and Exercises

Review Questions

1. Describe the communication cycle.
2. What are the relative advantages and disadvantages of written and oral communication?
3. Identify and describe the basic types of communication networks.
4. What is the informal communication network in organizations? How accurate is it?
5. Identify several barriers to effective communication, and then discuss how they can be overcome.

Analysis Questions

1. Have a brief conversation with the person sitting beside you. Then analyze that conversation in terms of the communication cycle pictured in Figure 20.1.
2. Think of recent examples of situations in which you used oral and written communication. Why did you choose one particular medium over the other? Did it offer the advantages and disadvantages discussed in the chapter? Explain.
3. Are you part of a communication network? If so, try to diagram it in the style of one of the networks illustrated in Figure 20.3.
4. Think of several bits of information that you have recently picked up from a grapevine. How accurate or inaccurate was each?
5. If you worked with a colleague who was a poor listener, what might you do to help the other person improve his or her listening skills?

Application Exercises

1. Identify all of the ways in which communication takes place in this class. For example, does your instructor lecture? Does he or she use an overhead projector? What forms of two-way communication are there? Characterize each type of communication in terms of other ways that the same message could be transmitted.
2. Visit a local organization, and interview a manager about the role that communication plays in her or his daily activities. Do your findings agree or disagree with what this chapter suggests?

Chapter Notes

1. "At Apple Computer Proper Office Attire Includes a Muzzle," *Wall Street Journal*, October 6, 1989, pp. A1, A5; "Computer Firm's Chief Faces Slowing Growth, Discord in the Ranks," *Wall Street Journal*, February 15, 1990, pp. A1, A4; "Mind What You Say; They're Listening," *Wall Street Journal*, October 25, 1989, p. B1.
2. John Huey, "The New Power in Black & Decker," *Fortune*, January 2, 1989, pp. 89–94.
3. See Karl E. Weick and Larry D. Browning, "Argument and Narration in Organizational Communication," *Journal of Management*, Summer 1986, pp. 243–259.
4. Henry Mintzberg, *The Nature of Managerial Work* (New York: Harper & Row, 1973).
5. Ibid.
6. "Executives Who Dread Public Speaking Learn to Keep Their Cool in the Spotlight," *Wall Street Journal*, May 4, 1990, pp. B1, B6.
7. Mintzberg, *The Nature of Managerial Work*.
8. Courtland L. Bovee and John V. Thill, *Business Communication Today* (New York: Random House, 1986), p. 147.

9. Robert H. Lengel and Richard L. Daft, "The Selection of Communication Media as an Executive Skill," *The Academy of Management Executive,* August 1988, pp. 225–232.

10. A. Vavelas, "Communication Patterns in Task-oriented Groups," *Journal of the Acoustical Society of America,* Winter 1950, pp. 725–730; Jerry Wofford, Edwin Gerloff, and Robert Cummins, *Organizational Communication* (New York: McGraw-Hill, 1977).

11. Brian Dumaine, "Corporate Spies Snoop to Conquer," *Fortune,* November 7, 1988, pp. 68–76.

12. Michael J. Glauser, "Upward Information Flow in Organizations: Review and Conceptual Analysis," *Human Relations,* August 1984, pp. 613–644.

13. Walter Kiechel III, "Breaking Bad News to the Boss," *Fortune,* April 9, 1990, pp. 111–112.

14. Keith Davis, "Management Communication and the Grapevine," *Harvard Business Review,* September–October 1953, pp. 43–49.

15. "Spread the Word: Gossip Is Good," *Wall Street Journal,* October 4, 1988, p. B1.

16. "Killing a Rumor Before It Kills a Company," *Business Week,* December 24, 1990, p. 23.

17. Albert Mehrabian, *Non-Verbal Communication* (Chicago: Aldine, 1972).

18. Michael B. McCaskey, "The Hidden Messages Managers Send," *Harvard Business Review,* November–December 1979, pp. 135–148.

19. Thomas Moore, "Make-or-Break Time for General Motors," *Fortune,* February 15, 1988, pp. 32–42; Brian O'Reilly, "How Jimmy Treybig Turned Tough," *Fortune,* May 25, 1987, pp. 102–104.

20. David Givens, "What Body Language Can Tell You That Words Cannot," *U.S. News & World Report,* November 19, 1984, p. 100.

21. Edward J. Hall, *The Hidden Dimension* (New York: Doubleday, 1966).

22. See Tom Peters and Nancy Austin, *A Passion for Excellence* (New York: Random House, 1985).

23. See Courtland L. Bovee and John V. Thill, *Business Communication Today,* 2nd ed. (New York: Random House, 1989) for a more detailed discussion of improving communication effectiveness.

24. See Otis W. Baskin and Craig E. Aronoff, *Interpersonal Communication in Organizations* (Glenview, Ill.: Scott, Foresman, 1980).

25. M. P. Rowe and M. Baker, "Are You Hearing Enough Employee Concerns?" *Harvard Business Review,* November–December 1984, pp. 127–133.

26. Joseph Allen and Bennett P. Lientz, *Effective Business Communication* (Santa Monica, Calif.: Goodyear, 1979).

27. See Eric M. Eisenberg and Marsha G. Witten, "Reconsidering Openness in Organizational Communication," *Academy of Management Review,* July 1987, pp. 418–426, for a recent discussion of these and related issues.

28. Walter Kiechel III, "Learn How to Listen," *Fortune,* August 17, 1987, pp. 107–108.

29. John J. Donovan, "Beyond Chief Information Officer to Network Manager," *Harvard Business Review,* September–October 1988, pp. 134–140.

30. "These Top Executives Work Where They Play," *Business Week,* October 27, 1986, pp. 132–134.

31. Robert Johansen and Christine Bullen, "What to Expect from Teleconferencing," *Harvard Business Review,* March–April 1984, pp. 164–174.

32. Walter Kiechel III, "Hold for the Communicaholic Manager," *Fortune,* January 2, 1989, pp. 107–108.

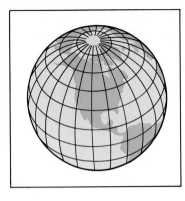

CASE 20.1

The Muppets Meet Mickey but They Don't Talk the Same Language

In late April 1991, almost a year after Jim Henson died of a massive bacterial infection, Walt Disney Company finally obtained the legal right to use Henson's famous characters, the Muppets, in its theme parks and movies. But the agreement — which settled lawsuits that Henson Associates Inc. and Disney had brought against each other — followed two years of poor communication that clouded the deal that Disney CEO Michael Eisner once characterized as "a business association made in family entertainment heaven."*

From the outside, the original deal seemed simple enough. In August 1989, Disney was to pay $150 million, partly in common stock, for Henson's film library and for merchandising rights to some of the Muppets, including Kermit the Frog and Miss Piggy. But at the negotiating table, things were far from simple. The cultures of the two organizations clashed badly. "It was," said one former Henson employee, "like the Grateful Dead going to work for IBM."†

There were also some sticky business issues. One concerned Big Bird and Cookie Monster, Muppets controlled not by Henson but by Chidren's Television Workshop on whose "Sesame Street" program they regularly appear. They weren't part of the deal, but Disney wanted to lower their profile, fearing that the popularity of those two big Muppets might diminish the value of the Muppets that Disney was buying.

As the months of negotiations dragged on, both Disney and Henson Associates carried on as though an agreement had already been reached. Henson's people were busy with a 3-D Muppet movie specially made for Disney World's multi-million-dollar theater. Shortly after Jim Henson's death, Disney World began running *Here Come the Muppets,* a live show featuring Kermit and Miss Piggy. Were they operating under an unofficial "gentleman's" agreement, or were they trying to capitalize on Henson's death and the uncertain state of the negotiations?

With the negotiations still apparently proceeding in good faith, two of Jim Henson's children, Lisa (an executive at Warner Brothers) and Brian, made plans to work for Disney, running the Muppet operation. For the Henson family, one of the complications of Jim's death was that now they wanted the negotiations to lead to a settlement that would reduce the estate-tax burden on the five Henson children. Meanwhile, Disney began producing Miss Piggy T-shirts with a Disney copyright.

Unfortunately, communication problems between the two companies abruptly deteriorated from talking with to swearing at each other. According to the Hensons, Disney had worked out a deal that would suit the Hensons' tax needs and had agreed to close the deal if the Hensons didn't ask for any further changes. As lawyers sweated over the details in a last frantic week, Henson engineers finished their work on the $90 million 3-D movie. Then, on the last day, everything fell apart. As the Hensons see it, Disney president Frank Wells suddenly asked Henson Associates to accept $25 million less than they had been expecting. According to Wells, the Hensons suddenly asked Disney for changes that would have forced Disney to assume $75 million in new liabilities. Wells says that Disney was willing to assume $50 million and that the Hensons refused to cover the remaining $25 million. In any case, negotiations broke off.

In a lawsuit filed April 17, 1991, Henson Associates contended that the ongoing negotiations were fraudulent and that Disney purposely attempted to drain Henson's "creative juices." The Hensons accused the larger company of "extreme arrogance," "corporate greed," and "exploiting" the legacy of the Muppets' founder. They pointed to the irony of Disney, well known for its strict protection of its own copyrights, infringing blatantly on Henson copyrights. Disney labeled the lawsuit "outrageous" and an "enormous distortion of the facts."

The Hensons figured that with a product as well known as the Muppets, they would have no trouble finding another buyer. But they soon discovered that MCA and other potential buyers didn't want to pay money to put a creation like Miss Piggy at Universal Studios when she was already performing for Disney World. In other words, without spending a cent for a Muppet copyright, Disney was both making money off the Muppets and keeping the Henson family from selling the Muppets to anyone else.

Just weeks before *Muppet-Vision 3-D* was to open in Disney World, Henson Associates sued Disney and Disney countersued. Then, finally, the two sides reached an agreement: Disney apologized for its past unauthorized uses of the Muppets and paid an undisclosed licensing fee to use them in the future. With so many conflicting stories and so much secrecy surrounding the conclusion, fans of Kermit, Miss Piggy, Mickey, and Minnie were left with the choice of concluding that one of their favorite all-American companies was full of lying scoundrels or that the whole thing was an example of miscommunication of gigantic proportions.

Discussion Questions

1. What possible sources of miscommunication were there in the Disney-Henson negotiations?
2. Can you think of a situation that was created by poor communication but that others interpreted as being caused by more malicious motives?
3. What could Henson or Disney have done to improve communications?
4. Why do you think the parties that had been unable to reach an agreement after two years of talking managed to come to terms within weeks after lawsuits were filed?

* Quoted in Lisa Gubernick, "Did Mickey Shaft Kermit?" *Forbes*, April 29, 1991, p. 44.
† Quoted ibid.

REFERENCES: Kent Gibbons, "Stage Set for Muppets," *USA Today*, May 1, 1991, p. A1; Lisa Gubernick, "Did Mickey Shaft Kermit?" *Forbes*, April 29, 1991, p. 44; Richard Turner, "Muppets Take Their Revenge Against Disney," *Wall Street Journal*, April 18, 1991, p. B1.

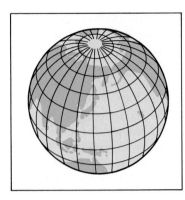

CASE 20.2

Talking It Up at ODS

Employees who like to have a say in their organization's decisions should try to get a job at Japan's ODS Corporation. All ODS employees spend as much as seven hours per week in meetings — team meetings about special projects, section meetings that discuss sales, managers meetings that formulate strategies, weekly meetings in which all employees discuss company rules, and marathon meetings every April and October.

Nothing, it seems, is beyond the scope of these meetings. At the annual three-day salary meeting, when sessions can stretch far into the night, employees get up and argue that they or their co-workers have been rated too low on the latest salary rankings. The company's 250 employees can debate the evaluations in all seven of the job and personality categories, and they can change the ratings. As an American ODS employee puts it, "It's an exhausting process, but it makes you think about yourself, your role in the company, and your relationships with your colleagues."* Employees also decide whom to appoint to the company board of directors.

And the company does make a profit, despite the hundreds of employee-hours it devotes each week to meetings. ODS does research, advertising, and consulting for other companies, designing products and creating logos for giants like Sony Corp. The founder of ODS, Takahiro Yamaguchi, modeled his company after the American ad agency Yankelovich Skelly & White Inc., and his clients consider him Japan's leading market survey specialist. Using Yankelovich's psychographic method of consumer research, Yamaguchi created the Japanese Life Style Indicator, and his clients say his research on young Japanese is especially accurate, perhaps because the average ODS employee is only 28. Besides selling its own research and ideas, ODS brings together Japanese clients and designers from around the world. For instance, Yamaguchi convinced Minolta Camera Company to hire Saul Bass of Los Angeles to create a new youthful corporate image. ODS 1989 sales were up 20 percent over the previous year's figures and were double 1986 sales.

Such success has won ODS respect in Japan even though many of Yamaguchi's ideas, especially about communication, violate the traditions of Japanese business and culture. The Japanese people have long been known for their reliance on nonverbal communication; they are more likely to sense or feel what someone is thinking than to ask a direct question or provide a direct answer. They learn to create *tatemae*, the mask that they show to the world, and in their own minds they make a clear distinction between that mask and *honne*, what they really think. Blunt, direct American business people often fail in their negotiations with their Japanese counterparts because they expect direct verbal responses and haven't learned how to read the nuances of Japanese nonverbal communication.

To most Japanese, therefore, Yamaguchi's approach is decidedly Western and somewhat suspect. Rivals describe him as very pushy and insistent on his point of view. Although Yamaguchi wouldn't deny that his communication style owes much to the non-Japanese, he insists that his goals are to make into a reality ideas that other Japanese companies merely preach. Japanese companies are world-famous for their participatory management and for instilling in workers the sense that what's good for the company is good for the worker. Yet Yamaguchi accuses many Japanese corporate leaders of being isolated from their employees, and he says that many workers are dissatisfied with their work and their lives. Current trends in Japanese life seem to support his criticism: many young Japanese now yearn for a more American lifestyle, and they're no longer content to spend their lives working for one company. One study found that 85 percent of current college graduates will put their families before their companies, and 60 percent don't expect to stay with one company for life.

If workers are truly to identify their own happiness with the company's success, Yamaguchi says, management must be flexible and adaptable, and employees must be "deeply involved with each other." In Yamaguchi's mind, "That demands strong and constant internal communication."† He feels that the interpersonal harmony that Japanese workers are known for can be made real only if conflicts are aired, as they are at ODS.

Of course the constant discussion of ODS isn't for some people: employee turnover is high. But others thrive on the atmosphere, especially women, who aren't normally granted a voice in conservative Japanese companies. At least for some employees, the constant communication enables ODS to live up to one of its teachings: "the company is a place where employees seek true happiness and satisfaction."‡

Discussion Questions

1. What is gained and lost by having employees spend so much time in meetings?
2. Do you agree with Yamaguchi that only "strong and constant internal communication" can lead employees to become deeply involved with each other and identify their happiness with their company's success?
3. Can you imagine American employees debating their own salary increases with their peers? Why or why not?
4. If the Japanese people gradually become more Westernized, do you expect the ODS communication style to become more popular?

* Quoted in Michael Berger, "Now the Japanese Bring Democracy to Salary Reviews," *International Management*, October 1986, p. 58.
† Quoted ibid., p. 59.
‡ Quoted in Yumiko Ono, "Sick of Meetings? Then ODS Is Not the Place for You," *Wall Street Journal*, September 12, 1989, p. A8.

REFERENCES: Michael Berger, "Now the Japanese Bring Democracy to Salary Reviews," *International Management*, October 1986, pp. 58–60; Phyllis Birnbaum, "What Makes Salaryman Run?" *Across the Board*, June 1988, pp. 14–21; Peter D. Miller, "Getting Ready for Japan: What *Not* to Do," *Journal of Business Strategy*, January–February 1991, pp. 32–35; Yumiko Ono, "Sick of Meetings? Then ODS Is Not the Place for You," *Wall Street Journal*, September 12, 1989, p. A8.

21

Conflict and Stress in Organizations

LEARNING OBJECTIVES

After studying this chapter, you should be able to:

1. Characterize the nature of conflict in organizations, and identify a few of its causes.

2. Describe the ways in which organizations may stimulate, control, and resolve conflict.

3. Characterize the nature of stress in organizations.

4. Identify and discuss the causes of stress in organizations.

5. Describe the consequences of stress for individuals and for organizations.

6. Explain some of the methods that individuals and organizations use to manage stress.

Safeway Stores Inc. is one of the largest grocery store chains in the United States. The chain was founded in 1926 by the Magowan family and by the mid-1980s had grown to more than two thousand stores in twenty-nine states and four foreign countries. In an effort to avert a hostile takeover, the firm's top management initiated a leveraged buyout in 1986.

At the time, managers and investors alike praised the move as a model of corporate efficiency. In the years since, however, evidence of the enormous human costs of the buyout has begun to pile up. More than sixty-three thousand employees were laid off or left the company as many individual stores were sold. Although many of these people eventually regained their jobs, most had to make do with lower pay or only part-time hours.

Many employees who were not able to regain employment have paid a high price indeed. One former Safeway truck driver with thirty years' experience with the firm committed suicide on the first anniversary of his dismissal. Another woman with fourteen years' experience died from a heart attack the day she was dismissed. Other former Safeway workers who have still not found new jobs are heavily troubled by a loss of self-esteem. Even those who remained or were rehired live in dread of the next economic downturn or family financial emergency. The company's corporate motto, formerly "Safeway Offers Security," has been changed. The new in-house slogan is "Targeted Returns on Current Investment."[1]

The experience of current and former Safeway employees can be summed up in one word: stress. Induced in this case by major organizational changes, stress can be caused by a variety of factors and can lead to numerous consequences. This chapter explores stress in detail. It also covers another important organizational phenomenon that is closely linked with stress — conflict. Stress is a frequent cause of conflict, and conflict can increase stress.

Below we explore the nature of conflict in organizations and describe how it can be stimulated, controlled, resolved, or eliminated. We then discuss stress and the individual. We examine some of the major organizational and life events that can cause stress, and we look at individual and organizational consequences of stress, including burnout. We conclude with a discussion of the ways in which individuals and organizations can manage stress.

Conflict in organizations can be either useful or destructive. In 1989 American Airlines fired Sherri Cappello from her job as a flight attendant because she was eleven pounds over the weight limit set by the organization. She sued American on the grounds of discrimination and won: the firm agreed to rehire Cappello and relax its weight standards for employees. In this instance, conflict was productive in that it forced the company to reassess a standard that had been in effect since 1959.

Conflict is a disagreement among two or more individuals, groups, or organizations.

Both too little and too much conflict within an organization can be dysfunctional. An optimal level of conflict can be beneficial.

Conflict in Organizations

Conflict has several implications for organizations. In this section we look at how conflict affects overall performance. We also explore the causes of conflict between individuals, between groups, and between an organization and its environment.

The Nature of Conflict

Quite simply, **conflict** is a disagreement among two or more individuals, groups, or organizations. The disagreement may be relatively superficial or very strong. It may be short-lived or exist for months or even years, and it may be work-related or personal. Conflict may manifest itself in a variety of ways. People may compete with one another, glare at one another, exchange angry words, or withdraw. Groups may band together to protect popular members. Organizations may seek legal remedy.

Most people assume that conflict is something to be avoided because it connotes antagonism, hostility, unpleasantness, and dissension. Indeed, managers and management theorists have traditionally viewed conflict as a problem to be avoided.[2] In recent years, however, we have come to recognize that although conflict can be a major problem, certain kinds of conflict may also be beneficial.[3] For example, when two members of a site selection committee disagree over the best location for a new plant, each may be forced to study and defend more thoroughly his or her preferred alternative. As a result of more systematic analysis and discussion on the part of the two members, the committee may make a better decision and be better prepared to justify the decision to others than it would have been if everyone had agreed from the outset and accepted an alternative that was perhaps less well analyzed.

As long as conflict is being handled in a cordial and constructive manner, it is probably serving a useful purpose in the organization. But when working relationships are being disrupted and conflict has reached destructive levels, it has likely become dysfunctional and needs to be addressed. We discuss ways of resolving or eliminating such destructive conflict later in this chapter.

Figure 21.1 depicts the general relationship between conflict and performance for a group or organization. If there is absolutely no conflict in the group or organization, its members may become complacent and apathetic. As a result, group or organizational performance and innovation may begin to suffer. A moderate level of conflict among group or organizational members can spark motivation, creativity, innovation, and initiative and raise performance. Too much conflict can produce such undesirable results as hostility and lack of cooperation, which lower performance. The key for managers is to find and maintain the optimal amount of conflict that fosters performance. Of course, what constitutes optimal conflict varies with both the situation and the people involved.

Figure 21.1

Relationship Between Conflict and Performance

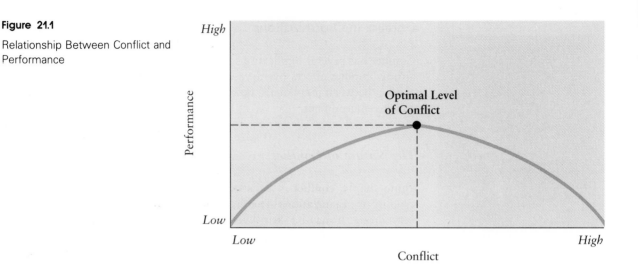

Causes of Conflict

Conflict may arise in both interpersonal and intergroup relationships. Occasionally conflict between individuals and groups may be caused by particular organizational strategies and practices. A third arena for conflict is between an organization and its environment.

Interpersonal Conflict   Conflict between two or more individuals is almost certain to occur in any organization, given the great variety in perceptions, goals, and attitudes among its members. William Gates, founder and CEO of Microsoft, and Kazuhiko Nishi, a former business associate from Japan, ended a long-term business relationship because of interpersonal conflict. Nishi accused Gates of engaging in too much political behavior, and Gates charged that Nishi's actions had become too unpredictable and erratic.[4]

A frequent source of interpersonal conflict in organizations is what many people call a personality clash — two people distrust each other's motives, dislike one another, or for some other reason simply can't get along. Conflict also may arise between people who have different beliefs or perceptions about some aspect of their work or their organization. For example, one manager may want the organization to require that all employees use IBM personal computers to promote standardization. Another manager may believe that a variety of equipment should be allowed in order to recognize individuality. Similarly, a male manager may disagree with his female colleague over whether the organization discriminates against women in promotion decisions.

Conflict also can result from excess competitiveness among individuals. Two people vying for the same job, for example, may resort to political behavior in an effort to gain an advantage. If either competitor sees the other's behavior as inappropriate, accusations are likely to result. Even after the "winner" of the job is determined, such conflict may continue to undermine interpersonal relationships, especially if the reasons given for selecting one candidate are ambiguous or open to alternative explanation.

Intergroup Conflict   Conflict between two or more organizational groups is also quite common. For example, the members of a firm's marketing group may disagree with the production group over product quality and delivery schedules. Two sales groups may disagree over how to meet sales goals, and two groups of managers may have different ideas about how best to allocate organizational resources.

Many intergroup conflicts arise more from organizational causes than from interpersonal causes. In Chapter 10 we described three forms of group interdependence: pooled, sequential, and reciprocal. Just as increased interdependence makes coordination more difficult, it also increases the potential for conflict. Recall that in sequential interdependence, work is passed from one unit to another. Intergroup conflict may arise if the first group turns out too much work (the second group will fall behind), too little work (the second group will not meet its own goals), or work of poor quality.

At a J. C. Penney department store, conflict recently arose between stockroom employees and sales associates. The sales associates claimed that the stockroom employees were slow in delivering merchandise to the sales floor so that it could be priced and shelved. The stockroom employees, in turn, claimed that the sales associates were not giving them enough lead time to get the merchandise delivered and failed to understand that they had additional duties besides carrying merchandise to the sales floor.

Just like people, different departments often have different goals, and these goals may often be incompatible. A marketing goal of maximizing sales, achieved partially by offering many products in a wide variety of sizes, shapes, colors, and models, probably conflicts with a production goal of minimizing costs, achieved partially by long production runs of a few items. Reebok recently confronted this very situation. One group of managers wanted to introduce a new sportswear line as quickly as possible; other managers wanted to expand more deliberately and cautiously. Because the two groups were not able to reconcile their differences effectively, conflict between the two factions led to quality problems and delivery delays that plagued the firm for months.

Competition for scarce resources can also lead to intergroup conflict. Most organizations — especially universities, hospitals, government agencies, and businesses in depressed industries — do not have unlimited resources. In one New England town, for example, the public works department and the library recently battled over funds from a federal construction grant. The Oldsmobile, Pontiac, and Chevrolet divisions of General Motors fought over the rights to manufacture the firm's new futuristic minivan.

Conflict Between Organization and Environment   Conflict that arises between one organization and another is called interorganizational conflict. A moderate amount of interorganizational conflict resulting from business competition is, of course, expected, but sometimes conflict becomes more extreme. For example, the owners of Jordache Enterprises Inc. and Guess?, Inc. have been battling in court for years over ownership of the Guess label, allegations of design theft, and several other issues.[5] H. Ross Perot and his old friends at Electronic Data Systems (EDS) are similarly at odds. After Perot sold EDS to General Motors, he resigned and started a new company to compete with his old firm. When he left GM, he signed a contract agreeing to not compete for a specified time and in specified areas. He contends that his new company lives up to that agreement, but EDS maintains otherwise. The result of their disagreement has been name-calling, lawsuits, and countersuits — with the end nowhere in sight. The strong personalities of the participants play a major role in their battles.[6]

Conflict can also arise between an organization and other elements of its environment. For example, an organization may conflict with a consumer group over claims it makes about its products. McDonald's faced this problem a few years ago when it published nutritional information about its products that omitted details about fat content. A manufacturer might conflict with a government agency such as OSHA. For example, although a firm's management may believe it is in compliance with OSHA regulations, officials from the agency itself may feel that the firm is not in compliance. Or a firm might conflict with a supplier over the quality of raw materials. The firm may claim the supplier is providing inferior materials, while the supplier thinks the materials are adequate. Finally, individual managers may have disagreements with groups of workers. A manager may think her workers are doing poor work and are unmotivated. The workers may believe that they are doing a good job and that the manager is doing a poor job of leading them.

Managing Conflict in Organizations

Managers may stimulate conflict for constructive purposes, control it before it gets out of hand, and resolve it if it does get out of hand.

How do managers cope with all this real or potential conflict? Fortunately, as Table 21.1 shows, there are ways to stimulate conflict for constructive purposes, to control conflict before it gets out of hand, and to resolve it if it does.

Stimulating Conflict

In some situations, an organization may stimulate conflict by placing individual employees or groups in competitive situations. Managers can establish sales contests, incentive plans, bonuses, or other competitive stimuli to spark competition. As long as the ground rules are equitable and all participants perceive the contest as fair, the conflict created by the competition is likely to be constructive because each participant will work hard to win (thereby enhancing some aspect of organizational performance).

Another useful method for stimulating conflict is to bring in one or more outsiders who will shake things up and present a new perspective on

Conflict can be stimulated by bringing in outsiders. Dow Chemical recently decided that it needed outside opinion if it was to be effective in monitoring its waste disposal practices. In several Dow locations, the firm has created panels of local community members to provide oversight review of the firm's operations. Seven participants in one such panel are shown here inspecting Dow's water treatment facility in Louisiana. The company has found that this cooperation is beneficial in creating public acceptance, planning for the future, and creating solutions to problems — as well as protecting the environment.

organizational practices. Outsiders may be new employees, current employees assigned to an existing work group, or consultants or advisers hired on a temporary basis. Of course, this action can also provoke resentment from insiders who feel they were qualified for the position. The Beecham Group, a British company, recently hired an American for its CEO position expressly to change how the company does business.[7] His arrival brought

Table 21.1

Ways of Managing Conflict

Stimulating conflict

- Increase competition among individuals and groups.
- Hire outsiders who will shake things up.
- Change established procedures.

Controlling conflict

- Expand the resource base.
- Enhance coordination of interdependence.
- Set supraordinate goals.
- Match personalities and work habits of employees.

Resolving and eliminating conflict

- Avoid the conflict.
- Convince the conflicting parties to compromise.
- Bring conflicting parties together to confront and negotiate the conflict.

with it new ways of doing things and a new enthusiasm for competitiveness. Unfortunately, some valued employees chose to leave Beecham because they resented some of the changes that were made.

Changing established procedures, especially procedures that have outlived their usefulness, can also stimulate conflict. Such actions cause people to reassess how they perform their jobs and whether they perform them correctly. For example, one university president announced that all vacant staff positions could be filled only after written justification had received his approval. Conflict arose between the president and the department heads, who felt they were having to do more paperwork than was necessary. Most requests were okayed, but because department heads now had to think through their staffing needs, a few unnecessary positions were appropriately eliminated.

Controlling Conflict

One method of controlling conflict is to expand the resource base. Suppose a top manager receives two budget requests for $100,000 each. If she has only $180,000 to distribute, the stage is set for conflict because each group will feel that its proposal is worth funding and will be unhappy if it is not fully funded. If both proposals are indeed worthwhile, it may be possible for the manager to come up with the extra $20,000 from some other source and thereby avoid difficulty.

As noted earlier, pooled, sequential, and reciprocal interdependence can all result in conflict. If managers use an appropriate technique for enhancing coordination, they can reduce the probability that conflict will arise. Techniques for coordination (described in Chapter 10) include making use of the managerial hierarchy, relying on rules and procedures, enlisting liaison persons, forming task forces, and integrating departments. At the J. C. Penney store mentioned earlier, the conflict was addressed by providing salespeople with clearer forms on which to specify the merchandise they needed and in what sequence. If one coordination technique does not have the desired effect, a manager might try another one.

Competing goals can also be a potential source of conflict among individuals and groups. Managers can sometimes focus employee attention on higher-level, or superordinate, goals as a way of eliminating lower-level conflict. When labor unions such as the United Auto Workers make wage concessions to ensure survival of the automobile industry, they are responding to a superordinate goal. Their immediate goal may be higher wages for members, but they realize that without the automobile industry, their members would not even have jobs.

Finally, managers should try to match the personalities and work habits of employees so as to avoid conflict between individuals. For instance, two valuable subordinates, one a chain smoker and the other a vehement antismoker, should probably not be required to work together in an enclosed space. If conflict does arise between incompatible individuals, a manager might seek an equitable transfer for one or both of them to other units.

Resolving and Eliminating Conflict

Despite everyone's best intentions, conflict sometimes flares up. If it is disrupting the workplace, creating too much hostility and tension, or otherwise harming the organization, attempts must be made to resolve it. Some managers who are uncomfortable dealing with conflict choose to avoid it and hope it will go away. Avoidance may be effective in the short run for some kinds of interpersonal disagreements, but it does little to resolve long-run or chronic conflict. Even more inadvisable, though, is "smoothing" — minimizing the conflict and telling everyone that things will "get better." Often the conflict only worsens as people continue to brood over it.

Compromise is striking a middle-range position between two extremes. This approach can work if it is used with care, but in most compromise situations someone wins and someone loses. Budget problems are one of the few areas amenable to compromise because of their objective nature. Assume that additional resources are not available to the manager mentioned earlier. She has $180,000 to divide, and each of two groups claims to need $100,000. If the manager believes that both projects warrant funding, she can allocate $90,000 to each. The fact that the two groups have at least been treated equally may minimize the potential conflict.

The confrontation approach to conflict resolution — also called interpersonal problem solving — consists of bringing the parties together to confront the conflict. The parties discuss the nature of their conflict and attempt to reach an agreement or a solution. Confrontation requires a reasonable degree of maturity on the part of the participants, and the manager must structure the situation carefully. If handled well, this approach can be an effective means of resolving conflict.[8]

Regardless of the approach, organizations and their managers must realize that conflict must be addressed if it is to serve constructive purposes and be prevented from bringing about destructive consequences. Conflict is inevitable in organizations, but its effects can be constrained with proper attention. For example, Union Carbide once sent two hundred of its managers to a three-day workshop on conflict management. The managers engaged in a variety of exercises and discussions to learn with whom they were most likely to come into conflict and how they should try to resolve it. As a result, managers at the firm later reported that hostility and resentment in the organization had been greatly diminished and that people in the firm reported more pleasant working relationships.[9] The Environmental Challenge describes how AT&T and NCR are attempting to manage the conflict created through the former's recent takeover of the latter.

Stress in Organizations

Conflict and stress are closely related behavioral phenomena in organizations. Conflict in the workplace may increase the stress felt by individual employees, and stress caused by personal problems may form the root of

THE ENVIRONMENTAL CHALLENGE

Managing Conflict at AT&T

In late 1990 AT&T announced that it wanted to acquire NCR. The telecommunications giant reached this decision only after careful consideration. In particular, AT&T had tried for years to break into the computer business but had never become a major player. It saw NCR as a natural avenue not only for entering the market but also for achieving synergies in a variety of areas. For example, AT&T thinks that it can add video connections to NCR's automatic teller machines and that the two firms can work well together on many different innovations.

Unfortunately, NCR wanted no part of AT&T. NCR CEO Charles Exley issued several scathing press releases that were highly critical of AT&T's management and its efforts to acquire NCR. NCR employees decorated their offices with anti-AT&T slogans and cartoons. Many NCR managers proclaimed that they would never work for AT&T.

After five months of debate, the two firms finally struck a deal on May 6, 1991. NCR would allow itself to be acquired for a staggering $7.4 billion. In addition, AT&T agreed to give a senior NCR manager a seat on its board of directors. It also promised that if any staff cuts were needed they would come from the ranks of AT&T managers.

On the surface the key players in the battle seemed to have put their differences behind them. At the press conference where the deal was announced, the CEOs of both companies smiled and said they would be able to work together harmoniously. It remains to be seen, however, if the anticipated synergies will come to pass and if other managers in the two firms will be able to work together without new conflicts arising.

REFERENCES: "Can 'Technie Bonding' Overcome Bad Blood?" *Business Week,* May 20, 1991, p. 39; "AT&T Believes Merger to Be Pooling of Interest," *Wall Street Journal,* July 2, 1991, p. A4; "AT&T, NCR Unveil Strategy of Merged Firm," *Wall Street Journal,* June 14, 1991, p. B3.

work-based conflict. The chapter-opening vignette about Safeway illustrates the pervasive effects of stress throughout an organization. Below we examine the nature and types of stress and discuss the ways in which different individuals respond to stress.

The Nature of Stress

Stress is an individual's adaptive response to a stimulus that carries excessive psychological or physical demands. The stimulus that causes this stress is called a *stressor.*

We define **stress** as an individual's adaptive response to a stimulus that carries excessive psychological or physical demands.[10] The stimulus that induces stress is usually called a **stressor.** As noted in the definition, the stressor can be either psychological or physical, and its demands must be excessive *for the individual.* If an individual does not experience the stressor as excessive, then he or she will not experience stress.

The *General Adaptation Syndrome (GAS)* is a cycle of response to stress that includes alarm, resistance, and exhaustion.

Stress generally follows a cycle referred to as the **General Adaptation Syndrome,** or **GAS,**[11] shown in Figure 21.2. According to this view, each of us has a normal level of resistance to stressful events. Some of us can tolerate a great deal of stress; others can handle much less. When an individual first encounters a stressor, the GAS is initiated and the first stage, alarm, is activated. The individual may feel panic, may wonder how to

Figure 21.2

The General Adaptation Syndrome

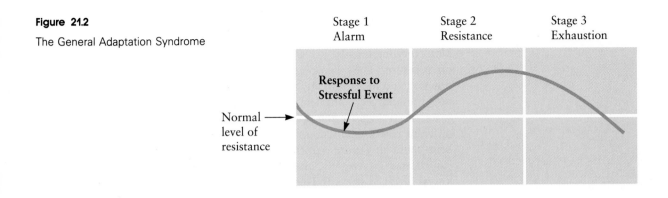

cope, and may feel helpless. For example, suppose a manager is told to prepare a detailed evaluation of a plan by his organization to buy one of its competitors. His first reaction may be, "How will I ever get this done by tomorrow?"

If the stressor is too intense, the individual may feel unable to cope and never really try to respond to its demands. In most cases, however, after a short period of alarm, the individual gathers some strength (physical or emotional) and starts to resist the negative effects of the stressor. For example, the manager with the evaluation to write may calm down, call home to say he's working late, roll up his sleeves, order out for coffee, and get to work. Thus, at stage 2 of the GAS, the person is resisting the effects of the stressor.

In many cases, the resistance phase may end the GAS. If, for example, the manager is able to complete the evaluation earlier than expected, he may drop it in his briefcase, smile to himself, and head home tired but satisfied. On the other hand, prolonged exposure to a stressor without resolution may bring on stage 3 of the GAS—exhaustion. At this stage, the individual literally gives up and can no longer resist the stressor. The manager, for example, might fall asleep at his desk at 3 A.M. and never finish the evaluation. (Long-term consequences of exhaustion are discussed later in this chapter.)

We should note that stress, like conflict, is not all bad.[12] Indeed, the relationship between stress and performance mirrors the relationship between conflict and performance, as illustrated earlier in Figure 21.1. In the absence of stress, we may experience lethargy, indifference, and stagnation. An optimal level of stress can result in motivation, excitement, and innovation. Too much stress, however, can have very negative consequences.

It is also important to understand that stress can be caused by "good" as well as "bad" things. Most people would agree that excessive pressure, unreasonable demands on our time, and bad news can all cause stress. But in similar fashion receiving a bonus and then having to decide what to do with the money can be stressful. So, too, can receiving a promotion, gaining recognition, getting married, and other "good" things.

Stress and the Individual

Not everyone handles stress in the same way. Some people seem to thrive on pressure. They get themselves "pumped up"; their adrenalin starts flowing; and they are ready to charge in. Other people panic at the slightest pressure and go to any lengths to avoid stress.

Research suggests that people from different cultural backgrounds exhibit different responses to stressors. One survey found that managers in Japan, Brazil, and Singapore report higher levels of stress than do managers in the United States, Germany, and Great Britain. Swedish managers reported the lowest levels of stress.[13] These differences are attributable to the differences in the pace of work that exists in different cultures as well as differences in the role of work in those cultures. The Global Challenge describes the stress experienced by Japanese managers who are working in the United States.

Type A and Type B Personality Profiles

Type A and *Type B* are two extreme personality profiles associated with stress-related behaviors.

One separate and important line of thinking about stress and the differences between people focuses on **Type A** and **Type B** personality profiles.[14] The Type A individual is extremely competitive and very devoted to work and has a strong sense of time urgency. Such individuals are likely to be aggressive, impatient, and very work-oriented. They have a lot of drive and want to accomplish as much as possible as quickly as possible. As a result, they may experience considerably more stress than the typical Type B individual.

The Type B individual is less competitive and less devoted to work and has a weaker sense of time urgency. Such individuals are less likely to experience conflict with other people and more likely to have a balanced, relaxed approach to life. They are able to work at a constant pace without a lot of time urgency. A Type B person is not necessarily more or less successful than is a Type A person, but he or she is less likely to experience stress.

Research suggests that few people are purely Type A or Type B. Instead, most people generally have tendencies toward one or the other personality type. An individual might exhibit marked Type A characteristics much of the time but still be able to relax occasionally. Likewise, a person tending toward the Type B profile might occasionally get caught up in a task or become especially conscious of time.

Early research on Type A and B personalities yielded some alarming findings. It was initially argued that Type A's were twice as likely as Type B's to suffer coronary heart disease.[15] In recent years, though, follow-up research by other scientists suggests that the relationship between Type A behavior and the risk of coronary heart disease is not as direct as once thought.[16] Some studies have found a stronger probability of heart disease for Type A people than have other studies. One school of thought suggests that the effects of being a Type A are felt only indirectly. For example, Type A's may experience more hostility and distrust than their Type B

THE GLOBAL CHALLENGE

Stress Among Japanese Expatriates

This could be Tokyo's Ginza nightclub district, but it's really midtown Manhattan. By 10:30 P.M., Club Albatross — a high-tech type of piano bar known as *karaoke* — begins to fill with Japanese men who gladly pay a cover charge that starts at $80. Many stayed late at the office to swap telexes with just-awakening Tokyo offices; now it's time to relax. One by one, customers take the microphone, stiffly rocking from side to side as they sing along with videos of Japanese favorites (including "My Way"). The others drink Chivas and talk with the modern equivalent of B girls. At 11:30 the staff puts a putting cup on the floor for the weekly golf contest. "This is totally Japan," says Naoko, an Albatross barmaid. "They can recognize again that they are Japanese."

As Japan's direct-investment binge in the United States picks up steam, the number of Japanese executives relocating to the United States grows apace. The 200,000 expatriates now working in America are corporate point men in the world's largest market. But even though their jobs have never been more important, companies have never had more trouble getting good people to fill them. The reason is simple: the difficulties "salarymen" — midlevel Japanese executives — face in the Untied States are immense.

At work, they struggle to cope with the soaring yen, which makes the price of Japanese-produced products less competitive. At home they worry that their children's American schooling will keep them out of Japan's top universities — potentially crippling the students' careers. And they often watch their wives suffer a brutally lonely existence. While Americans abroad voice similar concerns, the problems seem especially acute for the Japanese. "Everybody's having more difficulty," says psychiatrist Yukio Ishizuka, based in Rye, N.Y., who treats many Japanese for stress; before therapy some "beg the [company] president to send them home."

Though loath to talk about it publicly, many Japanese executives get quietly frustrated with American underlings. Americans, a Japanese boss often feels, need more supervision than their Japanese counterparts, who try to intuit their superior's desires. The executive is also cut off from the support of the *dokikai* — the fraternity of co-workers who joined the firm when he did. Most are still back home, sticking together, hammering out problems over drinks — and getting promotions.

In the small towns where many Japanese companies build plants, life is different. Managers urge employees and their families to assimilate as much as they can. Masako Takayasu, whose husband, Wako, is an executive of Diamond-Star Motors (a Chrysler-Mitsubishi joint venture based in central Illinois), serves on the board of the Bloomington-Normal Symphony and teaches Japanese cooking. Though the area has a single sushi restaurant and no karaoke bars, the Takayasus prefer the heartland to big cities. Says Wako Takayasu "In New York it's a helluva fight . . . Here it's more simple, straight through to the core of life."

counterparts. It may, therefore, be those characteristics that are actually the problem. If a Type A person can avoid such strong emotional reactions, he or she may not be as likely to experience heart problems.[17]

Causes of Stress in Organizations

Stress is obviously not a simple phenomenon. It can take a variety of forms and affect different people in very different ways. It should come as no surprise, then, that stress may be caused by a wide variety of things.[18] Some of the most common causes of stress are characteristics of organizations, or organizational stressors. Other common causes affect people outside of organizations and are called life stressors.

Organizational Stressors

Organizational stressors are task demands, physical demands, role demands, and interpersonal demands.

Organizational stressors, as shown in Figure 21.3, fall into one of four broad categories: task demands, physical demands, role demands, and interpersonal demands.

Task Demands   Task demands are stressors associated with the specific task or job that the person is performing. Some occupations are inherently more stressful than others. Having to make fast decisions, having to make decisions with less than complete information, or having to make decisions that have relatively serious consequences are some of the things that can make some jobs more stressful than others. The jobs of surgeon, airline pilot, and stock broker are relatively more stressful than are the jobs of general practitioner, airplane baggage loader, and office receptionist. Although a general practitioner clearly makes important decisions, he is also likely to have time to make a considered diagnosis and fully explore a number of different treatments. During surgery, in contrast, the surgeon must make decisions quickly while realizing that the wrong one may endanger her patient's life. Whatever the job, however, work overload also causes an individual to feel stress.

Physical Demands   Physical demands are stressors associated with the job setting. Working outdoors in extremely hot or cold temperatures, or even working in an improperly heated or cooled office, can lead to stress. A poorly designed office, which makes it difficult for people to have privacy or promotes too little social interaction, can result in stress, as can poor

Figure 21.3

Organizational Stressors

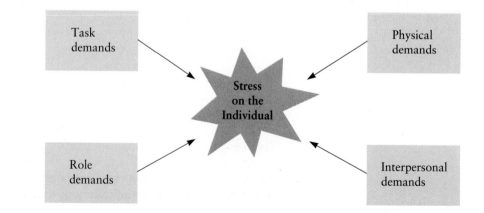

Stress can be caused by a variety of task, physical, role, and interpersonal demands. In response to the danger of infection from the AIDS virus — both to themselves and to their patients — medical professionals are having to adopt new procedures, such as wearing protective outfits designed for use during surgical procedures. Such measures, while increasing safety, may also add to the stress level of doctors and nurses by making the threat to their health more apparent.

Life change — any meaningful change in a person's personal or work situation — can be a significant source of stress.

lighting and inadequate work surfaces.[19] Even more severe are actual threats to health. Such conditions are found in jobs such as coal mining, toxic waste handling, and law enforcement.[20]

Role Demands   As discussed in Chapter 19, a role is a set of expected behaviors associated with a particular position in a group or organization. Stress can result from role ambiguity or from any of the varieties of role conflict that people can experience in groups.[21] For example, a student who is feeling pressure from her boss to work more hours while also having to study for exams and write term papers will almost certainly experience stress. Similarly, a new employee experiencing role ambiguity because of poor orientation and training practices by the organization will also suffer from stress.

Interpersonal Demands   Interpersonal demands are stressors associated with the characteristics of the relationships that confront people in organizations. For example, group pressures regarding restriction of output and norm conformity can lead to stress. Leadership style may also cause stress. An employee who feels a strong need to participate in decision making may feel stress if his boss refuses to allow participation. As noted earlier, individuals with conflicting personalities may experience stress if required to work too closely together. A person with an internal locus of control, who wants to be active in getting tasks finished, might be frustrated when working with someone who prefers to wait and just let things happen in their own time.

Life Stressors

The causes of stress may reside in events that are less connected to people's daily work lives. Some of these may have nothing to do with a person's work at all; others may only be work-related in a general sort of way. One early perspective on life stressors was called **life change** — any meaningful change in a person's personal or work situation.[22] According to this view, major changes in a person's life can lead to stress. For example, when many people finish college, they start their careers, have more responsibilities, usually have more money, and get married. Each of these events represents a significant life change.

Table 21.2 compares the effects of different types of life change, according to one research study. Some of these changes (such as marriage and outstanding personal achievement) are positive; others (such as the death of a spouse and serving a jail term) are negative. The research from which this set of changes is derived suggests that high total point values are likely to lead to health problems. The researchers suggested that a total of 150 "life change units" within a one-year period was associated with a 50 percent chance of major illness the following year.[23] Although this stress scale provides some instructive points, current theory and research portrays the effects of stress on people's lives as being more complex.

Table 21.2

Life Change and Stress

Rank	Life Event	Mean Value
1	Death of spouse	100
2	Divorce	73
3	Marital separation	65
4	Jail term	63
5	Death of close family member	63
6	Personal injury or illness	53
7	Marriage	50
8	Fired at work	47
9	Marital reconciliation	45
10	Retirement	45
11	Change in health of family member	44
12	Pregnancy	40
13	Sex difficulties	39
14	Gain of new family member	39
15	Business readjustment	39
16	Change in financial state	38
17	Death of close friend	37
18	Change to different line of work	36
19	Change in number of arguments with spouse	35
20	Mortgage over $10,000	31
21	Foreclosure of mortgage or loan	30
22	Change in responsibilities at work	29
23	Son or daughter leaving home	29

In addition to the types of change described in the table, other events in our daily lives can lead to stress, such as major historical disasters. During the days following the explosion of the U.S. space shuttle *Challenger* in 1986, many people felt unhappy, anxious, and tense. Similar feelings were experienced by people around the world during the Persian Gulf War in 1991.

Consequences of Stress in Organizations

Stress has consequences for both individuals and organizations.

As noted earlier, the results of positive stress may be increased energy, enthusiasm, and motivation. Of more critical concern, of course, are the consequences of negative stress. As shown in Figure 21.4 and discussed below, stress has consequences for individuals and for organizations.[24]

Table 21.2 (cont.)

Rank	Life Event	Mean Value
24	Trouble with in-laws	29
25	Outstanding personal achievement	28
26	Spouse beginning or stopping work	26
27	Beginning or ending school	26
28	Change in living conditions	25
29	Revision of personal habits	24
30	Trouble with boss	23
31	Change in work hours or conditions	20
32	Change in residence	20
33	Change in schools	20
34	Change in recreation	19
35	Change in church activities	19
36	Change in social activities	18
37	Mortgage or loan less than $10,000	17
38	Change in sleeping habits	16
39	Change in number of family get-togethers	15
40	Change in eating habits	15
41	Vacation	13
42	Christmas	12
43	Minor violations of the law	11

The amount of life stress that a person has experienced in a given period of time, say one year, is measured by the total number of life change units (LCUs). These units result from the addition of the values (shown in the right-hand column) associated with events that the person has experienced during the target time period.

SOURCE: Reprinted with permission from *Journal of Psychosomatic Research*, vol. 11, no. 2, Thomas H. Holmes and Richard H. Rahe. "The Social Adjustment Rating Scale," copyright 1967, Pergamon Press plc.

Individual Consequences

Stress has behavioral, psychological, and medical consequences for individuals. Although the organization may feel the effects of these consequences, the individual pays the real price.

Behavioral Consequences   Stress may lead some people to engage in detrimental or harmful behaviors, such as smoking, alcoholism, overeating, and drug abuse. Other stress-induced behaviors are accident proneness, violence toward self or others, and appetite disorders.

Psychological Consequences   Psychological consequences of stress interfere with an individual's mental health and well-being. These outcomes

Figure 21.4

Consequences of Stress

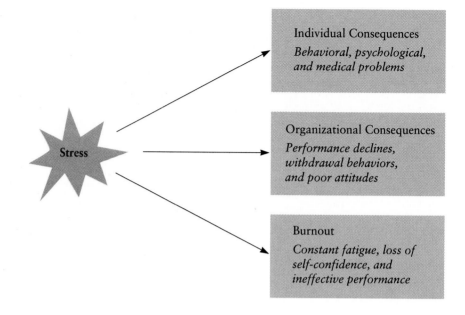

include sleep disturbances, depression, family problems, and sexual dysfunction. Managers are especially prone to sleep disturbances when they experience stress at work.[25]

Medical Consequences   Medical consequences of stress affect an individual's physiological well-being. Heart disease and stroke have been linked statistically to stress, as have headaches, backaches, ulcers and related stomach and intestinal disorders, and skin conditions such as acne and hives.[26]

Organizational Consequences

The stress experienced by individuals has direct consequences for organizations. The three effects discussed below are probably the most immediately noticeable.

Performance Declines   Too much stress can lower employee performance. For an operating employee, this may translate into poor work and decreased productivity. For a manager, it may mean faulty decision making and disruptions in working relationships. It can also mean less effectively run meetings and poor coordination of subordinates.

Withdrawal Behaviors   Withdrawal behaviors such as absenteeism and turnover can also result from stress. People who are having difficulties coping with stress in their jobs are more likely to call in sick or to consider leaving the organization for alternative opportunities. Other more subtle forms of withdrawal may occur. A manager may start missing deadlines, for example, or taking longer lunch breaks. Employees may also withdraw psychologically by developing feelings of indifference.[27]

Poor Attitudes   The irritation displayed by people under great stress can make them difficult to get along with. Job satisfaction, morale, and organizational commitment can all suffer as a result of excessive levels of stress. So, too, can motivation to perform.

Burnout

Burnout, a major consequence of stress, is a general feeling of exhaustion that results from too much pressure and too little satisfaction.

Another consequence of stress that has implications for both people and organizations is burnout. **Burnout** is a general feeling of exhaustion that may develop when an individual simultaneously experiences too much pressure and too few sources of satisfaction.[28] The most likely effects of burnout are constant fatigue and feelings of frustration and helplessness. Increased rigidity of thinking and feeling follows, as does a loss of self-confidence and psychological withdrawal. When this happens, the individual starts dreading going to work in the morning, often puts in longer hours but gets less accomplished than before, and generally exhibits mental and physical exhaustion.

Because of the potentially damaging effects of burnout, some organizations are taking active steps to help prolong its onset or avoid it altogether. For example, British Airways provides all of its employees with training designed to help them recognize the symptoms of burnout and develop strategies for avoiding it.[29]

Managing Stress in Organizations

Given the pervasiveness and potential consequences of stress, it follows that people and organizations should be concerned about how to limit its most damaging effects. Numerous ideas and approaches have been developed to help manage stress. Some are strategies for individuals; others are strategies for organizations.[30]

Individual Approaches to Managing Stress

One way people manage stress is through exercise. People who exercise regularly feel less tension and stress and are more self-confident and more optimistic than those who do not. Their better physical condition also makes them less susceptible to many common illnesses. People who don't exercise regularly tend to feel more stress and are more likely to be depressed.[31] They are also more likely to have heart attacks and to contract other illnesses.

Another method that people can use to manage stress is relaxation. Proper relaxation allows individuals to adapt to, and therefore better deal with, the stress they experience. Relaxation comes in many forms, such as taking regular vacations. A recent study found that people's attitudes toward a variety of workplace characteristics improved significantly following a vacation.[32] People can also learn to relax while on the job. Some experts recommend that people take regular rest breaks during their normal workday. Sitting quietly with eyes closed for ten minutes every afternoon is one popular method and can be quite effective.

The idea behind time management is that many daily pressures can be reduced or eliminated if individuals do a better job of managing time. One approach to time management is to make a list every morning of the things to be done that day. The items on the list are then grouped into three categories: critical activities that must be performed, important activities that should be performed, and optional or trivial things that can be delegated or postponed. The individual then performs the items on the list in their order of importance.

Individuals can use role management to avoid overload, ambiguity, and conflict. For example, an employee who doesn't know what is expected of him (and thus suffers role ambiguity) should ask for clarification from his boss rather than remaining silent and fretting. Another aspect of role management is learning to say no. As harmless as it might sound, a lot of people create problems for themselves by always saying yes to requests for their time. Besides their own regular job, they agree to serve on numerous committees, to volunteer for extra duties, and to accept extra assignments. Sometimes, of course, employees have no choice but to accept an extra obligation, but in many cases saying no is a viable option.[33]

Finally, people manage stress by developing and maintaining support groups. A support group may simply be a group of family members or friends with whom to enjoy leisure time. Going out after work with a couple of co-workers to a basketball game or a movie, for example, can help relieve stress built up during the day. Family and friends can help people cope with stress on an ongoing basis and during times of crisis. For example, an employee who has just learned that she did not get the promotion she has been working toward for months may find it tremendously helpful to have a good friend to lean on, to talk to, or to yell at.[34] People also may make use of formally constituted support groups. Community centers or churches may sponsor support groups for people who have recently gone through a divorce, the death of a loved one, or some other tragedy. A trained group leader helps the members of the group cope with their loss. The Entrepreneurial Challenge describes some small-business owners who have formed a support group for themselves.

Organizational Approaches to Managing Stress

Organizations are also beginning to become involved in helping their employees cope with stress. There are several different arguments for this activity. One is that because the organization is at least partially responsible

THE ENTREPRENEURIAL CHALLENGE

Support Group Helps Entrepreneurs Cope with Stress

Several entrepreneurs in Palo Alto, California, take part in a support group they call Master-Mind. The group was formed by psychologist Richard Borough, who felt that small-business owners needed help in coping with the stress that they encounter as part of their work. He recognized that managers in big companies can talk to each other but many entrepreneurs have no one to go to for relief from work pressures.

Master-Mind meets twice a month. Anywhere from six to ten people attend each meeting. Members pay $225 a month, and in return they attend two 3-hour meetings. They are also entitled to several individual counseling sessions with Borough.

During each meeting, members are encouraged to share any problems they are confronting and their attempts to solve them. The other members listen and offer advice or suggestions. One member, for example, recently complained that she never had any leisure time. After some discussion, the other group members agreed that she was not managing her time properly and suggested that she force herself to stop working every weekend. Another member used the group for support when he divorced his wife, who also happened to be his business partner. Because of this arrangement he had to cope with a breakup of both his family and his business at the same time. Still other members simply appreciate the chance to unload their emotional baggage among sympathetic peers. Borough feels that the Master-Mind concept has been very successful, and he intends to establish similar groups in other parts of the country.

REFERENCES: "Entrepreneurs Cope with Stress in a Self-Help Group," *Wall Street Journal,* April 27, 1989, p. B2; Walter Kiechel III, "12 Reasons for Leaving at Five," *Fortune,* July 16, 1990, pp. 117–118; Walter Kiechel III, "Overscheduled, and Not Loving It," *Fortune,* April 8, 1991, pp. 105–107.

for creating the stress, it should help relieve it. Another is that stress-related insurance claims by employees can cost the organization considerable sums of money. Still another is that workers experiencing lower levels of detrimental stress will be able to function more effectively. AT&T has initiated a series of seminars and workshops to help its employees cope with the stress they face in their jobs. The firm was prompted to develop these seminars for all three of the reasons noted above. Although no formal evaluation was done, people who attended the seminars found them to be useful.[35]

Institutional Programs   Institutional efforts to manage stress are based on established organizational mechanisms.[36] Poorly designed jobs and work schedules, and shiftwork in particular, often cause stress for individuals. People who work on rotating shifts have to continually adjust their personal life to fit with their work schedule and may suffer from sleeping disorders and feel alienated from their family. Thus one possibility is for organizations to change the design of especially stressful jobs, to rearrange work schedules, and to eliminate rotating shifts.[37]

Organizational culture itself can help manage stress. Some organizations convey strong norms against taking time off or going on vacation. Because such practices can be a major source of employee stress, organizations should strive instead to foster a culture that reinforces a healthy mix of work and nonwork activities. In addition, supervisors should be aware of the part they play in raising employee stress levels and try to limit these effects by better managing work assignments.

Wellness Programs   A wellness program is a special part of the organization specifically created to help deal with stress. Organizations have adopted stress management programs, health promotion programs, and other kinds of programs for this purpose. The AT&T seminar program noted earlier is similar to this idea, but true wellness programs are ongoing activities that have a number of different components. These components commonly include exercise-related activities as well as classroom instruction programs dealing with smoking cessation, weight reduction, and general stress management.

More and more companies are developing their own programs or using existing programs of this type.[38] Johns-Manville, for example, has a gym at its corporate headquarters. Other firms negotiate discounted health club membership rates with local establishments. For the instructional part of the program the organization can either sponsor its own training or perhaps jointly sponsor seminars with a local YMCA, civic organization, or church. Organization-based fitness programs facilitate employee exercise, a very positive consideration, but such programs are also quite costly. Still, more and more companies are developing fitness programs for employees.[39]

Organizations also help address employee stress through career development programs such as the one offered by General Electric. GE managers are given detailed information on career options available to them and instructions on how to keep track of their own career progress. As a supplement to regular performance evaluations, this program helps managers maintain a clear understanding of where they are in their career relative to where they would like to be. Other programs used by organizations promote everything from humor to massage as an antidote for stress.[40] Little or no research supports the claims made by many advocates of these programs, so managers must be careful to balance costs and benefits when developing any form of stress management program.

Learning Summary

Conflict is a disagreement between two or more people, groups, or organizations. Too little or too much conflict may hurt performance, but an optimal level of conflict may improve performance. Interpersonal and intergroup conflict in organizations may be caused by personality differences or by particular organizational strategies and practices. Organizations may conflict with one another and with various elements of the environment. Three methods of managing conflict are to stimulate it, control it, or resolve and eliminate it.

Stress is an individual's adaptive response to a stimulus that carries excessive psychological or physical demands. Like conflict, stress can be either positive or negative. Individuals respond to stress in different ways.

The General Adaptation Syndrome describes one normal pattern of stress-related behavior. Type A and Type B personality profiles also represent contrasting behavioral responses to stress.

Organizational stressors arise from task demands, physical demands, role demands, and interpersonal demands. Life stressors may arise from any meaningful changes in an individual's personal or work situation. Stress has consequences for individuals and for organizations. One consequence is burnout, which is a general feeling of exhaustion that may develop when an individual simultaneously experiences too much pressure and too few sources of satisfaction. There are a variety of individual and organizational approaches to managing stress.

Questions and Exercises

Review Questions

1. What are some of the causes of conflict?
2. Identify and describe ways that conflict can be stimulated, controlled, resolved, and eliminated.
3. What is stress? How does it affect an individual?
4. Identify the most common organizational and life stressors.
5. What are some individual consequences of stress? What are some organizational consequences?
6. What can people do to help manage their own stress?

Analysis Questions

1. Given that conflict and stress can each be either beneficial or harmful, what cues might a manager look for to determine whether each is present at an optimal level?
2. Think of recent situations in which you experienced conflict. What caused the conflict? Was it beneficial or harmful? How was it resolved?
3. Are you more of a Type A or a Type B person?
4. Think of things that cause stress for you. Are they rooted in organizational causes or associated more with your personal life?
5. How do you cope with stress?
6. Assume you are a manager with a subordinate who is obviously suffering from excessive stress. He or she denies the problem, however, and does not seem to want your help or concern. What should you do?

Application Exercises

1. Interview an employee or manager of a local organization. Ask about a recent situation that involved conflict. Find out what caused the conflict and how it was resolved.

2. During the next few years you will be going through major changes in your life — finishing school, starting or changing your career, moving, making new friends, and so forth. Given that you now know that all these changes can produce stress, how might you go about managing your life to minimize stress's potentially damaging effects?

Chapter Notes

1. "Safeway LBO Yields Vast Profits but Exacts a Heavy Human Toll," *Wall Street Journal,* May 16, 1990, pp. A1, A10; "Supermarket Darwinism: The Survival of the Fittest," *Business Week,* July 9, 1990, p. 42; "Stress: The Test Americans Are Failing," *Business Week,* April 18, 1988, pp. 74–76.
2. Clayton P. Alderfer, "An Intergroup Perspective on Group Dynamics," in *Handbook of Organizational Behavior,* ed. Jay W. Lorsch (Englewood Cliffs, N.J.: Prentice-Hall, 1987), pp. 190–222. See also Eugene Owens and E. Leroy Plumlee, "Intraorganizational Competition and Interorganizational Conflict: More Than a Matter of Semantics," *Business Review,* Winter 1988, pp. 28–32.
3. Catherine Alter, "An Exploratory Study of Conflict and Coordination in Interorganizational Service Delivery Systems," *Academy of Management Journal,* September 1990, pp. 478–502.
4. "How 2 Computer Nuts Transformed Industry Before Messy Breakup," *Wall Street Journal,* August 27, 1986, pp. 1, 10.
5. "A 'Blood War' in the Jeans Trade," *Business Week,* November 13, 1989, pp. 74–81.
6. "Perot War with EDS Pits Former Friends in High-Stakes Affair," *Wall Street Journal,* October 6, 1988, pp. A1, A12.
7. Joann S. Lublin, "Beecham's Chief Imports His American Ways," *Wall Street Journal,* October 27, 1988, p. B9.
8. "Battling Executives Seek out Therapists," *Wall Street Journal,* November 7, 1988, p. B1.
9. "Teaching How to Cope with Workplace Conflicts," *Business Week,* February 18, 1980, pp. 136, 139.
10. James L. Gibson, John M. Ivancevich, and James H. Donnelly, Jr., *Organizations — Behavior, Structure, Processes,* 6th ed. (Plano, Tex.: BPI, 1988), p. 230.
11. Hans Selye, *The Stress of Life* (New York: McGraw-Hill, 1976).
12. Ibid.
13. "U.S. Executives Less Stressed Than Those of Other Nations," *Chicago Tribune,* March 31, 1988, p. B1.
14. M. Friedman and R. H. Rosenman, *Type A Behavior and Your Heart* (New York: Knopf, 1974).
15. Ibid.
16. Joshua Fischman, "Type A on Trial," *Psychology Today,* February 1987, pp. 42–50.
17. "Hostility, Distrust May Put Type A's at Coronary Risk," *Wall Street Journal,* January 17, 1989, p. B1.
18. Selye, *The Stress of Life.* See also Stephan J. Motowidlo, John S. Packard, and Michael R. Manning, "Occupational Stress: Its Causes and Consequences for Job Performance," *Journal of Applied Psychology,* August 1986, pp. 618–629,

and James C. Quick and Jonathan D. Quick, *Organizational Stress and Preventive Management* (New York: McGraw-Hill, 1984).

19. Robert I. Sutton and Anat Rafaeli, "Characteristics of Work Stations as Potential Occupational Stressors," *Academy of Management Journal,* June 1987, pp. 260–276.

20. John M. Jermier, Jeannie Gaines, and Nancy J. McIntosh, "Reactions to Physically Dangerous Work: A Conceptual and Empirical Analysis," *Journal of Organizational Behavior,* January 1989, pp. 15–33.

21. John Schaubroeck, John L. Cotton, and Kenneth R. Jennings, "Antecedents and Consequences of Role Stress: A Covariance Structure Analysis," *Journal of Organizational Behavior,* January 1989, pp. 35–58.

22. T. H. Holmes and R. H. Rahe, "Social Readjustment Rating Scale," *Journal of Psychosomatic Research,* August 1967, pp. 213–218.

23. Ibid.

24. Quick and Quick, *Organizational Stress and Preventive Management.* See also John M. Ivancevich and Michael T. Matteson, *Stress and Work: A Managerial Perspective* (Glenview, Ill.: Scott, Foresman, 1980); and Paul E. Spector, Daniel J. Dwyer, and Steve M. Jex, "Relation of Job Stressors to Affective, Health, and Performance Outcomes: A Comparison of Multiple Data Sources," *Journal of Applied Psychology,* February 1988, pp. 11–19.

25. Walter Kiechel III, "The Executive Insomniac," *Fortune,* October 8, 1990, pp. 183–184.

26. Quick and Quick, *Organizational Stress and Preventive Management.* See also Brian D. Steffy and John W. Jones, "Workplace Stress and Indicators of Coronary-Disease Risk," *Academy of Management Journal,* September 1988, pp. 686–698.

27. Quick and Quick, *Organizational Stress and Preventive Management.*

28. Leonard Moss, *Management Stress* (Reading, Mass.: Addison-Wesley, 1981).

29. Thomas A. Stewart, "Do You Push Your People Too Hard?" *Fortune,* October 22, 1990, pp. 124–128.

30. Quick and Quick, *Organizational Stress and Preventive Management.*

31. C. Folkins, "Effects of Physical Training on Mood," *Journal of Clinical Psychology,* April 1976, pp. 385–390.

32. John W. Lounsbury and Linda L. Hoopes, "A Vacation from Work: Changes in Work and Nonwork Outcomes," *Journal of Applied Psychology,* May 1986, pp. 392–401.

33. "Eight Ways to Help You Reduce the Stress in Your Life," *Business Week Careers,* November 1986, p. 78.

34. Daniel C. Ganster, Marcelline R. Fusilier, and Bronston T. Mayes, "Role of Social Support in the Experiences of Stress at Work," *Journal of Applied Psychology,* February 1986, pp. 102–110.

35. Quick and Quick, *Organizational Stress and Preventive Management.*

36. Randall S. Schuler and Susan E. Jackson, "Managing Stress Through PHRM Practices: An Uncertainty Interpretation," in *Research in Personnel and Human Resources Management,* vol. 4, ed. K. Rowland and G. Ferris (Greenwich, Conn.: JAI Press, 1986), pp. 183–224.

37. Quick and Quick, *Organizational Stress and Preventive Management.*

38. Ibid.

39. Richard A. Wolfe, David O. Ulrich, and Donald F. Parker, "Employee Health Management Programs: Review, Critique, and Research Agenda," *Journal of Management,* Winter 1987, pp. 603–615.

40. "A Cure for Stress?" *Newsweek,* October 12, 1987, pp. 64–65.

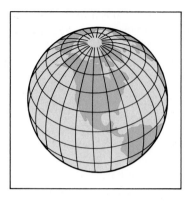

CASE 21.1

Family Conflict and Stress Reduction at U-Haul

To most Americans, the name U-Haul is as familiar and seems as generic as Xerox and Kleenex. Since 1945, U-Haul has dominated the self-moving business, renting trucks and trailers to people who have the great American urge to move on. The company is huge now — worth $1 billion, by some estimates — and rents everything from Roto-Rooters to recreational vehicles. But recently U-Haul has been making news not for its business innovations but for the conflict among members of its controlling family and for a controversial program to try to change how its employees handle stress.

Founder Leonard S. Shoen started U-Haul in 1945 with a good idea, very little capital, and a lot of 16-hour days. The company grew because Shoen persuaded thousands of gas stations around the country to act as U-Haul agents. When full-service gas stations began to disappear as a result of the oil crisis of the mid-1970s, U-Haul had to buy its own dealerships and began to diversify into renting almost anything. But diversification didn't work, and soon U-Haul began falling apart from the inside as a result of Shoen family battles.

Leonard Shoen had twelve children with three of his four wives, and all twelve worked for U-Haul. Trouble started in 1958, when Shoen remarried after his first wife's death. The two of Shoen's sons who were living at home at the time, Mark and Joe, hated the new Mrs. Shoen; police were actually called to the house in Phoenix after Mark punched his stepmother. Despite these signs that family loyalty was already strained, Leonard went through with his plan to give almost all of his stock in U-Haul's parent company, Amerco, to his children.

The Shoen children gradually rose to the top of U-Haul's executive ranks, and in the late 1970s four sons quit, tired of their father's control. Then as U-Haul's financial situation worsened, Shoen fired seven of his children from Amerco's board and hired nonfamily vice presidents. But the elder Shoen seemed to have forgotten that he had given his children more than 90 percent of the company stock, and a year later the children ousted their father from his own company, leaving two of the oldest brothers, Sam and Joe, in charge.

The problems might have ended there if the brothers could have agreed on a strategy. But chairman Joe wanted to refocus on the moving business, and president Sam wanted to keep a hand in other kinds of rentals. Sam quit in 1987 and eventually formed a dissident group of family members — including Leonard. The dissidents thought they could wrest control of the company until they discovered that Joe and the company board had secretly issued more shares of stock, diluting the ownership rights of the dissidents.

Under Joe's leadership, the company has become profitable again, but the dissidents say they have a right to their fortune and want to get some of their money out of the company. Unfortunately for them, U-Haul shares are not publicly traded. Only the company itself can buy them, and it can set the price. When a family meeting turned into a fight in 1989, Leonard lamented, "I've created a monster."*

Perhaps if Sam and Joe Shoen had been hired by some other large company to work together, they would have had no problems. But sibling rivalry can be a powerful and deeply ingrained source of conflict. No doubt Leonard envisioned his children carrying on his mission in harmony, all enjoying the fruits of their collective labors. If so, he seems to have ignored human nature and the certainty that a sibling struggle for power would lead to corporate conflict.

With its history of conflict-related stress at the highest levels, it seems ironic that U-Haul has been making headlines recently for its battle to change the ways its workers cope with stress. In 1990, it announced that it would begin deducting $5 from the biweekly paychecks of any employee who smokes or is seriously overweight or underweight. The company said it wanted to reduce its own bloated $17 million annual health insurance bill and was quick to point out that its insurance plan would cover weight-loss and smoking-cessation programs for employees. When executive vice president Harry DeShong made the announcement, he may have been more aware of the ironies than anyone else. DeShong was a key recipient of stock when Joe Shoen made the play for company control that resulted in a fistful of lawsuits. And he's also a pack-a-day smoker. According to one source, DeShong "hopes to stop smoking soon."† But the Shoens may have to make peace with each other before he'll feel calm enough to succeed.

Discussion Questions

1. Judging from U-Haul's experience and from your knowledge of other family-run businesses, do you think that a family empire is doomed to failure?
2. What kinds of conflict endured by the Shoens are unique to family-run businesses?
3. How do you think the Shoen family conflict affected U-Haul employees?
4. Do you think it's fair of U-Haul to penalize workers for smoking or being overweight?

* Quoted in Susan Skorupa, "U-Haul Founder's Children Slug It Out at Meeting," *USA Today,* March 7, 1989, p. 3B.
† Rhonda L. Rundle, "U-Haul Puts High Price on Vices of Its Workers," *Wall Street Journal,* February 14, 1990, p. B1.

REFERENCES: Jan Par, "King Lear," *Forbes,* February 23, 1987, p. 84; David Pauly, "U-Haul Hits the Skids," *Newsweek,* September 14, 1987, pp. 54–55; Rhonda L. Rundle, "U-Haul Puts High Price on Vices of Its Workers," *Wall Street Journal,* February 14, 1990, pp. B1, B5; Susan Skorupa, "U-Haul Founder's Children Slug It Out at Meeting," *USA Today,* March 7, 1989, p. 3B; Robert Tomsho, "U-Haul's Patriarch Now Battles Offspring in Bitterest of Feuds," *Wall Street Journal,* July 16, 1990, pp. A1, A8; Stewart Toy, "A New Generation Takes the Wheel at U-Haul," *Business Week,* March 28, 1988, p. 57; Stewart Toy, "The Family That Hauls Together Brawls Together," *Business Week,* August 29, 1988, pp. 64–66.

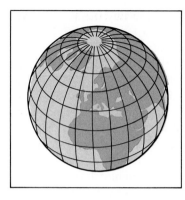

CASE 21.2

Grand Met's Troubled American Subsidiaries

Great Britain's Grand Metropolitan company supplies the world with more alcoholic beverages than any other company and is one of the world's leading food processors. It built a reputation for being an overly diversified conglomerate; but when Allen Sheppard took over in 1987, he set out to concentrate on Grand Met's three major businesses: alcoholic beverages, food, and restaurants. In his first two years at the helm, Sheppard sold off more than $4 billion of subsidiaries and spent about $8 billion buying other companies in Grand Met's key areas. The largest of those purchases was Pillsbury, the American food giant and owner of Burger King fast-food restaurants. Sheppard is known for being a tough boss who thrives on conflict, but in acquiring Pillsbury and Burger King, he may have gotten more than he bargained for.

To the public, Pillsbury is a familiar friendly giant, maker of those "ho-ho-ho" vegetables from Green Giant and symbolized by the Pillsbury Doughboy, a squishy little man with a childish laugh. But behind this warm and friendly front, Pillsbury has been managed for the last two decades by a succession of men who have left it with a sense of distrust and political intrigue that may haunt it for years.

From 1973 to 1985, the company was run by William H. Spoor, a man known for both his success and his temper. The former director of Pillsbury's investor relations remembers hiding under his desk one day to avoid an angry Spoor who was stomping toward his office, fuming about the poor price of Pillsbury stock. Spoor's hand-picked successor, John M. Stafford, lasted only three years, a time when Pillsbury's sales, earnings, and market share all declined. The tone for Stafford's tenure was set early, during a meeting on the fate of Pillsbury's J. J. Muggs chain. Insiders had been assured that Stafford supported the chain, but after Spoor, by then a director, attacked the chain and called for its closing, Stafford switched sides and joined the attack.

Thereafter, many at Pillsbury viewed Stafford as both weak and untrustworthy, and all sense of top management working as a team vanished. Pillsbury's top people spent much of their time and energy trading political gossip and jockeying for Stafford's position. The future briefly looked better when Pillsbury replaced Stafford with Philip L. Smith, a man with both vision and a winning personality, but he had no chance to turn the company around, for it was almost immediately bought by Grand Met. With a management style that he once described as "a light grip on the throat,"* Allen Sheppard did not look like the man to bring peace to Pillsbury.

The conflicts were somewhat different at Burger King. To run the company, Sheppard chose Barry J. Gibbons, who had helped Grand Met's restaurant operations double their profits in two years. Gibbons promised to improve product consistency, and he set out to focus Burger King on relations with customers and on cleanliness.

But his problems, and the unhappiness at Burger King, originated not with the executives but with the franchisees, who own their own stores.

They felt neglected by Pillsbury and called for the new boss to improve Burger King's image.

Franchisees were particularly incensed about Burger King's national ads. From 1976 to 1990, Burger King went through eight major national ad campaigns created by four different agencies. Some of them, like 1986's "Herb the Nerd" campaign, were spectacular flops; others, like "This Is a Burger King Town," were simply forgettable. But any hope the frustrated franchisees may have had that the Grand Met takeover would mean fresh, successful campaigns faded when Grand Met's Gary L. Langstaff unveiled his first major promotion, "Sometimes You've Gotta Break the Rules." Franchisees complained that neither they nor their customers understood the concept. Some wondered, "Are we telling our kids to go out and buy drugs?"† Langstaff defended the ads by saying that the slogan was a remake of the successful mid-1970s "Have It Your Way" campaign, which differentiated Burger King from archrival McDonald's. But unhappy critics felt the slogan didn't really separate Burger King from McDonald's and lacked the punch and clarity of the original slogan.

The problems that Allen Sheppard and Grand Met face in dealing with their two new American subsidiaries highlight the difficulties of running huge conglomerates. Both Pillsbury and Burger King are plagued by internal conflict that calls for management intervention, but it seems quite possible that the interventions that the two companies need are very different. The big question for Grand Met now is, Can one management team solve two such different kinds of conflict?

Discussion Questions

1. What do you think would help to resolve the conflicts at Pillsbury? At Burger King?
2. What issues are involved in the conflict between franchisees and a national company?
3. Would you expect that a manager like Allen Sheppard, who has a reputation for making smart deals and for trimming the fat, would be able to resolve the kinds of conflicts found at Pillsbury and Burger King?
4. Does Grand Met's status as a "foreign" company make it easier or harder for its managers to solve the problems of American subsidiaries?

* Quoted in Richard I. Kirkland, Jr., "Grand Met's Recipe for Pillsbury," *Fortune*, March 13, 1989, p. 61.
† Quoted in Mark Landler, "Tempers Are Sizzling over Burger King's New Ads," *Business Week*, February 12, 1990, p. 33.

REFERENCES: Harris Collingwood, "Grand Met Shakes Up Pillsbury," *Business Week*, March 20, 1989, p. 46; Richard Gibson and Robert Johnson, "Why Pillsbury's Chief from the '70s Is Again Taking Firm's Helm," *Wall Street Journal*, March 1, 1988, pp. 1, 21; Richard I. Kirkland, Jr., "Grand Met's Recipe for Pillsbury," *Fortune*, March 13, 1989, pp. 61–68; Mark Landler, "Tempers Are Sizzling over Burger King's New Ads," *Business Week*, February 12, 1990, p. 33; Russell Mitchell, "The Gods Must Be Angry at Pillsbury's Phil Smith," *Business Week*, November 14, 1988, pp. 61–62; "Trying to Get Burger King Out of the Flames," *Business Week*, January 30, 1989, pp. 29–30.

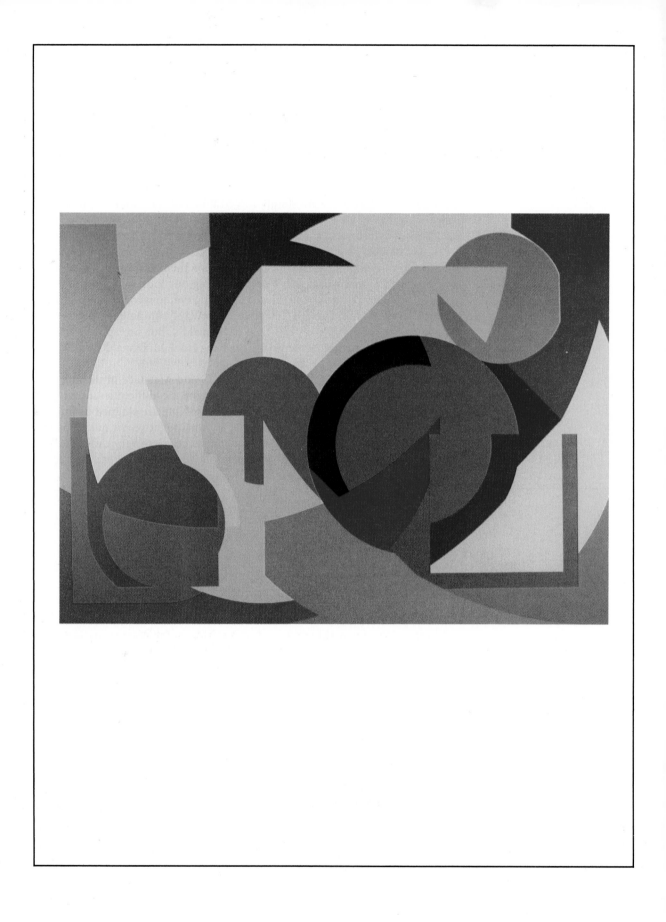

V Integrating Strategy, Structure, and Behavior

In addition to the basic functions of managing strategy, managing structure, and managing behavior (discussed in Parts II, III, and IV, respectively) organizations must address several other challenges. The common thread that unites these challenges is their relation to all three of the basic functions. The first set of integrative challenges involves ethics and social responsibility. As we learn in Chapter 22, ethics and social responsibility are related to strategy, structure, and behavior in organizations. Similarly, organization change, development, and revitalization, the topics of Chapter 23, also span the three core organizational functions. And effective entrepreneurship and small business management, addressed in Chapter 24, require that the organizational functions be addressed in a logical and integrated fashion.

22

Ethics and Social Responsibility in Organizations

LEARNING OBJECTIVES

After studying this chapter, you should be able to:

1. Discuss the formation of individual ethics, and describe three areas of special ethical concern for managers.

2. Trace the development of the concept of social responsibility, and specify to whom or to what an organization may be considered responsible.

3. Identify and describe four types of organizational approaches to social responsibility.

4. Explain the relationship between the government and organizations regarding social responsibility.

5. Describe some of the activities that organizations may engage in to manage social responsibility.

CHAPTER OUTLINE

S purred on by a rising tide of environmentalism and social consciousness during the last several years, many businesses have begun
to realize that being good to the environment can be good for
business. By trying to position their products as being good for the environment (or at least not as bad for the environment as alternative products),
dozens of businesses have achieved significant gains in both market share
and profits.

One notable example of this trend is in the trash business itself — in the
making of plastic trash bags. Mobil Chemical Co. started the practice when
it began to advertise its line of Hefty trash bags as being biodegradable.
Almost as soon as Mobil unveiled this new advertising campaign and
started putting biodegradability claims on Hefty packages, sales of the trash
bags increased significantly. So did criticisms of the firm and its claims.

Mobil's trash bags are indeed biodegradable — but only if they are left
in direct sunlight. Since most trash bags end up in landfills covered with
other trash, few of Mobil's bags will actually decompose as the term
"biodegradable" implies. Thus states and the Federal Trade Commission
are trying to force not only Mobil but all firms that make environmental
claims in their advertising to be more truthful. The state of Texas, for
example, filed a lawsuit against Mobil because of its exaggerated claims.
Although Mobil did not admit guilt, it did provide a cash settlement and
agreed to drop the claims from its advertising campaign.[1]

Mobil Chemical Co. has confronted one of the most challenging and controversial areas that organizations must face today — the relationship
between the organization and the social environment in which it functions.
Every society prohibits organizations from engaging in certain types of
activities. Organizations that violate these social proscriptions may face
dire consequences ranging from public humiliation to loss of business to
legal sanctions. The two ingredients that determine how an organization
responds to its social environment are the ethics of individuals within the
organization and the social responsibility of the organization itself.

This chapter explores issues of ethics and social responsibility in detail.
We first look at the ethics of individuals in organizations and then expand
our discussion to the somewhat controversial topic of social responsibility.
Next we explore some of the ways in which government attempts to
persuade organizations to adopt socially responsible practices, and finally
we examine how organizations themselves manage these activities through
both formal and informal approaches.

The Ethics of Individuals in Organizations

Ethics are an individual's personal beliefs about right and wrong behavior.

We define **ethics** as an individual's personal beliefs about right and wrong behavior.[2] Although this simple definition communicates the essence of ethics, three implications of it warrant additional discussion. First, notice that ethics are individually defined — people have ethics; organizations do not. Second, what constitutes ethical behavior can vary from one person to another. For example, one person who finds a twenty-dollar bill on the floor may pocket it without guilt; another may feel compelled to turn it in to the lost-and-found department. Third, ethics are relative, not absolute. This means that although ethical behavior is in the eye of the beholder, it is usually behavior that conforms to generally accepted social norms. (Social norms differ from group norms as discussed in Chapter 19. Group norms relate to behavior within a small group; social norms relate to an entire society or to a major segment of a society). Unethical behavior, then, is behavior that does not conform to generally accepted social norms.

In the sections that follow, we discuss factors that influence the formation of individual ethics and consider ethical behavior in an organizational context. Throughout the discussion we refer to higher and lower ethical standards and to behavior that is more or less ethical. Keep in mind that these distinctions are relative, as discussed above, not absolute.

The Formation of Individual Ethics

Various factors are instrumental in the formation of an individual's ethics.

As Figure 22.1 shows, an individual's ethics are shaped by a combination of family influences, peer influences, life experiences, personal values and morals, and situational factors.

Family Influences   Individuals start to form ethical standards as children in response to their perceptions of the behavior of their parents and the behaviors their parents allow them to choose. Children are more likely to adopt high ethical standards if they see that other family members adhere to high standards (such as being truthful) and if they receive rewards for conforming, and punishment for not conforming, to these standards. If family members engage in unethical behaviors (such as being untruthful) and allow children to do the same, those children are likely to develop lower ethical standards.

Peer Influences   As children grow and enter school, they are influenced by peers with whom they interact every day. For example, if a child's friends engage in shoplifting, vandalism, or drug abuse, the child may decide to engage in those activities. Conversely, if the child's peers have higher ethical standards and reject such behaviors as drug abuse and theft, the child is likely to adopt those standards.

Life Experiences   Dozens of important events, both positive and negative, shape people's lives and influence their ethical beliefs and behavior. These

Figure 22.1

Determinants of Individual Ethics

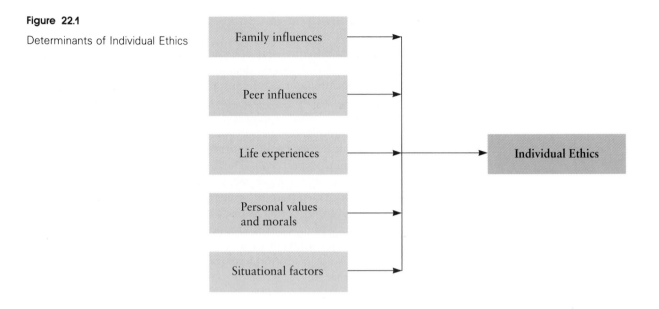

events are a part of growing up and maturing. For example, a person who steals something and does not get caught may feel no remorse and continue to steal. But a person who is caught stealing may feel guilty enough to revise her or his ethical standards and not steal in the future.

Personal Values and Morals   Values and morals also influence a person's ethical standards.[3] A person who places financial gain and personal advancement at the top of her list of priorities, for example, will adopt a personal code of ethics that promotes the pursuit of wealth. Thus she may be ruthless in efforts to gain these rewards, regardless of the costs to others. A person who puts his family at the top of his priority list will adopt different ethical standards.

Situational Factors   A final determinant of an individual's ethics is situational factors. Sometimes people unexpectedly find themselves in situations that cause them to act against their better judgment. For example, some people who pad their expense accounts do so because of personal financial difficulties. Although this does not justify their dishonesty, it does provide some context for understanding that people may behave unethically if they feel they have no other choice.

Managerial Ethics

Managerial ethics are standards of behavior that guide individual managers in their work.

Managerial ethics are standards for behavior that guide individual managers in their work. Ethics can affect managerial work in any number of ways. Three areas of special concern for managers are summarized in Table 22.1 and discussed below.

Relationship of the Firm to Its Employees   The behavior of managers defines the ethical standards according to which the firm treats its employees. These standards pertain to such areas as hiring and firing, wages and working conditions, and employee privacy. For example, most people consider it unethical for a manager to hire a family member or other close relative who is unqualified for the job or to fire someone because of her or his religion (the latter action is illegal in the United States).

Similarly, taking advantage of an individual worker's need for income by paying wages below those received by others in the organization is usually considered unethical. Spreading the word that an employee has AIDS or is alcoholic is also generally seen as an unethical breach of privacy.

Relationship of Employees to the Firm   Numerous ethical issues also surround the relationship of the employee to the firm, especially in regard to conflicts of interest, secrecy, and honesty in keeping expense accounts. A conflict of interest occurs when a decision potentially benefits the individual to the possible detriment of the organization. For example, if a manager responsible for selecting a new supplier accepts gifts from one potential supplier, he may decide to award the contract to that supplier even though another one might have offered the firm a better deal. To avoid such conflicts of interest, Wal-Mart does not allow its merchandise buyers to accept meals or gifts from sales representatives.[4]

Divulging company secrets to someone from a competing organization is also unethical, as is padding an expense account. Even so, some managers routinely add false meals, service charges, and car mileage to their expense account reports. They may do so out of greed or because they feel they are entitled to higher pay and see this tactic as one way to get it.

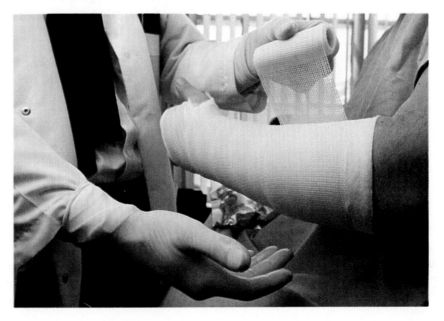

A key component of managerial ethics is the relationship of employees to the firm. An employee at 3M recently violated this relationship by stealing samples of a new casting tape the firm was developing; mailing them to competitors; and offering to explain 3M's technology in return for cash. The problem grew when one competitor, Johnson & Johnson, kept the samples rather than returning them. 3M alleges that its rival analyzed the stolen samples and used the results to create a new product for itself. Johnson & Johnson denies the allegations and is appealing a lower court ruling in favor of 3M.

Table 22.1

Three Areas of Ethical Concern for Managers

Area of Concern	Ethical Issues
Relationship of the firm to its employees	Hiring and firing Wages and working conditions Privacy
Relationship of employees to the firm	Conflicts of interest Secrecy Honesty in keeping expense accounts
Relationship of the firm to other economic agents	Customers Competitors Stockholders Suppliers Dealers Unions

SOURCE: Adapted from Thomas M. Garrett and Richard J. Klonoski, *Business Ethics,* 2nd ed. (Englewood Cliffs, N.J.: Prentice-Hall, 1986). Adapted by permission.

Relationship of the Firm to Other Economic Agents   Managerial ethics come into play in the relationship between the firm and other economic agents such as customers, competitors, stockholders, suppliers, dealers, and unions. Normal business ethics in customer relations suggest that products or services offered to the public be safe; be accompanied by appropriate information about product features, uses, and limitations; and be reasonably priced.[5] (Of course, like discrimination, many of these practices are covered by legislation.) The behavior of managers toward competitors is also dictated by ethical standards. Unfair business practices (such as pricing products so as to drive a competitor out of business) and denigration of competitors (by starting false rumors or making false claims in advertising about a competitor's products) are examples of unethical treatment of competitors.

Ethical standards also dictate that managers be truthful with their firm's stockholders. Misleading stockholders by telling them that the company is going to report record profits next year when management really expects only a modest profit is generally considered unethical, as is paying excessive compensation to the firm's management team. The CEO of Regina Co. was recently charged with violating regulations of the Securities and Exchange Commission. He allegedly altered financial records to make it seem as though the firm had more cash reserves than was actually the case, and he allegedly told investors that the firm was making high profits when it was really operating at a loss.[6]

Similarly, managers need to be fair and honest in their agreements and negotiations with suppliers, dealers, and unions. Convincing a supplier that a price break is needed or convincing a union that wage concessions are needed because of impending losses is unethical managerial behavior if the firm actually expects to make a profit. Likewise, shutting down a plant or office without giving workers adequate advance notice is considered to be unethical by many people.

Ethics in an Organizational Context

It is vital to note that ethical or unethical actions by particular managers do not occur in a vacuum.[7] Indeed, they most often occur in an organizational context that is conducive to them. Actions of peers and top managers, as well as the organization's culture, all contribute to the ethical context of the organization. A recent Dean Witter scandal, for example, took place in an office where over one hundred stockbrokers were supervised by a single branch manager. One broker started violating securities regulations, and others began to follow suit when the original perpetrator started talking about how easy it was and how much extra money he was making. As more and more brokers started participating, they encouraged others to join in. Since each broker had ample freedom to do whatever he or she wanted with little fear of being monitored (because of loose supervision), the illegal practices went on for several months before they were detected.

The starting point in understanding the ethical context of management is the individual's own personal ethical standards. Some people are willing to risk personal embarrassment or to lose their job rather than do anything unethical. Other people are easily swayed by the unethical behavior around them and by other situational factors, and they may be willing to commit significant crimes to further their own careers or for financial gain. Organizational practices may strongly influence the ethical standards of employees. Some organizations openly permit, and may even encourage, unethical business practices that are in the best interests of the firm.

A manager who becomes aware of an unethical practice but allows it to continue is contributing to the organizational culture that says such activity is permitted. For example, when the CEO of Beech-Nut discovered that his firm was using additives in apple juice that was being advertised as 100 percent pure, he decided to cover up the deception until the remaining juice could be disposed of. Many Beech-Nut employees participated in his plan. When the cover-up was finally discovered, the company suffered grave damage to its reputation and had to pay several million dollars in fines. In addition, the CEO was sentenced to a jail term.[8]

The organization's environment also contributes to the context for ethical behavior. In a highly competitive or highly regulated industry, for example, a manager may feel great pressure to achieve high performance by any methods possible. In Japan managerial success is often determined by the kinds of connections the manager is able to establish with important people. One Japanese manager, Hiromasa Ezoe, CEO of the Recruit Company conglomerate, was recently found guilty of giving lucrative stock options to a variety of well-placed government officials to facilitate this process of networking.[9]

Managing Ethical Behavior

Spurred partially by recent scandals over insider trading and similarly dishonorable acts, and partially by a sense of enhanced corporate consciousness about the importance of ethical and unethical behaviors, many organizations are re-emphasizing ethical behavior by employees.[10] The emphasis takes many forms, but any effort to enhance ethical behavior must begin with top management — the group that establishes the organization's culture and defines what behavior will and will not be acceptable. Some executives have even gone so far as to charge a subordinate with responsibility for helping them maintain appropriate ethical standards by periodically questioning the executives' motives, challenging their reasons for certain decisions, and raising other ethical questions.[11]

Some companies have started offering employees training in how to cope with ethical dilemmas. At Boeing, for example, line managers lead training sessions for other employees, and the company has an ethics committee that reports directly to the board of directors. The training sessions involve discussions of different ethical dilemmas that might be faced and how different managers might handle those dilemmas. Chemical Bank, Xerox, and McDonnell Douglas have also established ethics training programs for their managers.[12]

Organizations are also going to greater lengths to formalize their standards for ethical behavior. Some, such as General Mills and Johnson & Johnson, have prepared guidelines that detail how employees are to treat suppliers, customers, competitors, and other constituents. Others, such as Whirlpool, Hewlett-Packard, and Raytheon, have developed and publicized formal **codes of ethics** — written statements of the values and ethical standards that guide the firms' actions. The Whirlpool code of ethical conduct is reproduced in Figure 22.2.

A formal *code of ethics* is a written statement of the values and ethical standards that guide a firm's actions.

Of course, no code, guideline, or training program can truly make up for the quality of an individual's personal judgment about what is right or wrong behavior in any particular situation. Such devices may prescribe what people should do in a particular circumstance, but they often fail to help people understand and live with the consequences of their choices. Making ethical choices may lead to very unpleasant outcomes — firing, rejection by colleagues, the forfeiture of potential monetary gain, to name a few. The manager at Beech-Nut who finally alerted authorities to the apple juice deception eventually resigned because others thought he was a traitor. Thus managers must be prepared to confront their own consciences and weigh the options available when making difficult ethical decisions.[13]

Social Responsibility and Organizations

Social responsibility is the set of obligations that an organization has to protect and contribute to the society in which it functions.

Only individuals have ethics. Organizations themselves do not have ethics, but their relationships to their various environments often pose ethical dilemmas and call for ethical decisions. **Social responsibility** is the set of

Figure 22.2

The Whirlpool Code of Ethical
Conduct

The question of ethics in business conduct has become one of the most serious challenges to the business community in modern times.

At Whirlpool, we share with millions of other Americans a deep concern over recent revelations of unethical and often illegal conduct on the part of some of this nation's most prominent business people and corporations.

The purpose of this message is not to pass judgment on any of these occurrences; each must and will be judged on its own merits by those charged with that responsibility.

Rather this message is intended to place firmly on record the position of Whirlpool Corporation regarding business ethics and the conduct of every Whirlpool employee. It represents an irrevocable commitment to our customers and stockholders that our actions will be governed by the highest personal and professional standards in all activities relating to the operation of this business.

Over the years, circumstances have promted us to develop a number of specific policies dealing with such critical elements of ethical business practice as conflicts of interest, gifts, political activities, entertainment, and substantiation of claims.

We also have a basic statement of ethics which places the ultimate responsibility for ethical behavior precisely where it belongs in any organization. . . on the shoulders of the person in charge:

"No employee of this company will ever be called upon to do anything in the line of duty that is morally, ethically or legally wrong.

Furthermore, if in the operation of this complex enterprise, an employee should come upon circumstances of which he or she cannot be personally proud, it should be that person's duty to bring it to the attention of top management if unable to correct the matter in any other way."

Every Whirlpool manager carries the dual responsibility implicit in this policy statement, including the chairman of the board.

Our written policies deal with nearly all facets of business experience. We review, revise and recommunicate them to our managers on a regular basis. . . and we see that our managers carry on the communication throughout the company.

But as a practical matter, there is no way to assure ethical behavior with written policies or policy statements.

In the final analysis, "ethical behavior" must be an integral part of the organization, a way of life that is deeply ingrained in the collective corporate body.

I believe this condition exists at Whirlpool, and that it constitutes our greatest single assurance that this company's employees will conduct the affairs of this business in a manner consistent with the highest standards of ethical behavior.

At Whirlpool we have certain ways of doing things. They are commonly accepted practices, enforced not by edict, but rather by a mutual conviction that they will, in the long term, work in the best interest of our customers, our stockholders, the company and all its employees.

In any business enterprise, ethical behavior must be a tradition, a way of conducting one's affairs that is passed on from generation to generation of employees at all levels of the organization. It is the responsibility of management, starting at the very top, to both set the example by personal conduct and create an environment that not only encourages and rewards ethical behavior, but which also makes anything less totally unacceptable.

I believe this has been achieved at Whirlpool. The men who founded this company back in 1911 were individuals possessed of great integrity and honor. They fostered a tradition of ethical conduct in their business practices, and they perpetuated that tradition through careful selection of the people who would one day fall heir to leadership of the company.

The system works. Time and time again I have witnessed its efficacy. It shows no hospitality whatsoever to those not willing to abide by its standards, and unerringly identifies and purges them.

Unfortunately, the system is not automatically self-sustaining; it must be constantly reaffirmed by each new generation of leaders. In the position I now occupy, I view this as one of my most important responsibilities.

As this company grows, and as the pressures upon it increase, maintaining our tradition of ethical conduct becomes an increasingly difficult task. But I am confident it will be maintained, because it is necessary for continued growth, profitability and success.

SOURCE: From "Ethics as a Practical Matter: A Message from David R. Whitwam, Chairman of the Board." Used by permission of Whirlpool Corporation.

obligations that an organization has to protect and contribute to the society in which it functions.[14] In the sections that follow we trace historical views of social responsibility, identify organizational constituencies, and describe the approaches that organizations might take toward the social or environmental consequences of their practices.

Historical Views of Social Responsibility

Historical views of social responsibility have passed through the *entrepreneurial era,* the *Depression era,* and the *social era.*

Views of social responsibility held by organizations, the government, and the public at large have changed dramatically over the last hundred years. In particular, there have been three critical turning points in the evolution of thinking about social responsibility.[15]

The first turning point in the United States occurred during the late 1800s and is generally associated with what many now call the **entrepreneurial era.** During this time so-called captains of industry, including John D. Rockefeller, Cornelius Vanderbilt, J. P. Morgan, and Andrew Carnegie, were amassing fortunes and building empires in industries ranging from oil to railroads to banking to steel. Prior to their day and age, virtually all businesses were small, so these men were truly the first executives to control power and wield influence at a national level. Unfortunately, in many instances they chose to abuse their power through such practices as labor lockouts, discriminatory pricing policies, kickbacks, blackmail, and tax evasion. Eventually, outcries from public officials and other leaders forced the federal government to step in and pass laws that outlawed some business practices and restricted others. These laws were significant in that they acknowledged a relationship among business, the government, and society and indicated for the first time that business had a role to play in society beyond the pure maximization of profit.

Subtle changes in views toward social responsibility continued throughout the early part of the century, but the next turning point did not occur until the **Depression era** of the 1930s. By this time, large organizations had come to dominate the American economic scene, and many people criticized them for irresponsible financial practices that led to the stock market crash of 1929. As a part of Franklin Roosevelt's New Deal, the government passed several laws to protect investors and smaller businesses, and the Securities and Exchange Commission was created in 1934 to regulate the sales of securities and curb unfair stock market practices. As an outgrowth of these and other actions, the social responsibility of organizations was more clearly delineated. In particular, the new government actions insisted that organizations take an active role in promoting the general welfare of the American public.

The third major turning point in views of social responsibility came during the **social era** of the 1960s. This period of American history was characterized by a great deal of social unrest. The civil rights movement and widespread opposition to the war in Vietnam energized the American public to examine the nation's values, priorities, and goals. Students and other activists accused big businesses such as McDonnell Douglas and Du Pont of trying to promote and extend the Vietnam War in order to increase profits. Ralph Nader began his historic battle for automobile safety during this period. A strong push in consumerism that started with Nader prompted a great deal of action.

President John Kennedy proclaimed four basic consumer rights — the right to safe products, the right to be informed about all relevant aspects of a product, the right to be heard in the event of a complaint, and the right of consumers to choose what they buy. Government once again took a closer look at organizational practices. Tighter restrictions on pollution, consumer warnings on products such as cigarettes and flammable children's clothing, and increased regulation of many other industries all grew from concerns raised during this period. Kennedy's proclamation also brought to the fore the fact that organizational practices were being observed and evaluated — rightly or wrongly — by sections of the American public with many different interests and concerns.

This growing trend toward social responsibility raises two important questions: exactly to whom is business responsible, and who in an organization is ultimately accountable for the organization's practices? We address these questions in the next section.

Areas of Social Responsibility

Basic areas of social responsibility include constituents, the natural environment, and the general social welfare.

As Figure 22.3 shows, organizations may exercise social responsibility toward their constituents, toward the natural environment, and toward the general social welfare. Social entities closest to the organization (such as constituents) have the most immediate stake in what the organization does. Those farther removed (such as the general social welfare) have a more ambiguous and longer-term stake in the organization and its practices.

Organizational constituents are the people and organizations that are directly affected by the practices of a specific organization and have a stake in its performance.

Organizational Constituents   In Chapter 4 we described the task environment as the individuals, groups, or organizations that directly affect a particular organization but are not part of the organization. Now we can identify a broader network of **organizational constituents,** the people and organizations that are directly affected by the practices of a specific organization and have a stake in its performance. The major types of organizational constituents are depicted in Figure 22.4.

The interests of people who own and invest in an organization are affected by virtually anything the firm does. If the firm's managers are caught committing criminal acts or violating acceptable ethical standards, the resulting bad press and public outcry are likely to hurt the organization's profits, stock prices, and so forth. Organizations also have a responsibility to their creditors. If poor social performance hurts an organization's ability to repay its debts, those creditors and their employees also suffer. In similar fashion, the actions of an organization toward its social environment also affect each of the other constituents noted in Figure 22.4.

Figure 22.3

Areas of Social Responsibility

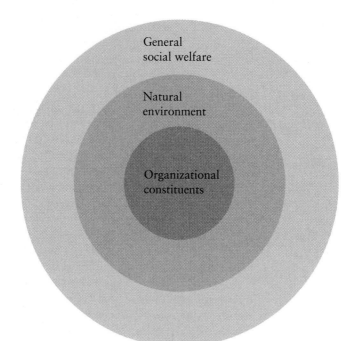

A firm that engages in socially irresponsible practices toward some of its constituents is asking for trouble. For example, managers at Allegheny International spent a half-million dollars to buy a lavish Pittsburgh home in which to entertain clients. The company maintained a fleet of five corporate jets so that its managers could travel anywhere, anytime. Although entertaining and travel are normal parts of doing business, Allegheny went too far. The company also made large loans to employees at an interest rate of only 2 percent. Nepotism in hiring was rampant. A close analysis of Allegheny's performance during this period suggested that it spent too much on executive perquisites, that conflicts of interest clouded executive judgment, that improper accounting methods were employed, that managers withheld information from shareholders, and that the board of directors inadequately monitored top management. Consequently, investors (who received lower dividends), the government (which received fewer tax dollars), the court system (which was eventually forced to deal with Allegheny's improprieties), and employees (who might have been paid higher wages under other circumstances) all were affected.[16]

In contrast, consider the case of Levi Strauss. The company gives 2.4 percent of its pretax earnings to social causes, treats its employees and suppliers with dignity and respect, plays an active role in important trade associations, has had no major ethical scandals, is respected by competitors, maintains good relations with government regulatory agencies, and contributes to college and university scholarship programs. This record suggests that managers at Levi Strauss are doing an excellent job of maintaining good relations with the firm's constituents.[17]

Figure 22.4

Organizational Constituents

Not all organizations can do as well as Levi Strauss in attending to constituents, but most make an effort to take a socially responsible stance toward three main groups: customers, employees, and investors. Land's End, a fast-growing mail-order house, has profited from good customer relations. Its operators are trained to be completely informed about company policies and products, to avoid pushing customers into buying unwanted merchandise, to listen to complaints, and to treat customers with respect. As a result, sales have been increasing 20 percent each year.[18]

Organizations that are socially responsible in their dealings with employees treat workers fairly, make them a part of the team, and respect their dignity and basic human needs. Companies such as 3M and Golden West Financial go to great lengths to find, hire, train, and promote qualified minorities.[19]

To maintain a socially responsible stance toward investors, managers should maintain proper accounting procedures, provide appropriate information to shareholders about the current and projected financial performance of the firm, and manage the organization in such a way as to protect shareholder rights and investments. Insider trading, illegal stock manipulation, and the withholding of financial data are examples of recent wrong-doings attributed to many different businesses. The former chairman of Ashland Oil, for example, was accused of selling important Ashland documents to Iran in order to manipulate the supply and price of oil for personal gain.[20]

The Natural Environment   A second critical area of social responsibility is the natural environment. Not long ago, many organizations regularly and indiscriminately dumped sewage, waste products from production, and trash into streams and rivers, into the air, and on vacant land. Now, however, many laws regulate the disposal of waste materials. In many instances, companies have seen the error of their ways and have become more socially responsible in their release of pollutants. Consequently, air and water pollution have decreased, although there is still widespread ocean dumping of sewage sludge.

Much remains to be done. Companies need to develop economically feasible ways to avoid contributing to acid rain, to depletion of the ozone layer, and to global warming, and alternative methods are required for handling sewage, hazardous wastes, and ordinary garbage.[21] Procter & Gamble, for example, is an industry leader in using recycled materials for containers, and Hyatt operates a new subsidiary to help recycle waste products from its hotels. Concern for the natural environment is also providing business opportunities for new firms. The Global Challenge describes how one European firm is profiting in this area.

Companies also need to develop safety policies that cut down on accidents that have potentially disastrous environmental results. When an Ashland Oil storage tank ruptured, spilling over 500,000 gallons of diesel fuel into Pennsylvania's Monongahela River, the company moved quickly to clean up the spill but was still indicted for violating U.S. environmental laws.[22] After the Exxon oil tanker *Valdez* spilled millions of gallons of oil off the coast of Alaska, Exxon adopted new and more stringent procedures to prevent another disaster.

General Social Welfare   Some people feel that in addition to treating constituents and the natural environment responsibly, business organizations also should promote the general welfare of society. Examples of such practices include contributions to charities, philanthropic organizations, and not-for-profit foundations and associations; support for museums, symphonies, and public radio and television; and taking a role in improving public health and education.[23] Some people also believe that organizations should act to correct, or at least not contribute to, political inequities. A well-publicized expression of this viewpoint in the late 1980s was the argument that U.S. businesses should end their operations in South Africa to protest that nation's policies of apartheid.[24] Companies like Eastman Kodak and IBM responded to these concerns by selling their operations in South Africa. This area of social responsibility, in particular, is a source of much controversy for the managers of modern organizations.

THE GLOBAL CHALLENGE

They Cart Waste Away, Treat It — and Then Sell It

When BUS Berzelius Environmental Services became the first green stock to be listed on the Frankfurt exchange in January, investors went wild. On the first day of trading, they bid the share price up from $196 to $310. Investors believe BUS is poised to turn Europe's mountains of toxic industrial waste into gold.

The three-year-old company has developed new technology to process hazardous wastes for less than half of what it now costs companies to dump them. Then, BUS sells the raw materials that it has refined from the waste back to industry. "Customers pay us twice — to cart the waste away and then to buy it back," says BUS Chief Executive Helmut Maczek.

BUS is a spin-off of West German metals-trading giant Metallgesellschaft. The parent company floated 25 percent of BUS stock to raise $130 million for an ambitious expansion drive, covering Germany and the rest of Europe with its new recycling plants. But BUS is already on the fast track. This year, sales are forecast to double, to $43 million, while gains of 70 percent are expected for each of the next three years. Earnings will triple in 1990, to $5.4 million, and should double

the next year, to more than $10 million. "We have the potential to become bigger than the parent company," says Maczek, a metallurgist who was a Metallgesellschaft senior manager before being tapped to run BUS.

Already, BUS plants in Germany, Spain, and Sweden are recycling one-third of Western Europe's noxious steel-furnace dust. Maczek is currently negotiating joint ventures with partners in France, Italy, and the Soviet Union, with hopes of doubling the company's capacity by 1993. And the choking industrial pollution in Eastern Europe could mean an additional huge market right on Maczek's doorstep.

BUS could be vulnerable to a drop in metals prices. Some 40 percent of revenues and a big chunk of profits flow from the resale of metals to industry. But its cleanup knowhow should ensure that Germany's first green stock keeps growing like a beanstalk.

SOURCE: "They Cart Waste Away, Treat It — and Then Sell It," by Gail E. Schares. Reprinted from May 21, 1990, issue of *Business Week* by special permission, copyright © 1990 by McGraw-Hill, Inc.

Arguments For and Against Social Responsibility

On the surface, there would seem to be little disagreement about the need for organizations to act responsibly not only toward their constituents but toward the natural environment and the wider society in which they operate. In truth, though, several convincing arguments are used by those who oppose these wider interpretations of social responsibility.[25] Some of the most salient arguments on both sides of this contemporary debate are summarized in Table 22.2 and explained below.

Arguments Against   Some people, including the famous economist Milton Friedman, argue that widening the interpretation of social responsibility will undermine the American economy by detracting from the basic mission of business: to earn profits for owners. For example, money that Chevron or General Electric contribute to social causes, programs, or charities is money that could otherwise be distributed to owners as a dividend. Another objection to deepening the social responsibility of businesses points out that corporations in America already wield enormous power and that pushing them to be more active in social programs gives them even more power. Without some system of checks and balances, the chances for corporate abuse of power through social programs increase.

Other arguments against social responsibility focus on the potential for conflict of interest. Suppose, for example, that one manager is in charge of deciding which local social program or charity will receive a large grant from her business. The local civic opera company (a nonprofit organization that relies on contributions for its existence) might offer her front-row tickets for the upcoming season in exchange for her support. If opera is her favorite form of music, she might be tempted to direct the money toward the local company even though it might do more good elsewhere.

Finally, critics argue that organizations lack the expertise to understand how to assess and make decisions about worthy social programs. How can a company truly know which cause or program is most deserving of its support? People who ask this question also see an alarming trend on the part of organizations to tie products to social causes. This practice began in 1983 when American Express pledged to donate one cent to the Statue of Liberty restoration project each time one of its credit cards was used. More recently MCI Communications has begun to contribute a share of its long-distance telephone profits to a reforestation program, and several other firms have employed similar promotional activities. Critics fear that this practice will enable companies to exert too much influence over the charitable causes with which they become associated and that charities will begin to function merely as marketing agents to help firms sell products.[26]

Arguments For   People who argue in favor of social responsibility claim that because organizations create many of the problems that need to be addressed, such as air and water pollution and resource depletion, they should play a major role in solving them. They also argue that because

Table 22.2

Arguments For and Against Social Responsibility

Arguments For Social Responsibility	Arguments Against Social Responsibility
1. Business creates problems and should therefore help solve them.	1. The purpose of business in American society is to generate profit for owners.
2. Corporations are citizens in our society.	2. Involvement in social programs gives business too much power.
3. Business often has the resources necessary to solve problems.	3. There is potential for conflicts of interest.
4. Social responsibility can enhance profits.	4. Business lacks the expertise to manage social programs.

THE ENTREPRENEURIAL CHALLENGE

Green Issues and Greenbacks

The environmental problems that bring headaches to most people create opportunities for some. Every environmental problem begs for a solution, and entrepreneurs who develop such solutions can turn today's "green" issues into profits. But environmentally oriented companies, like those in any new industry, suffer many setbacks as they grow.

Safer, Inc., for instance, recognized that many people want environmentally benign pesticides so that they don't poison themselves as they kill garden pests. Responding to that desire, Safer now sells some fifty types of biodegradable pesticides, and its sales have been doubling annually. However, Safer has been having trouble making a profit. It has had to contend with commercial growers' reluctance to try new pesticides that cost more than traditional chemicals and kill a narrower range of bugs. And because federal laws prohibit pesticide advertising from making safety claims, Safer has had some trouble differentiating its products from more environmentally destructive ones.

The country's growing environmental consciousness has also focused attention on what to do with the 160 million tons of solid waste that Americans throw out each year. A number of entrepreneurs have become rich by getting rid of that waste, but they often make enemies as fast as they make money. In 1980, Alan McKim borrowed $13,000 to start Clean Harbors, a toxic waste disposal company that now does over $100 million in business annually. McKim's

holdings are worth over $80 million, but he may be the most unpopular person in Braintree, Massachusetts, where his company wants to build a hazardous-waste incinerator.

Similar problems have plagued Wheelabrator Technologies, one of the first companies to get into the business of burning solid waste to produce energy. Wheelabrator builds incinerators and charges anyone who wants to get rid of garbage a per ton fee that varies depending on the local availability of landfills. But now that incineration has been linked to its own environmental problems, Wheelabrator's growth has slowed.

Ogden Projects is a latecomer to the waste-to-energy business, but it may have found a way to avoid the not-in-my-backyard syndrome. It signs long-term contracts with municipalities, assuring Ogden of profit and the cities of a solution to their garbage problem. Ogden's lesson may be an important one for other entrepreneurs trying to profit from environmentalism: it's much easier to succeed if you're perceived as supplying a service to local governments rather than as simply making a profit.

REFERENCES: James Cook, "Garbage into Gold," *Forbes*, January 22, 1990, pp. 48–49; Joshua Hammer, "The Big Haul in Toxic Waste," *Newsweek*, October 3, 1988, pp. 38–39; David Stipp, "Trying to Ride the Environmental Boom to the Big Green," *Wall Street Journal*, January 16, 1990, p. B2.

corporations are legally defined entities that have most of the same privileges as private citizens, they should not try to avoid their obligations as citizens. Advocates of social responsibility point out that although government budgets are stretched to the limit, many large businesses have surplus revenues that could be used to help solve social problems. For example, IBM routinely donates surplus computers to schools. Increased attention to social responsibility has also provided many new business opportunities, as described in The Entrepreneurial Challenge.

Although each of the arguments summarized above is a distinct justification for socially responsible behavior on the part of organizations, another basic reason for social responsibility is profit itself. Organizations that make clear and visible contributions to society can achieve enhanced reputations and garner greater market share for their products. Exaggerated or untrue claims such as those made by Mobil about the biodegradability of Hefty bags can haunt a company, but true and accurate claims can work to the benefit of both the organization and society. For example, during MCI's campaign for contributions to reforestation, the spokesperson acknowledged that MCI was trying to get more business. But she argued that everybody could win: the consumer would get a good product for a competitive price; the firm would increase its profits; and the natural environment would get more trees.

Organizational Approaches to Social Responsibility

Some people advocate an expanded social role for organizations, and others argue that their social role is already too large. Not surprisingly, organizations themselves have a wide range of positions on social responsibility. As Figure 22.5 illustrates, the four stances that an organization can take vis-à-vis social responsibility fall along a continuum ranging from a low to a high degree of socially responsible practices.

A *social obstruction* approach to social responsibility involves doing as little as possible to solve social or environmental problems.

Social Obstruction   The few organizations that take a **social obstruction** approach to social responsibility usually do as little as possible to solve social or environmental problems. When they cross the ethical or legal line that separates acceptable from unacceptable practices, their typical response is to deny or cover up their actions. We noted earlier Beech-Nut's attempt to hide the truth about its apple juice additives. Ashland Oil also has an unfortunate history of alleged social wrongdoing followed by less-than-

Figure 22.5

Organizational Approaches to Social Responsibility

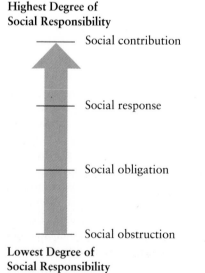

**Highest Degree of
Social Responsibility**

——— Social contribution

— Social response

— Social obligation

— Social obstruction

**Lowest Degree of
Social Responsibility**

model responses. For example, Ashland was found guilty of rigging bids with other contractors in order to charge higher prices for highway work in Tennessee and North Carolina.[27] It was also recently charged with wrongfully firing two employees because they refused to cover up illegal payments that the company made overseas.

A social obligation approach to social responsibility involves doing everything that is legally required to solve social or environmental problems but doing nothing more.

Social Obligation   One step removed from social obstruction is **social obligation,** whereby the organization does everything that is required of it legally but does nothing more. This approach is most consistent with the arguments against social responsibility described above. Managers in organizations that take a social obligation approach insist that their job is to generate profits. A firm with this approach to social responsibility will install the pollution-control equipment that is dictated by law but will not install higher-quality equipment even though it might limit pollution more. Tobacco companies such as Philip Morris take this position regarding their international marketing efforts. In the United States, they are legally required to include warnings to smokers on their products and to limit their advertising to prescribed media. At home they follow these rules to the letter of the law, but they use stronger marketing methods in countries that have no such rules. In many African countries, for example, cigarettes are heavily promoted, may contain higher levels of tar and nicotine than those sold in the United States, and carry few or no health warning labels on the packages.

A social response approach to social responsibility involves meeting legal and ethical requirements and going beyond those requirements in selected cases.

Social Response   A firm that adopts the **social response** approach meets its legal and ethical requirements and goes beyond these requirements in selected cases. Such firms voluntarily agree to participate in certain limited social programs, but solicitors must convince the organization that they are worthy of support. Both Exxon and IBM, for example, match contributions made by their employees to selected charitable causes. And many organizations respond to requests for donations to Little League, Girl Scouts, the local symphony orchestra, and so forth. However, someone has to knock on the door and ask; the organizations do not proactively seek such avenues for contributing.

A social contribution approach to social responsibility goes far beyond minimal requirements and involves proactively seeking opportunities to contribute to society.

Social Contribution   The highest degree of social responsibility that a firm can exhibit is the **social contribution** approach. Firms that adopt this approach take to heart the arguments in favor of social responsibility. They view themselves as citizens in a society and, as a result, proactively seek opportunities to contribute. An excellent example of social contribution is the Ronald McDonald House program undertaken by McDonald's. Generally located in urban areas and close to major medical centers, Ronald McDonald Houses are houses in which families can stay for minimal cost while their sick children are receiving medical treatment nearby. Both Sears and General Electric have established programs to help promote artists and cultural performers. These and related activities and programs exceed the social response approach — they indicate a sincere and powerful commitment to improving the general social welfare.

The government can influence organizations in a variety of ways. For years the Swiss banking system has been renowned as a haven for secret bank accounts —accounts that could be opened anonymously by depositors' attorneys or other representatives. Many of the accounts were set up by honest people who simply wanted privacy; others were opened by drug dealers, racketeers, and crooked government officials from other countries. In an attempt to drive out such unsavory business, the Swiss government has directed that all current secret account holders must identify themselves and that future account holders must be known by name to two bank officials.

Remember that these categories are not discrete but merely define stages along a continuum. Organizations do not always fit neatly into one category. The Ronald McDonald House program has been widely applauded, for example, but McDonald's also came under fire a few years ago for allegedly misleading consumers about the nutritional value of its food products.[28] And even though Beech-Nut and Ashland Oil took a social obstruction approach in the cases we cited, many individual employees and managers at both firms have no doubt made substantial positive contributions to society in a number of different ways.

The Government and Social Responsibility

We saw earlier in our historical overview the government's increasing influence in shaping the role of organizations in contemporary society. The relationship between organizations and government is two-way, however. As Figure 22.6 shows, organizations and the government use several methods in their attempt to influence each other.

How Government Influences Organizations

Regulation is the establishment of laws and rules that dictate what organizations can and cannot do in certain circumstances.

Direct Regulation   The government most often attempts to influence organizations through **regulation,** the establishment of laws and rules that dictate what organizations can and cannot do in certain circumstances. In terms of social responsibility, most regulatory control of organizations focuses on two of the areas of social responsibility discussed earlier: organizational constituents (especially customers, employees, and investors) and the environment.

To implement legislation, the federal government has created special agencies to monitor and control certain aspects of business activity. The Environmental Protection Agency handles environmental issues. The Federal Trade Commission and the Food and Drug Administration focus on consumer-related concerns. The Equal Employment Opportunity Commission, the National Labor Relations Board, and the Occupational Safety and Health Administration help protect employees. The Securities and Exchange Commission deals with investor-related issues. These agencies have the power to levy fines and bring civil or even criminal charges against organizations that violate regulations.[29] At both federal and state levels, there are many other, more specialized agencies.

Indirect Regulation   Other forms of regulation are indirect. The government can indirectly influence how organizations spend their social responsibility dollars by providing greater or lesser tax incentives. If the government wanted organizations to spend more on training the hard-core unemployed, Congress could pass laws that provide tax incentives to companies that open new training facilities. Some critics argue that regulation is already excessive. They maintain that a free-market system will eventually accomplish the same goals as regulation with lower costs to both organizations and the government.

Figure 22.6

How Organizations and the Government Influence Each Other

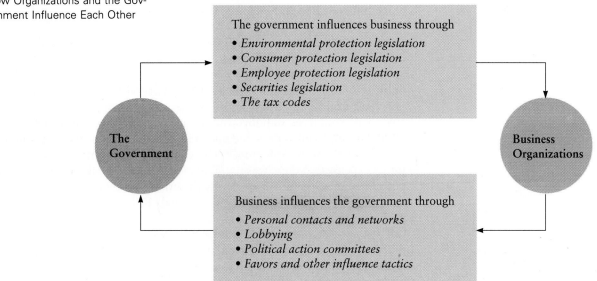

How Organizations Influence Government

As we saw in Chapter 4, organizations can influence their environment in many different ways. They have four main methods of addressing government pressures for more social responsibility.

Personal Contacts   Many corporate executives and political leaders travel in the same social circles. Thus personal contacts and networks offer one method of influence. A business executive may be able to contact a politician directly and present his or her case regarding a piece of legislation being considered.

Lobbying is an attempt by individuals or groups to influence legislation.

Lobbying   **Lobbying** is an attempt by individuals or groups to influence legislation. A lobbyist formally represents an organization before a law-making body. For example, a few years ago Congress was close to passing the Family and Medical Leave Act, which would have required organizations to give unpaid leave to parents. Over 150 businesses and trade associations joined forces and sent lobbyists to Washington to argue against the proposed law. As a result, passage of the bill was blocked.[30]

Political action committees (PACs) are created by organizations to funnel donations to political candidates.

Political Action Committees   **Political action committees (PACs)** are special organizations created to solicit and then distribute money to political candidates, because companies themselves cannot legally make direct donations to political campaigns. Employees of a firm may be encouraged to make donations to a particular PAC, because managers know that the PAC supports candidates with political views similar to their own. The PAC, in turn, makes the contribution itself, usually to a broad slate of state and national candidates. For example, the Federal Express PAC is called Fepac. In recent years it made most of its donations to Democrats, because that party controlled both the House and the Senate.[31]

Favors   Organizations sometimes rely on favors and other influence tactics to gain support. A few years back, two key members of a House committee attending a fund-raising function in Miami were needed in Washington to finish work on a piece of legislation that Federal Express wanted passed. (The law being drafted would allow the company and its competitors to give their employees standby seats on airlines as a tax-free benefit.) As a favor, Federal Express provided one of its corporate jets to fly the committee members back to Washington.[32] The company was eventually reimbursed for its expenses, so there was nothing technically illegal about its assistance, but some critics would argue that such actions are dangerous because they can easily lead to practices that are illegal. Bribes, blackmail, and other unseemly tactics have been part of the arsenal that businesses sometimes call on to make their wishes known in Washington. To combat illegal practices, numerous federal regulations have been passed in recent years stipulating what kinds of services organizations can and cannot provide for government officials.

Managing Social Responsibility

The demands for social responsibility placed on contemporary organizations by an increasingly sophisticated and educated American public are probably stronger than ever. As we have seen, there are pitfalls for managers who fail to adhere to high ethical standards and for companies that try to circumvent their legal obligations. Organizations therefore need to fashion an approach to social responsibility the way they would develop any other business strategy. They need to view social responsibility as a major challenge that requires careful planning, decision making, consideration, and evaluation. They may accomplish this through both formal and informal approaches.[33]

Formal Organizational Approaches

Three formal methods that organizations can use to manage social responsibility are *legal compliance, ethical compliance,* and *philanthropic giving.*

Formal (specifically planned and instituted) organizational approaches that can help manage social responsibility are legal compliance, ethical compliance, and philanthropic giving.[34]

Legal Compliance   **Legal compliance** is the extent to which the organization complies with local, state, federal, and international laws. The task of managing legal compliance is generally assigned to the appropriate functional managers. The organization's top human resources executive is generally responsible for ensuring compliance with regulations concerning recruiting, selection, pay, and so forth. The top finance executive generally oversees compliance with securities and banking regulations. The organization's legal department is also likely to contribute to this effort by providing general oversight and answering queries from managers about the appropriate interpretation of laws and regulations.

Ethical Compliance   **Ethical compliance** is the extent to which the members of the organization follow basic ethical (and legal) standards of behavior. We have already noted that organizations have started doing more in this area — providing training in ethics and developing guidelines and codes of conduct, for example. These activities serve as vehicles for enhancing ethical compliance. Many organizations also establish formal ethics committees, which may be asked to review proposals for new projects, help evaluate new hiring strategies, or assess a new environmental protection plan. They might also serve as a peer review panel to evaluate alleged ethical misconduct by an employee. The Environmental Challenge illustrates another fairly new approach to ethical compliance.

Philanthropic Giving   **Philanthropic giving** is the awarding of funds or other gifts to charities or other social programs. Dayton-Hudson Corporation, for instance, routinely gives 5 percent of its taxable income to such causes. Unfortunately, in this age of cutbacks, many corporations have

Philanthropic giving is one expression of social responsibility. Soft Sheen Products Company, a hair-care products firm based in Chicago's South Side, has adopted two elementary schools and two high schools in its neighborhood. The company regularly gives equipment and supplies to each of the four schools. In addition, its employees often donate their own time to help out with special programs in the schools. Frances William Gutter (r.), a Soft Sheen executive, is shown here along with Laurel Bennett, a volunteer, and some students.

Two informal methods that organizations can use to manage social responsibility are providing appropriate leadership and culture and allowing for whistle blowing.

Whistle blowing is the disclosure by an employee of illegal or unethical conduct by others in the organization.

limited their charitable gifts over the past several years as they trim their own budgets. For example, Atlantic Richfield's corporate giving decreased from $37 million in 1983 to $11.4 million in 1987. It dropped again to $10 million in 1990.[35] Firms that do engage in philanthropic giving usually have a committee of top executives who review requests for grants and decide how much and to whom money will be allocated.

Informal Organizational Approaches

In addition to formal approaches for managing social responsibility, there are also informal approaches. Two of the more effective are to provide appropriate leadership and culture and to allow for whistle blowing.

Organization Leadership and Culture   Leadership practices and organization culture can go a long way toward defining the social responsibility stance that an organization and its members will adopt. For example, Johnson & Johnson executives for years have provided a consistent message to employees that customers, employees, communities where the company does business, and shareholders — in that order — are all important. Thus, when packages of poisoned Tylenol showed up on store shelves in the early 1980s, Johnson & Johnson employees did not need to wait for orders from headquarters to know what to do: they immediately recalled all the packages before any other customers could buy them.[36] By contrast, the message sent to Beech-Nut employees by the actions of their top managers communicates much less regard for social responsibility.

Whistle Blowing   **Whistle blowing** is the disclosure by an employee of illegal or unethical conduct by others within the organization. An organization's response to this practice is likely to indicate its stance toward social responsibility. Whistle blowers may have to proceed through a number of channels to be heard and may even be fired for their efforts. Many organizations, however, welcome their contributions. Individuals who observe questionable behavior typically first report the incident to their boss. If nothing is done, the whistle blower may then inform higher-level managers or an ethics committee if one exists. Eventually, the person may have to go to a regulatory agency or even to the news media in order to be heard.[37] The apple juice scandal at Beech-Nut started with a whistle blower. Jerome LiCari, who managed the firm's research and development department, began to suspect that its apple juice was not "100% pure." His boss was unsympathetic and the president of the company turned a deaf ear. LiCari then resigned and took his message to the media.

Evaluating Social Responsibility

Any organization that is serious about social responsibility must ensure that its efforts are producing the desired benefits. Essentially this requires

THE ENVIRONMENTAL CHALLENGE

The "Green" Executive

As organizations become increasingly aware of and concerned about environmental issues and other aspects of social responsibility, they are also seeking new ways to manage their social responsibilities effectively. An approach used by several organizations is to appoint a senior manager to be in charge of all aspects of social responsibility, especially as it pertains to the environment.

The Walt Disney Company recently appointed Kym Murphy to the position vice president of environmental policy. Her primary task is to help set Disney's policies regarding environmental issues and concerns. Some of her activities include publishing an environmental policy statement for the firm and creating environmental affairs departments within each of the six Disney business units.

Another firm that has adopted this approach to managing its social responsibility is Lever Brothers, a unit

of Unilever. The firm expected the job to occupy only about one-fourth of Melinda Sweet's time when it named her as its environmental affairs director. In short order, however, both Sweet and the organization realized that it was a full-time job.

Other companies that are experimenting with this new type of management position include S. C. Johnson & Son Inc., the Kraft General Foods Division of Philip Morris, Colgate-Palmolive, and Turner Broadcasting System. During the years ahead, more and more firms will almost certainly be following in the footsteps of these pioneering organizations.

REFERENCES: "'Green' Executives Find Their Mission Isn't a Natural Part of Corporate Culture," *Wall Street Journal,* March 5, 1991, pp. B1, B6; Jeremy Main, "Here Comes the Big New Cleanup," *Fortune,* November 21, 1988, pp. 102–118; Shawn Tully, "What the 'Greens' Mean for Business," *Fortune,* October 23, 1989, pp. 159–164.

---

applying the concept of control to social responsibility. Many organizations require current and new employees to read their guidelines or code of ethics and then sign a statement agreeing to abide by it. An organization should also evaluate how it responds to instances of questionable legal or ethical conduct. Does it follow up immediately? Does it punish those involved? Or does it use delay and cover-up tactics? Answers to these questions can help an organization form a picture of its approach to social responsibility.

A corporate social audit is a formal and thorough analysis of the effectiveness of the firm's social performance.

Additionally, some organizations occasionally conduct corporate social audits. A **corporate social audit** is a formal and thorough analysis of the effectiveness of the firm's social performance. It requires the organization to define all its social goals clearly, analyze the resources devoted to each goal, determine how well the various goals are being achieved, and make recommendations about which areas need additional attention. Unfortunately, such audits are not conducted very often because they are expensive and time consuming. Indeed, most organizations probably could do much more to evaluate the extent of their social responsibility than they do.

Learning Summary

Ethics are an individual's personal beliefs about what constitutes right and wrong behavior. Ethics are formed by family and peer influences, life experiences, personal values and morals, and situational factors. Important areas of ethical concern for managers are the relationship of the firm to employees, the relationship of employees to the firm, and the relationship of the firm to other organizations. The ethical context of organizations consists of each manager's individual ethics and messages sent by organizational practices. Organizations use leadership, culture, training, codes. and guidelines to manage ethical behavior.

Social responsibility is the set of obligations that an organization has to protect and enhance the society in which it functions. Views of social responsibility have developed from the entrepreneurial era, through the Depression era and the social era, up to the present time. Organizations may be considered responsible to their constituents, to the natural environment, and to the general social welfare.

Organizations present strong arguments both for and against social responsibility. The approach that an organization adopts toward social responsibility falls along a continuum ranging from social obstruction, social obligation, and social response, to social contribution.

Government influences organizations through regulation, which is the establishment of laws and rules that dictate what businesses can and cannot do in prescribed areas. Organizations, in turn, rely on personal contacts, lobbying, political action committees, and political favors to influence the government.

Organizations use three formal approaches to manage social responsibility: legal compliance, ethical compliance, and philanthropic giving. Leadership and allowing for whistle blowing are informal means for managing social responsibility. Organizations should evaluate the effectiveness of their socially responsible practices as they evaluate any other strategy.

Questions and Exercises

Review Questions

1. What are ethics? How are an individual's ethics formed?
2. Summarize the basic historical views of social responsibility.
3. What are the arguments for and against social responsibility?
4. How does the government influence organizations? How do organizations influence the government?
5. What formal organizational approaches can be used to manage social responsibility?
6. What is a corporate social audit?

Analysis Questions

1. What is the relationship between the law and ethical behavior? Is it possible for illegal behavior to be ethical?

2. How are the ethics of an organization's CEO related to social responsibility?
3. Which set of arguments — those for or those against social responsibility — do you think are the strongest and most convincing?
4. Do you think that it is appropriate for an organization to attempt to influence key decision makers in the government? Explain.
5. How do you feel about whistle blowing? If you were aware of a criminal activity taking place in your organization, and if reporting it might cost you your job, what would you do?

Application Exercises

1. Refresh your memory about the Exxon *Valdez* oil spill. Evaluate the social responsibility dilemmas facing the company. For example, if Exxon had pledged unlimited resources to the cleanup, would this commitment have been fair to the company's stockholders?
2. Research the approach to social responsibility taken by ten large companies. What is your personal assessment of each?

Chapter Notes

1. "A New Sales Pitch: The Environment," *Business Week,* July 24, 1989, p. 50; "Environmentalists, State Officers See Red as Firms Rush to Market 'Green' Products," *Wall Street Journal,* March 13, 1990, pp. B1, B5; "Suddenly, Green Marketers Are Seeing Red Flags," *Business Week,* February 25, 1991, pp. 74–76.
2. See Thomas M. Garrett and Richard J. Klonoski, *Business Ethics,* 2nd ed. (Englewood Cliffs, N.J.: Prentice-Hall, 1986), for a review of the different meanings of the word "ethics."
3. John Snarey, "A Question of Morality," *Psychology Today,* June 1987, pp. 6–8.
4. John Huey, "Wal-Mart — Will It Take over the World?" *Fortune,* January 30, 1989, pp. 52–61.
5. Patricia Sellers, "Getting Customers to Love You," *Fortune,* March 13, 1989, pp. 38–49.
6. "How Don Sheelen Made a Mess That Regina Couldn't Clean Up," *Business Week,* February 12, 1990, pp. 46–50.
7. Linda Klebe Trevino, "Ethical Decision Making in Organizations: A Person-Situation Interactionist Model," *Academy of Management Review,* July 1986, pp. 601–617; Bart Victor and John B. Cullen, "The Organizational Bases of Ethical Work Climates," *Administrative Science Quarterly,* September 1988, pp. 101–125.
8. "What Led Beech-Nut down the Road to Disgrace," *Business Week,* February 22, 1988, pp. 124–128.
9. "The Dark Side of Japan Inc.," *Newsweek,* January 9, 1989, p. 41.
10. Archie B. Carroll, "In Search of the Moral Manager," *Business Horizons,* March–April 1987, pp. 7–15; William D. Litzinger and Thomas E. Schaefer,

"Business Ethics Bogeyman: The Perpetual Paradox," *Business Horizons,* March–April 1987, pp. 16–21.

11. Joseph A. Raelin, "The Professional as the Executive's Ethical Aide-de-Camp," *The Academy of Management Executive,* August 1987, pp. 171–182.

12. "Businesses Are Signing Up for Ethics 101," *Business Week,* February 15, 1988, pp. 56–57; "Ethics on the Job: Companies Alert Employees to Potential Dilemmas," *Wall Street Journal,* July 14, 1986, p. 17.

13. Sir Adrian Cadbury, "Ethical Managers Make Their Own Rules," *Harvard Business Review,* September–October 1987, pp. 69–73.

14. Jerry W. Anderson, Jr., "Social Responsibility and the Corporation," *Business Horizons,* July–August 1986, pp. 22–27.

15. See Archie B. Carroll, *Business and Society: Ethics and Stakeholder Management* (Cincinnati: Southwestern, 1989), for a review of the evolution of social responsibility.

16. "Big Trouble at Allegheny," *Business Week,* August 11, 1986, pp. 56–61.

17. Edwin M. Epstein, "The Corporate Social Policy Process: Beyond Business Ethics, Corporate Social Responsibility, and Corporate Social Responsiveness," *California Management Review,* Spring 1987, pp. 99–114.

18. "A Mail-Order Romance: Land's End Courts Unseen Customers," *Fortune,* March 13, 1989, pp. 44–45.

19. Alan Farnham, "Holding Firm on Affirmative Action," *Fortune,* March 13, 1989, pp. 87–88.

20. "Ashland Just Can't Seem to Leave Its Checkered Past Behind," *Business Week,* October 31, 1989, pp. 122–126.

21. Jeremy Main, "Here Comes the Big New Cleanup," *Fortune,* November 21, 1988, pp. 102–118.

22. "Ashland Just Can't Seem to Leave Its Checkered Past Behind."

23. Nancy J. Perry, "The Education Crisis: What Business Can Do," *Fortune,* July 4, 1988, pp. 71–81.

24. Anthony H. Bloom, "Managing Against Apartheid," *Harvard Business Review,* November–December 1987, pp. 49–56.

25. For discussions of this debate, see Abby Brown, "Is Ethics Good Business?" *Personnel Administrator,* February 1987, pp. 67–74; Jean B. McGuire, Alison Sundgren, and Thomas Schneeweis, "Corporate Social Responsibility and Firm Financial Performance," *Academy of Management Journal,* December 1988, pp. 854–872; "Business Ethics for Sale," *Newsweek,* May 9, 1988, p. 56; Kenneth E. Aupperle, Archie B. Carroll, and John D. Hatfield, "An Empirical Examination of the Relationship Between Corporate Social Responsibility and Profitability," *Academy of Management Journal,* June 1985, pp. 446–463; and Margaret A. Stroup, Ralph L. Neubert, and Jerry W. Anderson, Jr., "Doing Good, Doing Better: Two Views of Social Responsibility," *Business Horizons,* March–April 1987, pp. 22–25.

26. "Doing Well by Doing Good," *Business Week,* December 5, 1988, pp. 53–57.

27. "Ashland Just Can't Seem to Leave Its Checkered Past Behind."

28. "Fast-Food Chains Draw Criticism for Marketing Fare as Nutritional," *Wall Street Journal,* April 6, 1987, p. 23.

29. "Make the Punishment Fit the Corporate Crime," *Business Week,* March 13, 1989, p. 22.

30. "Should Business Be Forced to Help Bring Up Baby?" *Business Week,* April 6, 1987, p. 39.

31. "How to Win Friends and Influence Lawmakers," *Business Week,* November 7, 1988, p. 36.

32. Ibid.
33. Steven L. Wartick and Philip L. Cochran, "The Evolution of the Corporate Social Performance Model," *Academy of Management Review*, October 1985, pp. 758–769; Anderson, "Social Responsibility and the Corporation"; Epstein, "The Corporate Social Policy Process."
34. Anderson, "Social Responsibility and the Corporation."
35. "Corporate Giving Is Flat, and Future Looks Bleaker," *Wall Street Journal*, October 17, 1988, p. B1; "Oil Firms Cut Gifts," *Wall Street Journal*, February 24, 1991, p. B16.
36. "Unfuzzing Ethics for Managers," *Fortune*, November 23, 1987, pp. 229–234.
37. Janelle Brinker Dozier and Marcia P. Miceli, "Potential Predictors of Whistle-Blowing: A Prosocial Behavior Perspective," *Academy of Management Review*, October 1985, pp. 823–836; Janet P. Near and Marcia P. Miceli, "Retaliation Against Whistle Blowers: Predictors and Effects," *Journal of Applied Psychology*, February 1986, pp. 137–145.

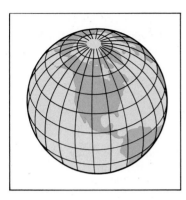

CASE 22.1

GM's High-Tech Headache

When General Motors bought Hughes Aircraft Company for $5.2 billion in 1985, it seemed like a good opportunity for the auto giant to gain a substantial share of the lucrative aerospace defense business and to develop high-tech gadgets for future GM cars. But within a week, some at GM must have been having second thoughts about the deal, for it took only that long for the new parent company to begin paying for the past ethical lapses of its subsidiary.

GM must have been shocked when, a week after closing the deal, it learned that Hughes had to pay a $200 million penalty for irregularities in its program to provide satellite links for U.S. Navy radar operations. Since then, Hughes has been the target of a number of federal grand jury investigations, and its CEO resigned amid the controversy.

One investigation involves top Hughes officials and Intelsat and includes allegations of kickbacks. The Justice Department has been looking into a whistle blower's charge that Hughes sold $3 billion worth of defective torpedoes to the Navy. And Hughes itself has asked the government to scrutinize the bidding on a $3.6 billion Federal Aviation Administration contract to overhaul the nation's air-traffic-control equipment. Hughes lost the contract to IBM, but in its complaint to the General Services Administration, Hughes complained that IBM, which supplies Hughes with some of its equipment, had quoted Hughes much higher figures for the equipment in question than it used in its own bid.

Furthermore, Hughes's expertise with radar and satellite technology has so far yielded only minor additions to GM's cars. A "head-up display" projects on the windshield the speed at which some Oldsmobile and Pontiac drivers are going. But really impressive high-tech products, such as a radar system that will help cars avoid a collision, are still in various stages of research and development.

The most enduring damage to the Hughes/GM name may come from a scandal involving Hughes's chairman Malcolm Currie. Because the five-year statute of limitations has run out and because investigators seemed reluctant to follow the scandal to the top, Currie will probably never be charged with anything. But the scandal has tarnished the reputation of a man who some viewed as the kind of person who could rebuild the defense industry's image.

Currie's style and breadth of experience earned him a high profile and interest from outside the defense establishment. He has a Ph.D. in engineering. He knows how to deal with Washington's politicians, having served as the Pentagon's chief of research, and he seems comfortable and unusually candid in the spotlight.

The scandal that tainted Currie occurred before he became chairman. It involves questions of who knew what and when. Such questions seldom lead to criminal charges outside the defense industry; but among those who stay in business by selling equipment to the Pentagon, knowledge is often the competitive edge. A company that can discover what systems the Pentagon intends to buy and how much it plans to spend can target its own research and marketing efforts most effectively and get a head start on its competitors.

According to government prosecutors, that's precisely what Hughes and other defense contractors did — illegally obtaining and distributing documents that outlined Pentagon spending plans. The government got charges to stick against six marketing managers from five companies. Hughes pleaded guilty and agreed to pay $3.6 million in fines. But according to some of those already convicted, Currie himself approved a system that routinely channeled government documents to Hughes, working around Hughes's own security system.

A group of document-swappers that government prosecutors called "The Clique" used elaborate methods to obtain the documents and keep them hidden. At Hughes, members of The Clique logged documents under phony names, slipped them past security guards with special courier passes, and kept them in personal drawers not subject to Pentagon inspection. Although no one alleges that Currie took part directly in such activities, considerable evidence indicates that he knew that his company was using information from illegally obtained documents and even encouraged the practice.

Why did the government let Currie get away? The most incriminating memoranda turned up late in the investigation, after the statute of limitations had run out and after prosecutors had already announced that they wouldn't seek indictments against Hughes's top officials. Investigators did interview Currie once but, unaccountably, didn't put him under oath. Some observers wondered whether Currie's connections with top Pentagon brass kept him safe. Such close scrapes with the law don't give General Motors the kind of progressive high-tech image it was hoping for.

Discussion Questions

1. Why do you think some defense contractors have a history of being involved in ethical scandals?
2. If you were on General Motors's board of trustees, what action would you want to take toward Malcolm Currie?
3. Why do indictments seldom reach the top executives of companies charged with criminal activities?
4. What could the Pentagon do to improve the ethical conduct of contractors who consistently violate its rules?

REFERENCES: Andy Pasztor and Rick Wartzman, "Hughes Aircraft Chief Is Implicated Belatedly in Defense-Secret Case," *Wall Street Journal,* July 3, 1990, pp. A1, A4; Eric Schine, "GM and Hughes: Is the Marriage Fizzling?" *Business Week,* February 12, 1990, pp. 54–55; Jacob M. Schlesinger, "GM's Hughes Unit Asks GSA to Review Bid Won by IBM for Air-Traffic System," *Wall Street Journal,* August 8, 1988, p. 3.

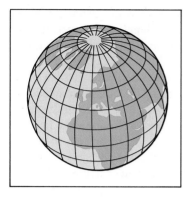

CASE 22.2

Will Environmental Concerns Slow Coke's European Takeover?

As far as Coca-Cola Company is concerned, these days, Europe is "it." European sales are growing at twice the rate of American sales, and they contribute almost one-third of Coke's operating profits. In fact, four-fifths of Coke's profits now come from overseas sales. You can buy Coke in Norwegian towns above the Arctic Circle, where "warmers" keep it from freezing. In South Korea, your snack at a baseball game will probably be Coke and squid. Coke is the best-known brand name in the world, and people everywhere who want to act like Americans find that the cheapest way to do so is to drink Coke.

Yet despite the ubiquity of Coca-Cola, the company feels that its future growth will come from overseas. The average inhabitant of planet Earth drinks about one-seventh as much soda pop as the average American consumes. Europeans drink only about 30 percent as much soda as Americans, preferring coffee, milk, and beer. So Coke figures it has a lot of growing to do.

Coke has already started an aggressive campaign in Europe. For years it let its local bottlers run the show, but now the parent company is taking over. In France, where Coke consumption is lower than in the rest of Europe, Coke bought the bottling operation from its long-time French bottler, Pernod Ricard. It built a huge new plant in Dunkirk, which allowed it to increase production suddenly when the iron curtain started falling. When the first East Germans began pouring through the Berlin Wall, Coca-Cola employees were on hand, handing out cans, six packs, even cases, hoping to infuence the life-long buying habits of these new consumers. The company quickly made plans to invest $140 million in East German bottling plants.

Although soft drinks seem to be harmless products and bottling is a clean process, Coke's huge worldwide success has provoked objections. A United Nations report recently criticized Coke and Pepsi for changing the drinking tastes of Filipinos so radically that indigenous Philippine beverages have virtually disappeared. Some Filipino children who can afford Coke suffer from vitamin deficiencies, the report said, because they prefer Coke to milk.

Coke may find its expansion in Europe hindered by similar concerns coupled with environmental objections to Coke's throwaway packaging. Although American-style "convenience" beverage packaging dominates the market in Britain, France, Italy, and Spain, in Germany, Switzerland, Denmark, and the Netherlands, most beverages still come in reusable glass bottles.

Germany and Switzerland, in particular, are crowded with local brewers who often bottle their own soft drinks and mineral water. Coke sees this fragmented market as a great opportunity for a big national brand to take over. Local bottlers, fearing that they will go out of business if Coke becomes too successful, have teamed up with members of Europe's "Green" movement to slow the tide of foreign beverages. The Greens, once thought of as environmental fanatics, now hold a good deal of power in Europe, and especially in Germany. Germans can purchase more than three thousand products stamped with the Blue Angel seal of environmental friendliness, but they may have trouble finding a plastic Coke bottle. The German government has imposed a 25-cent deposit on every plastic beverage bottle and may limit the total percentage of beverages that can be bottled in plastic.

Denmark has gone even further and banned all disposable cans for beer, mineral water, and soft drinks. As Europe moves toward economic unification, such trade restrictions are supposed to be disappearing, so the European Community sued Denmark over the ban in the European Court of Justice. But the court ruled that Denmark could restrain trade for environmental reasons, and that ruling may encourage other countries to make laws protecting their bottlers and their environment.

Coke's response is to try to persuade Europeans that one solution can please everyone. Aluminum cans are both disposable and totally recyclable, and the cans are worth enough as scrap to encourage businesses and community groups to collect them. Sweden already leads the world by recycling 80 to 85 percent of its aluminum cans, but so far the cans haven't caught on in the rest of Europe. Coke is hoping that other countries will follow Sweden's lead.

Coke became the number-one soft-drink maker in Europe by winning the right people to its side, lowering the initial resistance of Spanish wine makers, for instance, by making them local Coke bottlers. So the chances are good that environmental concerns won't slow Coke's European progress for long. But because of the pressure being put on beverage makers by European environmentalists, Coke's future victories in Europe may allow both the company and the environment to profit.

Discussion Questions

1. If you were a Coca-Cola executive, how would you feel about the possibility that increasing your company's sales might lead children to be malnourished?
2. What would Germany and Switzerland lose if national and international brands replaced local brands?
3. Do you think aluminum cans provide the perfect combination of disposability and environmental friendliness? Explain.
4. Do you think governments should get involved in issues like how to package beverages? Explain.

REFERENCES: Michael J. McCarthy, "As a Global Marketer, Coke Excels by Being Tough and Consistent," *Wall Street Journal,* December 19, 1989, pp. A1, A6; Patricia Sellers, "Coke Gets Off Its Can in Europe," *Fortune,* August 13, 1990, pp. 68–73; Shawn Tully, "What the 'Greens' Mean for Business," *Fortune,* October 23, 1989, pp. 159–164.

23

Organization Change, Development, and Revitalization

LEARNING OBJECTIVES

After studying this chapter, you should be able to:

1. Identify the sources of external and internal forces for change in organizations.

2. Describe a useful model for organization change, and explain why people tend to resist change.

3. Describe four areas of organization change.

4. Discuss the assumptions, techniques, and effectiveness of organization development.

5. Explain the need for organization revitalization.

When Drew Lewis was named CEO of Union Pacific Corp. in 1987, he knew he had a big challenge ahead of him. Union Pacific started as a railroad in 1862. As the railroad industry gradually declined during the twentieth century, Union Pacific branched out into trucking, natural resources, refining, real estate, and hazardous-waste management. But poor attention to operations and a lethargic organization were resulting in slow growth and minimal profits.

One of the first things Lewis did was to redirect the firm's strategy. He sold Union Pacific's refining operations and then its real estate business. He committed the money earned from those sales to the transportation and natural resources businesses.

Lewis also changed the firm's design. He felt it was too bureaucratic and needed to be made more responsive. Thus he eliminated half of the layers in the Union Pacific structure and tried to open up communication through all remaining levels of the hierarchy.

Finally, Lewis has been trying to change the behavior of Union Pacific employees. For one thing, he feels they are too passive and deferential to authority. He also thinks everyone behaves too formally. To change these behavioral patterns, he has done such things as occasionally wearing shorts and sneakers to work. He also drives himself to work in an old pickup truck. And he fines subordinates one dollar every time they call him Mr. Lewis.[1]

Drew Lewis was forced to grapple with something that all managers must eventually confront: the need for change. The inability of Union Pacific to remain competitive and profitable presented a significant set of challenges that had to be addressed. Some might argue that if Union Pacific had anticipated these problems and planned its response the company might have avoided the necessity for the kind of drastic action that Lewis eventually invoked. Understanding when and how to implement change is a vital part of good management.

This chapter explores the management of change. We start by examining some of the forces that provide a stimulus for that organization change. We then look at a model organizations may use to bring about effective change, and we discuss ways to overcome people's resistance to change. We then examine the major organizational areas in which change occurs. In subsequent sections we discuss organization development and organization revitalization, two particular approaches to making change happen.

Change in Organizations

Organization change is any substantive modification to some part of an organization.

Very broadly, **organization change** is any substantive modification to some part of an organization.[2] Many large organizations are not nearly as static as they may seem from the outside. Most companies or divisions of large companies must implement some form of moderate change at least every year and one or more major changes every four to five years.[3] Recent evidence suggests that this magnitude of change is increasing and that change occurs in organizations around the world. For example, one recent survey found that 44 percent of Japanese firms, 59 percent of American firms, 60 percent of German firms, 71 percent of South Korean firms, and 63 percent of Mexican firms surveyed had significantly changed their organization's structure within the period between 1989 and 1991.[4]

Changes may be made in any organizational area at any level — for example, in work schedules for a small group, in bases for departmentalization, in span of management, in machinery or equipment, in overall organization design, in organizational strategy. Any change in an organization, no matter how small, may have widespread effects. When Westinghouse installed a computerized production system at one of its plants, not only did employees have to be trained to operate the equipment, but the compensation system had to be adjusted to reflect new skill levels, the span of management of several supervisors needed to be altered, and a number of related jobs had to be redesigned. Selection criteria for new employees were also revised, and a new quality-control system was installed.[5]

Why do organizations find it necessary to change in the first place? Organization change is most often a response to an existing or anticipated change in the environment. Typically the organization has little choice but to change accordingly, either sooner or later. Indeed, the primary reason cited for organizational problems is the failure by managers to properly anticipate or respond to forces for change. These forces may originate in an organization's external or internal environment.

External Forces for Change

External forces for change come from outside the organization and relate to the organization's alignment with its environment.

As we saw in Chapter 4, organizations seek to maintain an effective alignment with their environment. The general environment includes broad trends and forces that indirectly affect an organization. The task environment consists of the individuals, groups, and organizations that directly affect a particular organization but are not part of it. When change occurs in either or both of those environments, an organization must change to maintain its alignment.

For example, two energy crises, a maturing Japanese automobile industry, and fluctuating currency exchange rates and international interest rates — all aspects of the international environment — induced major changes in the general environment faced by Ford Motor Company. New concerns about fuel efficiency, increased competition from Nissan and Toyota, and

External forces are vital stimuli for planned organization change. One such force is the economic unification of the European Community, which will create one vast single market. This major change in the general environment has caused businesses worldwide to focus on opportunities in Europe. Japanese industries, in particular, have entered European markets to a degree that has made some European leaders anxious. One example of the inroads made by the Japanese: every major Japanese carmaker except Mazda has announced plans for European factories.

varying costs of doing business abroad all served to define new rules of production and competition and forced the company to dramatically alter the way it does business.[6] Ford has had to introduce more fuel-efficient cars, improve the quality of its products to compete with the Japanese, and improve its accounting system to address currency fluctuations.

Equally significant are developments in the political arena, such as new laws, court decisions, and regulations, and developments in the economic climate, such as changes in inflation rates, in the cost of living, and in money supplies. Add to this our rapidly changing technology, which yields new production and communication capabilities that organizations need to explore. Unpredictable trends in cultural and societal values, which help determine what kinds of products or services find a ready market, also constitute a source of change.

Because the task environment is so directly related to the organization, it also represents a powerful force for change. Competitors influence an organization by means of their price structures and product lines. When Dell Computer Corp. began to compare their computers to those made by Compaq and then stress their lower prices, Compaq had two basic choices: lose market share to Dell or cut its prices (it chose the latter). Suppliers also affect organizations by raising or lowering prices, changing product lines, or even severing trade relations with a company. When a key supplier raises its prices, for example, the organization can cut costs elsewhere, pass on price increases to customers, or look for an alternative supplier.

Regulators can have dramatic effects on an organization. For example, if OSHA rules that a particular production process is dangerous to workers, it can force a plant to close until it meets acceptable safety standards.

THE ENVIRONMENTAL CHALLENGE

Global Giving on the Upswing

Corporations are often asked to make contributions to various charities and social programs. American corporations are beginning to learn, however, that although charity may begin at home it certainly doesn't end there. As U.S. firms become increasingly global, they are finding that external forces in foreign markets are beginning to pressure them for the same sorts of social support that they provide back home in the United States. Thus they are having to change their approach to social responsibility.

Consider, for example, the case of Aluminum Company of America (Alcoa). The firm operates a manufacturing facility in the small Brazilian town of Pocos de Caldas. The town's mayor recently asked Alcoa for $112,000 to build a sewage treatment plant. The firm felt that since the treatment plant would benefit everyone in the town, including its own workers, it was a worthy enough cause to justify the contribution.

In 1989, U.S. firms budgeted about 6 percent of their total giving for overseas causes. More recently,

however, many American firms, including Alcoa, American Express, Du Pont, Hewlett-Packard, and IBM, have significantly increased their overseas giving. For example, Hewlett-Packard made a large donation of computers to the University of Prague. Du Pont donated 1.4 million water-jug filters to eight African nations to help them rid drinking water of parasitic worms.

American firms are not the only ones changing their giving strategies. Japanese foreign giving increased by two-thirds in 1991 from the previous year, and European firms are also starting to increase foreign giving as well. Thus, just as we are moving toward a global economy, we also seem to be developing a global perspective on social responsibility.

REFERENCES: "Charity Doesn't Begin at Home Anymore," *Business Week,* February 25, 1991, p. 91; "Japanese Firms Embark on a Program of Lavish Giving to American Charities," *Wall Street Journal,* May 23, 1991, pp. B1, B5; William Miller, "Doing Well by Doing Good," *Industry Week,* November 5, 1990, pp. 54–55.

Unions may negotiate for higher wages, win a certification election, or go out on strike. Stockholders may threaten actions against the board of directors if they feel the board is not acting in their best interests, and joint-venture partners can attempt to modify or even cancel working relationships because they want to explore different opportunities elsewhere. In each instance the organization has choices, but each of those choices is likely to represent a change of some sort. The Environmental Challenge describes how another set of external forces has necessitated change by some U.S. organizations.

Internal Forces for Change

Internal forces for change come from inside the organization.

A variety of forces inside the organization may also cause change. Of course, the distinction between external and internal forces is blurred because an internally induced change may be prompted by the perception of an external event. However, an externally induced change is generally reactive, and an internally induced change is more likely to be proactive.

If top management decides to revise the organization's strategy in order to position the organization better in its market, the decision is an internally induced change. A decision by an electronics company to enter the home computer market or a decision to increase a ten-year product sales goal by 3 percent would occasion many organization changes. Sweeping changes may be brought about by CEOs themselves.[7] In 1987, when John F. McGillicuddy, head of Manufacturers Hanover, decided that the firm needed a major overhaul to face the banking environment of tomorrow, he decentralized the organization, changed its basic control systems from bureaucratic to clan, and altered the compensation system for managers so that pay was more directly tied to performance.

Shifts in sociocultural values may influence workers' attitudes toward their jobs, resulting in demands for new working hours or working conditions. In such a case, the organization must respond directly to the internal pressure generated by external change. For example, some organizations have chosen to provide on-site day care facilities for the children of single parents and dual-career parents who might otherwise be unable to work.

Approaches to Organization Change

Planned change is designed and implemented in an orderly and timely fashion in anticipation of future events.

Reactive change is a piecemeal response to circumstances as they develop.

Because organization change is a complex undertaking, managers must approach it systematically and logically in order to bring it to fruition. Some organization change is planned well in advance; other change comes about as a reaction to unexpected events. **Planned change** is designed and implemented in an orderly and timely fashion in anticipation of future events. Planned change is generally induced by internal forces as a way of preparing for anticipated environmental change. Thus a CEO who envisions a future environmental change and decides how to best address it is engaging in planned change.

Reactive change, in contrast, is a piecemeal response to circumstances as they develop. Reactive change is almost always induced by external forces that the organization either failed to anticipate or misinterpreted. Since reactice change may have to be carried out hastily, it increases the likelihood of a poorly conceived and poorly executed program.

Planned change is almost always preferable to reactive change. For example, as a result of the deregulation of the telephone industry and the subsequent breakup of AT&T, Southwestern Bell had to prepare to function as an independent corporation. To this end, top managers developed a plan for comprehensive change that identified two thousand major activities needing to be modified or replaced. Southwestern accomplished its plan remarkably well, with only a few slip-ups along the way.[8] By contrast, Union Pacific was forced to undergo several major reactive changes because its previous management had failed to anticipate the impending need for change.

Managers who sit back and respond to change only when they can no longer avoid it are likely to waste a lot of time and money trying to patch together a last-minute solution. The more effective approach is to anticipate the significant forces for change working on an organization and plan ways to address them. To accomplish this, managers must understand the steps needed for effective change.[9] Two models outlining the steps in organization change have been developed over the years. We look at these next.

The Traditional Model of Change

Lewin's traditional model of change consists of three steps: unfreezing, change implementation, and refreezing.

Kurt Lewin, a noted organizational theorist, was one of the first to address the process of change. He suggested that change requires three steps.[10] In the first step, called unfreezing, individuals who will be affected by the impending change must be led to recognize why the change is necessary. In the second step, the change is implemented. In the third step, called refreezing, the change is reinforced as part of the new system.

Caterpillar recently went through a major program of change that followed this pattern. Management's first step (unfreezing) was convincing the United Auto Workers (UAW) to support a massive work-force reduction to improve the firm's long-term effectiveness. Once union support was achieved, thirty-thousand jobs were eliminated (implementation). Then Caterpillar worked to improve its damaged relationship with remaining workers (refreezing) by guaranteeing future pay hikes and promising no more cutbacks.

As valuable as Lewin's model is in describing a general picture of change, it is not very helpful to people faced with the detailed task of bringing change about. A more comprehensive model, containing some specific procedural guidelines, is often required.

A Comprehensive Model of Change

The model of change shown in Figure 23.1 outlines seven steps that can lead to effective change.[11] This comprehensive model of change is quite similar to the model of classical decision making discussed in Chapter 5. The similarity is due in part to the fact that managing change is actually making a series of decisions about the change process. We should also note that this comprehensive model is useful for both planned and reactive change.

The first step in this approach is recognizing the need for change. Managers who merely react to the need for change might wait until numerous employee complaints, declines in performance indicators such as productivity or turnover, court injunctions, sales slumps, or labor strikes make action necessary. For managers who anticipate needed change, recognition is likely to come much earlier, as the result of marketing forecasts indicating new market potential, expert predictions about impending social or economic change, a cash surplus for possible investment, or a perceived opportunity to capitalize on a key technological breakthrough. These managers tend to initiate change because they expect it to be necessary in the near future in any case.

The manager must then set goals for the proposed change. It is important for the manager to specify from the outset what the change is supposed to accomplish. To maintain or increase market standing, to enter new markets, to restore employee morale, to reduce turnover, to settle a strike, to identify good investment opportunities — all these are possible goals. If the stimulus for change is an increase in turnover, a precise goal that might be adopted is to bring turnover back to its previous level.

An important next step is diagnosing what organizational variables have brought about the need for change. Turnover, for example, may be caused by a variety of factors, including low pay, inferior working conditions, poor supervision, better alternatives in the job market, or employee job dissatisfaction. Thus, if turnover is the recognized stimulus for change, the manager must understand what has caused it in this particular situation in

Figure 23.1

A Comprehensive Model of Change

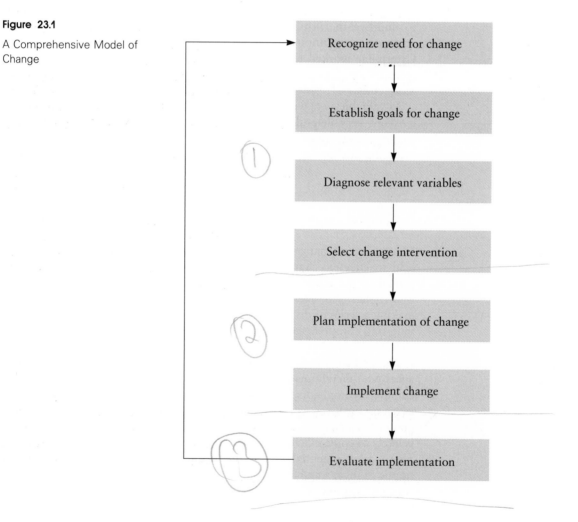

order to make the right changes. To carry out this diagnosis, the manager may discuss the situation with employees and other managers, compare wages with those offered by other organizations, and so forth.

After the manager has developed an understanding of the problem and its causes, he or she must select a change intervention that will accomplish the intended goal: to reduce turnover. An **intervention** is a specific change induced in an organization with the intention of solving a particular problem or accomplishing a specific objective. The selection of an intervention might be done by the individual manager in consultation with others, or it might be delegated to those most directly affected by it. If turnover is being caused by low pay, a new reward system may be needed. If the cause is poor supervision, interpersonal skills training for supervisors may be required.

The manager must then carefully plan the implementation of change. Issues to consider include the costs of the change, how the change will affect other areas of the organization, and the degree to which employees should participate in bringing change about. Hastily implemented change can result in more harm than good. For example, if the change involves the use of new equipment, the manager should not make any changes that rely on the use of that equipment until it has arrived and been installed and workers know how to use it. Moreover, as we discuss in the next section, people often resist change. If change is thrust upon them too quickly, their resistance may stiffen. Quite simply, a systematically implemented change is more likely to proceed smoothly and to encounter fewer obstacles than is a change that is implemented too quickly and without adequate preparation.

Finally, after the change has been implemented, the manager should verify that it has accomplished its intended goals. A change may fail to bring about the intended results. The original goal may have been inappropriate. The situation may have been inaccurately diagnosed. The wrong change intervention may have been selected. The intervention may have been improperly implemented. If the institution of a new reward system is the selected intervention, after it is planned and implemented the manager should determine whether turnover has in fact declined. If turnover is still too high, other changes may be necessary.

An intervention is a specific change induced in an organization with the intention of solving a particular problem or accomplishing a specific objective.

Why People Resist Change

When Westinghouse replaced all its typewriters with computer terminals and personal computers, most employees responded favorably. One manager, though, resisted the change to the point that he began leaving work every day at noon! It was some time before he began staying in the office all day. Managers need to know why people resist change and what can be done about it. Figure 23.2 summarizes the major reasons for resistance to change. These factors serve as barriers to the effective implementation of even planned change.

There are several reasons that people resist change: uncertainty, threatened self-interests, conflicting perceptions of the problem, and feelings of personal loss.

Figure 23.2

Major Reasons for Resistance to Change

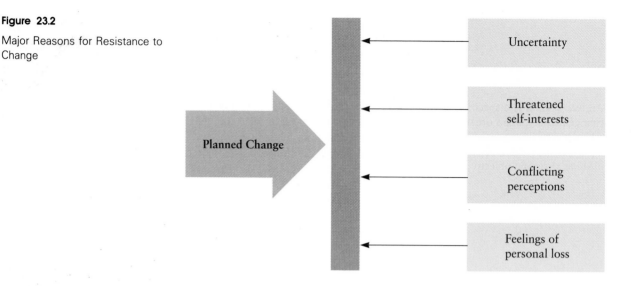

Uncertainty   Perhaps the biggest cause of employee resistance to change is uncertainty. In the face of impending change, employees are likely to become anxious and nervous. They may worry about their ability to meet the new job demands; they may think their job security is threatened; or they may simply dislike ambiguity. During the last few months of 1988, when RJR Nabisco was the target of an extended, bitter, and confusing takeover battle, the nerves of the firm's employees began to fray. The *Wall Street Journal* described Nabisco workers this way: "Many are angry at their leaders and fearful for their jobs. They are swapping rumors and spinning scenarios for the ultimate outcome of the battle for the tobacco and food giant. Headquarters staffers in Atlanta know so little about what's happening in New York that some call their office 'the mushroom complex,' where they are kept in the dark."[12]

Threatened Self-Interests   Many impending organization changes threaten managers' political self-interests. A change might seem to have the potential to diminish their power or influence within the company, so they fight the change to protect their status. A few years ago, managers at Sears developed a plan calling for a new type of Sears store. The new stores would be somewhat smaller than existing stores and would be located not in large shopping malls but in smaller plazas. They would carry clothes and other "soft goods" but not hardware, appliances, furniture, or automotive products. When executives in charge of the excluded product lines heard about the plan, they objected so strenuously that the entire idea was dropped.[13]

Conflicting Perceptions of the Problem   People may resist change because their perceptions of underlying circumstances differ from the perceptions of those who are promoting change. A manager may recommend a plan on the basis of her own assessment of a situation, but others in the organization may resist the plan because they do not agree with the manager's view. This type of problem is one reason the diagnosis phase of change is so important: conflicting perceptions can be identified and, perhaps, resolved before they have a chance to disrupt the change process. Drew Lewis encountered this problem with some executives at Union Pacific. One of his changes was to move the firm's headquarters from New York City to Bethlehem, Pennsylvania. He says he made the move to save money on rent, but some managers think he was partially motivated to be closer to a farm that he owns in Pennsylvania. Because of this difference in perception, one manager left the company and others remain skeptical about the move.

Feelings of Personal Loss   Some people resist change to avoid feelings of loss. For example, many organization change interventions alter work arrangements and thus disrupt existing social networks. Social relationships are important to most people, so they resist any change that might adversely affect those relationships. Change may also threaten people's feelings of familiarity and self-confidence. When conditions are stable, people grow accustomed to set patterns of interaction and understand their role in the organization. With change, however, these interactions may be disrupted and roles redefined.

Overcoming Resistance to Change

Managers need not abandon planned change in the face of resistance. Although there are no sure-fire cures, several techniques have some potential to overcome resistance.[14] Several of these are shown in Figure 23.3 and discussed below.

Participation   Participation is generally considered the most effective technique for overcoming resistance to change. Employees who take part in planning and implementing a change are better able to understand the reasons for the change than those who are not involved. They become committed to the change and to making it work. Employee participation reduces uncertainty and the threat to self-interest and social relationships. Employees who have the opportunity to express their own ideas and to understand the perspectives of others are likely to accept change gracefully.

The value of participation was shown in a classic study by Coch and French, who monitored the introduction of a change in production methods among four groups in a Virginia pajama factory.[15] One group was given no voice in the change. Its members responded with no change in performance and a high level of hostility and turnover — 17 percent of its members quit within forty days. In another group, which was allowed to send representatives to help plan the change, efficiency increased somewhat and no turnover occurred. Two other groups that were allowed to participate fully in planning and implementing the change improved production, morale, and cooperation significantly. More recently, 3M attributed $10 million in cost savings to employee participation in several different organization change activities.[16]

Figure 23.3

Overcoming Resistance to
Change

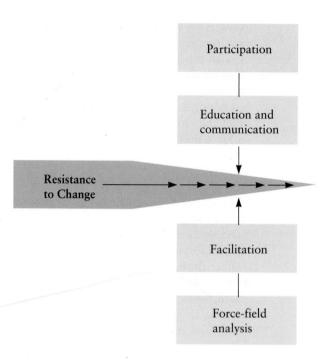

Education and Communication   Educating employees about the need for
and the expected results of an impending change should reduce their resistance. Managers can minimize uncertainty by establishing and maintaining
open channels of communication (as discussed in Chapter 20) while planning and implementing change. Caterpillar used these methods to reduce
resistance to its recent work-force reduction. First, UAW representatives
were informed of the need for and potential value of the planned changes.
Later, all employees were told about the change, when it would happen,
and how it would affect them individually.

Facilitation of Change   Knowing ahead of time that people are likely to
resist change, managers should do as much as possible to help them cope
with uncertainty and feelings of loss. Introducing change gradually, making
only necessary changes, announcing changes in advance, and allowing time
for people to adjust to new ways of doing things can help reduce resistance.
One manager at a Prudential Insurance regional office spent several months
systematically planning a change in work procedures and job design. He
then decided to implement the change rapidly. Over a weekend he came
into the office with a work crew and rearranged the office layout. When
employees walked in on Monday morning and saw the new arrangement,
they were anxious and resentful. A promising organization change became
an interpersonal disaster, and the manager had to scrap the entire plan.

Force-Field Analysis   Although it may sound like a technique from *Star
Trek,* force-field analysis can help overcome resistance to change. In almost

Force-field analysis is a method of overcoming resistance to change that involves removing or minimizing some of the forces acting against the change.

any situation where a change is being planned, there are forces acting for and forces acting against the change (these forces are not the same as the internal and external forces for change discussed earlier). In **force-field analysis,** managers list each set of forces and then try to remove or at least minimize some of the forces acting against the change.

Texas Instruments (TI) successfully used this approach during a period of cutbacks and retrenchment in the mid-1980s. At one point, the firm needed to close several plants. As shown in Figure 23.4, three factors reinforced the change: TI needed to cut costs; it had excess capacity; and the plants had outmoded production facilities. Forces acting against the change were employee resistance, concern that workers would lose their jobs, and the argument that a plant might be needed again in the future. TI first convinced workers that the closing was necessary by presenting profit and loss figures. As part of this effort, the firm also offered relocation or retraining to many displaced workers. In addition, instead of selling the plants, TI merely shut them down so they could be renovated and reopened if necessary. As a result, TI minimized the three major forces hindering the change, and the subsequent closings went off as planned.

Major Areas of Organization Change

Although change can be brought to virtually any part of an organization, most planned change occurs within the context of the basic organizational functions of managing strategy, managing structure, and managing behavior.[17] Table 23.1 lists the most common areas of change within each of these broad categories. Given the great array of change interventions that focus on structure, we break our discussion of that function down into two levels: change focused on structure and design per se and change focused on technology and operations.

Changing organizational strategy is a planned attempt to alter the organization's alignment with its environment.

Changing Strategy

A change in organizational strategy is a planned attempt to alter the organization's alignment with its environment.[18] As noted in Table 23.1, change

Figure 23.4

Force-Field Analysis at Texas Instruments

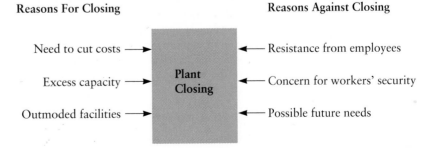

Reasons For Closing

Need to cut costs ⟶

Excess capacity ⟶

Outmoded facilities ⟶

Plant Closing

Reasons Against Closing

⟵ Resistance from employees

⟵ Concern for workers' security

⟵ Possible future needs

might be focused on any area of strategy. An organization might change its strategic goals. A multidivisional corporation might add to or subtract from its business portfolio, or it might revise a particular business strategy — for example, by dropping a differentiation strategy and adopting cost leadership. An altered functional strategy might reflect changes in debt or changes in spending on research and development. Other changes in organizational strategy would be to enter into a joint-venture partnership or to move into international markets. The Global Challenge describes how Airbus Industrie changed its strategy to become the number-two manufacturer of commercial airplanes in the world.

Changing Structure and Design

Changing structure and design can focus on some component of the organization's structure or on its overall design.

A change in organizational structure and design focuses on some component of the organization's structure or on its overall design. Thus the organization might change the design of its jobs by decreasing specialization, or the organization might change its bases of departmentalization by moving from functional to product. Likewise, it might change reporting relationships by eliminating a layer of management, and it might change the distribution of authority by becoming more decentralized. Also subject to change are coordination mechanisms (perhaps by the addition of some rules and procedures) and line/staff configurations (perhaps by the transfer of some staff managers to line positions).

On a larger scale, an organization might change its overall design. An expanding business might drop its functional design and adopt a divisional design to enable further growth. Or it might transform itself into a matrix to better cope with environmental uncertainty. An organization might also try to change its culture to clarify its understanding of what it expects of its employees. Finally, the organization might change some part of its human resources management system, such as selection criteria, methods

Table 23.1

Areas of Organization Change

Strategy	Structure and Design	Technology and Operations	Behavior
Strategic goals	Job design	Machinery and equipment	Abilities/skills
Business portfolio	Departmentalization	Work processes	Performance
Business strategy	Reporting relationships	Work sequences	Perceptions
Functional strategy	Distribution of authority	Information systems	Expectations
Partnerships	Coordination mechanisms	Control systems	Attitudes
Internationalization	Line/staff structure	Automation	Values
	Overall design		
	Culture		
	Human resource management		

THE GLOBAL CHALLENGE

Airbus Takes Off

Airbus Industrie is a unique organization. It has no real corporate headquarters and is jointly owned and operated by the governments of Germany, Britain, France, and Spain. The firm manufactures and markets aircraft to major airlines around the world. Its major competitors are Boeing and McDonnell Douglas.

For years, however, Airbus provided only token competition. Most of its orders were from small airlines, and its planes had a reputation for poor quality. Indeed, if Airbus had been a private corporation rather than a government-subsidized organization, it would almost certainly have folded years ago. Although its records are not available for public scrutiny, most experts believe that Airbus has lost money every year of its existence.

In 1988 a new director, Robert Smith, was appointed and given a mandate to make Airbus profitable. Smith embarked on several major programs aimed at cutting costs, improving quality, and streamlining operations.

He also set a new strategy for the organization. Rather than go after small orders and leave the big ones for Boeing and McDonnell Douglas, he decided that Airbus would attack the industry giants head-on. Under his leadership, Airbus introduced several new models to compete directly with planes made by the two U.S. firms and began to provide competitive financing. The firm also became much more aggressive in its sales efforts.

By 1991 Smith's efforts were beginning to pay off. Airbus passed McDonnell Douglas to become the number-two firm in the industry. In 1985 the firm had a backlog of 200 planes to build. Now that backlog is 1,600 planes worth $70 billion. Clearly the new Airbus strategy is working.

REFERENCES: "Zoom! Airbus Comes on Strong," *Business Week,* April 22, 1991, pp. 48–50; "Is Airbus Pushing the Envelope?" *Business Week,* October 8, 1990, p. 42; "Planemakers Have It So Good, It's Bad," *Business Week,* May 8, 1989, pp. 34–36.

of performance appraisal, or compensation and benefits, to better address staffing needs or to comply with a new government regulation.[19]

Changing Technology and Operations

Changing technology and operations focuses on the conversion process that the organization uses to transform inputs into outputs.

A change in technology is a planned attempt to alter the conversion process that the organization uses to transform inputs into outputs. Because of the rapid rate of all technological innovation in our society, technological and operations changes are becoming increasingly significant to organizations.[20] Table 23.1 lists several areas in which technological change is likely to occur.

To keep pace with competitors, firms find it necessary to periodically replace existing machinery and equipment with newer models. A change in work processes and activities may also be necessary if new equipment is introduced or new products are manufactured. In manufacturing industries, the major reason for changing a work process is to accommodate a change in the materials used to produce a finished product. Consider, for instance, a firm that manufactures battery-operated flashlights. For many years flashlights were made of metal, but most are now made of plastic. A firm that decides to move from metal to plastic flashlights because of consumer

Changing technology and operations is a critical area of organization change. General Electric recently collaborated with SNECMA of France, IHI of Japan, and Fiat Avio of Italy to construct this new aircraft engine, the GE90. GE relied on new manufacturing technology to plan and construct the engine. The creation of the new engine defines a new type of technology that aircraft manufacturers such as Boeing and Airbus cannot ignore.

preferences, raw materials costs, or other reasons faces a major shift in technology. It also must determine the extent to which it will automate work processes.

Of course, work process changes may occur in service organizations as well as in manufacturing firms. As traditional male barber shops and female beauty parlors are replaced by hair salons catering to both sexes, for example, these hybrid organizations have to develop new methods for handling appointments and setting prices.

A change in work sequence may or may not accompany a change in equipment or a change in work processes. Essentially, making a change in work sequence means altering the order of the workstations used in a particular manufacturing process. For example, two parallel assembly lines produce two similar sets of machine parts. The lines converge at a central quality-control unit where inspectors verify adherence to standards. To improve quality, the production manager might decide to change to periodic rather than final inspection. Under this arrangement, one or more inspections are established earlier in the manufacturing process.

Work sequence changes can be made in settings other than manufacturing, such as in the processing of insurance claims. The sequence of logging claims, verifying claims, requesting checks and countersignatures, and mailing checks might be altered in several ways, such as combining the first two steps or routing the claims through one worker while another worker handles checks.

One form of technological change that has been especially important in recent years is the revolution in information systems. Simultaneous advances in large mainframe computers, personal computers, and network tie-in systems have created vast potential for change in most workplaces. The main reason to adopt computers in offices is to create an information-processing station for each employee. The person at each workstation may manipulate ideas and drafts that are still in preliminary form, create, store, and retrieve documents, and distribute final copies. Both the initial implementation of such a system and its subsequent refinements constitute forms of organization change.

Systems of control constitute another area of technological and operations change that has emerged in recent years. New and more efficient methods of monitoring inventory, tracking production processes, and assessing quality have all been adopted in organizations during the last several years. For example, a new inventory-control system at Caterpillar has greatly reduced the time required to move components through the plant. In one instance, the time necessary to assemble a clutch was reduced from more than twenty days to just four hours.[21]

Changing Behavior

Changing behavior is a planned attempt to alter the way people in the organization feel or perform.

A change in behavior is a planned attempt to alter the way people in the organization feel or perform. Prompted by changes in technology, for example, an organization might need to upgrade the abilities and skills of its work force. It might do so by instituting training programs for existing workers and new selection criteria for potential workers. An organization that wants to improve employee performance might develop a new incentive system or performance-based training.

As we discussed in several chapters of Part IV, organizations must often address the perceptions and expectations of people. If an organization's workers feel that their wages and benefits are not as high as they should be, a manager might be able to allay their concern by showing evidence that the firm is paying a competitive wage and providing a superior benefit package. The change in perception, then, is brought about by informing and educating the work force about the comparative value of its compensation package. A common method for doing this is to publish a statement that places an actual dollar value on each benefit provided and comparing that figure to benefits provided by other local organizations.

Change might also be directed at employee attitudes and values. In the "old days" at many U.S. organizations, for example, labor and management worked together only grudgingly. Workers were told what to do and were expected to obey. Today, labor and management are more inclined to work together as partners. Each employee may be expected to offer insights into how to accomplish his or her responsibilities more effectively and efficiently, and management is more likely to listen to employees' ideas than in the past. In many ways, changing people's attitudes and values is the most difficult goal for organizations to achieve. Indeed, there is a separate body of thought that explores this task: organization development. Our next section examines this concept.

Organization Development

Organization development activities are principally directed at improving the behavioral or interpersonal side of organization life. Moreover, organization development reflects a broad, comprehensive approach to individual-organization relationships.[22] In this section, we explore the assumptions, techniques, and effectiveness of organization development.

OD Assumptions

Organization development (OD) is a planned organization-wide effort, managed from the top, that attempts to increase organization effectiveness through planned interventions in the organization's "process," using behavioral science knowledge.

The purpose of organization development is to change people's attitudes, perceptions, behaviors, and expectations. More precisely, **organization development** (OD) can be defined as a planned organization-wide effort, managed from the top, that attempts to increase organization effectiveness through planned interventions in the organization's "process," using behavioral science knowledge.[23] Any attempt to use OD in an organization needs to be systematic, must be supported by top management, and should be broad in its application.

The theory and practice of OD are based on several very important assumptions: (1) people have a desire to grow and develop; (2) people have a strong need to be accepted by others within the organization; and (3) the total organization and the way it is designed will influence the way individuals and groups within the organization behave. Some form of collaboration between managers and employees is necessary to (1) take advantage of employee skills and abilities and (2) eliminate aspects of the organization that retard employee growth, development, and group acceptance. Because of the intense personal nature of many OD activities, large organizations often rely on one or more OD consultants (either full-time employees assigned to this function or outside experts hired specifically for OD purposes) to implement and manage their OD program.

OD Techniques

Wendell L. French and Cecil H. Bell, Jr., have identified several types of interventions or activities generally considered to be part of organization development.[24] Some OD programs may use only one or a few of these; other programs use several of them simultaneously.

Diagnostic Activities   Just as a medical doctor examines a patient to diagnose her or his current condition, diagnostic OD activities analyze the current condition or welfare of an organization. Diagnostic activities rely on such techniques as questionnaires, opinion or attitude surveys, interviews, archival data, and meetings. The results from this diagnosis may generate profiles of the organization's operating procedures and growth patterns, which can then be used to identify problem areas in need of correction.

Education is an important organization development technique used by most organizations. Grace Pastiak is a plant manager for Tellabs, Inc., a firm that makes sophisticated telephone equipment. Pastiak is a firm believer in the value of education; she devotes several days each month to teaching classes, an activity that many managers assign to subordinates. She is shown here conducting a class in problem solving for a group of Tellab employees.

Team Building   Team-building activities are intended to enhance the effectiveness and satisfaction of individuals who work in groups or teams and to promote overall group effectiveness. Project teams in a matrix organization are good candidates for these activities. An OD consultant might interview team members to determine how they feel about the group; then an off-site meeting could be held to discuss the issues that surfaced and to iron out any problem areas or member concerns. Caterpillar has used team building as one method for changing the working relationships between workers and supervisors from confrontational to cooperative.[25] Managers report that the team-building effort has been successful and that working relationships have indeed become more cooperative.

Survey Feedback   In survey feedback, each employee responds to a questionnaire intended to measure perceptions and attitudes (for example, satisfaction and supervisory style). The results of this survey are then provided to everyone involved, including the supervisor. Thus all participants learn how others perceive them. This approach focuses on changing the behavior of supervisors by showing them exactly how their subordinates perceive them. After the feedback has been provided, workshops may be conducted to evaluate results and suggest constructive changes.

Education   Educational activities focus on classroom training. Although such activities can obviously be used for technical or skill-related purposes, an OD educational activity typically focuses on sensitivity skills. It teaches people to be more considerate and understanding of the people they work with. Participants often go through a series of experiential or role-playing exercises to learn how others in the organization feel. Many organizations use education to help develop skills for dealing with diversity.

Intergroup Activities   The purpose of intergroup activities is to improve the relationships between two or more groups. Recall from Chapter 10 that as group interdependence increases, so do coordination difficulties. Intergroup OD activities are designed to promote cooperation or to resolve conflict that may have arisen as a result of interdependence. Again, experiential or role-playing activities are often used to bring this about.

Third-Party Peacemaking   Another approach to OD is third-party peacemaking. It is most often used when substantial conflict exists within the organization (recall that we discuss conflict in Chapter 21). Thus third-party peacemaking can be appropriate for individuals, groups, or the entire organization. The third party, usually an OD consultant, uses a variety of mediation or negotiation techniques to resolve problems or conflicts between individuals or groups.

Technostructural Activities   Technostructural activities focus on the design of the organization, its technology, and how both of these influence people in their jobs. A structural change such as decentralization, a job design change, an increase in the use of automation, or a technological change involving a modification in work flow all qualify as technostructural OD activities if the objective is to improve group and interpersonal relationships within the organization.

Process Consultation   In process consultation, an OD consultant observes groups in the organization to develop an understanding of their communication patterns, decision-making and leadership processes, and methods of cooperation and conflict resolution. The consultant then provides feedback to the involved parties about the processes that he or she has observed. The goal of this form of intervention is to improve those processes. A leader who is presented with feedback outlining deficiencies in his or her leadership style, for example, might be expected to change in order to overcome them.

Life and Career Planning   Life and career planning helps employees formulate their personal goals and evaluate strategies for integrating these goals with the goals of the organization. Activities could include specification of training needs and plotting a career map. General Electric does an outstanding job in this area. The firm has an elaborate tracking system that keeps employees informed about their career path opportunities. The system also provides performance appraisal information so that people can monitor where they are in the hierarchy relative to where they would like to be or think they should be.

Coaching and Counseling   Coaching and counseling provide nonevaluative feedback to individuals. The purposes are to help people develop a better sense of how others see them and to help people learn behaviors that will assist them in achieving work-related goals. The focus of this technique is not on how individuals perform today but on how they can perform better in the future.

Planning and Goal Setting   More pragmatically oriented than many other interventions are activities designed to help managers improve their planning and goal setting (recall the discussion of goal-setting theory in Chapter 17). Emphasis still falls on the individual, however, in that the intent is to help individuals and groups integrate themselves into the overall planning process. The OD consultant might use the same approach as in process consultation, but the focus is more technically oriented on the mechanics of planning and goal setting.

Grid OD   The grid approach to OD is based on the Leadership Grid®, first developed by Robert Blake and Jane Mouton.[26] The Leadership Grid provides a means for evaluating leadership styles and then training managers to move toward an ideal style of behavior. The most recent version of the Leadership Grid, as developed by Blake and Anne Adams McCanse, is shown in Figure 23.5. The horizontal axis represents concern for production, and the vertical axis represents concern for people. Notice the five basic combinations of managerial behavior: the 1,1 manager (impoverished management) who exhibits minimal concern for both production and people; the 9,1 manager (authority-compliance management) who is highly concerned about production but exhibits little concern for people; the 1,9 manager (country club management) who has the exact opposite concerns from the 9,1 manager; the 5,5 manager (middle of the road management) who maintains adequate concern for both people and production; and the 9,9 manager (team management) who exhibits maximum concern for both people and production.

According to Blake and Mouton, the ideal style of managerial behavior is 9,9. They have developed a six-phase program (seminar training, team building, intergroup interventions, organizational goal setting, goal attainment, and stabilization) to assist managers in achieving this style of behavior. Many companies, including Pillsbury, Union Carbide, and Exxon, have used the Leadership Grid. However, there is little published scientific evidence regarding its true effectiveness.

The Effectiveness of OD

Organizations that actively practice OD include American Airlines, Tenneco, Texas Instruments, Toyota, Procter & Gamble, ITT, and Polaroid. B. F. Goodrich has trained sixty individuals in OD processes and techniques; these people have become internal OD consultants to assist other managers in applying the techniques.[27] Many other organizations report that they tried OD but discarded it because it didn't work or produced mixed results.[28] Given the diversity of activities encompassed by the term "organization development," it is not surprising that managers report mixed results from the various OD interventions.

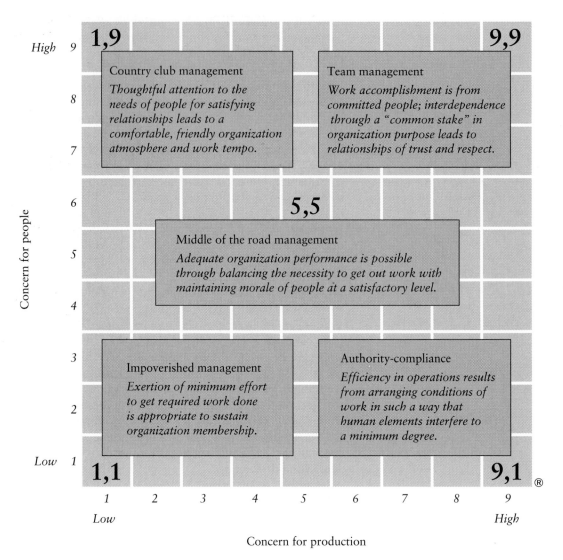

Figure 23.5

The Leadership Grid® Figure

SOURCE: The Leadership Grid® figure from *Leadership Dilemmas — Grid Solutions*, by Robert R. Blake and Anne Adams McCanse. Houston: Gulf Publishing Company, p. 29. Copyright © 1991 by Scientific Methods, Inc. Reproduced by permission of the owners.

There are no sure things when dealing with complex social systems such as organizations, so the effectiveness of many OD techniques is difficult to evaluate. Because all organizations interact with their environments, an improvement in an organization after an OD intervention may be attributable to the intervention. But it may also be attributable to changes in economic conditions, luck, or other factors.[29] Nevertheless, OD will probably remain an important part of management theory and practice because so many people believe that understanding human behavior in organizations is a critical ingredient for organizational effectiveness. This is one

Many organizations go through a period of revitalization to regain lost effectiveness. Leaders at the Wharton School (the school of business at the University of Pennsylvania) recently concluded that their course of study was not providing the best training for tomorrow's managers. As a result, they studied their MBA program and decided to overhaul it completely. The new MBA at Wharton will focus more on providing people skills, developing a global perspective, managing creativity and innovation, promoting real-world problem solving, and integrating diverse business perspectives than it has in the past.

reason that the University of Chicago's Business School, famous for focusing on quantitative skills, recently took steps to increase its students' awareness of OD.[30]

Organization Revitalization

Revitalization is a systematic and concentrated attempt to infuse new energy and strength into an organization.

Another perspective on organization change that warrants attention is revitalization. **Revitalization** can be defined as a systematic and concentrated attempt to infuse new energy and strength into an organization.[31] Like OD, revitalization may involve any number of different techniques. But unlike OD, revitalization is not focused on one specific organizational function (managing people); instead, it focuses on the management of strategy, structure, and behavior.

The Need for Revitalization

Why do organizations find it necessary to revitalize themselves? Because the environment of most organization shifts so rapidly, and because it is difficult for managers to always understand and predict what is going on in their environment, virtually all organizations occasionally find themselves misaligned. As a consequence, disorder and decline set in. The organization may start losing money; its effectiveness begins to suffer; and other indicators such as market share and profitability decline.

Only truly exceptional companies are able to avoid this sort of decline completely. Even such well-managed firms as Merck and Disney have gone through periods of stagnation. The key is to recognize when decline starts and to move immediately toward revitalization. In many instances the organization may be able to make quick changes to get its performance back on track and to regain proper environmental alignment. The major problems occur when managers either do not recognize the onset of disorder and decline until it is well advanced or are too complacent to correct it.

Approaches to Revitalization

To resuscitate a flagging organization, managers must have an understanding of the three basic stages of revitalization. These are shown in Figure 23.6. The first stage is contraction. During contraction the organization decreases in size and scope, cutting back on expenses, work force, facilities, and so forth. The basic purpose of contraction is to generate resources that can be used for new initiatives. At Union Pacific, for example, contraction involved eliminating jobs, closing some facilities, and developing new methods for cost control.

The next stage is consolidation. During this period the organization learns to live with a leaner, tighter way of doing things. Union Pacific managers, for example, have been forced to learn the real value of customer service and service quality. Many of their former rail customers had switched to trucks because they were cheaper and more reliable. Only by focusing on genuine improvements in price and reliability has Union Pacific been able to win back some of its customers.

In the third stage, expansion, true revitalization occurs. The firm can begin to build on its new base for operations, perhaps entering new markets, gradually expanding production again, adding to its work force as the need arises. To this end, Union Pacific has initiated more upgrades in its equipment and services.

Figure 23.6

Stages of Revitalization

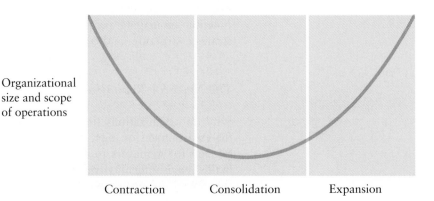

Organizational size and scope of operations

Contraction   Consolidation   Expansion

THE ENTREPRENEURIAL CHALLENGE

Turnaround at Navistar

Sometimes a start-up isn't a start-up at all. Take the case of Navistar International Corporation, formerly known as International Harvestor (IH). The firm can trace its roots back to 1846 when Cyrus McCormick built a factory to make reapers. IH was formed in 1902 when McCormick's operations were merged with those of several other farm equipment companies.

For years IH dominated the markets for both farm equipment and trucks. During the boom years following World War II, IH was selling everything it could make. As a result, the firm neglected new-product development and gradually began to lose its technological edge. IH eventually lost its leadership position in the farm equipment industry to John Deere and its leadership position in the truck industry to Ford.

A six-month labor strike in 1980, combined with a major economic recession, drove IH to the verge of bankruptcy. Between 1980 and 1982, for example, the firm lost $2.3 billion. Its managers knew that IH had to undergo a major transformation if it was to be revitalized. Accordingly, IH sold its construction equipment business to Dresser Industries and its agricul-tural equipment business (and its name!) to Tenneco in 1985.

The firm was reborn as Navistar International Corporation in 1986. From day one, managers treated Navistar like a new business. Gone were 85 percent of the IH employees and 42 of the 48 IH manufacturing plants. The new Navistar has not yet become profitable but does appear to be on its way to new financial health. Navistar now controls over 27 percent of the combined medium and heavy truck market in the United States. It is also one of Ford's biggest suppliers of diesel truck engines. And Navistar controls the U.S. market for school bus chassis. Although the firm isn't out of the woods yet, it does appear to be on the right road.

REFERENCES: Gary Hoover, Alta Campbell, and Patrick J. Spain, eds., *Hoover's Handbook — Profiles of Over 500 Major Corporations* (Austin, Tex.: The Reference Press, 1990), p. 395; Chet Borucki and Carole K. Barnett, "Restructuring for Self-Renewal: Navistar International Corporation," *The Academy of Management Executive,* February 1990, pp. 36–49; "Jim Cotting's Love Affair with Cash," *Forbes,* March 19, 1990, pp. 50–55.

Union Pacific has gone through a modest period of revitalization. Other firms have gone through similar processes to varying degrees. Disney's recent revitalization, for example, was fairly significant. The firm's movie division had declined in market share and profitability, and everything else was standing still. Hiring new talent, committing to more movies, exploiting the video market, and opening new hotels and theme parks turned things around. The revitalization of Navistar — formerly International Harvester — is discussed in The Entrepreneurial Challenge.

Once they understand the general pattern of revitalization, managers must usually rely on their own experience and analysis of specific situations when planning revitalization efforts. Any area of organization change or combination of OD techniques described earlier could be the basis for revitalization. Typically, such efforts involve a new or reoriented strategy, a new or significantly altered organization structure, and a new pattern of behavior among all managers and employees of the organization. A new set of cultural values or a company-wide organization development program might re-energize a firm's people and practices and set the organization on a road to new growth.

Learning Summary

Organization change is any substantive modification to some part of the organization. Change may be prompted by forces internal or external to the organization. Planned change is usually preferable to reactive change. The traditional model devised by Kurt Lewin gives a general perspective on change, but the more comprehensive seven-step model provides managers with guidelines for action. These steps are recognizing the need for change, establishing goals for the change, diagnosing relevant variables, selecting the change intervention, planning for implementation, implementing the change, and evaluating the results.

People tend to resist change because of uncertainty, threatened self-interests, conflicting perceptions of the problem, and feelings of personal loss. Participation, education and communication, facilitation, and force-field analysis are techniques for overcoming this resistance. Change may be brought to any organizational area: strategy, structure and design, technology and operations, and behavior.

The purpose of organization development is to change people's attitudes, perceptions, behaviors, and expectations. It is based on the assumption that people have a desire to grow and to be accepted by others. Another assumption of OD is that the design of the organization influences the behavior of people within the organization. There are many types of OD techniques, and organizations have used them with varying degrees of success.

Revitalization is the infusion of new energy and strength into the organization. It is occasionally needed to counter the effects of decline and disorder. The stages in revitalization are contraction, consolidation, and expansion.

Questions and Exercises

Review Questions

1. Distinguish between external and internal forces for change.
2. What are the seven steps in the comprehensive change model?
3. Why do people resist change? How can this resistance be overcome?
4. What are some basic aspects of strategy, structure, and behavior that can be changed?
5. What are some basic OD techniques? What is their common purpose?
6. Why do organizations need to revitalize themselves? What stages do they typically go through during revitalization?

Analysis Questions

1. What current environmental forces do you think are causing the most changes in organizations?
2. Do you resist change? Why or why not?

3. Assume your instructor wants to implement some significant change in this class. How might he or she proceed in order to minimize resistance?
4. Select any area of change from Table 23.1. How might a change in that area necessitate changes in other areas of the table?
5. Were you ever the subject of any of the OD techniques discussed in the chapter? If you were, were your experiences generally favorable or unfavorable?
6. What might be the likely consequences of a failed or unsuccessful revitalization effort?

Application Exercises

1. Find a recent article about a business in *Fortune* or *Business Week*. Describe a hypothetical scenario in which the organization featured in the article might use the comprehensive model of change to improve its operations.
2. Interview the manager or owner of a local business. Ask about any recent changes that the organization has made. Why were they undertaken? How were they managed? How successful have they been?

Chapter Notes

1. Based on material from "Union Pacific Changes Its Hidebound Ways Under New Chairman," January 18, 1989. Used by permission of *The Wall Street Journal* © 1989 Dow Jones & Company, Inc. All Rights Reserved Worldwide. Also from Gary Hoover, Alta Campbell, and Patrick J. Spain, eds. Hoover's Handbook — Profiles of Over 500 Major Corporations, © 1990. Used by permission of the Reference Press.
2. See Roy McLennan, *Managing Organizational Change* (Englewood Cliffs, N.J.: Prentice-Hall, 1989), and Richard Beckhard and Reuben T. Harris, *Organizational Transitions,* 2nd ed. (Reading, Mass.: Addison-Wesley, 1987), for recent reviews of this area.
3. John P. Kotter and Leonard A. Schlesinger, "Choosing Strategies for Change," *Harvard Business Review,* March–April 1979, p. 106.
4. Rosabeth Moss Kanter, "Transcending Business Boundaries: 12,000 World Managers View Change," *Harvard Business Review,* May–June 1991, pp. 151–164.
5. See Robert H. Hayes and Ramchandran Jaikumar, "Manufacturing's Crisis: New Technologies, Obsolete Organizations," *Harvard Business Review,* September–October 1988, pp. 77–85, for additional insights into how technological change affects other parts of the organization.
6. Allan D. Gilmour, "Changing Times in the Automotive Industry," *The Academy of Management Executive,* February 1988, pp. 23–28.
7. "The Turnaround Trauma at Manufacturers Hanover," *Business Week,* August 24, 1987, pp. 68–69.
8. Kenneth Labich, "Was Breaking Up AT&T a Good Idea?" *Fortune,* January

2, 1989, pp. 82–87; Zane E. Zarnes, "Change in the Bell System," *The Academy of Management Executive,* February 1987, pp. 43–46.

9. See Gloria Barczak, Charles Smith, and David Wilemon, "Managing Large-Scale Organizational Change," *Organizational Dynamics,* Autumn 1987, pp. 22–35, and Thomas H. Fitzgerald, "Can Change in Organizational Culture Really Be Managed?" *Organizational Dynamics,* Autumn 1988, pp. 4–15.

10. Kurt Lewin, "Frontiers in Group Dynamics: Concept, Method, and Reality in Social Science," *Human Relations,* June 1947, pp. 5–41.

11. For another approach see David A. Nadler and Michael L. Tushman, "Organizational Frame Bending: Principles for Managing Reorientation," *The Academy of Management Executive,* August 1989, pp. 194–204.

12. "RJR Employees Fight Distraction Amid Buy-Out Talks," *Wall Street Journal,* November 1, 1988, p. A8.

13. Patricia Sellers, "Why Bigger Is Badder at Sears," *Fortune,* December 5, 1988, pp. 79–84.

14. See Paul R. Lawrence, "How to Deal with Resistance to Change," *Harvard Business Review,* January–February 1969, pp. 4–12, 166–176, for a classic discussion.

15. Lester Coch and John R. P. French, Jr., "Overcoming Resistance to Change," *Human Relations,* August 1948, pp. 512–532.

16. Charles K. Day, Jr., "Management's Mindless Mistakes," *Industry Week,* May 29, 1978, p. 42.

17. Harold J. Leavitt, "Applied Organization Change in Industry: Structural, Technical, and Human Approaches," in *New Perspectives in Organization Research,* ed. W. W. Cooper, H. J. Leavitt, and M. W. Shelly II (New York: Wiley, 1964), pp. 55–71.

18. Warren Boeker, "Strategic Change: The Effects of Founding and History," *Academy of Management Journal,* September 1989, pp. 489–515.

19. David A. Nadler, "The Effective Management of Organizational Change," in *Handbook of Organizational Behavior,* ed. Jay W. Lorsch (Englewood Cliffs, N.J.: Prentice-Hall, 1987), pp. 358–369.

20. Paul D. Collins, Jerald Hage, and Frank M. Hull, "Organizational and Technological Predictors of Change in Automaticity," *Academy of Management Journal,* September 1988, pp. 512–543.

21. Henkoff, "This Cat Is Acting Like a Tiger," *Fortune,* December 19, 1988, pp. 71–76.

22. For recent reviews, see Marshall Sashkin and W. Warner Burke, "Organization Development in the 1980s," *Journal of Management,* Summer 1987, pp. 393–417, and Richard Woodman, "Organization Change and Development," *Journal of Management,* June 1989, pp. 205–228.

23. Richard Beckhard, *Organization Development: Strategies and Models* (Reading, Mass.: Addison-Wesley, 1969), p. 9.

24. Wendell L. French and Cecil H. Bell, Jr., *Organization Development: Behavioral Science Interventions for Organization Improvement,* 2nd ed. (Englewood Cliffs, N.J.: Prentice-Hall, 1978). See also McLennan, *Managing Organizational Change.*

25. William G. Dyer, *Team Building Issues and Alternatives* (Reading, Mass.: Addison-Wesley, 1980).

26. Robert R. Blake and Jane S. Mouton, *The Managerial Grid* (Houston: Gulf Publishing Company, 1964); Robert R. Blake and Jane S. Mouton, *The New Managerial Grid* (Houston: Gulf Publishing, 1978); Robert R. Blake and Anne Adams McCanse, *Leadership Dilemmas — Grid Solutions* (Houston: Gulf Publishing Company, 1991).

27. Roger J. Hower, Mark G. Mindell, and Donna L. Simmons, "Introducing Innovation Through OD," *Management Review,* February 1978, pp. 52–56.

28. "Is Organization Development Catching On? A Personnel Symposium," *Personnel,* November–December 1977, pp. 10–22.

29. For a recent discussion on the effectiveness of various OD techniques in different organizations, see John M. Nicholas, "The Comparative Impact of Organization Development Interventions on Hard Criteria Measures," *Academy of Management Review,* October 1982, pp. 531–542, and Richard W. Woodman and Sandy J. Wayne, "An Investigation of Positive-Findings Bias in Evaluation of Organization Development Interventions," *Academy of Management Journal,* December 1985, pp. 889–913.

30. "Chicago's B-School Goes Touchy-Feely," *Business Week,* November 27, 1989, p. 140.

31. Michael Beer, "Revitalizing Organizations: Change Process and Emergent Model," *The Academy of Management Executive,* February 1987, pp. 51–55; Willem Mastenbroek, "A Dynamic Concept of Revitalization," *Organizational Dynamics,* Spring 1988, pp. 52–61.

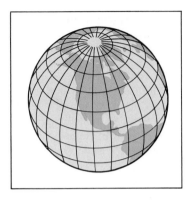

CASE 23.1

Looking for Change? Try United Air Lines

The airline industry in the United States has been in a state of flux ever since it began to feel the effects of federal deregulation in the early 1980s. At first deregulation seemed to open the door for a number of new, small entrants. But then the great shakeout began as first some of the small airlines and then former world leaders like Pan Am, Continental, and Eastern filed for bankruptcy and began selling off their routes.

In this volatile environment, no airline has experienced more change for more reasons than United. Changes at United have been both reactive and planned, resulting both from environmental pressures and from internal problems and strategies. The ultimate goal of United's changes is to make the airline the leader in the world. But a wrong move or bad luck could leave it fighting for survival.

United's recent turmoil began in 1985, when chairman Richard J. Ferris bought Pan Am's Pacific routes. Ferris's move turned out to be a real coup in United's competition with American Airlines, whose president, Robert L. Crandall, had decided that the routes were overpriced. Because of bilateral treaties and space limitations at some airports, the right to fly only certain routes is a major factor limiting the growth of every airline. Since 1985, American has been buying up routes from troubled airlines, but it can't match United in the Pacific.

And the Pacific is where the action is. U.S. airlines can no longer count on domestic travel to earn them profits. In 1990, domestic air traffic grew by only 3 percent, but airlines increased their capacity by 7 percent. With the airlines trying to fill all those domestic seats, price wars were inevitable. Those wars were a major reason that both United and American lost approximately $250 million in the last quarter of 1990.

Contrast that situation with the one in the Pacific. In 1990, Pacific air traffic increased 24 percent, and much of that traffic consists of business travelers who pay top fares. Because treaties often set rates for international travel, fare wars are not a problem.

But while United was doing well by expanding overseas, internal strife was leading to change of a different sort. Airlines' biggest single expense is labor, and United has had to contend with unrest in its three largest unions, representing pilots, flight attendants, and machinists. In 1990, at the tail end of the great merger and buyout spree of the 1980s, United's unions tried to buy the airline and make it into the largest employee-owned company in the world. But they should have learned a lesson from their own management. A year earlier, United's chairman Stephen Wolf had tried and failed to engineer a management buyout of the airline, and to many his failure was a sign that money for buyouts was getting tight. The unions found a top manager, former Chrysler executive Gerald Greenwald, to head their effort, but by the fall of 1990 the idea was dead.

The attempt, however, may have proved worthwhile for at least the pilots. To the surprise of many in the industry, Wolf gave in to the pilots' demands for pay hikes in a round of negotiations that ended in April 1991. Wolf agreed to raise pilots' pay to equal that of American Airlines pilots immediately and to reach the pay level of Delta pilots by 1993 (American had rejected similar demands by its pilots' union). Wolf seemed to be betting that United could pay for the hefty raises through increased growth. For while he was negotiating with the pilots, he was also placing orders for $22 billion of new planes and buying Pan Am's routes to London.

Although such purchases result from careful planning, no one in the industry could have planned for the most important environmental change of 1990 — Iraq's invasion of Kuwait and the resulting increases in the price of jet fuel. Some airline executives have months or years to make decisions, but those who buy jet fuel need to be ready to change course on a minute's notice. Even when the world's oil-producing regions are politically stable, United's fuel buyers have to be on their toes, making sure United's airports have sufficient fuel to satisfy the company's 6.3-million-gallon-per-day appetite and deciding how full to keep the company's 126-million-gallon-capacity storage tanks. Every cent that the price of jet fuel increases costs United $22.5 million over a year's time. So if a fuel bargain appears at any time, anywhere in the world, United's fuel buyers must be ready to take advantage of it.

By the minute and by the decade, at home and overseas, in response to union demands, Wall Street's woes, governments' regulations, and wars, United changes. But if it can continue to make the right decisions about change, it may enter the twenty-first century as the world's largest airline.

Discussion Questions

1. How would you categorize the various changes that United has recently experienced?
2. Is it possible for a company to develop a coherent strategy in an industry as radically affected by environmental change as the airline industry? Explain.
3. United's unions wanted to buy the company to stabilize it. How could union ownership achieve that result?
4. What kind of organizational structure, culture, and strategy does a company like United need to deal with change most effectively?

REFERENCES: Doug Carroll, "United's Fuel Buyers Ride Currents," *USA Today*, September 17, 1990, pp. B1, B2; Gerald Greenwald, "The United Job Is History-Making," *Fortune*, July 2, 1990, pp. 53–54; Kevin Kelly and Aaron Bernstein, "Why United Is Putting Pilots on the Gravy Train," *Business Week*, April 29, 1991, p. 32; Kenneth Labich, ". . . There Will Be No Soft Landing at United," *Fortune*, July 2, 1990, p. 57; Michael Oneal, Kevin Kelly, Wendy Zellner, and Seth Payne, "Dogfight!" *Business Week*, January 21, 1991, pp. 56–62.

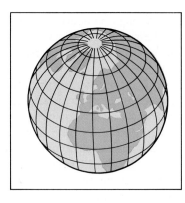

CASE 23.2

Westernizing Hungary's Tungsram

When the Berlin Wall came down in 1989 and revolutions transformed eastern Europe, thousands of American companies began to look for profitable business ventures in this newly opened territory. General Electric, which had actually begun the search for an eastern European subsidiary in 1987, was one of the first to commit itself to a major investment on the other side of what used to be the iron curtain: it paid $150 million for a controlling interest in Hungary's Tungsram Company. Thus began an experiment that will reveal to the rest of the world how well American capital and management techniques can transform one of the relics of communism.

The transformation is not going to be easy. GE certainly knows Tungsram's business — light bulbs — for the American company is the world's second largest maker of light bulbs, after Philips Lighting. But many of the conditions in the Hungarian company are alien to any American manager. Some of Tungsram's factories date back to the turn of the century. The company still keeps track of its accounts with pencil and paper and employs 150 people just to stuff cash into seventeen thousand pay envelopes each month. Years of being a state-run industry led the company and its employees to adopt strange habits: some workers lined cartons of bulbs with rocks so they could be paid extra for the volume they shipped, and the company's warehouses were packed with unsold and in some cases unsalable products, shipped to warehouses because company executives got bonuses for moving the goods along. Perhaps most appalling from an American manager's point of view, Tungsram's workers regularly produced about one-seventh as much as their American counterparts.

To deal with such problems, GE needed someone familiar with Hungarian culture yet schooled in American management techniques and in the GE philosophy. It found the perfect chief executive in George Varga, who had been working for GE for twenty-eight years after fleeing his native Hungary as a college student in 1956 and later earning an economics degree from Stanford. To assist in his mammoth undertaking, Varga passed over the kind of cocky, arrogant young managers for which GE is known. Instead, he chose veterans who would, he thought, be sensitive to the particular needs of a company trying to achieve a "cultural marriage."

The new managers had to work on many fronts at once. They had to explain to Hungarian engineers what profit is and why the company was interested in it. They had to start pouring capital into Tungsram to upgrade its equipment. The trickiest part of the transformation has been dealing with the Hungarian labor force.

One of the reasons American companies are so eager to set up operations in eastern Europe is that the cost of labor there is so low. Hungarian workers typically earn about one-tenth as much as their American counterparts. Labor therefore accounts for only about one-quarter of the cost of making a Hungarian light bulb (it eats up about half of every dollar spent producing bulbs in the United States). But although Hungarian workers are not used to making much money, they are also not used to losing their jobs, and fear of such losses under the new American leadership quickly eroded morale in some Tungsram factories.

American managers assigned to trim costs in an American factory are likely to look first at cutting the labor force. But GE's Tungsram managers are moving cautiously. They hoped to reduce the work force by about two thousand during the first year, simply through attrition and early retirement. After that, the going will become more difficult. Tungsram's union is already asking for a 30 percent pay raise in return for higher productivity, and the company is anxious not to alienate workers by appearing insensitive to their need for job security. GE's managers are looking to cut other costs — particularly those associated with materials — in order to make Tungsram's factories more efficient. And they hope that they can quickly convince Hungarian workers of a lesson that many American workers treat with skepticism — that what's good for the company (increased worker productivity, for example) is good for the workers.

Every company with a stake in Europe must plan for the changes sure to follow the elimination of the European Community's trade barriers in 1992. This major step toward the formation of a global economy will no doubt change many of the trading relationships in Europe and will likely give large, established companies an edge. GE's purchase of Tungsram is part of GE's overall strategy of becoming number one or number two in a business. Other American companies are watching GE's experiment closely to see what they can learn about how to manage the kind of transformation sure to become common as eastern Europe welcomes a flood of Western capital and companies.

Discussion Questions

1. How are the Tungsram workers' views of the changes in their company likely to be different from GE's views?
2. Would other managers transforming a company be smart to take Varga's approach and hire mostly older, more experienced executives? Explain.
3. Do you think GE should consider the changes it is making at Tungsram a revitalization? Explain.
4. How do you think Tungsram's new managers can best work with employees to lower workers' resistance to the changes?

REFERENCES: Jonathan B. Levine, "GE Carves Out a Road East," *Business Week*, July 30, 1990, pp. 32–33; Jeremy Main, "How to Go Global—and Why," *Fortune*, August 28, 1989, pp. 70–76; Amal Kumar Naj and Barry Newman, "GE to Buy 50% of Hungarian Lighting Firm," *Wall Street Journal*, November 16, 1989, pp. A2, A4; Shawn Tully, "GE in Hungary: Let There Be Light," *Fortune*, October 22, 1990, pp. 137–142.

24

Entrepreneurship and Small Business Management

LEARNING OBJECTIVES

After studying this chapter, you should be able to:

1. Discuss the nature of entrepreneurship.

2. Describe the roles of entrepreneurs in society.

3. Understand the key issues in choosing strategies for small firms.

4. Discuss the structural challenges unique to entrepreneurial firms.

5. Describe the special behavioral challenges facing small firms.

6. Understand the determinants of the performance of small firms.

The Nature of Entrepreneurship

The Role of Entrepreneurship in Society

Innovation

Job Creation

Contributions to Large Businesses

Strategy for Entrepreneurial Organizations

Choosing an Industry

Emphasizing Distinctive Competencies

Writing a Business Plan

Structure of Entrepreneurial Organizations

Forms of Ownership and Sources of Financing

Methods for Starting a New Business

Methods of Organizational Control

Sources of Management Help

Behavior in Entrepreneurial Organizations

Providing Motivation and Leadership

Group Dynamics

The Performance of Entrepreneurial Organizations

The Life Cycle of Entrepreneurial Firms

Reasons for Entrepreneurial Success

The Gentile boys always had a reputation for being a little different. It wasn't only that the two older boys, John and Anthony, were identical twins and bore a striking resemblance to Woody Allen. Nor was it that their younger brother, Chris, excelled so in school. What made the Gentiles different was that as they grew older, they never lost their ability to play or their ability to imagine.

In the late 1980s, John and Anthony were designing a new video game system. Frustrated and bored with the fundamental two-dimensional character of video games, they were looking for ways to make the game player feel more involved in the action. While warriors battled forces of evil and spaceships dodged exploding missiles, the game player remained all too aware of standing outside the screen and looking in. Inveterate video game players themselves, Anthony and John wondered, "What can we do to break through the wall of that TV?" Unlike most video game players, the Gentile brothers developed the technology to answer this question.

Their technology was the Power Glove, a video game controller that fits over a player's hand, much like a glove. Video game players wearing a Power Glove control the on-screen action by moving their hand through space, three dimensionally. The technological secret behind the Power Glove is a complex but relatively inexpensive position-sensing system. With this computer-controlled system in place, the video game always knows the exact location of the Power Glove. Movements in the position of the Power Glove trigger movements in key figures in the video game.

Although the technology of the Power Glove is an important component of the Gentiles' success, the entrepreneurial insight and drive that led them to identify the limitations of previous video game systems, as well as to recognize a way around those limitations, are as significant. In 1989 Mattel sold over $50 million worth of Power Gloves, and 1991 sales projections exceeded $100 million. The licensing arrangement between the Gentiles (through their company Abrams/Gentile Entertainment Inc.) and Mattel generated approximately $12 million in just two years for John, Anthony, and Chris.[1]

Like John, Anthony, and Chris Gentile, thousands of people all over the world start new businesses every year. Many of these people succeed in their enterprise, but many others fail. Some who fail try again, and sometimes it takes two or more failures before a new business gets under way. Henry Ford, for example, went bankrupt twice before succeeding with the Ford Motor Company.

This chapter examines the nature of entrepreneurship. The challenges involved in conceiving of and forming a new business are in many ways the same as the challenges of managing an established business. The management issues of choosing a strategy, implementing an organizational structure, and encouraging appropriate behavior are just as important to the success of small firms as they are for large firms.

The Nature of Entrepreneurship

Entrepreneurship is the process of organizing, operating, and assuming the risk of a business venture. An *entrepreneur* is someone who engages in entrepreneurship.

Entrepreneurship is the process of organizing, operating, and assuming the risk of a business venture.[2] An **entrepreneur** is someone who engages in entrepreneurship. The Gentile brothers were entrepreneurs because they recognized a consumer need, developed a technology to address that need, then developed an organization to exploit the market potential of their technology. Business owners who hire professional managers to run their businesses and then turn their own attention to other interests are not entrepreneurs. Although they are assuming the risk of the venture, they are not actively involved in organizing or operating it. Likewise, professional managers whose job is running someone else's business are not entrepreneurs, for they assume less-than-total personal risk for the success or failure of the business.

A *small business* is one that is privately owned by one individual, or by a small group of individuals, and has sales and assets that are not large enough to influence its environment.

Entrepreneurs start small businesses. We define a **small business** as one that is privately owned by one individual, or by a small group of individuals, and has sales and assets that are not large enough to influence its environment. The U.S. Small Business Administration (SBA), which was created in 1953 by Congress to improve the managerial skills of entrepreneurs and to help them borrow money, has drafted more specific definitions to fit virtually every industry.[3] A partial list appears in Table 24.1. Notice that some definitions go far beyond what many people think of as "small." For example, a petroleum refiner with 1,500 employees probably has sales of several million dollars each year.

The Role of Entrepreneurship in Society

The history of entrepreneurship, and of the development of new businesses, is in many ways the history of great wealth and of great failure. Some entrepreneurs have been very successful and have accumulated vast fortunes from their entrepreneurial efforts. For example, when Microsoft sold its stock to the public in 1986, Bill Gates, then just 30 years old, received $350 million for his share of Microsoft.[4] Many more entrepreneurs, however, have lost a great deal of money. Research suggests that the majority

Table 24.1

SBA Standards for "Small Businesses" by Industry

Manufacturers	Fewer employees than
Petroleum refining	1,500
Electronic computers	1,000
Macaroni and spaghetti	500
Wholesalers	**Fewer employees than**
Sporting goods	500
Furniture	500
Paints and varnishes	500
Retailers	**Annual sales less than**
Grocery stores	$13.5 million
Automobile agencies	11.5 million
Restaurants	10.0 million
Services	**Annual sales less than**
Computer-related services	$12.5 million
Accounting services	4.0 million
Television repair	3.5 million

SOURCE: "U.S. Small Business Administration: Small Business Size Standards," *Federal Register,* vol. 49, no. 28 (Washington, D.C.: Government Printing Office, February 9, 1984), pp. 5024–5048.

of new businesses fail within the first three years of founding.[5] Many that last longer do so only because the entrepreneurs themselves work long hours for very little income.

The experiences of individuals who win (and lose) fortunes as a result of their entrepreneurial activities may make fascinating stories, but the vital role that entrepreneurship plays in our society and our economy is even more telling. More than 99 percent of the nation's 16 million businesses are small. Over six hundred thousand new businesses are incorporated each year. Their vibrant, almost countless activities influence a number of economic areas, including innovation, job creation, and contributions to large businesses.[6]

Entrepreneurs and small businesses play three vital roles in society: (1) they foster innovation; (2) they provide jobs; and (3) they contribute to the success of large businesses.

Innovation

The resourcefulness and ingenuity typical of small business have spawned new industries and contributed a great many innovative ideas and technological breakthroughs to our society. Small businesses or individuals working alone invented, among other things, the personal computer, the

Entrepreneurship is an important source of innovation in society. In the 1950s Jack O'Neill, president and founder of O'Neill Inc., began manufacturing wet suits using plastic, foam rubber, and a soldering iron. Advances in design and materials have made it possible to tailor wet suits for different water sports and different environments. New colors and patterns have also made wet suits into fashion items.

transistor radio, the photocopying machine, the jet engine, and the instant photograph. They also gave us the pocket calculator, power steering, the automatic transmission, air conditioning, and even the nineteen-cent ballpoint pen. There are some scholars who believe that entrepreneurs and small businesses are the driving force behind innovation in a society. In Chapter 9, this driving force was called the "cycle of creative destruction." As entrepreneurs seek the income and wealth associated with successful innovation, they create new technologies and products that displace older technologies and products.[7]

Job Creation

Small businesses create more new jobs than do larger businesses. One study suggested that small businesses may account for as much as 66 percent of all new employment in the United States each year. In another study, the U.S. Department of Commerce found that small, young, high-technology businesses created new jobs at a much faster rate than did larger, older businesses.[8]

The new jobs created by small businesses come in small bites. When a new restaurant opens, it may employ fifteen people. When a new retail specialty store opens, it may employ twenty people. However, because so many new businesses are created each year, the cumulative impact on employment can be very significant.

Contributions to Large Businesses

It is primarily small businesses that supply and distribute the products of large businesses. General Motors, for example, buys materials from over twenty-five thousand suppliers, most of them small businesses. GM also distributes its products through small businesses — independent dealers. An organization like Sony buys supplies from thousands of small businesses, distributes its electronics products through numerous small distributors and its movies through numerous independent movie theaters, and sells its records through independent record stores.

Although entrepreneurship and new-business development have an important impact in many economies, their impact in Japan is less than might be expected. The reasons are discussed in The Global Challenge.

Strategy for Entrepreneurial Organizations

Like managers in any organization, entrepreneurs in small businesses must choose a strategy, create an appropriate structure, and motivate required behavior.

The three challenges that face any organization — choosing a strategy, creating an appropriate structure, and motivating required behavior — also face entrepreneurial organizations. In this section, we discuss some of the unique strategic problems facing small businesses. Subsequent sections discuss small-business structure and behavior. The three strategic challenges facing small firms discussed in this section are choosing an industry, emphasizing distinctive competencies, and writing a business plan.

Choosing an Industry

Porter's five forces framework can be applied by small businesses to choose an industry within which to compete.

As Chapters 4 and 7 discussed, we can apply Michael Porter's five forces framework to estimate the average economic performance of the firms in an industry. In general, an industry characterized by high levels of rivalry, strong substitutes, a strong threat of entry, and powerful suppliers and buyers has lower return potential for firms than do industries without these characteristics.[9] Entrepreneurs seeking to begin small-business operations should generally look to industries with favorable industry attributes. Thus, for example, entrepreneurs who start a business based on a technology with few rivals or substitutes and a low threat of entry usually earn higher rates of return than entrepreneurs who start a business without these advantages.

Examples of small businesses that chose a high-potential industry are Microsoft and Lotus, both very successful computer software companies.[10] These companies have developed personal-computer software that dominates their respective market segments (Microsoft in operating systems, Lotus in spreadsheet software). Because these firms are so dominant in their segments, there is low rivalry in their industries. Because of the skills that computer users have developed in applying these particular software packages, there are few substitutes. And because of the reputation and

THE GLOBAL CHALLENGE

Entrepreneurship in Japan

In the United States and most of the rest of the economically developed world, entrepreneurship and small business formation play vital roles in economic development. Indeed, economic scholars have suggested that entrepreneurship and small business formation are the single most important cause of economic development in a society.

However, this generalization — like so many others — does not fully apply in Japan. The number of entrepreneurs and new small businesses in Japan is far smaller than what one would expect, given the size of its economy. Moreover, the small firms that do exist do not seem to play a major role in technical innovation. In the past fifty years, only a handful of Japanese companies (including Honda and Sony) have grown from small entrepreneurial businesses to worldwide corporations. Even in industries dominated by entrepreneurial organizations throughout the world — such as microelectronics — one finds mostly large corporations in Japan.

There are several possible explanations for the relative unimportance of entrepreneurship and small business development in Japan. First, most small- and medium-sized firms are relegated to a secondary status as suppliers to large organizations. Large organizations are able to attract the best engineers and managers and thus have the human resources required to be innovative and entrepreneurial. As suppliers, most small- and medium-sized Japanese firms are unable to be innovative and creative *and* meet the demands of the large firms they supply.

Second, history has shown that large Japanese firms are often able to duplicate the innovative conditions of small entrepreneurial organizations. In particular, these firms are able to discover new markets as well as niches and established markets, and they are able to move quickly to create first-mover opportunities. In large Japanese firms, when a manager sees an opportunity to be innovative and creative, he is often able to obtain the resources needed to take advantage of that opportunity while remaining in the large corporation.

Third, the culture in Japan tends to discourage Western-style entrepreneurship and new-business development. Overall, the Japanese people tend to value conformity and "fitting in" more than individuality and "breaking away." In Japan, the saying is, "If one nail sticks up higher than other nails, pound that one nail down." This emphasis on staying in the group, fitting in, and working together does not encourage the independent risk taking that is usually required to start a new business.

REFERENCES: William G. Ouchi, *The M-Form Society* (Reading, Mass.: Addison-Wesley, 1986); Takeru Ohe, Shuji Oliva, and Ian MacMillan, "Entrepreneurs in Japan and Silicon Valley: A Study of Perceived Differences," *Journal of Business Venturing,* March 1991, pp. 135–144; Takeru Ohe, Shuji Honjo, and Ian MacMillan, "Japanese Entrepreneurs and Corporate Managers: A Comparison," *Journal of Business Venturing,* May 1990, pp. 163–176; Joel Kotkin, "Creators of the New Japan," *Inc.,* October 1990, pp. 90–110.

success of these firms, entry into these software segments is unlikely (although certainly not impossible).

An example of small businesses that begin operations in industries with lower return potential is independent video rental stores. Because of the large number of video rental stores, and the fact that all stores carry many of the same videos, rivalry in this industry is intense. Substitutes in the form of cable television, movie theaters, network television, and even books are common. Because the cost of entering this industry is relatively low (the cost of videos plus a lease and computer software), entry into the video rental business is easy. For these reasons, independent video retail operations are often marginal financial performers, although as members of national chains, video stores can be profitable.[11]

Small businesses are often strong in service, retail, and wholesale industries.

Industries in Which Small Businesses Are Strong   Small businesses tend to do well in the service, retail, and wholesale industries. Service organizations are perhaps the most common type of entrepreneurial business because they require a fairly small capital investment to start up. A certified public accountant, for example, can open a business simply by renting an office and hanging out a sign. Small businesses ranging from video rental shops to hair salons and tax preparation services have significantly increased in numbers in recent years, all because the costs of the physical assets needed to start these businesses are relatively low.

Entrepreneurs are also effective in the area of specialty retailing. Specialty retailers cater to specific customer groups such as golfers, college students, and people who do their own automobile repairs. Often, the number of these special consumers is relatively small, and thus the dollar size of the market associated with these consumers is small. Although large organizations may be unwilling to enter a business where the market is so small, small businesses may be very successful in these industries.[12]

Wholesalers buy products from large manufacturers and resell them to retailers. Small businesses dominate the wholesale industry because they are often able to develop personal working relationships with several sellers and several buyers. A wholesale supplier of computer equipment may have to develop supply relationships with five or six floppy disk manufacturers, six or seven hard disk manufacturers, five or six video screen manufacturers, and so forth, to have the inventory it needs to respond to the needs of its retail customers. If this wholesaler was not "independent" but instead was part of a larger electronics company, it would have supply relationships with only one supplier of floppy disks, one supplier of hard disks, one maker of video screens, and so forth. As long as end users want more supply options than this, the independent wholesaler can play an important economic role.[13]

Small businesses have strategic weaknesses in industries with large economies of scale, such as heavy manufacturing. Agriculture used to be dominated by small family farms but is now coming to be dominated by large corporate farms.

Industries in Which Small Businesses Are Weak   Small organizations have difficulty succeeding in certain other industries. Industries dominated by large-scale manufacturing are particularly difficult for small organizations. Agriculture is an industry in transition from being dominated by small family farms to being dominated by large corporate farms.

Research has shown that manufacturing costs often fall as the number of units produced by an organization increases. This relationship between cost and production is called an "economy of scale."[14] Small organizations usually cannot compete effectively on the basis of economies of scale. As depicted in panel A of Figure 24.1, organizations with higher levels of production have a significant cost advantage over those with lower levels of production. Given the cost positions of small and large firms when there are strong economies of scale in manufacturing, it is not surprising that small manufacturing organizations generally do not do as well as large ones.

Interestingly, when technology in an industry changes, it often shifts the economies-of-scale curve, thereby creating opportunities for smaller organizations. For example, steel manufacturing was historically dominated by a few large companies that owned several huge facilities. However, with the development of mini-mill technology, it became possible to extract economies of scale at a much smaller level of production. This type of shift is depicted in panel B of Figure 24.1. Point A in this panel is the low-cost point with the original economies of scale. Point B is the low-cost point with the economies of scale brought on by the new technology. Notice that the number of units needed for low costs is considerably lower for the new technology. This has allowed the entry of numerous smaller firms into the steel industry. Such entry would not have been possible with the older technology.[15]

Of course, not all manufacturing is capital-intensive. Some manufacturing can be done with minimal plant and equipment. This kind of light industry is typical of some parts of the computer industry and some parts of the plastic fabrication industry, in printing, and elsewhere. Small organizations can excel in these industries.[16]

Agriculture is an industry in transition. Small family farms were among the first small businesses in the world, and until recently they were among the most successful. Economies of scale and high equipment prices, however, have forced many small farmers out of business. Giant agribusiness enterprises and corporate farms are gradually replacing them. These multifarm businesses own and farm millions of acres and are large enough to fully exploit economies of scale by purchasing and sharing the most modern farm equipment, applying the latest scientific methods in farming, and even influencing government policy to favor farmers.[17]

Figure 24.1

Economies of Scale in Small Business Organizations

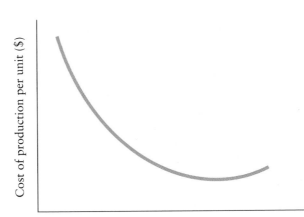

Standard Economies of Scale Curve

(A)

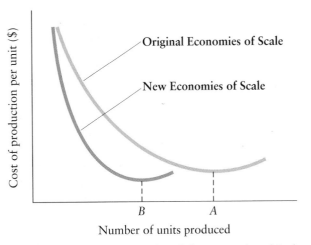

Change in Technology That Shifts Economies of Scale and May Make Small Business Production Possible

(B)

Entrepreneurs are often able to move quickly to identify niches in markets and to exploit first-mover advantages. This is true in Japan, where Reiko Sudo, founder of Nuno Corporation, has used her specialized knowledge of textiles and fashion to carve out a niche in the highly competitive textile industry. Her company produces, sells, and distributes textiles based on traditional Japanese design.

Emphasizing Distinctive Competencies

As defined in Chapter 7, an organization's distinctive competencies are the aspects of business that the firm performs better than its competitors. The distinctive competencies of small business usually fall into three areas: the ability to identify new niches in established markets, the ability to identify new markets, and the ability to move quickly to take advantage of new opportunities.

Small businesses often possess the ability to (1) identify niches in established markets, (2) identify new markets, and (3) move quickly to take advantage of opportunities.

Identifying Niches in Established Markets   An **established market** is one in which several large firms compete according to relatively well-defined criteria. For example, throughout the 1970s several well-known computer-manufacturing companies, including IBM, Digital Equipment, and Hewlett-Packard, competed according to three product criteria: computing power, service, and price. Over the years, the computing power and quality of service delivered by these firms continued to improve, while prices (especially relative to computing power) continued to drop.

Enter Apple Computer and the personal computer. For Apple, user friendliness, not computing power, service, and price, was to be the basis of competition. Apple targeted every manager, every student, and every home as the owner of a personal computer. The major entrepreneurial act of Apple was not to invent a new technology (indeed, the first Apple computers used all standard parts) but to recognize a new kind of computer and a new way to compete in the computer industry.[18]

A *niche* is a segment of a market that is not currently being exploited.

Apple's approach to competition was to identify a new niche in an established market. A **niche** is simply a segment of a market that is not currently being exploited. In general, small entrepreneurial businesses are better at discovering these niches than are larger organizations. Large organizations usually have so many resources committed to older, established business practices that they may be unaware of new opportunities. Entrepreneurs can see these opportunities and move quickly to take advantage of them.[19]

Identifying New Markets   Successful entrepreneurs also excel at discovering whole new markets. Discovery can happen in at least two ways. First, an entrepreneur can transfer a product or service that is well established in one geographic market to a second market. This is what Marcel Bich did with ballpoint pens, which occupied a well-established market in Europe before Bich introduced them to this country. Bich's company, BIC Corp., eventually came to dominate the U.S. market.[20]

Second, entrepreneurs can sometimes create entire industries. Entrepreneurial inventions of the dry paper copying process and the semiconductor have created vast new industries. Not only have the first companies into these markets been very successful (Xerox and National Semiconductor, respectively), but their entrepreneurial activity has spawned the development of hundreds of thousands of other companies and hundreds of thousands of jobs. Again, because entrepreneurs are not encumbered with a history of doing business in a particular way, they are usually better at discovering new markets than are larger, more mature organizations.

A *first-mover advantage* is any advantage that comes to a firm because it exploits an opportunity before any other firm does.

First-Mover Advantages   A **first-mover** **advantage** is any advantage that comes to a firm because it exploits an opportunity before any other firm does. Sometimes large firms discover niches within existing markets or new markets at just about the same time as small entrepreneurial firms do but are not able to move as quickly as small companies to take advantage of these opportunities.

There are numerous reasons for this difference. For example, many large organizations make decisions slowly because each of their many layers of hierarchy has to approve an action before it can be implemented. Also, large organizations may sometimes put a great deal of their assets at risk when they take advantage of new opportunities. Every time Boeing decides to build a new model of a commercial jet, it is making a decision that could literally bankrupt the company if it does not turn out well. The size of the risk may make large organizations cautious. The dollar value of the assets at risk in a small organization, in contrast, is quite small. Managers may be willing to "bet the company" when the value of the company is only $100,000. They might be unwilling to "bet the company" when the value of the company is $1 billion.[21]

Writing a Business Plan

Once an entrepreneur has chosen an industry to compete in, and determined which distinctive competencies to emphasize, these choices are usually

A *business plan* is a document that summarizes the business strategy and structure.

included in a document called a business plan. In a **business plan** the entrepreneur summarizes the business strategy and how that strategy is to be implemented.[22] The very act of preparing a business plan forces prospective entrepreneurs to crystallize their thinking about what they must do to launch their business successfully and obliges them to develop their business on paper before investing time and money in it. The idea of a business plan is not new. What is new is the growing use of specialized business plans by entrepreneurs, mostly because creditors and investors demand them for use in deciding whether to help finance a small business.

The plan should describe the match between the entrepreneur's abilities and the requirements for producing and marketing a particular product or service. It should define strategies for production and marketing, legal aspects and organization, and accounting and finance. In particular, it should answer three questions: (1) What are the entrepreneur's goals and objectives? (2) What strategies will the entrepreneur use to obtain these goals and objectives? (3) How will the entrepreneur implement these strategies?

Some idea of the complexity of planning a new business may be gleaned from the PERT diagram shown in Figure 24.2.[23] The diagram shows the key steps in planning the launch of a new business. Notice that the development of a business plan consists of a set of specific activities, perhaps none of which is more pivotal than marketing research — the systematic and intensive study of all the facts, opinions, and judgments that bear on the successful marketing of a product or service.

Figure 24.2 also demonstrates the sequential nature of much strategic decision making in small businesses. For example, entrepreneurs cannot forecast sales revenues without first researching markets. The sales forecast itself is one of the most important elements in the business plan. Without such forecasts, it is all but impossible to estimate intelligently how large a plant, store, or office should be or to determine how much inventory to carry or how many employees to hire.

Another important activity is financial planning, which translates all other activities into dollars. Generally, the financial plan is made up of a cash budget, an income statement, balance sheets, and a breakeven chart. The most important of these statements is the cash budget because it tells entrepreneurs how much money they need before they open for business and how much money they need to keep the business operating.

Structure of Entrepreneurial Organizations

With a strategy in place and a business plan in hand, the entrepreneur can take the second major step in creating a new business: devising a structure that turns the vision of the business plan into a reality. Many of the same concerns in structuring any business, which were described in Part III of this book, are also relevant to small businesses. For example, entrepreneurs need to consider organization design and develop job descriptions, organization charts, management control systems, and so forth. However, small

Figure 24.2

A PERT Diagram Showing the Steps in Planning the Launch of a New Business

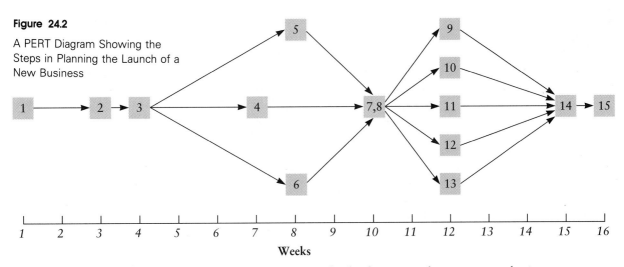

Weeks

Shown here at 16 weeks for illustrative purposes. Clearly, the time it takes to prepare a business plan may take less or much more than 16 weeks, depending on the complexity of the venture.

Key:

1 Make commitment to go into business for yourself
2 Analyze yourself
3 Choose product or service
4 Research markets
5 Forecast sales revenues

6 Choose site
7 Develop production plan
8 Develop marketing plan
9 Develop organizational plan
10 Develop legal plan

11 Develop accounting plan
12 Develop insurance plan
13 Develop computer plan
14 Develop financial plan
15 Write cover letter

SOURCE: From Nicholas C. Siropolis, *Small Business Management: A Guide to Entrepreneurship,* 4th ed. (Boston: Houghton Mifflin, 1990). Copyright © 1990 by Houghton Mifflin Company. Used with permission.

Some structural concerns unique to small businesses include (1) the form of ownership, (2) methods for starting the business, and (3) methods of organizational control that are appropriate in a small-firm context.

businesses do have some special concerns relating to structure, including the form of ownership and sources of financing, methods for starting the business, methods of organizational control, and sources of management help.

Forms of Ownership and Sources of Financing

Ownership structure specifies who possesses legal title to all of an organization's assets and who has a claim on any economic profits generated by a firm. Financing a small business involves decisions concerning the sources of capital that will be used to start the business and what claims (if any) these sources have on the organization's profits. There are a number of alternatives for both ownership structure and sources of financing, and each of them has advantages and disadvantages.[24]

The major forms of ownership available to small businesses are *sole proprietorships, partnerships, corporations, master limited partnerships, sub-chapter S corporations,* and *cooperatives.*

Forms of Ownership   A popular form of legal ownership for many new businesses is the **sole proprietorship,** in which legal title to all assets and claims on all future economic profits are controlled by a single individual. About 70 percent of all American businesses are sole proprietorships. The major advantages of a sole proprietorship are that the individual entrepreneur has total freedom in conducting business, start-up is simple and inexpensive, and business profits are taxed as ordinary income to the proprietor. The disadvantages are that the proprietor has unlimited liability (his or her personal assets are at risk to cover business debts) and the business ends when the proprietor retires or dies.

Another form of ownership is the **partnership,** in which two or more people agree to be partners in a business, share title in the assets of the firm, be held jointly liable for a firm's debts, and share a firm's profits. The least common form of ownership, partnerships are often used by accounting, legal, and architectural firms. These types of organizations are highly dependent on the professional skills of individuals, and partnerships tend to foster the professional mutual respect that is essential in these business activities. Partnerships provide a larger pool of talent and capital to start a business than do sole proprietorships, but they are just as easy to form and they offer the same tax benefits. They also have similar disadvantages: liability and no legal continuance if the partnership is dissolved. An added difficulty may be conflict or tension between partners.

Most large organizations, and some smaller organizations, use the corporation as the basis for ownership. A **corporation** is a legal entity created under the law that is independent of any single individual. Like an individual, a corporation can borrow money, enter into contracts, own property, sue, and be sued. Its owners are the stockholders. An advantage that distinguishes the corporation from sole proprietorships and partnerships is that it is responsible for its own liabilities, so the owners have limited liability. A corporation continues to exist despite the retirement or death of any of its owners, and it can often borrow money easily. However, corporations have higher start-up costs and are subject to more regulation and to double taxation (the corporation pays taxes on its profits, and then stockholders pay taxes on their dividends).

A few other special forms of ownership exist. **Master limited partnerships** and **sub-chapter S corporations** provide many of the advantages of corporations but without double taxation. **Cooperatives** enable a number of small organizations to pool resources and share markets. Ocean Spray Cranberries is a cooperative that is made up of 700 independent cranberry growers and 100 citrus growers.

The major sources of financing for new businesses are personal resources, funding from banks and government agencies, and venture capital firms.

Sources of Financing   An important issue confronting all entrepreneurs is locating the money necessary to open and operate the business. Personal resources (savings and money borrowed from friends or family) are the most common sources of new-business financing. Personal resources are often the most important source because they reinforce the entrepreneur's personal commitment to the venture.[25] Many entrepreneurs also take advantage of various lending programs and assistance provided by lending

THE ENTREPRENEURIAL CHALLENGE

"Vulture" Capitalists

Venture capital has been cited as one of the most important sources of capital for entrepreneurship and new business development. Indeed, there is little doubt that the growth of "Silicon Valley" in California and "Route 128" in Massachusetts was directly tied to the investment of venture capital firms in numerous high-technology start-up companies.

But despite the importance of venture capital firms as a source of capital, entrepreneurs and new-business managers do not always "like" working with them. Venture capitalists have been accused of being interested only in a short, three- to five-year payout on their investment and are thought to be willing to do anything necessary to make sure they receive it. This reputation has earned some venture capitalists the nickname "vulture capitalists."

Part of the pressure that venture capitalists put on small businesses is attributable to the structure of the venture capital investment. A venture capital firm usually joins together with several other such firms to purchase a share of the equity in a small business. The more equity these firms purchase, the more influence they have over how the small business should be managed. Recent research suggests that venture capital investments in small businesses average just over 50 percent of the equity in a small business.

With this 50 percent share, venture capitalists obtain seats on the small organization's board of directors, where they can influence hiring and promotion decisions, help decide when the business should introduce its products and in which markets, and influence how

much money the organization will spend on research and development. Venture capitalists can even decide to replace the founder of a small business with a manager of their own choosing. When asked, most venture capitalists admit that the question is not whether they should replace the founder but more frequently when they will do it. Obviously, this degree of power can make an entrepreneur uncomfortable. After all, many entrepreneurs begin their businesses to escape this kind of external control.

Despite the tension that might exist between venture capital firms and the small businesses they invest in, research seems to suggest that — on average — venture capitalists and entrepreneurs enjoy respectful, even friendly relationships. In the end, venture capitalists and entrepreneurs alike recognize that it is best to develop cordial relationships. For entrepreneurs, harmony increases the chances of remaining with the organizations they founded. For venture capitalists, it increases the chances that they will receive a positive return on their investment.

REFERENCES: Jay Barney, Lowell Busenitz, James Fiet, and Doug Moesel, "The Structure of Venture Capital Governance," *Academy of Management Proceedings: "Best Papers 1989,"* Meeting of the Academy of Management, Washington, D.C., 1989; Swee-Sum Lam, "Venture Capital Financing: A Conceptual Framework," *Journal of Business Finance and Accounting,* January 1991, pp. 137–149; Edward Roberts, "High Stakes for High-Tech Entrepreneurs: Understanding Venture Capital Decision Making," *Sloan Management Review,* Winter 1991, pp. 9–20.

institutions and government agencies.[26] Government programs are especially interested in helping women and minority entrepreneurs.

Another common source of funds is venture capitalists. A **venture capitalist** is someone who actively seeks to invest in new businesses. The advantage of this approach is that it gives entrepreneurs access to a large resource base with fewer restrictions than might be imposed by the government or by banks. In return, however, the entrepreneur must relinquish to the venture capitalist a portion of the profits or share ownership.[27] The relationship between new businesses and venture capital firms is discussed in The Entrepreneurial Challenge.

Methods for Starting a New Business

The major options for starting new businesses are (1) buying an existing business, (2) starting from scratch, and (3) franchising.

Another set of organizational questions that an entrepreneur must address when organizing a business is whether to buy an existing business, start a new one, or seek a franchising agreement.

Buying an Existing Business   Buying an existing business offers a strong set of advantages. Because the entrepreneur can examine historical records for the business to determine the pattern of revenue and profit and the type of cash flow, much guesswork about what to expect is eliminated. The entrepreneur also acquires existing supplier, distributor, and customer networks. On the negative side, the entrepreneur inherits whatever problems the business may already have and may be forced to accept existing contractual agreements.

Starting a New Business   Starting a new business from scratch allows the owner to avoid the shortcomings of an existing business and to put his or her personal stamp on the enterprise. The entrepreneur also has the opportunity to choose suppliers, bankers, lawyers, and employees without worrying about existing agreements or contractual arrangements. However, there is more uncertainty involved in starting a new business than in taking over an existing one. The entrepreneur starts out with less information about projected revenues and cash flow, has to build a customer base from zero, and may be forced to accept unfavorable credit terms from suppliers. It is also hard for a new business to borrow money because it is an unknown quantity.

A *franchising agreement* is a contract between an entrepreneur (the *franchisee*) and a parent company (the *franchiser*). The entrepreneur pays the parent company for the use of the trademarks, products, formulas, and business plans.

Franchising   An alternative to buying an existing business or starting one from scratch is entering into a **franchising agreement**. The entrepreneur pays a parent company (the **franchiser**) a flat fee or a share of the income from the business. In return, the entrepreneur (the **franchisee**) is allowed to use the company's trademarks, products, formulas, and business plan. Industries within which franchising is common include fast foods (e.g., McDonald's), specialty retail clothing stores (e.g., Benetton), personal computer stores (e.g., ComputerLand), and local automobile dealerships.[28]

Franchising may reduce the entrepreneur's financial risk because many parent companies provide advice and assistance. They also provide proven production, sales, and marketing methods; training; financial support; and an established identity and image.

On the negative side, franchises may cost a lot of money. A McDonald's franchise costs several hundred thousand dollars. Also, the parent company often restricts the franchisee to certain types of products. A McDonald's franchisee cannot change the formula for milkshakes, alter the preparation of Big Macs, or purchase supplies from any other company. Some franchise agreements are difficult to terminate.

Despite the drawbacks, franchising is growing by leaps and bounds. Presently, one-third of U.S. retail sales go through franchises, and that figure is expected to climb to one-half by the end of this century.[29] Much

THE ENVIRONMENTAL CHALLENGE

When the Franchise Relationship Breaks Down

Franchising agreements, like any cooperative relationships between independent organizations, are based on mutual respect, trust, and open communication. Of course, these relationships are supplemented by numerous legal contracts that list specific obligations for both the franchiser and the franchisee. However, although the explicit contract is important, the relationship that underlies that contract is perhaps even more important for parties in a franchising agreement.

Some franchising organizations, like McDonald's, spend a great deal of time and money developing the "right" relationships with their franchisees. McDonald's requires their franchisees to learn the business "from the ground up" by cooking hamburgers and french fries and cleaning up in another McDonald's before they are able to purchase their own franchise. Potential franchisees are also trained at "Hamburger University" to understand corporate policy and to develop close relationships with individuals in the McDonald's organization.

Despite these efforts to build close relationships, conflicts sometimes emerge between franchisees and franchisers. Benetton, the clothing manufacturer, is an organization that had very cooperative relationships with its franchisees. Indeed, relationships between Benetton and its franchisees were so positive that the legal contracts drawn up to manage this relationship were not well developed. Benetton operated on the basis of handshakes and trust — and this seemed to work well.

But the relationship changed as Benetton began to face some financial challenges. In order to continue growth and profitability, Benetton began to pressure its franchisees to increase sales, to accept more and more inventory, and in other ways to move more product. Benetton even began shipping inappropriate types of clothing to some of its franchisees, just to move inventory. When the owner of a Benetton outlet in Atlanta received a huge shipment of sweaters in June, the positive relationship that had existed suddenly ended in a series of lawsuits.

Since then, Benetton has made an effort to repair relationships with its franchisees. It has also adopted a new, strict contract to help define this relationship. Both sides fondly recall the "good old days" when trust and cooperation were the basis of the franchise relationship.

RESOURCES: Sara Jackson, Andy Simmonds, Christopher Ellerten, and Michael Hesketh, "The European 500," *Director,* December 1990, pp. 41–88; Edmund Andrews, "European Franchisers Go Global, " *Europe,* June 1988, pp. 18–19; Amy Dunkin, "Why Some Benetton Shopkeepers Are Losing Their Shirts," *Business Week,* March 14, 1988, pp. 78–79.

of the attraction of franchising is that this approach to starting a new business involves limited risks. However, it is not risk-free. Some of the risks are discussed in The Environmental Challenge.

Methods of Organizational Control

Methods of control in small businesses include accounting control and budget controls.

Organizational control, despite its importance, tends to be ignored by many entrepreneurs in the belief that control is a function practiced only by large businesses. Considering this attitude, it is hardly surprising that so many small businesses falter almost from the start. Some entrepreneurs fail to see that control is simply the process by which they may ensure that their actions, as well as those of their employees, conform to plans and policies.

Accounting Control Accounting information is especially necessary for effective control because it allows entrepreneurs to compare actual performance with expected performance. This information allows them not only to measure their performance but also to determine the appropriateness of their goals and actions and, if necessary, to adjust them. To grasp the importance of control to the small business, consider the experience of one small contracting firm, Elling Brothers Mechanical Contractors, which specializes in the design and installation of piping systems. After expanding into the installation of custom and made-to-order systems, the company lost $250,000 on small cost overruns that snowballed over the course of one fifteen-month job. Following a set of guidelines developed by a consultant, the firm implemented a new accounting control system that saved it from bankruptcy.[30]

Budget Control Another important control tool for small business, the budget translates operating plans into dollar terms or other quantitative measures. To see how budgets help entrepreneurs control business operations, consider the case of Georgia Qua, the owner of a Buick dealership in Ohio. As the budget in Table 24.2 shows, Qua expresses new-car sales in units. The unit budget is used by her sales manager to monitor the performance of salespeople. However, it alone does not provide complete sales control because the sales manager might instruct salespeople to increase unit sales by selling cars at a discount or by offering high prices for trade-ins. Both of those practices would erode profit margins. To avoid that problem, Qua prepares a second budget, which translates units into dollars. This budget is shown in Table 24.3. But the control system is still incomplete because the sales manager may overspend in advertising in order to reach his unit goal of selling $27,500,000 worth of cars in a year. So

Table 24.2

New Car Sales Budget — Units

| Model | Quarter | | | | |
	First	Second	Third	Fourth	Total
Small	200	300	300	200	1,000
Medium	100	150	150	100	500
Large	200	250	250	200	900
	500	700	700	500	2,400

SOURCE: From Nicholas C. Siropolis, *Small Business Management: A Guide to Entrepreneurship*, 4th ed. (Boston: Houghton Mifflin, 1990). Copyright © 1990 by Houghton Mifflin Company. Used with permission.

Table 24.3

New Car Sales Budget — Net of Trade-in

Model	Quarter				
	First	Second	Third	Fourth	Total
Small	$1,600,000	$2,400,000	$2,400,000	$1,600,000	$ 8,000,000
Medium	1,200,000	1,800,000	1,800,000	1,200,000	6,000,000
Large	3,000,000	3,750,000	3,750,000	3,000,000	13,500,000
	$5,800,000	$7,950,000	$7,950,000	$5,800,000	$27,500,000

SOURCE: From Nicholas C. Siropolis, *Small Business Management: A Guide to Entrepreneurship*, 4th ed. (Boston: Houghton Mifflin, 1990). Copyright © 1990 by Houghton Mifflin Company. Used with permission.

Qua prepares a third budget, which covers selling expenses. This budget is shown in Table 24.4. Armed with all three of these budgets, Qua is adequately prepared to control the performance of her new-car sales department. The budgets enable Qua to evaluate the performance of the sales manager, and they enable the sales manager to evaluate the performance of the sales force.[31]

Table 24.4

New-Car Selling Expense Budget

Model	Quarter				
	First	Second	Third	Fourth	Total
Salaries	$600,000	$600,000	$600,000	$600,000	$2,400,000
Commissions	300,000	450,000	450,000	300,000	1,500,000
Advertising	60,000	120,000	180,000	120,000	480,000
Telephone	3,000	3,000	3,000	3,000	12,000
	$963,000	$1,173,000	$1,233,000	$1,023,000	$4,392,000

SOURCE: From Nicholas C. Siropolis, *Small Business Management: A Guide to Entrepreneurship*, 4th ed. (Boston: Houghton Mifflin, 1990). Copyright © 1990 by Houghton Mifflin Company. Used with permission.

Table 24.5

Sources of Help for Entrepreneurs

Management Help Offered by	Where Available	Before they go into a business whose technology is		After they go into a business whose technology is	
		High	Low	High	Low
U.S. Small Business Administration					
Counseling by:					
Staff	N		✓		✓
Service Corps of Retired Executives	N		✓		✓
Active Corps of Executives	N				✓
Small Business Institutes	N			✓	✓
Small Business Development Centers	S	✓	✓	✓	✓
Pre-business workshops	N		✓		
Nonaccredited courses and seminars	N				✓
Publications	N		✓		✓
U.S. Department of Commerce					
Seminars and workshops	N			✓	✓
Publications	N	✓	✓	✓	✓
Other federal agencies (example: Internal Revenue Service)					
Seminars and workshops	N				✓
Publications	N				✓
State, county, and local governments					
Counseling	S				✓
Seminars and workshops	S				✓
Publications	S				✓
Local development corporations and similar companies					
Counseling	N				✓
Seminars and workshops	N				✓

Sources of Management Help

Since the 1950s, the idea that small businesses benefit from management assistance has grown widely. Table 24.5 lists the many sources of management help now offered at little or no cost to entrepreneurs, both before and after they embark on a new business. Because of the extent of management sophistication needed to launch a venture such as microcomputer manufacture, special services are available to entrepreneurs who go into a high-technology business.

Table 24.5 *(cont.)*

Management Help Offered by	Where Available	Before they go into a business whose technology is		After they go into a business whose technology is	
		High	Low	High	Low
Universities					
Accredited courses	S	✔	✔	✔	✔
Nonaccredited courses and seminars	S	✔	✔	✔	✔
Publications	S	✔	✔	✔	✔
Counseling	S	✔	✔	✔	✔
Community colleges					
Accredited courses	S		✔	✔	✔
Nonaccredited courses and seminars	N		✔	✔	✔
Counseling	S		✔	✔	✔
Small-business groups (example: National Federation of Independent Business)					
Seminars and workshops	S				✔
Counseling	S				✔
Publications	N				✔
Large corporations (example: Bank of America)					
Publications	N		✔		✔
Counseling	S				✔
Trade associations					
Publications	N			✔	✔
Seminars and workshops	N			✔	✔

N = Nationally
S = Some parts of nation

SOURCE: From Nicholas C. Siropolis, *Small Business Management: A Guide to Entrepreneurship,* 4th ed. (Boston: Houghton Mifflin, 1990). Copyright © 1990 by Houghton Mifflin Company. Used with permission.

Table 24.5 covers not only federal help but also help from such sources as community colleges and universities, chambers of commerce, and other organizations made up of small businesses. Heading the list is the Small Business Administration (SBA). Many entrepreneurs have the mistaken view that the SBA only lends money or guarantees repayment of loans made by commercial banks. Even more important are SBA efforts to help entrepreneurs manage their businesses effectively and spend their money wisely.

The SBA offers entrepreneurs four major cost-free management-assistance programs: SCORE (Service Corps of Retired Executives), ACE (Active Corps of Executives), SBI (Small Business Institutes), and SBDC (Small Business Development Centers). Under the SCORE and ACE programs, the SBA tries to match an expert to the need. If an entrepreneur needs a marketing plan but does not know how to put one together, the SBA pulls from its list of SCORE or ACE counselors someone with marketing knowledge and experience. SCORE counselors are retired executives. ACE offers the assistance of currently practicing executives. The SBI program taps the talents available at colleges and universities. This program involves not only professors of business administration but also students working for advanced degrees. Under a professor's guidance, such students work with entrepreneurs to help solve their management problems. Finally, the SBDC program brings resources and skills needed by entrepreneurs together at a single location where entrepreneurs can go to receive instruction and training in management and technical skills.

Behavior in Entrepreneurial Organizations

The same challenges that face all managers in leading and motivating workers face entrepreneurs in small businesses. Unlike many managers, however, entrepreneurs must set and adjust business strategy and choose and adjust organizational structure as well. In larger organizations, many of the latter tasks are managed by specialists. IBM has a full-time manager whose sole responsibility is to keep track of changes in the firm's organization chart, and General Motors has numerous managers who focus only on planning. In small business, the entrepreneur may sometimes rely on specialists but generally does all these tasks plus many more. For this reason, entrepreneurs need a wider variety of management skills than do managers in large organizations.

Providing Motivation and Leadership

To provide effective motivation and leadership, an entrepreneur should enable employees to satisfy their own personal goals while performing organizational responsibilities well. Entrepreneurs may approach this task in several ways. First, an entrepreneur must sincerely desire to help employees become achievers. As leaders, entrepreneurs can help employees achieve job status and gain a positive opinion of themselves and their jobs by sharing decision-making responsibilities, taking employees' suggestions to heart, and judging employees rigorously on merit and rewarding them accordingly.

Second, to be effective leaders, entrepreneurs must have a knack for clearly communicating assignments to employees and for creating an atmosphere of fairness, confidence, and camaraderie in the workplace. Creating such a work atmosphere is difficult. As we saw in Chapter 16 and elsewhere, no two employees are exactly alike, and what appeals to one may discourage another. Because all employees are unique and complex, entrepreneurs must take their individual needs into consideration.

Entrepreneurs who are successful at creating a positive work environment have, in a sense, created a corporate culture. The values and beliefs of this corporate culture can guide behavior over a long period of time. Indeed, research suggests that the culture created by a firm's founders can have an impact on the firm for decades, long after the founders have died.[32]

Of all the traits that entrepreneurs must possess if they are to be effective leaders, perhaps none is so vital as the willingness to set high standards and demonstrate a personal commitment to excellence. Entrepreneurs who expect excellent performance from employees often receive it. Only highly motivated employees are likely to make and sell superior products that earn the loyalty of customers.

> Entrepreneurs need to realize that they are likely to be more highly motivated and committed to the success of their company than are their employees.

The leadership and motivation tasks of managers in small businesses are distinct from those of managers in large firms in two ways. First, entrepreneurs in small businesses are, themselves, almost always highly motivated and committed to the success of their firm. In this circumstance, it is not uncommon for entrepreneurs to simply assume that other employees in the organization are equally motivated and committed. It is usually wiser for the entrepreneur to assume that his or her employees are *not* motivated and committed to the same extent. The entrepreneur might want to engage in specific activities to help employees satisfy their own personal goals, communicate expectations to employees, and create a positive organizational culture.[33]

> As small organizations grow, the leadership and motivational tools used by managers must change.

Second, in a large firm, the tools and techniques that managers can use to lead and motivate workers are relatively fixed. For example, they can use formal training sessions, taped messages from the CEO, and in-house newspapers to communicate throughout the organization. In contrast, the techniques and tools that entrepreneurs can use to motivate and lead evolve over time. When a firm is very small, most communication can be face to face and very hands-on. However, as the firm becomes successful and grows in size, many informal techniques and tools for leading and motivating are no longer applicable. Thus, as the organization evolves, entrepreneurs need to modify the tools and techniques they use to lead and motivate the organization.

Group Dynamics

> Two group dynamics issues unique to small firms are relationships between (1) employees who own stock in the company and those who do not and (2) employees who are family members and employees who are not.

Many of the challenges of managing individuals in groups and managing relations between groups in large organizations exist small businesses. Conflicts between different functions (for example, engineering versus manufacturing) that are endemic in large organizations exist in small organizations too.

Some group dynamics issues are peculiar to small businesses, however. One of the most important involves status differences created by degrees of ownership. When a small business is first founded, it is usually the case that all the firm's assets, including its stock, are owned by a very small number of individuals — often no more than one or two original founders. However, in the early history of a company, it is not uncommon for new employees to receive some ownership position in the company upon accepting employment. They may also receive additional equity ownership in the company as part of their compensation.

Broadening the ownership base has several advantages, but over time it can complicate group dynamics within a firm, for it creates two classes of individuals — those who own part of the company and those who do not. These ownership groups do not necessarily parallel hierarchical lines of authority. For example, if a company's founder retires and brings in a new president from the outside, the new president may own less stock in the company than a low-level engineer who has worked there from the beginning. Obviously, this type of discrepancy can cause conflict and confusion within an organization. Managers in small businesses must anticipate these group dynamics and seek ways of managing them effectively.[34]

A second challenge involving group dynamics in small firms concerns status differences linked to family relationships. Founders of small companies often employ family members because they may be willing to work for less than a market wage, they may be motivated to work very hard, and they may be especially committed to the success of a firm. However, having family members as employees can create difficulties, because in some cases family loyalties conflict with business loyalties, putting nonfamily managers in a difficult position. Even relationships within a family can be strained when family members are employees. Sometimes, for example, young siblings may be more skilled managers than older siblings, yet tradition in many families suggests that older siblings should be the senior managers. Small business managers need to seek ways to take advantage of family members as a resource for the firm without allowing family relationships to interfere with the efficient operation of the company.[35]

The Performance of Entrepreneurial Organizations

The choice of organization strategy, its implementation through structure, and the behavior that supports this implementation — these three elements determine the overall performance of an entrepreneurial organization. This section examines how entrepreneurial firms evolve over time and the attributes of these firms that enhance their chance for success.

The Life Cycle of Entrepreneurial Firms

The entrepreneurial life cycle that small businesses pass through consists of three stages: (1) acceptance, (2) breakthrough, and (3) maturity.

The entrepreneurial life cycle is a series of predictable stages that small businesses pass through. A common pattern of evolution for entrepreneurial organizations is depicted in Figure 24.3.[36] This pattern is similar to the

The acceptance stage, the first in the life cycle of entrepreneurial firms, is critical to the long-term success of small businesses. Alambic Inc., a small California distiller, faces many of the challenges of acceptance as it attempts to market a cognac distilled in the United States. Using the skills of its distiller, Hubert Germain-Robin, Alambic hopes to convince consumers that high-quality cognac come from places other than Europe.

product life cycle discussed in Chapter 7 as well as to the innovation process presented in Chapter 9, but it refers specifically to the challenges and changes in small entrepreneurial firms.

First comes the acceptance stage, in which the small business struggles to break even and survive. Entrepreneurial firms are usually small enough at this stage that they can spot obstacles to success and act quickly to remove them. Moreover, entrepreneurs usually have the skills needed to modify their products or services as required by customers during this stage. Such modifications are often necessary for small firms struggling to obtain enough cash from sales and other sources to continue operations. Many small organizations, despite the skill and effort of entrepreneurs, never emerge from the acceptance stage.

Next follows the breakthrough stage. In the preceding stage, the rate of growth is slow — so slow that it is often unnoticed. But in the breakthrough stage, growth is so fast and so unpredictable that many entrepreneurs fail

Figure 24.3

Stages of Evolution for Entrepreneurial Firms

Acceptance	Breakthrough	Maturity
• Firm struggles to break even • Low cash flow • Entrepreneur uses skills to adjust product and processes to meet market demands	• Rapid sales growth • Challenges in managing cash flow, production, quality, delivery	• Stable balanced growth • Entrepreneur must develop management skills

to keep pace with it. Caught unprepared, they blunder. Sales revenues spiral upward as problems begin to surface with cash flow, production, quality, and delivery. At the same time, competition may become more severe.

In the face of these pressures, entrepreneurs may apply hasty, ill-conceived solutions to problems. For example, if sales begin to level off or slip, they may hire specialists such as an accountant, a quality-control analyst, or a customer services representative to relieve the problem. As a result, costs go up, squeezing profits further.

Perhaps the best way to head off the problems presented by rapid growth is to continue updating the business plan. With a thorough, updated business plan in place, entrepreneurs are less likely to be surprised by breakthroughs.

In the mature stage, the lack of control of the breakthrough stage is replaced by a more stable, balanced period of steady growth. Organizations that survive to this stage can continue to grow for many years. However, in this last stage entrepreneurs often face another challenge. Although they usually have the technical skills required during the acceptance stage, they often do not possess the managerial skills required during the mature stage. Entrepreneurs without these skills either have to develop them or turn the day-to-day operations of their organization over to professional managers and concentrate on new business opportunities or the creation of new organizations.[37]

Reasons for Entrepreneurial Success

Many organizations successfully move through the stages listed in Figure 24.3 to become stable and mature organizations. Many factors contribute to this success. Six of the most common ones are described below.

Reasons for the success of small firms include (1) the entrepreneur's hard work, drive, and dedication, (2) market demand for products or services, (3) managerial competence, (4) luck, (5) strong control systems, and (6) sufficient capitalization.

Hard Work, Drive, and Dedication   An individual must have a strong desire to work independently and be willing to put in long hours in order to succeed as an entrepreneur. Successful entrepreneurs tend to be reasonable risk takers, self-confident, hard working, goal setters, and innovators.[38] In addition, small businesses generally benefit if the owner attends well to detail. Some entrepreneurs fail because they neglect the details of business operations. They may open a business for the glamour and excitement of it, but as the concomitant drudgery of entrepreneurship builds, they may ignore key areas such as inventory control and collections. They may also ignore customer dissatisfaction, worker unrest, or financial difficulties, preferring to think that problems will solve themselves. Over time, though, they rarely do.

Market Demand for Products or Services Provided   For any business to succeed, there must be sufficient demand for the product or service it provides. If a college community of 50,000 citizens and 15,000 students has one pizza parlor, there is probably sufficient demand for more. However, if fifteen pizza parlors are already in operation, a new one will have to serve especially good pizza or offer something else unique if it is to succeed. Liz Claiborne's clothing business was successful because there was unmet demand for clothing for working women; Apple Computer was successful because there was unmet demand for personal computers.

Managerial Competence   It is necessary for the entrepreneur to possess basic managerial competence. He or she needs to know how to select business locations and facilities, how to acquire financing, and how to hire and evaluate employees. The entrepreneur must also be able to manage growth, control costs, negotiate contracts, and make difficult choices and decisions. An entrepreneur who has a product for which there is tremendous demand might be able to survive for a while without managerial skills. Over time, and especially in the mature stage of the life cycle, however, the manager who lacks these skills is unlikely to succeed.

Luck   Some small businesses succeed purely because of luck. There was an element of luck in Alan McKim's success with Clean Harbors, an environmental "clean-up" organization based in New England. McKim formed this business just as the federal government committed $1.6 billion to help clean up toxic waste. Although McKim might have succeeded anyway, the extra revenue generated by the government Superfund no doubt contributed to this success.[39]

Strong Control Systems   As we saw earlier in this chapter, small businesses, like all organizations, need strong control systems. Small businesses can be ruined by weak control. For example, too many slow-paying customers can reduce a small business's cash flow to a trickle. Excess inventory, employee theft, poor-quality products, plummeting sales, and insufficient profit margins can have equally disastrous effects. If the control system does not alert the entrepreneur to these problems, or alerts the entrepreneur too late, recovery may be difficult or impossible.

Sufficient Capitalization   Small businesses need sufficient funds to survive start-up and growth. One rule of thumb is that an entrepreneur should have sufficient personal funds when starting out so as to be able to live with no business income for a year.[40] The entrepreneur needs to be able to maintain his or her personal life, cover all operating expenses, and still have an allowance for unexpected contingencies. An entrepreneur who is planning to pay next month's rent from a new business's profits may be courting disaster.

Learning Summary

Entrepreneurship is the process of organizing, operating, and assuming the risk of a business venture. An entrepreneur is someone who engages in entrepreneurship. In general, entrepreneurs start small businesses. Small businesses are an important source of innovation, create numerous jobs, and contribute to the success of large businesses.

Entrepreneurs seeking to start small businesses face the same three challenges as any managers in any organization: choosing a strategy, implementing that strategy through structure, and motivating behavior. In choosing strategies, entrepreneurs have to consider both the characteristics of the industry in which they are going to conduct business and their organization's distinctive competencies. Entrepreneurs can use Porter's five forces framework to choose their industry.

Small businesses generally have several distinctive competencies that they should exploit in choosing their strategy. Small businesses are usually skilled at identifying niches in established markets, identifying new markets, and acting quickly to obtain first-mover advantages. Small businesses are usually not skilled at exploiting economies of scale.

Once an entrepreneur has chosen a strategy, the strategy is normally written down in a business plan. Writing a business plan forces an entrepreneur to plan very thoroughly and to anticipate problems that might occur.

With a strategy and business plan in place, entrepreneurs must choose a structure to implement them. All the structural issues summarized in Part III of this book are relevant to the entrepreneur. In addition, the entrepreneur has some unique structural choices to make. In determining ownership and financial structure, the entrepreneur can choose between a sole proprietorship, a partnership, a corporation, a master limited partnership, a sub-chapter S corporation, and a cooperative. In determining financial structure, an entrepreneur has to decide how much personal capital to invest in an organization, how much bank and government support to obtain, and whether to encourage venture capital firms to invest in the firm. Finally, entrepreneurs have to choose among the options of buying an existing business, starting a new business from scratch, or entering into a franchising agreement.

Whatever decisions an entrepreneur makes, it is very important that he or she also implement a variety of organizational controls, including accounting and budgeting controls. Entrepreneurs have several sources of management help and assistance.

With a strategy and structure chosen, the entrepreneur must next develop systems and procedures that encourage appropriate behavior in the firm. In particular, entrepreneurs need to create a work setting that enables workers to derive personal satisfaction from their jobs, that encourages clear communication, and that creates high standards of performance for employees. In addition, the entrepreneur often faces unique behavioral challenges in the areas of leadership and motivation, and group dynamics.

Most small businesses pass through a three-phase life cycle: acceptance, breakthrough, and maturity. There are several reasons why successful small businesses are able to move through all three of these stages of development: hard work, drive, and dedication; market demand for products or services provided; managerial competence; luck; strong control systems; and sufficient capitalization.

Questions and Exercises

Review Questions

1. How are entrepreneurs and small businesses important to society?
2. In which types of industries do small firms often excel? In which types of industries do small firms struggle?
3. List several distinctive competencies and a strategic weakness that are typical of small businesses.
4. List the ownership options available to entrepreneurs. What are the advantages and disadvantages of each?
5. Evaluate the advantages and disadvantages of using venture capital as a source of capital for a small firm compared to other alternatives.
6. What behavioral and group phenomena are managers more likely to face in small businesses than in large organizations?
7. What are the major stages of the life cycle of entrepreneurial organizations? What are the characteristics of each stage?
8. What are the elements of success for small businesses?

Analysis Questions

1. Entrepreneurs and small businesses play a variety of important roles in society. If these roles are so important, do you think that the government should do more to encourage the development of small business? Why or why not?
2. Franchising agreements seem to be particularly popular ways of starting a new business in industries where retail outlets are geographically widely spread and where the quality of goods or services purchased can be evaluated only after the purchase has occurred. For example, a hamburger may look tasty, but you know for sure that it is well made only after you buy it and eat it. By going to a McDonald's, you know exactly the kind and quality of hamburger you will receive, even before you walk in the door. What is it about franchise arrangements that makes them so popular under these conditions?
3. If employing family members can cause problems in a small organization, why is this practice so common?

Application Exercises

1. Interview the owner of a small business in your town. Evaluate how successful this small business has been. Using the criteria presented in this chapter, explain its success (or lack of success).
2. Using the information about managing a small business presented in this chapter, analyze whether you would like to work in a small business — either as an employee or as a founder. Given your personality, background, and experience, does working in or starting a new business appeal to you? What are the reasons for your opinion?

Chapter Notes

1. John Birmingham, "Boys and Their Toys," *Continental Profiles,* June 1990, pp. 30+; Carla M. Tuzzolino, "Nintendo Zaps the Consumer Market," *Incentive,* May 1991, pp. 103–104; Cleveland Horton, "Nintendo Paces Videogames," *Advertising Age,* January 30, 1989, p. 77; Thane Peterson and Maria Shao, "But I Don't Wanna Play Nintendo Anymore," *Business Week,* November 19, 1990, pp. 52, 54.

2. Murray B. Low and Ian C. MacMillan, "Entrepreneurship: Past Research and Future Challenges," *Journal of Management,* June 1988, pp. 139–159; Barbara Bird, "Implementing Entrepreneurial Ideas: The Case for Intention," *Academy of Management Review,* July 1988, pp. 442–453.

3. "U.S. Small Business Administration: Small Business Size Standards," *Federal Register,* vol. 49, no. 28 (Washington, D.C.: Government Printing Office, February 9, 1984), pp. 5024–5048.

4. Bro Uttal, "Inside the Deal That Made Bill Gates $350,000,000," *Fortune,* July 21, 1986, pp. 23–33.

5. Low and MacMillan, "Entrepreneurship"; Arnold C. Cooper and William C. Dunkelberg, "Entrepreneurship and Paths to Business Ownership," *Strategic Management Journal,* January/February 1986, pp. 53–56.

6. See David L. Birch, *The Job Creation Process* (Cambridge, Mass.: MIT Program on Neighborhood and Regional Change, 1979); Nicholas C. Siropolis, *Small Business Management: A Guide to Entrepreneurship,* 4th ed. (Boston: Houghton Mifflin, 1990); Stuart Gannes, "America's Fastest-growing Companies," *Fortune,* May 23, 1988, pp. 28–40.

7. "Big vs. Small," *Time,* September 5, 1988, pp. 48–50; J. A. Schumpeter, *Capitalism, Socialism, and Democracy,* 3rd ed. (New York: Harper & Row, 1950).

8. Birch, *The Job Creation Process;* Siropolis, *Small Business Management.*

9. Michael Porter, *Competitive Strategy* (New York: Free Press, 1980).

10. Uttal, "Inside the Deal That Made Bill Gates $350,000,000"; Keith Hammonds, "Spreadsheet Wars: When Will Lotus Do Windows," *Business Week,* January 14, 1991, p. 42.

11. Erik Calonius, "Meet the King of Video," *Fortune,* June 4, 1990, p. 208.

12. See Faye Brookman, "Specialty Cosmetics Stores: A Hit with Frustrated Consumers," *Advertising Age,* March 4, 1991, p. 32; Laurie Freeman, "Department Stores in Fight for Their Lives," *Advertising Age,* March 4, 1991, p. 29.

13. See Steve Zurier, "Distribution's Perfect Example," *Industrial Distribution,* April 1991, pp. 18–22; and Donald A. Duscheseneau and William B. Gartner, "A Profile of New Venture Success and Failure in an Emerging Industry," *Journal of Business Venturing,* September 1990, pp. 297–312.

14. F. M. Scherer, *Industrial Market Structure and Economic Performance,* 2nd ed. (Boston: Houghton Mifflin, 1980).

15. Thomas Rohan, "Maverick Remakes Old-Line Steel," *Industry Week,* January 21, 1991, pp. 26–30.

16. See Candace Campbell, "Change Agents in the New Economy," *Economic Development Review,* Spring 1989, pp. 56–59.

17. See Kenneth Harling and Phoebe Quail, "Exploring a General Management Approach to Farm Management," *Agribusiness,* September 1990, pp. 425–441; and Charles Silear, "Where Did All the Pigs Go?" *Forbes,* March 19, 1990, pp. 152–156.

18. See Richard Pastore, "Small Is Big in PC Land," *Computerworld,* December 24, 1990, pp. 27, 29; and Pat Sweet, "The Evolution of the PC's," *Director,* March 1990, pp. 101–107.

19. The importance of discovering niches is emphasized in Charles Hill and Gareth Jones, *Strategic Management: An Integrative Approach,* 2nd ed. (Boston: Houghton Mifflin, 1992).

20. C. Roland Christensen, Norman A. Berg, and Malcolm Salter, "BIC Pen (A)," *Policy Formulation and Administration,* 8th ed. (Homewood, Ill.: Irwin, 1980), pp. 146–171.

21. See Siropolis, *Small Business Management;* Richard M. Hodgetts and Donald F. Kuratko, *Effective Small Business Management,* 3rd ed. (Chicago: Harcourt Brace Jovanovich, 1989). The risks run at Boeing are described in "Running Ahead, but Running Scared," *Forbes,* May 13, 1991, pp. 38–40.

22. Siropolis, *Small Business Management.*

23. Ibid.

24. See Thomas E. Copeland and J. Fred Weston, *Financial Theory and Corporate Policy,* 2nd ed. (Reading, Mass.: Addison-Wesley, 1983), for a discussion of the different kinds of claims that sources of capital can have on a firm. Eugene Fama and Michael Jensen discuss the advantages and disadvantages of various forms of corporate ownership in E. Fama and M. Jensen, "Agency Problems and Residual Claims," *Journal of Law and Economics,* June 1983, pp. 327–349; and E. Fama and M. Jensen, "Separation of Ownership and Control," *Journal of Law and Economics,* June 1983, pp. 301–325. A more practical guide to choosing ownership structure is found in Hodgetts and Kuratko, *Effective Small Business Management.*

25. Jay Barney, Lowell Busenitz, James Feit, and Doug Moesel, "The Structure of Venture Capital Governance," *Academy of Management Proceedings: "Best Papers 1989,"* Meeting of the Academy of Management, Washington, D.C., 1989, pp. 64–68.

26. "Persistence Pays in Search of Funds," *USA Today,* May 11, 1987, p. 3E.

27. Barney et al., "The Structure of Venture Capital Governance."

28. Faye Rice, "How to Succeed at Cloning a Small Business," *Fortune,* October 28, 1985, pp. 60–66; "Franchising Tries to Divvy Up Risk," *USA Today,* May 11, 1987, p. 5E.

29. Rice, "How to Succeed at Cloning a Small Business."

30. Mathew Berke, "Elling Brothers Got Costs Under Control," *Inc.,* June 1982, pp. 64–74.

31. Siropolis, *Small Business Management.*

32. See Lynn Zuker, "The Role of Institutionalization in Cultural Persistence," *American Sociological Review,* October 1977, pp. 726–743.

33. Siropolis, *Small Business Management.*

34. See John P. Thornton, "Saving the Family Business," *Life Association News,* May 1991, pp. 78–87, for a discussion of the practical implications of these conflicts.

35. See Cheryl Holland, "Passing on the Family Business," *Business and Economic Review,* April–June 1991, pp. 37–39.

36. Siropolis, *Small Business Management.*

37. Ibid.

38. Ibid.

39. See Jay Barney, "Strategic Factor Markets: Expectations, Luck, and Business Strategy," *Management Science,* October 1986, pp. 1231–1241.

40. Siropolis, *Small Business Management.*

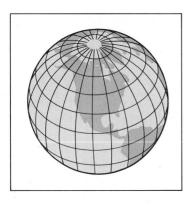

CASE 24.1

Growing Big Without Losing Touch

One of the unsettling aspects of starting a new business is the tendency of companies to lose their personal touch, their responsiveness, and their uniqueness as they grow large. But as L. L. Bean proves, it doesn't have to be that way.

Leon Leonwood Bean, orphaned at age 12, survived by working on the farms of friends and relatives in western Maine. He eventually earned enough money to pay for two years of schooling, and by 1907 he had begun working at his brother's store in tiny Freeport.

One of L. L.'s passions was hunting, and like most of the hunters of the time, he felt dissatisfied with the footwear available to him. He could choose either clumsy rubber boots or comfortable leather loggers' boots that were far from waterproof. The idea that made him famous was to combine the two, sewing leather uppers to rubber soles, creating the Maine Hunting Shoe. In 1912, he mailed advertisements to holders of Maine hunting licenses, guaranteeing his new shoes "to give perfect satisfaction in every way."*

Honoring that guarantee turned out to be costly but earned Bean a reputation that has endured. When the leather separated from the rubber in ninety out of the first one hundred pairs of boots sold, Bean refunded the customers' money, borrowed more, and persuaded a leading rubber company to come up with a better sole. After that first difficult year, word of mouth and Bean's clever use of mail-order selling helped the company grow rapidly.

Bean gradually added items to his catalog, first hand-knit stockings, then other hunting gear. He tested each item himself, selling only things that he felt would be genuinely useful to other hunters. In the 1920s, he added fishing and camping gear, boasting that fishermen no longer had to experiment with dozens of flies because "We have done that experimenting for you."†

Bean's mail-order business became famous for service and efficiency. The morning's orders were mailed out in the afternoon. Bean did not neglect customers who wanted to make their way to Freeport, and beginning in 1951 he kept the store open twenty-four hours a day. It has closed only twice since: once in 1963 after the death of President John Kennedy, once in 1967 after the death of L. L. himself at age 94.

The founder's death was a critical event for the company, as it is for any organization created by one person. L. L.'s grandson, Leon A. Gorman, made sure that his grandfather's business would not become just a memory. He woke the sleepy company up and brought it into the age of computers. Bean's sales grew rapidly and its catalogs proliferated, until by the end of the 1980s it was shipping twenty-four different catalogs aimed not just at hunters but at people who enjoy the outdoors in any way or just like to look as though they do. Although almost 90 percent of the company's business comes through the mail, its store in Freeport is now the second largest tourist attraction in the state (after the Atlantic Ocean), drawing some 3.5 million people per year.

Despite its tremendous growth, Bean is still the kind of company that its founder could take pride in. The people who answer the phone still provide advice about where to fish in Maine or what kind of gear to take to the Himalayas. Employees still test Bean's products, and customers can still get their money back any time for anything they have bought from Bean.

Bean's catalog operations are so efficient that companies from Xerox to J. C. Penney have flocked to Freeport to study them. Yet the secret of Bean's success is still people, not machines. Computers keep track of where merchandise is and help employees choose the most efficient way to gather the items for an order. But there are no robots in Bean's warehouse, and compared with many fully automated warehouses, Bean's is rather old-fashioned.

Perhaps the most remarkable aspect of Bean's performance is its ability to handle the Christmas rush, when it adds more than two thousand workers and sends out as many as 134,000 packages per day. Even these temporary, part-time workers uphold Bean's reputation for excellent service. They are well trained, steeped in the Bean ethic, and in general feel a strong loyalty to the company. Their productivity and accuracy help determine their pay rates. They receive bonuses and profit sharing at the end of the year, and part-timers know that Bean usually hires permanent workers from its pool of temporaries. Although these employees can now send you anything from wet suits to dress loafers, they'll still be glad to box up a pair of L. L.'s rubber-and-leather innovations to keep your feet dry in the woods.

Discussion Questions

1. How has L. L. Bean managed to avoid the common pitfalls of becoming a big company?
2. In what ways was L. L. Bean a typical entrepreneur? In what ways was he unusual?
3. How does L. L. Bean ensure that its service will continue to be outstanding?
4. What, in your opinion, are the most important keys to Bean's success?

* Quoted in Leon A. Gorman, *L. L. Bean, Inc.* (New York: Newcomen Society, 1981), p. 8.
† Quoted ibid., p. 9.

REFERENCES: Beverly Geber, "Training at L. L. Bean," *Training,* October 1988, pp. 85–90; Leon A. Gorman, *L. L. Bean, Inc.* (New York: Newcomen Society, 1981); "L. L. Bean Information," March 1990; Steven E. Prokisch, "Bean Meshes Man, Machine," *New York Times,* December 23, 1985, pp. B1+; John Skow, "Using the Old (L. L.) Bean," *Reader's Digest,* June 1986, pp. 25–26+.

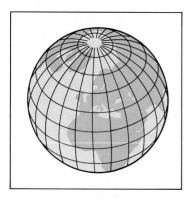

CASE 24.2

A Passion for Musicals and Money

Cameron Mackintosh was only eight when he settled on his life's work. His aunt took him to see *Salad Days,* a London musical, and afterward he wandered backstage and demanded to see the author and composer, Julian Slade. After that experience, he spent every possible minute in and around theaters, taking any theater-related job he could get before he was finally given a chance to do what he really wanted to do — produce musicals.

But this is not the story of a struggling artist and the cold cruel world that wouldn't accept him. Mackintosh and the musicals he produced were not instant successes, but for the past decade, Cameron Mackintosh Ltd. and his musicals have been doing well enough to rank Mackintosh among Britain's two hundred wealthiest men and to earn his musical *Cats* the honor of being the most successful production in history.

Mackintosh's success relies on a mixture of intuition, hard work, and good business sense. Mackintosh spent four years working on one of his most recent productions, *Miss Saigon,* before it was ready for the stage, and during that time he went through two directors and eight versions of the script. Mackintosh first stages his plays in London's West End before taking them to New York's Broadway and around the world. He never starts a Broadway run until he has a hit in London, and he thinks far ahead. He sent posters for *Miss Saigon* to ticket agents two years before the show was to open, and he invested $450,000 in last-minute publicity for the show even though it was sold out for the next six months. "There's no better time to beat the drum than when people can't buy tickets," he explains. "You have to let them know they can't buy a ticket. That's what the difference between a hit and a megahit is all about."*

Just as important as Mackintosh's business sense is his intuition, his artistic temperament. He seems to retain much of the eight-year-old's appreciation for what happens on the stage, and usually what pleases him ends up pleasing audiences. Critics don't always like Mackintosh's elaborate sets and dramatic technical feats, like bringing a helicopter on-stage to rescue Americans fleeing Vietnam in *Miss Saigon.* But such touches get audiences talking and add to the publicity. "My own tastes happen to be in tune with what the public wants," he says.†

Intuition also helps Mackintosh choose the right people to work with. A lunch with composer Andrew Lloyd Weber in 1980 turned into an all-afternoon meeting, at the end of which Mackintosh suggested to Weber making a musical of T. S. Eliot's poems about cats. Weber liked the idea, and *Cats* has since grossed close to a half-billion dollars.

Despite his reputation for driving hard bargains, extracting every cent he can get from local presenters, and switching theaters or directors when he is not satisfied, Mackintosh has earned almost universal respect within the theatrical community. The only complaint among Mackintosh's friends in the community seems to be that he makes them struggle as much as anyone else to get a piece of his next show.

Miss Saigon, however, did create some problems for Mackintosh, proving that he is human, but he seems to have turned the controversy to his benefit. When Mackintosh was preparing to bring *Miss Saigon* from London to New York, the Council of Actors Equity Association objected to the casting of British actor Jonathan Pryce as one of the play's main characters, a Eurasian. Pryce had played the role in London, but the Equity Council throught that Asian and Eurasian actors in the United States should be given a chance to play the role. Mackintosh felt that the Council's stand amounted to an accusation that he was racially insensitive, and he canceled the show. The Council, which has long supported blacklisted and minority actors, received a lot of criticism for its position on Pryce and eventually backed down. Mackintosh's reputation may have been somewhat tarnished by the controversy, even though supporters pointed out that a year before the dispute he had opened a *Miss Saigon* school in London, providing free singing and dancing lessons for Asian actors, eight of whom made it into the London production. But of course all the uproar in the press provided the best advance advertising a producer could hope for.

Mackintosh shares with many entrepreneurs at least one trait: the ability to use his own creativity to spark the creativity of others. He hunts down problems in a production and comes up with numerous solutions. His solutions are rarely the best ones, but they, as he puts it, "invariably prompt [someone] to come up with the right solution, usually one I would never have dreamt of myself."‡

Discussion Questions

1. In what ways does Mackintosh fit the definition of an entrepreneur given in this chapter? In what ways is he different?
2. What skills does a theatrical producer like Mackintosh need in order to be successful?
3. To some, having a Caucasian playing the role of a Eurasian seems racist. Do you feel that government or professional organizations should have the power to influence the hiring decisions that an entrepreneur makes?
4. What difficulties do you imagine Cameron Mackintosh Ltd. will face if it continues to be successful?

* Quoted in Ed Behr, "The 'Middlebrow' Maestro of Megahits," *Newsweek,* October 2, 1989, p. 69.
† Quoted in Mervyn Rothstein, "The Musical Is Money to His Ears," *New York Times Magazine,* December 9, 1990, p. 84.
‡ Quoted ibid., p. 98.

REFERENCES: Ed Behr, "The 'Middlebrow' Maestro of Megahits," *Newsweek,* October 2, 1989, pp. 68–69; Richard Hummler, "'Saigon' Vote, Round 2: Will Reversal Save It?" *Variety,* August 15, 1990, p. 69; Jack Kroll, "The Chutzpah of 'Miss Saigon,'" *Newsweek,* October 2, 1989, pp. 68–69; Mervyn Rothstein, "The Musical Is Money to His Ears," *New York Times Magazine,* December 9, 1990, pp. 48+; William Stevenson, "3 Make a Winning Hand for Cameron Mackintosh," *Variety,* August 15, 1990, pp. 51, 68.

PHOTO CREDITS, continued

Chapter 5: p. 144, courtesy of Goodyear Tire & Rubber Co.; p. 148, courtesy of Johnson & Johnson; p. 159, courtesy of General Mills, Inc. **Chapter 6:** p. 183, Jim Wilson/NYT Pictures; p. 188, Antinea; p. 195, © Pascal Sittles/REA/SABA. **Chapter 7:** p. 223, © Andy Freeberg; p. 226, courtesy Matson Navigation Co., San Francisco; p. 233, courtesy Dairy Crest Limited & *Quality Update.* **Chapter 8:** p. 249, courtesy of Chevron Corporation; p. 260, © David E. Klutho; p. 262, left: courtesy of Columbia Pictures, center: Courtesy of Tri-Star Pictures, right: courtesy of Columbia Pictures Television. **Chapter 9:** p. 283, courtesy of Carolina Herrera; p. 295, George Lange/Outline Press; p. 299, © John S. Abbott. **Chapter 10:** p. 317, courtesy of Lufthansa; p. 323, © Bob Firth/ Photobank; p. 326, © Breton Littlehales/Gianni & Talent. **Chapter 11:** p. 347, Terrence McCarthy/NYT Pictures; p. 365, Susan May Tell/Picture Group; p. 366, photograph by Photogroup, Portland, OR 97202, (503) 239-7817. **Chapter 12:** p. 389, Lisa Dennis/Spot (The Image Bank) Benelux, Brussels.; p. 390, © Shonna Valeska; p. 404, © Larry Maglott. **Chapter 13:** p. 416, courtesy of Union Pacific Corporation. Photo by Ovak Arslanian; p. 422, Dick Luria/FPG International; p. 429, Digital Equipment Corporation. **Chapter 14:** p. 452, Louis Psihoyos/Matrix; p. 461, © R. Ian Lloyd; p. 469, © Nancy Lane Photo/The Boston Herald. **Chapter 15:** p. 484, © John Madere; p. 501, courtesy of Digital Equipment Corporation. Photo © Carol Kaplan; p. 505, © John S. Abbott. **Chapter 16:** p. 521, Karen Kasmauski/Woodfin Camp & Associates; p. 531, courtesy of The Procter & Gamble Company; p. 538, Courtesy SATURN Corporation/Photo by Robin Hood. **Chapter 17:** p. 553, courtesy of Grand Trunk Corporation; p. 562, © James Schnepf; p. 571, © Pat Davison. **Chapter 18:** p. 588, © Estée Lauder; p. 591, © Rob Kinmonth (212) 475-6370; p. 610, © Barbara Reis (202) 328-1993. **Chapter 19:** p. 626, © Steve Hill; p. 631, M. Richards/Sipa Press; p. 643, courtesy Volvo, Kalmar, Sweden. **Chapter 20:** p. 656, © David Klutho; p. 659, courtesy of Knight-Ridder, Inc. Photo © George Schiavone; p. 675, courtesy Hewlett-Packard Company. **Chapter 21:** p. 687, Phil Huber/Black Star; p. 691, courtesy of Dow Corning Corporation; p. 699, © Nina Barnett. **Chapter 22:** p. 721, © Steve Winter; p. 736, © H. Mark Weidman; p. 740, Steve Shay/NYT Pictures. **Chapter 23:** p. 754, Ken Kerbs/DOT; p. 766, courtesy of General Electric; p. 769, Steve Kagan/NYT Pictures; p. 773, © 1991 by David Fields. **Chapter 24:** p. 789, Gerry Gropp/Sipa Press; p. 794, © Torin Boyd; p. 809, NYT Pictures.

Name Index

Organization and Product Index

Subject Index